Beginning SQL Server 2000 Programming

Robin Dewson

Wrox Press Ltd. ®

Beginning SQL Server 2000 Programming

Latest Reprint November 2002

Published by Wrox Press Ltd,
Arden House, 1102 Warwick Road, Acocks Green,
Birmingham, B27 6BH, UK
Printed in the United States
ISBN 1-861005-23-7

Trademark Acknowledgements

Credits

Author
Robin Dewson

Additional Material
Tony Bain
Christopher Graves
Hope Hatfield
Brian Knight

Technical Reviewers
Michael Benkovich
Jim W. Brzowski
James R. de Carli
John Fletcher
Damien Foggon
Christopher Graves
Hope Hatfield
Ian Herbert
Jody F. Kerr
Rick Leander
Don Lee
Dianna Leech
Larry McCoy
Frederick O'Leary
Troy Proudfoot
David Schultz
Keyur Shah
Helmut Watson
Andrew Watt
Thearon Willis
Sakhr Youness

Category Manager
Bruce Lawson

Technical Architect
Catherine Alexander

Index
Michael Brinkman
Andrew Criddle

Technical Editors
Victoria Blackburn
Claire Brittle
Benjamin Egan
Paul Jeffcoat
Fiver Locker
Douglas Paterson
Andrew Polshaw

Author Agents
Tony Berry
Avril Corbin
Chandima Nethisinghe

Project Administrators
Rob Hesketh
Cilmara Lion
Chandima Nethisinghe

Production Manager
Simon Hardware

Production Coordinator
Tom Bartlett

Production Assistant
Natalie O'Donnell

Figures
Paul Grove

Additional Artwork
Chris Matterface

Proofreader
Chris Smith

Cover
Dawn Chellingworth

About the Author

Robin has been working with Wrox Press for over two years now as a technical reviewer, and recently was invited to provide additional material for Professional Access 2000 Programming, Professional SQL Server Development with Access 2000, Professional SQL Server DTS, and Professional SQL Server 2000 Programming.

He has built up a good rapport with Wrox Press over this time and from his working experience was invited to write this book concerning SQL Server 2000.

Robin has written articles for Pinnacle publications on Visual FoxPro and Visual Basic which gave him a taste of writing and from that point felt that helping to write a book one day was a goal.

Before leaving school, he was introduced to computing while on a university visit where he saw a Commodore Pet. From there he knew that computing was the area to move in to, and worked very hard during the summer of 1980 to buy his very first computer, the Sinclair ZX80. The ZX81 and the Sinclair Spectrum soon followed this. (What ever happened to Jet Set Willy?)

His working background, though, does not come from PC's, but from mainframes where he was introduced to an ICL mainframe at Ravenscraig Steel Works in Motherwell, Scotland, while on day release from his college. This then moved on to IBM mainframes at his second college, the Scottish College of Textiles in Galashiels, Scotland, where he spent many hours playing games when he should have been working on his project! Another passion of Robin's is rugby and he was glad when he was accepted to S.C.O.T. as this was right next door to Galashiels rugby ground.

Before leaving college, a job offer was made from Texas Instruments who were based in Bedford, England at the time and it was here that he started his working life, still very wet behind the ears. After a couple of more jobs, it was time to become a consultant where he was in more control of his life and how things developed and he then spent over 8 years at Save & Prosper, working mainly on a financial system, still on mainframes.

However during this time, it was soon clear that mainframes were not the area to be in for him, and so he started looking at working with PC's. This all came about from inheriting a postal soccer game called Sick Parrot which was written in FoxBase.

His first main application of his own was a Visual FoxPro application that could be used to run a Fantasy League system. It was at this point he met up with a great help in his PC development life, Jon Silver at Step One Technologies where in return for training, he helped Jon with some other Visual FoxPro applications.

From there, realizing that the market place for Visual FoxPro in the United Kingdom was limited, decided to learn Visual Basic and SQL Server. Starting out with SQL Server 6.5 he soon moved to SQL Server 7 and Visual Basic 5 where he became involved in developing several applications for clients both in the UK and the US ranging from a supplier and analysis system for Rohbe Inc. through to a membership system for AJS & Matchless Motorcycles. From there he moved to SQL Server 2000 and Visual Basic 6.

Robin currently is consulting at Lehman Brothers in the City of London using Visual Basic 6 and Sybase on a trading system called Kojak, where he has been for nearly 5 years.

Unbeknown to him also at Lehman Brothers working at the same time, was a current Wrox employee, Cilmara Lion who Robin has worked with for almost a year at Wrox.

When he has a spare moment, he is also beta testing .NET technologies and is looking forward to the next generation of technologies.

Dedication

Without wishing to read like one of those boring Oscar speeches, where everyone in the world is mentioned through floods of tears, and then the main person who should be thanked is missed, there are quite a large number of people I really would like to thank. Without them, I would not be where I am today, and this book would never exist. No doubt I will miss a few, and to those, I apologize.

I would like to start with Tony Berry, who over the past 2+ years has been a brilliant person to work with and who I would classify as one of my greatest friends. He has stuck with me and had the courage to give his support in allowing me to write this book. His only downfall is that he is a Manchester United supporter. Tony, everyone has their faults!

Also within Wrox, another great person has been Cilmara Lion. She allowed me to technically review some very good books within Wrox in the past 12 months, and from this, and her faith in persuading others to allow me to write within a few of these books, has all accumulated in the writing of this book all on my own. And to show how small a world it really is, unbeknown to either of us, we actually worked for the same company at the same time before meeting up with each other at Wrox! I hope motherhood is working out well for you Cil.

Finally, but far from least, is **Catherine Alexander**. This is her book as much as it is mine. Her skill and dexterity in pulling my technical ramblings into proper English and ensuring that the book made it out on time, is invaluable. In working with her when helping out in other SQL Server books I knew how brilliant Catherine was, and I was so pleased when Catherine was assigned to this book.

Moving on to others who have influenced me, I must start with **Thearon Willis** whom I respect and admire, and whose input into my book proposal has been invaluable. **Rob Vieira's Professional SQL Server 2000 Programming** book is constantly by my side in the work place and is a great source of reference. You will find this out too by the time you come to the end of this book and are ready to move on.

Having been a technical reviewer on many Wrox books, I know how hard these people work and in some respects are the backbone of a good book. No matter how good the author, the technical architect or any others, without the **technical reviewers**, books would fall flat on their face. I cannot thank you all enough. Each has given their own individual input which really has made a difference. **Sakhr Youness** though, thanks for your help when I became stuck! Then so many others at Wrox, each and every one is a star. As a reader, you just don't know what these people do and the time they spend giving up weekends, holidays, to ensure that what you read is enjoyable and understandable. Techies are the worst at grammar!

To everyone at **Bedford Rugby** club, for supplying great rugby while writing this book; it has given me an escape and relaxation when I needed it the most. **Colin Jackson, Dave Shawl, Lee Smith**, the players and staff, *Up the Blues.*

I then need to thank those people at Save & Prosper. There are many there I need to thank, but in my eight and a half years there, there are three people who really stand out above them all. **Roger Finch, John Wheatley,** and **Derek Lakin** are all people who looked after me, and ensured that my time with them was memorable and a great experience. However I cannot leave Save & Prosper without mentioning **Glen Harding**, **Dave Eling**, **Paul Cohen**, **Penny Trim**, **Ken MacKenzie**, **Mike Patterson**, **John Wellman,** and **Tony Best**

To **Jon Silver** who spent time and had patience to teach me the different techniques in programming PC's to mainframes, and also the intricacies of Visual FoxPro and to a lesser extent Visual Basic, many thanks.

When I moved from using mainframes as my main form of revenue generation to PC's at Lehman Brothers, there were three people who took a massive gamble on me, and I hope I repaid them back over the time I worked with them. Without these friends I might still be stuck in mainframes. To **Annette** "they wouldn't put me in charge if I didn't know what I was doing" **Kelly**, **Daniel** "The Dream Sequence" **Tarbotton**, **David** "Its almost as if it's trading itself" **Antinori**, and **Andy** "I don't really know, I've only been here for a week" **Sykes**, I thank you. We had many laughs and many memorable moments, even more so when **Stephen Richards** who knew where that "line" was and knew the best way to cross it, joined us.

Also from Lehman Brothers, **Tom Carroll**, my boss for many of my important years there and **Jack Mason,** who has really had to put up with quite a lot, but has always been so supportive and for whom nothing has ever been too much trouble. Without his understanding and letting me have holiday when deadlines were looming, this book would not have gone to press on time. I really cannot thank you enough Jack.

To my mum and dad, **Scott and Laura**. When I left school, I was about to just drift in my life. Not once, but twice they steered me back on to the correct course. Their help and perseverance with me has ensured I have a good life. Oh and yes dad, I do permanently smell of "roses", no matter what I fall in. Where I cannot thank them enough was in organizing and sending me to first of all Motherwell Technical College, and then on to the Scottish College of Textiles in Galashiels in Scotland. The best 2 years of my life were spent at S.C.O.T, where I studied Computer Data Processing, and my greatest regret are the many friends I made there, I have lost contact with them all and I wish I hadn't. So many to mention, but if you are out there **Robert "Toad" McMillan**, do drop me a line!

Then there are my father-in-law and mother-in-law, **David and Jean**. Before David passed away, he helped my family and myself in so many different ways. Nothing was too much trouble, and so many times, he was there when I needed him most. I miss him immensely. My mother-in-law Jean, has been brilliant with us and our children and has been a great help in allowing me to get on with this book when my wife has been busy.

Finally, but far from least, my wife, **Julie** and three wonderful kids, **Scott**, **Cameron** and **Ellen**. Julie is the best mother ever and the kids are very lucky to have her. She has gifted to this world, and then developed and allowed to grow within their own independence, three great children. I constantly am so grateful for her fairness, even handedness, and resourcefulness in keeping three children on an even keel. Scott, you constantly surprise me as to what sports you enjoy and partake in; however, rugby being your love, I hope you do well. Cameron, I would never have thought you would enjoy horse riding so much, but you do. Stick with it, for someone of your young years, you are excellent. Ellen "catch that kiss daddy", the terror, but I mean this in the nicest way. Never the ballet dancer, always the rugby player. Rarely Barbie, more Action Man. Already I feel sorry for the man you marry! However, you are my little cutie, and you constantly make me laugh. Julie, you are a star.

As I say so often to my children, as long as you try your hardest then we can never ask or expect more. To you, reader, keep that in mind.

> *Life is not a dress rehearsal. Live it, enjoy it. You don't get a second chance. Never think that "there is always tomorrow". One day, tomorrow won't come. Ensure that at the end of the day, you can look back and say, "If that was my last, it couldn't have been better".*

Table of Contents

Introduction

Microsoft SQL Server for Windows has been around for a number of years now, starting out with version 4.2, which ran on Windows NT. There were prior versions to this; however, these were based around OS/2 as the operating system and were built in collaboration with another database company called Sybase. The Microsoft/Sybase connection continued up to the release of SQL Server 6.0, where the two companies went their own ways. Sybase is still a major database contender and is mainly found on Unix boxes. However, from SQL Server 6.0 came a version upgrade/bug fix to version 6.5, which was mainly aimed at upgrading SQL Server and altering some of the areas that developers didn't like about how it worked. This was also the first Microsoft-only version of SQL Server.

SQL Server 6.5 didn't take off as fast as might be expected, for many reasons, but Microsoft, responding to the market, took SQL Server 6.5 and rewrote many parts of the system and changed the design quite drastically. There was a product in the market place that had a much better database engine and technologically developed method for searching data. This was bought by Microsoft and used as the basis of its engine, not only for SQL Server, but also Access. That product was FoxPro, which still lives on as Visual FoxPro. This used a database technology called Rushmore Technology, which made it the fastest desktop database in the market place.

This new database engine and architecture was all built up and released as SQL Server version 7.0, which not only ran on Windows NT, but also Windows 98. This was the stepping stone to today's SQL Server 2000, which has become a much more secure, feature rich, and easily developed system available on many different Windows operating platforms.

What's Covered in this Book

As the book progresses, a simple example application will be built taking you stage by stage through how the example is created and developed, in a clear, but simple, manner that is easy to follow and understand.

First of all, we must be sure that our machine will allow us to run SQL Server 2000, and choose the version we wish to use. To this end, **Chapter 1** covers choosing the right version of SQL Server 2000 and installing it onto your system.

As with any program, you need a way to use it, and a graphical user interface is often the best choice. **Chapter 2** looks at the Enterprise Manager, the tool that allows us to manipulate the data held within our SQL Server databases. It has many features to learn about, which are covered in this chapter.

Chapter 3 then goes on to look at Query Analyzer, the tool that allows us to get more out of the data we have. If you use Access, you will be familiar with queries – Query Analyzer is the tool that allows us to build sophisticated queries to manage our data.

As previously mentioned, this book builds up a simple example through which we can learn the techniques that will help us to use SQL Server 2000 more effectively. **Chapter 4** looks at why we need the sample database we build up, covering the basics of design and normalization, which is where the design is such that the database operates more efficiently, with particular focus on our chosen database solution.

Chapter 5 then looks at setting up the sample database that we will use throughout the book, while **Chapter 6** goes on to create and modify the tables that will hold the data that we need in our solution. Again, this is building on the knowledge of our solution that we have gained from previous chapters.

Another way to make our database more efficient is to give it a way in which it can identify data more easily – **Chapter 7** covers the topic of indexing data, which does just that. As the idea of a relational database is that the tables held within it are related to each other, we move on to look next at defining relationships between the tables in our database in **Chapter 8**. **Chapter 9** covers the topic of database diagrams, which is a graphical way of understanding how the tables, and therefore the data, within our database are related.

Now that we have a database, we don't want to have to build it all up again from the beginning if something should happen to get rid of it. So, **Chapter 10** covers backing up and restoring the data, just in case there are times in the future that our database mysteriously gets lost! In the same vein, we don't ever want to lose our database, or the data within it, so we need to come up with a plan to make sure that this never happens. To this end, **Chapter 11** looks at the topic of a database maintenance plan.

We now have a database, with tables, we have a plan to make sure we never lose it, and we know how to get it back if we ever do – but what about putting some data into the database to make it actually useful? **Chapter 12** moves on to looking at the different ways that data can be inserted into our tables in our database. In the same way, now that we have data, we want to be able to look at it in the future, so **Chapter 13** looks at how we can retrieve data from our solution according to our needs.

To err is human, and if it should ever happen that some data is incorrect, or has perhaps changed since we first put it into our database, we need a way of changing the data to reflect any changes. This is called updating, as we don't want to start again from scratch, simply update a record or two at a time. Updating data is covered in **Chapter 14**. Of course, it may be that updating is just not enough, and it would be better to start from scratch, so **Chapter 15** looks at the different ways of deleting data if it should no longer reflect our needs.

Now that we have our tables in place and populated with data, we may find ourselves frequently accessing a certain set of data, or we may want to exclude certain people from looking at some sensitive data that our database may contain. One way to do this is to create a view, which is a virtual table – it is simply a representation of the data in the tables, in which we can specify exactly which data should, and shouldn't, be seen by certain users. Views are the topic of **Chapter 16**.

Chapter 17 then moves on to look at stored procedures. Similar in some ways to a view, you will learn here exactly what a stored procedure is, how to use it, and how to build your own for your own purposes. As they are so useful and there are so many ways to use them, **Chapter 18** goes on to look at some more advanced areas of stored procedures as well.

SQL Server 2000 incorporates many new features, not least of which is the capability to use XML to retrieve data within our database. Using XML is not only new and exciting, but it means that we can take the interface to our data to the web, making our data a truly global affair. XML as a way of data retrieval is covered in **Chapter 19**.

The last chapter in the book, **Chapter 20**, looks at triggers, which are statements you can place in your database to automatically manage updating data. Basically, when an event that we have specified occurs, a trigger will fire another event that we have said should happen automatically. As you can imagine, the correct use of triggers can save us hours of work in updating the data if something should change, and reduces the risk of human error missing an update out, as we will have specified everything that should happen, and the trigger won't miss a thing.

Who is this Book For?

There are many reasons why you would want to read this book: perhaps you have seen the job market move from your chosen database to SQL Server 2000 and you need to know SQL Server 2000 to ensure that you continue to be a marketable commodity in the job market; or perhaps you wish to build on the skills you have acquired from your existing database knowledge, like Oracle, Sybase, Microsoft Visual FoxPro, Microsoft Access, etc.

This book is designed for novice database programmers or people familiar with a desktop solution, such as Access, who would like to scale up to SQL Server 2000.

What You Need to Use this Book

Ideally you will be running one of the following:

- Windows 2000 (Professional)
- Windows NT Workstation 4.0 with SP 5
- Windows 2000 Server
- Windows 2000 Advanced Server
- Windows NT Server 4.0 with SP5.

If so, everything you need is on the CD included at the back of the book. The CD contains an 120 day Evaluation edition of Microsoft SQL Server 2000 (Enterprise Edition). Steps and information on how to install this software and get started can be found in Chapter 1, *SQL Server 2000 Installation*, along with further information about the recommended hardware to run SQL Server 2000.

If you're running Windows 98, you will need the following:

- Microsoft Access
- MSDE (Microsoft Data Engine) – This is the stripped and scaled-down version of a SQL Server database engine. It comes with Microsoft Office 2000 Premium or Developer editions or can be freely downloaded from www.Microsoft.com if you have a license for Microsoft Visual software, such as Visual Studio, Visual Basic, Visual C++ etc.

Conventions

To help you understand what's going on, and in order to maintain consistency, we've used a number of conventions throughout the book:

When we introduce new terms, we **highlight** them.

> *Advice, hints, and background information comes in an indented, italicised font like this.*

Try It Out

After learning something new, we'll have a *Try It Out* section, which will demonstrate the concepts learned, and get you working with the technology.

How It Works

After a *Try It Out* section, there will sometimes be a further explanation within a *How It Works* section, to help you relate what you've done to what you've just learned.

Words that appear on the screen in menus, like the File or Window menu, or URLs for web sites that contain further information, are in a similar font to what you see on screen.

Keys that you press on the keyboard, like *Ctrl* and *Enter*, are in italics.

We use two font styles for code. If it's a word that we're talking about in the text, for example, when discussing `functionNames()`, `<ELEMENTS>`, and `ATTRIBUTES`, it will be in a fixed pitch font. File names are also displayed in this font.

If it's a block of code that you can type in and run, or part of such a block, then it's also in a gray box:

```
SELECT EmployeeName
FROM Employees
```

Sometimes you'll see code in a mixture of styles, like this:

```
SELECT DISTINCT
   ShipCity,
   ShipRegion,
   ShipCountry
FROM
   Orders
WHERE
   ShipCountry = 'USA'
   OR ShipCountry = 'Canada'
```

In this case, we want you to consider the code with the gray background in particular, for example to modify it. The code with a white background is code we've already looked at, and that we don't wish to examine further.

Downloading the Source Code

The source code for all of the examples is available for download from the Wrox site (see below). However, you might decide that you prefer to type all the code in by hand. Many readers prefer this, because it's a good way to get familiar with the coding techniques that are being used.

Whether you want to type the code in or not, we have made all the source code for this book available at our web site, at the following address:

http://www.wrox.com

If you're one of those readers who likes to type in the code, you can use our files to check the results you should be getting – this should be your first stop if you think you might have typed in an error. If you're one of those readers who don't like typing, then downloading the source code from our web site is a must!

Either way, it'll help you with updates and debugging.

Tell Us What You Think

We've worked hard to make this book as relevant and useful as possible, so we'd like to get a feel for what it is you want and need to know, and what you think about how we've presented things.

If you have anything to say, let us know at:

`feedback@wrox.com`

Errata & Updates

We've made every effort to make sure there are no errors in the text or the code. However, to err is human, and as such we recognize the need to keep you informed of any mistakes as they're spotted and amended.

More details on obtaining support, finding out about errata, and providing us with feedback, can be found in Appendix G.

SQL Server 2000 Installation

Welcome to the Beginning to SQL Server 2000. I assume that as you are reading this book you are interested in learning how to create solutions with Microsoft SQL Server 2000, but have no prior knowledge of SQL Server 2000. The aim of this book is to bring you up to a level at which you will very quickly become a competent developer with SQL Server 2000, and be ready to move on. This book is specifically dedicated to beginners, and to those who at this stage wish to only use SQL Server 2000. If you wished to use Visual Basic as well, I wholly recommend **Thearon Willis's** "*Beginning SQL Server 2000 for Visual Basic Developers*" (Wrox Press, IBSN 1-861004-67-2). By the end of this book, you will be ready to move on to what I consider to be the bible on SQL Server 2000, and that is "*Professional SQL Server 2000 Programming*" (Wrox Press, ISBN 1-861004-48-6), by **Robert Vieira**.

But let's get back to this book. I suspect that many of you are either new to developing on a database, or have experience with another database, but wish to learn SQL Server 2000.

In this chapter the following areas will be covered:

- Why SQL Server 2000?
- Now I have chosen SQL Server 2000, which edition should I choose?
- What hardware do I need?
- Can I just confirm that I have the right operating system?
- How do I know if my hardware meets the requirements?
- What can I do with SQL Server 2000?

We will also then look at installing our chosen edition – this section will cover:

- Installing SQL Server 2000 on a Windows 2000 platform
- Options not installed by default
- Where to install SQL Server physically
- Multiple installations on one computer
- How SQL Server runs on a machine
- How security is implemented
- Log on IDs for SQL Server, especially the `sa` (system administrator) logon

Why SQL Server 2000?

The following discussion is my point of view, which will no doubt differ from other viewpoints; however, the basis of the discussion will hold true. There is competition from other databases, not only from other Microsoft products, but also from competitors like Oracle, Sybase, DB2, and Infomix to name a few. Looking at Microsoft's own offerings, the other choices are Microsoft Access and Microsoft Visual FoxPro.

Access is a very prolific desktop database found on a very large number of users' PCs. The fact that it is packaged with Office 2000 has helped this; however, a great number of people actually do use the software. Unfortunately, it does have its limitations around scalability, speed, and flexibility, but, for many systems, these areas of concern are not an issue as the systems are small, in house, and do not require major database functionality. Access can also be used as a front end to SQL Server and Wrox have a book "*Professional SQL Server Development with Access 2000*" (Wrox Press, ISBN 1-861004-83-4), which shows how Access and SQL Server can be used together to make a very professional system.

Moving on to Visual FoxPro, this is the language with which I made my breakthrough into PCs in 1995. It's a good system that has the database and the GUI built in together, not unlike Access, but having the power of a GUI that you would find in Visual Basic. It is also very much Object Orientated and has beaten its other Microsoft rivals in this area over many years. It is only now with Visual Studio .Net that Visual Basic is catching up. Many Visual Basic programmers will find the previous statement controversial, but Visual FoxPro has been a stronger development platform than Visual Basic from many viewpoints.

Now we come to the competition, Oracle and Sybase. Oracle is seen as perhaps the market leader in the database community, and has an extremely large user base. There is no denying it is a great product to work with, and fits well with large companies with large solutions. There are many parts to Oracle, which make it a powerful tool, including scalability, and performance. It also gives flexibility in that you can add on tools as you need them, with more flexibility in that area than SQL Server. However, it isn't as user friendly from a developer's point of view, in areas like its ad hoc SQL Query tool, its XML and web technology tools, as well as in how you build up a complete database solution; other drawbacks include its cost and the complexity involved in installing and running it effectively.

Then there is Sybase. Yes it is very much like SQL Server with one major exception: the GUI front end – there isn't one. Sybase Adaptive Server Anywhere, which is mainly used for small installations, does have a front end, but the top of the range Sybase does not. To the purists, there is no need for one and GUI front ends are for those who don't know how to code in the first place – well, that's their argument of course, but why use 60+ keystrokes when a point, click, and drag is all that is required?

Sybase is also mainly found on Unix, although there is an NT version around. You can get to Sybase on an NT machine as well, using tools to connect to it, but you still need to use code purely to build your database solution. It is very fast, very robust and it is only rebooted about once, maybe twice a year.

Another thing about Sybase is that it isn't as command and feature rich as SQL Server. Each database has its own SQL syntax, although they all will have the same basic SQL syntax known as the **ANSI-92 standard**. This means that the syntax for retrieving data, and so on, is the same from one database to another. However, each database has its own special syntax to maintain it, and trying to use a feature from this SQL syntax in one database, may not work, or work differently, in another.

So SQL Server seems to be the best choice in the market place, and in many scenarios it is. It can be small enough for a handful of users, or large enough for the largest corporations.

Now that you know the reasons behind choosing SQL Server, you need to know which versions of SQL Server are out there to purchase, what market each version is aimed at, and which version will be best for you, including which version can run on your machine.

SQL Server Versions

There are seven different SQL Server flavors of the 2000 version around, plus another database engine, which is very similar to SQL Server 2000. Don't break out in a cold sweat – the next section will go through these editions simply and clearly, which will enable you to know exactly what each edition consists of, and what would be most suitable in specific work scenarios. The seven versions are:

- Enterprise
- Enterprise Evaluation
- Developer
- Standard
- Personal
- SQL Server CE
- Desktop

Although this may seem like a lot of choice, each version is specifically targeted to its own market place and has been developed, tuned, and priced to suit that area's needs.

Each edition in the following section will be described so that you know which edition will suit you best in your scenario if you need to go out and purchase for yourself, or your organization. Let's dive straight on in with the first edition, the Enterprise Edition.

Enterprise Edition

This is the Rolls Royce of SQL Server. This edition is the most powerful and will be the version installed in many large production environments. It is powerful, supports multiple processors and hardware options, includes Data Transformation Services, and gives developers everything that they may need. From your point of view, it will be when you move on to having a solution on the Internet, and when you use web development and have SQL Server as the back end to that site, that this edition is the one recommended for you. Don't worry if you have already bought the Standard or Developer Edition and you want to use the Enterprise Edition, as you can upgrade from any version to this version without any worries.

The **Enterprise Edition** includes every feature that comes with SQL Server. This ranges from the necessary Enterprise Manager, which is the main front-end tool for building your database solutions using a GUI, to Query Analyzer, which is a useful tool for entering code to work with data, as well as building database solutions. Also included are more complex tools that include the ability to set complex search criteria on your information, and areas concerning networks and multiple server based solutions. These last, more complex, items are way beyond the scope of this book, and are more for those who become much more advanced in SQL Server and perhaps take on more of a SQL Server management or database administrator role than that of a developer. There is also for a first time SQL Server developer a great deal in the Enterprise Edition, which could cloud your view on the more simple tasks that you will want to perform while getting up to speed.

I could be really boring and list all of the features and functions within the Enterprise Edition but this would get long winded as it would be necessary to explain what these functions are, which for someone reading a Beginners' book, at this point, would just fly straight over your head. After reading this book, if you want to learn more, there are many different ways you can progress: Wrox, as I will mention occasionally in this book at the right time, produces many high quality books that will be at your new level of understanding; there is also the Microsoft site dedicated to SQL Server, found at http://www.microsoft.com/sql/default.asp. These and other sources of help and further reading can be found in Appendix A.

The only other edition that comes close is the **Developer Edition**, which only really loses out on a single graphical interface for helping set language settings. So why pay a lot more money for Enterprise Edition when it seems that Developer Edition will do just as well?

It is not just the powerful utilities that have to be considered: it is also the scalability of the product. First and foremost, the Enterprise Edition has been developed for implementation on a server. Also, there is more memory required, or more memory is at least highly recommended, to run the Enterprise Edition. But where the real differences can be found is in the operating system requirements. To be able to run the Enterprise Edition must be installed on Microsoft Windows NT Server 4.0 (SP5), Microsoft Windows NT Server Enterprise Edition 4.0 (SP5), Windows 2000 Server, Windows 2000 Advanced Server, or Windows 2000 Data Center Server. Windows NT 4 Workstation is not supported. Also, you will find that only Enterprise Edition can run databases greater than 2GB. This sounds a lot, but once you get in to a live environment, you may well find that data gets close to that maximum. Finally, this book revolves around Windows 2000 Professional, and again, Enterprise Edition does not install on this operating system (although the Enterprise Evaluation Edition provided with this book will work on this OS).

These limitations aside, there is no real difference between Enterprise and Developer Editions, so unless you need to purchase Enterprise, I think you will find the Developer Edition to be just as good.

Enterprise Evaluation Edition

This edition can be used to evaluate the Enterprise Edition and has exactly the same power as the Enterprise Edition but with one exception: the Evaluation Edition does not have the single graphical interface for helping to set language settings, as found in the Developer Edition. This version will expire after 120 days of being installed. You may wish to start with this edition (especially as it comes free on the CD at the back of this book!) if you are unsure as to which edition of SQL Server you may require, as you do have 120 days to see what tools you will use and from there make your purchase decision. This edition will work on all operating systems except for Windows 98 and Windows CE.

Developer Edition

Moving on to inspecting the Developer Edition itself, as we have just discussed, there are few differences between this edition and the Enterprise Edition. There are two remaining items I have found to differ which have not been mentioned: the cost and licensing. The Enterprise Edition is a great deal more expensive than the Developer Edition. I will avoid quoting figures as each country will differ, as well as difference in prices between different suppliers, but that aside, for someone starting out on SQL Server, unless you have a big enough budget, then you will find the Developer Edition will work perfectly well and be powerful enough for your needs for this book, and beyond.

Secondly, if you install the Developer Edition on a server as opposed to a desktop, then you are in fact breaking the Microsoft licensing agreement, as this edition is only licensed for workstation use.

As I have mentioned, this is the edition that will be used within the book. It has almost the complete functionality of Enterprise Edition but is customized for the desktop and so will suit a developer perfectly without being clouded by network and server issues, as these will not be implemented.

Standard Edition

The standard edition doesn't have many of the server and network features found in the editions described above, although it does have a feature called replication.

Replication is where there are two identical databases and any modifications made in one database are copied to the other. This is found mainly when there is a need for an immediate backup of the data, or where there are offices in different locations, but you don't have a fast, or any, link between the offices all the time.

There are one or two major limitations though with this version, which make it unsuitable for this book. However, there is no reason that you couldn't buy this version if funds are limited. The only area that you will miss out on is working with indexed views. First of all, as I have indicated, this book revolves around Windows 2000 Professional, and Standard Edition does not install on this operating system. It does install on the three Windows 2000 Server editions and the two Windows NT Server editions. The operating system considerations for each edition come in a few minutes time. The second point involves an area that is covered much later in the book, where we cover taking a view of data, and making that view faster by indexing the data on it.

The Standard Edition is a much reduced version of SQL Server 2000, but if you are starting out, then it is an option to consider; however, it is only recommended that you choose this if you are unsure about whether you do really want to work with SQL Server, or if you are totally new to computing and unsure if you wish to pursue this path, or if money is a major issue.

Personal Edition

The Personal Edition is almost exactly the same as the Standard Edition, except that this edition does run on Windows 2000 Professional, Windows NT Workstation, and Windows 98. The feature list is the same as Standard Edition so again you come across the option, if you have Windows 2000 Professional and you have the same constraints or considerations as that for the Standard Edition, then the Personal Edition is the edition you need. Finding a common theme so far? However, I don't know the reason for these slight variations; the underlying SQL Server model exists no matter what edition, on whatever operating system, but these differences exist, so from these differences the choices have to be made.

If you are also a Visual Basic developer then this is the edition Thearon Willis uses in "*Beginning SQL Server 2000 for Visual Basic Developers*" (Wrox Press, ISBN 1-861004-67-2), which you should also read.

SQL Server CE Edition

Do you have a hand held computer that runs Windows CE? Do you need to have a database on it that is very limited in its functionality but will connect and work with a major database holding the full amount of information? Then look no further than Windows CE Edition of SQL Server. This version is really an organized repository for data for users on the move, for example, a traveling salesman who needs to keep product information close to hand. There isn't much to say about this edition, as there is not a great deal to it; after all, it has to fit on to a machine that may have very limited capacity.

Desktop Edition

So, you have written a SQL Server database solution on the Developer Edition, or any other suitable edition. You have a moderately large client base, but all are small independent vendors, for example. Perhaps the application is for a small sports club, a set of local hardware stores or something similar. They don't want to spend hundreds of dollars on just the database, never mind the solution you have built. So what do you do? This is where the Desktop Engine comes into the picture.

The Desktop Edition was known as Microsoft Data Engine (MSDE) in SQL Server 7.0. If you have used SQL Server 7.0, don't get confused by thinking that this is still the same version as the SQL Server 7.0 Desktop Edition, as it isn't. What was the Desktop Edition in SQL Server 7.0 is now the Personal Edition that we looked at a few moments ago in SQL Server 2000.

This is a version of SQL Server that has no interface, no administration facilities, and is purely capable of manipulating the information contained within it from the distributed databases built beforehand using another edition of SQL Server. Therefore it is used for running database solutions only and is not capable of administering the contents within it. It is installed along with your application and uses the Windows Installer service, which is a separate process within Windows, to install itself. So, no matter if your application uses InstallShield, Windows Installer or any install package, SQL Server 2000 Desktop Edition will install, as long as the Windows Installer is on the machine in question. There are a number of issues surrounding installation of this Edition for which, if this is an option to consider, I would read Books Online, and consult with the application developer, as it is outside the scope of this book.

Books Online is an optional addition that it is highly recommended that you install, as it is a very comprehensive help file for SQL Server.

Hardware Requirements

Now that you know which editions of SQL Server the book could use, the next big question on your list may well be: "Do I have a powerful enough computer to run these editions on? Will this help me refine my decision?"

Judging by today's standards of minimum specification hardware that can be bought, the answer will in most cases be "Yes" to most editions. However, you may have older hardware (things move so fast that even hardware bought a couple of months ago can quickly be deemed below minimum specification), so let's take a look at what the minimum recommendations are, and how you can check your own computer to ensure that you have sufficient resources.

CPU

The minimum recommended **CPU** that SQL Server will run on is an Intel Pentium 166 MHz processor, a compatible processor, or similar processing power. However, as with most minimums listed here, I wholly recommend a faster processor. The faster the processor the better your SQL Server will perform and from this the fewer bottlenecks that could surface. Many of today's computers start at 500 MHz or above and 166 MHz has not been the standard installation for a couple of years now. If you have a lower speed processor, try to invest in upgrading it. You will find your development time reduced for it.

However, it is not processor alone that speeds up SQL Server. A large part is also down to the amount of memory that your computer has.

Memory

Now that you know you have a fast enough processor, it is time to check if you have enough **memory** in the system. All the editions of SQL Server, with the exception of the Windows CE version, require a minimum of 64MB of **RAM** onboard your computer. Many of the editions that could be used will run with this, although you shouldn't have too many more applications open and running as they could easily not leave enough memory for SQL Server to run fast enough.

The Personal Edition and the Desktop Engine do have a minimum of 32MB of RAM if you are on Windows 98 or Windows NT, but I very much doubt if you will have 32MB of RAM on Windows NT as this is below the minimum for that operating system's requirements. So, if you do have NT and 32 MB of memory, this may explain a few things for you!

Moving the other way, if you wanted to run the Enterprise Edition, then a minimum, and I mean a bare minimum, of 128MB really should be installed, especially if you want to use any of the more advanced features.

The more memory the better: I really would recommend a minimum of 128 MB on any computer that a developer is using, with 256 MB ideal and sufficient to give good all round performance. If a process can be held in memory, rather than swapped out to hard drive or another area while you are running another process, then you are not waiting on SQL Server being loaded back into memory to start off where it left off. This is called **swapping** and the more memory, the less swapping could, and should, take place.

Taking CPU speed and memory together as a whole, it is these two items that are crucial to the speed that the computer will run and having sufficient will let you develop as fast as possible.

Hard Disk

Lots! But name a major application these days that doesn't need lots! For SQL Server alone, ignoring any data files that you are then going to add on top, you will need **250MB** of space. Certainly, the installation options that will be used later in the chapter will mean you need this amount of space. You can reduce this by opting not to install certain options, for example Books Online, however, even most notebooks these days come with a minimum 10GB, and 20GB is not uncommon either. Hard disk space is cheap as well and it is better to buy one disk too large for your needs than have to have one hard drive that suits now, and then buy another later with all the problems then of moving information to clear up space on the original drive.

Again, you will need spare space on the drive for the expansion of SQL Server and the databases, as well as room for temporary files that you will also need in your development process. So think big – big is beautiful!

Screen Resolution

Talking of big is beautiful, the larger the screen and the higher the screen resolution the better as well. The barest of minimums is 800x600 VGA, but I really do think this should be **SVGA** and at least **1024x768**. As you go through the book, you will see that the wider the screen, the easier it is to see things and figure out what is going on. The other side to the coin with this, though, is that by increasing the resolution, the characters may be too small and you have to struggle to see the screen; if this happens, by all means choose a resolution that is comfortable to you.

Other Hardware Considerations

Of course, SQL Server comes as standard on a **CD-Rom**, so a CD-Rom player or a **DVD** player that can read CD-Roms (I am referring to some external models here mainly that don't read CD-Roms), is essential, if not connected to your computer, then at least accessible over the network that your computer can attach to.

It is also useful to have some sort of **backup** device handy for when you want to perform a backup of a single, or several databases.

If you are connected to a network, be aware that SQL Server cannot backup to a tape device that is not directly connected to your computer.

NTFS, FAT, and Compressed File Systems

In Chapter 5 you will come across two terms, **Data files** and **Transaction Logs**. In essence, they record the data within the database, and what the database does. These files can quite happily sit on an **NTFS** file system, and also a **FAT** file system – these are two different ways of storing data physically on a hard drive, used by differing operating systems, but you find that, these days, you have a choice. It is not worth discussing these file systems here, as you will have already made your choice on your computer; however, you may also be short on spare disk space, so you may be thinking of compressing your hard drive. Well, I hate to be the bringer of bad tidings, but you cannot install SQL Server on a compressed file system. If you are really that short of disk space, you will have to find something already installed that you can remove, or get another hard drive. To be honest, as I have said, disk space is so cheap these days, getting another hard drive should be an available option to you, and compressed drives do slow down system performance.

Operating System Requirements

You will find that SQL Server 2000 is no longer supported on a Windows 95 operating system, with the exception of **Client Tools** or **Connectivity Only**. In plain English, what this means is that on a Windows 95 machine there is a limited functionality available to you. Taking the easiest option first, Connectivity Only: by installing this option, this will just allow the computer to connect to SQL Server for application development. There will be no SQL Server interface, therefore no development of a database solution can take place, only connection to an existing solution. The second option, Client Tools, gives a limited amount of SQL Server functionality: for example, tools to allow access to SQL Server through URLs, or even ad hoc queries. There is also limited availability for managing SQL Server. However, in essence, this allows a computer to interact with a SQL Server database on a different computer or server.

Windows 98 will only support installations of the Personal and Desktop Edition. SQL Server utilities are supported on Windows 98, so it is possible to develop a full solution using Windows 98. You will also find that the only way to log on to SQL Server 2000 with the server installed on Windows 98 is to use the security within SQL Server itself, and there will be no security available through the operating system. This is called **SQL Server Authentication** or **standard authentication**. There will be more on this when you read about Windows NT/2000. However, if the SQL Server installation is itself on Windows NT/2000 and you are logging in on a Windows 98 machine, then it is possible to use operating system security, known as **Windows Authentication,** or **trusted authentication**. Don't worry too much about the authentications discussed here, as there is more about this later.

You can run SQL Server 2000 on Windows NT 4 providing that you have installed service pack 5, or above, and where you see Windows 2000 Professional, this relates to Windows NT Workstation.

Finally, Windows 2000 Professional can have Personal and Developer installed. This operating system, along with any of the Windows 2000 versions can have SQL Server or Windows Authentication on it, which is a crucial security issue that will be mentioned later.

However, I haven't covered every combination, so here is a table detailing which edition works with which operating system. This is probably the last item of information determining which edition you will in fact install on your computer.

SQL Server Edition	Operating Systems that can have the edition installed
Enterprise	Microsoft Windows NT Server 4.0
	Microsoft Windows NT Server Enterprise Edition 4.0
	Windows 2000 Server
	Windows 2000 Advanced Server
	Windows 2000 Data Center Server
Standard	Microsoft Windows NT Server 4.0
	Windows 2000 Server
	Microsoft Windows NT Server Enterprise Edition
	Windows 2000 Advanced Server
	Windows 2000 Data Center Server
Developer	Microsoft Windows NT4.0 (Server and Workstation)
	Windows 2000 (all editions)
Personal	Microsoft Windows Me
	Windows 98
	Windows NT Workstation 4.0
	Windows 2000 Professional
	Microsoft Windows NT Server 4.0
	Windows 2000 Server
	and all the more advanced Windows operating systems
Desktop	Microsoft Windows NT Workstation 4.0
	Windows 2000 Professional
	and all other Windows NT and Windows 2000 operating systems

Obviously, Windows CE will only support SQL Server 2000 CE.

How Can You Tell?

I have thrown many pieces of information at you that you need to know about your computer. So how do you go about finding out if you have the necessary setup for SQL Server? Luckily Windows provides utilities that can help you out. This section will take you through how to find out the necessary information on your computer. Although this will be completed on a Windows 2000 Professional machine, the principles and area to look at are similar on all the other Microsoft operating systems.

Try It Out – Finding Your Computers Setup

1. We are first going to check our screen resolution. So, from the Start button, click Settings | Control Panel.

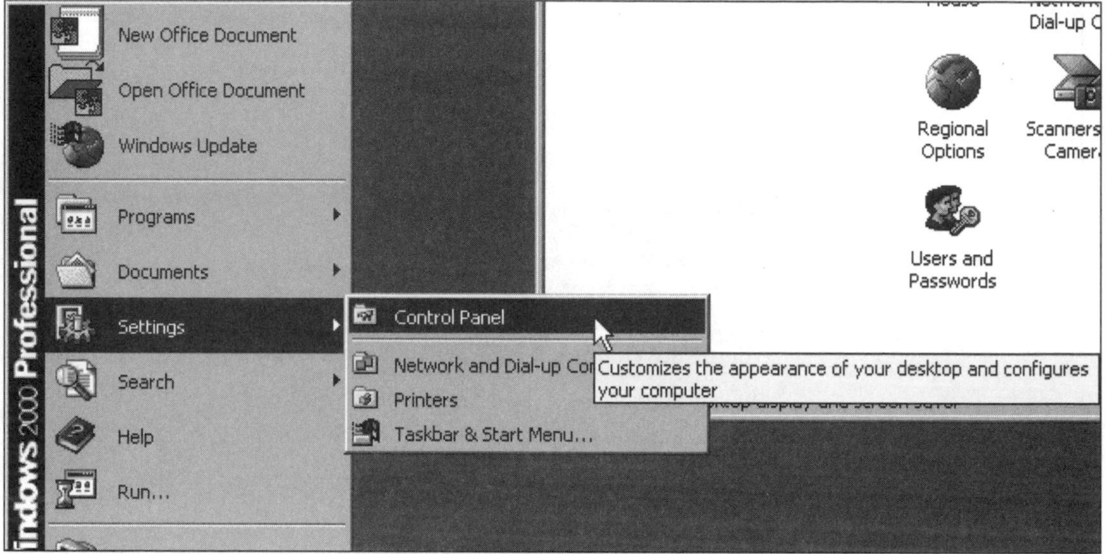

2. Within the panel, you will find an icon called Display. Double click on this.

3. This brings up the Display Properties form, which is shown after this text. As you can see, clicking on the Settings tab, reveals that I am running with a resolution higher than the recommended minimum and it is at a safe level for me.

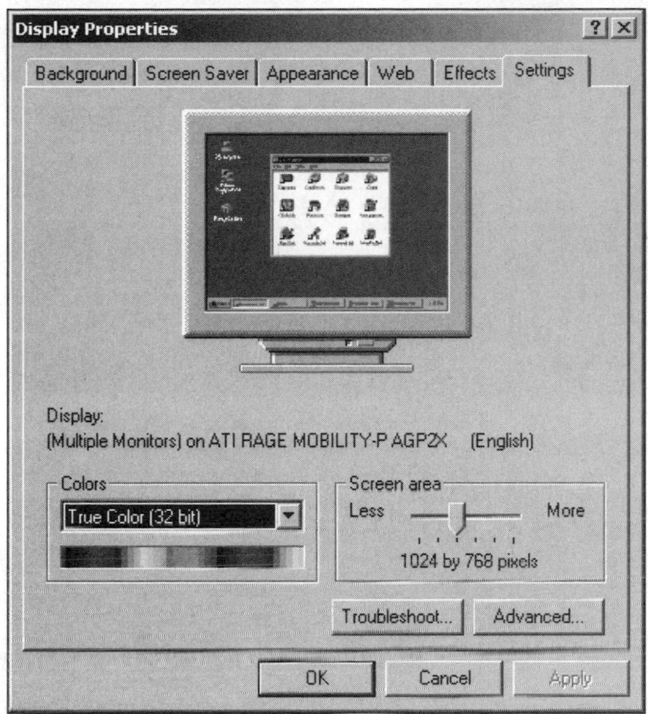

4. So that's the easiest one covered, screen resolution. If you close that down by clicking OK, and move back to the control panel, you will see the Administrative Tools icon.

5. We are now going to check our resource requirements. Double click the Administrative Tools icon, which brings up the Administrative Tools panel. Locate the Computer Management icon and double click on this.

6. After a few moments this gives a whole raft of information. First of all, you will notice near the bottom Total Physical Memory, which shows the memory defined as 130,544 KB. This equates to 128MB, which is ample for my needs. Above this and half way down, the next two pieces of information are about the CPU. System Type is demonstrating that it is X86-based, which means that it is an Intel, and then the Processor, at the end of the line of information, confirms that it is a GenuineIntel running at approximately 600 Mhz.

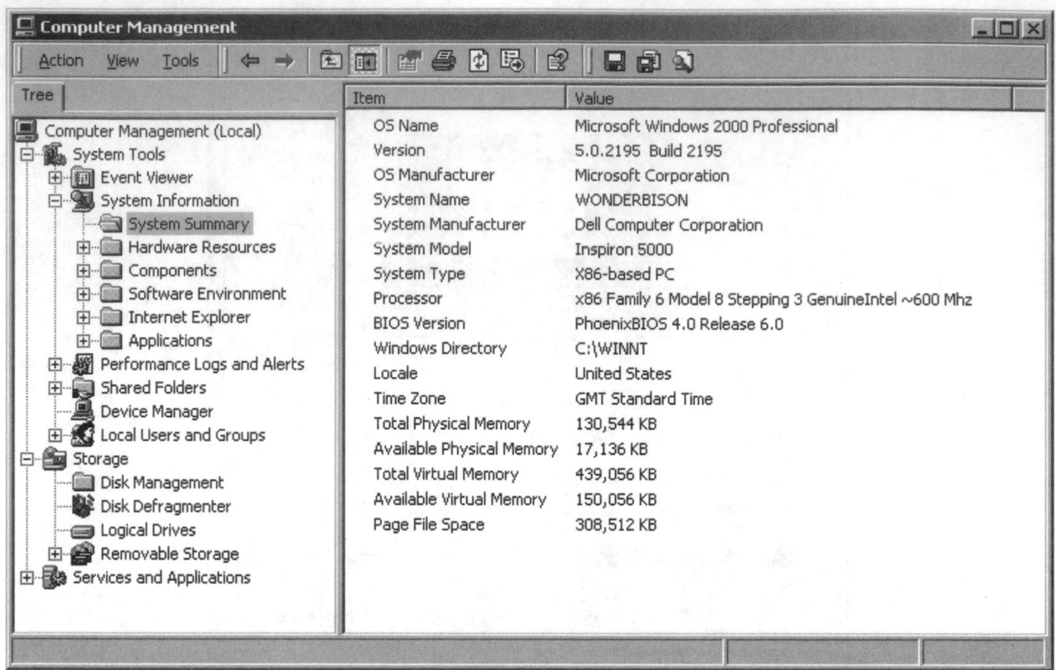

7. Staying within the **Computer Management** form, move to the **Components** node, and then down to **Storage** and the **Drives**. This will then bring up the information about your hard drive(s). Notice that I have highlighted the **Size** of the hard drive, and just below, how much is left, **Free Space**; just over three and a quarter gigabytes, well over the 250 MB recommended, so I have more than enough.

Item	Value
Drive	A:
Description	3 1/2 Inch Floppy Drive
Drive	C:
Description	Local Fixed Disk
Compressed	False
Size	8.89 GB (9,543,557,120 bytes)
Free Space	3.38 GB (3,624,853,504 bytes)
Drive Description	Disk drive
Drive Manufacturer	(Standard disk drives)
Drive Model	IBM-DARA-212000
Drive MediaLoaded	True
Drive MediaType	Fixed hard disk media
Drive Partitions	2
Drive Size	12068904960 bytes
Drive	E:
Description	Local Fixed Disk
Compressed	False
Size	2.34 GB (2,511,011,840 bytes)
Free Space	1.51 GB (1,626,632,192 bytes)
Drive Description	Disk drive
Drive Manufacturer	(Standard disk drives)
Drive Model	IBM-DARA-212000
Drive MediaLoaded	True
Drive MediaType	Fixed hard disk media
Drive Partitions	2
Drive Size	12068904960 bytes

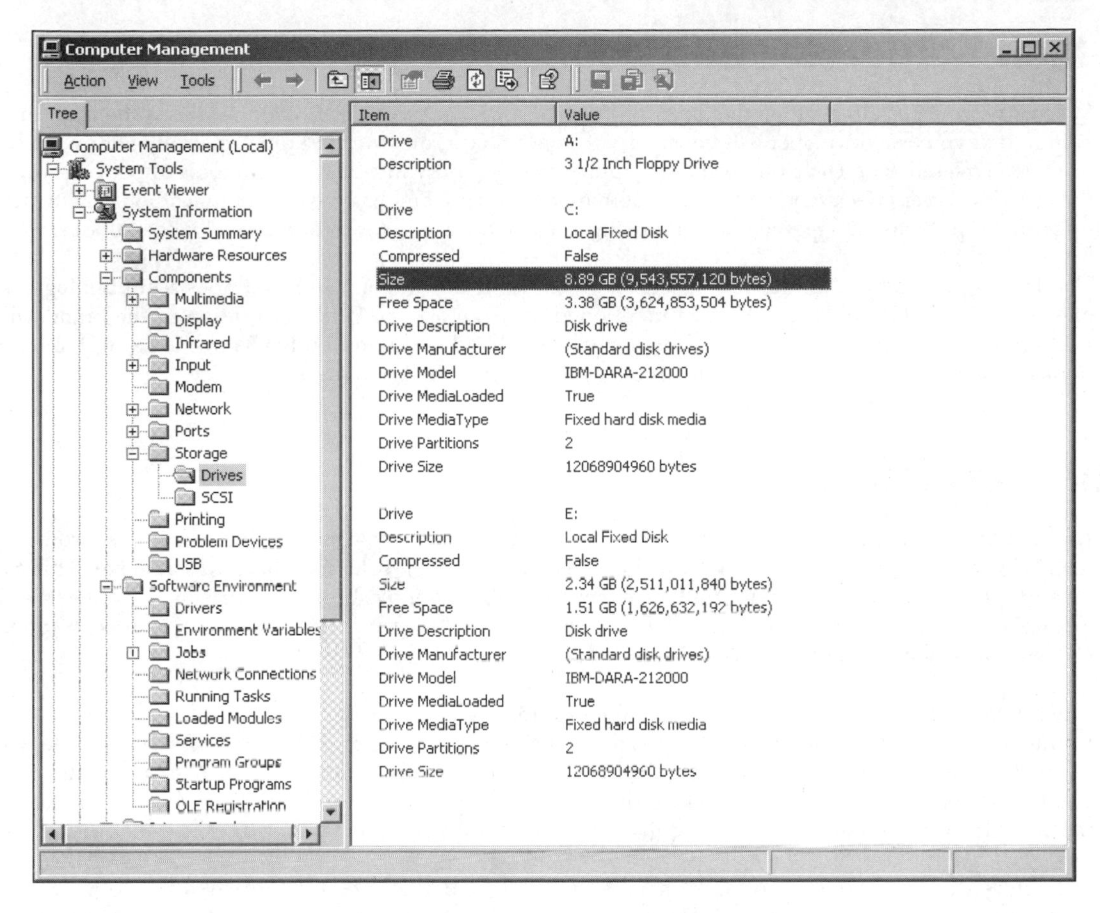

8. Finally, I need to check if I have a CD or DVD ROM on my machine. By moving to Components/Multimedia/CD-ROM you will see that I do have a TOSHIBA DVD-ROM, which is capable of CD-ROM capabilities, as the Media Type has defined. Of course, I could always look at the front of the machine, but that wouldn't tell me if it was suitable or not!

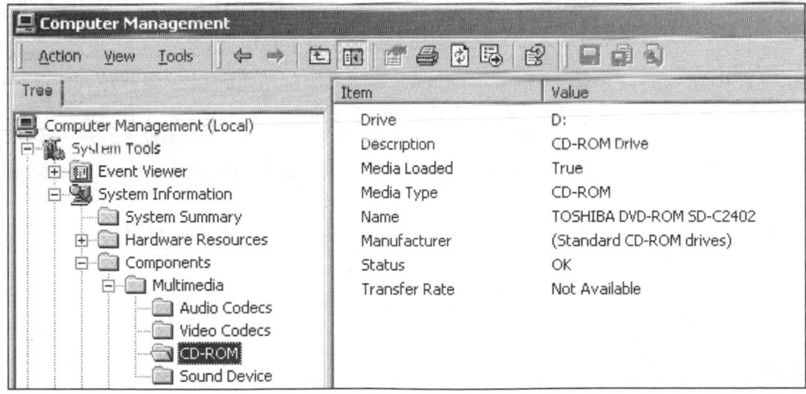

So, my computer is more than capable of meeting the requirements to run SQL Server.

Which Edition for this Book?

We will be concentrating within this book on the SQL Server Developer Edition, as this is the most likely edition that you as a developer will have, or will want to have, on your desktop, especially after what has just been covered. The Developer Edition supplies the necessary information and tools to perform your job as a developer effectively, on the most common platforms, and has the capability without having to upgrade, or purchase an upgrade, when moving to more advanced tasks, or more advanced books.

The Developer Edition, as the name suggests, really is for developers, and so it does seem the logical choice, and it is. However, as has been mentioned, you can use the Personal Edition or the Standard Edition for nearly all of this book, but then when you do advance on to other Wrox Press SQL Server books, you may find that there is functionality missing on your installation.

The Example

In order to demonstrate SQL Server 2000 fully, we have decided to develop a system for recording details about a sports club, the players within the club, and the results that the teams achieve. This can be any sports club, from rugby to football, soccer to netball, ten pin bowling to baseball. So, even if the example in the book is not about your favorite sport, it will be very easy for you to alter it. The sport chosen for this book is golf.

The book builds on this idea and develops the example demonstrating how to take an idea and formulate it into a design with the correct architecture. It should be said though, that the example will be the bare minimum to make it run, as I don't want to detract from SQL Server. The book will give you the power and the knowledge to take this example, expand it to suit your sports needs, and give it the specifics and intricacies that are required to make it fully useful for yourself.

But before we can get to this point, we need to install SQL Server, and then discuss the two most important tools that come with SQL Server so that you know what is happening. All of this follows in the rest of the book.

Installation

Now that you are aware which SQL Server version can perform which tasks on the relevant operating systems, it is now time to install this from the CD-ROM. This book will be concentrating on the Developer Edition.

This chapter will guide you through the installation process and cover many of the options and combinations that can be completed within an installation. A number of different tools are supplied with SQL Server to be included with the installation. We will look at these tools so that a basic understanding of what they are will allow us to decide which to install.

Installation covers a great many different areas:

- Security issues
- Different types of installation – whether this is the first installation and instance of SQL Server or a subsequent instance, for development, test, or production
- Custom installations

Most of these areas will be covered so that by the end of the chapter we can feel confident and knowledgeable to complete any subsequent installations that suits our needs.

Installing SQL Server 2000 Developer Edition

Let's now take the time to **install** SQL Server 2000 on our machines. As we discussed earlier, the Developer Edition is probably the best edition for the needs of most developers. Although this book comes with the Enterprise Evaluation Edition, as this is free to use for a time limited period, the differences between this and the Developer Edition, at least from a beginner's viewpoint, are very limited and it is only when you move into very advanced topics that there are the couple of differences. Therefore, there is no conflict if you install the Enterprise Edition or the Developer Edition.

The Developer Edition is most suited to our needs as there is no need for all the functionality of the Enterprise Edition or some of the advanced features that may be used in a production environment. The Developer Edition is also a great deal cheaper than the Enterprise Edition if we decide to buy it. The Enterprise Edition, or even the Personal Edition, should be sufficient for most of this book if you already have them installed.

Insert the Microsoft SQL Server 2000 Developer Edition CD in your CD-ROM drive and start the installation. What we will cover is a standard installation, which most of you will also go through.

Try It Out – Installing SQL Server

1. Ensure that if you are using Windows NT or Windows 2000, you have logged on to your machine with administrative rights. Administrative rights will allow files and folders to be created on your machine, which is obviously required for installation to be successful.

2. If, when placing the CD-ROM into your computer, the installation process does not automatically start, open up Windows Explorer and double-click on **autorun.exe**, found at the root level of the CD-ROM.

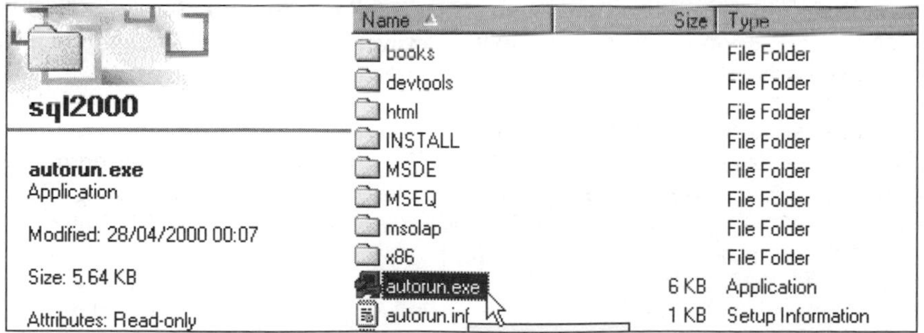

3. You are now presented with the Microsoft SQL Server 2000 Developer Edition installation screen. Select **SQL Server 2000 Components**. We only need to be concerned with the SQL Server 2000 Prerequisites option if we are running on Windows 95. This allows components required for SQL Server Client Connectivity to be installed onto a Windows 95 machine. As this book is based on a Windows 2000 installation with Windows 98 in mind, as well as Windows NT, then this option can be ignored, because the required components are already installed.

   It is also possible to read documentation about SQL Server before installing, and this can be accessed through the Browse Setup/Upgrade Help and the Read the Release Notes options on the right. If you don't wish to read these notes now, you can come back to them later. Finally, if the web site is where you would like to go, you can click on the Visit Our Web Site link. Alternatively, you can visit the site at any time with the URL: http://www.microsoft.com/sql/default.asp.

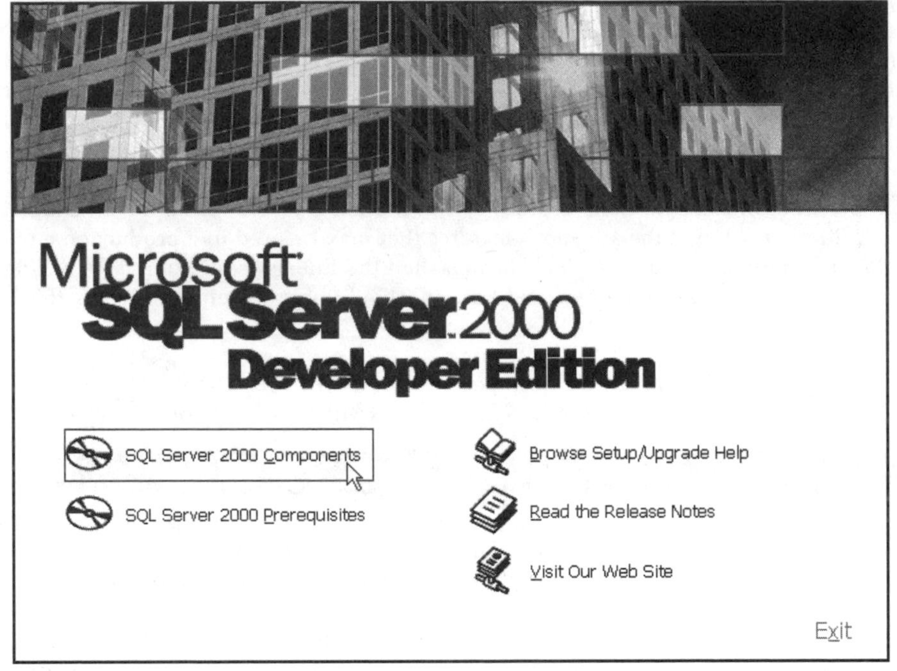

4. The next screen lists the SQL Server Components. Choose Install Database Server. The only option that this book is concerned with is the installation of SQL Server, and so the Install Database Server option will do just that. However, it is worth taking a moment to briefly explain what the other two options are, even though we will not use them.

   Selecting the Install Analysis Services option gives SQL Server the tools to perform **OnLine Analysis Processing** (**OLAP**). OLAP allows complex analysis of data stored in SQL Server databases. This area is covered in "*Professional SQL Server 2000 Programming*" (Wrox Press, ISBN 1-861004-48-6) as well as "*Professional Data Warehousing with SQL Server 7.0 and OLAP Services*" (Wrox Press, ISBN 1-861002-81-5).

Selecting **Install English Query** will give SQL Server the ability – after a fair amount of work by the developer on a fair sized database – to allow users to create queries on the data that are phrased very much like the English language. A user could enter something like, "Supply a list of customers that have bought the Acme Roadrunner Seed Enticer in the last month, who live in Warner Brothers Village" – as you can see, there is a lot of information that SQL Server would have to interpret. However, it is possible, and English Query is the tool that can do this. English Query works by taking an English Query, using the model and information built up within an English Query application, and turning the English Query into an equivalent SQL statement to provide the answers that the users are looking for.

5. After a few moments, once InstallShield has completed its own set up, you will be presented with the Welcome screen. Click **Next** to continue with the installation or **Cancel** if you decide not to continue with the installation at this time.

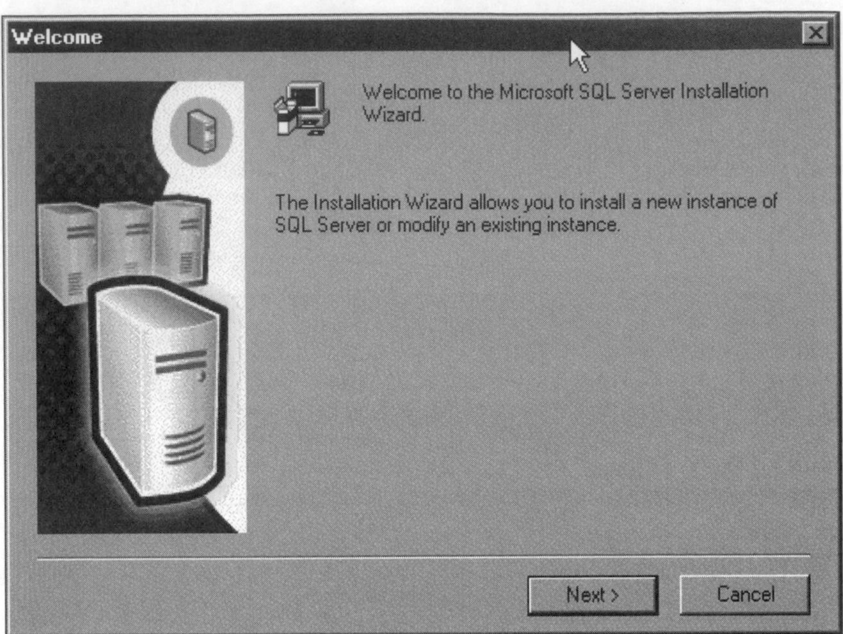

6. You now have the choice to install SQL Server on your local computer or on a remote computer located on the network.

   There are three types of SQL Server Installations – these are on the **Local Computer**, which is the option that this book will be following, on a **Remote Computer**, and on a **Virtual Server**. Installing on a local computer means that SQL Server will be installed on the computer that the setup is running on. By the way, if you are installing SQL Server client tools, installation on a local computer is the only option available.

   The second available option is to install on a **Remote Computer**. If the installation is to be placed on a computer other than your own, but one that can be accessed by your computer, then the **Remote Computer** option should be selected. Choosing this option will physically place the SQL database on the remote computer, and doing so requires a networked connection to that remote computer. From there it is possible to either enter the computer name, or to browse for the computer. This option is used when SQL Server is installed in a clustered environment.

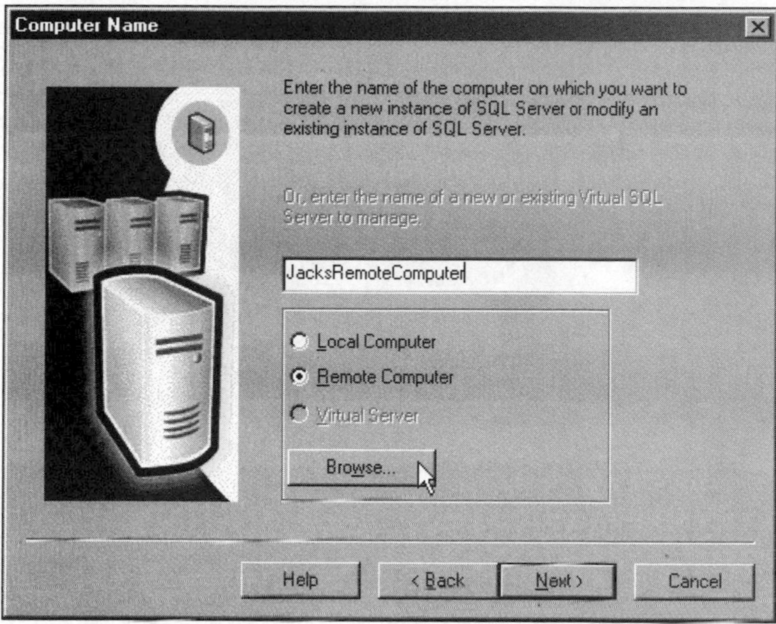

The final option, Virtual Server, deals with the ability to resort to a second computer when the first computer fails. To define this second computer, also known as a failover, you would use this option. If you wish to know more about this, then check out "*Professional SQL Server 2000 Programming*" (Wrox Press, ISBN 1 861004-48-6). Virtual Servers require that Microsoft Cluster Services (MSCS) be installed.

Let's leave the options as they are, so that a local installation is created.

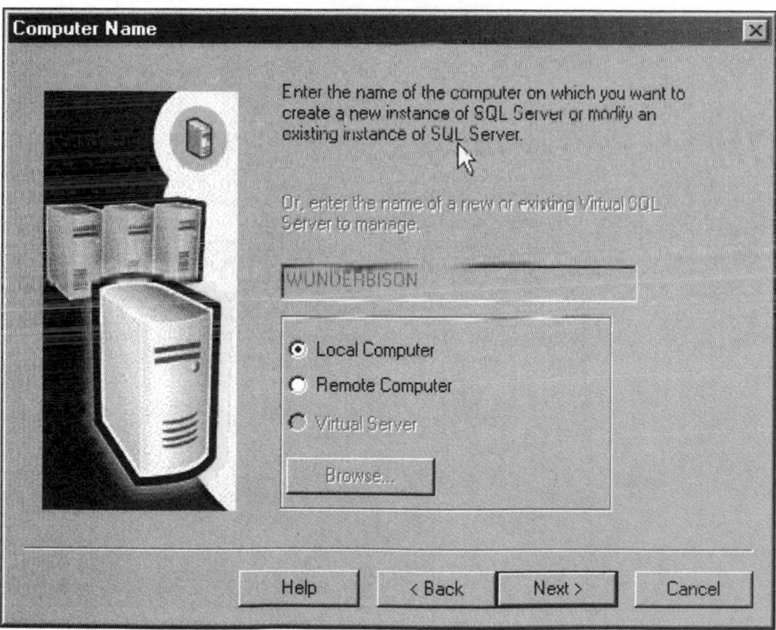

7. If you are upgrading from a previous version of SQL Server, then the upgrade option will be selected. Otherwise select: Create a new instance of SQL Server, or install Client Tools.

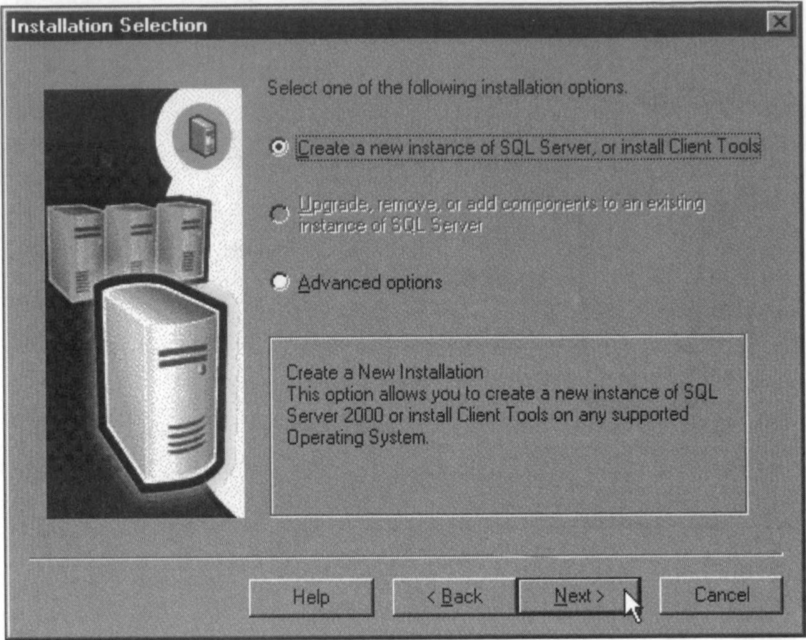

8. It is now time to enter your name, and any company name. As you can see, the relevant fields have already been populated. You may find that the details are pre-filled from the registry – using data from either a previous installation of SQL Server, or other Microsoft products.

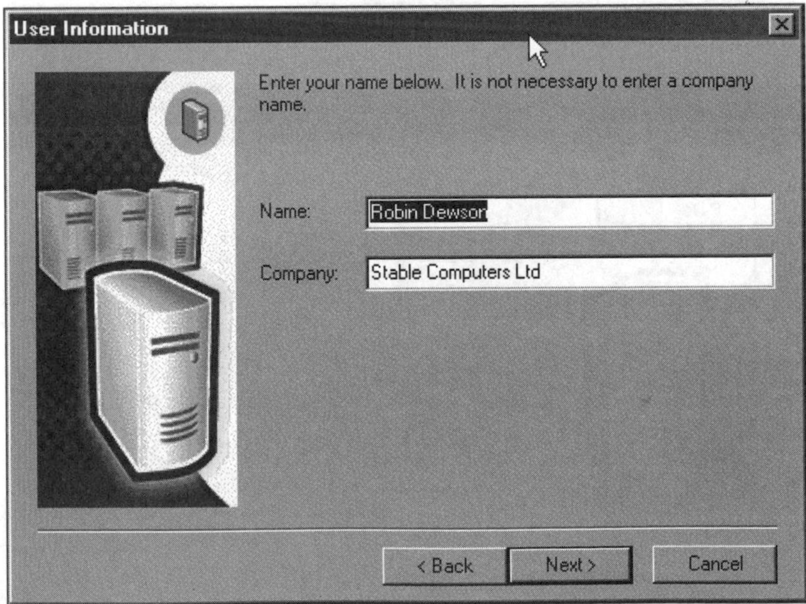

9. After accepting the software license agreement you will be given a choice of three different installations that can be performed. Providing you are on a Windows 2000 or Windows NT box, Server and Client Tools should already be selected for you. This is the option that will install SQL Server on any computer specified, remote or local, and will also install all the tools to connect to a SQL Server installation on a remote computer and administer SQL Server.

Performing a remote installation requires admin privileges on the remote computer.

10. Click Next. The other two options will be discussed later, in the section titled *Other Types of Installation.*

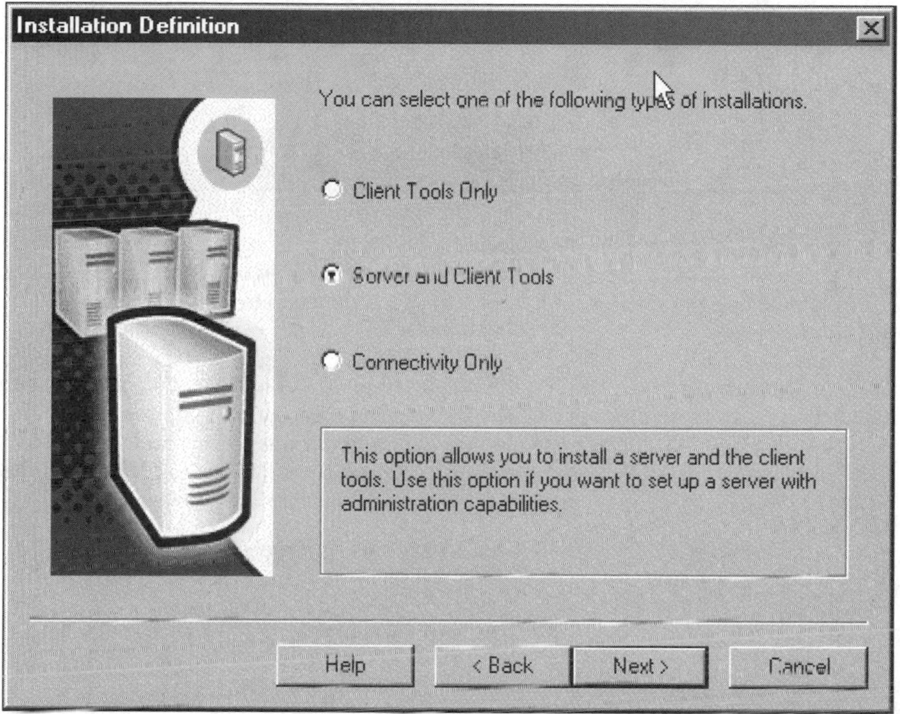

11. The next screen asks for the name of the SQL Server instance. Leave the selection as Default, unless you already have a version of SQL Server installed that you wish to keep, or you want to install more than one instance of the server. More on this later in the chapter where we cover multiple installations.

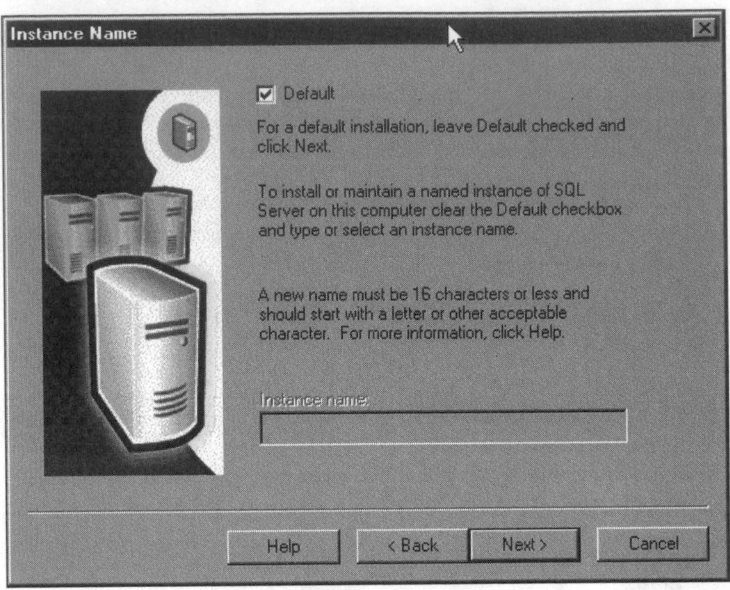

12. We are almost at the end of the setup instructions now. This next screen concerns which parts of SQL Server we wish to install. Leave Typical installation selected as this installs all of the components. See the section on *Other Types of Installations* later in this chapter for details on the other options.

Change the directories if you do not wish to use these defaults (that is, if you need to install to somewhere with more disk space – see the previous section on system requirements). The Program Files and the Data Files are two independent directories and will hold their own specific information. It is strongly advised not to place the program files within the same folder as the data files for several reasons – mainly backup and security.

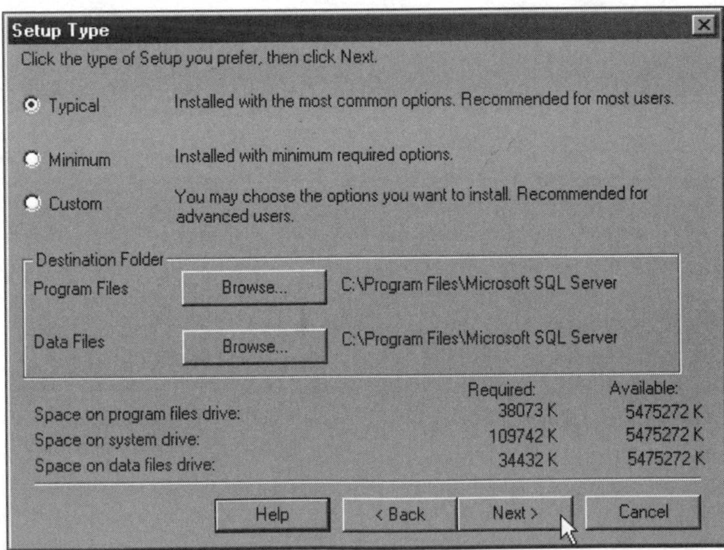

13. The Services Accounts screen sets up security preferences and will be explained further in the *Security* section later on in this chapter. For now use the defaults that the installation suggests, not forgetting to enter a password for the Domain account. You may find, though, that you wish to use the local system account if you are on a standalone machine.

If you think that you are not going to be using SQL Server on a regular basis after installation, then you may wish to use Customize the settings for each service option and leave the Auto Start Service box at the foot of the screen unchecked. This will stop SQL Server being started each time your computer reboots. We demonstrate how to start SQL Server in Chapter 2 if you don't have SQL Server already started when you reboot your computer. By turning off the Auto Start Service, you will reduce the amount of time it takes to boot up your computer and also increase the amount of resources left, as SQL server will slow down boot up and use up resources on the computer, even if it is doing nothing.

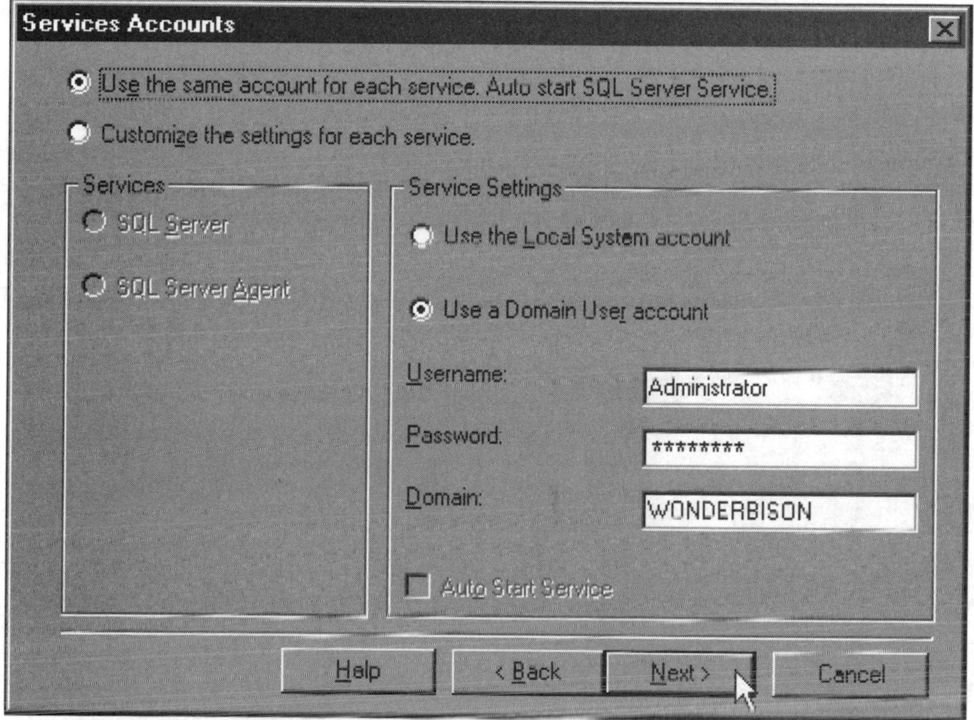

14. The next screen is one of the most important screens in the installation process. This covers what type of access to SQL Server you want to allow. Select Mixed mode (more on this later). It is also recommend to enter a strong password for the sa login.

> **Never, ever leave the password blank for the sa login! It is just asking for trouble and leaving a big security hole in your system. Also, never make the password one that can be easily guessed. The stronger the password – for example, using letters and numerics in any combination is perhaps the strongest method – the better!**

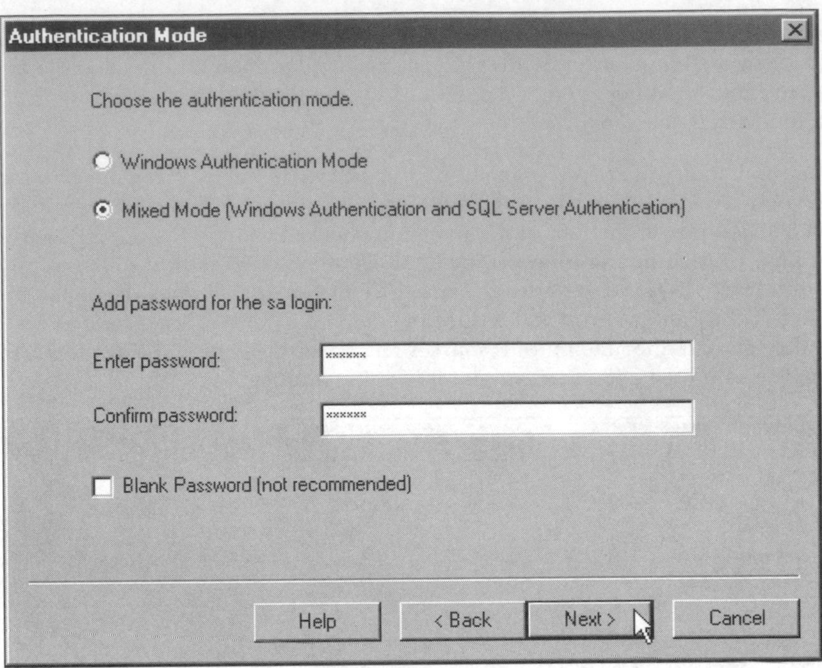

15. You are now at the final screen. When you click **Next** InstallShield will start copying files onto your computer.

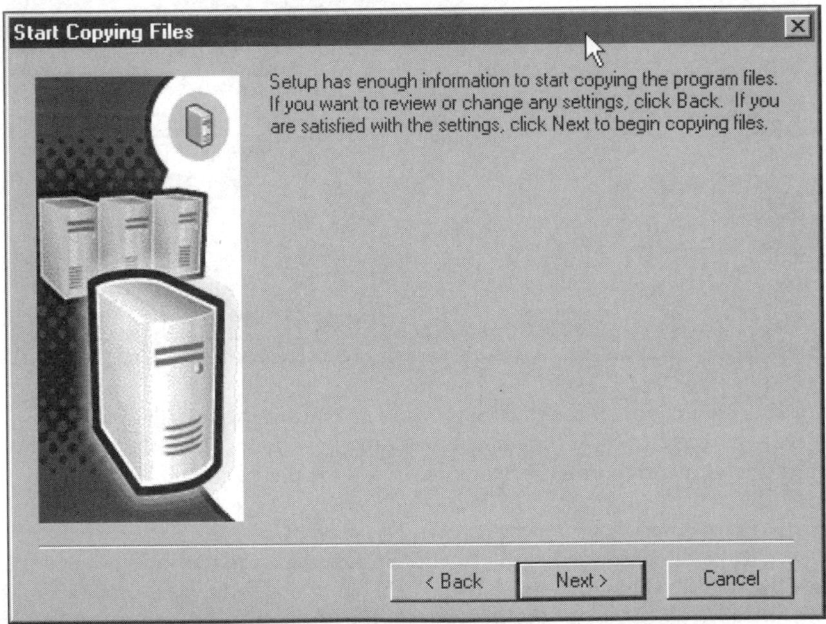

16. You will see a few pop-up screens like the following (which is in fact installing **Microsoft Data Access Components, MDAC**, a form of data access)..

MDAC is the data access method for SQL Server and other data connections such as Excel, which enables a computer to access data using ADO, OLE DB, or ODBC as the programming interface to the data from an application. It is important to keep up to date with this technology, and any updates can be found at http://www.microsoft.com/data.

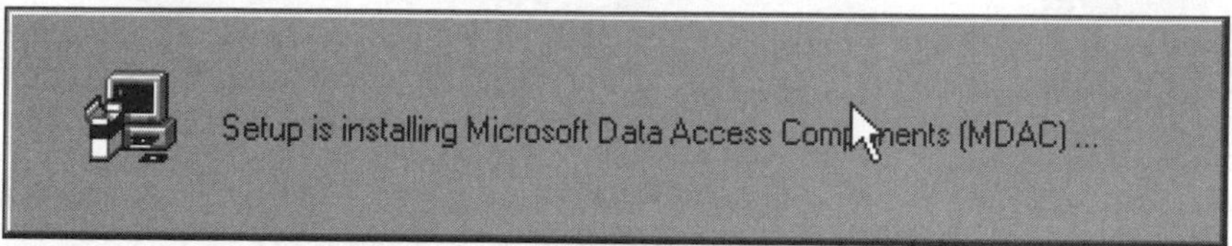

17. Once everything is installed, you should see an information screen.

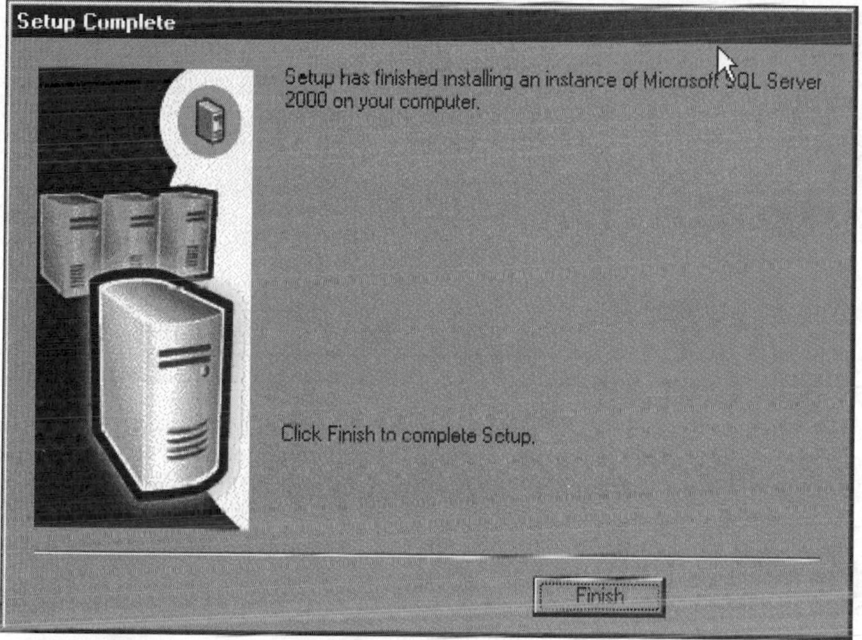

Now that you have successfully installed SQL Server, let's go through the installation in detail and cover what the options are and how it works. If you are not advised by the setup to reboot, then it may be advisable to do so anyway to ensure that you are starting with a clean machine.

Advanced Options

The Installation Selection screen is used to determine what sort of installation to perform.

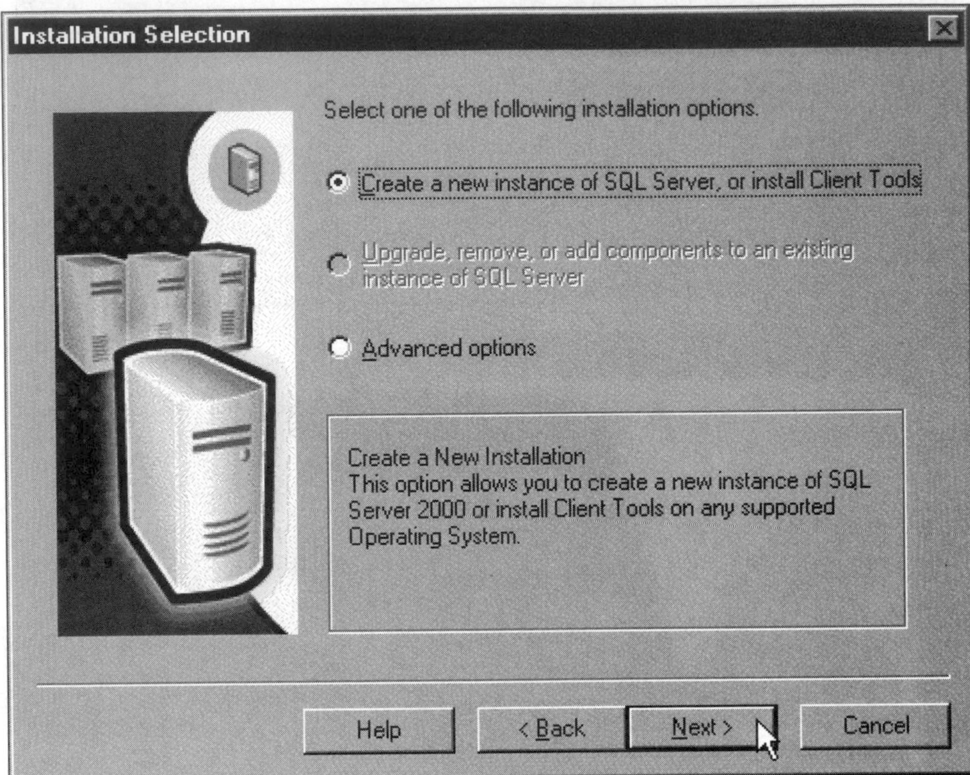

On first install only two options will be available to you. However, if there was already an installation of SQL Server, the middle option – Upgrade, remove, or add components – would be available. This would allow the modification of the existing installation, including the addition of components. Keep this in mind for the following screens, so that you realize how to upgrade the installation. We cover looking at installing second and subsequent installations later in the chapter.

Before looking at the first option, we'll take a moment to cover the Advanced options. Selecting this option and clicking Next will display the following dialog:

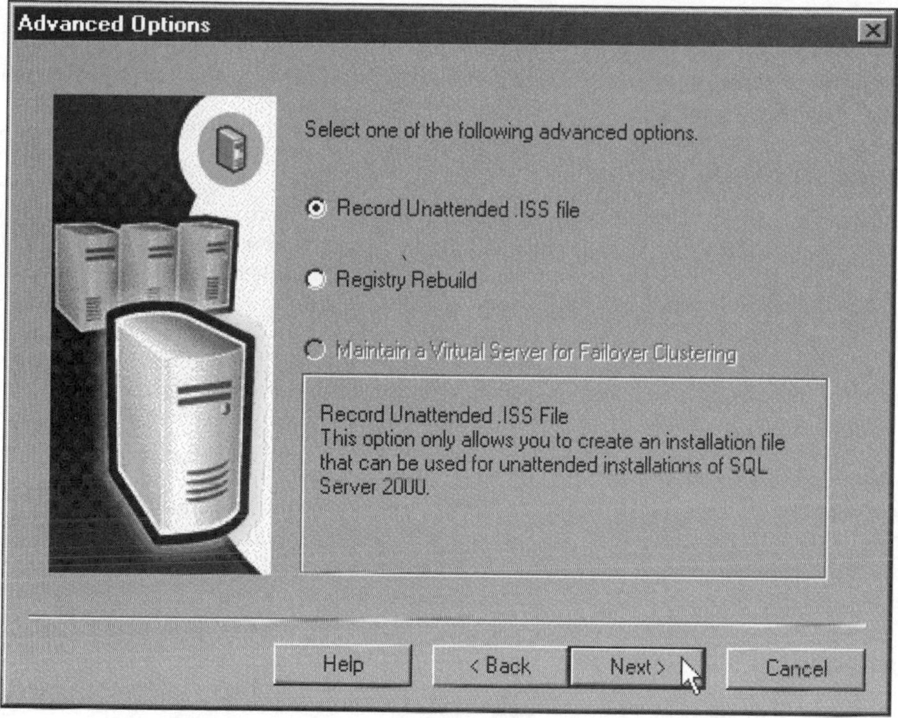

If it was one of our tasks to create an instance that other users in your company could use to install SQL Server, then this is possible from the **Advanced options** selection. We will still go through the remainder of the installation process, but instead of installing SQL Server an unattended installation file will be created by selecting the **Record unattended .ISS file** option. This is of great use should you need to perform several identical server installations, because each unattended installation will proceed without requiring any additional setup information.

If you find that the SQL Server entry in the registry has been corrupted, then it is possible – by selecting the **Registry Rebuild** option and going through the remainder of the installation process – to rebuild the registry, rather than install a new instance of SQL Server. Note that this option doesn't repair corrupted databases, just a damaged registry.

At this point we won't worry about the third option: **Maintain a Virtual Server for Failover Clustering**. This is a large area in itself, and Failover clustering is quite an advanced topic, which is covered in "*Professional SQL Server 2000 Programming*" (Wrox Press, ISBN 1-861004-48-6).

Let's now get back to the first option on the previous screen. This will be the option to select for the installation required in this book, which is a new instance of SQL Server.

> *It is possible to have more than one SQL Server instance installed on your computer, each holding its own information. This would allow a development server and perhaps a system testing server. Using the* **Create a new instance** *option would allow these two servers to be installed. This would then allow two separate instances of data that are totally separate from one another and so provide two separate environments for specific types or instances of testing. Also, you will no doubt have a second instance for production!*

Other Types of Installation

We discussed installation types previously, as well as options for connecting to a SQL Server database, or installing client tools only.

The Connectivity Only Option

The easiest option – Connectivity Only – installs only the software components needed to connect to SQL Server. These are the ODBC drivers and Microsoft Data Access (MDAC) components. Taking this a bit further, the SQL Server installation would add to the computer **ODBC drivers** and **MDAC 2.6**, which must be installed to connect to SQL Server. But what are these?

ODBC is an open industry standard; it is short for Open DataBase Connectivity. This is a method that computer programs use to connect to any sort of data source that has an ODBC **driver**. You can have ODBC drivers for any data source, not just SQL Server. ODBC drivers exist for Oracle, Sybase, Visual FoxPro, Access, Excel, even text files. Connecting to text files is a method for connecting to legacy data stored in very old systems, but it is still used in database systems like Access, and Visual FoxPro. You can, in fact, use ODBC from most languages currently commercially available, especially those you are likely to use with SQL Server. ODBC allows applications to communicate with different databases without the applications needing to pay any attention to which particular vendor database they are connected to. ODBC is the link between the program and the data.

Client Tools Only

The Client Tools Only option will only install the tools that deal with the Client side of SQL Server 2000. These tools include Enterprise Manager, Query Analyzer, connectivity through MDAC, and Books Online. This also includes the ability to connect to a client version of SQL Server or to connect to a SQL Server on a remote computer. SQL Server is not installed and therefore you have to connect to an existing SQL Server installation.

Multiple Instances

SQL Server 2000 permits multiple instances to be installed on the same computer. Typically you would install a Default instance and add additional named instances as required. This would be done when you get to the Instance Name screen.

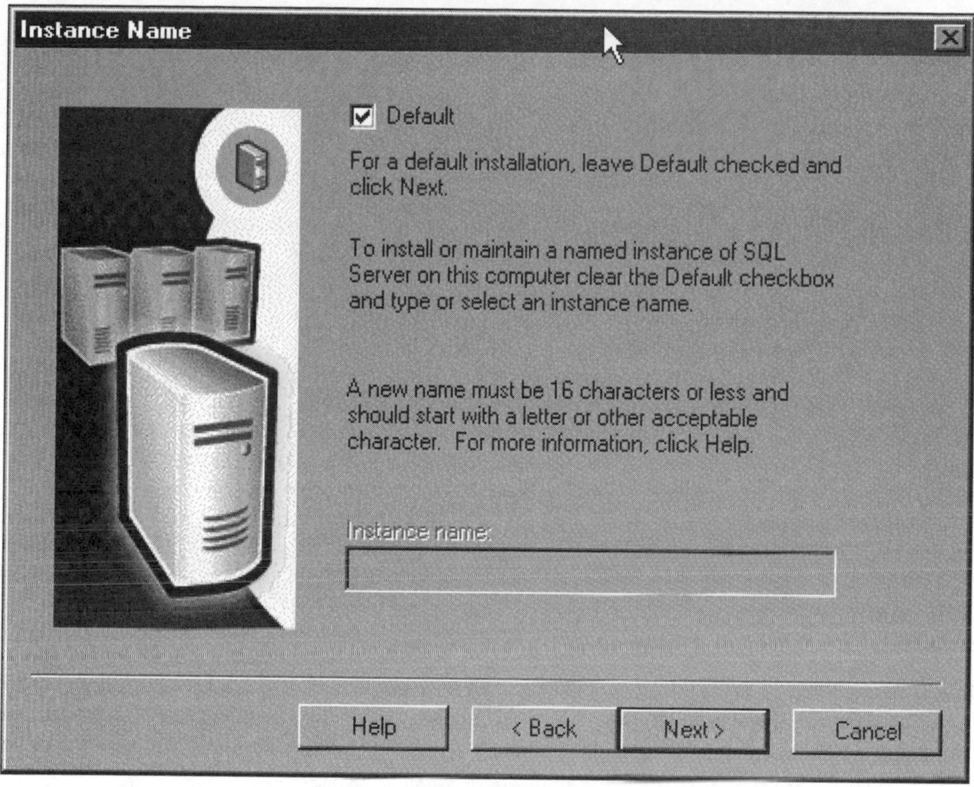

This is a simple screen that allows an installation to have a specific name attached to it. This can be useful if we want to run a development server and system test server on the same machine. By unchecking the **Default** box (if this is a subsequent installation this box will be unchecked and disabled already) the second instance name of SQL Server can be entered.

The two different instances of SQL Server will run separately, and are in fact, placed in separate directories. As you can see in the following view of the directory structure in Windows Explorer, a second instance of SQL Server has been installed on one machine. This was achieved by having already installed SQL Server for this book, and then going through the installation process again. The name SYSTESTSERVER was entered in this dialog. You will see in the following screenshot that this name is prefixed with MSSQL$. This is a naming standard used by SQL Server for installations.

Any new installation has its own directory structure in the Microsoft SQL Server directory. Therefore we can be safe in the knowledge that any modifications to the data or structures in one database will not filter through to any other instances. This is all controlled through **Enterprise Manager**, which is the tool used by DBAs to work in SQL Server most of the time.

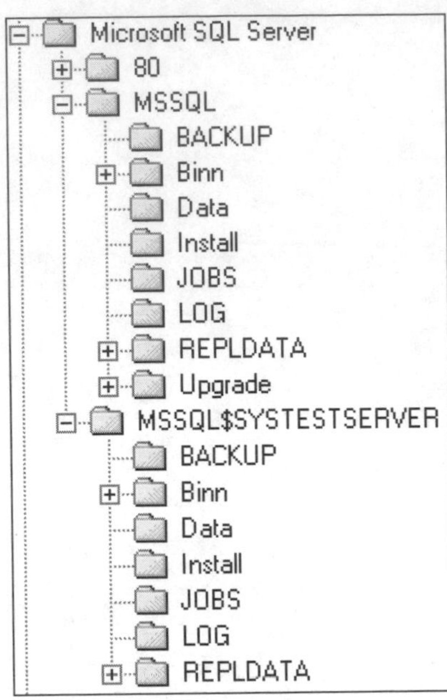

However, one instance of Enterprise Manager will run both servers. There is a bit of fiddling to be done, which will be covered in the next chapter, so that you know how to use a development server as well as a test server. Enterprise Manager can manage multiple instances of SQL Server, as seen in the next screenshot:

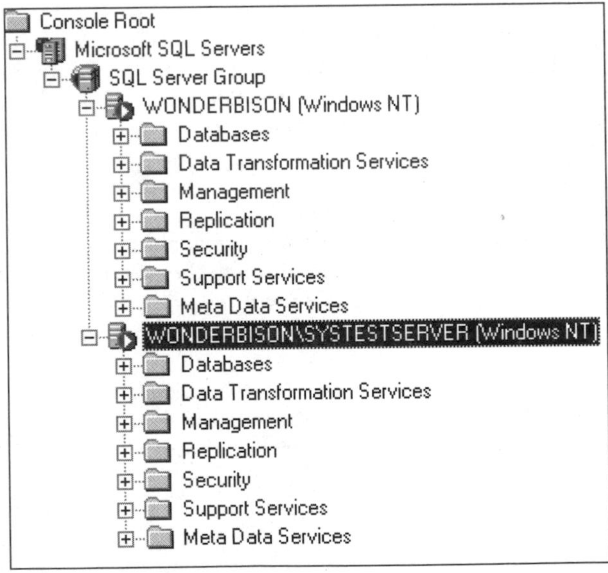

Now that you have chosen the type of installation, and the instance information, the whole installation process needs specific information for that installation process to complete. The first items of information concern what options you wish to be installed, as well as where this instance of SQL Server will be installed.

Typical, Minimum, or Custom?

SQL Server allows some control over the components installed with each instance. The **Setup Type** screen allows us to set different choices.

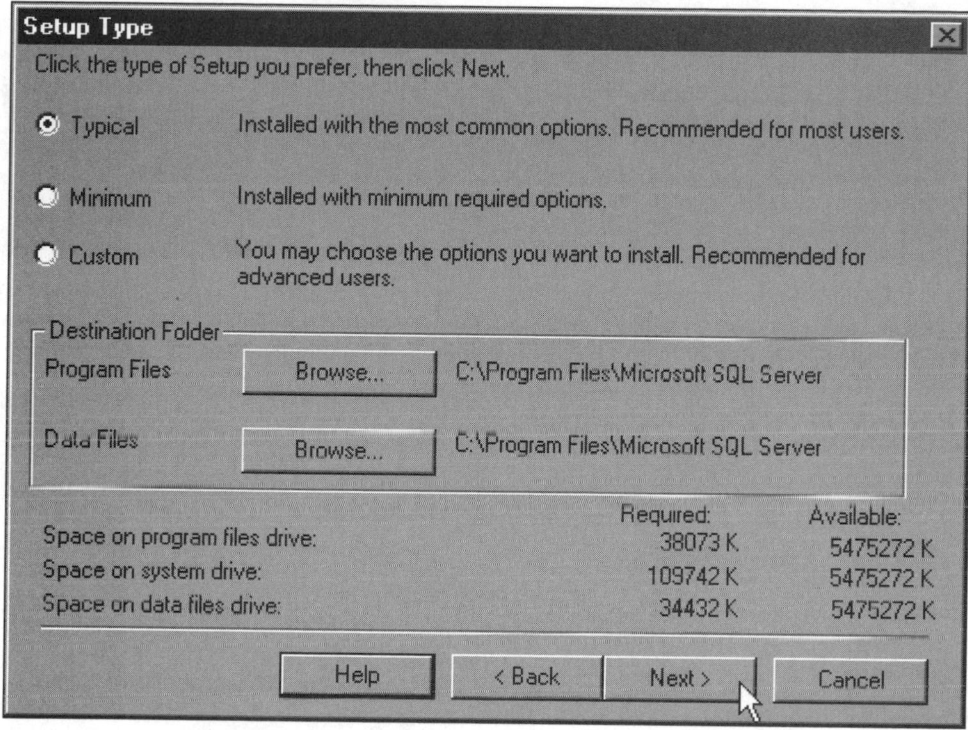

This section will cover the tools installed so that you can make an informed and knowledgeable judgment on which option suits you now and for the immediate future. We can use the installer to update components at a later date.

Typical

By selecting this option the following tools will be installed:

- Database Server – this is the SQL Server Engine itself. Without it, you won't have SQL Server installed on your machine.
- Upgrade Tools – used to upgrade data from a previous version of SQL Server (such as SQL 6.5 or 7) to this one.
- Replication Support – we can use this tool to mirror everything happening in one SQL Server. This is an advanced feature and not covered in this book.
- Full Text Search – allows advanced search features. This is covered in "*Professional SQL Server 2000 Programming*" (Wrox Press, ISBN 1-861004-48-6).

- Client Management Tools – this includes Enterprise Manager, which is perhaps the most important tool as it is the interface with SQL Server. There are also a few other tools, including Query Analyzer. This tool is covered in Chapter 3, and it is the second most important tool. These are the tools that will be installed with the Client Tools Only option shown earlier in the chapter.
- Client Connectivity – this is software that is used as the interface between software on a client machine and a SQL Server database on a server. The data and instructions have to be marshaled between these two entities and it is the Client Connectivity tools that perform this function.
- Books Online – online help when you can't put your hands on a good Wrox book!
- Development Tools – most of these items are for developers of C or Visual Basic code. They include an interface that can be used for debugging stored procedures in a program.
- Code Samples – samples demonstrating how to write programs that use SQL Server.
- Collation Settings – defines how the data is stored within a database. Collations can be case sensitive or non case sensitive, among many other characteristics, which then defines in which order the data is stored. More on this in Chapter 6 when the database for our example is created.

The Typical Installation will install enough tools for us to work with, plus a few more when we are ready for them. Providing you have plenty of disk space, this is the best option to go for, and the option recommended. The only options not installed is program examples for developers. and program examples for developers.

Minimum

Minimum Installation installs the following:

- Database Server
- Replication Support
- Full Text Search
- Client Connectivity
- Collation Settings

All of these have been discussed previously. Even for a minimum installation, which is usually chosen when disk space is short, or when you only require the minimum tools of SQL Server, there are still some powerful tools installed, specifically Replication Support and Full Text Search. They only take up 7MB of space; however, this might be the difference between a successful installation, and an unsuccessful installation. By selecting this option, not all of the tools necessary to use this book to its fullest potential will be installed. Minimum installation could also be installed when you have a production server that only requires the minimum tools for the developed solution to work.

Custom

Finally we come to the Custom Installation. The Typical Installation provides all the tools we need to use this book. On the other hand, by selecting this option, space could be saved on the Typical Installation detailed above. The options selected are detailed below, with an indication of which ones could be de-selected while still having the right tools installed to use this book. Again, like the Minimum Installation, you would use this to install the tools necessary for your production server for the developed solution.

- Management tools
  - Enterprise Manager – essential. This is the application used to configure SQL Server.
  - Profiler – used to interface with SQL Server system tables detailing major "events" which have happened (for example logins etc). Optional; not covered in this book, but handy to have at times.
  - Query Analyzer – essential. This is the second main interface used in this book.
  - DTC Client Support – optional. Only used to extend transactions across multiple servers (advanced).
  - Conflict Viewer – mandatory. You cannot de-select this. It is used when you have replicated servers and when there is a conflict of data updates.
- Client Connectivity – optional. Depends if SQL Server is on a remote server and you are connecting from a client. Uses the MDAC components installed.
- Books Online – optional, but if you can afford the disk space, about 35MB, then it is recommended to install this.
- Development tools – optional. Unless you wish to use VB or C++ or another language, then these tools are not required and could be de-selected.
- Code Samples – optional – but use the same arguments as the Development Tools if you wish to install them.

Destination Folder

When selecting what type of installation to perform, you can also alter the destination folder for the installation. In the previous screenshot, you will see that both the program and the data files are set to be installed on the `C:` drive of the local computer. If you are performing a local installation then these two options are best left as they are, or if you have more than one drive or partition on your computer, then you may wish to have the program files on one partition and the SQL Server data files on another.

When installing on a remote computer on a network then you may have on the server different partitions, or anchor points, for specific functions. For example, if the remote computer was called `RCNY05` for remote computer New York, number 5, then you may find that this has a partition called `APPS` and another partition called `APPSDATA`. You would then place the program files on `\\RCNY05\APPS\Microsoft SQL Server 2000` and the data on `\\RCNY05\APPSDATA\Microsoft SQL Server 2000`. This all depends on how your organization has servers defined and set up.

Security

To discuss the Services Accounts dialog properly we need to delve into the area of Windows security.

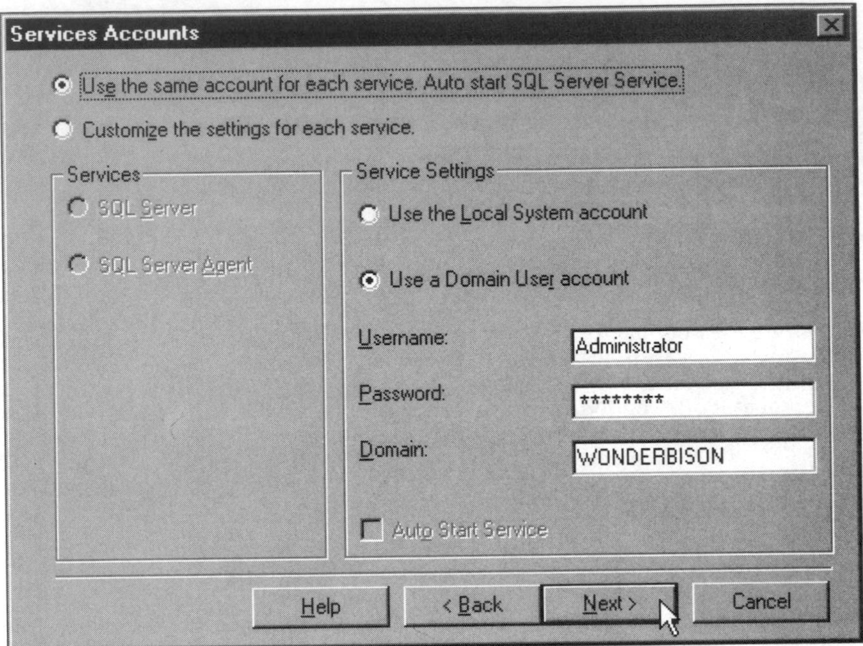

In this section we will first discuss the concept of Windows services as opposed to programs. We will then see how the fact that SQL Server is run as a service influences security settings. Later we will be discussing different types of authentication we can choose when installing SQL Server.

Services Accounts

On Windows NT/2000 machines, SQL Server runs as a Windows **Service**. So what is a service? First and foremost, a service has absolutely no user interface. There will be no form to display, and no user input to deal with at run time. The only interaction with the process runs either through a separate user interface, which then links in to the service, but is a totally separate unit of work (for example, Enterprise Manager), or from Windows management of that service itself. Any output that comes from the service must go to the Event Log, which is a Windows area that stores any notification from the services that Windows runs.

A service can be set to start automatically before any user has even logged on; all other programs require a user to be logged in to Windows in order for them to start. A good example of a service is be any anti virus software that runs continuously from when the user restarts the computer to the point that the computer shuts down. A program, on the other hand, either runs, or it doesn't. It is either loaded in memory and running, or not started. So what is the advantage of running a service? When you have a unit of work that can run as a service, Windows can control a great deal more concerning that process. Having no interface means that the whole process can be controlled without human intervention. This then means that, providing the service is designed well, Windows can take care of every eventuality itself, and can also run it before anyone has even logged into the computer.

In most production environments SQL Server will be running on a remote server, one probably locked away in a secure and controlled area, possibly where the only people allowed in are hardware engineers. There probably isn't even a remote access program installed as this could give unauthorized access to these computers. SQL Server will run quite happily and hopefully never give an error. But what if, one day, there is an error? If this was written as a program, some sort of decision has to be taken. Even if SQL Server crashed, there at least has to be some sort of mechanism to restart it. This means another process needs to be run, a monitoring process, which in itself could give a whole ream of problems. However, as a service SQL Server is under Windows control. If a problem occurs, whether with SQL Server, Windows, or any outside influence, Windows is smart enough to deal with it through the services process.

Let's take a moment to see more about Windows services. Understanding this will help slot the first part of the security jigsaw into place.

A few prerequisites before we start the example:

- The following section only applies to Windows NT/2000 (since services aren't supported under Windows 9x). The specific examples are for Windows 2000 (the screens will be slightly different for Windows NT).

> **Within a Windows 95/98/ME machine, you don't have the luxury of services, as the operating system is built differently so that everything has to run as a program.**

- Make sure that the installation is complete before you attempt this example.
- This example will only work if the user logged into the machine has local admin rights assigned to them.

Try It Out – Windows Services

1. Click Start | Settings | Control Panel.

2. Find and double click Administrative Tools.

3. Find and double click Services.

4. Scroll until you see MSSQLSERVER.

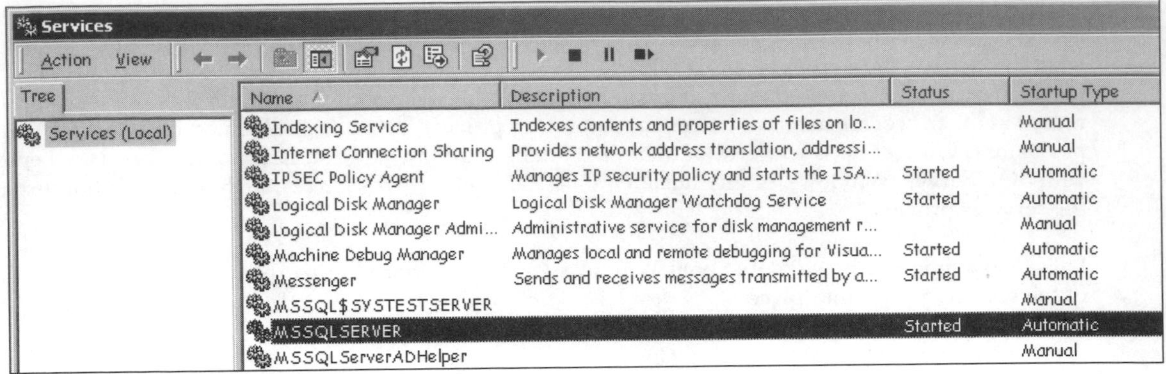

5. Right-click and select Properties.

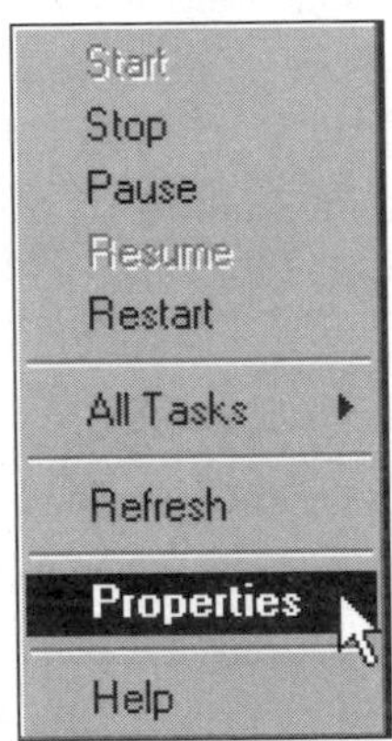

6. The first tab (General) we see contains the name of the service, the component that implements it, and the ability to start, stop, pause, and resume it.

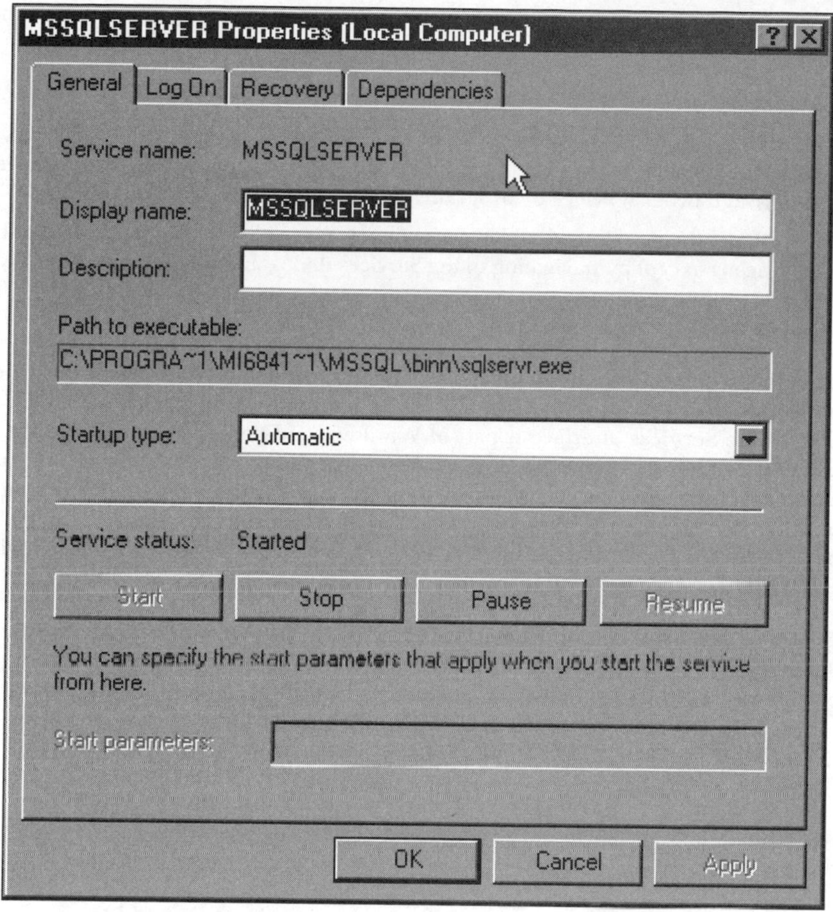

The Service name is the physical name given to the service that SQL Server can link to an actual executable. This is the name that you will see in SQL Server Service Manager as well as Enterprise Manager.

The Display name is the actual name that is listed in the Services Management Console only. Although it is possible to alter this, unless the service is a service built within your organization that you are in control of, leave this as it is. Altering the name could in fact confuse any one else wishing to investigate the service at a later stage. For services built within the organization, placing some details in the Description: field is probably a wise move. If nothing else, it helps others to understand the service.

Path to executable is the physical location where you will find the program that is run as a service. You will notice that good old MS-DOS naming convention regarding long filenames still survives in the executable name. I still haven't figured out why!

The next section is the interesting part of this dialog. The Startup Type determines how the service will start up when Windows restarts. There are three possible options:

- Automatic – when Windows reboots this service will start.
- Manual – when Windows boots up this service is not started. We could start the service either by moving to the Services screen and then starting up the service using the buttons or through other services or programs (for example Query Analyzer).
- Disabled – this service is disabled and will not start with Windows, and cannot be started by any means except by navigating to the Services dialog and altering the startup type to Manual.

The Service Status gives information about the state the service is in.

Next comes a set of four buttons that allow manual control over the service, which are all self-explanatory. However, doesn't it go against the grain of a service to have a GUI interface to it? No, as the Services interface is part of Windows and passes commands to the service, which acts on them. There is also the occasional need for manual control. For example, you can access services on one computer remotely with the same interface. Users with this control tend to be system administrators who stop the service if they are doing a full back up. The service itself will determine the level of security, but for SQL Server you may wish to ensure that security is tight to stop unwanted access stopping a SQL Server.

Some services can take in options at run time that will determine actions that they take, for instance how they start up, and it would be here that you define those. So, if the service accepted any Start parameters, the grayed out box at the bottom would be available for use.

7. The second tab is titled Log On, and shows security information. The username and password are the ones entered during the installation process.

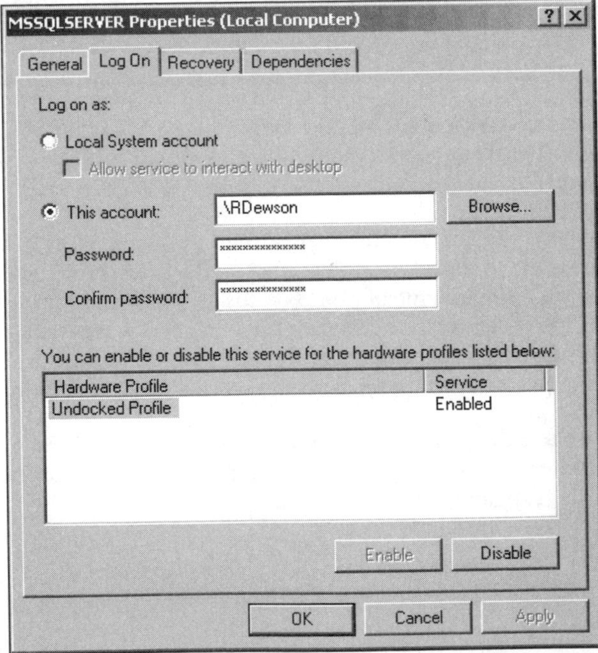

The Log On tab is the place where the first security issues are dealt with. As we know SQL Server runs as a service on Windows NT/2000 machines, and there is no interface. However, it is still necessary for the service to log on to SQL Server to run anything as a service. It is possible for the service to log on to SQL Server in two ways. Don't forget that no user needs to be logged in to the operating system, and the username used here must be a valid SQL Server login.

The first way is as a **Local System** account. This is a simple logon which has no password. Obviously, if this ID has no password it would be easy for anyone to log on to a SQL Server database using this ID. To cover this scenario Microsoft has limited the functionality to only allow access to the local machine. There is no possibility if you used this account that this service could log on to a SQL Server database on a remote machine. By changing a log on to a Local System account we can also ensure that any development work can only be done on the local machine and therefore stop any inadvertent work being completed on a production database on a server. People do log on to SQL Server using this method as a way of knowing that they are not working on a remote server, and it is very effective.

The other method that can be used to start SQL Server as a service is to use what is called a **domain account**. Logging on to the service using this method means that the service will check the Windows NT security model to ensure that the username and password entered is valid. If you are on a network instead of a standalone machine and have .\ as the prefix to the user name, then you will see the network name of the ID.

The Windows NT Security Model ensures that the domain account setting in the service matches a valid account and password on the Windows PDC (Primary Domain Controller).

It doesn't matter whether SQL Server is installed locally on your machine, or remotely on a network; if you wish to adopt some sort of security for starting up the service, then select this option, and ensure that the username is that of a Windows NT username that has been set up specifically and uniquely to run SQL Server. By adopting this method rather than using a Local System account, there will at least be the security of the Windows Security Model – as well as your password – securing the account.

You may work in an installation where your own NT username does not allow you full **administration rights** to your machine (in this case you probably won't be able to follow the rest of this section as you will have no access to services). Administration rights allow the user to create folders, add and remove files, and basically administer their own computer. Also the ID needs to have the ability to alter the registry. If this is the case, then you will need to create a user account that has these rights for SQL Server to be able to log on using a domain account. You should have administration rights on your machine if you have just performed a local installation; however, if you are using a SQL Server on a network, then you may have to ask a network administrator to either create an account for you on your machine or give you administration rights.

If you adopt this method, ensure that the username has a password that never expires or can be locked out. If it is ever locked out, try not to get the password reset on the account: if you do, then you will need to also alter the password within this dialog.

As we can see this tab is the security between SQL Server and the server being visible to the outside world. Take care with it.

8. The third tab deals with what actions have to be taken when the service fails. As you can see, you can set specific actions determined by the number of errors that have occurred.

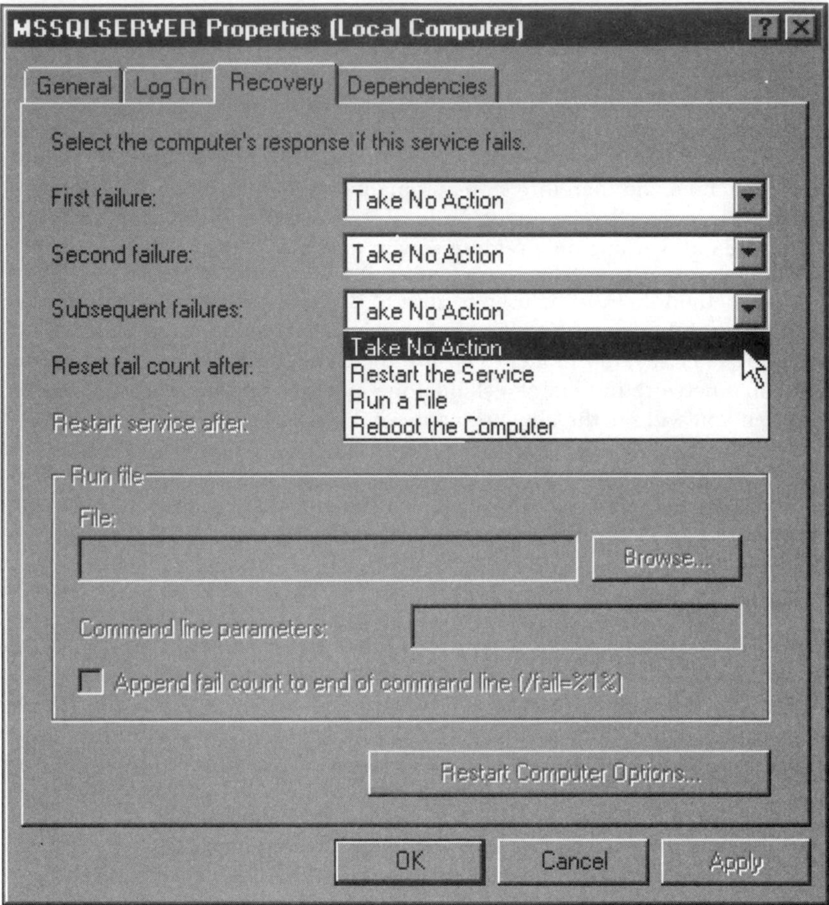

The best option is to set this to the following:

- First failure – Restart the Service. Quite simply this will attempt to restart SQL Server and will not affect the server itself.
- Second failure – Run a File, which is usually some sort of mail program informing you that there have been problems. When selecting run a file, you can then enter in the area below the action commands the name of the file that you wish to run when the service hits a problem.
- Subsequent failures – Reboot the Computer. Choose this carefully as you may find many different servers or services running on this computer if it is a server, therefore rebooting the computer may not only affect you, but possibly the whole corporation.

As you can see, the implications of each of these settings are quite varied. In other words, Take No Action is a non-invasive action, and at the other end of the spectrum Reboot the Computer is an invasive action that may affect other services and programs running on the computer.

9. The final tab shows any processes that must be running before the selected service can start, and also which processes are dependent on this process for their execution to take place. This tab is a trouble-shooting mechanism.

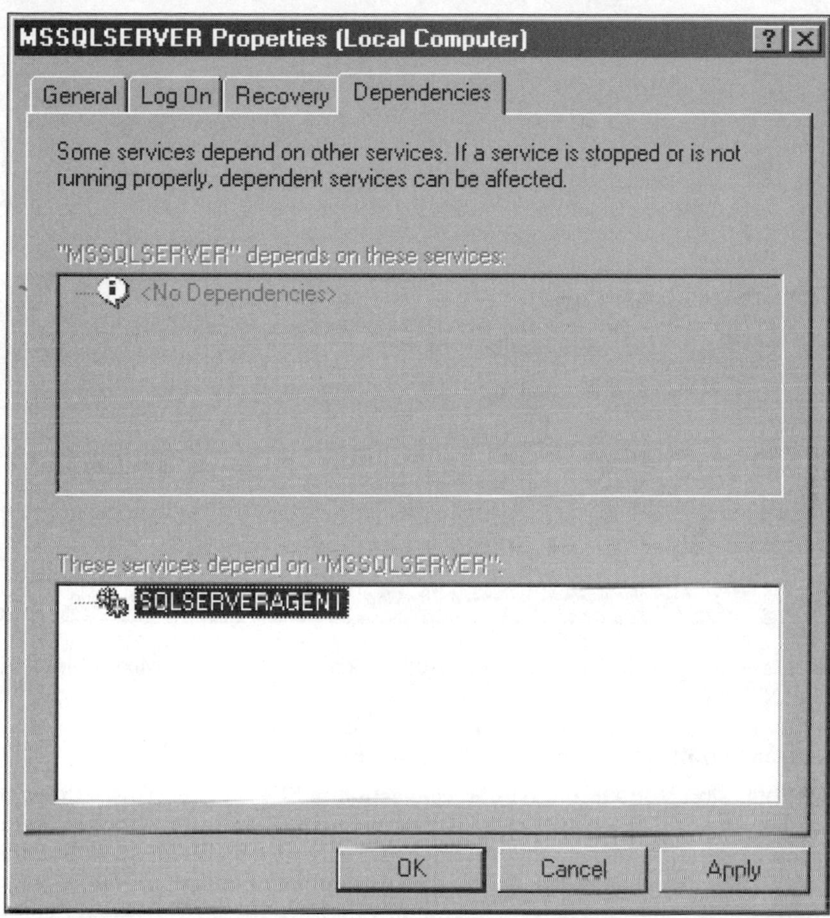

Now that you know what a service is, and how important security is when you set up a service, and realize how crucial the accounts are for logging on, it's time to move on to the options we are given during installation regarding Authentication Mode.

Authentication Mode

Probably the most crucial information in the whole setup process, and also the biggest decision that has to be made, is done in the Authentication Mode screen.

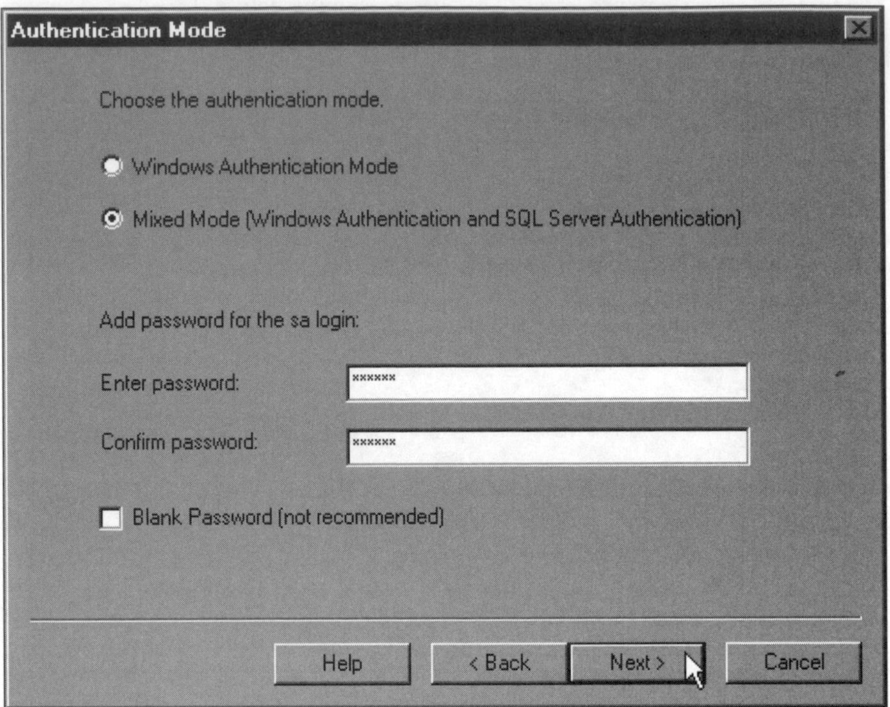

As we can see there are two choices, Windows Authentication Mode and Mixed Mode. This is on a Windows 2000/NT machine.

Windows Authentication Mode

Windows Authentication Mode uses a **trusted connection** to SQL Server. This is the preferred Windows method to connect to a SQL Server database. When people use the term Windows Authentication Mode, confusion can arise as to what this statement actually means. Windows Authentication Mode actually applies to the operating system SQL Server is running on rather than the operating system the user is on. Therefore, if you have clients who run on Windows 98, but SQL Server is installed on a Windows NT or 2000 server, then Windows Authentication is a perfectly valid method of connecting to the data. But how does Windows Authentication work?

To log on to a Windows NT or Windows 2000 machine, a username must be supplied. There is no way around this (unlike Windows 9x where a username is optional). So, to log on to Windows2000/NT the username and password have to be validated within Windows before the user can successfully log in. When this is done, Windows is actually verifying the user against username credentials held within the domain controller. These credentials check the access group the user belongs to (their **user rights**). The user could be an administrator, who has the ability to alter anything within the computer, right the way down to a basic user who has very restricted rights.

Once we have logged into Windows, SQL Server uses a **trusted connection**. This means that SQL Server is trusting that the username and password have been validated. If, however, the username does not exist – for example, you type in the username and there is an error – SQL Server will attempt to take the user rights of the invalid username and see if there is a group setting within SQL Server that matches the user rights. Obviously the name will not exist and a log on could not be completed. Let's look at an example.

> **This example is Windows 2000 specific. There are differences between this and Windows NT.**

Try It Out – Windows Authentication Mode.

1. Ensure that you are logged on to your machine as an administrator. If you are on a local computer, the chances are that your log in is in fact an administrator ID. If this computer is on a network and you are unsure about your access rights ask your PC support desk to help you out with the ID and password.

2. From Start | Settings | Control Panel select Users and Passwords.

3. When the Users and Passwords dialog comes up click Add.

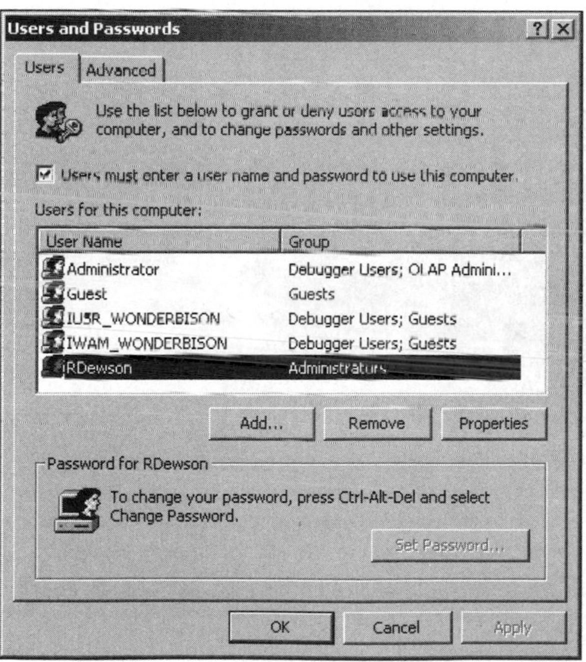

4. Once the Add New User dialog comes up, enter the User name, the Full name, and a Description. When done, click Next.

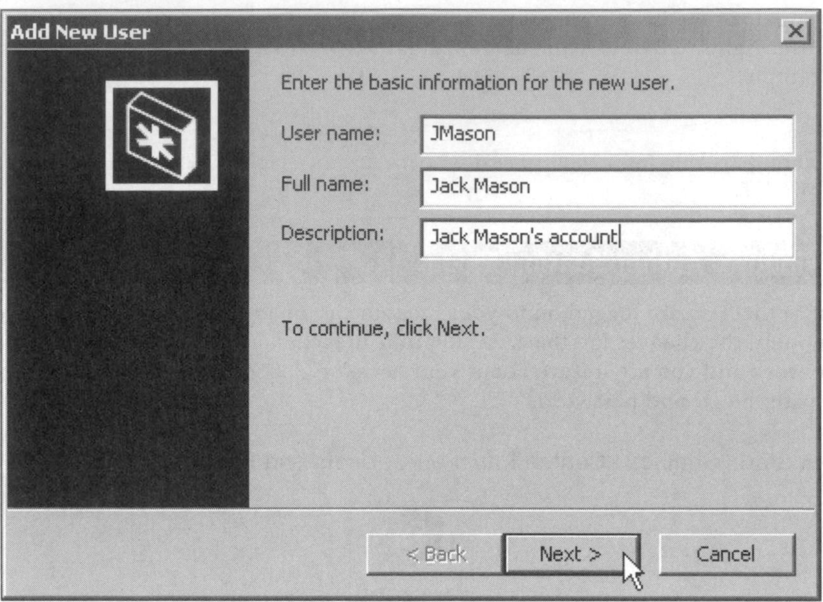

5. It is important that you enter a Password when adding a new user. This is not a SQL Server restriction, it is just a good security practice. When you have entered and confirmed a Password click Next.

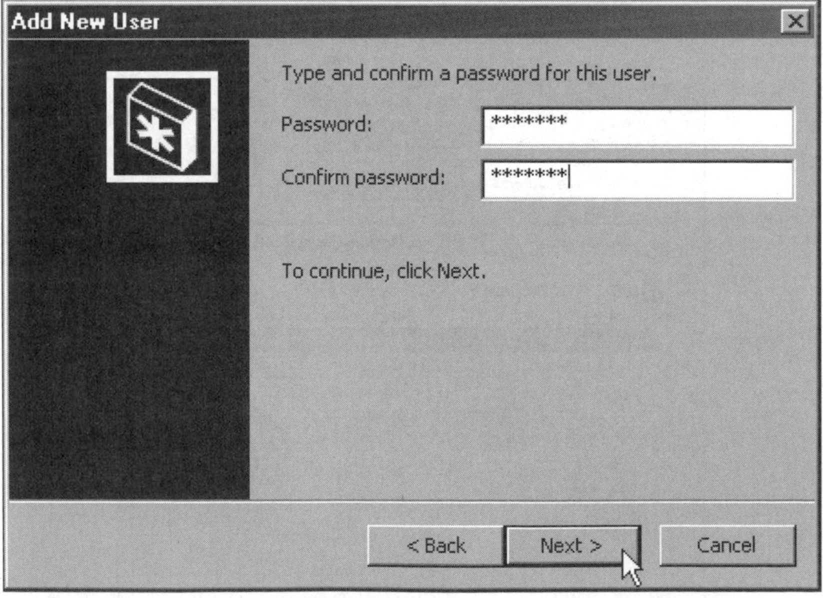

6. Click on the Restricted user button, then click Finish.

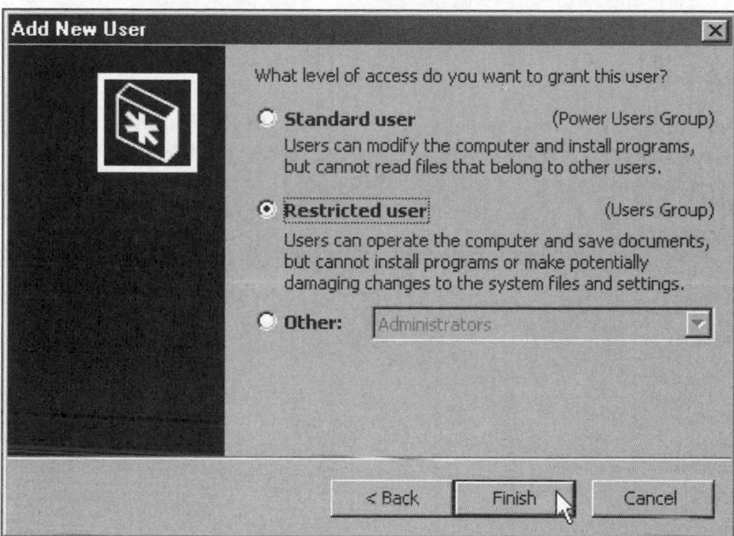

7. Stay in the Users and Passwords screen, as a second username will be added. Repeat the above process using the following details:

    - User name: AKelly
    - Full Name: Annette Kelly
    - Description: Annette is an Administrator

    Ensure that a Password is entered.

8. This time, click on the Other option button and ensure that Administrators is selected.

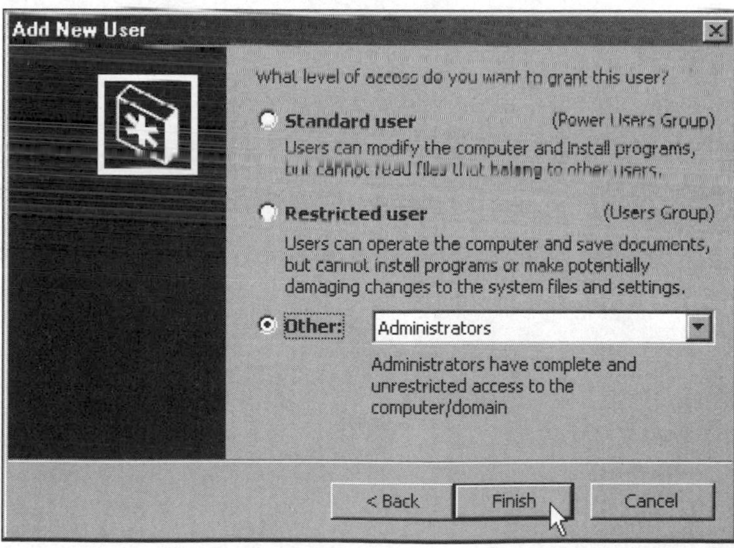

9. Log off from Windows and then log on using the first ID that you created: JMason.

10. Once logged in, start up SQL Server Enterprise Manager, which is found under Start | Programs | Microsoft SQL Server | Enterprise Manager.

11. Keep expanding the nodes (the + signs) because with this username, an error will be produced. Although a slightly misleading message, it is informing you that the login has failed. However, it is pointing you in the direction of SQL Server itself or the registration of the server. It is assuming that the username built is valid and should work.

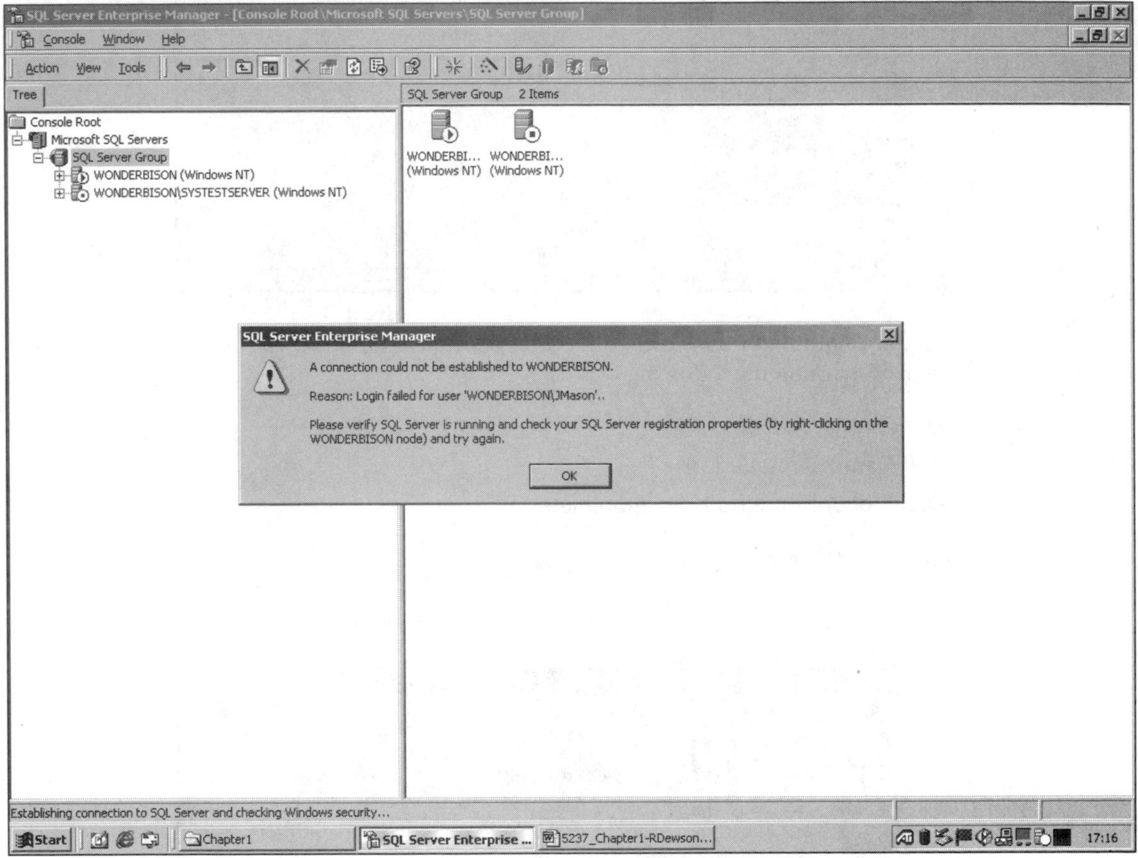

12. We will now try out the other user we created. Close down SQL Server, log off Windows and log on using the second ID we created – AKelly. Once logged in, start up SQL Server Enterprise Manager again.

13. Keep expanding the nodes until you see the following screen. Access was successful!

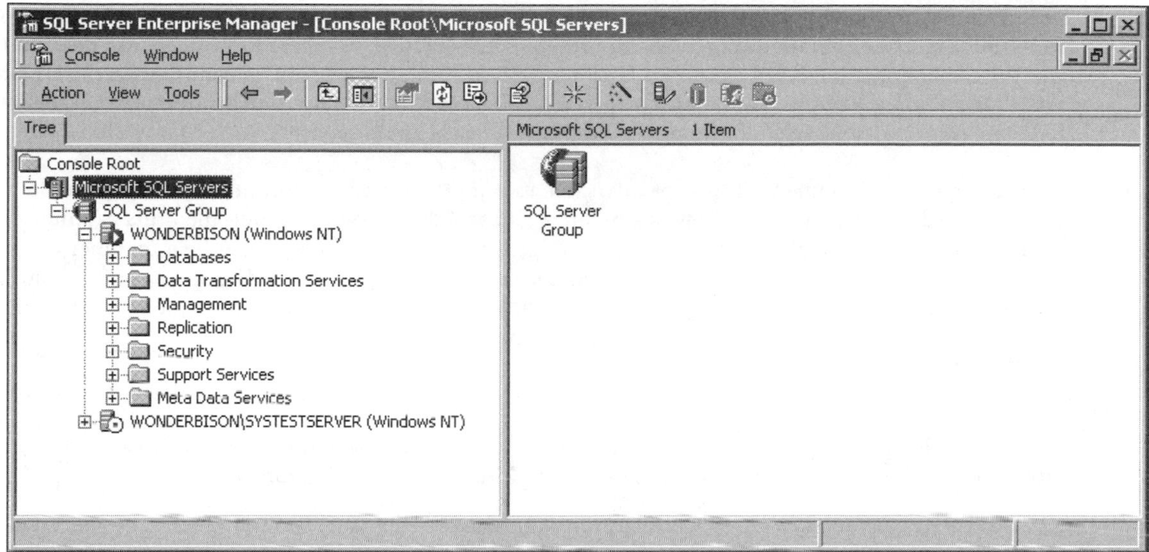

14. Expand the Security node and click on the Logins.

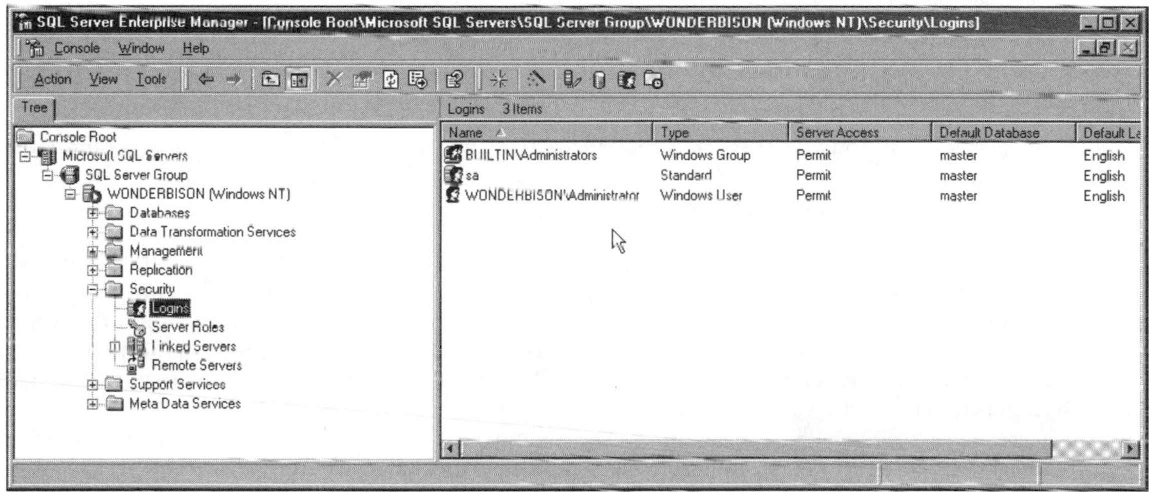

We have created two usernames: one that has restricted access (JMason), while the other has administration rights (AKelly). However, neither of these specific usernames exist within SQL Server itself: after all, we haven't entered them and they haven't appeared as if by magic. So why did one succeed and one fail?

Windows NT/2000 has ensured that both IDs are valid. If the ID or password were incorrect, there is no way that you could be logged in to Windows. Therefore, when you have tried to start SQL Server, the only check that is performed is whether the username exists, or if the type of user exists. As we can see in the last screenshot, neither AKelly nor JMason exist. However, if we look at the top item on the right we can see that there is a Windows Group called Administrators. This means that any username that is set up as an Administrator within NT/2000 will have the capacity to log on to this SQL Server. Hence avoid if possible setting up users as Administrators of their own PC.

In a production environment, it may be advisable to remove this group from the system if you do allow users to be Administrators. As AKelly is a member of the Administrators group then this username will also be a member of the BUILTIN\Administrators group. However, she will also be a member of the WONDERBISON\Administrators group. So what is the difference? When defining a specific group login that also relates to a Windows group, like Administrators, Power Users, and so on, it is best to define the prefix of the group as BUILTIN rather than the machine name.

Mixed Mode

If we installed SQL Server with Mixed Mode this means that we can either use Windows Authentication, as has just been covered, or use SQL Server Authentication.

First a word of caution. Microsoft has stated that this has only been included as backward compatibility, so therefore, it may not exist in future versions. Microsoft state that this is for backward compatibility only because Windows ME is the last version of Windows that will be separate from the NT/2000 architecture (although this was supposed to be true with Windows 98 and potentially Windows 95; however, the time is approaching).

How does Mixed Mode differ from Windows Authentication? To start with, there is no assumption that the username entered is a valid ID; therefore Mixed Mode is only really effective for the 9x/ME operating system where it is possible to access the machine without being logged in.

There is also another argument for Mixed Mode. There may be some reason (for example, for auditing purposes) that we wish the user to log on to SQL Server using a different username from that of their Windows NT account. We could be working on a large SQL Server development project that will have developers coming in and out of the team as the need arises. In this case it might be necessary to create temporary usernames, as opposed to permanent IDs linked to the developer's Windows username. In SQL Server we could create usernames of `Developer1`, `Developer2`, etc. These usernames can have different access rights within SQL Server. Another situation would be the case of an internet-based application where there is just no way we could create a username for every visitor to our site. Therefore we would create generic login ID using a specific ID created for a web site. Whatever the reason there is a need to have usernames not linked with the Windows username.

We will cover adding usernames to SQL Server (as opposed to adding Windows users) in the next chapter when we look closely at Enterprise Manager. It is necessary to be comfortable with this tool first.

There is one area of security left that needs to be discussed. This is the `sa` login.

The sa Login

The sa login is a default login that has full administration rights for SQL Server. Therefore, if you logged in to SQL Server as sa you will have full control over any aspect of SQL Server. SQL Server inserts this ID no matter which authentication mode you install. If you have an NT/2000 account defined as sa, for example, for Steve Austin, then this user will be able to log in to the server if you have set the server up as Windows Authentication. Try to avoid login IDs of sa or set up SQL Server as Mixed Mode.

In a Mixed Mode installation sa will be a valid username and validated as such. As you can guess, if any user gets hold of this username and the password they will have full access to view and amend or delete any item of data. At worst, they could corrupt any database, as well as corrupt SQL Server itself. They could even set up tasks that e-mail data to a remote location as it is being processed.

> **It is essential to set up a strong password on the sa account in the Authentication mode screen if you choose Mixed Mode. You should never have a blank password on the sa account! You would be surprised how many people have blank passwords, and this is why so many people are leaving their database open to attack. Always keep the password safe, but also make a note of it in a safe place. If you forget the sa password and this is the only administration ID that exists you will need to re-install SQL Server to get out of this problem.**

There is also another reason not to log on to SQL Server with the sa username. There will be times when it is essential to know who is running a particular query on a SQL Server database. In a production database someone may be running an update of the data, which is filling up the disk space. We need to contact that person to check if they can stop their process. If they log in as sa, we will have no idea who that person is. However, if they logged on with an identifiable name they would have an ID in SQL Server, which we could track. By restricting the sa login so that people have to use their own accounts, we can ensure a much higher degree of system monitoring and integrity.

So, there may be times that we want Mixed Mode authentication; it is perfectly acceptable to wish this. We have also decided not to have sa as an administration logon after reading the sections so far. So what do we do? Well, we create a logon ID that will have the same access privileges as the sa logon. In the above example, AKelly would have full system administration rights. In the next chapter we will go through this when talking about the Enterprise Manager.

> **No matter what you decide to do within the whole setup process, if a choice of Mixed Mode is made it is imperative from a security point of view that the sa login password is set. It is crucial that this password is secure.**

Summary

By this point you should understand the small differences between each version of SQL Server and why we chose the Developer Edition for this book. You should also know how to check your computer to see if it is suitable for a SQL Server installation.

By following the steps you should have a successful installation of SQL Server on your computer. You may even have completed the installation twice so that you have a development server as well as a test server. This is a good idea, and something to consider if you have only one installation so far.

Security has been introduced so that we can feel comfortable knowing which way we want to implement this and how to deal with different usernames. We may not have any data yet, but we want to ensure that when we do only the right people get to look at it!

You are now ready to explore SQL Server 2000 – one of the best ways of managing SQL Server is by using the Enterprise Manager, which we will now move on to discuss.

Managing SQL Server

Now that SQL Server 2000 is successfully installed on your machine, it is time to start exploring the various areas that make this an easy and effective product to use. In this chapter, the main focus will be on Enterprise Manager, which is the heart of the GUI interface between the developer – or database administrator – and the SQL Server engine. This is an easy-to-use and intuitive tool, and before long, you will feel confident in using it to work with SQL Server quickly and efficiently.

The properties of the SQL Server installation will also be explored through Enterprise Manager, and it will become clear how to configure SQL Server for your own use. Exploring and finding out what is contained within Enterprise Manager will demonstrate how to examine and work with property settings and configurations.

Then it will be time to look at the SQL Server Service Manager. This is a front-end tool that deals with the run state of SQL Server, and allows us to start, stop, and pause the engines that drive SQL Server.

From there the chapter will move back to Enterprise Manager and deal with looking at the properties of your SQL Server installation, and also how to configure SQL Server.

Finally, it is possible to have multiple installations (or instances) of SQL Server that you also wish to use, and this chapter will explain how you would go about getting Enterprise Manager to recognize these instances.

Enterprise Manager is crucial to your success as a developer. Therefore, by the end of this chapter you will have gained experience with it and be proficient in the following areas:

- Enterprise Manager – a front-end tool to SQL Server
- Finding your way around the Enterprise Manager Console
- Service Manager – a front-end tool that works with SQL Server engine and other services installed along with the SQL Server installation
- Configuring Enterprise Manager and SQL Server
- Dealing with 2-digit year issues
- Registering future or other SQL Server instances and installations

Let's start straight away, and have a look at Enterprise Manager and how this is used to work with SQL Server 2000…

Enterprise Manager

As you have read in the previous chapter, SQL Server engine runs as a separate process on a suitable Windows based computer, be it on a standalone desktop machine, or on a server or network. When you install SQL Server, depending on your selections, you will have one or more services running. One of these services is the SQL Server service that runs in its own process space, and is isolated from other processes on the machine. What this means is that SQL Server engine should not be affected by any other piece of software that does not talk to any SQL Server component. If you have to end-task any othercomponent, the SQL Server engine should, and will, continue to run.

When this book mentions SQL Server engine, it can also mean SQL Server itself, as there could be many SQL Server engines, depending on what components have been installed. Each engine communicates with the others to make a full SQL Server process. From this point we will just use the term SQL Server when we mean the whole engine process.

On a Windows 2000 or Windows NT machine, SQL Server runs as a service that is controlled and monitored by Windows itself. Windows ensures that it is given the right amount of memory, processing power and time, and that everything is working well. Because SQL Server runs as a service, it has no interface attached to it for a user to interact with. As a result, there needs to be at least one separate utility that can pass commands and functions from a user through to the SQL Server service, which then passes them through to the underlying database.

One interface that accomplishes this is **SQL Server Enterprise Manager**. This is the front end, or **GUI** tool that will be discussed in this chapter. In Chapter 3 there will be a discussion of another useful tool – **SQL Server Query Analyzer**. For now, let's just start off with Enterprise Manager.

GUI is short for Graphical User Interface. This is a program with a user-friendly front-end, allowing developers to easily work with the database engine, without the need to know complex sets of commands.

Enterprise Manager can be used to develop and work with several installations of SQL Server in one application. These installations can be on one computer, or on many computers connected through an internal network (**LAN**), a wide area network (**WAN**), or even the Internet. Therefore, it is possible to deal with your development, system testing, user testing, and production instances of SQL Server from one instance of Enterprise Manager. EM can help the development of database solutions including creating and modifying components of a database, amending the database itself, and dealing with security issues. Getting to know this tool well is crucial to the success of becoming a professional SQL Server developer, as well as a database administrator.

Enterprise Manager is powerful enough to complete any task and build any component we may require within a database, as well as tasks like sending mail or backing up data. Before we try out Enterprise Manager, let's have a quick look at the framework it runs in.

Microsoft Management Console (MMC)

This product is a graphical tool that is used to plug-in other management tools such as SQL Server Enterprise Manager, and IIS Manager. The Management Console is the whole crux of Enterprise Manager, and it is from here, whether it be from icons, nodes, or the menu, that we operate our SQL Server instances. Almost anything that we do in Management Console is actually done with other SQL Server tools such as the Query Analyzer (covered in the next chapter), but the Management Console gives us a common interface. Throughout the book we will cover areas such as creating databases, tables, and so on in both Query Analyzer and Enterprise Manager within the MMC. Management Console is the wrapper for the graphical interface that allows the developer to perform the operations that are required for a SQL Server instance as well as other Microsoft or indeed third party products.

We saw a quick splash of Enterprise Manager when demonstrating security in the last chapter, next, let's spend some time taking a look at Enterprise Manager in more detail...

Try It Out – Enterprise Manager

1. To start up SQL Server Enterprise Manager, select Start | Programs | Microsoft SQL Server | Enterprise Manager. We will cover some of the other options that you see here later on in this chapter and in the next one.

2. This should start up Enterprise Manager, which will look similar to the following screenshot:

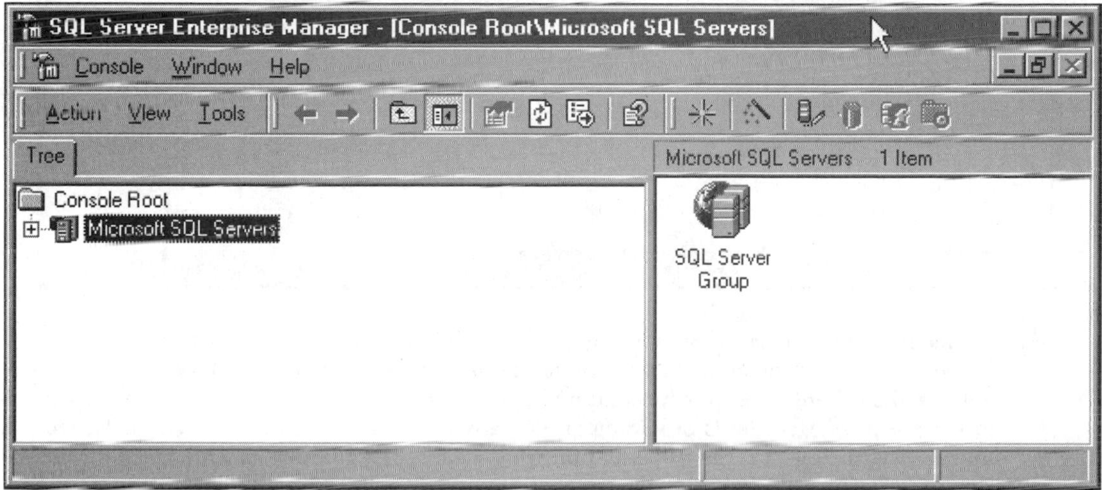

3. You will see that Enterprise Manager uses **nodes** (the + signs) to keep much of the layout of the server (the **hierarchy**) compacted and hidden until needed. This works in much the same way as Windows Explorer. Expand your SQL Server installation found under the Microsoft SQL Servers node (by clicking on the + sign), and keep expanding down the tree to display the Databases structure as seen overleaf. Don't forget that your installation of SQL Server will not be called WONDERBISON, but will instead be based on the name you gave it during installation.

Providing that you are still logged in to the computer where you completed the installation of SQL Server, you should have no problems connecting to SQL Server when expanding each of these nodes. If you have problems connecting, refer back to Chapter 1 to see where your problems might lie. One problem could be that you have since logged off and now logged back on, and SQL Server was not set up to restart automatically. Alternatively, there could have been a change in your access privileges.

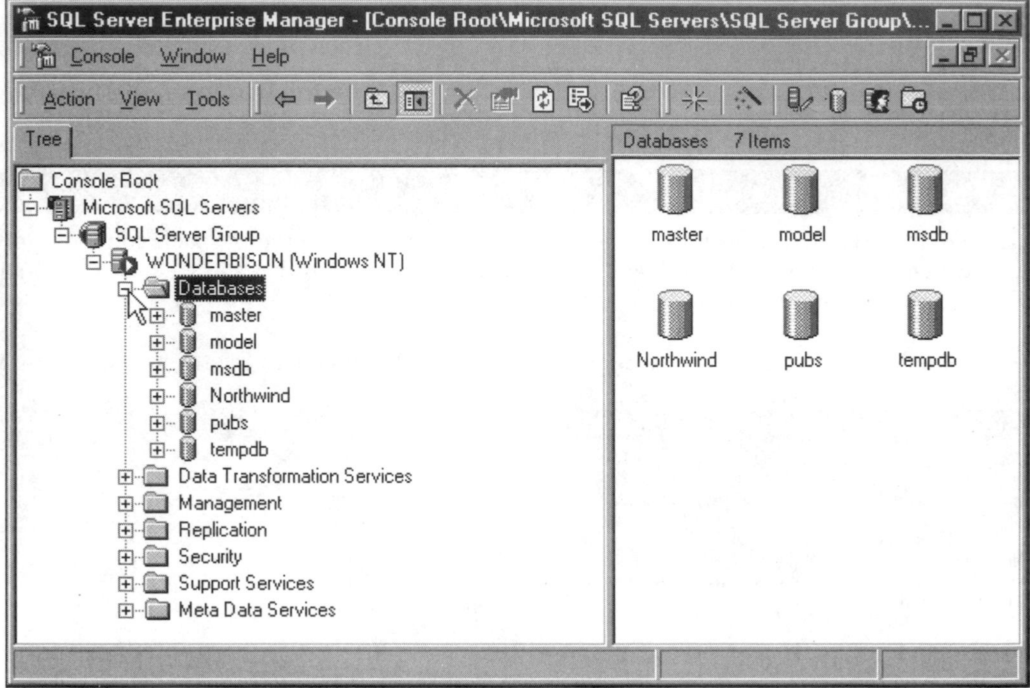

4. Notice how the title bar of SQL Server has now altered to show the path down the SQL Server structure, depending on your preferences. Now that Enterprise Manager is open we will see the different components that make up a SQL Server installation. Already, we can see how Enterprise Manager is providing us with a whole host of useful information. The first area that we will deal with is the Security node that we discussed in the last chapter. Find the Security node, and then expand it.

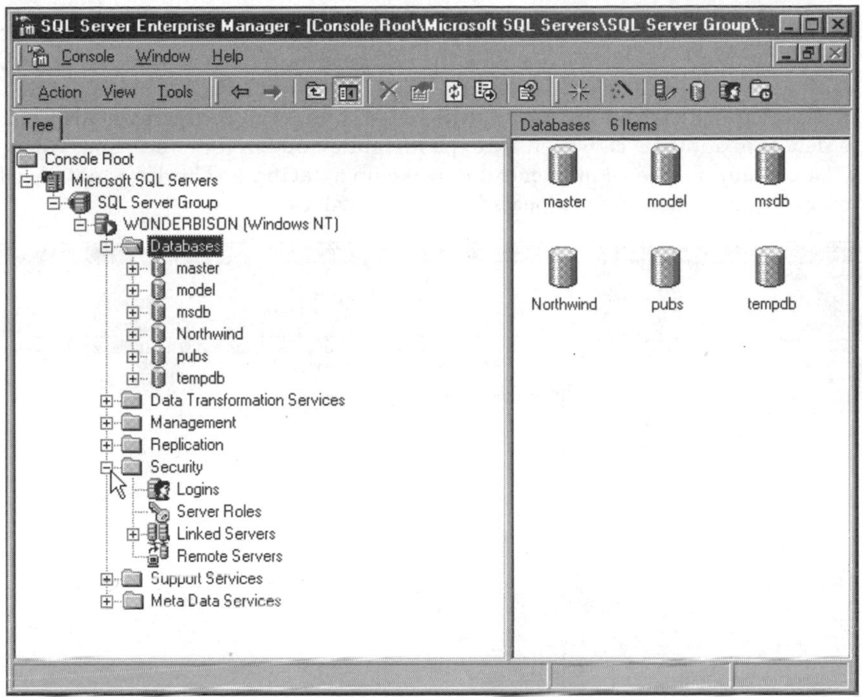

5. There are four areas within this node that revolve around security: Logins, Server Roles, Linked Servers, and Remote Servers. Security is a major issue, and as it is an advanced topic, we will continue to cover it throughout the book. Click on Logins and you will see that the right-hand pane – the **View pane** – changes to show more details about this node. You should see a list of three logins, sa, an Administrators login, and a login defined when you installed SQL Server. Chapter 1 covered these three logins and their access rights. The third login – unlike sa and Administrators – is not going to be the same on every SQL Server installation as it refers to the user ID that was logged in to Windows at the time the installation took place.

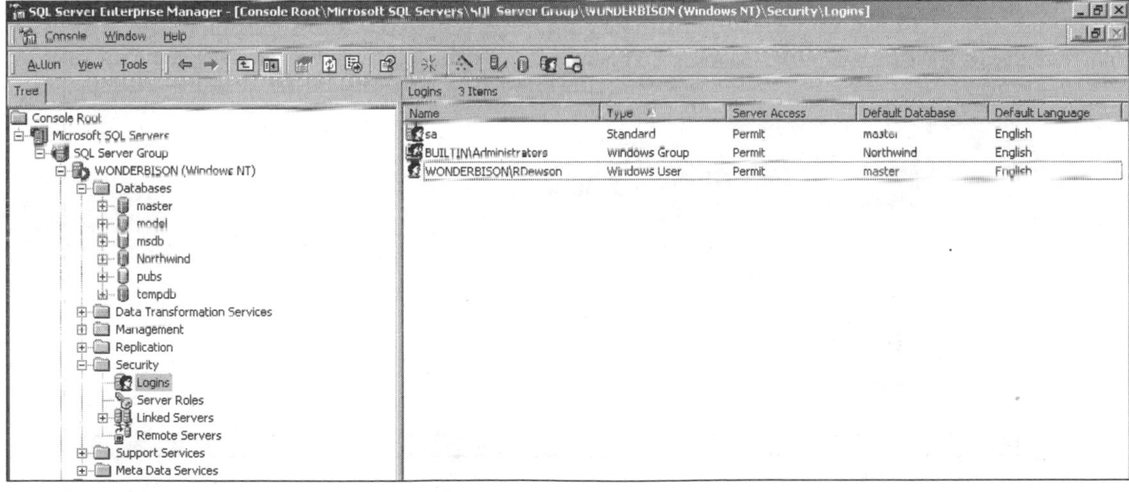

6. Let's now move back to the **Databases** node, and expand the **Northwind** database node. Although the node has been expanded, the database hasn't actually been selected, and so the details in the View pane have not altered. SQL Server quite deliberately does not alter this pane until explicitly requested to, allowing the developer to compare details from one node with details in another. However, by expanding the node in the **Tree** pane, you will see that this list contains all the components that make up a database. This list is not specific to the `Northwind` database, but is repeated for each database.

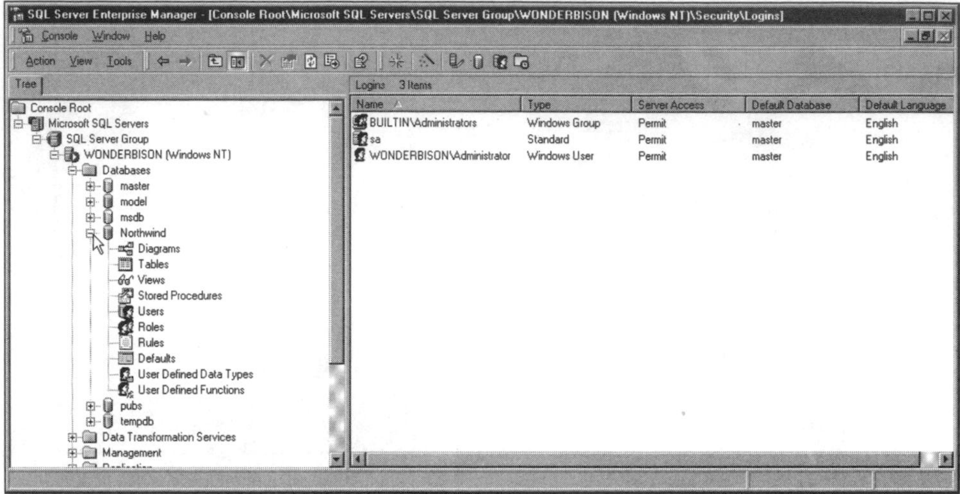

7. If you now click on the actual database name, **Northwind**, you will see the right-hand pane alters to show the database components, as illustrated in the screenshot below. The available view options are identical to the ones you would find in Windows Explorer: **Large Icons**, **Small Icons**, **List**, or **Details**. There is also another option, covered later, which is the **Taskpad** option, which is a tabbed view of the database. Note that this option is only available at the database level.

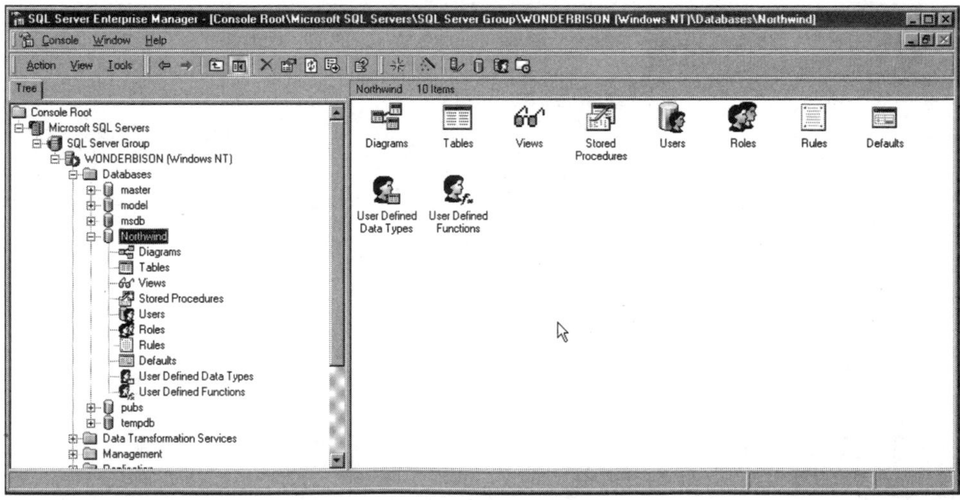

8. By clicking **View** on the menu bar, it is possible to alter the display shown on the right-hand side to one of the options listed above. Now, if you click on the **Tables** node within the **Tree** view on the left, you should see some tables from the `Northwind` database, which will be familiar to you if you have used MS Access before.

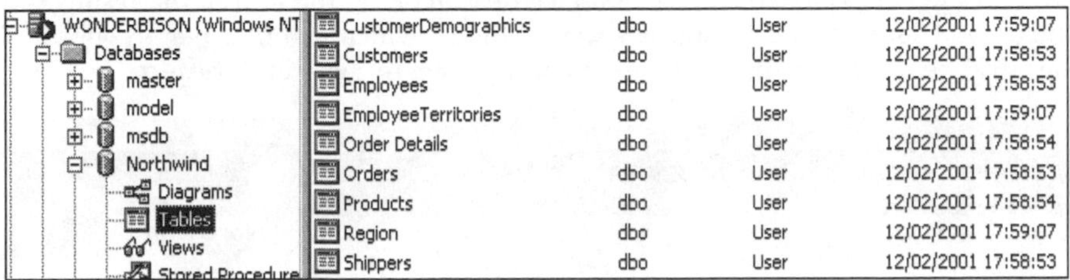

9. By clicking on the **Taskpad** option, the Details pane on the right-hand side alters to show a summary of information concerning the database in question. Details about the `Northwind` database are immediately visible, including who the **Owner** of the database is, the **Date Created**, and perhaps most importantly, the **Space Allocated** and the amount **Used**. These are very important, as you will find out if ever you experience space problems and need to expand the size of the database.

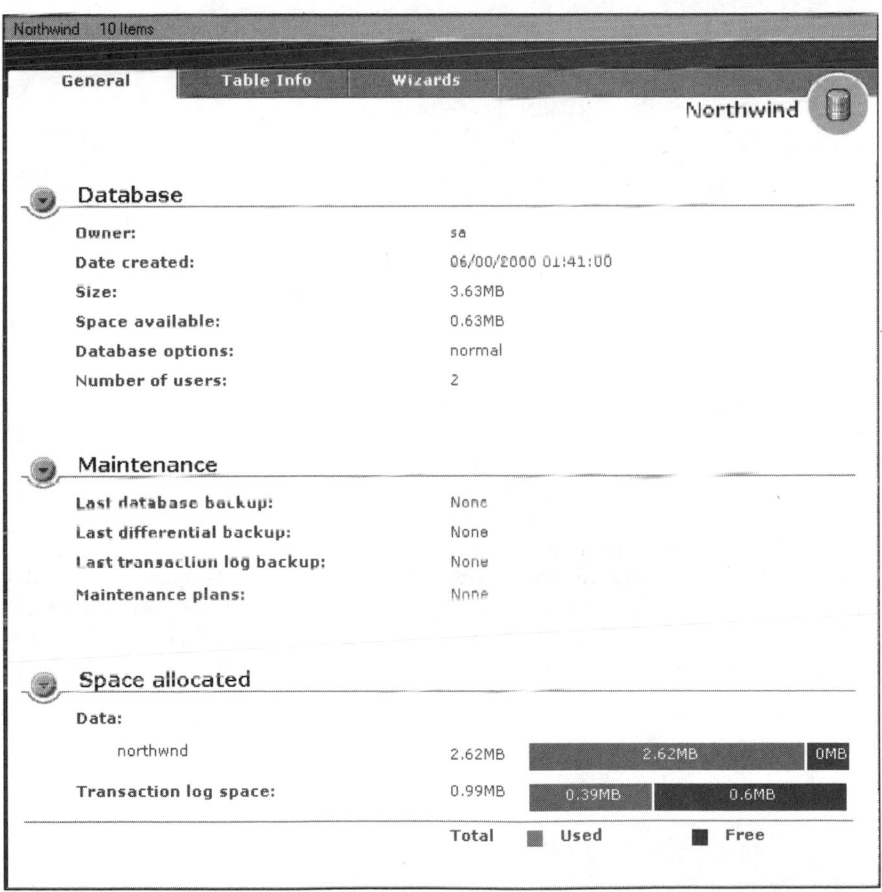

10. Clicking on the **Table Info** tab alters the display to list the tables and information related to these tables. The screenshot below demonstrates how you can restrict this display to show only a specific table, or search for a table in a large database by using the **Search** option. When you search the database objects (for example, by typing "**Orders**" into the **Search for** field and then clicking **Go**), you will notice three icons at the foot of the results screen: **Table**, **Index**, and **Clustered** – a cluster is a special index, which will be covered later in the book). They are the legend for the icon next to each object in the search results.

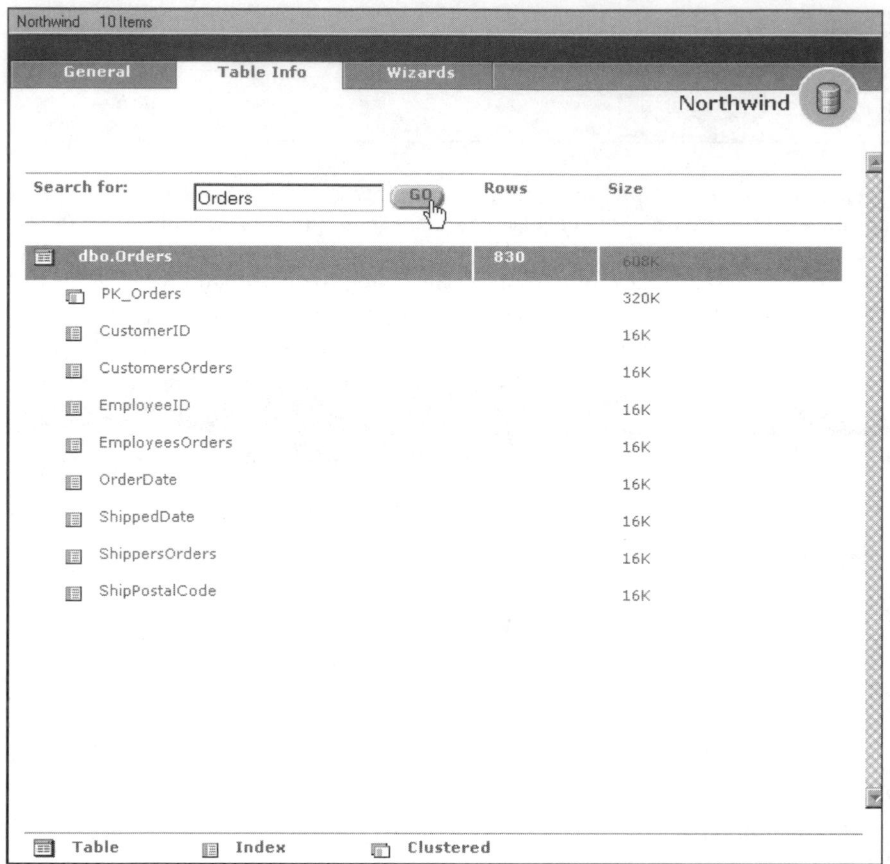

11. Finally, the **Wizards** tab allows access to some of the great utilities already built in to SQL Server that aid a developer or administrator in building items and tasks for the database. Many of these wizards can also be accessed from the toolbar at the top of the screen, but don't worry about these for the moment, as they will be covered later in the book. For example, creating a database is covered in Chapter 5, and creating an index is detailed in Chapter 7.

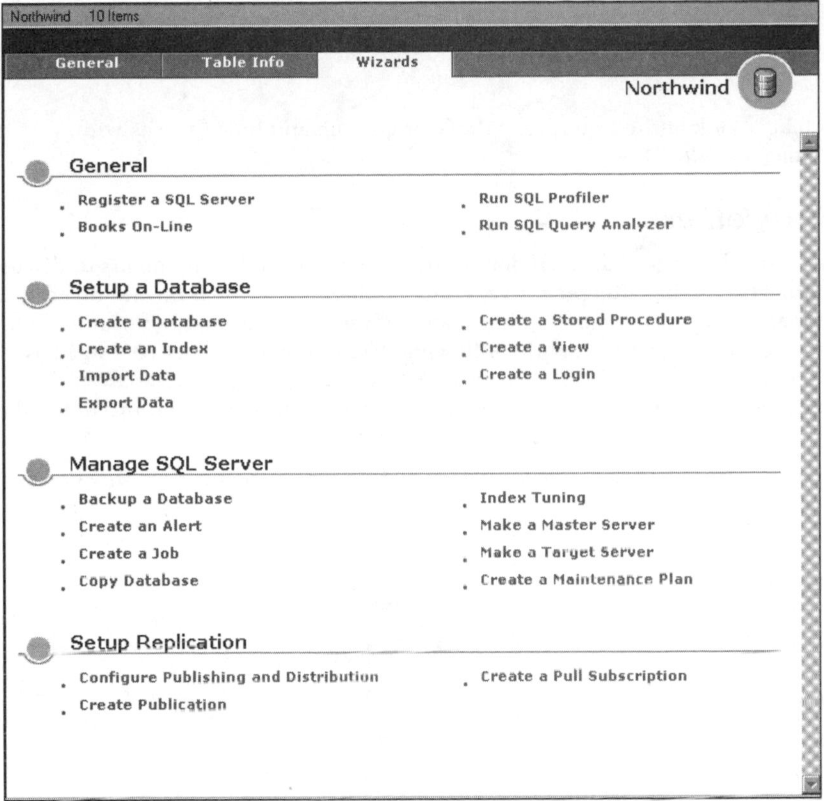

12. The View menu option allows us to customize the type of information that we wish to see, by clicking on View | Customize. You may find the best thing is to keep all the options available and on display, and then close them as necessary.

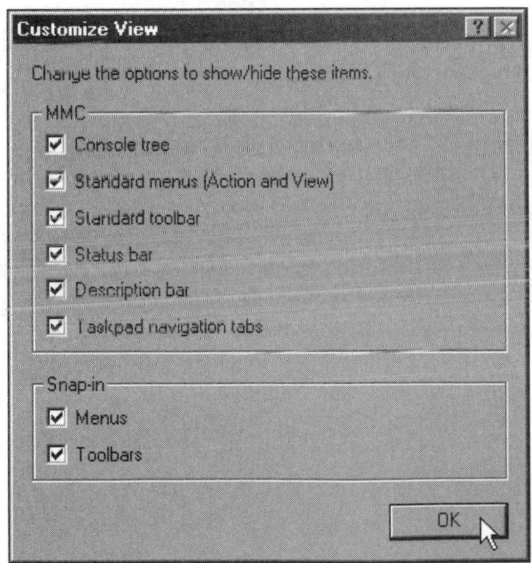

By this point you should know how to alter the display of Enterprise Manager, know where some of the basic information is stored and how to find it, and finally, how to retrieve vital information about a specific database.

Time now to take a look at the Enterprise Manager console and how this sits within Enterprise Manager itself.

Pulling It All Together

Now that Enterprise Manager has been demonstrated, let's take a few moments to discuss how the whole operation sits together. Keeping it very simple, there are three levels involved from data to Enterprise Manager. This is a logical (rather than a physical) representation of how Enterprise Manager will work with the data. If you look at the following diagram, you will notice that I have used the `Northwind` database an example. To clarify, `Northwind` is a sample database that is supplied with SQL Server as a demonstration database (see Chapter 5 for information on pre-defined databases).

Don't forget that when adding a new database to SQL Server, the data is physically stored on the machine with an `MDF` file extension.

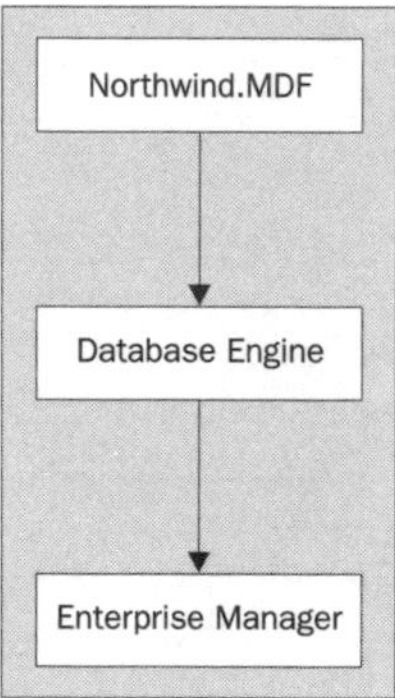

When Enterprise Manager has to complete any work, it is not Enterprise Manager itself that deals with the data. There is a separate process, the **database engine**, that takes all requests from Enterprise Manager, administers and deals with the requests themselves, or passes the requests on to another manager specifically built for a set task, such as querying data.

Service Manager

It is possible to control the actual SQL Server service itself using the Services control screen within the Administrative tools of the Control Panel, which was covered in Chapter 1, under the section *Services Accounts*. At times, however, this method can be a little cumbersome and confusing, as every service running on a machine is listed, especially as some services can have pretty obscure names! The Services control also opens up a lot more functionality and information than we need.

Therefore, Microsoft has supplied a utility, called Service Manager, which can be used as a quick and useful front-end to SQL Server services. It runs in the background on your machine with a minimum amount of interface displayed, and therefore you will need to use the Start menu button to see the Service Manager interface.

Service Manager is an interface to the services that run on a Windows NT/2000 machine. We discussed services on NT in Chapter 1 where we demonstrated how they run on a Windows machine.

The way the Service Manager works is by interfacing directly with the Windows operating system and not the database engine or the services that it is controlling at all. Each service running in Windows has its own user account that is allowed to start and stop the service, and the SQL Server services are no different. Among other information, the information for each service is stored in the Windows Registry. So, when we issue a command to stop or start a service, say the SQL Server Service, for example, Windows looks at the credentials of the user that is logged-in to the system, and decides if this user is authorized to do this. If so, Windows shuts down or starts the service accordingly. SQL Server has absolutely nothing to do with this, and this tool is simply provided to target services that relate directly to SQL Server.

Let's take a first look at the Service Manager utility, and then see what it can do…

Try It Out – Service Manager

1. In the bottom right-hand side of the screen, in the area set aside for icons that show running processes, you should be able to see the Service Manager icon.

2. If it is not visible then it could mean SQL Server is not running, or that you have chosen not to have the icon display in your Taskpad. If there is no icon, then select Start | Programs | Microsoft SQL Server | Service Manager on your machine. If there is an icon in Taskpad, then double-click it to open Service Manager.

3. The Service Manager window should look similar to the following screenshot. This screen is showing that server WONDERBISON has a SQL Server service of SQL Server selected, and that this service is running. On the bottom left of the window you will see that the option to Auto-start service when OS starts is checked. Therefore, this means that SQL Server will be started every time the computer is booted up.

4. Select the server that you wish to investigate (in my case, this was WONDERBISON).

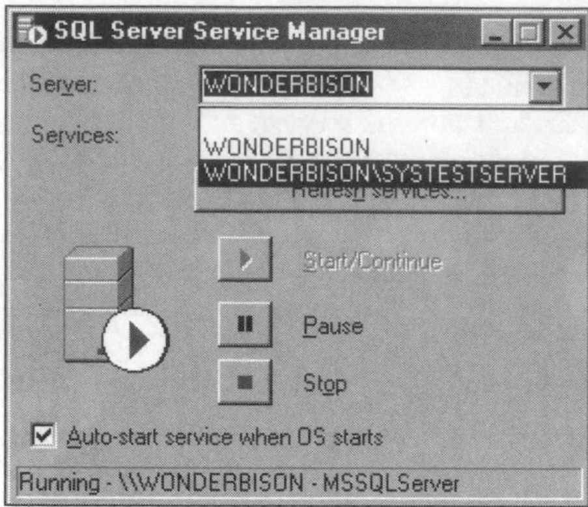

5. Select the service to alter the state of:

6. Now that you have made your selections you can start, stop, or pause SQL Server running at your slightest whim.

Configuring SQL Server Installations

We will now look at configuring SQL Server specifications such as memory, security, mail, and connections. This can be done from Enterprise Manager, or through SQL Server Query Analyzer, which is covered in the next chapter. In this next section, the configuration options will be covered to help you understand how to configure SQL Server for your own, specific needs.

Try It Out – Configuring SQL Server

1. Ensure that SQL Server Enterprise Manager is running. If not, go to Start | Programs | Microsoft SQL Server, and then select Enterprise Manager.

2. Navigate to the server you wish to configure. In our example, I will be working with the WONDERBISON installation.

Don't forget that if you installed more than one SQL server, for example a production and test server, you need to configure these separately.

3. Select SQL Server Configuration Properties from the Tools menu in Enterprise Manager. You can also get to the next screen by right-clicking the server instance and choosing Properties.

4. After selecting this menu option, the following dialog should be displayed. This is the main dialog for configuring the SQL Server installation. The following few sections will review each of the tabs in turn, so as to make you a little more familiar with the contents of each tab.

5. This first tab gives a General summary of SQL Server and the computer it is installed on.

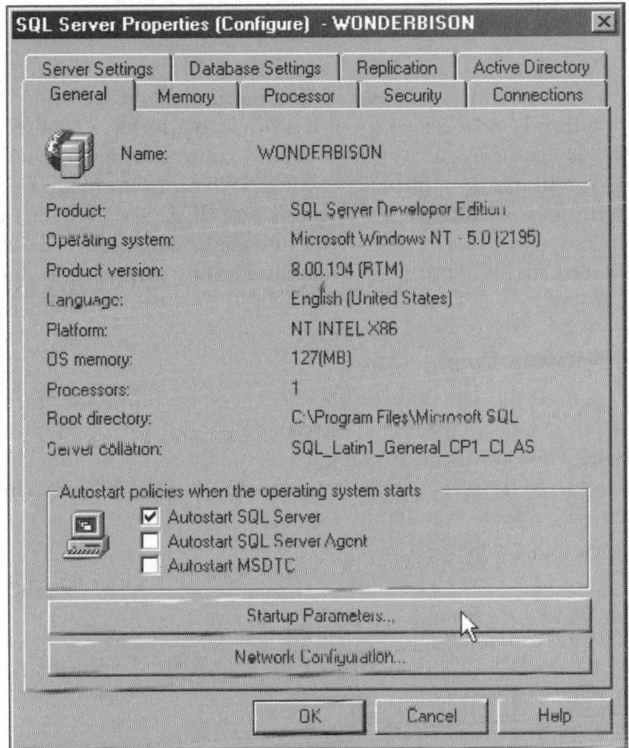

Let's look at this tab in more detail:

- Name – The name of the server that is being interrogated.
- Product – The edition of SQL Server currently installed.
- Operating System – The name of the operating system that the server is running on. In this case NT 5.0 does in fact refer to Windows 2000.

- Product Version – Which version of SQL Server this is. This is different from the edition version, of 2000, in that it this shows version 8.00, sub-version, or build number 194, and it is the RTM, the retail version, rather than a beta.
- Language – The language dialect built-in to the server. This could be any spoken, supported language.
- Platform – This describes which processor platform the server is running on. Alternatives here could be AMD or RISC processors.
- OS Memory – How much memory is available to the operating system.
- Processors – The number of processors within the machine. This is a single processor installation, but it could just as well be a server with multiple processors.
- Root directory – Where SQL Server is installed.
- Server collation – How the data is stored within SQL Server.

Autostart Policies

These three checkboxes denote which processes will automatically start when the computer is rebooted. If the SQL Server installation is on a server, then it is advisable to have, at the minimum, SQL Server start automatically. If SQL Server is on a desktop, then it is optional as to whether it should start automatically or not, as it will use up a little processing power and memory running in the background, even if nothing is happening. I would advise always having SQL Server start automatically, due to the small amount of resources it uses; that is unless you find that you will not be using SQL Server for a number of days. If you are using a Windows 9x machine, then you will find that these boxes are grayed out, and not available to you.

Startup Parameters and Network Configuration

These options are not covered here as they are too advanced for someone starting up in SQL Server development. However, they can be used to specify the SQL Server log file, the location of the master database, and the network configuration covering areas such as determining the network protocols by which clients can connect to SQL Server. However, these topics are beyond the scope of this book as we are really only discussing a local installation here.

6. Clicking on the **Memory** tab displays, and allows you to alter, any memory configuration options for SQL Server. This is quite a hot topic.

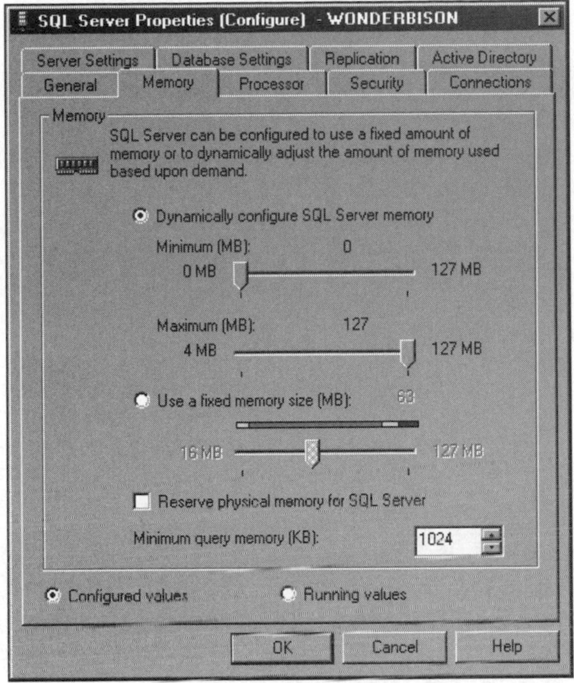

Let's look in more detail at the options available on this tab:

- **Dynamically configure SQL Server memory** – If we change any of the minimum or maximum values in the associated slider controls, then this will immediately adjust the amount of memory that SQL server can use. It really should not be necessary to restrict the memory ranges of SQL Server, as Windows and SQL Server should manage memory well enough by themselves. However, if we did decide that we specifically wanted to set limits, for whatever reason, then we could do that here.

- **Use a fixed memory size** – As above. Should we wish to define a fixed amount of memory for SQL Server to use, we can define this here. Notice the color-coding, which denotes: safe (green), warning (yellow), and dangerous (red) areas. If you do wish to use this option, then do not stray in to the red (danger) areas.

- **Reserve physical memory for SQL Server** – This option is used to inform Windows that no matter what it thinks, the amount of memory defined in the box below this option will always remain in physical memory, and will never be swapped out to disk. This will result in performance enhancements in the running of SQL Server, at the cost of other items on the computer. Use with extreme care. I advise that this is left alone until you become more proficient in the use of SQL Server and Windows.

- **Configured values** or **Running values** – At present, this option is showing what the values are that have been configured for SQL Server. If you click on the **Running values** option, you will see what memory is actually being used at the time. Obviously, if nothing is happening with SQL Server, then the amount of memory will be minimal.

7. Click on to the Processor tab. This tab really only comes into its own on computers with multiple processors, and even more so on servers. We won't be covering this tab, as this is a more advanced topic, and I recommend that the default settings are left alone, as in the wrong hands, playing with these settings can do more damage than good.

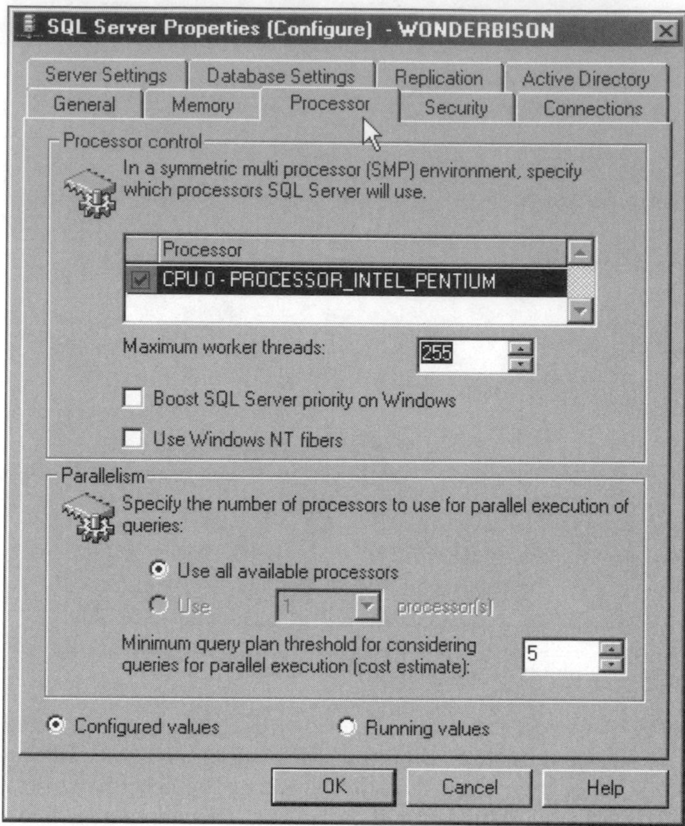

8. Now click on to the Security tab. Remember our discussion earlier in the chapter, about SQL Server Service Manager, and the security of logging on? Well, it would be here that any changes to that account are implemented.

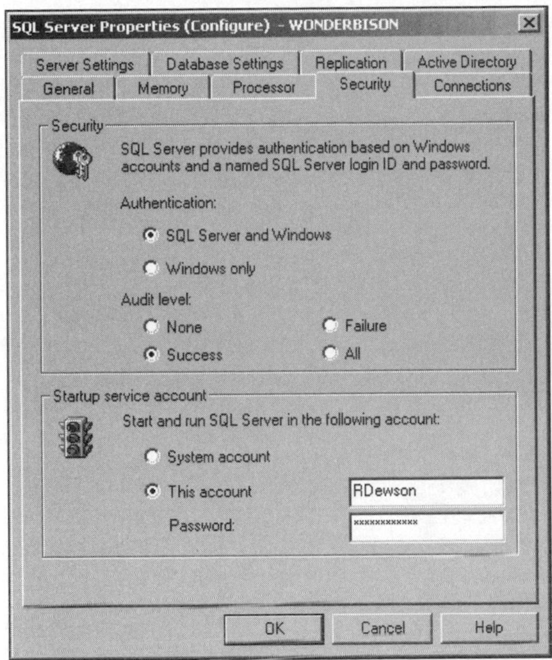

Security will crop up time and again with SQL Server, and so it should. After all, the last area we want to get wrong is the security of our database, which could possibly result in allowing anyone to inspect, or worse, corrupt the data within. This tab is one area that we have to get right. Authentication has been covered in Chapter 1, and therefore there is no need to cover it again. However, the next option, Audit level, is very interesting, and does require a bit of thought about our SQL Server installation, and how SQL Server is being used.

By choosing one of the four audit level options, we can use this to determine which login attempts will be logged to either the Windows Application Log, or the SQL Server log. The screen shown in the earlier Security tab illustration shows that there was no auditing in progress. However, to demonstrate logging, alter the Audit level option to Success. What this means is that for every successful login to SQL Server, an entry will be logged to the specific log. For this alteration to take place, SQL Server has to be stopped and started through SQL Server Service Manager.

Query Analyzer is then started by selecting Start | Programs | Microsoft SQL Server | Query Analyzer. After selecting your database and ensuring Windows Authentication is selected, pressing enter will login to SQL Server! This would be seen as a successful log in attempt. To check this, view the **Windows Application Log**, which you can find on a Windows 2000 machine first by clicking Start | Programs | Administrative Tools | Event Viewer (you can also get at this via the Control Panel), which will then show the Event Viewer for Windows. Select the Application Log, as shown below:

If you then take a look at the last event entry, providing nothing else that generates entries is working on your computer, you should see the successful login to SQL Server logged in the Application Log. If you then double-click on the event, the dialog should look very similar to that shown here:

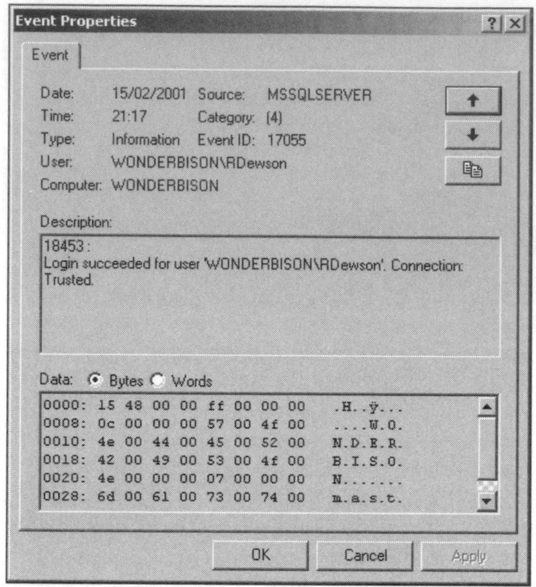

Taking this a stage further, it is important to sit back and think about the security on your site. Take in to consideration the amount of events logged, and whether it is better to log just failures, or failures and successes. Personally, I think that logging failures is a must in a productive environment, as it enables us to check if anyone is trying to force their way into the system. Logging successes may also be useful for checking that no single user has had their own security compromised, for example, in the event of their User ID being logged in when the user is in fact not present in the office. However, I tend to feel that the logging of any successful login should reside within any application written in languages such as Visual Basic, Visual FoxPro, etc. that are accessing SQL Server, rather than at the SQL Server level.

It is possible to alter the Service Manager account startup User ID and password, as was mentioned earlier. This can be done from the Security tab in the Startup service account section. If the password expires on the ID that is currently used to log in, or is altered for any other reason, then it is imperative that you come to this tab and match up the passwords. SQL Server will not start until this is done, and using Enterprise Manager is a great deal easier than using the Services applet in Administrative Tools from the Control Panel.

The ability to alter the User ID and password here is only valid if you have the required administration rights on your computer.

> **You should always use an ID with Administrator privileges to the machine, and the corresponding password to start up and run SQL Server, as it is this ID that logs SQL Server on to the machine. Without administration rights, SQL Server will not be able to update or create security IDs.**

9. Now click on the Connections tab. Again, this is an advanced topic, and we won't be covering this in detail. This tab would be used if we wished to limit the number of connections to the database at any one time.

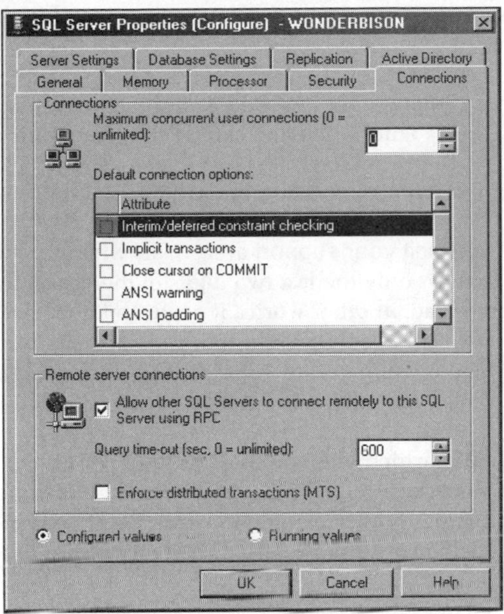

10. Moving on to the second row of tabs, we come to the Server Settings. Not the best named tab in the world, as all of these tabs can alter any of the server settings, but as you can see, there are certain settings that can be altered here. For example, we can specify how to deal with years that are stored as two digits.

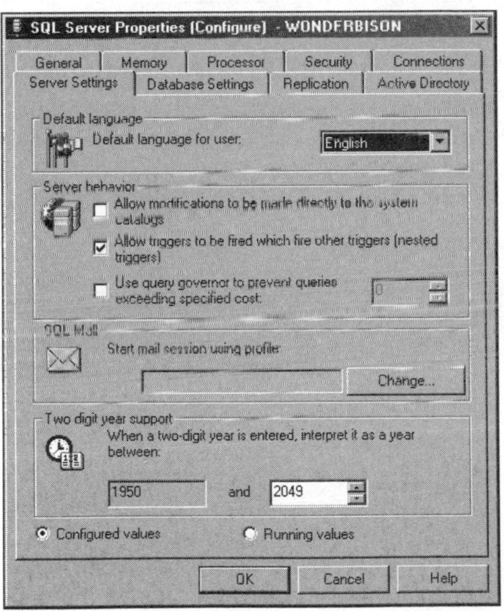

Looking at the Server Settings tab, notice that the default language is the language chosen at install time. The screenshot shows English as this is my native language, but it could easily have been French, German, Chinese, British English, or even Traditional Chinese. However, this option only applies to the messages sent back from SQL Server, and not to the data contained within, or how it is stored. That relates to **SQL Server collation**. This was mentioned in Chapter 1 when SQL Server was installed, and is covered further in Chapter 6.

The next section of the Server Settings tab, the Server behavior section, refers to some quite advanced subject areas, so for the time being ignore this and skip to the next section.

SQL Mail, SQL Servers own mail service, is also not used in this book, so skip that section as well.

However, moving on to the Two digit year support area, deals with the situation of a query or any other data entry into SQL Server, that has only the last two digits of the year number entered. SQL Server needs to know how this will be represented, in other words, it needs to know whether to use a prefix of 19, or a prefix of 20, and this section is where this decision is made. At present, the dialog informs us that if a two-digit year of 99 is entered, then this will be set to 1999. If 02 is entered, then the year will be set to 2002. Just to clarify, if 50 is entered, the year will be 1950, if 49 is entered, then if will be set to 2049.

We can change one of the values, which will automatically set the first value displayed, in this case 1950, to being one year less than the altered value, and as such, it is therefore possible to have different cut-off dates. So, we could alter the right-hand side to being 2099, and therefore the left-hand side would be set to 2000. This would mean that we are only dealing with dates in the range of 2000-2099, and all dates would be prefixed with 20.

If a four-digit date is passed in, these tests are bypassed, and the date passed is accepted for what it is. I also strongly recommend that 4-year digit years should be stored, as that the space saving associated with switching to 2 digit years can be more trouble than it is worth.

11. We now come to the Database Settings tab, which dictates how the databases within SQL Server are dealt with.

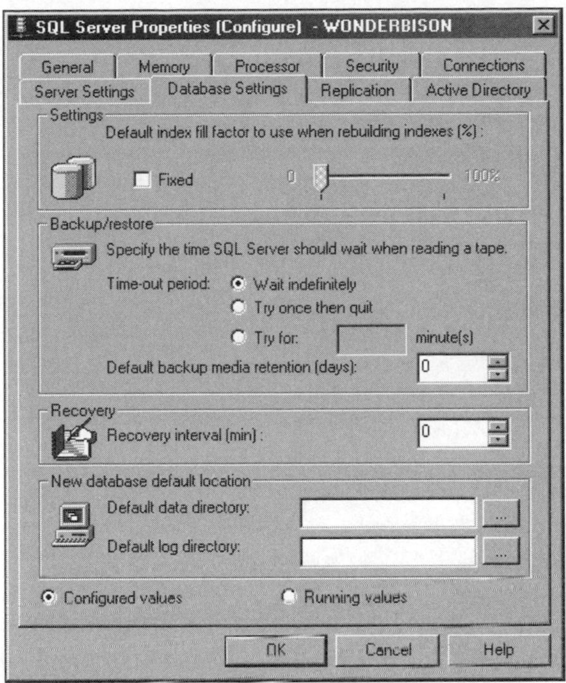

The first area that concerns us with our study will be the Backup/restore area, as the Settings frame should only really be altered by an experienced database administrator.

This section deals with when we are performing a backup to a tape drive, and the settings here are used to determine how SQL Server will perform when writing to a tape drive. This needs some careful thought. For example, do we really need to ensure SQL Server waits indefinitely for a tape drive to become ready? Is there a better option? Obviously, we have to think about what is going on with our backup, and there is a whole chapter dealing with backups later in the book. Waiting on a tape drive indefinitely should only be chosen if it is crucial that a backup be performed, and that it would be potentially disastrous if a backup was not taken. This would probably be found in a monitored production scenario, and a better option for a non-critical production environment could be to skip the backup.

There is also an option that allows us to say that a tape is only valid for a certain number of days. During this time, SQL Server will see the tape as a valid backup tape, and will therefore not overwrite the data backed-up on it. However, once the tape is set as being old, in other words, once the set number of retention days have elapsed, then the backed-up data can be overwritten.

The Recovery frame is quite an advanced system administration option, so it won't be covered here. Now, move on to the last section, New database default location. If this is populated, then we are informing SQL Server that the directories specified will be the default file location when creating a new database.

12. The next two tabs won't be covered, as these deal with areas that you should really only tackle when you have become more knowledgeable about SQL Server. The Replication tab deals with the replication, or copying, of data between two SQL Server installations. This is mainly used for security or performance reasons.

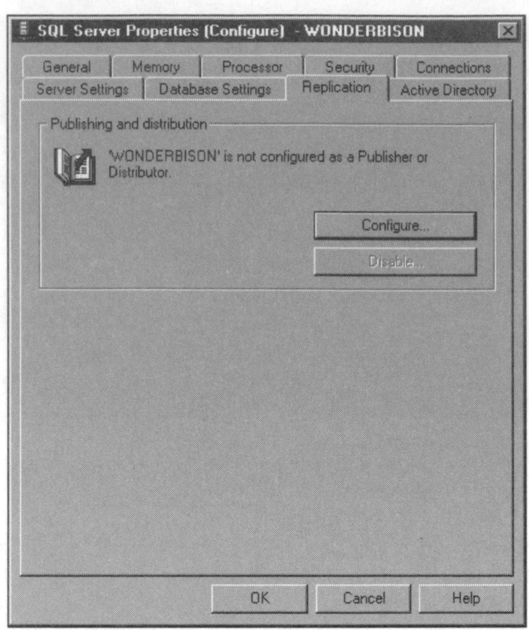

13. Finally, Active Directory is a security feature introduced in Windows 2000. Although security is a major issue for SQL Server, Active Directories is a very large topic, which is oriented more towards Windows 2000.

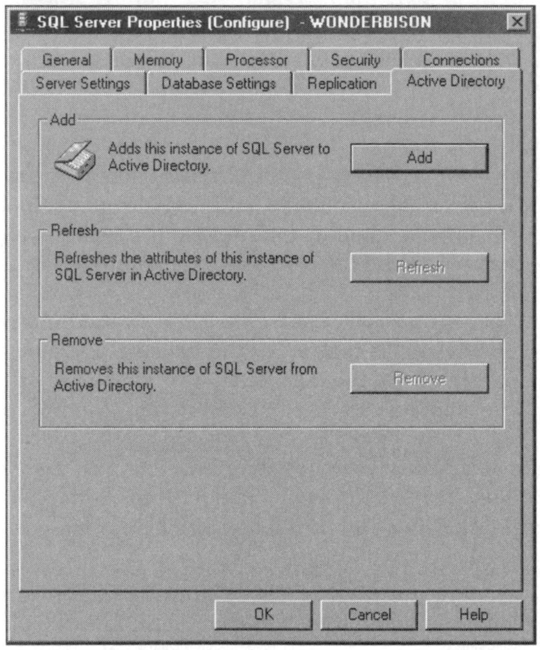

So, by now you should now be fully conversant with setting up the necessities of SQL Server, and now that you know how to set up a SQL Server, it's time to now add a new SQL Server instance, which will be used for system testing.

Registering a New SQL Server

Enterprise Manager needs to know what installations of SQL Servers it has to work with. When SQL Server is first installed, a default server is registered, and Enterprise Manager is informed of this server, and registers it. However, any subsequent installations, whether remote or local, will need to be registered with Enterprise Manager.

If you recall, in Chapter 1, we mentioned that it was possible to install more than one SQL Server on the same machine, so for example, a development server and a system test server could be installed on a single desktop. In this next section, we will assume that a second installation has been made, keeping in mind the points made about two installations in Chapter 1.

Just to recap, you need to install another SQL Server instance using the setup CD. A name needs to be given to this extra instance, which has to be different from the name assigned to any other SQL Server installed on that computer, so, for our example, let's choose SYSTESTSERVER. We will then be able to use this as a new registration within SQL Server, and this installation will be registered and displayed within Enterprise Manager.

If you are working with an existing setup you may find that the second installation is already within Enterprise Manager, but if it isn't, or a subsequent installation is required, then you may find that you have to go through this process in this section.

This time, a built-in wizard will be used to set up a registration to a new SQL Server instance (installed from the CD), and then the result will be inspected in Enterprise Manager.

Try It Out – New SQL Server Registration

1. Ensure Enterprise Manager is up and running by checking that the Service Manager tool has a green arrow displayed. Navigate to the SQL Server Group within Enterprise Manager, and then right-click on it. You will see a context menu, from which select New SQL Server Registration...

2. It is also possible to click on the Wizards button on the toolbar (depicted by a magic wand), which brings up the Select Wizard dialog. Select the first option, Register Server Wizard.

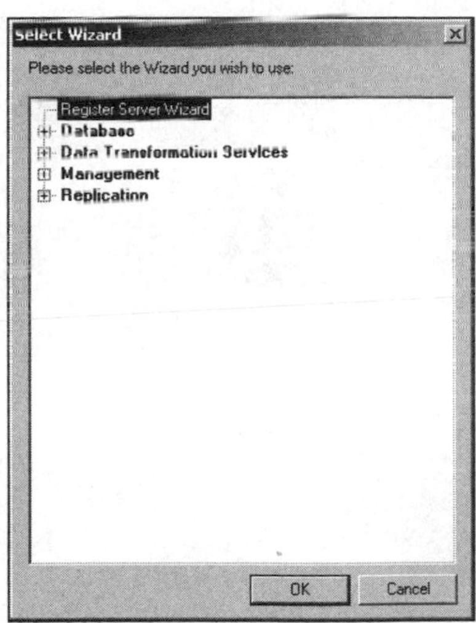

3. Either of these options, starts the **Register SQL Server Wizard**. You should see a check box, informing us that it is possible from here on, to complete registration without a wizard. Yes this is possible, but I suspect that you, like me, will register a server so few times that it's simply easier to use the wizard. Click **Next**.

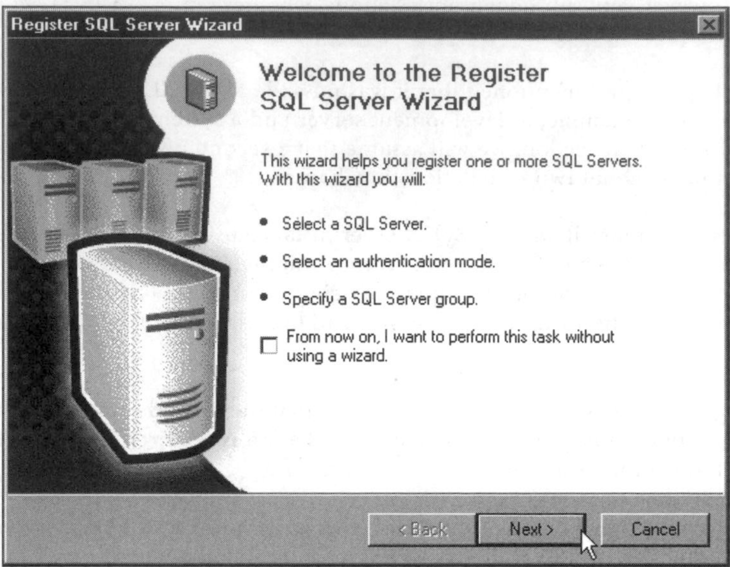

4. You are now at the point to register a new SQL Server. The list of available servers will show the server boxes available, or it is possible to simply enter the desired server name. As you can see, there is nothing listed here, so we will have to type in the server name manually. The name I used was **WONDERBISON\SYSTESTSERVER**, which relates directly to the instance name used during the physical installation. Once done, click **Add**.

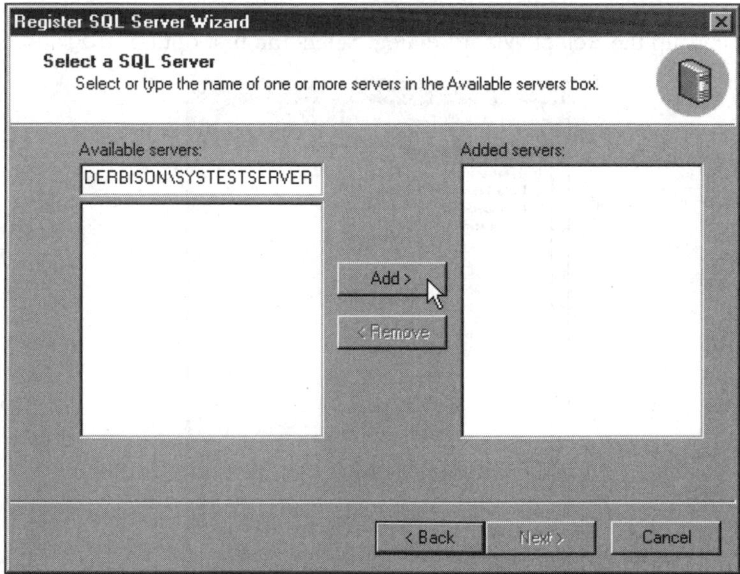

5. On clicking **Add**, the server that we've just specified will be placed in the **Added Servers:** list box, which will list all of the servers to be added. We can actually add more than one server at a time if so desired. Once done, click **Next**.

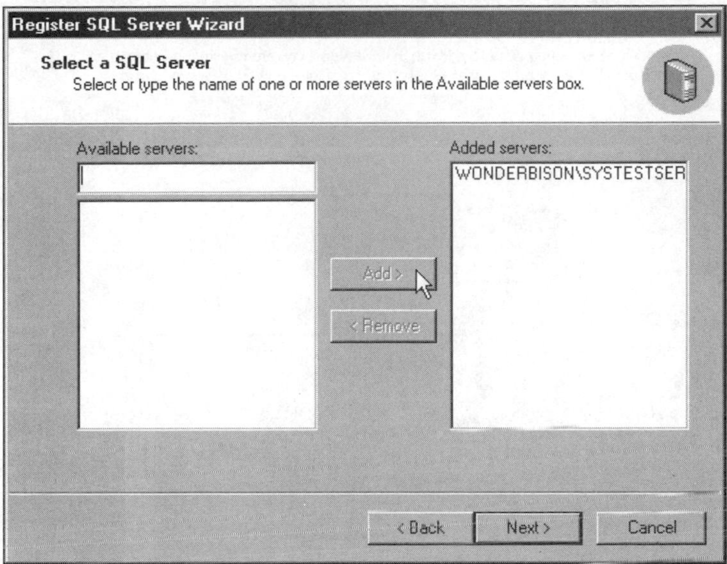

6. This now asks what sort of authentication we wish to use for the server. Here we will choose **Windows Authentication**. You would be best to use the same authentication as the other SQL Servers in the Server Group. If you wish to change authentication modes for this server, it might be better to put this in a different group so that maintenance of the servers is a bit easier. After making the selection, click **Next**.

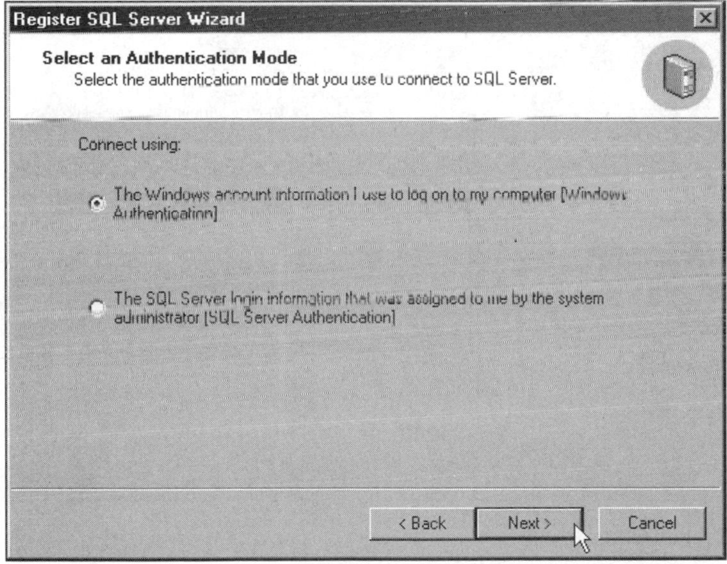

7. We can add the SQL Server instance to any group that exists within SQL Server, or we can create a new group. We will discuss what a SQL Server group is later. Once done, click **Next**.

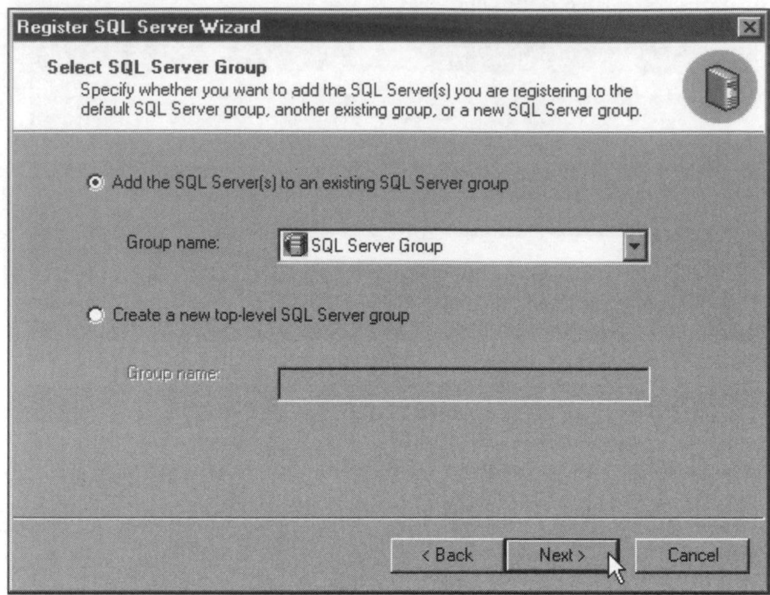

8. The last dialog gives us a chance to change our mind. This lists the SQL Servers that will be registered. If we're happy, we simply click **Finish**. This will then start the registration process.

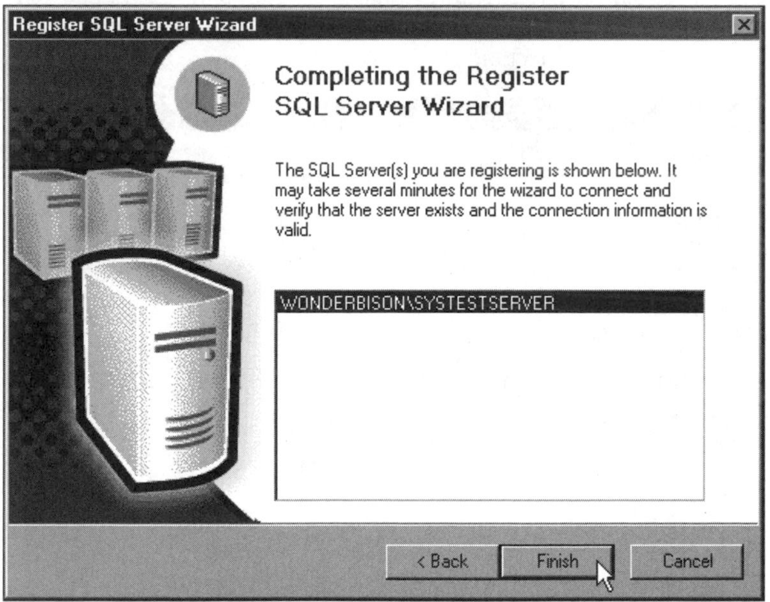

9. Once the registration of the new SQL Server instance in Enterprise Manager is complete, you will hopefully see the following success message. As you can see, this entry registered successfully, but in the event of a failure, say for example because of an authentication problem, then we could simply select it and alter the properties, as in such a case, the Properties button would become enabled.

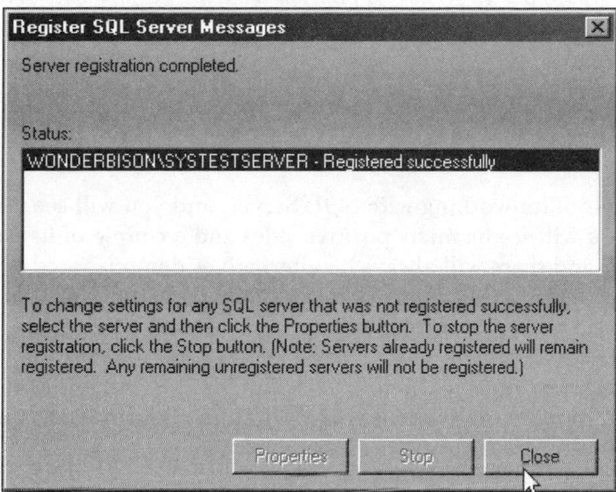

10. Click on Close, and then navigate to Enterprise Manager. You may have to refresh the Tree view; however, you should find the new server(s) listed as I have here:

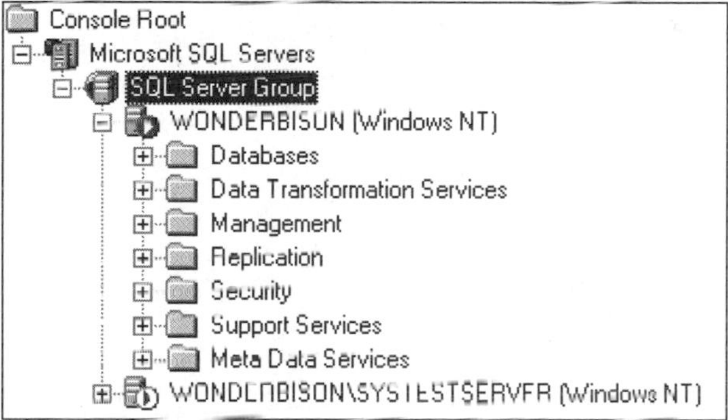

This process will not install a new instance of SQL Server on your machine, but will merely register within Enterprise Manager any installation that Enterprise Manager did not know about.

One of the first areas that require thought deals with SQL Server groups. These are logical groupings within Enterprise Manager, and have no real overall use within SQL Server. However, what groups are excellent for, is collating databases that have similar attributes or uses as a group, so that we can point to any server within that group, and inherently know certain facts about it.

As such, you can imagine that it might be useful to have a group for development servers, a different group for testing servers, and finally another group for production databases. Similarly, if perhaps you were to have different physical servers for production, testing, and development, you may well create groups for different projects.

It is possible to have groups within groups, so that you could have a production group, and then a sub-group within that for each project.

Summary

Enterprise Manager is a tool for working with SQL Server, and you will see it in action throughout the book, and from there you will see its many positive sides and a couple of its flaws. However, you will not be left high and dry, and there will always be alternatives demonstrated where Enterprise Manager is not available to you. Enterprise Manager is an extremely powerful tool, and this book will be discussing its behavior and attributes throughout.

Upon completing this chapter, you should now have an idea as to what information is available through tools such as Enterprise Manager, and where you can find the information you need to deal with any development issues that may arise.

This chapter has demonstrated how Enterprise Manager will aid you with your development, and in the next chapter an alternative, called Query Analyzer, will demonstrated. At then end of that chapter you will have more of an idea as to where we might use Enterprise Manager over Query Analyzer, and also be aware of just how Enterprise Manager saves us from having to remember specific commands.

Query Analyzer

Now that SQL Server is installed, and that Enterprise Manager and SQL Server Service Manager have been demonstrated, there is one front-end tool interacting with the SQL Server engine left to discuss. Some people will argue that it is the most important tool within SQL Server, especially those who prefer to type in command syntax rather than burrowing through Enterprise Manager. This tool is SQL Server **Query Analyzer**. What this tool provides is effectively a command-line interface to databases within SQL Server. But there is a lot more to this tool. It is extremely useful, powerful, and informative. This chapter won't demonstrate this power, but will demonstrate what features are included to allow that power to be used to its full effect. The power demonstration will come as you progress through each chapter of the book, starting at Chapter 5 where the first stages of building the database example begin.

There will also be the ability to demonstrate how Query Analyzer can be used to help with interrogating data, using system functions, and displaying results. It is quite a powerful command-line interface. So why have I called it a command-line interface, when the tool obviously is not that at all?

When Query Analyzer was first developed, it *was* a simple command-line interface. You went to a MS-DOS box and logged in to a server using a utility called ISQL, which is short for Interactive Structured Query Language. Just as a reminder, SQL is the language used to interrogate and manipulate data, as well as build and manipulate databases and the information contained within them. Microsoft has its own proprietary dialect of SQL called **Transact SQL**, or **T-SQL**.

> *ISQL and OSQL (Object-oriented SQL) are both command-line utilities for entering T-SQL commands for a SQL Server database. ISQL uses an old method of data access known as DB-Library, and is only fully compatible with SQL Server 6.5. It has not been updated with the functionality found in subsequent SQL Server versions. OSQL is an upgrade of ISQL that uses ODBC for data access. ODBC is also quite an old method of data access, but it has been kept up to date and, therefore, the full functionality of T-SQL commands is supported by OSQL.*

We will explore and explain each area that is contained within Query Analyzer so that, when each area is used later in the book, you will instantly recognize it. Covering each area now will provide an excellent reference point to come back to later, if you need to.

So what exactly does this chapter cover and what are these areas in Query Analyzer? By the time you reach the summary, you will:

- Know what Query Analyzer is
- Know how to start Query Analyzer and log in successfully
- Have learned how to use the Object Browser to find database objects
- Have explored the templates tab and learned what templates are
- Know how to use the menu and know where to find specific commands
- Have learned how to change the database you are working with
- Have seen the different methods of displaying output
- Have figured out how to customize Query Analyzer
- Have learned what options are available on the toolbar
- Be able to create a new login account
- Be able to change which database a user is automatically connected to

This list demonstrates what a powerful tool Query Analyzer is, and gives us quite a large amount of information to cover in one chapter but, trust me, it's not all that bad.

So, without further ado, let's dive right in and have a look at how to start Query Analyzer.

Starting Query Analyzer

Query Analyzer can be started in two different ways, from within Enterprise Manager and from the Start menu button. In this section of the chapter, both of these methods will be demonstrated, as each does have minor idiosyncrasies concerning logging in to SQL Server. First of all, let's take a look at how to start Query Analyzer from Enterprise Manager.

Starting from Enterprise Manager

Probably the most common way to start Query Analyzer is from within Enterprise Manager. You will have navigated to your server in Enterprise Manager, and then will realize that you need Query Analyzer to perform some function or other.

As soon as you open up Enterprise Manager and select a server, a connection attempt is made to that server through SQL Server Service Manager. If the connection is successful then, of course, you can proceed with using the databases, etc. within that server. You should not have any problems with your connections to the server installation built in this book.

If you have not highlighted a node in Enterprise Manager at the server level (for example, if you are at the SQL Server Group level, or above), then Query Analyzer will not log on to a server automatically. This is covered in the next section.

Also remember that Enterprise Manager will display multiple servers. I would expect that, as a developer, you would have at least two servers: your development server and your test server. So take care that you are working with the right one.

Try It Out – Starting Query Analyzer from Enterprise Manager

1. SQL Server should be up and running at this point. If not, then start up SQL Server as you were shown in Chapter 2. Now start up Enterprise Manager and navigate to the server that you want to have Query Analyzer connect to at its startup, by default. As you can see, I have chosen the initial WONDERBISON server, built when SQL Server was installed.

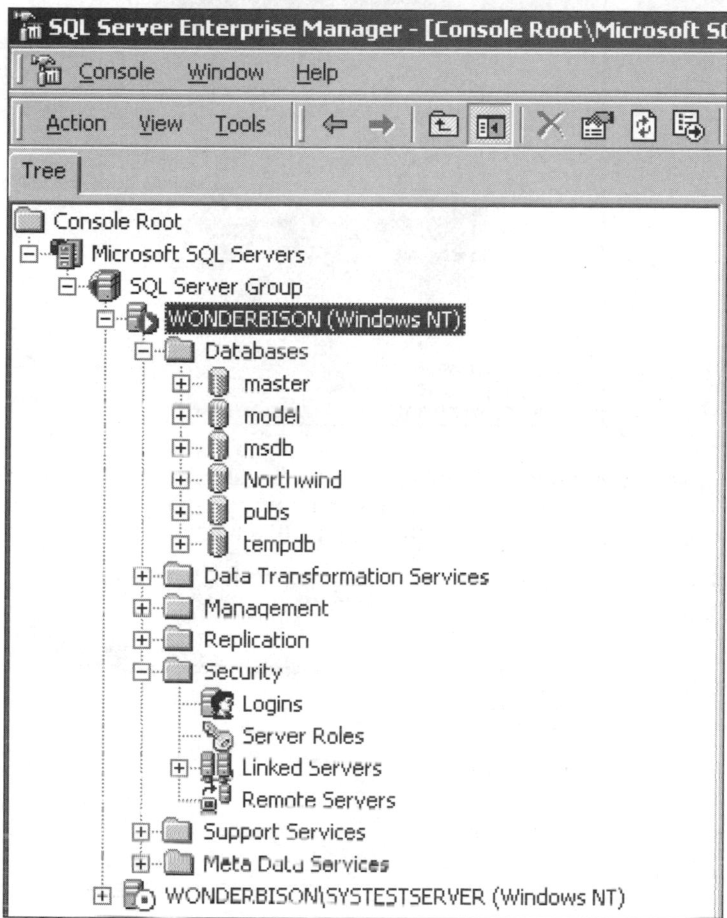

2. From the Tools menu, select SQL Query Analyzer:

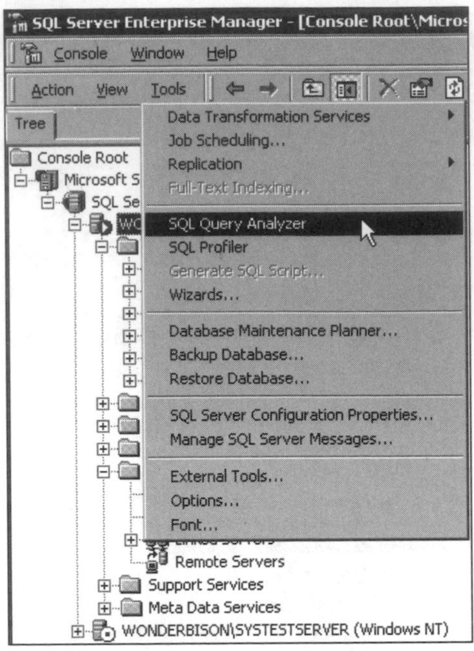

3. From here, you should find that Query Analyzer has started up, is in the correct server, and is ready to accept any instructions that you wish to pass to it. You can tell that it is the correct server by the first WONDERBISON listed in the title bar.

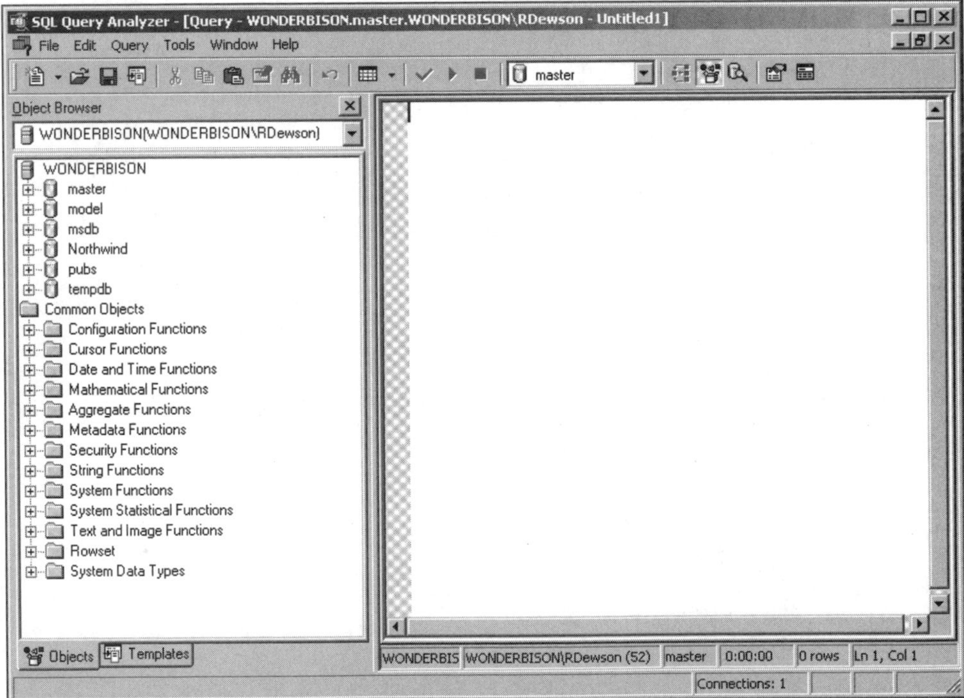

So, a connection has been made and it is valid. You have also explicitly said to Enterprise Manager that you wish to use the Query Analyzer tool. Therefore, Enterprise Manager quite rightly makes the assumption that it is the current login that wants to start up Query Analyzer, and that Query Analyzer is required for work with the server that is currently highlighted in Enterprise Manager. Consequently, Enterprise Manager passes the current connection information through to the SQL Server engine as parameters with the command to start Query Analyzer. These parameters allow Query Analyzer to log in and be ready for work on the right server without any input from you.

4. The next screenshot shows how the title bar differs when Query Analyzer is connected to a different server. Notice how master in the title bar is prefixed with SYSTESTSERVER now:

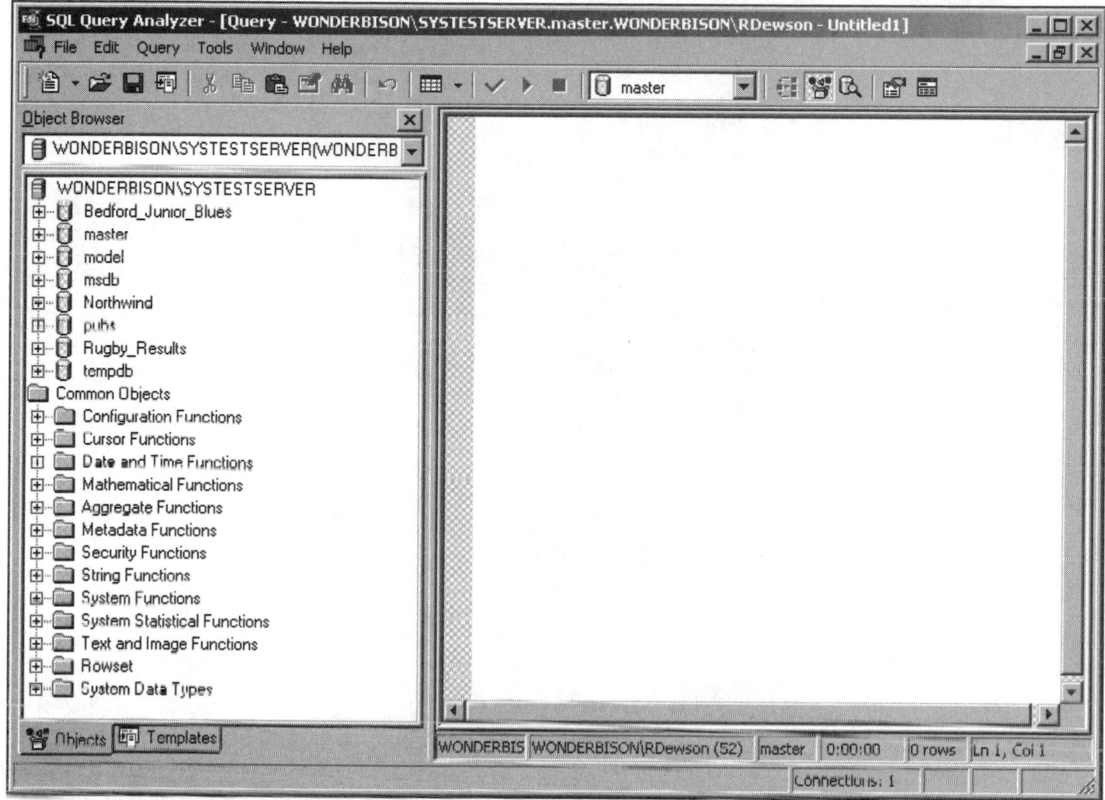

Starting from the Start Button

The second possible way of starting Query Analyzer is from the Start button on the taskbar. Let's have a look at this.

Try It Out – Starting Query Analyzer from the Start Button

1. By selecting Start | Programs | Microsoft SQL Server | Query Analyzer, Query Analyzer will start up on your machine. However, this time, you will have a login screen to contend with. You should see either of the two screens below, depending on how you have installed SQL Server, and defined the login options for the server. The first screen is attempting to log on through **SQL Server Authentication**, while the second is attempting to log on through **Windows Authentication**. Recall Chapter 1, where Windows Authentication and SQL Server Authentication were discussed. Both screens are valid.

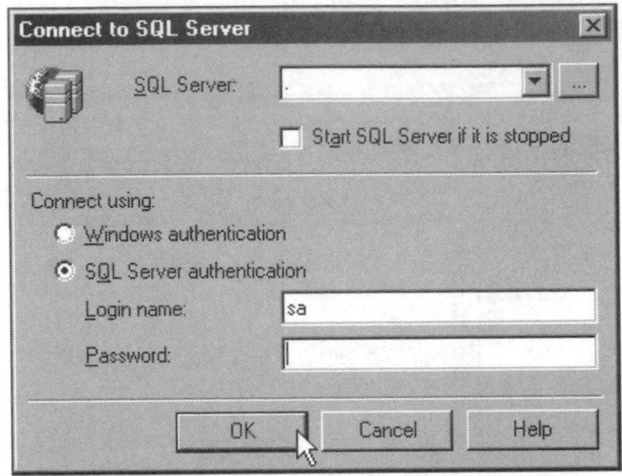

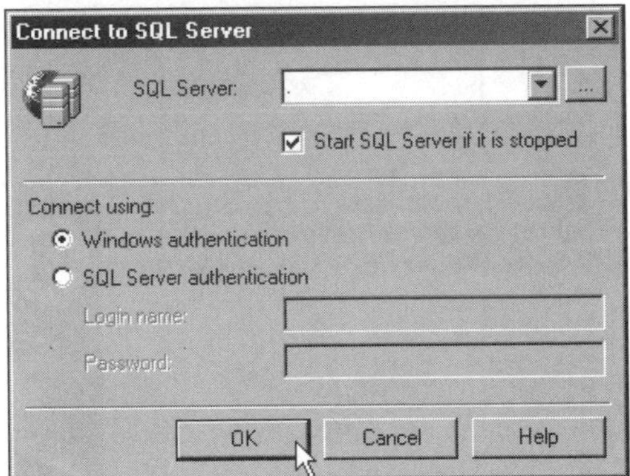

2. If you make sure that you have entered the right Login name and Password for the first of these windows, and that the Start SQL Server if it is stopped check box is checked in both cases, when you click on OK, you will log in to SQL Server exactly as if you went through Enterprise Manager. However, things are working a bit differently behind the scenes, so let's go through that now.

In the first screenshot of the two above, you will see that SQL Server authentication is being used, and that the sa User ID is used as the login name. If you remember, in Chapter 2 I mentioned that the `sa` login should not be used unless absolutely necessary, and it should also be password protected. `sa` is the default login name when Query Analyzer opens, but if everyone uses it, it becomes very difficult to track who is actually doing what in SQL Server and who is causing problems.

This is where using Windows Authentication comes in to play, especially where SQL Server is on an NT or 2000 machine. By logging in to SQL Server using Query Analyzer with Windows Authentication, you are logging in to the server as yourself, with the correct credentials. Even when more than one person is logged in to SQL Server, with Windows Authentication, it is possible to track the users and the processes that they are running. Of course, people can still log on using SQL Server Authentication – they just shouldn't do it with the `sa` login. The best method, as was described in Chapter 1, is to place a secure but memorable password on the `sa` account, and tell nobody what it is.

A major point to note in both screens is the top **SQL Server** combo box. Notice the period (`.`) where the name of the server should be. This is what will be seen for a local SQL Server. You can also type in: **(local)**. If, however, the SQL Server were on a remote computer, then you would enter the name of this remote computer in this box, or click the ellipsis (...) button on the right. This would bring up a list of SQL Servers on remote computers that you had access to, and you could select which installation to connect to:

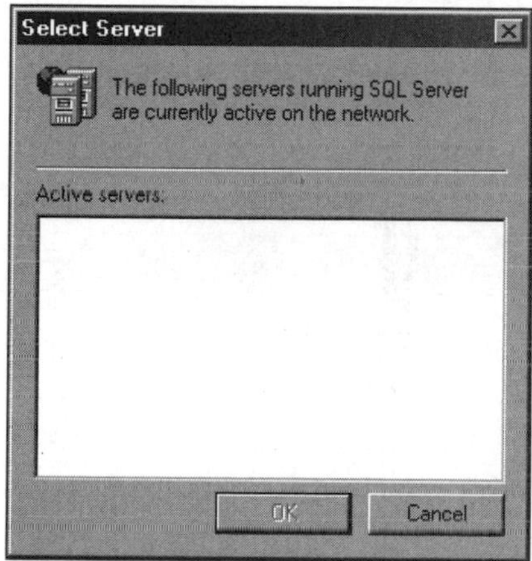

As you can see, in this local installation there are no active servers on the network.

The final point to note is the **Start SQL Server if stopped** check box. It could be that SQL Server is not running when you start up Query Analyzer from the **Start** button. This box is checked by default, which means that Query Analyzer will start SQL Server for you. Really you would only check this if you wanted to use Query Analyzer without the need to find out any information from any SQL Server database, which would be pretty rare.

Now that you know how to start Query Analyzer and have it started on your desktop, we can take a look at what makes up Query Analyzer, starting with the Object Browser.

The Object Browser

As you can see in the screenshot below, the Object Browser is located on the left-hand side of Query Analyzer. If it is not immediately visible, you will need to go to Tools | Object Browser | Show/Hide. Note the two Objects and Templates tabs at the bottom of the screen:

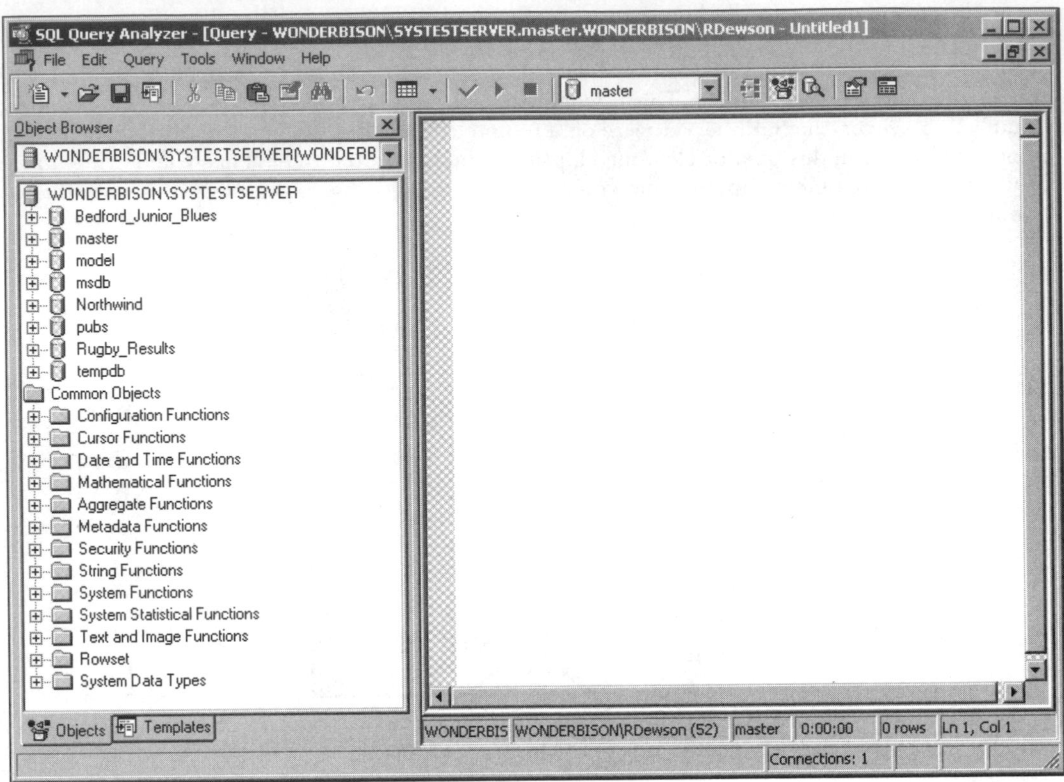

The Object Browser shows a list of objects within the SQL Server you have connected to. It also provides a list of functions that can be used for constructing queries and stored procedures, and help in using these functions. Finally, all the system data types that are valid within SQL Server are also available for inspection through this pane.

This all helps you, as a developer, to know what functions are available for use within your queries, and to demonstrate the syntax and parameters to be passed in to them. The next section will look at these objects in a bit more detail. First of all, let's take a look at the Objects tab and the objects within SQL Server.

System Objects

SQL Server comes installed with a number of built-in databases – four are required to make SQL Server work and two others created as example databases. These were discussed in Chapter 1 when the installation process of SQL Server was demonstrated. However, no matter whether the database is a system database, an example database, or even your own database, there will be specific objects within every database that make that database function in the correct manner. These are all known as **system objects**, and includes user and system tables, views, and even the databases themselves.

When you first open Query Analyzer, the system objects tree nodes will all be collapsed such that no individual item within any node can be seen: The root object nodes within the tree are the databases of the SQL Server installation, and when you expand these nodes, you will see other system objects, which are grouped together.

> *You may have noticed the* Common Objects *node situated below these system objects. This is something quite separate, which we will discuss shortly.*

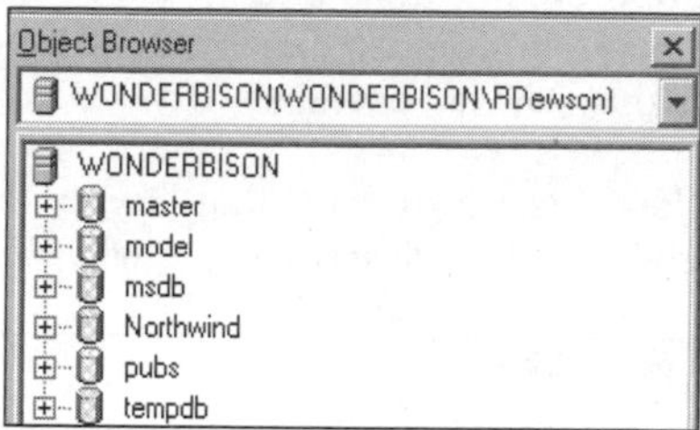

These nodes can then be expanded, by clicking on the + signs, so that you can see whatever information you require at any given time. Imagine, for example, that you want to explore what information is within a `Northwind` table. You can't remember whether a column called `OrderDate` is within a table called `Orders` or `OrderDetails`. By expanding the nodes in the Object Browser, you can see exactly where that piece of information is. The screenshot below shows the columns in the `Orders` and `OrderDetails` tables expanded:

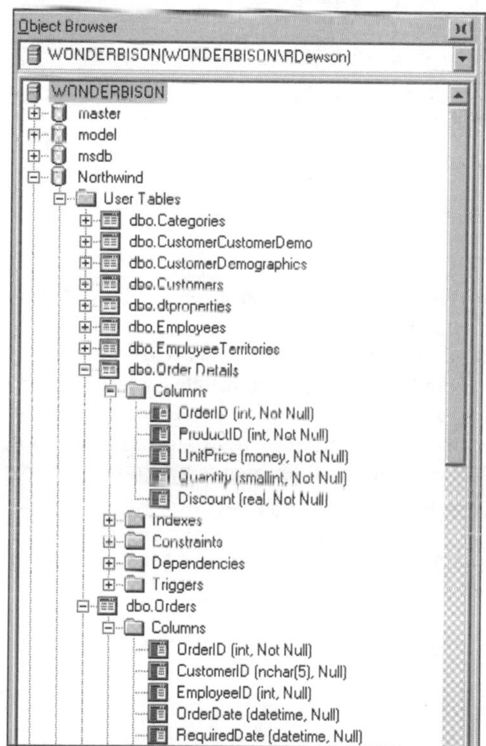

As you can see, the `OrderDate` column is in the `Orders` table and not in `OrderDetails`.

Common Objects

Common objects – under the Common Objects folder, are those objects that are not specific to a particular database. The items within this part of the Object Browser are not tables, etc., but are the functions that you can perform within SQL Server, or the system data types that are available to you. These are aids to help you with SQL Server commands within Query Analyzer, a sort of quick reference guide if you like.

Query Analyzer has grouped all of these functions into areas of similar functionality, so that specific functions are easy to locate. For example, you can expand the String Functions node to find a list of all the string manipulation functions that you can use.

What is great about this part of the Object Browser is that, if you place the cursor over a specific function, a tool tip is displayed giving a short description of what the function does.

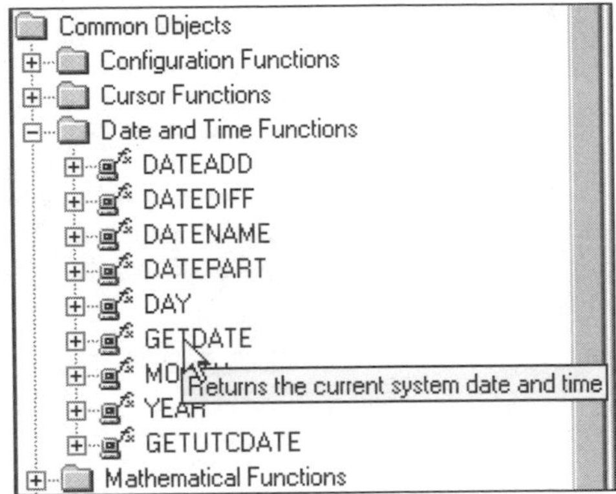

Let's now take a look at the other tab – Templates.

Templates

The Templates tab is used for holding SQL Server and user-built templates. A template is a file which holds the basics of a function used in Query Analyzer, which can either manipulate databases, manipulate database objects, or server objects, or work with the data within a table in a server. When I say manipulate here, I also mean that there are templates that exist for the creation of databases, objects, and so on. Notice that I said "the basics". This is the whole essence of what a template is – it provides the basic template for a function. Some templates contain more information, and more built-in functionality than others. However, with all templates, there are parameters that must be set to allow the template to become a fully functional piece of code.

If you move on to the Templates tab you will see many template groups, which give us a quick overview of the areas that we may apply templates to.

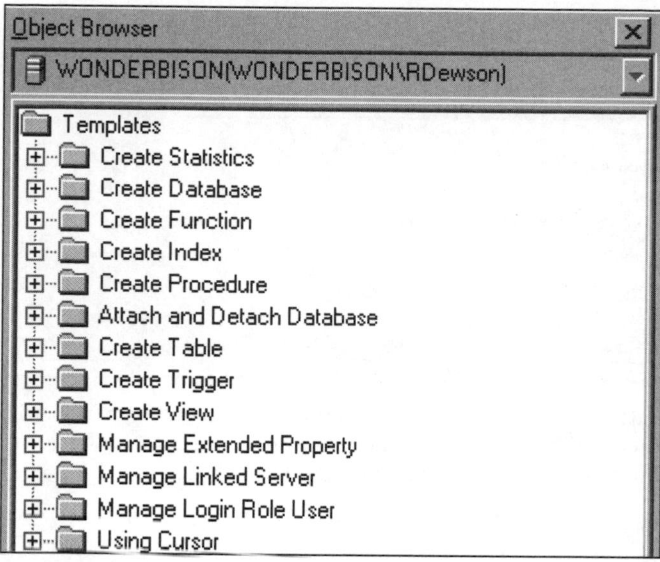

This may seem a little confusing and, although templates will be covered in more detail in Chapter 6 when we look at the creation of tables, it would be useful to see the contents of a template right now.

Click on the Create Table node to expand it and double-click on Create Table Basic Template. The following code will appear in the main pane of Query Analyzer. Don't worry if you don't understand it all yet, as this specific code is covered in Chapter 6:

```
-- =============================================
-- Create table basic template
-- =============================================
IF EXISTS(SELECT name
   FROM  sysobjects
   WHERE name = N'<table_name, sysname, test_table>'
   AND type = 'U')
   DROP TABLE <table_name, sysname, test_table>
GO

CREATE TABLE <table_name, sysname, test_table> (
   <column_1, sysname, c1> <datatype_for_column_1, , int> NULL,
   <column_2, sysname, c2> <datatype_for_column_2, , int> NOT NULL)
GO
```

If you look closely, you will see a number of lines of code with greater-than and less-than signs surrounding three comma separated names. These are the parameters that were referred to above. By using the template replacement facility, *Ctrl+Shift+M*, or Edit | Replace Template Parameters from the menu, you can very quickly alter these parameters to make the template complete. The dialog for setting these parameters is shown overleaf:

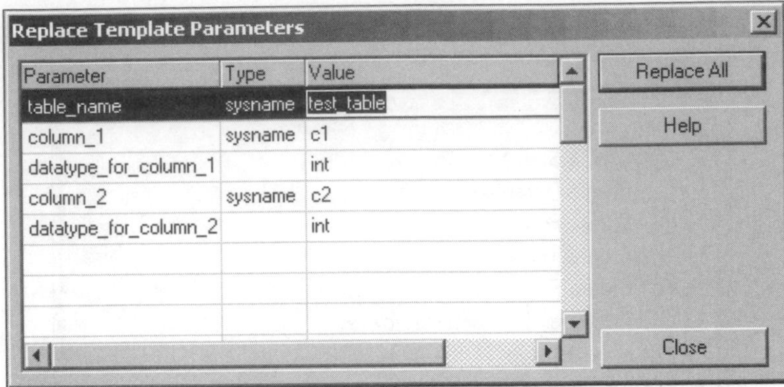

You can directly relate what you see in this dialog to necessary information within the template. This makes the whole process of building a useful query to perform potentially complex functions a great deal easier. Click Close to remove the dialog for the time being.

The Query Pane

The **Query pane** sits on the right of the Object Browser and, as you can see in the screenshot below, I have placed some text within it to denote where it is. When you enter SQL code to run against your SQL Server instance, database, tables, or any other valid query statement, you enter the code in the Query pane:

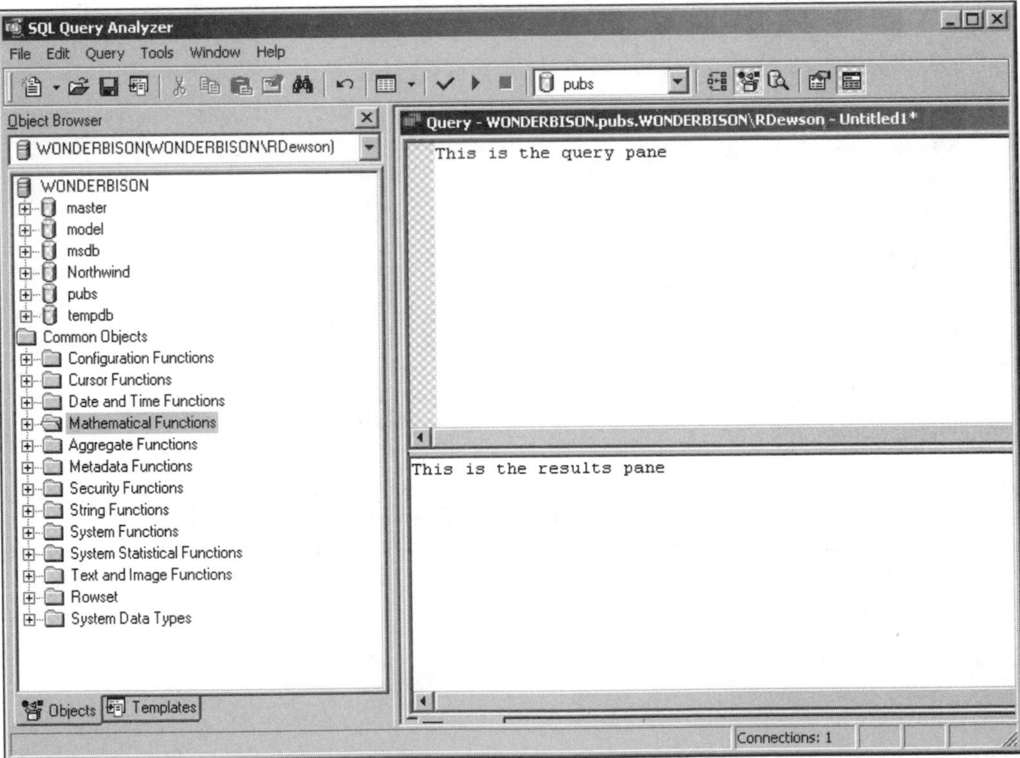

> **Note that, when you close a pane, if that is the last pane that is connected to a specific server, the connection to that server will be ended.**

The Results Pane

The **Results pane** is used to display any results and messages from running SQL code placed in the Query pane. It is always found below the Query pane. I have added text to show its location in the screenshot above. The Results pane doesn't display by default. You need to switch it on by actually running a query, by the toolbar button, or through the menu: Window | Show Results Pane. *Ctrl+R* toggles the Results pane on and off.

Menu Options

Like every Windows-based product, Query Analyzer comes with a menu containing the necessary functionality to make it work. In this next section, the menu items will be described so that you know what is available to you, and why. Some menu choices are standard to Windows products, for example, File | Exit, and we will not cover them here.

The File Menu

The menu will be discussed from left to right. Let's start with the File menu.

File | Connect (Ctrl+O)

Use this if you have disconnected from a server and wish to either reconnect or connect to a different server entirely. You can also add a server, which is not listed, to the Object Browser. When you select this item, you will be presented with the Connect to SQL Server dialog that you would see if starting Query Analyzer from the Start menu.

Query Analyzer allows you to connect to different servers at the same time with each connection having its own Query and Result panes.

File | Disconnect (Ctrl+F4)

Use this if you wish to disconnect and lose the connections that you have with the server that has the connection in the current Query pane. As I said previously, more than one server can be connected to at any one time. By selecting a Query pane that is connected to the server, and disconnecting by selecting this menu item, all connections to that server will be lost. The Query pane with the connection will be closed, and you will be prompted to save any code that you have entered or changed.

File | Disconnect All

As you might expect, this option is very much like Disconnect, except every connection to every server is lost. All Query panes are closed and, again, you will be prompted to save any code that you have entered or changed.

File | New (Ctrl+N)

File | New through the menu allows the creation of a new blank query pane, or a template for one of several functions. Don't worry about templates for the moment – they are covered later in the chapter. When you select File | New, a pop-up dialog appears, allowing you to select an item to create in a new query pane. Here, I've selected Blank Query Window:

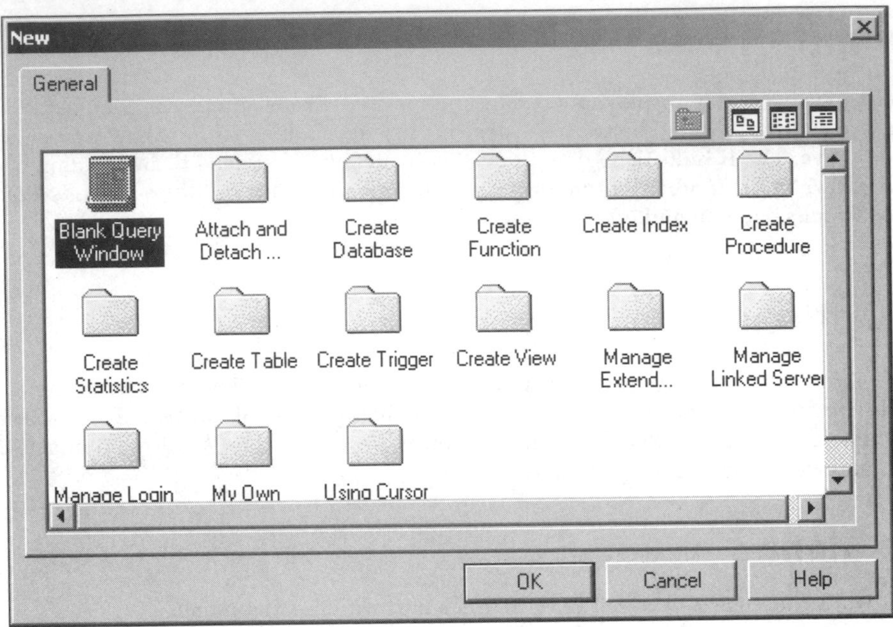

> **Using File | New through the menu works differently to pressing *Ctrl+N*, even although the two are linked on the menu. Hitting *Ctrl+N* simply creates a new blank Query pane and does not bring up the dialog.**

File | Open (Ctrl+Shift+P)

Open opens a selected file in the active Query or Results pane, overwriting anything already entered there. Of course, if you have any unsaved items, you will be prompted to save these first.

File | Save (Ctrl+S)

This will save the query text from the Query pane, or the results from the Results pane, to a file on your disk. Only the query text *or* the results produced will be saved, depending on which pane the active cursor is in at that time. If you want to save the query *and* the results, then you have to do this in two separate actions.

Just like any other Save command, if this is the first time that this item has been saved, you will be prompted with a Save Query or Save Results dialog box, looking not dissimilar to this:

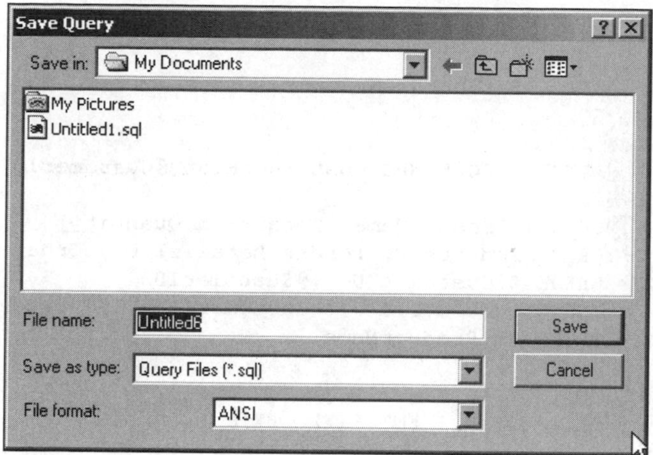

As you can see, I have already saved a file called `Untitled1.sql`. It is sensible to save your queries with meaningful names.

Once a query has been saved, *Ctrl+S* or the **Save** menu option overwrites the original file.

File | Save All Queries

Save and **Save As** only work with the current Query or Results pane. **Save All Queries** will save the details in every Query pane. Nothing from any Results panes will be saved with this option.

File | Print (Ctrl+P)

Print can only be used against a single Query pane. It cannot be used against a result set if it is displayed as a grid or multiple Query panes.

File | Exit (Alt+F4)

Exit will disconnect the connection to any SQL Server instance that you are connected to, as you can be connected to multiple SQL Server instances at once, and close down Query Analyzer.

The Edit Menu

Now we look at the Edit menu.

Edit | Clear Window (Ctrl+Shift+Delete)

This command will remove all code from the active Query pane only.

Edit | Bookmarks (Shift+F2)

A bookmark is a temporary marker, placed within a Query pane, used to mark specific areas of code that you wish to return to or highlight. This is usually used when you have more than one piece of code within a Query pane that you wish to run, or perhaps a large stored procedure that you wish to mark and then move through using the **bookmarks**. A bookmark is denoted by a light blue rectangular shape placed in the gray column to the left of the code:

```
SET QUOTED_IDENTIFIER ON
GO
SET ANSI_NULLS ON
GO

ALTER  PROCEDURE CustOrderHist @CustomerID
AS
SELECT ProductName, Total=SUM(Quantity)
FROM Products P, [Order Details] OD, Order
WHERE C.CustomerID = @CustomerID
AND C.CustomerID = O.CustomerID AND O.Orde
GROUP BY ProductName

GO
SET QUOTED_IDENTIFIER OFF
GO
SET ANSI_NULLS ON
GO
```

There are the following commands, which allow you to navigate around and use these bookmarks.

Command	Keyboard Shortcut	Description
Toggle Bookmark	*Ctrl+F2*	This will toggle a line of code between being bookmarked and not being bookmarked.
Next Bookmark	*F2*	This will move you to the next bookmark down from the point you are at. This will loop around to the first bookmark if it reaches the end of the code.
Previous Bookmark	*Shift+F2*	This will move you to the previous bookmark upwards from the point you are at. This loops around back to the last bookmark if the search reaches the top.
Clear All Bookmarks	*Ctrl+Shift+F2*	Removes all bookmarks from the Query pane.

Edit | Insert Template (Ctrl+Shift+Insert)

Earlier on, the definition of a template was mentioned. Templates are quite simply files holding templated code; saved on a hard disk that Query Analyzer knows the path to. To use a template, which is demonstrated later in the book in Chapter 14, when we look at updating rows of information within a table, you can use this command to insert the template into the active Query pane, with the contents of the template inserted where the cursor is currently positioned.

By selecting this option, a dialog box is displayed requesting you to select which template you wish to include from a selection of template groups. By navigating to the correct folder, it is possible to select a specific template.

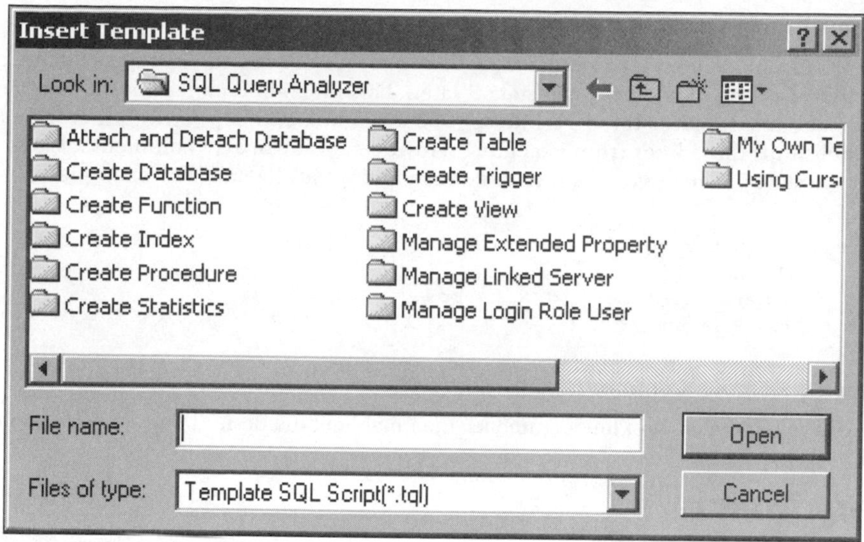

Edit | Replace Template Parameters (Ctrl-Shift+M)

This was discussed in the Templates section previously.

Edit | Advanced

The Advanced menu option leads to a set of sub-menu options, which are covered here.

Edit | Advanced | Make Selection Lower Case (Ctrl+Shift+L)

By highlighting a section of text and then using this option, all of the selected text becomes lower case. This option has limited use unless you have chosen a language installation that has mandatory case sensitivity.

Edit | Advanced | Make Selection Upper Case (Ctrl+Shift+U)

Making all SQL commands and functions upper case helps to make your code more readable.

Edit | Advanced | Increase Indent (Tab)

You should indent your code at appropriate places to make it more readable, as well. As the book progresses and the demonstration code becomes more and more complex, you will see these indentations in action.

This option will only work when more than one line of code is selected. If only one line, or part of one line is selected, then that *selection* of code is lost and the cursor is moved across by one tab.

Edit | Advanced | Decrease Indent (Shift+Tab)

As you would expect, this is the opposite of Increase Indent.

Edit | Advanced | Comment Out (Ctrl+Shift+C)

While you are testing, you may have several different pieces of code in your query pane, or perhaps you wish to remove a chunk of code but reinstate it later. This function enables you to comment out many lines of code at once. It places the SQL line comment symbol, two hyphens (`--`), at the start of each line of code, which stops those lines from executing. However, you can also comment a block of code out by using `/*` at the start of where you want to comment, and `*/` at the end. For example:

```
/* This is the start of some code here
And on to the next line
And it ends here with the next line code to run */
SELECT * FROM Players
```

Edit | Advanced | Remove Comments (Ctrl+Shift+R)

Once you wish to remove a set of line comments, then highlight the desired lines of code and use this action.

The Query Menu

The basis of a query is a set of commands and options used to create a way of inspecting or manipulating data within a database. The Query menu is where perhaps the most useful options within Query Analyzer are found. Most of these options will be used very early on in your career as a SQL Server developer, so this section is very important.

A few of the options in this menu are very complex and are discussed in Robert Vieira's "Professional SQL Server 2000 Programming" (Wrox Press, ISBN 1-861004-48-6).

Query | Change Database (Ctrl+U)

The first option gives the ability to change which database is being used within your query. At present, you will find that your login ID is currently pointing to the `master` database. Recall that you really ought not to alter this database. So, how do we change this selection?

Try It Out – Change Database

1. Ensure that Query Analyzer is running and that you are successfully logged in. In this demonstration, I am logged in as the Administrator, which has a default database of `master`. You can check this by looking at the combo box on the right side near the top of the screen.

2. From the Query menu, select Change Database. You can also press *Ctrl+U*.

3. This then brings up a dialog, which allows a different database to be selected. Notice that you also get two other useful pieces of information: Compatibility Level and Status.

Compatibility Level

The Compatibility Level displays the version of SQL Server that the database listed is backwardly compatible with. A value of 80 actually relates to SQL Server 2000, the current version, so the databases in the screenshot are not compatible with SQL Server 7.0, for instance. Values of 70 or 65 relate to version 7.0 and 6.5, respectively. Of course we're really using SQL Server 8, but in keeping with Microsoft's current naming strategy, it is called SQL Server 2000. Compatibility levels refer to many areas of the database, from functionality, to what is valid and what is not. Within this book, all the databases will be compatible with SQL Server 2000. However, if you are working with a SQL Server upgrade, you may see a database like `Northwind` set to a compatibility level other than 80.

Status

The second column is Status. You will find, as you work through the book, that a database can have several different statuses – online or offline, for example. This column shows exactly what status the database has. A status of online, or blank, means the database is up, running, and ready for updates, interrogations etc. But if status is offline the database will not accept any changes, as it has been shut down.

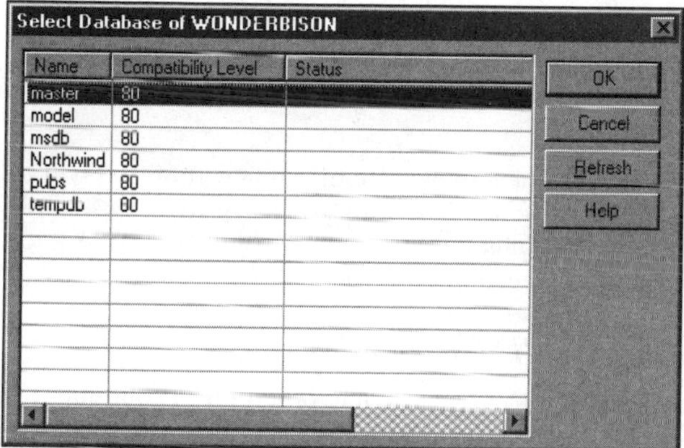

4. Select any one of the other databases. Don't worry – we won't be doing anything with it. This is just to demonstrate altering which database you are potentially going to use. In my case, I have chosen Northwind. Notice, though, that the current database is shown in light blue. Now click OK.

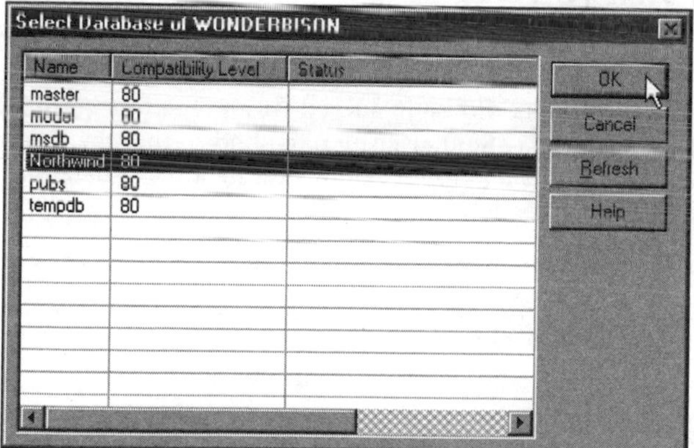

5. Notice that the combo box on the right, which shows the current database, has now altered to Northwind. This also demonstrates that you are now pointing at the new database.

Changing database like this alters the database that Query Analyzer is pointing to for the active Query pane only. If you have more than one Query pane, the non-active ones will remain pointing to the database that they were originally connected to.

By altering the database displayed in the database selection dialog, you need to remember that this is not a permanent change and, therefore, when you restart Query Analyzer, you will be back with your default database. We will cover changing the default database later in this chapter.

Time to move on to some of the other options under the Query menu.

Parse (Ctrl+F5)

This option will take any code entered in to the active Query pane, and will parse it for any errors. It will not actually execute the code, but will check it for syntax errors only. It will not validate database objects or ensure that variable settings are correct. This is very useful when wishing to check that your query syntax is valid before execution to remove typing errors.

Execute (F5 or Ctrl+E)

This will take the active Query pane and execute the code within it. It will not execute any other pane that is within Query Analyzer, only the pane with focus. We will be using this very exhaustively throughout the book, as this is the method for running examples placed into Query Analyzer. This will be used a great deal so there's no need to bore you with it now.

Cancel Executing Query (Alt+Break)

If you have a query that is running and you no longer wish it to continue, you can cancel, or attempt to cancel the query by pressing these commands. If you are on a locally installed SQL Server, then the cancellation should happen; however, if you are connecting to a remove server, you are sending the cancel to that server and you are then relying on the server to cancel the task in time. This may or may not happen depending on what process the server is running. Then you get into more complex areas of having to cancel your task by issuing specialized commands, which require a great deal of care.

Query | Results in Text (Ctrl+T)

The three Results in... options are properly demonstrated later in the book. However, we will quickly explain what these options are now. The first option, Results in Text, shows any results in the Results pane in a textual format. The results will be in a fixed-width type font so that characters can be lined up, and the data will be presented in a columnar fashion, tabbed so that the data from the correct column is under the correct heading. Below is a graphic demonstrating a set of data brought back from the pubs database using the Results in Text option:

```
au_id       au_lname                                 au_fname             phone
----------- ---------------------------------------- -------------------- ------------
172-32-1176 White                                    Johnson              408 496-7223
213-46-8915 Green                                    Marjorie             415 986-7020
238-95-7766 Carson                                   Cheryl               415 548-7723
267-41-2394 O'Leary                                  Michael              408 286-2428
274-80-9391 Straight                                 Dean                 415 834-2919
```

Query | Results in Grid (Ctrl+D)

The previous option leaves a lot of wasted space. Therefore, you may wish to select the Results in Grid option. The one area you have to be careful with this option though, is that the messages returned from queries are placed in a separate tab. Here is the same data from the pubs database, shown in a grid format. You will notice that more data is displayed, as the grid takes the item with the longest length for that column and makes this the column width:

	au_id	au_lname	au_fname	phone	address	city	state	zip
1	172-32-1176	White	Johnson	408 496-7223	10932 Bigge Rd.	Menlo Park	CA	94025
2	213-46-8915	Green	Marjorie	415 986-7020	309 63rd St. #411	Oakland	CA	94618
3	238-95-7766	Carson	Cheryl	415 548-7723	589 Darwin Ln.	Berkeley	CA	94705
4	267-41-2394	O'Leary	Michael	408 286-2428	22 Cleveland Av. #14	San Jose	CA	95128
5	274-80-9391	Straight	Dean	415 834-2919	5420 College Av.	Oakland	CA	94609

Query | Results to File (Ctrl+Shift+F)

This is quite simply a method for placing the results from a query directly into a file. I won't say much more about this now, as it is covered in detail later in the book. Suffice to say that the data returned from the query is not displayed on screen, but saved to a file that can be opened outside of Query Analyzer.

Query | Current Connection Properties

The connection to the SQL Server instance can be tailored to meet your specific needs. For example, it is possible to build a query and check its validity without actually running it, or to check how well it will perform when it is run.

The Current Connection Properties dialog, reached via Query | Current Connection Properties, allows you to tailor such options. At this juncture, I won't go through all the options as some are too advanced for this stage of the book. However, I will go through the options that you will use most frequently.

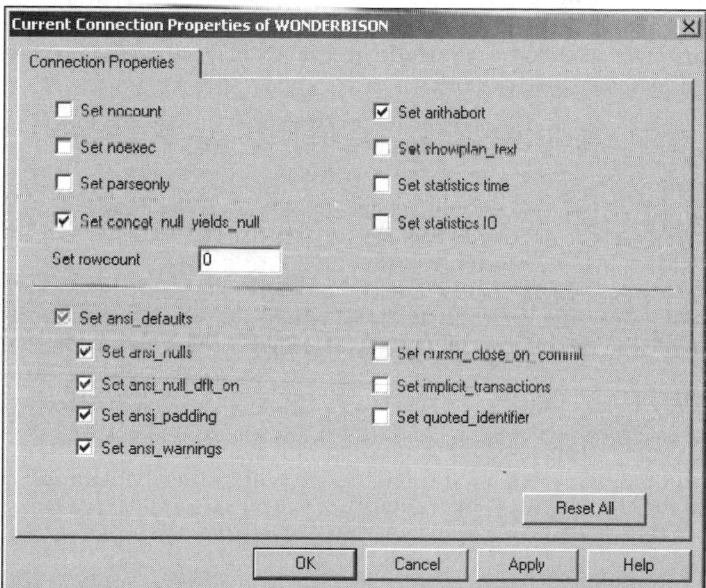

Set noexec

This will take the code entered, parse it, and ensure the code is valid. If there are any syntax errors then you will see the relevant error message returned. Ignore the minor detail that you may not know what the following command means, but enter it in to a Query pane and execute it.

```
SELECT * FORM Customers
```

You will then see the following error message:

Server: Msg 170, Level 15, State 1, Line 1
Line 1: Incorrect syntax near 'Form'.

It will also check any objects listed, to be sure that they are valid within the database or server. It compiles the code to achieve this.

This option can also be set directly with SQL query commands. You would enter the following into the Query pane:

```
--To turn set noexec on
SET noexec ON

--To turn set noexec off
SET noexec OFF
```

Using Current Connection Properties *dialog is simpler if you want to alter several different properties at once, but using SQL query syntax is better if you are switching an option on and off frequently while testing code in Query Analyzer.*

Set parseonly

Set parseonly differs from Set noexec in that it does not compile the code, and also does not check that any objects specified in the code are valid. However, it does check if the code parses correctly. For example, it will ensure that the SQL commands are spelled correctly but, if you misspell a column name in a table, it will still pass the code as valid.

The query syntax for this command is:

```
SET parseonly ON
SET parseonly OFF
```

Set rowcount

This will set the number of rows shown in the Results pane that a query returns. This is useful if you have a very large table, but you only wish to return the first `n` rows.

The syntax for this command is.

```
SET rowcount n
```

where `n` is the number of rows you want to return:

Set ansi_defaults

This box is grayed by default. All of the options below the Set ansi_defaults check box if checked would make the Query Analyzer comply with a standard set by ANSI, called ANSI SQL-92 compliance. ANSI is the American National Standards Institute, which discusses and ratifies standards for the industry. So, to comply with the ANSI SQL-92 standard, these check boxes have to be all checked. If you alter any, you are making your database non SQL-92 compliant. That said, there is no problem if your database is compliant or not from your own viewpoint, but if you moved to another database, then you might be used to non-compliant settings and therefore confusion may arise, or vice versa. Also, not all the commands within SQL Server meet the ANSI standard anyway, which is also the case for most databases. Each database system has its own proprietary code to complete specific functions.

Set quoted_identifier

I find that this is my favorite, but most troublesome option. This option sets whether two double quotes delimit the contents of a string, or whether double quotes define identifiers (for example, the name of a column within a table). `SET QUOTED_IDENTIFIER OFF` allows double quotes to be used to define string static values within a query. There are pros and cons for both choices, which I will demonstrate shortly.

First of all, the syntax for this command is:

```
SET quoted_identifier ON
SET quoted_identifier OFF
```

I run with this set to `OFF` so that I can use single and double quotes in my code to define strings. This allows me to use `"O'Malley"` as a valid string, because `'O'Malley'` would not be valid. But, be warned! There are a couple of areas in which you cannot use this option and have to resort to single quotes for string identifiers; see below:

Try It Out – Quoted_Identifier

1. To demonstrate what I mean, enter the following code into a new Query pane.

```
SET QUOTED_IDENTIFIER OFF
GO

DECLARE @surname VARCHAR(20)
SELECT @surname = "O'MALLEY"
PRINT "This will work...." + @surname
GO

SET QUOTED_IDENTIFIER ON
GO

DECLARE @surname VARCHAR(20)
-- This next line will produce an error
SELECT @surname = "O'MALLEY"
PRINT 'This will NOT work....' + @surname
GO
```

```
DECLARE @surname VARCHAR(20)
-- This next line will produce an error
SELECT @surname = 'O''MALLEY'
PRINT 'However this does work as I have a second single quote in the
   name....' + @surname
GO

SET QUOTED_IDENTIFIER OFF
GO
```

2. Now execute it, either by using the menu (Query | Execute), by pressing Ctrl+E or F5, or by clicking on the Execute Query button on the toolbar (the green triangle). You will see the following results:

```
SET QUOTED_IDENTIFIER OFF
GO

DECLARE @surname VARCHAR(20)
SELECT @surname = "O'MALLEY"
PRINT "This will work...." + @surname
GO

SET QUOTED_IDENTIFIER ON
GO

DECLARE @surname VARCHAR(20)
-- This next line will produce an error
SELECT @surname = "O'MALLEY"
PRINT 'This will NOT work....' + @surname
GO

DECLARE @surname VARCHAR(20)
-- This next line will produce an error
SELECT @surname = 'O''MALLEY'
PRINT 'However this does work as I have a second single quote in the name....' + @surname
GO

SET QUOTED_IDENTIFIER OFF
GO
```

```
This will work....O'MALLEY
Server: Msg 207, Level 16, State 3, Line 4
Invalid column name 'O'MALLEY'.
However this does work as I have a second single quote in the name....O'MALLEY
```

Don't worry too much about understanding the code but, as you can see, I had to alter O'Malley to make it work when I had `Quoted_Identifier` set to `ON`. However this is all covered later in the book when inserting data in Chapter 12.

The Tools Menu

In this there are a few useful options, and some that we will not cover in this book. Many are detailed below.

The Tools | Options Menu (Ctrl+Shift+O)

Selecting Tools | Options brings up a multi-tabbed dialog box which is used for setting up many different options within Query Analyzer. We'll look at three tabs with the most frequently used options in this section.

The General Tab

This tab is perhaps one of the more informative and useful tabs for you as a new SQL Server developer. It is concerned with where and how files are stored.

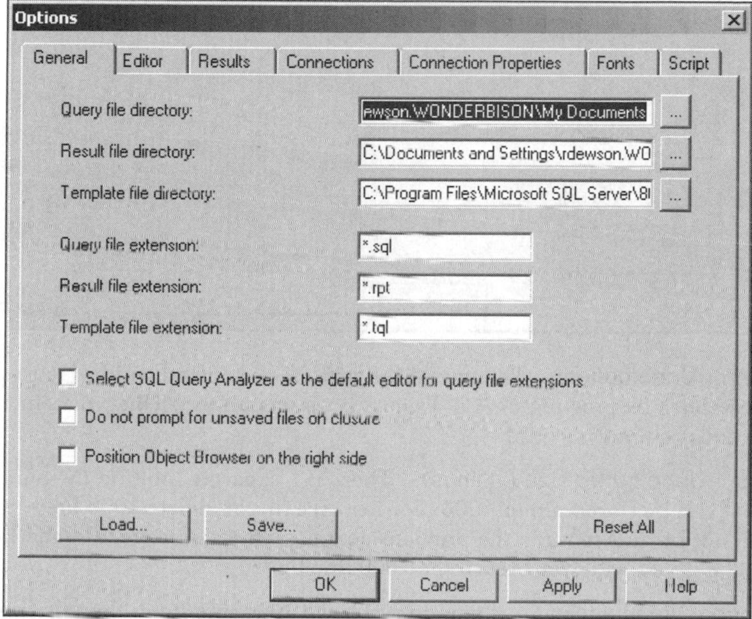

The first three options define where specific files, which have been or will be saved, are located. The default is for the local user's hard drive. However, you may find that your organization has a central folder on a network drive where it stores queries, etc., so that they are available to all. You may wish to alter these directories to point to an area in your organization like this.

Move on to the three extension boxes. These are the default extensions placed on files when they are saved. Personally, I would not alter these, as they are standard extensions.

The three check boxes at the bottom are fairly self-explanatory.

The Load and Save buttons, at the bottom on the left, allow the whole configuration tool to be saved to a configuration file, with a `.sqc` extension. Again, this allows one configuration file to be set up and distributed to every user, to assist with implementing standards within an organization.

The Editor Tab

While using the Query pane to edit your SQL code, there will be times when you need to alter certain aspects of the editing process.

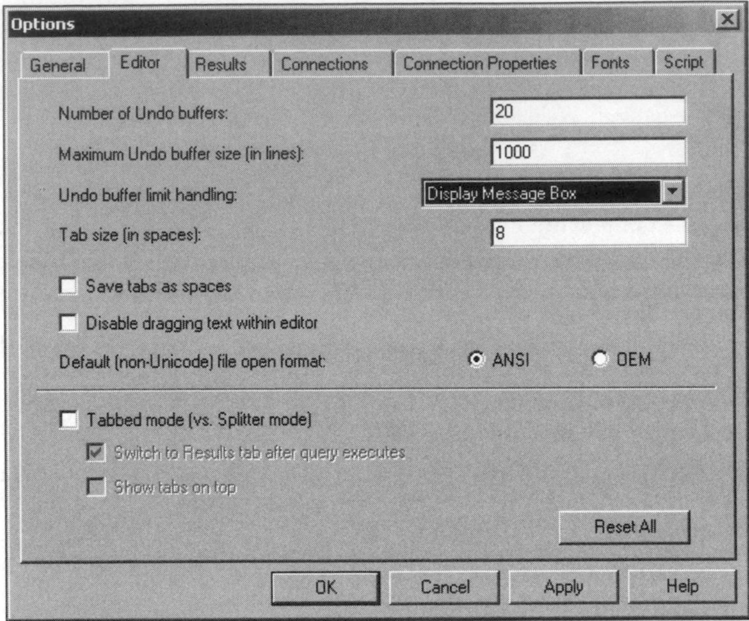

- Number of Undo buffers – The number of actions performed within Query Analyzer that can be moved back by pressing *Ctrl+Z*. Twenty is the maximum. This works in conjunction with the next two options.
- Maximum Undo buffer size (in lines) – There is a separate limit on the number of lines of code that can be stored, up to 1000. For instance, if you delete 1000 lines in a single action, you will not be able to undo the previous action even if you have 20 undo buffers. I doubt very much if you will ever breach the 1000 line limit.
- Undo buffer limit handling – If you do reach the 1000 line limit, though, this box determines what happens in QA. The two options are to Display Message Box or Default to Discard. The latter means that the lines of data in the undo buffer will be lost. I recommend that you leave this option as it is.
- Tab size (in spaces) – The number of characters inward that are moved when a tab function is performed within the Query pane.
- Save tabs as spaces – Select this option if you wish to convert tab characters to spaces. In this instance, a single tab would be converted to eight spaces. I tend to leave this unchecked in case other people have different tab settings and then open up a saved query.

- **Disable dragging text within editor** – If you want to avoid accidentally moving code with a drag operation, select this option.
- **Default (non-Unicode) file open format** – Whether you wish to open files in **ANSI** format or **OEM** format. With traditional formats for defining characters, only 1 byte of data is used, therefore you can only have up to 256 different characters. The Unicode format takes up 2 bytes of data and therefore you can have up to 65,536 characters. By why do you need so many when there are only 26 letters in the alphabet? Because using Unicode allows you to have multiple languages stored as one set of data. OEM is a different type of code page to ANSI, for example MS-DOS code page 437 uses OEM.
- **Tabbed mode (vs. Splitter mode)** – At present, the Results pane sits below the Query pane but it is possible, by selecting this option, to have the Query pane and Results pane separated onto separate tabs. Selecting this option opens up the last two options.
- **Switch to Results tab after query executes** – Once you execute a query, you will immediately find yourself on the **Results** tab if you select this.
- **Show tabs on top** – Quite simply, whether the **Query** and **Results** tabs are displayed at the top of the window. Personal preference.

The Results Tab

This whole tab is concerned with how results are displayed within Query Analyzer. The first option is just like the **Query** menu options, which declare whether the results are displayed in text or grid, or saved to a file.

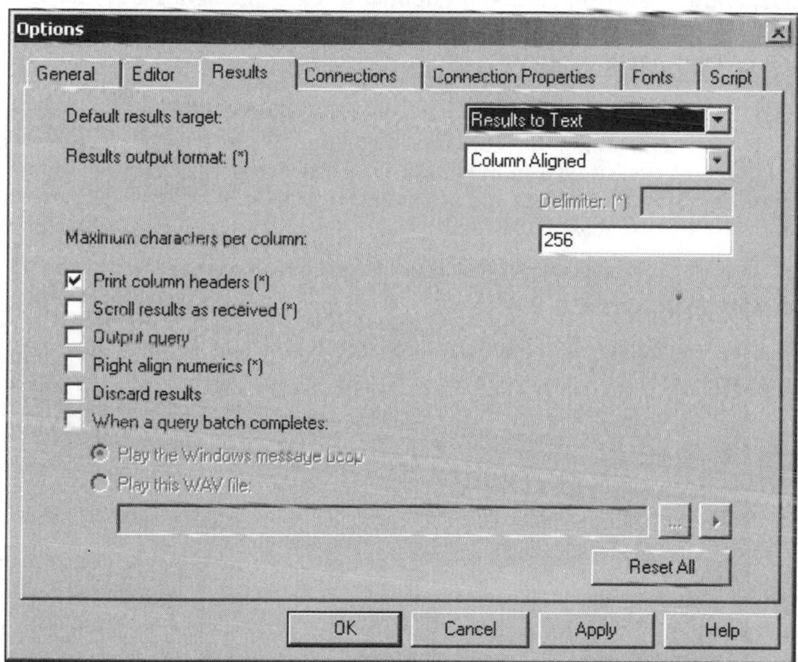

The next option, **Results output format**, is probably best left as it is. I have found that altering this, to tab delimited, perhaps, is more troublesome than what it is worth. However, do experiment so that you know what each of the options does.

Here is a quick summary of each of the other options:

- Maximum characters per column – The maximum number of characters per column on any output. For wider columns if you want a larger output, then increase this value.
- Print column headers – When this option is selected, each column of results has a header indicating what the information in that column relates to, and which column it relates to in the relevant table(s). *Very* useful.
- Scroll results as received – As each line of results is returned to the Query pane, a scroll action occurs if the Results pane is full. With this option on, once the query has run, you will be at the end of the set of results.
- Output query – Will print up to the first three lines of the query in the Results pane.
- Right align numerics – Any numerics are right aligned in the Results pane, rather than the default of left aligned.
- Discard results – When a query has finished, no results are displayed in the Results pane if this option is checked. I am not sure when you would ever use this option!
- When a query batch completes – This will play a tone to alert you that a query has finished.

The Connections Tab

This tab is not covered here because it deals with quite advanced settings for connecting to the server. Perhaps the only option that might be of interest is Use regional settings when displaying currency, number, dates, and times. By checking this option, you are instructing QA that any output received from SQL Server will respect the locale settings on the computer that SQL Server is installed on. If the option is off, no conversion takes place.

> **This option only affects the display of data, and not data entry. It can cause confusion if this option is switched on and the machine on which Query Analyzer is running has a different locale setting to that which was installed with SQL Server. Consequently, I tend to keep this switched off.**

The Connection Properties Tab

This is exactly like the Current Connection Properties dialog in the Query menu, as shown above, except that this manages the default settings when you log in to SQL Server each time.

The Fonts Tab

This deals with the fonts you wish to use in Query Analyzer.

The Script Tab

These are options that you can set when outputting any objects as a script. For example, you can output the SQL required to build the `Northwind` database to a SQL script file. These options are all self-explanatory. I recommend leaving them as they are.

The Tools | Customize Menu

The options in this menu enable you to associate particular functions or key combinations with specific combinations of keys. This cuts down the amount of time required to perform actions in Query Analyzer, and reduces the potential for typos when running frequent commands. Similar simple macros exist in other products like Word and Excel.

> **When executing sequences of commands stored in this way, it is impossible to combine them with the input of extra values. Consequently, this functionality is different to that of templates, which allow you to input values for specified options before execution.**

The next *Try It Out* section demonstrates how to customize keystrokes and then use them in Query Analyzer. Two different keystroke commands will be created – one to change the default database for a specific user, and one to go back to the `Northwind` demonstration database for the same user. This is NOT altering the database that you are working with, just the database that will be connected to when that specific user logs in to Query Analyzer.

So far there are only two main User IDs in our SQL Server. One is the `sa` login, which was covered in Chapter 1 and which is added to SQL Server by default. The second ID is the Administrator login ID, in the case of the book, `RDewson`, which was used to install SQL Server and which is the login ID on my machine, and has full administration rights. There will be new IDs later but, for the moment, I will still be working with the Administrator login.

Try It Out – Customizing Function Keys

1. Ensure that Query Analyzer is running. In this case, I have logged in as Administrator. It is important to know as whom you have logged in, so that you can create the correct information in the key assignments.

2. From the menu, select Tools | Customize:

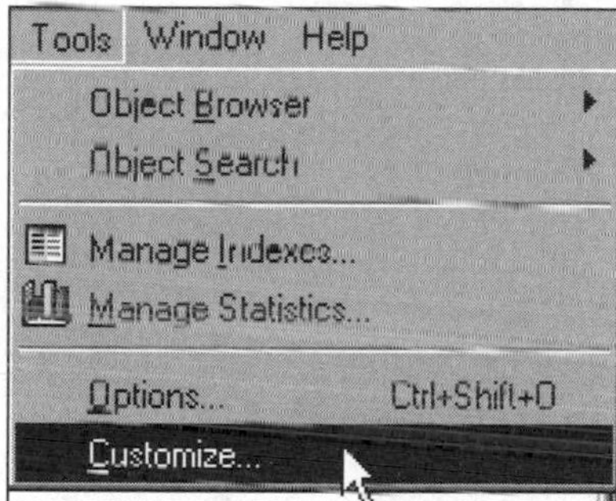

3. This brings up the Customize dialog, which can be used to customize key combinations. Notice that there are a few key combinations populated already:

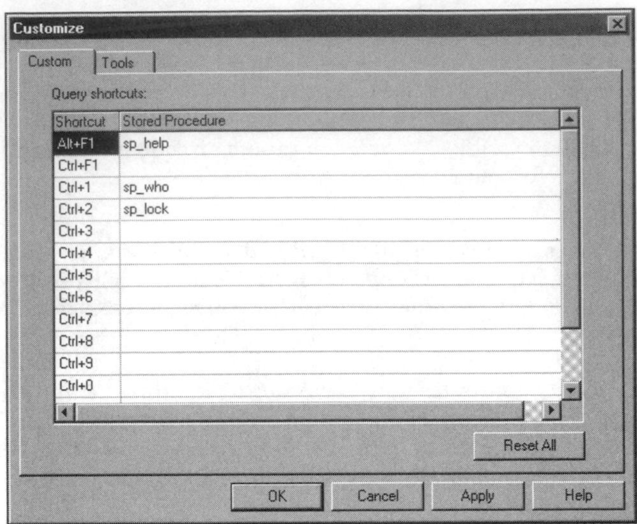

4. Edit one of the empty assignments. I will choose *Ctrl+3* for the following code:

```
sp_defaultdb "WONDERBISON\RDewson","pubs"
```

Obviously, alter the `WONDERBISON\RDewson` login to one that is valid for your machine. You should end up with something like this:

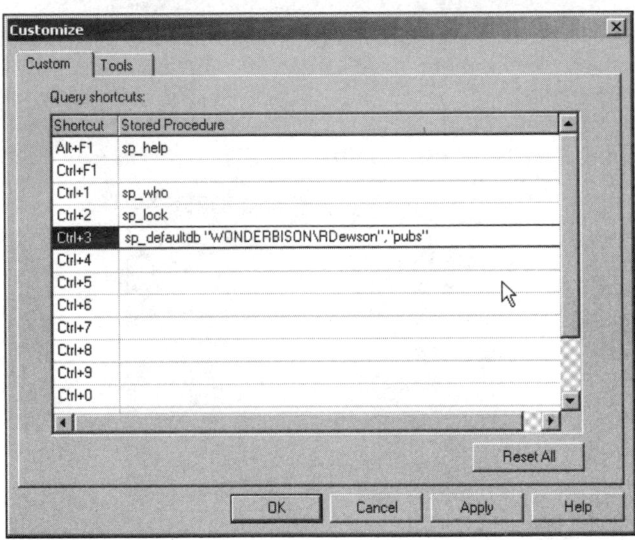

5. Enter the following code against another empty key assignment:

```
sp_defaultdb "WONDERBISON\RDewson","Northwind"
```

This time I chose *Ctrl+4*:

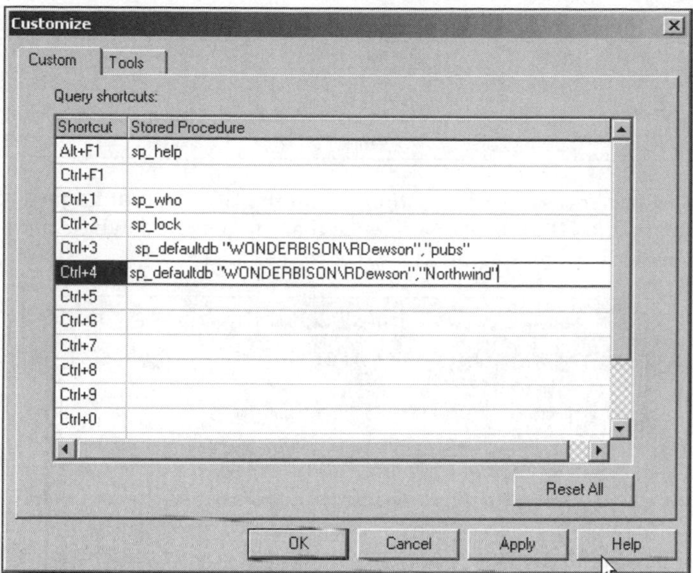

6. Now click OK, which will apply the changes and remove the dialog.

7. Now move to Enterprise Manager and expand the server nodes until you get to the Security node on the installation of SQL Server. Expand this node and click on Logins:

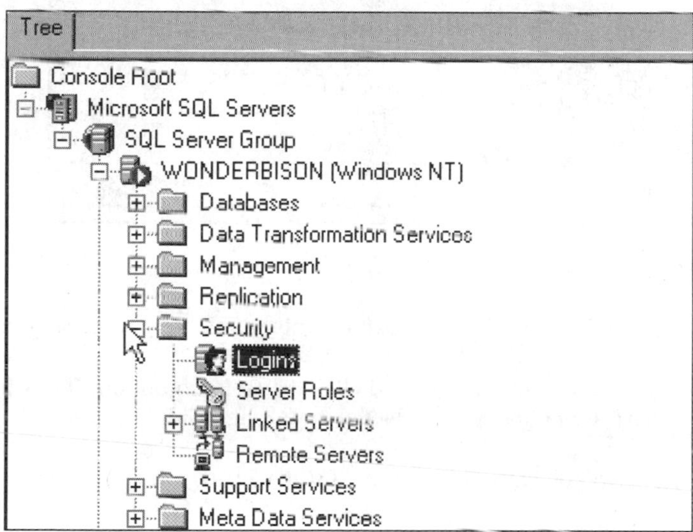

8. On the right-hand side, the Details pane, find the ID that you have set up to alter the default database with. In my case, it is the RDewson ID. Notice that, in this row, the Default Database is set to master:

Logins 3 Items				
Name	Type	Server Access	Default Database	Default Language
sa	Standard	Permit	model	English
BUILTIN\Administrators	Windows Group	Permit	master	English
WONDERBISON\RDewson	Windows User	Permit	master	English

9. You can also find this same information within the SQL Server Login Properties dialog; double-click on the ID to display it. Notice that the default database at the bottom of this screen is currently set to master:

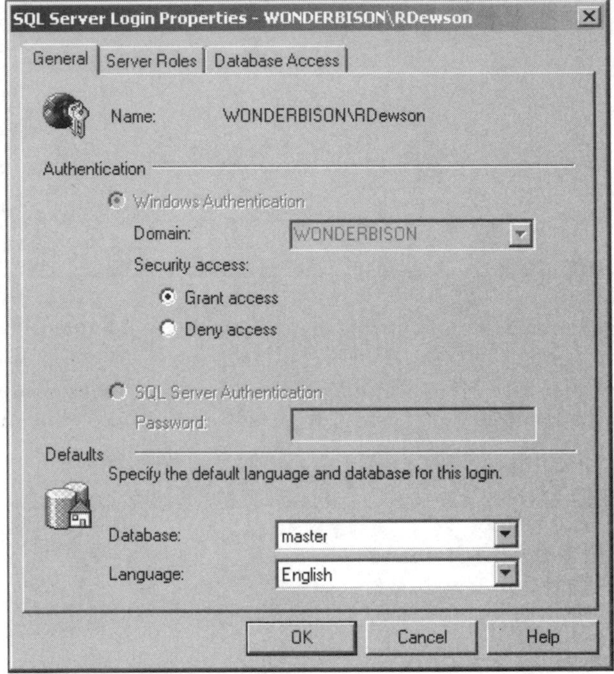

10. Click Cancel, and switch back to Query Analyzer.

11. Now press *Ctrl+3*. You should see a Default database changed message in the Results pane.

12. Switch back to Enterprise Manager and click the Refresh button. If this button is not visible, ensure that there are no login IDs selected on the right side.

13. Notice that the Default Database column for the RDewson ID is now set to pubs, just as we expected:

Logins 3 Items				
Name	Type	Server Access	Default Database	Default Language
sa	Standard	Permit	model	English
BUILTIN\Administrators	Windows Group	Permit	master	English
WONDERBISON\RDewson	Windows User	Permit	pubs	English

14. Now hit *Ctrl+4* to switch back to `Northwind`.

The Query Analyzer Toolbar

Now that the menus have been covered (with the exception of standard ones like Help and Windows), let's take a quick look at the toolbar buttons. There are many toolbar buttons in Query Analyzer and, like other Microsoft products, these buttons can be removed or new ones added. As you would expect, these toolbar buttons are shortcuts to other options, either found on the menu or in other areas within Query Analyzer. The toolbar is shown below:

To add new buttons, or remove existing buttons, move the mouse pointer over the toolbar,and right-click, which will automatically bring up the Customize Toolbar screen. This screen allows you to move the toolbar buttons around; or by clicking Reset, place the original toolbar buttons back on the toolbar. You may wish to alter your toolbar, but throughout the book, the original toolbar buttons are kept.

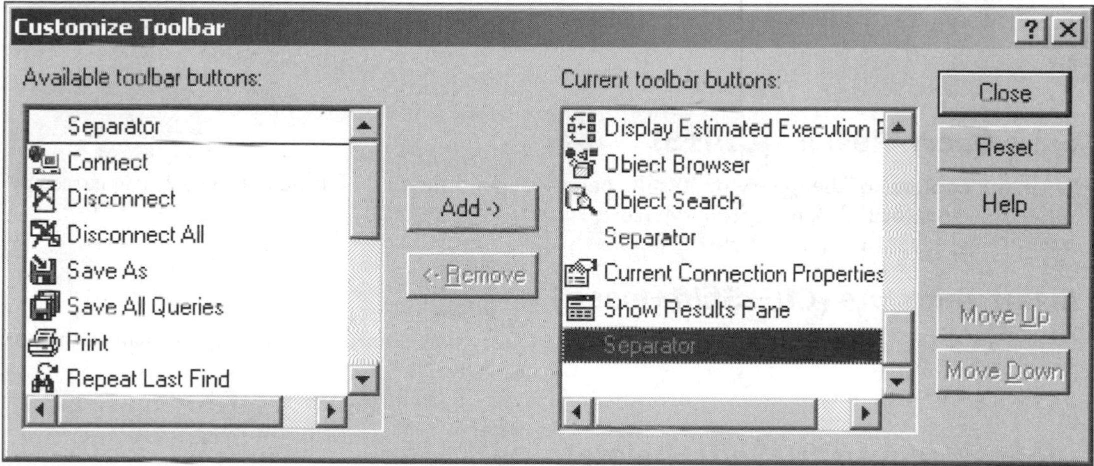

We will quickly work through each button next, going from left to right (again, skipping the standard icons like cut and paste).

New Query (Ctrl+N)

Pressing this button allows you to create a new empty query window (which includes a Query pane and a Results pane, as normal). If you press the black drop-down triangle next to the button instead, then you receive a list of options of more than just a Blank Query Window. The other options will create a new query window with the relevant template:

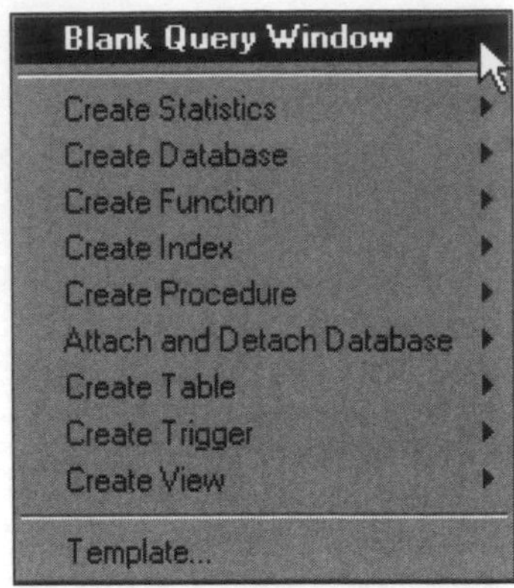

Load SQL Script (Ctrl+Shift+P)

Finds a SQL script on the local hard drive or on a remote computer, and loads this in to a fresh query window.

Save Query/Results (Ctrl+S)

Saves the contents of the Query or Results pane – depending on which pane the cursor is currently active in – to a local disk or remote device.

Insert Template (Ctrl+Shift+Insert)

Inserts a predefined SQL template into the active Query pane, starting to the right of where the cursor is currently located.

Clear Window (Ctrl+Shift+Delete)

Will clear the contents of the pane where the cursor is currently active. This could be the Query pane or the Results pane.

Find (Ctrl+F)

Will bring up a Find dialog form, allowing you to enter a string to search for in the active Query or Results pane.

Execute Mode

Clicking the black drop-down arrow next to this button produces the menu shown overleaf. The first three options define how any results from a query will be displayed. We won't cover the last three options, as they are quite advanced functions:

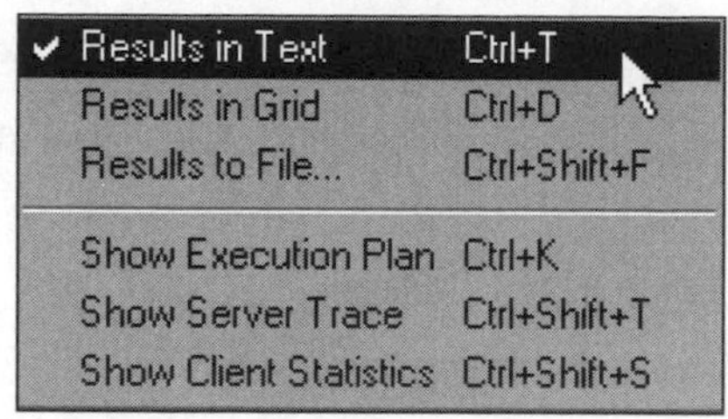

Parse Query (Ctrl+F5)

Takes the code in the active Query pane and parses it to ensure that it is syntactically correct. Does not check that any objects listed are valid.

Execute Query (F5)

Compiles and executes the SQL code in the current Query pane.

Cancel Query Execution (Alt+Break)

This will cancel any query running against a server. However, be wary of this. When you run a query, as mentioned earlier, it doesn't run locally but runs on the SQL Server that you are connected to. Therefore, you are actually sending a command to the server to cancel the execution. If the server is busy running your query, and is not pausing to look to see if there are any other commands to complete, your cancel command will not be dealt with immediately. Therefore, you may find that the cancellation is not instant in some circumstances. Also, this is issuing a command to SQL Server to inform it to rollback the changes applied within the query. This can also make it look as if it is taking a long time to cancel the query when in fact it is working.

Database Combo Box

The database combo box is used by Query Analyzer to inform the user which database is currently connected to. This also provides a quick method for changing databases when your work requires you to do so. It is also very similar to the function keys demonstration earlier in the chapter.

The next section will show you how easy it is to use this combo box to alter the database that you are working with.

Try It Out – Altering the Database

1. Ensure that Query Analyzer is running. It doesn't really matter who you are logged in as at the moment.

2. You should be connected to the `Northwind` database from the earlier example. Just to prove that `Northwind` is the current database, enter the following code in a new query pane and then execute it:

```
sp_tables
```

3. You should see something like the following in the Results pane (the width has been shrunk so it fits on the page):

```
TABLE_QUALIFIER  TABLE_OWNER  TABLE_NAME
---------------  -----------  ------------
Northwind        dbo          syscolumns
Northwind        dbo          syscomments
Northwind        dbo          sysdepends
Northwind        dbo          sysfilegroups
Northwind        dbo          sysfiles
...
```

4. Click the down arrow on the right side of the database combo box. This will bring up a list, as shown below:

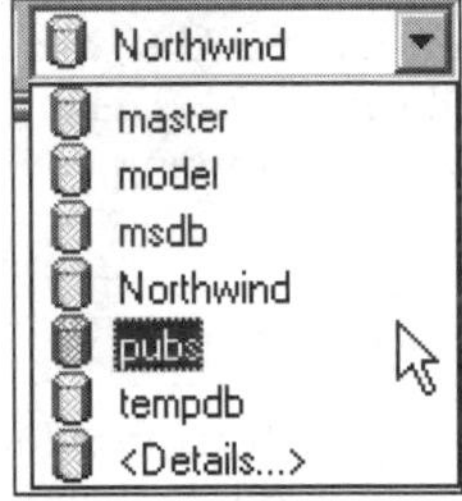

5. Select **pubs**. This will alter the database that you are pointing to.

6. Now execute the `sp_tables` code again, and you will see the following results:

```
TABLE_QUALIFIER  TABLE_OWNER  TABLE_NAME
---------------  -----------  ------------
pubs             dbo          syscolumns
pubs             dbo          syscomments
pubs             dbo          sysdepends
pubs             dbo          sysfilegroups
pubs             dbo          sysfiles
...
```

7. Once you are done, select the Northwind database in the combo box again.

There is another method for altering databases within Query Analyzer. It is possible to use a command, `USE`, which when combined with the name of the database will also alter which database the Query pane is working with. So, `USE Northwind`, which is then executed, would change to the `Northwind` database from that point onwards. Keep in mind though, that it is for that Query pane only.

Display Estimated Execution Plan (Ctrl+L)

When you have built a set of code, which is going to access data in a database, it is possible to check how well the query should run using this option. We won't go into any more detail here, except to say that this option shows how well your code has been built, and highlights areas that could be optimized.

Object Browser (F8)

This is used to toggle the display of the Object Browser on or off. Useful for creating more screen space when writing lengthy queries.

Object Search (F4)

This helps you search for particular objects. An object can be a table, a column, or any other piece of information that is stored in a database. The Object Search utility is a savior when using large or unfamiliar databases.

Let's take a look at how this works.

Try It Out – Object Search

1. Imagine that we have just received a call requiring us to find out the year-to-date sales of books. We know the name of the column, `ytd_sales`, but can't remember which table or database it is in.

2. Click the Object Search button, which brings up the Object Search screen:

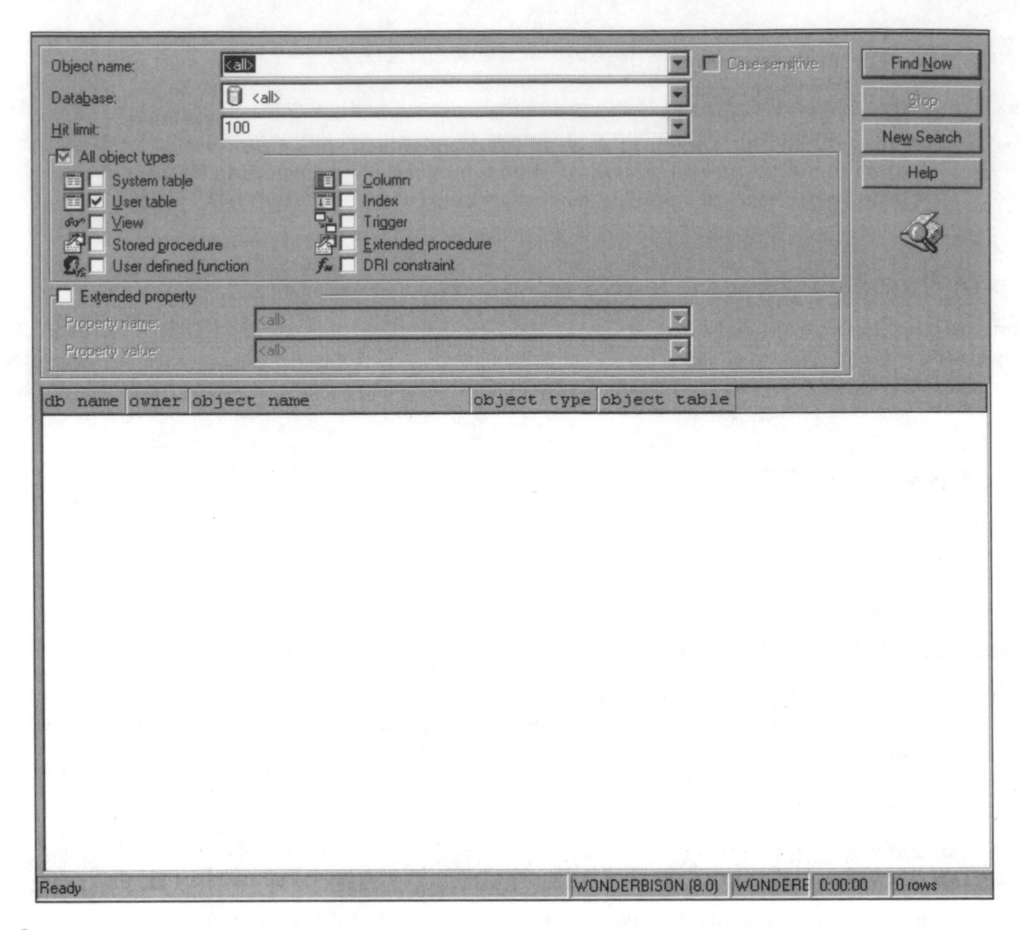

3. In the **Object name** combo box, enter **ytd_sales**. You can also place wildcard characters if required, for example you could have entered `ytd_sal*`.

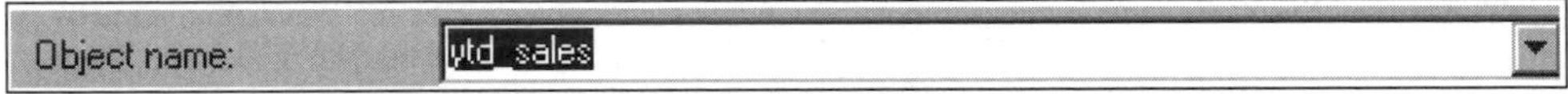

4. If we knew that we had to look within the `pubs` database, we could select **pubs** in the **Database** combo box. For the moment, leave it as **<all>**:

5. Leave the **Hit limit** set to **100**. We know that we want to find a column so, in the **object types** check boxes, uncheck the **User table** check box and select **Column** instead.

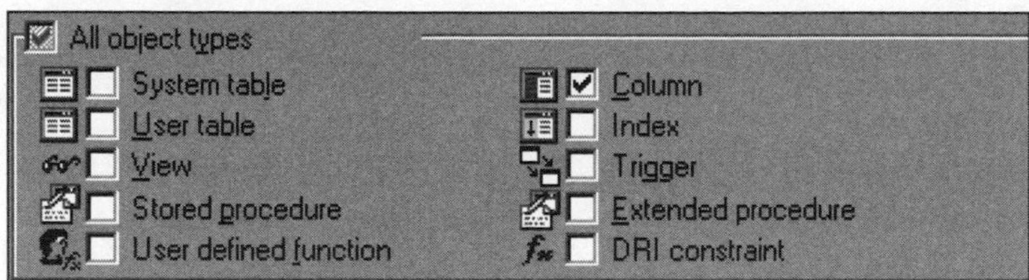

6. Click the Find Now button on the top right side.

7. When the search is finished, you should see two items listed as the Object Search has found two object_names matching the search:

db name	owner	object name	object type	object table
pubs	dbo	ytd_sales	column	titleview
pubs	dbo	ytd_sales	column	titles

Current Connection Properties

This is exactly as was discussed earlier in the chapter; it shows the current settings for the current server connection.

Show Results Pane

This toggles whether you see the Results pane or not. Good when you are not running any query and are building up a large amount of SQL.

Using Query Analyzer

By this stage, you should know your way around Query Analyzer and should be ready to start using it properly. Let's start using it in earnest. I won't show you any queries dealing with data yet; there are plenty of examples of that later in the book. The first example will show you how to create a new login account.

Creating a New Login Account

You will have noticed that the only IDs seen so far in this chapter are `RDewson`, `sa`, and `Builtin\Administrator`. Do you remember that, in Chapter 1, new User IDs were created when we demonstrated the authentication modes? Well, it's time to allow a specific User ID to be placed into SQL Server. If you remember, Annette Kelly was an NT administrator, so she could log in to SQL Server already because there is an administrator login. However, Jack Mason couldn't. I think it is time to let User ID `JMason` log in.

Try It Out – Creating a New Login Account

1. Ensure that Query Analyzer is up and running and that you are logged in to an account, which has administrator privileges. I will use the login created when SQL Server was installed, `RDewson`.

2. In the Query pane, enter the following code not forgetting to change `WONDERBISON` to your own computer, or network name. Once entered, run this code by either pressing *Ctrl+E*, *F5*, or the Execute button on the toolbar:

```
EXEC sp_grantlogin "WONDERBISON\JMason"
USE Northwind
GO
EXEC sp_grantdbaccess "WONDERBISON\JMason","JMason"
EXEC sp_addsrvrolemember  'WONDERBISON\JMason',"sysadmin"
```

> **This example uses double and single quotes, so you may get an error when running it. If you do, check back to the `Set quoted_identifier` subsection of the Query | Current Connection Properties section to see where you are going wrong.**

3. You should see the following in the Results pane:

```
Granted login access to 'WONDERBISON\JMason'.
Granted database access to 'WONDERBISON\JMason'.
'WONDERBISON\JMason' added to role 'sysadmin'.
```

4. Now move to Enterprise Manager and find the Logins node within the Security node. Refresh by right-clicking on the Logins node and selecting the Refresh option. You will then see the new `JMason` ID listed alongside the other login IDs. If you then right-click on the `JMason` login ID and select Properties, you will see the following dialog:

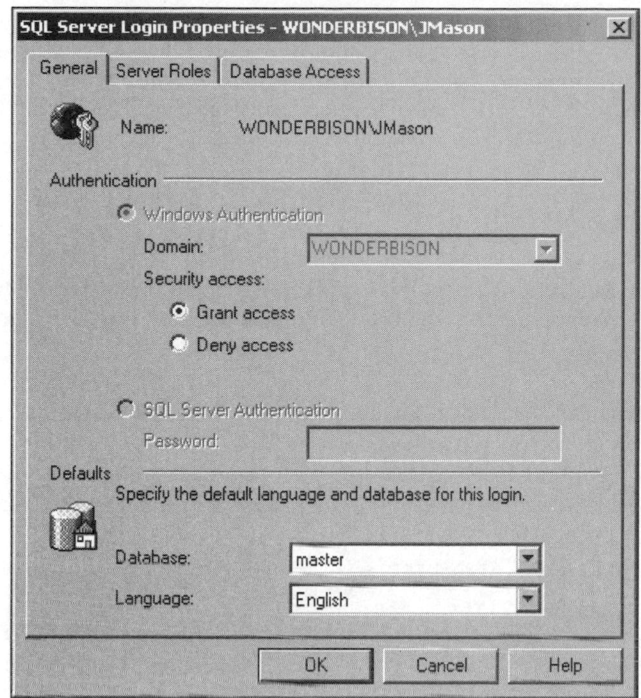

5. If you want to modify or inspect this login ID further, you may get the following error message. However, if you leave Enterprise Manager and start it up again, the message disappears. This seems to be a timing issue within all the processes, which shouldn't exist, but unfortunately does when adding a user through Query Analyzer.

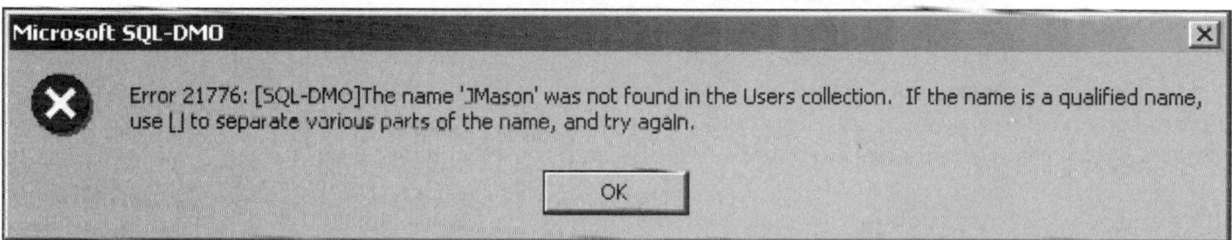

How It Works

Query Analyzer is performing several actions over several lines of code to achieve a full new login for Jack Mason. First of all, it takes the User ID of `JMason`, found in the Users and Passwords section of Windows NT/2000, and then grants this user with a specific login to SQL Server, and therefore once again, removes the need to log in with a generic ID, or worse still, "`sa`". In the past, Jack would not have been able to log in either under his own ID or with a group ID, as there is only an Administrator group ID set up and Jack does not have an Administrator User ID. Therefore, to allow Jack to use SQL Server using Windows NT Authentication, we have to grant him a log in. We created a SQL Server account in the previous chapter for `DTarbotton` so you can compare the differences. So, the `sp_grantlogin` gives Jack a User ID in to SQL server.

```
EXEC sp_grantlogin "WONDERBISON\JMason"
```

However, as it is, this is still not of much use. Yes, Jack could log in to SQL Server, but he would not be able to complete any work because he still does not have any rights to any of the databases. All he has is a login. This is where the remaining lines of code come in to action. I would like Jack to be able to use the Northwind database. Therefore, I have to specifically tell SQL Server that this is to be the case. Query Analyzer is moved to the correct database using the USE command:

```
USE Northwind
GO
```

Once the Northwind database is selected, it is possible to begin the actions required to give Jack full rights to the database. Without getting into too many technicalities here, the next line grants Jack access to Northwind:

```
EXEC sp_grantdbaccess "WONDERBISON\JMason","JMason"
```

The final line of code gives him a **role** within SQL Server, which grants him full system administration privileges. Jack can now perform any action that he likes within the Northwind database:

```
EXEC sp_addsrvrolemember  'WONDERBISON\JMason',"sysadmin"
```

Once all of these lines of code have executed, Jack is a valid member of SQL Server and the Northwind database.

Altering the Default Database for a User

When you enter Query Analyzer, there is always a database selected. This is called the **default database**, and it is the database that has been defined as the main database that this user will be working with. Don't worry – it isn't saying that this is the only database that you can work on. It's just one way of saving a few seconds by having a specific database selected and ready to start dealing with. You can change the default database for a user within Enterprise Manager, or through a command in Query Analyzer. This process was covered to some extent earlier when using key shortcuts to run system commands. We also saw how to alter the database that is being used temporarily, using the database combo box. This will not affect the user's default database setting.

By setting the default database, not only will you be saving yourself time when you open up Query Analyzer, but it will also help you to avoid developing solutions in the wrong database and then apparently losing your changes when you do move to the right database.

First of all, let's check out the first of these methods, which is within Enterprise Manager.

Try it out – Altering the Default Database in Enterprise Manager

1. Start up Enterprise Manager and navigate to your SQL Server installation. In my case, this is WONDERBISON.

2. Expand the Security tab and click on Logins icon:

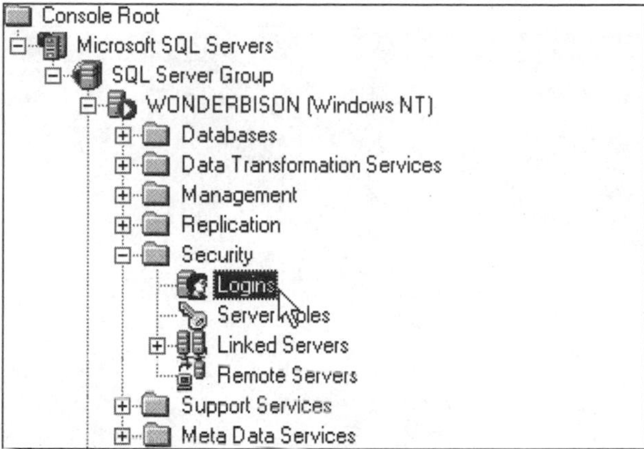

3. Find the User ID to alter and double- click on it. I chose `BUILTIN\Administrators`, which relates to any User ID defined in Windows 2000 as an Administrator, but is without a specific User ID within SQL Server. I could have chosen my login, `RDewson`, but I am saving this for later. As you can see, the Database defined in this dialog is set to master:

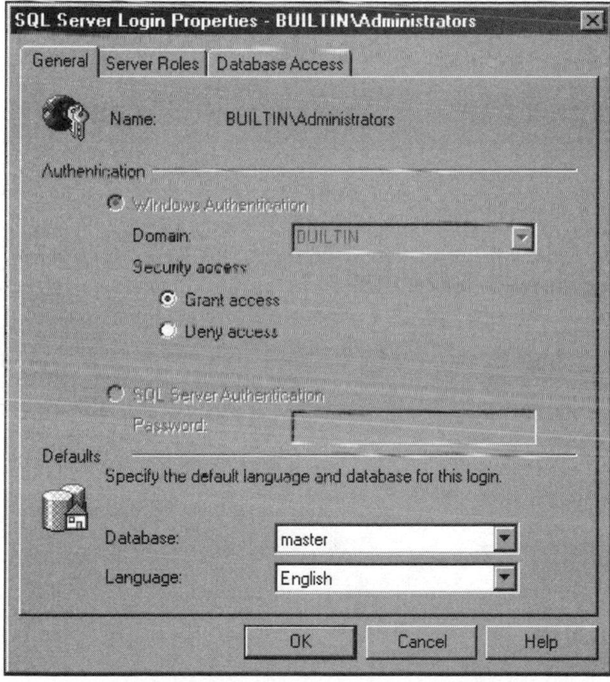

> **As you read in Chapter 1, `master` is a major system database and you should never really be in it, so let's alter this default straight away.**

4. Under Defaults, change the Database to another database. There are only two non-system databases at the moment: `pubs` and `Northwind`. Select one of these. I have chosen Northwind:

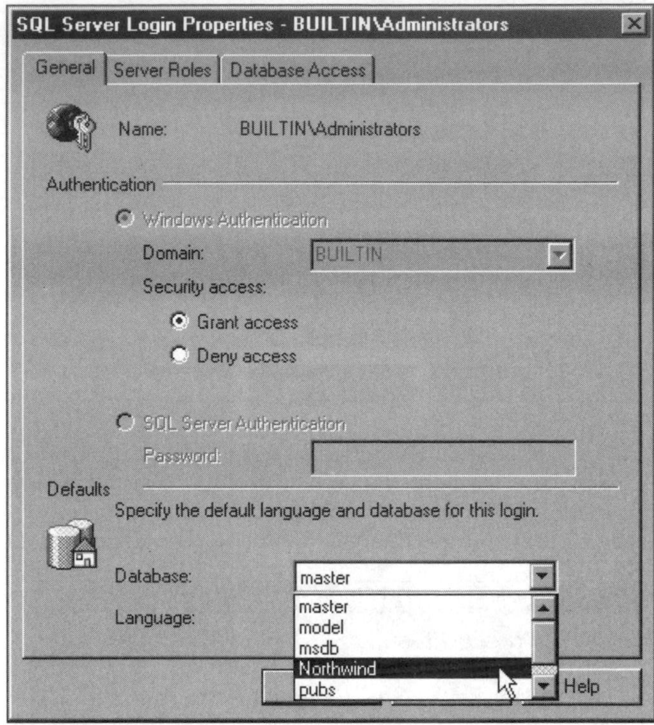

5. Once you have made you selection, click OK.

6. This will take you back to Enterprise Manager. Check the Enterprise Manager Details pane and you will see the Default Database has altered and will now show the database you chose – in my case, Northwind.

Logins 3 Items

Name	Type	Server Access	Default Database	Default Language
sa	Standard	Permit	master	English
BUILTIN\Administrators	Windows Group	Permit	Northwind	English
WONDERBISON\RDewson	Windows User	Permit	master	English

That's all there is to it. Now, when I log in to Query Analyzer using an NT account that belongs to the Administrators' group, then SQL Server will log me in as `BUILTIN\Administrators` and will default to the `Northwind` database. For example, if Annette Kelly logged in with her User ID of `AKelly`, then, as she is not specifically listed in SQL Server, and as she was set up as an Administrator user in Chapter 1, she will automatically be pointed towards `Northwind` to start with.

What Enterprise Manager is, in fact, doing is altering a system table within the `master` database to reflect these changes, as Query Analyzer refers to this system table to know what the default database is for each user. It is as simple as that.

Earlier on, we created a new login called `RDewson`. The default database was set to `master`. It is now time to alter that database to be `Northwind` too. This is an even simpler process in QA.

Try It Out - Altering the Default Database in Query Analyzer

1. Ensure that Query Analyzer is still running.

2. In the Query pane, enter the following:

```
EXEC sp_defaultdb "WONDERBISON\RDewson","Northwind"
```

3. You should see the following result:

   Default database changed.

4. If you check in Enterprise Manager, and complete a refresh, you will see that `RDewson` now has a default database of `Northwind`:

Logins 3 Items

Name	Type	Server Access	Default Database	Default Language
sa	Standard	Permit	master	English
BUILTIN\Administrators	Windows Group	Permit	Northwind	English
WONDERBISON\RDewson	Windows User	Permit	Northwind	English

This works in exactly the same way as altering the default database did in Enterprise Manager, but without the pretty interface. Under the hood, Enterprise Manager runs the same piece of code that you saw above, but it just hides this from you.

Of course, you can also alter the database temporarily within Query Analyzer, without affecting the defaults at all. We have seen this when we looked at the database combo box before.

This next section will show you how to temporarily alter `RDewson` from `Northwind` to the `pubs` database, and will check that this is only a temporary change.

Try It Out – Temporarily Change Databases

1. Ensure that Query Analyzer is running and that you are logged in as `RDewson`. This equates to the User ID that you installed SQL Server with.

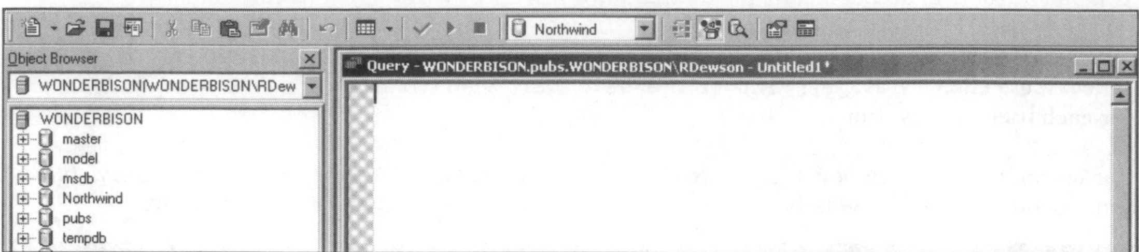

2. From within Query Analyzer, use the Database combo box and select **pubs** from the dropdown list. This now means that any work within any Query pane in Query Analyzer is done within the `pubs` database. Recall from earlier in the chapter the mention of the `USE` command for altering the database? This is performing the same process.

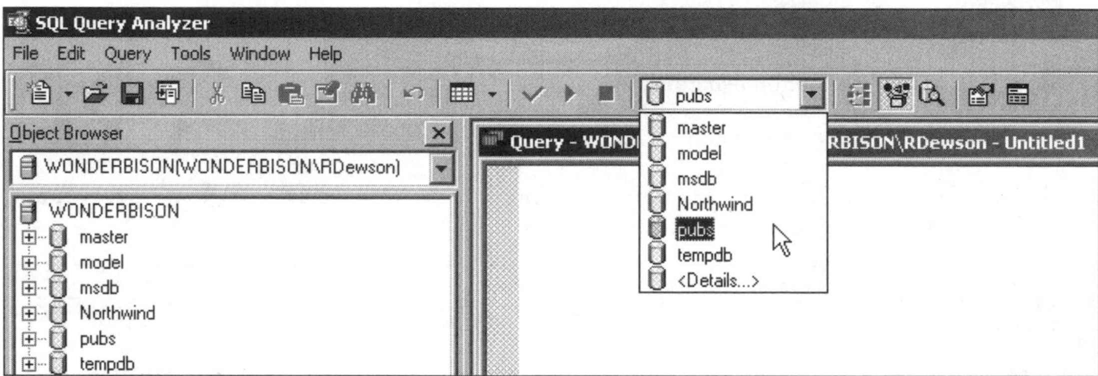

3. To prove that this alteration is only temporary, switch to Enterprise Manager and go to the **Logins** icon. You will see that nothing has altered and that **Northwind** is still the **Default Database** for **RDewson**:

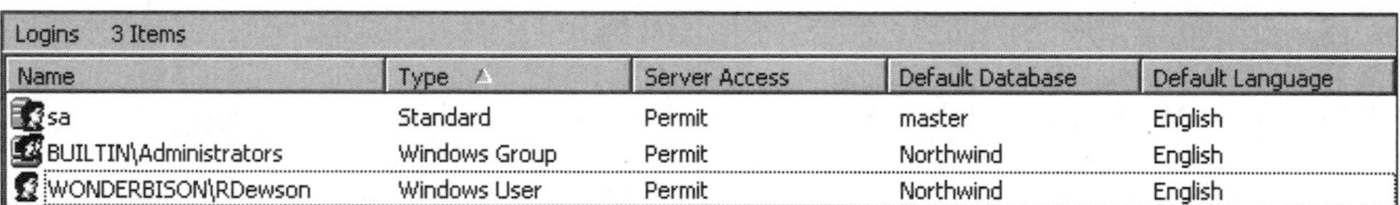

Logins 3 Items

Name	Type	Server Access	Default Database	Default Language
sa	Standard	Permit	master	English
BUILTIN\Administrators	Windows Group	Permit	Northwind	English
WONDERBISON\RDewson	Windows User	Permit	Northwind	English

Using the Database combo box does not run the same line of code that we saw earlier when changing the default database in Query Analyzer. So Query Analyzer just keeps track of the database change under its own hood so that, when you do any work within Query Analyzer, it always knows which database to point to. Then, when Query Analyzer is finished with, it throws away its knowledge of which database it was working on so that, next time it is started, it will revert back to the default database.

Summary

Query Analyzer has been thoroughly covered and when you read through the rest of the book, you should feel comfortable with your knowledge of where everything is within it. Also, if you wish to alter any item to suit your own method of working, you should be able to find out what to do from the relevant section in this chapter.

We have also seen how Enterprise Manager relates to Query Analyzer. We permanently changed the default database associated with a user and added a new user. We saw that we can use Enterprise Manager to check that commands in Query Analyzer have run successfully.

You should be able to deduce from this that Query Analyzer and Enterprise Manager are quite closely linked. Well, this is sort of true. What actually links them is the server engine that runs within Windows itself and deals with the SQL Server databases installed on the computer. Enterprise Manager is a GUI to this engine, designed for managing the overall maintenance of a server, its databases and their objects, security, etc. Query Analyzer uses the same engine, but is used primarily for running and developing scripts to maintain the database. A less graphical UI, it requires more keystrokes and perhaps a better memory on your part to remember which command completes which action. At the end of the day, Query Analyzer and Enterprise Manager really serve different purposes. You will very quickly find out which tool is best for which task.

One last advantage for Query Analyzer; you can have Query Analyzer on a machine without the need for Enterprise Manager. It installs quite happily on any operating system and can connect to the data source allowing you to work with databases, whereas Enterprise Manager will only install on specific operating systems, depending on which version of SQL Server you have purchased. Query Analyzer will run on Windows 95 and upwards.

It's now time to move on and look at how we deal with the book's main example.

Database Analysis and Design

Now that SQL Server is installed and the main tools that we will use in our life as a SQL Server developer or administrator have been demonstrated, it is almost time to start building the `Wrox_Golf_Results` database solution. However, we cannot do this yet because we still don't know what will be within the database. At this point in time, all the information that we have so far is that we will be building a database that will hold golf society results for an organization called Wrox. This is the information that we have been given, and we now have to gather enough information about the requirements of the solution, and about what information require to be stored.

The aim of this chapter is to gather information so that we know what needs to be stored, and what needs to be done to retrieve the data from the system. This is a whole book in itself and in fact Wrox have a great book, *"Professional SQL Server 2000 Database Design" (Wrox Press, ISBN 1-861004-76-1)*. However, this chapter will give an insight in to the vast area that design is. Armed with this information, we need to proceed through arranging the data so that retrieval is as efficient as possible – called normalizing the data – and ensuring that data duplication is as little as possible, or ideally that no data duplication exists. It is also necessary to know how the system and the data within it will be used on a day-to-day basis. Finally, we need to know what type of system is being built, for instance, whether it will receive instant data updates, or just be used to analyze already defined data.

Although the methods and processes involved may not meet the needs of every organization and their methods, this chapter is an overview of the processes involved, and also shows how to build up information and ensure that the design is well thought out.

The aim of this chapter is to:

- Demonstrate the gathering process for collecting data about the current system
- Seek out information about the new system
- Detail what data will be recorded in our example
- Normalize the information from our data gathering
- Show the relationships between tables
- Define the type of system, whether transactional or analytical

This chapter discusses the data gathering and methods, but will be building a logical design rather than a physical design: that is left to the rest of the book. Also no specific formal techniques will be used in this exercise, as this is not a book on design. However, the processes, both physical and logical, to get to the final design of the database will be the same. First of all, taking the information that has been given to us, it is necessary to gather enough data to then move on to placing that information into a database.

Gathering the Data

One of the first tasks before building the database is to find out what information the database system has to hold and also how that information should be stored, for example, numerical or text, length, and so on. To achieve this, we would perform a data gathering exercise, which could involve talking with those people who would be the owners of the system and those who will be using the system.

For larger systems, several meetings would take place where one area of the system would be pinpointed and that area discussed and researched. Even then it may take several meetings of going back and discussing those areas. We could also conduct interviews, distribute questionnaires, or even just observe any existing processes in action, all to try to gather as much of the information that we need as possible.

The main area that defines whether a database solution is successful or not is not so much the building of the system, but the information gathering process before the first line of code is written. If we get the wrong item of information or are missing an area that might be crucial to the final solution, then already our system is flawed. Involving the users as much as possible at the earliest stage, and then including them as the design progresses should result in a significant reduction of errors and missing parts.

Taking the example of golf, or any sports society results, the first people to include in the information gathering stage would be those people within the society who currently record the scores of matches, probably by hand, or perhaps on an Excel spreadsheet. It will be these people who know what information is currently recorded, and what information they are currently missing that would be good to have.

So, at the first meeting we would take these recording documents and see what information is currently stored. We find out at the meeting that the current system is storing information in an Excel spreadsheet where details of the previous season are shown to you. A snippet of the details is shown below:

Wrox Golf Society				
Match v The Laurel & Hardy's	23rd September 2000	Match 1	Cath Alexander	Won
Match v The Laurel & Hardy's	23rd September 2000	Match 2	Claire Brittle	Lost
Match v The Laurel & Hardy's	23rd September 2000	Match 3	Douglas Patterson	Drawn
Match v The Laurel & Hardy's	23rd September 2000	Match 4	Cilmara Lion	Won
Match v The Laurel & Hardy's	23rd September 2000	Match 5	Fiver Locker	Drawn
Total Score	Won	8-5		
Match v Bedford Junior Blues	15th October 2000	Match 1	Fiver Locker	Lost
Match v Bedford Junior Blues	15th October 2000	Match 2	Claire Brittle	Won
Match v Bedford Junior Blues	15th October 2000	Match 3	Cilmara Lion	Won
Match v Bedford Junior Blues	15th October 2000	Match 4	Douglas Patterson	Lost
Match v Bedford Junior Blues	15th October 2000	Match 5	Cath Alexander	Lost
Total Score	Lost	6-9		

Even before any further discussion takes place there are many items of information within this spreadsheet. It would be our job as a designer to gather that information from the spreadsheet – so let's do this now.

The first item of information at the top of the spreadsheet is the name of the golf society. This is only recorded once in the whole of the spreadsheet and therefore would only need recording once within the system.

The next item of information is the details of each game within the match. We can see who the opposition is, the date it was played, the order of the games, who the player from the society was that played that game, and whether it was a win, a loss, or a draw. All of these items still need to be recorded but we can see that there is duplication of the match details with the opposition and the date the match was played. There is also duplication of players between the different matches. However, for the moment, the only goal is to collect the necessary information about the system we are going to build. Removing duplication comes later.

The final item of information is the final result of the match and whether it was a win overall.

Now that we have this, we start discussions about what is required from the system we are to build. Obviously a great deal will be discussed and there will be useful information as well as insignificant information passed across.

However, out of the discussion the following points are made:

1. The system has to be expanded to cater for more than one golf society group.
2. The system has to be able to display details of the club, results, and players on the Web.
3. Details of the club the societies play at also need to be recorded for the Web.
4. More in-depth details of the players are required. Some of these details include their photo, date of birth for aged events, and whether they have left the society or not. Handicap is not required as the main club records this centrally.
5. Further information for the players is the number of games played, and the number of points they have gained. This will then be used to get to an average points gained.
6. Due to the expansion to more than one society group, a league table will be set up.
7. It is a wish to keep track of the society groups' financial position.
8. A newsletter providing information to the members will also be produced.

Notice how the information is in no set order as this is how information tends to come out. Due to the size of the system being quite small, this will be the only data gathering exercise to be performed. However, what has been gathered will be cross-checked later in the design phase, although this is outside the scope of this book.

The Information to Record

Looking at the list of areas that require information to be recorded, it is necessary to start to arrange these into some sort of order. First of all, it is necessary to scan through the bullet points and try to group the information into specific related areas. The bullet points above have been numbered so that this can be used to demonstrate how the groupings have occurred.

- Club Details – 2, 3
- Players – 2, 4, 5
- Matches – 2, 6
- League n – 6
- Society Groups – 1, 6, 7
- Newsletters – 8

As we seem to have six distinct groups, these could translate into being six distinct tables within our proposed database. From here it is then possible to start to look at what information could go within these tables. We will look at it should in turn with a list of the information to hold. The information listed is taken from the discussion with the users, and a list of the columns will be supplied that may initially form the basis of the tables. Each column has a description against it so that when we go back to the users they know what each column is about. Also at this stage we will add in columns to hold any identifiers for finding the records – in the following they are denoted with (K).

Club Details

The aim of this table is to hold the details of the club where the societies play. There will only be one record as this system is only going to hold details for the one golf club. There is, therefore, no need to relate this table to any other as all the tables within this system relate automatically to a single record within the table. If we were to deal with more than one club – for example, a central database, perhaps held by the Royal and Ancient at St. Andrews in Scotland, the headquarters for golf – then it would be necessary to take the `Club Details` table to a stage where an ID did exist to make the record unique.

- Club Name (K) – the name of the golf club that the society clubs meet.
- Address – the address of the club excluding state, zip and country.
- Phone Number – the club's phone number.
- Fax Number – the fax number, although at present the club does not have a fax, but it is necessary to cater for one.
- Zip Code – the zip code for any mail.
- State – the US. state in which the club resides.
- Country – the country that the club resides for when foreign societies wish to come to play.
- E-mail address – again not available to receive e-mails, but this is in progress, so required for future development.

- Web Site – the URL of the web site for the club and the societies.
- Chairperson – the name of the chair.
- Vice Chair – the name of the vice-chair.
- Secretary – the name of the secretary.
- Last Updated – when the web site was last updated.

Players

This table will hold each of the players within each different society. No player can play for more than one society.

- Player Id (K) – a unique ID for each player.
- Society Id – the ID to link the player to a society.
- First Name – player's first name.
- Last Name – player's last name.
- Number of games played – number of matches the player has played.
- Number of points scored – the number of points scored.
- Date of Birth – date of birth.
- Left the club – whether the player has left the club or not.
- Photograph – the photograph of the player if one exists.

Matches

This table will hold the matches and the results of the matches played.

- Match Id (K) – a unique ID for each match.
- Society Id – an ID to link in to the Society Groups table.
- Opposition – the name of the opposition. Quite often it will be societies within the same club that will play one another; however, it is possible to play societies outside the club. Provision has been made for both types.
- When match played – the date of the match.
- At home – whether the team is the home team or the away team.
- Player – the name of the player.
- Result – what their result was.

League

This table will not exist as the information can be derived from the `Society Groups` table. This can be done when we look at the `Society Groups` table next, by working with the points for and points against.

Society Groups

This table exists to hold details of each society group. There will be one record per society group. This will also hold a summary of the overall match scores, which can then be used to provide a league.

- Society Id (K) – a unique ID for each society. Used to link in to the Matches and Players tables.
- Group name – the full name of the group.
- The leader's name – each society will have a contact, or a leader.
- Games played – number of games played.
- Games won – number of games won.
- Games drawn – number of games drawn.
- Games lost – number of games lost.
- Points for – the number of points won in each individual match and so becomes the total won for the society.
- Points against – number of points lost in each individual match.
- Points difference – the number of points between those gained and lost. A negative number denotes more points lost than won.
- Society Group bank balance – will hold the current state of the bank balançe.

Newsletters

A simple table that will hold details of newsletters to be sent out.

- Society Id (K) – an ID to link in with the society group.
- Date to be sent out – the date the newsletter should be sent out. Along with society ID, this will make this record unique.
- Contents – what is to be said within the newsletter.

Now that the first cut of the tables has been made there is one more piece of information that we need to know, which concerns information not recorded as it won't be included within this database.

External and Ignored Information

The database in this example will not hold every item of information that is required to make the system complete. This is to keep the example simple and to avoid having extra tables, which would not be used within the book. For example, some systems would use an external addressing system and rather than holding the whole club address within the system, would use a cross reference ID, and also use this for holding the address for each of the players. A table would also exist to hold all of the financial transactions, but this will not form part of this solution.

Now that all the information has been gathered, it is now time to look at normalizing the data to provide a good solution.

Normalization

Normalizing a database is the art of reducing any duplication of data within tables and building multiple tables related to one another through keys or indexes to achieve this goal.

There are a number of levels of normalization, called **normal forms**, each focusing on a specific part of reducing data duplication. We will look at these more a little later in the chapter.

However, a database designer should not normalize with impunity, as this may have an effect on speed within the database and the retrieval of data. Good normalization will produce faster sorting of data, queries will run faster, and it will also allow a larger number of **clustered indexes** in the database, which, as we will see when we come to the indexing chapter, Chapter 7, can improve performance. Although normalization will produce an efficient database, it is possible to over normalize data by creating too many relationships and too many slim, small tables, so that to retrieve one piece of information requires access to many tables and many joins between these tables. A good designer knows when to stop normalizing, and does not take things just that stage too far.

In logical modeling, the term **entity** is used to mean a conceptual version of a table. As we are still in the logical modeling stage of designing our database, we will use the term entity rather than table in our discussions here, since it is less tied to implementation.

The question remains as to what should be contained in an entity? There are three principles that should govern the contents of an entity:

- Each entity should have an unique identifier
- Only store information that directly relates to that entity
- Avoid repeating values or columns

Each Entity Should Have a Unique Identifier

It must be possible to find a unique row in each table. This can be completed through the use of a unique identifying column, or the combination of several columns. However, no matter which method is used, it must be impossible for two rows to contain the same information within the unique identifying column(s).

Consider the possibility that there is no combination of columns in a table that can make a row unique, or perhaps we wish to build a single value from a single column. SQL Server has a special data type, called **uniqueidentifier**, that can do this, but a more common solution is to build a column with an integer data type, and then set this up as an **identity** column. This will be covered in the book when building the tables in Chapter 6.

Only Store Information that Directly Relates to that Entity

It can be very easy in certain situations to have too much information in one entity and therefore almost change the reason for the existence of the specific entity. This could reduce efficiency in an On-Line Transaction Process, or OLTP system (discussed later) where duplicate information has to be inserted. It could also lead to confusion when an entity that has been designed for one thing actually contains data for another.

Avoid Repeating Values or Columns

Having columns of data where the information is an exact copy of another column within either the same table or a related table is a waste of space and resources. However, what tends to happen is that you have repeated values or columns within two or more tables and therefore the information is duplicated. It would be in this scenario that you would be expected to avoid the repeating values and move them out elsewhere.

Now that we know what should be contained within a table, how do we go about normalizing the data? The normalization forms that will be addressed within this chapter are the **First Normal Form**, the **Second Normal Form,** and the **Third Normal form**. There are a number of other, "higher" normal forms, but they are rarely used outside academic institutions, and so will not be covered here.

Before looking to normalize our own data, it is first necessary for us to know what each of the normalization forms means.

First Normal Form (1NF)

To achieve the first normal form within a database, what is required is to eliminate any repeating groups of information. Any groups of data found to be repeated will be moved to a new table. Looking at each table in turn we will see if all the tables meet the first requirement of first normal form.

Players

There are five columns that could contain repeating data. These are first name, last name, number of games played, number of points scored, and date of birth – for example, there may be two players called Fred, the Smith family may have three players, and a set of twins could also be players! Therefore we should look at moving these pieces of information out to a separate table to meet the first normal form criteria. Taking the description literally, this is what we should do; however, we have already hit the first problem with normalization. Remember that speed is the essence of a good system – in our case, almost all of the players will have different first names, last names, and dates of birth; therefore, moving these out to a separate table just for a few, if any, records does not seem logical, as the chances of repeating values are very low indeed. So, this then leaves number of games played and points scored. These could be moved out to a new table, linked to the players information by the player ID, but again, in our case, the incidences of repeating values would be low. So, given that we have few records, it is decided that the table will stay as it is.

Matches

There are four columns that will have repeating values: the Society Id, Opposition, when the match is played, and whether the game was at home or not. There would be a high incidence of repetition of these values as there would be duplication on each individual player with each game played. Therefore these columns should be moved to another table, or the remaining columns be moved. This would then give the following result:

Matches	**Match Scores**
Match Id	Match Id
Society Id	Player
Opposition	Result – Points
When match was played	Result – Win/Draw/Loss
At home	

These two tables will now work such that the `Matches` table will have one record per match, and each individual match will be recorded in the `Match Scores` table.

Looking at the remaining tables, there are no more occurrences of repeating values.

Second Normal Form (2NF)

> **To achieve second normal form, each column within the table must depend on the whole primary key.**

In other words what this means is that if we looked at any single column within a table, you need to ask if it is possible to get to this information using the whole key, or just part of the key? If only part of the key is required, then we must look to splitting the tables so that every column does match the whole key. So, you would look at each column within the table and ask, can I reach the information contained within this column from just using part of the key? All of our tables use an ID as the primary key, and only one column. Therefore, to break 2NF with this is almost impossible. Where you are more likely to break 2NF would be where the primary key uses several columns.

If we take all the tables within our example, every column within each table does require the whole key to find it.

Third Normal Form (3NF)

> **To achieve third normal form, we must now have no column dependant on any other column within the table that is not defined as a key, and that no data is derived from other data within the table.**

When splitting the `Matches` table, notice that there are two result columns: one for the points, and one for whether the result was a win, a draw, or a loss; this means that one column is deriving its information from another column. Therefore it is possible, and a requirement to meet third normal form, to remove one of the columns. The best column to remove would be the Result – Win/Loss/Draw as the number of points is used to build up the information within the `Society Groups` table.

This leaves looking at derived data. The only table with derived data is `Society Groups` where there is a column called Points difference. This is derived by taking the Points against column away from the Points for column. This can be completed within code: therefore this column is redundant and should be removed.

We have now reached full normalization to 3NF of the tables within our database.

Time to re-visit our tables and ensure that all the information within each of the tables meets the needs of the system.

Let's take a look at each bullet point from the investigation and ensure that each point is met and where it is met:

1. The system has to be expanded to cater for more than one society group – the `Society Groups` table.
2. The system has to be able to display details of the club, results, and players on the Web – the `Clubs` table, the `Matches` table, the `Match Scores` table, and the `Players` table.
3. Details of the club the societies play at also need to be recorded for the Web – the `Clubs` table.
4. More in-depth details of the players are required. Some of these details include their photo, date of birth for aged events, and whether they have left the society or not. Handicap is not required as the main club records this centrally – the `Players` table.
5. Further information for the players is the number of games played, and the number of points they have gained. This will then be used to get to an average points gained – the `Players` table.
6. Due to the expansion to more than one society group, a league table will be set up – this will be derived from the records within the `Society Groups` table.
7. It is a wish to keep track of the society groups' financial position – held within a bank balances column within the `Society Groups` table.
8. A newsletter providing information to the members will also be produced – this is fully contained in the `Newsletter` table.

Denormalization

Despite having normalized our data to be more efficient, there will be times that denormalizing the data is a better option. Denormalization is the complete opposite of normalization and it is where you introduce data redundancy within a table to reduce the number of table joins and potentially speed up data access.

This can be found in production systems where the join to a table is slowing down queries, or perhaps when normalization is not required, for example, when working with a system where the data is not being regularly updated. We cover more on this in the OLAP section a bit later on.

Just because people say your data should be totally normalized, this is not necesserily quite true, so don't feel forced down that route. The drawbacks of denormalizing your data is the fact that you will be holding duplicate and unnecessary information that could be normalized out to another table and then just joined during a query. This will therefore have performance issues as well as using a larger data storage space. However, this can be overridden if queries do run faster.

However, denormalization is not the route we want to take, so now that we know we have all the data to produce the system, it's time to look at how these tables will link together.

Relationships

Within a database system most of the tables will be related to one another between primary and foreign keys, otherwise we would just have a collection of single table objects with nothing linking them together. There are several types of relationships that can exist and this is covered in depth in Chapter 8, where relationships between tables are demonstrated. These relationships can be when there is one record in one table joining on to multiple records in another table, or vice versa. This is known as a **one-to-many** relationship and is perhaps the most common type of relationship, and is seen within all the related tables within our solution. The other types of relationships are **one-to-one** and **many-to-many**.

A foreign key is a key on a child table that is used to link to a primary key on a master table. More on this in Chapter 8, when we discuss relationships in detail.

Database Diagram

Taking the information built about the relationships between the tables, and what we know about the tables themselves, it is now possible to build a database diagram. This will show the links between the tables but not how the relationships work. This is covered in Chapter 9 where we cover the building of the relationships within the database using the SQL Server Database Diagramming tool.

The diagram below will show the tables within the database solution we are creating, as well as showing the external tables and how they would fit in to the whole model if they were also included.

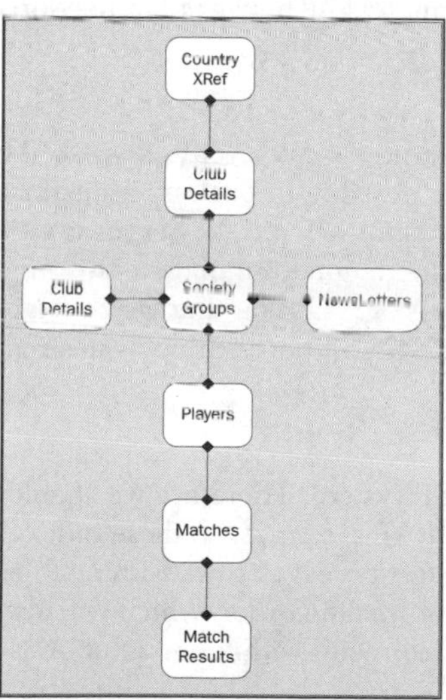

Now that the diagramming is completed, the final stage of the design process is to decide what type of system the solution will be; whether it is one used for analytical processing, or one that will take and deal with real-time updates still needs to be determined.

Using the System, OLTP or OLAP?

Now that we have the database designed, one of the major design decisions is whether the system will be an **On-Line Transaction Processing** (**OLTP**) system, or an **On-Line Analytical Processing** (**OLAP**) system.

Before making the decision, it is necessary to know what these two key types of systems are.

OLTP

The first type of system to look at will be an OLTP system, which is a system designed where there will be instant updates of data. This will be our system. There is a fair chance that an OLTP database system will have a separate part that will be the user front end written in a language such as Visual Basic, Visual FoxPro, or Visual C++, among many others. This user front end will call through to the database and make instant updates of any changes a user has made to the underlying data.

A system built as an OLTP has to have many considerations to ensure that it is fast, reliable, and keeps the data integrity intact. When designing an OLTP system, it is not only the database structure that it is crucial to get right, but also where the data physically resides. You will also tend to find that OLTP systems are normalized to 3NF, although this may not happen in every case. By normalizing your data you will aid the achievement of a main goal of OLTP systems, which is to keep data updates as short as possible. By normalizing your data – removing redundant or duplicate columns – you should ensure that the data to be written is as compact as possible. In many OLTP systems, normalization is king.

Data Placement

Although our system is not going to produce large data updates, if we do design a system that does, then it is crucial that we place our data and indexes on a fast and reliable computer to avoid any bottlenecks, down time, or slow data access through slow network connections.

Backups

Many OLTP systems are in use 24 hours a day, 7 days a week. Therefore backing up the database is a hazardous, and necessary, task. It is possible to back up a database while SQL Server is in use, although, if possible, it is best to perform a backup when SQL Server is either not in use or when there will be a small amount of activity updating the data taking place – this might be in the middle of the night or even during a break period. However it is crucial that we constantly monitor and check any backup within an OLTP system to see that it is still performing as desired.

Indexes

Speed is crucial to a successful OLTP system. Therefore we should see a higher number of indexes within an OLTP system compared to an OLAP system, with these indexes not only used to help relate data from one table to another, but also allow fast access to rows within tables themselves. This also stretches to using an index to hold the information in a specific order, which will also aid data retrieval. Building indexes and how they work and should be dealt with within our solution is covered in detail in Chapter 7.

OLAP

With an OLTP system, what must be kept in mind is that an update to the database could happen at any moment in time, and that update must be reflected within the database instantly. It is also crucial that the system can perform many updates simultaneously and that by doing so, will not corrupt any data.

Moving on to an OLAP system, this is where a system has been designed with the data remaining pretty static with very infrequent updates. These updates could be overnight, weekly, monthly, or any other time variant as long as there are not updates happening on a high frequency basis like an OLTP system. As the name suggests, a system that can be defined as an OLAP system is one where a large amount of the processing is analysis of the existing data. There should be little or no updating of that data, ostensibly only when the data within the analysis is found to be incorrect, or as mentioned above, when more data is being applied for analysis.

Systems designed for OLAP sometimes do not follow any design standards or normalization techniques and most certainly have fewer indexes than an OLTP system. You tend to see no normalization, as it is easier to take data and to slice and dice it without have to bring in data from a normalized table. There are few, or no updates taking place on an OLAP system, so transactions and keeping these compact are not a concern. Most OLAP systems will contain no normalization. Quite often we will find one or two large flat files rather than several files related together, and therefore, as there are fewer relationships, there will be fewer indexes.

> *OLAP systems are also known as data warehouses although data warehousing is only one part of the overall OLAP system design. Put simply, the data warehouse is the database that holds the information used within the OLAP system.*

There is a lot more to analysis systems and if this is an area that you need to know more about, make sure you read *"Professional Data Warehousing with SQL Server 7.0 and OLAP Services" (Wrox Press, ISBN 1-861002-81-5)*

So, when we take into consideration all of the above information, it is fairly obvious that although the data updates will be relatively infrequent – in other words, only when a match is in progress or completed – there will be updates occurring online with instant results expected. Therefore, our system will be an OLTP system.

Summary

There is a lot of theory within this chapter but it is crucial to getting the design of a database right as early as possible. The later the design is left, or if the design is made while development is in progress, we have a recipe for disaster.

If you are building your own large system, then a true modeling technique using full diagrams and perhaps a diagramming software package is a must.

Design is not an area that can be skipped or taken lightly and within this chapter you have seen a flavor of what is required to get the right information from the right areas, take that information, and build a good table design, and from there, normalize the information so that you have a tightly built, fast, and efficient solution.

Now the design is out of the way, it is possible to move on and start building the `Wrox_Golf_Results` database solution.

5

Creating the Sample Database

By now we should know our way around SQL Server and its components that make it easy to use and understand. It's now time we started building our example application.

Earlier in the book we saw that this example is based on a small sports club that wants to keep track of its fixtures and results, along with a note of the players and further statistics. To be a bit more specific, the sports club that we will be looking at is a golf society.

Before we can build this example application, the very first action we must complete is to construct the sample database. This chapter will take us through the following:

- Defining and building the database to be used for our example
- Ensuring that it exists within SQL Server
- Checking the details of the database
- Demonstrating how to remove an unwanted database

By the end of this chapter we will know:

- What a database is, and what one consists of
- What a transaction log is
- Where a database is stored
- How to create a database through either Enterprise Manager, a Wizard, or Query Analyzer
- How to set database options in Enterprise Manager and Query Analyzer
- How to review the database details
- How to remove a database using Enterprise Manager and Query Analyzer

First of all, it is important to know and understand the basics, and what better place to start than knowing what a database is.

Defining a Database

A SQL Server database is a container for objects that not only store data but also enable data storage and retrieval to operate in a secure and safe manner. A SQL Server 2000 database will hold the following:

- The **table** definitions
- The **columns** within those tables, which make up **rows** of data
- Any programs – which are called **stored procedures** – used to access the data
- Any **indexes**, which are used to speed up the retrieval of data
- Any **views**, which are specialized ways of looking at the actual data

This list contains a fair number of technical terms, so let's take a few moments to go through what they mean:

- **Tables** – This is where data is kept within the database. A database must contain at least one table to be of use, although you can have a database with no user tables and only system tables. Tables contain information within rows and columns.
- **Columns** – These provide a definition of each single item of information that builds up to a table definition. A column is pre-defined as to what the data within it relates to, what type of data it is, and how large the information stored in it can be. Each table must have at least one column, although the column doesn't need to hold any information within it.
- **Rows** – Each row is made up of one instance of every column defined for the table, and their amalgamation makes up one row. There can be any number of rows in a table; you are only limited by your disk space. A row will define a single unit of information built up from the information contained within the columns of the table. A row can also be called a record. Tables, Columns, and Rows are all covered in Chapter 6.
- **Stored Procedures** – When it comes to requiring a program to manipulate or work with data, or perform the same task repeatedly, it is often better to store this code in a program called a stored procedure. Stored procedures contain one or more T-SQL statements, which are compiled and are ready to be executed when required. The program is permanently stored in the database, ready for use. We will be using stored procedures in Chapter 17.
- **Indexes** – These can be regarded as pre-defined lists of information that inform the database how the data is physically sorted and stored, and can be used by SQL Server to find rows of data quickly using information supplied, and matching this to data within columns. An index consists of one or more columns from the table it is defined for, but it is not possible for an index to cover more than one table. An index in SQL Server is very much like the index of a book, which you would use to locate a piece of information faster than going through every page in the book. We will look at indexes in Chapter 7.
- **Views** – Views can be thought of as virtual tables. Views can contain information combined from several tables, and can present a more user-friendly interface to the data. Views can also add a great deal of security to an application, but do give reduced functionality over the use of stored procedures or direct access to the tables. Views are covered in Chapter 16.

Also within every database, there is a set of system tables that SQL Server uses to maintain that database. These hold information about every column, every user, and many other pieces of information (metadata). These tables should be treated with the greatest of care, and should never be modified directly.

There is another crucial area to know about databases, which helps them to work in the most extreme conditions. It's time to learn about Transaction Logs.

Transaction Logs

Data within the database is stored, of course, on your hard drive, or on a hard drive on the server. Imagine the work involved on the disk controller, and imagine the work SQL Server has to do every time data is added, amended, or removed. Writing data is a slow process so, inevitably, every time data is written, SQL Server slows down. What if part of the way through writing the data, there was a power cut and you had no uninterruptible power supply (UPS) in place? What a mess you would be in, not knowing what had been written to disk, and what hadn't!

It is also possible in SQL Server to update several tables at once. How would you work around the fact that some of the tables had been updated but when it came to updating a specific table, the update failed? Well, this is where transaction logs come into play. **Transactions** themselves are covered in Chapter 14, but very simply, a transaction is a single unit of work that can contain one or more table modifications that are either all successful and committed to the database, or if some are unsuccessful all the modifications are discarded. It is also possible to roll back a transaction so that no changes are made to the database. However, it is useful to know at this time what the Transaction Log is.

The first item to note is that every database within a SQL Server instance has its own transaction log, you will see how to create the transaction log for the example database a bit later on in the chapter. Every time SQL Server is requested to do any data modifications – whether these are additions, deletions, or modifications – a record is kept of the action. These recorded actions are kept in a place called a **Transaction Log**. There are several reasons for this.

First of all, a piece of code could in fact do several different updates at once. If one of the updates fails, then you may wish to return the values in all the updated fields to their original value. This is called **rolling back** a transaction. SQL Server achieves this, in part, by looking at the data held in the transaction log. However, any successful action where all the updates are valid would be permanently stored on file, called **committing** a transaction. After a specific number of successful transactions have been placed in the transaction log, with this number having been defined in the SQL Server configuration, the transaction log is **checkpointed**. The use of a checkpoint ensures that any data modifications are actually committed to the database and not held in any buffers, so that if a problem occurs, such as a power failure, there is a specific point that you can start from. Therefore, at the end of a checkpoint transaction, you know the database is in a consistent and valid state. As SQL Server knows that at a checkpoint all is well within the database, there is no need to keep the completed transactions recorded in the transaction log stored up to the checkpoint. SQL Server will therefore issue a truncation of the transaction log to remove these records, minimizing the size of the log on the computer. This is known as **truncating** the transaction log.

If you had a power failure, you might have to "replay" all the work completed since the last backup, and the transaction log could also be used to do this, in certain scenarios. SQL Server doesn't write data immediately to disk. It is kept in a **disk cache** until this cache is full or SQL Server issues a checkpoint, and then the data is written out. If there was a power failure while the cache was still filling up, then that data is lost. Once the power came back though, SQL Server would start from its last checkpointed state, and from the transaction log, any updates after the last checkpoint, that were logged as successful transactions, will be performed.

> *A disk cache is a space in the system where changes to the tables within the database are held. By doing so, a whole block of data can be written at once, saving on the slow process of disk head movement.*

Transaction logs are best kept, if at all possible, on a separate hard drive to the data. The reason for this is that, when data is written to a transaction log, it is written serially. Therefore, if there is nothing else on the hard drive except the transaction log, the disk heads will be in the right place to continue writing each time. A minor overhead, but if performance is an issue, this is worth considering.

Backing up of the Transaction Log needs a little care, and is covered in Chapter 10, *Database Backups and Recovery*.

It's now time to look at the databases that are included when you install SQL Server.

Databases within SQL Server

Within SQL Server, there are several databases installed and displayed when SQL Server is first installed. In this section, we will explore each of these databases so that you will know what each does and will feel comfortable when you come across them outside of this book. Let's first look at the most important database in SQL Server, the **`master`** database.

master

As the `master` database is the most important one in SQL Server, the first area that must be covered are the warnings, dire warnings! Directly alter this database at your peril! There should be no justifiable reason to go in to any of the tables within this database and alter the records or column information directly. There are system functions that allow a constructive alteration of any of the data in an orderly fashion, and these should be used if you wish to alter the `master` database.

The `master` database is at the heart of SQL Server, and if it should become corrupted, there is a very high chance that SQL Server will not work correctly. The `master` database holds the following crucial information within it:

- All user login IDs, or roles that the user IDs belong to
- Every system configuration setting (for example, how the data is to be sorted, how security is implemented, what the default language is)
- The names of and information about the databases within the server
- The location of databases
- How SQL Server is initialized

- Specific system tables holding the following information (this is not an exhaustive list)
    - How the cache is used
    - Which character sets are available
    - A list of the available languages
    - System error and warning messages

The `master` database is like the security guard of SQL Server and it uses this information to ensure that everything is kept in check.

> **It is crucial that you keep a regular backup of this database. Ensure that it is part of your backup strategy. Backups are covered in Chapter 10.**

tempdb

The **`tempdb`** database is – as its name suggests – a temporary database, which has only a lifetime of the duration of a SQL Server session. Once SQL Server stops, the `tempdb` database is lost. When SQL Server starts up again the `tempdb` database is re-created, fresh and new, ready for use. There is more to this, but first, you also need to know what the `tempdb` database is used for.

As you know, a database can hold data, and that data can be held in many tables. You use commands and functions to retrieve and manipulate that data. However, there may be times when you wish to temporarily store a certain set of data for processing at a later time, for example, when passing data from one stored procedure to another that is going to run straight after the first one. One area that you may look towards, is storing that data within the `tempdb` database. Any temporary table created within a stored procedure or query will be placed within the `tempdb` database. This is fine, as long as the `tempdb` database is not refreshed. If it is, then your data will be gone, and you will need to rebuild it.

You may be thinking that this is not an ideal solution. After all, wouldn't it be wonderful if temporary information could be stored somewhere outside of the database. Well, that's not really where the `tempdb` would be used. It really should only be thought of as transitional storage space. We don't need to use this database until much later in our SQL Server development life, anyway.

Another reason the `tempdb` is refreshed, is that not only is it available for a developer to use, but SQL Server itself also uses `tempdb`: SQL Server uses `tempdb` all the time, and when we re-initialize SQL Server, it will want to know that any temporary work it was dealing with is cleaned out. After all, there could have been a problem with this temporary work that caused us to restart the service in the first place.

Being just like any other database, `tempdb` it has size restricitions and you must ensure that it is big enough to cope with your applications and any temporary information stored within it. As we go through the next sections, we will see that a database has a minimum and a maximum size. This includes `tempdb` and you should ensure that there are good settings for expansion so that the `tempdb` can grow as required.

> **A word of warning here. Because `tempdb` has a limited size, care must be taken that when you do use it, it doesn't get filled with records in tables from rogue procedures that indefinitely create tables with too many records. If this were to happen, then not only would your process stop working, but the whole server could stop functioning and therefore impact on everyone on that server.**

As indicated in the first paragraph of this section, there is more to be said on the refresh of the `tempdb`, which is covered under the `model` database section.

model

Whenever you create a database, as we will be doing shortly in this chapter, it has to be modeled on a pre-defined set of criteria. For example, if you want all your databases to have a specific initial size, or perhaps to have a specific set of information, you would place this information into the **`model`** database, which acts as a template database for further databases. If you wanted all databases to have a specific table within them, then you would put this table in the `model` database.

As you have just seen, there is a `tempdb` database, which is used when you need to place information into a temporary storage place, and it is re-created every time SQL Server starts up. This could be after a couple of hours, days or weeks. It doesn't matter when this happens, SQL Server will always re-create it. Being an automatic process, there are no prompts or questions so that SQL Server can rebuild this database. The `model` database is used as the basis of the `tempdb` database. Thus a little bit of care and thought needs to be used if you do alter the `model` database, because any changes will be mirrored within the `tempdb` database.

msdb

This is another crucial database to SQL Server. If you recall from Chapter 2, a process called **SQL Server Agent** was introduced. Just to recap, this process runs scheduled **jobs** and looks after the error logs as well as other system processes. A job is a process defined in SQL Server that runs automatically without any manual intervention to start it. It is from `msdb` that SQL Server Agent retrieves the necessary information to run these processes. Again, this is a database that really should not be amended directly, and there is no real need to do so. There are many other processes that use `msdb`. When creating a backup or performing a restore, `msdb` is also used to store information about these tasks as well as many other areas.

This database is for more advanced use, and is covered in more detail in *"Professional SQL Server 2000 Programming"* (Wrox Press, ISBN 1-861004-48-6).

pubs

Here you will come across the first example database found in SQL Server. The `pubs` database has been around as the sample database for SQL Server for quite some time now, is fully functional, and is provided for developers to view and test existing work. This database can be used, and is used, not only by SQL Server developers, but also by developers in Visual Basic, Visual C++, etc.

This database is based on an example of a (fictitious) book publishing house, where the database records contain details of books, authors, employees, and a whole host of other information.

It doesn't have any purpose in helping make SQL Server run, but is a useful point of reference when you are developing your own solutions and you just need to look up an example. If you wished, you could remove it from your installation, and we will see how to remove databases later in this chapter, but it may as well be left alone. It doesn't do any harm, takes up very little hard drive space, and you never know, may be useful to you. If you do remove it, there is not a problem in re-installing it later on if you realize you need it after all.

Time to look at the second sample database, and also the last standard database within SQL Server.

Northwind

If you have come from a Visual Basic or Access background, then you will instantly recognise this database. This is the second sample database, is based on a (fictitious) product supply company, and has tables for customer orders and shipping details, among others. For example, there is a `Customers` table that is related to the `Orders` table, which is in turn related to not only the `Order Details` table, but also to the `Products` table. All of these tables hold relevant information to ensure that the database can cater for dealing with building a set of orders and then shipping these once ready.

As with `pubs`, unless you absolutely need the space, keep this database with SQL Server. Especially if you're from an Access or Visual Basic background, knowing this database may give you that extra confidence boost you need at a certain time.

Now that we know what databases are in SQL Server, we can start building our own.

Creating our Sample Database

We will begin to create our own example database. In this chapter we will be covering three different ways to create a database in SQL Server:

- Using Enterprise Manager
- Using Query Analazyer
- Using the Create Database Wizard from Enterprise Manager

Each method has its own merits and pitfalls for creating databases as we will discover, but these three methods (Enterprise Manager, Query Analyzer, and the wizards) are used whenever possible throughout the book, and where you might find one method is good for one task, it may not be ideal for another. Within these chapters we will point out, where appropriate, the advantages or disadvantages of one method over another, and which method may be most suited to a particular task. None of these methods is right or wrong for every task, and it basically comes down to a personal preference, and what you are trying to do at the time. For example, if the syntax for the commands is not familiar to you, you may well choose to use a wizard or the Enterprise Manager. One you become more comfortable with the syntax, then Query Analayzer might become your favored method.

Creating a Database in Enterprise Manager

The first method of creating a database we encounter will be to use Enterprise Manager, which we looked at in Chapter 2.

Try It Out – Creating a Database in Enterprise Manager

1. Before we can create our database, we need to start up Microsoft SQL Server 2000 Enterprise Manager. To do this, select Start|Programs|Microsoft SQL Server|Enterprise Manager.

2. In the **console tree** on the left, expand all the nodes, until you see the individual databases themselves. If the SQL Server service was not previously started, it will automatically be done as you expand the tree, which may take a while. Ensure that the Databases folder is highlighted ready for the next action.

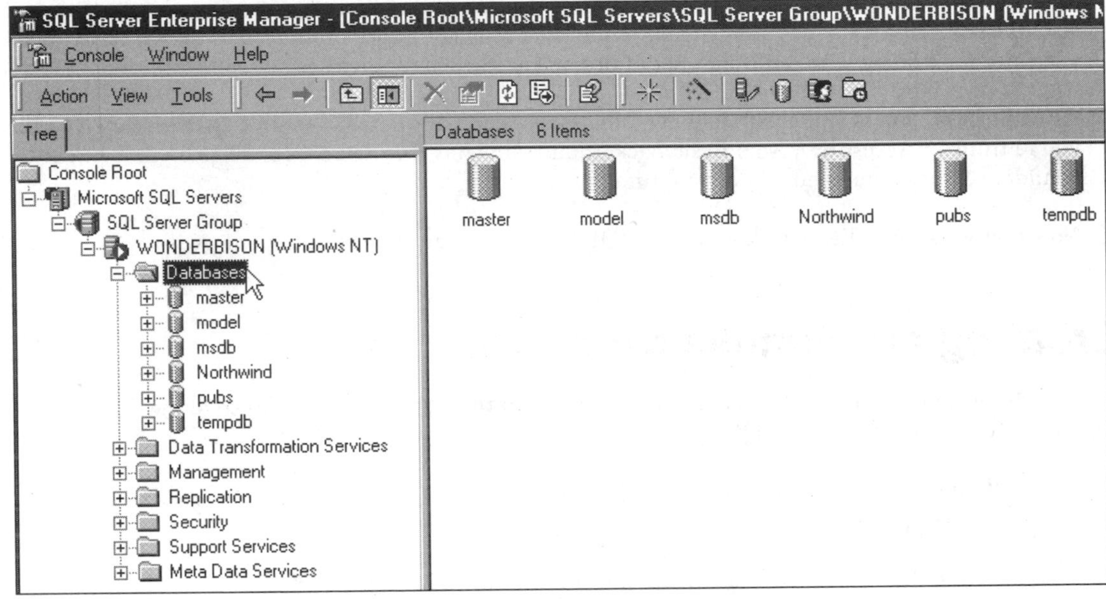

There is a minimum amount of information required to create a database:

- The name the database will be given
- How the data will be sorted
- The size of the database
- Where the database will be located
- The name of the files used to store the information contained within the database

Enterprise Manager gathers this information using the New Database... menu option.

3. Right-click on the **Databases** folder. This will bring up a context-sensitive menu with a number of different options. Select **New Database…**

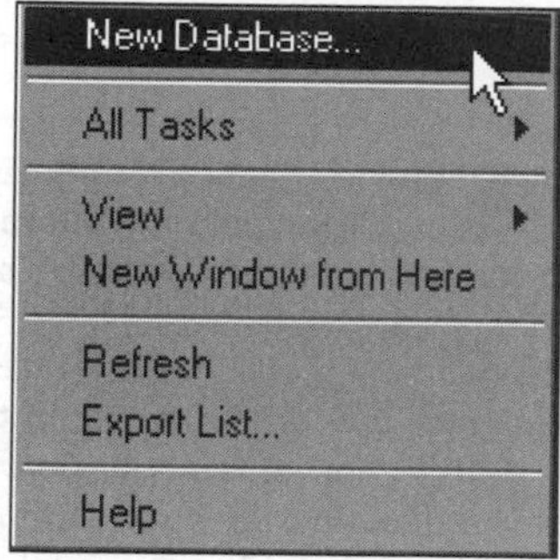

You can get the same result by selecting the menu option **Action|New Database…** or by clicking the **New** toolbar button.

4. You are now presented with the **Database Properties** screen, set to the **General** tab. First enter the **Name** of the database you want to create, in this case **Wrox_Golf_Results**. Leave the combo box at the bottom of the screen as **(Server Default)** for this database.

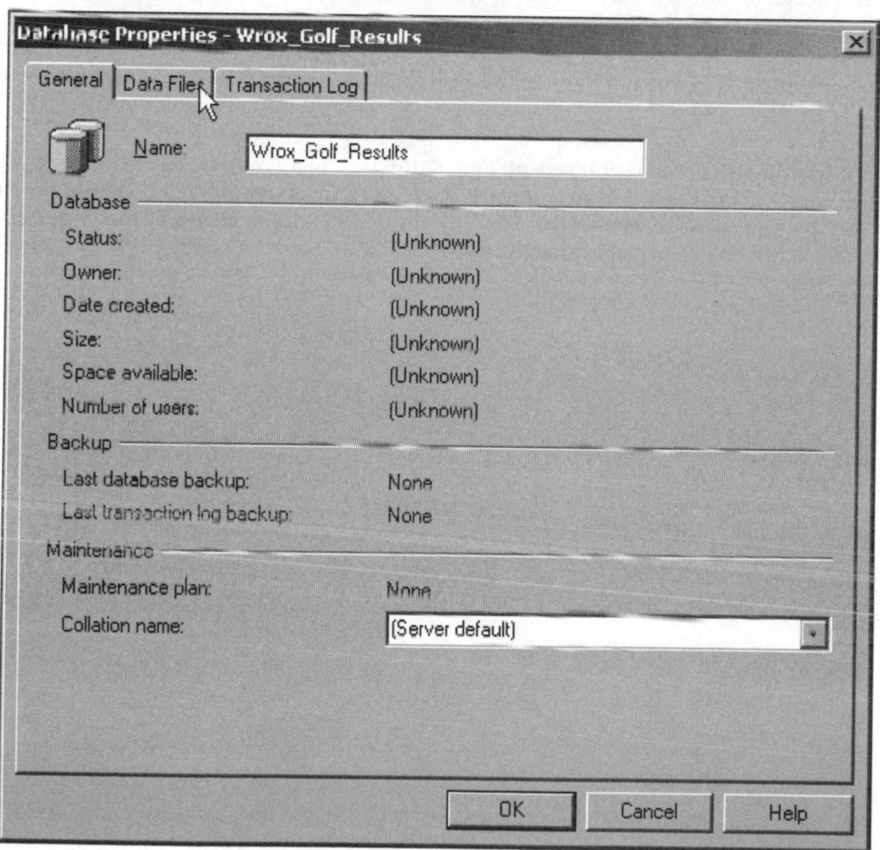

The General dialog within this option collects the first two pieces of information. The first piece of information required is the database Name. No checks are done at this point as to whether the database exists or not (this comes when you click OK), however, there is some validation in the field so that certain illegal characters will not be allowed.

> **Illegal characters for a database name are " ' */?:\<> - keep to alphabetic, numeric, underscore, or dash. Also, you may want to keep the database name short, as the database name often has to be entered manually in many parts of SQL Server.**

Once the database name has been entered, it's time to move on to the Collation name: field at the bottom of the tab. This item defines to SQL Server the **collation** that will be applied to the database, in other words, the sorting sequence of the data and how one item of data is compared to another. A definition of (Server default) informs SQL Server that the database will have the same collation sequence as the SQL Server instance, and you can use the combo box in the database creation dialog to set a different collation sequence. For example, the whole SQL Server instance may ignore case sensitivity for data and commands, but for a specific database you may need to say that all the data must be matched including the case. In SQL Server 2000, you can define different collations for each different database. Thus in one database, you can have a collation of Central European, and in another, a collation perhaps of Hebrew_CS_AS which means a Hebrew collation sequence which is case sensitive and accent sensitive. If we choose a collation of Hebrew_CS_AS, it doesn't mean that all of our data is altered from English to Hebrew, it is purely a method of sorting and collating the data. Another setting is to change from case sensitive to case insensitive for working with data that may or may not require the right casing. There is more on this in Chapter 13 when searching for data.

> **If you need to alter a collation setting on a database, then it can be done but care is required. Altering the collation sequence on a Server is even worse and should only be tackled by the SQL Server System Administrator who will be aware of the issues and have the authority to perform specific tasks.**

5. Now click on the second tab, Data Files.

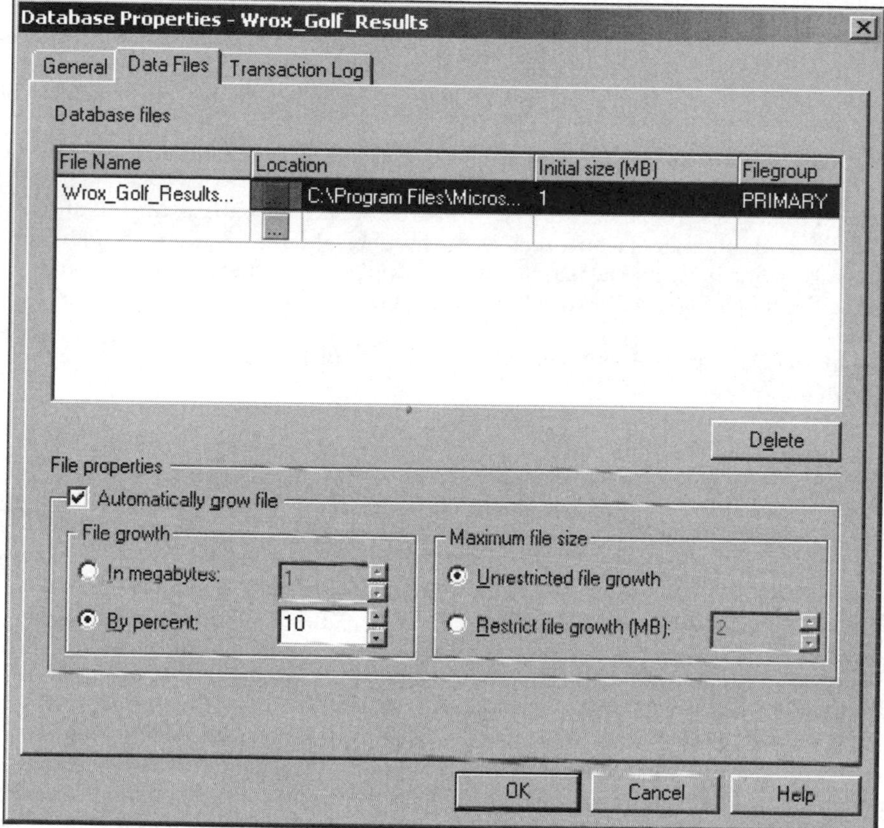

Let's inspect the Data Files tab. The File Name entry is the name of the physical file that will hold the data within the database you are working with. As you can see, by default, SQL Server has taken the name of your database, and placed a suffix of _Data to create this name.

The database files are stored on your hard drive with an extension of **MDF**. Therefore, you would see Wrox_Golf_Results_Data.MDF. In this case, MDF is not something used by DIY enthusiasts, but actually stands for **Master Data File** and is the name of the **primary data file**. Every database **must** have at least one primary data file. This file not only holds the data for the database, but also the startup information.

It is also possible to have **secondary data files**. These would have a suffix of **NDF**. Again, you could use whatever name you wished, and in fact could have an entirely different name from the primary data file. However, if you did so, the confusion that would abound is not worth thinking about.

You would place the file name for a secondary data file in the row below the Wrox_Golf_Results_Data entry on the Data Files tab. We will come back to why you can have a secondary data file when talking about File properties further down in this section.

The next column, Location, defines where the database files will reside on your hard drive. If SQL Server is installed on your C drive and none of the paths for the data were changed, you will find that the default is `C:\Program Files\Microsoft SQL Server\MSSQL\Data`. The command button with the ellipsis ... (to the left of the path) brings up an Explorer-style dialog that allows you to change the location of the database files. For example, if you move to a larger SQL Server installation, moving the location of these files to a server relevant to the needs of your database will probably be a necessity.

The next item is the Initial size (MB) column. The initial size of the database is its size when empty. Don't forget that the database won't be totally empty, and some of the space will be initially taken up with the system tables. It is impossible to say, "you are creating a database, the initial size must be nnMB", it all depends on many factors, such as the number of tables, how much static information is stored, how large you expect the database to grow to, and so on. When starting out and learning SQL Server, setting the Initial Size to 20MB will be sufficient.

If you navigate to C:\Program Files\Microsoft SQL Server\MSSQL\Data you will see that a 1MB file has been created.

The final column is the Filegroup, and this column allows you to specify the PRIMARY filegroup and any SECONDARY data files. Every database must have a primary filegroup, and to designate secondary data files, enter SECONDARY into this column. You may use any name for secondary data files, but it is advisable to choose a name that closely resembles the primary filegroup name.

The logic behind secondary data files is relatively straightforward. A primary filegroup will always, and must always, contain the system tables that hold the information about the database, the tables, the columns, and so on. If you had Automatically grow file (covered below), switched off, then the primary filegroup is likely to run out of space at some point. If this happens, and no secondary data files are specified, then the database will grind to a halt until some space is added. However, in most instances, especially when starting out, you can leave the database with only a primary filegroup. Don't misunderstand filegroups and space though. Filegroups are there to help you organize your files within your database storage and may span several disks for a performance issue. You will move files around filegroups for speed, efficiency, security, backups, and a number of other reasons. However, you can still hold all the files in one filegroup, the primary, which is what we will do through the book.

> **Remember that the primary filegroup may not only hold data, but also the system tables, so the primary filegroup could fill up purely with information about tables, columns etc.**

The Delete button allows any entries in the Database Files list to be removed. A database always requires a primary data file, and at least this file must be present in the list, otherwise an error message will be returned.

It's now time to take a look at File properties on this tab.

The first area and perhaps the most important is the Automatically grow file checkbox. Selecting this box – which is recommended, especially while you are starting out – means that SQL Server will automatically handle the situation that arises if your database reaches the Initial Size limit. If you don't check this, you will have to monitor your database and expand its size manually. Think of the overhead in having to monitor, never mind having to increase the size! It is so much easier and less hassle, and much less of a risk, to let SQL Server handle this.

While SQL Server handles increasing the size of the database for you, it has to know by how much. This is where the File growth options come in. You can either let SQL Server increase the database by a set amount each time in megabytes or by a percentage. The default is By percent, and at this stage it doesn't really matter. In our example, the first increase will be 102KB, the second increase by 112KB (don't forget that 10% of 1MB is 102KB, and 10% of 1.126MB is 112KB). For our example, this is sufficient as there won't be a great deal of data being entered. However, the percentage option does give uneven increases and if you like order, then In megabytes is the option for you.

Maximum file size sets a limit on how large the database is allowed to grow. The default is Unrestricted file growth – in other words, the only limit is the spare space on the hard drive. This is good as you don't have to worry about maintaining the database too much. But what if there is a rogue piece of code that is entering an infinite loop of data? Pretty rare; but not unheard of. It might take a long time to fill up, but fill up it will, and with a full hard drive purging the data will prove troublesome. When it is time to start moving the database to a production environment, the Restrict file growth (MB): option should be set, to guard against such problems. In *"Professional SQL Server 2000 Programming"* (Wrox Press, ISBN 1-861004-48-6) you will find techniques that can be adopted so that warnings appear when the database is approaching its maximum size.

6. Click on the last tab, Transaction Log settings. The Transaction Log settings tab is similar to the Data Files tab shown in the previous screen shot. Again, for the moment, just leave the defaults as they are.

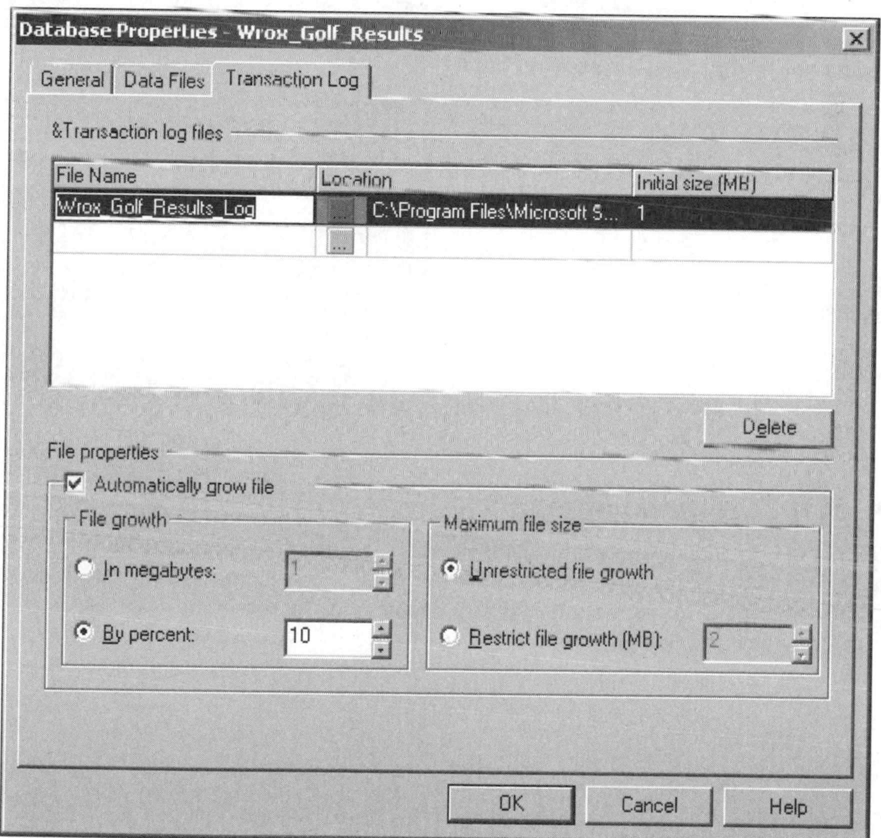

The Transaction Log tab includes the same information as the Data Files tab with one or two minor exceptions. The File Name places a suffix of _Log onto the database name, and there is no Filegroup column, since the Transaction Log doesn't actually hold system tables, and so would only fill up through the recording of actions. It is possible, however, to define multiple log file locations. The reason for this is that if we do fill a transaction log, then we do have space and a file to fail to, probably on another machine. Filling the transaction log and not being able to process any more information because the log is full will cause your SQL Server to stop processing. The use of a failover log file in larger production systems is advisable.

7. Now click on OK.

SQL Server then performs several actions. First it checks whether the database already exists, and if so, you will have to choose another name. Once the database name is validated, there is a security check to make sure that the user has permission to create the database. This is not a concern here, since by following this book, you will always be logged on to SQL Server with these permissions. Now that you have security clearance, the data files are created and placed on the hard drive. Providing there is enough space, these files will be successfully created, and it is not until this point that SQL Server is updated with the new database details in the internal system tables.

Once this is done, the database is ready for use. As you can see, this whole process is relatively straightforward, and simple to complete. Congratulations!

8. When you now return to Enterprise Manager, you will see the new database listed in both the Tree pane and the Details pane on the right.

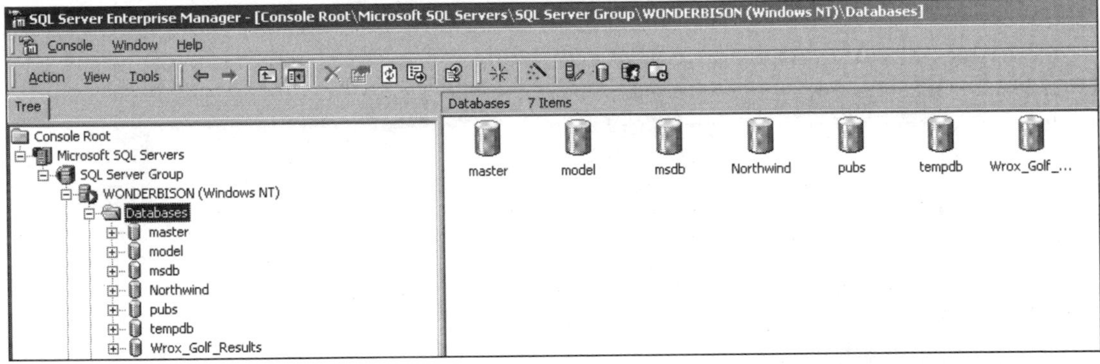

Viewing within Enterprise Manager

So now that we have created the database, and looked at Enterprise Manager building and registering the database, let's take a few moments to review our database and check that everything is OK. By following these actions at any time in the future, you can ensure that your database is still in good health. Let's now view the database details and see what we have defined.

Try It Out – Verifying the Database

1. Find the database `Wrox_Golf_Results`, and right-click on it.

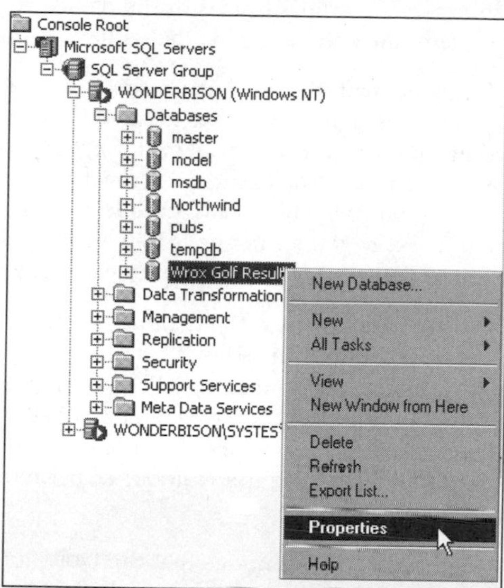

2. Select Properties. This will bring up the database details summary dialog.

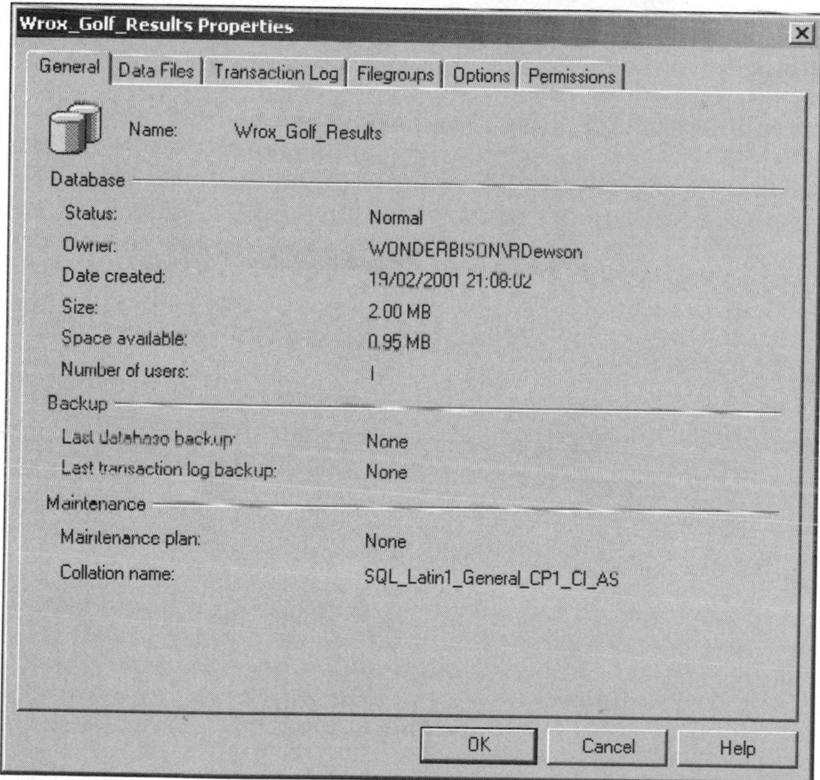

3. On the General tab you will see a summary of the database including Status, Backup, and Maintenance Plan.

The General tab provides a summary of certain aspects of the database. You may find this to be quite useful in getting a quick run down of the database and what is happening at a specific point in time.

We'll look at the Database information first: the database in this instance is Normal. This is the status that you would expect in most circumstances. There are other statuses which you may well see, for example, if the database was **Loading**, **Offline**, or on **Standby**. Normal is informing you that the database is running and is ready for work. When a database is in Loading state, it means that the database is in the process of being made available to SQL Server, but is being loaded. Offline means that the database is valid, but is not available for receiving any work, since it does not have a live connection to the server. Finally, Standby mode is inferring that the database is in read only mode on a secondary server.

The Owner is the user ID of the login that created the database. This is useful to know, as it is possible from this to find out whom to contact with any queries. This also highlights another reason why a database should be created under an ID that is meaningful rather than the generic `sa` login. Date Created is obvious, but you may be surprised that the Size is 2.00MB, as the database was created with a size of 1MB. This figure is the sum of the sizes of the data file and the transaction log, giving 2MB. Space available is the space left in the data file, and Number of users shows how many different users are currently connected to the database.

The remaining sections are straightforward, but notice that the Collation name has changed from (Server default) to that of the actual collation involved (Latin1_General_CI_AS).

4. Click on the Data files tab. This tab gives all the information about the files holding the actual data and indexes of the database. This is just like the tab that we saw when we were defining the database.

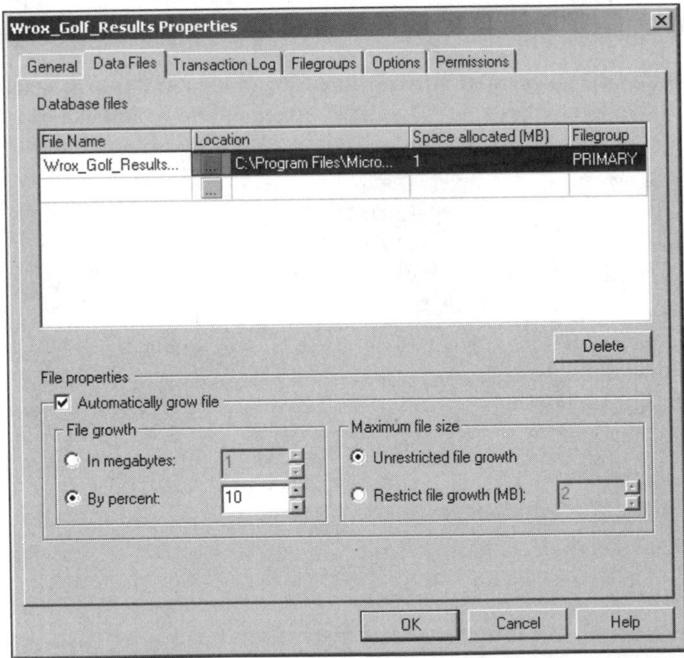

5. Click on the **Transaction Log** tab. The **Transaction Log** tab again is just as it was when you were defining the database earlier. The **Data Files** and **Transaction Log tabs** don't alter from the database creation layout. Again, take a quick look and we'll move on to the last three tabs, which are more interesting.

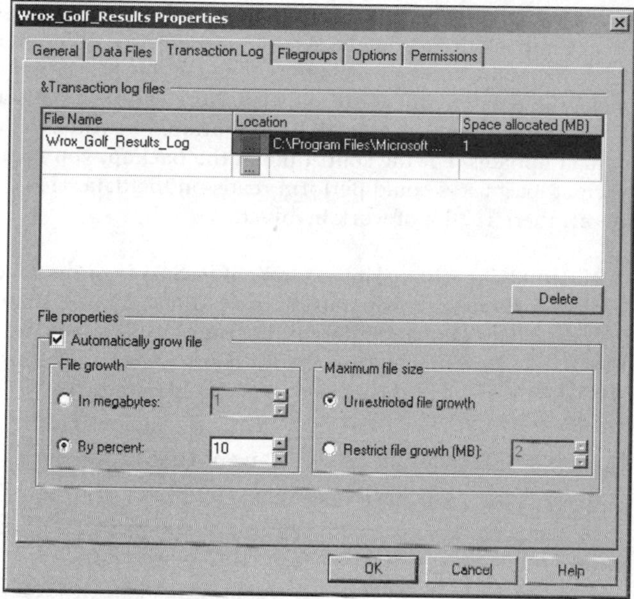

6. Click on the fourth tab, **Filegroups**. This tab is showing information that you won't have seen before. Recall that when setting up the database we had to ensure that the data had a primary filegroup, and the **Filegroups** tab summarizes information relevant to this.

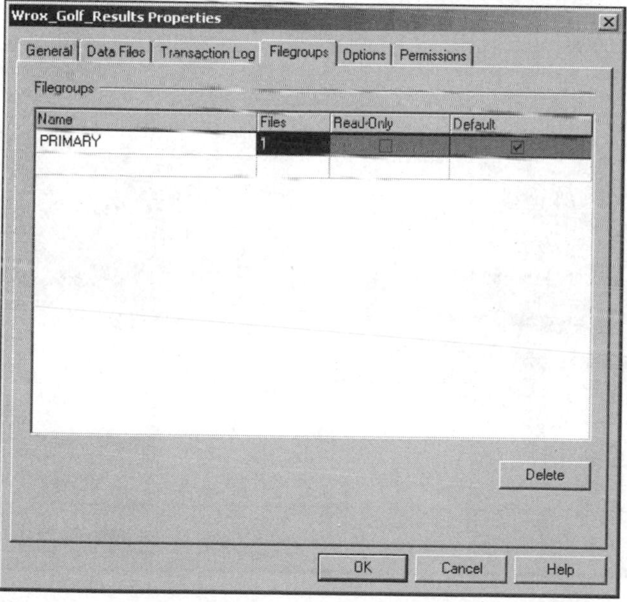

The **Filegroups** tab displays a bit more information than on the database creation screen. It specifies the physical number of files in that filegroup. The **Read-Only** box is quite interesting. Every database must have a primary filegroup, but it is also possible to have secondary filegroups, and selecting the **Read-Only** box allows you to make the secondary filegroups read only. You are now probably wondering: "Why would I want to do that?" Imagine that you had a production database and you also had a number of procedures that were accessing the data needing read-only access to compute statistics, reports, and so on. You could back up the database and restore it to a different server for the read-only activities. Then, instead of having to run a process to make everybody's access read only, it would be much simpler just to make the database files read only, so there can be no mistake of updates happening to the wrong database. Or perhaps you are in a 24/7 installation, but you need to have the database backed up without any data updates. For the short time of the backup, you could make the files on all filegroups read only, then at least users could perform reads on the data. However, if your filegroups span more than one server, there is a lot of work involved.

Finally on this tab is the **Default** checkbox. This informs SQL Server of the filegroup into which any user defined tables are placed. By default, when using the `CREATE TABLE` statement, which we will see in the next chapter, it is possible to define a different filegroup for a table to be placed into. It is not mandatory for any tables to be placed in any specific filegroup. Altering the filegroup for table creation is something that is used when spreading the workload over separate servers.

7. Click on the **Options** tab. This tab allows the setting of various options specifically for this database.

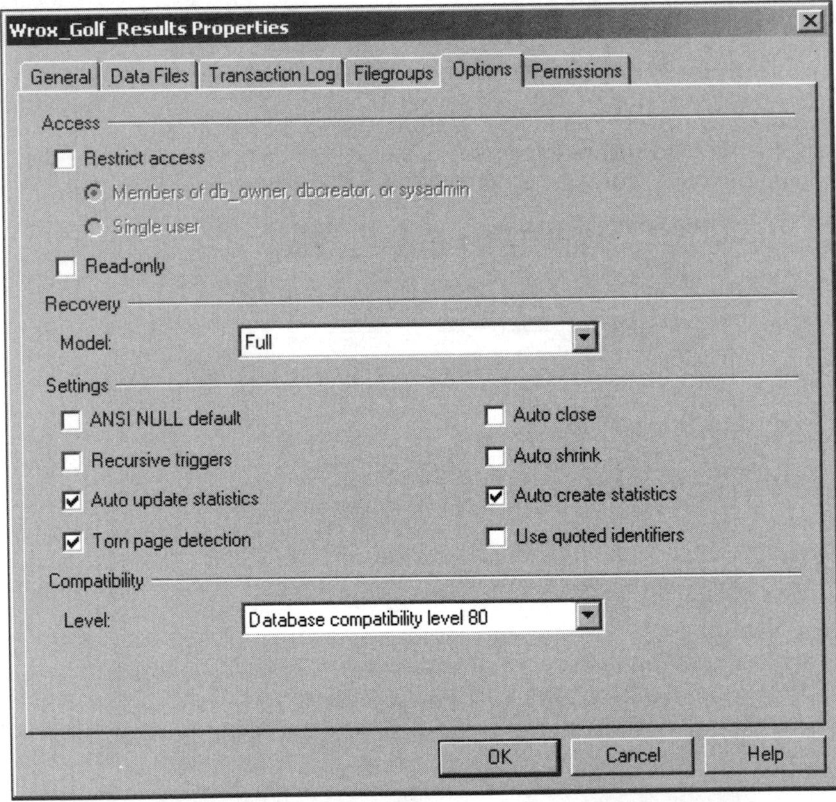

By changing any of these options and then clicking OK we will immediately set the changes that we have made on this tab, and all the others. It is also possible to alter options manually through SQL Query Analyzer, but setting the options from within this dialog means that we don't have to remember the commands' syntax. This will be covered when creating the database using Query Analyzer later on in this chapter.

In the Access area it is possible to set the users who have access to the database. This is also possible in the next tab, Permissions. However, using this area is a fast method that allows you to restrict the database objects that can be created by the listed roles or users. By default these options are not set so that we can achieve a more flexible approach to setting permissions. If the database is in development, or is in the process of being moved to the production server, then it might be worthwhile restricting the access to the specific user IDs of the **database owner**, **database creator**, and **sysadmin**. By setting this option, you will stop anyone getting into the database while you set it up, with the exception of database owner, database creator, and sysadmin. Another time you might want to use this option is during any system maintenance, where you don't want to allow any user to work on the database. Without this option, it would be necessary to remove the permissions of all users, complete the work, and then reapply the permissions, which would be cumbersome.

> *A sysadmin role (`sa`) is someone who has full system administration rights, which means they can do anything, creating databases, creating users, deleting databases, in fact, any task at all.*

The Single User option informs SQL Server that only one person can access the database at any one time. This is one way of ensuring that the user logged in has exclusive use, and that there can be no other users working on the database or the data. This option is ideal for backups. It is also useful for moving data to a data warehouse.

The final option is Read-only, and it does what it says. This option will allow no modifications, perfect for a database set up to archive data.

> **Don't forget that Read-only should not be set when updating the archive with more information from the production database, or else the updates will fail. And then don't forget to re-set it back on!**

The Recovery option will be covered later in the book, and the Settings options will be covered shortly in this chapter when we create a database though Query Analyzer.

Finally, there is the option of database Compatibility. With SQL Server 2000, it is possible to have a database created that is compatible with previous versions of SQL Server. You can be compatible with SQL Server versions 6.0, 6.5, 7.0, or 8.0 (which is in fact SQL Server 2000). Setting this option will determine the compatibility level that the database will be set to (for example, Database Compatibility Level 60 equals compatibility with SQL Server 6.0). For the moment, leave the option set as it is.

8. The final tab displays the Permissions, in other words which user IDs are allowed to access the database.

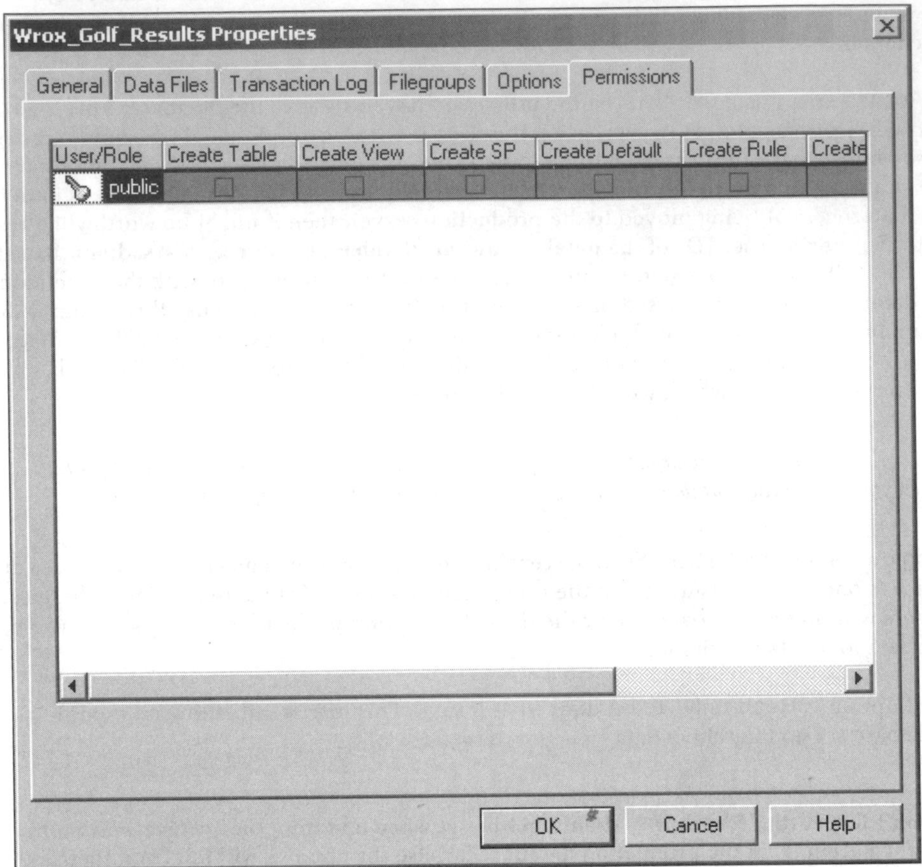

This tab deals with security issues that are beyond the scope of this book. Security is a deep topic, and there is good coverage in *"Professional SQL Server 2000 Programming"* (Wrox Press, ISBN 1-861004-48-6). However, we do take a higher-level look at security in the appendix at the rear of the book.

That aside, at the moment, the Permissions tab is displaying that only the sa login, or someone with sa rights, has the ability to do anything with this database. The `sa`, or `sysadmin` account always has full access to the database at all times. This is easy to tell, as no options are selected and therefore are not enabled.

Dropping the Database in Enterprise Manager

In order to follow the next examples properly, it is necessary to remove the database just created. It is also handy to know how to do this anyway, for those times that you have made an error or because you wish to remove a database that is no longer in use. Deleting a database is also known as **dropping** a database.

Try It Out – Dropping a Database in Enterprise Manager

1. If Enterprise Manager is not started, then start it up now, and expand the nodes until you see the database, Wrox_Golf_Results.

2. Right-click Wrox_Golf_Results to bring up the options menu.

3. Click the option to Delete.

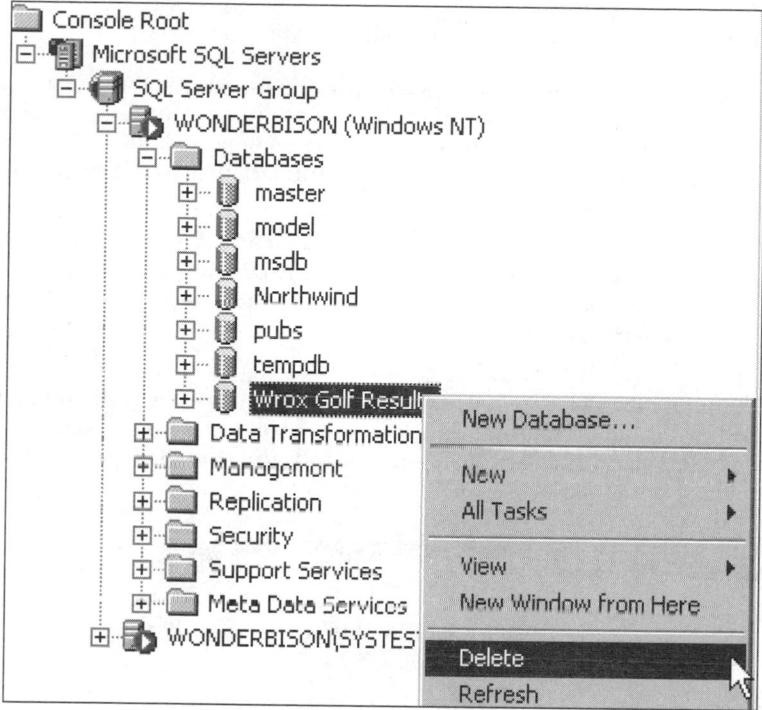

4. The following dialog will be displayed. Click Yes.

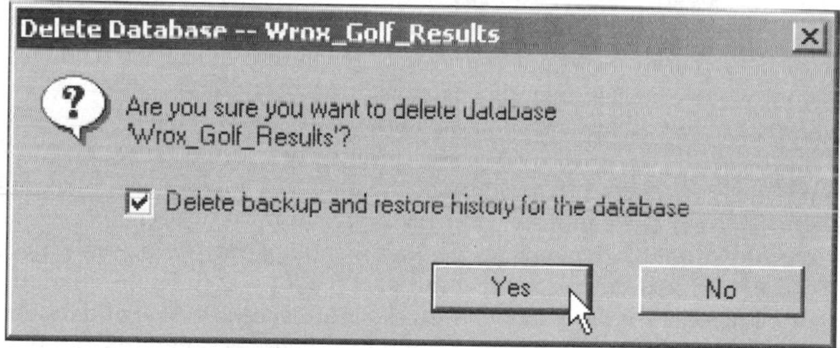

The check box in the dialog gives you the option of keeping or removing the history information that was generated when completing backups or restores. If you wished to keep this information for audit purposes, then uncheck the box.

A word of warning: while there is a dialog that gives you the opportunity to change your mind, the default key is the Yes button. So, if you do want to change your mind then it is imperative you click No. Pressing a key, or getting it wrong is bad news. It will be too late! Backing up the database is covered in Chapter 10, and it is a crucial chapter. The check box asking if you want to also remove all the backups and restores for this database is also set to the affirmative. It is these default settings that should encourage you not to use Enterprise Manager to delete databases!

5. The database is now permanently removed.

When the Yes button is clicked, SQL Server actually performs several actions. First of all a command is sent to SQL Server informing it of the name of the database to remove. SQL Server then checks that nobody is currently connected to that database. If someone is connected, through either SQL Server Query Analyzer or a data access method like ODBC or OLE-DB, then SQL Server will refuse the deletion.

ODBC is one of several methods of connecting to data, not just SQL Serve databases. Visual Basic programmers might connect to a database via ODBC or OLE-DB using technologies such as ADO, RDO, or a number of third-party tools. These connections provide a simple and unified method of retrieving and manipulating data.

For SQL Server to refuse the deletion, it does not matter if anyone connected to the database is actually doing anything, all that is important is the existence of the connection. For example, if you selected Wrox_Golf_Results in Query Analyzer, then returned to Enterprise Manager and tried to drop the database, you would see the following error:

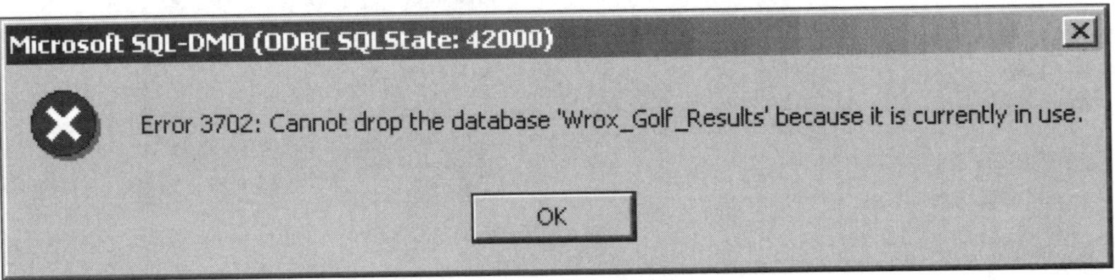

Once SQL Server has checked that nobody is connected to the database, it then checks that you have **permission** to remove the database. SQL Server will allow you to delete the database if it was your user ID that created it, in which case you own this database, and SQL Server allows you do what you want with it. However, you are not alone in owning the database.

If you recall from Chapter 1, there was mention of the sa account when installing SQL Server. Since it is the most powerful ID, and has control over everything within SQL Server, there were warnings about leaving the sa account without any password, and also, about using the sa account as any sort of login ID in general. This section also mentioned that the sa account was in fact a sysadmin server role. A role is a way of grouping together similar users who need similar access to sets of data. Anyone in the sysadmin role has full administrative privileges – and this includes removing any database on the server.

So whether you are logged in as yourself, or a sysadmin, just take care when using Enterprise Manager to drop a database. A better method will be demonstrated later in the chapter.

Creating a Database – Using a Wizard

This section will build the Wrox_Golf_Results database using the **Create Database wizard**.

Try It Out – Using a Wizard

1. From Enterprise Mangage, you can either start the wizard selection from the menu bar options: Tools/Wizards… or by clicking on the wizard button on the toolbar at the top of Enterprise Manager.

2. You are now presented with a list of SQL Server's built-in wizards. If you expand the Database node, you will see at the top of the list, Create Database Wizard. Select this and click on OK.

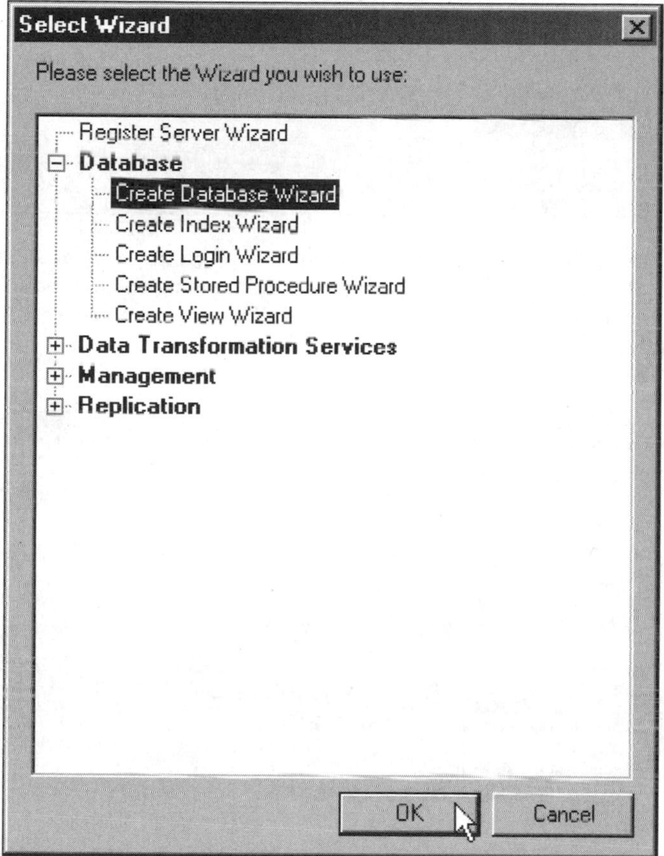

3. Once you have clicked OK you are presented with the Welcome screen. It doesn't really tell you much, apart from what is about to happen. Click Next, and let's get moving right along.

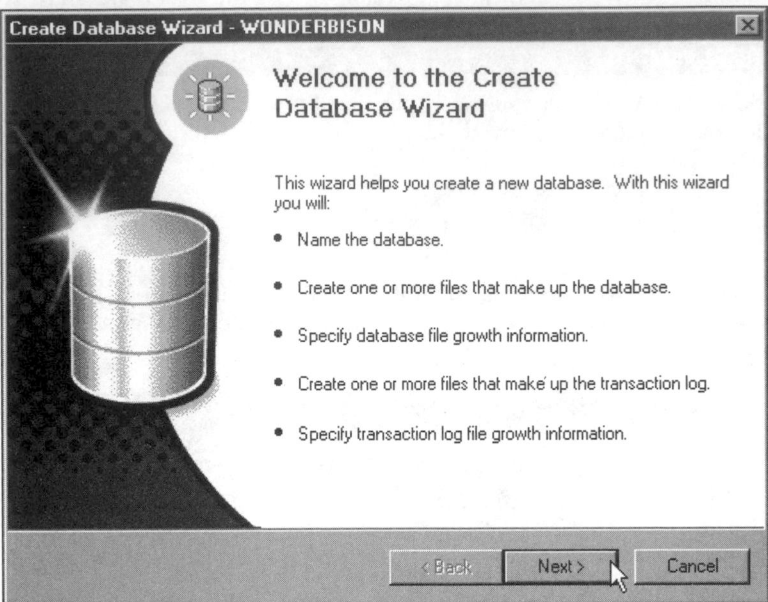

4. You are presented with the initial details required to build your database. Again, put in Wrox_Golf_Results, and since we have covered changing the database locations earlier in the chapter, you can alter where the data is stored, if you want. Here we will leave the defaults so that all our database files are saved in the same place. Once you have entered the database name, click Next.

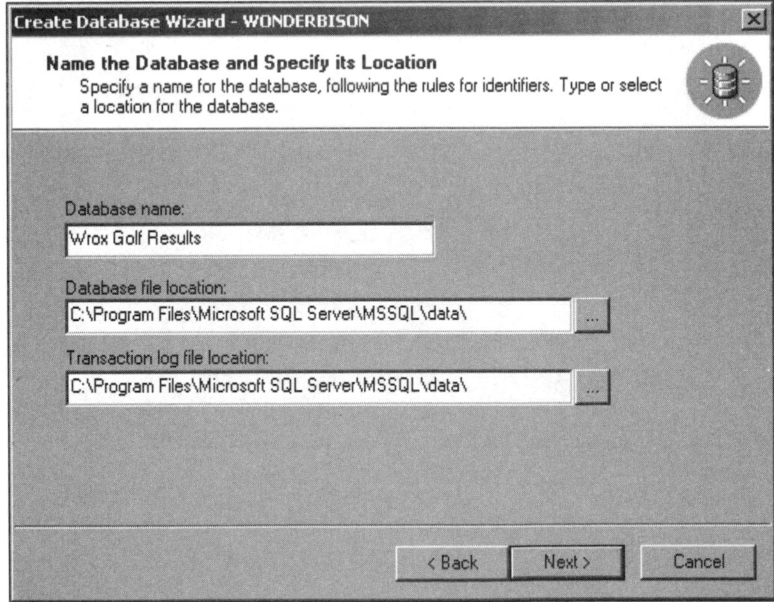

5. Now the wizard presents you with a dialog that is actually the top half of the **Data Files** dialog we saw earlier when creating the database with Enterprise Manager. The wizard is simply presenting less information at this point, to try to make creating a database easier. Once again, just leave the defaults as they are and click **Next**.

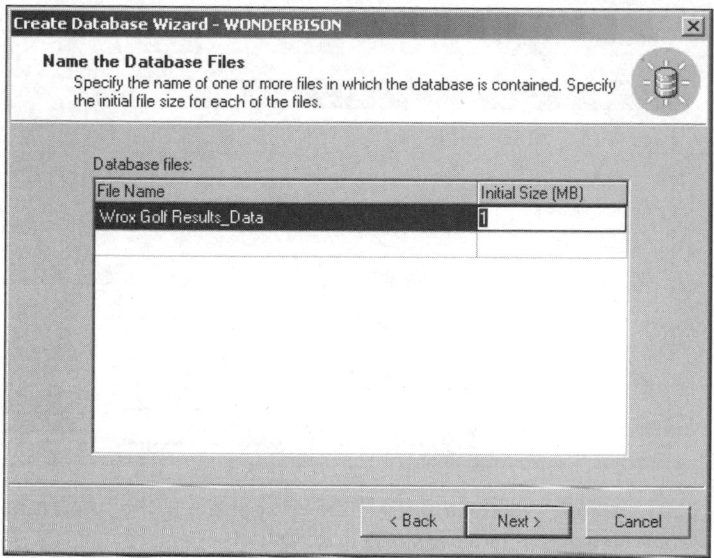

6. The following screen is just the lower half of the data files dialog. Leave the defaults as they have been presented and click **Next**.

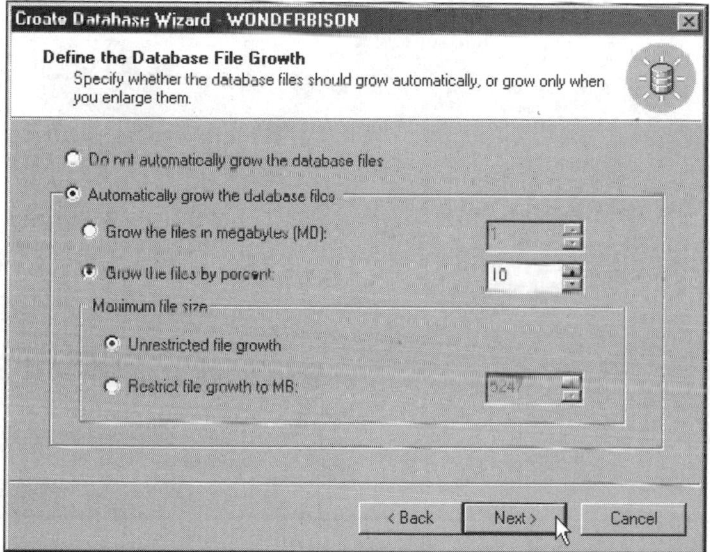

7. Again the wizard is just presenting the top half of a dialog that was presented earlier in Enterprise Manager. Click **Next**.

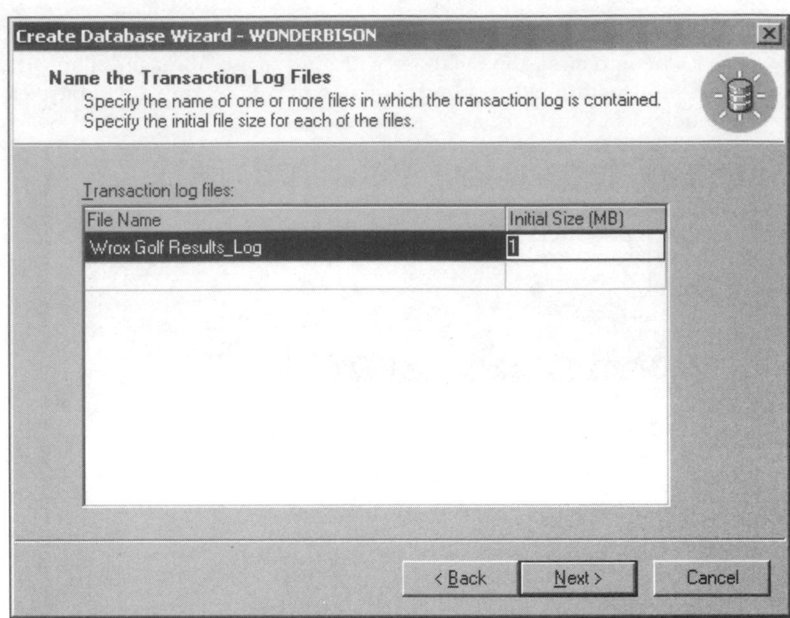

8. Now the wizard presents a screen that is from the bottom half of the Transaction Log dialog. Again leave the defaults as they are and click Next.

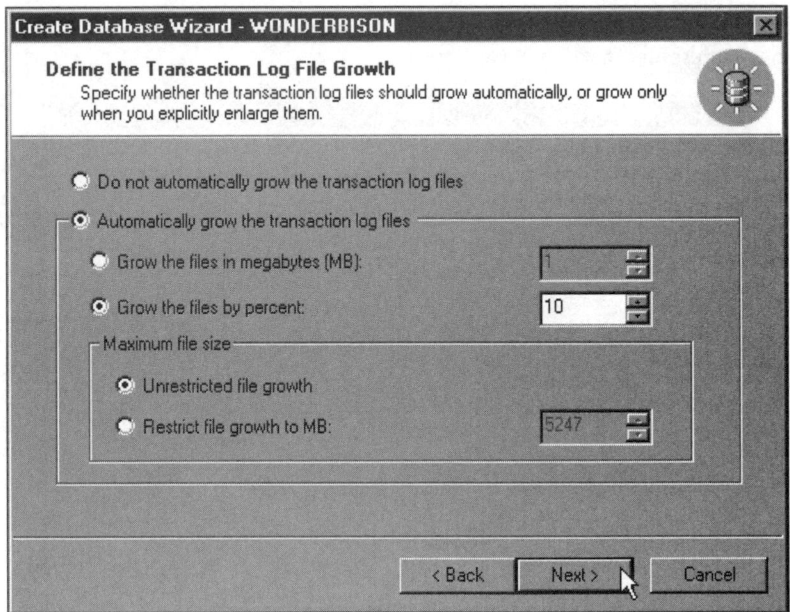

9. The final screen is your last chance to cancel the creation of the database. You can review the summary report before you finally decide all is OK. If you don't want to proceed any further, click Cancel. If you have seen problems you can click the Back button until you reach the point in the wizard needing changes. Otherwise, click Finish, and the database will be created.

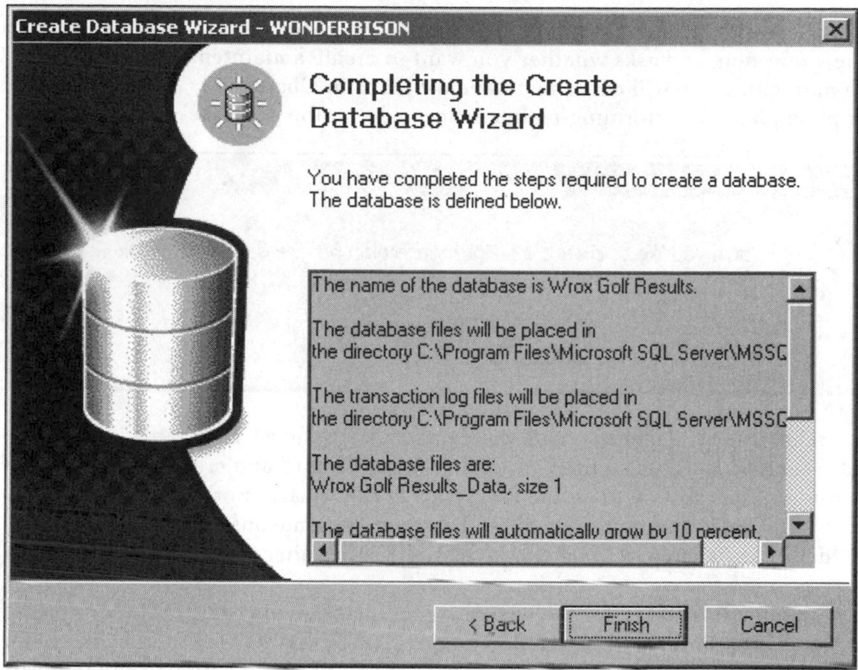

10. If all has gone well you will see the dialog informing you that the database has been created. You will see in the background as well, that the database has actually been created and is in Enterprise Manager. Click OK.

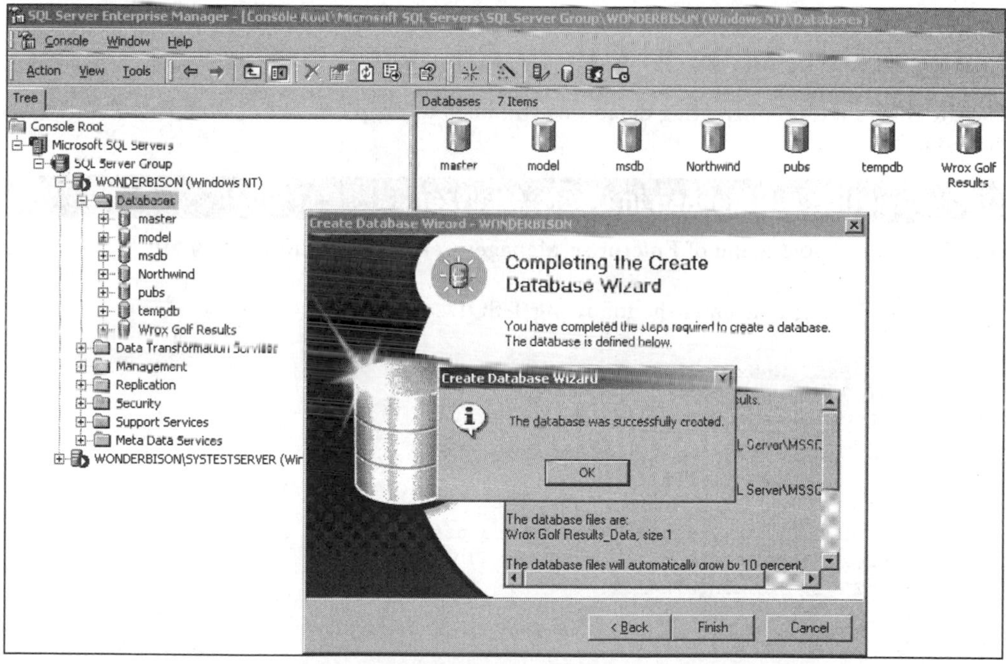

11. Unlike creating a database through Enterprise Manager, using the wizard takes you through to a new question, and asks whether you want to create a **maintenance plan** or not. Click No for the moment, as we will cover maintenance plans in Chapter 11. A maintenance plan is quite simply a plan for performing maintenance tasks on the database.

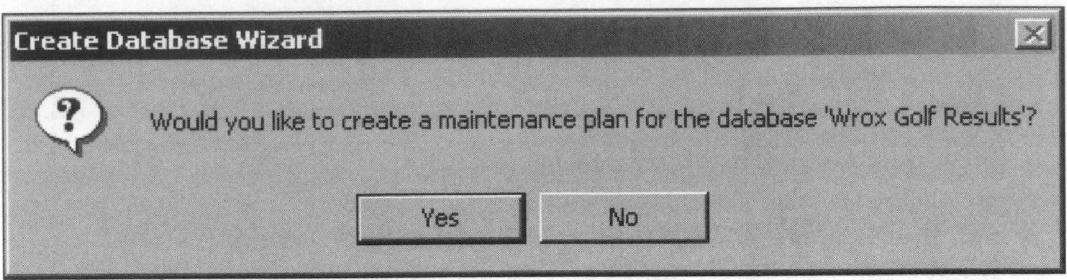

As you have seen, it took longer to create the database with the wizard than with Enterprise Manager. Another difference between using the Create Database Wizard and creating a database with Enterprise Manager is that there is no way to define filegroups in the wizard. Both methods complete the same work, ask the same basic questions, and should receive the same answers. It is necessary to define the name of the database, where it will be stored, as well as the other setup information.

Validation of the details entered for the wizard doesn't happen until the Finish button is pressed, at which point the validation is performed. So you don't really have a way of knowing beforehand if there is a problem with what has been entered. However, if you do spot an error, then you can use the Back button to rectify the mistake.

Now that we have created a database through the wizard, we'll look at creating a database by "hand", from within Query Analyzer.

Creating a Database in Query Analyzer

To use the third method of creating databases you need to drop the Wrox_Golf_Results database as described above.

Try It Out – Creating a Database in Query Analyzer

1. From the Tools menu of Enterprise Manager, select SQL Query Analyzer.

2. In the Query pane, enter the following T-SQL script:

```
CREATE DATABASE Wrox_Golf_Results
ON (NAME='Wrox_Golf_Results_Data',
    FILENAME='C:\Program Files\Microsoft SQL
Server\MSSQL\data\Wrox_Golf_Results_Data.MDF',
    SIZE=1, FILEGROWTH=10%)
LOG ON (NAME='Wrox_Golf_Results_Log',
        FILENAME='C:\Program Files\Microsoft SQL
Server\MSSQL\data\Wrox_Golf_Results_Log.LDF',
        SIZE=1, FILEGROWTH=10%)
COLLATE SQL_Latin1_General_CP1_CI_AS
GO
```

Execute this code, either by pressing *F5*, or *Ctrl+E*, or by pressing the Execute Query toolbar button

3. Once the code is executed you should see the following results:

```
The CREATE DATABASE process is allocating 1.00 MB on disk 'Wrox_Golf_Results_Data'.
The CREATE DATABASE process is allocating 1.00 MB on disk 'Worx_Golf_Results_Log'.
```

How It Works – Creating a Database in Query Analyzer

The main focus of this section of the chapter is the code listed above: the `CREATE DATABASE` command.

When placing code in the Query Analyzer, you are building up a set of instructions for SQL Server to act on. As you progress through the book, there will be many commands that can be placed in Query Analyzer, which build up to provide powerful and useful utilities or methods for working with data. An in-depth discussion of Query Analyzer took place in Chapter 3, so if you need to refresh your memory, take a quick look back.

Before actually looking at the code itself, it is necessary to inspect the syntax of the `CREATE DATABASE` command.

```
CREATE DATABASE <database name>
[ON
   ( [ NAME = logical_name, ]
       FILENAME = physical_file_name
     [, FILESIZE = size ]
     [, MAXSIZE = maxsize ]
     [, FILEGROWTH = growth_increment] ) ]
[LOG ON
   ( [ NAME = logical_name, ]
       FILENAME = physical_file_name
     [, FILESIZE = size ]
     [, MAXSIZE = maxsize ]
     [, FILEGROWTH = growth_increment] ) ]
[COLLATE collation_name ]
```

There are a number of parameters that will be covered now, so that when you want to create your own database, you will know what is happening.

- `database name` – The name of the database that the `CREATE DATABASE` command will create within SQL Server
- `ON` – The use of the `ON` keyword informs SQL Server that the command will specifically mention where the data files are to be placed, their name, size, and filegrowth. With the `ON` keyword comes a further list of comma separated options. These options are listed below:
  - `NAME` – The logical name of the data file that will be used as the reference within SQL Server
  - `FILENAME` – The physical file name and full path where the data file will reside. You must include the suffix `.mdf`.

- SIZE – The initial size, in megabytes by default, of the data file specified. This parameter is optional, and if omitted, will take the size defined in the model database. You can suffix the size with KB, MB, GB, or TB (TerraBytes)
- FILEGROWTH – The amount that the data file will grow each time it fills up. You can either specify a value that indicates by how many megabytes the data file will grow, or you can specify a percentage as discussed earlier when creating a database with Enterprise Manager.

- LOG ON – The use of the LOG ON keyword informs SQL Server that the command will be specifically mentioning where the log files will be placed, the name, size, and filegrowth.
  - NAME – The name of the log file that will be used as the reference within SQL Server
  - FILENAME – The physical file name and full path to where the log file will reside. You must include the suffix .ldf. This could be a different name to the FILENAME specified above.
  - SIZE – The initial size, in megabytes by default, of the log file specified. This parameter is optional, and if omitted, will take the size defined in the model database. You can suffix the size with KB, MB, GB, or TB (TerraBytes)
  - FILEGROWTH – The amount by which the log file will grow each time the data file fills up, which has values as for the data file's FILEGROWTH above.

- COLLATE – This will be the collation used for the database. Collation was also discussed earlier in the chapter when creating a database with Enterprise Manager.

It's now time to inspect the code that has been entered into Query Analyzer that will create the Wrox_Golf_Results, database.

Commencing with CREATE DATABASE, you are informing SQL Server that the following statements are all parameters to be considered for building a new database within SQL Server. Some of the parameters are optional and SQL Server will include default values when these parameters are not entered. But how does SQL Server know what values to supply? Remember at the start of this chapter there was a discussion about the built-in SQL Server databases, specifically the model database. SQL Server takes the default options for parameters from this database unless they are specified. Thus it is important to consider carefully any modifications to the model database.

The database name is obviously essential, and in this case, Wrox_Golf_Results is the chosen name.

The ON parameter provides SQL Server with specifics about the data files to be created, rather than taking the defaults. Admittedly in this instance, there is no need to specify these details, as by taking the defaults, SQL Server would supply the parameters as listed anyway.

This can also be said for the next set of parameters, which deals with the Transaction Log. In this instance, there is no need to supply these parameters, as again, the listed amounts are the SQL Server defaults.

Finally, the collation sequence we specify is actually the default for the server.

Taking all this on board, the command could be actually be entered as the following, which would then take all the default settings from SQL Server to build the database:

```
CREATE DATABASE Wrox_Golf_Results
```

When viewing the database within Enterprise Manager, we discussed that the options of the database could be set, and that this can also be achieved from SQL Server Query Analyzer. The following section sets these options in Query Analyzer.

Try It Out – Setting Database Options

1. Start Query Analyzer.

2. In the Query Pane enter the following code:

```
EXEC sp_dboption 'Wrox_Golf_Results', 'autoclose', 'True'
GO
EXEC sp_dboption 'Wrox_Golf_Results', 'read only', 'False'
GO
EXEC sp_dboption 'Wrox_Golf_Results', 'dbo use', 'False'
GO
EXEC sp_dboption 'Wrox_Golf_Results', 'single', 'False'
GO
EXEC sp_dboption 'Wrox_Golf_Results', 'autoshrink', 'False'
GO
EXEC sp_dboption 'Wrox_Golf_Results', 'ANSI null default', 'False'
GO
EXEC sp_dboption 'Wrox_Golf_Results', 'quoted identifier', 'True'
GO
```

3. Now that you have entered the code it needs to be executed. Once the code has executed, you should see the following result:

```
The command(s) completed successfully.
```

How It Works – Setting Database Options

There are a lot of options to set, and as you can tell, a good deal of typing.

First of all, we will cover the basic syntax of the code, and then move on to each option.

`sp_dboption` is a system function that allows a specific database option to be set. However, it can also display the settings of specific properties, or for a whole database it can show which options have been set.

Before exploring the three different methods of running this function, let's take a look at its syntax:

```
sp_dboption ['database name']
            [,'option name']
            [,'value to set']
```

It's a simple function, taking three parameters. The first parameter is the name of the database that you wish to set the database option in. The second parameter is the name of the option itself, and the third parameter is the option setting. If you omit the third parameter, the current setting of that option is *returned.*

If we ran the following in a Query Analyzer Query pane:

```
EXEC sp_dboption 'Wrox_Golf_Results', 'auto create statistics'
GO
```

we would see the following output in the Results pane.

```
OptionName                          CurrentSetting
----------------------------------- -------------------
auto create statistics              ON
```

The above code is asking SQL Server to query the `auto create statistics` option and to check its setting, which in this case is the default value, ON. Notice as well that there is a `GO` statement after each command. `GO` is a special command that will be covered in more detail in Chapter 14, but basically it is informing SQL Server to perform the command.

If we reduce the function further to the following:

```
EXEC sp_dboption 'Wrox_Golf_Results'
GO
```

Then we can see which settings have been set (in other words, which are not set to the default), which on my computer produced the following output with three settings listed. Depending on your computer and the defaults set up at installation, this list may vary.

```
The following options are set:
-----------------------------------
torn page detection
auto create statistics
auto update statistics
```

Let's now take a quick look at each of the options that we set in the *Try It Out – Setting Database Options* code:

- `autoclose` – A setting of `True` ensures that the database is cleaned up. In other words: the resources are cleared when the last user logs off.
- `read only` – If set to `True`, no modifications to the data can be made. Only data reads are allowed.
- `dbo use` – If set to `True` means that only the user ID that created the database has access and can use the database. Any other ID will be refused.
- `single` – When set to `True`, only one user has access to the database at a time. Any subsequent users will be refused. It doesn't matter who the user is, but only one is possible.
- `autoshrink` – A setting of `True` indicates that if SQL Server believes that this database can be shrunk in size safely.

- `ANSI null default` – When set to `True`, SQL Server follows the SQL 92 rules to see if a column can allow `NULL` values.
- `quoted identifier` – This is a favourite and can catch many people out. Using this option, it is possible to say that only single quotes are allowed when using this database. By setting this to `OFF`, you can delimit a string by either a single quote or a double quote. However, when set to `ON`, you cannot use double quotes around string variables as double quotes will be signifying a SQL Server identifier.

Now that the database has been created, and all the options are set, it is possible to view the databases through Query Analyzer.

Viewing in Query Analyzer

There are two ways of viewing the Wrox_Golf_Results database within Query Analyzer. The first, and probably the most used way, is through the Object Browser. Through this, there are many options and actions that are available. It's time to take a look at our example datbase with this:

Try It Out – Displaying Database Info in Query Analyzer

1. Start SQL Query Analyzer

2. On the left-hand side there should be the Object Browser. It will look like the following:

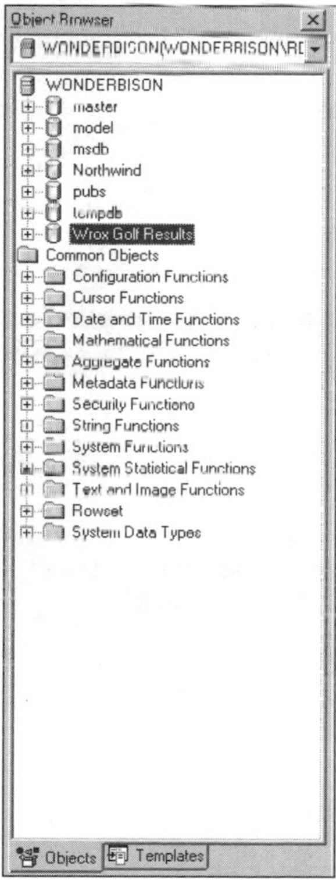

If it doesn't exist, then you can bring up the Object Browser by pressing *F8* or clicking the Object Browser toolbar button.

3. Now that we have the Object Browser displayed, you will see the Wrox_Golf_Results database listed.

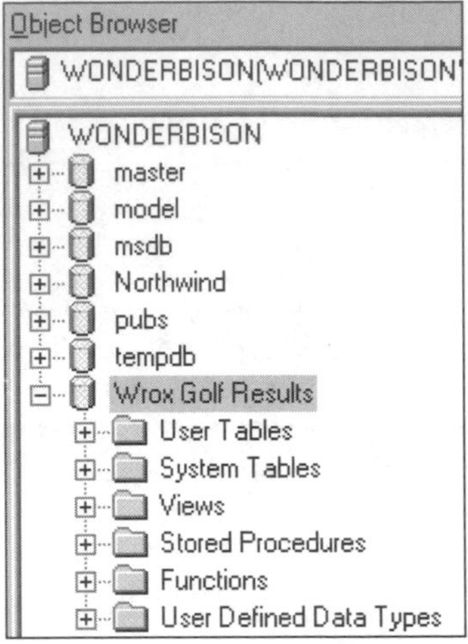

That is all that there is to it. The second method is to type in a system function.

Using Commands – Query Analyzer

The system commands that we look at here are powerful, built-in stored procedures, which return a predefined set of information. They are not always the best way to find out certain information, as there are times when we would get information overload, or perhaps its not as well presented as it would be in SQL Server, but they do form the basis of SQL Server.

Try It Out – Displaying Database Info in Query Analyzer

1. Start SQL Query Analyzer.

2. Enter `sp_helpdb Wrox_Golf_Results` in the Query Pane.

3. Execute the code. The information produced is just far too large and wide to fit on a page, but if you look at the results pane, and scroll right to left, you will see exactly the same information as you did through the properties dialog in Enterprise Manager.

```
      db_size       owner
----- ------------- ------------------------------------------------------------------
          2.00 MB WONDERBISON\RDewson


      fileid filename
----- ------ -----------------------------------------------------------------------
           1 C:\Program Files\Microsoft SQL Server\MSSQL\data\Wrox_Golf_Results_Data.MDF
           2 C:\Program Files\Microsoft SQL Server\MSSQL\data\Wrox_Golf_Results_Log.LDF
```

sp_helpdb is a system function, in fact, a system-built stored procedure. What this function does is to take information from certain tables in the master database, discussed earlier in the chapter, and display the output in the results pane of Query Analyzer.

There were dire warnings about touching the master database earlier in the chapter, and this is where system functions come in to their own, as they can safely retrieve and alter information in these tables. By using such system functions, there is no need to remember the name of the tables that hold the information. In fact, these tables hold more information than we would probably need, and some of the information can be confusing to the untrained eye. The two tables from the master database that are here are **sysdatabases**, and **sysfiles**.

Dropping a Database in Query Analyzer

Probably the safest method within SQL Server to remove a database is to use Query Analyzer. The reasoning behind this is that you have to definitely type in the database name and then execute the command. Once the command is executed there is no going back, but at least you have to be pretty certain as to what you are doing at the time.

> **This statement isn't quite true. We will cover an even safer method later on, in Chapter 15.**

It's time to see how to drop a database from within Query Analyzer.

Try It Out – Dropping a Database in Query Analyzer

1. Start SQL Query Analyzer

2. Ensure that the database you want to delete is not selected in the database combo box. As you can see in the graphic, the master database is the database selected. If you find that the database you want to delete is the database listed in this combo box, then just change it first. If you don't change it, you won't be able to delete the database as there is still a connection being held, and it is only when all connections are removed that a database can be deleted.

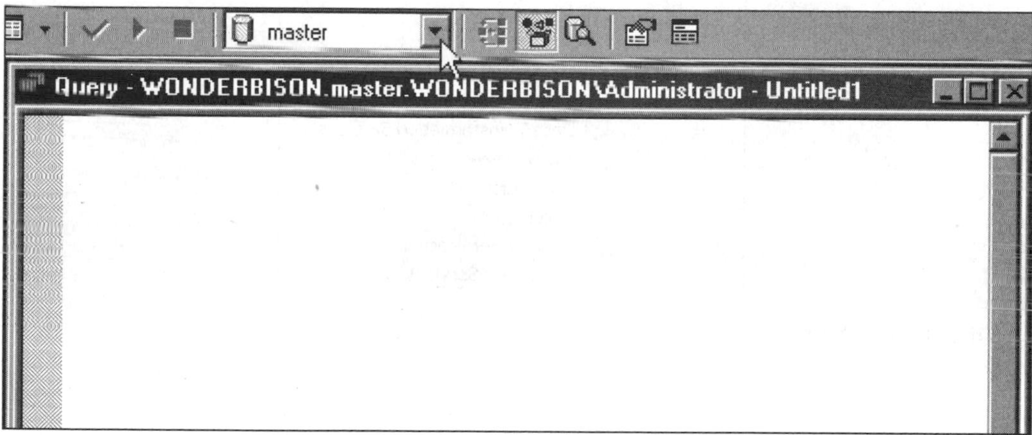

3. Now we move to the query entry screen, and enter the code to drop the database. In this example, we'll drop the Wrox_Golf_Results database. It will be easy to add in the database again later.

4. The code to enter into the Query screen is the following. Although this example is only showing one database being dropped, it is possible to drop more than one database in one single execution.

```
DROP DATABASE Wrox_Golf_Results
GO
```

5. Once this code is executed, its effect will be immediate with no "last warning" dialog as we saw in Enterprise Manager. You should see the following in SQL Query Analyzer Results window:

```
DROP DATABASE Wrox_Golf_Results
GO
```

```
/*-----------------------------
DROP DATABASE Wrox_Golf_Results
GO
-----------------------------*/
Deleting database file 'C:\Program Files\Microsoft SQL Server\MSSQL\data\Wrox_Golf_Results_Log
Deleting database file 'C:\Program Files\Microsoft SQL Server\MSSQL\data\Wrox_Golf_Results_Dat
```

6. You can see that in the **Object Browser** on the left of the screen, the database is still listed, and if we switch to Enterprise Manager, you will see that here also, **Wrox_Golf_Results** is still listed.

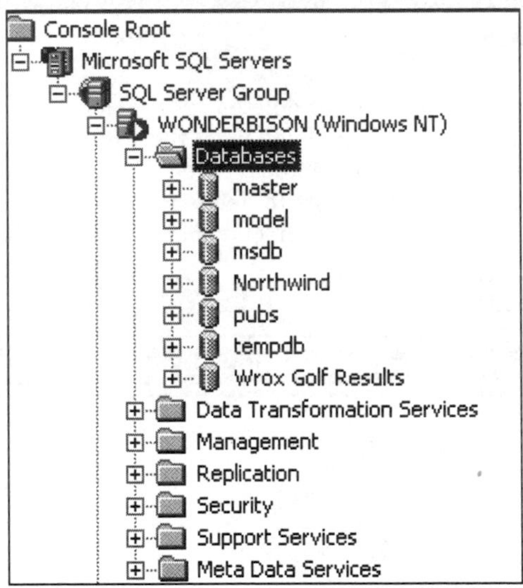

Press the **Refresh** button

on the toolbar, or press *F5*, which has the same effect.

7. You should now see that the database has disappeared.

How It Works – Drop Database in Query Analyzer

Dropping a database in Query Analyzer is just like using Enterprise Manager to remove a database. When the `DROP DATABASE` command is used, SQL Server first checks that the name supplied is valid. This means that if there is a space in the name of the database, it must be surrounded by [], and that only valid characters are contained. The next check it performs is to see if the database actually exists. It does this by checking against the **`sysdatabases`** table in the `master` database, to see if there is a record stored for the name passed in. The next check is to ensure that either the ID logged in is the owner of the database, or that the ID logged in has enough privileges to remove the database.

Once all these tests are passed, SQL Server then removes the database from the `sysdatabases` table, and also removes the files created to hold the data and the transaction log.

It's as simple as that.

> **Before leaving this chapter, don't forget to recreate the Wrox_Golf_Results database ready for the following chapters and to do this under your own user ID!**

Summary

We have now successfully built and removed a database in SQL Server 2000 using three different methods. This chapter should have clarified for you exactly what a database is, and where a SQL Server database sits on your computer.

The chapter then moved on to discussing data files and transaction logs and why it is best to keep these separate from each other. In a local installation, or even for a small database, there isn't really much to be gained from this, and the database overhead perhaps doesn't make it worthwhile, but in a medium, or especially in a large installation, it really should be considered.

Finally, having demonstrated different methods to create and delete databases, this chapter should have given an insight as to what happens in the background of SQL Server when actions are performed. By knowing this, and the three different methods, we can figure out which method is best for certain circumstances.

6 Defining Tables

Now that the database is created, it obviously needs to have the ability to store information, after all, without this, what is the point of a database, and then what is the point of this book? The first area that needs to be worked on is the table definitions.

To be functional, a database needs at least one table, but it can have many, and depending on the solution you are working on building, the number of tables can become quite large. Therefore, it is imperative that you as a developer know as much about tables, their structures, and their contents as possible. The aim of this chapter is to teach just that, so that we have a sound base to work from, regarding tables, and then to use this with the creation of other objects associated with tables.

The design of a table is crucial. Each table needs to contain the correct information for its collection of columns to allow the correct relationships to be established. One of the skills of a database developer, or administrator, is to ensure that the final design is the correct solution, hence avoiding painful alterations once further development of the system is in progress. For example, if we designed a system where the table definitions had some major problems, and required columns to be moved around tables, then every aspect of an application would have to be revisited. This would mean quite a large re-design, which would have to be catered for. Chapter 4 covers this, although there is a great SQL Design book, "*Professional SQL Server 2000 Database Design*" *(Wrox Press, ISBN 1-861004-76-1)*, which you can use to help you through your design process.

Before we create a table, it is necessary to know certain information about the database: Which ID is logged in, and what administrative rights within SQL Server it has. Providing that everything is valid, you can go ahead and create your table.

So that we can achieve the successful creation of a table, this chapter will cover the following:

- The definition of a table
- How and where a table is stored
- Searching for necessary information before creating a table, and database ownership
- Server roles, and allowing user IDs the ability to create table objects
- Creating a table using Enterprise Manager and Query Analyzer

- Dealing with more advanced areas of table creation including:
  - How to make a row unique
  - Special data states
- Dealing with pictures and large text data
- What data types are available to use, and what do they mean

First though, it is necessary to know what a table is.

What is a Table?

A table is a repository for data, with items of data grouped in one or more columns. Tables contain zero or more rows of information. An Excel spreadsheet can be thought of as a table, albeit it a very simple table with few or no rules governing the data.

What sets a table inside SQL Server apart from other potential tables, is that a table will have specific types of data held in each column, and that a pre-determined type of data defined for a column can never change without affecting every row of data within that column for that table. If we use Excel, in a specific column you could have a character in one row, a number in the next row, a monetary value in the following row, and so on. That cannot happen in a database table. You can store all of these different values, but they would all have to be stored as a datatype that holds strings, which defeats the object. At the time the table is created, every column will contain a specific datatype. Therefore, very careful consideration has to be made when defining a table to ensure that the column datatype is the most appropriate. There is no point in selecting a generic data type (a string, for example) to cover all eventualities, as we will probably have to revisit the design later anyway.

A table's purpose is to hold specific information. The table requires a meaningful name and one or more columns defined, each given a meaningful name and a datatype; in some cases, we want to set a restriction on the maximum number of characters that the column can hold.

> **Like a database, a table has a specific owner. In most cases, the owners will be the same. However, you do need to have specific permissions to create tables in the database. As soon as you can create a table, if you are not within the database owners' role, then the database will belong to your login ID.**

Some datatypes have fixed storage occupancy specifications that are assigned to the column, whereas with other datatypes, we have to decide for ourselves how many characters the maximum will be. If we had a column, which was defined for a surname, it would hold character values. There would also be no sense in setting the maximum length of this column at 10 characters, as many surnames are longer than this. Similarly there would be little sense in saying the maximum should be 1000 characters. A sensible balance has to be reached.

The rows of data that will be held in a table should be related logically to each other. If a table is defined to hold customer information, then this is all it should hold. Under no circumstances would we consider putting, within the table, information that was not about a customer. It would be illogical to put for example, details of customer's orders within it.

Before You Can Define a Table

Creating a table is not that difficult; however, we need to clear a couple of obstacles before we get there. First, you must be using a login account, that has the authority to add tables, not only to SQL Server, but also to the specific database. This is another security issue, which we need to cover. First, we also need to have access to that specific database. Let's take the issue of access to the database if we are using a user ID that did not create the database.

The database was re-created at the very end of the previous chapter under user ID `RDewson`. Be careful here, as throughout the chapter, the login ID of "`sa`" was being used, but do use your own ID to create the database at the end. The reason to change to your own ID is that the user who creates the database is seen as the database owner, also known as **dbo**. So how can you check?

Every object that is created within SQL server needs to be associated with an owner. This starts right at the top with a database. Why do you need to have owners?

When a database is created, it is necessary to know who created it. This is so that this person - the database owner - can determine which user, or group of users can develop it, access the data, modify the data, and perform tasks that are more complex. This is a security issue.

When having a database owner, a specific name is crucial (rather than a generic name, like "`sa`", the catch-all name SQL Server provides) so that it is possible to know who to approach to amend security rights. In a large organization with many different development teams, there is just no way it would be possible to track down the owner. At the end of the last chapter, I asked you to create the database under your own user ID, which if you followed the instructions so far and you are a local administrator of the machine SQL Server is installed on, you should have the right privileges within SQL Server to do.

If you are working with SQL Server already installed on an NT/2000 machine, you need to ensure that your user ID is set up as an `Administrator` user ID, as demonstrated in Chapter 1, or set up specifically as an Administrator within SQL Server Security Logins.

This next section will demonstrate how you check the identity of the database owner.

Try It Out – Checking the Database Owner

1. Ensure that Enterprise Manager is open.

2. Navigate to the database that you wish to check on, in this case, Wrox_Golf_Results.

3. Click on the Wrox_Golf_Results node in the console tree on the left-hand side of the screen once, and then right-click.

4. Select Properties. On the General tab there will be an item that says Owner. This is the fully qualified NT account preceded by the domain or local machine name.

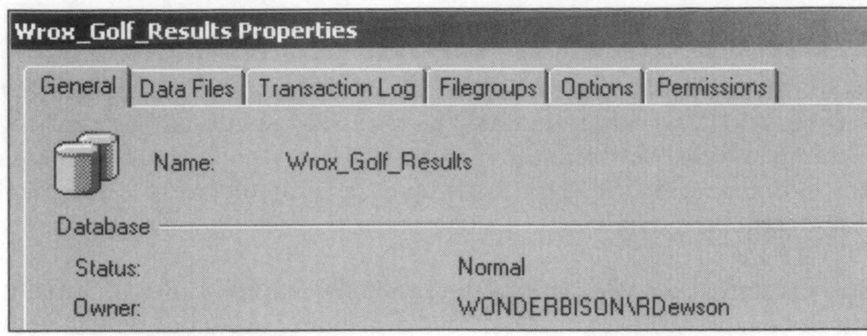

5. Click **Cancel** to close this dialog.

6. You can now move to **Security | Logins** on the console tree to find **RDewson**, or in your case, the login ID on the machine that installed SQL Server.

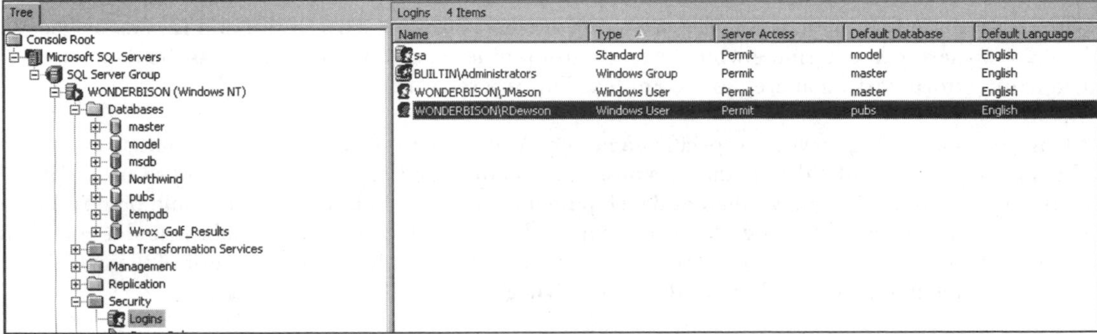

7. Double-click the login ID, which will bring up its **Properties**.

8. Take the opportunity to alter the default database permissions for this user to **Wrox_Golf_Results**. This will help when using Query Analyzer throughout the rest of this book. By pointing to the right database as a default, when you start up Query Analyzer you will be set up ready to start working within the **Wrox_Golf_Results**, and you won't have to move to that database first.

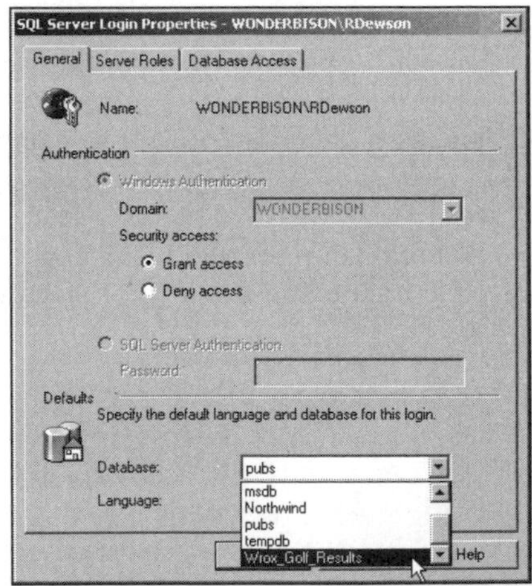

9. Next move to the **Database Access** tab, and click on the **Wrox_Golf_Results** database. You will see the **Database roles** at the bottom. A database role is, quite simply, a method of grouping users in to a specific single group, which you can then apply permissions to. Being the owner means that the **db_owner** role has a conformation tick as well as the **public** role.

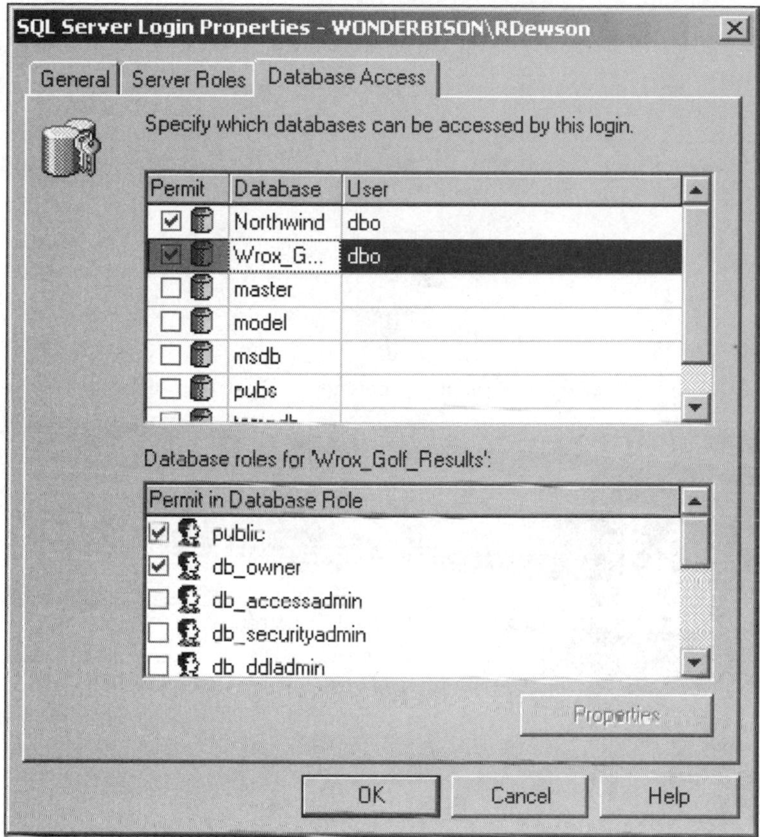

10. Click **Ok** to save the changes. We have now checked that the database owner is **RDewson**, and you have now changed the default database for **RDewson** to **Wrox_Golf_Results**.

Ownership of tables and other database objects is just as important. If you create a table using the same login ID as that which created the database with, the table will have a prefix of `dbo`. This denotes database owner. However, if you logged in with a different user ID, the table would have that user ID as the prefix to the table name, replacing the `dbo` prefix.

Now we know who the database owner is, it is up to that person, or another user ID that has system administration rights, to allow any other specified user the ability to create tables within the database. We have a user called Daniel Tarbotton (`DTarbotton`), who is not a system administrator, but a developer. The next section will go through a scenario where as a developer, he had no rights to create any new items, however, we will alter this so that he has. This next section will set up Daniel as an NT user as well as set him up as a SQL Server user, and then we will demonstrate his login.

Try It Out – Allowing a User To Create a Table

1. Adding in new users is only required if we wish to log in to Windows using the new user ID. This has been covered before in Chapter 1, but let us quickly go through it again in regard to Daniel. Just to remind you, adding a user in to the Windows Users section is not required if your server has been installed with Mixed Mode, and you wish to log in with SQL Server authentication. Join in at point 8 if you are in Mixed Mode and logging in with SQL Server authentication.

2. First, the new user will be created. If you are on a Windows 2000 machine then click Start | Settings | Control Panel | Users and Passwords. On Windows NT, select Start | Programs | Administrative Tools (Common) | User Manager.

3. Click Add, and then enter the details of the new user. Once completed, click Next.

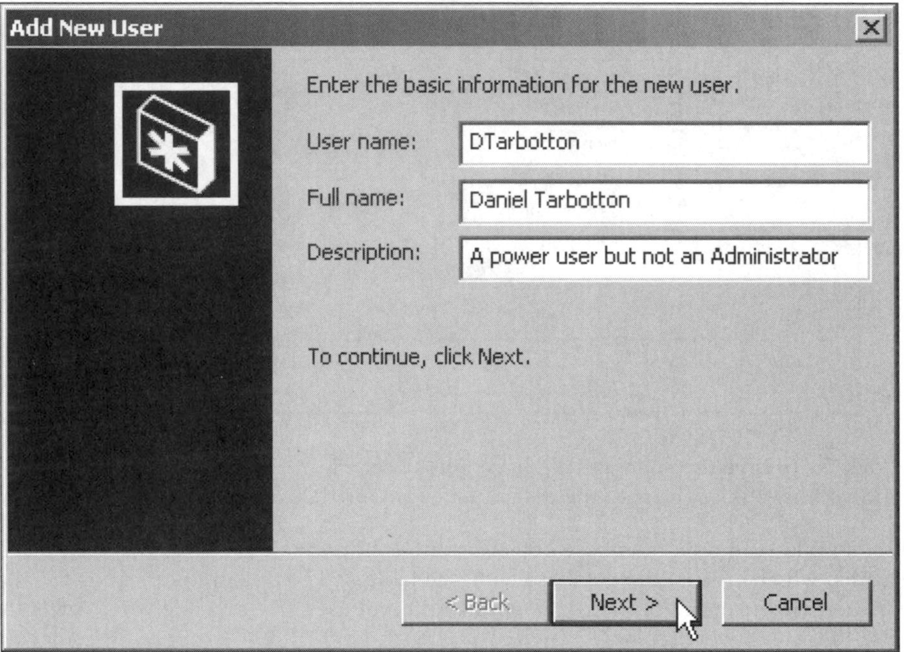

4. On the next screen, we set up a password. Once finished, click Next.

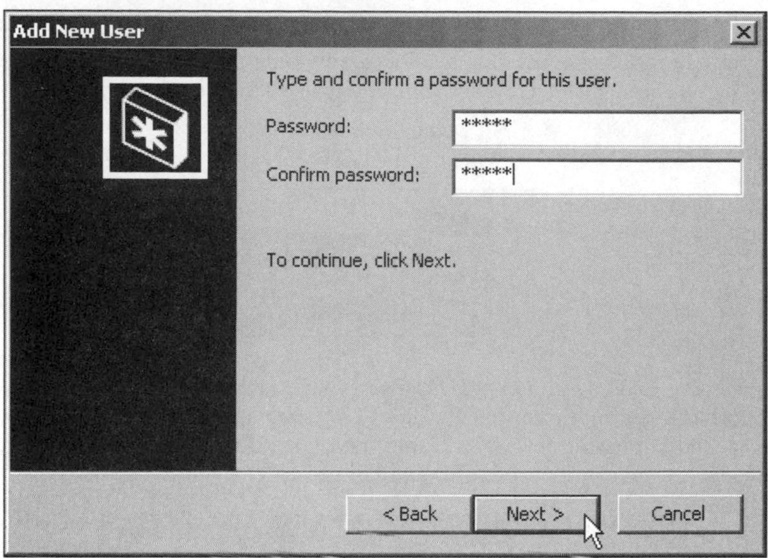

5. On the next screen, select Power User. This gives the user ID the ability to run SQL Server Enterprise under this ID, but not with full Administrative rights.

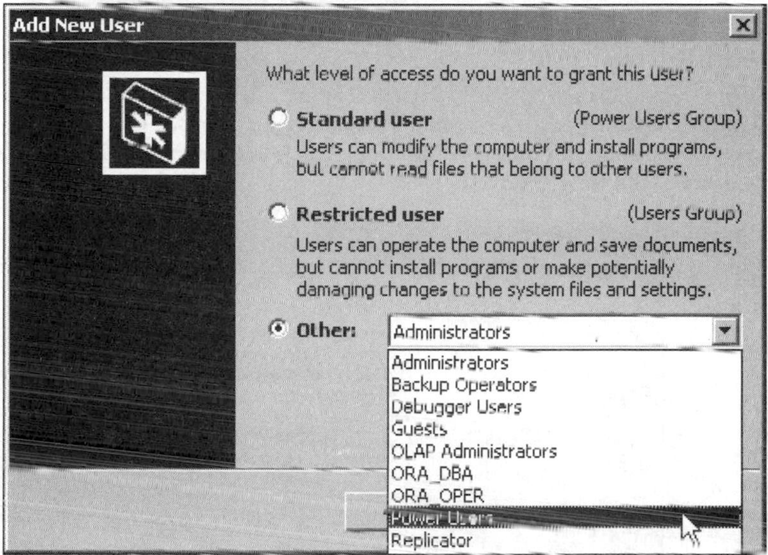

6. Once done, click Finish, and then OK, which will leave the Users and Passwords setup screen.

7. Now that the user is set up for those with Windows NT Authentication, it is necessary to add them to SQL Server.

> **If you are joining from a Mixed Mode setup, and you are logging in with SQL Server Authentication, you need to start from the next step.**

8. Ensure SQL Server Enterprise Manager is running, and that you log in with an account that has full administration rights; in my case it is RDewson, but in your case it will probably be the account that you installed SQL Server with. Navigate to the Security option and select Logins.

9. Right-click and select New Login...

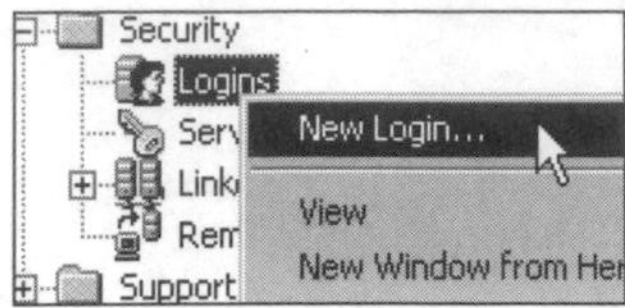

10. If you are going to create the user ID to use Windows Authentication, then you can search for a user that has been built into the Windows User management area by clicking on the ellipsis button on the right hand side of the Name: text box. If this new ID is to use SQL Server authentication, then skip the next three bullet points.

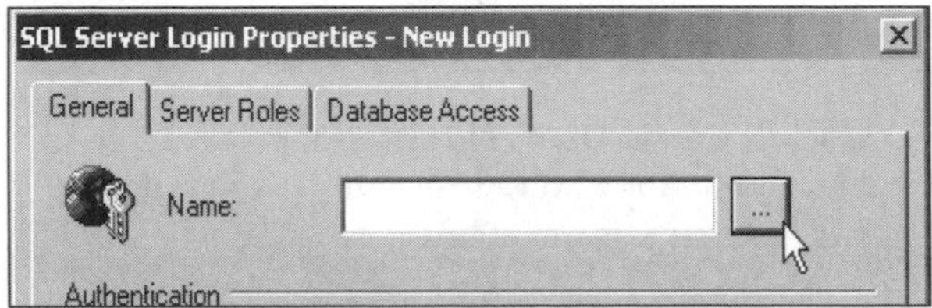

11. Clicking the ellipsis brings up a list of users that are contained within our computer. On a network, we will see the network domain that we belong to, which we can then use to find the user. Scroll down until you find DTarbotton, click Add, which fills Daniel's name into the Add Name: text box, and then click OK.

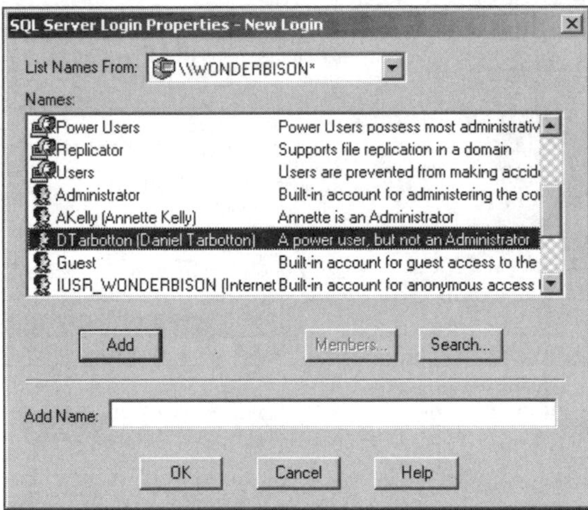

12. This will now populate the New Login front screen. At the same time, alter the default Database to Wrox_Golf_Results.

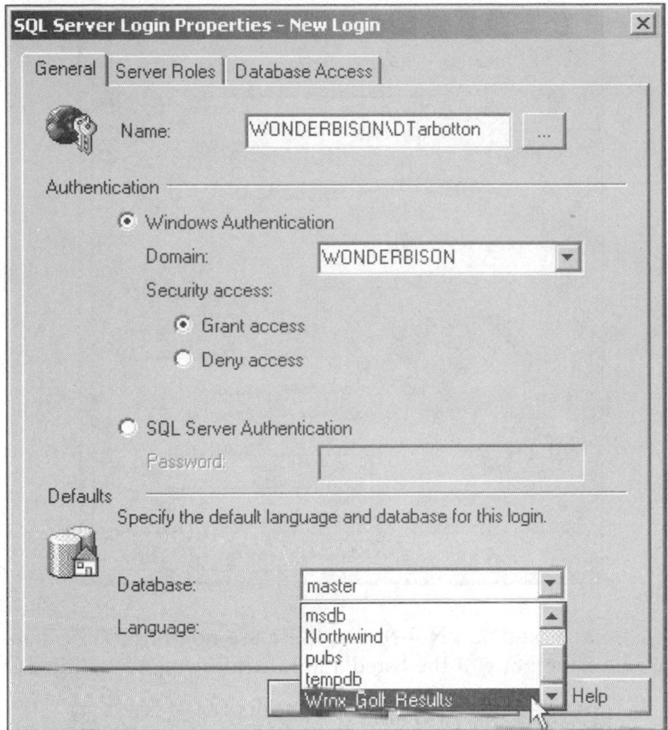

13. If you click OK at this point, you will receive the following message box informing you that although you have chosen Daniel to have the Wrox_Golf_Results as his default database, in fact, you haven't given him access to it. So, click No on the dialog. Don't worry about fixing this, as we start to do this in step 15.

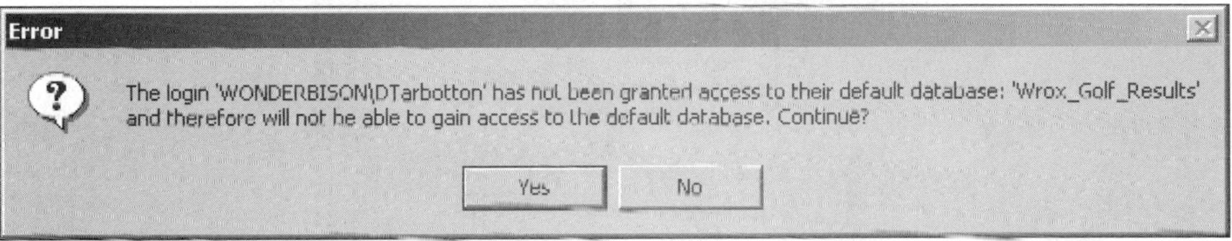

14. To use SQL Server authentication (for those who have Mixed Mode Authentication installed) enter the SQL Server user ID and the password, and alter the default Database to Wrox_Golf_Results. For those trying out both of these methods, you should not have DTarbotton as a user ID twice, so think up another name.

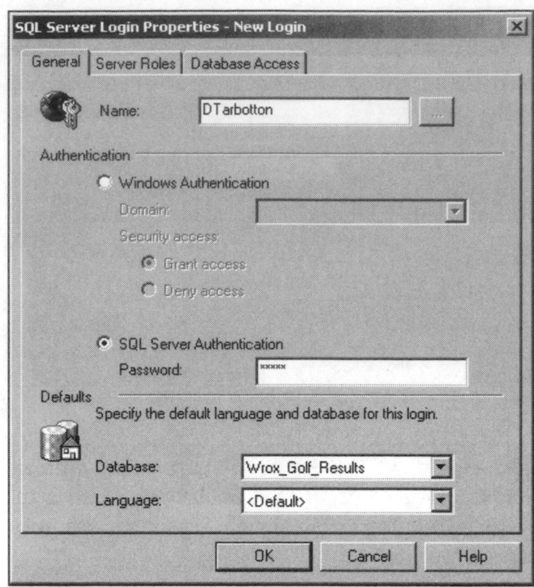

15. Click on the Server Roles tab. Notice that there are no options checked. This is indicating that this user will have none of the listed administration rights within SQL Server.

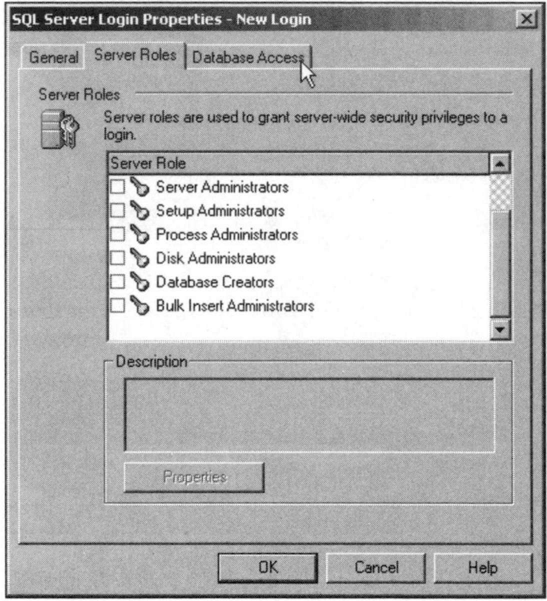

16. Click on the Database Access tab at the top. At first, there will be no database selected. The user is not a system administrator, so if the ID were left like this, this user would not be able to do anything within SQL Server. Therefore, click on Wrox_Golf_Results to give the user access to the database.

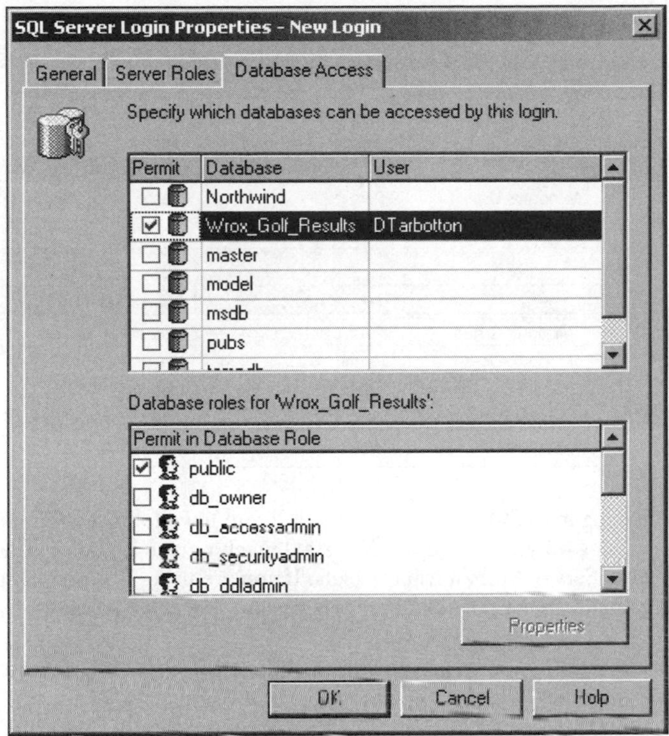

17. By clicking on Wrox_Golf_Results, you will see that the Database Roles in the section below the list of databases alter, and that the public role is selected. More on roles at the end of this section. For now, we leave these options as they are and click OK.

18. If we are using SQL Server Authentication, we will get an extra dialog box to confirm the SQL Server password.

19. Daniel is now created as a user within the Wrox_Golf_Results database. You can find the screenshots below from Security | Logins within Enterprise Manager. The following screenshot is for Windows NT Authentication, with the screenshot below that for SQL Server Authentication. You can tell the difference between users with two methods. The first is that the NT user ID is prefixed with the domain name and the type of icon is single head. If there is an icon, then they are set up as a SQL Server user ID.

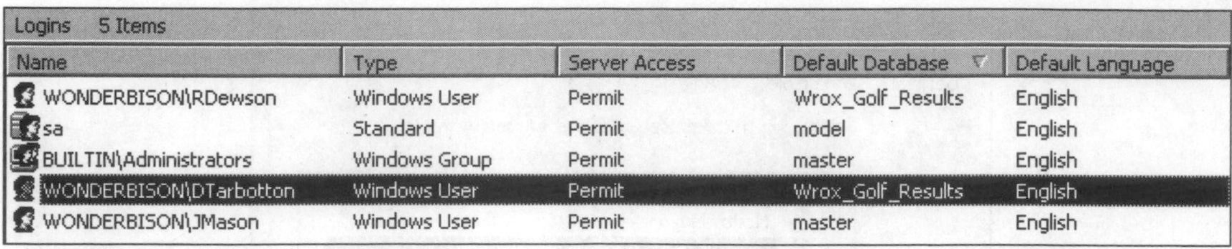

Logins 5 Items

Name	Type	Server Access	Default Database	Default Language
WONDERBISON\RDewson	Windows User	Permit	Wrox_Golf_Results	English
sa	Standard	Permit	model	English
BUILTIN\Administrators	Windows Group	Permit	master	English
WONDERBISON\DTarbotton	Windows User	Permit	Wrox_Golf_Results	English
WONDERBISON\JMason	Windows User	Permit	master	English

Logins 5 Items

Name	Type	Server Access	Default Database	Default Language
BUILTIN\Administrators	Windows Group	Permit	master	English
WONDERBISON\JMason	Windows User	Permit	master	English
sa	Standard	Permit	model	English
DTarbotton	Standard	Permit	Wrox_Golf_Results	English
WONDERBISON\RDewson	Windows User	Permit	Wrox_Golf_Results	English

20. We now need to log in to SQL Server as Daniel. If you have followed this example exactly so far, then you need to log off your Windows NT/2000 machine and log in as DTarbotton. This next section is for SQL Server Authentication users. If you are using Windows NT Authentication, then skip down to point 27, where the example reaches the new table creation.

21. It is not necessary to log off Windows NT to change the SQL Server user ID when using SQL Server Authentication. This can be achieved within Enterprise Manager. This is a great piece of information to know when testing out user access, as the next part of this *Try It Out* will demonstrate. Move to the SQL Server installation name, and right-click. Then select Edit SQL Server Registration properties...

22. You should see something like the following screenshot (altered for your own installation details). Notice that the server is set up with Windows NT authentication. In Chapter 1, we set up this SQL Server 2000 installation as Mixed Mode, and here is one benefit of this. By allowing Mixed Mode, I can log in as a user ID that differs from my Windows NT user ID.

> **We can only do this with any user ID set up for SQL Server authentication, and not any user ID that is set up for Windows Authentication. If the installation were by Windows NT Authentication only, then we would need to log in to Windows NT as that user (and have all the security issues that go with that).**

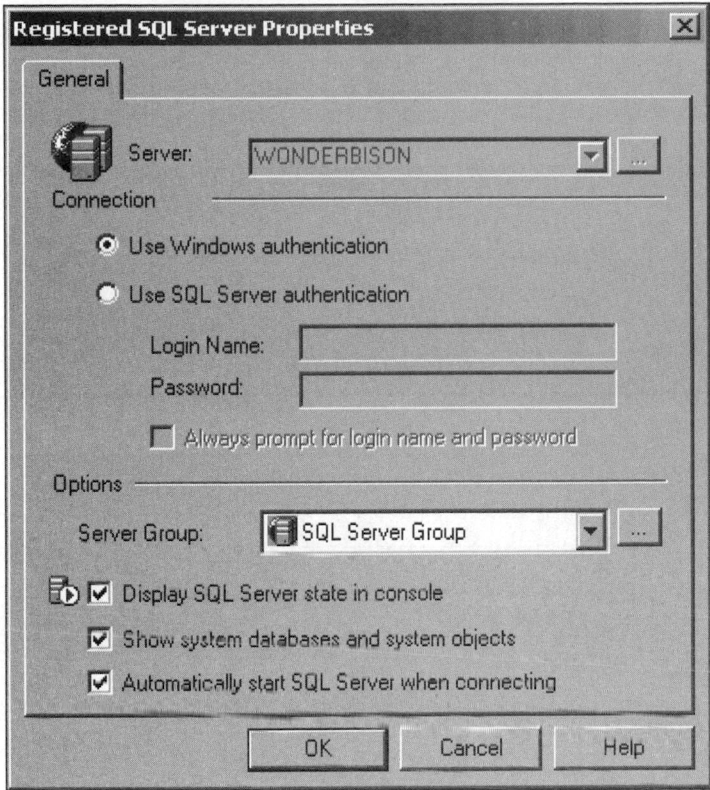

23. Alter the Connection to Use SQL Server Authentication, enter DTarbotton as the user ID, and click on Always prompt for login name and password. Click OK.

24. You will then be prompted to confirm the password for the SQL Server account. Enter the password with the user ID and click Connect.

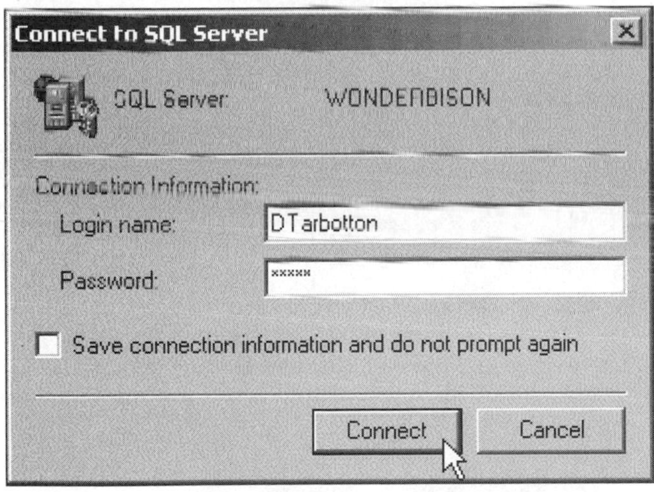

25. This will bring up the final dialog for this process. Be warned, this *will* disconnect your session, so make sure you know the SQL Server password for that user, and also the password for the connection you are removing; which in this instance should not be too much of a worry, as it will be the login user that created SQL Server.

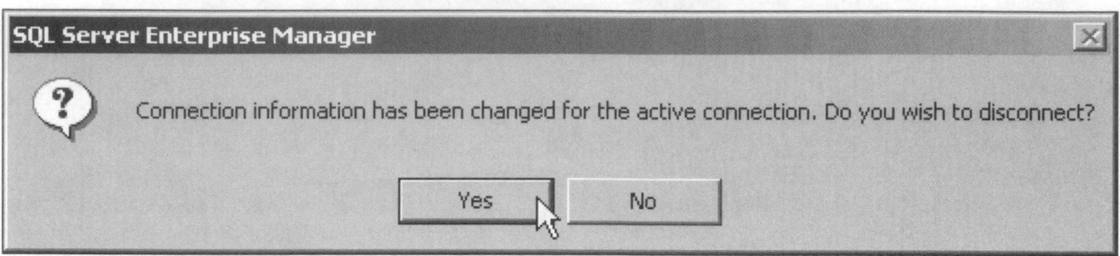

26. After clicking Connect, we will be logged on as `DTarbotton`. As we have access to Wrox_Golf_Results, we can navigate to this database without any problems. Navigate to the Tables option and notice that there is a list of tables on the right-hand side in the Details pane.

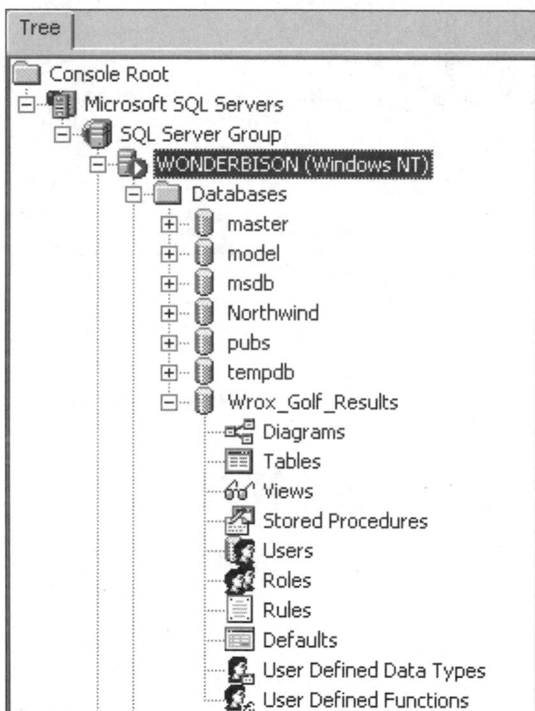

27. This point is for both Windows authentication, and SQL Server authentication users. If you right-click on the Tables icon in the Wrox_Golf_Results database, you will notice that the New Table... option is grayed out and disabled. This means that this user ID does not have the authority to add tables. This is because of the role that this SQL Server Authenticated user ID is given.

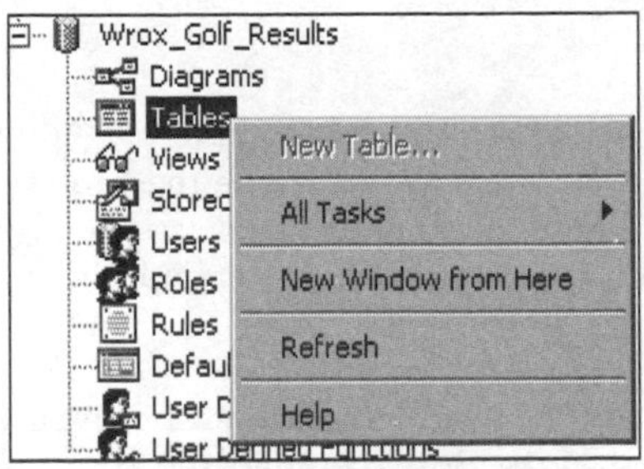

We have demonstrated that a user can connect to a database, but not necessarily create new objects within it. This will be discussed in the *Security* appendix.

> **Don't forget before going on further to ensure that you alter the SQL Server Registration Properties to what they were before, so that when you move to the next section of the chapter, you can build tables. This is easiest if you go back to the original user ID (the equivalent of `RDewson`).**

The whole essence of this section revolves around the ability of a user ID to have enough security rights to add tables to a database. It doesn't matter which type of Authentication we use within the database for any user inserted, if that user doesn't have the privilege, they can't execute their tasks.

In Windows Authentication the setting up of user IDs is done within Control Panel | Users and Passwords icon. Daniel was set up as a user type of Power User. Annette Kelly - who was set up in Chapter 1 as an Administrator. Also, the same was completed with Jack Mason, also in Chapter 1. Annette was set up as an Administrator. This automatically gave her full access rights to SQL Server. With Jack Mason, we had to go to the Server Roles tab, and specifically click the System Administrators option. This then gave Jack the same rights within SQL Server, as Annette. This is where you discover what a role is within SQL Server. It is from these roles, that you define what each user ID can perform. Finally, if you are using Windows NT/2000, every Windows account belonging to a certain Windows group will also belong to a certain role within SQL Server by default. Let's look at server roles from both a Windows and SQL Server Authentication perspective to start with.

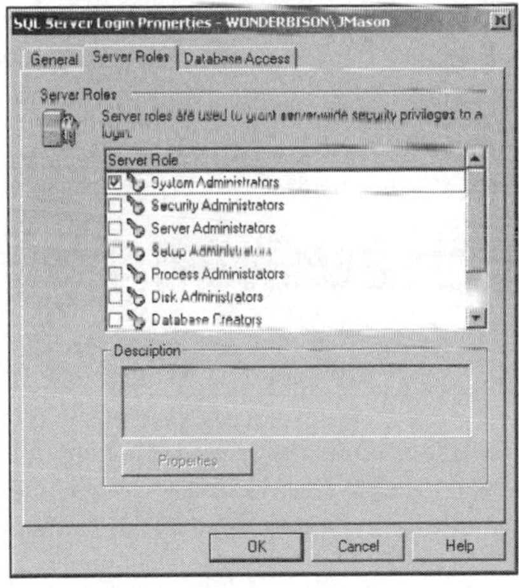

Server Roles

How do you know that someone who has been added in to the Administrators groups is able to perform their tasks? Within SQL Server, there are specific pre-defined roles, which are set up to allow certain tasks, and to restrict other tasks. These roles can then be assigned by someone with the right permissions, for example, the database owner or a system administrator, to any user ID, or group of user IDs within SQL Server.

If you look at the Server Roles tab in the previous screenshot, you will see that there are System Administrators, Security Administrators, Server Administrators, and so on, giving a total of eight different roles. But what do they mean? You get a little hint if you move to the Server Roles node within Enterprise Manager.

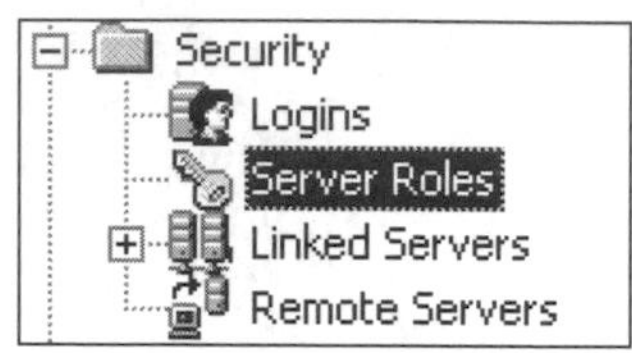

If you then move to the Details pane on the right, you will see the eight Server Roles listed. Most of these roles are specialist tasks and are defined to cater for specific issues. For example, you could set up someone as a Security Administrator only, which means that the only action within SQL Server that they can perform is to create and manage logins for SQL Server.

Server Roles 8 Items

Full Name	Name	Description
Bulk Insert Administrators	bulkadmin	Can perform bulk insert operation.
Database Creators	dbcreator	Can create and alter databases.
Disk Administrators	diskadmin	Can manage the disk files.
Process Administrators	processadmin	Can manage the processes running in SQL Server.
Security Administrators	securityadmin	Can manage the logins for the server.
Server Administrators	serveradmin	Can configure the server-wide settings.
Setup Administrators	setupadmin	Can manage extended stored procedures.
System Administrators	sysadmin	Can perform any activity in the SQL Server installation.

However, it was the System Administrators login that all of our users have been added to presently. To confirm, you can highlight System Administrators, and right-click, and then select Properties.

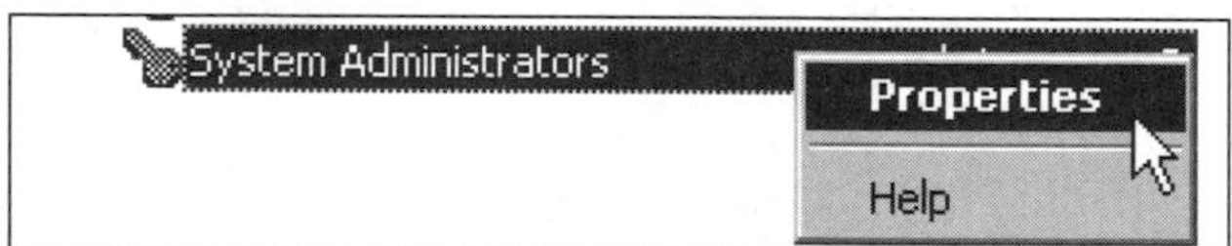

This brings up a tabbed dialog. The first tab informs you which user IDs are currently assigned to this server role. As you can see, there is a specific user ID of JMason; however, there is also the user ID of sa, as well as a group of users who fit in as Administrators. These are any Windows login IDs defined as Administrators.

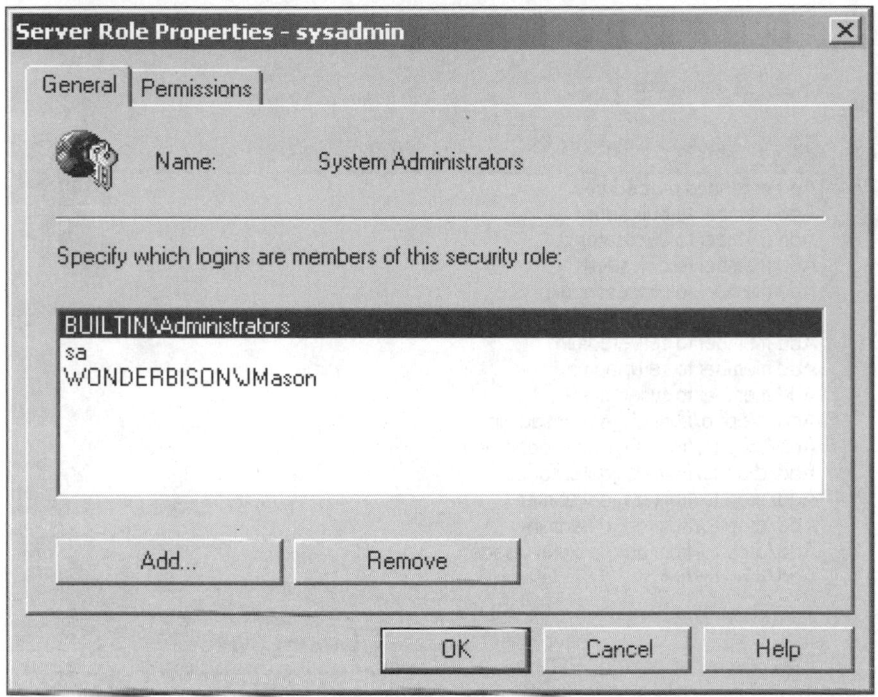

Although I am not going to alter this for my database, having Windows NT administrators automatically being administrators for SQL Server can be a bit of a security issue for you within your own environment. Many companies batten down their computers so that no user is an administrator of their local machine. By doing this, they are stopping people adding their own software, shareware, games, or whatever, to a machine that is administrated and looked after by a support team. This helps the machine to remain stable, and throughout your organization everyone will know that a piece of software developed on one machine will work on any other. Therefore, users won't have Administrator rights on their NT/2000 machine and will therefore not fall into this group. This is not the case in all organizations. By leaving the Administrator group in the System Administrators role, everyone who has Administrator rights on their PC will have System Administrator rights within SQL Server. You, as the owner of your database, have now lost control of the security and development of your SQL Server database.

Because this book assumes that we're using either a standalone PC or a secure set of users, it is safe to keep the Administrator group. However, you will find that this group is usually removed from database setups, to keep the security of the database intact. If you are on a Windows 9x machine, the whole issue of Administrators etc. does not exist because there are no such things as account groups.

If you now click on the Permissions tab, you will see a whole list of what this role is allowed to do within SQL Server.

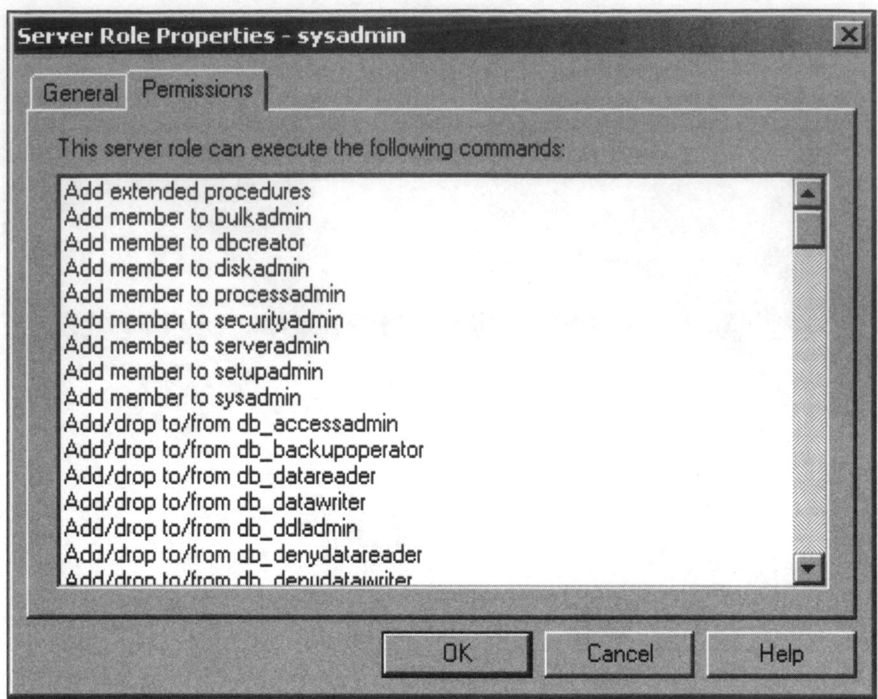

We already know from previous experience that the role can achieve a number of tasks. However, the **sysadmin** role can do anything at all within SQL Server. A great deal of the commands the System Administrator can perform will not mean a great deal, and there is no need within this book to know specifics. Just be aware that any user ID assigned to this role has complete authority to perform any action within your database.

Defining a Table – Enterprise Manager

We have covered quite a lot before even getting to create the first table. However, all of these points are essential to knowing the background of creating a table, and the ramifications of going horribly wrong. We also now know why we have to be careful with login user IDs to ensure that the ID has enough security privileges to build tables.

Defining a table can be completed either in Enterprise Manager or Query Analyzer. We can also create a table through a number of other means using developer tools and languages, but these two methods will be the ones this book will focus on. We will create the first table with Enterprise Manager. This is the `Club_Details` table. It will hold specific details about the golf club, including the name of the club, the address at which the club is located, and the e-mail address for general enquiries, among others.

This is the first table in the example. Every club has to have some sort of headquarters, and therefore every club will need to store these details. If you recall back to Chapter 4 where the data layout for the example was shown, you will see that this table has no direct links with any other table. This is known as a **standalone** table. There could be a link to another table, for example one that held country identifiers. In Chapter 4 we saw an external table link with a `country` table. If you want to include this information, then you can include this in the table later.

Try It Out – Defining a Table

1. Ensure that Enterprise Manager is running.

2. Expand the Tree pane so that you can see the Wrox_Golf_Results database, created in the last chapter.

3. Expand the Wrox_Golf_Results database so that you can see the Tables node.

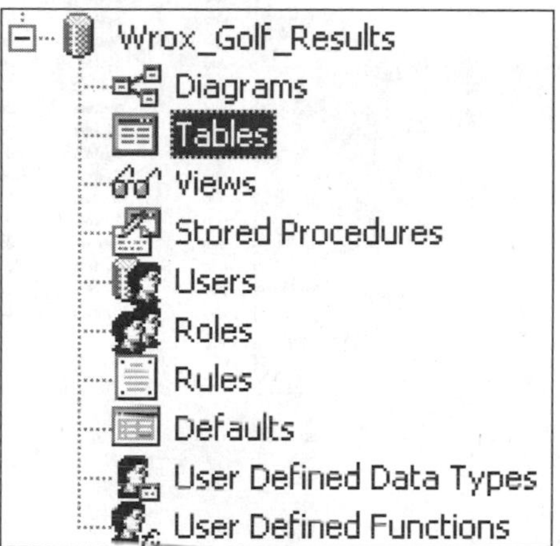

4. Right-click the Tables node. This will bring up the following context menu.

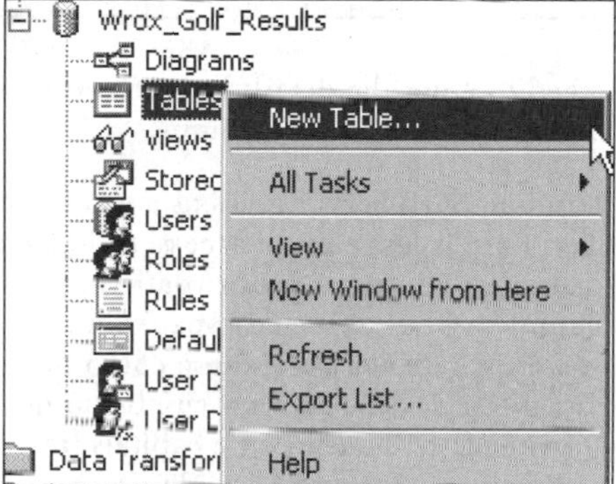

5. From the context menu, select New Table... This will then take you into the Table Designer. If you have used Microsoft Access before, you will notice some similarities. There are also major differences when it comes to datatypes, perhaps the biggest being that all strings in Access are of a fixed length, but in SQL Server strings can have a varying length. The following screenshot shows how the Table Designer looks when you first enter it.

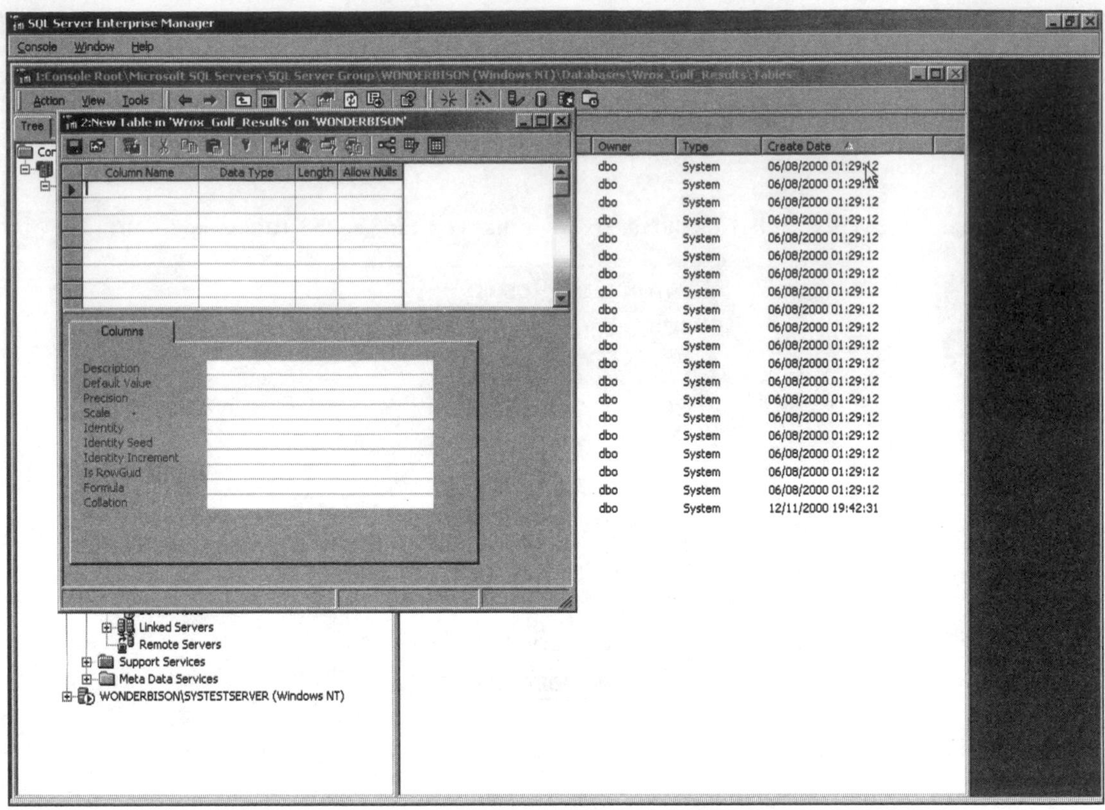

6. From this screen, you need to enter the details for each column within the table. Enter the first column, Club_Name, in the Column Name column.

When selecting the New Table option, SQL Server gives us a screen that is very similar to those used in Microsoft Access. The Description field is less easy to access, as it is not listed alongside the other column information, but make sure that you enter proper data there as it makes it easier to document the database. When naming columns, try not to include spaces in them. It is perfectly valid to have column names with spaces, however, whenever using these columns in SQL code, we will have to surround the names by square brackets: `[]`. This is very cumbersome. Split up the names of the columns by using underscores _ instead, or by using title capitals (for example, `Club_Details`). This will make writing SQL code much easier and more portable.

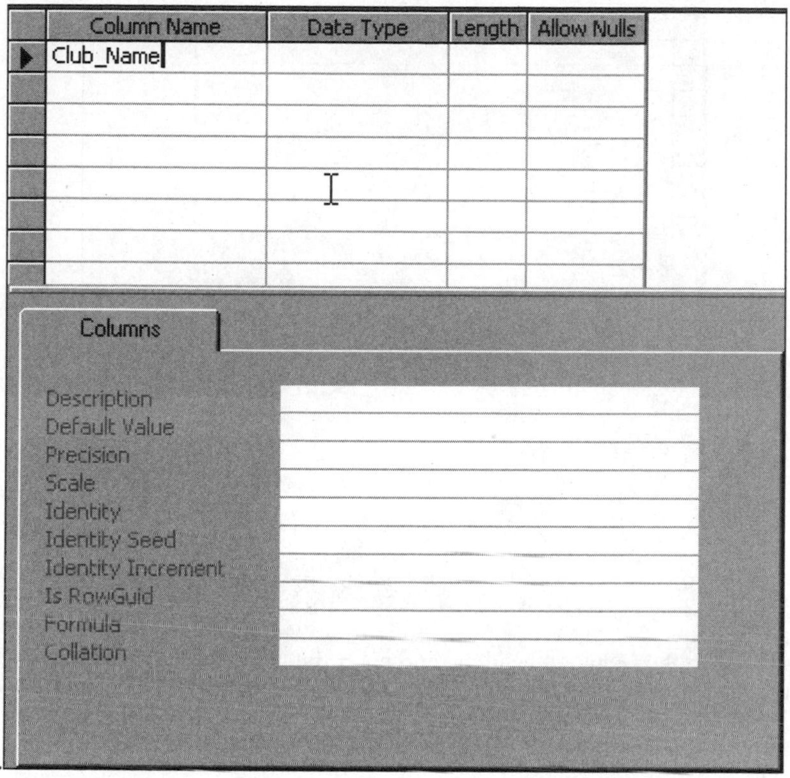

	Column Name	Data Type	Length	Allow Nulls
▶	Club_Name			

Columns

Description
Default Value
Precision
Scale
Identity
Identity Seed
Identity Increment
Is RowGuid
Formula
Collation

7. Press the *Tab* key and change the value in the **Data Type** column to **varchar**. You can do this by typing in varchar or by scrolling down through the combo box and finding **varchar**.

8. Tab out of the **Data Type** combobox, and move to the **Allow Nulls** column. Alter this so that the check box is empty. Leave the **Length** at **50**, which is the default length for `varchar` types.

One of the first areas in which SQL Server helps us with table creation, is the drop-down combo box that lists the datatypes. This way we don't have to remember every datatype there is within SQL Server, and then having to enter that datatype correctly. By having all the necessary values listed, it is simple enough to just select the best one.

The final major area of creating a column within a table is the **Allow Nulls** check box. If the box is not ticked it is obligatory that some sort of data is placed in this column. Leaving the check box in the default state will allow blank fields in the table. This is not recommended if the data is required (name, order number, etc.). You can also allow `Nulls` for numeric columns as well, so instead of needing to enter a zero, you can just skip over that column when it comes to entering the data. The **Club_Details** table has been set up so that the **Club_Name**, **Country**, and the **Address** fields must have data entered into them. In all the other columns, data entry is optional.

9. Move to the **Description** box, which should be found in the bottom half of your screen, and enter an appropriate description. By entering a description you are aiding documentation of your system so that any future developer can instantly see what each column is actually for. It just gives that further clarification.

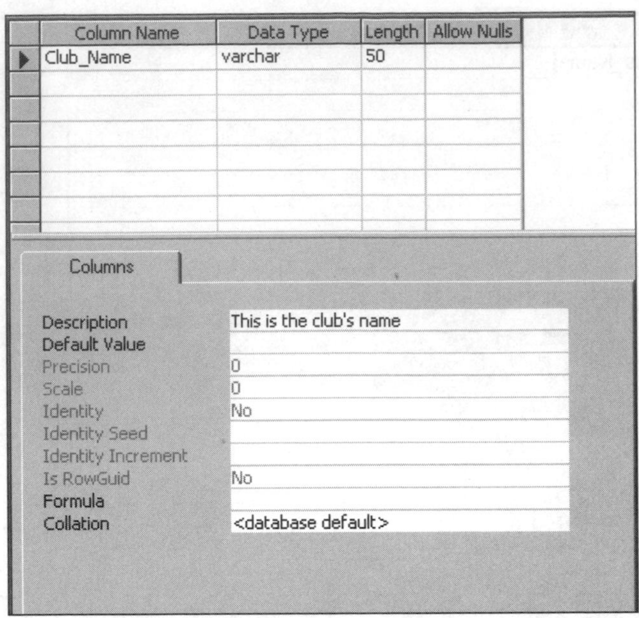

10. Move back to the **Columns** heading, and enter the next column, which is **Address**. Set the datatype to **varchar**, the **Length** to **200**, and remove the **Allow Nulls** check. By removing the **Allow Nulls** check, you are informing SQL Server that this column must have a value placed within it. Also enter a **Description**.

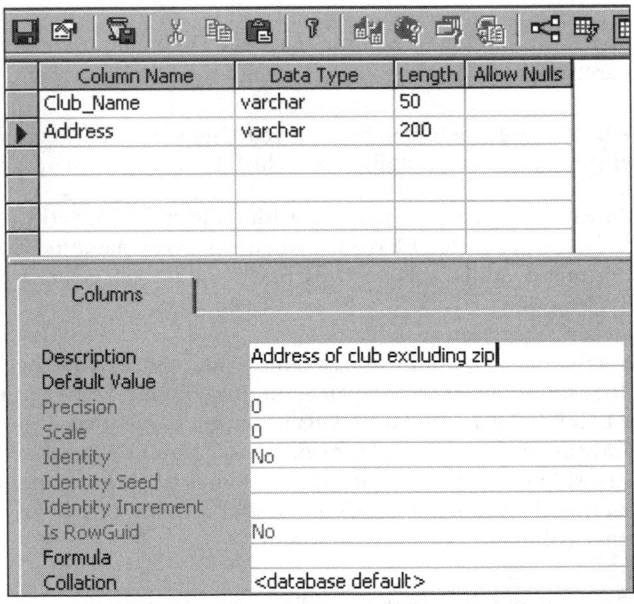

11. Enter the remainder of the fields as shown in the screenshot. Notice that some of the fields have a check in the **Allow Nulls** column. Ensure that you duplicate this. Also you may be wondering why the **Country** column is an integer. More on this later.

Column Name	Data Type	Length	Allow Nulls
Club_Name	varchar	50	
Address	varchar	200	
Phone_Number	varchar	20	✓
Fax_Number	varchar	20	✓
Club_Email	varchar	50	✓
Web_site	varchar	50	✓
Zip_Code	varchar	10	✓
State_US_Only	char	2	✓
Country	int	4	

12. Once all the details are entered, close the windows, which will start the save process. You could also click the floppy disk icon on the toolbar, which will also start the process. If you use the Close icon, you will end up at the following dialog. If you don't wish to save the changes, then obviously click No, otherwise click Yes.

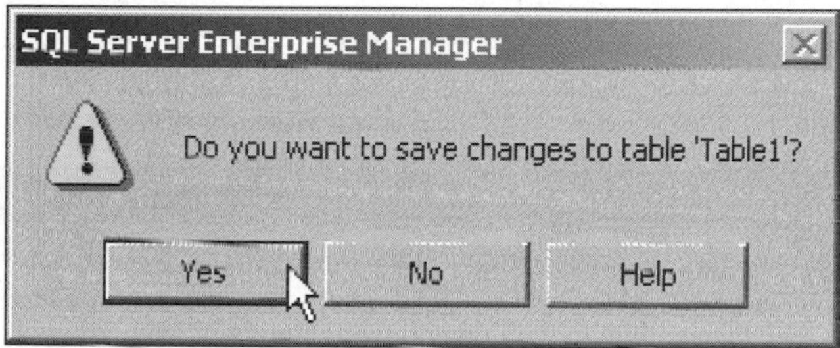

13. The next dialog is prompting you for the name of the table. Enter Club_Details. This dialog is only displayed the first time the table is saved.

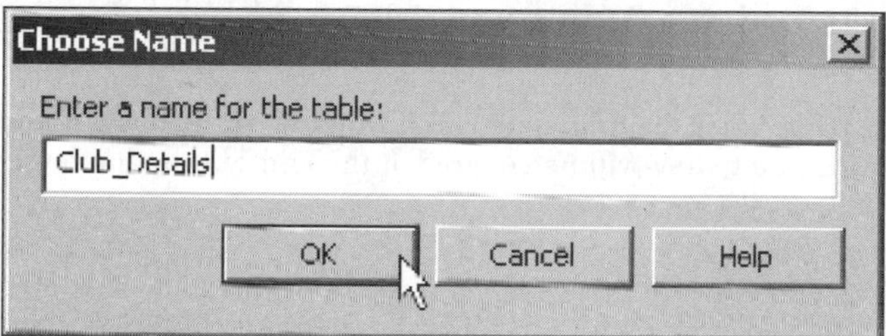

Congratulations. Your first table has been created within the `Wrox_Golf_Results` database. This table is now ready for data. There will be no primary key, nor any key for this table. You will find out more about indexes in Chapter 7, but this table will only hold one record, and an index would in fact be a performance hindrance.

If you check out the Details Pane in Enterprise Manager, you will see the table listed with a few details:

Name	Owner	Type	Create Date
Club_Details	dbo	User	25/02/2001 20:14:56

As you can see, the Owner of the table is not RDewson as you might expect, as it was this ID that created the table, but dbo. Recall I mentioned that the database owner for Wrox_Golf_Results was RDewson, who belongs to the dbo role. However, it could as easily have been AKelly, who is also a member of the dbo role. It doesn't matter if either of these two created the table – the table was still built by a database owner. Therefore SQL Server is indicating that it was the database owner that created the table. However, this is where SQL Server can be confusing. The owner, dbo, covers more than just the actual creator of the database. It also covers any user who has administration rights to the SQL Server database. Therefore, any table that JMason creates will show the owner of that table as dbo. However, if you were logged in as DTarbotton and his login credentials were altered so that he could create tables, but was not a system administrator, the table would have an owner ID of DTarbotton.

Now that a table has been created in Enterprise Manager, let's look at another way to create a table, and that is within Query Analyzer.

Defining a Table Through Query Analyzer

The next table that needs to be created is the table that will hold the details of the society groups. This is a summary record of how the society has performed, as well as holding specific details about it. This table will be used in several places within the book when working with the results of the golf club.

Try It Out – Defining a Table Through Query Analyzer

1. Ensure that Query Analyzer is running. The user ID that is logged into Query Analyzer must have the ability to create tables and to work on this database. In this case, user ID RDewson is being used.

2. Ensure that you are pointing to the Wrox_Golf_Results database in Query Analyzer.

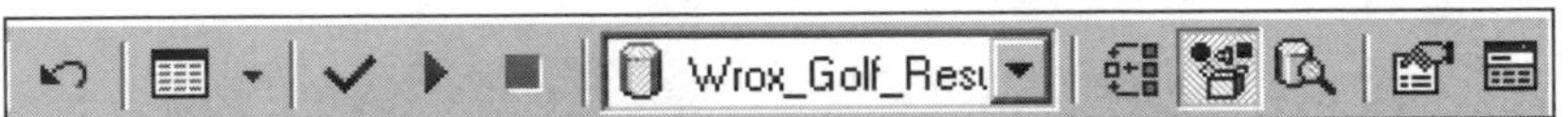

3. In the Query pane, enter the following code. Don't worry about not understanding the datatypes at this point; they will be covered at the end of this chapter.

```
CREATE TABLE Society_Groups (
   Society_Group_Id int IDENTITY (1, 1) NOT NULL ,
   Society_Group_Desc varchar (20) NOT NULL ,
   Society_Leader_Name varchar (50)  NOT NULL ,
   Games_Played int NOT NULL ,
   Games_Won int NOT NULL ,
   Games_Drawn int NOT NULL ,
   Games_Lost int NOT NULL ,
   Scored_For int NOT NULL ,
   Scored_Against int NOT NULL ,
   Bank_Balance money NOT NULL
)
```

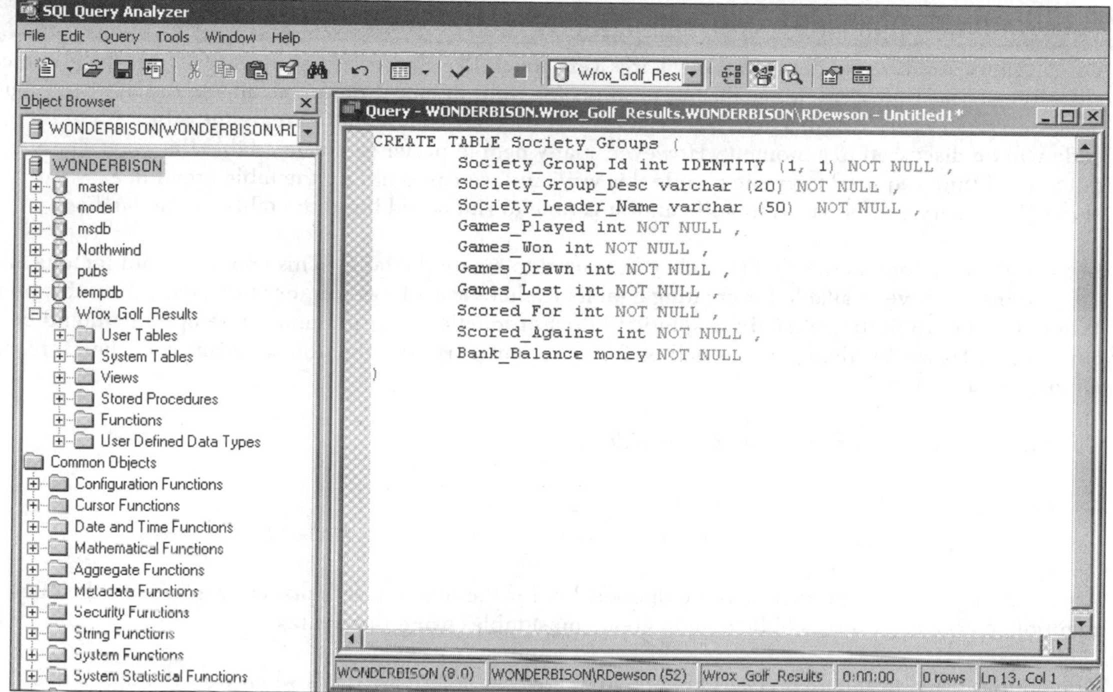

4. Execute the code by either pressing *CTRL+E* or *F5* or the toolbar Execute button.

5. You should now see the following message in the Results pane:

   The command(s) completed successfully.

6. However, you may have received an error message instead. This could be for a number of reasons from a typing mistake, through to not having the authority to create tables. We could list every message that you could receive at this point, but we would be doing this for many pages. Taking one example below, as you can see, the error messages generated are usually self-explanatory. This is informing me that I have a typing error on line 5.

   Server: Msg 170, Level 15, State 1, Line 5

   Line 5: Incorrect syntax near 'NUL'.

7. Now move to Enterprise Manager. If it is already open you will have to refresh the Details pane (by right-clicking on the Tables node and selecting Refresh). You should then see the Society_Groups table:

Tables 22 Items			
Name	Owner	Type	Create Date
Society_Groups	dbo	User	26/02/2001 19:10:50
Club_Details	dbo	User	25/02/2001 20:14:56

How It Works - Defining a Table Though Query Analyzer

Using Query Analyzer to define a table works very much like Enterprise Manager without the graphical aids. Recall that Enterprise Manager has prompts for column name, datatype, and so on, but here you have to type in every detail. There has even been extra code to type in to create the table. All of the code will be discussed in a moment. However, many people prefer to create a table this way. There is not a lot of time required to create a table this way, and we can build up the table creation as we go along. The query can be saved to a file until it is time to run it and build the table in the database.

Let's now take a look at the T-SQL code that is used to create the table. This code does not include all the options we have available for creating a table, as there are a large number not used within this book. When it comes to putting a database solution into a production environment, these options should be considered. However, these options will be for larger enterprise production solutions and, therefore, are a more advanced topic.

The basic syntax for creating a table is as follows:

```
CREATE TABLE [database_name].[owner].table_name
   (column_name data_type [length] [IDENTITY(seed, increment)] [NOT NULL])
```

There are a greater number of possible options, but for the moment let's just concentrate on the ones mentioned above. You should be able to create most tables using this syntax.

The options listed in square brackets are optional; however, there are times when we will require them. Let me explain. Take the first option, `database_name`: if you are in the `Pubs` database and you wish to create a table in the `Wrox_Golf_Results` database, it would be mandatory to either switch to that database, or use the `database_name` option. The `Owner` option allows us to assign a different owner, rather than who is currently logged in. There are three points to keep in mind here. The first is that any ID entered into the query, must be a valid ID within SQL Server. The second point is that if the user ID that is logged in executing the `CREATE TABLE` script is a SQL Server administrator, then the table will be given an owner of any ID, but if one is not entered then it will have an owner ID of `dbo`, as has been shown earlier. Finally, if the user currently logged in is not a member of the `dbo` roles, but does have table creation rights, then there is no option – the table created will be owned by the login ID that created it

Therefore, the syntax for the creation of `Society_Groups` could have read:

```
CREATE TABLE Wrox_Golf_Results..Society_Groups
```

Note that there are two period marks between the database name and the table. Recall I said that the database owner was optional. So that SQL Server can figure out the correct parameters, and which part of the statement means what, if you declare the database, you will have to either declare the table owner, or denote where the table owner should be. If you didn't, and the query looked like the following:

```
CREATE TABLE Wrox_Golf_Results.Society_Groups
```

SQL Server would attempt to create the `Society_Groups` table in the current database, with an owner of `Wrox_Golf_Results`. Therefore you have to take some care.

It is now time to define the columns. Column name and datatype are mandatory, however, depending on the datatype, the length is optional. At the end of the chapter is a reference showing when length is a required attribute, and when it is optional.

You must prefix the first column with an opening parenthesis, `(`, and once you have defined the last column, close the list with a closing parenthesis, `)`. Each column should be separated from the previous column by a comma. There is a limit of 1024 columns for a table. If you get anywhere close to that number, you should sit back and re-evaluate your table design, because chances are that the design needs to be revised.

In the following sections, the other two options shown in the syntax for the column definition will be covered, which are the **IDENTITY** keyword and dealing with `NULL` values. First of all, let's cover the `IDENTITY` keyword.

Generating IDENTITY values

The next option deals with the `IDENTITY` keyword. For those readers who have used MS Access, this option is similar to `AutoNumber`.

When adding a new row to a SQL Server table, you may wish to give this row a unique but easily identifiable ID number that can be used to link a row in one table with a row in another. Within the `Wrox_Golf_Results` database there will be a table holding a list of players, who need to be linked to their match scores. Rather than trying to link on specifics that cannot guarantee a unique link (first name and surname, for example), a numeric ID value gives that possibility, providing it is used in conjunction with a unique index. If you have a player with an ID of 100 in the `Players` table (that we'll create shortly), and you have linked to the results table via the ID, you could retrieve all the results for that player where the foreign key is 100. However, this could mean that when you want to insert a new player, SQL Server would have to figure out which ID is next. But fear not, this is where the `IDENTITY` option within a column definition is invaluable.

By defining a column using the `IDENTITY` option, what you are informing SQL Server is that:

- The column will have a value generated by SQL Server
- There will be a start point (seed)
- An increment value is given, informing SQL Server by how much each new ID should increase
- SQL server will manage the allocation of IDs
- Values cannot be modified, as the column is totally controlled by SQL Server internally
- Each row will be unique by virtue of the ID being unique

All of the tasks above would need to be performed by yourself if SQL Server did not do this for you. So by using this option on a column definition, you can use the value generated to create a solid, reliable, and unique link from one table to another, rather than relying on more imprecise selection criteria.

The Use of NULL Values

As you have seen from the table definitions above, there are columns defined as **Allow Nulls** and columns that have Allow Nulls unchecked. But what does all this mean? In T-SQL terms, as you will see shortly, it means placing either `NULL`, or `NOT NULL` at the end of a column definition. These two different statements define whether data must be entered into the column. A `NULL` value means that there is absolutely nothing entered in that column, no data at all. A column with a `NULL` value is a special data state, with special meaning. This really means that the type of data within the column is unknown.

If a field has a NULL value, no data has been inserted into the column. This also means that you have to perform special function statements within any T-SQL code to test for this value. Take the example of a column defined to hold characters, but where one of the rows has a NULL value within it. If you completed a SQL function based around string manipulation, then the row with the NULL value would cause an error, or cause the row not to be included in the function being performed. However, there are times when the use of NULL is a great advantage.

Why Define a Column to Allow NULL?

So what advantages are there to allowing data columns to hold NULL values? Well, perhaps the largest advantage is that if a field has a NULL value, you know for a fact that it has a value that is unknown. If there was no ability to define a column as having NULLs, when a column was defined as numeric, and the column had a value of 0, you could not be sure if this meant that the column had no value, or that the column does have a valid value of 0. Instantly you will know that the column has no data, and you can then work with the data in that knowledge.

Another advantage is the small space that a NULL column takes up. To be precise, it takes up no space whatsoever, again unlike a 0 or a single space, which do take up a certain amount of space. In this age of inexpensive hard drives, this is less of an issue, but if you extrapolate for a database with a million rows, and 4 columns have a space instead of a Null, that's 4 million bytes (4MB) of space used up unnecessarily.

There will be more on NULL values when the book covers working with data. Time to move on and create some more tables using different techniques.

Defining a Table – Using a Template

Now we have seen how to add a table in Query Analyzer entering the code line by line. If you recall back in Chapter 3, we saw that Query Analyzer also has some inbuilt templates to help create the code for such tasks. The next table, the Players table, which holds specific details of each individual player on separate rows, is going to use the Create Table template in Query Analyzer.

Try It Out – Creating a Table Using a Template

1. First of all, ensure that Query Analyzer is running.

2. In the Object Browser within Query Analyzer, you will see two tabs at the bottom. One of these is the Templates tab. Click on this.

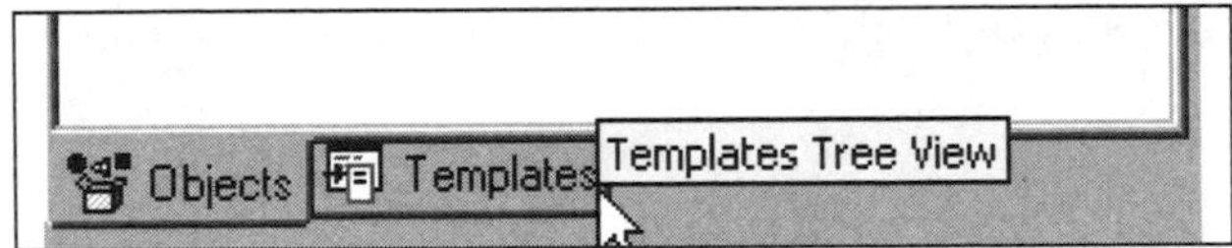

3. This lists all the templates within Query Analyzer. Locate and expand the Create Table node in the Object Browser.

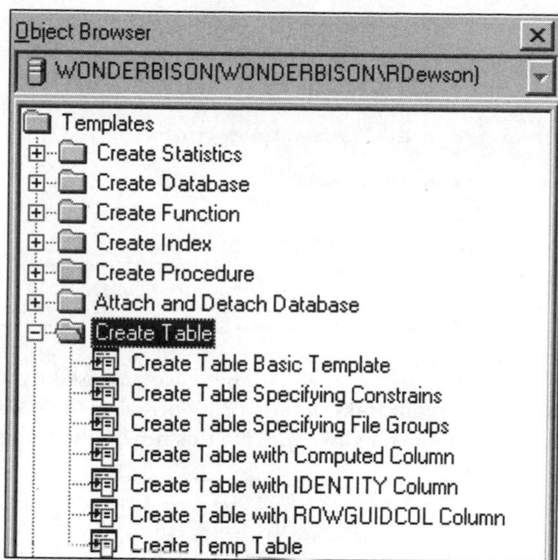

4. Now find the **Create Table with IDENTITY column** option, and double-click on this.

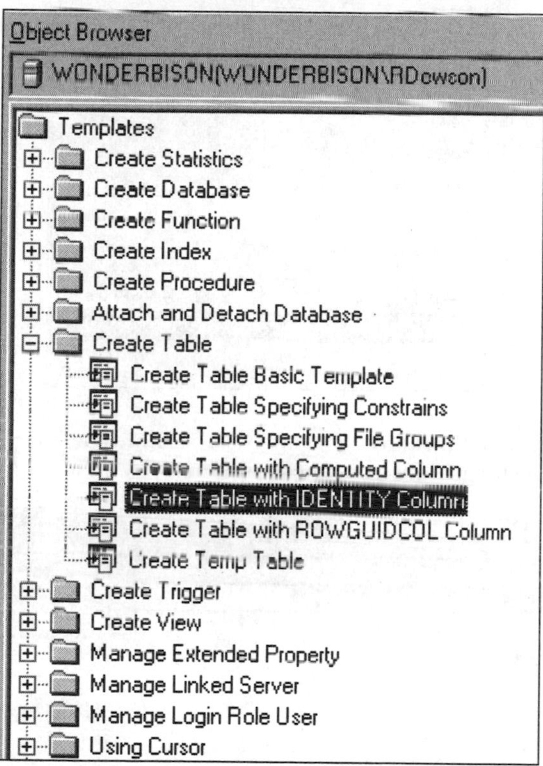

5. This will open up a new query window with some T-SQL code in it. Take a look at the code in the Query pane. There is a fair amount of code we have not come across before. We will cover this later.

```
-- =============================================
-- Create table with IDENTITY column
-- =============================================
IF EXISTS (SELECT name
           FROM   sysobjects
           WHERE  name = N'<table_name, sysname, test_table>'
           AND    type = 'U')
    DROP TABLE <table_name, sysname, test_table>
GO

create table <table_name, sysname, test_table> (
<column_1, sysname, c1> <datatype_for_column_1, , int> IDENTITY(<seed, , 100>, <increment, , 1>),
<column_2, sysname, c2> <datatype_for_column_2, , int> NOT NULL)
GO
```

6. A template includes a number of parameters. These are enclosed by angle brackets (<>). By selecting Edit/Replace Template Parameters, or by pressing *Ctrl+Shift+M*, you can alter these parameters to make a set of meaningful code. Do this now, so that the parameters can be altered.

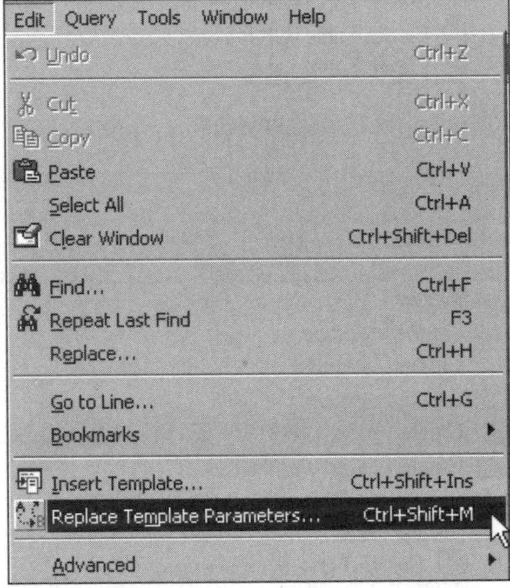

7. This brings up a dialog that allows the parameters within the query template to be replaced. As you can see, the template is populated with the default values from the template.

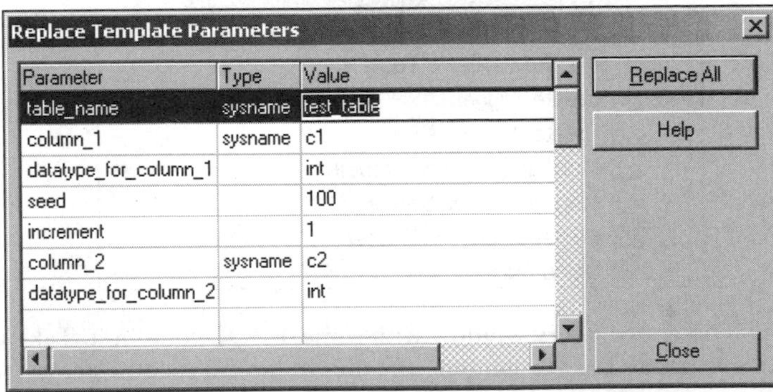

8. Alter all the entries in the **Value** Columns to those shown in the screenshot below. These are the actual values that will be used in place of the parameter names to define the table. Once complete, click **Replace All**, which replaces the parameters and closes this dialog. Any mistakes or missed updates to the parameters after clicking **Replace All** will have to be altered directly in Query Analyzer.

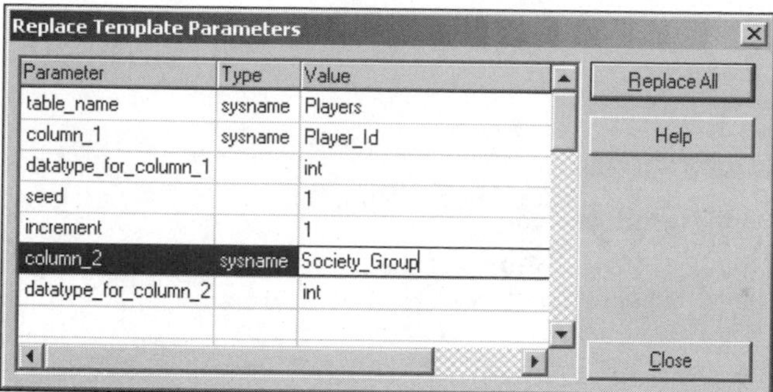

9. The Query pane will now look as follows:

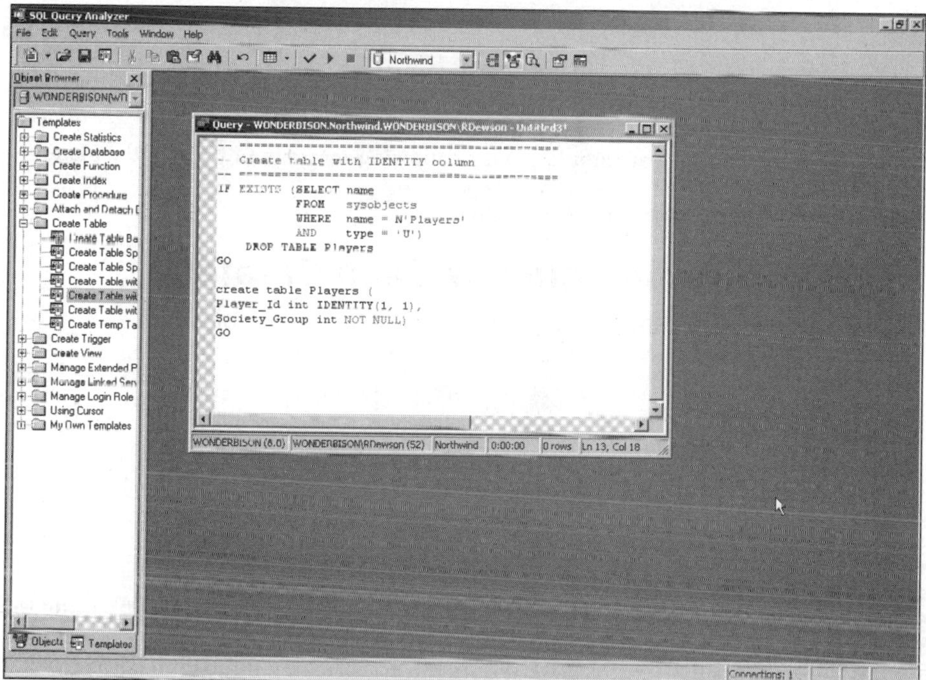

10. The query is missing a few column definitions and this is where the templates let themselves down a little. A few more columns within the template would not go amiss, as it is quicker and easier to remove extra items than it is to add them in later. You can alter the Query Analyzer templates to suit your regular requirements, but more on that in another chapter. For the moment, enter the extra column information so that the final query looks as shown overleaf. Do take care when entering definitions and, if in doubt, look at how the other definitions have been created. If you get it wrong, then you will get an error, as you saw earlier on in the chapter.

```
-- =============================================
-- Create table with IDENTITY column
-- =============================================
IF EXISTS (SELECT name
   FROM sysobjects
   WHERE name = N'Players'
   AND type = 'U'
)
DROP TABLE Players
GO

create table Players (
   Player_Id int IDENTITY (1, 1) NOT NULL ,
   Society_Group int NOT NULL ,
   Player_First_Name varchar (50) NOT NULL ,
   Player_Last_Name varchar (50) NOT NULL ,
   Date_Of_Birth smalldatetime NOT NULL ,
   Games_played tinyint NOT NULL ,
   Points_Scored smallint NOT NULL ,
   Has_Left_The_Club bit NOT NULL ,
   Photograph image NULL
)
GO
```

11. Now that all the code is entered, execute the code.

12. Once this has been run you should see the following message in the Results pane:

The command(s) completed successfully.

Checking if a Table has Already Been Created

In the above section of code within the template, you see a new section of code:

```
IF EXISTS (SELECT name
   FROM sysobjects
   WHERE name = N'Players'
   AND type = 'U'
)
DROP TABLE Players
GO
```

This code tests to see if the `Players` table has already been created. It does this by using the `SELECT` function to interrogate a system table to check whether the table that is defined in the `CREATE TABLE` statement below it has already been created; it does this by checking if the table already `EXISTS` from the data returned from the `SELECT`. If the table does exist, Query Analyzer will execute the `DROP TABLE` statement. You can then safely and successfully run the `CREATE TABLE` statement.

> **The `DROP TABLE` statement will delete the table and all the data contained within it.**

The ALTER TABLE Command

There is an alternative: the ALTER TABLE statement, which will allow restrictive alterations to a table layout but keep the contents:

- Any new columns created using the ALTER TABLE statement, where a value is expected (or defined as NOT NULL) will take time to implement. This is because any existing data would have NULL values; after all, SQL Server can decide what value to enter. When altering a table and using NOT NULL, you need to complete a number of complex processes, which include moving data to an interim table and then moving it back. The easiest solution is to alter it with NULLs allowed, then alter the columns within the rows that already existed before the change, place a default value within them, and then alter the column to NOT NULL.
- If you really need to delete the table, but want to keep the contents, then you can do this, but this requires a few statements to complete.

If you need to modify a table once it has been created, then the ALTER TABLE statement may be the best option. This will be covered later in the book, in Chapter 8 when I define relationships.

Defining the Remaining Tables

Now that three of the tables have been created, we need to create the remaining three tables. We will do this as code placed in Query Analyzer. There is nothing specifically new to cover in this next section, and therefore only the code is listed. Enter the following code in Query Analyzer Query pane, and then execute the code as before. Once finished, you can move in to Enterprise Manager, refresh it, and then you should see the new tables created and displayed.

```
CREATE TABLE dbo.Matches (
   Society_Group_Id int NOT NULL ,
   Match_Id int IDENTITY (1, 1) NOT NULL ,
   Date_Played smalldatetime NOT NULL ,
   Opposition_Name varchar (50) NOT NULL ,
   Home bit NOT NULL ,
   Points_For smallint NOT NULL ,
   Points_Against smallint NOT NULL
)
GO

CREATE TABLE dbo.Match_Scores (
   Match_Id int NOT NULL ,
   Player_Id int NOT NULL ,
   Score_Time datetime NOT NULL ,
   Score_Points tinyint NULL
)
GO

CREATE TABLE dbo.Newsletters (
   Society_Group_Id int NOT NULL ,
   Date_Published smalldatetime NOT NULL ,
   Contents text NULL
)
GO
```

Different Data Types

SQL Server has many different data types that are available for each column of data. This next section will explain the different data types and help you down the path of choosing the right type.

You will find that several data types may look similar, but keep in mind that each data type has a specific use. For example, unless you really need to define characters to be stored as Unicode, then don't use the `n` prefix data types. Also when looking at numerics, if the largest value you will store in a column is 100, then don't go for the data type that will allow the largest number to be stored. This would be a bit of a waste of disk space.

Let's take a look at the data types.

char

This is a data type, that is fixed in length. If you define a column to be of length 20 characters, then 20 characters will be stored. If you enter less than the number of characters defined, the remaining length will be space filled to the right. Therefore, if a column were defined as `char (10)`, "aaa" would be stored as "aaa   ". Use this data type when the column data will need to be of fixed length. This tends to be in customer IDs, bank account IDs, or similar columns where the length of the information stored *must* be of a fixed length.

nchar

The `nchar` type is exactly the same as `char`, but will hold characters in Unicode format rather than ANSI. The Unicode format has a larger character set range than ANSI. ANSI character sets only hold up to 256 characters. However, Unicode can hold up to 65,536 different characters. However, Unicode defined data types do take up more storage in SQL Server, in fact we would need to double the space, so unless there is a need in your database to hold this type of characters, it is easier to stick with ANSI.

varchar

This holds alphanumeric data, just like `char`, however, each field in that column, can hold a different number of characters up to the maximum length defined. If a column is defined as `varchar(50)`, this means that the data in the column can be up to a maximum of 50 characters long; however, if you only place a string of three characters, then only three spaces are used up. This definition is perfect for scenarios where there is no specific length of data; for example, people's names, descriptions where the length of the stored item does not matter. The maximum size of a varchar column is eight thousand characters long.

nvarchar

The `nvarchar` type is defined very similarly to varchar, except this uses Unicode and therefore doubles the amount of space required to store the data.

text

If you need to hold any text longer than 8,000 characters, then you cannot use `varchar`. This is where the `text` data type comes in to play. These data types can hold up to two gigabytes of data. However, `text` data types are usually different to other data types. Because such a large amount of data can be stored in this data type, it doesn't make sense to store this data within each row of SQL Server. If you think about it, you would very quickly have a vast database holding very little data. Therefore, if you are storing data within this data type, the data itself is held elsewhere. A pointer is held within SQL Server in the column defined as a text data type, pointing to where the data is physically held. However, we can store up to 7000 characters of physical data, if we wish, within this data type, but really if we have decided to use text as a data type, we are expecting large amounts of data and therefore it would be best to keep the data outside the database. This data type could be used to hold notes about customers in a call center, for example

ntext

Very similar to the `text` data type, with the exception that the data is stored as Unicode, and only 1GB of characters can be stored because this datatype takes double the amount of space to store 1 character of text.

image

`Image` is very much like the `text` data type except this is for any types of images. This datatype is used later in the book when building the tables and dealing with images.

int

The `int`, or integer, data type is used for holding numeric values that do not have a decimal point, or whole numbers. There is a range limit to the value of the numbers held: `int` will hold any number between the values of -2,147,483,648 and 2,147,483,647.

bigint

A `bigint`, or big integer, is very similar to `int`, except that much larger numbers can be held. A range of -9,223,372,036,854,775,808 through to 9,223,372,036,854,775,807 can be stored.

smallint

The `smallint` datatype, or small integer, holds small integer numbers in the range of -32,768 through to 32,767. Do take care when defining columns with this data type that there really is no possibility of exceeding these limits. There is always a large danger when creating a column with this datatype that you have to go back and change the datatype so, if in doubt, select `int`.

tinyint

The tinyint datatype, or tiny integer, is even smaller than `smallint`, and holds numbers from 0 through to 255. It could be used to hold a numerical value for each US or Canadian state, or perhaps every county in the United Kingdom

decimal/numeric

Both of these data types hold the same precision and ranges of data. The range is from –10 to the power 38 +1 through to 10 to the power 38 –1. These are quite large ranges, from -0.00000000000000000000000000000000000001, through to 10,000,000,000,000,000,000,000,000,000. However, do take care with this, as you cannot store 38 digits to the right and left of the decimal point. You can only store up to and including 38 digits. So, the greater the precision required to the right of the decimal point, the less digits are left to represent the whole number.

float

This is used for numbers where the decimal point is not fixed. `Floats` hold very large numbers in the range of -1.79E+308 through 1.79E+308. There is a warning with this datatype and that is that the values cannot always be seen as 100% accurate, as they can be approximate. The approximation arises from the way the number is physically stored as binary code. You will have problems where a number ends in .3, .6s or .7. The value stored has to be approximated, or rounded, as some values could not be stored accurately for they may have more decimal places than can be catered for. A well-known example is be the value of Pi.

real

The `real` data type is very much like `float`, except that real can store only numbers, in the range of -3.40E+38 through 3.40E+38. This will data type also hold an approximate value.

money

The `money` data type is used for holding numeric values up to four decimal places. If we need to use more than four decimal places, we look to another data type, such as `decimal`. This data type doesn't actually store the currency symbol to signify the monetary type, therefore you cannot use this data type for different currencies. The `money` data type has a range of -922,337,203,685,477.5808, through to 922,337,203,685,477.5807. If you need to store the currency that is held here, then you would need to store this separately, as the `money` datatype does not hold the currency symbol. A column defined as `money` will hold the money to 1/10000 of a decimal unit, which is a bit of a waste if you are storing the values as Turkish Lira.

smallmoney

Similar to `money` with the exception of the range, which lies between -214,748.3648 and 214,748.3647.

datetime

This will hold any date and time from January 1st, 1753, through to December 31st 9999. However, it not only stores a date, but also a time alongside it. If you just populate a column defined as `datetime` with a date, a default time of 12:00:00 will be stored as well.

smalldatetime

Very much like `datetime`, except the date range is January 1st, 1900, through to June 6th, 2079. The reason for this strange date lies in the binary storage representation of this `datetime`.

timestamp/rowversion

This is an unusual data type as it is not a column for which you will be expected to supply a value. The `timestamp` data type holds a binary number generated by SQL Server, which will be unique for each row within a database. Every time a record is modified, this column will be modified and a new value placed within this column. Therefore, you can use these values in more advanced techniques where you want to keep a version history of what has been changed.

> **Timestamp in SQL Server 2000, is not SQL-92 compliant, which means that it does not follow the rules imposed by ANSI, so use timestamp with care. I recommend that you use `rowversion` instead. To make `timestamp` SQL-92 compliant would mean altering the data type to hold a `datetime` instead of a binary value generated by SQL Server. This may well happen in the next release of SQL Server.**

uniqueidentifier

This holds a **Globally Unique Identifier**, or **GUID**. This is similar to the `timestamp/rowversion` data type, in that the identifier has to be initiated by a SQL Server command, and not when a record is inserted or modified. The identifier is generated from information from the network card on a machine, processor ID, and the date and time. If you have no network card, then the uniqueidentifier is generated from information from your own machine information only. These IDs should be unique throughout the world.

binary

Data held in this data type is held in binary format. This data type is mainly used for data held as flags or combinations of flags. For example, perhaps you wanted to hold flags about a customer. You need to know if the customer is Active (value=1), ordered within the last month (value=2), last order was for more than $1,000 (value=4), meets loyalty criteria (value=8). This would add up to 4 columns of data within a database. However, by using `binary` values, if a client had a value of 13 in `binary`, then they would have values 1+4+8, which is Active, last order more than $1,000 and meets the loyalty criteria. When you define the column of a set size in `binary` all data will be of that size.

varbinary

Very much like `binary`, except the physical column size per row will differ depending on the value stored.

bit

Holds a value of `0` or `1`. Usually used to determine True (1), or False (0) values.

These are the main datatypes within SQL Server. There are a few more, like `cursor`, `table`, and `sql_variant` but these are for more advanced development and so are not discussed in this book.

Image and Large Text Storage in SQL Server

Storing pictures and large amounts of text, is very much different from storing other kinds of information within SQL Server. Pictures can take up large amounts of space. The following also holds true for large amounts of text.

Several scenarios exist where, by holding large amounts of data, SQL Server and the SQL Server installation will just end up running into problems. I'll explain why in a minute, but first of all we will see what SQL Server does instead.

If you wish to store large amounts of images, or large amounts of text (by large, I mean more than 8KB – 4K characters if you want to store the Unicode version of the text) you should store these outside SQL Server on the hard drive somewhere. SQL Server then holds a pointer in the column to the location where the image, or text file is held. From there you can retrieve the information and use it as necessary. This gives you as a developer or database administrator the ability to store large amounts of data on a different volume to the SQL Server installation, on a different server, or even just in a different directory. However, having this control of the storage of the information allows SQL Server to run without taking up vast amounts of the database space declared at setup. After all, if you set your database initial size to 20MB with 5 MB extensions, it would not take too many pictures to fill this up. But by using a pointer, you will not be taking up much space at all, and so will allow your database to still fulfill maximum space requirements. Not only that, SQL Server has in-built functionality, called **transactions**, where a copy of the data can be taken before and after any modification. If that data included a 5MB graphic, or volume of text, then SQL Server would have to deal with keeping track of that information while the transaction was in progress.

> **Transactions are covered later in the book in Chapter 14 when looking at table updates. When executing a transaction, SQL Server takes a copy of the data, and then applies your changes. If everything looks OK, you can inform SQL Server to save them or, if there are problems, you can inform SQL Server to roll back those changes. Therefore, SQL Server needs to keep copies of all the data changed in the transaction.**

If your application does use images or large amounts of text, then keep a close eye on disk space where the information is stored, so you can avoid your SQL Server database stopping when the limit of disk space is met either on your hard drive, or from SQL Server with no growth options left.

Later in the book, there will be discussions about images, manipulating and inserting these into the database, and how this works. However, just keep in mind the information given above so that you can start planning now what solution would be best for your database.

Summary

So, now you know how to create a table. This chapter has covered several options on how to achieve this. Later in the book you will learn how to alter a table, but for the moment, we just concentrated on getting the tables defined correctly.

There is one point that you should keep in mind when building a table, whether you are creating or modifying them. If creating tables in Enterprise Manager, always save the table first by clicking on the Save toolbar button. If you have made a mistake when defining the table and you close the table, and so save in one action, then you will get an error message informing you that an error has occurred, but all your changes will be lost. You will then have to go back in to the table designer and re-apply any changes made.

Try also to get used to using both Enterprise Manager and Query Analyzer as you may find that Query Analyzer gives you a more comfortable feel to the way you want to work. Also you will find that in Query Analyzer, you can save your work as you go along. You can also do this within Enterprise Manager; however, the changes are saved to a text file as a set of SQL commands which then need to be run through Query Analyzer anyway.

Defining tables is the most crucial area to get right within your design of your database solution. If you are getting involved in design, take a look at Louis Davidson's book *"Professional SQL Server 2000 Database Design" (Wrox Press, ISBN 1-861004-76-1)* concerning design with SQL Server. Take time, ensure that the data is normalized (Chapter 4) and that you can justify that each column is in the right table. Keep in mind the old adage, "Get it right first time!"

At this point in the book you should feel confident with knowing how to build a table, creating the columns, and which datatype to put against each column. Your solution is now coming together nicely, however, there are still many hurdles to jump. The next area will be dealing with is accessing the data faster, and this is where indexes come in.

Creating Indexes

Now that we have created the tables, it would be possible to stop at this point and just work with our data from here. However, this would not be one of our better decisions. As soon as any table contained a reasonable amount of information, and we wished to find one particular record, it would take a fair amount of time to locate it. Not really a good idea for performance and our users would soon get annoyed with how slow it is to work with our data. Think of it as a large filing cabinet, in which we had to find one piece of paper, with no help.

However, if we had some sort of cross-reference facility, then things might be easier. If that cross-reference were in fact an index, then this is even better, as we might even be able to find the piece of paper almost instantly. And it is this theory that needs to be put in to practice in our SQL Server database tables. Generally, indexing is a conscious decision to favor conditional selection of records over modification or insertion of records.

There are many ways to create an index and this chapter will cover each of these different methods. First of all, we really need to know what an index is and how it is held within SQL Server. Once we know the difference between data in a table and in an index, the chapter then takes us through what makes a good index and what makes a bad index. A great deal of thought about the way the data is accessed needs to be given before building our indexes, and this section will provide the required information.

There are many different types of index that can be created, from ones that store the data in the table in the same physical order as the index, through to indexes that force each row of information to be unique. All of these indexes have special names and we will go through each of the indexes with an in depth explanation of what they are for. Also we will see how an index in one table can be used to link up with information within another table.

Finally it will then be time to demonstrate the SQL syntax for creating indexes, as well as building them using tools such as Enterprise Manager and Query Analyzer. The chapter also covers what needs to be done when we want to alter an index.

So by the end of this chapter you will know:

- What an index is
- How to determine when you need an index, and how to determine when you don't
- How to avoid data retrieval from a table when a covering index can do the job
- What the names of all the different types of indexes are and what they mean
- How to build an index in Enterprise Manager using the different methods available to us
- How to build an index in Query Analyzer using the different methods available to us
- Why statistical information is essential to SQL Server and indexes in record retrieval
- What a primary key is and how the setting of this differs from building other keys/indexes
- What the `CREATE INDEX` syntax is for building indexes through SQL commands
- Finally, how to alter and drop an index

Let's take the first point and begin by looking at what an index is and how it stores data.

What is an Index?

In the previous chapter, we looked at what a table was. This is in essence a repository that holds data and information about that data; what it looks like and where it is held. However, a table definition is not a great deal of use in getting to the data quickly or storing the data in a specific order. What is required is some sort of cross-reference facility where for certain columns of information within a table, it should be possible to get to the whole record of information quickly. If you think of a table as a very large filing cabinet, and each row as a separate piece of paper within that filing cabinet, you need some sort of cross-reference to get to a file quickly. This is where an index within your SQL Server database comes in.

You define an index in SQL Server so that it can locate the rows it requires to satisfy database queries faster. If an index does not exist to help find the necessary rows SQL Server has no other option but to look at every row in a table to see if it contains the information required by the query. This is called a table scan and by its nature adds considerable overhead to data retrieval operations.

However, there are good indexes, and unfortunately, there are also bad indexes. In the next section both of these areas will be covered so that you will know how to create an index that is of use and enhances your database's performance.

When an index is created, the information used to build the index is placed separate to the table, and therefore can be stored on a different physical disk if required. When a record is added to a table that has at least one index on it, the data is placed into the table, and the indexes are then updated with a copy of the necessary information, plus a pointer to where the physical data is stored. Then when searching a table using the index, you are not going through the whole data stored in the table, but a much smaller subset of that data, which obviously is faster, and once the record is found in the index, there is a pointer to say where the data for that row can be found in the relevant table.

When defining an index, there are different types of index that can be built on to a table. An index can be created on one column, a **simple** index, or on more than one column, a **compound** index. The circumstances of the column or columns chosen, and the data that will be held within these columns will lead to choosing a particular type of index.

What Types of Indexes are There?

SQL Server has two types of index, **clustered** and **non-clustered**. The index type refers to the way the index is stored internally by SQL Server. However the difference is an important one so it is worth our while to describe these differences.

Clustered

An index defined as being **clustered**, defines the physical order that the data in the table is stored. Only one clustered index can be defined per table, obviously, as it would be impossible to store the data in two different physical orders. As we have said, do not choose columns that will have a lot of updates performed on them to make a clustered index, as this will mean SQL Server having to constantly alter the physical order of the data and so use up a great deal of processing power.

As the clustered index contains the table data itself SQL Server would perform less I/O operations to retrieve the data using the clustered index than it would using a non-clustered index. Therefore if you only have one index on a table make sure it is a clustered index.

Non-Clustered

Unlike a clustered index, the non-clustered index does not store the table data itself. Instead the non-clustered index stores pointers to the table data as part of the index. Therefore many non-clustered indexes can exist on a single table at one time.

As a non-clustered index is stored in a separate structure to the base table it is possible to create the non-clustered index on a different file group to the base table. If the file groups are located on separate disks data retrieval can be enhanced for your queries as SQL Server can use parallel I/O operations to retrieve the data from the index and base tables concurrently.

Primary

This is probably the most important definition within SQL Server for the viewpoint of an index. A **primary key** within a table makes several statements to you as a developer, and to itself in ensuring data integrity. First and foremost, the primary key is informing you that the data defined within the column definitions for the key will return a unique row of data from the table. A primary key cannot be defined on a column, or sequence of columns that do not return a single row. To meet this end, it is not possible to define a primary key for any columns that allow `NULL` values.

Also a primary key is used to link up data from one table with data from another. To explain further, if you had two tables, one holding Customers, and then another holding customer Orders, you would define a primary key on the Customers table on the customer ID that is generated uniquely each time a new customer record is inserted. This would then be used to link up to the many records within the customer Orders table, to return all the customer orders for that customer ID. The link, or **join**, between these two tables would be the customer ID, which would be defined as a primary key in the Customers table. Later on in the book you will see how to join tables together and define a **relationship** between them.

> **A join and a relationship essentially mean the same thing. These key words mean that there is a logical link between two or more tables, which can be defined through a specific column or set of columns between these two tables.**

Foreign/Referencing Key

As has just been discussed, there will be times when two or more tables will be linked together. The example above has demonstrated this. The link between the Customer and the customer Orders table would be the customer ID column. This column will return a unique row in the Customers table, and hence it is defined as the primary key of the Customers table. However, to link to the customer Orders table, there has to be a corresponding foreign key, which would be the customer ID column in the customers Order table. Unlike a primary key though, a foreign key is not held as an index.

When it comes to creating relationships within our database in Chapters 8 and 9, you will see how a foreign key is created that will create a link, or a relationship, between the two columns. This is created through a **constraint**, which is a method SQL Server uses to check the details built into the relationship. From the viewpoint of a foreign key, this constraint, or check, will ensure that the relationship follows the conditions set with it. There is more on foreign keys in Chapters 8 and 9.

Candidate/Alternate Key

A table can only have one primary key. However, there may be another index created which could also be defined as a primary key. This is known as a candidate key, as it is a candidate for being the primary key. There is no difference at all between the definition of a candidate key and a primary key. For example, if you had a table that held spare parts for a General Motors' vehicle, you could have an internal G.M. part number, so that when ordering parts at head office for branches, you would order by the G.M. internal part number. This would be unique and probably the primary key. However, there will also be the part number created by each of the manufacturers, which will be unique to them. These too could be a primary key if you include the supplier identifier as well. You can't have two primary keys and you have chosen the G.M. part number as the primary key. Therefore you would create a key using the manufacturer's part number and their identifier, and this would be a candidate key.

Unique Key

This is where the index defined will return a unique row from the table the index it is associated with. This sounds very much like the primary key definition above, but there are differences. A unique key may return a single row; however, the index is not necessarily used to link two or more tables together. For example, you may have a table of customers. The primary key would be the column holding the unique identifier generated by SQL Server every time a new customer is inserted. However, you could have a unique key on the customer name and depot location. This would not be a primary key as it did not then link in to any other table. Also a unique key can contain `NULL` values; however `NULL` is treated as any other value within a column, and therefore the columns used to make a unique key must remain unique, including the `NULL` value, when looking to insert data.

Uniqueness

An index can either be defined as unique or non-unique. A unique index ensures that the values contained within the unique index columns will appear only once within the table, including `NULL`.

SQL Server automatically enforces the uniqueness of the columns contained within a unique index. If an attempt is made to insert a value that already exists in the table an error will be generated and the attempt to insert the data will fail.

A non-unique index is perfectly valid. However, as there can be duplicated values, a non-unique index has more overhead than a unique index when retrieving data. Unique indexes are commonly implemented to support constraints such as the primary key. Non-unique indexes are commonly implemented to support the locating of rows using a non-key column.

Determining What Makes a Good Index

To create an index on a table, you have to specify which columns are within the index. As you will see later in the chapter, not every data type can be indexed, but within Enterprise Manager, SQL Server does point these data types out to you. An index can be created on columns that have valid data types, but the columns in the index do not have to all be of the same data type. There is also a limit of 16 columns on an index and the total amount of data for the index columns within a row cannot be more than 900 bytes. To be honest, if you get to an index that contains more than four or five columns, you should stand back and re-evaluate the index definition. There may be times that there will be more than five columns, but you really should double check.

We will look at some factors that can determine what makes a good index:

- Using "Low maintenance" columns
- Being able to find a specific record
- Using covered indexes
- Looking for a range of information
- Keeping the data in order

Low Maintenance

As we have indicated, for non-clustered indexes the actual index data is separate from the table data, although both can be stored in the same area, or in different areas, for example on different hard drives. To reiterate, what this first statement means is that when inserting a record in to a table, the information from the columns included in the index is copied and inserted in to the index area. So, if you alter data in a column within a table, and that column has been defined as making up an index, SQL Server also has to alter the data in the index. Thus, instead of just completing one update, there will be two. If the table has more than one index, and in more than one of those indexes there is a column that is to be updated a great deal, then there may be several disk writes to perform when updating just one record. While this will result in a slight performance reduction for data modification operations, appropriate indexing will balance this out by greatly increasing the performance of data retrieval operations.

Therefore, data which is "low maintenance", namely columns that are not heavily updated, could become an index, and would make a good index. The fewer disk writes that SQL Server has to do, the faster the database will be, as well as every other database within that SQL Server instance. Don't let this statement put you off. If it is felt that data within a table is retrieved more often than it is modified, or the performance of the retrieval is more critical than the performance of the modification, then do look at including the column within the index.

To give an example, suppose you have a bank system. Each month you need to update a customer's bank balance with any interest gained, or charged. However, you have a nightly job that wants to check for clients who have between $10,000 and $50,000 as the bank can get a higher rate of deposit with the Federal Reserve bank on those sort of amounts. A client's bank balance will be constantly updated, however, an index on this sort of column could speed up the overnight deposit check program. Before the index in this example is created it should be determined if the slight performance degradation in the updating of the balances is justified by the improvement of performance of the deposit check program.

Primary and Foreign Keys

One important use of indexes is on referential constraints within a table. In fact in SQL Server a primary key constraint is always accompanied by a unique index. You are able to select if this primary key index is clustered or non-clustered, but you cannot drop it.

SQL Server does not automatically create indexes on your foreign keys. However as the foreign key column values need to be identified by SQL Server when joining to the parent table it is almost always recommended that an index be created on the columns of the foreign key.

Finding Specific Records

Ideal candidates for indexes are columns that allow SQL Server to quickly identify the appropriate rows. In Chapter 13, where we look at retrieving data, we will meet the `WHERE` clause of a query. This clause lists certain columns in your table and is used to limit the number of rows returned from a query. It is these columns used in the `WHERE` clause of your most common queries that make excellent choices for an index. So for example, if you wanted to find a customer's order for a specific order number, an index based on `customer_id` and `order_number` would be perfect, as all the information needed to locate a requested row in the table would be contained in the index.

If this is going to make up part of the way the application works, then do look at this scenario as an area for an index to be created.

Covered Indexes

As this section has said, when you insert or update a record, any data in a column that is included in an index, is not only stored in the table, but also in the indexes. From finding an entry in an index, SQL Server then moves to the table to locate and retrieve the record. However, if the necessary information is held within the index, then there is no need to go to the table and retrieve the record, giving much speedier data access. To expand further, look at the `authors` table in the `Pubs` database. Suppose that you wanted to find out where a specific author lived. If an index was placed on the columns `au_lname` and `city`, and knowing that the last name was unique, you would ask SQL Server to find a record using the last name supplied, and it would then be able to retrieve the city. Well, SQL Server is smart enough to find out the city information directly from the index, based on `au_lname`. It would not have to go to the table for this information.

This is called a **covered index**, since the index covers the relevant columns for data retrieval.

Looking for a Range of Information

In the same scenario as above, you may wish to try and find a set of authors between two sets of values, for example, a list of authors between Carson and Karsen. The index defined above would be ideal for this, as when it is used to find a range of records , an index speeds up data retrieval.

It should be noted that SQL Server Indexes are not useful when attempting to search for characters embedded in a body of text. Suppose we wanted to find all authors whose last name contained the letters "ab".

```
SELECT *
FROM Authors
WHERE LastName LIKE '%ab%'
```

As you can see this query does not provide a means of determining where in the index tree to start and stop searching for appropriate values. The only way SQL Server can determine which rows are valid for this query would be to examine every row within the table; depending on the amount of data within the table, this can be very slow. If you have a requirement to perform this form of wildcard text searching you should take a look at the SQL Server Full-text feature, as this will provide better performance for such queries. The following query:

```
SELECT *
FROM Authors
WHERE LastName LIKE 'ab%'
```

gives SQL Server a start and end point within the index tree to search for the appropriate rows, therefore an index defined on the `LastName` column would be used. Don't worry if you don't fully understand the SQL code above just yet, we will take a detailed look at the `SELECT` syntax in Chapter 13.

Keeping the Data in Order

As mentioned earlier, there is also a special type of index that actually keeps the data in the table in a specific order. This is called a **clustered index**. When you specify a column, or multiple columns, as a clustered index, on inserting a record, SQL Server will place that record in a physical position to keep the records in the correct ascending or descending order that corresponds to the order defined in the index. To explain this a bit further, if you have a clustered index on customer numbers, and the data currently has customer numbers 10,6,4,7,2,5, then SQL Server will physically store the data in the following order, 2,4,5,6,7,10. If a process then adds in a customer number 9, then it will be physically inserted between 7 and 10, which may mean that the record for customer number 10 needs to move, physically. Therefore if you have defined a clustered index on a column, or a set of columns where data insertions cause the clustered index to be reordered, this is going to greatly affect your insert performance. SQL Server does provide a way to reduce the reordering impact by allowing a fill factor to be specified when an index is created.

Determining What Makes a Bad Index

Now that you know what makes a good index, you really need to know what makes a bad index. There are several "gotchas" to be aware of.

Poor Choice of Columns

If a column isn't used by a query to locate a row within a table then there is a good chance that the column does not need to be indexed, unless it is combined with another column to create a covering index as we described earlier. If this is the case the index will still add overhead to the data modification operations but will not produce and performance benefit to the data retrieval operations.

Poor Selectivity of Data

Indexes work best when the data contained in the index columns is highly selective between rows. The optimal index is one created on a column that has a unique value for every row within a table, such as a primary key. If a query requests a row based on a value within this column SQL Server can quickly navigate the index structure and identify the single row that matches the query predicate.

However if the selectivity of the data in the index columns is poor, the effectiveness of the index is less. For example, if an index is created on a column which only contains three distinct values the index would only be able to reduce the number of rows to a third of the total before applying other methods to identify the exact row. Therefore, when deciding on appropriate index columns you should examine the data selectivity to estimate the effectiveness of the index.

Including Many Columns in an Index

The more columns in an index, the more data writing has to take place when a process completes an update or an insertion of data. Although in SQL Server 2000 these updates to the index data take a very small amount of time, it can add up. Therefore, each index that is added to a table will incur extra processing overhead, so it is recommended that you create the minimum number of indexes needed to give your data retrieval operations acceptable performance.

Small Number of Records in the Table

There is also absolutely no need to place an index on a table which has only one row. SQL Server will find the record first time of asking without the need of an index to get there.

This also holds true where a table has only a handful of records. So again, there would be no reason to place an index on these tables. The reason behind this is that SQL Server would go to the index, use its engine to make several reads of the data to find the correct record, and then move directly to that record using the record pointer from the index to retrieve the information. There are several actions involved in this, as well as passing data between different components within SQL Server. When you execute a query SQL Server will determine if it is more efficient to use the indexes defined for the table to locate the necessary rows, or if it is more efficient simply to perform a table scan and look at every row within the table.

In this case it would be better to not have an index on the table. If you have no indexes on a table, and SQL Server has to go through every record on a table checking to see if the data you wish to retrieve is contained within that row, this is called a table scan, as mentioned earlier. From the `Wrox_Golf_Results` example, there are two tables on which there would be no reason to place an index, namely the `Club_Details` and `Society_Groups` tables. `Club_Details` will only have one record, and `Society_Groups` will have only a handful of records.

Constantly Review

It is highly advisable to set up tasks that constantly review your indexes and how they are performing. Every so often it should be necessary for you as an administrator or a developer to review the indexes built on your table to ensure that yesterday's good index is not today's bad index.

When a solution is built, what is perceived to be a good index in development may not be so good in production, for example, the users maybe performing one task more times than we expected. Therefore constantly review the indexes built to ensure that everything remains as it should be.

Good, Bad, How do I Tell?

If you are unable to determine what would make a good index , SQL Server 2000 provides the Index Tuning wizard to help. This wizard takes your table(s), a file holding a representative amount of information which will be processed through the table, and uses this to figure out what indexes to place within the database. At this point, we haven't actually covered data in the book, and so going through this wizard could just lead to confusion. There is a great deal more on the wizard in *"Professional SQL Server 2000 Programming" (Wrox Press, ISBN 1-861004-48-6)* and some experience is required to deal with the information returned.

> **Getting the indexes right is crucial to the optimal running of your SQL Server database. Spend time thinking about these, trying to get them right, and then reviewing them at regular intervals.**

Creating an Index

Now that we know what an index is, and the various types of index, we will proceed to create some in SQL Server. There are many different ways to create an index within SQL Server as you might expect. This chapter will cover these, and it is time to look at the first method, which is to use the table designer in SQL Server Enterprise Manager.

The first index that will be placed in to the database will be on the `Player_ID` field within the `Players` table.

Creating an Index – Table Designer

If you recall in the previous chapter when the `Player_Id` column was set up, SQL Server automatically generates the data within this field whenever a new record is inserted in to this table, and this data will never alter, as it uses the `IDENTITY` function for the column. Thus the `Player_Id` column will be updated automatically whenever a player is added. An application, for example written in Visual Basic, Visual C++, or VB.NET, could be used as the user front end for updating the remaining areas of the player's data and the application could also display specific player details, but it would not know that the `Player_Id` requires updating for each record.

The first index created will be used to find the record to update with a player's information. Instead of looking for the player by first name, last name, and date of birth, the application will know the `Player_Id` and use this to find the record within SQL Server. It will be this that is used to specifically locate the record to update. The next section will add this index to the `Players` table.

Try It Out - Creating an Index in Enterprise Manager

1. Ensure SQL Server Enterprise Manager is running, and that you have expanded the nodes in the Tree View so that you can see the tables node within the Wrox_Golf_Results database.

2. Find the first table that the index is to be added to, which is the Players table. Right-click, and select Design table.

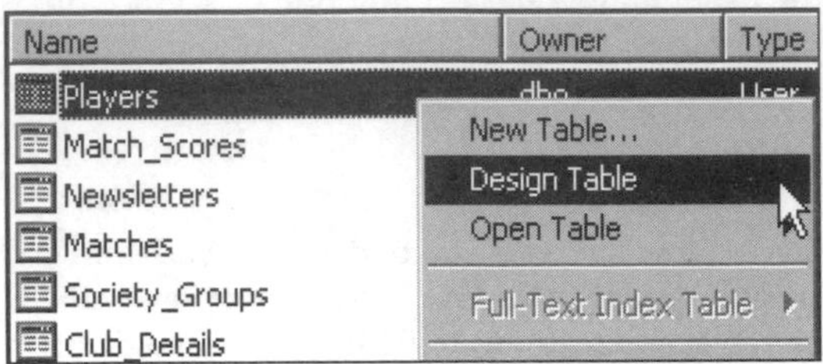

This will bring you into the table designer. Right-click and select Properties or alternatively click the second to last icon on the toolbar, the Manage Indexes icon

This icon will bring up the table Properties dialog that gives access to the Indexes/Keys tab. Click on this tab.

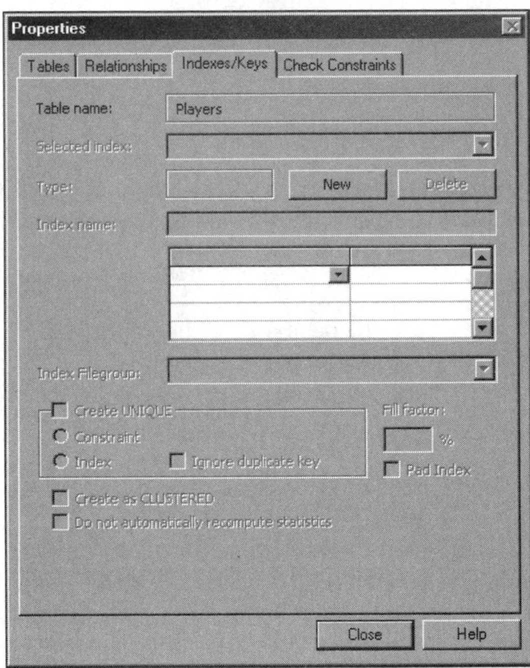

3. As you can see, there is nothing entered, and a lot of the dialog is grayed out. To create the index, click the New button. This automatically creates the basics of a new index for you, and populates and enables the necessary fields and options that you might wish to use. However, no matter what indexes have been created already, the initial column chosen for the index will always be the first column defined in the table.

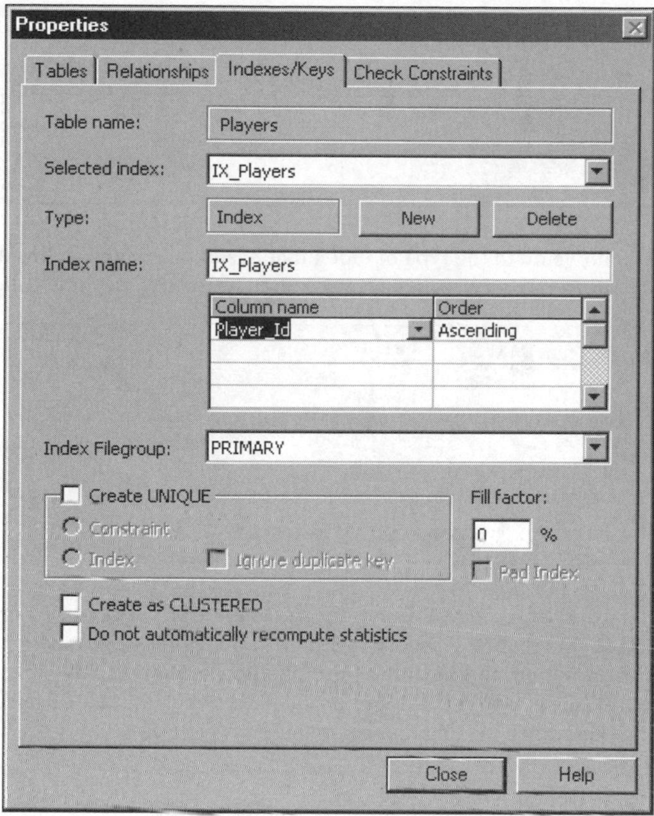

4. The first area to change is the name of the index. Notice in the Index name: textbox, SQL Server has created a possible value for you. The name is prefixed with IX, a good naming system to use. It is also good to keep the name of the table, and then a useful suffix, such as the name of the column. In this case, the index will be called IX_Players_PlayerId.

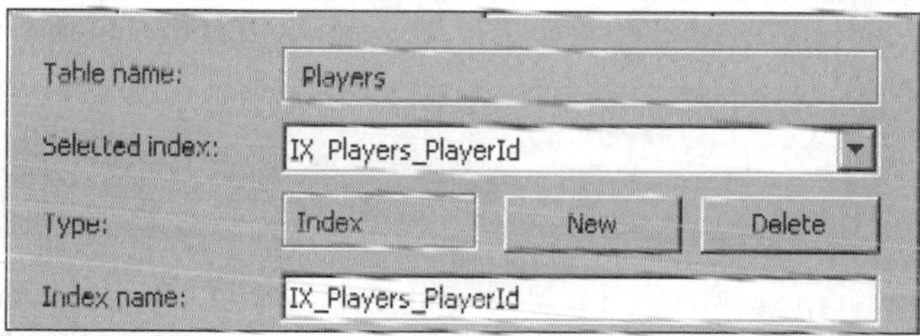

5. SQL Server has, in this instance, correctly selected Player_Id as the column that will make up the index, and that the index will be Ascending. For this example the default sort order is appropriate. The sort order of the index column is useful when creating an index on the columns that will be used in an `ORDER BY` clause of a query, a topic which we will cover in Chapter 13. If the sort order of the columns within the index matches the sort order of those columns specified in the `ORDER BY` clause SQL Server may be able to avoid performing a internal sort, resulting in improved query performance.

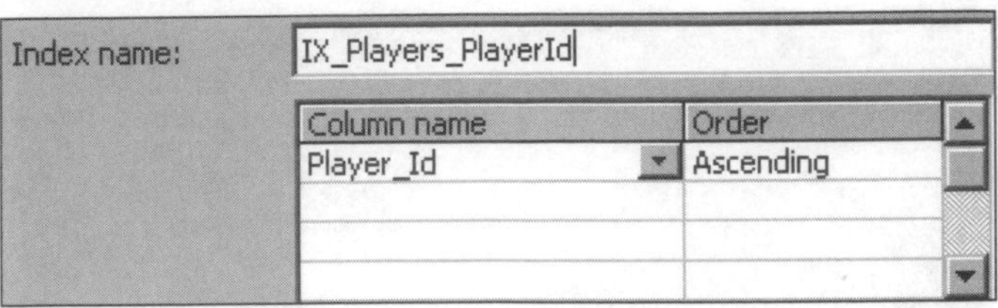

6. Now it's time to move on to the type of index that has to be created in this example. The following figure demonstrates SQL Server's default suggestion as to how this index should be built.

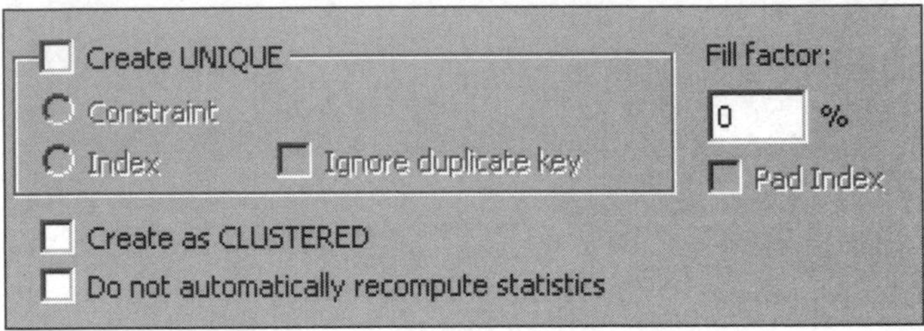

7. As indicated earlier, SQL Server generates the value of the **Player_Id** column with the next number in a sequence, when a record is added. This value can't be altered, and so taking these two items of information and putting them together, you should be able to deduce that this value will be unique. There is therefore no need to tick the **Create UNIQUE** box in this instance. However, more on this in a moment.

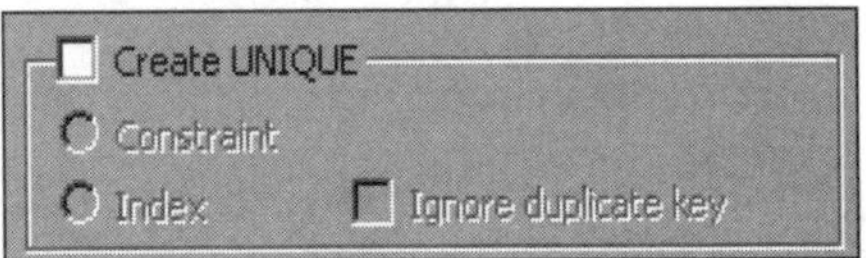

8. The final part of creating the index is to tick the **Create as CLUSTERED** check box. The order of the records inserted into SQL Server won't change, and by using the **Player_Id** as the basis of the clustered index will speed up access for the scenario that the index is being created for.

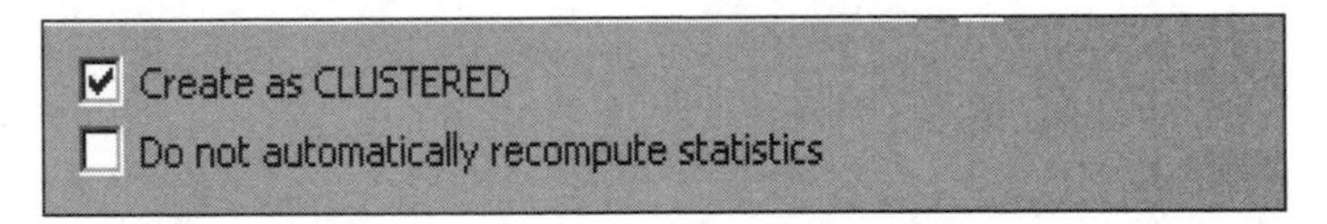

Building an index in Enterprise Manager is a straightforward set of actions as you have just seen. Although this is the first index that you have created yourself, it has only taken a few moments to achieve and there were only a couple of areas where any reasonable amount of decision making had to be completed. We will cover those areas now.

Choosing the name of the index, and the columns to include is easy and it is not worth dwelling on. You should know which columns to include from the discussions at the start of the chapter where the basics of building indexes were covered.

As you move down the index creation process you come across the first real area to cover, which is the Create UNIQUE area. The column chosen for this index is an identity column which, if you recall, is a column that cannot have data entered in to it by any SQL command, as the data entered in to this column is completed automatically by SQL Server itself. Also as an identity column, by default, no two rows can have the same value in this column. Therefore, there is no need to inform SQL Server that the index will be unique. If you did, then you are including unnecessary processing on your table every time a record is added.

Moving on further down to the Create as CLUSTERED area, the data in this table would be best held in `Player_Id` order. This is because records will be inserted each time with a higher `Player_Id` number than the previous record. Therefore each time a record is added it will be added to the end of the table. By having this incrementing number as the clustered index, the data will be stored in the same order as it is inserted. As with the Create Unique option, the Create as CLUSTERED option doesn't need to be checked, however, there is a more advanced setting within SQL Server for when a record is deleted and a hole is created in the sequence, any new record added will fill this hole. By having the index clustered, the data will remain in sequential order. If you do not create a clustered index for a table, the table is referred to as a heap. The data within a heap is not stored in any particular order.

The final check box, Do not automatically recompute statistics, should always remain unchecked. If you ever build or alter an index, then SQL Server should always be allowed to recompute the statistics on the table. You are probably wondering why that is.

Indexes and Statistics

When retrieving data, SQL Server obviously has to make some decisions as to the best way to get to that data and return it to the query requesting it. Even if an index has been created on a set of columns, SQL Server may feel that it is better and faster to use another method to retrieve the data, through a table scan perhaps. Or perhaps there are a couple of indexes that could be chosen to retrieve the same data. No matter what the scenario, SQL Server has to have some basis of information to make sensible and accurate choices. This is where statistics come in.

SQL Server keeps statistics on each column, which are updated over a period of time and over a number of inserts or modifications. The specifics of how all of this works in the background, and how SQL Server keeps the statistics up to date is an advanced topic. However, what we do need to know is that if you alter or build an index on a table that has data in it, and don't let SQL Server recompute the statistics on the table, then SQL Server could be using inaccurate information when it is trying to decide how to retrieve the data. It could even mean that the index change you thought would improve performance has in fact made the performance much slower. Therefore, always let SQL Server recompute the statistics when building or altering an index. The option to turn off the automated re-computation of statistics is included for special situations where it is more appropriate for the statistics to be regularly manually maintained by an administrator.

Setting a Primary Key

Setting a primary key can be completed in Enterprise Manager with just a couple of mouse clicks. This section will demonstrate how easy this actually is.

Try It Out – Setting a Primary Key

1. Ensure that SQL Server Enterprise Manager is running and that you have navigated to the Wrox_Golf_Results database. Find the Society_Groups table, and right-click. This will bring up the dialog that you can see in the figure below. Select Design Table and click.

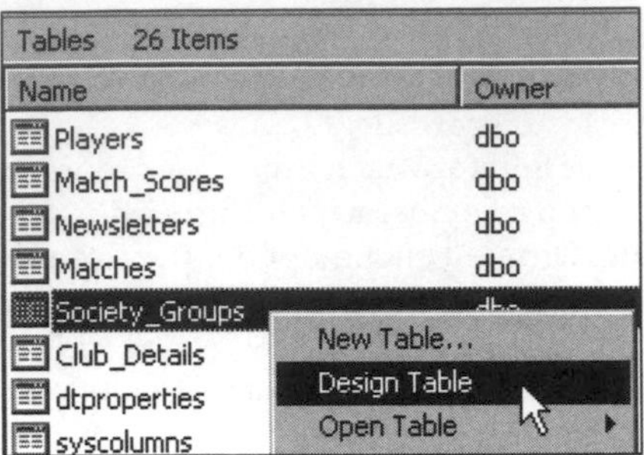

2. This then opens up the Society_Groups table within SQL Server. Ensure that the Society_Group_Id column is selected, as this will be the column on which we define our primary key. Our key will only contain this column, but if you wanted to define your primary key on more than one column, you would press the *Ctrl* key while clicking on the other desired columns.

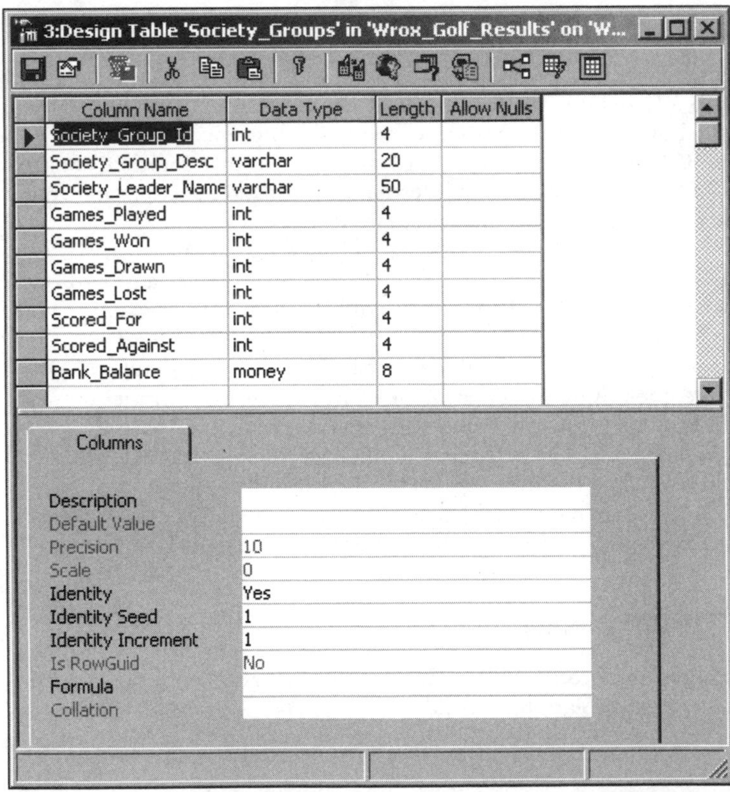

3. A right-click on the selected Society_Group_Id field will bring up the pop-up menu shown next. Notice that the first option is to Set Primary Key. Select this and click on it.

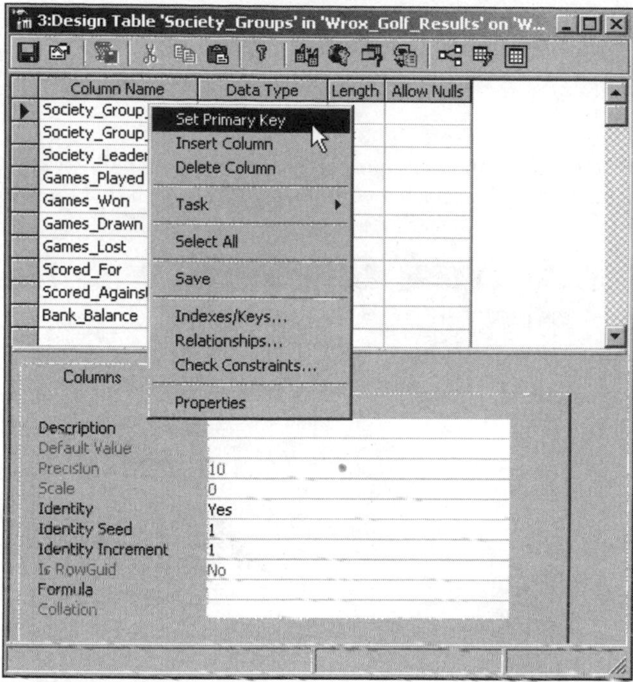

4. This will then set a yellow coloured key against the column or columns making up the primary key. However, this is not all that goes on in the background, as you will see.

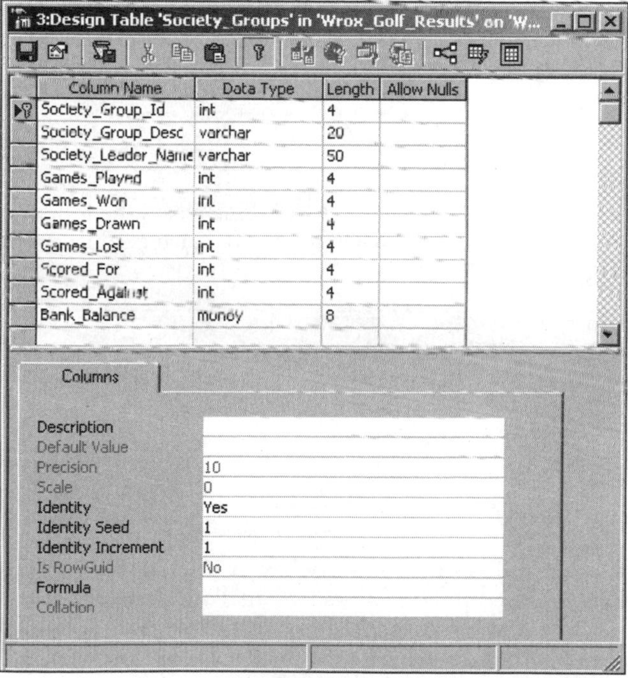

5. Clicking on the **Manage Indexes** icon:

brings up the **Indexes/Keys** tab on the table properties screen. Notice that a key definition has been created for you, with a name and the selected column, informing you that the index is **Unique** and **Clustered**.

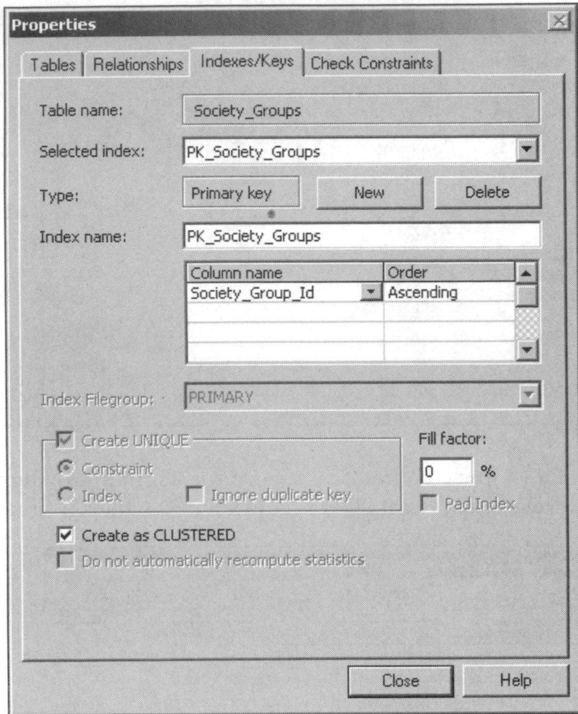

6. Once done in the screen above, click **Close**, which closes the indexes dialog. Saving the table will prompt you as to whether you want to save the changes incorporated. Click **Yes** to save your changes.

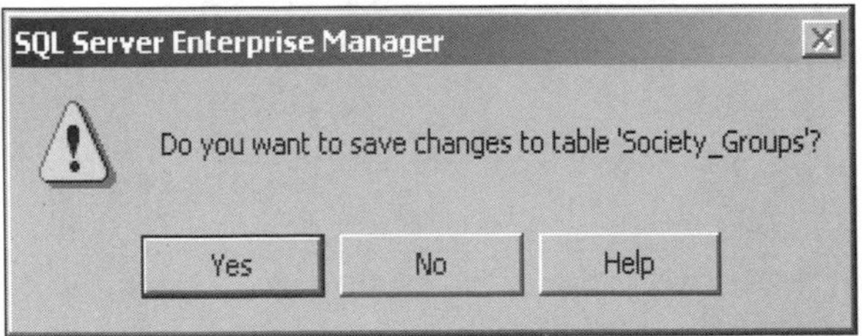

That's all there is to creating and setting a primary key. A primary key has now been set up on the `Society_Groups` table. In this instance, any record added to this table will ensure that the data will be kept in `Society_Group_Id` ascending order, and it is impossible to insert a duplicate row of data. This key can then be used to link to other tables within the database at a later stage, which will be demonstrated in the next chapter on Relationships.

Now we look at using a wizard in SQL Server to help build an index.

Creating an Index – Using a Wizard

The next index we require will give the database the ability to search for a player by their surname. In Chapter 13, where we cover retrieving data from SQL Server, we will look at how to search for a name when you only know part of that name. In the meantime, to allow this to happen, an index is required on a player's last name. In the following section, an index will be created on this column to allow this sort of search to take place.

Try It Out – Creating an Index using a Wizard

1. Ensure that SQL Server Enterprise Manager is running. It is not necessary to be sited on Wrox_Golf_Results database, just ensure that you are successfully connected.

2. Either select Wizards from the Tools menu, or press the wizards toolbar option. This then brings up the Wizards dialog. Expand the Database node and select the Create Index Wizard, then click OK. This starts the index wizard that steps you through the building of an index.

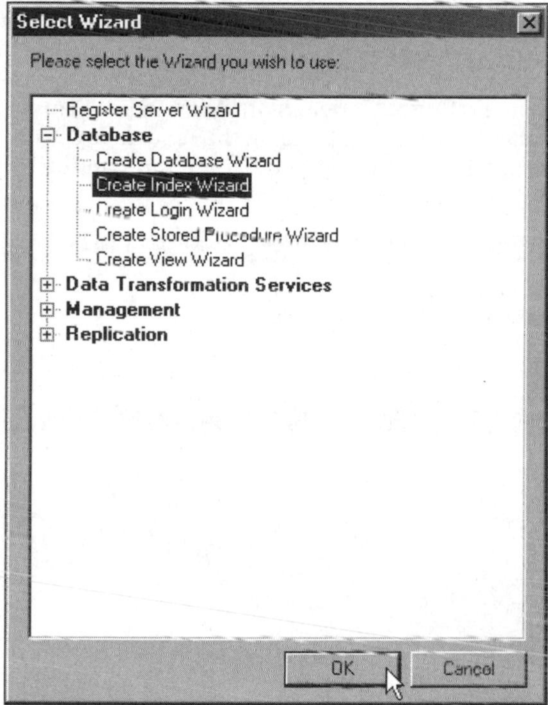

3. The first screen is just the wizard's introductory screen. Click Next to move to the screen shown overleaf, from which you can select the database that the index is for, and the table that the specific index will be placed in. Ensure that Wrox_Golf_Results is the selected database, and that Players is the chosen table. Once completed, click Next.

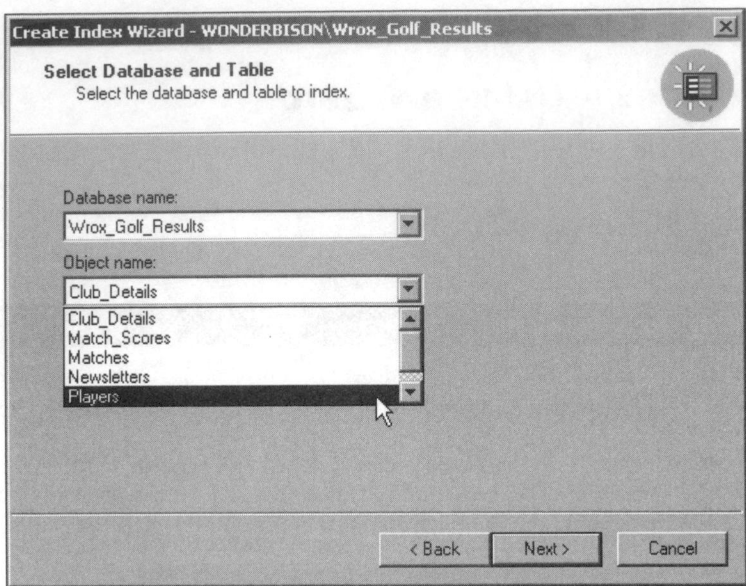

4. The indexes that have been created so far on the table are now listed for you to see, in a summary fashion on the Current Index Information screen. This is a handy little reminder that can save you making the mistake of building the same index twice! Unlike the other methods of creating an index, it is actually a great deal easier to find such information in this way. Once you have finished, click Next.

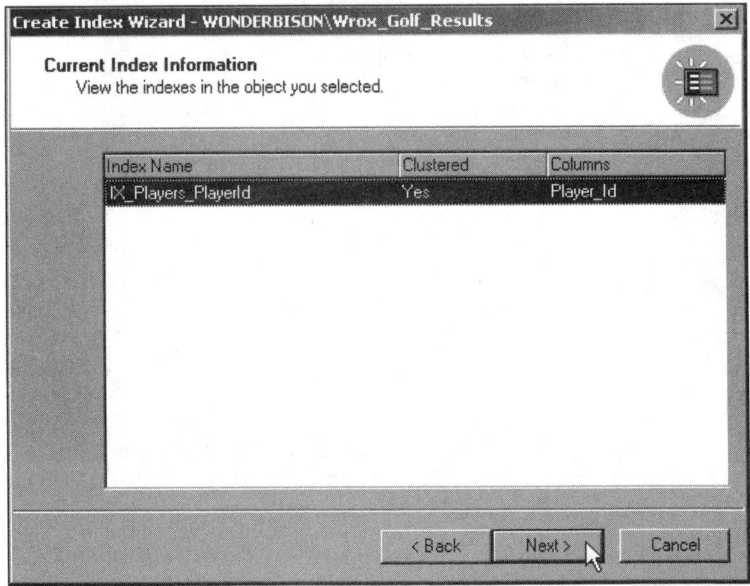

5. The next dialog is the most important in this wizard; it is on this screen that we select the columns that will make up our index. Notice that the last two columns have a big red cross against them: this indicates that they cannot be included in the index due to their data types.

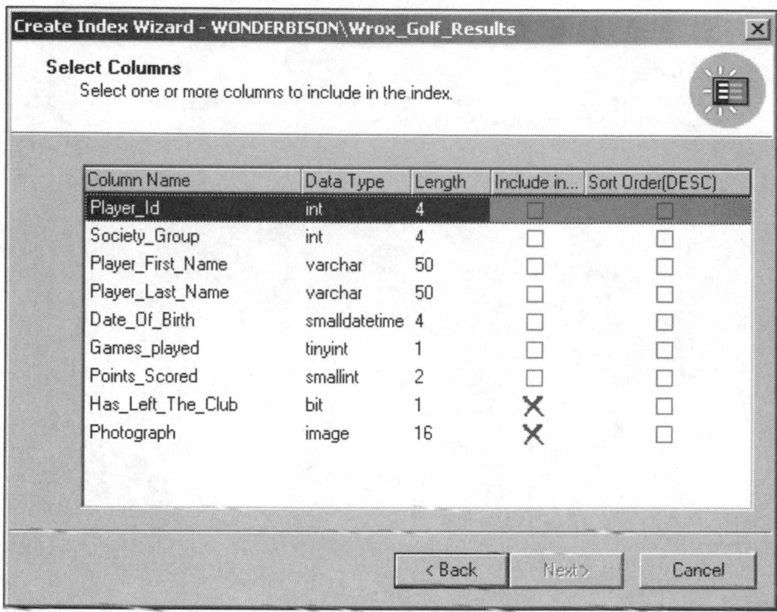

6. For the moment, as we discussed at the top of this section, the index will be based around the player's last name. So, select Player_Last_Name by clicking in its Include in... column, then click Next.

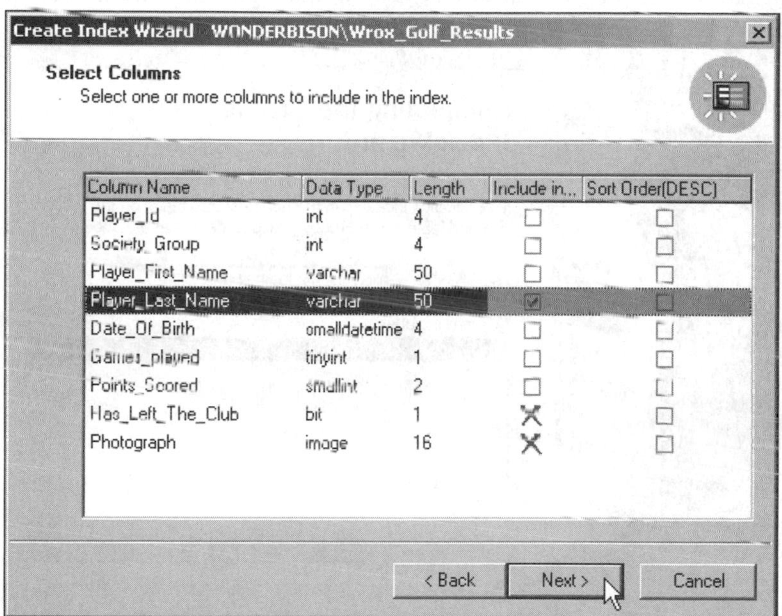

7. On the next page, all the options will be left as they are. There is no guarantee that Player_Last_Name will always be unique, so that option cannot be selected, and Fill Factor is not needed for this example, so we will skip that as well. Click Next.

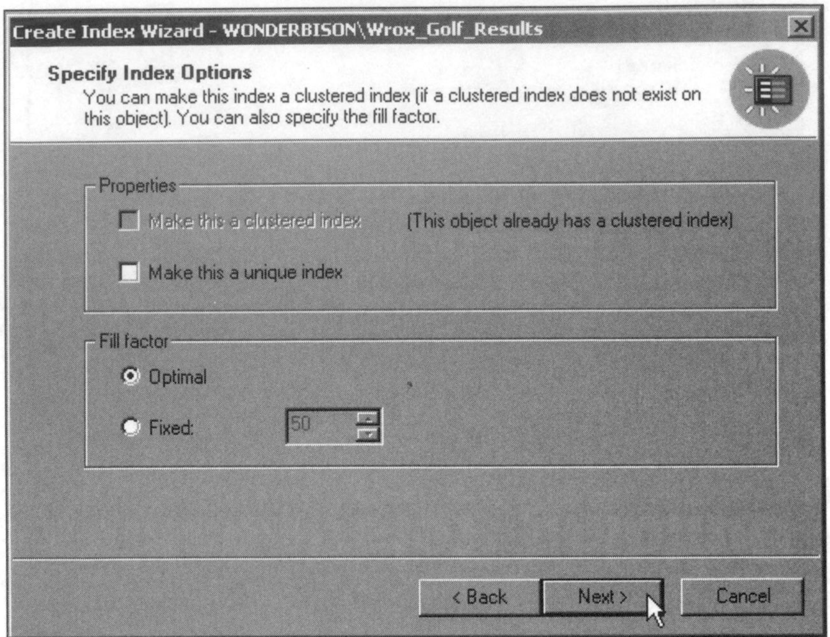

8. The next dialog is the last screen of any real note in this wizard, and this is where the index is given its name, IX_Players_Last_Name. As mentioned before, try to employ a meaningful naming convention for your indexes; here we will be using the convention of IX_table_column.

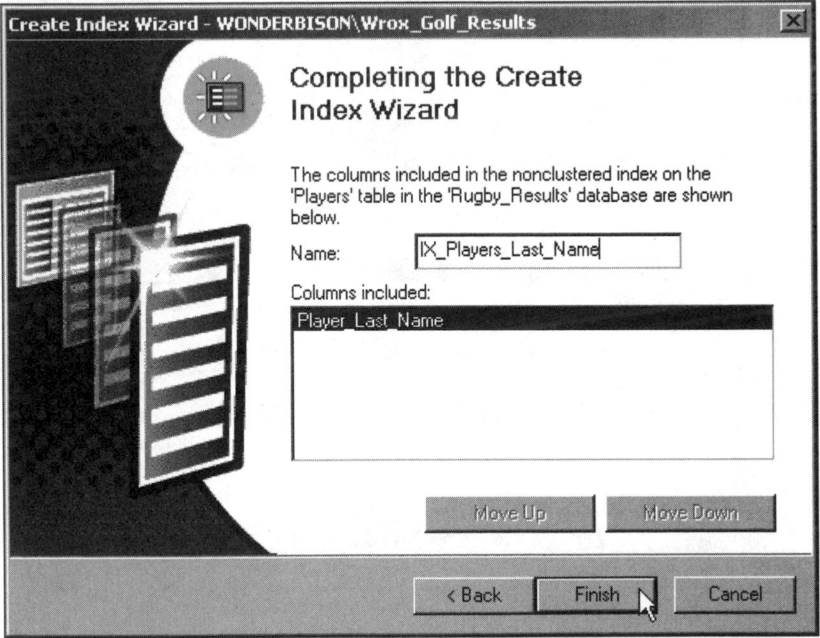

9. The index has now been created and placed in to the Players table. Click OK, which ends the wizard.

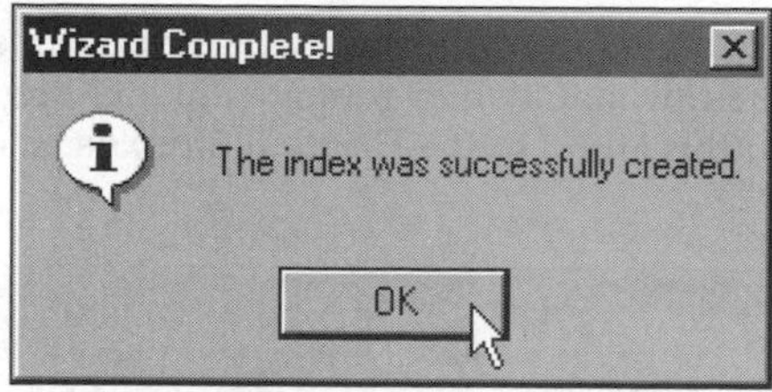

That's it, the index has been created and is ready for use.

Creating an Index – Tasks

Now we will change tables and create an index on the `Matches` table. There are three indexes to be created on this table, although only one is covered in this chapter. The other two indexes will be created in the next chapter, when demonstrating building relationships between tables and will show why indexes are important in this process.

The index that we are covering will use two columns, which will be the `Society_Group_Id` and the `Date_Played`. This is so that a score can be found on a specific date for a particular Society Group. Also, this index will allow us to perform a search of games for a society, starting from a specific date and going forward, or starting with the latest games and working back match by match. This section will build this index from Enterprise Manager from the All Tasks option.

The All Tasks option of building an index is probably the best way of creating an index, especially when starting out. It seems that this option has all the good bits from all the other methods of creating an index. First of all, it displays any indexes that have already been created for that table. This will help in deciding the name of the index and which columns to place into the index as well.

Try It Out – Using the All Tasks Option

1. In SQL Server Enterprise Manager, ensure that you have navigated to the `Wrox_Golf_Results` database.

2. Find the Matches table, right-click, select All Tasks, and then Manage Indexes...

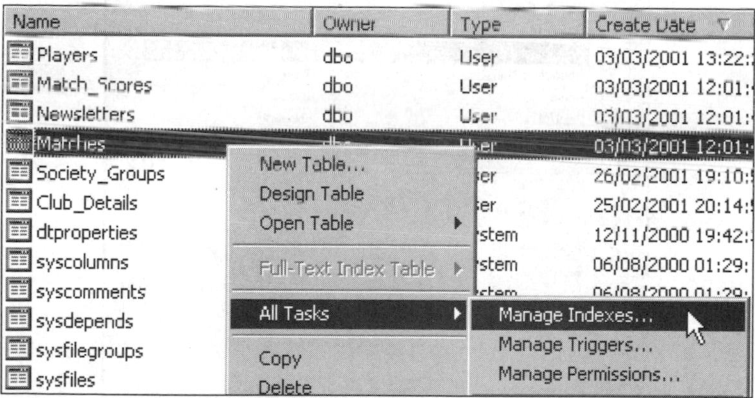

3. This brings up the main dialog to this section where you can see any indexes already created, and also create new ones, or maintain or remove any existing ones selected. We haven't yet created any indexes on this table, so the **Existing Indexes:** section is empty. To create a new index, click on **New...**

4. By clicking on the **New** button, a dialog is displayed that allows the selection of the columns to be placed into an index. You can see that the two columns discussed at the top of this section are shown as selected. Also this will be the **Clustered index** for this table, so ensure that this option is selected under **Index options**. Finally, don't forget to create an **Index Name:** at the top of the dialog.

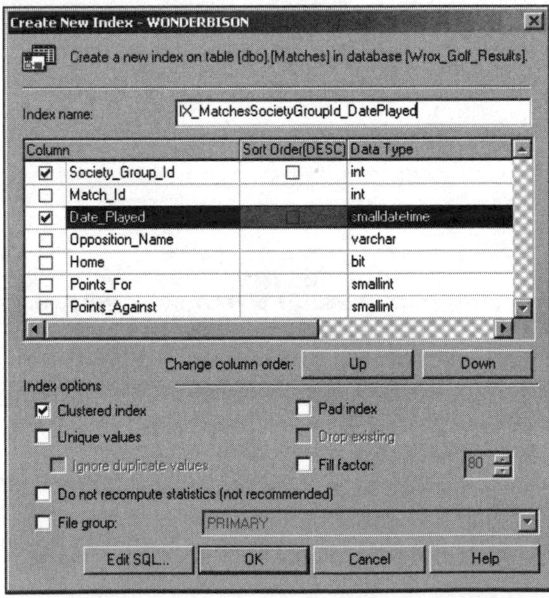

5. There is a button down at the bottom of the dialog titled **Edit SQL**... This will allow us to inspect the SQL statements that our actions have generated. Let's take a quick look at this, although, at the moment, we won't be touching the actual code listed: click on **Edit SQL**... The SQL shown may confuse you at the moment, but shortly we will explore it in more detail, so that you could write your own SQL, or modify what is here, if you so desire. As you can see, this is not the best editor as the code has moved off the screen. For the moment, just click **Cancel**. This will take you back to the screen shown above, so click **OK** so that we can proceed.

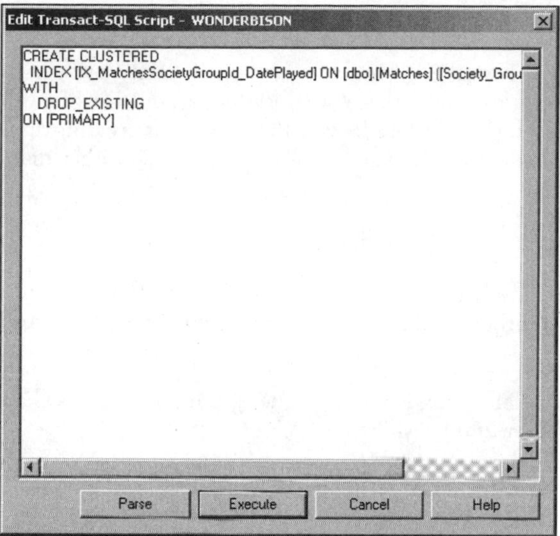

6. Clicking **OK** at the index setup screen, brings you back to the first dialog in this section, which shows the indexes to manage. The index just created is now displayed; if you have made any mistakes just click **Edit**... to get back to it. If you have finished, then click **Close**.

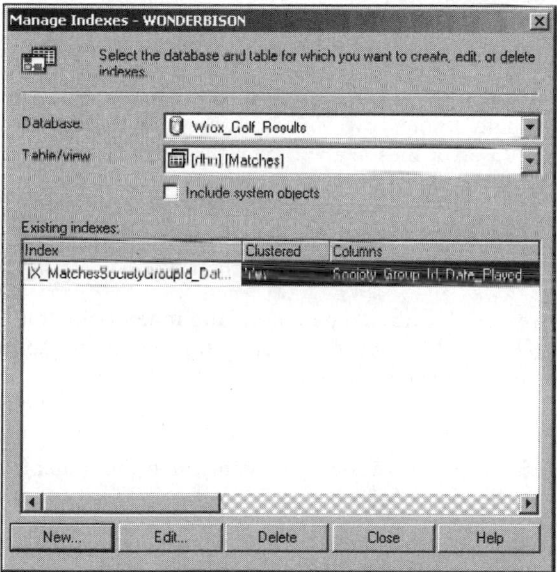

You have now just created another index in your ever-expanding SQL Server solution. Although this solution has the same result as what has been covered, there are one or two areas that it would be useful to cover further.

All Tasks provides all the necessary options to build your index. The only real options that you will be interested in are Clustered index and Unique values.

Clicking the Edit SQL... button exposes the actual SQL command that Enterprise Manager will run to create the index. Don't worry too much about the syntax, as in the very next section the syntax will be examined in detail.

That just about finishes this example. Again, you can see that Enterprise Manager has made it as simple as it can be to build an index graphically; therefore, building an index using this method should be relatively straightforward. As promised though, let's look at the syntax for creating an index as it has been displayed above; the next sections all deal with creating indexes using code rather than a graphical front end.

The CREATE INDEX Syntax

Creating an index is a lot easier than creating a table. This section will only cover indexes on tables, although there is a special object within SQL Server called a **view** that can also be indexed. Views are covered in Chapter 16.

The full syntax for creating an index is not listed here, but a reduced version that will be sufficient while you are learning SQL Server 2000 is shown:

```
CREATE [UNIQUE] [CLUSTERED|NONCLUSTERED]
INDEX index_name
ON table (column [ASC|DESC] [ ,...n ] )
[WITH {IGNORE_DUP_KEY|DROP_EXISTING|SORT_IN_TEMPDB}]
[ON filegroup ]
```

As you can see, there is not a great deal to learn about the syntax for building an index. However, let's take you through each point one by one.

- `CREATE` – Required. Keyword to inform SQL Server that you will be building a new object
- `UNIQUE` – Optional. If used, it will inform SQL Server that the columns listed in the index will bring back a single unique row. This is enforced by SQL Server when attempting to insert a duplicate row, as an error message will be returned.
- `CLUSTERED` or `NONCLUSTERED` – Optional. If neither `CLUSTERED` or `NONCLUSTERED` are explicitly listed, the index is created as `NONCLUSTERED`.
- `INDEX` – Required. This informs SQL Server that the new object will be an index.
- `index_name` – Required. This is the name of the index being built. This name must be unique for the table, and it is advisable to keep this name unique for the database, using the naming method we discussed earlier of `IX_table_column`.
- ON – Required.
- `table` – Required. The name of the table with which the index is associated. Only one table can be named.
- `column`– Required. The name of the column(s) in the table that we wish to include in the index. This is a comma-separated list.

- ASC – Optional, default. If neither ASC nor DESC is mentioned then ASC is assumed. ASC informs SQL Server that it should store the column named in ascending sequence.
- DESC – Optional. Informs SQL Server that the column is to be stored in descending order.
- WITH – Optional. It is, however, required if any of the following options have to be used:
  - IGNORE_DUP_KEY – only available when the index is defined as UNIQUE. If this option has not been used earlier, then this option is not available to you. More on this in a moment.
  - DROP_EXISTING – used if there is an existing index of the same name within the database. This will then drop the index before re-creating it. This is useful for performance if you are not actually changing any columns within the index. More on this in a moment.
  - SORT_IN_TEMPDB – when building an index where there is already data within the table, it may be advisable, if the table is a large table, to get the data sorted for the index within the temporary database, tempdb, as mentioned in Chapter 5. Use this option if you have a large table, or if tempdb is on a different hard disk from your database. This may speed up the building of the index as SQL Server can simultaneously read from the disk device where the table is located and write to the disk device where tempdb is located.
- ON – Optional. However, it is required if you are going to specify a filegroup. This is not required if you wish the index to be built on the PRIMARY filegroup.
- filegroup – the name of the file group on which the index should be stored. At the moment there is only one file group set up, which was covered when installing SQL Server. That filegroup is PRIMARY. PRIMARY is a reserved word and is required to be surrounded by square brackets, [ ], if used.

There are two options needing further clarification.

IGNORE_DUP_KEY

If you have an index defined as UNIQUE, then no matter how hard you try, it is impossible to add a new row whose values in the index columns match the values of any current row. However, there are two actions that can be performed depending on this setting within an index.

When performing multi-row inserts, if the IGNORE_DUP_KEY option is specified, then no error is generated within SQL Server if some of the rows being inserted violate the unique index, only a warning message. The rows that violated the Unique index are not inserted; however, all other rows are inserted successfully.

When performing multi-row inserts, if the IGNORE_DUP_KEY option is omitted, then an error message is generated within SQL Server if some of the rows violate the unique index. The batch is rolled back and no rows are inserted into the table.

There is a system variable called @@ERROR (discussed in more detail in Chapter 18) that can be tested after every SQL Server action to see if there has been an error in any item of work. If there has been an error, some sort of error handling within the batch will usually be performed. If you have IGNORE_DUP_KEY then no error will be produced when there is an attempt to insert a duplicate row, and so the batch will run as if everything has been inserted. So, take care! It may look as if everything has worked, but in fact, some rows were not inserted.

DROP_EXISTING

With data being inserted and modified, there will be times when an index bloats to a less than ideal state. This is a bit like an Access database that needs to be compacted. The same is true for indexes within SQL Server and you will get indexes that need to be compacted. Compacting the index, will speed up performance, as well as reclaim disk space by removing fragmentation of the index. Therefore, to complete a compaction of the index, you re-create an index without actually modifying the columns, or in fact starting from scratch and having to build the whole index from the start visiting every row within the table.

The `DROP_EXISTING` clause provides enhanced performance when rebuilding a clustered index over the `DROP INDEX`, `CREATE INDEX` method. Non-clustered indexes are rebuilt every time the clustered index for a table is rebuilt. So, if you drop a clustered index, then recreate it, the existing non-clustered indexes are rebuilt twice: once from the drop and once for the creation.

`DROP_EXISTING` also allows an existing index to be rebuilt without explicitly dropping and recreating the index. This is particularly useful for rebuilding primary key indexes. As other tables may reference a primary key, it may have been necessary to drop all foreign keys in these other tables prior to dropping the primary key. By specifying the `DROP_EXISTING` clause SQL Server will rebuild the index without affecting the primary key constraint.

Creating an Index in Query Analyzer – Template

Not surprisingly, there is a template within Query Analyzer that can be used as a basis for the creation of an index. This will be demonstrated first, before building an index natively in Query Analyzer, as this creates the basis of the SQL syntax for the creation of the index.

However, this example will demonstrate when a template may not be as useful as other methods as there is more to take out of the template than to put in.

Try It Out – Using a Query Analyzer Template to Build an Index

1. Ensure that SQL Server Query Analyzer is running and that you are logged in with an account that has the authority to update databases.

2. At the bottom of the Object Browser, you will see two tabs. Click on the Templates tab

3. This brings up the Templates that have been created and are found within SQL Server. The template that will be used here is a template for creating indexes, so expand the Create Index node. Two templates are available by default from Query Analyzer. The Create Index Basic template contains the minimum syntax required by SQL Server to create an index: you simply enter an index name, a table name, and column names. The Create Index Full Syntax template contains all the various syntax options available when creating an index. This is what we want to look at, so double-click on the Create Index Full Syntax option.

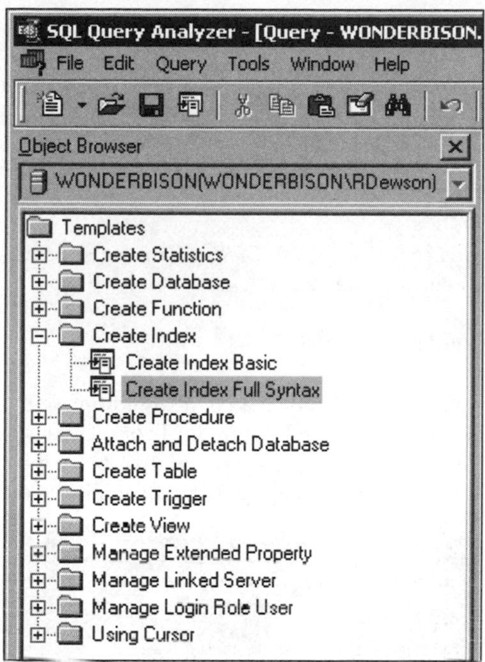

4. Once you have double-clicked the option, you will see the full syntax for creating an index in a new Query pane within Query Analyzer. There is a lot in here that is not used for this example, and may not be used by you for a while, but it is useful to see what needs to be entered for an index.

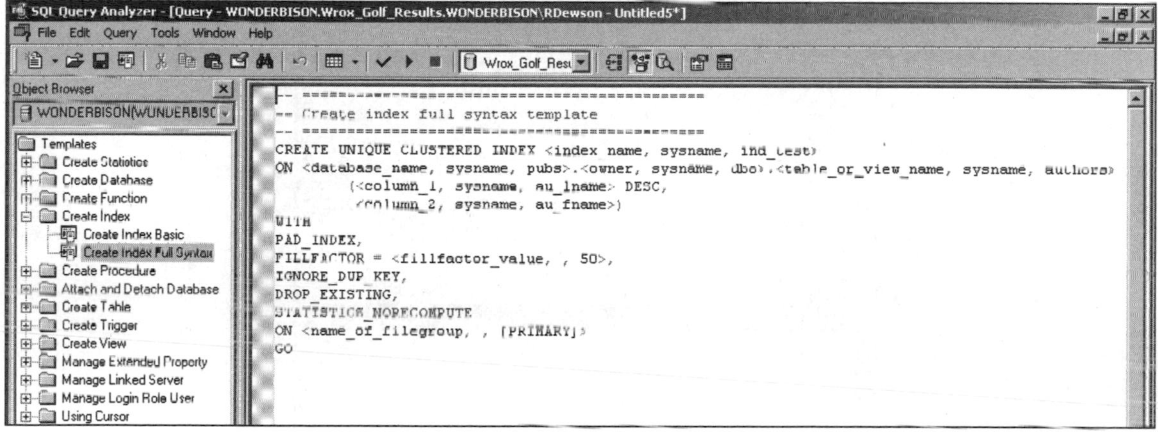

5. Alter the above template, either by physically altering the code, or by using the **Replace Template Parameters** option from the **Edit** menu, demonstrated in the previous chapter, so that the template now reads like the code overleaf. As you can see, a great deal of the template has been removed.

```
-- =============================================
-- Create index full syntax template
-- =============================================
CREATE UNIQUE CLUSTERED INDEX IX_Newsletters_AgeGroup_Published
  ON Newsletters
  ([Society_Group_Id], [Date_Published] DESC )
GO
```

6. Execute the above code by pressing *F5*, *CTRL+E*, or the execute toolbar button. You should then see the following success message:

```
The command(s) completed successfully.
```

7. Now that the index has seemingly been created, it would be useful to check that the index has actually been created and is as expected. From the Tools menu, select Manage Indexes. If you find that the Manage Indexes option is grayed out, then place the cursor in the Results pane where you saw the successful completion message and try it again. The option will then be available.

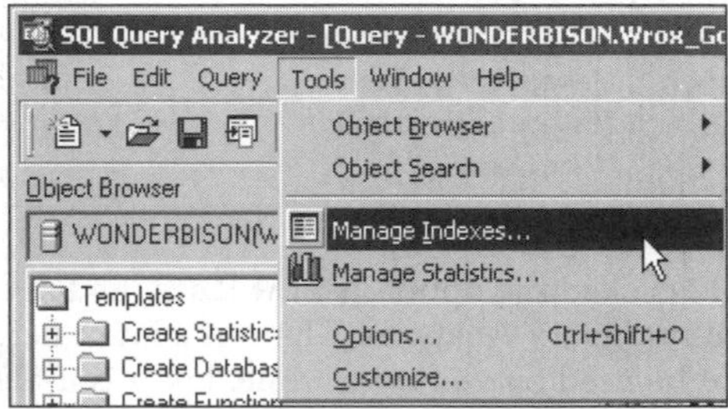

8. This then brings up the Manage Indexes dialog that is used to build or check on indexes within a database. Select the Newsletters table.

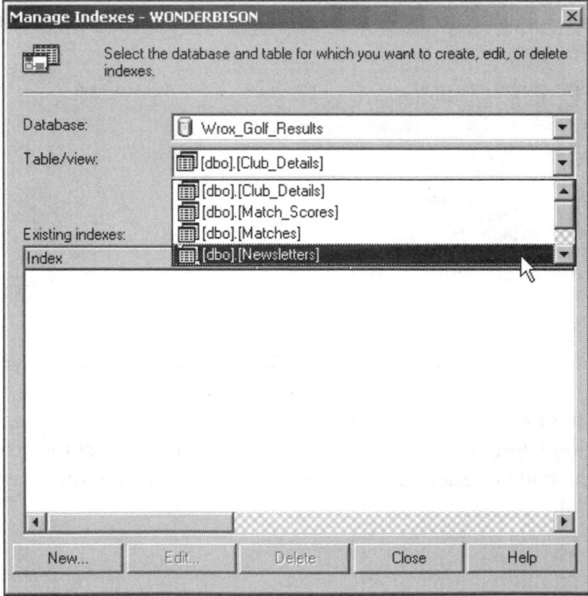

9. This will then bring up the index that has just been created. Click on the **Edit** button to reveal more details about the index.

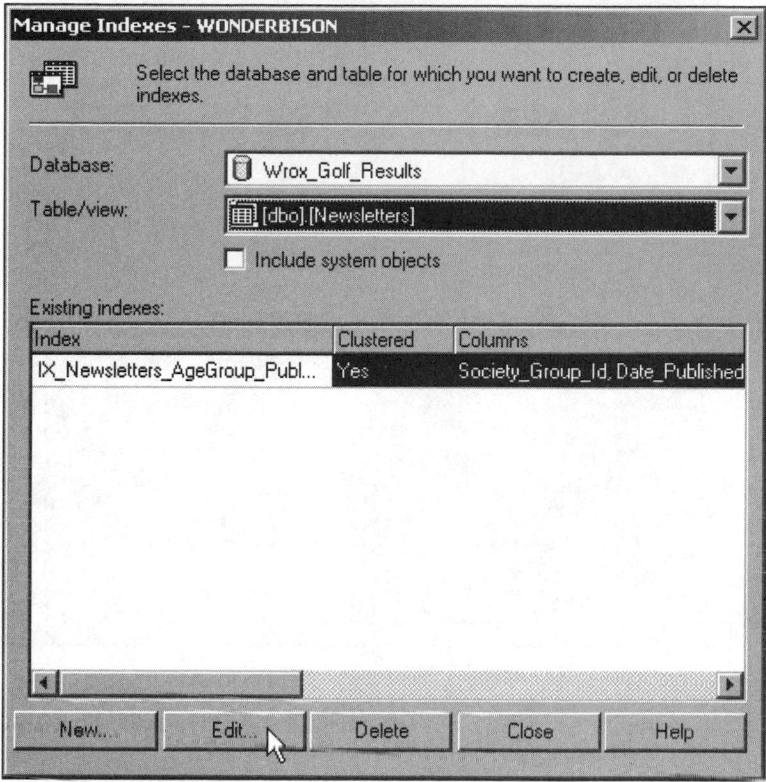

10. As you can see overleaf, there are two columns that have been selected – that is, have a tick against them – and the **Date_Published** column has been selected so that it will be sorted in descending order. Let's check to see if the SQL stored in SQL Server resembles the SQL that was created earlier. Click on the **Edit SQL...** button.

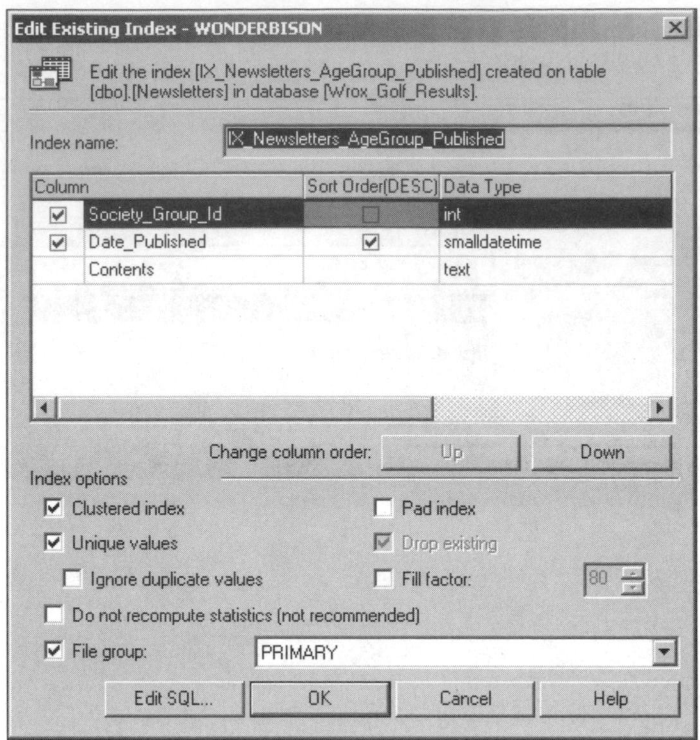

11. The SQL that is displayed looks as follows:

```
CREATE UNIQUE CLUSTERED
  INDEX [IX_Newsletters_AgeGroup_Published] ON [dbo].[Newsletters]
      ([Society_Group_Id], [Date_Published]  desc )
  WITH
    DROP_EXISTING
  ON [PRIMARY]
```

That's it! Another index created.

Creating an Index – Query Analyzer – SQL Code

In the following section, we will create two separate indexes for a single table within the Query Analyzer tool. The table will be the `Matches_Played` table.

Try It Out – Creating an Index with Query Analyzer

Using Query Analyzer within a Query pane to create an index doesn't differ much, if at all, from using a template as a basis.

1. Enter the following code into an empty Query pane of Query Analyzer:

```
USE Wrox_Golf_Results
CREATE CLUSTERED INDEX
   IX_Match_Scores_InScoreOrder
   ON Match_Scores (Match_Id, Score_Time)
   ON [PRIMARY]
GO
CREATE UNIQUE INDEX
   IX_Match_Scores_PlayersScoresInOrder
   ON Match_Scores (Player_Id, Match_Id, Score_Time)
   ON [PRIMARY]
GO
```

2. Execute the above code by pressing *F5*, *CTRL+E*, or the execute toolbar button. You should then see the following success message:

```
The command(s) completed successfully.
```

There are two different indexes created in this example; the first one is a clustered index, so that any golf matches inserted into the `Match_Scores` table are stored in match order when the score is entered. The other cannot be a clustered index as the first index already has that privilege, so it has to be a non-clustered index. However, it is still possible to make this index unique. It is impossible for a player to play two golf matches at once, and, even if it wasn't, it would be impossible to enter two scores at the same time. Therefore, it is possible to inform SQL Server that the second index will create unique values. This is crucial, as it will help SQL Server find the right record straightaway.

What is interesting though about this example is that two indexes are being created at once, whereas in the previous examples only one index was created at one time. Notice the keyword `GO` between the two `CREATE` statements creating the index; each index creation has to be completed on its own without any other SQL statements included. Such a grouping of SQL statements is known as a **batch**, with the end of a batch indicated by the `GO` statement. Therefore, if you need to create more than one index, but would prefer to build them at the same time, then this may be the solution you need.

An area we have not yet covered is what happens if you try to create an index twice using the same index name. The indexes above have already been created, but if you run the query again, SQL Server will produce error messages informing you that the index already exists. You should see messages like the following:

```
Server: Msg 1913, Level 16, State 1, Line 2
There is already an index on table 'Match_Scores' named 'IX_Match_Scores_InScoreOrder'.
Server: Msg 1913, Level 16, State 1, Line 1
There is already an index on table 'Match_Scores' named
'IX_Match_Scores_PlayersScoresInOrder'.
```

Even if you altered the contents of the index and included different columns, but still used the same name, it would not be possible to create another index with the same name as an existing one.

Once again there are a couple of new areas to be covered in this section, but this now completes the information needed to be able to create the most common indexes. Indexes need a lot less coding than tables and can be created quickly and easily. However, if you are adding a new index to an existing table that has a substantial amount of information, adding this new index could take a few minutes to complete, depending on the scenario. Take care when doing this, as your table will be locked from updates while the index creation is taking place. So, try to build indexes during scheduled down times.

Dropping an Index

Dropping an index is simply a case of executing the DROP INDEX statement followed by the table name and the index name.

If the index is used by a primary key or unique constraint you cannot drop the index directly: in this case you must use the DROP CONSTRAINT command. The removal of this constraint will also remove the index from the table.

Try It Out – Dropping an Index in Query Analyzer

If we wish to drop the indexes we created in the last section all we need to do is execute the following code:

```
USE Wrox_Golf_Results
DROP INDEX MatchScores.IX_Match_Scores_InScoreOrder
GO
DROP INDEX MatchScores.IX_Match_Scores_PlayersScoresInOrder
GO
```

But what do you have to do to alter an index?

Altering an Index in Query Analyzer

Unlike a table, it is not possible to use an ALTER command to change the columns contained in an index. To do this, you first have to DROP the index, and then re-CREATE it. The DROP command will physically remove the index from the table; therefore you should ensure that you know what the contents of the index are before dropping the index, if you want to re-create a similar index. In Enterprise Manager you can add and remove columns from an index's definition without dropping and recreating the index, as this is all done for you behind the scenes.

This next section will demonstrate the code needed to remove an index and then re-create it.

Try It Out – Altering an Index in Query Analyzer

1. Using the basis of the query built in the previous example, alter the code so that it looks like that below:

```
USE Wrox_Golf_Results
DROP INDEX Match_Scores.IX_Match_Scores_InScoreOrder
GO
CREATE CLUSTERED INDEX
   IX_Match_Scores_InScoreOrder
   ON Match_Scores (Match_Id, Score_Time)
   ON [PRIMARY]
GO
```

```
DROP INDEX Match_Scores.IX_Match_Scores_PlayersScoresInOrder
GO
CREATE UNIQUE INDEX
   IX_Match_Scores_PlayersScoresInOrder
   ON Match_Scores (Player_Id, Match_Id, Score_Time)
   ON [PRIMARY]
GO
```

2. Now execute the code using your chosen method and you should see the following results:

```
The command(s) completed successfully.
```

The only code change to discuss is the DROP command. Like the CREATE INDEX command, a DROP command has to be within its own batch and no other SQL commands can be part of that batch; hence, at the end of the DROP INDEX command, there is a GO statement.

When dropping an index, it is necessary to prefix the name of the index with the table that the index is associated with. This allows SQL Server to avoid any instances of two indexes with the same name on different tables. In a professional environment, such name problems should not arise; however, SQL Server can never be sure and so it covers itself by insisting on the table prefix.

We could also recreate the indexes by using the DROP_EXISTING clause of the CREATE INDEX command we described earlier. The code would look like the following:

```
USE Wrox_Golf_Results
CREATE CLUSTERED INDEX
   IX_Match_Scores_InScoreOrder
   ON Match_Scores (Match_Id, Score_Time)
WITH DROP_EXISTING
   ON [PRIMARY]
GO

CREATE UNIQUE INDEX
   IX_Match_Scores_PlayersScoresInOrder
   ON Match_Scores (Player_Id, Match_Id, Score_Time)
WITH DROP_EXISTING
   ON [PRIMARY]
GO
```

Take care when building indexes. It is possible to use the same columns in the same order, thus creating the same index twice, but under two different index names. This is a pure waste of time and it will place unnecessary overhead on SQL Server.

Summary

So, another major building block in creating a SQL Server solution has been covered. The last few chapters have covered how to store the data, and in this chapter we have learned about indexes and how they are used to quickly and efficiently retrieve the data stored in the table.

There are many different types of index, and choosing the right one at the right time to complete the right job is quite an art. This chapter has taken you through the steps to decide which columns will make an efficient index, and then build those columns in the right type of index to make the most of the information.

One of the most efficient methods of retrieving data is to use a covering index, but do take care and heed the warnings of not putting too many columns in the index just for the sake of it.

By this point you should now be comfortable with building an index, and, as you have seen, it is possible to build a table and an index at the same time. However, you should also feel confident in building an index separately from building a table, and also building an index within code.

In the next chapter you will also see how indexes can be used to build relationships and to join tables together logically to enforce data integrity and also learn how data should be stored logically.

Building Relationships

Introduction

Like people, databases can be temperamental creatures and need a bit of loving and caring, and good relationships are the basis of this sustenance. At the moment, our tables could just be seen as single, unrelated items. Of course, there are columns that have the same name in different tables, however, there are no specifics tying them together. This is where defining relationships between the tables is crucial to the glue that binds the tables together. Binding the tables together will ensure that changes in one table do not cause data in another table to become invalid.

This section of the book looks at building relationships between tables, and how relationships enforce checks on the data to ensure that the data remains in a valid state. This is referred to as **Referential Integrity** (also known as R.I.), and is crucial to maintaining data integrity, now, and always.

By implementing relationships between tables within SQL Server, and using referential integrity as the basis of any relationships, we are removing the burden of keeping the data valid from any front-end system, perhaps one written in Visual Basic, to the back-end, SQL Server system. By placing the referential integrity within the database, we are empowering SQL Server with the ability to check any data entered that could affect a key or a relationship between two tables, and then act on any problems or potential problems found. Installing referential integrity is a quick and straightforward process, as this chapter will demonstrate.

This chapter will cover:

- The definition of a relationship
- Referential Integrity, what it is, and how it works
- The different types of relationship, and when they would be found
- How a foreign key is crucial to building relationships
- Building a relationship correctly, and how it is possible to make mistakes when building relationships
- How to find out which objects depend on information in others

Where better to start but with the definition of a relationship, the basis of this chapter...

What is a Relationship?

A relationship in a SQL Server database is a logical link between two tables. It is impossible to have a physical link, although, as you will see later, a physical line is drawn between two tables. To have a physical link would mean the actual data linking the two tables would only be stored once in a central location, and that information within the keys linking the tables would be stored more than once, which is just not the case. When defining a logical relationship, we are informing SQL Server that we will be linking a primary key from the master table, to a foreign key in another table. So already there is a need for two keys to be created, one on each table. From the last chapter you should know what a primary and foreign key are, as they were described quite early on.

Such a relationship could be drawn between one record in the `Matches` table, and none, one, or many records within the `Match_Scores` table. The primary key of `Match_Id` within the `Matches` table must relate to a key on the `Match_Scores` table.

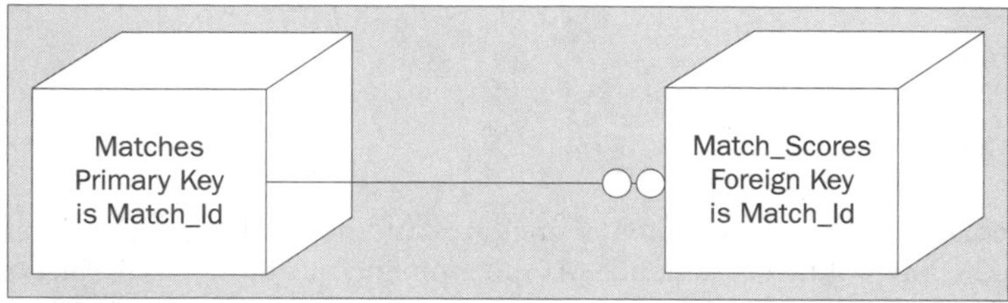

In the following sections you will see more specific details about relationships and why they exist. First of all though, let's start with a look at how relationships work...

What is Referential Integrity?

A relationship can be used to enforce data integrity. In other words, if we are expecting data in one table because there is data in another, we can place a relationship between these two tables to ensure that no SQL command breaks this rule. However, don't confuse this with other processes that are associated with maintaining data integrity, such as placing checks or default values on columns to ensure that values for a specific column are valid. Referential integrity revolves around the idea that there are two tables in the database that contain the same information, and referential integrity requires that the duplicated data elements are kept consistent. For example, if we have a primary key on one table, and a foreign key in another table that has exactly matching data, then it is important that both pieces of data either both change together or don't ever change at all. Relationships are not the only way the referential integrity can be enforced, as you can use triggers to ensure that data remains valid, as will be demonstrated in Chapter 20.

To give an example, a banking system might include `customer` and `customer transactions` tables. It is not possible to record customer transactions without a customer record. As a result, we would have to use referential integrity to enforce data integrity between these two tables, so that a customer record could not be removed from the database while there are customer transaction records for that customer. Similarly, this same rule should allow the removal of a customer record when there are no customer transaction records.

Another result of enforcing this referential integrity is that it would not be possible for a customer transaction to be entered using a customer reference number that did not exist within the `customer` table. Instead, to enter a customer transaction in this situation, we would first have to create the customer record, and then go about carrying out the transaction. Finally, if we had a customer record and related customer transaction records, we could not alter the customer reference number in the customer record without first altering the customer transaction records, and checking that the reference that we are altering the customer transaction records to, already exists.

So, there are quite a few rules to follow if we want to maintain the integrity of our data. If we so desired, we could use referential integrity to enforce this. However, there is a flip side to all of this, which we need to be aware of, and that is that we can keep data integrity within a system, and not use referential integrity to do this. Instead, we could create **stored procedures** or **triggers**, which are covered in Chapters 17, 18, and 20, or leave it up to an application to ensure that the data is kept valid. This is a perfectly suitable solution, but it does leave our system open to instances where data integrity is not kept, due to holes within the design of the system, or perhaps because a developer does not have the correct processing sequence to ensure that all data is always valid. That said, having the data integrity checks completed in an application, does lead to less traffic flow over the network as all the validation is done in the front end.

There is one more point about referential integrity; if you want to maintain referential integrity by creating a relationship between two tables, then these two tables must be in the same database. It is not possible to have referential integrity over two databases. This is one area that I am hoping that future versions of SQL Server will address, as there are many valid circumstances when this would be useful. For example, when completing data archiving, you would want to ensure that what you are archiving remains valid during the archiving process

Types of Relationships

There are three main types of relationship that can exist in a database, and they are:

- **One-to-One**
- **One-to-Many**
- **Many-to-Many**

We'll be taking a look at each of these different types so that when it comes to creating a relationship, you know which one to create, when, and why. The first relationship that we will look at is the one-to-one relationship. This is perhaps the easiest type of relationship to understand, although it is one of the least used.

One-to-One

This type of relationship is very uncommon within a working database. Typically, there is no real reason for only one record in one table to match just one record in another. This scenario would only really exist, for example, if we were splitting a very large table into two, separate tables. To illustrate this, imagine that we had a bank database, in which there is a table that holds PIN numbers for electronic cards, keeping them completely separate from the remainder of the customer records. In most cases there would be one PIN number record to one customer record, but there may be exceptions, for instance, a high deposit account may not carry a card, and therefore there would be no associated PIN number record.

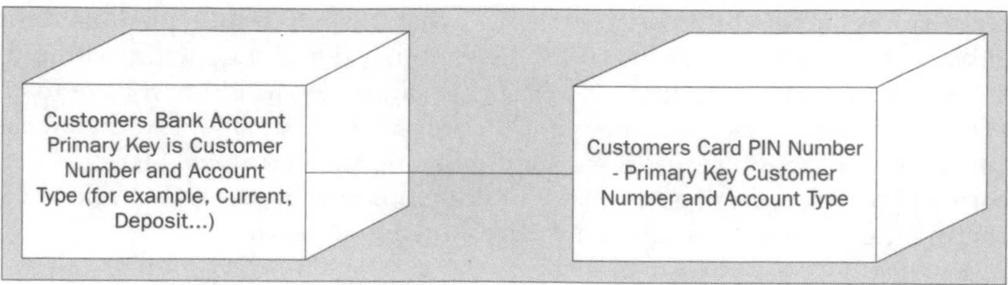

The next two types of relationship are far more common...

One-to-Many

Perhaps the most common relationship that will be found in a database is that found in the one-to-many scenario. This is where there is one master record linked with zero, one, or more records in a child table. Thinking back to our earlier banking example discussion, we had a customer master record along with any number of associated transaction records. The number of these transaction records could range from none, which would correspond to when a customer is new to the bank, to one or more, corresponding to when there has been an initial deposit, and then after that, further deposit or withdrawal transactions.

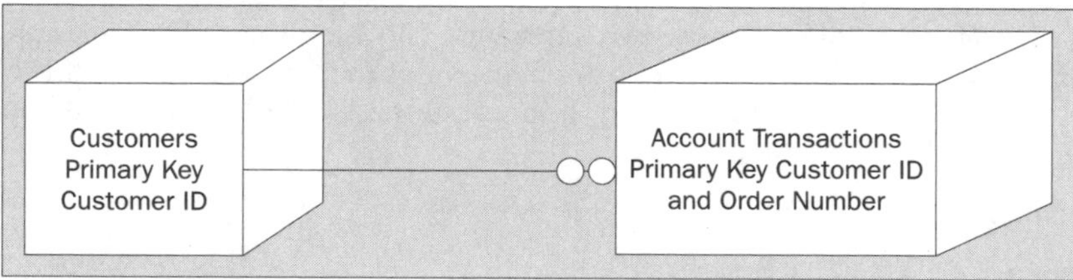

Many-to-Many

A many-to-many relationship is the final type of relationship that can exist in a database. This can happen relatively frequently where there are zero, one, or indeed, many records in the master table related to zero, one, or many records in a child table. By way of illustration, an example scenario might be where a company has several depots for dispatching goods, seen as the master table, which then dispatch goods to many stores, seen as the child table. If the depots were located and organized so that different depots could all supply the same store, for example, if the depots were arranged in groups of for example, produce, frozen, perishables, and bonded, then in order for a store to be supplied with a full complement of goods, it would need to be supplied by a number of different depots, which would typically be in different locations.

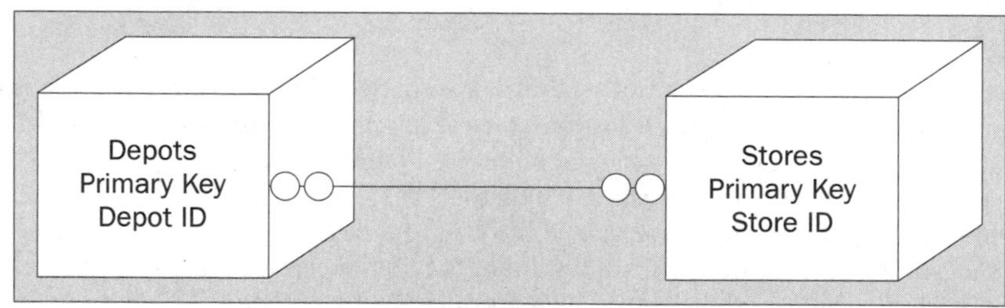

What is a Foreign Key?

In the previous chapter we introduced the idea of a foreign key, and now we shall take a more in-depth look at what a foreign key actually is, and what makes a foreign key. Specifically, a foreign key is any key on a child table, where a column, or set of columns can be directly matched with exactly the same number and information from the master table.

However, a foreign key does not have to map to a primary key on a master table. It is much more common to see a foreign key mapped to a primary key, but as long as the key in the master table that is being mapped to is a unique key, then we can build a relationship between a master and child table.

The whole essence of a foreign key is the mapping process, and the fact that it is on the child table. A foreign key will only exist when a relationship has been created from the child table to the parent table. But what are the master table and the child tables? Well, recall that a few moments ago, the chapter defined the different types of relationship. Take for example, the one-to-many relationship. The master table would be on the left-hand side, or the *one* side of the relationship, and the child table would be on the right-hand side of the relationship, or the *many* side of the relationship.

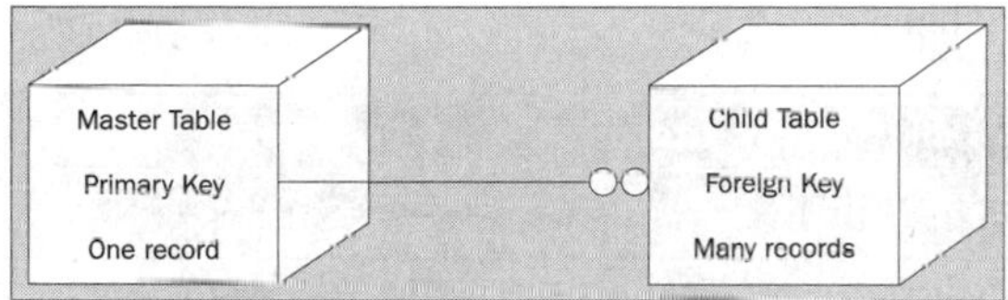

There is one final point concerning foreign keys and relationships, master and child tables, which is that it is totally possible for the master table and the child table to be the same table, and that the foreign key and the unique key are both defined within the same table. This is called a **self-join** or a **reflexive relationship**. You don't tend to see this much within a database as it is quite an unusual situation, although we could use it to ensure that the data in one column exactly matches the information in another column, just as in any other join. For example, if we had a table that was built around customers, and we had two columns, one of which was parent customer ID, which held an ID for the head office, and was used to link all the branches, then if the head office was also seen as valid branch of the conglomerate, the second column would be the specific branch ID, and we would put a link between these two columns so that there was still a valid link for the head office as a branch as well.

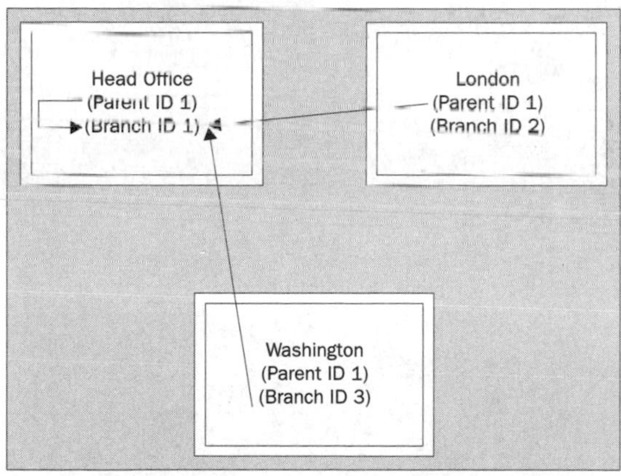

Creating a Relationship

The first relationship that we will create will be between the `Society_Groups` table and the `Matches` table. This will be a one-to-many relationship where there is one `Society_Groups` record to many `Matches` records. In the previous chapter, a primary key was created on the `Society_Groups` table using the `Society_Group_Id`, and then on the `Matches` table there was a key that had two columns, `Society_Group_Id` and `Date_Played`. As mentioned earlier, for a foreign key, there doesn't have to be a one-to-one match, as long as there is a matching column in the foreign key. We will now build that first relationship.

Try It Out – Building a Relationship

1. Ensure that SQL Server Enterprise Manager is running, and that **Wrox_Golf_Results** is selected and expanded. Find and select the **Society_Groups** table, and then right-click. Select **Design Table** to invoke the Table Designer.

2. Once in the **Design Table** mode, find the **Manage Relationships...** toolbar button and click it. You can also get to the relationships menu by right-clicking within the table and then selecting **Relationships...**

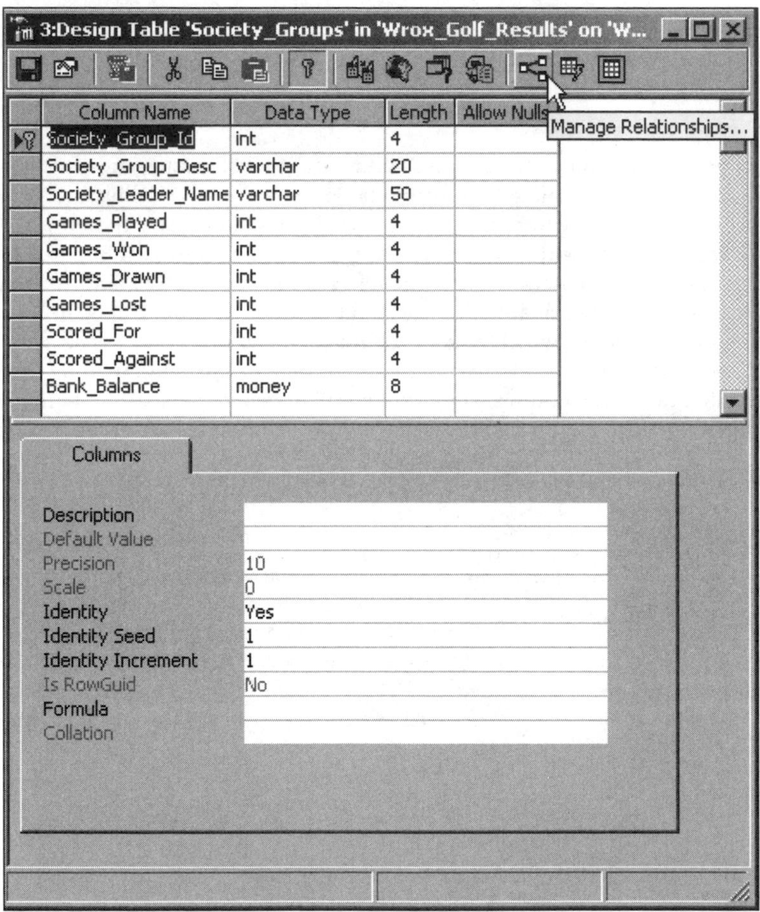

3. This then brings up the Properties dialog for the table, and you will find the Relationships tab has been selected. Notice that there are no relationships yet defined.

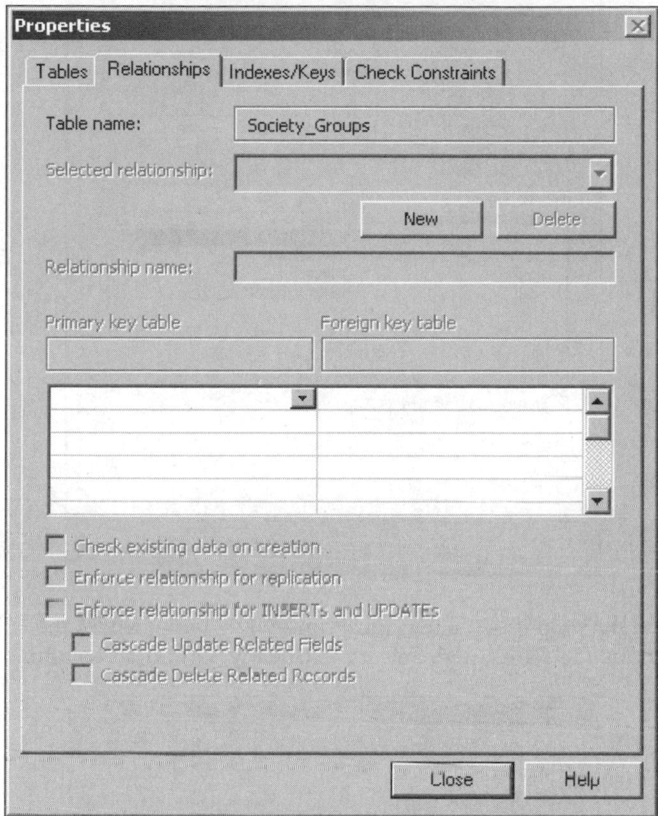

4. Click the New button as there is a relationship to be created.

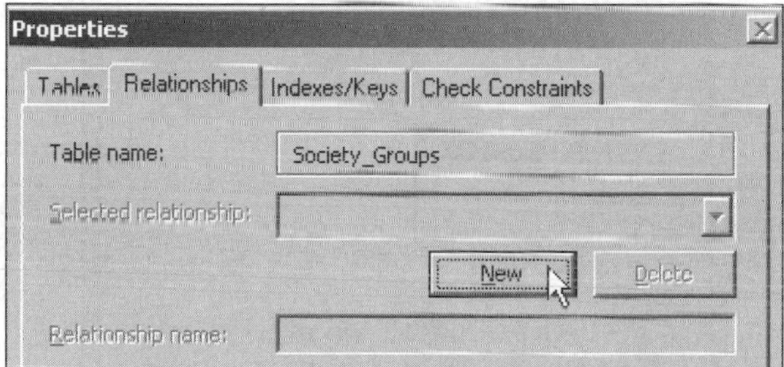

5. This then populates the details in the Relationships tab. The Primary key table will always default to the first table (in alphabetical order) that is stored within our database. Use the drop-down combo box to change this to Society_Groups. Also select Matches as the Foreign key table. As you can also see, by clicking New, a name is created. This changes automatically to a name describing the two tables involved in the relationship.

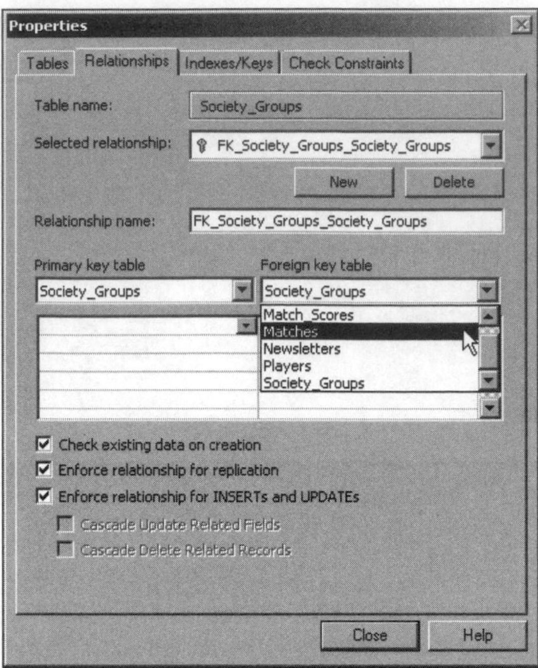

6. Now move to the drop-down under the **Primary key table**, where the columns of the **Society_Groups** table are listed. Select the **Society_Group_Id** column.

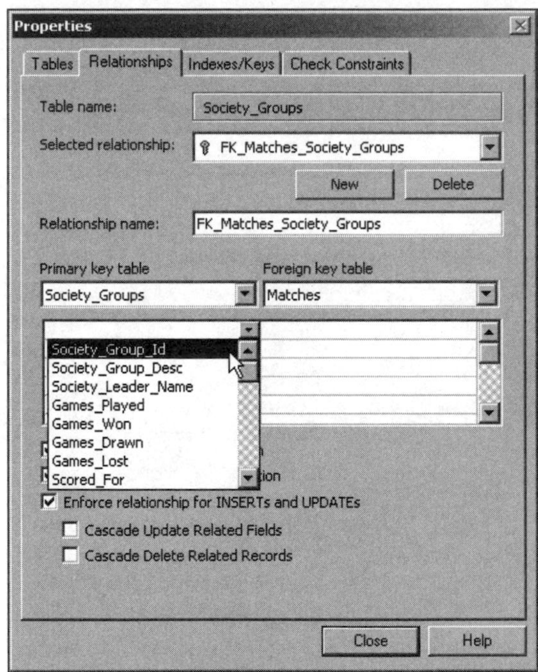

7. Under the **Foreign key table**, select the drop-down, which will then list the columns in the **Matches** table. Notice that there is also a column named **Society_Group_Id**. Select this. If in either case you needed to create keys that were for multiple columns, then it is just a matter of moving to the next row below the chosen column to add in more columns for the foreign key.

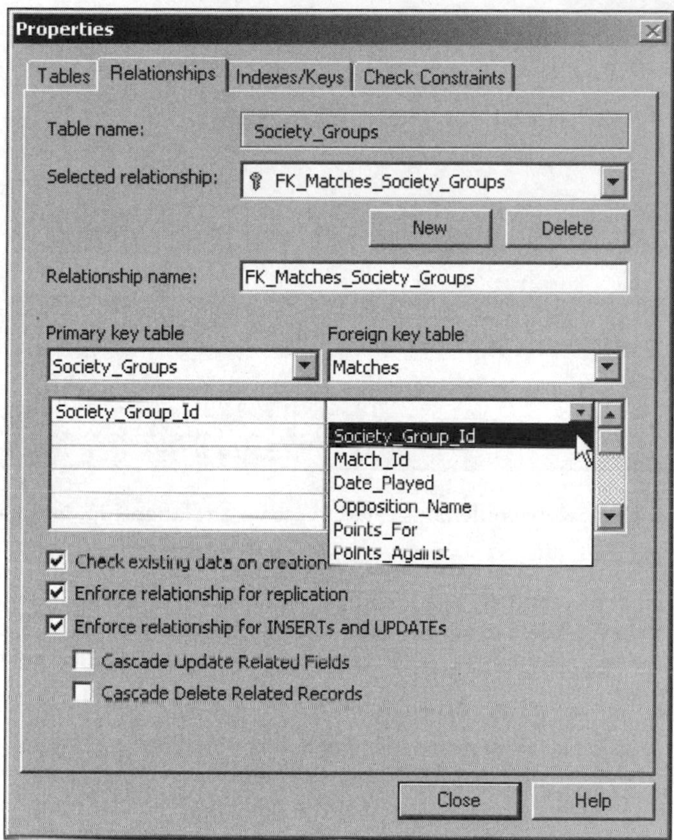

If you look towards the bottom of the dialog, you will see two check boxes: **Cascade Update Related Fields** and **Cascade Delete Related Records**. These two check boxes can be quite crucial in the development of a database. If we were in a scenario where the primary key of the primary key table can be altered, then of course, we would not want to have any records in any child tables associated with the primary key table to become **orphan records**, in other words, records in the child table with no primary table record. By checking these boxes, we can ensure that if we alter or delete a primary key value in a primary key table, then SQL Server will automatically update or delete any records in the child tables.

8. Now we have created the relationship in the window, we are ready to start committing these to the database. Don't worry about the various check boxes within the dialog; leave them set as they are. Click **Close** to let us continue through to working on the database. When you close down the table you'll be presented with a **Save** dialog; simply click **Yes** to continue.

9. This then brings up a further **Save** dialog. As you can see, both the tables involved in the relationship building exercise are listed. Click **Yes** to finally commit the changes into the database.

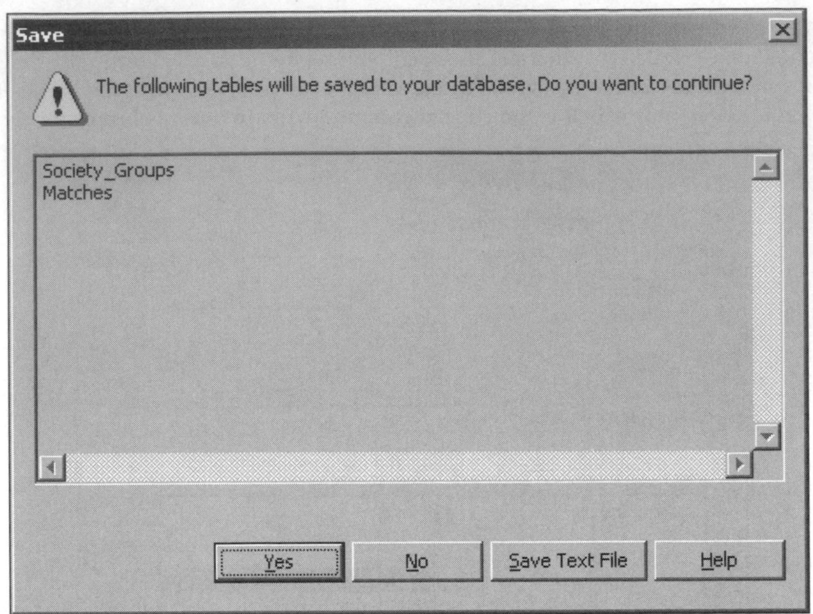

So, now that all the steps have been demonstrated to create a relationship, let's have an in-depth look at what is going on.

We have covered a great deal of the background earlier on in the book, and so you know what information has to exist within the database, and more specifically, the tables involved in the relationship, before we can get down to building a relationship. In this case, the two keys were built in the previous chapter.

As a result, setting up the actual relationship is a simple and straightforward process. However, if the information is not already there to build the relationship, you will get into trouble, and the next section will demonstrate this. But first, let's go back to this section and go about building a successful relationship.

When creating a new relationship by clicking the New button, SQL Server very kindly puts in two table names, one within the Primary key table, and one in the Foreign key table. The way SQL Server seems to complete this is by placing the first table (as I said before, determined by alphabetical order) in the Primary key table, regardless of whether it is impossible for a link to exist as the table has no primary key, with the table you are altering in the Foreign key table tab.

> *Even if you swap the tables around so that the table you are designing is in the Primary Key table, the table you are modifying must be mentioned in one of the two sides.*

However, it is the check boxes at the foot of the Relationships tab that are of interest to us, and it is here that decisions can be made that will affect how SQL Server works with your table join. Each of these options will be covered now; so that it is clear what each option means, and what action it performs.

Check Existing Data on Creation

This is actually one of the simplest and easiest options to decide on. If there is data within either of the tables, by checking this box we instruct SQL Server that when the time comes to physically add the relationship, the data within the tables is to be checked. If the data meets the definition of the relationship, then the relationship is successfully inserted into the table. However, if any data fails the relationship test, then the relationship is not applied to the database. An example of this would be when it was necessary to ensure that there was a customer record for all customer orders, but there are customer order records that don't have a corresponding customer record, and this would cause the relationship to fail. Obviously, if you come across this, there is a decision to be made. Either, correct the data by either adding master records or altering the old records, and then re-apply the relationship, or re-visit the relationship to ensure it is what you want.

Enforce Relationship for Replication

Being honest, for now we can ignore this option, as this book does not cover replicating databases.

Replication is quite simply where a replica of a database is made and is stored elsewhere within an organization, and any changes to the main database are copied (replicated) to the replicated database.

Enforce Relationship for INSERTs and UPDATEs

If you want to implement referential integrity through a relationship, this is the check box for you! By selecting this option we can request that at the end of a process of either inserting or updating data, also known as a **transaction**, this data will still meet the rules of the relationship. As a result, it will be impossible to insert records into the `Matches` table when there is no matching `Society_Group_Id` in the `Society_Groups` table. Similarly, we would not be able to modify the `Society_Group_Id` field in either table to that of a value that did not exist in the other table (if we were allowed to do that, anyway, in the first place). Finally, we would not be allowed to delete a record from the `Society_Groups` table while there are still matches set up for that `Society_Group_Id` in the `Matches` table. Basically, if our action will cause problems in linking up our tables afterwards, we can't do it!

The next two check boxes don't implement referential integrity; they simply maintain it once it is in place. Let's see how these two check boxes differ from the Enforce check box that we've just discussed.

Cascade Update Related Fields/Cascade Delete Related Records

As indicated just a minute ago, we cannot change the key data in one table alone. This would break the rules of referential integrity, and would therefore lose the data integrity that we were trying to enforce. If it was possible to change the key information, and we wished to, how could we go about this? Well, we must change both tables at once, as otherwise we will get an error, and also, we need to remember to do both tables in the first place, and not to change one but not the other!

But why not let SQL Server do the work for us? Well, this is what these two check boxes are for. If we change the key information in one table, SQL Server will automatically cascade these changes through to the other table, keeping both tables in alignment. To expand on this, if the Cascade Delete Related Records box is checked, and at some later time we decide to remove a `Society_Group` record, then all the `Matches` associated with that `Society_Group_Id` would also be deleted. Similarly, with an update on one table's `Society_Group_Id`, if the Cascade Update Related Fields box was checked, then SQL Server would automatically alter the table not directly modified by us. Cascades will only happen when the data in the master table is modified, and are not cascaded upwards in the event of child table records being modified.

> **If at any point you do decide to implement cascade deletion, then please do take the greatest of care, as it can result in deletions that you may regret. For instance, say you had cascading deletes linked on: `Parts` to `OrderDetails`, `Parts` to `PurchaseOrderDetails`, `Parts` to `QuoteDetails`, and `Parts` to `ShipmentReceiptDetails`. If, by some chance, the person responsible for maintaining the parts were to delete a part, every Order Detail, Purchase Order Detail, Quote Detail, and Shipment Receipt that uses that part would be deleted. Not a good idea, to say the least!**

Instantly, you can see how this will keep the data integrity intact, and if that is a goal of your system, there are few, if any, better ways of achieving this.

Creating a Relationship – Missing Keys

This section will address the case when a relationship can't be built because there is a key missing on one of the tables. In this section a relationship between the `Players` table and the `Match_Scores` table will be built, or at least, an attempt will be made to build it. The problem is that the `Players` table does not have a primary key built within it to be used as a foreign key to the `Match_Scores` table. Obviously this is a problem, so let's see what happens and how problematic it can be for you to rectify it.

Try It Out – Relationships with Missing Keys

1. Ensure that SQL Server Enterprise Manager is running, and that you are at the Tables node. Also, ensure that you have Query Analyzer running, as this will be used in a few moments as well.

2. Find the Match_Scores table, select it, right-click, and then select Design Table.

3. Now click on the Manage Relationships… button, this will take you again into the Relationships tab of the Table Properties dialog.

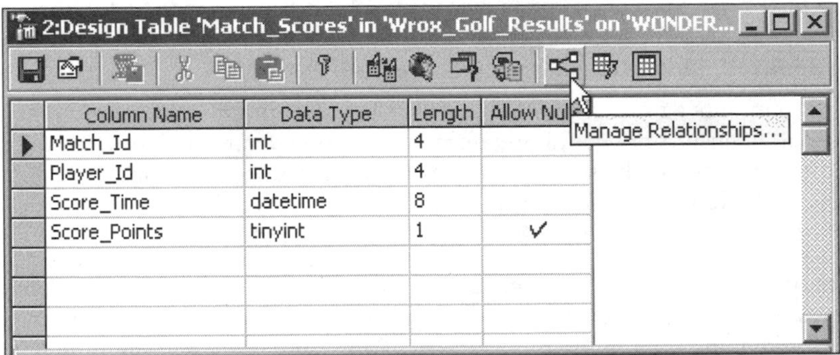

4. The next screenshot shows one of the later stages of building the relationship. The New button has been pressed, the two tables selected, and the columns chosen.

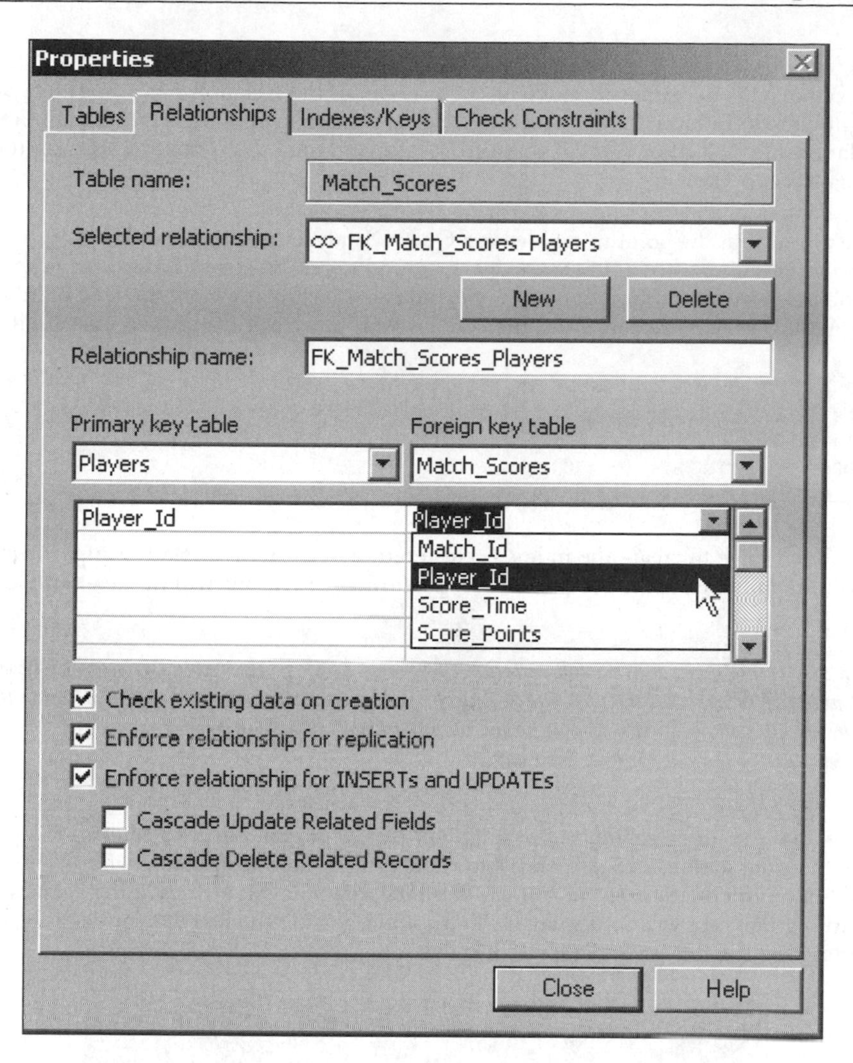

5. Now when you click the Close button, you'll receive the following dialog box indicating that there is a problem. This is quite correctly informing us that there is no primary key on the Players table that meets the requirements to build a relationship on a foreign key in another table. Although there is a field called Player_ID in the Players table, we haven't yet set this up as a primary key and/or unique indexed field to map to the Player_ID foreign key in the Matches table. We need to do this before we can create the required one-to-many relationship. For our purposes here, click OK.

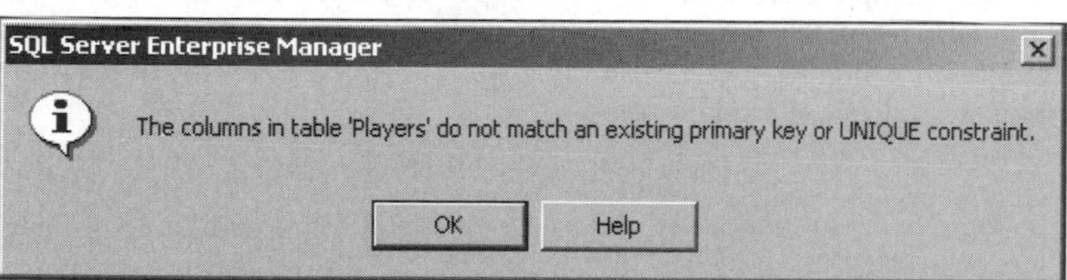

6. So, what do we do? First of all clicking OK above will bring us back to the Relationship Designer. It is necessary to move all the way out of the Relationship and Table Designers, right back to Enterprise Manager itself. To do this we need to delete the attempted relationship being built by clicking the Delete, and then the Close, buttons on the Relationship Designer.

7. We are now at the point though where Query Analyzer could come into play, so that we could create the index without having to work around open screens in Enterprise Manager (and the problems that are around due to the invalid relationship anyway). So, let's build the necessary index in Query Analyzer. Enter the code as it is shown here, and then execute it.

```
CREATE UNIQUE CLUSTERED INDEX IX_Players_PlayerId
ON Wrox_Golf_Results.dbo.Players
   (Player_Id)
WITH DROP_EXISTING
ON [PRIMARY]
```

We don't have to create the index as clustered to perform in a relationship; however, we do wish the index to be clustered for other performance reasons within the example.

We can also create the index through Enterprise Manager by using the Table Designer, and we would not have to move all the way out to Enterprise Manager to do so; we could just create the index by clicking on the Index *tab, and then working from there. The method we're using here was chosen in order to show what had to be done.*

8. Now that the index is built either in Query Analyzer or Enterprise Manager, move through the first four actions detailed above to rebuild the relationship. Now when you click the Close button on the relationship tab, you will notice that you can now save the relationship and no warning message will be displayed. You should be able to close down the table, and you should see the following dialog. Click Yes.

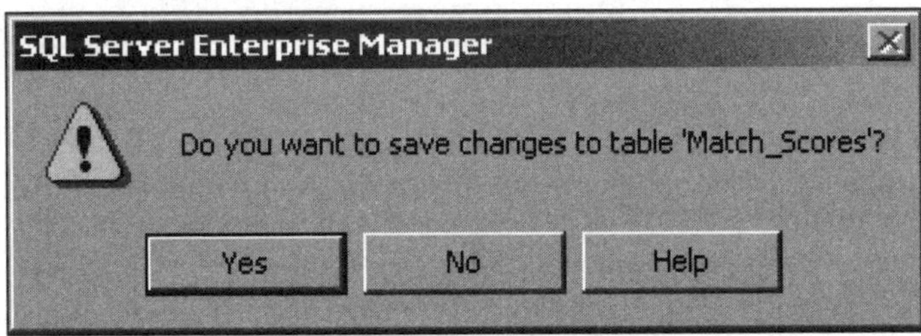

9. This then brings up the tables involved in building the relationship to give you the ability to save the relationship. Click Yes to save them. Two tables are mentioned within the list because a relationship has been created between them and modifications to the tables have been made to indicate the relationship.

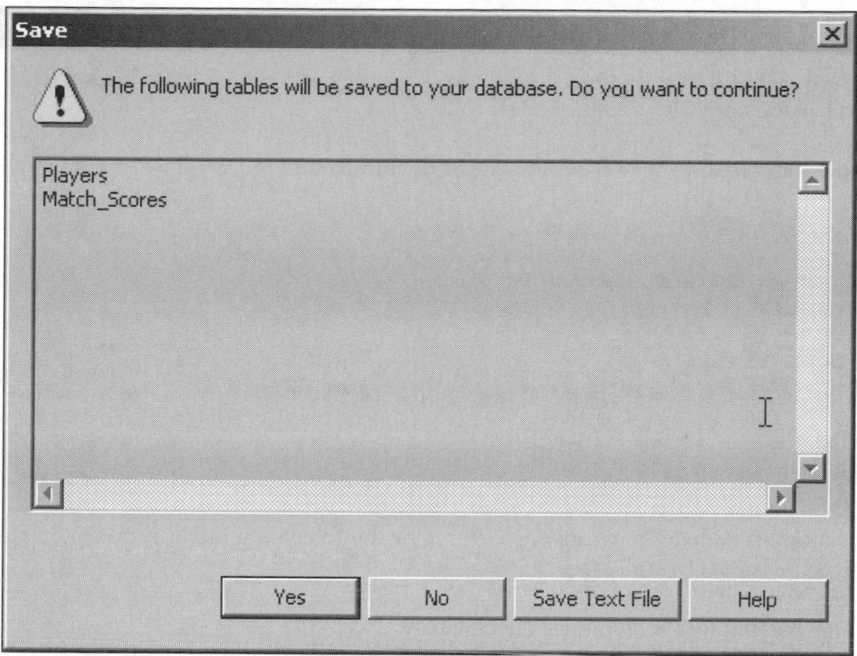

At last! The relationship is created, but see how problematic it can be at the moment if we forget to build an index, and then try to use Query Analyzer to get ourselves out of trouble. This would not have arisen if we had just used Enterprise Manager to build the index rather than Query Analyzer, so this would be a trouble when things don't go right when they should.

The next section demonstrates how to alter a table to build a relationship using T-SQL commands. This would have alleviated the problem in the section above as there was a missing index, and this solution demonstrated next, might have been a better solution to adopt.

Using the Alter Table SQL Statement

It is also possible to complete the building of a relationship, or constraint, through a SQL statement. This would be done using an `ALTER TABLE` SQL command run through Query Analyzer. This time, a relationship will be created between the `Matches` table and the `Match_Scores` table. There is no index on the `Matches` table for the `Match_Id` column, so this has to be completed first of all. This will then demonstrate how to get over the problem in the previous section. After the index has been created, the relationship can then be built.

Try It Out – Using SQL to Build a Relationship

1. Ensure that SQL Server Query Analyzer is running and that you are logged in as an account that has the authority to alter tables.

2. In the Query pane enter the following SQL commands:

```
USE Wrox_Golf_Results
GO
CREATE UNIQUE INDEX IX_Matches_MatchId
   ON Matches ([Match_Id]) ON [PRIMARY]
GO
ALTER TABLE Match_Scores
   ADD CONSTRAINT [FK_Match_Scores_Matches] FOREIGN KEY
                  (Match_Id)
   REFERENCES [Matches] ([Match_Id])
GO
```

3. Execute this code by pressing *F5*, *CTRL+E*, or the Execute toolbar button. You should then see the following success message:

   The command(s) completed successfully.

That's it. The index is created in the second batch of T-SQL code, the first batch ensuring that we are pointing to the right database. Once the index is built, it is possible to alter the table to add the relationship.

How It Works – Using SQL to Build a Relationship

The first section of code is straightforward and is covered in the previous chapter, which dealt with building of indexes, and so there is little point in going over old ground. Moving to the second major coding area, which covers the alteration of the `Match_Scores` table, no columns are being altered, but a **constraint** is being added. A relationship is a special type of constraint, and it is through a constraint that a relationship is built.

A constraint is in essence, a checking mechanism, checking data modifications within SQL Server and the table(s) that it is associated with. The code you see here is what went on behind the scenes in the first and second examples when the relationship was being built within Enterprise Manager. Let's now take a few moments to check the syntax for building a constraint within T-SQL code.

```
ALTER TABLE child_table_name
      ADD CONSTRAINT [Constraint_Name] FOREIGN KEY
                     (child_column_name, …,)
      REFERENCES [master_table_name] ([master_column_name, …,])
```

As you can see, we have to use an `ALTER TABLE` command to achieve the goal of inserting a constraint to build the relationship. After naming the child table in the `ALTER TABLE` command, we then move on to building the constraint. To do this, we must first of all instruct SQL Server that this is what we are intending to complete, and so we will need the `ADD CONSTRAINT` command.

Next, we name the constraint we are building. Again, I tend to use underscores instead of spaces, however, if you do wish to use spaces, which I wholeheartedly do not recommend, then you'll have to surround the name of the key using the `[ ]` brackets. I know I mentioned this before, but it's crucial to realize the impact of having spaces in a column, table, or constraint name. Every time you wish to deal with an object which has a name separated by spaces, then you will also need to surround this with square brackets. Why make extra work for yourself?

Now that the name of the constraint has been created, the next stage is to inform SQL Server that it is a `FOREIGN KEY` that is being defined next. When defining the foreign key, ensure that all column names are separated by a comma, and surrounded by normal curved parentheses. The final stage of building a relationship in code is to specify which master table the constraint is being built on to, and the columns involved.

The rule here is that there must be a one-to-one match on columns on both the child table, and the master table, and that all corresponding columns must match on data type.

It is as simple as that. When building relationships, you may wish to use Enterprise Manager as there is a lot less typing involved, and you can also instantly see the exact correspondence between the columns and if they match in the same order.

Display Dependencies

Now that relationships between tables have been built, the database has reached a point where one table is now dependent on details within another table. Yes, another administration headache. For example, if you wanted to alter a column in one table, you need to ensure that there are no dependencies on the column, in any other part of the database.

It is quite possible to see if a table is dependent on another. Now that we have built the relationships between some of the tables, we will complete the remainder of the relationships in the next chapter. If we take a look at the `Matches` and the `Match_Scores` tables, the `Match_Scores` table is dependent on the fact that a value in the `Match_Id` for each row in that table has a corresponding record on the `Match_Id` column in the `Matches` table. By building constraints before any data is inserted, we ensure that this will always be the case. The same can be said for the `Matches` table and the `Society_Groups` table, where there has to be a `Society_Groups` record for every `Matches` record.

However, there will be times when as a SQL Server developer or administrator, you will pick up a database that you don't know much about, and you'll probably wish to see what relationships do exist. This next section will demonstrate how simple it is to find out this information.

Let's now see how we can display the dependency between the four tables using the dependency between matches and match scores as the basis of the demonstration.

Try It Out – Displaying Dependencies

1. Ensure that SQL Server Enterprise Manager is running, and that you can see the tables under the Wrox_Golf_Results database.

2. Highlight the Matches table, right-click, select All Tasks, and then at the bottom you will see Display Dependancies..., which you should then select.

3. This then brings up the following dialog, in which you can see the tables that depend on Matches, and the tables that Matches itself is dependent upon.

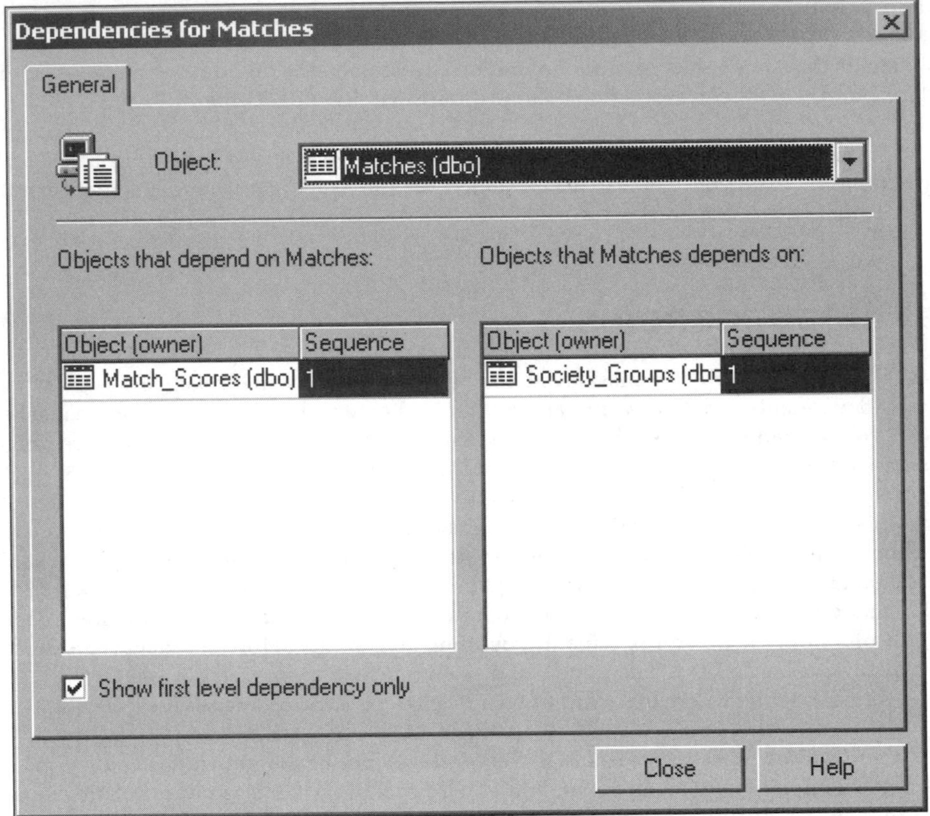

Displaying dependencies is, as you can see, very straightforward, and it does give a whole host of information about the objects within a database. It is possible to get similar information concerning relationships using a database diagram; however, showing dependencies like this does show how other database objects are also dependent on each other. You may be asking why this matters? Well, it's crucial to know when altering a property of an object, what, if any, knock-on effects there will be. For example, suppose we wished to alter a column of a table, and that we wanted to change, say, the name, or perhaps the data type. So why not just go ahead and get the job done? Well we can't just do that, because there may be relationships, stored procedures (which are stored SQL code), and views, all of which use this column and so, these too will all need to be altered. Use this tool to find out that information.

Summary

Building relationships between tables is one of the easiest jobs to complete for a SQL Server administrator or developer. Having said that, it is crucial that you get it right, otherwise you could be placing erroneous constraints on data modification, or in fact, leaving holes within your whole data integrity architecture. This would just be storing up problems for later when you discover that data you expect to be there, isn't there.

A point to note: If you are loading up tables that require referential integrity to be inserted, but you are in a scenario where you must load a great deal of information into a database, one table at a time, rather than following the path of one row at a time, then you should consider removing any referential integrity created; validating the data so that there are no records breaking the referential integrity that has to be applied, and then, providing that the data is valid, re-creating the referential integrity once the data is in. There is one method that is not covered in this book for loading in the data, which is known as BCP, or Bulk Copy Program. When loading data using this method, which you can see in "*Professional SQL Server 2000 DTS*" (Wrox Press, ISBN 1-861004-41-9), any constraints are ignored, and therefore the data inserted may have invalid entries.

Now let's see another method to build a relationship, but also at the same time, how to diagram, and in essence document, the SQL Server database solution for your problem.

Diagramming the Database

Now that the database has been built, tables have been created, indexes inserted have been, and relationships link some of the tables, it is time to start documenting. To help with this, SQL Server offers us the **database diagram** tool, which is the topic of this chapter.

One of the worst things about documentation is documenting tables, and showing how they relate to one another in a diagram. The diagramming tool can do all of this very quickly and very simply with one caveat: if more than one person is using the diagramming tool on the same database and there are two sets of changes to be applied to the same table, the person who saves their changes last will be the person who creates the final table layout. In other words, the people who save before the last person will lose their changes.

As you developed tables within your database, you have commented the columns as you have gone along to say what each column is. This is one major part of documentation anyway, and providing that you comment columns at the start, then it is less of a chore when adding new columns to add in further comments. If you do have comments on each of your columns within a table, then this will help overall with the documentation that is seen within the diagram.

This said, SQL Server's database diagram feature is more than just a documentation aid. This tool provides us with the ability to develop and maintain database solutions. It is perhaps not always the quickest method of building a solution, but it is one that allows the entire solution to be completed in one place, or can build up sections of a database into separate diagrams, breaking the whole solution into more manageable parts, rather than switching between nodes in Enterprise Manager.

In this chapter you will learn:

- What a database diagram is
- What the diagramming tool is
- The default database diagram – what is it and what it is used for
- How to create a database diagram
- How to alter the layout of the diagram
- That the diagram can be used as a basis of your development
- How to create the default database diagram

This is perhaps one of the book's easiest chapters to pick up and learn and feel confident with. All this is down to the groundwork you have completed so far in the book, but more importantly the simplicity and ease with which the database diagramming tool works, and that it allows developers and administrators to work with their database solutions. Let's plow on and look at what a database diagram is.

What is a Database Diagram?

In the book so far, with the creation of databases, tables, indexes, and relationships, naming standards have been kept, and as much documentation as SQL Server will allow has so far been maintained. However, there is no documentation demonstrating how the tables relate to one another within the database. This is where the database diagram comes in.

A database diagram is a useful and easy tool to build simple, but effective documentation on these aspects, and as the old saying goes, "a picture is worth a thousand words", and this is no exception. You build the diagram yourself, and you control what you want to see within the diagram. When you get to a large database solution, you may want diagrams for sections of the database that deal with specific aspects of the system, or perhaps you want to build a diagram showing information about process flows. Although there are other external tools to do this, none are built into SQL Server that can allow diagrams to be kept instantly up to date. Below is a sample diagram taken from the `Northwind` database using the SQL Server diagramming tool.

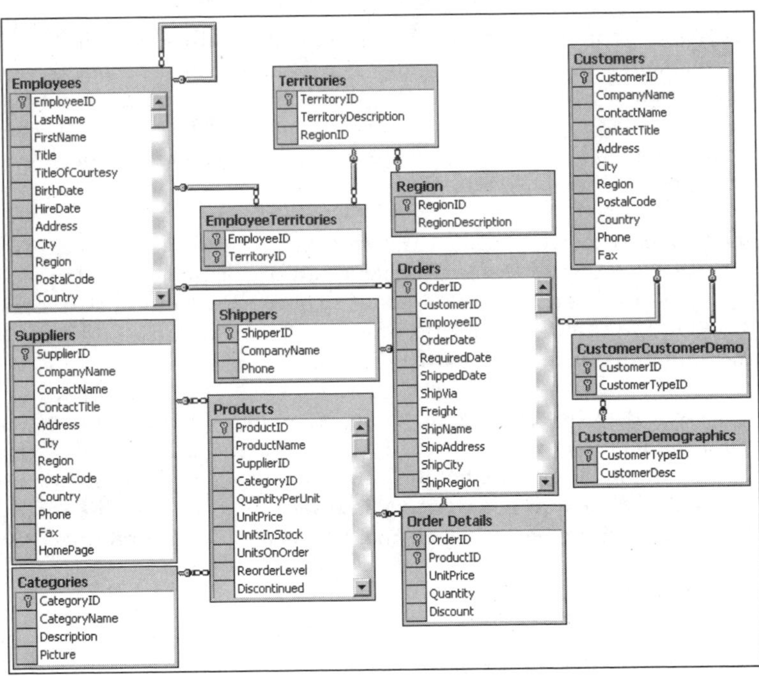

A diagram will only show tables, columns within those tables, and the relationships between tables, in a bare form. You will also see the yellow "key" which denotes a primary key on the table, where one has been defined, but that is all the information displayed. It is possible to define the information that is to be displayed about the columns in the table, whether it is just the column name, or more in-depth information such as a column's data type and length, comments, etc. However, to display more than just the bare essentials, a little bit of work is required.

Although the diagram shows the physical and logical attributes of the database that is being built, or has been built, it also allows the developer or administrator to see exactly what is included with the database at a quick glance, and how the database fits together.

The first area that we will look at is what the diagramming tool is about.

The Database Diagramming Tool

Enterprise Manager's database diagramming tool aids the building of diagrams that detail aspects of the database that a developer wishes to see. Although it is a simple and straightforward tool, and not as powerful as some other tools in the marketplace for building database diagrams, it is perfect for SQL Server. For example, one of the major market leaders in database design tools is a product called **ERWin**. ERWin is a powerful database utility that not only builds diagrams of databases, but also provides data dictionary language output, which can be used to build database solutions. Through links such as ODBC, these tools can interact directly with databases and so can be used as a front-end for creating databases. They can also, at the same time, keep the created source in alignment and under control from a change control perspective, so ensuring that not only does the code exist within the database, but also if it was necessary to create a new database quickly, issuing a command could complete this. An example of when this might be useful is when creating a new test database. Perhaps SQL Server could benefit from this sort of control, perhaps being tightly integrated with Visual SourceSafe, but at the moment, there is no need for this from the diagramming tool. If you want to go further than the SQL Server diagramming tool provides, and within this chapter you will see what the boundaries are with the tool, then you should be looking at more powerful tools, which do cost a great deal of money.

SQL Server's database diagramming utility offers more than just the ability to create diagrams; as mentioned earlier, it can also be used as a front-end for building database solutions. Through this utility, SQL Server allows you to add and modify tables, build relationships, add indexes, and much more information. Any changes built in the tool are held in memory until they are committed using a save command within the tool. However, before you are wondering why this whole book doesn't cover working with this tool, there are limitations to its overall usefulness.

First of all, the biggest restriction of any diagram-based database tool comes down to the amount of screen space available to see the diagram. As soon as your database solution goes over more than a handful of tables, you will find yourself scrolling around the diagram trying to find the table you are looking for.

Secondly, you cannot add stored procedures, users, views, or any object that is not a table. However, other products can allow you to include these objects, or even build some of them for you.

Finally for the moment, when altering any of the information you can alter within this tool, you are usually using the same dialogs and screens as you would in Enterprise Manager.

As you will see as you go through the chapter, the database diagram tool is quite powerful in what it can achieve, but there are some areas of concern that you have to be aware of when working with diagrams. Keep in mind however that the database diagram tool is holding all the changes in memory until you actually save the diagram away.

If you have a database diagram open, and a table within that diagram is deleted outside of the diagram, perhaps in Query Analyzer or Enterprise Manager by yourself or another valid user ID, then there are two scenarios that can occur. First of all, if you have unsaved changes to the deleted table, saving your diagram will recreate the table, but don't forget that through the earlier deletion, all the data will be removed. If however, you have no changes pending to that table, then the table will not be recreated. When you come to re-open the diagram, the table will have been removed.

With several developers working on the database at once, any changes made from the diagram tool of your Enterprise Manager will not be reflected in any other developers' diagrams until their changes are saved and their diagrams refreshed. If you have multiple diagrams open, and you alter a table and insert or remove a column, then this will reflect immediately in all the open diagrams within your own Enterprise Manager. Don't forget this is an in-memory process and so this process cannot reflect on anyone else's diagrams until the changes are saved and their diagrams refreshed.

Also if you remove an object in your diagram, when you save your diagram the object will be removed and any changes completed by others will be lost. Effectively, last person who closes their diagram wins!

To summarize, if you use the diagram, use it with care. Because many of the processes are in memory, you could be inadvertently causing problems.

The Default Database Diagram

Although not mandatory, I do feel every SQL Server database solution should have a default database diagram built in to it so that any developer new or old can instantly see how the database being inspected fits together.

A **default database diagram** should include every table and every relationship that is held for that database. Unlike other diagrams that may take a more sectionalized view of things, the default database diagram should be all encompassing.

But how does the default database diagram differ from any other diagram? There is only one true attribute that makes the difference, and that is how it is viewed. As you will see, every database diagram built, except for the default diagram, is held within the diagram node of the database. To view the contents of the diagram, you have to specifically select the diagram and open it up.

The default database diagram sits at the root level of the database. Therefore, when you click on the database name, the default database diagram will be displayed instead of the task pad, which lists the tables, and other information about the database that we saw in Chapter 2. You will see this later in the chapter when the default diagram is built.

Therefore, whenever someone moves onto your database, they have, without any further actions, the ability to see exactly what is happening in your database solution.

As mentioned earlier, it is imperative to keep this diagram up to date. You will notice this statement repeated a few times in this chapter. Don't use the default diagram as the source of development for your database solution. The default diagram includes all the tables, which means that if you are using the diagramming tool for development, you are potentially locking out all other users from touching any other table as part of their development, in case their changes are lost. Only update the diagram with tables and relationships once they have been inserted in the database. More on this later when we discuss the dangers of using the database diagramming tool as a source of development.

Now that you know what diagrams are, it's time to create the first diagram for this database.

Creating a Database Diagram

When creating a database diagram, SQL Server does a lot of the initial work for you. The building of the initial diagram through the wizard is a great start, and this is where our example starts. The diagram that we create will hold all the tables within the Wrox_Golf_Results database. To be honest, there isn't another way to create a diagram except through a wizard, but once a diagram is built, it is easy to work on it, as you will see later on in the chapter. Back to the present though, and let's build the first diagram.

Try It Out – Creating a Database Diagram

1. Ensure that SQL Server Enterprise Manager is running and that the Wrox_Golf_Results database is expanded so that you see the diagrams and tables nodes.

2. Select the Diagrams node and then right-click. Select New Database Diagram...

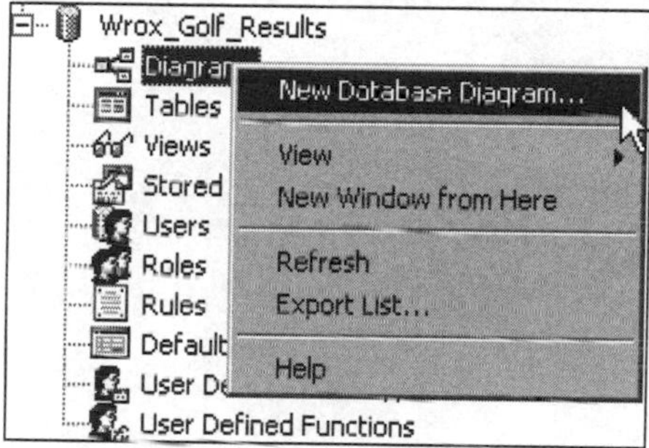

3. This starts up the database diagram wizard that exists within Enterprise Manager. As usual, the first screen can be skipped after the first time of reading. Click Next.

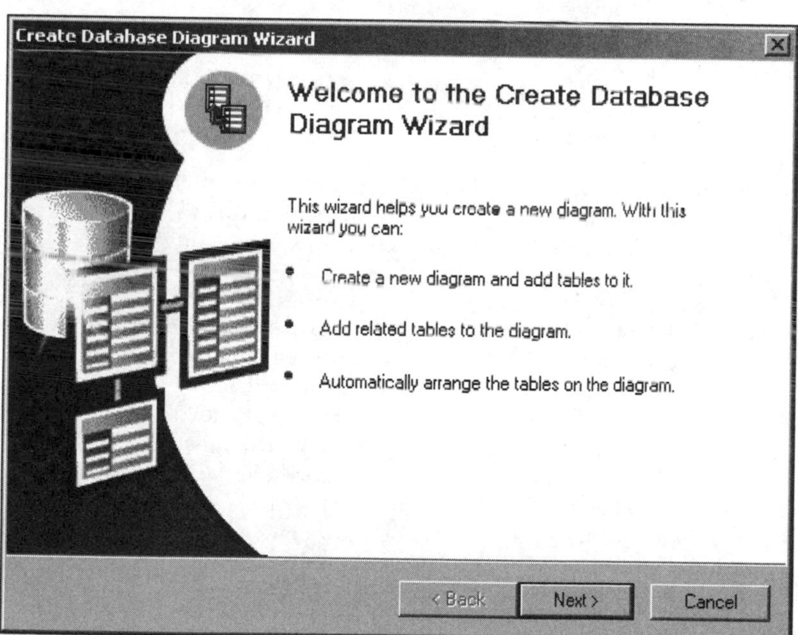

4. This then brings up the next screen in the wizard where the list of available tables can be seen.

There are no tables initially selected, but you will also notice that there are a number of tables listed, which you haven't explicitly created, namely the system tables that reside in the database as well. These system tables also form part of the database and for all SQL Server knows, you may want a diagram of the system tables and how they link. There is no reason not to do this, except that you should not be dealing directly with the system tables in the first place! However, from a learning point of view, this is a perfectly valid action.

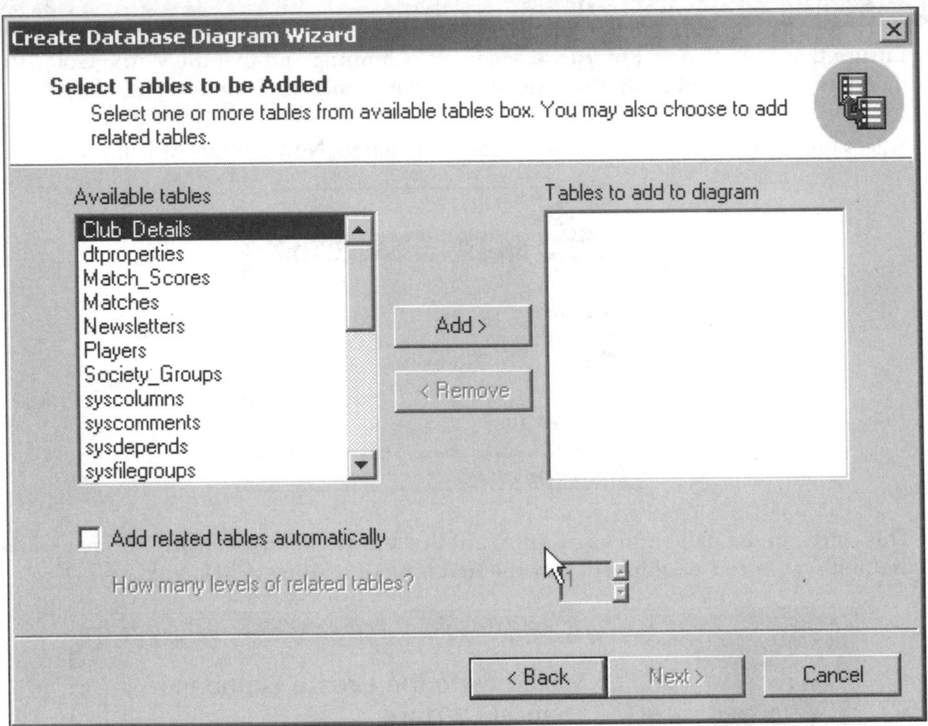

5. Before selecting any tables, select Add related tables automatically. This will enable the How many levels of related tables? spinner control. Ensure that the number is set to 3 in this case. Click the Society_Groups table and then click Add. You should then see four tables as listed in the screenshot.

Remember that some of the tables have a relationship defined. Therefore we select the Add related tables automatically option, and when you click to move your chosen table across to the selected Tables to add to diagram column, it checks to see if any relationships exist on that table, and if so, it will then also move across the related tables. The number that is entered for How many levels of related tables will decide how many relationships down through the architecture will be examined before this wizard stops looking further. For example, a level of 1 will take the tables mentioned in the Tables to add to diagram list box, and then check to see what tables they are linked to. A value of 2 would then take these tables and check which tables they are then related to. So it is all about how many tables you move away from the root table in the Tables to add to diagram list box. This is a quick and easy way of getting tables across to the selected tables column, and so aids the building of the database by making it just that little bit faster.

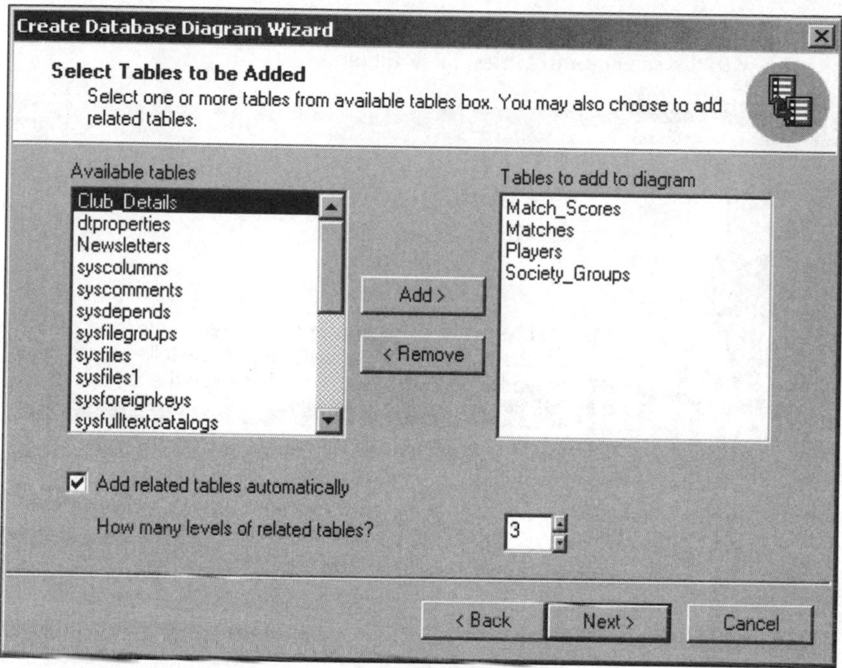

6. However, this isn't a list of all the tables that should be in the diagram. Find and select Club_Details and Newsletters in the Available tables column, and click Add. When done, click Next.

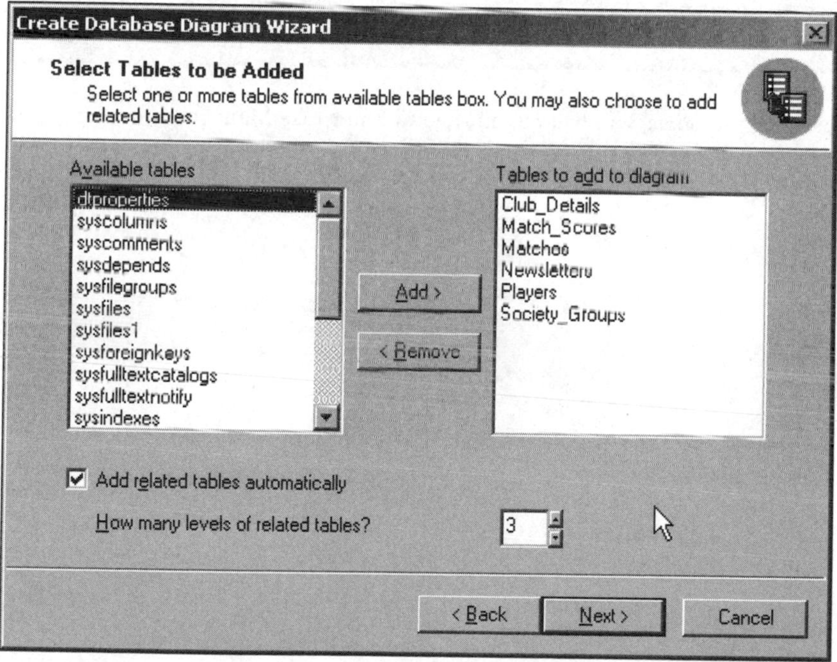

7. This brings you to the final screen, which confirms the tables that make up the diagram. If you are happy with the selection of tables, click Finish.

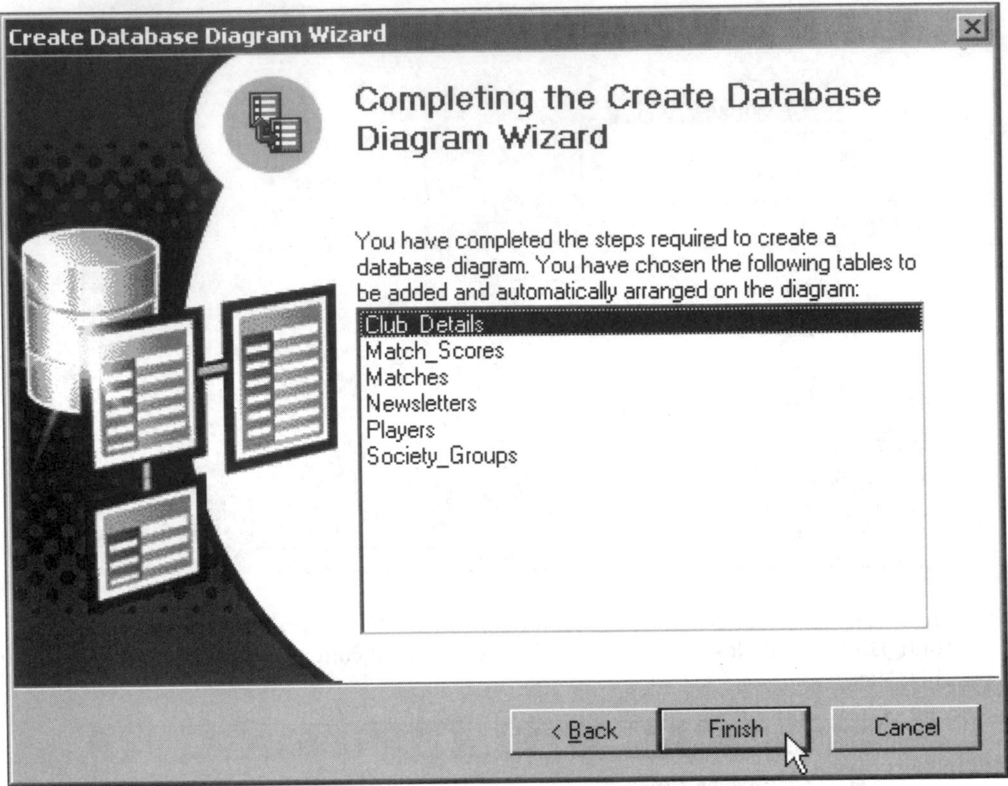

8. After a few moments, you will be returned to Enterprise Manager, but with the database diagram now built. A little small to read don't you think? Don't worry; sorting this out will come in the next section. Don't close this diagram just yet – we'll be altering it in the next section.

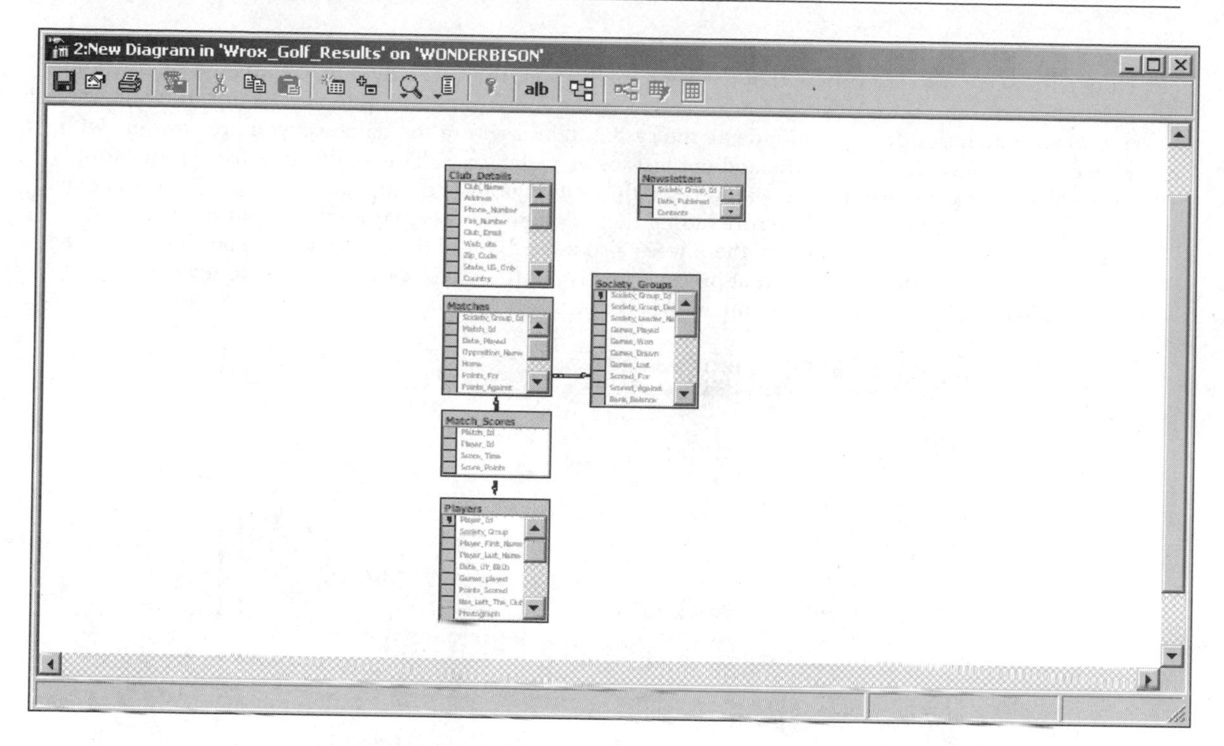

9. At this point, it is worth pointing out how to stop the display within SQL Server of the system databases and system tables. If you move to your server registration node within Enterprise Manager and right-click, a pop up menu appears.

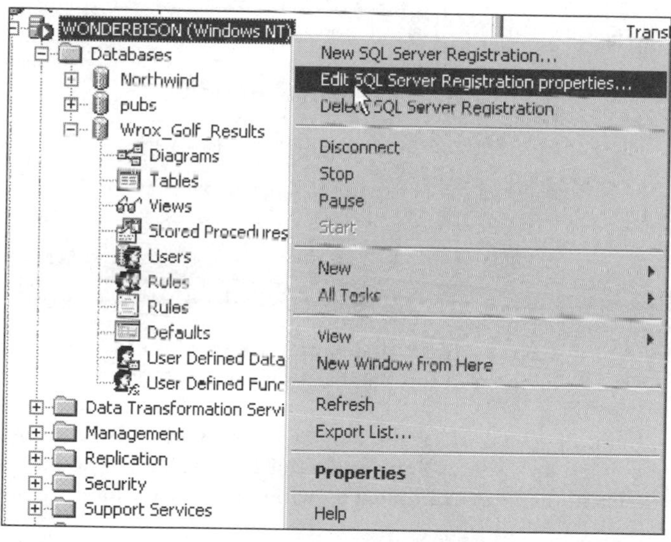

Select Edit SQL Server Registration properties, which takes you to the SQL Server properties dialog. Notice the second-to-last option that has been unchecked, the Show system databases and system objects check box. Setting this as unchecked as in the screenshot will hide the master, tempdb, model and msdb databases. It will also hide all the system tables within the database you are working with. However, it does this server-wide, and not just for your database. This is also true for system stored procedures and views where you will also see the system objects disappear from view (they still exist, they are just not displayed). Therefore hiding these system objects may suit you, but may not suit everyone. Yes, it would be better if there were also a database option, so that you could just hide the system tables at database level, but at present, this is not the case. It's a good idea to leave this box checked just in case you are impacting on what others want to see.

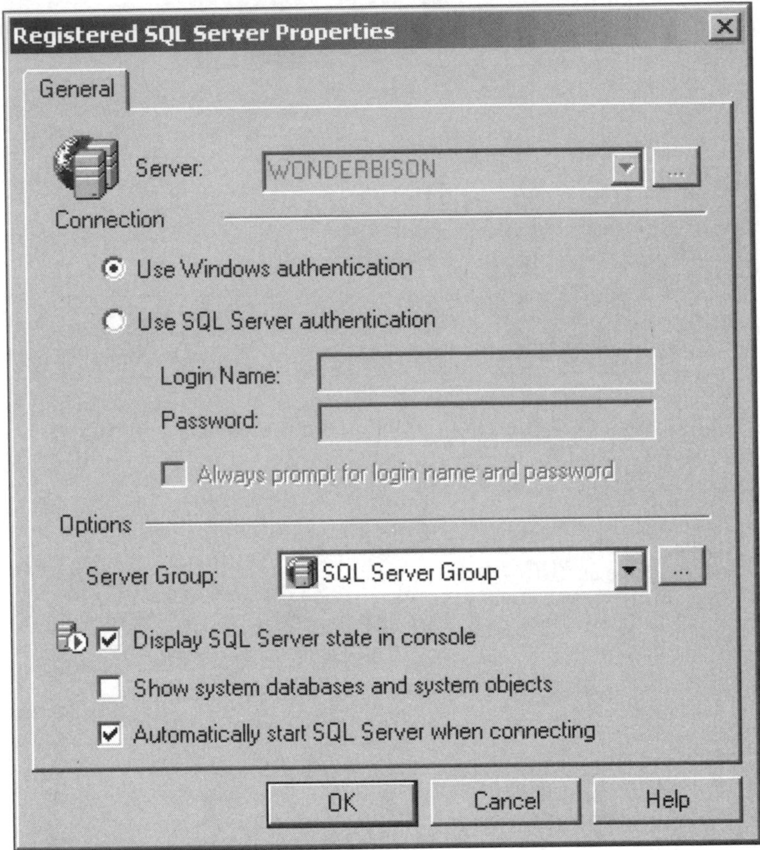

Getting back to building the diagram, the system tables are mixed in with our example tables, so just deal with the tables that are involved in this database solution.

That is all there is to building a basic diagram. However, as an administrator or a developer, it is crucial to keep any diagram created up to date. You can do this by altering the layout, and although we won't be adding any new tables in the next example, you will see how easy altering the table can be.

Altering the Layout

Now that the initial database diagram has been created, as you can see, SQL Server doesn't do the best job at laying out the tables for display that perhaps it could. The layout is almost unreadable due to the zoom level being too small, and the tables could perhaps have been arranged in a better order. However, this does give us a good opportunity to demonstrate how to alter the layout to suit your needs or preferences. This next section will demonstrate how to move tables around, annotate the diagram, and then save it away before further work is completed. In fairness to Microsoft, creating a diagram with everything in the right place and at the right zoom level is a pretty difficult job and, if they did spend a long time getting it right, there will still be a large number of people who want to modify the layout anyway.

Altering the layout of a database diagram is a very easy process and is just like using many other products in the marketplace. There is the ability to zoom, drag and drop, group items together, and print. It is also possible to add database objects such as tables and relationships as well as columns. In fact, from a database diagram, you can complete a whole database design and implementation since it is possible to add the full range of database objects.

It's now time to alter the layout of the diagram created earlier.

Try It Out – Altering the Layout

1. You should still be at the diagram created above. The diagram layout that SQL Server built didn't suit the best way of laying out the scheme of the database and where it would be best for the tables to be. As you can see, the tables aren't exactly clear to see. It would be better to zoom in on the diagram first, which can be done by selecting the magnifying glass on the toolbar, and then select To Fit. You could also right-click and select this option from the Zoom option from the pop-up menu.

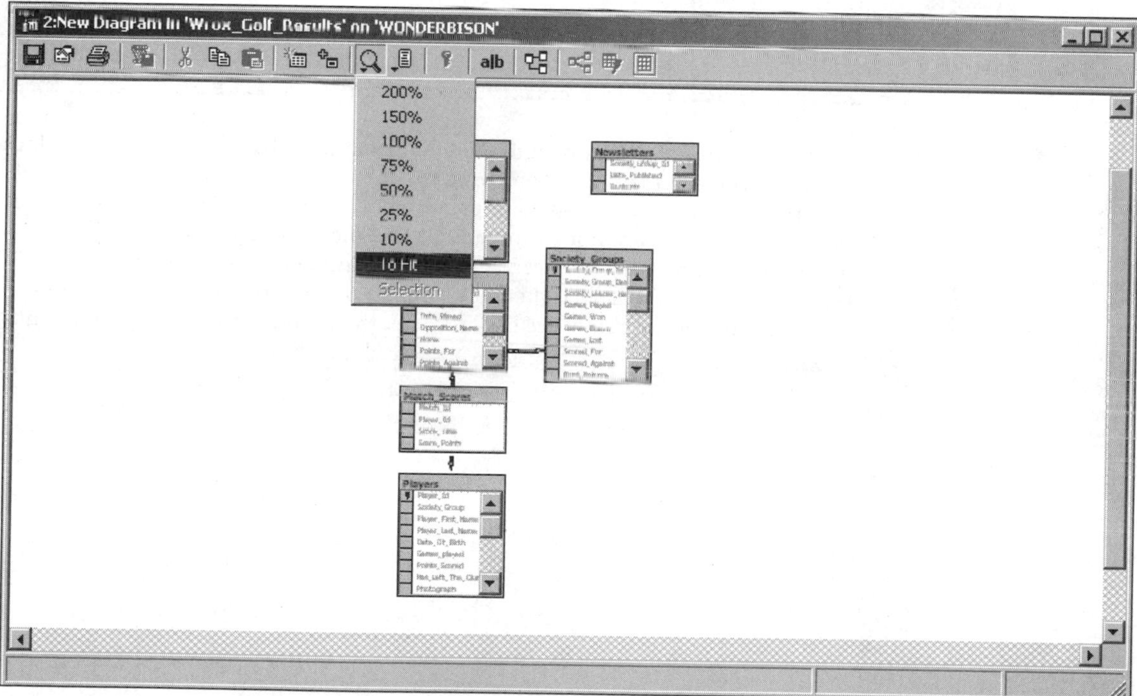

2. After the zoom, the diagram now looks like the screenshot below, still not ideal, but you can read parts of the table names. This will be fixed next.

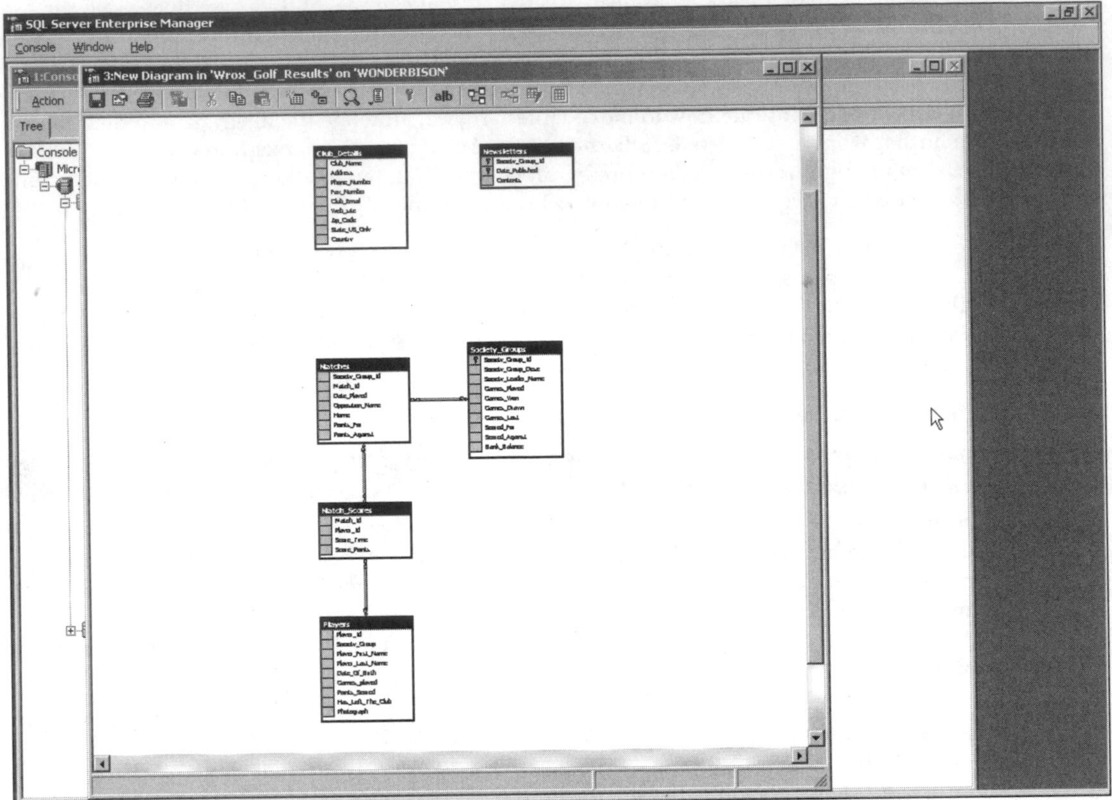

3. The next layout change will involve moving the tables around, so that the Zoom To Fit does a much better job. However you may also be moving the tables around to keep specific areas together, or perhaps to ensure that the diagram prints well. No matter what the reason, you can move the tables so that they are not so spread out and therefore too small to read. Highlight the tables shown opposite. You can see the selection being made by placing the cursor in the top left of the area to select, then keeping left the mouse button pressed down dragging it until the tables shown below are covered. Let the mouse button go and the tables should be highlighted.

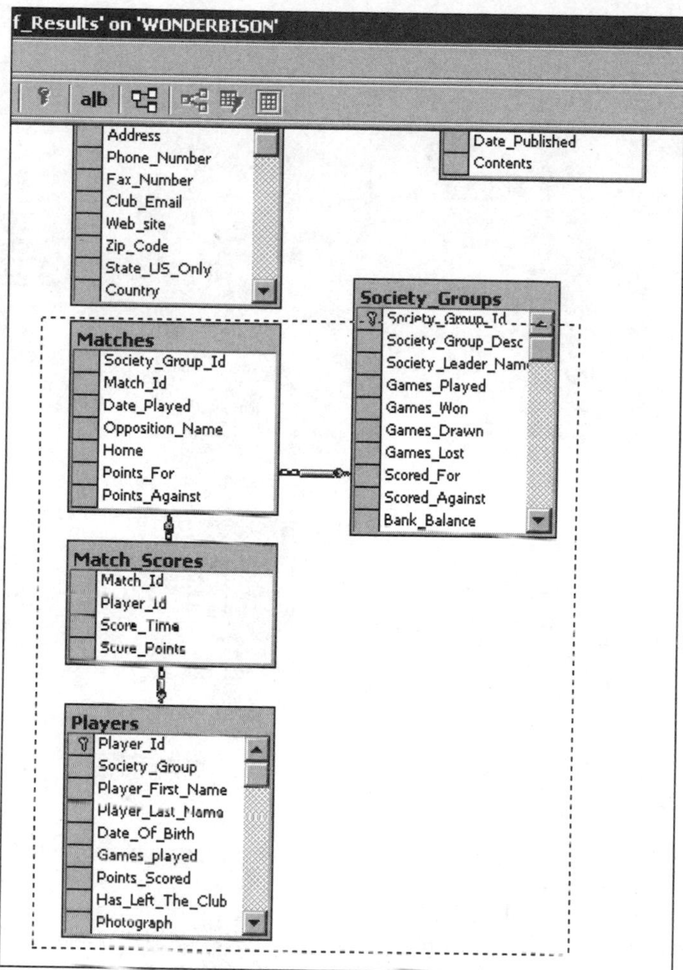

4. By clicking on one of the highlighted tables and holding down the mouse button, you can drag these tables around the screen, so drag them to the right of the Newsletters table, and release the mouse button. Again select the magnifying glass and select Zoom to Fit. The screenshot overleaf shows how the diagram will look after all of these actions have taken place. As you can see, all the tables and columns are much easier to read. From this point, the example can move forward. The first things to notice are the lines that connect the four tables on the right of the diagram. The lines connecting the tables are the relationships defined in the previous chapter. More on this later in the chapter.

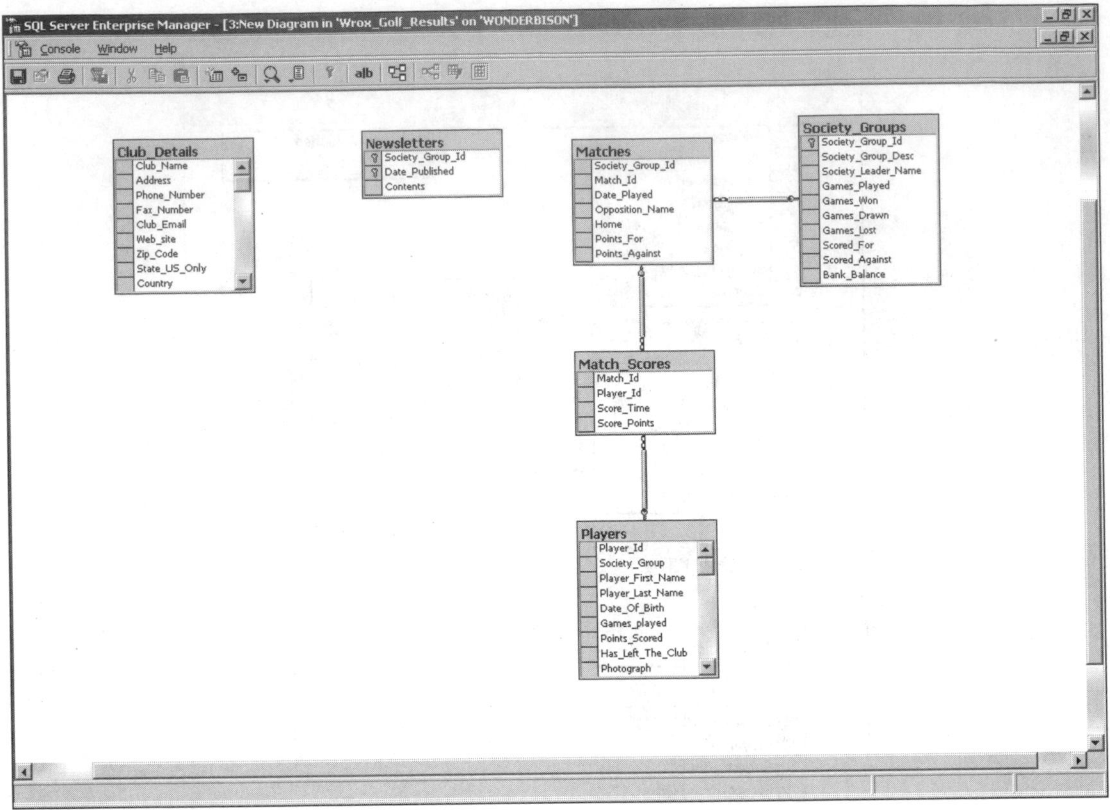

5. When looking at the individual tables, only the column names are displayed. In some instances, this may not be enough information. It is possible to show more than just the column names for a table. In the next screenshot, by selecting the Show… icon, we can alter the layout of the tables from Column Names to Standard. This function is also available by right-clicking on the table, and selecting the Table View menu item that is within the pop-up menu. This then brings up more details about the columns. Do take care with this. Only the tables selected at the time of using the Show… icon will alter. The menu will be disabled if no tables are selected at the time. In the screenshot, just two tables have been altered.

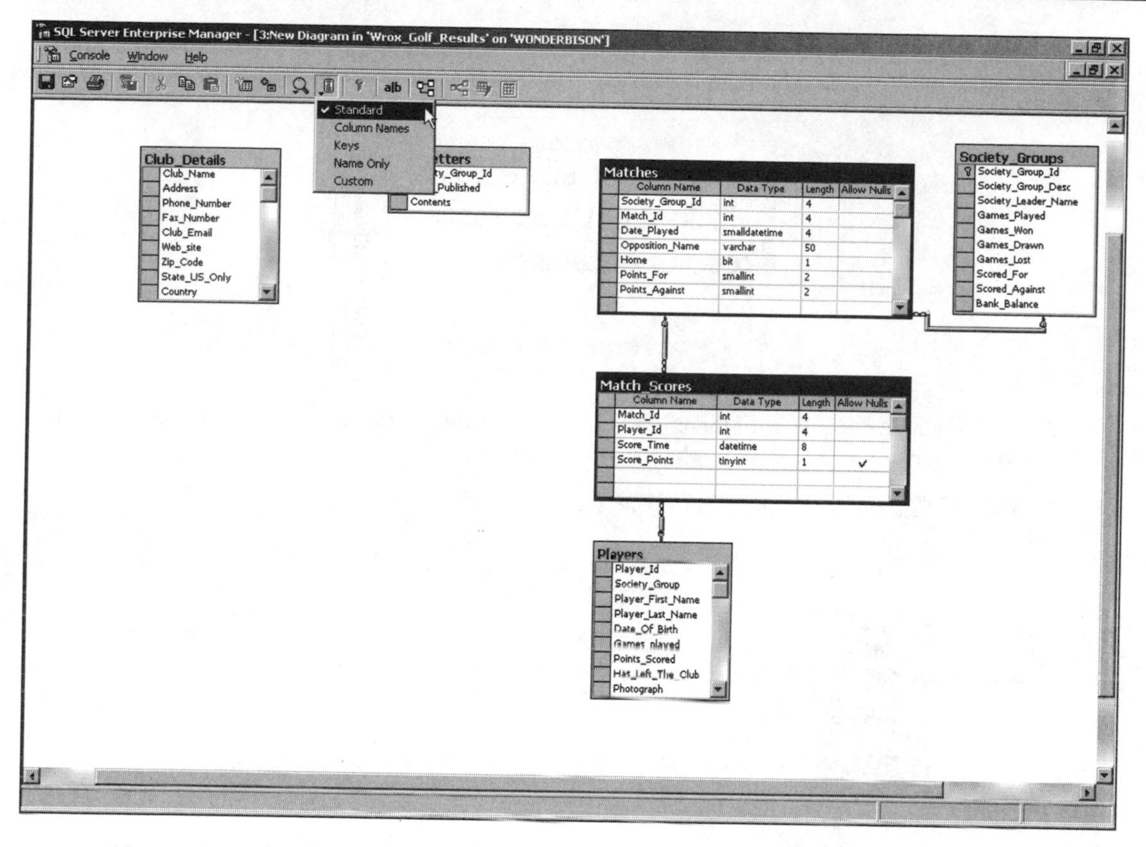

After making these alterations above, it is possible to let SQL Server automatically arrange the tables within the diagram in the best way that it thinks. This is completed through the Arrange tables icon:

However, SQL Server doesn't always make a good job of this, or produce an arrangement that suits you. When completing this for the above diagram, SQL Server arranged the tables so that it was spread over two pages and so it wasn't possible to get a full screenshot for you to see.

6. The main point about diagramming is that it is used as a source of documentation. Therefore, it is important that once a diagram is created, for future reference it is known what the diagram is trying to illustrate. This is what the Annotate icon is for, and allows a plain text box to be positioned within the diagram for any notes. In this case, the Annotate icon

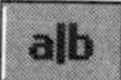

will be used to just label the diagram. Click on this, and a text box will be inserted in to the middle of the diagram.

7. Enter a meaningful description. In this instance, enter a description of Diagram of all tables within the Wrox Golf Results database. You may find you have to alter the size of the text box.

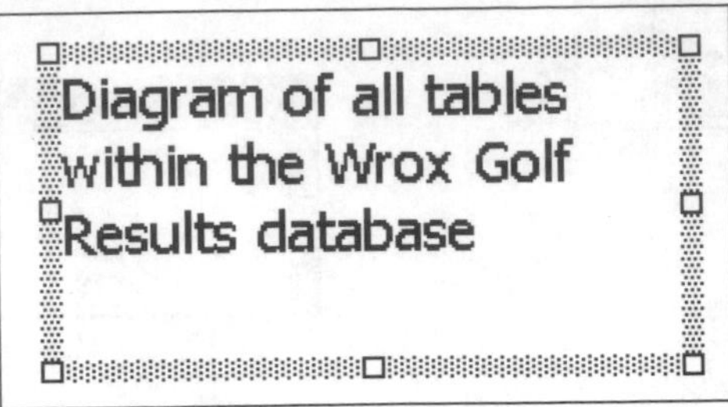

8. Once you are happy with the contents and readability of the annotation, then you can move the description to a sensible place on the diagram.

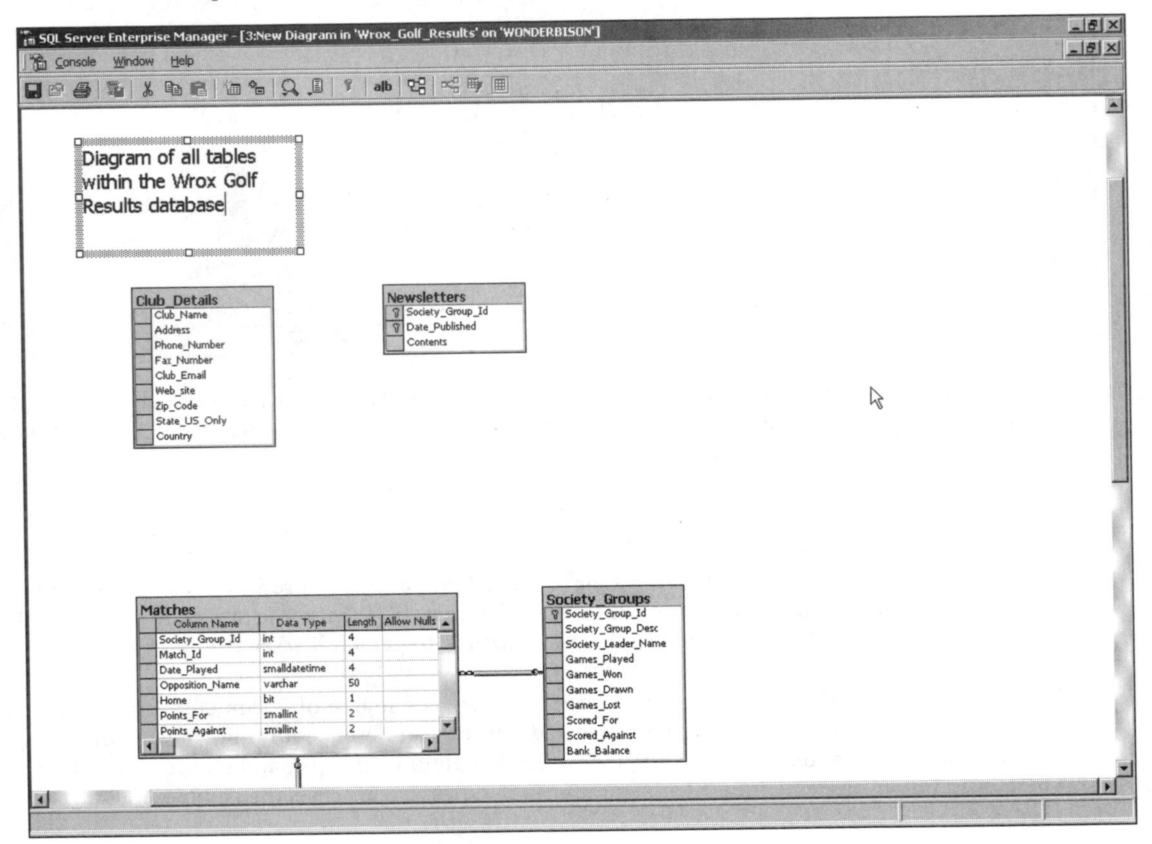

9. If you wanted to insert an existing table into the diagram, perhaps because one has been added to the database and you are now updating the diagram, then there is a toolbar button to allow you to do this. Adding a table to a diagram is just as simple as using the wizard, and adding a table through this button, just as adding tables through the wizard, won't alter the database. However, in the next bullet point, things are different.

10. It is also possible to use the diagram to add a new table to the database. There is also a toolbar button for this. Creating a new table is as straightforward. Although we will create a table, we will not store it in the database as this is demonstrating how easy it is to add a table (but also to remove it). Click on the New table icon.

11. This then brings up a screen asking you to enter a new name for the table. The table name cannot already exist within the database. Because this table will never actually make it into the database, enter a name demonstrating that this is for demo. Then click OK.

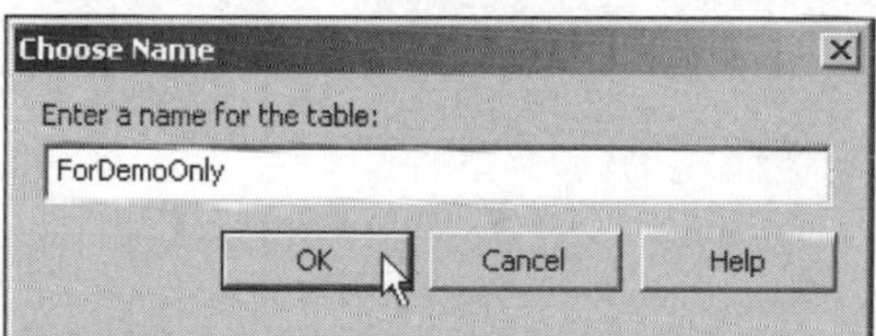

12. This will then create a new table dialog, which looks just like all of the other table dialogs that use the current Table View layout. The table below is displayed as Standard. The table comes up blank, but for demonstration, two column values have been entered. You would enter the table details as required.

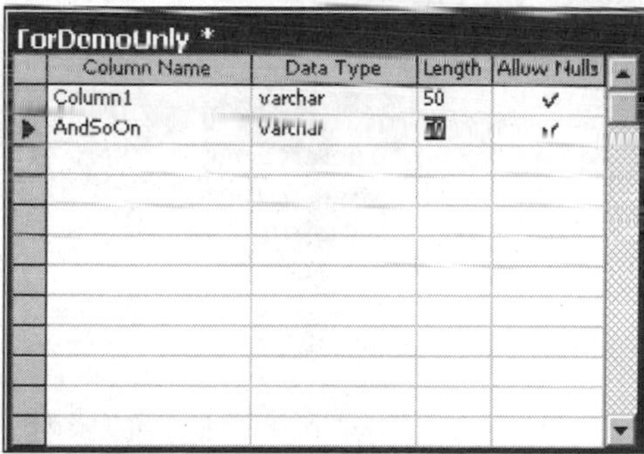

13. Although the table is still not saved in to the database, when you right-click, you are given the option to Delete Table from Database. This is still a valid option, but to demonstrate what happens, select it.

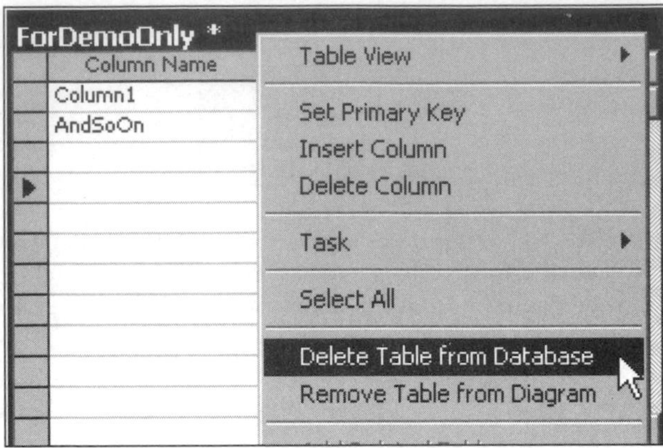

14. You are then presented with a message box, which seems to indicate that the table has been inserted in to the database. It has not. It is still in memory and has not been committed; therefore this is really ambiguous. Clicking Yes will remove the table from the diagram and will therefore not commit it to the database.

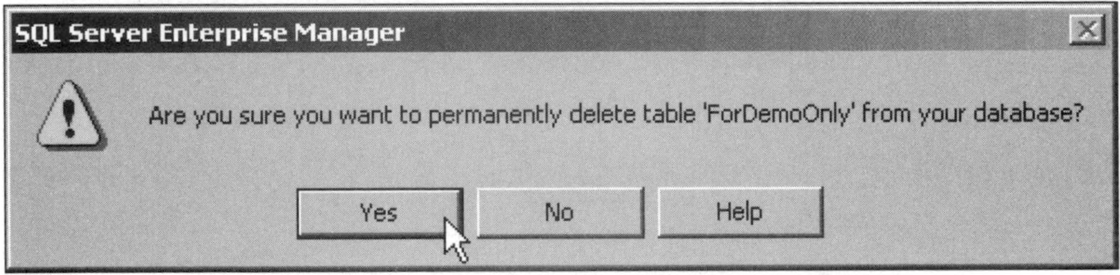

15. By right-clicking again, select the more appropriate Remove Table from Diagram option, as this really is what we want to do.

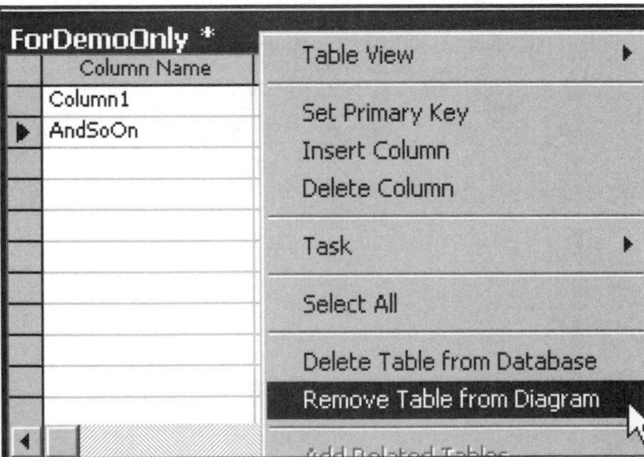

16. This message box is much more realistic as it still is giving you the option to save the created table, but just not in this diagram. We don't want the table so click No to discard the changes.

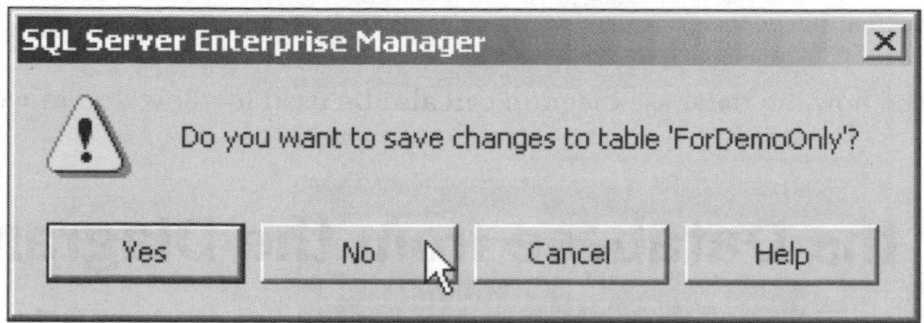

17. Now that we are happy with everything, save the diagram by clicking on the Save icon on the toolbar.

18. This brings up the Save As dialog, which allows you to enter a name for the diagram. When saving a second or subsequent database diagram, if you try to save the diagram using an existing diagram name, you will be asked if you want to replace the existing diagram. The diagram name has to be unique within the database, but you can have the same name in different databases. Also the name of the diagram can also include spaces just like any other object.

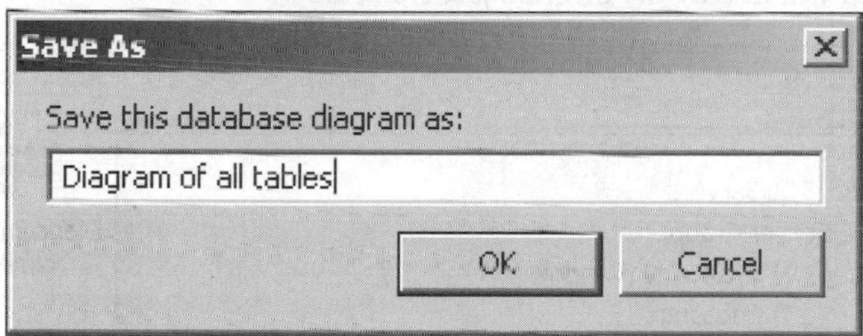

19. If you then close down the diagram, returning you to SQL Server Enterprise Manager, you will see the diagram listed.

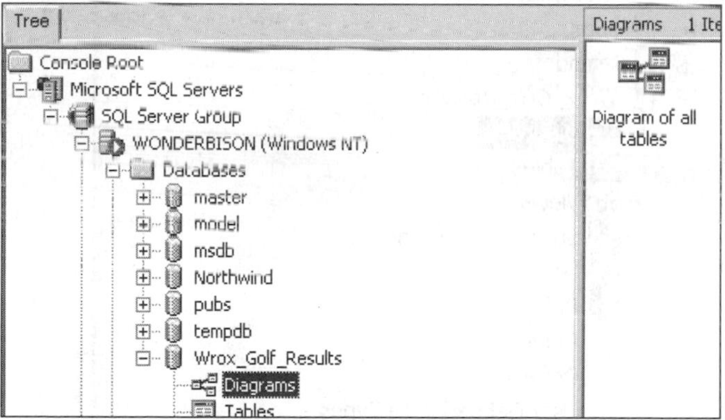

Working in a diagram is very simple. The main area that really has to be remembered is what the diagram is there for. As you will see in the next section, this can be to maintain the database and work with it, but it is best to see a diagram as a useful documentation tool. Microsoft has made the diagramming very easy and simple to do, and so even for those who are against documentation, there is no real excuse not to use it.

However, let's now see how the database diagram can also be used to allow you to work with your database.

Working on the Database from the Diagram

As ever, Microsoft has not limited its product to completing just a single task. It quite often comes up with more than one way to skin a rabbit, and this is no exception.

The next section will show how to complete some changes to the Club_Details table to prove the point that the diagramming tool can be just as powerful as Enterprise Manager itself.

Try It Out – Altering the Database with the Diagram Designer

1. Ensure that SQL Server Enterprise Manager is still running, and ensure that you have navigated to the Wrox_Golf_Results database, and expanded it. Then click on the diagrams node, which will display the diagram just created.

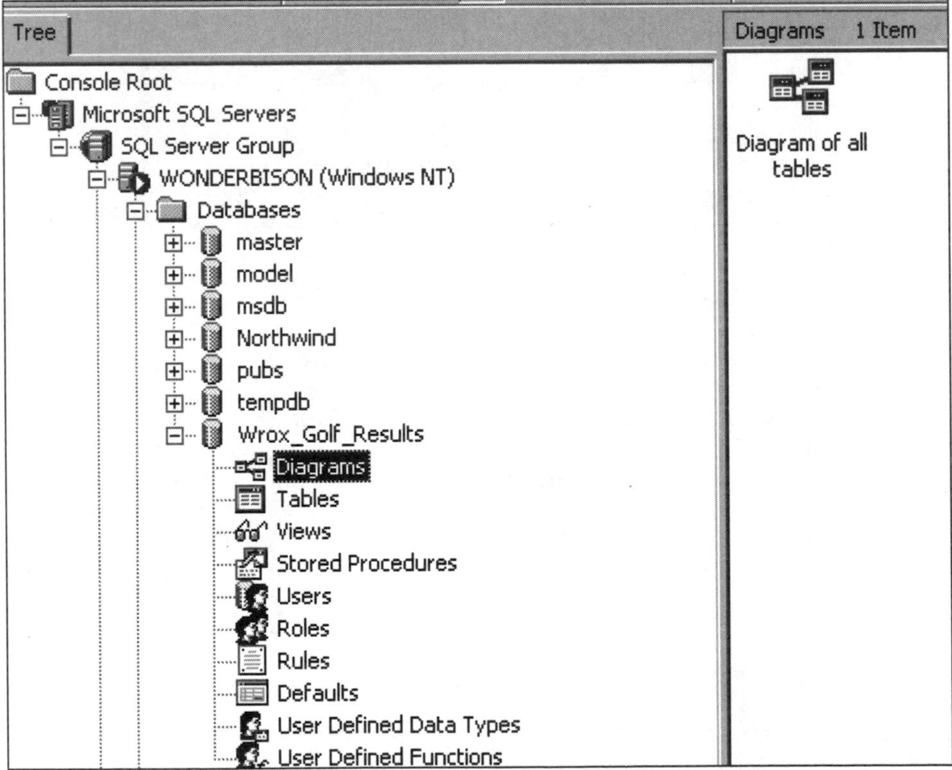

2. On the diagram, right-click and select Design Diagram. You can also simply double-click on the diagram icon.

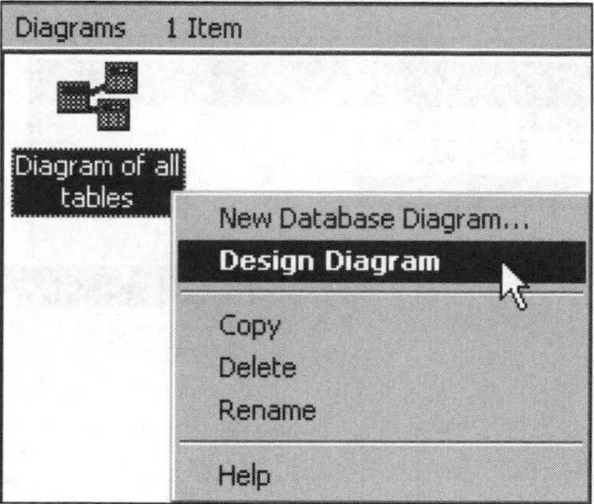

3. The Club_Details table is still showing only the column names, so select the Club_Details table, click on Show... on the toolbar and select Custom from the drop-down menu, or you can right-click on the table, select Table view and then click Custom. Selecting Standard does not give enough information in the table for our needs.

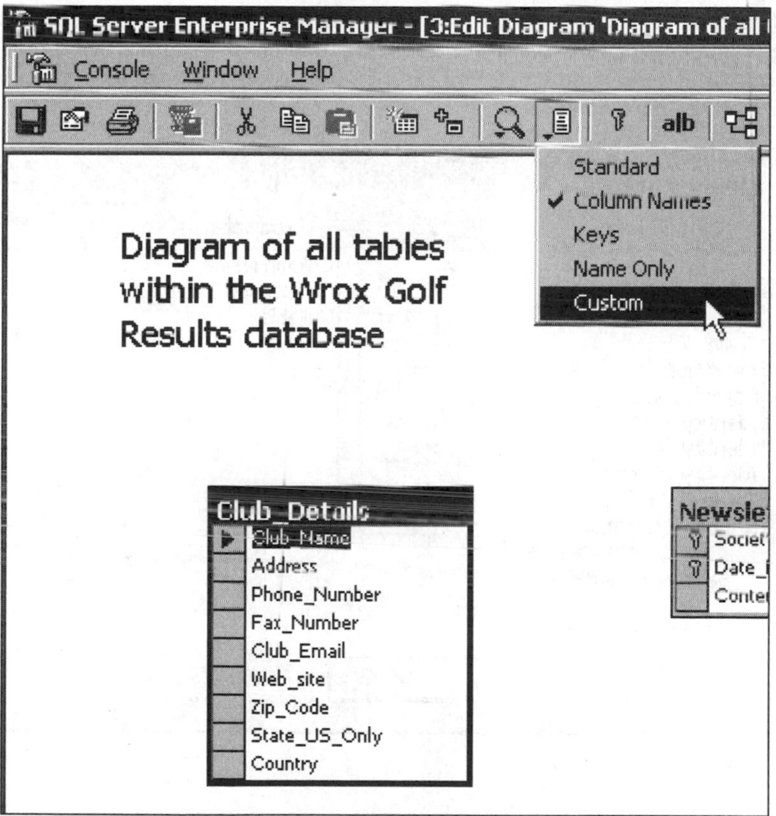

4. This will initially give the view of the columns that you would see if Standard had been selected. To add more information to each column, ensure that Club_Details is still selected, right-click, and select Table View and then Modify Custom...

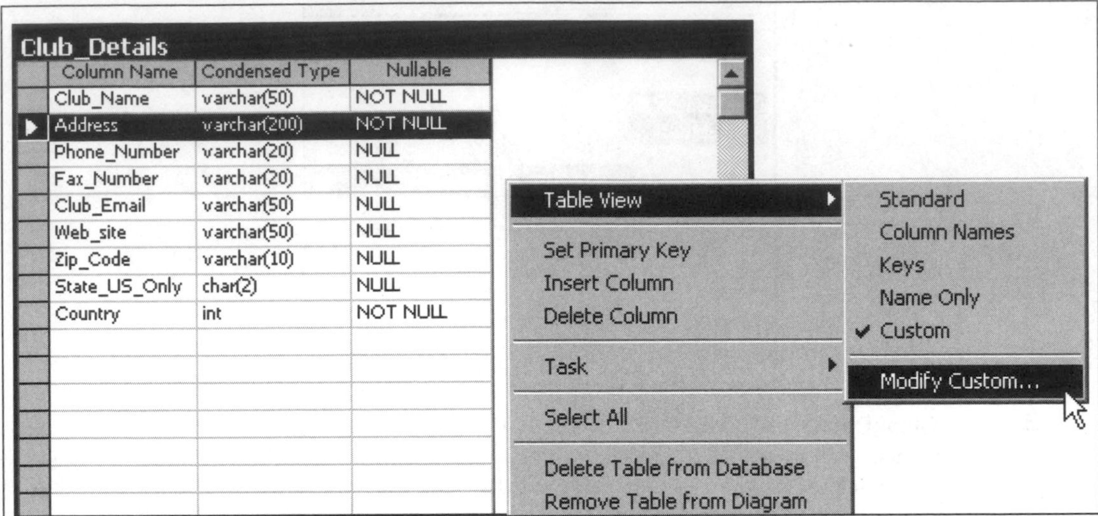

5. This brings up the Column Selector dialog, where the columns that you want to see can be chosen. Don't get confused with this referring to columns within a table; these are the columns of information about a table. As you can see, only three columns have been selected, and can be seen on the right-hand side.

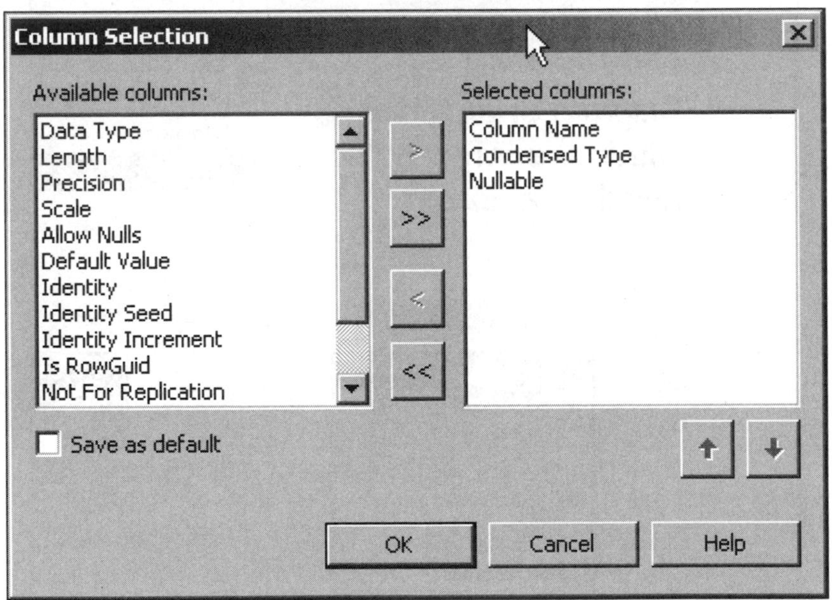

6. From the Available columns dialog, select Data Type, Length, Precision, Scale, Allow Nulls, Default Value, and Description, ensuring that Save as default is checked. This will ensure that the Custom view from this point on will now show these columns of information as default. Tables displayed using the Custom view will alter in display to reflect these changes as well. Don't forget that you can move columns between the two lists by double-clicking on the relevant item. Once done click OK.

> **Note that any tables that have been set up to view their information in Custom mode will reflect the changes just applied through this dialog.**

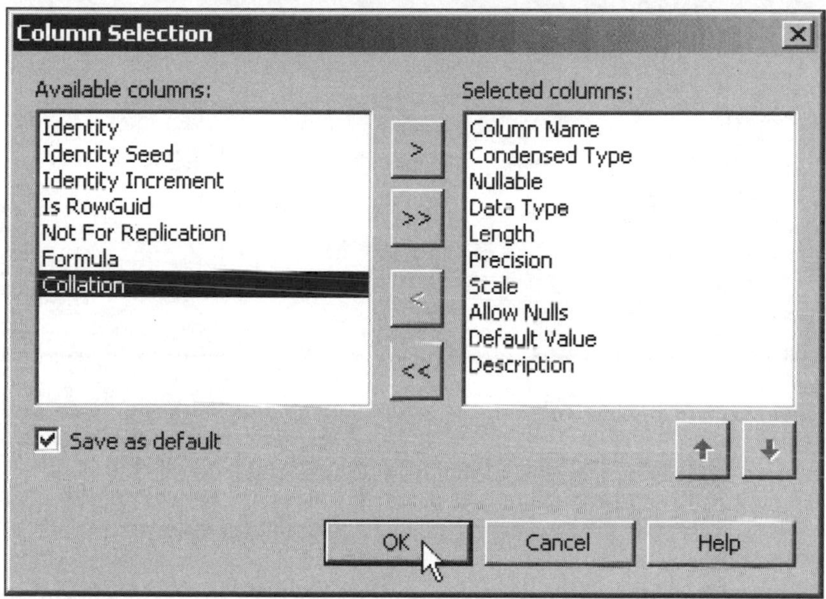

7. On clicking OK, the size of the Club_Details table should automatically expand to give you some leeway to add some new table columns. If not, then expand the table by dragging the bottom bar of the table downwards to add a bit more room.

Club_Details

Column Name	Condensed Type	Nullable	Data Type	Length	Precision	Scale	Allow Nulls	Default Value	Description
Club_Name	varchar(50)	NOT NULL	varchar	50	0	0			This is the clubs name
Address	varchar(200)	NOT NULL	varchar	200	0	0			Address of club excluding zip
Phone_Number	varchar(20)	NULL	varchar	20	0	0	✓		Phine number of club
Fax_Number	varchar(20)	NULL	varchar	20	0	0	✓		Fax number of club
Club_Email	varchar(50)	NULL	varchar	50	0	0	✓		The full email address
Web_site	varchar(50)	NULL	varchar	50	0	0	✓		Where the clubs web site is he
Zip_Code	varchar(10)	NULL	varchar	10	0	0	✓		The Zip Code
State_US_Only	char(2)	NULL	char	2	0	0	✓		The US state
Country	int	NOT NULL	int	4	10	0			Which country the club resides

8. It is now possible to add in three new columns to the end of the table. These are **Club_Chairperson**, **Club_ViceChair**, and **Club_Secretary**. These are straightforward columns, and we also add the description for these columns, keeping the documentation up to date. Notice that at the top of the table designer for this table, there is now an asterisk (*) after the **Club_Details** table name. This is signifying that there have been table changes that have not been physically placed in the database as yet. To enter the details, you would just move across each row for every new column to add. There is one area to point out, which concerns the **Condensed Type** column. If you skip over this and enter the necessary information about the column **Data Type** and **Length**, **Precision**, and **Scale**, then the **Condensed Type** will automatically populate itself with the correct information.

Club_Details *

Column Name	Condensed Type	Nullable	Data Type	Length	Precision	Scale	Allow Nulls	Default Value	Description
Club_Name	varchar(50)	NOT NULL	varchar	50	0	0			This is the clubs name
Address	varchar(200)	NOT NULL	varchar	200	0	0			Address of club excluding zip
Phone_Number	varchar(20)	NULL	varchar	20	0	0	✓		Phine number of club
Fax_Number	varchar(20)	NULL	varchar	20	0	0	✓		Fax number of club
Club_Email	varchar(50)	NULL	varchar	50	0	0	✓		The full email address
Web_site	varchar(50)	NULL	varchar	50	0	0	✓		Where the clubs web site is he
Zip_Code	varchar(10)	NULL	varchar	10	0	0	✓		The Zip Code
State_US_Only	char(2)	NULL	char	2	0	0	✓		The US state
Country	int	NOT NULL	int	4	10	0			Which country the club resides
Club_Chairpersor	varchar(50)	NULL	varchar	50	0	0	✓		Club Chair person
Club_ViceChair	varchar(50)	NULL	varchar	50	0	0	✓		Club Vice Chair Person
Club_Secretary	varchar(50)	NULL	varchar	50	0	0	✓		Club Secretary

9. It is also possible to add a column half way through the table layout, where perhaps it would make more sense to be located and found by developers or future database owners. The new column we add will record when the web site was last updated. Inserting this new column is quite a simple operation; we simply place the cursor below the column that requires the insert to be after, as the new column is inserted above the highlighted column. Then right-click and select the **Insert Column** option.

Club_Details *

Column Name	Condensed Type	Nullable	Data Type	Length	Precision	Scale	Allow Nulls	Default Value	Description
Club_Name	varchar(50)	NOT NULL	varchar	50	0	0			This is the clubs name
Address	varchar(200)	NOT NULL	varchar	200	0	0			Address of club excluding zip
Phone_Number	varchar(20)	NULL	varchar	20	0	0	✓		Phine number of club
Fax_Number	varchar(20)	NULL	varchar	20	0	0	✓		Fax number of club
Club_Email	varchar(50)	NULL	varchar	50	0	0	✓		The full email address
Web_site	varchar(50)	NULL	varchar	50	0	0	✓		Where the clubs web site is he
Zip_Code	varchar(10)	NULL	varchar	10	0	0	✓		The Zip Code
State			char	2	0	0	✓		The US state
Cour			int	4	10	0			Which country the club resides
Club			varchar	50	0	0	✓		Club Chair person
Club			varchar	50	0	0	✓		Club Vice Chair Person
Club			varchar	50	0	0	✓		Club Secretary

Table View
Set Primary Key
Insert Column
Delete Column
Task

10. Notice that there is a blank line, ready for your input.

Club_Details *

Column Name	Condensed Type	Nullable	Data Type	Length	Precision	Scale	Allow Nulls	Default Value	Description
Club_Name	varchar(50)	NOT NULL	varchar	50	0	0			This is the clubs name
Address	varchar(200)	NOT NULL	varchar	200	0	0			Address of club excluding zip
Phone_Number	varchar(20)	NULL	varchar	20	0	0	✓		Phine number of club
Fax_Number	varchar(20)	NULL	varchar	20	0	0	✓		Fax number of club
Club_Email	varchar(50)	NULL	varchar	50	0	0	✓		The full email address
Web_site	varchar(50)	NULL	varchar	50	0	0	✓		Where the clubs web site is he
Zip_Code	varchar(10)	NULL	varchar	10	0	0	✓		The Zip Code
State_US_Only	char(2)	NULL	char	2	0	0	✓		The US state
Country	int	NOT NULL	int	4	10	0			Which country the club resides
Club_Chairpersor	varchar(50)	NULL	varchar	50	0	0	✓		Club Chair person
Club_ViceChair	varchar(50)	NULL	varchar	50	0	0	✓		Club Vice Chair Person
Club_Secretary	varchar(50)	NULL	varchar	50	0	0	✓		Club Secretary

11. Fill out the row as highlighted in the screenshot below. This will add the new column into the table in the correct place.

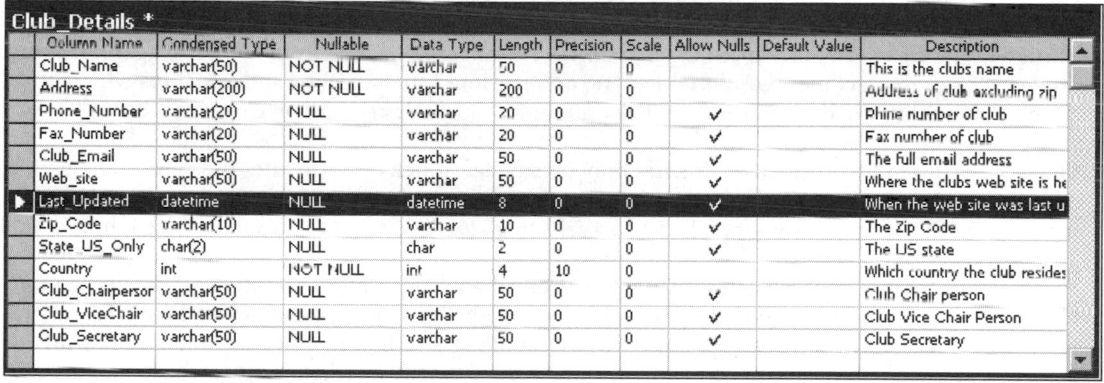

Club_Details *

Column Name	Condensed Type	Nullable	Data Type	Length	Precision	Scale	Allow Nulls	Default Value	Description
Club_Name	varchar(50)	NOT NULL	varchar	50	0	0			This is the clubs name
Address	varchar(200)	NOT NULL	varchar	200	0	0			Address of club excluding zip
Phone_Number	varchar(20)	NULL	varchar	20	0	0	✓		Phine number of club
Fax_Number	varchar(20)	NULL	varchar	20	0	0	✓		Fax number of club
Club_Email	varchar(50)	NULL	varchar	50	0	0	✓		The full email address
Web_site	varchar(50)	NULL	varchar	50	0	0	✓		Where the clubs web site is he
Last_Updated	datetime	NULL	datetime	8	0	0	✓		When the web site was last u
Zip_Code	varchar(10)	NULL	varchar	10	0	0	✓		The Zip Code
State_US_Only	char(2)	NULL	char	2	0	0	✓		The US state
Country	int	NOT NULL	int	4	10	0			Which country the club resides
Club_Chairpersor	varchar(50)	NULL	varchar	50	0	0	✓		Club Chair person
Club_ViceChair	varchar(50)	NULL	varchar	50	0	0	✓		Club Vice Chair Person
Club_Secretary	varchar(50)	NULL	varchar	50	0	0	✓		Club Secretary

12. Now that all the changes have been made, it's time to save and close the diagram. This time, click the Windows standard close button. This then brings up the Save dialog. Click Yes, obviously.

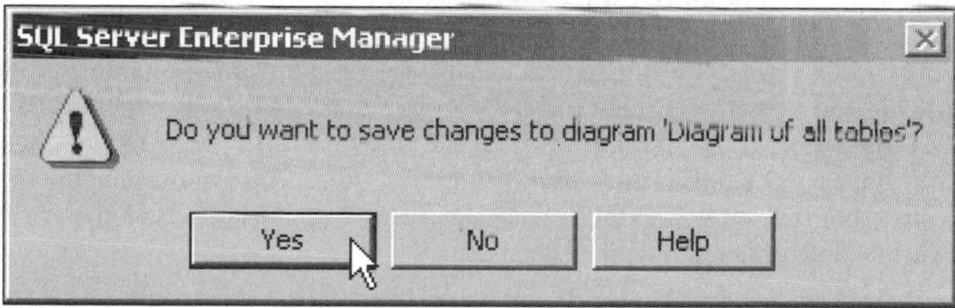

13. SQL Server notices that in fact, the Club_Details table has been altered, and brings up a prompt asking whether the table changes should be saved to the database. This would list all the tables that have been altered, including those that have a relationship to the table you are altering, if changes have been replicated through to them as well. Again, click Yes.

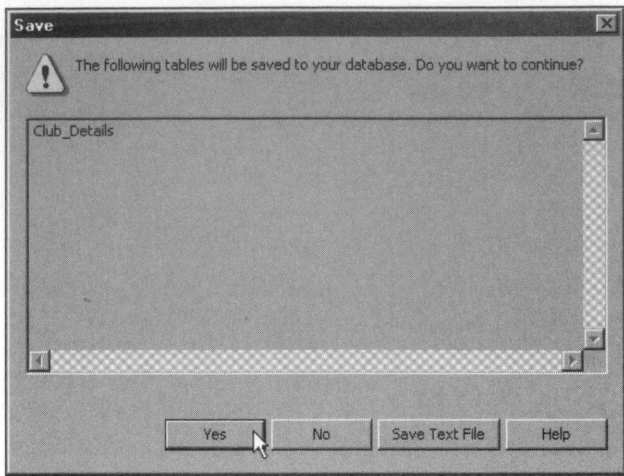

As you have just seen through one example, it is possible to alter the database using the database diagramming tool. Although all we have demonstrated is the alteration of the table, it should be evidence that the tool is powerful enough to complete the most complex tasks. This can be combined with the next example, where further relationships are added. All of this is done without having to change nodes or environments to get to complete two separate tasks. However, once again, it comes down to what you feel most comfortable with, and no doubt there will be some readers who will prefer developing within the diagramming tool as opposed to other development areas.

Once the diagram has been opened, it has only taken a few quick clicks to alter the view of the necessary table to see the relevant information; in this case we want to add new columns. This is all performed through the Show toolbar option, followed by selecting and modifying the Custom selection from that.

However, using this option is more than is required when using Enterprise Manager to alter a table. The list of information required to add in the columns already exists within Enterprise Manager, but you have to alter the view of the table within the diagramming tool before you have enough information to complete these changes effectively. However, once the Custom view is set up, it is just a matter of selecting the necessary table and then selecting Custom from the Show toolbar. So after the initial selection of which columns need to be displayed for the custom view, the task will be completed much faster in future. Therefore, it is important that the most frequently used columns are selected for the Custom view. However, there is no real reason against selecting every column to be displayed in the Custom view, it just means that more room is taken up within the designer.

Adding, removing, and altering columns is just as easy in the diagram as it is in the table designer within Enterprise Manager, and this is how it should be. There would be no advantage if this were not the case. It just so happens that in the diagramming tool, all the information is on one row; however in the table designer, it is split between two different areas, the main column information such as name, data type, and length is grouped at the top of the table designer, and then areas such as the default value, and description are at the bottom. Again, this is cosmetic.

Although we have only shown the Zoom To Fit option, you can zoom in on a diagram to see a specific table with great clarification. You will find that the Zoom To Fit option is the most commonly used option; but don't forget that these other zoom levels are also there to help.

By now you should be comfortable with what has been demonstrated in this example and so let's move on to a more complex task, which will add further relationships between tables within the database.

Adding in Further Relationships

In the previous chapter, a number of relationships were built between tables within the database. This was a straightforward exercise where it was possible to start with either of the two tables involved in the relationship and use this starting point to build a relationship between the two tables.

There is a need for a relationship between the Players table and the Society_Groups table. It is important to establish a relationship between these tables so that a player is associated with a particular golf society. In real life of course, not all golf players are associated with a society, however, the example within the book does deal with societies as a whole, and therefore it is important to keep this relationship alive. It is crucial to the database's data integrity that a society cannot be removed until all the players have been removed first, and working the other way, every player must be associated with a society.

Try It Out – Adding Further Relationships

1. Ensure that SQL Server Enterprise Manager is running. Navigate to the initial diagram created earlier. Right-click, and select Design Diagram...

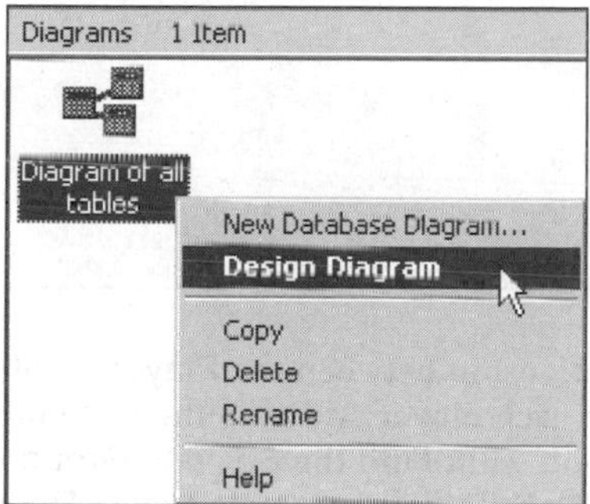

2. This brings up the initial diagram. If you find the layout has altered, to make things easier, change it so that it looks like the layout overleaf. Do this by dragging the tables around, and selecting the Zoom To Fit mode.

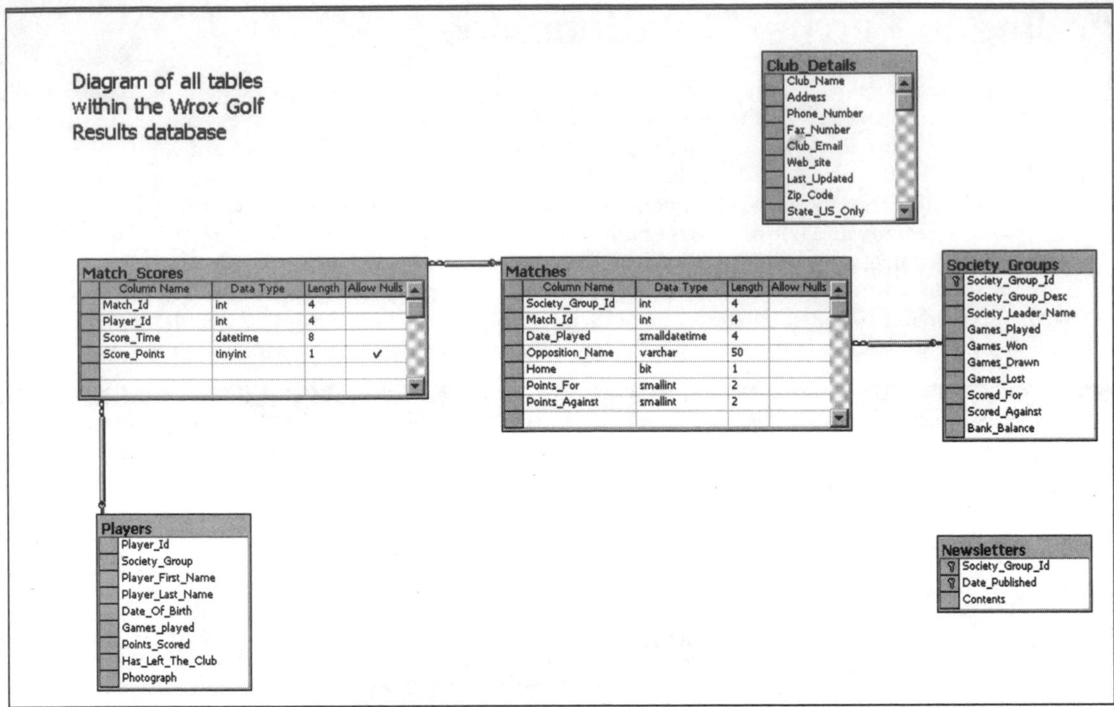

3. It is time to create a relationship between the Players table and the Society_Groups table. This is to ensure that for each player added to the system, a valid society will be assigned to them, for them to play golf with. Find the Society_Group within the Players table, and the Society_Group_Id within the Society_Groups table. The diagram should change to look like the diagram opposite. To complete this, click on the Society_Group_Id column within the Society_Groups table, and while keeping the mouse button down, drag the mouse pointer over to the Players table and release the mouse button when the pointer is over the Society_Groups column. Be warned, that you need to click on the Society_Group_Id column in the gray column marker to the left of the column name.

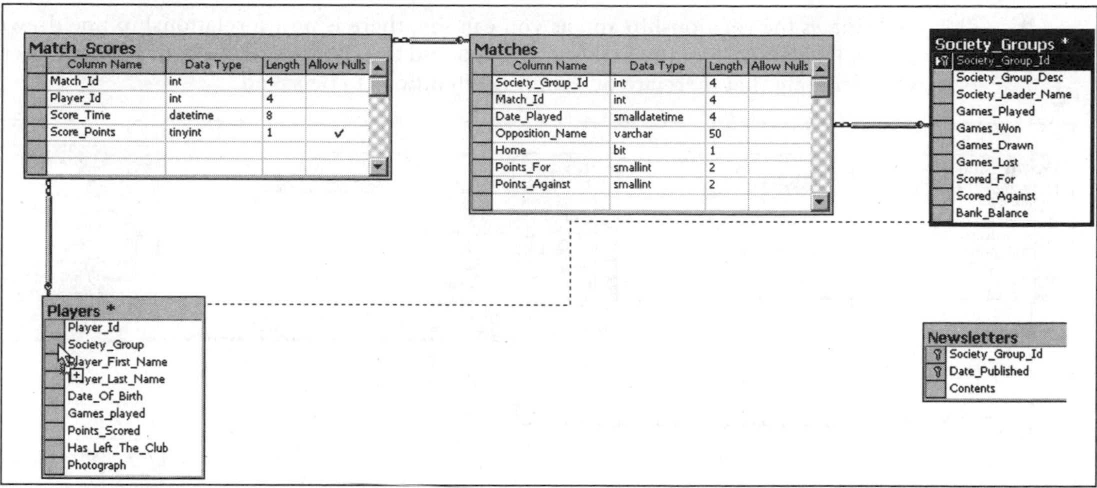

4. Dragging between the tables, and releasing the mouse button, brings up the **Create Relationship** dialog. Notice in this case that the two columns are called by different names and there is no problem in doing this. This emphasizes the fact that it is not necessary to have a relationship between columns that have identical names. Saying that, it is important that you do try to keep column names the same when they hold the same information. If you have not managed to select the two correct columns for your relationship, it is possible to alter them before clicking **OK**. You can do this by using the drop down list, which will display the list of column objects within the relevant table. You can then select the relevant column to join to. However, we have selected the correct columns so click **OK**.

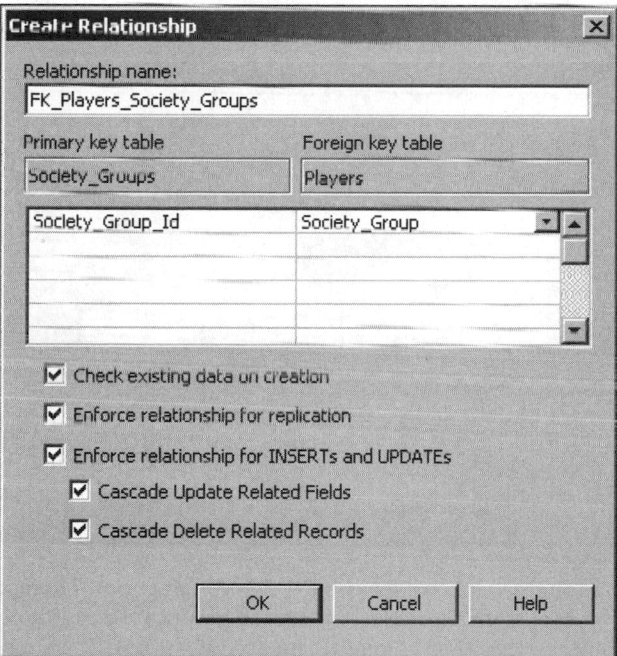

5. This now creates the relationship and as you can see, there is now a relationship line drawn between the two tables, and the **Society_Groups** and the **Players** tables both have an asterisk as a suffix denoting that there are outstanding alterations to be saved.

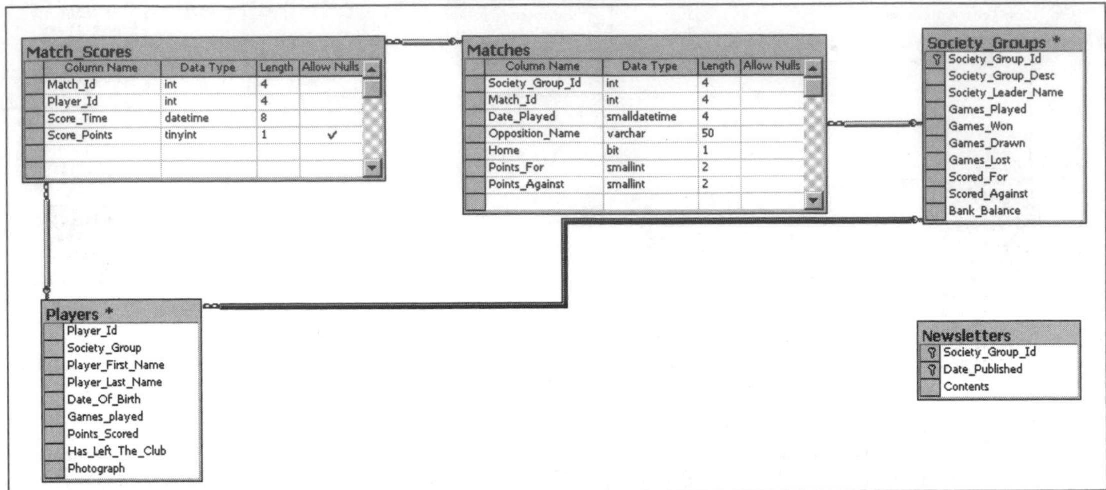

6. Now you can click on the **Save** button in the left hand side of the toolbar. This will then confirm that there are outstanding changes to be saved for the two tables mentioned. Click **Yes** to commit the changes.

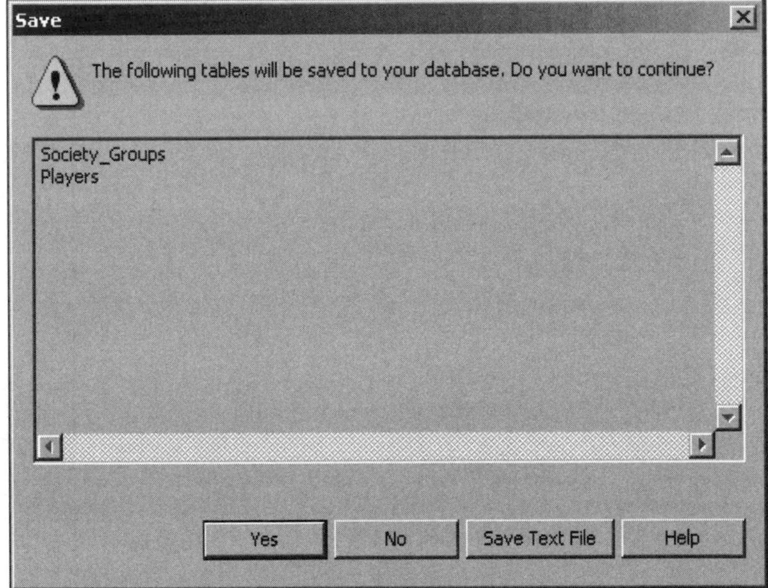

That's all there is to building a relationship with the digramming tool. There are not too many differences between this tool and Enterprise Manager as you can see, but it is important to realize these differences because they can lead to problems if you do not work with the diagramming tool correctly.

If you recall, when building a relationship diagram within Enterprise Manager, you could initially choose either table to get to the relationship dialog to build the relationship between two tables. Once into the dialog, you could swap around which table was the primary key table, and which was the foreign key table. This is not the case with the diagramming tool. The primary key table is always located where you start the dragging action from, and the foreign key table is where the dragging action stops. Once done, there is no going back except to cancel the relationship and start again. So, before starting to build the relationship, ensure that you do have the dragging action the correct way about.

The next area to look at is the actual diagram itself. You will see that there are lines joining the two tables involved in the relationship, where one end has a yellow key, and the symbol on the other end is an infinity symbol. These symbols are denoting the primary key table, which is denoted by the yellow key, and the foreign key, which is denoted by the infinity symbol. Because there is only one infinity symbol, this is denoting that the relationship is a one-to-many relationship. An infinity symbol on both sides would be a many-to-many relationship, and no infinity symbol would mean a one-to-one relationship

However this is all that there is different to working within the diagram from using native Enterprise Manager, so again Microsoft has given you as a developer or administrator the ability to work in two different environments with ease.

Now that you have seen how to work with a diagram and how useful it is, there is another area where creating a diagram comes in to its own and where a diagram will really help every developer using your database; this is the default diagram.

Creating the Default Diagram

Near the beginning, we discussed the database's default diagram, and why it should exist. This next example will demonstrate the building of that default diagram for the `Wrox_Golf_Results` database.

This is a very simple process, and follows many of the details covered when building a normal diagram earlier in the chapter. There are one or two specific anomalies to the default database diagram that you have to be aware of, which is why this example is being demonstrated.

Try It Out – Creating the Default Database Diagram

1. Ensure that SQL Server Enterprise Manager is still running and that you have clicked and highlighted the Wrox_Golf_Results database. You must be on the database itself and not any of the nodes below.

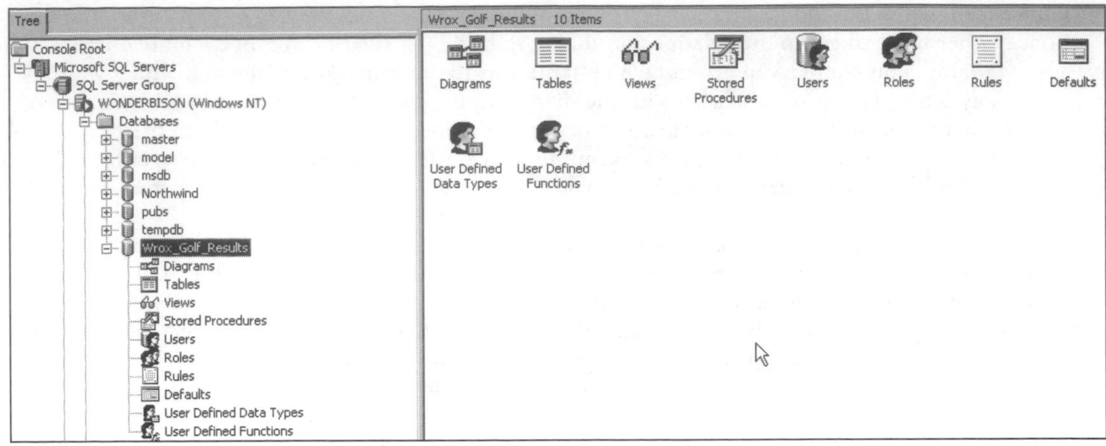

2. From the menu, select View and then you will see Default database diagram. As there has been no default database diagram already created, selecting this will start the process of building the default diagram. Go ahead and select Default database diagram.

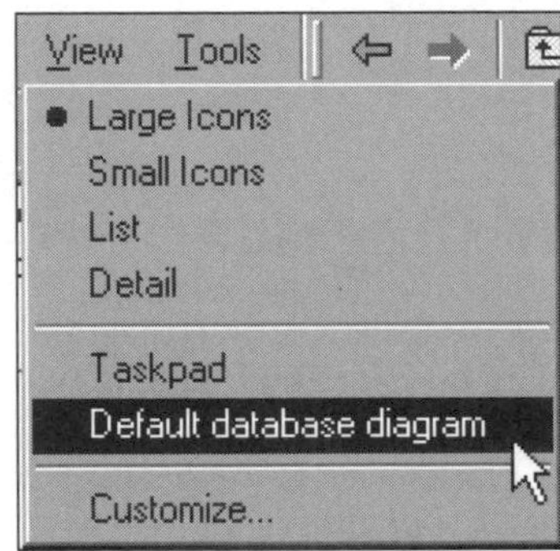

3. You are prompted by Enterprise Manager that no default diagram has been created, and if you wish to create a diagram, click Yes. This will move you on to the creation of the database diagram.

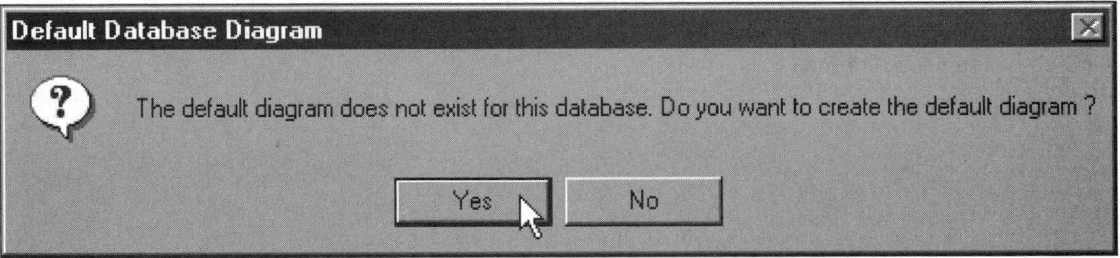

4. This starts the Create Database Diagram Wizard as before. As expected, the first screen is just a quick summary of what is going to happen next. Click Next. As before, you are presented with an empty dialog to add in the relevant tables. Add in all the tables just as in the previous example. To recap, the tables to add in are Club_Details, Match_Scores, Matches, Newsletters, Players, and Society_Groups. Once you are finished the dialog should look like the screenshot opposite . Click Next.

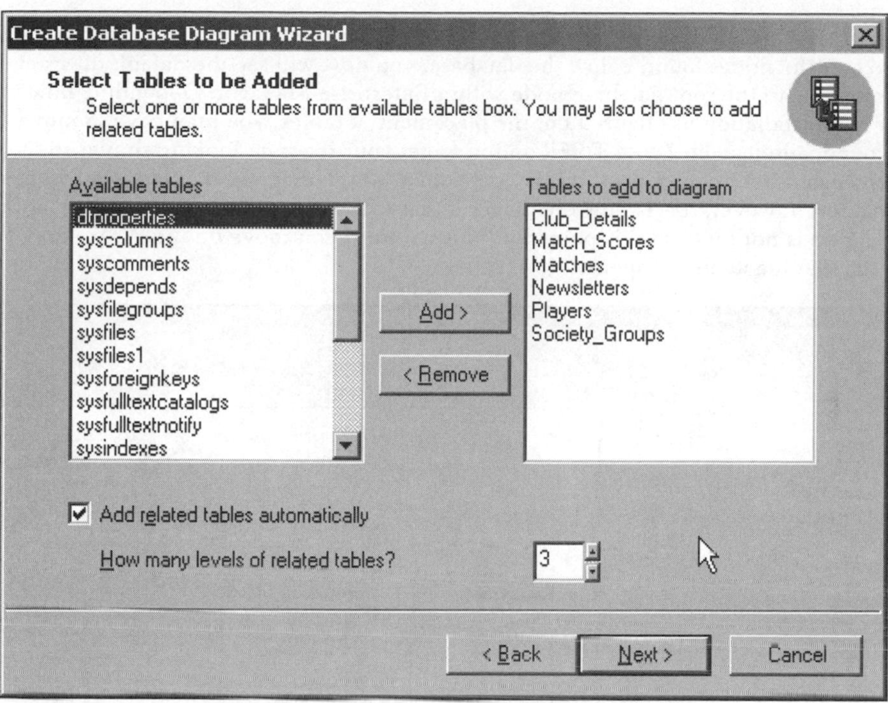

5. As before the final dialog appears, confirming what is going to happen. Click Finish.

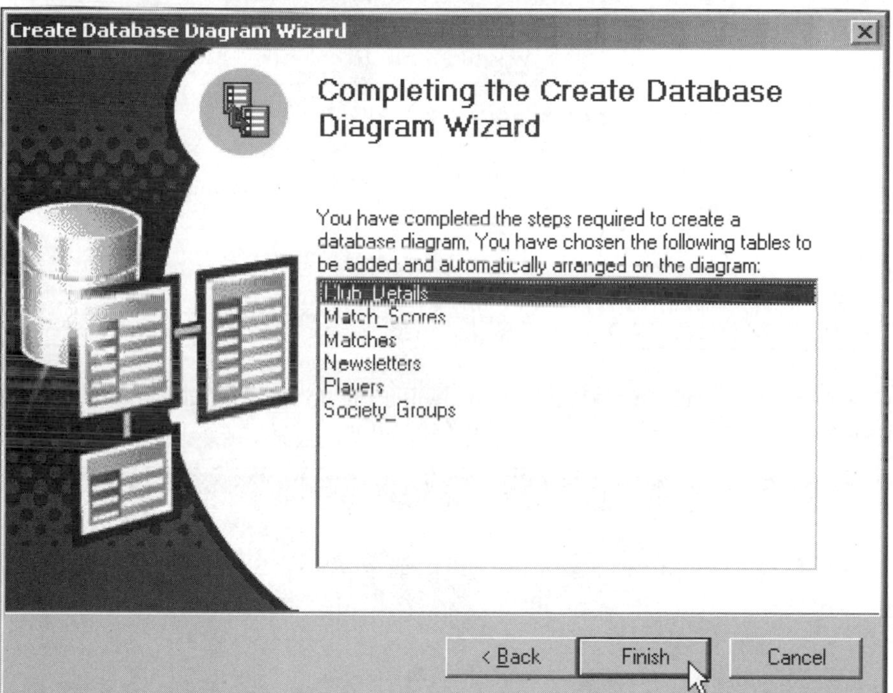

6. Enterprise Manager now looks like the following screenshot. Instead of displaying icons for each of the nodes found below the database, you now will see the default diagram each time you move to the root database node within Enterprise Manager. Depending how your SQL Server installation has figured out the placement of tables, you may have to move the tables around, and use the Zoom To Fit option to get your diagram looking similar to the one in the screenshot below. That said, this is very similar to the diagram that was created earlier in the chapter, however, this is now the diagram that will be used as the default for the database. The diagram is not saved at this point, and it is not until you move off the Wrox_Golf_Results node that it actually happens.

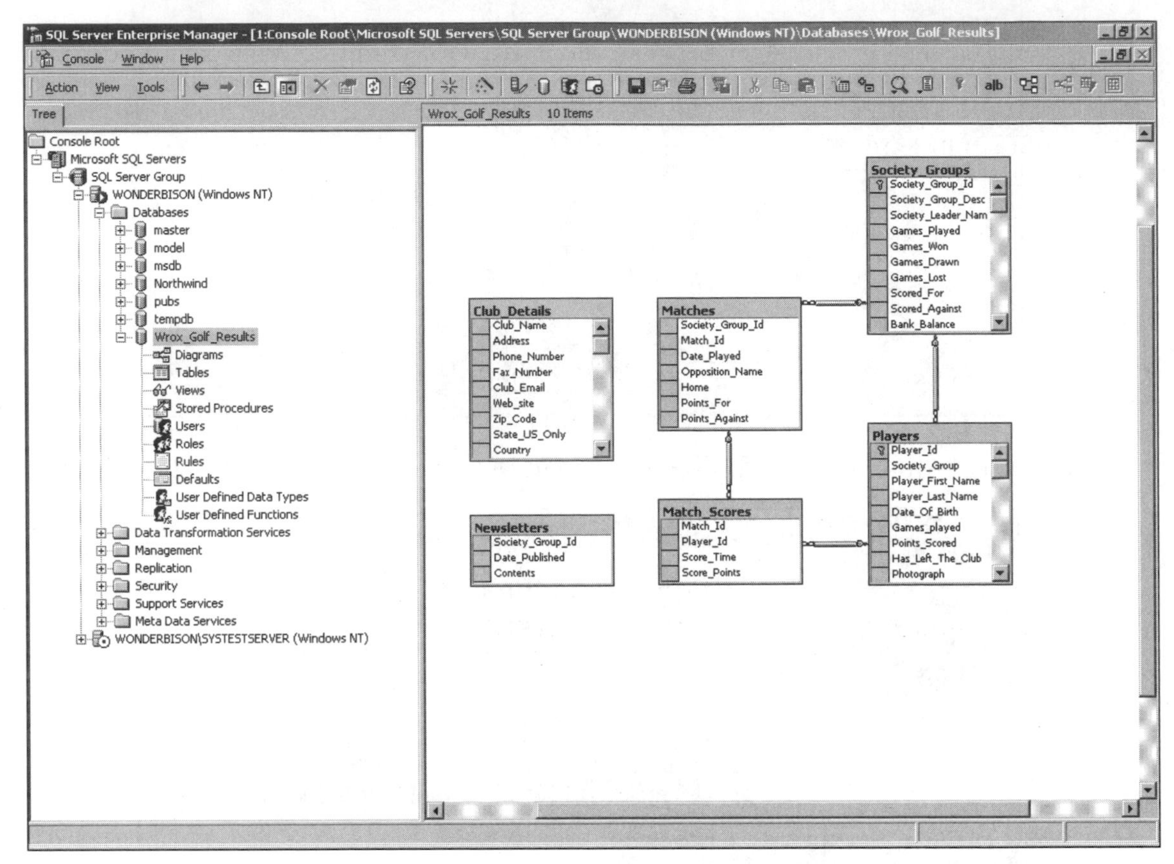

7. Moving off the Wrox_Golf_Results node, will bring up the Default Database Diagram Save prompt. If you are happy, then click the Yes button.

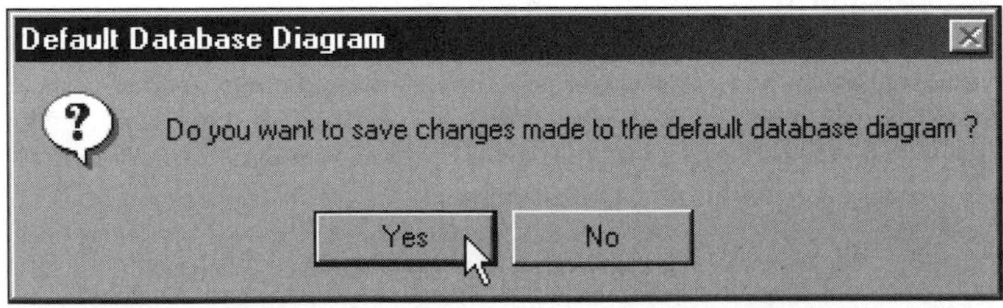

8. If you now move to the diagrams node of the **Wrox_Golf_Results** database, then you will notice that the default diagram is not listed. Only the initial diagram created earlier in the chapter is displayed. Just to remind you, you can see the initial diagram, by having the database as the anchor point in the tree view on the left, and having the **Default database diagram** option selected from the **View** menu.

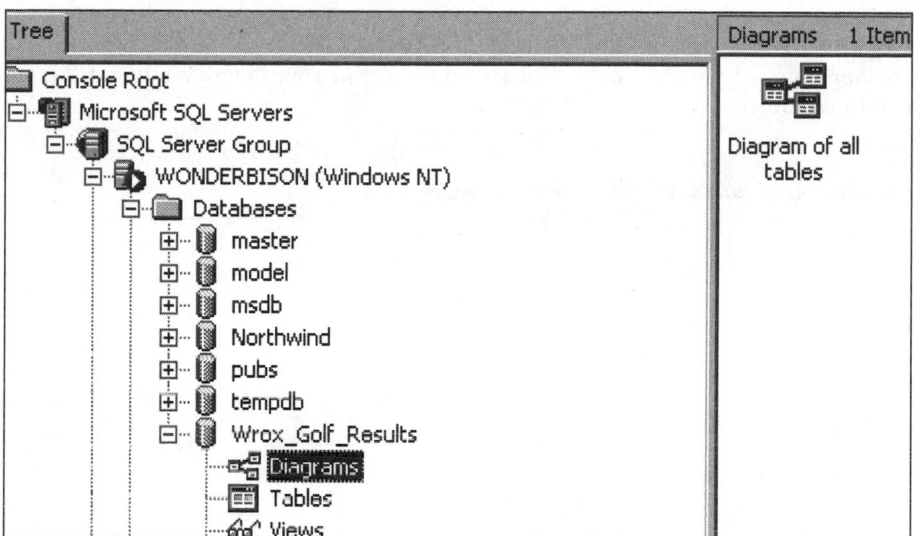

Summary

This chapter has been about another tool that gives you the ability to complete your job in an efficient manner, as well as looking at the whole process of working with your database from a different angle. Database diagrams should initially be thought of as a form of documentation. Keep in mind though, that the diagramming tool may expand in future versions of SQL Server to become much more sophisticated and powerful than it is now, although even now, it is quite a powerful utility. It is possible that Microsoft will take the diagramming tool and use this as a replacement for much of Enterprise Manager. Saying that, if it did, there would be a great deal of work involved, as well the issue of screen space occurring. Therefore out of all of this, knowing the diagramming tool and using it has more importance than you may well think at this moment in time, and so it is useful to become familiar with it and to use the power that it already has, not just as a documentation tool, but also as a development tool.

Don't get caught out by the fact that changes in the diagram are not applied until the diagram is saved, and that your changes could overwrite another's changes. If you are using the database diagram tool for development in any sort of multi-user environment, take the greatest of care when completing updates. Unless you split your database solution into multiple diagrams, with any table being found in at most one diagram, do not use the database designer as a development tool.

The database diagram tool is ideal for printing diagrams that will be used in any planning or team meetings that discuss updates to the database, including new columns, new tables, and relationships. A picture can convey this information very effectively, and the SQL Server database diagramming tool can certainly help in achieving this.

Always keep the default database diagram up to date and concurrent so that the whole database solution can be seen from a design or documentation view point, but don't use it as the diagram used in development as it encompasses everything. When adding new tables or removing redundant ones, try to ensure that the diagram is well laid out to view as much as possible.

If you do wish to use the diagramming tool as a development platform, try to divide up the database into logical sections and build diagrams for those sections. At least then you are minimizing any possible conflict with other designers, and it is also easier to corner an area for your development within your team. By having your area of the whole database set up within your diagram you can then inform others not to touch those tables.

> **Remember, they who save last, save the changes.**

Database Backups and Recovery

Now that a major part of the database has been created in the previous chapters, and before moving on to inserting and manipulating the data, this is a good point to take a moment's breath to backup the database, just so that if things go wrong, it is possible to recover back to a stable point.

What is really abundantly clear when working with any sort of system where data is held must be that there is a clear and workable backup and recovery strategy in place when things go wrong. It may also be required that not only should this recovery cater for hardware failure, but for anything up to an act of God should the whole building collapses around us. It is in this instance that we would move to an "offsite", which is a building a safe distance away from our current building housing the computing equipment. That is quite a dramatic step and is a decision that would be taken at a higher level than we probably could affect, however, we must create a backup of our system and store it according to the recommendations of our Board of Directors, whether they are for in-house or offsite storage.

This chapter looks at different backup strategies that can be implemented by us as a developer or an administrator, and how they would be implemented. We also look at scenarios where the database is in use 24 hours a day, 7 days a week, and how a backup strategy needs to be formed around such scenarios. From there, we will see how to perform an adhoc backup of the database as well as scheduled transaction log backups. It will be made clear in this chapter when we would perform both of these types of backups and when they would be useful. Of course after the backup, then there is the necessity to test that the backup can be restored. Generally, this backup will be restored onto a non production system. Some companies have complete environments established to test their disaster recovery scenarios.

What we have to realize, and what will be demonstrated, is that there are different methods of taking backups depending on what we are trying to achieve. The most common scenarios are discussed and demonstrated in this chapter, but we also have to look at the next chapter where database maintenance plans are also covered.

It is imperative that we get the correct backup strategy in place, and that it works. This point will be repeated throughout the chapter.

So, in this chapter we will learn:

- Backup strategies
- When a problem might occur during the backup and restore process
- How to take a database offline, and then bring it back online
- How to create a backup
- Different media for building a backup – what needs to be considered
- Backing up the transaction log
- When to back up the data, and when to back up the transaction log
- Scheduling backups and what happens if the server isn't running at the scheduled time
- Restoring a database
- Detaching and attaching a database
- How to work with users still attached to the database when we need them not to be connected
- How to build SQL statements for backing up the database structure, and when it is useful to have them

The first one to look at is the backup strategy that we want to adopt.

Backup Strategies

Backing up a database, no matter how large or small, should form part of our database solution. Even if a backup is only taken once a week, or even once a month, it is crucial that we sit down and decide which backup strategy is right for us. Much of this decision lies in the hands of the product owners for our company since they must weigh the risk they're willing to take against the cost of minimizing that risk. There are also many different strategies that can be adopted within our overall main backup strategy, depending on days of the week, or perhaps period within the month.

Based on the strategy that we choose, we will have to decide what type of backup we will need. Full database backups take a complete snapshot of a database at any given point. A differential backup will backup only the data that has changed since the last full backup. Finally, a transaction log backup only backs up the data in the transaction log, which consists of transactions that were recently committed to the database. All of these types of backups can be done while our SQL Server is online and while users are actively hitting our database. To be able to restore a database to any point-in-time, we will have to use a combination of these backup types. We will go into much more detail about each of these later in this chapter.

The first place to start with the strategy is to look at the application and ask ourselves the following questions:

- How much of the data can be lost, if any? In other words, how crucial is it that no data is lost? (This could cover where a database could be re-populated with information.)
- How often is the data updated? Do we need regular backups from a performance viewpoint as well as recovery viewpoint?

- Do we need to back up all the data all of the time, or can we do this periodically, and then only back up the data that has altered in the meanwhile?
- How much data needs to be backed up and how long do we need to keep the copies of the backups?
- In the event of catastrophic failure, how long will it take to completely rebuild the database, if it's even possible?

There are many more questions that can be asked, but for the moment, these are the most crucial questions that need answers.

If we can afford to allow data updates to be lost, then this is a straightforward periodic database backup; for example, backup the whole database once a week. This is simple and easy to complete and requires little thought. This is a rare scenario and found usually in data warehousing systems or those with a large amount of static data that can be rebuilt.

Looking at the next question, if there are a large number of updates that take place, then a more complex solution is required. For every update, a record is kept in the transaction log file. This log file has a limited amount of space, as does the data file. If we backed up and cleared the transaction log file, this would free up the space and also aid performance. The smaller the transaction log file, the better. However, the downside to that is that is will take longer to recover from a corrupt database. This is due to the fact that a restore will have to restore the data, and then every transaction log backup to the point of failure. That is, each transaction log will have to be restored to update the database, not just the latest log file.

The third question, though, covers the real crux of the problems. If we need to back up all the data each time, how often does that need to take place? This could well be every night, and many production systems do just this. By completing a full data back up every night, we are allowing ourselves to be in a state where only one or two restores need to occur to get back to a working state. This would be the data backup, followed by the single transaction log backup, if one was taken in the mean time, to be restored. Much better than having one data backup to be restored, and then a log file for every day since the data file backup. What happens if the failure is on a Friday and we complete a whole database back up on a Saturday? That would take one data file and six transaction log file restores to complete.

Therefore sit down and take stock. As often as we can, take a full database backup, then from there take a differential backup, followed by transaction log backups. However, we have to weigh this against the time that a full backup takes over a differential backup or a transaction log; how large a window in processing time we have to complete these backups, and what is the risk level on having to complete, for example, six transaction log restores.

The problem is, there is no universally right answer. Each situation is different, and it is only through experience, which comes from testing our solution thoroughly, that we find out what is best for that situation.

Whatever our backup strategy, the best possible scenario is to complete a backup when there is nobody working within the database. If there are times when we can make the database unavailable then this is an ideal opportunity to take the backup. Although SQL Server can perform full backups while the database is online and active, we will gain performance benefits by having an inactive database. The first example, shortly, demonstrates one method of doing this.

When Problems May Occur

Obviously, when taking a backup it must work; otherwise we have wasted our time, but, crucially, we are leaving our database and organization in a vulnerable position. If we have time within our backup window to verify that a backup has been successful; then do it how to do this will be shown later in the chapter. It cannot be stressed strongly enough that verifying a backup is just as crucial as taking the backup in the first place. There have been situations where a backup has been taken every night; however, it has not been noticed that the backup has failed and there has been a hardware failure, and so no backup to revert back, to use as a restore on a new machine.In one case almost a week's worth of data was lost. Luckily, the weekend backups had succeeded; otherwise the company would have been in a major data loss situation. The cause was that the tapes being inserted for the backup were not large enough to hold the backup being performed. Therefore the tape became full, and so the backup failed. Obviously this was a case of where the company not only failed to verify the backup, but also failed to have processes in place to check that their backup strategy was still working after a period of implementation.

We should always review our backup strategy on a regular basis. Even better, put in place jobs that run each day, giving some sort of space report so that it is possible to instantly see that there is a potential problem looming. This is quite an advanced task and may be completed by a more senior developer. In *"Professional SQL Server 2000 Programming" (Wrox Press, ISBN 1-861004-48-6)*, creating jobs is covered in more detail, although they are touched on here.

Taking a Database Offline

As we have just discussed in the Backup Strategies, *if it is possible to shut down the database then do so.* Doing this will ensure that all the data that needs to be flushed out from any buffers is, and that the data is physically written to the database. This will then allow a backup of the database to be taken without any fear of anyone working within the database at the time.

Keep in mind that SQL Server does not have to be offline to perform a backup. In most environments, we will not have the luxury of taking a database offline before backing it up, because users are constantly making data changes. Backing up a database can take a long time when we have databases over a gigabyte in size. SQL Server has implemented a failsafe to make sure that no transactions are lost. Say, for example, that we begin a database backup at 7 a.m. and a user updates 1000 records before the backup is complete. The user's updates are appended to the end of the backup when the backup completes.

By taking our database offline, we do not have to use SQL Server to perform the backup. What this strategy is for is to take a disk backup. This means the hard drive is being backed up, rather than a specific database within a server. However, don't forget that by taking our database offline, it means we will have to take a backup of the directory using some sort of drive back up, even if this is file copy.

If we have our database on a server, no doubt there is some sort of server backup strategy in place, and so our database would be backed up fully and successfully through this method, so if we can take our database "out of service" in time for those backups, then we should do so.

Taking the database offline means taking our database out of service. Nobody can update or access the data, and nobody can modify table structures, etc. In this next section, we will take Wrox_Golf_Results offline before backing up the database. There isn't a great deal to this section, as it is a straightforward process, however let's go through it, as it will form part of many readers' backup strategies.

Try It Out – Taking a Database Offline

1. Open the SQL Server Enterprise Manager and navigate to the Wrox_Golf_Results database.

2. Right-click on our database, select All Tasks, and then click Take Offline.

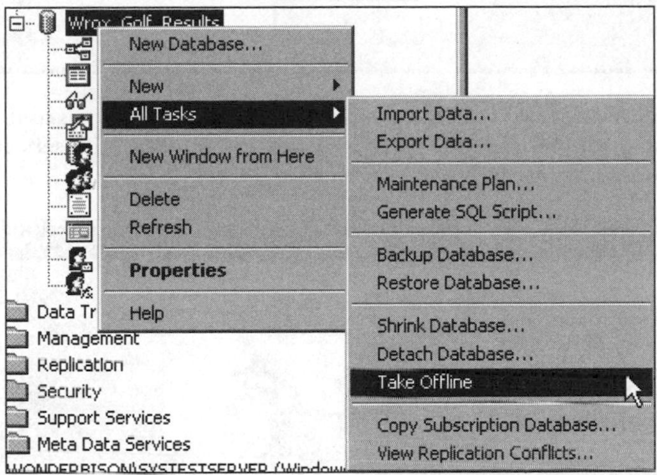

3. That's it. After a few moments, and some hard drive activity, Enterprise Manager will show the Wrox_Golf_Results as (Offline).

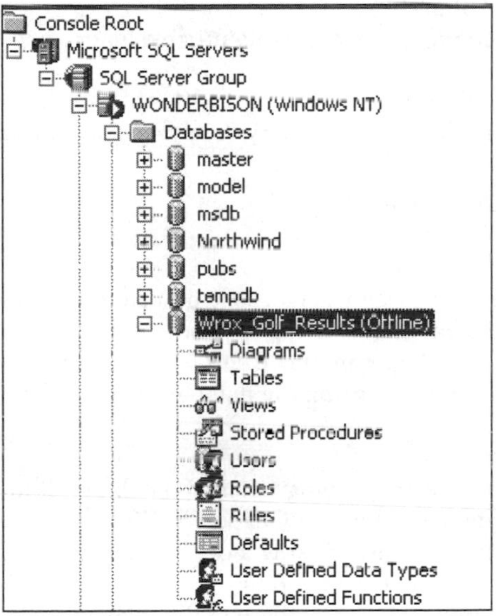

4. If we then try to click on some of the nodes for the Wrox_Golf_Results database, for example, the Tables node, we will be reminded that the database is offline, and therefore cannot be viewed or modified. We will also not be able to access the database through any application such as Query Analyzer.

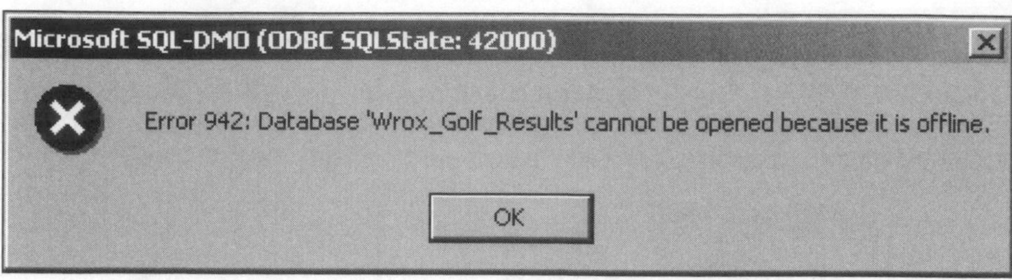

To take a database offline, SQL Server must be able to gain exclusive access to the database. This means that no user can be in the database when we issue the command. If users are connected, then we will receive the following message in Enterprise Manager:

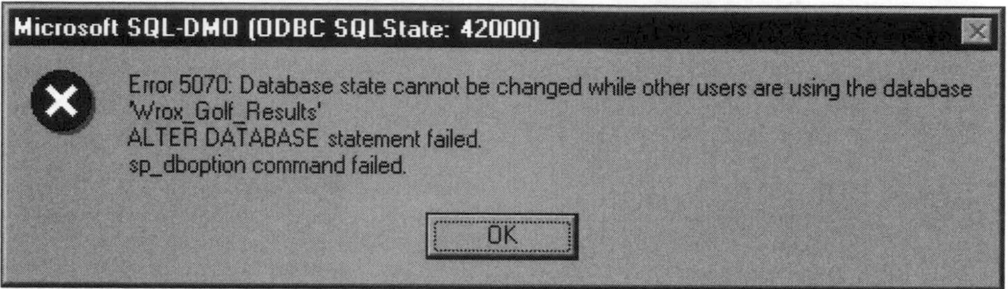

To take the database offline, we'll first have to disconnect every user connected to that database. We will cover this in detail later in this chapter. A quick way, though, to disconnect all the users in a database can be found at the URL http://www.sqlservercentral.com/columnists/bknight/uspkillusers.asp.

We can also take a database offline in T-SQL by using the `ALTER DATABASE` syntax, shown below. To do this, connect to the `master` database in Query Analyzer and run the following query:

```
ALTER DATABASE World_Golf_Results
SET OFFLINE
```

As said earlier, that's all there is to it. Our database is now no longer available for any updates of data, or modifications, and so can be backed up using any backup utility that takes files from a hard drive. If we have to ever restore from a backup completed this way, don't forget to take the database offline first, then restore from the backup, and then bring the database back online, ready for use, which is covered in the next section.

There is also one strange side issue concerning taking a database offline, petty as it may seem. If we recall, a default database diagram was built in Chapter 9. Well, when we take the database offline, then this diagram is no longer available to us. What is more, we are prompted that there is no default database diagram, and asked if we would like to build one, but then when we do try to build a diagram, as we would expect, there are none of the database tables available to us to build a diagram! Click Cancel to exit this. The database is offline. This is more an oversight by Microsoft than a bug, as there is really no point of having a default database diagram for a database that is offline.

However, let's now look at how to bring the database back online so it is possible to look more at backup strategies.

Bringing a Database Back Online

Now that the database is offline, and we assume that the backup has been performed on the server, it is time to bring the database back online and ready for any modifications required of it. With the database offline, we can copy it into multiple locations and "clone" our database multiple times as we bring it online. If we try to copy a database file while SQL Server is running normally, we will receive a sharing violation. Make sure we keep a copy of the database in its original location though: if we don't do this, the database will appear corrupt when it is brought back online.

Taking a database online is a simple process once again and can be completed very quickly.

Try it Out – Bringing a Database Online

1. Ensure the SQL Server Enterprise Manager is running and that we have navigated to the Wrox_Golf_Results database.

2. Right-click, select All Tasks, and then click Bring Online.

3. That's it. After a few moments, and a bit more disk activity, then Enterprise Manager will show Wrox_Golf_Results as being back online.

We can also take a database online using T-SQL and the `SET ONLINE` syntax, as shown below:

```
ALTER DATABASE World_Golf_Results
SET ONLINE
```

There is one area of note about having backup strategies that employ these methods. If we have a server backup that runs, for example at 0200 hours, do you fancy getting up every night, just before 2 a.m., taking the database offline, and then bringing the server back up once the backup is complete? No – not many people would. Of course, there are installations where people are working through the night so this is less of a problem, but what if they are busy? Or forget? Then our whole backup will fail because the files are in use, and therefore the server will not backup these files.

There is quite a lot of third-party software out there that claims to have the ability to backup "open files", like databases. Essentially, they claim that we can back up the data and log files for SQL Server while the database is still online and active. Stay clear of these products: if we back up a database using a program like this, we risk losing transactions that are "in flight" and when we restore the database, it could be in an unstable state.

So let's now look at a more friendly method of backing up the data by using SQL Server instead.

Backing Up the Data

Using SQL Server to back up the database will be the method used by the majority of readers. By using SQL Server, we are keeping the backup of the database under the control of an automated process that can control its own destiny, and as we will find out later, it can also control the system when things go wrong.

The backup will be split into two parts. The first part, which will be covered here, will be when we perform the backup manually each time. Obviously this could be placing us in the scenario where we have to be available to perform the backup, but this can be rectified quite easily. Once this has been covered, the next section will schedule a backup to run at a specific time, which will relieve us of needing to be available to complete a backup at the specified time.

Let's start by looking at the manual backup.

Try it Out – Backing Up the Data

1. Ensure SQL Server Enterprise Manager is running. Find our database, right-click, select All Tasks, and then click on Backup Database….

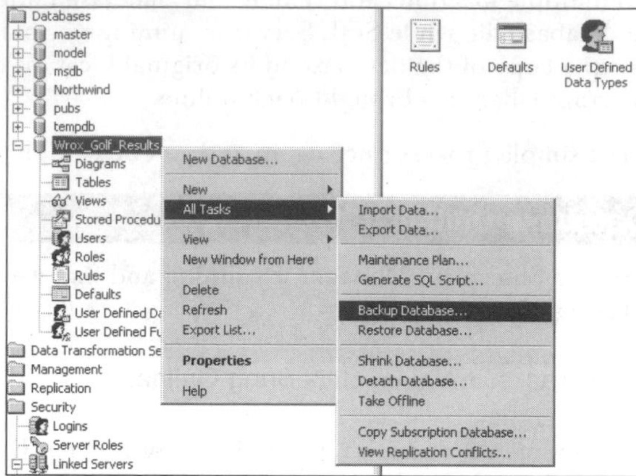

This then brings up the SQL Server Backup dialog. There is a lot on this screen, which will be dealt with a section at a time. This is what the dialog looks when it is first displayed:

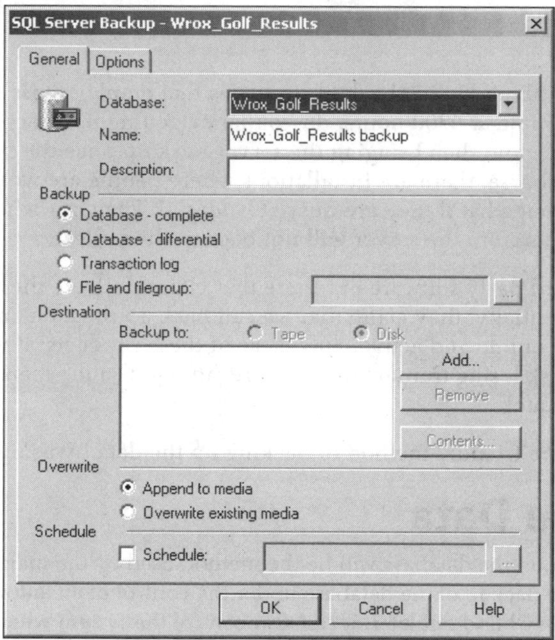

2. Ensure that a sensible name is placed in the Name box, as this forms the name in the logs that are created when the backup runs. It is recommended that the database forms part of the name of the backup; this will then allow us to distinguish between other similar backups on other databases. In this instance, there is no data in the database, so this will be a structure only backup and hence it is named as such Many people will append a timestamp to the end of the name to distinguish when the backup was created easily.

3. A Description is always useful. There will be different backups that we create through time, so a good description is always something that will help at a later date.

4. The next area of the dialog is a very crucial dialog that does require an amount of thought. These options are discussed below. For the moment, take the default of Database – complete. Some of these options may be grayed out by default. The options we see here are based on the recovery model we have selected for the given database. We'll cover the other options and recovery models in a moment.

   If we were backing up the `master` database, then the only option that would be available to us would be a complete database backup. However, looking at these four options together, the first option is straightforward. Selecting this option will ensure that the whole database will be backed up. All the tables, the data, and so on are all backed up if we use this option.

   The Database – differential option, also known as an interim backup, is the backup we would complete when the circumstances are such that a full backup is either not required or not possible. This just performs a backup on data changed since the last backup. For example, we may take a full backup at the weekend, and then a differential backup every night. Then when it came to restoring, we would restore the weekend full backup, and then add to that the latest differential backup taken from that point. A word of warning here, if you do take a week's worth of differential back ups, and you back up to magnetic tape rather than a hard drive, do keep at least enough different tapes for each differential back up. So therefore, use a complete backup when necessary and then in the interim, use a differential backup.

   The next option, the Transaction log, will be covered in the next section.

   The final option, File and filegroup, is for when we have our data split over more than the primary filegroup, or if it is a specific file that we wish to back up. As backing up individual files and filegroups is a more advanced topic, see "*Professional SQL Server 2000 Programming*" (*Wrox Press, ISBN 1-861004-48-6)* for more information on these options.

5. In the next section, the Destination section, there are no entries. This means that there has not been an area selected for the database to be backed up to. So click Add..., which will take us into the dialog to select an area.

6. The Select Backup Destination dialog allows us to decide where to place the backup, or which backup device to use. In this case, the backup will be placed onto the local hard drive. It is possible to back up to a different drive, perhaps on another server, or to back up on to a tape backup device.

   This name will be used every time a backup is taken if we set the backup as a schedule, but more on that in a moment when we talk about backing up the transaction log.

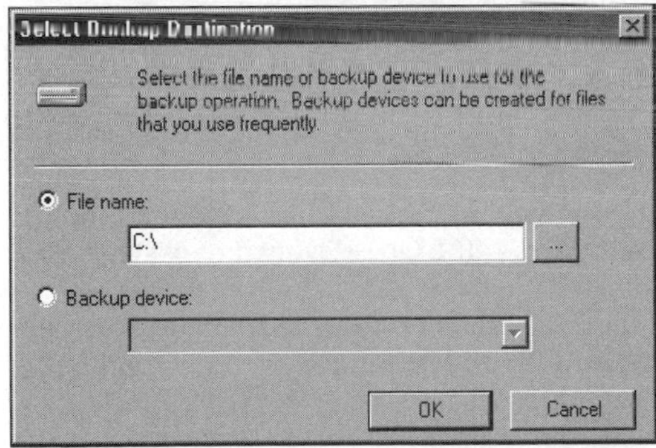

7. Find a suitable area on the hard drive for the backup to be placed in. It is best to have a directory set aside for backups so that they are easy to find, perhaps with a name such as `SQL Server Backups`. It is also advisable to give the backup file a meaningful name. In this instance, it has been given the name of the database, `Wrox_Golf_Results`. Once done, click OK. We can gain a substantial performance improvement by backing the database up to a separate disk or to a RAID 1 drive if it is available. This is because data is written to the backup file in a sequential manner.

8. If we enter an invalid path, the directory doesn't exist for example, then we will be warned about this. If we click No, then we will be taken back to enter a valid data path.

9. After clicking OK on the Edit Backup Destination modal screen, the Contents... button within the destination section has now become enabled. This looks at the contents of the file listed as the area to backup, so that SQL Server can look at the file to determine what is contained within it. If you don't have Service Pack 1 for SQL Server 2000 installed, this action may take some time to display.

10. Moving on to the Overwrite section of the dialog, there are two options that we can choose. We have to make a careful choice here, which we will cover later as this is quite a crucial area. Remember where the company lost a week's worth of data? It was here that they made their mistake! If we overwrite our media, the old backups on the file will be purged before backing up the new database. Select Overwrite existing media. Below is the now completed dialog box:

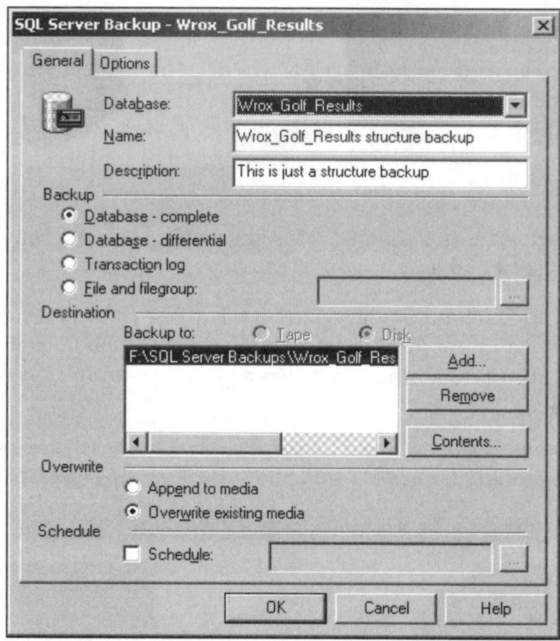

As we have seen above, there are two options: Append to media and Overwrite existing media. You may be thinking, "If I select Overwrite existing media, does this mean my whole hard drive is wiped out?" Well, it is nice to know that it doesn't. What this means, is if we are using a tape drive, then the contents of the tape will be overwritten. If we're backing up to disk, then the old backup file will be purged.

11. This brings to an end the General tab. Click on the Options tab, which brings up a few useful options. Some of the options are disabled due to the media that has been selected, which is a hard drive rather than a tape. The following dialog demonstrates how the dialog looks when we first see it. Some options may not be grayed out on your screen based on what you selected in the General tab. For example, if you selected the Overwrite option earlier, then the Initialize and Label Media option will be available.

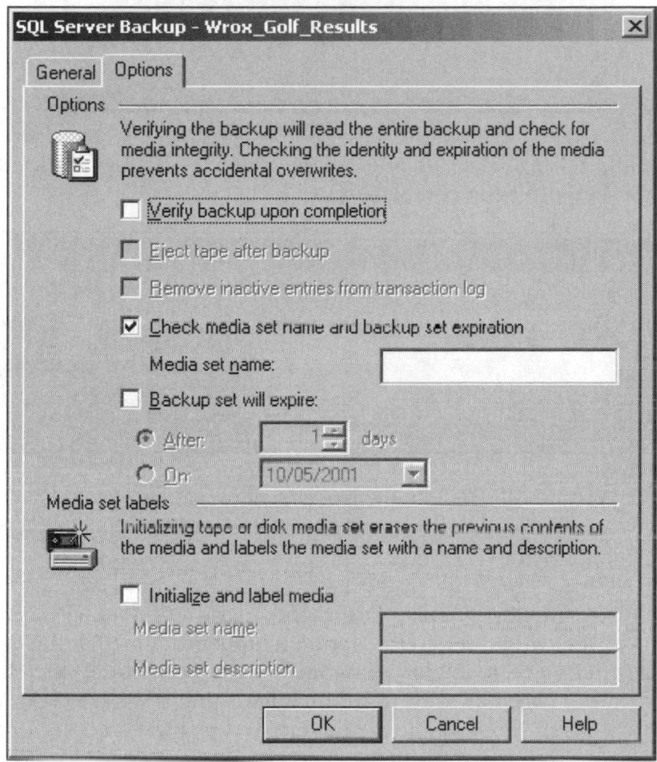

12. Taking the first part of this tab, it is recommended that we always check the Verify backup upon completion option. This means the backup takes that little bit more time, but this will cover the times when a backup on a tape media failed and also when a tape becomes full.

The Options tab has a great deal of options for tape backups. If we are performing a tape backup, the tape backup device must be directly connected to the computer or server that SQL Server is situated on, and we are not allowed to connect to a tape backup device across the network! If we want to back up to a disk on a remote server, keep in mind that SQL Server cannot see mapped drives. We will need to use the UNC path of the remote server and directory (for example, \\ServerName\backups).

13. This is the only change to be made in this instance, so when we click OK, the backup will start. We should see the following Backup Progress modal dialog, but depending on how large our database is, then we may only see this for a couple of seconds. If we have a large multi-gigabyte database, it may take a few minutes to see the first bar.

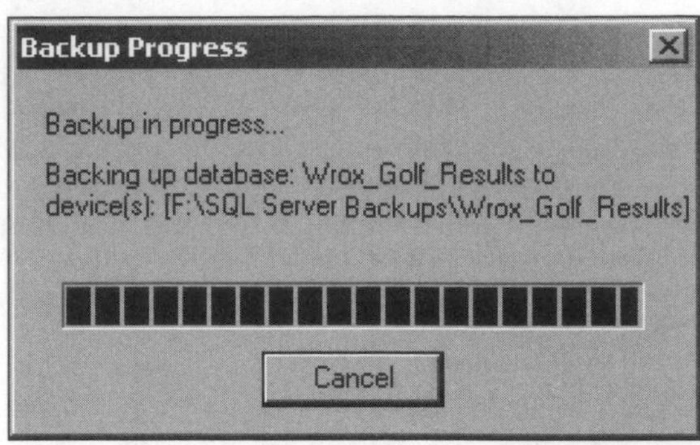

14. Once the backup is finished we should see the following dialog. Notice that it mentions that the verification has also been completed.

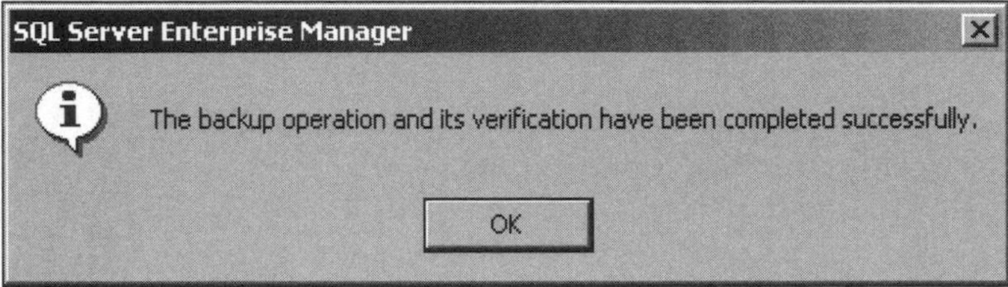

The first backup of the **Wrox_Golf_Results** database has now taken place and should have been successful. If we now move to the directory on the hard drive where the backup took place, then we will see the `Wrox_Golf_Results` file.

Recall that it was mentioned that a company lost a week's worth of data when explaining the example? What had happened was it they had set up the option to append to media, the tape had become full and if had not set up the proper scenario to alert someone when a problem occurred. So there was not just one failure in the system but two; however, it still highlights that if we are using append to media, we mustcheck that there is enough room on the media that we are appending to for the back up to succeed.

Creating a backup of our database and the data is the most crucial action in building a database solution. Get it wrong and we may as well go home. Well not quite, but if (or when) things go wrong, and we don't have a valid or recent enough backup that is acceptable to the users of our database, it will take a long time for us as a developer to recover from that situation and get back to the excellent working relationship we had beforehand.

The backup taken in the above example is the simplest backup to perform. It is a complete backup of our particular SQL Server database, which happens while we are watching. If it goes wrong we will instantly see and be able to deal with it. However, most backups do not happen when we are there and will happen through the night. In the next section we will see more about scheduling jobs and how to schedule a task to run through the night. However, it doesn't cover what to do when things go wrong. This is a difficult area to cover and should be integrated with our database maintenance plan, which is covered in the next chapter. What this example is demonstrating is how to complete a backup manually rather than as an automated process.

Before moving on, there are a couple more points concerning backups that we must keep in mind and it is recommended strongly that these directions are followed. First of all, keep a regular and up-to-date backup of the `master` and `msdb` system databases. SQL Server very rarely becomes corrupted, but it can happen for any number of reasons, from a hard drive failure, to a developer altering the database in error. It really doesn't matter, but if we don't have a backup of the `master` database we could find ourselves in trouble. However, be warned. Restoring the `master` database should not be performed unless we really have to, and only if we are experienced with SQL Server. Restoring the `master` database is not like restoring other databases, and has to be completed outside Enterprise Manager. This book quite deliberately does not cover having to restore the `master` database since it is a very advanced topic. For more on that discussion, read "*Professional SQL Server 2000 Programming*" *(ISBN 1-861004-48-6).*

When it comes to the `msdb` database and when to back this up, it could be that a daily backup is required. If we recall, this database holds job schedules, and other information pertinent to the SQL Server Agent for scheduling. If we have jobs that run each day, then if we need to keep information about when jobs were run a daily backup, may be required. However, if we only wish to keep a backup of jobs etc. that are set up and there is no need to know when certain jobs ran and whether they were successful or not, then perhaps look at backing up this database weekly.

The `model` database should be backed up if any details within the model database have been altered. This should be pretty infrequent and therefore backing up this database need not be as regular as any other database. Once a week is probably frequent enough. Backing up `tempdb` is not necessary, as this should be seen as a transient database, which has no set state.

As we can see, it is not just our own databases that need to be considered and remembered when it comes to dealing with our backup strategy. A database within SQL Server is not an insular arrangement and affects the system databases just as much.

> **If in doubt, back it up more frequently than is required!**

Backing up the Transaction Log with a Wizard

It is not only the data that can be backed up, but also, and just as importantly, so can the transaction log for the database. Just to recap, the transaction log is a file used by databases to log every transaction including DML actions like rebuilding indexes. In other words, every data modification that has taken place on any table within the database. The transaction log is then used in many different scenarios within a database solution, but where it is more useful, from a database recovery point of view, is that if the database crashes, then the transaction log can be used to move forward from the last data backup, using the transactions listed within the transaction log.

Backing up the transaction log is a good strategy to employ when we can only get to the database to complete a data backup once a week, perhaps at a weekend. Or perhaps more commonly, a transaction log backup will take place at set times throughout the day so that the transaction log is kept small, and therefore will give a more efficient and faster overall database performance. It also gives us point-in-time recoverability; this means that we can quickly restore to any time in the past where the transaction was backed up. The next section demonstrates how to backup the transaction log using an inbuilt Enterprise Manager wizard. The only problem with transaction log backups is that we will have to manage lots of files. When we restore the files, Enterprise Manager is intelligent enough to chain those files together in the appropriate order.

Try It Out – Backing Up the Transaction Log with a Wizard

1. There is a wizard that can be used to backup the data, rather than the more manual process covered in the previous section. The following wizard being used to backup the transaction log can be altered to backup the data. However, it is also necessary to backup the Transaction Log within our database, and in this section, it will be the transaction log that will be selected. From the SQL Server Enterprise manager, select the Wizards toolbar button

or select from the menu Tools | Wizards... This will then bring up the following dialog:

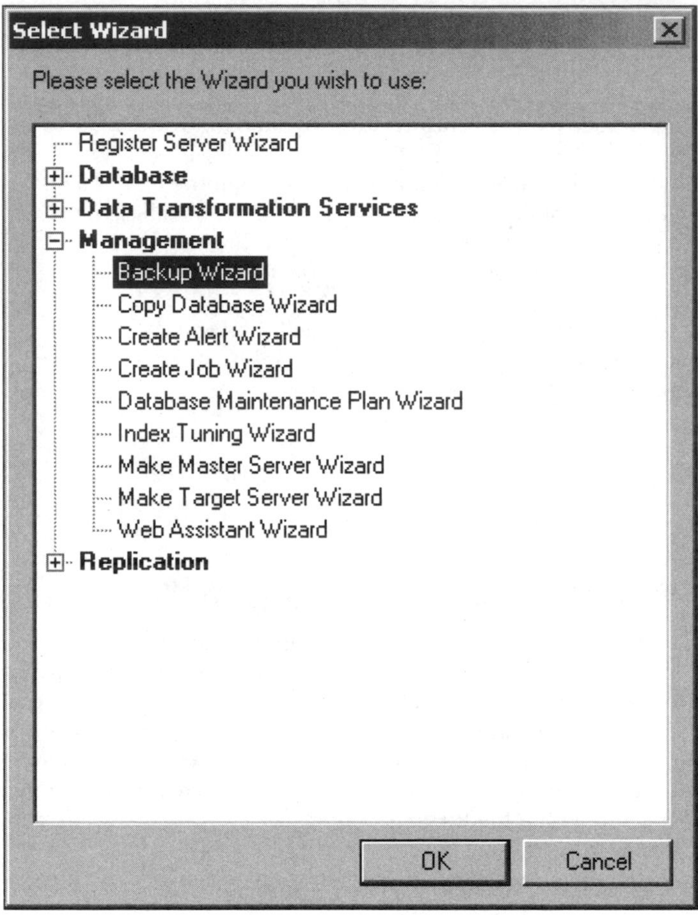

2. Expand the Management group and select Backup Wizard. The opening screen is just an introduction, worth reading only once. Click Next.

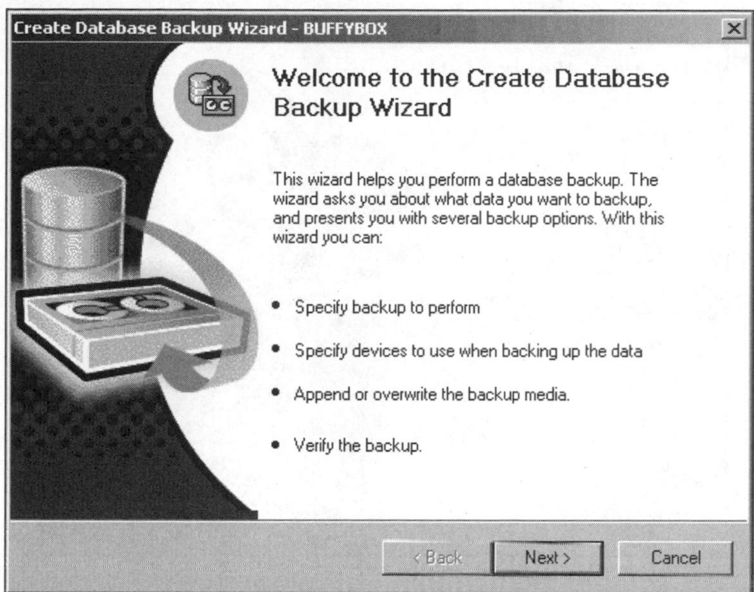

3. This then brings us to the screen where we select which of the databases in the SQL Server we wish to backup. Select Wrox_Golf_Results.

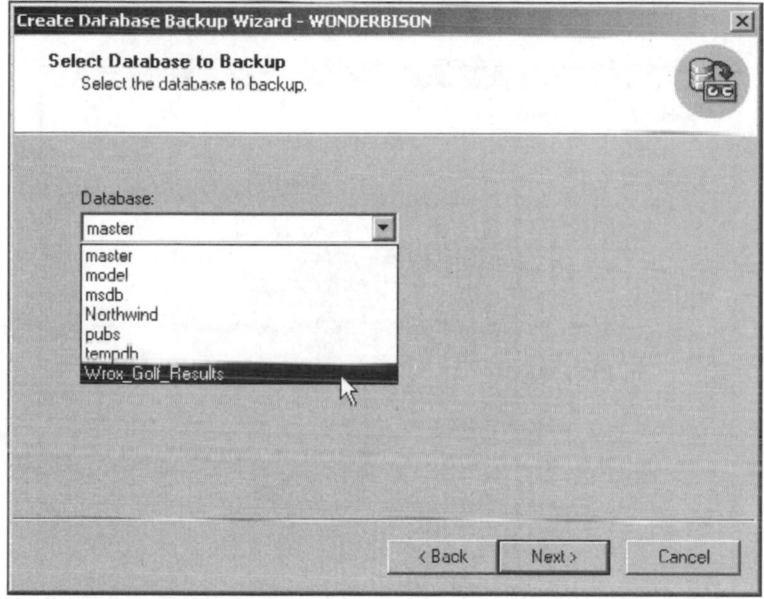

4. In the next dialog we need to define the **Name** of the backup as well as an optional **Description**. Note that we can place spaces in the name without any problems at this stage. However, the usual warning over using spaces still applies as we can perform backup and restores using SQL Server's native query language, T-SQL, to back up the database. Once done, click **Next**.

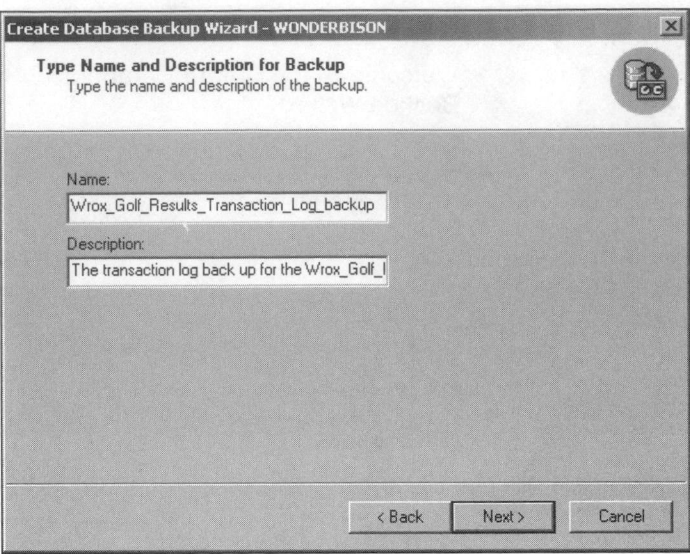

5. The next dialog is where it is possible to select what kind of backup we wish to perform. In this instance, it is the transaction log, so select the third option, Transaction log. This option will be grayed out if our database is in the simple recovery model. If this is the case, we will need to change the recovery model for our database to full or bulk-logged by clicking the right mouse button on the database in Enterprise Manager and selecting Properties. We can change the recovery model under the Options tab with the Recovery drop-down box.

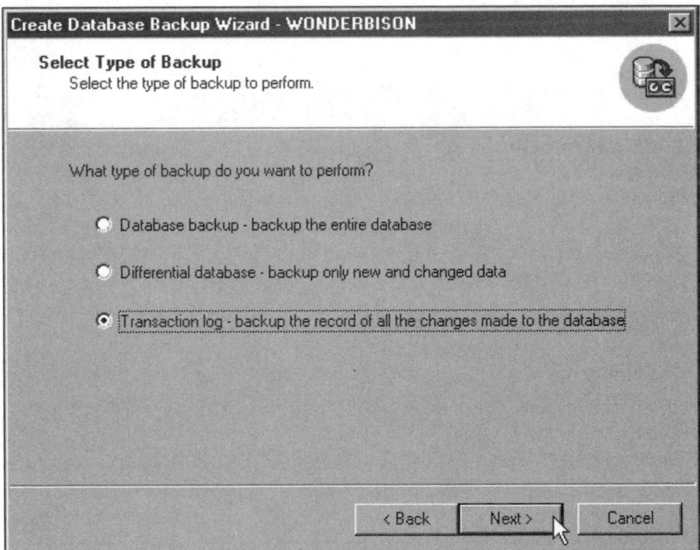

6. Once we have clicked Next, we need to make the decision of where to backup the transaction log. The next screen is how the dialog is as we first come to it. As we can see, the File option is selected, and the destination is where the data is currently residing. Not good if we have a media failure, as we will not only lose the database, but also lose our backup. Click on the button to the right, so that a different location can be chosen.

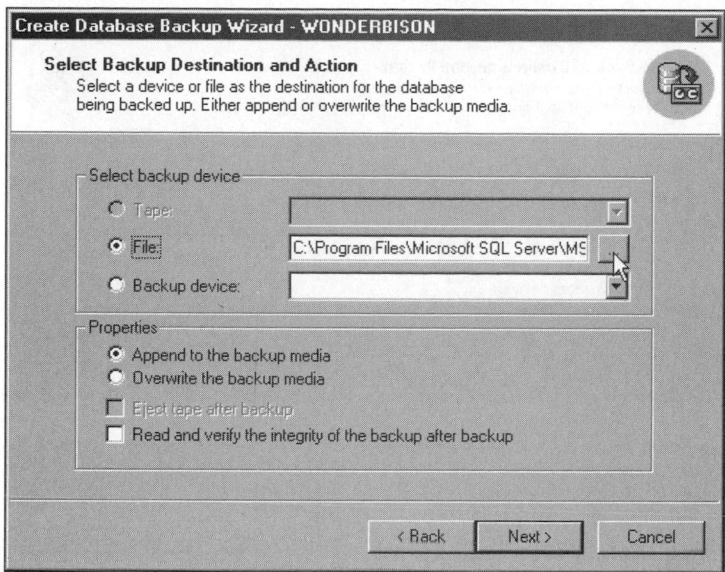

7. The following dialog comes up for us to specify where we wish to place our backup. Select the directory where we wish it to be located, or if we are going to overwrite an existing backup, then we can also select the file that will be overwritten. In this instance, the SQL Server backups directory has been selected and the name of the backup file is in the File Name: text box at the bottom. Once complete, select OK.

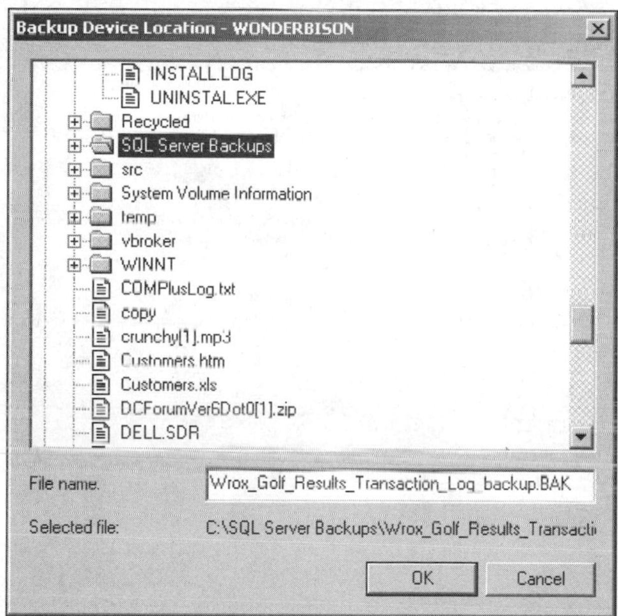

8. This then brings us back to the Select Backup Destination and Action screen with the File property filled out. The Read and Verify check box should be selected. The rest of the properties are left alone. Click Next.

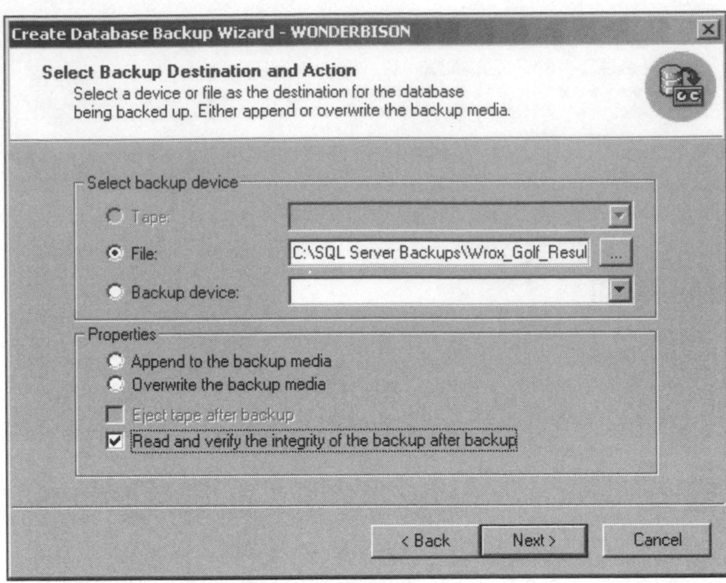

9. The next screen displayed concerns the media and the schedule that the backup should run. If we selected Overwrite the Backup Media option in the previous screen we may be seeing a different screen asking us to initialize the media. The screenshot below shows how this page of the wizard is displayed as a default. As we can see, there is already a schedule put in place for the backup to run weekly. This is Microsoft's way of prompting us to complete regular backups. To demonstrate how easy it is to alter the back up schedule, click on the Change... button.

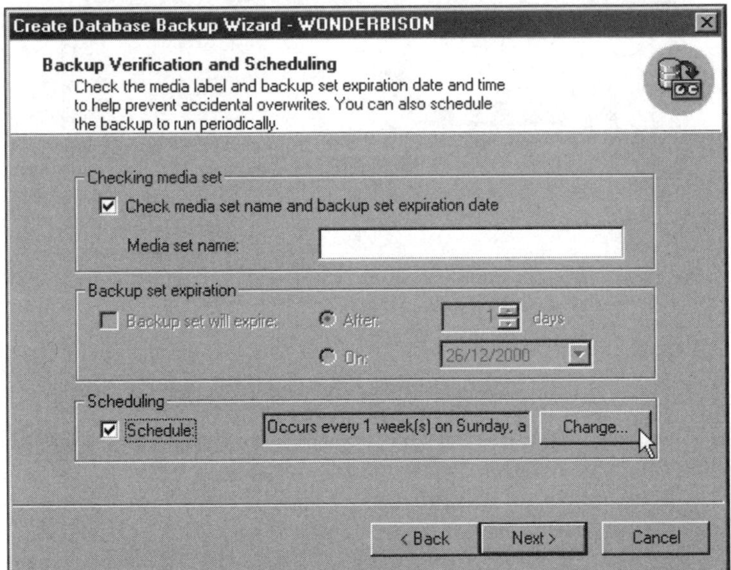

10. Clicking Change brings up the initial schedule dialog. Enter a meaningful Name, ensure that the Enabled box is checked so that the backup will run on the scheduled dates. Then we need to click the Change... button again.

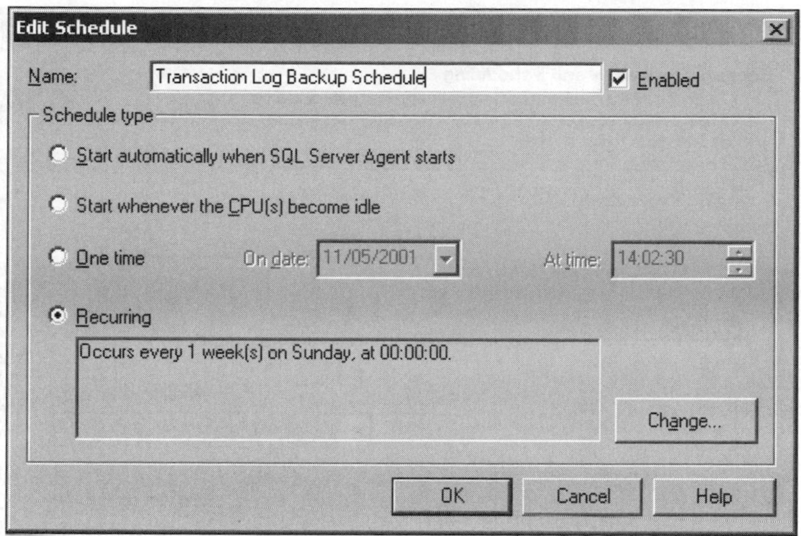

11. The wizard has now moved to a dialog used for setting up the Recurring Job Schedule. It is a fairly straightforward and simple form and it is very easy to set up a schedule for regular backups. We know that the database is likely to be unused at 0200 every weekday, Monday to Friday. The recurring job schedule is set up as such, which will allow the job to run at the time specified. The backup will also run indefinitely, by setting No end date. This means that every Monday to Friday, until it is told otherwise, this backup will run once. When finished, click OK.

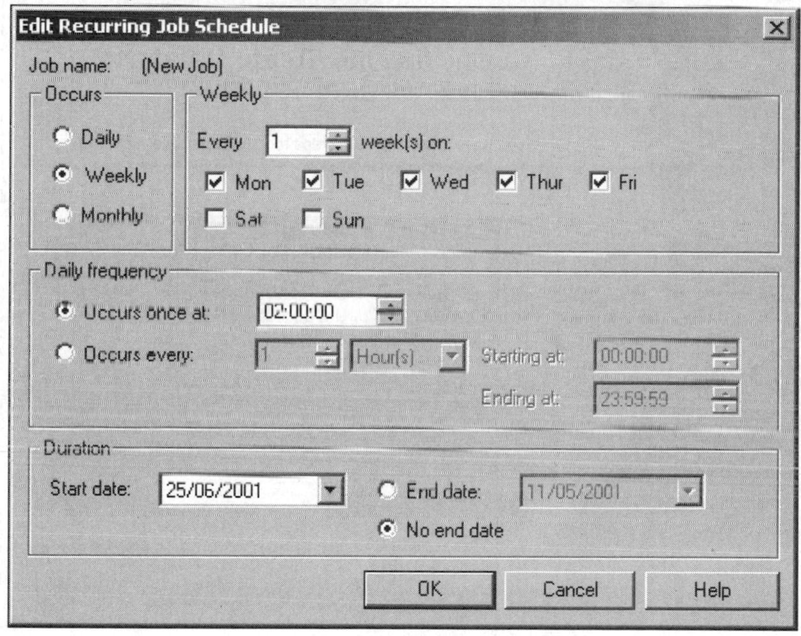

12. Click the next OK button – this brings us back to the wizard and the schedule details at the bottom have been updated. Once we are happy with the schedule, click Next.

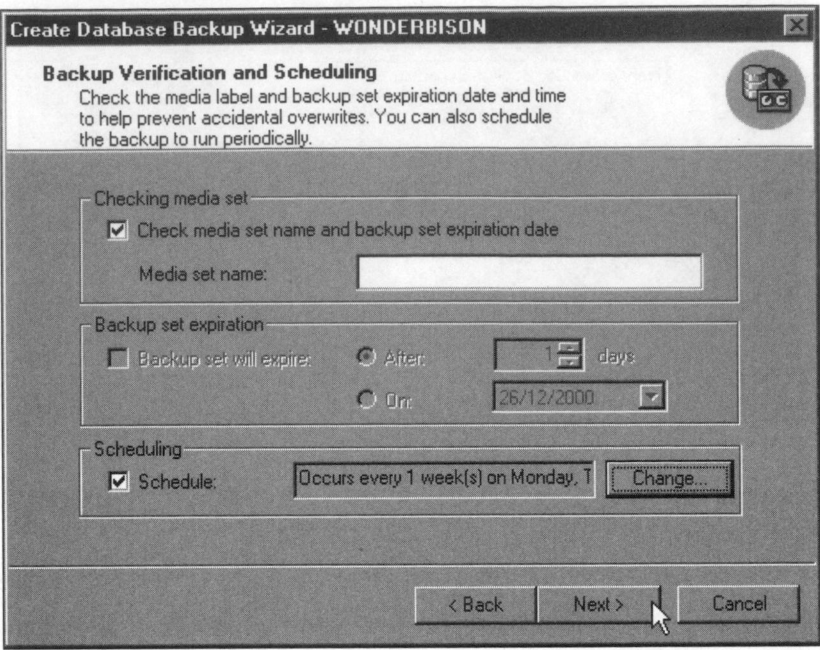

13. The final screen is a summary of everything so far. Click Finish to set up the backup.

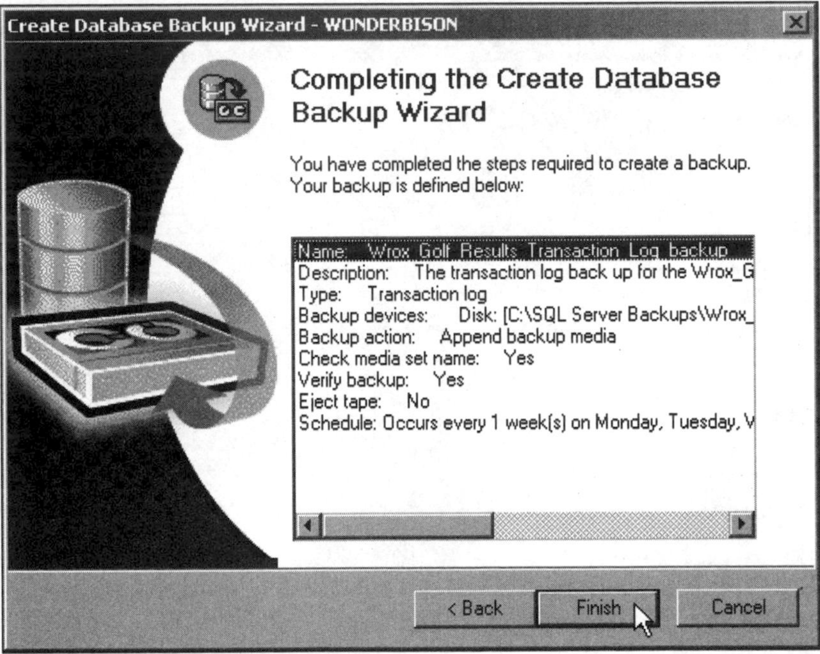

14. If we have followed these instructions, after a short pause, we will see the following success message. Click OK..

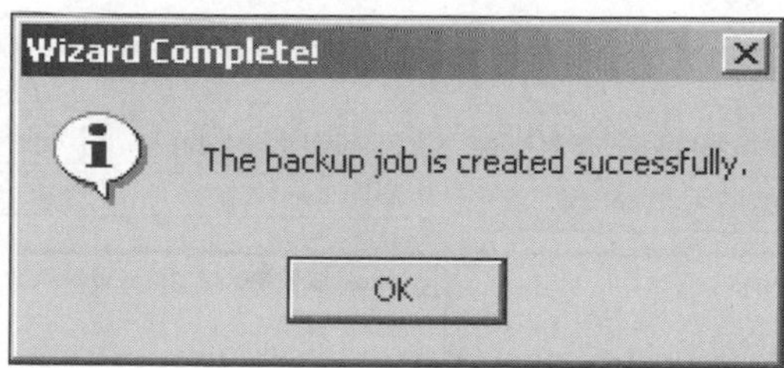

15. However, it is quite possible that we did not see the above message informing us that the backup job had been set up correctly. We may well see the error message below. This is informing us that SQL Server Agent, which is used to run scheduled jobs, is not started. We will need to go to SQL Server Service Manager to start up the agent.

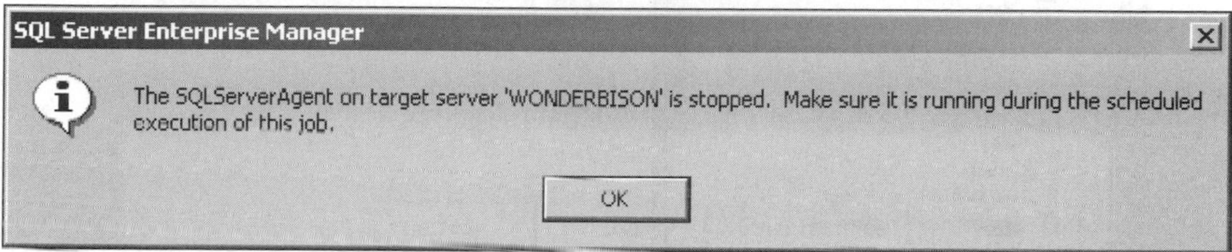

16. To start up SQL Server Service Manager, double click on the Service Manager icon on the toolbar.

This will then bring up the Service Manager, from where we can select the SQL Server Agent service, and then click on the **Start/Continue** button.

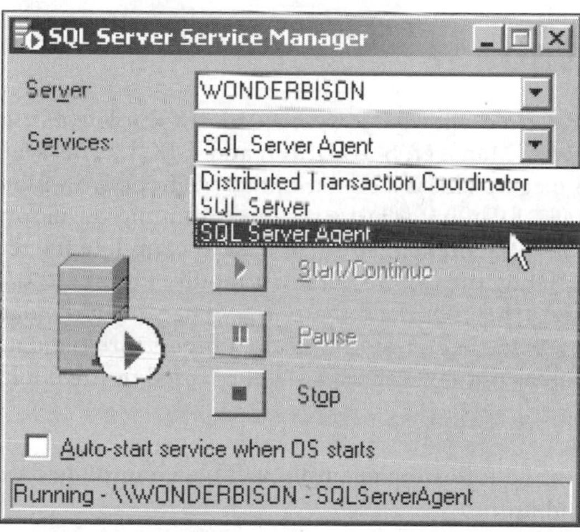

17. If things went well, we will see a new object within the database under the **Jobs** node, below the **Management** and **SQL Server Agent** nodes. We may have to **Refresh** for the job to be displayed, but it will be there. There will be a bit more on all of this in a moment, but jobs and schedules are covered in much more detail in the next chapter, where it is more pertinent.

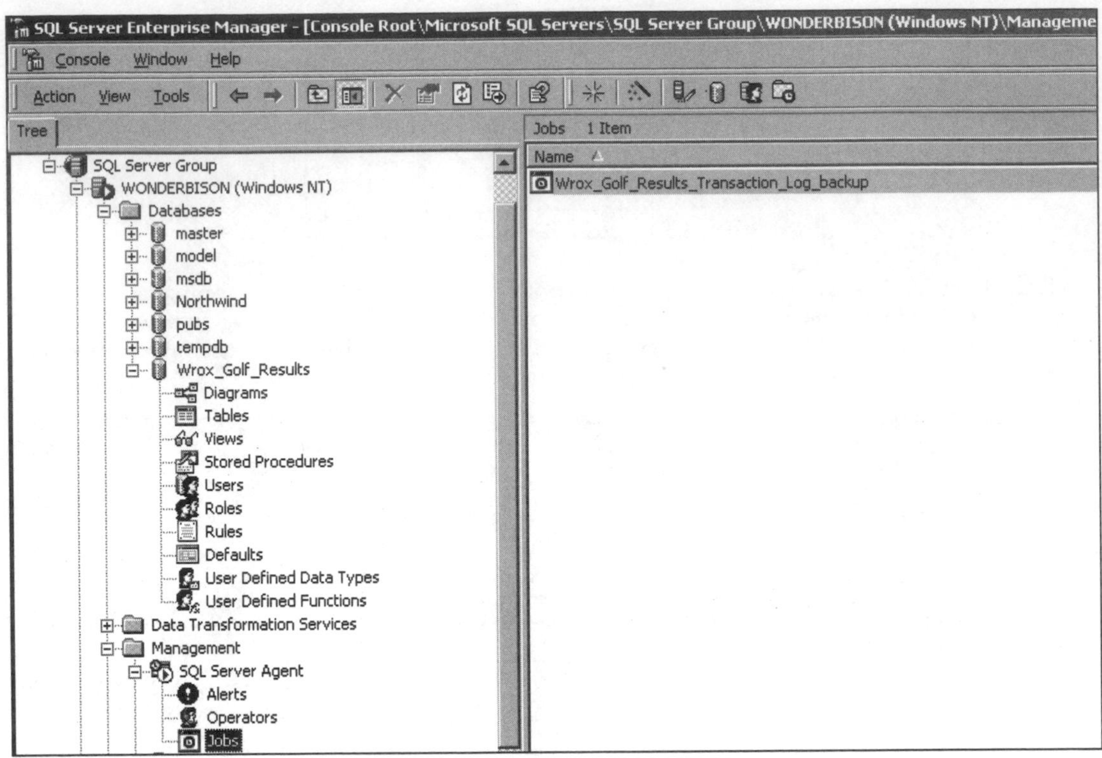

Although a backup has not been performed at this point in time, it is scheduled to run at 2 a.m. every morning, Monday to Friday.

Restoring a Database

Now that the data has been backed up, what if we needed to complete a restore? There are three ways to restore the database: Enterprise Manager, SQL-DMO, and T-SQL. This section will only discuss restoration in Enterprise Manager. This is a scenario, that we hope we will never perform, but it would be surprising if this were the case. Even if it is just a restore within the development environment to remove test data and to get back to a stable predefined set of data to complete the testing, then this next section should help us. Before completing the restore, let's first modify the `Wrox_Golf_Results` database to prove that the restore worked. This is because there is no data within the database yet to prove the restore that way. Keep in mind, however, that a restore will not only restore the data structures, but also the data, the permissions, and other areas of the database not yet covered in the book, for example, views, stored procedures, and so on.

The restore demonstrated in the following example will be a complete database restore of the `Wrox_Golf_Results` database.

Try It Out – Restoring a Database

1. With SQL Server Enterprise Manager running, expand the server, and select the `Wrox_Golf_Results` database. Expand **Tables**, select **Club_Details**; right-click and select **Design Table**.

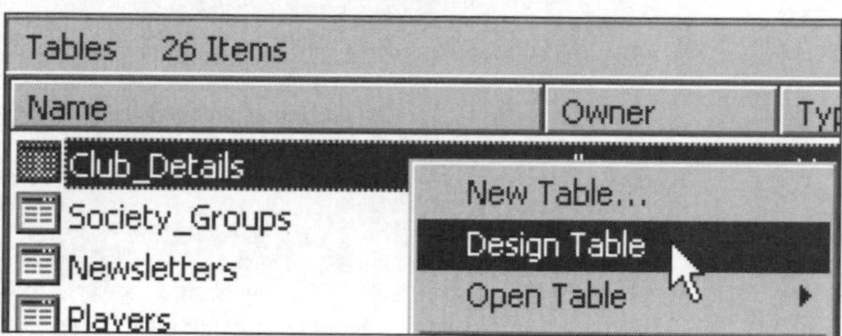

2. Select any column from the table, for example **Fax_Number**. Right-click again, and select **Delete Column** to remove the column from the table.

Column Name	Data Type	Length	Allow Nulls
Club_Name	varchar	50	
Address	varchar	200	
Phone_Number	varchar	20	✓
Fax_Number	varchar	20	✓
Club_Er		50	✓
Web_si		50	✓
Zip_Coc		10	✓
State_L		2	✓
Country		1	

Set Primary Key
Insert Column
Delete Column
Task
Select All
Save

3. Now that the column is removed, close the table down. This will then bring up the dialog to save our changes. Click on **Yes**.

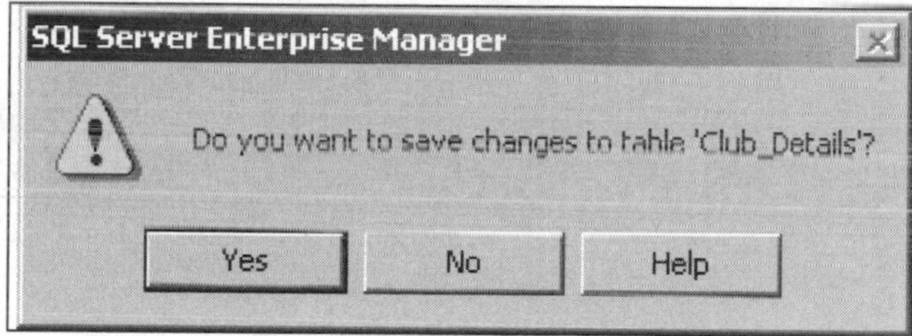

4. Now that there is proof to test that the restore worked, right-click on the **Wrox_Golf_Results** database, select **All Tasks**, and then select **Restore Database**.

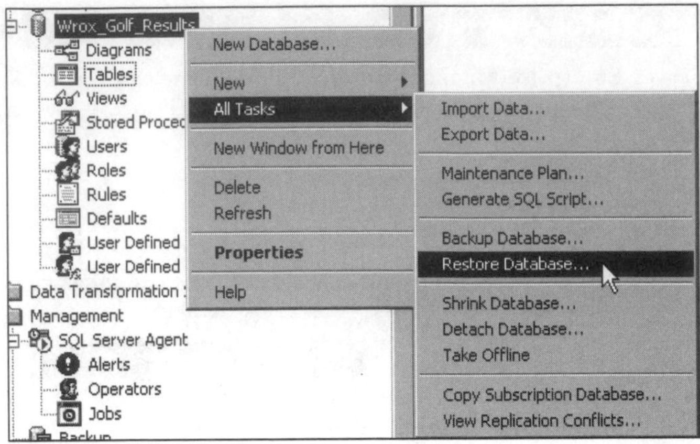

5. This then brings up the dialog that will be used for restoring the database from the backup. All the backups taken that are still valid will be listed within this dialog, and it will be up to us as the database administrator to select the backup that we wish to use to restore the data. Notice that the phrase "database administrator" was used, not developer. The reason for this is that this action, although it can be done by developers, should only really be completed by an administrator. When we restore a database, it wipes out the old data and loads it with the data from the backup. This could be quite dangerous if not done properly. As there has only been one database backup taken, then this will be the only option that will yield any backups that can be restored from the First backup to restore: combo box. Click OK.

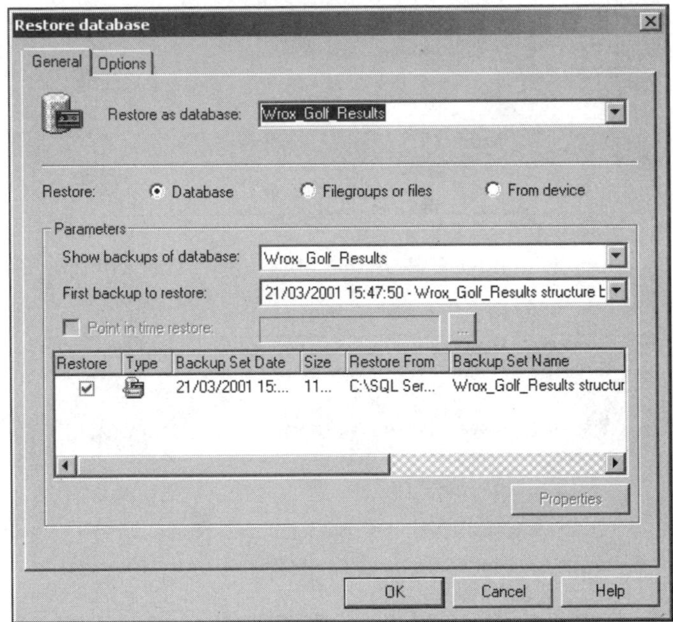

6. The restore will be from the Structure backup taken earlier in this chapter. To ensure we are happy with the backup selected, and that the right backup has been chosen, highlight the Backup Set and then select the Properties... button.

7. These are as many details as we should need to know about to ensure that the correct backup is chosen. Using these and the details in the previous graphic, we should know that the correct backup is about to be used as the restore. Click **OK** both on this dialog, and the **Restore database** dialog.

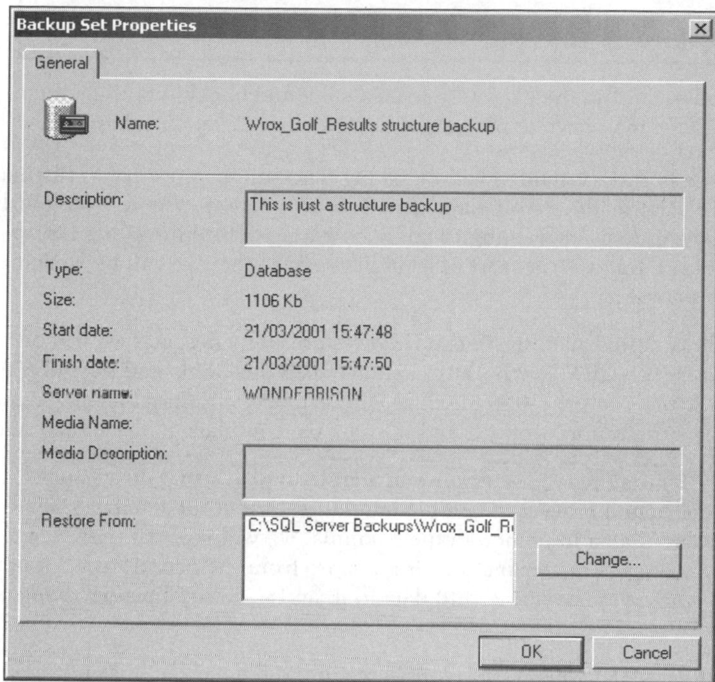

8. The restore should then commence. This process will take longer than the backup, but to demonstrate that the restore is happening, the progress bar will show how near completion the restore is. Don't forget that a restore could be happening on a server, so it may not be possible to just check the hard drive light on the computer!

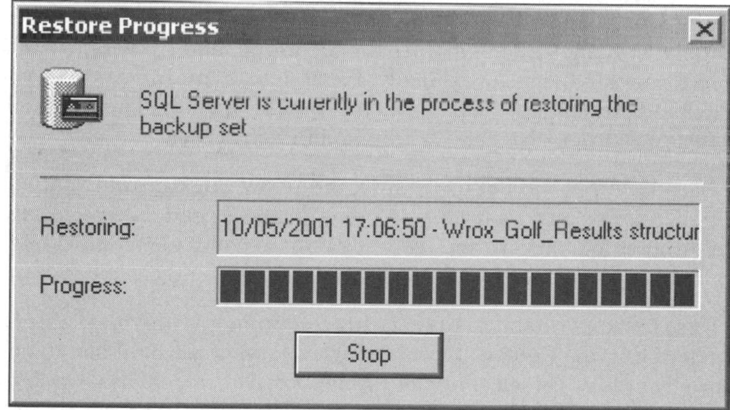

9. Once the restore is complete, we should see the following message:

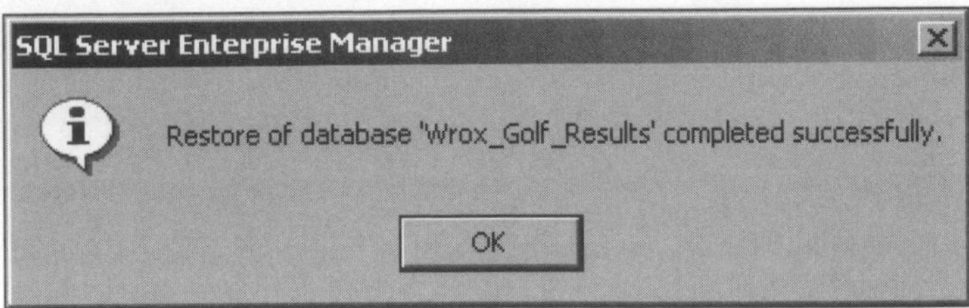

We can now move back to the `Club_Details` table and check that the column removed has now been reinstated. We may have to perform a Refresh first to see the changes.

Restoring a database in most instances will be taking place under pressure as the database will have become corrupt, or been inadvertently damaged. The production system is obviously down and not working and we have irate users wanting to know how long before the system is up. This is hopefully the worst-case scenario, but it is that sort of level of pressure that we will be working under when we have to restore the database.

However, we will have tested all of the backup and restore strategies, and we will be confident that it will all work, and of course, it will! Why? Because we have read this book, and possibly "*Professional SQL Server 2000*" *(Wrox* Press, ISBN 1-861004-48-6*)*, and we will be totally comfortable and confident that we have done all we can to get the restore working and the data back in place in the shortest time possible.

This example starts by making a modification to a table to prove that the restore actually has worked. It then moves on to the actual process of completing the restore of the database. If we take another look at the Restore Database dialog in point 5 of the example, we will see that there are a few options and decisions to make. It doesn't matter that this is a restore from the Structure back up; it would be the same if we were restoring the database with data in it, and we would just be choosing a different backup file to work from.

The first point to note is that when completing a restore, the database does not have to exist. If we want to create a different database out of our backup, simply type in the new name in the Restore as Database drop-down box in the General tab. When we try to restore the database, the database will be created automatically then loaded with data.

The next point in the dialog asks what type of restore to perform. We have three choices, Database, Filegroups or files, or From device. The Database option would restore the whole database from the backup. Filegroups or files would allow selective data (certain tables, records, etc.) to be restored. If we recall, this book is only working with the PRIMARY file group, and so therefore this would be the only option to be catered for within the restore. Finally, From device informs SQL Server that we will be restoring from a backup place on a device, like a tape, or a hard drive. This is usually what we'll have to select when we're restoring from a backup file from a different server.

Moving on to the Parameters section of the restore, the Show Backups of Database option would only differ if we wanted to restore a backup from a different database on the server. If, for example, we were restoring into test a production backup, and the test database had a name indicating that this was a test version of the database. In most instances these two options will be the same.

Moving on to the First backup to restore option, this combo box is only available when we have the Database option selected in the Restore section. However, what it would like to know is which backup task it should restore from first. By selecting the combo box, we can choose which backups to restore first. Once choosing the backup group, the list of backups available to us, shown in the grid at the foot of the dialog, will change to show what backups can be chosen.

Restoring to the Failure Point

The final option to look at is the most crucial option here. It is the Point in time restore option. This is useful when we have the scenario where we have a transaction log backup that completed at 10 a.m. in the morning and someone updates every employee record accidentally to have the CEO's salary. We can restore to the point in time before the accident occurred by using this method. There has been a data backup, followed by further transaction log backups. In the graphic below, the latest data backup has been chosen, which has one transaction log backup taken after that point. We would like to restore to that point in time. We can just select these two backups and leave it at that, which will restore to the point in time that we desire. However, what do we do if we want to make the time earlier than that?

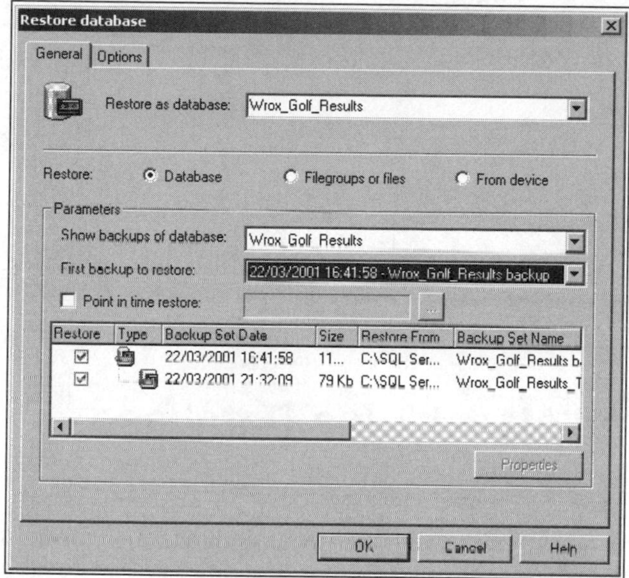

By selecting the Point in time restore option, it enables the ... button to the right of that option. Clicking on that button brings up the Point in time restore dialog. We should be able to enter any time previous to the time that the transaction log backup was taken.

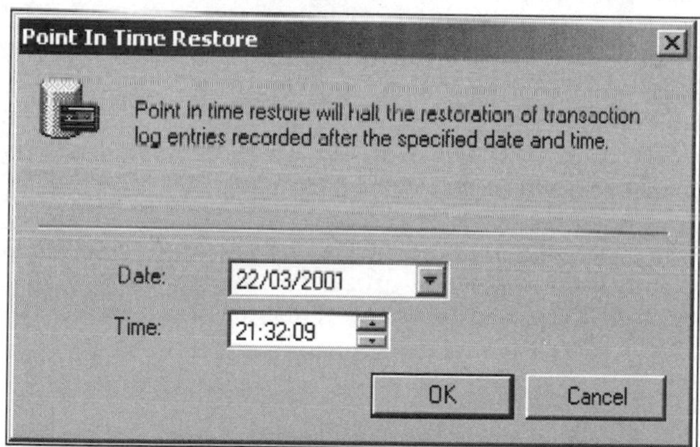

However, if we set the time later than the time the transaction log was backed up to, we will receive the following message. Obviously we cannot restore past the time that the last back up was taken. So ensure that the date and time in the previous dialog are set correctly.

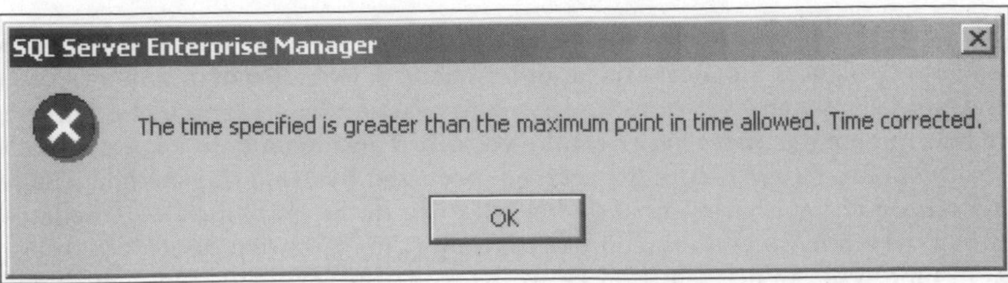

From this point the restore should work perfectly. Well, the dialog box below is what should happen:

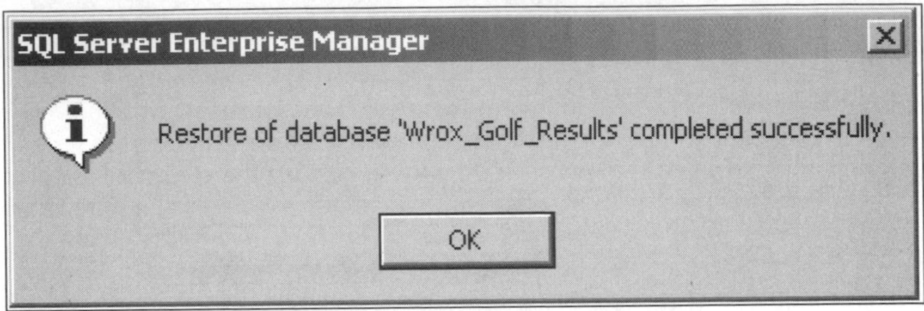

Detaching and Attaching a Database

There may be a time in the life of our SQL Server database when we have to move it from one server to another, or in fact just from one hard drive to another. For example, we currently have `Wrox_Golf_Results` on our C drive and this is getting full, so we would like to move our database to another hard drive. Or perhaps we are moving from an old slower server to a new faster server, or a server on a better network. By detaching and re-attaching the database, we can do this simply and easily.

There are a couple of obvious points to be made; they may seem straightforward and really obvious, but better to mention them than cause problems at a later stage. First of all, no updates can be occurring, no jobs can be running, and no users can be attached. Secondly, just in case, do take a backup before moving the database. This may add time to the process but it is better to be safe than sorry. Ensure that where we are moving the database to has enough disk space, not only for the move, but also for expected future growth, otherwise we will be moving our database twice. We should not attach our database to a server without immediately completing a backup on the new server afterwards; this way we can ensure that the databases are protected in their new state.

Detaching a database physically removes the details from the server, but does not remove the data from the disk that it resides on. However, detaching the database from the server will then allow a safe moving, copying or deletion of the files that make up the database, if we so desired. This is the only way that a database should be physically removed from a server.

Try It Out – Detaching a Database

1. First of all, it is necessary to ensure as well as possible that nobody is logged into the database, and even if there is, that they are not doing any updates. You can refer to the earlier section in the chapter about disconnecting users if you need help on this. Ensure that SQL Server Enterprise is running and that the `Wrox_Golf_Results` database is selected. Right-click and select **Properties**.

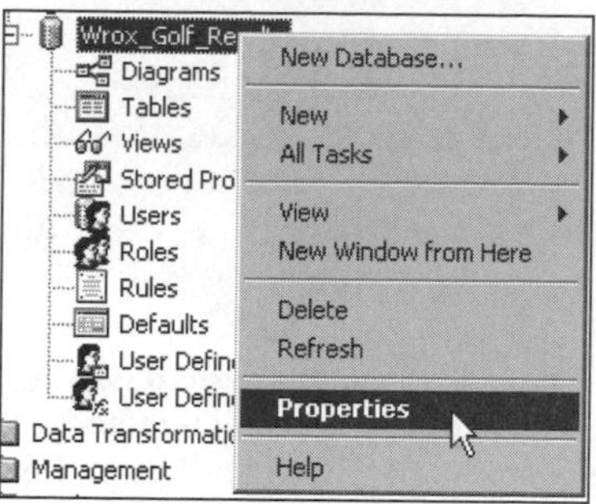

2. This then brings up the **Properties** for the `Wrox_Golf_Results` database. Select the **Options** tab. Notice that at the top there is the **Access** section of the properties. All will be explained later; however, select **Restrict Access** and ensure that the **Single user** option is selected; it is also imperative that the **Read-only** option is selected. When done click **OK**.

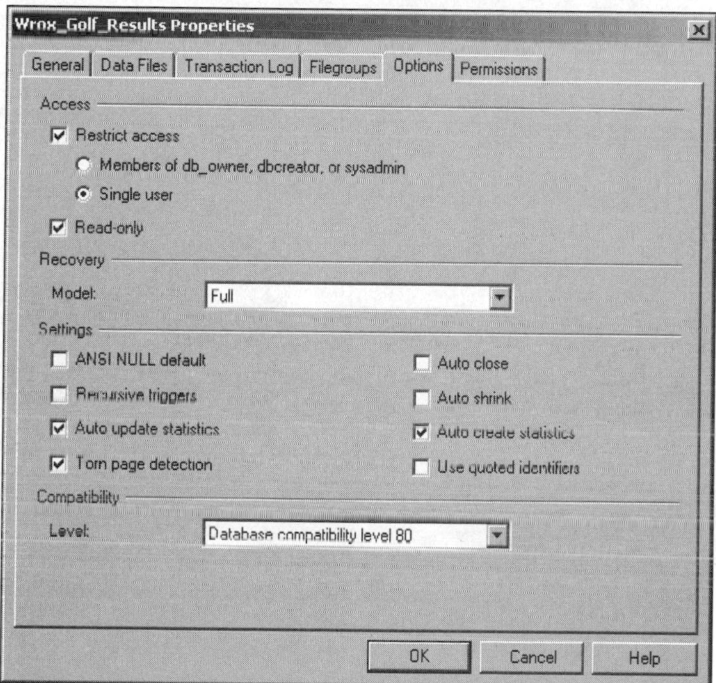

3. If there are in fact no users connected to the database at this time, then all will go well. However, if there are still users connected, using this option is not possible. If we get the following error message, then we cannot use this method initially to restrict connections. More on this later.

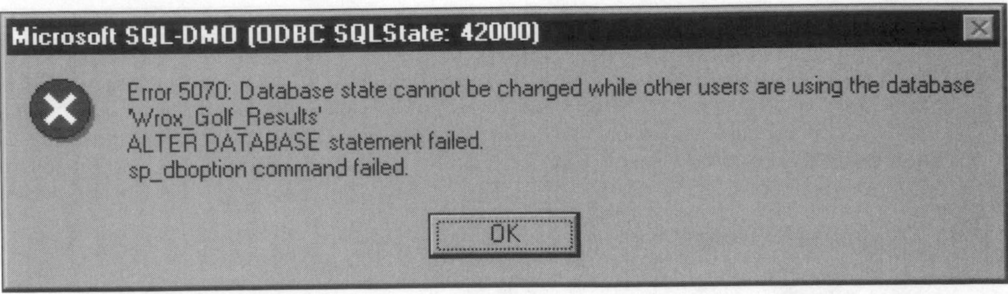

4. Now move back to the database and right-click, select All Tasks and then the Detach Database… option.

5. This then brings up the dialog for detaching the database. As we can see in the following screenshot, there are no users connected to the database at this moment. This is quite true because it was possible to see the database options earlier in the example. This is a simple process, and in this instance, we just click OK.

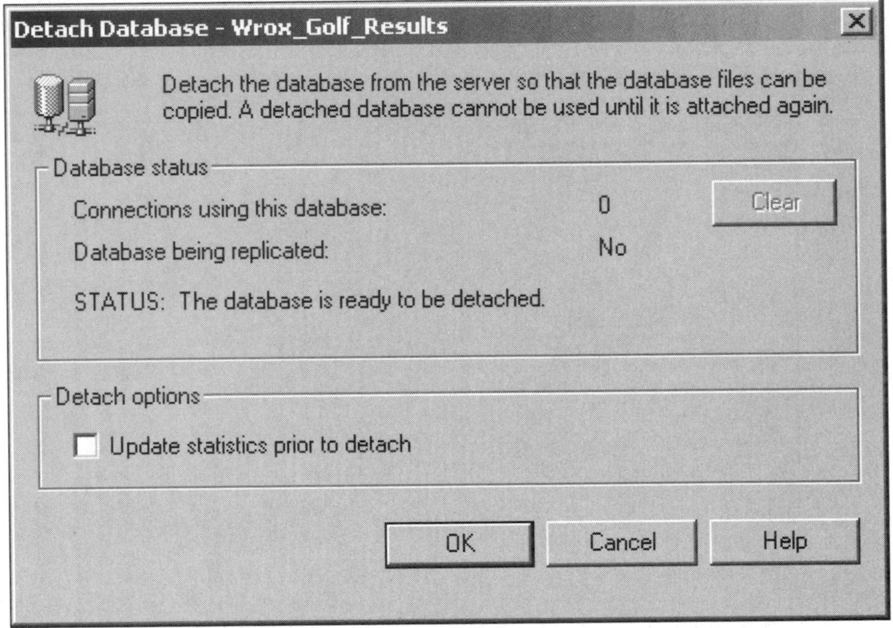

6. However, if there are still users connected to the database, the above dialog will look different. In the following example there was still one person connected to the database – giving the dialog shown.

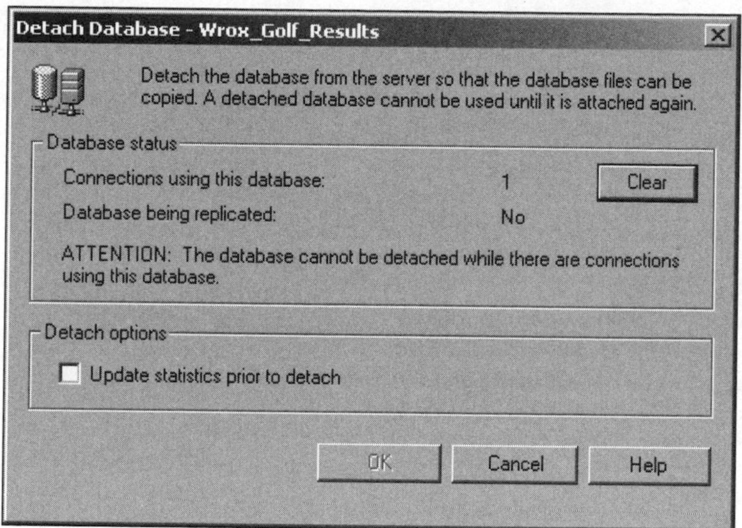

7. To remove these connections, we have to click the Clear button on the dialog. On clicking this, we will receive the following warning message. If it is ok to proceed, then click OK. This will disconnect all the connections from the database except us. This can be a very risky maneuver if a user is performing a crucial job like updating massive amounts of data when they're disconnected.

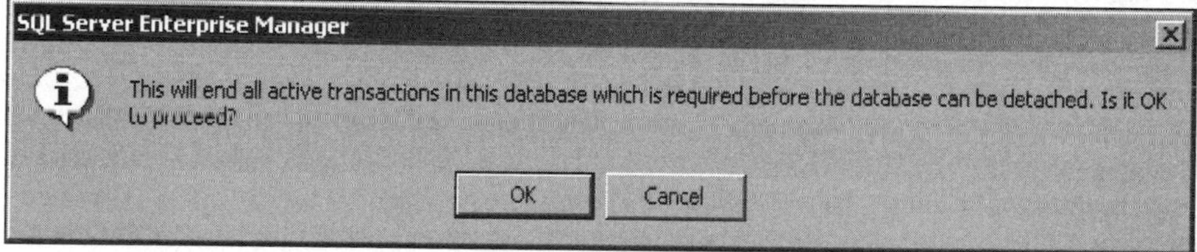

8. Finally we will be asked if we want to notify the currently connected users. Now, if we click Yes on this, there is no guarantee that we would receive a notification. It is very likely that some sort of notification goes out on a network, but on a single user machine not connected to a network, it is doubtful if this is the case. Click Yes or No depending on which option we require:

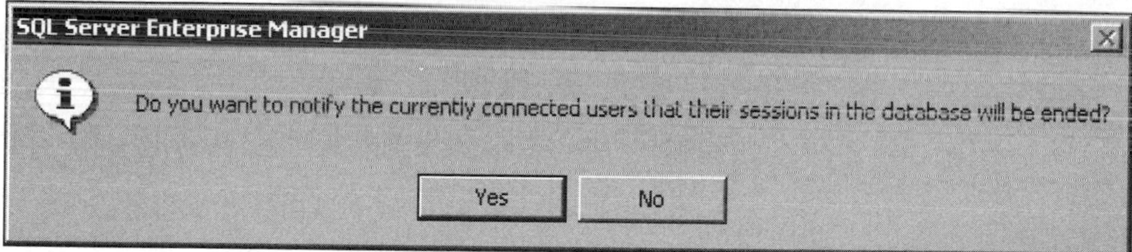

9. The last option is the Update Statistics Prior to Detach option. By selecting this option, we ensure that when we attach the database, the statistics for the database are up-to-date and can make the database perform faster when it's first attached.

10. Whether we had connections or not, the database is then detached and we should see the following message box saying everything has finished successfully. Click OK.

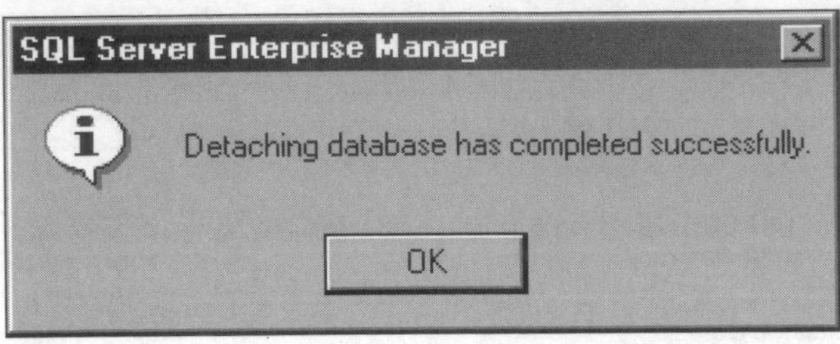

That's it. The database is detached, is no longer part of SQL Server and is ready to be removed or even deleted.

Detaching a database, although seemingly a simple and innocuous operation, is in fact potentially fraught with problems and worries. As the example demonstrated, ensuring that there are no users attached to the database at the time of detaching is not as easy as it first may seem. Setting up the database options to eliminate connections or to stop updates is only possible once everyone has been removed from connections to the database. Even to set the database to read only is hard. There is no easy way of removing connections safely as we never know what an application with a connection to the database is doing. We could remove a connection that is in mid processing. Even broadcasting a message informing users that they are about to be disconnected by using the Clear button does not allow people to say "just 5 more minutes and I will be finished". It is just too late by that point. The only real way to control removing connections is within Query Analyzer and using a system stored procedure called `sp_who`. This command will list all connections to the current database. However, it does also include our login in the list, which can cause a bit of confusion.

In the next screenshot `sp_who` has been run on the WONDERBISON server, and these are the results that have been produced. This is quite an advanced topic but to briefly cover it, we will see that under the column dbname, which is short for database name, there is one login, Rdewson, which is working on the Wrox_Golf_Results database. From this information it may be enough to contact this log in ID, and ask that they remove themselves from the application pointing to the database so we can reattach the database elsewhere.

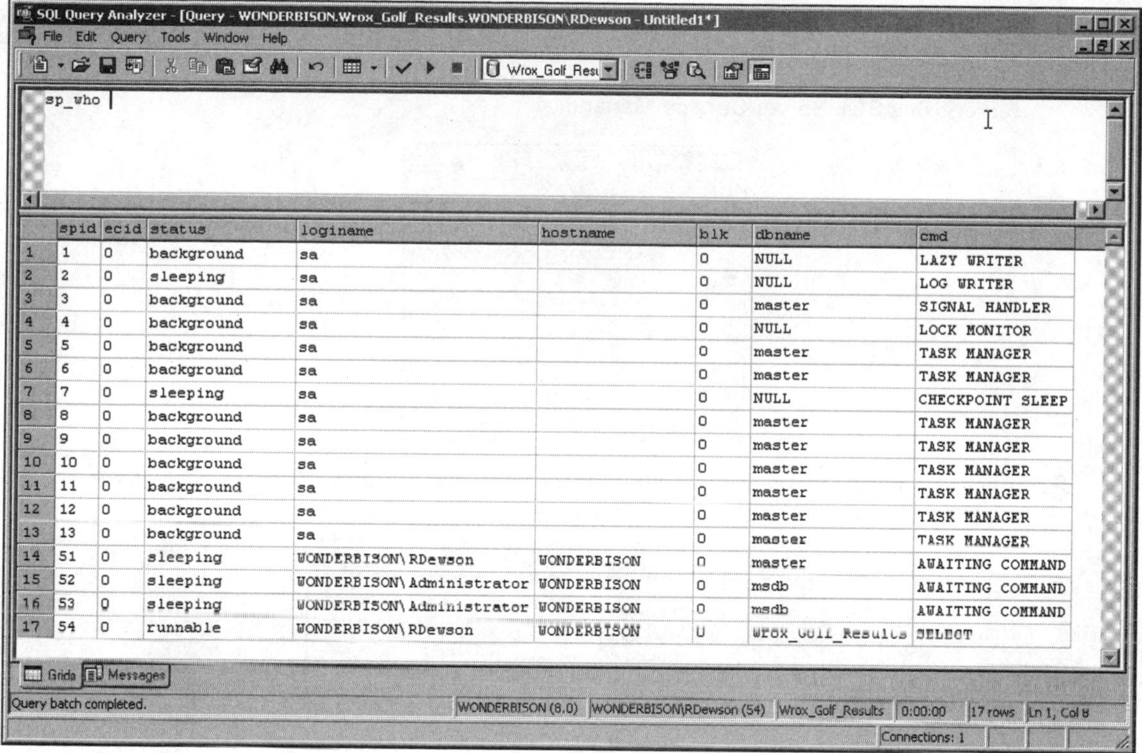

	spid	ecid	status	loginame	hostname	blk	dbname	cmd
1	1	0	background	sa		0	NULL	LAZY WRITER
2	2	0	sleeping	sa		0	NULL	LOG WRITER
3	3	0	background	sa		0	master	SIGNAL HANDLER
4	4	0	background	sa		0	NULL	LOCK MONITOR
5	5	0	background	sa		0	master	TASK MANAGER
6	6	0	background	sa		0	master	TASK MANAGER
7	7	0	sleeping	sa		0	NULL	CHECKPOINT SLEEP
8	8	0	background	sa		0	master	TASK MANAGER
9	9	0	background	sa		0	master	TASK MANAGER
10	10	0	background	sa		0	master	TASK MANAGER
11	11	0	background	sa		0	master	TASK MANAGER
12	12	0	background	sa		0	master	TASK MANAGER
13	13	0	background	sa		0	master	TASK MANAGER
14	51	0	sleeping	WONDERBISON\RDewson	WONDERBISON	0	master	AWAITING COMMAND
15	52	0	sleeping	WONDERBISON\Administrator	WONDERBISON	0	msdb	AWAITING COMMAND
16	53	0	sleeping	WONDERBISON\Administrator	WONDERBISON	0	msdb	AWAITING COMMAND
17	54	0	runnable	WONDERBISON\RDewson	WONDERBISON	0	Wrox_Golf_Results	SELECT

To be perfectly honest, however, if we are detaching a database to move servers, then there will have to be application updates anyway, but that aside, we may have a SQL Server developer working on the database as we are trying to detach it to promote it into another region.

However, the actual detaching of the database is purely removing entries within the SQL Server system tables to inform SQL Server that this database is no longer within this instance of SQL Server and therefore cannot be used. It is as simple as that.

> **One real word of warning is to use the Clear button to clear connections with the greatest of caution. It is only as a last resort that this button should be used.**

Now that the database is detached, it's time to re-attach the database to another server. In the next section, we will be demonstrate how easy this is. The `Wrox_Golf_Results` database is going to be re-attached to the System Test Server created earlier in the book, to simulate transferring the database from development to system test.

Try It Out – Attaching a Database

1. Ensure that the System Test Server is running and available. We may have to start up the test server using SQL Server Service Manager.

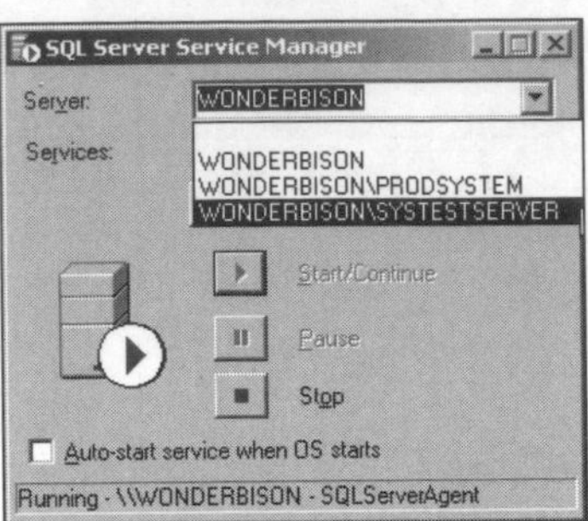

2. Expand the Databases node within Enterprise Manager, and the SYSTESTSERVER instance. As we can see, there is no `Wrox_Golf_Results` database.

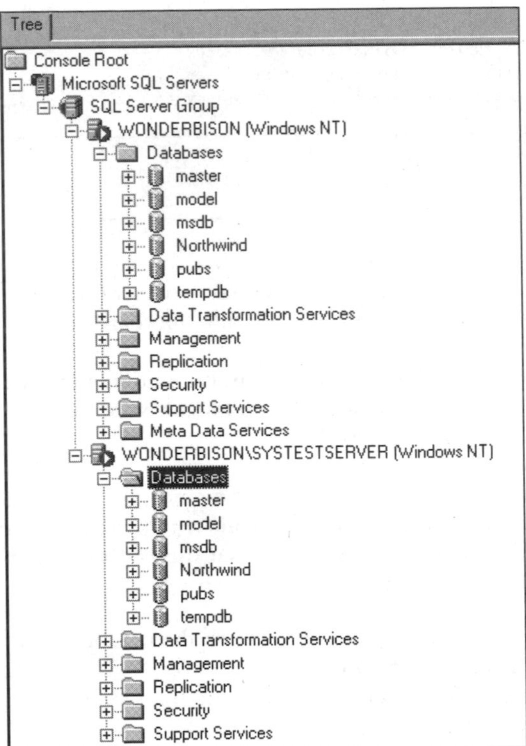

3. The database is still detached, from the previous section. Therefore no updates can be performed, so a simple file copy is possible and safe to complete. Navigate through Windows Explorer to where the data files are kept. Highlight both the `mdf` and the `ldf` files for the `Wrox_Golf_Results` database and copy them to a new location. One thing to note is that if you copy a file from a CD, make sure you take them out of read-only mode in Windows Explorer before attaching them.

4. Now that the files are in the correct location, the Wrox_Golf_Results database can now be attached to the System Test Server. From the Databases node that we navigated to at the start of this section, right-click, select All Tasks, and then the Attach Database... option.

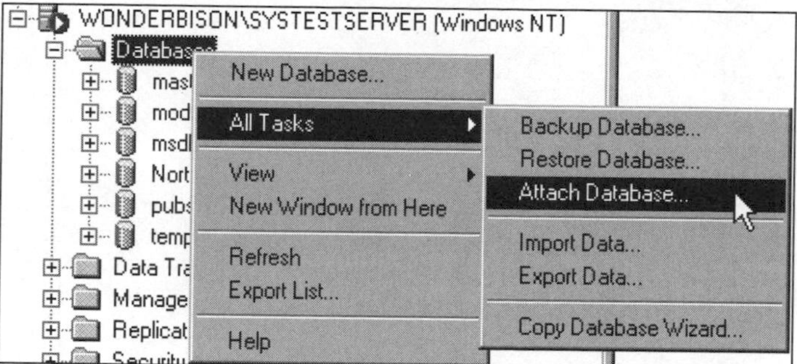

5. This then brings up the dialog for attaching a database to a server. As we can see, it is pretty empty at present. To find the database to attach, click the Elipsis (...) button at the top right of the dialog.

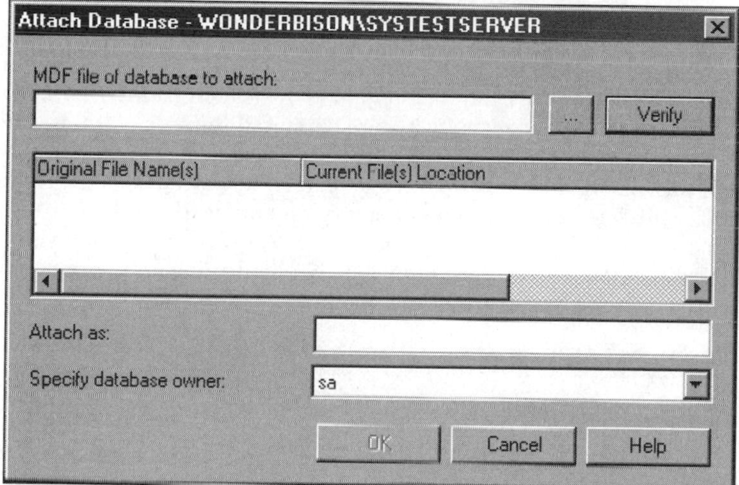

6. This then brings up a search dialog to allow finding the database through a local machine or on a server. This is being run on a local machine not connected to a network, and so only the two hard drives are listed.

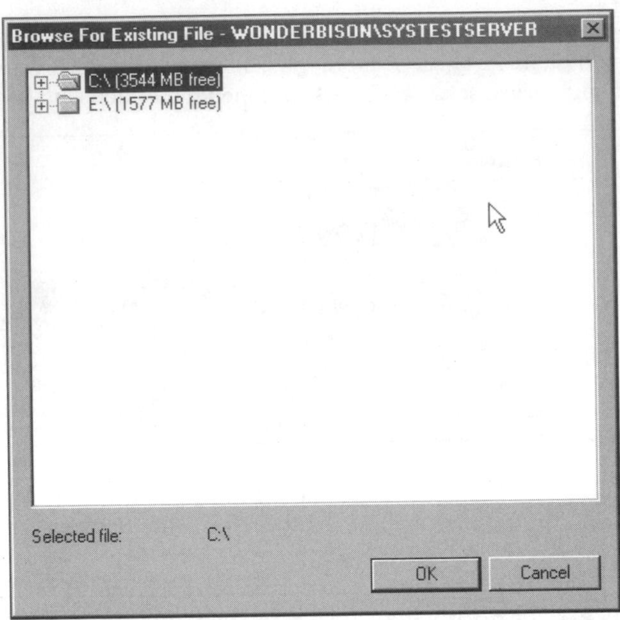

7. Expand the node to where the data is stored, and double-click on the `mdf` file of `Wrox_Golf_Results`. This will then populate the Attach dialog with data similar to that seen below, depending, of course, on where we stored the data. Also, it is not desirable to have the sa login as the database owner because we must be a member of the sysadmin role to perform this action. The only option available in this instance is the Administrator login, which is the only login created in the System Test Server. If you type in the path and file name to the `mdf` file, then you may want to click Verify to ensure that you typed it correctly. The Attach as option will also be automatically populated with the right database name. If you want to attach the files as a different name, type in the new name here.

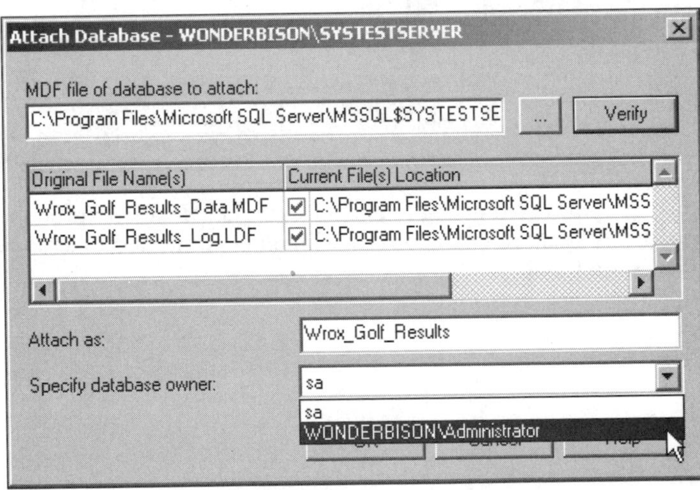

8. Once you are happy with the details, click OK, which will then attach the database, and the success dialog will be displayed. Click OK.

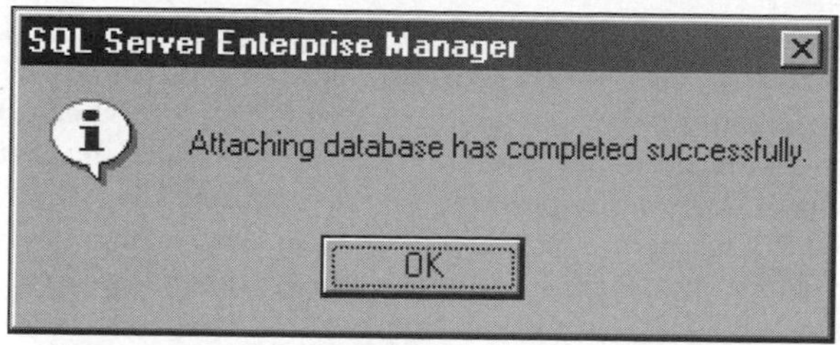

9. This then brings back Enterprise Manager, and the Wrox_Golf_Results database can now be clearly seen as attached.

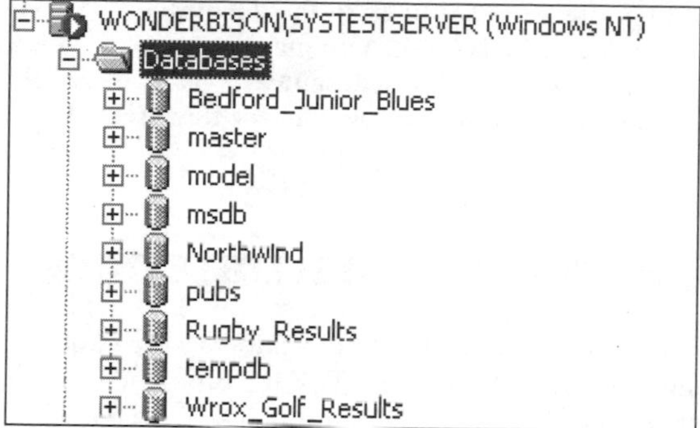

This example showed moving the detached database to a new instance of SQL Server. Hopefully you will also have at least two instances of SQL Server. When installing SQL Server in Chapter 1 of the book, two instances were demonstrated. If you do not have a second instance, pop back to Chapter 1 and revisit installing a second instance.

The detached database will be going into the System Test Server instance of the WONDERBISON server, as this is moving the development process from a plain development environment into system testing. It is possible that the second instance of SQL Server is not up and running. If it is not, and you are the owner of the SQL Server installations, then go ahead and start up this instance. However, if you are learning SQL Server in the work place where there many people using the database, do seek permission before using SQL Server Service Manager to start up this instance.

Attaching a database involves informing SQL Server of the name and the location of the data files and the transaction log files. This data can be placed anywhere on a computer or a network but it is recommended to place the data in a sensible location. The data also does not need to be in a subdirectory of Microsoft SQL Server installation found under Program Files. In fact, in production environments, this is the last place we would locate the data. We would generally want to keep these files away from any program files or the `pagefile.sys`. This is because SQL Server's performance can be maximized when these files are separated. However for the purpose of this book, placing the data in the `DATA` directory under the instance of SQL Server is perfectly valid and acceptable.

Once the two data files have been copied, it is a simple process of using a couple of mouse clicks to attach these files into the instance. What happens in the background, very basically, is that SQL Server takes the information of the name of the database and the location of the data files, and places this into internal tables that are used to store information about databases. It then scans the data files to retrieve information such as the names of the tables, to populate the system tables where necessary.

The main point to keep in mind is the database owner. If you remember back to Chapter 5 when the database was created, and even more so to Chapters 1 and 2 in the book where database owners were mentioned, then it is just as important in attaching a database as it is when creating a database, that we get a valid database owner, and not to use the `sa` login. We may find that before attaching the database we need to create the user ID within the instance we are attaching that will be, the login ID that the database will be assigned to. When moving a database to a new instance there are a number of other steps you will have to perform. For more information on this, see "*Professional SQL Server 2000 Programming*" *(Wrox Press, ISBN 1-861004-48-6).*

It's now time to look at how to create a structure backup of the database using T-SQL commands.

> **Don't forget to re-attach the database back to the normal SQL Server server to continue with the remainder of this book. You may notice after you attach the database that you may have to refresh the database tree. Enterprise Manager uses extremely aggressive caching and the only way to see new items is to refresh the appropriate tree.**

Producing SQL Script for the Database

The next section demonstrates a different method of backing up the structure of the database and the tables and indexes contained within it; this is using T-SQL commands to complete this. Do note that it is only the structure that will be generated as T-SQL commands; no data will be backed up – only the schema that is needed to recreate the actual database can be scripted here. The usefulness of this procedure is limited and really is only useful for keeping structure backups or producing an empty database for whatever reason, but it is useful to know rather than going through the process of copying the database with all the data when the data is not required.

This method is very useful for setting up empty databases when moving from development to test, or into production.

Try It Out – Producing the Database SQL

1. Ensure that SQL Server Enterprise Manager is running and that you have expanded the server so that you can see the `Wrox_Golf_Results` table. Right-click, select All Tasks and then select Generate SQL Script...

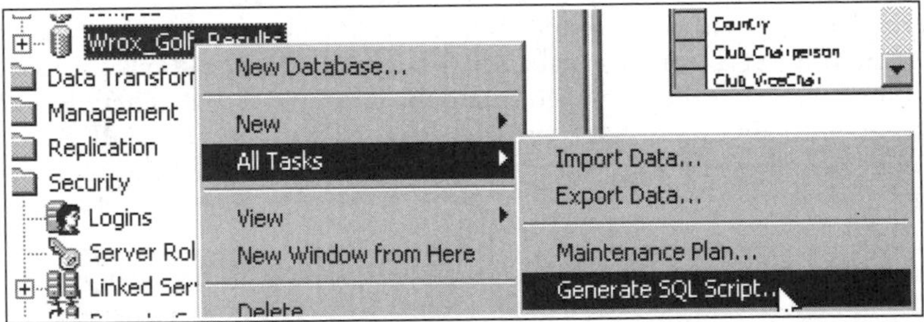

2. This then brings up a dialog that allows the database to be scripted. Initially there are no objects listed, so click the Show All button.

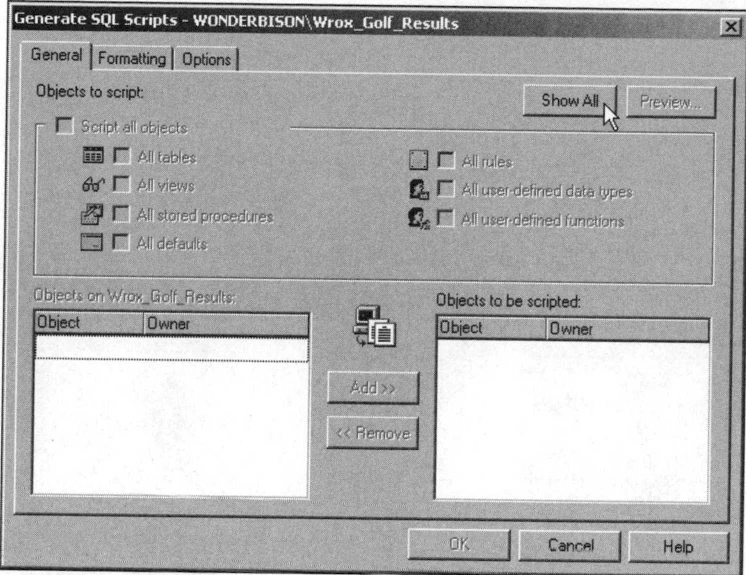

3. This then lists all the tables and views that are found within the database that have been created in the book so far. Selecting **Script all objects**, will produce a script for all the objects within the `Wrox_Golf_Results` database. This does not include the systems tables as they have been found to get in the way in other examples.

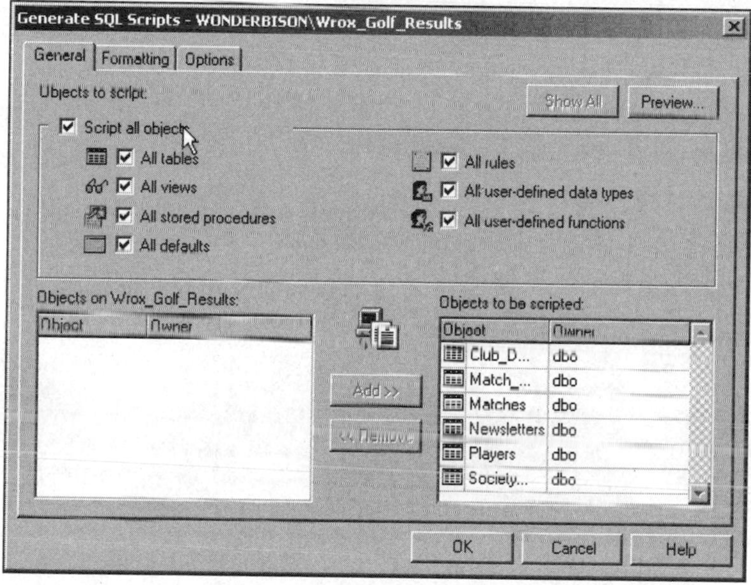

4. It is possible to stop here and generate the T-SQL from this point; however, it would be nice to apply some formatting to the SQL script that will be produced, so that it is neat and tidy. Click on the **Formatting** tab. The only check box that needs to be altered is **Include descriptive headers in the script files**, which should be checked as this does help with the documenting of the script file produced. Tick this box.

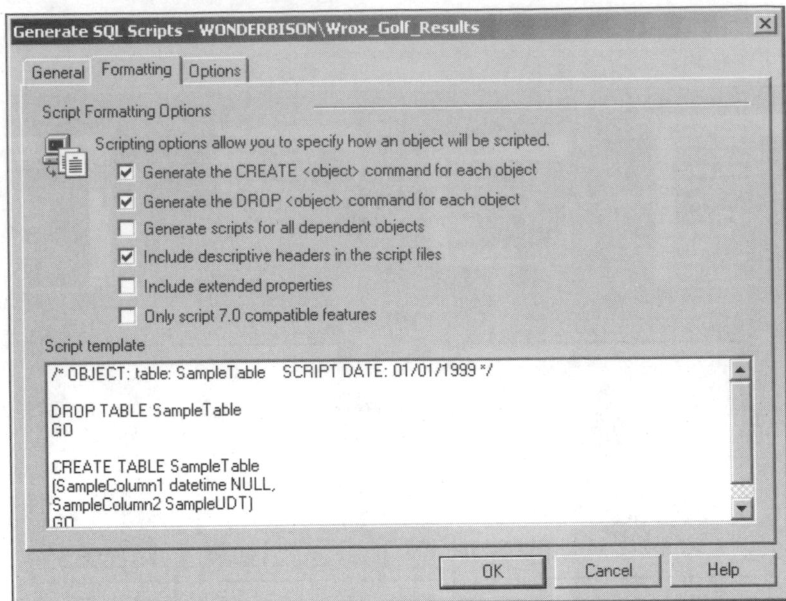

5. Click on the Options tab. As it is the whole database that should be scripted and this is forming part of the documentation and backup strategy for the database, ensure that all the check boxes are ticked. Leave File options as they are and then click OK.

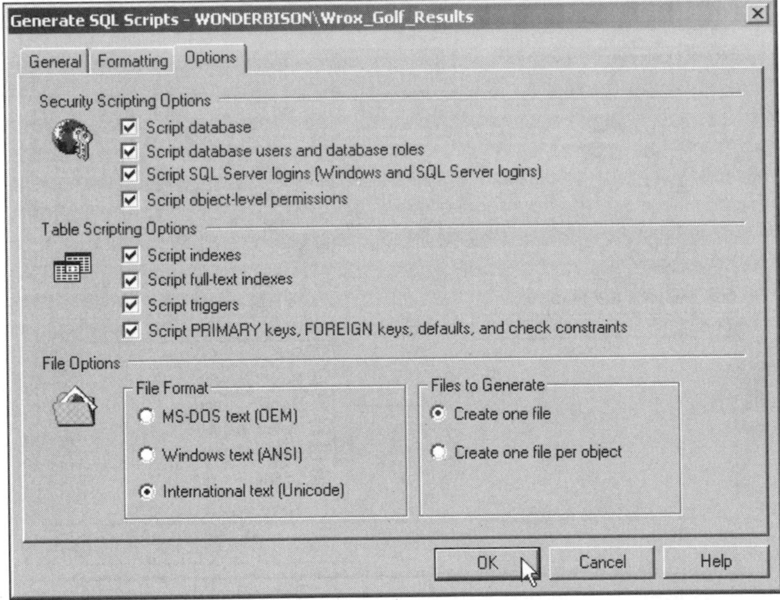

6. Clicking OK, will display a form for saving the SQL code to a file somewhere on your computer or network. Choose a suitable name, and a suitable location, and click Save. It is recommended, if this is forming part of our backup strategy, that we save the SQL script file in the same location as the backup files taken earlier in the chapter.

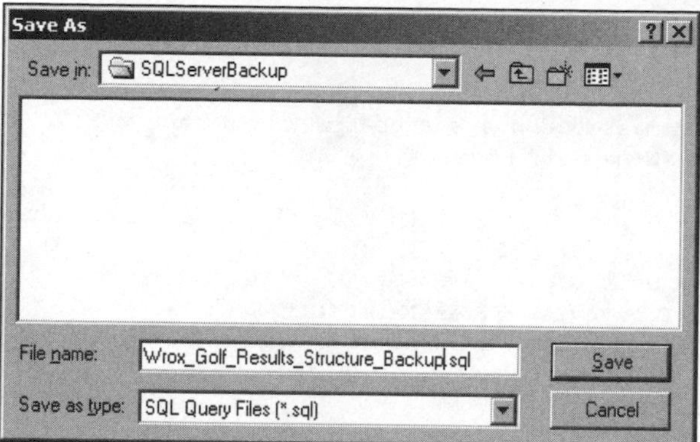

7. Once **Save** has been clicked, a progress dialog will be displayed showing the progress of the scripting of the database. This should only take a few moments on our database; however, as the database grows this process can reach several minutes long.

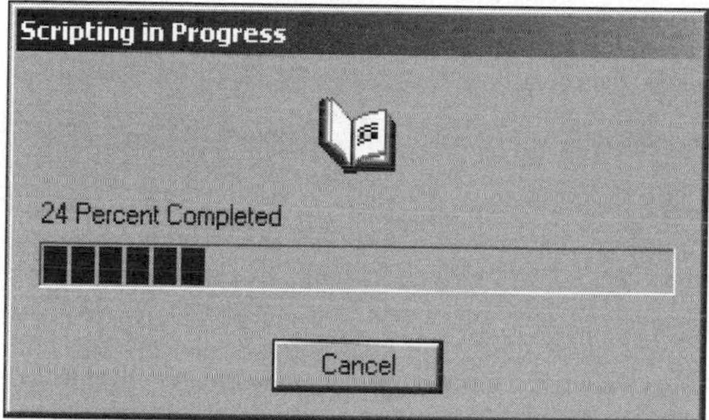

8. Once completed, the expected success message box is displayed.

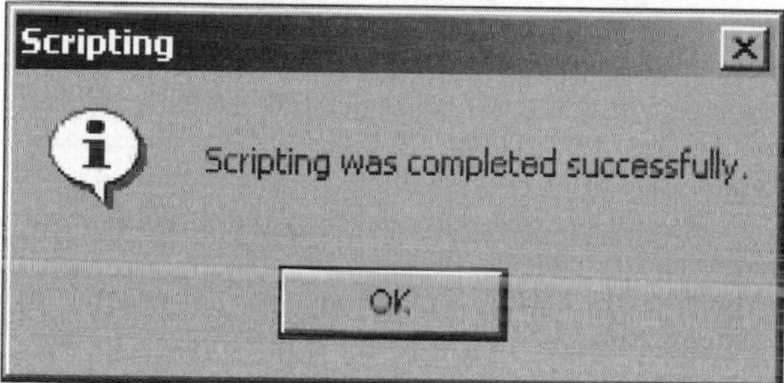

9. Locate the file placed in the location specified in the save dialog, and open it up in WordPad, Notepad, or the text editor of your choice. A selection of the code is below. There are a few pieces of SQL within the full file that have not been demonstrated or discussed in the book. Be warned though, that the selected code below will drop any database named `Wrox_Golf_Results` and recreate it without any data.

```
/****** Object:  Database Wrox_Golf_Results   Script Date: 22/03/2001 14:52:55
******/
IF EXISTS
(SELECT name FROM master.dbo.sysdatabases WHERE name = N'Wrox_Golf_Results')
   DROP DATABASE [Wrox_Golf_Results]
GO

CREATE DATABASE [Wrox_Golf_Results]
ON (NAME = N'Wrox_Golf_Results_Data',
    FILENAME = N'C:\Program Files\Microsoft SQL
      Server\MSSQL\Data\Wrox_Golf_Results_Data.MDF' ,
    SIZE = 1,
    FILEGROWTH = 10%)
LOG ON (NAME = N'Wrox_Golf_Results_Log',
        FILENAME = N'C:\Program Files\Microsoft SQL
          Server\MSSQL\Data\Wrox_Golf_Results_Log.LDF' ,
        SIZE = 1,
        FILEGROWTH = 10%)
COLLATE SQL_Latin1_General_CP1_CI_AS
GO
```

Summary

Phew! We covered a great deal in this chapter, but as has been said within the chapter, getting a backup and a backup strategy right is probably more important than getting the database architecture correct. All it needs is for you to get the backup wrong or the strategy wrong and then when things do go wrong with the database you will be at a loss.

The best you can do is to review the backup strategy at least every six months, even if it is only for a few short minutes, but also, to complete a recovery from a backup into a test system as well. This may take a couple of hours out of your day every six months, but one day you may well be glad that you did. A backup and restore that has been working for a couple of years, may, for whatever reason, suddenly stop working. It is also essential that you ensure that if a backup goes wrong, you are notified. As already mentioned, there will be more on this in the next chapter where the whole maintenance plan of the database is dealt with; however, test this out. If it means one night in production staying late to check what happens if a tape is not in the tape drive, again, you may well be glad of it.

These may seem like extreme measures, and no doubt some of you will be thinking that all of these measures are over the top. Well, perhaps in some cases they are, for example when the data is not critical and can be started from scratch again. However, look at it from the other side of the coin: if you do have a problem, and don't have a backup to restore, what will this mean to your corporation, and what will it mean to your reputation?

There is more on backups in the next chapter, where we look at a more overall picture and look at maintenance plans for databases.

11 Maintaining Your Database

At this point, we have now created a backup and performed a restore of the example database. We have also covered the different methods to back up and restore the database. However, we have no real plan for maintenance and detection of problems in our database strategy. Any jobs for backup of the database or transaction log are held as single units of work called steps. Not only that, but there is nothing in place that will look after the data and indexes held within the database to ensure that they are still functioning correctly and that the data is still stored in the optimal fashion.

This chapter will demonstrate building a plan and then checking on the plan after it has run to ensure that all has gone well with it. To do this, we will use the Database Maintenance Wizard, which will monitor any type of corruption in the database, optimize how the data is stored, and back up both the database and transaction logs. Finally, the wizard will schedule all of this to occur on a regular interval. Some areas of this chapter, like the backup screens, are straightforward as they were covered in the previous chapter concerning backups and restores; however, this now brings the whole maintenance of the database into one wizard.

In this chapter you will learn

- How to create a database maintenance plan
- Why to use a plan instead of single units of work
- What is contained within the database once a plan has run
- How to send notifications when any problems occur

Database Maintenance

Many of you are probably wondering what the term database maintenance actually means. Part of a maintenance plan includes corruption "health checks", but because SQL Server databases so rarely corrupt, this is a minor feature. The other features of the wizard include:

- Rebuilding indexes for a database
- Complete database backups
- Transaction log backups
- Shrinking the database if necessary
- Updateing the database statistics

As mentioned in Chapter 7, SQL Server stores data based on what clustered index is defined for the table. Indexes use fill factors to determine how much data will fit on each page before a new page is created. If we have an index factor of 90%, then a data page is 90% full before another is created. When the indexes are rebuilt on an index with a fill factor of 90%, the data pages are "shuffled" around into an optimal order, creating the needed 10% of free space on each data page. This can be seen to be by far the best feature of the maintenance plan wizard. The statistics are optionally updated when a plan is run, which will make sure SQL Server uses the indexes it has properly.

Creating a Database Maintenance Plan

Now that the database is up and built and the tables are there, it really is time to start considering a whole database maintenance plan before data is entered. This will cover database corruption through to inadvertent errors in development. Even though corruption is rare in SQL Server, it can be caused when the SQL Server is powered off abruptly.

There are many areas to building a maintenance plan, and this chapter covers many of them. There are one or two areas that are only touched on as they are quite advanced and will not be covered in this book. We will still need a little background so that we can see how crucial this area is and we can move on to those more advanced areas a bit later on.

A single maintenance plan can be built for one database or several databases. A single plan can be set up for system databases and all user databases by selecting those options at the start of the maintenance plan wizard. However, it is recommended that you create a plan for all system databases, but should have a separate maintenance plan for each separate user database. The logic behind this is that each user database will have its own needs, its own overnight routines, and even its own people for callout when things go wrong. Even if you are a one-man band, each user database should still have a maintenance plan. Therefore, in keeping with this, only the `Wrox_Golf_Results` database will be selected.

Try It Out - Creating a Database Maintenance Plan

1. Click on the wizard button on the toolbar to bring up the wizards dialog. Expand the Management node and select the Database Maintenance Plan Wizard. You can also access the wizard by right-clicking on the database and selecting All Tasks | Maintenance Plan.

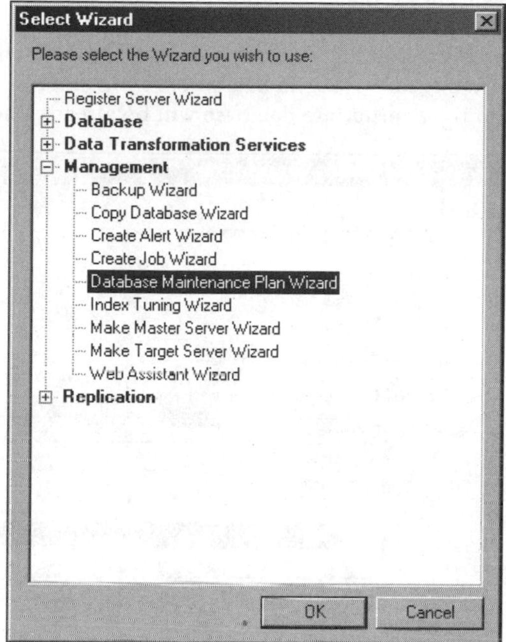

2. This is the first screen of the wizard. Once you have read it, click Next.

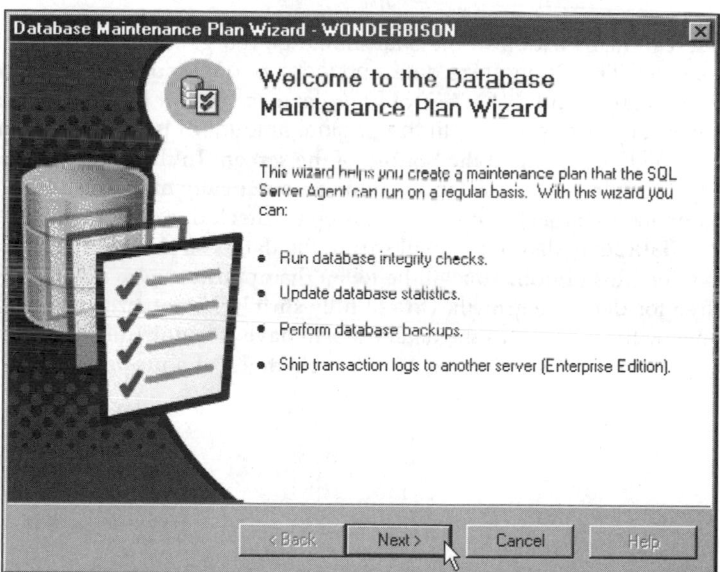

3. This next screen allows us to select the databases that we wish to create a maintenance plan for. It is best to have separate maintenance plans for the user databases, and one separate maintenance plan for the system databases. This not only splits up the workload into sizeable, useful, and easy-to-understand units of work, but also into logical components as each database may have a different maintenance plan. You will also have different requirements for the system databases from for the user-defined databases. It is preferable not to select the All User Databases option because SQL Server will automatically begin running the maintenance plan on databases that may have been added without prior knowledge. For our example, select the Wrox_Golf_Results database. If you entered the wizard by right-clicking on the database, then the appropriate database will be already checked. Click Next.

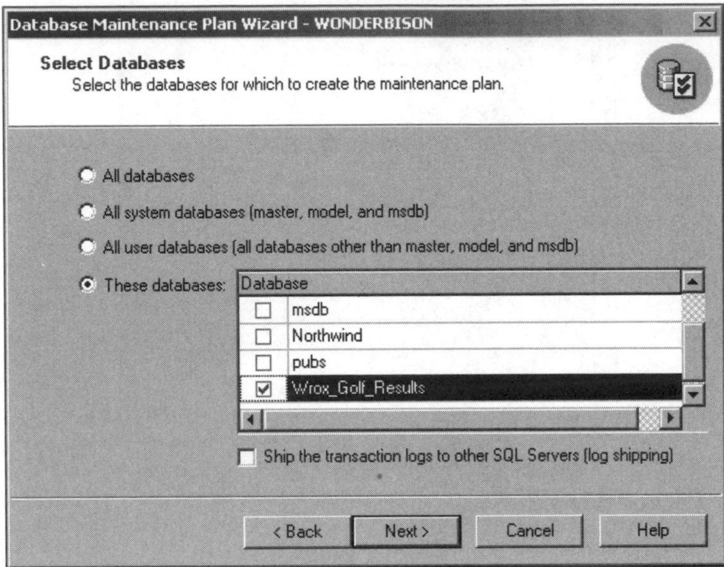

4. The next screen deals with how the data should be reorganized. Initially this will have no options selected. The Reorganize data and index pages option should be checked to ensure that the performance and disk usage of your database is kept healthy, so select this option and ensure that Reorganize pages with the original amount of free space is checked. This will enable the schedule section at the bottom of the screen. In this screen you can also have the statistics updated. In most cases, this is done automatically unless you have selected otherwise. As this is done automatically, it is unnecessary to check this option. The Remove unused space from database files option will shrink the database if it has space it is not fully using. After you select this option, you will be given the opportunity to still leave a given percentage of space free for database growth. Do not fully shrink the database to 0% of free space or your performance will be worse, as the database will have to automatically grow. Click on the Change... button, as this action needs to be scheduled at a proper time.

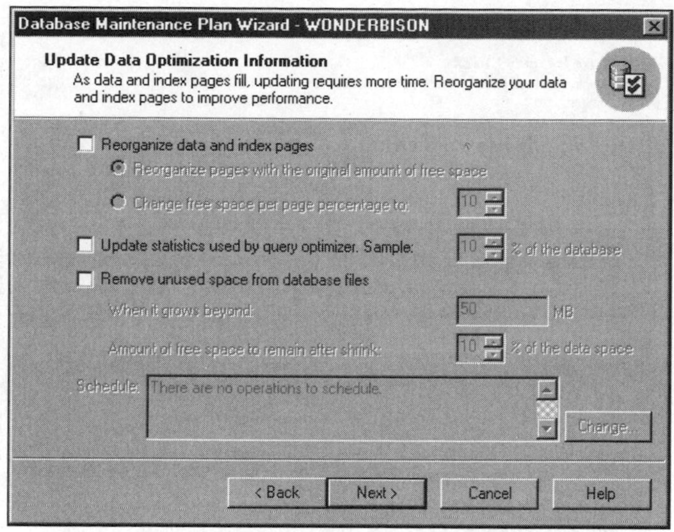

5. By now we should be familiar with this dialog, as we have come across it before in the previous chapter. However, in the next section there will be more on schedules, how they work and what to do when things go wrong. The scheduling of the data optimization should be at a quiet time and unless the database is updated heavily, this maintenance plan choice will only be required infrequently. Running a maintenance plan can be quite intense for the server and should only be done during low usage hours. For the sake of Wrox_Golf_Results, it could be as infrequent as monthly; however, for the moment, in the initial setup of the database, while the input of data might be heavy, set this up as a weekly task for now. It can easily be altered later. Once done, click OK. This then brings you back to the data organization screen, and as we are done, click Next.

6. We are now at the Database Integrity Check form. Of course, it is up to you as to how much you wish to ensure that the database data and indexes are still ok, but I would recommend that as much as possible is checked. Select the options as overleaf, which will also enable the schedule option. The integrity checks will perform checks on the database to ensure that the pages are properly linked. If you do this, it makes sense to include indexes in these checks. SQL Server can also repair some minor problems. If you uncheck this, the problems are logged and will require manual intervention.

   A nice feature of this screen is the Perform these checks before doing backups option: this allows you to ensure that the backup you create is good before wasting the media. This is generally not a problem unless you have huge databases. It is important to note here that for large databases, the process of checking the database integrity can take hours, even days. For databases like this, it is best to run these checks manually. Rather than demonstrating the same schedule dialog each time, if you wish to alter the schedule that SQL Server has chosen, then click the Change... button, and once the schedule has been altered, click the Next button.

Warning: Only select the Attempt to repair any minor problems option if you have SQL Server 2000 Service Pack 1 or greater installed. Otherwise, you risk your database being placed in single-user mode and not taken out. This could be a huge problem if you have a database that's accessed around the clock.

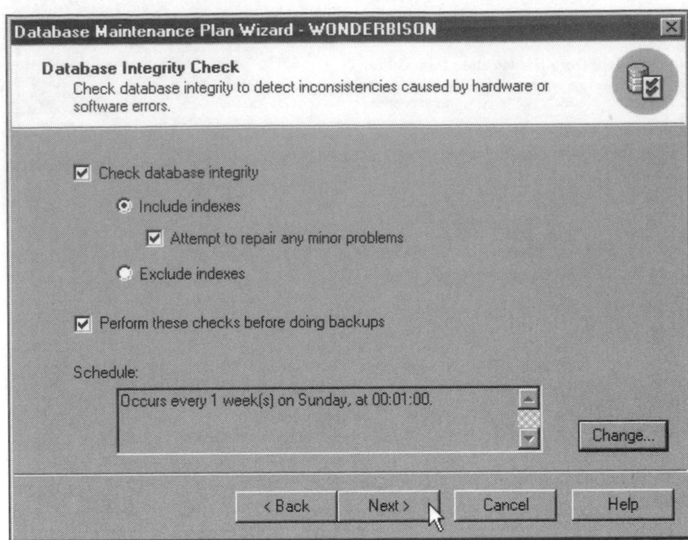

7. This then moves the wizard into the Database Backup Plan screen. This is similar to the previous chapter where a backup is built. However, it does bring the backup in as part of the whole plan, rather than as a separate entity of its own. This has some merit as the whole plan is kept as one. Again alter the schedule as you wish, and when done, click Next.

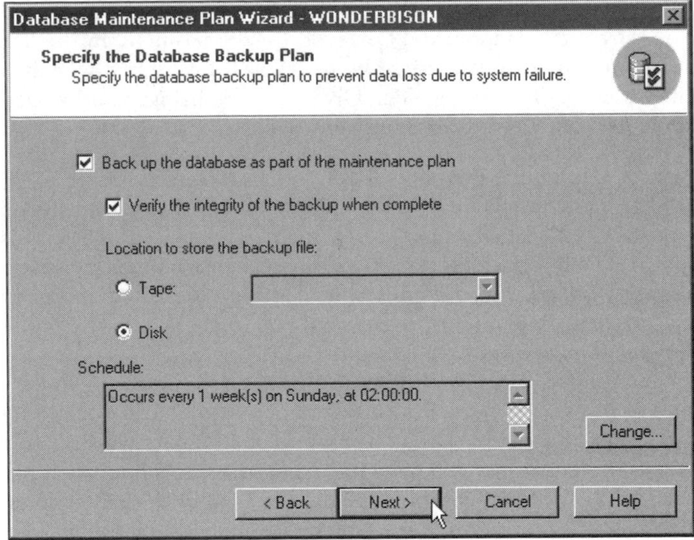

8. Having chosen for the backup to go to disk, before you move on to the Transaction Log Backup Plan, you have to specify the Backup Disk Directory, so that SQL Server knows where to put the database backup. Don't forget that once you back up your databases locally, you will want some system (likely a tape backup system) to pick up those files. Select Use this directory and then click the ellipsis to the right. On systems with lots of databases, it makes sense to select the Create a subdirectory for each database option so that you can organize your databases cleanly.

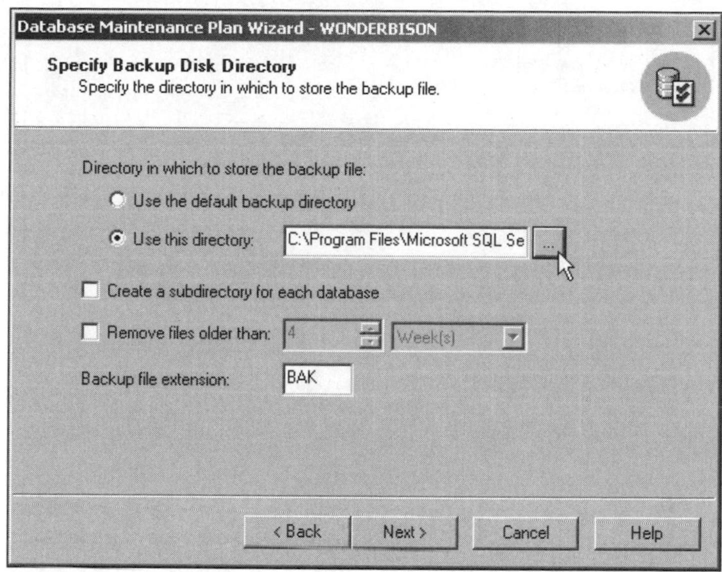

9. Select the directory that you wish the backup to be placed into. In the screenshot, the same directory as used in the previous chapter will be used, SQL Server Backups. Once you have selected your desired directory, click OK.

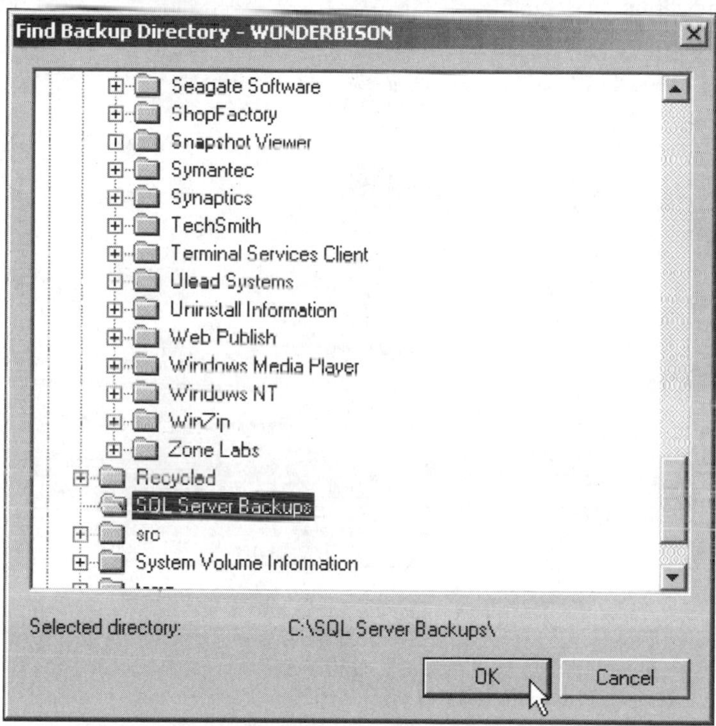

10. The Remove files older than 4 weeks option will cause the maintenance job to purge old backup files as they become obsolete. Once done, click Next.

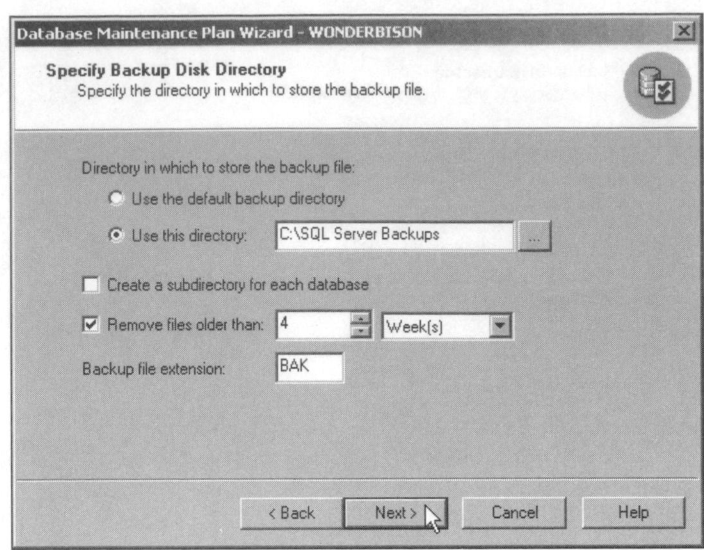

11. Again like the last chapter, the Transaction log can also be unified with the rest of the database maintenance plan. In the following screenshot, the Verify the integrity of the backup when complete option was selected to ensure that our backup is good. If the integrity check fails, the job will fail and the problem will be logged. Once you have selected the options as shown and set up the schedule, click Next.

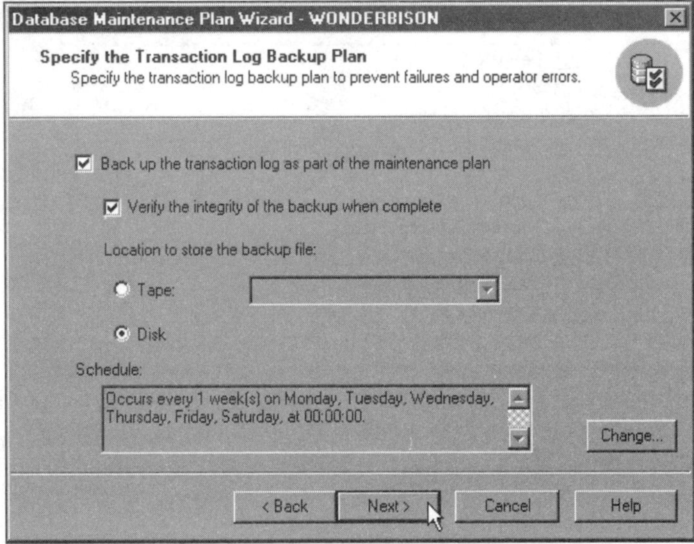

12. If you select to have the Transaction Log backed up to disk, then the following dialog will appear in the wizard. This is just as before with the database, and it requires details of where the data is to be located. As you can see, the details are similar to those of point 10. The only option that may require changing occasionally is how many intervals of the backup you keep. If you're doing regular transaction log backups, you may not require more than a week's worth of backups. The only change is in the Backup file extension, which the wizard has changed to TRN to denote a transaction log. When done, click Next.

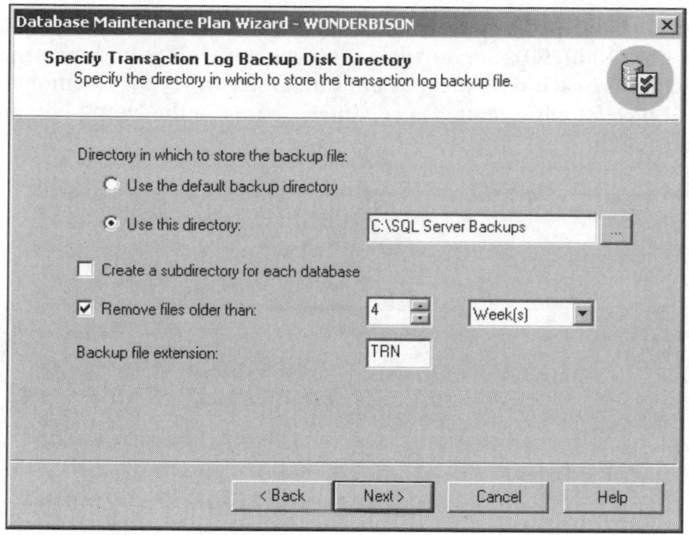

13. The wizard now brings in what is probably one of the most important areas of this whole wizard. This screen concerns the reporting of what the plan has completed, and when. This is a very important area as it records what is happening within SQL Server without any manual intervention, and therefore it allows you as a DBA, or developer, to see what has happened, especially when things have gone wrong and you need to determine where to get back to. Don't treat the reporting of the maintenance plan as immaterial because it is not. Some companies have not kept reports for any length of time, and it was impossible to know what had happened from day to day. The backup directory is generally the best place to store the reports, and it is best to keep, as the barest minimum, one month's (shown in the screenshot as 4 weeks) worth of information. However, it would be good if people were notified of success or failure of the plan. If no operators exist on your system, then you will have to add a new one by clicking on New Operator....

14. This then will bring up the option of creating a new operator within SQL Server. An operator is a person defined in SQL Server who will receive warnings and messages. In our case, they will receive the log each time the jobs are run. Don't worry for the moment what this is about, as there will be a lot more on this later. Enter a name in the **Name** box and an **E-mail name** as well. Then click the **Test** button.

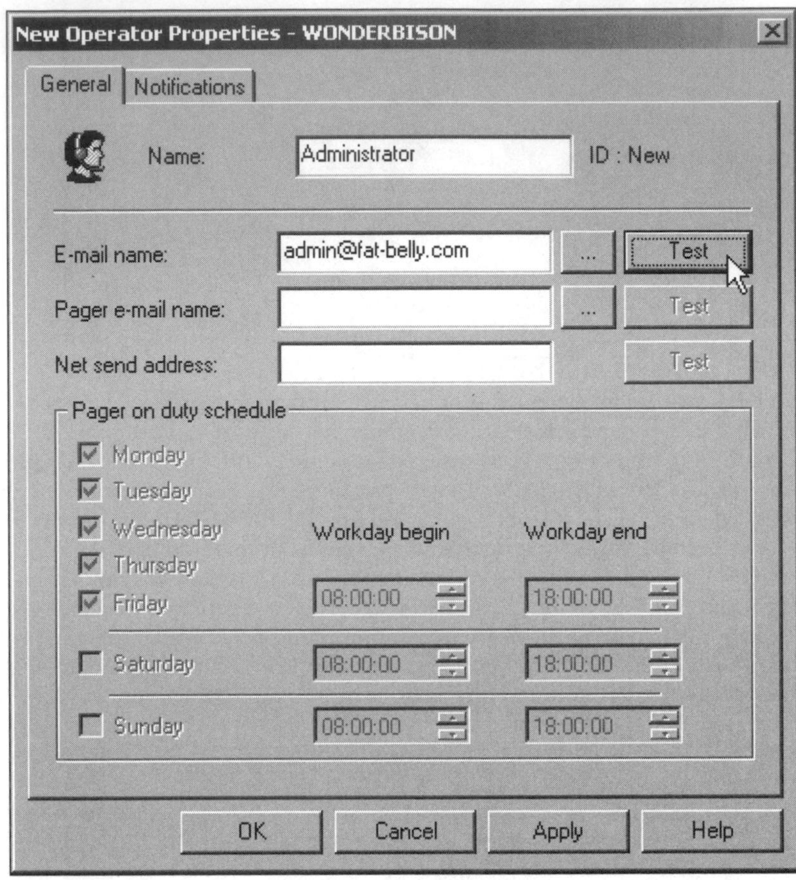

15. You are then informed about a test e-mail that will be sent. Providing the address is ok, then click **OK**. If SQL Server Agent is not running, then you will receive a warning asking you to start the service.

16. On clicking **OK**, you may well get the following error message. This is because sending mail through SQL Server has not been set up within the book. Click **OK**.

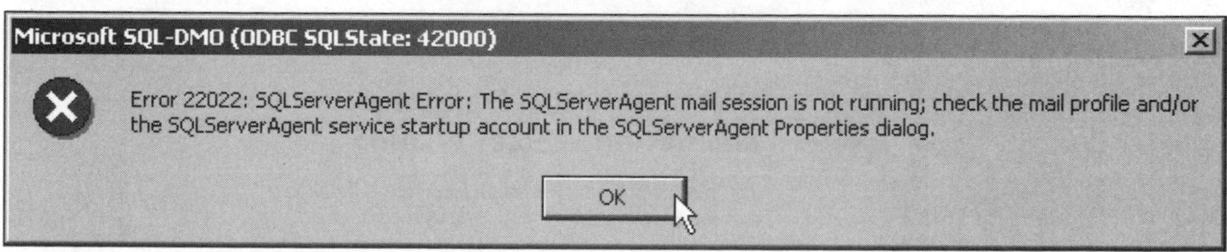

17. You are then returned back to the New Operator screen, where you must click OK to get back to our maintenance plan. Clicking Next on the dialog brings you to a form that deals with the generation of records each time the maintenance plan runs, detailing successes and failures. Don't alter anything on this screen: just click Next.

Database Maintenance Plan Wizard - WONDERBISON

Maintenance Plan History

Specify how you want to store the maintenance plan records.

Local server

☑ Write history to the msdb.dbo.sysdbmaintplan_history table on this server

☑ Limit rows in the table to: 1000 rows for this plan

Remote server

History is added to the msdb.dbo.sysdbmaintplan_history table on the remote server. Windows Authentication is used to log on to the remote server.

☐ Write history to the server: ...

☑ Limit rows in the table to: 10000 rows for this plan

< Back | Next > | Cancel | Help

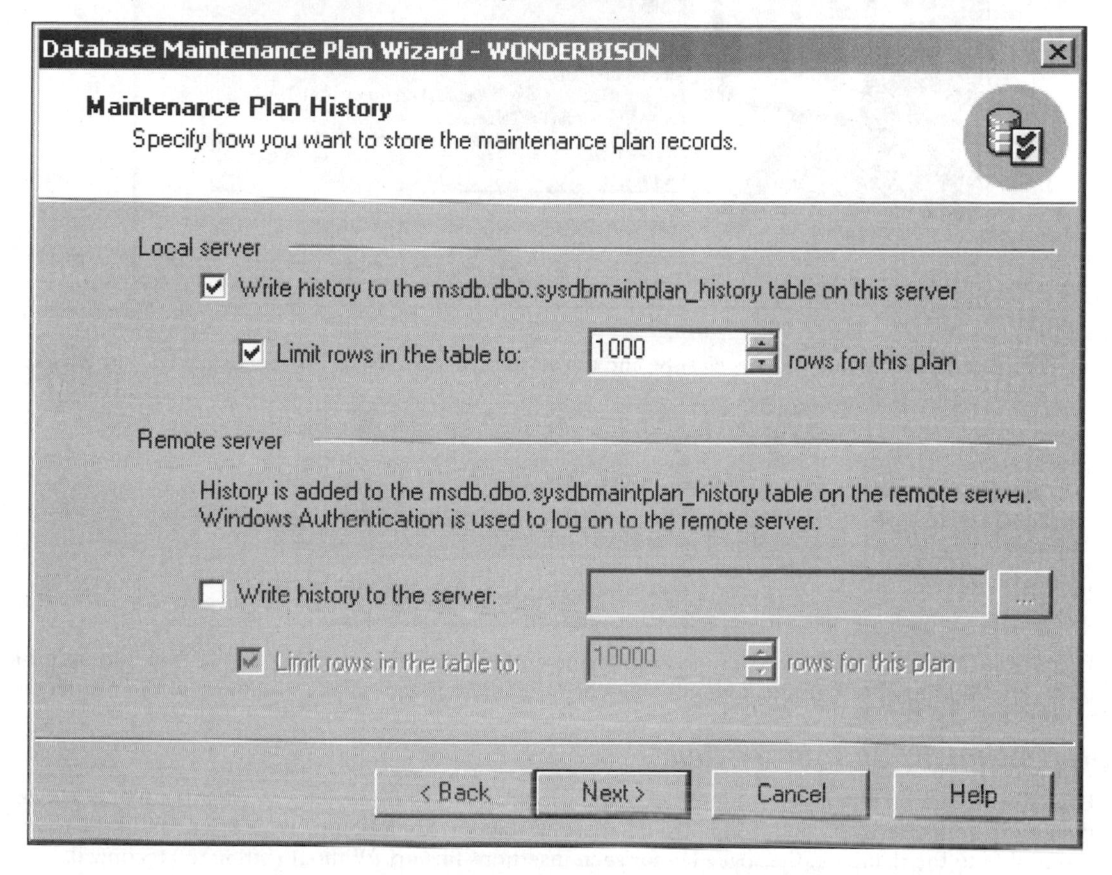

18. This now brings you to the end of the wizard where it is essential, as ever, to give the plan a clear and meaningful name. This name can be changed later. Just quickly scroll through the plan options to ensure that you are happy with everything before clicking Finish.

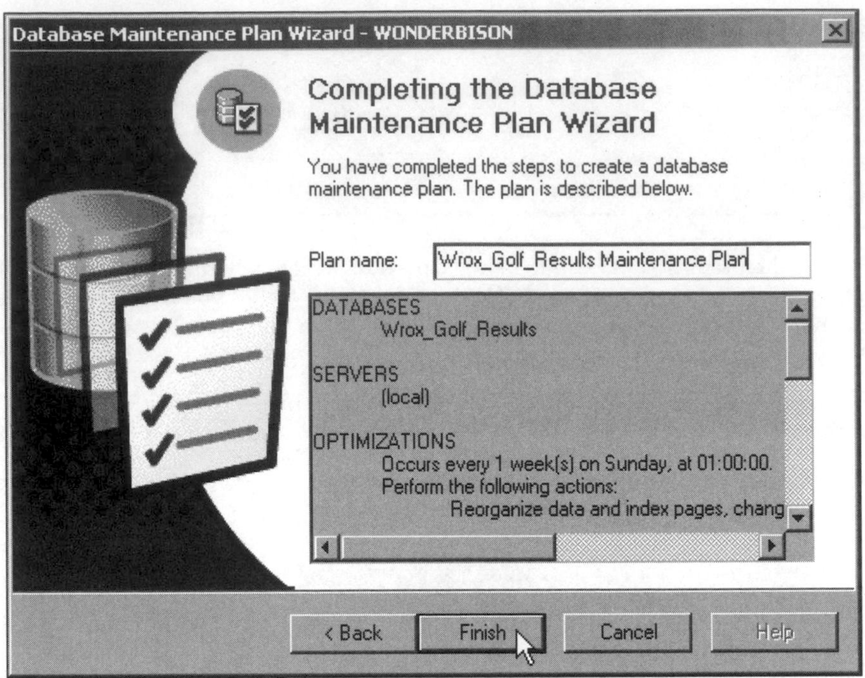

19. Everything should process cleanly, and the usual success message box be displayed. Just click OK.

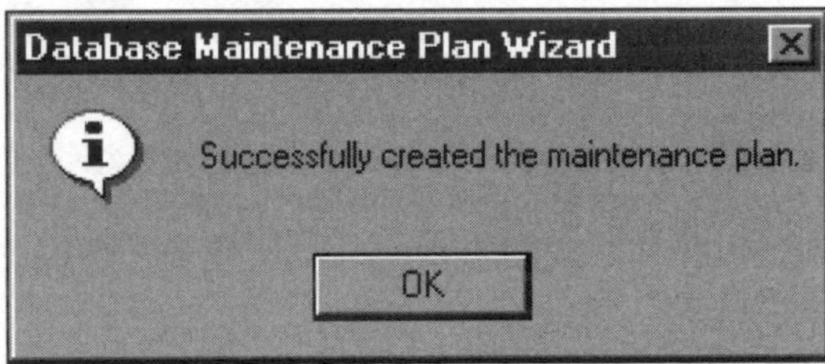

If you want to access the plan later, go to Enterprise Manager, and select Database Maintenance Plans under the Management group. Then double-click the maintenance plan to edit any of the properties.

Data Optimization Information

Under the Update Data Optimization step of the wizard, you will find what you want the maintenance plan to do concerning the data within the database. Databases are a bit like hard drives and as data is inserted in to the database, the space left for such insertions fills up. Without getting too technical, as pages fill up, then the potential for SQL Server to do a lot of background processing moving data around grows. Reorganizing the data will allow the free space required for insertions to be regained by doing the background processing in one hit in the reorganization, rather than during each insertion and slowing down SQL Server when the processing is required most. Figuring out how much space to leave and create is quite an advanced technique, therefore, for the moment, just leave all this as default.

The rest of the options should be left, as once again they are for more advanced users.

Database Integrity Check

The Database Integrity Checks screen deals with how you wish the maintenance plan to deal with checking the data and indexes within the database. Problems may arise within your database, for whatever reason, from a hardware failure or a bug within SQL Server, to the possibility of a SQL Server user meddling with system tables, and this tab will to find such problems and try to fix them. The likeliness of this occurring on a properly secured server is very minimal. There are T-SQL commands that can complete specific database integrity checks and this wizard uses the T-SQL command `DBCC CHECKDB`, which is an all encompassing database integrity check.

By also including the Attempt to repair any minor problems, you are going to cover the majority of (the few) problems that occur within SQL Server. Some of these problems may include linkage problems where one data page is improperly linked to another. Problems that are left not repaired will be those that require intervention by the database administrator. Some major problems like database corruption cannot be fixed here and will require manual intervention.

It is also best to perform this check before performing any backup, so that you are not backing up a corrupt database.

> **Even though it may seem like a good idea to enable the Repair Minor Problems option, it is not recommended. It is sometimes better to know about the problem and fix it manually: SQL Server 7.0 and 2000 have both had bugs where SQL Server would place a database that it's trying to repair in single user mode and not take it out.**

Database Backup Plan and Transaction Log Backup Plan

This is very much like the last chapter that dealt with backing up the data and the transaction log. This whole section has no real surprises or changes from this process and therefore we won't be going into detail again.

Reports

Every time that an option within the database maintenance plan runs, whether it is the database integrity check, or a backup, then there is the ability to write a report to a text file of exactly what went on and when, along with other information. This will on many occasions point out problems that aren't viewable in your regular logs. We will see information from a backup report towards the end of the chapter. By opting to have a report written out, we will always have a copy of what has gone wrong that is viewable by outside viewers such as Notepad in the event that SQL Server becomes unavailable. Keep no more than a month's worth of reports unless there is some sort of auditing requirement to keep reports longer, but even then you should look to archive them anyway.

New Operator

Moving on to the New Operator function, this is where you set up a user within SQL Server to receive notifications of jobs that have completed or when there have been problems.

Most of you at this point may find that SQL Mail does not work on your computer. The easiest route to installing SQL Mail is to first install Outlook 2000; earlier versions of Outlook have problems with SQL Server 2000 until SQL Server 2000 Service Pack 1. You will then need to configure a MAPI profile name to be set up on your computer, which can be configured from Outlook or Exchange. This configuration can also be done in Control Panel under the Mail icon.

The key point to remember when you're setting up a profile to be used by SQL Mail is that you must be logged in as the Windows user that starts SQL Server. With that said, this would mean to fully utilize SQL Mail, you couldn't have the System account start SQL Server or SQL Server Agent.

If you do have MAPI then you need to set up SQL Mail first with the relevant MAPI profile. We won't go into too many details, as there is a fair amount to know about SQL Mail; however, if you do wish to know where to set up SQL Mail, the following figure shows that SQL Mail sits under the **Support Services** node, and by right-clicking and selecting **Properties**, you will get to the screen for setting up the MAPI profile. If you need more information about SQL Mail, read *"Professional SQL Server 2000 Programming" (Wrox Press, ISBN 1-861004-48-6)*.

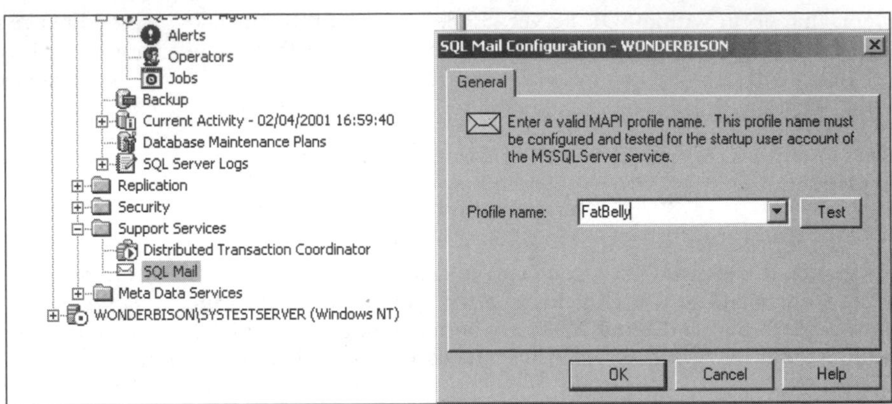

However, you do also have the option of sending a pager e-mail if you have the relevant pager software installed, or, perhaps the final possible method, through a **net send**. For those not familiar with net send, this is a network command that will allow the sending of a message, usually from a command prompt or from the run command, to another user on the network. Of course, this command will not work for those who are not hooked up to a network.

You can have many different operators set up for different jobs and there is a whole complex myriad of different combinations that you can set up for different operators. This book is not here to teach you this, as it would need to have many pages on this area on its own.

Maintenance Plan History

Each time the maintenance plan is run, a log is kept of when it ran along with other pertinent information. Not only will this be placed in any reports created earlier, but a record is also kept within the `msdb` database, which is the database used for SQL Server Agent scripts, of which the maintenance plan is one. You can store this information on a Local server as well as a Remote server. This allows maintenance plans run on remote systems to be placed in one central server where all maintenance plans for an organization could be viewed.

At the end of all of this setup you have a single contained plan rather than individual jobs that need to be maintained and dealt with one at a time. A maintenance plan is just as it suggests, a plan of how the whole database will be maintained and kept in good order. If you have to alter how your database is maintained, for example, the overnight batch window alters for one reason or another, then by dealing with the plan you know that all the processes will have been covered and re-visited to ensure that no job runs outside the window. With individual jobs, there is always the danger that you will miss one.

Now that a plan has been built, revisiting this plan displays the information about the plan differently from how it has just been viewed within the wizard.

Checking the Maintenance Plan

Once the plan has run several times, (if you want to cheat, just move your computer's clock forward to the required time and date!) then it is worthwhile checking out the maintenance plan so that it is possible to see what has happened.

Try It Out - Checking the Maintenance Plan

1. Expand the Tree nodes down to the Maintenance plan node. You will then see the maintenance plan created earlier in the chapter. Double-click on the maintenance plan; you can also right-click on the maintenance plan and select Properties.

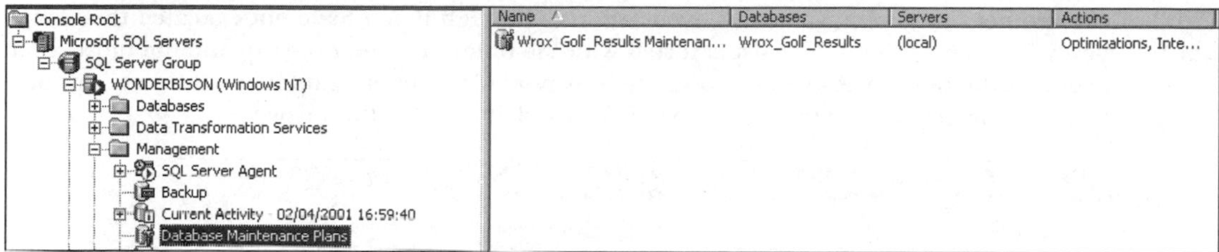

2. This brings up the maintenance plan form with several tabs. These tabs bring together the details entered in the wizard. There is not a great deal to be gained from going through these tabs, as all the relevant details are exactly those that were covered in the wizard. Have a look through and alter any information that requires attention. For our example, we'll skip any modifications. When completed, click OK.

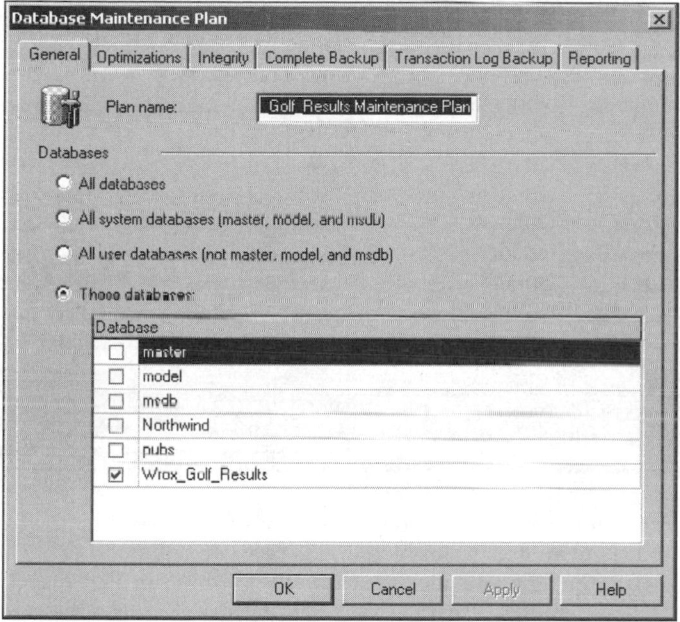

3. Moving back to the maintenance plan within Enterprise Manager, select the maintenance plan, right-click, and select Maintenance Plan History...

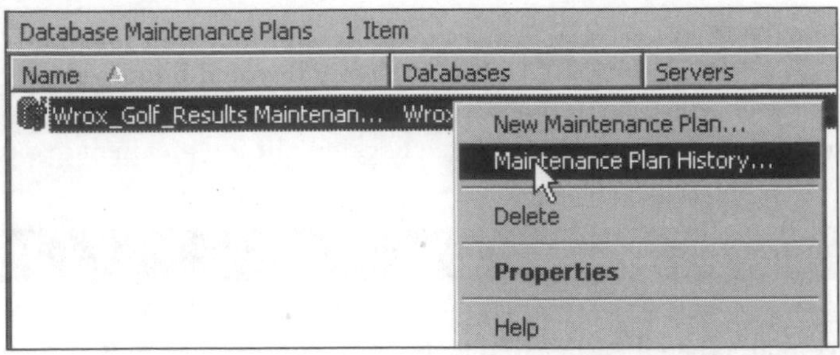

4. This brings up the history of what has happened within the maintenance plan so far. As you can see below, there have been eleven actions, although if you have not executed the plan, you will see no actions. The list is sorted with the oldest action at the top and the most recent action at the bottom. As you can also see, it is possible to filter using many different options to find the correct activity for the correct database that you want to inspect.

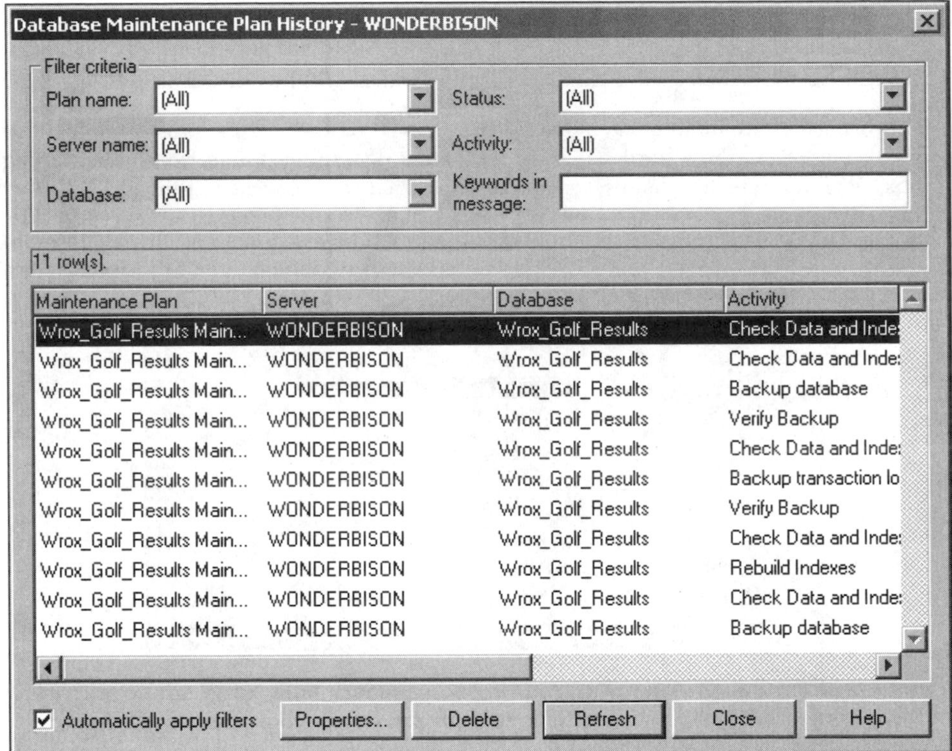

5. The next area that the example is going to demonstrate is looking at what details are stored with an action. Find an item to inspect; in this case, we will check a backup to see what has happened. Select the item and click the Properties... button. This displays exactly what has gone on with that item in the maintenance plan history. You can see that, the backup was successful, when it started and completed, along with other details that could be useful. Once you are done, click the Close button.

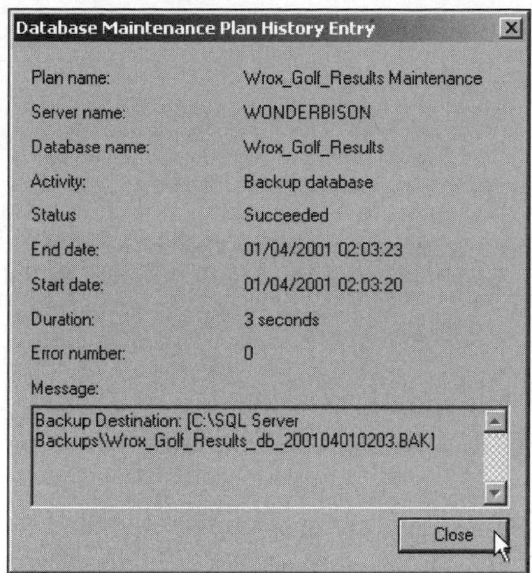

6. It is also possible to check out the reports that have been produced. Start up Windows Explorer and navigate to the directory where the reports are kept. Remember that in the case of the book, these are being stored in `C:\SQL Server Backups`. Select a report to inspect, and open this up in WordPad or Notepad.

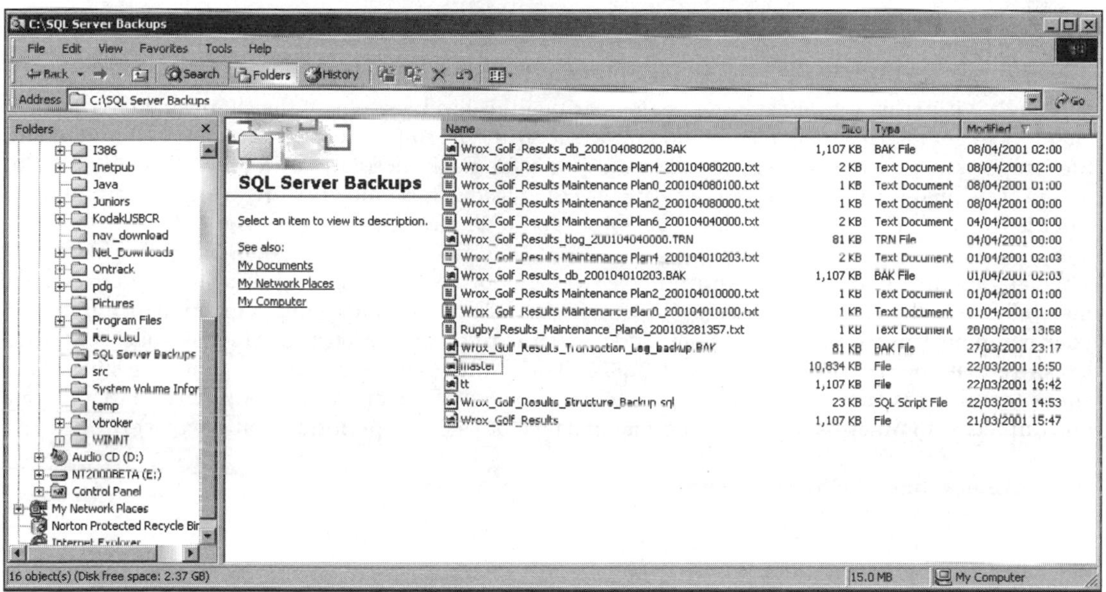

7. Below is an excerpt of a report created from the selected backup from earlier in the example. This was the database backup on April 1st. The line to especially watch for on a regular basis is the line that says [1] Database Wrox_Golf_Results: Check Data and Index Linkage. If problems were to appear, it would usually be there. If any one of the steps were to fail, then the entire job would fail and you would have to go to a log to see where the problem occurred.

```
Microsoft (R) SQLMaint Utility (Unicode), Version Logged on to SQL Server 'WONDERBISON'
as 'WONDERBISON\RDewson' (trusted)
Starting maintenance plan 'Wrox_Golf_Results Maintenance Plan' on 01/04/2001 02:03:20
[1] Database Wrox_Golf_Results: Check Data and Index Linkage...

   ** Execution Time: 0 hrs, 0 mins, 1 secs **

[2] Database Wrox_Golf_Results: Database Backup...
   Destination: [C:\SQL Server Backups\Wrox_Golf_Results_db_200104010203.BAK]

   ** Execution Time: 0 hrs, 0 mins, 3 secs **

[3] Database Wrox_Golf_Results: Verifying Backup...

   ** Execution Time: 0 hrs, 0 mins, 1 secs **

[4] Database Wrox_Golf_Results: Delete Old Backup Files...
   0 file(s) deleted.

Deleting old text reports...   0 file(s) deleted.

End of maintenance plan 'Wrox_Golf_Results Maintenance Plan' on 01/04/2001 02:03:24
SQLMAINT.EXE Process Exit Code: 0 (Success)
```

Summary

Although it is perhaps a relief to you as a reader that this has been one of the shortest and easiest chapters to get to grips with, this should not detract from the importance. It cannot be said often enough how important a backup strategy is towards a successful database solution. Couple this with a sensible and professional maintenance plan, where areas such as database integrity are just as important to as trouble free a time as possible with the database, and it all makes common sense.

The database maintenance plan wizard makes so many of the decisions easy and simple to make. This may lull some of you into a false sense of security in which you do not build a maintenance plan that fits your company's needs or perhaps your servers' restrictions. Always keep in mind, as you would with backups, that you must revisit the maintenance plan, ensure that the scheduling times are still valid, and check that there is enough time in the plan to complete all of the operations. Also ensure that there are no conflicts with other backups or other maintenance tasks being performed on the server.

We move now onto the topic of inserting data into our database.

Inserting Data

It has been a long time getting to this point, with many examples, and a lot of work, but at last, it is time to populate our tables with some data. The many tables within the database cover a number of different types of data that can be stored. The range is from characters and numbers, through to images. This chapter will show how to insert data into columns defined with all of these data types.

Not all the tables will be populated with data at this point. Data will be inserted in other tables later on in the book when different functionality of SQL Server is being demonstrated. Although data is being inserted, the database is still at the stage of being set up, as we are inserting static information at this point. To clarify, static data is data that will not change very often, if at all, once it has been set up.

Not everyone who is allowed to access our database may be allowed to insert data into all of the tables. Therefore, you need to know how to set up the security to grant permission to specific user logins for inserting the data. It is possible to have different permissions for different users on different tables to really make your database secure, and on many systems this may be what is implemented.

Once we have set up users correctly it is time to demonstrate inserting data into SQL Server. It is possible to insert data using SQL commands through Query Analyzer, or through Enterprise Manager. Although both of these tools will have the same final effect on the database of data inserted, each works in its own unique way. When inserting data, we don't have to insert data into every column. There are many different methods that surround how to avoid inserting data into every column. This section will demonstrate the varyious different methods we can use to avoid having to use `NULL` values and default values. By using these methods, you are reducing the amount of information that it is necessary to include with a record insertion. This method of inserting data uses special commands within SQL Server called constraints. You will see how to build a column constraint through T-SQL in Query Analyzer as well as in Enterprise Manager.

We will also see how to insert and deal with images within SQL Server and what the issues are with inserting images. When more and more Internet sites are being built with SQL Server as the back end, images are all important to the success of a site, and this area of SQL Server is becoming a crucial functionality.

Finally the chapter will demonstrate how to insert several records or several images at once.

To recap, we will deal with

- Finding out who can add data
- How to protect your data from unwanted intrusions by users who should not be inserting data
- The `INSERT` command in T-SQL
- Adding data into selective columns
- Inserting data using Enterprise Manager
- Dealing with `NULL`s and default values
- What a constraint is and how to create a constraint using T-SQL commands
- How images are stored within SQL Server and how to work with them
- Inserting several records at once

Let's first look at security within tables and look at who can insert data by default, and how to change who can insert data.

Who Can Add Data

In this chapter, you will be asked to insert a certain amount of data. In most cases, all will go well and the data will be inserted easily. This does not mean that anyone who has access to our database could also add data, as easily as we can. In Chapter 1 we set up several different users for the system. To recap on this here are the users and their authority:

- `RDewson` – Administrator/database owner
- `AKelly` – Administrator
- `DTarbotton` – Developer
- `JMason` – Developer
- `sa` – Administrator, SQL Server's default user

The *security* appendix at the rear of this book covers looking at a users' initial permissions when they have their login first placed into SQL Server, and how to add a user to a role to give them the right permissions for the task you wish them to perform. Please refer to there for setting up a developer's role for `DTarbotton`, which will be used to demonstrate tightening security.

By setting up the role of Developer as described in the *Security* appendix you should now know which users can access the data, and how to set up groups of users to protect your data at this point. It is now time to move on and look at inserting data into the database. Of course, it is normal practice to set up several roles within your database for each area of the business. There would be a role for Supervisors, and perhaps another for Line Managers, and another for Directors and so on. It all depends on your database and the solution you are providing as to how many different roles are required.

The T-SQL INSERT Command Syntax

Before it is possible to demonstrate how to insert data using T-SQL code, it is necessary to look at the INSERT command and its structure first of all.

The INSERT command is very simple and straightforward in its simplest and minimalist form, which is all that is required to insert a record.

```
INSERT [INTO]
   {table_name|view_name}
   [{(column_name,column_name,...)}]
   {VALUES (expression, expression, ...)}
```

Obviously, we are required to start the command with the type of action we are trying to perform, for example, insert data. The next part of the command, INTO, is optional. It serves no purpose, but you will find several people do use it to ensure their command is more readable. The next part of the statement deals with naming the table or the view that the insertion has to place the data into. If the name of the table or view is the same as that of a reserved word or contains spaces we have to surround that name with square brackets or double quotation marks.

> **I cannot stress enough that really, there is nothing to be gained by using reserved words for table, views, or column names. Deciding on easy-to-use and unambiguous object names is part of a good design.**

Column names are optional, but most times, it will be necessary to place the column names in a comma-delimited list. The only time that column names are not required is when the INSERT statement is inserting data into every column that is within the table in the same order as they are laid out in the table. However, this is a potentially dangerous scenario when this is completed in a query built earlier, which was saved and is now being used later, or within a stored procedure. If we expect the columns to be in a specific order because that is the way they have always been and then someone comes along and adds a new column, or perhaps alters the order, your query or stored procedure will either not work, or give erroneous results. Therefore, I recommend, that you always name every column in anything but a query, which is built, run once, and thrown away. The list of column names must be surrounded by parentheses, ().

The VALUES keyword, which precedes the actual values to be entered, is mandatory. SQL Server needs to know that the following list is a list of values, and not a list of columns. Therefore we have to use the VALUES keyword, especially if we omit the list of columns as explained above.

Finally you will have a comma-separated list surrounded by parentheses, covering the values of data to insert. There has to be a column name for every value to be entered. To clarify, if there are ten columns listed for data to be entered, then there must be ten values to enter.

Now that the INSERT command is clear, time to move on and use it.

INSERT SQL Command

The first method of inserting data is to use the `INSERT` SQL command as described above. This example will insert one record into the `Club_Details` table using Query Analyzer. When inserting the data, the record will be inserted immediately without any opportunity to roll back changes. This command does not use any **transaction processing** to allow any change of mind to take place. However, this will be covered in Chapter 14. You will also see with this example how Query Analyzer can aid you as a developer in building the SQL command for inserting a record. Let's dive straight in and create the record.

Try It Out – Query Analyzer Scripting

1. Ensure that Query Analyzer is running and that you are logged in with an account that has insert permissions on the Club_Details table. This will be any member of the Administrator's or database owner's role.

2. In the Object Browser window, expand the nodes until you can see the Club_Details node.

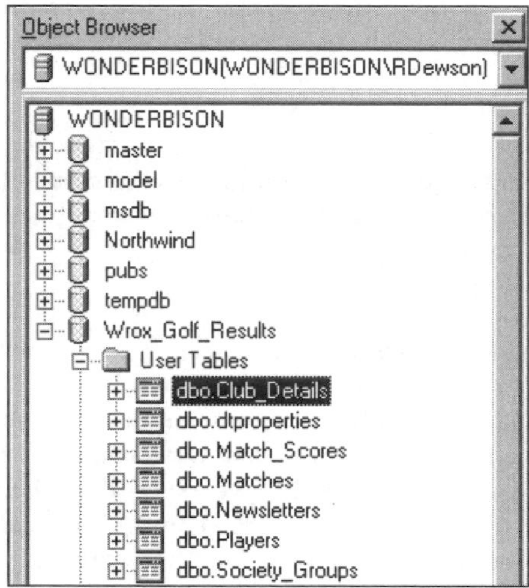

3. Right-click, select Script Object to New Window As, which will bring up another sub-menu, and from there select the Insert option.

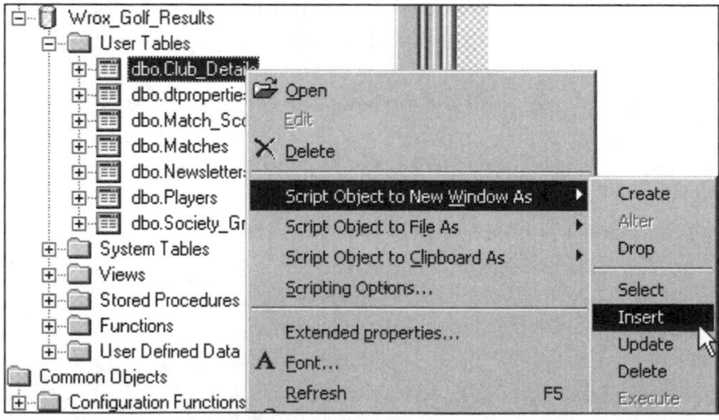

4. This brings up a section of code, which would be too wide to fit on a page (note that Query Analyzer does not have a word-wrap function).This is the code that within the Query Pane of Query Analyzer ready for altering is generated:

```
INSERT INTO [Wrox_Golf_Results].[dbo].[Club_Details]([Club_Name], [Address],
[Phone_Number], [Fax_Number], [Club_Email], [Web_site], [Last_Updated], [Zip_Code],
[State_US_Only], [Country], [Club_Chairperson], [Club_ViceChair], [Club_Secretary])
VALUES(<Club_Name,varchar(50),>, <Address,varchar(200),>,
<Phone_Number,varchar(20),>, <Fax_Number,varchar(20),>, <Club_Email,varchar(50),>,
<Web_site,varchar(50),>, <Last_Updated,datetime,>, <Zip_Code,varchar(10),>,
<State_US_Only,char(2),>, <Country,int,>, <Club_Chairperson,varchar(50),>,
<Club_ViceChair,varchar(50),>, <Club_Secretary,varchar(50),>)
```

5. There is a modification to place at the top of this code, just to ensure that Query Analyzer has a setting to allow double quotes to be used to surround strings. This was covered in Chapter 5 when discussing database options. To cover yourself though, you can always place the following code at the start of queries where quotation marks will be used. There is one hidden downfall that we will cover at the end. Notice as well, that there is a `GO` command at the end of the `SET` command. This is because this command must take place in its own transaction.

```
SET QUOTED_IDENTIFIER OFF
GO
```

6. By altering the code within the query analyzer pane, you will see that the next section of code actually inserts the data into the `Club_Details` table. Notice that there is no `GO` statement at the end of this code. There is no need because there is only one `INSERT` and no other commands that need to form part of this same transaction.

```
INSERT INTO [Wrox_Golf_Results].[dbo].[Club_Details]([Club_Name], [Address],
[Phone_Number], [Fax_Number], [Club_Email], [Web_Site], [Last_Updated], [Zip_Code],
[State_US_Only], [Country], [Club_Chairperson], [Club_ViceChair], [Club_Secretary])
VALUES("Bedford Golf Society","c/o Bedford Golf Club, Wenworth Drive, Bedford, Beds.", "No
phone", "No Fax", "bedford@wrox-golf.co.uk", "www.wrox-golf.co.uk", "12 May 2001", "MK41
0PU", NULL, 42, "Andy Illingworth", "", "Lee Smith")
```

7. Now that all the information has been entered into the query pane, it is time to execute the code. Press *F5*, or *CTRL+E*, or click on the Execute button on the toolbar. You should then see the following result. This indicates that there has been one row of data inserted into the table.

```
(1 row(s) affected)
```

This now sees the first record of information placed into the database in the Club_Details table. It is simple and straightforward. All the columns have been listed and a value has been inserted.

How It Works

Query Analyzer itself allows the ability to create template scripts for several T-SQL commands. You have come across templates earlier in the book, which hold parameter placeholders that required modification to build up the whole command. These differ from actual templates as the information created within Query Analyzer for these templates is for one command only. Therefore what you are actually seeing is the template for a one-line script.

When using the scripting options within Query Analyzer, it is possible to build the script as you have just seen for inserting a record in to the `Club_Details` table, and save the T-SQL within a new Query Analyzer pane, to a file, or even to a clipboard. This would then allow the data to be reinserted instantaneously should the table be deleted. To an extent, scripting to files or clipboard is not as useful as scripting to a Query pane. By scripting to files or a clipboard, you would need to move back into these files to make the necessary changes for data insertion. As you saw, when the script is placed in the Query pane, the table and the columns are listed, but obviously the values need to be altered. This would have to be completed in a file or a clipboard, by re-opening these contents and making modifications after the event.

The scripting template does build the whole `INSERT` command and lists all the columns as well as - in the `VALUES` section of the command – the name of the column and its data type definition. From there it is easier to know what value is expected within the `INSERT` command line.

The example mentions that using `SET QUOTED_IDENTIFIER OFF` does have one hidden downfall: In many cases, when using T-SQL commands, it is possible to surround reserved words with double quotation marks, rather than square brackets; however with the `QUOTED_IDENTIFIER` set to off, you will only be able to surround reserved words with square brackets. To clarify this point the `INSERT` command could have been written as follows if the `QUOTED_IDENTIFIER` was set to `ON`. Notice that there are double quotes instead of square brackets surrounding the names of columns as well as the table. In the example above, comparing the snippet below with the code above, you will see the difference:

```
SET QUOTED_IDENTIFIER ON
GO
INSERT INTO "Wrox_Golf_Results"."dbo"."Club_Details" ("Club_Name", "Address",
"Phone_Number", "Fax_Number", "Club_Email", "Web_Site", …
```

Square brackets and double quotes are actually only required to surround words that are reserved. The insert statement above also could be written like that below. Notice the distinct lack of quotes or square brackets.

```
SET QUOTED_IDENTIFIER ON
GO
INSERT INTO Wrox_Golf_Results.dbo.Club_Details (Club_Name, Address, Phone_Number,
Fax_Number, Club_Email, Web_Site, Last_Updated, Zip_Code, …
```

Now that you know several different valid ways of constructing an `INSERT` statement, it is time to look at how we need not define all the columns within a table.

Using NULL and Default Values

As you have just seen, every column in the table has been specified within the insert statement. You are now probably wondering if you have to specify every column every time a record is inserted into a table. The answer is: No. However, there are a few areas to be aware of. The following sections will show when the table definitions allow columns to be left out, and the first section deals with `NULL` values as there are a couple of points to consider with them.

Allowing NULLs and the Allow Nulls Option

One method for avoiding having to fill in data for every column is to allow NULL values in the column. Ensuring that the column's Allow Nulls option is checked can complete this. If you take a look at the figure below on the Club_Details table, a number of the columns do allow a NULL value to be entered into the column.

2:Design Table 'Club_Details' in 'Wrox_Golf_Results' o...

Column Name	Data Type	Length	Allow Nulls
Club_Name	varchar	50	
Address	varchar	200	
Phone_Number	varchar	20	✓
Fax_Number	varchar	20	✓
Club_Email	varchar	50	✓
Web_site	varchar	50	✓
Last_Updated	datetime	8	✓
Zip_Code	varchar	10	✓
State_US_Only	char	2	✓
Country	int	4	
Club_Chairperson	varchar	50	✓
Club_ViceChair	varchar	50	✓
Club_Secretary	varchar	50	✓

Therefore the previous example could only have placed data in the Club_Name, Address, and Country fields, as all of the others could have been left empty. If the Club_Details record had only been inserted with those three columns, the data would have looked like the next screenshot. The T-SQL statement to add in a record, which would produce the following results, would look as follows:

```
INSERT Club_Details (Club_Name, Address, Country) VALUES ('Bedford Golf
Society','c/o Before Golf Club, Wenworth Drive, Bedford, Beds.',0)
```

Club_Name	Address	Phone_Number	Fax_Number	Club_Email	Web_site	Last_Updated	Zip_Code	State_US_Only	Country
Bedford Golf Societ	c/o Bedford Golf Cl	<NULL>	<NULL>	<NULL>	<NULL>	<NULL>	<NULL>	<NULL>	0

To see the above screenshot you would view this table in Enterprise Manager. This is covered shortly, as unfortunately we are in the chicken and egg scenario of showing an area before it has been discussed. As you can see, the columns that had no data entered have a setting of <NULL>. A NULL setting is a special setting for a column. The value of NULL requires special handling within SQL Server or applications that will be viewing this data. What this value actually means is that the information within the column is unknown. It is not a numeric, or an alphanumeric value. It is unknown. Therefore because you don't know if it is numeric or alphanumeric you cannot compare the value of a column that has a setting of NULL, to the value of any other column, and this includes another NULL column.

There is one major rule surrounding NULL values, which is that a primary key cannot contain any NULL values.

There will be more on NULL values later on within the book, for example in Chapter 14 when dealing with data updates.

Default Values

Another method for avoiding having to enter a value is to set a column or a set of columns with a default value. Setting up a default value will be demonstrated in the next example. However, the basis of giving a column a default value setting is to give the column a value when a new row of information is added, without the query having to specifically define this value.

Default values are used when a large number of `INSERT`s for a column would have the same value entered each time. Why have the overhead of passing this information, which would be the column name, plus the value, through to SQL Server, when SQL Server could perform the task quickly and simply for you? Network traffic would be reduced and accuracy ensured as the column information would be completed directly by SQL Server.

Although it has been indicated that default values are best for a large number of `INSERT`s, it can also be argued that this need not be the case. Some people will argue that all that is required is a significant number of rows to be affected from a default value setting for the use of default values to be an advantage. It does come down to personal preference as to when you think setting a default value will be of benefit. However, if there are times when you wish a column to start with a specific value, then it is best to use a default value.

Getting it Wrong

But what happens if we don't follow these guidelines and we try to insert data that is not allowed, and therefore the `INSERT` query fails? Well, the record will not be inserted. The *"Try It Out – Inserting with Default Values"* example that comes later will demonstrate what happens when you don't enter data into a field that requires it, in other words, it is defined as not allowing `NULL` values, and finally, what happens when you do try to enter data into a column whose values are automatically generated, in this case an **identity** column (explained in Chapter 6).

If we try to complete an erroneous insert, in so much as a query tries to insert an alphanumeric character into a numeric field, SQL Server will inform us of the fact, and *not* insert just part of the data, which would leave our table in an inconsistent state.

Allowing Defaults to Populate Columns

This next section will demonstrate how to use a default value to populate specific columns. This will be completed after altering the `Society_Groups` table to set up specific columns for a default value to be entered when no value is passed. In the next section, a second table will be altered to demonstrate creating T-SQL code for allowing defaults to populate columns.

Altering the Table

First of all, there are two tables that need to have columns defined to allow default values when no value is passed in. The two tables in this case are the `Society_Groups` table and the `Players` table, which is altered in a few pages time once we have finished with the `Society_Groups` table. The `Society_Groups` table will be altered in Enterprise Manager, and the `Players` table will be altered using Query Analyzer. So let's press on and alter the `Society_Groups` table first.

Try It Out – Altering a Table for a Default Value: Enterprise Manager

1. Ensure that SQL Server Enterprise Manager is running. Expand on the `Wrox_Golf_Results` database, and the **Tables** node, so that you can get to the `Society_Groups` table. Right-click and select **Design Table...**

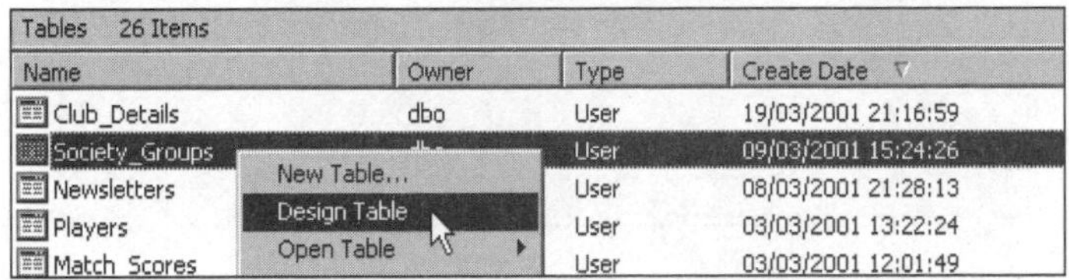

2. This brings up the familiar table designer. We are now going to give certain columns a default value. Like all the other columns that are about to be modified, the first column, `Games_Played`, will have a default value of `0`. The following screenshot demonstrates how to achieve this. Find the necessary column and alter the **Default Value** setting, which can be found in the lower half of the screen.

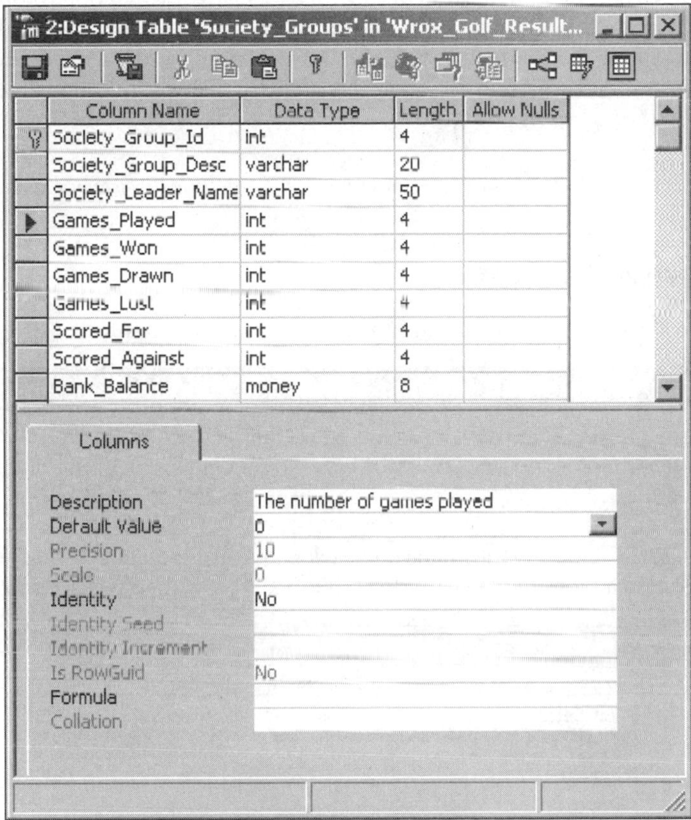

3. The other columns that require a similar action are **Games_Won**, **Games_Drawn**, **Games_Lost**, **Scored_For**, **Scored_Against**, and **Bank_Balance**. Set the **Default Value** to **0** for all of these columns.

4. Once completed, click the cross in the top right hand corner of the designer, which will prompt you to save the table changes. Click **Yes**.

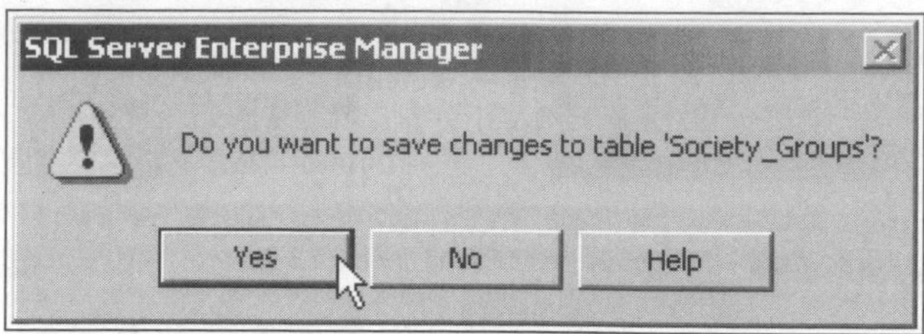

Inserting Data Using Default Values

Now that the `Society_Groups` table have been altered, it is possible to demonstrate inserting data using a default value. As has been mentioned, it would have been necessary before to insert a value for those columns where a default value will be used now, since the insertion of a `NULL` value was not allowed. As we said earlier, by having a default value, especially a value that the majority of new inserts will require anyway, we will reduce the amount of code within a program and cause a reduction in network traffic from application to server, because those columns and values do not have to be passed, and so produce a speed increase on insertion as those default values will be inserted by SQL Server itself, right at the heart of the processing.

Whenever possible, do use default values for record insertion. Every little performance improvement helps

Using Enterprise Manager

The first example will use Enterprise Manager as the tool for data addition.

Try It Out – Inserting with Default Values: Enterprise Manager

1. Ensure that Enterprise Manager is running and that you are logged in with an account that allows the insertion of records. This would be someone who is in the database owners' role, for example `RDewson`.

2. Expand the **Wrox_Golf_Results** node and click on the **Tables** node so that you have access to the **Society_Groups** tables. Right-click, select **Open Table**, and then select **Return all rows**.

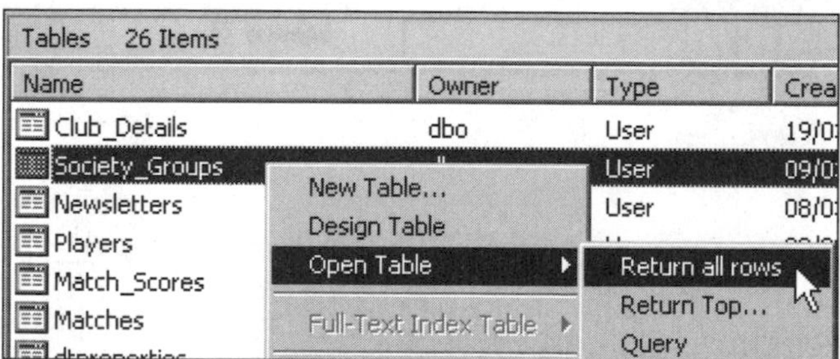

3. This brings up an empty grid like the figure below. This grid would show all the rows of data that are within the table, however, as this table contains no data yet the grid is empty and ready for the first record to be entered. Notice that on the far left-hand side there is a black arrow pointing to the right. This is the record marker and denotes which record the grid is actually pointing to. Perhaps not so relevant in this screenshot; however, very useful when there are several records being displayed.

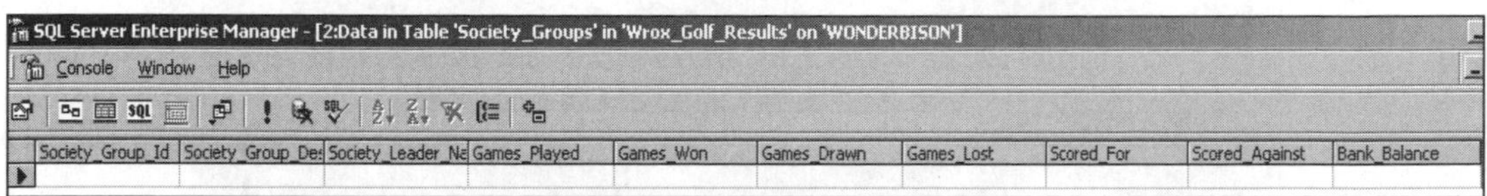

4. It is a simple process to enter the information into the necessary columns as required. However, if you don't enter the data into the correct columns and leave a column empty, when in fact it should have data, you will receive the following error message. To see this, I only entered data in the Society_Group_Desc column and then pressed the down cursor. SQL Server is expecting data within the Society_Leader_Name column and therefore throws an error.

Pressing the down *arrow moves you to the next record. By default, SQL Server will then try to update the record you are moving from.*

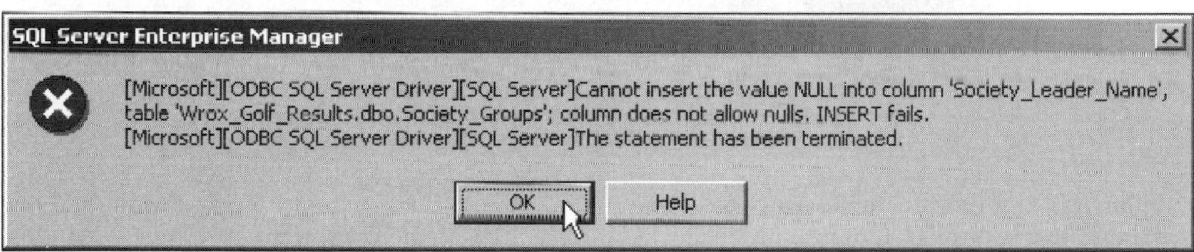

5. By clicking OK we can go back and enter the data in the necessary columns, in this case, the Society_Group_Desc and the Society_Leader_Name columns. Once completed you can once again press the *down* arrow. This will then update the database, and you should see the following screen.

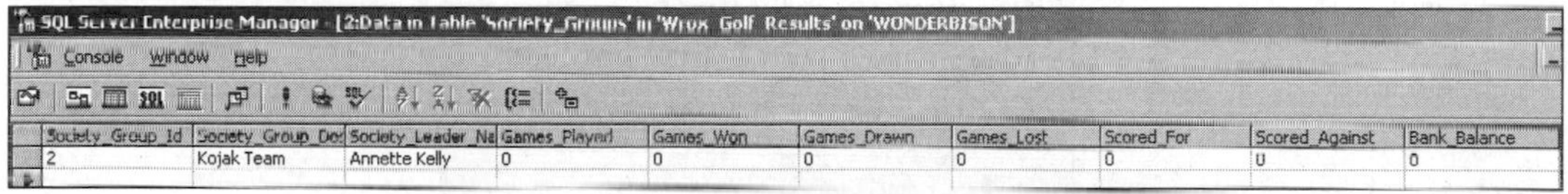

The thing to notice is that although this is the first record entered, the Society_Group_Id is set to 2. Whether insertion of a record is successful or not, an identity value is generated. This can and will cause gaps within your numbering system. You can see how quickly data can be entered now with defaults being used as initial values for columns. This `INSERT` literally took seconds, compared to a few minutes when entering data into the Club_Details table. However, where the real benefit of default values lies, is in ensuring that specific columns are populated with the correct default values. Of course we aren't comparing like with like, but there is not a great deal of difference between the two examples. As soon as we moved off fromthe new row, the default values were inserted and ready to be modified.

There is one more item to notice within the last screenshot. In the first column, Society_Group_Id, there is now a value of 2 entered within this column. There was no default value set up, but in the table design, this column was set up as an identity column. To remind you, there is a screenshot below showing the column in question.

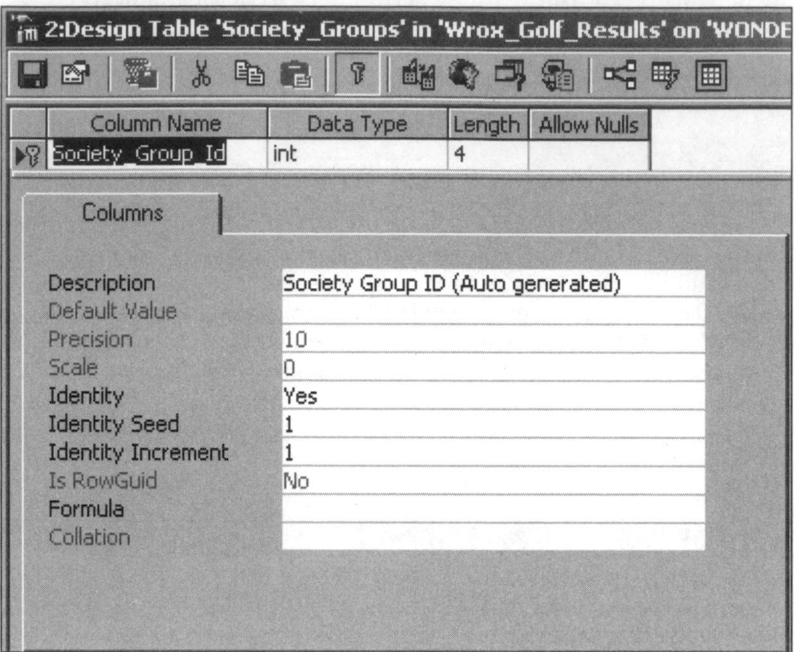

By having an Identity column, every time a record is entered or an attempt is made to enter a record – whether this is through Enterprise Manager or an INSERT statement – the column value within the table will be incremented by the Identity Increment amount. This is also another column that doesn't require data to be entered, but unlike columns with default values we will not be able to enter a value at all. If we do try to enter data within Enterprise Manager, we will instantly receive the following error message as soon as a key is pressed.

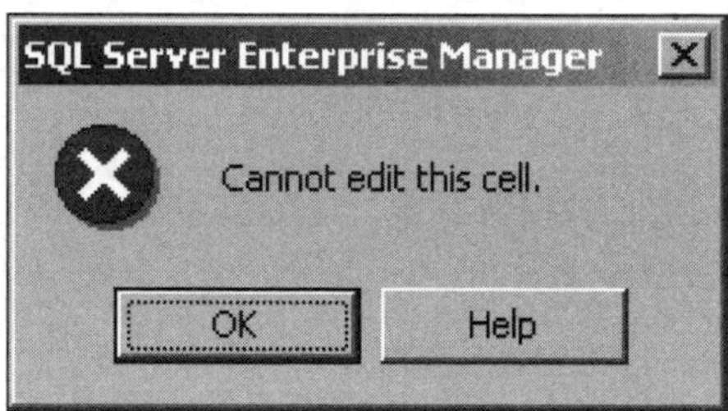

We now have a slight problem in that already there is a gap in the table. This can be remedied easily within Query Analyzer.

DBCC CHECKIDENT

If you find that when testing out identity columns you receive a number of errors, and the identity number has jumped up further than you wished, it is possible to reset the seed of the identity column so that Query Analyzer starts again from a known point. The syntax for this command is very simple

```
DBCC CHECKIDENT ('table_name'[,{NORESEED |{RESEED[,new_reseed_value]}}])
```

There are only three areas of the syntax that need to be discussed:

- The name of the table that you wish to reset the identity value for is placed in quotation marks.
- You can then use `NORESEED` to return back what SQL Server believes the current identity value should be, in other words, what the current maximum identity value is within the identity column.
- The final option is the one we are interested in. You can either reseed a table automatically by simply specifying the `RESEED` option with no value. This will look at the table defined and will reset the value to the current maximum value within the table. Or optionally, you can set the column of the table to a specific value by separating the value and the option `RESEED` by a comma.

> **If you use `RESEED` and there are no records in the table, then the value will still be set to the last value entered, so take care.**

Resetting the seed for an identity column though does have a danger, which you need to be aware of. If you reset the point to start inserting values for the identity column back past the greatest number on the given table, you will find that there is the potential of an error being produced. When a value that already exists, is generated from an `INSERT` after resetting the identity column value, then you will receive an error message informing you the value already exists. To give an example, you have a table with the values `1,2,5,6,7,8` and you reset the identity value back to `2`. You insert the next record, which will correctly get the value `3`, and work. The insertion will still work the same with the next insertion, which will receive the value `4`. However, come to the next record, and there will be an attemp to insert the value `5`, but that value already exists; therefore, an error will be produced. However, if you had reset the value to `8`, the last value successfully entered, then everything would be OK.

We need to do this to the `Society_Groups` table now. The code below will remove the erroneous record entry and reset the seed of the identity column back to `0`, to a value indicating that no records have been entered. Enter the following code, place the code into Query Analyzer, and execute. The first line removes the record from `Society_Groups` and the second line resets the identity. Don't worry too much about it, as deleting records is covered in detail in Chapter 15.

```
DELETE FROM Society_Groups
DBCC CHECKIDENT (Society_Groups,RESEED,0)

INSERT INTO Society_Groups (Society_Group_Desc, Society_Leader_Name)
VALUES('Kojak Team','Annnette Kelly')
```

When the code is run, you should see the following information output to the query Results pane:

(1 row(s) affected)

Checking identity information: current identity value '2', current column value '0'.
DBCC execution completed. If DBCC printed error messages, contact your system administrator.

(1 row(s) affected)

It is also possible to enter data through Query Analyzer where a default value exists, and the next example will demonstrate this.

Using Query Analyzer

This example will insert a second golf society record into the `Society_Groups` table. However, the example will also demonstrate the types of errors received in Enterprise Manager to show that Query Analyzer handles these errors differently.

Try It Out – Inserting With Default Values: Query Analyzer

1. Ensure that Query Analyzer is running and that you are logged in using an account, that has permissionto insert records.

2. Enter the following code into the Query pane. Don't forget when setting up Query Analyzer that we allowed double quotation marks to be used when defining literals to be inserted. If you did not select this option, or it is now switched off, then you need to prefix this code with:

   ```
   SET QUOTED_IDENTIFIER OFF
   ```

```
USE Wrox_Golf_Results
GO
INSERT into Society_Groups
(Society_Group_Desc)
VALUES ("Bedford Junior Blues")
```

3. Now execute this by pressing *CTRL+E*, *F5*, or the Execute button on the toolbar. This code will generate an error because there is no data entered for the `Society_Leader_Name`. You should see the following results, indicating that it is necessary to insert data into the `Society_Leader_Name` column. This is a very similar error message to that when using Enterprise Manager.

   Server: Msg 515, Level 16, State 2, Line 1

   Cannot insert the value NULL into column 'Society_Leader_Name', table Wrox_Golf_Results.dbo.Society_Groups'; column does not allow nulls. INSERT fails.

   The statement has been terminated.

4. If the INSERT statement now tries to insert a value into the identity column, an error will also be produced, just as before. Enter the following code:

```
USE Wrox_Golf_Results
GO
INSERT into Society_Groups
(Society_Group_Id, Society_Group_Desc)
VALUES (20, "Bedford Junior Blues")
```

5. Now execute this in the usual way. You should see the following results, providing you with more information than the "Cannot edit this cell" Enterprise Manager error message. More on the error message at the end of this section.

   Server: Msg 544, Level 16, State 1, Line 1

   Cannot insert explicit value for identity column in table 'Society_Groups' when IDENTITY_INSERT is set to OFF.

6. This final example will work successfully. However, note that the Society_Leader_Name is before that of the Society_Group_Desc column. This demonstrates that it is not necessary to name the columns within the insertion in the same order as they are defined within the table. It is possible to place the columns in any order you desire.

```
USE Wrox_Golf_Results
GO
INSERT INTO Society_Groups
(Society_Leader_Name, Society_Group_Desc)
VALUES ("Jack Mason", "Bedford Junior Blues")
```

7. This time when you execute the code, you should see the following results, indicating the record has been inserted successfully:

   (1 row(s) affected)

That is all there is to it. Just as simple as using Enterprise Manager, but you did get more informative error messages. Notice as well that this time we did not use the scripting tool within Query Analyzer, as this would mean more deleting of information than typing in the query.

Dragging and Dropping Column Names

Another method to build up a query is to drag and drop column names from the Object Browser into the Query pane. This can reduce the time to build a query as well as avoid spelling mistakes. There is still a small amount of work that needs to be completed, however, by dragging and dropping columns, your time spent building the queries should drop. This section won't build an executable example, but will just quickly demonstrate dragging and dropping.

Try It Out – Dragging Column Names

1. Find an empty Query pane within Query Analyzer and ensure that the **Object Browser** is visible. If it is not, then you can display it by pressing *F8*. Within the empty Query pane, you need to start the code example, so, as this is an insert chapter, enter the following code. There must be a space after the word INTO otherwise the information you will be dropping in to the code will append directly onto the INTO keyword.

```
INSERT INTO
```

2. Ensure that you can see the Wrox_Golf_Results database, along with the Society_Groups table within the Object Browser. Highlight the Society_Groups table by left-clicking on it with your mouse, and then keeping the button down, drag the mouse pointer to the Query pane. You should see the mouse pointer look like it does below.

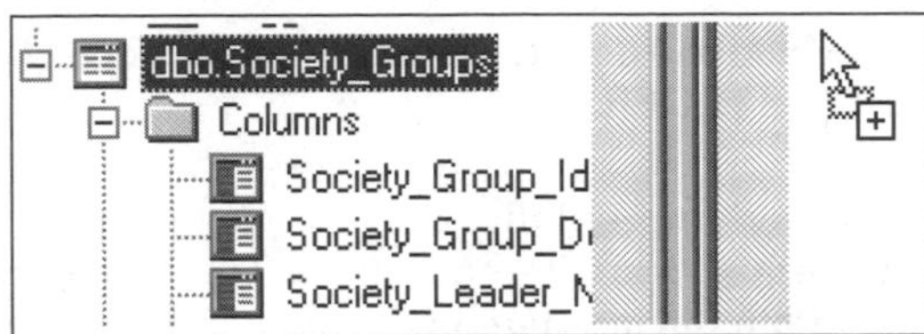

3. Drag the mouse so that the mouse pointer passes the keyword into it. It should look like the graphic below. When you have done this, release the left mouse button.

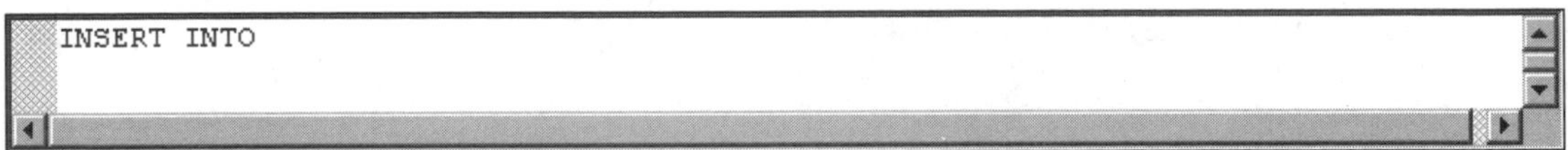

4. The query pane should now look as follows. Of course, you can carry on dragging and dropping columns or tables from the object browser as much as you wish.

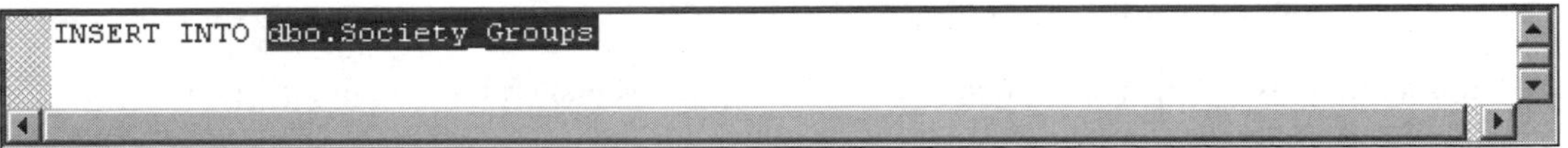

Now that the basics of record insertion have been covered, we can move on to more complex areas, and look at how column constraints can aid column validation.

Column Constraints

A **constraint** is essentially a check that SQL Server places on a column to ensure that the data to be entered in the column meets specific conditions. This will keep out data that is erroneous, and therefore avoid data inconsistencies. Constraints are used to keep database integrity by ensuring that a column only receives data within certain parameters.

We have already built constraints earlier on in this chapter when we added default values to the Society_Groups table. From this you can see that constraints are not only used to validate data, but also to insert default values. Constraints are quite flexible tools to use and can complete a number of different tasks, from data integrity through to inserting a default value.

However, when using constraints within SQL Server, you do have to look at the whole picture, which is the user graphical system with the SQL Server database in the background. If you are using a constraint for data validation, some people will argue that perhaps it is better to check the values inserted, within the user front-end application rather than SQL Server. This has some merit but what also has to be kept in mind is that you may have several points of entry to your database. This could be from the user application, to a web-based solution, and also inserting the data through other applications if you are building a central database. Many people will say that all validation, no matter what the overall picture is, should always be placed in one central place, which is the SQL Server database. Then there is only one set of code to alter if anything changes. It is a difficult choice and one that you need to look at carefully.

This part of the chapter will demonstrate how to do this through code in Query Analyzer. First of all it is necessary to look at the code that is used to build the constraint.

Add Constraint

There are two ways to add a constraint onto a table:

- Through Enterprise Manager using the **Table Properties** dialog, just like creating a relationship, by using the **Constraint** tab or the Table Designer shown above when creating a default value
- By using T-SQL commands through Query Analyzer

The following example shows the T-SQL method of adding a constraint. This is achieved through the ALTER TABLE command

The ALTER TABLE command can cover many different alterations to a table, but in this instance, the example just concentrates on adding a constraint. This makes the ALTER TABLE statement easy, as the only real meat to the clause comes with the ADD CONSTRAINT syntax. This is all covered at the end of the example in the *How It Works* section.

The next example will work with the Players table, and you will see three different types of constraints added, all of which will affect insertion of records. Once the constraints have been added you will see them all in action, and how errors are generated from erroneous data input.

Try It Out – Altering a Table for a Default Value: Query Analyzer

1. Ensure that Query Analyzer is running and that you are logged in with a user ID that can alter a table's definition. To demonstrate more areas on security and how other user IDS can also fit in to the picture, this time why not log in to Windows and then Query Analyzer using an Administrator ID, for example AKelly.

2. Although all the examples deal with the Players table, each constraint being added to the table will be created one at a time, which will allow a discussion for each point to take place. In the Query pane, enter the following code, which will add a primary key to the Players table. This will place the Player_Id column within the key, which will be non-clustered; in other words, the data will not be stored in this order.

```
USE Wrox_Golf_Results
GO
-- This will add a primary key to the Players table
ALTER TABLE dbo.Players ADD CONSTRAINT
   PK_Players PRIMARY KEY NONCLUSTERED
   (
      Player_Id
   ) ON [PRIMARY]
GO
```

3. The next constraint to add is a CHECK constraint on the Points_Scored column. The Players table is once again altered, and a new constraint added called CK_Players_PointsCheck. This constraint will ensure that for all records inserted into the Players table from this point on, the score must be equal to or greater than 0. Notice as well that the NOCHECK option is mentioned, detailing that any records already inserted will not be checked for this constraint. If they have invalid data, which they don't, then the constraint would ignore them and still be added.

```
/*
 This will ensure that when the Points_Scored column is updated
 the value will be positive
*/
ALTER TABLE dbo.Players WITH NOCHECK ADD CONSTRAINT
   CK_Players_PointsCheck CHECK (([points_scored] >= 0))
GO
```

4. Moving on to the third constraint to add to the Players table, we have a DEFAULT value constraint. In other words, this will insert a value of 0 to the Games_Played column if no value is entered specifically into this column.

```
-- This will add a default value of 0 if no value specified
ALTER TABLE Players WITH NOCHECK
   ADD CONSTRAINT DF_Players_Games_Played DEFAULT (0) FOR Games_Played
GO
```

5. Just like the previous example, this is adding a DEFAULT value constraint but this time for the Points_Scored column.

```
-- This will add a default value of 0 if no value specified
ALTER TABLE Players WITH NOCHECK
   ADD CONSTRAINT DF_Players_Points_Scored DEFAULT (0) FOR Points_Scored
GO
```

6. And finally another DEFAULT value constraint for the bit flag to indicate that the player has not left the club. After all, when inserting a player, they aren't likely to have left the club, therefore to aid integrity, a default value of 0 is set to indicate that they are still in the club. There is one last thing about all of these constraints. Each constraint is independent and there is no link between any of them.

```
-- This will add a default value of 0 if no value specified
ALTER TABLE Players WITH NOCHECK
   ADD CONSTRAINT DF_Players_Left_Club DEFAULT (0) FOR Has_Left_The_Club
GO
```

7. Execute the three batches of work by pressing *F5*, *CTRL+E*, or clicking on the Execute button on the toolbar. You should then see the following result:

   The command(s) completed successfully.

8. There are two methods to check that the code has worked before adding in any data. Move to the Object Browser in Query Analyzer. This isn't refreshed automatically, so you do need to refresh it.

9. You should then see the five new constraints added under the constraints node, and also the existing constraint that exists for a foreign key, which was built when building the relationships in Chapter 8.

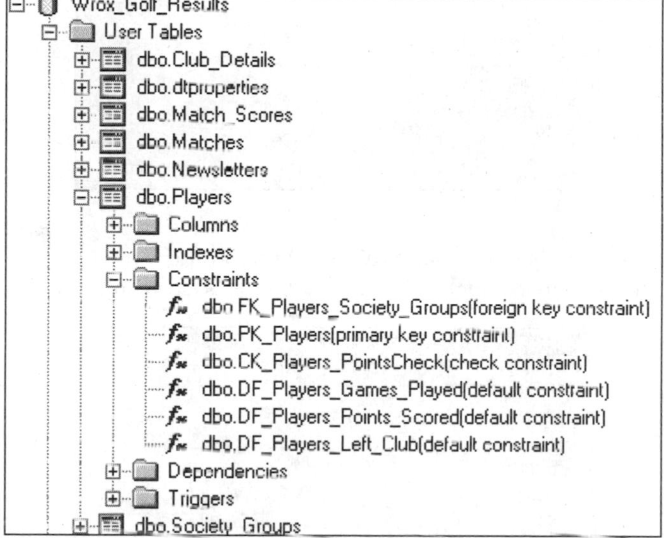

10. Another method is to move to Enterprise Manager, find the `Players` table, right-click and select Design table...

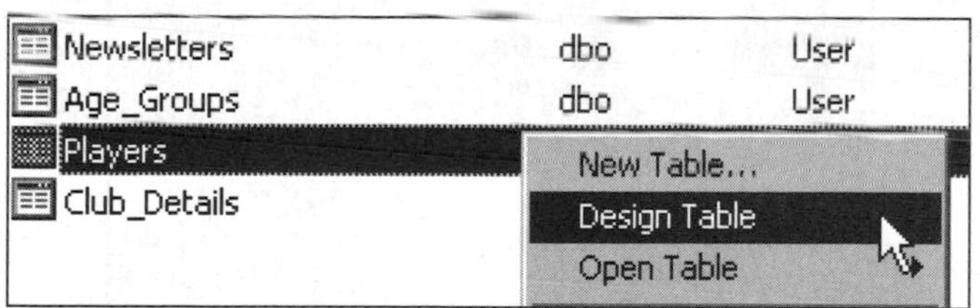

11. This brings us into the table designer, where we can navigate to the necessary column to check out the default value, in this case **Games_Played**. Also notice the yellow key against the **Player_Id** signifying that this is now a primary key.

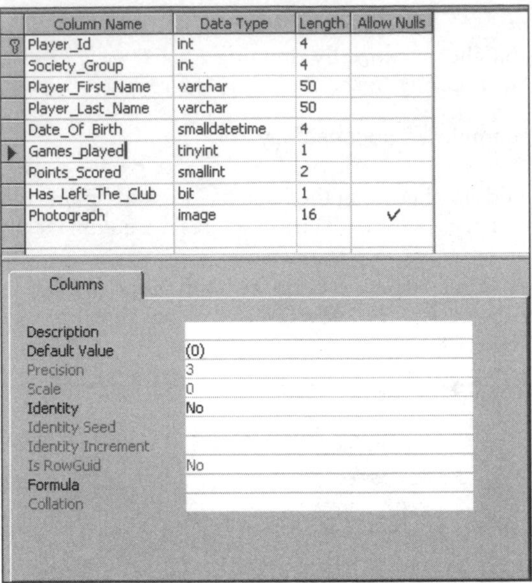

12. If you then select the **Manage Constraints…** button on the toolbar you will be able to see the last constraint added, which was for the **Points_Scored** column.

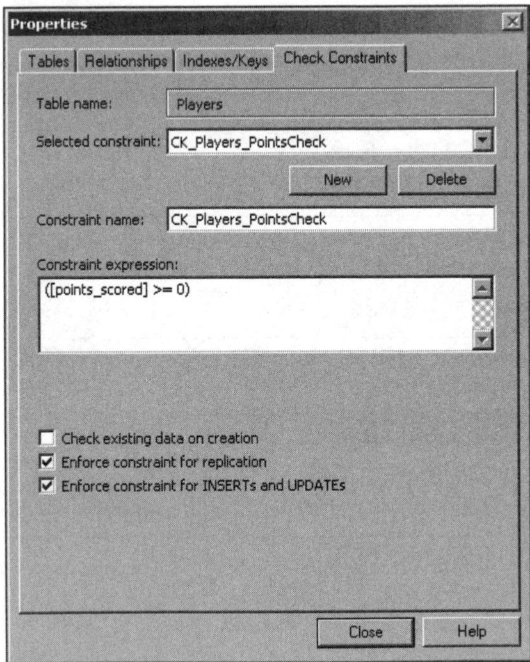

13. Now it's time to test the constraints to ensure that they work. First of all, the only constraint added that can be checked is the `Points_Scored` column constraint. The Primary Key constraint is an identity column. The default value constraint has been demonstrated earlier. The first player to add will be Daniel Tarbotton. With Daniel, the example will break the `Points_Scored` column constraint as I will try to say that Daniel has a negative point score. Enter the code below:

```
INSERT INTO Players(Society_Group, Player_First_Name, Player_Last_Name,
Date_Of_Birth, Games_played, Points_Scored, Has_Left_The_Club)
VALUES (1, "Daniel", "Tarbotton", "24 Mar 1964", 1, -3, 0)
```

14. When you execute the code in Query Analyzer, you will see the following result. Instantly you can see that the constraint check (`DF_Players_Points_Scored`) has cut in and the record has not been inserted.

    Server: Msg 547, Level 16, State 1, Line 1

    INSERT statement conflicted with COLUMN CHECK constraint 'CK_Players_PointsCheck'. The conflict occurred in database 'Wrox_Golf_Results', table 'Players', column 'Points_Scored'.

    The statement has been terminated.

Building constraints through Query Analyzer is a straightforward process.

How It Works – Adding Constraints

Adding a constraint occurs through the `ALTER TABLE` statement as we have just demonstrated. However, the `ADD CONSTRAINT` command is quite a flexible command and can achieve a number of different goals.

The example above has used the `ADD CONSTRAINT` to insert a primary key, which can be made up of one or more columns, none of which can contain a `NULL` value, and also to insert a validity check and a set of default values. The only option not covered in the example is the addition of a foreign key, but this is very similar to the addition of a primary key.

The first constraint added was the primary key. The syntax for this command is as follows:

```
ADD CONSTRAINT key_name PRIMARY KEY [CLUSTERED|NONCLUSTERED] (column[,column,…)
   ON filegroup
```

The only real decision in using this command is to whether you wish the primary key to be clustered or non-clustered. The differences in these two key types were covered in the indexing chapter earlier in the book, Chapter 7. However, as a quick reminder, a clustered index will store the data in the physical order defined for that index. There can only be one clustered index for a table. However, the clustered index does not need to be on the primary key.

The second constraint definition was building a column check to ensure that the data entered is valid:

```
ADD CONSTRAINT constraint_name CHECK (constraint_check_syntax)
```

The syntax for a CHECK constraint is a simple true or false test. When adding in a constraint for checking the data, the information to be inserted is valid, true, or invalid, false, when the test is applied. As you will see, by using mathematical operators to test a column against a single value or a range of values, this will determine if the data can be inserted.

If you notice in the example, the ADD CONSTRAINT command is preceded with a WITH NOCHECK option on the ALTER TABLE statement. This is informing SQL Server that any existing data in the table will not be validated when it adds the table alteration with the constraint, and that only data modified or inserted after the addition of the constraint will be checked. If you do wish the existing rows to be checked, then you would use the WITH CHECK option. The advantage of this would be that the existing data would be validated against that constraint, and if the constraint was added to the table successfully, then you would know your data is valid. If any error was generated, then you would know that there was erroneous data and that you would need to fix that data before being able to add the constraint. This is just another method of ensuring that your data is valid.

Finally, for adding a default value, the ADD CONSTRAINT syntax is very simple.

```
ADD CONSTRAINT constraint_name DEFAULT default_value
   FOR column_to_receive_the_value
```

The only part of the above syntax that requires further explanation is the default_value area. The default_value can be a string, a numeric, NULL, or a system function (for example GETDATE(), which would insert the current date and time). So the default value does not have to be fixed, it can be dynamic.

Inserting Images

There are times when text up to 7KB in size is included with the row of data, and times when the text is kept separate from the table. With images, the same restrictions apply. However, unless the image is extremely small (below 7KB), or you increase the size of the data held within the column, then you will find that images are kept separate from the data. Instead, the column defined as image, text, or ntext will hold a pointer to another page of data within SQL Server where the information is stored. The confusion that arises with images, is in dealing with how to get the image data into the column. Throughout the book, the image column will hold the directory path and the name of the actual image that is to be used. If you wanted SQL Server to store the actual image itself, you have to break down the image into binary data format, and it is the binary data that has to be placed in to the column. This is just not physically possible within this book; otherwise the binary values would take up about ten pages. Even when Microsoft inserts images to demonstrate Northwind, the length of the binary data takes up quite a large amount of data. So to avoid having to type in binary values, the column will hold the path to the graphic instead. If you wish to store the image physically, then you must pass in the binary values of the image.

Where to Store Images

As you have just read, images are not physically stored within the database. Unless they are very small images where the size of the image is below 7KB, you will find the images are stored outside of the database. But where is the best place to store the images?

There are a number of factors to consider before deciding on this option:

- With the addition of images, will there still be sufficient room on the server for growth within any systems stored on that server?
- If it is possible to store images on another server, will the network traffic be too great when dealing with the images?
- Does the server backup allow sub-directories to hold the images below the directory where the SQL Server database files are defined? For example, a backup of a server may mean that a server backup is split by directories due to the amount of data that can be held on a server's hard drives, and as such, a backup may not allow sub-directories of the main data path in case this exceeds the amount of space in the backup device.

These are questions that can really only be answered by yourself. If possible it is best to keep the images in a directory separate from that where the data is stored so that full access rights can be given to that directory while still protecting the directories where the SQL Server data files are kept.

In this example, a player will be inserted into the `Players` table. Then a photograph of the player will be added.

Try It Out – Inserting Images

1. Ensure that Query Analyzer is running and that you are logged in with an account that allows data to be inserted into the table. Any Administrator ID would be valid. You may still be logged in as `AKelly`, if you are, then stay with that ID.

2. First of all, insert the details for the player, remembering that some columns have default values. Note the strange entry for the `Photograph` column. More on this in a moment.

```
SET QUOTED_IDENTIFIER OFF
GO
USE Wrox_Golf_Results
GO
INSERT INTO Players
(Society_Group,Player_First_Name,Player_Last_Name,Photograph,Date_Of_Birth)
VALUES (1,"Annette","Kelly",0xFFFFFFFF,"23 Sep 73")
```

3. Now execute the code. This should be the first data that you have entered into this table, and therefore this will generate a `Player_Id` of 1. It is now time to insert the picture for Annette. I have placed this picture into the directory: `C:\Program Files\Microsoft SQL Server\MSSQL\Data\Wrox_Golf_Results\Images`

4. Now that you can see where the picture is stored, it is possible to use this information to insert the player's picture to the record created.

5. It is necessary to insert the photograph (or the pointer to it) for Annette Kelly into the table.

6. Clear the contents of the Query Analyzer pane. The fastest way I have found to do this is by pressing *Ctrl+Shift+Del*. Once this is empty, enter the following SQL code (you will need to amend the path according to your own storage location). Don't worry too much about the contents of this code, all will be revealed shortly!

```
DECLARE @Pointer_Value varbinary(16)
SELECT @Pointer_Value = TEXTPTR(Photograph)
FROM Players
WHERE Player_ID = 1
WRITETEXT Players.Photograph @Pointer_Value
   "C:\Program Files\Microsoft SQL Server\
      MSSQL\Data\Wrox_Golf_Results\Images\ak.bmp"
```

7. Now all you need to do is execute the code, by the usual methods. This should now have the path to the photograph within the table. We will see the following SQL Server message:

   The command(s) completed successfully

How It Works

Inserting an image, or for that matter text, is not a simple process. However because it is essentially data that is being inserted it is better to include this example in this chapter.

The first part of the example is pretty straightforward as it is a simple `INSERT` that is being performed, with one major exception; and that is the initial insert of information into the `Photograph` column. This column will hold a pointer to where the data actually resides. We cannot insert the pointer directly with an `INSERT` statement. However, the column does need to have a value inserted it into it. Later on in the example we saw how to insert the actual photograph. What we inserted, `0xFFFFFFFF`, is in fact a **high value**. This means that we have placed the largest value possible into this column. It is also not a real value of a pointer to where the data is kept. It doesn't have to be this value, it could be any hexadecimal value; however, by using any other value, there is the danger that you could create a valid pointer to data that already exists. The whole reason behind placing a hexadecimal value like this within the `Photograph` column is that the `WRITETEXT` function, which is used a few lines later in the T-SQL code, must have a pointer value passed as one of its parameters for it to work. There is more on this in a moment.

If we now move on to where the actual insertion of the picture takes place and look at the code to see what is happening there; we will see a fair amount of code that is unfamiliar. Firstly, it is necessary to have a variable declared to hold the pointer value for the `WRITETEXT` function. This has to be a variable length binary data type.

WRITETEXT and TEXTPTR

As has been said, when storing image or text information outside of the row of data that holds the rest of the row information, it is a pointer that is stored within that column. It is necessary to convert that pointer to a binary value to store it within a variable. This is just how SQL Server works when dealing with this sort of data. To change a pointer that is stored as hexadecimal within the row, it is necessary to use the `TEXTPTR` command to alter that to a binary value.

Once this is done, then the `WRITETEXT` command can take that pointer to overwrite the information that has already been stored, and generate a new pointer, which is stored within the image or text column.

This is the first time that you will have come across using a variable within this book. Defining a variable is very simple and straightforward. First of all, the keyword `DECLARE` has to be defined and it must prefix the name of the variable. Variable names must be directly prefixed with an @ sign and are then seen as defined locally to this transaction of code. In other words, the variable below, `@Pointer_Value`, is only available in this transaction. If we tried to access this variable in another transaction we would receive an error message. Finally we name the data type of the variable and its length. These data types and lengths were all covered in Chapter 6.

```
DECLARE @Pointer_Value varbinary(16)
```

In the second line of code a SELECT statement is used. A SELECT statement, as you will see in the next chapter, is used to retrieve a value from a table. In this instance the SELECT is retrieving the pointer value from the Photograph column. We know that this is a meaningless pointer value; however, this doesn't matter because the WRITETEXT command is going to overwrite this value anyway. However, the WRITETEXT command does need a pointer, and the TEXTPTR function will take the information found within the Photograph column and build a pointer. So why not leave the Photograph column with a NULL value? Recall an earlier discussion about NULL values and how a NULL isn't any real data information. Therefore, it is necessary to place some sort of hexadecimal value within the Photograph column, and to be sure safe, a high value was entered. Although not done in this chapter, this column would be an ideal candidate for a constraint to add a default value of 0xFFFFFF to the column.

```
SELECT @Pointer_Value = TEXTPTR(Photograph)
```

This next section will find the specific player record to which to add the player's photograph. There will be more on this in the next chapter when dealing with the syntax of SELECT statements.

```
FROM Players
WHERE Player_ID = 1
```

The final section of code will insert a pointer value generated by the WRITETEXT command into the Players table's Photograph column, using the information supplied to it. I must admit, I am at a bit at a loss explaining why the WRITETEXT command needs any sort of pointer when in fact it overwrites this value, and I would have thought just naming the column the pointer has to be placed into, as well as where the image resides, would have been sufficient and a lot less work; however, that is the way it has to be. So, the code preceding this final statement built up a pointer in a local variable called @Pointer_Value. WRITETEXT then builds a pointer and inserts that pointer into the relevant column.

```
WRITETEXT Players.Photograph @Pointer_Value
   "C:\Program Files\Microsoft SQL Server\
      MSSQL\Data\Wrox_Golf_Results\Images\ak.bmp"
```

Dealing with Several Records at Once

It is now necessary to enter a few more players so that there is a reasonable amount of data within the Players table to work with later on in the book. We need to do the same with the Society_Groups table. This section will also deal with inserting a number of images as well. This section will prove that there is no extra or specialized processing required when inserting several records. When working with data, there will be many times that several records of data may be inserted at the same time. This could be to initially populate a table, or when testing. In this sort of situation, where you are repopulating a table, it is possible to save your query to a text file, which can then be re-opened in Query Analyzer and executed without having to re-enter the code. This is demonstrated at the end of the example.

Inserting Several Records in a Query Batch

This next example will demonstrate inserting several records. The work will be completed in batches. There is no transaction processing surrounding these INSERTs and therefore each insertion will be treated as a single unit of work, which either completes or fails.

> **A transaction allows a number of INSERTs or modifications to be treated as one unit, and if any insertion failed within the transaction, all the units would be returned back to their original value and no insertions would have taken place. Transactions will be seen in more detail in Chapters 14 and 15.**

Try It Out – Insert Several Records At Once

1. Ensure that SQL Server Query Analyzer is up and running and that you are logged in as an Administrator or database owner.

2. In the query window, enter the following code. Notice at the start there is a command dealing with quoted identifiers again. Notice how there are two GO commands within this set of INSERTs. Although each INSERT is its own self-contained unit, a GO command also determines the end of a batch, or unit, of work. Therefore, here we have the two INSERT statements actually being treated as a single unit of work from a SQL Server viewpoint. What this means is that SQL Server ignores the fact that each INSERT has no relationship with the other, it takes the two statements, and executes them in one single execution.

```
SET QUOTED_IDENTIFIER OFF
GO
INSERT INTO Society_Groups (Society_Group_Desc, Society_Leader_Name)
   VALUES("The Upmarket Traders","Jason Atkins")
INSERT INTO Society_Groups (Society_Group_Desc, Society_Leader_Name)
   VALUES("Gilbert's Golfers","Martin Aynsley")
GO
INSERT INTO Society_Groups (Society_Group_Desc, Society_Leader_Name)
   VALUES("Security Blankets","Dave Shawl")
INSERT INTO Society_Groups (Society_Group_Desc, Society_Leader_Name)
   VALUES("The Chieftan Coach","Colin Jackson")
GO
```

3. Now just execute the code in the usual way. You will see the following output in the Results pane. This indicates that four rows of information have been inserted into the database, one at a time.

```
(1 row(s) affected)

(1 row(s) affected)

(1 row(s) affected)

(1 row(s) affected)
```

4. Now there is a slight variation on the theme where the remaining players will be inserted into the Players database. There is no GO statement and therefore all of the statements will be treated as one single execution. However, another issue with the GO statement, and the reason that it has been left out, is that when a GO statement is issued, any variable defined prior to the GO statement is then invalid and non-existent after the GO statement. Therefore, you would need to continually re-define the @Pointer_Value variable for each player. Type the following code into the Query pane and execute. Don't forget that photographs will also be inserted for these players as well. Also one final point, and that is that the Society_Group_Id values associated with the players match the values of existing Society_Group_Ids that exist within the Society_Groups table.

```
INSERT INTO Players
(Society_Group,Player_First_Name, Player_Last_Name,Photograph,Date_Of_Birth)
VALUES (3,"Jason","Atkins",0xFFFFFFFF,"15 Oct 81")

DECLARE @Pointer_Value varbinary(16)
SELECT @Pointer_Value = TEXTPTR(Photograph)
FROM Players
WHERE Player_ID = 2
WRITETEXT Players.Photograph @Pointer_Value
   "C:\Program Files\Microsoft SQL Server\
      MSSQL\Data\Wrox_Golf_Results\Images\ja.bmp"

INSERT INTO Players
(Society_Group,Player_First_Name, Player_Last_Name,Photograph,Date_Of_Birth)
VALUES (2,"Ian","McMahon",0xFFFFFFFF,"3 Feb 82")

SELECT @Pointer_Value = TEXTPTR(Photograph)
FROM Players
WHERE Player_ID = 3
WRITETEXT Players.Photograph @Pointer_Value
   "C:\Program Files\Microsoft SQL Server\
      MSSQL\Data\Wrox_Golf_Results\Images\im.bmp"
```

5. After executing the code, you should see the following information:

   (1 row(s) affected)

   (1 row(s) affected)

6. To cater for when the table is completely emptied, for example when testing removing rows within a table that contains data that is no longer desired, it would be best to save the above query to a text file on the hard drive, ready to use again. To do this, ensure that it is the Query pane that has the focus within Windows, rather than any other pane – especially the Results pane. Then you can either select File | Save or File | Save As to save the query, or press *Ctrl+S*.

7. This then brings up the Save Query window where you would enter the File name that you wish to store the query as, and then once happy, click the Save button.

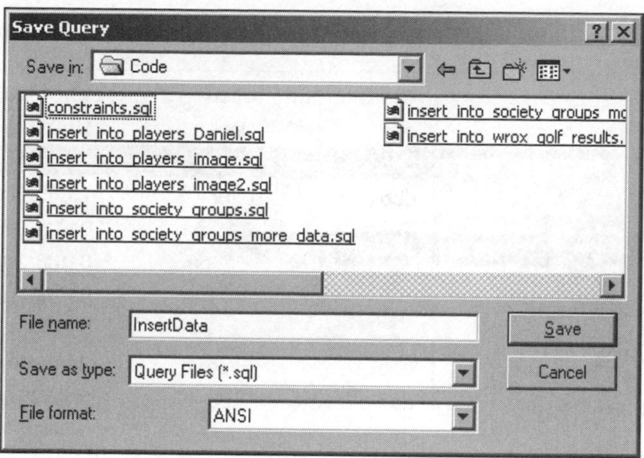

No Permissions for INSERT

If you check in Appendix E at the end of the book, you will see that we have set up a Developers role that only has access to work with the `Society_Groups` table. A user within that group is `DTarbotton`, and so therefore, this user only has access to the `Society_Groups` table. So how do you prove the fact that they cannot insert a record in to another table, like the `Players` table?

This following section demonstrates how, by combining the information of the role's security permissions and the information of which role a user is a member of, SQL Server does not allow a user to perform actions that have not allowed.

Try It Out – No INSERT Permission

1. Login to Windows NT/2000 as `DTarbotton`. This user ID was set up as a Developer and therefore does have access to `Wrox_Golf_Results`, but can only work with the `Society_Groups` table. This user has no access to any other table.

2. Start up Enterprise Manager and navigate to the Wrox_Golf_Results database. Then move to the Players table and right-click. Notice that you are not allowed to create a new table, or to open this table for design purposes. You can open the table to view the rows though, or so you are led to believe.

3. If you now select Open Table, Return all rows, you will receive an error message.

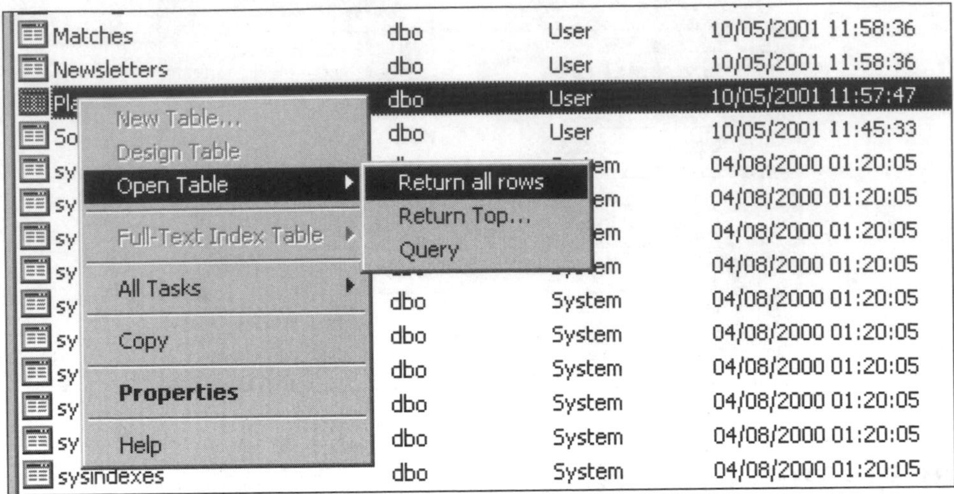

4. You will see the following dialog informing you that either you don't have permission, or that the table may no longer exist within the database. This is a bit of a misleading error message as of course the table does exist.

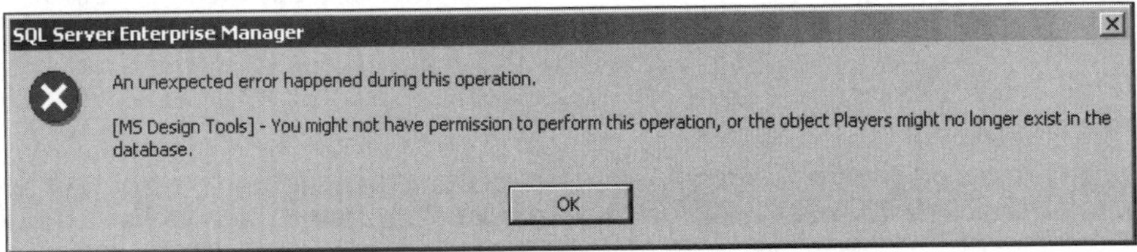

5. A better message comes from SQL Server if you use Query Analyzer to insert a record. From Tools | Query Analyzer, you should find that Query Analyzer starts up and that you are logged in as `DTarbotton`. You can check that you are who you think you are from the title bar of the query pane.

Query - WONDERBISON.Wrox_Golf_Results.DTarbotton - Untitled1

6. If you now insert the following code into a Query pane, and try to execute it, you will receive an error message.

```
SET QUOTED_IDENTIFIER OFF
GO
Insert Into dbo.Players
(Society_Group,Player_First_Name,Player_Last_Name,
Date_Of_Birth) values (1,"Lee","Smith","1 Mar 1954")
```

7. The error message you receive informs you that `DTarbotton` does not have permission to insert into the `Players` table. The message should read like this:

   Server: Msg 229, Level 14, State 5, Line 1

   INSERT permission denied on object 'Players', database 'Wrox_Golf_Results', owner 'dbo'.

This section demonstrated how security could be tied down in SQL Server for the right roles.

Summary

The `Players` table has now had some extra security placed on it by building column constraints for checking that the correct values are inserted in to the columns, and you should go through the remainder of the tables if you are going to go further with this solution yourself.

This chapter also demonstrates the syntax for the `INSERT` command. This command can become a great deal more complex than has been demonstrated here. We will find that this syntax will be used most often, especially while you are still building up your knowledge of SQL Server. Building an `INSERT` command has also been made simpler for you by Query Analyzer with its scripting options allowing an `INSERT` to be built from a given table. We may find that for an `INSERT` at least, we will not actually use the scripting option much, especially once we get used to coding the `INSERT` command directly.

We have also seen how it is possible to not have to insert data into every column but instead let SQL Server insert data for you. This is achieved through column constraints, a task demonstrated using Enterprise Manager and Query Analyzer.

Finally, images. These can be very awkward in their use; however, they are being used more and more in SQL Server solutions involving web sites. There was a great deal of code needed to insert an image Later on in the book we will see how to view these images as well as update them. So to summarize, we have covered:

- The `INSERT` command
- Using default values and `NULL` values
- Inserting data, with and without default values
- Auto-numbering and its settings
- Adding constraints
- Inserting images
- Multiple record insertions

So now that we are fully up to speed with inserting all different kinds of data, it is time to move on and find out how to retrieve any data that has been inserted into the database.

13

Retrieving Data

This chapter will demonstrate how to view the data that has been placed in the tables so far. There are many ways of achieving this, from using Enterprise Manager, through to T-SQL commands, and as you would expect, they will all be covered here.

The positioning of this chapter in the book may seem awkward, as retrieving data has been covered already in a number of places in other chapters, although we haven't really coded any SQL `SELECT` statements to return rows for display.

The aim of this chapter is to enable us to get data, using the fastest retrieval manner possible, from a table. We can retrieve data from one or more tables through joining tables together within our query syntax; all of these methods will be demonstrated.

The simplest method of retrieving data is using Enterprise Manager, and we demonstrate this method first. There is no need to know any query syntax: it is all done for us. However, we are left with a limited scope for further work.

We can alter the query built up within Enterprise Manager to cater for work that is more complex, but we would then need to know the `SELECT` T-SQL syntax; again, this is explained and demonstrated. This can become very powerful very quickly, especially when it comes to selecting specific rows to return.

The results of the data can also be displayed and even stored in different media, like a file. It is possible to store results from a query and send these to a set of users, if so desired.

Initially the data returned will be in the arbitrary order stored within SQL Server. This is not always suitable, so another aim of this chapter is to demonstrate how to return data in the order that is desired for the results. Ordering the data is quite an important part of retrieving meaningful results and this alone can aid the understanding of query results from raw data.

Retrieving images is not as straightforward as retrieving normal rows of data so there is a section specifically about this.

Finally, it is also possible to build a new table from data returned in a SELECT statement. Care has to be taken with this command, but all of this is covered at the end of the chapter. To recap, the aims of this chapter are to:

- Use Enterprise Manager to retrieve data and limit the rows returned
- Familiarize ourselves with the SELECT statement
- Limit the columns returned
- Name the tables involved
- Display the results in different formats
- Limit the search to specific sets of records
- Concatenate columns
- Order the data in the sequence required
- Limit the number of rows returned
- Find records from partial information
- Learn how to use Books Online when an error occurs
- Return an image
- Create a new table from returned rows
- Demonstrate the joining of two tables

Starting with the simplest of methods, let's look at Enterprise Manager and how easy it is for us to retrieve records.

Using Enterprise Manager

The first area that will be demonstrated is the simplest form of data retrieval, but it is also the least effective. Retrieving data using Enterprise Manager is a very straightforward process with no knowledge of SQL required in the initial stages. Whether it has to return all rows, or even when we want to return specific rows, using Enterprise Manager makes this whole task very easy. This first example will demonstrate how flexible Enterprise Manager is in retrieving all the data from the Society_Groups table.

Try It Out – Enterprise Manager

1. Ensure that SQL Server Enterprise Manager is running. Navigate to the Wrox_Golf_Results database and click on the Tables node; this should then list all the tables in the right-hand pane. Find the Society_Groups table and right-click on it to bring up the pop-up menu we have seen a number of times before. Select Open Table, which then brings up another pop-up menu; select Return all rows.

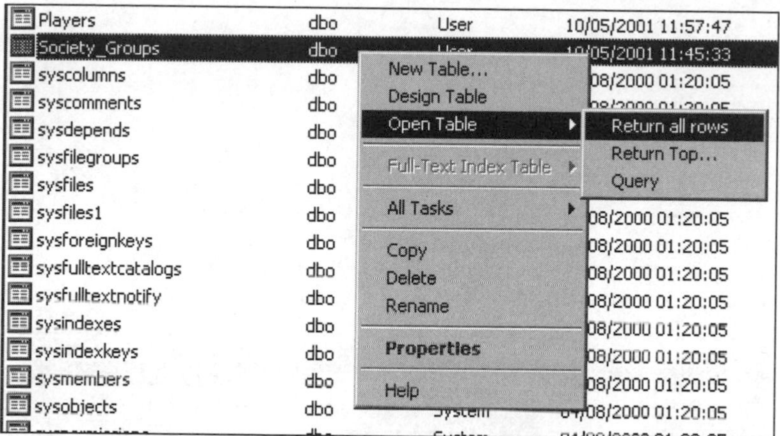

2. This instantly brings up the screen below, which shows all the rows that are in the Society_Groups table. But how did SQL Server get this data? Let's find out.

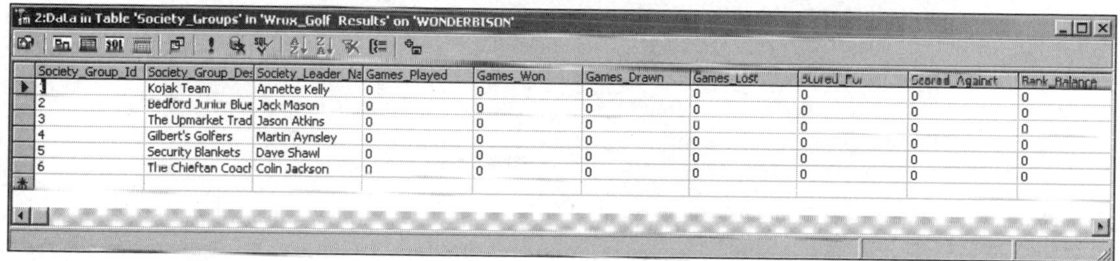

Society_Group_Id	Society_Group_De	Society_Leader_Na	Games_Played	Games_Won	Games_Drawn	Games_Lost	Scored_For	Scored_Against	Rank_Balance
1	Kojak Team	Annette Kelly	0	0	0	0	0	0	0
2	Bedford Junior Blue	Jack Mason	0	0	0	0	0	0	0
3	The Upmarket Trad	Jason Atkins	0	0	0	0	0	0	0
4	Gilbert's Golfers	Martin Aynsley	0	0	0	0	0	0	0
5	Security Blankets	Dave Shawl	0	0	0	0	0	0	0
6	The Chieftan Coach	Colin Jackson	0	0	0	0	0	0	0

3. On the toolbar, you will see a button that, when pressed, will show the SQL code that was built to create this query.

4. Clicking on the button alters the screen to that shown below. This is the SQL syntax generated by SQL Server Enterprise Manager to provide the information requested:

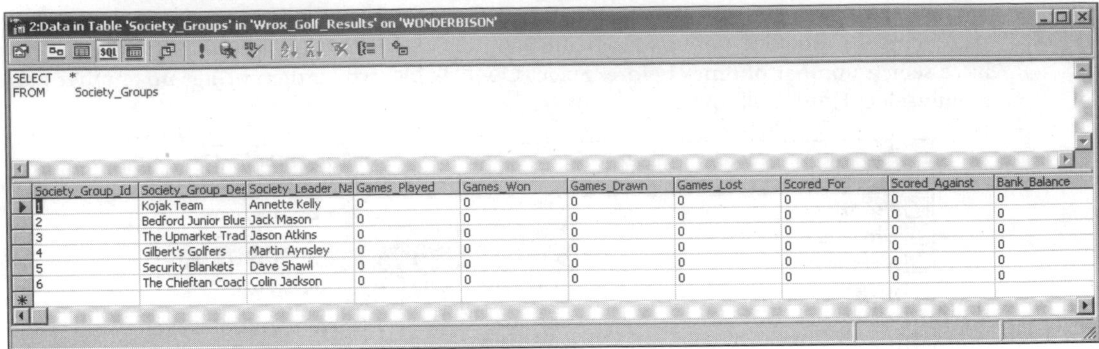

Society_Group_Id	Society_Group_Des	Society_Leader_Na	Games_Played	Games_Won	Games_Drawn	Games_Lost	Scored_For	Scored_Against	Bank_Balance
1	Kojak Team	Annette Kelly	0	0	0	0	0	0	0
2	Bedford Junior Blue	Jack Mason	0	0	0	0	0	0	0
3	The Upmarket Trad	Jason Atkins	0	0	0	0	0	0	0
4	Gilbert's Golfers	Martin Aynsley	0	0	0	0	0	0	0
5	Security Blankets	Dave Shawl	0	0	0	0	0	0	0
6	The Chieftan Coach	Colin Jackson	0	0	0	0	0	0	0

5. Close the query by pressing *Ctrl+F4*, which will take us back to Enterprise Manager. From there, right-click on the Society_Groups table, select Open Table and then Return Top...

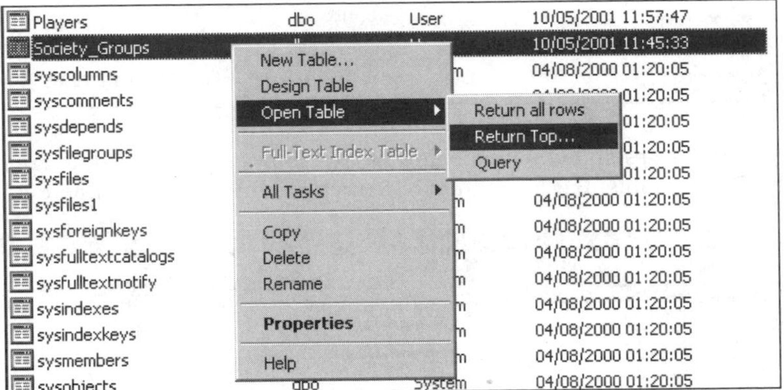

6. This then brings up a screen in which we enter the maximum number of records that we wish to return. The order of the records returned will be determined by the clustered index created on the table. However, if the table has no clustered index, then the order the records are returned is the order in which they were inserted into the table. This of course assumes that you have not placed any code to define an order to return the records in. We can enter any number we choose, but for this first time at least, enter 3 in the box. Before moving on, note that this option says Maximum number of rows. If we entered a value of 100, we would only get six rows returned, as that is the maximum number of rows in the table. You would use this perhaps when you don't know the number of records within a table, but you are only interested in a maximum number of 100 if there are more. This would be when you want to look at just a small selection of content in columns within a table.

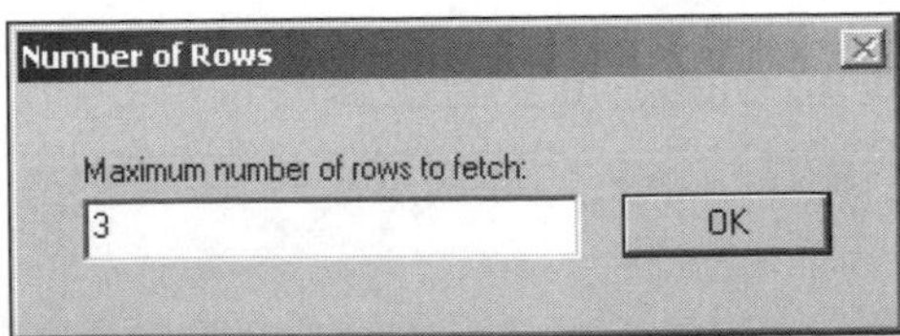

7. This will, as expected, bring up the first three rows found in the **Society_Groups** table in the order of the clustered index.

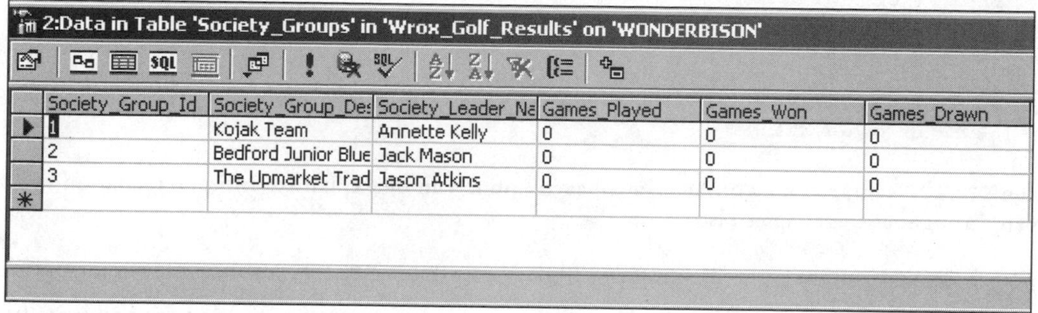

8. Again, by clicking the SQL button on the toolbar, the SQL code is exposed. Notice how this differs from the previous example in that `TOP 3` has been placed after the `SELECT` statement. Press *Ctrl+F4* to close the dialog.

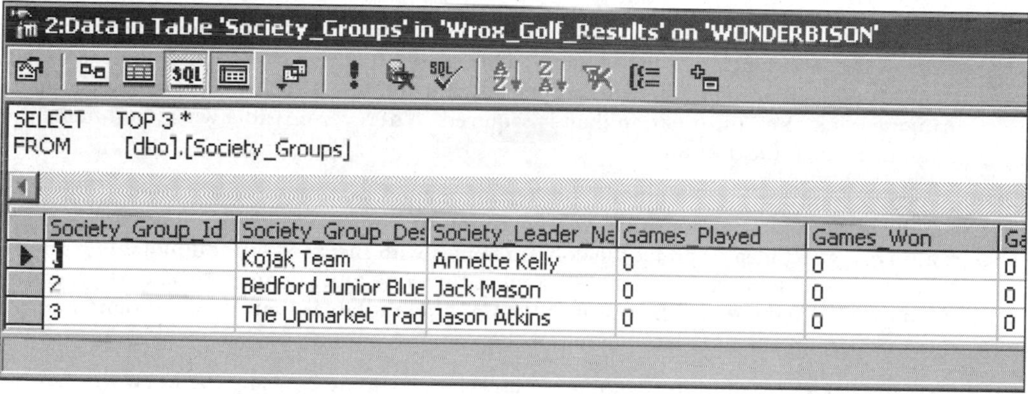

9. There is another option in Enterprise Manager, which is the **Query** option. However this is very similar to building a view, which we cover in Chapter 16.

The SELECT Statement

If we wish to retrieve data for viewing from SQL Server using T-SQL commands, then the `SELECT` statement is the command we need to use. This is quite a powerful command as it can retrieve data in any order, from any number of columns, from any table that we have the authority to retrieve data from, perform calculations on that data during data retrieval, and even include data from other tables! If the user does not have the authority to retrieve data from a table, then you will receive a similar error message to that which you saw in the last chapter, informing the user that permission is denied. `SELECT` has a lot more power than even the functions mentioned so far, but for the moment, let's concentrate on the fundamentals.

Let's take some time to inspect the simple syntax for a SELECT statement within SQL Server 2000.

```
SELECT [TOP n [PERCENT]
   *|column1, column2,….
[INTO new_table]
FROM table_name|view_name, table_name|view_name2,…
[WHERE where_clause]
[ORDER BY order_clause]
```

If the SELECT syntax is now broken down, each option can be explained. More explanation will be given throughout the chapter also:

- SELECT – Required – This informs SQL Server that a SELECT instruction is being performed.
- TOP *n* PERCENT – Optional – You can return the top number of rows as defined by either the order of the data in the clustered index, or if the result is ordered later, then the top number from that order sequence. You can also add the word PERCENT to the end: this will mean that the top n percent of records will be returned. If this is missed out, all the records will be returned (unless specific column names are given).
- * – Optional – By using the asterisk, you are instructing SQL Server to return all the columns from all the tables included in the query. This is not an option that should be used on large amounts of data, or over a network, especially if it is busy. By using this, we are normally bringing back more information than is required. Wherever possible we should name the columns instead (next option).
- column1, column2,… – Optional but recommended. Not required if * used – This option is where we name the columns that we wish to return from a table. When naming the columns, it is always a good idea to prefix the column names with their corresponding table name. This becomes mandatory when we are using more than one table in our SELECT statement and instances where there may be columns within different tables that share the same name. This is covered in an example later on in the chapter.
- INTO new_table – Optional – We can create a new table by using the keyword INTO. The table will have the layout of the SELECT statement column names and contain the data returned from the SELECT query. This is demonstrated at the end of the chapter.
- FROM table_name | view_name – Required – We have to inform SQL Server where the information is coming from. The list in the FROM section could mention one table, or several tables as a comma-separated list. When using multiple columns, then it would be necessary to issue some sort of JOIN statement between these tables. Joins are discussed at the end of the chapter.
- WHERE where_clause – Optional – If we want to retrieve rows that meet specific criteria, we need to have a WHERE clause specifying the criteria to use to return the data. The WHERE clause tends to contain the name of a column on the left-hand side of a comparison operator, like =, <, > and either another column within the same table, or another table, a variable, or a static value. There are other options that the WHERE statement can contain, where more advanced searching is required, but in the main these comparison operators will be the main constituents of the clause.

- ORDER BY order_clause – Optional – The data will be returned naturally in the physical order they are stored within the table if no ORDER BY clause is specified, which if we have a clustered index built on the table, will be that order; otherwise, it will be in the order in which they were inserted. However, you can alter the ordering by using the ORDER BY clause, which will determine the order of the rows returned, and you can specify whether each column is returned in ascending or descending order. Ascending, ASC, or descending DESC, is for each column and not defined just once for all the columns within the ORDER BY. Sorting is completed once the data has been retrieved from SQL Server but before any command like TOP.

Keep in mind that when building a SELECT statement, we do not have to name all the columns. In fact, we should only retrieve the columns that we do wish to see; this will reduce the amount of information sent over the network. There is no need to return information that will not be used.

Naming the Columns

When building a SELECT statement it is not necessary to name every column if we don't want to see every column. We should only return the columns that we need. It is very easy to slip in to using * to return every column, even when running one-time-only queries. Try to avoid this at all costs; typing out every column name takes time, but when we start dealing with more complex queries, and a larger number of rows, the few extra seconds is worth it.

Now we know not to name every column unless required, and to avoid using *, what other areas do we need to be aware of? First of all, it is not necessary to name columns in the same order that they appear in the table – it is quite acceptable to name columns in any order that we wish. There is no performance hit, or gain, from altering the order of the columns, but we may find that a different order of the columns might be better for any future processing of the data.

When building a SELECT statement and including the columns, if the final output is to be sent to a set of users, the column names within the database may not be acceptable. For example, if you are sending the output to the users via a file, then they will see the raw results set. Or if you are using a tool like Crystal Reports to display data from a SELECT statement within a SQL Server **stored procedure**, then naming the columns would help there as well. Not only are the column names less user friendly, but also some column names will be purely confusing for users; therefore it would be ideal to be able to alter the names of the column headings. Placing the alteration to the SQL Server column headings with the new, **alias** column headings desired, in either quotation marks or square bracket delimiters, is easily accomplished with the AS keyword. There is more on this later in the chapter.

Now we know about naming the columns, let's now take a look at how the SQL command can return data.

The First Searches

This example will revolve around the `Players` table, making it possible to demonstrate how all of the different areas mentioned above can affect the results displayed.

Try It Out – The First Set of Searches

1. Ensure that Query Analyzer is running and that you are within the Wrox_Golf_Results database. In the Query pane enter the following SQL code. As we can see, the code is all in lower case, just to prove that SQL Server, unlike other database systems, is not case sensitive for commands or definitions – however, it is usually the case, and from now on the SQL commands will be presented in upper case to make them stand out from the rest of the code.

```
select * from players
```

2. Execute the code using *Ctrl+E*, *F5*, or the Execute button on the toolbar. We should then see something like the results below.

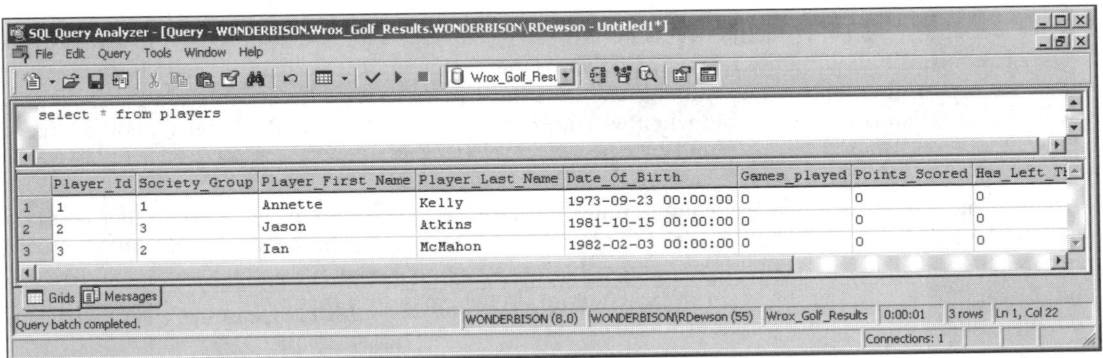

3. This is a simple `SELECT` command returning all the columns and all the rows from the `Players` table. Let's now take it to the next stage where specific column names will be defined in the query, which is a much cleaner solution. In this instance from the `Players` table, we would like to return a player's first name and the number of games that they have played. This would mean naming `Player_First_Name` and `Games_Played` as the column names in the query. The code will read as below:

```
SELECT Player_First_Name, Games_Played FROM Players
```

4. Now execute this code, which will return the following results. As we can see, not every column is returned.

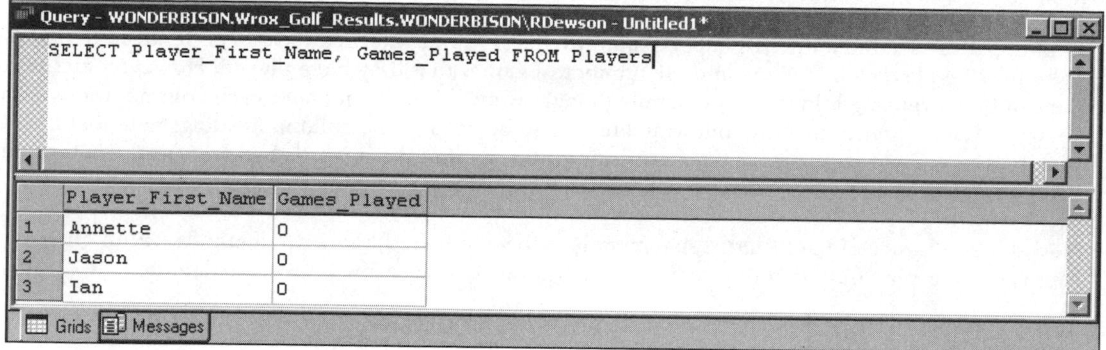

5. As we have seen from the examples so far, the column names, although well named from a design viewpoint, are not exactly suitable if we had to give this to a set of users; it would be better if the column titles had no underscores, for example. This can be accomplished by using column aliases and this next example demonstrates this. Using the same query as before, a couple of minor modifications are required to give the columns aliases. `First name` is in quotes as it contains a space.

```
SELECT Player_First_Name AS "First name", Games_Played AS Played
FROM Players
```

6. Execute this and the displayed output changes – much more friendly column names.

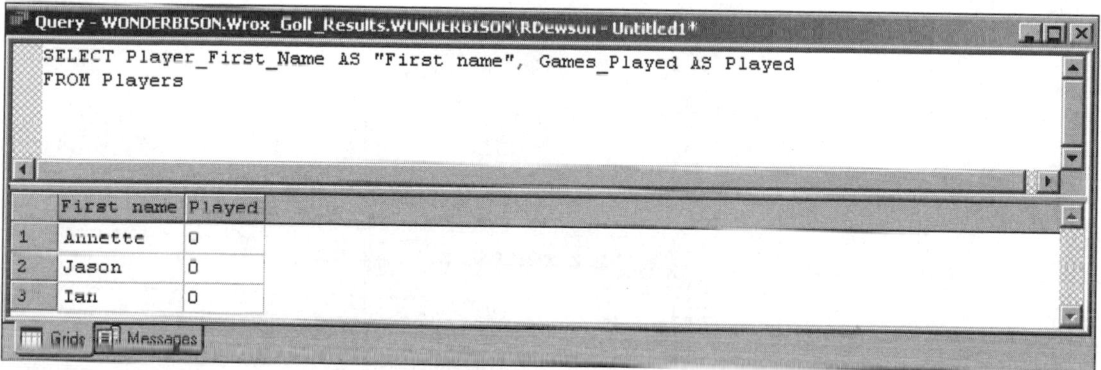

How It Works

The first `SELECT` statement demonstrates the fact that in most SQL Server instances, whether we use upper or lower case doesn't matter to our queries; however, some language installations are case sensitive. When installing SQL Server, if we chose a SQL Collation sequence that was case sensitive, as denoted by **CS** within the suffix of the collation name, `SQL_Latin1_General_Cp437_`**`CS`**`_AS`, for instance, then the first `SELECT` query would generate an error. The collation sequence for SQL Server was chosen in Chapter 1 when we installed the application. Changing a collation sequence within SQL Server is a very difficult task that requires rebuilding parts of SQL Server, so this book won't move into that area.

Moving back to discussing the first query, this query will select all columns and all rows from the `Players` table, ordered according to how the database sees it – looking at the figure, it has quite plainly done this.

Looking at the second and third query examples, the columns returned have been reduced to just two columns: the player's first name and the number of games that they have played. However, all the rows are still being returned. In the last example though, we will notice that after each column, there is an `AS` keyword. This signifies that the following literal is to be used as the column heading; note that if we wish to use two words separated by spaces, we must surround these words by identifiers, whether this is double quotes, as above, or square brackets.

Now that the basics of the `SELECT` statement have been covered, there are methods within Query Analyzer to display output in different manners, so this is what we will take a look at next.

Displaying the Output Differently

There are different ways of displaying the output: from a grid, as we have seen, a straight text file, still within a Query pane, or as pure text, just like a tabulated Word file. You may have found the results in the previous exercise laid out in a different format that shown above, depending on how you initially set up Query Analyzer. In the results so far, we have seen the data as a grid. This next section will demonstrate the tabular text, otherwise known as Results in Text, as well as outputting the data to a file. Let's get right on with the first option, Results in Text.

Try It Out – Putting the Results in Text and a File

1. We are still in Query Analyzer; from the Query menu option, select Results in Text, or press *Ctrl+T*.

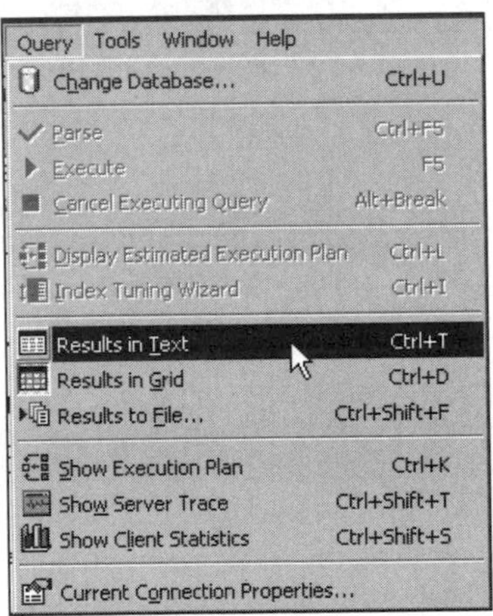

2. If we run the same query as earlier (the code is detailed again below), we will be able to see the difference. Once the code is entered, execute it.

```
SELECT Player_First_Name As "First name", Games_Played AS Played
FROM Players
```

3. As we can see, the output has changed a great deal. No longer is the output in a nice grid where the columns have been shrunk to a more manageable size, but each column's data takes up, and is displayed to, the maximum number of characters that each column could contain. This obviously stretches out the display, but from here we can see easily how large each column is supposed to be.

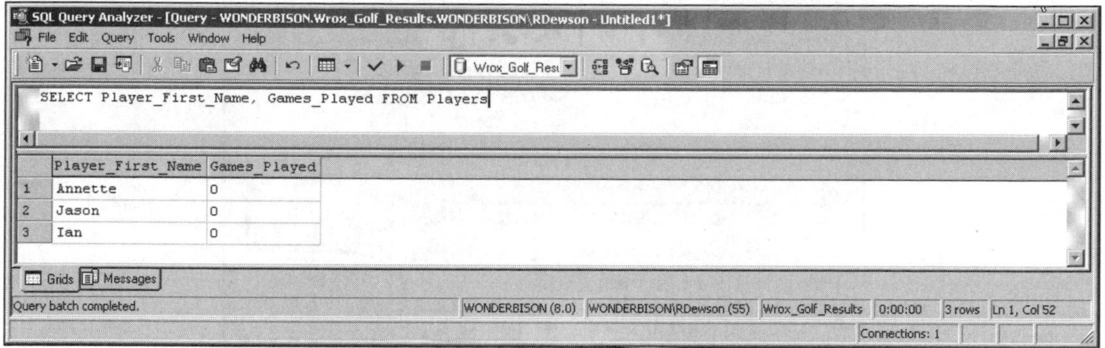

4. There will be times, though, when users require output to be sent to them. For example, they wish to know specific details from a set of records, and so you build a query and save the results to a file to send to them. Or perhaps they want output to perform some analysis of data within a Microsoft Excel spreadsheet. Again this can be achieved from the Query menu: Results to File, or *Ctrl+Shift+F*.

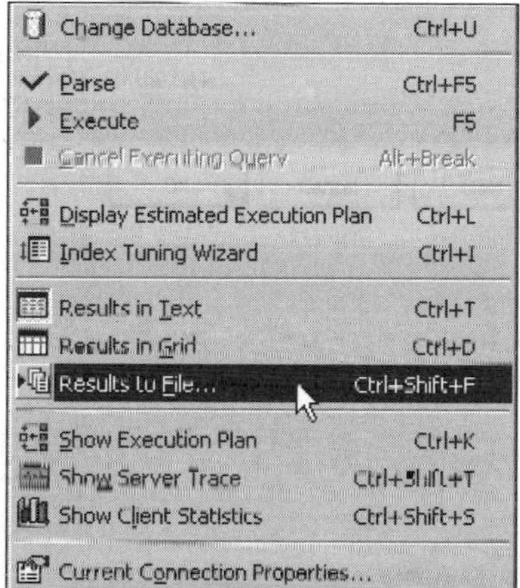

5. Using the code we should now be familiar with, again detailed below, execute the query.

```
SELECT Player_First_Name As "First name", Games_Played As Played
FROM Players
```

6. Once the code has been executed, a **Save Results** dialog box will appear: this could show any folder location initially – in this case, it shows the **My Documents** folder:

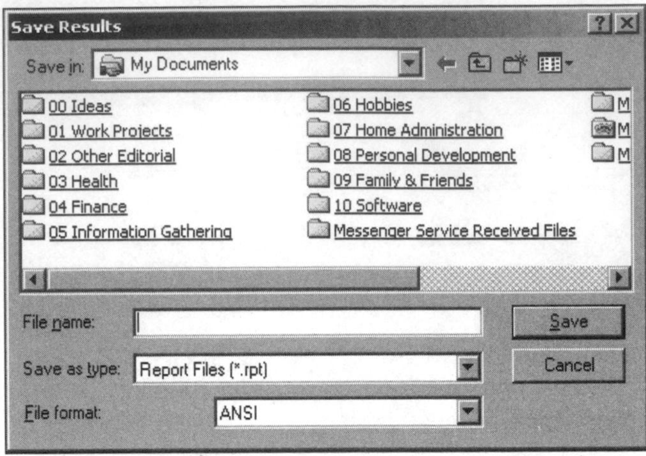

7. However, this may not be where the file needs to be saved, so navigate to the most suitable location where it is handy to pick up for mailing to the users and then deleting afterwards. The file name should be something meaningful; also, as in this case we don't want the output to have a suffix of `.rpt`, it is necessary to change the **Save as type**: to that of **All Files (*.*)**, then enter a suffix of `.txt` (or the suffix will default back to `.rpt` automatically).

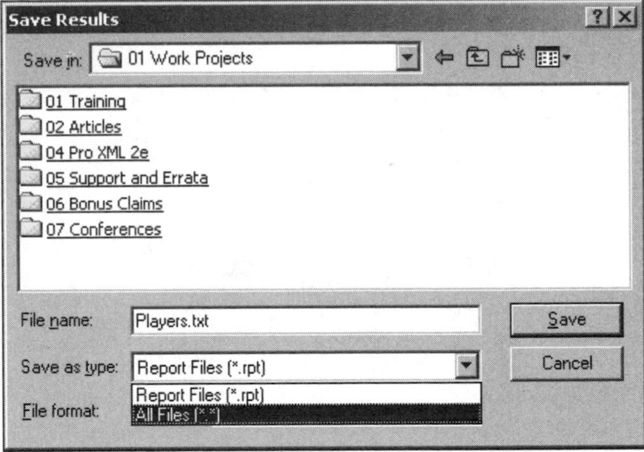

8. Once all the necessary information has been entered, click the **Save** button on the dialog.

9. This will then save the file to the location we specified, ready for us to distribute to the relevant people. Query Analyzer also presents us with some relevant and useful information about what we have just accomplished.

```
(3 row(s) affected)

The following file has been saved successfully:

E:\01 Work Projects\Players.txt 307 bytes
```

If we then look at the text file we created, it should look something like this:

```
First name                                      Played
----------------------------------------------- ------
Annette                                         0
Jason                                           0
Ian                                             0

(3 row(s) affected)
```

Limiting the Search

There are a number of different ways to limit the search of records within a query. Some of the most basic revolve around the three basic relational operators: <, >, and = (less than, greater than, and equal to). There is also the use of the keyword `NOT`, which could be included with these three operators, however, `NOT` does not work as in other programming languages that we may have come across: this will be demonstrated within this example so we know how to use the `NOT` operator successfully.

All of these operators can be found in the `WHERE` clause of the `SELECT` statement used to reduce the number of records returned within a query.

Try It Out – The WHERE Statement

1. Let's alter the query a bit now and limit the records to return by using the `WHERE` statement. We should still be in Query Analyzer but let's change how the output is displayed back to the grid, by pressing *Ctrl+D.*

2. The requirement for this section is to find a specific society group, using the name of the group as the criteria to search for. We will try to find the record for the Society_Group of the Gilbert's Golfers. We restrict the `SELECT` statement so that only the specific record comes back by using the `WHERE` statement, as can be seen in the code below. Notice the `QUOTED_IDENTIFIER` statement – this ensures that Query Analyzer will allow us to use the single quote in the name.

```
SET QUOTED_IDENTIFIER OFF
GO
SELECT * FROM Society_Groups
WHERE Society_Group_Desc = "Gilbert's Golfers"
```

3. Execute this code and we will see that the single record for **Gilbert's Golfers** is returned.

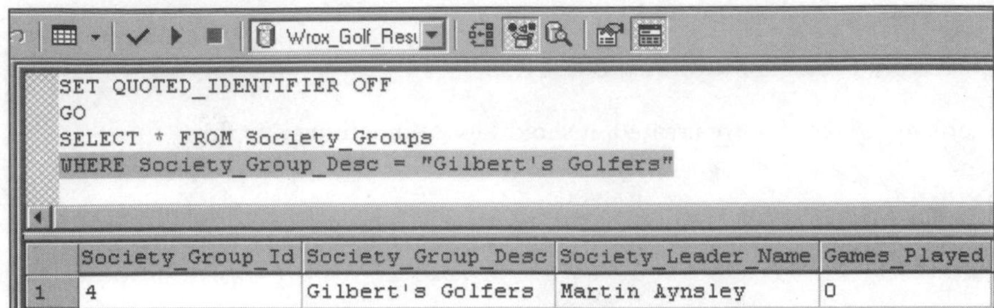

```
SET QUOTED_IDENTIFIER OFF
GO
SELECT * FROM Society_Groups
WHERE Society_Group_Desc = "Gilbert's Golfers"
```

	Society_Group_Id	Society_Group_Desc	Society_Leader_Name	Games_Played
1	4	Gilbert's Golfers	Martin Aynsley	0

4. To prove that we are working within an installation that is not case sensitive from a data perspective, unless you installed a different collation sequence to that described in Chapter 1, if you perform the following query, you will get the same results as in the point above (I've set the query output to be text in this case though).

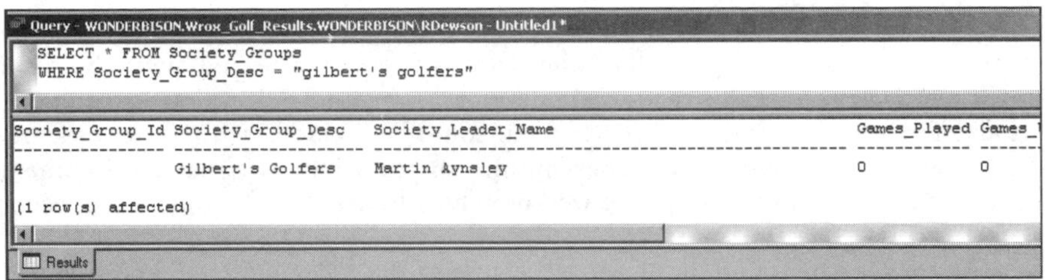

```
SELECT * FROM Society_Groups
WHERE Society_Group_Desc = "gilbert's golfers"
```

```
Society_Group_Id Society_Group_Desc   Society_Leader_Name                                 Games_Played Games_
---------------- -------------------- --------------------------------------------------- ------------ ------
4                Gilbert's Golfers    Martin Aynsley                                      0            0

(1 row(s) affected)
```

5. We have seen the `WHERE` in action using the equals sign; it is also possible to use the other relational operations in the `WHERE` statement. The next query demonstrates how SQL Server takes the `WHERE` condition and starts returning records after the given point. This query and the result provide an interesting set of results. Enter the code as detailed below:

```
SELECT * FROM Society_Groups
WHERE Society_Leader_Name > "Jack"
```

6. Once done, execute the code and check the results, which will be discussed in the *How It Works* section in a moment.

```
SELECT * FROM Society_Groups
WHERE Society_Leader_Name > "Jack"
```

	Society_Group_Id	Society_Group_Desc	Society_Leader_Name
1	2	Bedford Junior Blues	Jack Mason
2	3	The Upmarket Traders	Jason Atkins
3	4	Gilbert's Golfers	Martin Aynsley

7. Change the greater than sign to that of a less than sign, and we will get the remaining records left in the table. Enter the code below to see the results.

```
SELECT * FROM Society_Groups
WHERE Society_Leader_Name < "Jack"
```

8. Once the code is executed, as expected, the remaining three records from the `Society_Groups` table are displayed.

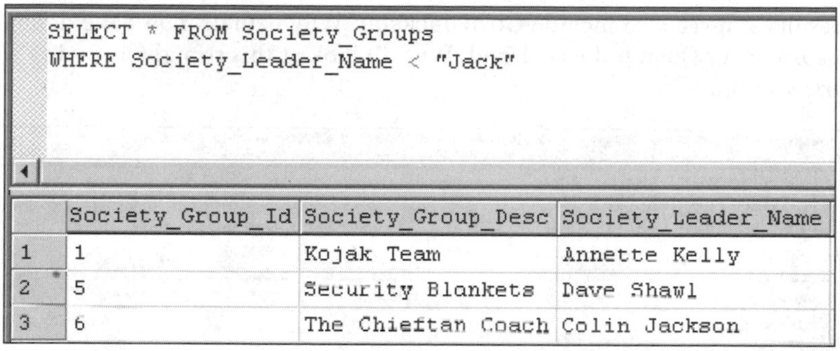

```
SELECT * FROM Society_Groups
WHERE Society_Leader_Name < "Jack"
```

	Society_Group_Id	Society_Group_Desc	Society_Leader_Name
1	1	Kojak Team	Annette Kelly
2	5	Security Blankets	Dave Shawl
3	6	The Chieftan Coach	Colin Jackson

9. Let's now bring in two further options in the WHERE statement: the use of AND, and where we don't want to return specific rows. This can be achieved in one of two ways: the first is by using the less than and greater than signs; the second is by using the NOT operator. Enter the code below, which will return two sets of results in one execution – this is also known as a **multiple result set**.

```
SELECT * FROM Society_Groups
WHERE Society_Group_Id <> 4 AND Society_Group_Id <> 6

SELECT * FROM Society_Groups
WHERE NOT Society_Group_Id = 4 AND NOT Society_Group_Id = 6
```

10. Executing this code will produce the output shown below. As we can see, both sets of results have not listed the groups with an ID of 4 or 6.

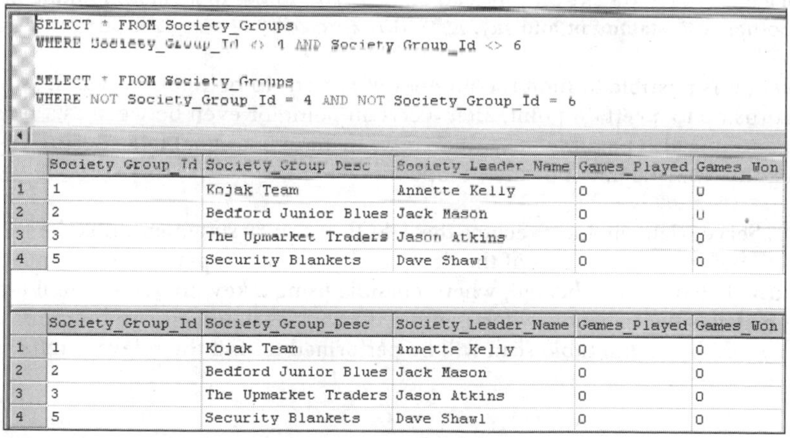

```
SELECT * FROM Society_Groups
WHERE Society_Group_Id <> 4 AND Society_Group_Id <> 6

SELECT * FROM Society_Groups
WHERE NOT Society_Group_Id = 4 AND NOT Society_Group_Id = 6
```

	Society_Group_Id	Society_Group_Desc	Society_Leader_Name	Games_Played	Games_Won
1	1	Kojak Team	Annette Kelly	0	0
2	2	Bedford Junior Blues	Jack Mason	0	0
3	3	The Upmarket Traders	Jason Atkins	0	0
4	5	Security Blankets	Dave Shawl	0	0

	Society_Group_Id	Society_Group_Desc	Society_Leader_Name	Games_Played	Games_Won
1	1	Kojak Team	Annette Kelly	0	0
2	2	Bedford Junior Blues	Jack Mason	0	0
3	3	The Upmarket Traders	Jason Atkins	0	0
4	5	Security Blankets	Dave Shawl	0	0

11. The final example that this section will touch on returns records between two sets of values. The query below will return results that you might find just a little surprising. What we wish to do is return the society leaders Jack Mason, Jason Atkins, and Lee Smith. Therefore you wish to retrieve all records between Colin Jackson and Martin Aynsley. Enter the following code and execute it.

```
SELECT Society_Leader_Name
FROM Society_Groups
WHERE Society_Leader_Name > "Colin" AND Society_Leader_Name < "Martin"
```

12. The results you see also include Colin Jackson. Why is that? You have defined that you wish the records after Colin to be returned. We will look at this straight away in the following *How it Works* section.

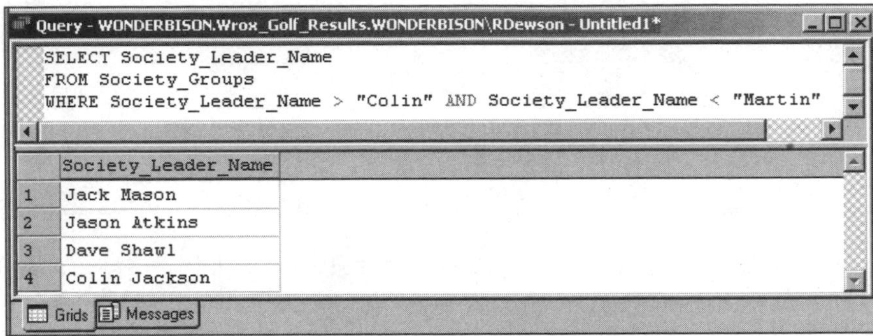

How It Works

As mentioned above, we will now look at the difference between using > `"Colin"` and < `"Martin"` in our query. When a query looks at the `WHERE` statement and there are mathematical operators included, for example > and <, SQL Server will where possible, use an index to search; inthis case for all the records where the first name of a player is alphabetically before Martin, `< "Martin"` or where they are alphabetically after Colin, `> "Colin"`. So why then, does Colin Jackson become listed in the output? This is because you have terminated the starting point for Colin at the end of the letter `n` within his name. Therefore a space, or another letter, or even a number, are alphabetically greater than nothing, which is what follows the letter `n`. Therefore Colin Jackson is listed. So how would you get around this? One way would be to place `"Colin Jackson"` instead of `"Colin"` in the first clause looking at the data. Or you could place another `AND` statement and say, `AND NOT Society_Team_Leader = "Colin Jackson"`.

As we have seen, it is possible to limit the number of records to be returned via the `WHERE` clause; we can return records up to a certain point, after a certain point, or even between two points with the use of an `AND` statement. It is also possible to exclude rows that are not equal to a specific value or range of values by using the `NOT` statement or the <> operator.

When the SQL Server data engine executes the T-SQL `SELECT` statement, it is the `WHERE` statement that is dealt with before any ordering of the data, or any limitation placed on it concerning the number of rows to return. The data is inspected, where possible using a key, to determine if a row stored in the relevant table matches the selection criteria within the `WHERE` statement, and if it does, to return it. If a key cannot be used, then a full table scan will be performed to find the relevant information.

Table scans can be a large performance problem within your system, and you will find that if a query has to perform a table scan, then data retrieval could be very slow, depending on the size of the table being scanned. If the table is small with only a small number of records, then a table scan is likely to retrieve data more quickly than the use of an index. However, table scanning and the speed of data retrieval will be the biggest challenge you will face as a SQL Server developer. With data retrieval, it is important to bear in mind that whenever possible, if you are using a `WHERE` clause to limit the records returned, you should try to specify the columns from an index definition in this `WHERE` clause. By doing this, you will be giving the query the best chance for optimum performance.

As discussed in Chapter 7, which dealt with indexes, getting the index right is crucial to fast data manipulation and retrieval. If you find you are forever placing the same columns in a `WHERE` clause, but those columns do not form part of an index, perhaps this is something that should be revisited to see if any gain can come from having the columns as an index.

For any table, ensuring that the `WHERE` clause is correct is important. As has been indicated from a speed perspective, using an index will ensure a fast response of data. This gains greater importance with each table added, and even more importance as the size of each table grows.

Finally, by ensuring the `WHERE` statement filters out the correct rows, we will ensure that the required data is returned, the right results are displayed, and less data is sent across the network as the processing is done on the server and not the client. Also, having the appropriate indexing strategy helps with this as well.

Now that simple `SELECT` statements have been built, let's look at making things slightly more complex with column manipulation and concatenation.

String Functions

There are a large number of system functions available for manipulating data. This section purely looks at the string functions available for use within a T-SQL command; later in the book we will look at some more functions that are available to us. This is not a comprehensive list of string functions – in fact, the list only covers four of the functions – but string functions, as well as date, time, and mathematical functions can be found in Appendix C at the back of the book. Below are the functions that are used in the next example.

LTRIM/RTRIM

`LTRIM` and `RTRIM` perform similar functionality. If we have a string with leading spaces, and we wish to remove those leading spaces, we would use `LTRIM` so that the returned `varchar` value would have a non space character as its first value. If we have trailing spaces, we would use `RTRIM`. We can only use this function with a datatype of `varchar`, or if a datatype is converted to `varchar` using the `CAST` SQL Server function.

> *`CAST` is a specialized function that will convert one datatype to another datatype. We don't cover this within the book, although an entry on `CAST` can be found in Appendix C. If you wish to convert datatypes, check on the command in Books Online, which can be found by selecting* Help *in Query Analyzer.*

LEFT/RIGHT

This function will return the left-most or right-most characters from a string. Passing in a second parameter to the function will determine the number of characters to return from whichever side of the string. The `LEFT` and `RIGHT` functions accept a `varchar` expression to perform the string manipulation, and return a `varchar` datatype as a result.

Try It Out – String Functions

1. Ensure that Query Analyzer is running and switch the display output to **Results in Text** by pressing *Ctrl+T*.

2. Empty the Query pane by pressing *Ctrl+Shift+Del*, and then enter the code below. Notice the use of the + operator within the `SELECT` query. This will concatenate the strings defined within the query in to one single string value. Unlike with some programming languages, you cannot use the & character, as this has a totally different meaning in SQL Server.

```
SET QUOTED_IDENTIFIER OFF
SELECT RTRIM(Player_First_Name) + " " + RTRIM(Player_Last_Name)
AS "Player name", Games_Played AS "Pld",Points_Scored AS "Scored"
FROM Players
```

3. Execute this code, which produces the following output:

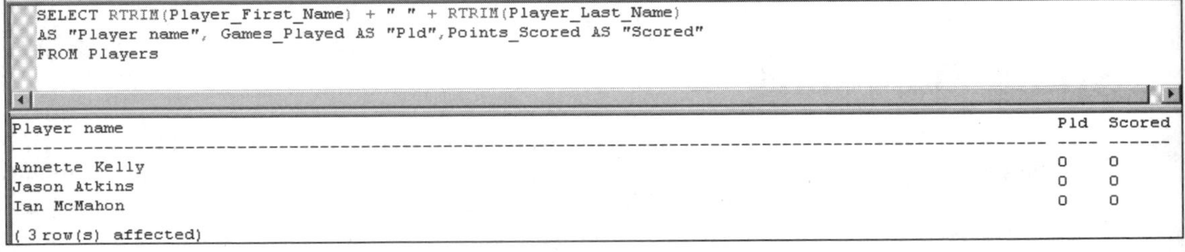
SELECT RTRIM(Player_First_Name) + " " + RTRIM(Player_Last_Name)
AS "Player name", Games_Played AS "Pld",Points_Scored AS "Scored"
FROM Players
Player name Pld Scored
Annette Kelly 0 0
Jason Atkins 0 0
Ian McMahon 0 0
(3 row(s) affected)

4. As you can see, it's a bit unwieldy. The **Player name** column name goes far wider than is required. There is a complex way of getting this right, but a much simpler method is to use the `LEFT` command. The sum of the two columns gives this column width; by using the `LEFT` command, it is possible to achieve something better. Clear the Query Analyzer Query pane and enter the following code:

```
SET QUOTED_IDENTIFIER OFF
SELECT LEFT(RTRIM(Player_First_Name) + " " + RTRIM(Player_Last_Name),30)
AS "Player name", Games_Played AS "Pld",Points_Scored AS "Scored"
FROM Players
```

5. This produces the following results. What the query above has done is to remove all trailing spaces from the `Player_First_Name` and `Player_Last_Name` columns through the use of the `RTRIM` command, and then concatenate the two columns together with a single space in between, by using the + operator. Then, it took the subsequent concatenation of the two columns with the space and requested only the first thirty characters. If the resulting string were greater than 30 characters, then the result would be truncated to those first 30 characters.

```
Player name                    Pld  Scored
------------------------------ ---- ------
Annette Kelly                  0    0
Jason Atkins                   0    0
Ian McMahon                    0    0
```

Order! Order!

Of course, retrieving the records in the order of the clustered index may not always be what is desired. However, it is possible to change the order in which you return records. This is achieved through the ORDER BY clause, which is part of the SELECT statement. The ORDER BY clause can have multiple columns, even with some being in ascending order and others in descending order.

If we should find that we are repeatedly using the same columns within an ORDER BY clause, or that the query is taking some time to run, we should consider having the columns within the query as an index. Indexes were covered in Chapter 7.

Before we can look further at the SELECT statement, we need to add in a few more players in to the Players table. These players will allow full demonstration of the ORDER BY clause and joining two tables together later on in the chapter. The insertion of players will occur at the start of the example.

Let's now take a look at building a query that uses an ORDER BY clause.

Try It Out – Altering the Order

1. Clear the query window in Query Analyzer by pressing *Ctrl+Shift+Del*, and set the display option back to grid by pressing *Ctrl+D*. Now enter the following code, which will enter the new players. Once you have entered the code, execute it.

```
SET QUOTED_IDENTIFIER OFF
GO
INSERT INTO Players (Society_Group, Player_First_Name, Player_Last_Name,
   Date_Of_Birth) VALUES(1,"Andrew","Kelly","12 Jan 1976")
INSERT INTO Players (Society_Group, Player_First_Name, Player_Last_Name,
   Date_Of_Birth) VALUES(2,"Justin","Mason","12 Jan 1976")
INSERT INTO Players (Society_Group, Player_First_Name, Player_Last_Name,
   Date_Of_Birth) VALUES(1,"Andy","MacKay","12 Jan 1976")
INSERT INTO Players (Society_Group, Player_First_Name, Player_Last_Name,
   Date_Of_Birth) VALUES(1,"Martin","Price","12 Jan 1976")
INSERT INTO Players (Society_Group, Player_First_Name, Player_Last_Name,
   Date_Of_Birth) VALUES(3,"Ian","Prentice","12 Jan 1976")
```

2. You should see the following results:

(1 row(s) affected)

(1 row(s) affected)

(1 row(s) affected)

(1 row(s) affected)

(1 row(s) affected)

3. Once complete, enter the following code into the Query pane.

```
SELECT LEFT(Player_First_Name,1) + " " + Player_Last_Name AS Name
FROM Players
ORDER BY Player_Last_Name
```

4. Execute the code; this will produce the following results:

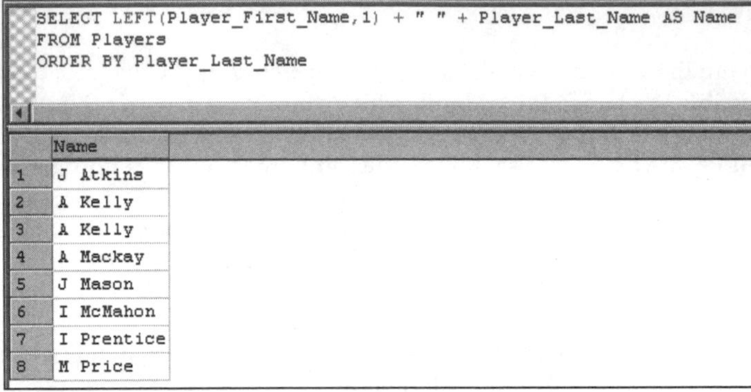

5. Of course, we can also complete the same query, but having the surname in descending order, rather than ascending order. This is simply done by placing `DESC` after the column name.

```
SELECT LEFT(Player_First_Name,1) + " " + Player_Last_Name AS Name
FROM Players
ORDER BY Player_Last_Name DESC
```

6. If you execute this changed code, the results end up in descending order, as expected.

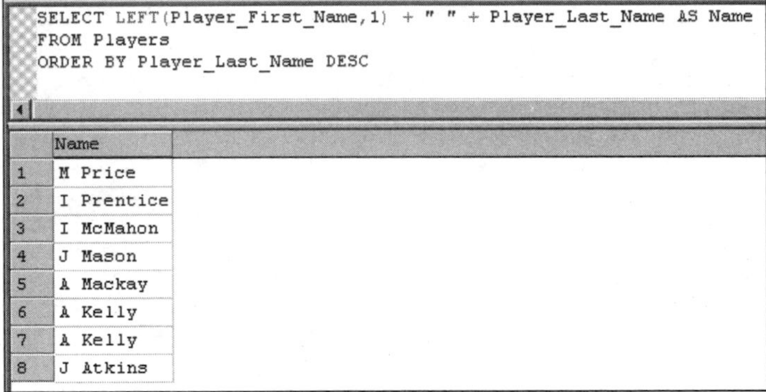

7. However, what if we want to sort by the first initial, and descending last name? We need to put the sort direction against each item in the `ORDER BY` clause, not forgetting that ascending is the default.

```
SELECT LEFT(Player_First_Name,1) + " " + Player_Last_Name AS Name
FROM Players
ORDER BY LEFT(Player_First_Name,1), Player_Last_Name DESC
```

8. This gives exactly the results that we want. Notice also the use of the string command, `LEFT`, in the `ORDER BY` clause, which returns the first character of `Player_First_Name`.

```
SELECT LEFT(Player_First_Name,1) + " " + Player_Last_Name AS Name
FROM Players
ORDER BY LEFT(Player_First_Name,1), Player_Last_Name DESC
```

	Name
1	A Mackay
2	A Kelly
3	A Kelly
4	I Prentice
5	I McMahon
6	J Mason
7	J Atkins
8	M Price

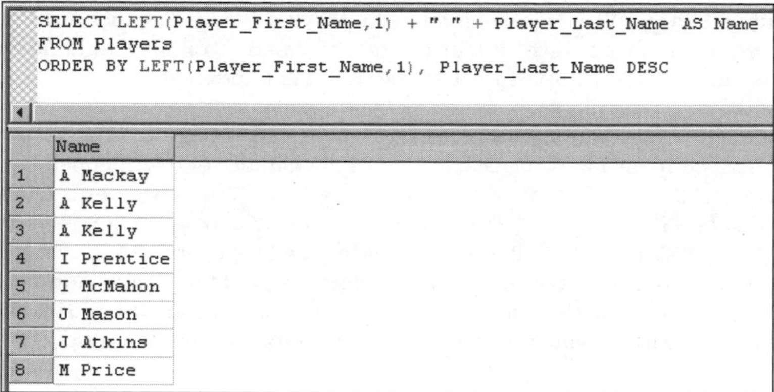

9. Again, just to make things clear, the final query of this section will sort the initial letter of the player in descending order, but have the last name in ascending order. This should be simple to figure out by now; to confirm the answer, here it is below.

```
SELECT LEFT(Player_First_Name,1) + " " + Player_Last_Name AS Name
FROM Players
ORDER BY LEFT(Player_First_Name,1) DESC, Player_Last_Name
```

10. Quickly execute this and check the results.

```
SELECT LEFT(Player_First_Name,1) + " " + Player_Last_Name AS Name
FROM Players
ORDER BY LEFT(Player_First_Name,1) DESC, Player_Last_Name
```

	Name
1	M Price
2	J Atkins
3	J Mason
4	I McMahon
5	I Prentice
6	A Kelly
7	A Kelly
8	A Mackay

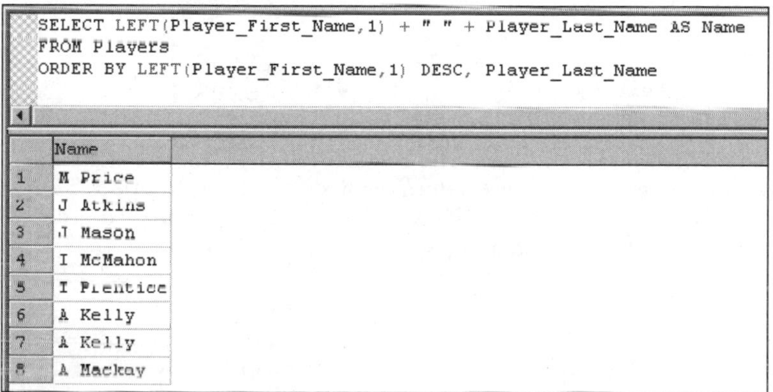

Other Limiting Methods

There are a few other methods to limit the number of records returned in a query, rather than having to use a `WHERE` statement. It is also possible to return a specific number of rows, or a specific percentage of the number of rows, based on either the order the records are stored in, or the order placed on the query by an `ORDER BY` statement. These statements are discussed below with a short code example demonstrating each in action. First of all, we will look at a statement that does not actually form part of the `SELECT` command itself.

SET ROWCOUNT n

This is a totally separate command to the SELECT statement and can in fact be used with other statements within T-SQL. What this command will do is for the session that the command is executed in, limit or reset the number of records that will be processed. Caution should be exercised if we have any statements that also use a TOP command, described in a moment.

The SET ROWCOUNT n function stops processing of the SELECT, or even UPDATE and DELETE commands, described in the following chapters, once the number of rows defined has been reached. The difference between SET ROWCOUNT and SELECT TOP n is that TOP n will perform one more internal instruction to that of SET ROWCOUNT. Processing halts immediately when the number of records processed through SET ROWCOUNT is reached. However, by using the TOP command, all the rows are returned internally, the TOP n are selected from that group internally, and then passed for display. Returning a limited amount of records is useful when you just want to look at a handful of data to see what values could be included, or perhaps you just wish to return a sample of rows for sampling the data.

You can set the number of rows to be affected by altering the number, *n*, at the end of the SET ROWCOUNT function. This setting will remain in force only within the query window in which the command is executed, or within the stored procedure in which the command is executed.

To reset the session so that all rows are taken in to consideration, we would set the ROWCOUNT number to 0.

Try It Out – SET ROWCOUNT

1. In Query Analyzer, enter the following code into a new Query pane; once entered, execute it.

```
SELECT * FROM Society_Groups
SET ROWCOUNT 3
SELECT * FROM Society_Groups
SET ROWCOUNT 0
SELECT * FROM Society_Groups
```

2. You should see three result sets. The first will return all six rows from the Society_Groups table. The second result set will return the first three rows from Society_Groups in the order of the clustered index, which is in the Society_Group_Id order. The third result set returns all the rows once again.

Query - WONDERBISON.Wrox_Golf_Results.WONDERBISON\RDewson - Untitled1*

```
SELECT * FROM Society_Groups
SET ROWCOUNT 3
SELECT * FROM Society_Groups
SET ROWCOUNT 0
SELECT * FROM Society_Groups
```

	Society_Group_Id	Society_Group_Desc	Society_Leader_Name	Games_Played	Games_Won	Games_Drawn	Games_Lost	Scored_
1	1	Kojak Team	Annette Kelly	0	0	0	0	0
2	2	Bedford Junior Blues	Jack Mason	0	0	0	0	0
3	3	The Upmarket Traders	Jason Atkins	0	0	0	0	0
4	4	Gilbert's Golfers	Martin Aynsley	0	0	0	0	0
5	5	Security Blankets	Dave Shawl	0	0	0	0	0
6	6	The Chieftan Coach	Colin Jackson	0	0	0	0	0

	Society_Group_Id	Society_Group_Desc	Society_Leader_Name	Games_Played	Games_Won	Games_Drawn	Games_Lost	Scored_
1	1	Kojak Team	Annette Kelly	0	0	0	0	0
2	2	Bedford Junior Blues	Jack Mason	0	0	0	0	0
3	3	The Upmarket Traders	Jason Atkins	0	0	0	0	0

	Society_Group_Id	Society_Group_Desc	Society_Leader_Name	Games_Played	Games_Won	Games_Drawn	Games_Lost	Scored_
1	1	Kojak Team	Annette Kelly	0	0	0	0	0
2	2	Bedford Junior Blues	Jack Mason	0	0	0	0	0
3	3	The Upmarket Traders	Jason Atkins	0	0	0	0	0
4	4	Gilbert's Golfers	Martin Aynsley	0	0	0	0	0
5	5	Security Blankets	Dave Shawl	0	0	0	0	0
6	6	The Chieftan Coach	Colin Jackson	0	0	0	0	0

Grids | Messages

TOP n

This option is found within the `SELECT` statement itself. This will return a specific number of rows from the `SELECT` statement and is very much like the `SET ROWCOUNT` function. In fact, the `TOP n` option is the preferred option to use when returning a set number of rows, as opposed to the `SET ROWCOUNT` function. The reason behind this is that the `TOP n` only applies to that query command; however, by using `SET ROWCOUNT n`, you are altering all commands until you reset SQL Server to act on all rows through `SET ROWCOUNT 0`. Any `WHERE` statements and `ORDER BY` statements within the `SELECT` statement are dealt with first, and then, from the resultant records, the `TOP n` function comes into effect. This will be demonstrated with the following example.

Try It Out – TOP n

1. In Query Analyzer enter into a new Query pane the following code, once entered, execute it.

```
SELECT TOP 3 * FROM Society_Groups
SET ROWCOUNT 3
SELECT TOP 2 * FROM Society_Groups
SET ROWCOUNT 2
SELECT TOP 3 * FROM Society_Groups
SET ROWCOUNT 0
SELECT TOP 3 * FROM Society_Groups WHERE SOCIETY_GROUP_ID < 6
ORDER BY SOCIETY_GROUP_ID DESC
```

2. The code returns four result sets. The first set is just the top three records. The second will only return two records, even though the ROWCOUNT is set to 3. The third recordset takes into account the ROWCOUNT setting, as this is the lesser value this time. Finally, the last recordset will have three records, which have been displayed after the WHERE and the ORDER BY clauses have been executed. When looking at SET ROWCOUNT and SELECT TOP n, it is always the smaller figure that will be chosen to return the number of rows. If there is a conflict, then the smallest number of rows is returned.

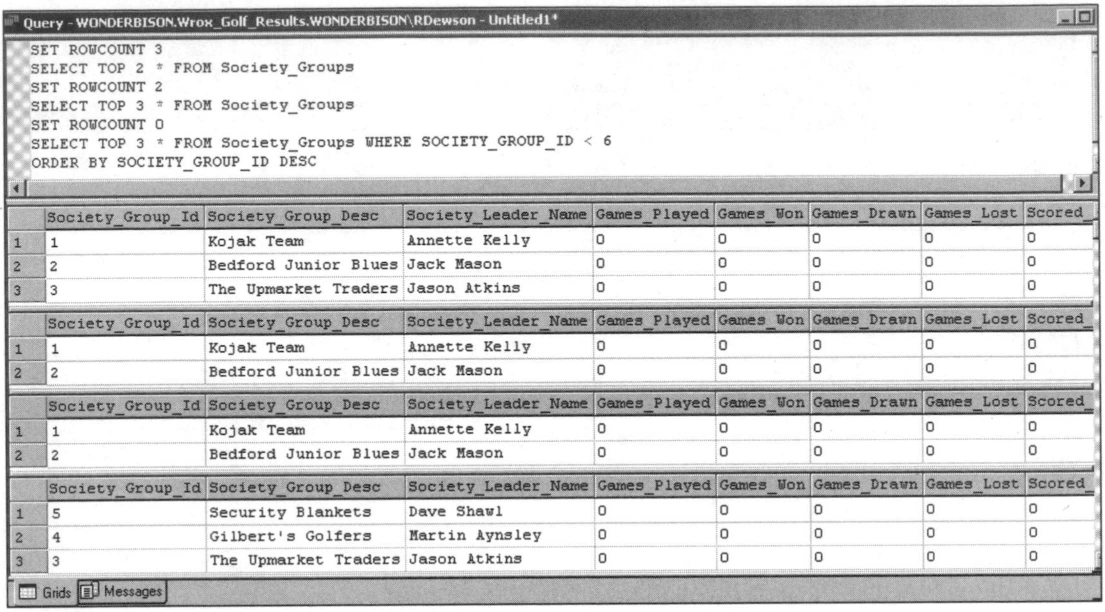

Query - WONDERBISON.Wrox_Golf_Results.WONDERBISON\RDewson - Untitled1*

```
SET ROWCOUNT 3
SELECT TOP 2 * FROM Society_Groups
SET ROWCOUNT 2
SELECT TOP 3 * FROM Society_Groups
SET ROWCOUNT 0
SELECT TOP 3 * FROM Society_Groups WHERE SOCIETY_GROUP_ID < 6
ORDER BY SOCIETY_GROUP_ID DESC
```

	Society_Group_Id	Society_Group_Desc	Society_Leader_Name	Games_Played	Games_Won	Games_Drawn	Games_Lost	Scored_
1	1	Kojak Team	Annette Kelly	0	0	0	0	0
2	2	Bedford Junior Blues	Jack Mason	0	0	0	0	0
3	3	The Upmarket Traders	Jason Atkins	0	0	0	0	0

	Society_Group_Id	Society_Group_Desc	Society_Leader_Name	Games_Played	Games_Won	Games_Drawn	Games_Lost	Scored_
1	1	Kojak Team	Annette Kelly	0	0	0	0	0
2	2	Bedford Junior Blues	Jack Mason	0	0	0	0	0

	Society_Group_Id	Society_Group_Desc	Society_Leader_Name	Games_Played	Games_Won	Games_Drawn	Games_Lost	Scored_
1	1	Kojak Team	Annette Kelly	0	0	0	0	0
2	2	Bedford Junior Blues	Jack Mason	0	0	0	0	0

	Society_Group_Id	Society_Group_Desc	Society_Leader_Name	Games_Played	Games_Won	Games_Drawn	Games_Lost	Scored_
1	5	Security Blankets	Dave Shawl	0	0	0	0	0
2	4	Gilbert's Golfers	Martin Aynsley	0	0	0	0	0
3	3	The Upmarket Traders	Jason Atkins	0	0	0	0	0

Grids | Messages

TOP n PERCENT

This is very similar to the TOP n clause with the exception that instead of working with a precise number of records, it is a percentage of the number of records that will be returned. Keep this in mind, as it is not a percentage of the number of records within the table, as the next example demonstrates. Also, the number of records is rounded up; therefore, as soon as the percentage moves over to include another record, then SQL Server will include this extra record. The following example demonstrates this where there are six records within the Society_Groups table. As soon as the percentage to return exceeds 16.6666* (recurring), we will have a second record returned.

Try It Out – TOP n PERCENT

1. In Query Analyzer enter into a new Query pane the following code; once entered, execute the code.

```
SELECT TOP 17 PERCENT * FROM Society_Groups
SELECT TOP 17 PERCENT * FROM Society_Groups WHERE SOCIETY_GROUP_ID < 6
   ORDER BY SOCIETY_GROUP_ID DESC
```

2. This will return two recordsets. The first will return two records, as discussed above, as the percentage exceeds the 16.6666* percentage. The second result set only returns one record; this is because only five records would be returned from the WHERE statement, so any number greater than zero and less than twenty percent, will return one record.

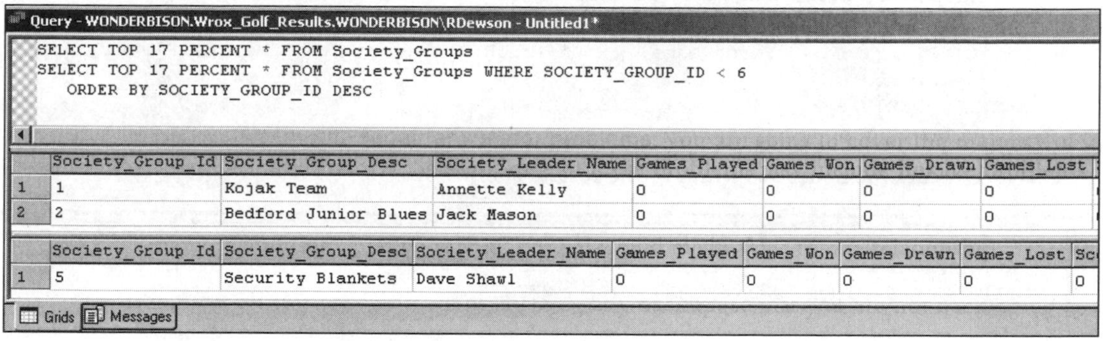

Query - WONDERBISON.Wrox_Golf_Results.WONDERBISON\RDewson - Untitled1*

```
SELECT TOP 17 PERCENT * FROM Society_Groups
SELECT TOP 17 PERCENT * FROM Society_Groups WHERE SOCIETY_GROUP_ID < 6
   ORDER BY SOCIETY_GROUP_ID DESC
```

	Society_Group_Id	Society_Group_Desc	Society_Leader_Name	Games_Played	Games_Won	Games_Drawn	Games_Lost
1	1	Kojak Team	Annette Kelly	0	0	0	0
2	2	Bedford Junior Blues	Jack Mason	0	0	0	0

	Society_Group_Id	Society_Group_Desc	Society_Leader_Name	Games_Played	Games_Won	Games_Drawn	Games_Lost	Sc
1	5	Security Blankets	Dave Shawl	0	0	0	0	0

Grids | Messages

The LIKE Operator

It is possible to use more advanced techniques for finding records where a mathematical operation doesn't quite fit; for example, someone is trying to track down a player, but doesn't know their full name – they know part of the surname, but not all of it, and the part they do know is the second half of the surname.

Suppose we know that the surname ends in "kins". So how would this to be put into a query? There is a keyword that can be used as part of the WHERE statement, called LIKE. This will use pattern matching to find the relevant rows within a SQL Server table using the information provided.

The LIKE operator can come with one of four operators, which are used alongside string values that we want to find. Each of the four operators is detailed below. They can be used together and using one does not exclude using any others.

- % – This would be placed at the end and/or the beginning of a string. The best way to describe this is through an example; if you were searching the players who had the letter "a" within their first name, you would search for "%a%", which would look for the letter "a" ignoring any letters before and after the letter "a", and just check for that letter within the first name column.
- _ – This looks at a string but only for a single character before, or after, the position of the underscore. Therefore looking in the first name column, by looking for "_a" would return any player who has two letters in their first name, where the second letter is an "a". In our example, no records would be returned. However, if you combined this with the % sign and search for "_a%" then you would get back Jason Atkins, Ian McMahon, Martin Aynsley and Ian Prentice. You would not get back Annette Kelly because "A" is the first letter.
- [] – Place a number of values or a range of values to look for. For example, if you were looking in the player's first name for the letters "c-f", you would use LIKE "%[c-f]%"
- [^...] – Similar to the option above, but would list those items that do **not** have values within the range specified.

The best way to learn how to use LIKE is to use an example.

Try It Out – The LIKE Operator

1. Query Analyzer should still be running. Clear the screen using *CTRL+D*. Once done, enter the following code in the Query pane. The sequence we are using isn't case sensitive, but if you happen to have installed a case-sensitive version, the UPPER keyword is used.

```
SELECT RTRIM(Player_First_Name) + " " + RTRIM(Player_Last_Name) As Player_Found
FROM Players
WHERE UPPER(Player_Last_Name) LIKE "%KINS"
```

2. Execute the code; this will give the results below:

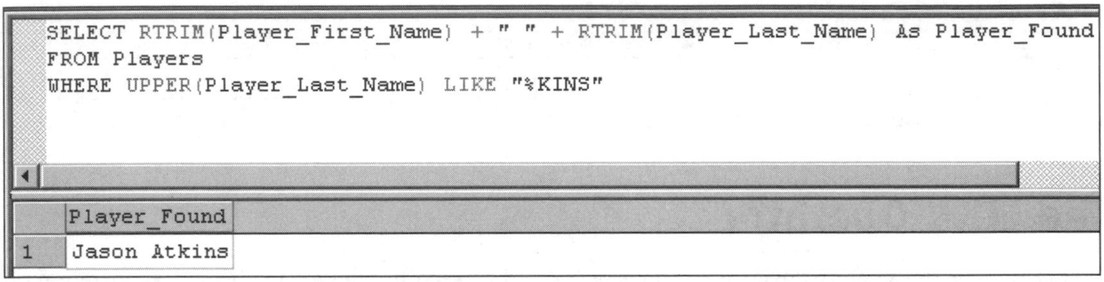

```
SELECT RTRIM(Player_First_Name) + " " + RTRIM(Player_Last_Name) As Player_Found
FROM Players
WHERE UPPER(Player_Last_Name) LIKE "%KINS"
```

	Player_Found
1	Jason Atkins

3. We can also go to extremes using the LIKE operator, for example, seeing which players have the letter "O" anywhere in their name. The code for this is shown below:

```
SELECT RTRIM(Player_First_Name) + " " + RTRIM(Player_Last_Name) As Player_Found
FROM Players
WHERE UPPER(Player_First_Name) like "%O%"
   OR UPPER(Player_Last_Name) like "%O%"
```

4. When you execute this, three players are returned as they have an "O" somewhere in their name.

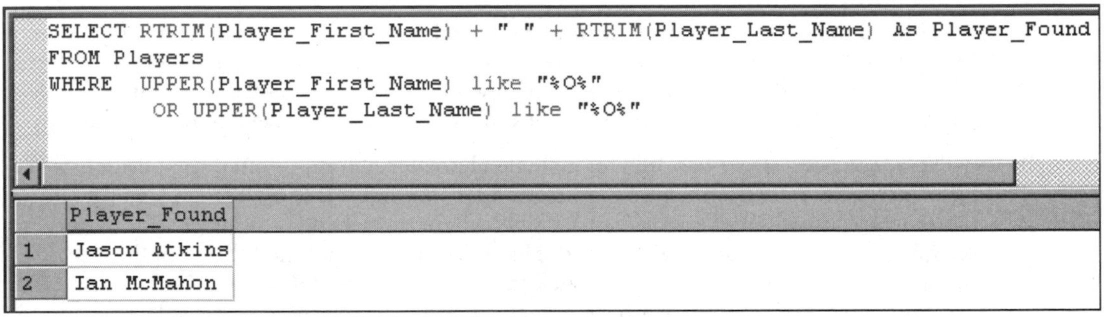

```
SELECT RTRIM(Player_First_Name) + " " + RTRIM(Player_Last_Name) As Player_Found
FROM Players
WHERE  UPPER(Player_First_Name) like "%O%"
        OR UPPER(Player_Last_Name) like "%O%"
```

	Player_Found
1	Jason Atkins
2	Ian McMahon

5. Why would we want to go to such lengths? Would it not have been possible to use the Player_Found alias, which is a combination of the first name and last name columns? Well, unfortunately not – the code we might expect to use would look something like the following

```
SELECT RTRIM(Player_First_Name) + " " + RTRIM(Player_Last_Name) As Player_Found
FROM Players
WHERE  UPPER(Player_Found) like "%O%"
```

6. When we execute this, instead of the success messages that we have become used to, an error message will be returned. We can only search on real column names, not aliases.

   Server: Msg 207, Level 16, State 3, Line 1

   Invalid column name 'Player_Found'.

7. Although we can probably figure out what the problem is here, it is also possible to use SQL Server help to provide more information. Of course, this does depend on having installed Books Online on our system (an option on the installation screen). Highlight the characters 207 in the error statement, as can be seen below.

```
Server: Msg 207, Level 16, State 3, Line 1
Invalid column name 'Player_Found'.
```

8. If we press *Shift+F1* we will find ourselves in Books Online, a very useful tool within SQL Server.

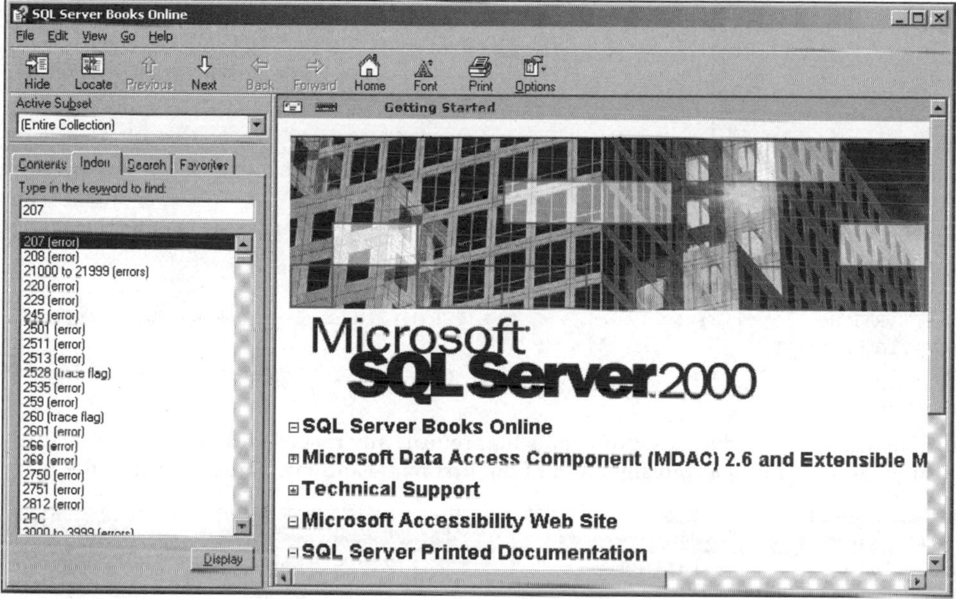

9. We may have to press *Enter* to get the actual help item displayed; sometimes we are taken straight to the error, sometimes we are not. On some systems, pressing *Shift+F1* doesn't take us straight to the help item – in this case, we would simply choose the Index option from the left-hand side of the screen, type in 207 and press *Enter*. Here is the error displayed below:

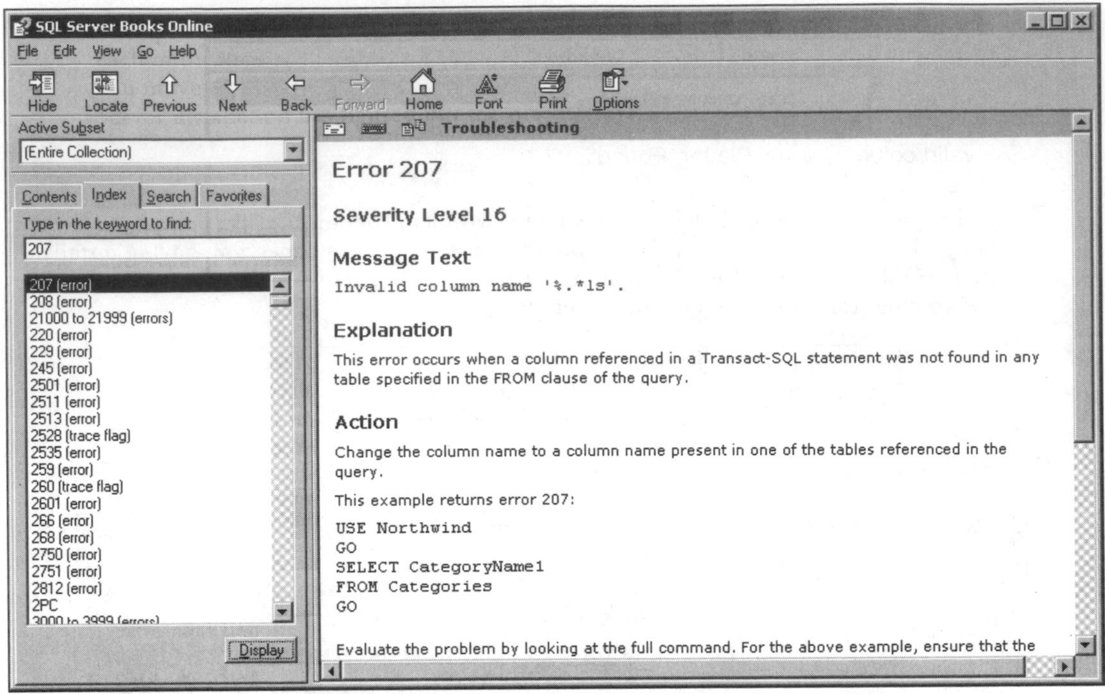

10. However, all of this said, you can use the `LIKE` operator on concatenated columns. For example, enter the following code and execute it.

```
SELECT RTRIM(Player_First_Name) + " " + RTRIM(Player_Last_Name) AS "Player"
FROM Players WHERE
RTRIM(Player_First_Name) + " " + RTRIM(Player_Last_Name) LIKE "%[k-l]%"
```

11. This will then produce a set of results that returns any record with the letters "k" through "l" anywhere within the concatenation of the first name and last name record of the players.

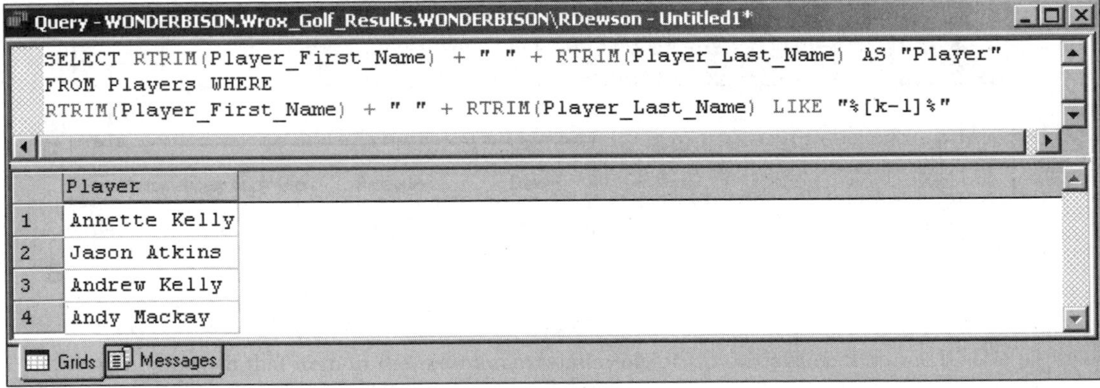

Retrieving Pictures

Retrieving pictures from a table is more complex than just retrieving normal columnar information. As we saw in the previous chapter, inserting images requires a few more statements than any other data that can be inserted in one single action. The actual data of the image is still stored in SQL Server, but in a separate data area to that of all the other information in the rows and columns for our database.

To clarify, the pointer that is inserted into a row is not a pointer to where the image is within our computer, network, or any other storage place, but a pointer to a new data page where the image is actually stored within SQL Server.

It is not possible to retrieve and display the image using T-SQL commands within Query Analyzer. Query Analyzer does not have the tools to display images. However when it comes to looking at the data when using XML and a web browser, then the image can be displayed. Therefore, there is no example here that shows retrieving pictures and displaying the results. But in our example, we have not actually stored the image, but the image path.

If we wish to know the location of an image, when storing the actual picture, we would have another column within the table, defined as `char` or `varchar`, and this column would hold the actual location. We still could not display the image using T-SQL commands, but at least we would know where the image was located when it was inserted in to SQL Server. Of course, there is no guarantee that it will still be there!

But, we have stored the path. So how do we go about getting that path out? Well, it is not as simple as you might think. The problem lies around the use of the `READTEXT` command. In the previous chapter, which dealt with inserting images, you read about the `TEXTPTR` command and how to insert text or image data using `WRITETEXT`. Well, `READTEXT` is very similar, but instead of writing data, it reads it. The downside is that it can read text back, but you cannot place what is read back into a variable. Why does this matter? Well, the data stored within the data page that the image data type has a pointer to, is stored in hexadecimal format. It is necessary to convert that byte-by-byte, into an integer data type, and then convert that in to an ASCII value. Rather a long-winded process, but this is because we are using an image data type. If we had used a text data type, then the information would have been stored as a text data type. The problem is that, as we discussed in the previous chapter, to store an actual image would mean transmitting all the binary values for the picture as one large item. Also this would then mean that retrieving information from the photograph column would be impossible, as Query Analyzer can't display images.

Lets see though how to get the path back to our image. I just would like to reiterate, you do not need to do the conversion in the second part of the example if you have a text data type here.

Try It Out – Retrieving Text From an Image Datatype.

1. First of all retrieve the pointer to where the path to the photograph path is held. Just the same as the chapter on inserting data, you define a variable to hold the pointer, which is then stored in the `@ptr` variable through a `SELECT` command.

```
DECLARE @ptr VARBINARY(16)
SELECT @ptr=TEXTPTR(Photograph)
FROM Players WHERE Player_Id = 2
```

2. Now use the `READTEXT` command to read the pointer from the column to retrieve the data path back. Once this is done, we will display the results from the information held within the data page in SQL Server that the pointer was pointing to. This will give the hexadecimal results of the path to the image. Once you have entered the above code and the line that follows, execute the code, ensuring that the output goes to text. You can ensure this by pressing *Ctrl+T*.

```
READTEXT Players.Photograph @ptr 0 79
```

3. You should see the following results. The value returned does go on further to the right, but there is not enough room to fit this onto the page.

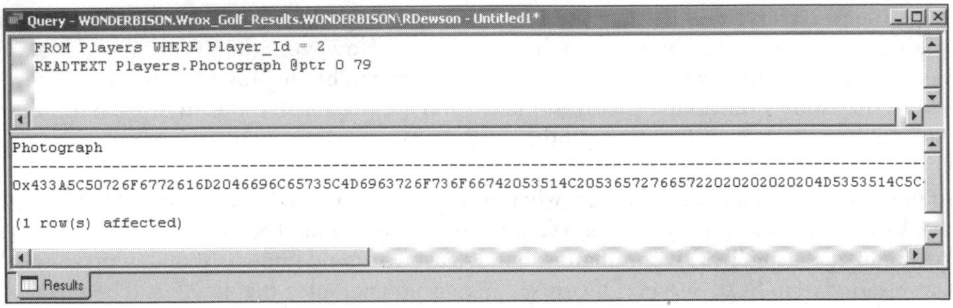

```
Query - WONDERBISON.Wrox_Golf_Results.WONDERBISON\RDewson - Untitled1*
FROM Players WHERE Player_Id = 2
READTEXT Players.Photograph @ptr 0 79

Photograph
---------------------------------------------------------------------------------------------------
0x433A5C50726F6772616D2046696C65735C4D6963726F736F66742053514C205365727665722020202020204D5353514C5C

(1 row(s) affected)

Results
```

4. Now comes the difficult part. There is a much better way to do this, by using flow control, but that topic will be covered in the stored procedures chapter, Chapter 17. By taking each value from the output, each value corresponds to two characters from the output, and using the `CAST` function, which will take one hexadecimal datatype and convert it to an integer, and then use the integer value to convert that to an ASCII value, you will slowly build up the path to where the picture is.

```
SELECT  CHAR(CAST(0x43 as int)) + CHAR(CAST(0x3A as int)) +
CHAR(CAST(0x5C as int)) + CHAR(CAST(0x50 as int)) + CHAR(CAST(0x72 as int))
   + CHAR(CAST(0x6F as int)) + CHAR(CAST(0x67 as int))
   + CHAR(CAST(0x72 as int)) + CHAR(CAST(0x61 as int))
   + CHAR(CAST(0x6D as int)) + CHAR(CAST(0x20 as int))
```

5. When you execute the code above, you will see the start of the path to the picture. If you had completed all of the values, it would have returned C:\Program Files\Microsoft SQL Server\ MSSQL\Data\Wrox_Golf_Results\Images\ja.bmp.

```
Query - WONDERBISON.Wrox_Golf_Results.WONDERBISON\RDewson - Untitled1*
SELECT  CHAR(CAST(0x43 as int)) + CHAR(CAST(0x3A as int)) +
CHAR(CAST(0x5C as int)) + CHAR(CAST(0x50 as int)) + CHAR(CAST(0x72 as int))
   + CHAR(CAST(0x6F as int)) + CHAR(CAST(0x67 as int))
   + CHAR(CAST(0x72 as int)) + CHAR(CAST(0x61 as int))
   + CHAR(CAST(0x6D as int)) + CHAR(CAST(0x20 as int))

-----------
C:\Program

(1 row(s) affected)

Results
```

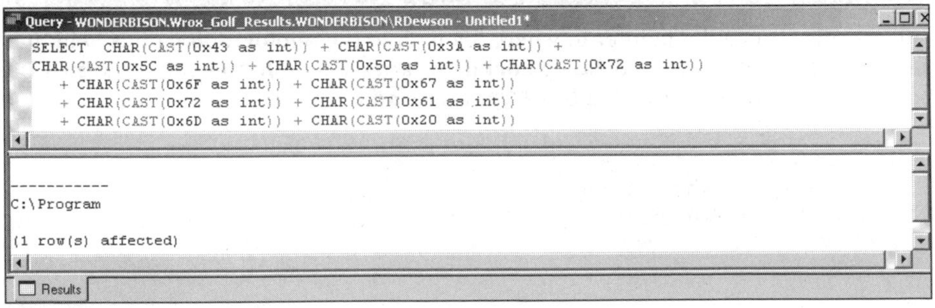

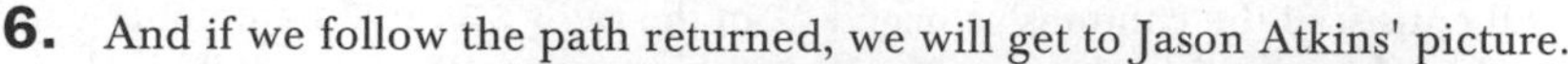

6. And if we follow the path returned, we will get to Jason Atkins' picture.

We have made things difficult for ourselves by using an image data type as we are storing a path and not the actual image, but just to reiterate again, it would have taken many pages of hexadecimal values to get the picture stored in to SQL Server. You will see more on images within the XML chapter as proof of how it is possible to retrieve images directly from SQL Server.

Creating Data – SELECT INTO

This is quite an advanced area to be getting in to, however, it not too advanced to be covered within this book. It is possible to create a new table within a database by using a keyword, `INTO`, within a `SELECT` statement, providing of course, you have the right database permissions to create tables in the first place. First of all, it is necessary to clarify the syntax of how the `SELECT INTO` statement is laid out; we simply add the `INTO` clause after the column names, but before the `FROM` keyword. Although the section of code shows just one table name, it possible to create a new table from data from one, or more tables.

```
SELECT *|column1,column2,…
INTO new_tablename
FROM tablename
```

The `INTO` clause is crucial to the success of the creation of the new table. The `SELECT` statement will fail if there is a table already in existence with the same name, for the same table owner. This will be demonstrated within the example.

The table generated will consist of the columns returned from the built `SELECT` statement, whether that is all the columns from the table mentioned within the `FROM` statement, or whether it is a subset. The new table will also only contain the rows returned from the `SELECT` statement. To clarify, this command is creating a new table using the structure within the `SELECT` statement. There will be no keys, no constraints, relationships, or in fact any other facet of SQL Server, except a new table. Hence creating tables using `SELECT ... INTO` should only be used with thought.

> **Two tables can exist with the same name within a database, providing that they have different owners. The tables in `Wrox_Golf_Results` all have the database owner as their owner, but it is possible for a `Society_Groups` table to exist for an owner like `DTarbotton`. Although possible, this is NOT recommended as it causes confusion.**

Let's look at the `INTO` statement in action.

Try It Out – SELECT INTO

1. In an empty Query Analyzer window, enter and execute the following code:

```
SELECT Society_Group_Id, Society_Group_Desc, Society_Leader_Name
INTO Society_Group_Temp
FROM Society_Groups
WHERE Society_Group_Id > 1
```

2. This will return the following message in the Results pane below.

   (5 row(s) affected)

3. If we now move to the Object Browser on the left-hand side (if the Object Browser is no longer there, press *F8*), and complete a Refresh by pressing *F5* while located on the Wrox_Golf_Results database, we should see a new table in the expanded User Tables node, called Society_Group_Temp.

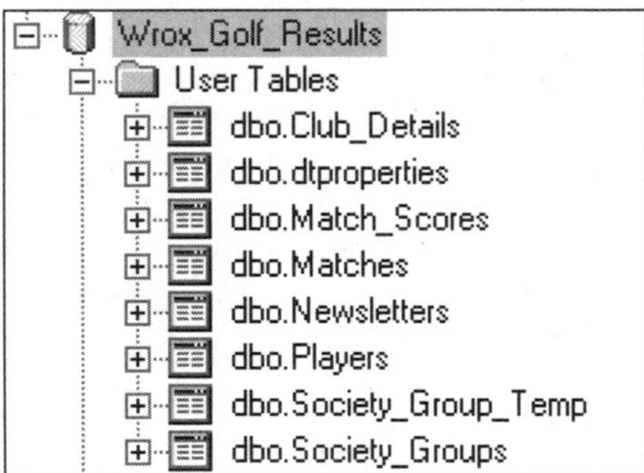

4. To prove that there are five records within this table, in a Query pane enter the following code:

```
SELECT * FROM Society_Group_Temp
```

5. This will produce and list the five records created in the first SELECT statement of this section, which did not copy to the new table the record with the Society_Group_Id of 1.

```
SELECT * FROM Society_Group_Temp
```

	Society_Group_Id	Society_Group_Desc	Society_Leader_Name
1	2	Bedford Junior Blues	Jack Mason
2	3	The Upmarket Traders	Jason Atkins
3	4	Gilbert's Golfers	Martin Aynsley
4	5	Security Blankets	Dave Shawl
5	6	The Chieftan Coach	Colin Jackson

6. If you run the code again to create the table, you will get an error message. Here is the code again:

```
SELECT Society_Group_Id, Society_Group_Desc, Society_Leader_Name
INTO Society_Group_Temp
FROM Society_Groups
WHERE Society_Group_Id > 1
```

7. You will now see the following error message informing you that the Society_Group_Temp object already exists.

   Server: Msg 2714, Level 16, State 6, Line 1

   There is already an object named 'Society_Group_Temp' in the database.

This new temporary table will be kept and used later on within the book when data needs to be removed. We should use the INTO clause with care. Security has not been set up for the table and we are also creating tables within our database that have not been through any normalization or development lifecycle. It is also very easy to fill up a database with these tables if we are not careful. However, it is a useful and handy method for taking a backup of a table and then working on that backup while testing out any queries that might modify the data. Do ensure though that there is enough space within the database before building the table.

Using More Than One Table

Throughout this chapter, the SELECT statement has only dealt with and covered the use of one table. However, it is possible to have more than one table within our SELECT statement, but we must keep in mind that the more tables included in the query, the more detrimental the effect on the query's performance. When we include subsequent tables, there must be a link of some sort between the two tables, known as a **join**. A join will take place between at least one column in one table, and a column from the joining table. The columns involved in the join do not have to be in any key within the tables involved in the join. However, this is quite uncommon, and if you do find you are joining tables, then there is a high chance that there is a relationship, which would mean you do require a primary key and a foreign key. This was all covered in the relationships chapter, Chapter8.

It is possible that one of the columns on one side of the join is actually a concatenation of two or more columns. As long as the end result is one column, this is acceptable. Also, the two columns that are being joined do not have to have the same name, as long as they both have similar data types. For example, you can join a `char` with a `varchar`.

Joining two tables together can become quite complicated, so this book will only cover the most basic join condition where there is a straight join between two tables. This is called an **INNER JOIN**. There are two ways to perform a join between two tables. You can use a `WHERE` statement or you can use the keyword, `JOIN`. Using the `WHERE` clause within a `SELECT` is much simpler to follow; however, the `WHERE` clause is very restrictive on how you join two tables together. To expand on this, when joining two tables, it is possible to retrieve information from one table when there is no information in another. This is called an **OUTER JOIN**. If there is no information on the left-hand table, but there are rows of information on the right-hand table of the join, then this is called a **RIGHT OUTER JOIN**. Vice versa, if there is information within the left-hand table, but none on the right, this is called a **LEFT OUTER JOIN**. Outer joins can become complex when dealing with the information returned and expected performance, and we won't be going any further into this topic here. Getting back to the `WHERE` clause, this can only support inner joins, in other words, where there are matching rows in both tables. We will demonstrate using the `WHERE` clause in this section. Some people see this as an outdated way of joining tables, but some people do prefer it, as it is simpler to code. The more up-to-date method, and the SQL-92 standard-compliant method, is to use the `JOIN` keyword.

We will use two tables to demonstrate the inner join in this example, `Society_Group` and `Players`. Every player must belong to a society group, although some society groups may not have any players at this point. There is a column within each table that allows this join to take place: the `Society_Group_Id` column from the `Society_Groups` table, and the `Society_Group` column from the `Players` table. Notice how they don't have exactly matching column names; this is not a problem, but it is not a desirable scenario and should be avoided, especially in any new system – although you may find this scenario within legacy systems. The only reason that there is inconsistency in any column names in this book is to demonstrate that it is possible to join two tables here, or within a relationship diagram, on columns that don't match on name.

Joining two tables could not be simpler. All the columns in both tables are available to be returned through the query, and so we can list the columns desired as normal. However, if there are two columns of the same name, they must be prefixed with the name, or the alias name, of the table from which the information is derived.

> **It is recommended that whenever a join does take place, whether the column name is unique or not, that all columns are prefixed with the table or alias name. This saves time if the query is expanded to include other tables, but it also clarifies exactly where the information is coming from.**

Moving on to the `FROM` clause. If you are using the `WHERE` statement to join the two tables, each table is separated by a comma. It does not matter what order the tables are named in. It is possible to supersede every table by a space and then an alias name. A table alias can be of any length following the naming standards within SQL Server; in most cases two or three letters are sufficient.

```
FROM tablea, tableb
```

The final, and most important, area is the `WHERE` statement. It is at this point that the tables are joined together and it is crucial that we get it right. An error here will bring back spurious results or even no results at all, and any results brought back might take a very long time to retrieve, especially on large tables. It is at this point that the one-to-one column match should take place between the two tables.

But if you are using the `JOIN` keyword, then in the `FROM` clause, you would name the table, then the type of join you are performing, in this case `INNER JOIN` followed by the second table:

```
FROM tablea INNER JOIN tableb
```

You would then use the `ON` keyword to define the columns that the join is taking place on:

```
ON tablea.column1 = tableb.column4
```

Let's look at an example, which will make all of this clear.

Try It Out – Joining Two Tables

1. With Query Analyzer, enter the following code, and then execute it. This will use the `INNER JOIN` keywords to join the two tables together. You can see that the join of the columns is successful even when the two columns do not have the same name. SQL Server is taking the query, noticing that there are two tables involved in the join by looking at the `FROM` clause, and then looking at the `ON` clause to see what columns are required to make the join work. The `INNER JOIN` keyword is also informing SQL Server that it should only return records where there is a match between the two tables.

```
SELECT sg.Society_Group_Id "ID", sg.Society_Group_Desc "Society",
   RTRIM(pl.Player_First_Name) + " " + pl.Player_Last_Name AS "Name",
   pl.Date_Of_Birth AS "DOB"
FROM Society_Groups sg INNER JOIN Players pl
ON sg.Society_Group_Id = pl.Society_Group
```

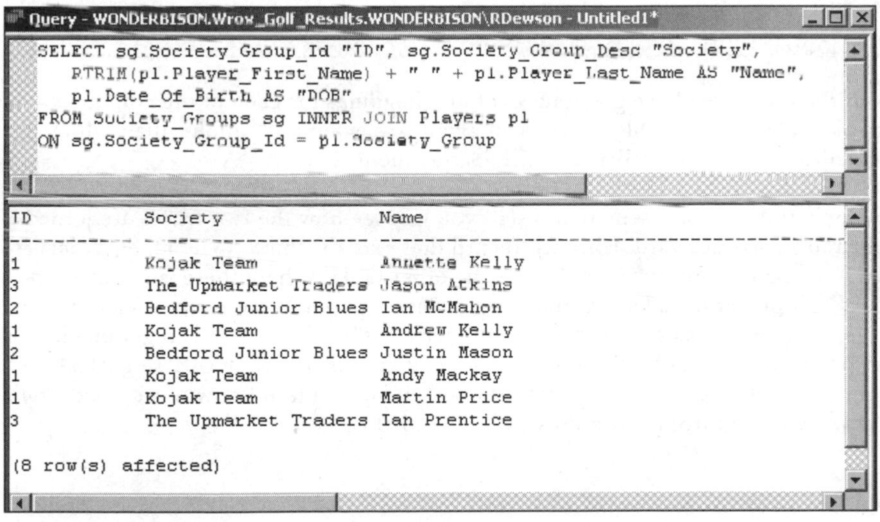

2. Now we can look at the same query as above, but this time using the `WHERE` statement instead. The theory is the same. SQL Server can see the two tables mentioned within the `FROM` clause and can see, from the `WHERE` clause, the two columns defined for the match to take place on. By default, as with any other `WHERE` clause, it is only where there is a match that you will have records returned.

```
SELECT sg.Society_Group_Id "ID", sg.Society_Group_Desc "Society",
   RTRIM(pl.Player_First_Name) + " " + pl.Player_Last_Name AS "Name",
   pl.Date_Of_Birth AS "DOB"
FROM Society_Groups sg, Players pl
WHERE sg.Society_Group_Id = pl.Society_Group
```

3. This will produce results as follows, and should match exactly the query using the `INNER JOIN` keyword.

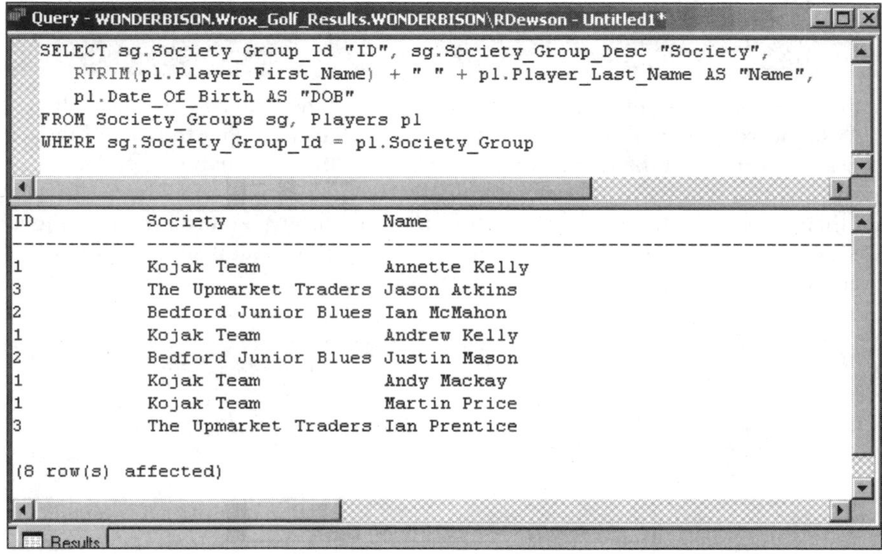

If we look at the query, we have given new column headings for each of the columns to make the output more readable. Also the two tables have been given a relevant and unique alias, which has then been used in the column names as well as the `WHERE` statement.

If you now look at the `WHERE` statement itself, you will see how the two tables are joined together – it's very simple and straightforward. For each record that exists within one table, SQL Server is trying to match it up to a corresponding record within the other table. Where there is a match, the record is printed out. Each player does have a matching society group, but not every society group has a player. For example, society groups 4, 5, and 6 do not have a listing above. We can get much more involved with joins, for example, in getting the missing society groups out using `OUTER JOINS`, but then this becomes quite complex, so let's leave that for now – if you want to know more, read *Professional SQL Server 2000 programming*, from Wrox Press, ISBN 1-861004-48-6.

Summary

Now that you have completed this chapter, you should be confident in retrieving data from any table within any database in a speedy and professional manner. Selecting data will probably be your most common action as your database develops, as you will be constantly investigating data and dealing with the contents of that data, whether it is for reports, updating information elsewhere, or even bug tracking. Ensuring that you know how to retrieve data in a timely fashion is crucial to ensuring that the server is not slowed down when dealing with awkward or ungainly data retrieval.

Constantly check indexes when dealing with queries to ensure that you have indexes that match your data retrieval. Keep in mind that only the columns required for the data information should be retrieved within your query. When dealing with multiple tables, it is imperative that you know how the tables are linked and how the join conditions within the T-SQL commands work, are effective, and retrieve the correct information.

Each of these points is as crucial as the others and by now you should be more than capable of dealing with requests from many different viewpoints. To summarize, in this chapter we have covered:

- Retrieving data from records using Enterprise Manager
- The `SELECT` statement
- Searching columns of data
- Formatting the output
- Limiting searches
- String functions
- Ordering the results
- Restricting the size of the returned data
- The `LIKE` operator – finding near matches
- Retrieving images
- Creating tables with `SELECT INTO`
- Using more than one table at once

There is one last area that we recommend that you keep in mind. If in doubt, limit the number of records that the query is to deal with by using the `SET ROWCOUNT` option, but also build up the query one step at a time so that you know exactly where a problem is introduced. While building up the query, return the smallest amount of information possible.

Now it's time to move on to updating the data.

Updating Data and Transactions

Now that data has been inserted into our database, and we have seen how to retrieve this information, it is now time to look at how to modify, or update the data. Ensuring that you update the right data at the right time is crucial to maintaining data integrity. You will find that when updating data, and also when removing or inserting data, it is best to group this work as a single, logical unit, called a **transaction**, thereby ensuring that if an error does occur, it is still possible to return the data back to its original state. This chapter features how a transaction works and how to incorporate this within your code.

Updating data is a relatively straightforward process, with some very simple T-SQL code being used to perform an update. However, updating images does require a little more work, and is not too dissimilar to inserting image information as demonstrated in Chapter 12, *Inserting Data*. This chapter will demonstrate updating the data in a column, which in our example will in fact end up overwriting the information contained in the column.

Dealing with images is quite a handful, and having a template to do this is very useful. There is no template that comes with SQL Server to perform this function; therefore, this chapter will show you how to build a template to update image data in a column.

This chapter aims to ensure that you:

- Know the syntax of the `UPDATE` command
- Are competent at updating data within a SQL Server table
- Are aware of transactions and how to use them effectively within SQL Server
- Can deal with updating images
- Are able to build your own template to save a large amount of coding for dealing with images

First of all, let's take a look at the syntax for the `UPDATE` command.

The UPDATE Command

The UPDATE command will update columns of information from rows returned from the selection criteria. The syntax of the UPDATE command has similarities to the SELECT command, which makes sense, as it has to look for specific rows to update, just as the SELECT statement looks for rows to retrieve. The syntax below is in its simplest form. Once you become more experienced, the UPDATE command can become just as complex and versatile as the SELECT statement.

```
UPDATE tablename
   SET column = value | variable | column
     [,column2 = value | variable | column]
       . . .
WHERE where_condition
```

The tablename clause is simply the name of the actual table on which to perform the update.

Moving on to the next line of the syntax we reach the SET clause. It is in this clause that any updates to a column take place. One or more columns can be updated at any one time, but each column to be updated must be separated by a comma.

When updating a column, there are three choices that can be made for data updates. This can be through a direct value setting, the value from a variable, or a value from another column, even from another table. We can even have mathematical functions or variable manipulations included in the right-hand clause, have concatenated columns, or have manipulated the contents through string functions. Providing that the end result sees the left-hand side having the same data type as the right-hand side, the update will then be successful. As a result, we cannot place a character value into a numeric data type field without converting the character to a numeric value.

If we are updating a column with a value from another column, the only value that it is possible to use, is the value from the same row of information in another column, provided this column has an appropriate data type.

Finally, the WHERE condition is exactly as in the SELECT command, and can be used in exactly the same way. Note that omitting the WHERE clause will mean the UPDATE statement will affect every row in the table.

Updating Data – Query Analyzer

To demonstrate the UPDATE command, the first update to the data will be to change the name of a society team leader. This uses the UPDATE command in its simplest form, by locating a single record and updating a single column.

Try it Out – Updating Data

1. Ensure that Query Analyzer is running, and that you are logged in with an account that can perform updates. In the query pane, enter the following `Update` command:

```
SET QUOTED_IDENTIFIER OFF
GO

UPDATE Society_Groups
   SET Society_Leader_Name = "Lee Smith"
WHERE Society_Group_Desc = "Security blankets"
```

2. It's as simple as that! Now that the code is entered, execute the code, and you should then see a success message like this:

   (1 row(s) affected)

3. Now enter a `SELECT` statement to check that Lee Smith is now leader of the Security Blankets, and not Dave Shawl as it was before. For your convenience, here's the statement, and the results:

```
SELECT * FROM Society_Groups
```

	Society_Group_Id	Society_Group_Desc	Society_Leader_Name
1	1	Kojak Team	Annette Kelly
2	2	Bedford Junior Blues	Jack Mason
3	3	The Upmarket Traders	Jason Atkins
4	4	Gilbert's Golfers	Martin Aynsley
5	5	Security Blankets	Lee Smith
6	6	The Chieftan Coach	Colin Jackson

4. Now here's a little trick that you should know, if you haven't stumbled across it already. If you check out that screenshot below, you will see that the `UPDATE` code is still in the query pane, as is the `SELECT` statement. No, we aren't going to perform the `UPDATE` again! If you highlight the line with the `SELECT` statement by holding down the left mouse button and dragging the mouse, then only the highlighted code will run when you execute the code again.

```
SET QUOTED_IDENTIFIER OFF
GO

UPDATE Society_Groups
        SET Society_Leader_Name = "Lee Smith"
WHERE Society_Group_Desc = "Security blankets"
GO

SELECT * FROM Society_Groups
```

5. On executing the highlighted code, you should only see the values returned for the `SELECT` statement, and no results saying that an update had been performed.

6. It is also possible to update data using information from another column within the table, or with the value from a variable. This next example will demonstrate how to update a row of information using the value within a variable, and a column from the same table. Notice how although the record will be found using the `Society_Group_Desc` column, the `UPDATE` command is also updating that column with a new value. Enter the following code and then execute it:

```
SET QUOTED_IDENTIFIER OFF
GO

DECLARE @ValueToUpdate VARCHAR(30)
SET @ValueToUpdate = "Mick Bagram"
UPDATE Society_Groups
   SET Society_Leader_Name = @ValueToUpdate,
       Society_Group_Desc = Society_Leader_Name
WHERE Society_Group_Desc = "Security Blankets"
```

7. You should then see the following output:

   (1 row(s) affected)

8. Now to check what has happened. You may be thinking that the update has not happened because you are altering the column that is being used to find the record, but this is not so. The record is found, then the update occurs, and then the record is written back to the table. Once the record is retrieved for update, then there is no need for that value to be kept. Just check that the update occurred by entering and executing the following code:

```
SELECT * FROM Society_Groups
```

9. You should now see the alteration in place, with Mick Bagram now the leader of the society which has a Society_Group_Desc of Lee Smith!

```
SELECT * FROM Society_Groups

Society_Group_Id Society_Group_Desc    Society_Leader_Name
---------------- --------------------  ------------------------------
1                Kojak Team            Annette Kelly
2                Bedford Junior Blues  Jack Mason
3                The Upmarket Traders  Jason Atkins
4                Gilbert's Golfers     Martin Aynsley
5                Lee Smith             Mick Bagram
6                The Chieftan Coach    Colin Jackson

(6 row(s) affected)
```

10. Now let's move on to updating columns where the data types don't match. SQL Server does a pretty good job when it can to ensure the update occurs, and these following examples will demonstrate how well SQL Server copes with updating an `integer` data type with a value in a `varchar` data type. The first example will demonstrate where a `varchar` value will successfully update a column defined as `integer`. Enter the following code and execute it:

```
SET QUOTED_IDENTIFIER OFF
GO
DECLARE @WrongDataType VARCHAR(20)
SET @WrongDataType = "12"
UPDATE Society_Groups
   SET Games_Won = @WrongDataType
WHERE Society_Group_ID = 5
SELECT Society_Group_Desc, Games_Won FROM Society_Groups
```

11. As you can see, the value 12 has been placed in to the `Games_Won` column. SQL Server has performed an internal data conversion, has come up with an `integer` data type from the value within `varchar` as this is what the column expects, and therefore can successfully update the column. Here is the output as proof:

(1 row(s) affected)

	Society_Group_Desc	Games_Won
1	Kojak Team	0
2	Bedford Junior Blues	0
3	The Upmarket Traders	0
4	Gilbert's Golfers	0
5	Lee Smith	12
6	The Chieftan Coach	0

12. However, in this next example, the data type that SQL Server will come up with is a non-integer as it has a decimal point defined. Therefore, we cannot put this value into an `integer` column. Enter the following code, and then execute it:

```
SET QUOTED_IDENTIFIER OFF
GO
DECLARE @WrongDataType VARCHAR(20)
SET @WrongDataType = "10.76"
UPDATE Society_Groups
   SET Games_Won = @WrongDataType
WHERE Society_Group_ID = 5
SELECT Society_Group_Desc, Games_Won FROM Society_Groups
```

13. Notice how SQL Server has generated an error message informing you of the problem. Hence, never leave data conversions to SQL Server to perform. Try to get the same data type updating the same data type.

Server: Msg 245, Level 16, State 1, Line 5
Syntax error converting the varchar value '10.76' to a column of data type int.

14. However, with the final value, SQL Server *does* manage to take the value and update the table. It takes the static value passed in, truncates it to an `integer`, and then updates the column. Once you enter the following code, execute it to prove the point:

```
UPDATE Society_Groups
   SET Games_Won = 15.75
WHERE Society_Group_ID = 5
SELECT Society_Group_Desc, Games_Won FROM Society_Groups
```

15. Sure enough, the value 15 has been placed in the column. This is because in this instance, 15.75 is of a similar data type for SQL Server to update the column with the value, but in the "10.76" example that failed, the data type, although converted by SQL Server, is still essentially a `varchar`. As a result, a failure occurred within the "10.76" example.

(1 row(s) affected)

	Society_Group_Desc	Games_Won
1	Kojak Team	0
2	Bedford Junior Blues	0
3	The Upmarket Traders	0
4	Gilbert's Golfers	0
5	Lee Smith	15
6	The Chieftan Coach	0

Updating data is very straightforward, as the example above has demonstrated. Notice how, in the `WHERE` clause in certain collation sequences, the exact casing of `Society_Group_Desc` doesn't matter. On this occasion, this does in fact involve a higher risk of causing problems both now, and in the future.

Take the scenario where there are two records, both with the same society group name, but one has the name in upper case, and the other as it is, mixed case. We would find that both records are updated with the new society group leader's name. This is probably not a desirable solution. Where at all possible, either use a unique identifier, for example the `Society_Group_Id`, or first of all ensure that the records that will be updated are the right ones. Before executing an `UPDATE` statement that cannot use a unique identifier data type, you may want to write a `SELECT` statement first, and then change this into an `UPDATE` statement once you are certain that the results returned are the correct ones. Even then, it is a good idea to wrap up the whole `UPDATE` within a transaction, just in case any data modifications have occurred since checking the data. Transactions are covered in the next section.

Getting back to the `UPDATE` command and how it works, first of all SQL Server will filter out from the table the first record that meets the criteria of the `WHERE` statement. The data modifications are then made, and SQL Server moves on to try to find the second row matching the `WHERE` statement. This process is repeated until all the rows that meet the `WHERE` condition are modified.

But what if you didn't want the update to occur immediately? There will be times when you will want to perform an update, and then check that the update is correct before finally committing the changes to the table. This is where **transactions** come in, and these are covered next.

Transactions

Transactions within a database are, like a number of areas, a very important topic but also one that requires a great deal of understanding. This chapter covers the basics of transactions, although to really do justice to this area so that the full picture is given, involves dealing with some very complex and in-depth scenarios, covering all manner of areas such as triggers, nesting transactions, and transaction logging. This is covered in an excellent manner in Rob Vieira's *Professional SQL Server 2000 programming* (Wrox Press, ISBN 1-861004-48-6*)*, and you should only tackle complex transactions once you really know how SQL Server works. As a beginner, it's possible that you could in fact create more problems than you solve; but with our rate of progress it won't be long before you're ready to confidently deal with transactions.

If you remember back to Chapter 12, when we were discussing the insertion of data, several records were inserted at the same time, separated by a `GO` command. To recap, this was called **batching**. The insertion of the data still took place straight away, but, if you recall, SQL Server reported back the number of inserts within the batch, rather than one record at a time.

Well, there is another way to batch your work, which also provides you with the option of changing your mind, or, in the event of an error occurring within data modifications, undoing the changes and restoring the columns and rows that have been modified to their original state. This method is used when we place our data modifications within a **transaction**.

A transaction can be placed around any data manipulation, whether it is an update, insertion, or deletion, and can cater for one row or many rows, and also many different commands. There is no need to place a transaction around a `SELECT` statement unless you are doing a `SELECT...INTO`, which is of course, completing data modifications. This is because a transaction is only required when data manipulation occurs such that changes will either be committed to the table or discarded. A transaction could cover several update, delete, or insert commands, or indeed a mixture of all three. However, there is one very large word of warning. Be aware that when creating a transaction, you will be keeping a hold on the whole table or specific rows of information in question, and depending upon how your SQL Server database is set up to lock data during updates, you could be stopping others from updating any information, and you could even cause a **deadlock**, which is also known as a **deadly embrace**.

A deadlock is where two separate data manipulations, in different transactions, are being performed at the same time. However, for each to complete its update within a transaction, it is waiting on the other to complete its transaction first. Neither manipulation can be completed because each is waiting for the other to finish. A deadlock occurs, and it can (and will) lockup the tables and database in question.

In the example below, Transaction 1 is updating the `Society_Groups` table, and now needs to update a record in the `Players` table. However, a second, independent transaction is currently updating the record required by Transaction 1 in the `Players` table, but it now needs to update the record that Transaction 1 is currently updating in the `Society_Groups` table. This is a deadlock, and what would then happen is that one or perhaps both transactions would fail and return an error.

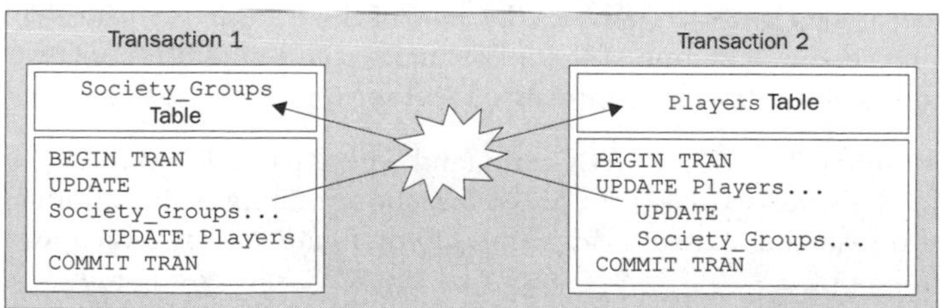

Therefore, it is advisable to keep transactions as small, and as short, as possible, and under no circumstances hold on to a lock for more than a few seconds. We can do this by keeping the processing within a transaction to as few lines of code as possible, and then either roll back or commit the transaction to the database as quickly as possible within code. With every second that we hold a lock through a transaction, we are increasing the potential of trouble happening. In a production environment, with every passing millisecond that we hold on to a piece of information through a lock, we are increasing the chances of someone else trying to modify the same piece of information at the same time, and the problems that would then arise.

A transaction forms a single unit of work, which must pass the **ACID test** before it can be classified as a transaction. The ACID test is an acronym for **Atomicity**, **Consistency**, **Isolation**, and **Durability**.

Atomicity

In its simplest form, all data modifications within the transaction must be both accepted and inserted successfully into the database, or none of the modifications will be performed.

Consistency

Once the data has been successfully applied, or rolled back to the original state, all the data must remain in a consistent state, and the data must still maintain its integrity.

Isolation

Any modification in one transaction must be isolated from any modifications in any other transaction. Any transaction should see data from any other transaction either in its original state, or once the second transaction has completed. It is impossible to see the data in an intermediate state.

Durability

Once a transaction has finished, all data modifications are in place, and can only be modified by another transaction or unit of work. Any system failure (hardware or software), will not remove any changes applied.

There are two parts that make up a transaction, the start of the transaction, and the end of the transaction, where we decide if we want to commit the changes or revert back to the original state. We will now look at the definition of the start of the transaction, and then the T-SQL commands required to commit or roll back the transaction. The basis of this whole section is that there is only one transaction in place, and that there are no nested transactions. Nested transactions are much more complex, and should only really be dealt with once you are confident and proficient with SQL Server.

BEGIN TRAN

The T-SQL command, `BEGIN TRAN`, denotes the start of the transaction processing. From this point on, until the transaction is ended with one of the following two commands, `COMMIT TRAN` or `ROLLBACK TRAN`, any data modification statements processed will form part of the transaction.

It is also possible to suffix the `BEGIN TRAN` command with a name of up to 32 characters in length. If you were to have nested transactions, with one transaction running inside another transaction, then it is only the outermost transaction that you can name. If you name your transaction, it is not necessary to use the name when issuing a `ROLLBACK TRAN` or a `COMMIT TRAN` command.

COMMIT TRAN

The COMMIT TRAN command will commit the data modifications to the database permanently, and there will be no going back once this command is executed. This function should only be executed when all changes to the database are ready to be committed.

ROLLBACK TRAN

If we wished to remove all the database changes that have been completed since the beginning of the transaction, say for example, because an error had occurred, then we could issue a ROLLBACK TRAN command.

To clarify a point, if we were to start a transaction with BEGIN TRAN, and then issue an INSERT which succeeds, and then perhaps an UPDATE which fails, we could issue a ROLLBACK TRAN to rollback the transaction as a whole. As a result, not only are the UPDATE changes rolled back, but because it forms part of the same transaction, the changes made by the INSERT are rolled back as well, even though that particular operation was successful.

> **To reiterate, keep transactions small and short. Never leave a session with an open transaction. Ensure that in your own code you will not cause a deadly embrace. If you issue a BEGIN TRAN then you MUST issue a COMMIT or ROLLBACK transaction as quickly as possible, otherwise the transaction will stay around until the connection is terminated.**

Locking Data

The whole area of locking data, how locks are held, and how to avoid problems with them is a very large, complex area not for the faint hearted. However, it is necessary to be aware of locks, and at least have a small amount of background knowledge so that when designing your queries, you stand a chance of avoiding problems.

The basis of locking is to allow one transaction to update data knowing that if it has to rollback any changes, no other transaction has modified the data since the first transaction did. To explain this with an example, if we have a transaction that updates the Players table, and then moves on to update the Society_Groups table, but hits a problem when updating the Society_Groups table, the transaction must be safe in the knowledge that it is only rolling back the changes it made, and not changes by another transaction. Therefore, until all the table updates within the transaction are either successfully completed or have been rolled back, then the transaction will keep hold of any data inserted, modified, or deleted.

However, there is one problem with this approach, and that is that SQL Server may not just hold the data that the transaction has modified. If it did just keep a lock on the data it had modified, which is called **row-level locking**, SQL Server may be set up to lock the database, which is known as **database-level locking**. There are several levels in between, and so we could lockup a large resource, depending on the task being performed.

This is about as deep as we will take talking about locks, so as not to add any confusion, or create a problematic situation. Dealing with locks is completed automatically by SQL Server, but it is possible to make locking more efficient by developing an effective understanding of the subject, and then customizing the locks within your transactions.

Updating Data – Using Transactions

Now, what if, in the first update query of this chapter, we had made a mistake, or an error occurred? For example, say we chose the wrong society group, or even worse, omitted the WHERE statement and therefore all the records were updated. By using a transaction, we would have had the chance to correct any mistakes easily, and could then revert to a consistent state. Of course, this next example is nice and simple, but by doing this, the subject of transactions will hopefully become a little easier to understand and appreciate.

Try it out – Using a Transaction

1. Query Analyzer should still be running. The first example will demonstrate COMMIT TRAN in action. There should be no difference from an UPDATE without any transaction processing, as it will execute and update the data successfully, however, this should prove to be a valuable exercise, as it will also demonstrate the naming of a transaction. Enter the following code, and then execute it. This will place Lee Smith back as the Society_Group_Leader for Society_Group 5, and also reset its name to Security Blankets. You will then see the Society_Groups table from the SELECT statement, and also that the update has taken place.

```
SET QUOTED_IDENTIFIER OFF
GO

BEGIN TRAN Restore_Value
DECLARE @ValueToUpdate VARCHAR(30)
SET @ValueToUpdate = "Security Blankets"
UPDATE Society_Groups
   SET Society_Group_Desc = @ValueToUpdate,
       Society_Leader_Name = Society_Group_Desc, Games_Won = 0
WHERE Society_Group_ID = 5
COMMIT TRAN

SELECT * FROM Society_Groups
```

2. Notice in the above code, that the COMMIT TRAN does not use the name associated with the BEGIN TRAN. The update has succeeded, and therefore the COMMIT must have worked. This is the output you should see:

```
(1 row(s) affected)

Society_Group_Id Society_Group_Desc   Society_Leader_Name
---------------- -------------------- ------------------------------
1                Kojak Team           Annette Kelly
2                Bedford Junior Blues Jack Mason
3                The Upmarket Traders Jason Atkins
4                Gilbert's Golfers    Martin Aynsley
5                Security Blankets    Lee Smith
6                The Chieftan Coach   Colin Jackson

(6 row(s) affected)
```

3. We are now going to demonstrate a ROLLBACK TRAN. We will take this one stage at a time so that you fully understand and follow the processes involved, and the code will look like that shown below. Note that the WHERE statement has been commented out with --, and that there is a BEGIN TRAN statement. By having the WHERE statement commented out, hopefully, you'll have already guessed that every record in the Society_Groups table is going to be updated. The example needs you to execute all the code, including the SELECT statement, so enter the following code into your query pane, and then execute it.

```
SET QUOTED_IDENTIFIER OFF
GO

BEGIN TRAN
UPDATE Society_Groups
   SET Society_Leader_Name = "Lee Smith"
-- WHERE Society_Group_Desc = "Security blankets"

SELECT * FROM Society_Groups
```

4. If you check on the **Messages** tab below the query pane in the **Results** pane, you will see that there are two messages, both informing you that 6 rows of data have been changed, a bit of a giveaway that something is wrong.

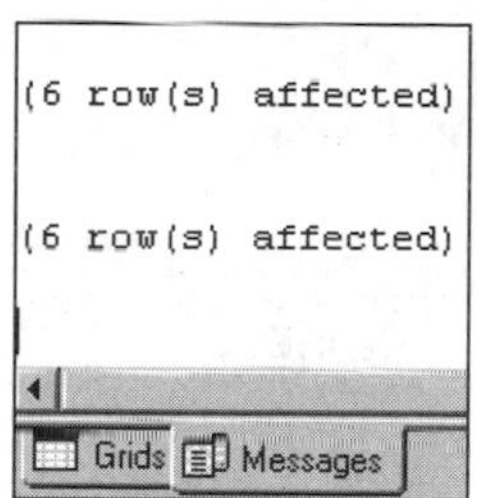

5. Moving back to the **Grids** pane, we see that there is another giveaway that things have gone wrong; all of the **Society_Leader_Names** now say **Lee Smith**. Oops!

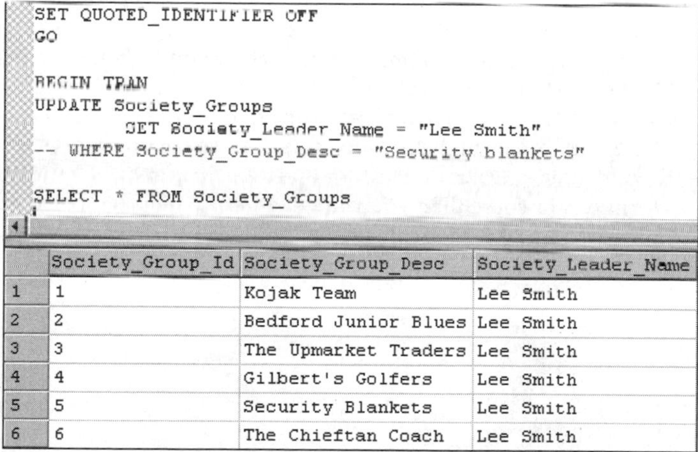

```
SET QUOTED_IDENTIFIER OFF
GO

BEGIN TRAN
UPDATE Society_Groups
        SET Society_Leader_Name = "Lee Smith"
-- WHERE Society_Group_Desc = "Security blankets"

SELECT * FROM Society_Groups
```

	Society_Group_Id	Society_Group_Desc	Society_Leader_Name
1	1	Kojak Team	Lee Smith
2	2	Bedford Junior Blues	Lee Smith
3	3	The Upmarket Traders	Lee Smith
4	4	Gilbert's Golfers	Lee Smith
5	5	Security Blankets	Lee Smith
6	6	The Chieftan Coach	Lee Smith

6. So how are we going to get out of this mess? The answer is the `ROLLBACK TRAN` command, which we discussed just above. Let's try it out right here and now. Enter the following code, which will rollback the changes and then display the contents of the `Society_Groups` table, just to confirm.

```
ROLLBACK TRAN

SELECT * FROM Society_Groups
```

Execute this code once you are ready, which should all be kept within the same query pane. Notice in the following screenshot how the code was entered, highlighted, and then run, as discussed earlier in the chapter. Notice how all the changes have reverted back to as they were.

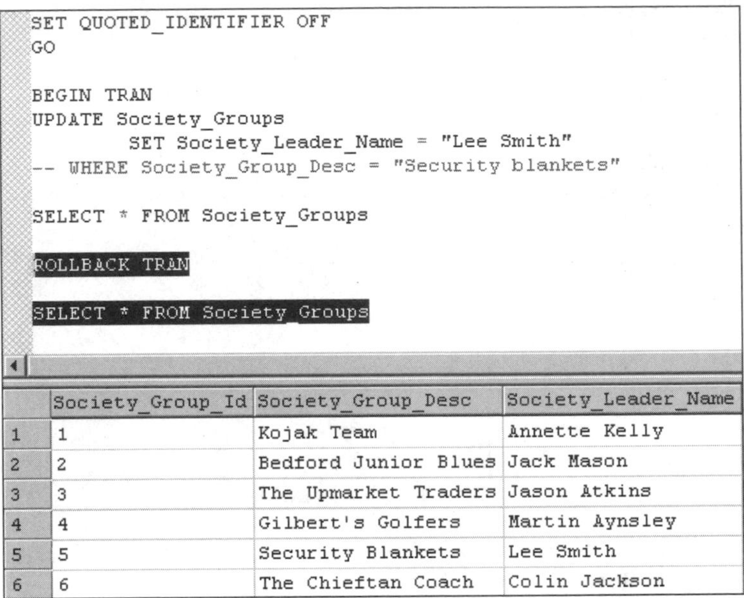

	Society_Group_Id	Society_Group_Desc	Society_Leader_Name
1	1	Kojak Team	Annette Kelly
2	2	Bedford Junior Blues	Jack Mason
3	3	The Upmarket Traders	Jason Atkins
4	4	Gilbert's Golfers	Martin Aynsley
5	5	Security Blankets	Lee Smith
6	6	The Chieftan Coach	Colin Jackson

7. There is one last example to give before moving on. If you have a `BEGIN TRAN` and then a `ROLLBACK TRAN`, there is just no point if in your code you then have a `COMMIT TRAN` command. The `ROLLBACK TRAN` will already have executed, and therefore by default, the end of the transaction will have occurred. This means that there is no corresponding `BEGIN TRAN` for the `COMMIT TRAN` to pair up with. Don't forget a transaction works as a pair of commands, `BEGIN TRAN` with either a `COMMIT TRAN` or a `ROLLBACK TRAN`. Getting back to the example, if you do perform this in code, then you will get an error message returned. Enter the following code, which I admit is simplistic, but demonstrates the problem without becoming confused with other issues.

```
SET QUOTED_IDENTIFIER OFF
GO

BEGIN TRAN Restore_Value
DECLARE @ValueToUpdate VARCHAR(30)
```

```
SET @ValueToUpdate = "Security Blankets"
UPDATE Society_Groups
   SET Society_Group_Desc = @ValueToUpdate
WHERE Society_Group_ID = 5
ROLLBACK TRAN
COMMIT TRAN

SELECT Society_Group_Desc FROM Society_Groups
```

8. When you execute the code above, you will see the following output:

```
(1 row(s) affected)

Server: Msg 3902, Level 16, State 1, Line 9
The COMMIT TRANSACTION request has no corresponding BEGIN TRANSACTION.
Society_Group_Desc
--------------------
Kojak Team
Bedford Junior Blues
The Upmarket Traders
Gilbert's Golfers
Security Blankets
The Chieftan Coach

(6 row(s) affected)
```

Now that you have updating of data sorted, let's now look at what could be a more problematic area, which surrounds the area of working with images.

Updating Image Data Types

Updating the image data type is slightly easier than inserting into the image data type for the first time. If you recall, when inserting into an image data type, a pointer had to already exist within the necessary column of the necessary row, before the data could be inserted. With an update, the pointer already exists, so that is one less hurdle to overcome. However, you will still have to return the row of information first, and retrieve the pointer within the column, before you can update it.

To update an image data type (or `text`, or `ntext` data type for that matter), we would use the `UPDATETEXT` command, however, it's not just an update that this command can perform. You see, we can also delete and insert text depending upon the parameters we use with the `UPDATETEXT` command

The syntax for `UPDATETEXT` differs from `WRITETEXT`, so let's take a look at it here:

```
UPDATETEXT {table_name.dest_column_name_desc_text_ptr}
           {NULL|insert_offset}
           {NULL|delete_length }
[WITH LOG]
   [inserted_data|{table_name.src_column_name src_text_ptr } ]
```

The first part of the syntax is very similar to the `WRITETEXT` command, where we name the column to receive the text, and then the pointer associated with the image, `text`, or `ntext` column. Next comes an optional parameter, `insert_offset`, where we can define the start position for the update to take place. If we specify `NULL`, then we are informing `UPDATETEXT` that we will be appending the new text to the end of the existing text within the column. A value of `0` indicates that we are inserting the data at the beginning, while any other value informs SQL Server that the update is to start at that point.

The next parameter covers the `delete_length`, in other words, the length of the text within the column that the new text is replacing. For example, if we are inserting a string of 10 characters long, but defined this parameter as 20, then the length of the text will drop by 10 characters. A value of `0` defines that no data is deleted, and a value of `NULL` indicates that all the data is deleted from the `insert_offset` to the end.

Finally, we can choose to insert the new data either as a static value, a variable, data from another column, or data from another image, `text`, or `ntext` column providing that we also get the length of the pointer of that column as well.

To replace existing data with new data, we have to define a non-zero value for both the `insert_offset` and the `delete_length`, and then define the text to replace. To delete data from the column, we define a non-zero `insert_offset`, and non-zero `delete_length`, but do not define any text. Finally, to insert new data, we define a non-zero `insert_offset` where the new text should start from, a zero value for `delete_length`, and then the new text.

This next example will demonstrate how simple it can be to insert a new image. You see; problems could arise if we were to get the wrong values in the two data length parameters, but don't fret, we will demonstrate how to get it right. This example will update Ian McMahon's picture with a new image.

Try it out-Updating Images

1. Ensure that Query Analyzer is running, and that you have an updated image to deal with. In this case we will be updating the photograph column with an updated image for Ian McMahon.

2. The following code should be entered in an empty query pane, and then executed. First of all, we will be getting the pointer to where the image path resides. Then we will update the `Photograph` column with the new value, replacing all the text with the new value. The two offset values are set so that the insert point is at character 0, and by using a `NULL` for the data length, we will then be replacing all the text to the end. As a result, we are overwriting all that was there with this new value, whether the string was shorter or longer.

```
DECLARE @Pointer_Value varbinary(16)

SELECT @Pointer_Value = TEXTPTR(Photograph)
FROM Players
WHERE Player_Id = 3

UPDATETEXT Players.Photograph @Pointer_Value 0 NULL "C:\Program Files\Microsoft
SQL Server\MSSQL\Data\Wrox_Golf_Results\Images\im_new.bmp"
```

3. This should return the following result:

    The command(s) completed successfully.

Updating images is very much like inserting an image as demonstrated in the earlier `INSERT` chapter, although instead of using `WRITETEXT`, you'll find that the example has used the `UPDATETEXT` command. Technically, this example should use the `WRITETEXT` command rather than the `UPDATETEXT` command, as `UPDATETEXT` is used to replace a portion of data. As the whole value in this case is to be updated, then the `WRITETEXT` command should have been used.

However, you *can* use the `UPDATETEXT` command. This command has two more parameters than the `WRITETEXT` syntax, and these two extra parameters define the start and end points of the update of the column to be updated.

This whole process can be seen as a bind, and a good deal of code has to be used. This is perhaps one area where a template would be useful, so let's look at that next…

Building Your Own Template

As we've seen, dealing with images can be a bit monotonous, and updating them could be seen as perhaps the most painful aspect of data updating, however, all is not lost! Building a template to insert this data type will lessen the burden, and this section of the chapter will demonstrate how easy it is to build your own template, and where to store it safely

Try it out – Building Your Own Template

1. First of all, we need to create the T-SQL code that will form the basis of the template. We can do this in Query Analyzer, and use it just as a text editor, or if you prefer, we can simply use a basic text editor such as Notepad. Once you've decided which editor to use, simply enter the code as shown below. Notice that there are three comma separated options between each < > pair. These options translate to the three columns displayed within the replace template parameters. The first option is the description of the parameter; the second option is the type of parameter to be defined (which is free formatted, but is used as an indicator of the data type, although the most common value seen is `sysname`). Finally, the third parameter deals with an example of the value to place within that parameter, and where possible, any default value that might be used, or a common value used for a significant number of template creations.

```
-- =============================================
-- Update an image, text or ntext column
-- =============================================
DECLARE @Pointer_Value varbinary(16)

SELECT @Pointer_Value = TEXTPTR(<column_to_update, sysname, Photograph>)
FROM <table_name, sysname, test_table>
WHERE <column_to_find, sysname, find> = <value_to_find_with, sysname, find_value>

UPDATETEXT <table_name, sysname, test_table>.<column_to_update, sysname,
Photograph> @Pointer_Value 0 NULL <where_image_is_stored, sysname, "Image Path">
```

2. Now click **File | Save as**. This should bring up the **Save as** dialog. Navigate to the following folder (or wherever you have installed SQL Server): `C:\Program Files\Microsoft SQL Server\80\Tools\Templates\SQL Query Analyzer`.

   Once there, click on the **Create New Folder** button.

3. Create a meaningful name for the folder. For our examples, we will create a folder called **My Own Templates**.

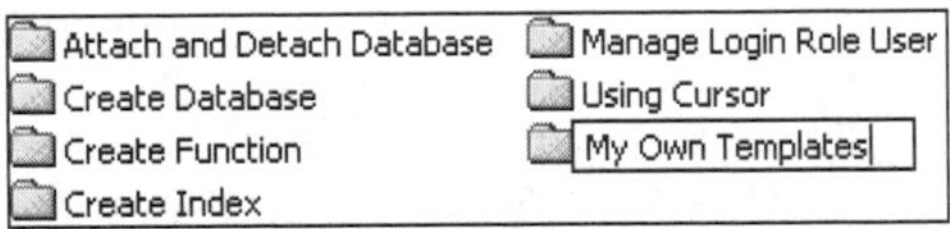

4. Now create a name for the template, change the save as type to Template, and click **Save**, noticing that this file has a `tql` file extension.

5. This saves the template in the correct tree structure for the SQL Server Query Analyzer to find the template. Although the process is just a little more involved, we can in fact save our template wherever we want. If we want to store our template in a different directory to the default, then we simply need to inform Query Analyzer where we've stored it. This can be done from **Tools | Options** on the menu bar, which brings up the **Options** dialog in which we would then need to alter the **Template file directory:** to that of our new directory. Once

Altering the directory will also remove the pointer to where the other templates are stored; as a result, you would either have to lose the other templates from within Query Analyzer, or move the templates to the new directory.

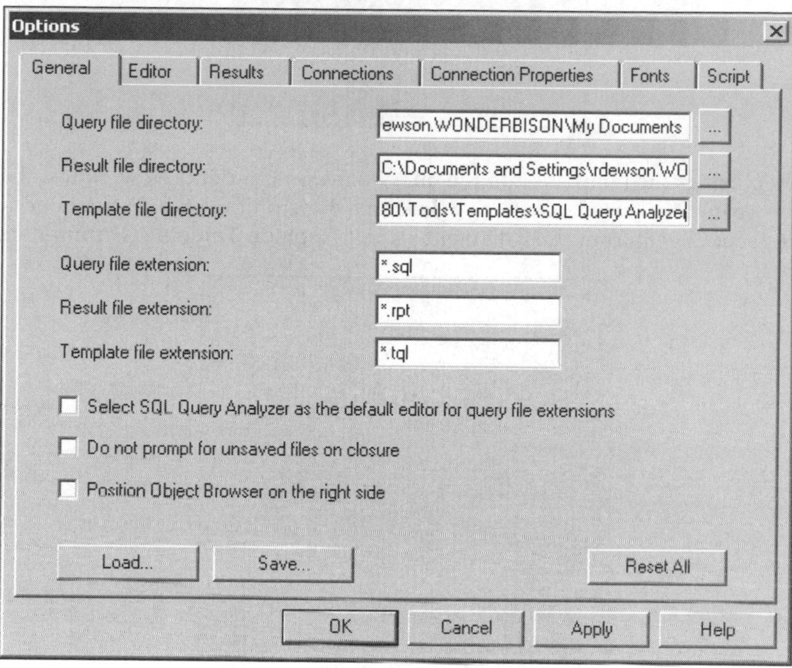

6. Switch to Query Analyzer, and select the **Templates** tab. On this tab, press *F5*, which will then refresh the browser to show the new template.

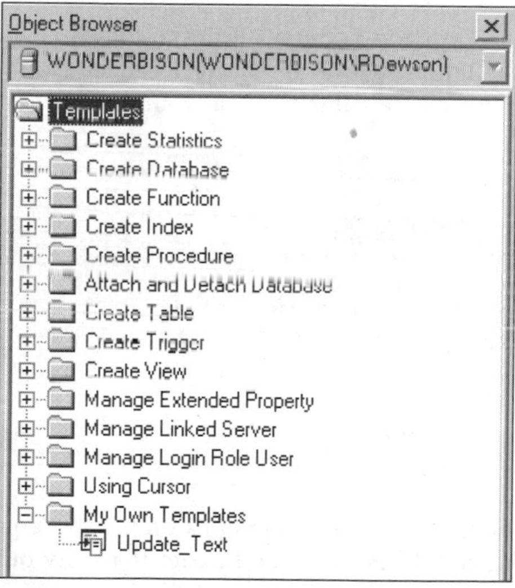

7. Notice that the Update_Text template is now sitting nicely within the My Own Templates node. Now select it, right click, and then select Open.

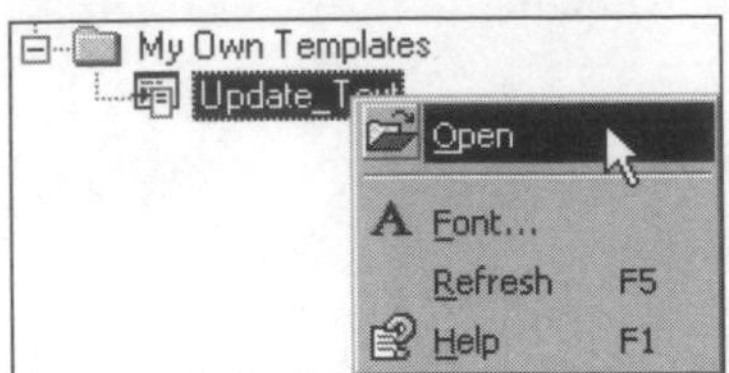

8. This then brings the template into the query pane on the right. Now, to test that the template that we created now works correctly, click anywhere on the code in the query pane, so that it has the focus. Then, from the Edit menu, select Replace Template Parameters.

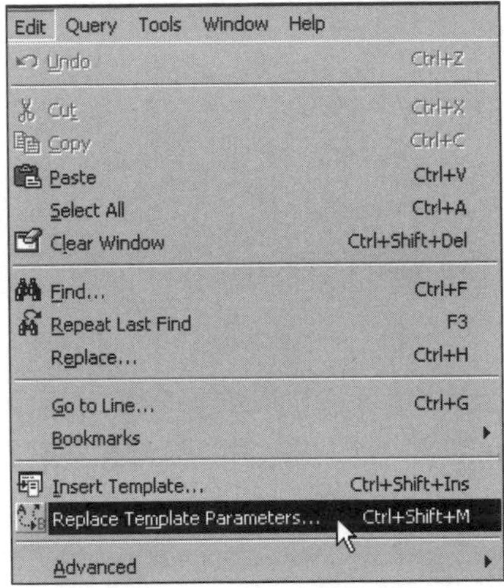

9. This then brings up the Replace Template Parameters dialog box. Alter the parameters as necessary to update the template with the correct values. Don't forget when entering the path to the image, that it requires the value to be surrounded by quotation marks.

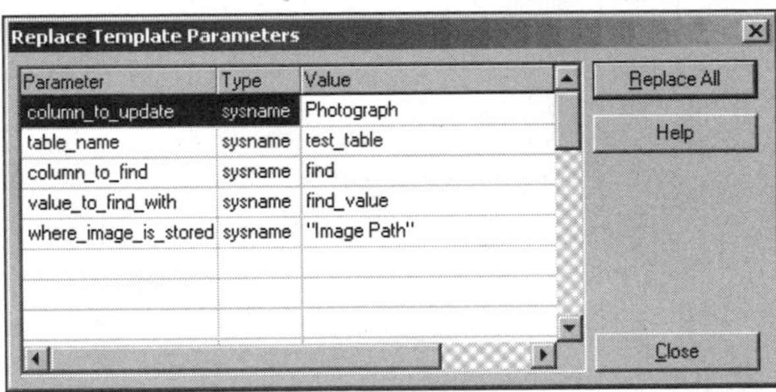

Parameter	Type	Value
column_to_update	sysname	Photograph
table_name	sysname	test_table
column_to_find	sysname	find
value_to_find_with	sysname	find_value
where_image_is_stored	sysname	"Image Path"

10. Once finished, click Replace All, and then click on Close. You will then have the right information. This should be faster and easier than any other method of coding the update of images.

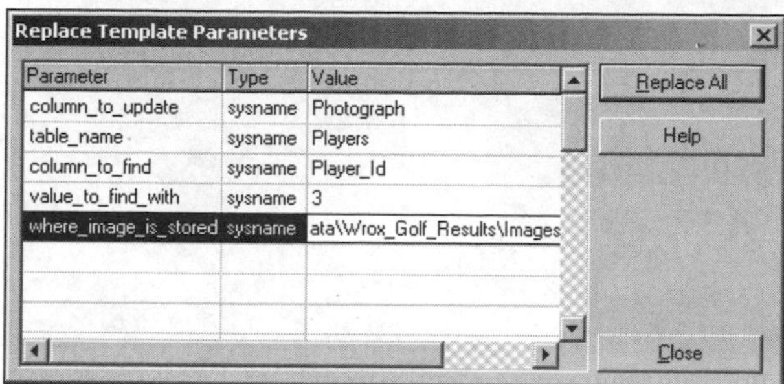

11. This will then create the following correct T-SQL code to update an image. Much faster!

```
-- =============================================
-- Update an image, text or ntext column
-- =============================================
DECLARE @Pointer_Value varbinary(16)

SELECT @Pointer_Value = TEXTPTR(Photograph)
FROM Players
WHERE Player_Id = 3

UPDATETEXT Players.Photograph @Pointer_Value 0 NULL "C:\Program Files\Microsoft SQL
Server\MSSQL\Data\Wrox_Golf_Results\Images\im_new.bmp"
```

Summary

Updating data can go wrong, and does, especially when you are working in a live environment and you wish to update data that is in flux. In such a scenario, getting the correct rows of information to update and then actually updating them is akin to a fine art.

Therefore, surrounding any of your work with a transaction will prevent any costly and potentially irretrievable mistakes from taking place, so always surround data modifications or deletions with a transaction. With data inserts, it is not quite so critical that you surround your work with a transaction, although it is recommended. For example, if you are inserting data within a test environment and the data insertion is easily removed if you have part of the insertion wrong, then perhaps it's not overly critical to use a transaction, although to be safe, really and truly, I still recommend that you use a transaction.

Updating columns within a table is very straightforward. As long as the data type defined for the column to update is the same as, or is compatible with, the data type of the column, variable, or static value that is being used to update this column, then you will find no problem. For example, you can update a `varchar` column with `char` data type values. However, it is not possible to update an `integer` column with a `varchar` value that has a non-integer value, without converting the `varchar` value to an `integer`. But don't be fooled, you can update a `varchar` with an `integer` or `numeric` data type. But if you do need to perform a conversion, then these commands and areas are covered in Appendix C where there are examples of not only data conversions, but also other data manipulation commands.

Now that updating data has been completed, the only area of data manipulation left is row deletion, which comes in the next chapter.

Deleting Data

This will perhaps be one of the shortest chapters in the book as deleting data is very straightforward, especially after covering all of the other data manipulation functions in other chapters, particularly transactions and basic SQL. Before delving into this chapter, we must be aware that deleting data without the use of a transaction is almost a final act: the only way to get the data back is to either re-enter it, restore it from a back up, or retrieve the data from any audit tables that had the data stored in them when the data was created. Deleting data is not like using the recycle bin on a Windows machine: unless the data is within a transaction, it is lost. Keep in mind that even if you use a transaction, the data will be lost once the transaction is committed also. That's why it's very important to back up your database before running any major data modifications.

This chapter will demonstrate the `DELETE` T-SQL syntax and then show how to use this within Query Analyzer. It is also possible to delete records from the results pane within Enterprise Manager; this will also be demonstrated.

However, what about when we want to remove all the records within a table, especially when there could be thousands of records to remove? We will find that the `DELETE` command takes a very long time to run. Luckily there is a command for this scenario, called `TRUNCATE`, which is covered at the end of the chapter. However, there are words of caution with the use of this command, and these also are covered at the end of the chapter.

The aim of this chapter is to ensure that we are aware of:

- The syntax for the `DELETE` command
- How to use this command in T-SQL
- How to remove records within Enterprise Manager
- The pitfalls of the `TRUNCATE` command

First of all, it is necessary to know the simple syntax for the `DELETE` command for deleting records from a table. Really, things don't come much simpler than this.

DELETE Syntax

The DELETE command is very short and sweet. To run the command, simply state the table you wish to delete records from, as shown below:

```
DELETE
FROM tablename
WHERE where_condition
```

The FROM condition is optional, so your syntax could easily read:

```
DELETE tablename
WHERE where_condition
```

There is nothing within this command that has not been covered in other chapters. The only area that really needs to be mentioned is that records can only be deleted from one table at a time.

As there is so little to say about the DELETE syntax, let's dive right in with an example.

The DELETE Statement

Rather than delete data from the tables built within the book, if we recall from Chapter 13, the *Retrieving Data* chapter, a table was created with the SELECT INTO command. This was the Society_Groups_Temp table. It is from this table that the data will be removed.

The second point to note is that transactions will be used a great deal here to avoid having to keep inserting data back into the table. It's a good idea to use transactions for any type of table modification in your application. Imagine that you're at the ATM and you deposit money. During that process, a transaction built up of many actions is used to make sure that your money doesn't credit one system and not the other. If an error occurs, the entire transaction rolls back and no money changes hands.

For another example, imagine that a user accidentally powers off their computer in the middle of an equally crucial process without a transaction. At that point, their data is logically corrupt. If this were to happen in an ordering system, we may have the accounting system showing a debit from the customer but the order table may not show an order.

Make sure you keep your SQL very clean when doing transactions. This means that if we begin a transaction, we must make sure that we always issue some type of COMMIT or ROLLBACK statement somewhere in the transaction. A COMMIT TRAN statement, as you may remember, writes the data to the database, while the ROLLBACK TRAN statement undoes the modification. If we run a query in Query Analyzer that modifies data and doesn't have one of these two commands somewhere in the transaction, we risk causing a locking problem in our database. For example, let's take a look at what happens if we were to run this statement:

Don't actually run this code or you'll delete all the records from our table!

```
BEGIN TRAN
   DELETE Society_Group_Temp
```

If we were to run this, we would open a transaction and then tentatively delete all the records from the `Society_Group_Temp` table. The records are not actually deleted until a `COMMIT TRAN` statement is issued. In the interim though, SQL Server will place a lock on the table and prevent other users from reading bad data that is in the process of being deleted. Because of this lock, all users trying to read or modify data from this table will have to wait until a `COMMIT TRAN` or `ROLLBACK TRAN` statement has been issued. If one is never issued, a user will have to wait indefinitely. This is known as a blocking, as discussed in the previous chapter. This problem is one of a number of issues frequently encountered in applications when analyzing performance issues.

So, time to start deleting records.

Try It Out – Deleting Records

1. First of all, let's switch to outputting **Results to Text** by pressing *Ctrl+T* in Query Analyzer.

2. Ensure that Query Analyzer is running and that the query pane is empty. Enter the following command, which will remove all the records within a transaction, prove the point by using a new command that can be included in a `SELECT` statement, and then roll back the changes so that the records are put back into the table. Once the code is entered, execute the code using the normal method.

```
BEGIN TRAN
   SELECT COUNT(*) FROM Society_Group_Temp
   DELETE Society_Group_Temp
   SELECT COUNT(*) FROM Society_Group_Temp
ROLLBACK TRAN
SELECT COUNT(*) FROM Society_Group_Temp
```

3. Once executed, you should see the following results. Notice that the number of records in the `Society_Group_Temp` table before the delete is 5, then after the delete the record count is tentatively set to 0. Finally, after the rollback it's set back to 5. If we were not to issue a `ROLLBACK TRAN` command in here we would see 0 records, but other connections would be deadlocked.

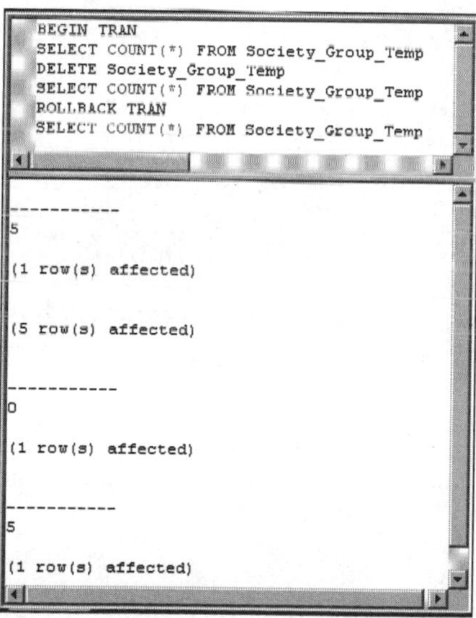

4. Let's take this a stage further and only remove the last three records of the table. Again this will be within a transaction. Alter the code that was there before, as indicated below, and then execute it.

```
BEGIN TRAN
SELECT * FROM Society_Group_Temp
DELETE FROM Society_Group_Temp
WHERE Society_Group_ID > 3
SELECT * FROM Society_Group_Temp
ROLLBACK TRAN
SELECT * FROM Society_Group_Temp
```

5. This will produce the following results:

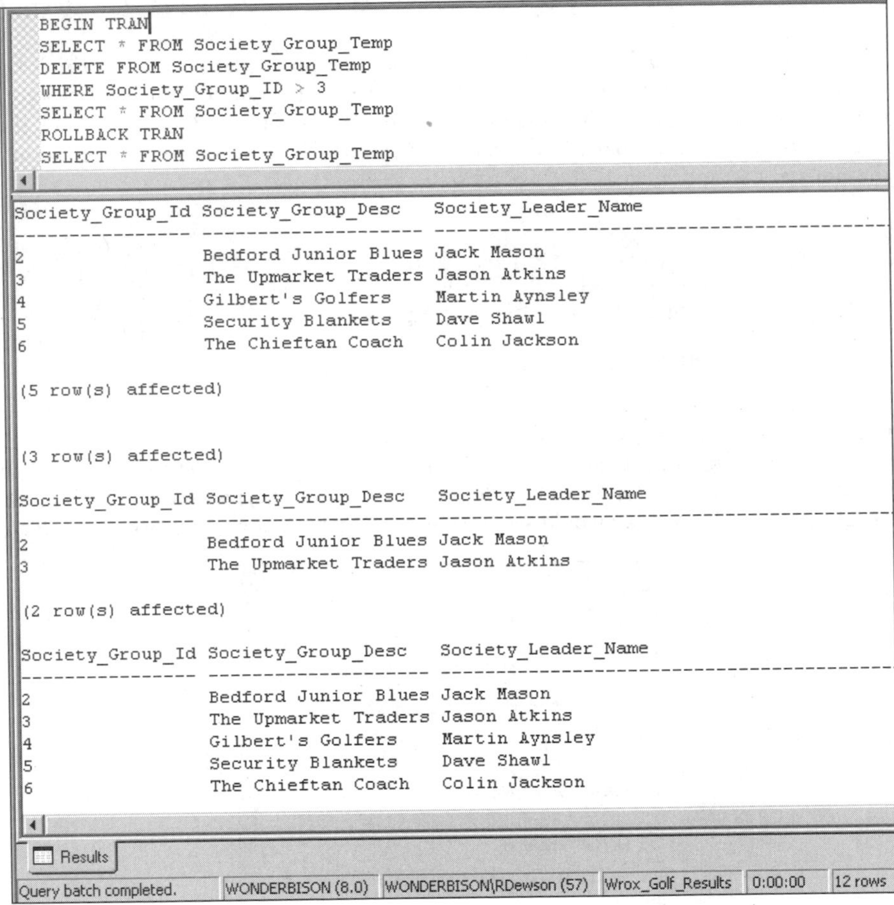

```
BEGIN TRAN
SELECT * FROM Society_Group_Temp
DELETE FROM Society_Group_Temp
WHERE Society_Group_ID > 3
SELECT * FROM Society_Group_Temp
ROLLBACK TRAN
SELECT * FROM Society_Group_Temp
```

```
Society_Group_Id Society_Group_Desc   Society_Leader_Name
---------------- -------------------- ------------------------------------------
2                Bedford Junior Blues Jack Mason
3                The Upmarket Traders Jason Atkins
4                Gilbert's Golfers    Martin Aynsley
5                Security Blankets    Dave Shawl
6                The Chieftan Coach   Colin Jackson

(5 row(s) affected)


(3 row(s) affected)

Society_Group_Id Society_Group_Desc   Society_Leader_Name
---------------- -------------------- ------------------------------------------
2                Bedford Junior Blues Jack Mason
3                The Upmarket Traders Jason Atkins

(2 row(s) affected)

Society_Group_Id Society_Group_Desc   Society_Leader_Name
---------------- -------------------- ------------------------------------------
2                Bedford Junior Blues Jack Mason
3                The Upmarket Traders Jason Atkins
4                Gilbert's Golfers    Martin Aynsley
5                Security Blankets    Dave Shawl
6                The Chieftan Coach   Colin Jackson
```

Results

Query batch completed. | WONDERBISON (8.0) | WONDERBISON\RDewson (57) | Wrox_Golf_Results | 0:00:00 | 12 rows

6. As you can see, any type of `WHERE` clause will work. If you wanted to use a `LIKE` qualifier, you could use a query like the one below, which would remove Bedford Junior Blues record in this case:

```
BEGIN TRAN
SELECT * FROM Society_Group_Temp
DELETE FROM Society_Group_Temp
WHERE Society_Group_Desc LIKE 'Bed%'
SELECT * FROM Society_Group_Temp
ROLLBACK TRAN
```

```
BEGIN TRAN
SELECT * FROM Society_Group_Temp
DELETE FROM Society_Group_Temp
WHERE Society_Group_Desc LIKE 'Bed%'
SELECT * FROM Society_Group_Temp
ROLLBACK TRAN
```

	Society_Group_Id	Society_Group_Desc	Society_Leader_Name
1	2	Bedford Junior Blues	Jack Mason
2	3	The Upmarket Traders	Jason Atkins
3	4	Gilbert's Golfers	Martin Aynsley
4	5	Security Blankets	Dave Shawl
5	6	The Chieftan Coach	Colin Jackson

	Society_Group_Id	Society_Group_Desc	Society_Leader_Name
1	3	The Upmarket Traders	Jason Atkins
2	4	Gilbert's Golfers	Martin Aynsley
3	5	Security Blankets	Dave Shawl
4	6	The Chieftan Coach	Colin Jackson

Transaction Log Activity

Once records are deleted and committed, they are gone. There is one last failsafe though: the action is recorded in the transaction log. That's why it is very important to keep regular transaction log backups so that you can undo to a given point in time. It is possible, using the MARK clause, to set a "bookmark" in your transaction log before you issue a large data update. This command provides you with a safety net when updating data. To use it, you would include the WITH MARK clause in your transaction as shown in the following syntax.

```
BEGIN TRAN MassDelete WITH MARK 'Update Mass Records'
GO
DELETE Society_Group_Temp
COMMIT TRANSACTION MassDelete
```

You can then restore the transaction log to the moment before or after the "bookmark". There are also programs like LogExplorer that can view the transaction log to rollback individual committed records. This comes in handy when an employee forgets his or her WHERE clause in their DELETE statement, inadvertently deleting all records in the table. Selectively marking transaction logs is an advanced topic and if you'd like more details on it, please read *"Professional SQL Server 2000 Programming" (Wrox Press, ISBN 1-861004-48-6).*

TOP Clause in DELETE Statements

Another handy clause you can use in delete statements is the TOP clause. As you may remember, the TOP clause will return a given percentage or exact number of records from a table. If you have a large table with millions of records in it from which you'd like to delete records in batches, you can use the TOP command to do so. There's a slight trick to it though. The following syntax shows how to delete the top 3 records from our table. The trick is that we must join the table to itself, as you can see with the Society_Group_Temp1 table join below:

```
DELETE Society_Group_Temp
FROM (SELECT TOP 3 * FROM Society_Group_Temp) AS Society_Group_Temp1
WHERE Society_Group_Temp. Society_Group_ID =
      Society_Group_Temp1. Society_Group_ID
```

This leaves the Society_Group_Temp table with only 2 records, which are displayed below:

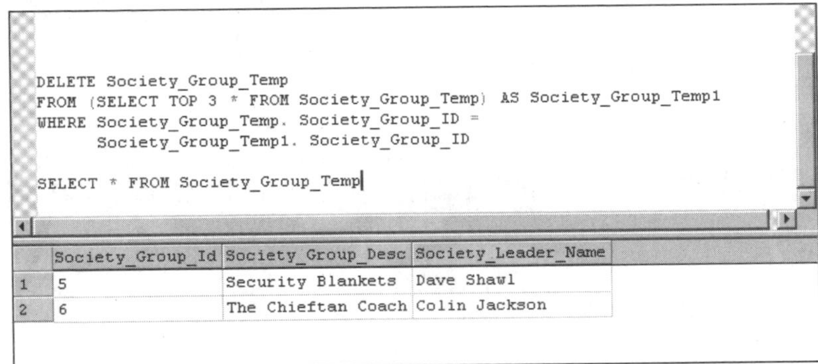

Using Enterprise Manager to Delete Rows

It is also possible to remove records from within Enterprise Manager. This is just as simple as using Query Analyzer, as the following example will demonstrate.

Try It Out – Deleting Rows in Enterprise Manager

1. Switch to Enterprise Manager, navigate to the Wrox_Golf_Results database and find the Society_Group_Temp table. Right-click on it, select **Open Table** and then **Return all rows**.

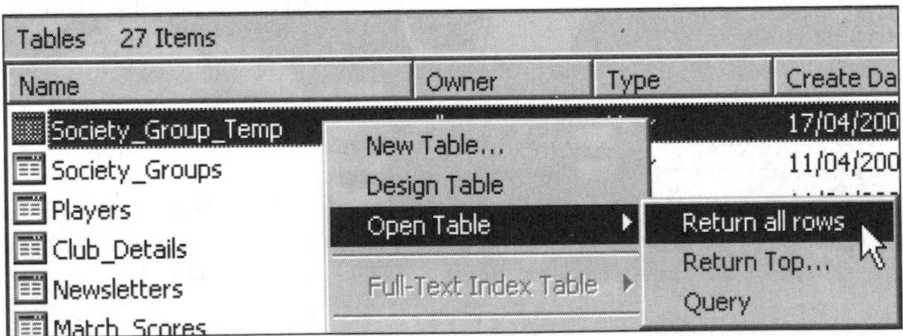

2. This will then return all the rows in the Society_Group_Temp table. Highlight the whole row of data by clicking in the grey column to the left of the Society_Group_Id of the row to delete. In the example, this is the top row.

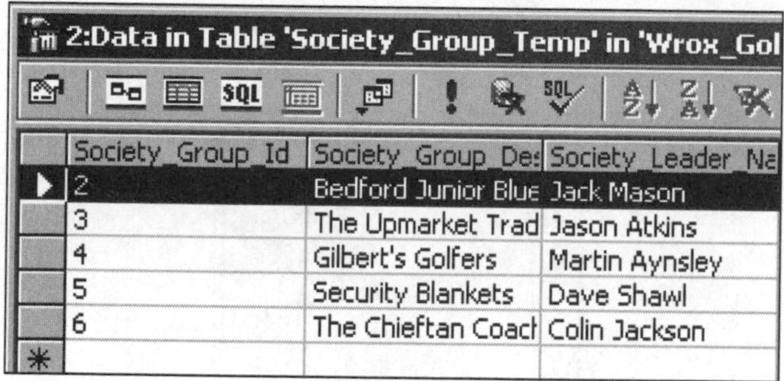

2:Data in Table 'Society_Group_Temp' in 'Wrox_Gol
Society_Group_Id
Society_Group_Des
Society_Leader_Na
2 Bedford Junior Blue Jack Mason
3 The Upmarket Trad Jason Atkins
4 Gilbert's Golfers Martin Aynsley
5 Security Blankets Dave Shawl
6 The Chieftan Coach Colin Jackson

3. Now press the *Delete* key on your keyboard. This will then bring up the following dialog. To remove the record, click Yes.

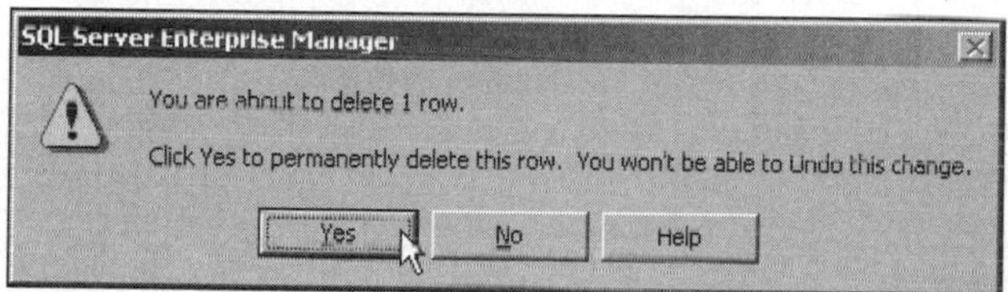

4. This will return you back to the queried data, but the row deleted will already be missing.

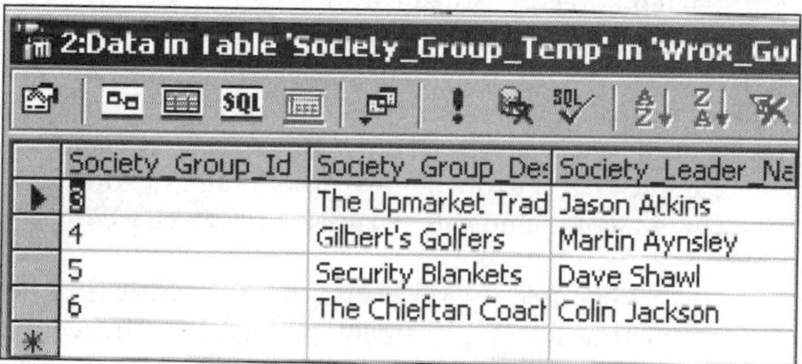

2:Data in Table 'Society_Group_Temp' in 'Wrox_Gol
Society_Group_Id
Society_Group_Des
Society_Leader_Na
3 The Upmarket Trad Jason Atkins
4 Gilbert's Golfers Martin Aynsley
5 Security Blankets Dave Shawl
6 The Chieftan Coach Colin Jackson

5. Another way to remove a record is to right-click on the record that you wish to delete and choose **Delete** from the pop-up menu that appears (near the bottom). Selecting this will indicate to SQL Server that it is this row that is to be removed.

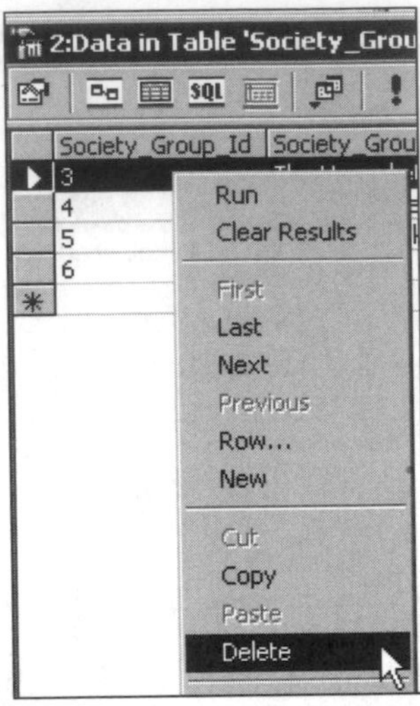

Truncate Table

As we have just seen, all delete actions caused by `DELETE` statements are recorded in the transaction log. Each time a record is deleted, a record is made of that fact. If you are deleting millions of records before committing your transaction, your transaction log can grow quickly. Recall the from the previous chapter the discussions about transactions; now think about this a bit more. What if the table we are deleting from has thousands of records? That is a great deal of logging going on within the transaction log. But what if the deletion of these thousands of records was, in fact, cleaning out all the data from the table to start afresh? Seems a lot of overhead when we don't really need to keep a log of the data deletions anyway. This is where a command called **`TRUNCATE TABLE`** comes in to its own.

By issuing a `TRUNCATE TABLE` statement, we are instructing SQL Server to delete every record within a database, without any logging or transaction processing taking place. In reality, minimal data is logged about what data pages have been de-allocated. The deletion of the records can be almost instantaneous, and a great deal faster than using the `DELETE` command.

The syntax for truncating a table is simple. To truncate a table, use the following command:

```
TRUNCATE TABLE Society_Group_Temp
```

Use the TRUNCATE TABLE statement with extreme caution: there is no going back after the transaction is committed; we cannot change our minds. Also every record is removed: we cannot use this command to selectively remove some of the records. Only use this command as a last resort.

This command is often used when trying to delete large tables (like a table that logs the amount of web hits). For example, `TRUNCATE TABLE` will delete data from a table with millions of records in only a few seconds, whereas using `DELETE` to remove all the records on the same table would take several minutes.

Another benefit to the `TRUNCATE TABLE` clause is that it reseeds any identity columns. For example, say that you have a table with an identity column that is currently at 2,000,000. After truncating the table, the first inserted piece of data will produce the value 1 (if the seed is set to 1). If you issue a `DELETE` command in order to delete the records from the table, the first piece of data inserted after the table contents have been deleted will produce a value of 2,000,001, even though this newly inserted piece of data may be the only record in the table!

One of the limitations with this command is that you cannot issue it against tables that have foreign keys referencing them. For example, the `Orders` table in the `Northwind` database has the `Order Details` table referencing it. If you try to issue the following command:

```
USE NORTHWIND
GO
TRUNCATE TABLE Orders
```

You will receive the following error message:

```
Server: Msg 4712, Level 16, State 1, Line 1
Cannot truncate table 'ORDERS' because it is being referenced by a FOREIGN KEY
constraint.
```

Dropping the Table

Another way to quickly delete the data in a table is to just delete the table and recreate it. Don't forget that if you do this, you will need to also recreate any constraints, indexes and foreign keys. When you do this, SQL Server will de-allocate the table, which is minimally logged. To drop a table in SQL Server, issue the following command:

```
DROP TABLE Society_Group_Temp
```

As with `TRUNCATE TABLE`, `DROP TABLE` cannot be issued against a table that has a foreign key referencing it. In this situation, either the foreign key constraint referencing the table or the referencing table itself must first be dropped, before it is possible to `DROP` the original table.

Summary

The DELETE command in this chapter completes the commands for data retrieval and manipulation. From this point, SQL Server is your oyster and should be no stopping you now. Deleting data is a very straightforward process, perhaps too straightforward, and with no recycle bin you really do have to take care. Having to reinstate data is a lot harder than having to remove records inserted incorrectly or changing back modifications completed in error.

Whenever deleting data (no matter how small the recordset is), it is strongly recommend that a transaction is used and this chapter has demonstrated how to use a transaction and also that a SELECT statement is included to check your work.

Finally the removal of every record within a table was also shown, along with the dire warnings if you got it wrong. Really, only use the TRUNCATE TABLE command in development or with the utmost extreme care within production.

So where can you go from here? The next chapter will look at views of data.

Building a View

A view is a virtual table that, in itself, doesn't contain any data or information. All it contains is the query that the user defines when creating the view. You can think of a view as a stored query. Views are used as a security measure by restricting users to certain columns or rows, as a method of joining data from multiple tables and presenting it as if it resides in one table, and to return summary data instead of detailed data.

Building a simple view is a straightforward process and can be completed in Enterprise Manager or Query Analyzer within SQL Server 2000. Each of these tools has two options to build a view, and all four options are covered in detail so that you are conversant with building a view no matter which tool is currently to hand.

To give things a bit more bite in this chapter, a query within a query, known as a **subquery**, will also be demonstrated, along with how to build a subquery to create a column.

Finally, placing an index on a view can speed up data retrieval but it also can give performance problems as well. An index on a view is not as quite as straightforward as building an index on a table.

The aim of this chapter is to:

- Make you aware of what a view is
- Inform you as to how views can improve a database's security
- Show how to encrypt your view so that the source tables accessed cannot be seen
- Demonstrate building a view using:
    - Enterprise Manager View Designer
    - Enterprise Manager Create a View Wizard
    - Query Analyzer and T-SQL
    - Query Analyzer, T-SQL using a Template
- How to join two tables within a view
- Demonstrate subqueries within a view
- Build an index on a view and give the reasons as to why you would or would not do this

What is a View?

There will be times when we want to group together data from more than one table, or perhaps only allow users to see specific information from a particular table, where some of the columns may contain sensitive or even irrelevant data. A view can take one or more columns from one or more tables and present this information to a user, without the user accessing the actual table itself. A view protects the data layer while allowing access to the data. All of these scenarios can be seen as the basis and reason for building a view rather than another method of data extraction. If you are familiar with Access, views are similar to "Queries".

Let's take a look at how a view works. Let's assume that you have an Employee table that holds information about an employee such as their first name, last name, social security number, date of birth, address, and telephone number. There will be times when you want your users to have access to only the first and last names but not the other sensitive data like social security numbers and addresses. This is where a view comes into play. You would create a view that returns only an employee's first and last name but no other information. Look at the following diagram. The Employee table holds the physical data. We create the Employee Information View that will return the employee's first and last names but not the other data. When we run the view, a virtual table is returned that only contains the first and last names.

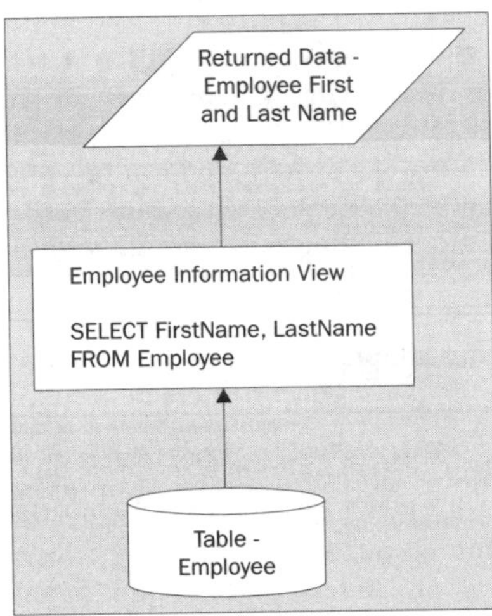

Creating a view can give a user enough information to satisfy a query they may have about data within a database without them having to know any T-SQL commands. A view actually stores the query that creates it and when you execute the view the underlying query is the code that is being executed.

From a view, in addition to retrieving data, you can also modify the data that is being displayed, delete data, and in some situations insert new data. There are several rules and limitations for deleting, modifying, and inserting data from multitable views. We will cover some of these limitations in a section later in the chapter.

However, what a view is not, is a tool for being able to process data using a number of T-SQL commands, like a stored procedure can. A view is only able to hold one query at a time. Therefore a view is more like a query than a stored procedure. Just like a stored procedure or a query within the Query Analyzer, you can also include tables from databases that are running on different servers. Providing the user ID has the necessary security, it is possible to include tables from several databases.

So to summarize, a view is a virtual table created by a stored SQL statement that can span across multiple tables. They can be used as a method of security within your database, and provide a simpler front end to a user when they are querying the data.

Later in the chapter you will see how to build a view and how all of these ideas are put into practice. However, let's look in more depth at how a view can be used as a security vehicle.

Using Views as Security

Security is always an issue when building your database. So far the book has covered the different roles, when to use them, how to set up different types, and how powerful they are. In Chapter 12, security was discussed further, as well as how these roles could be used to tie down access to tables. By restricting all users from accessing or modifying the data in the tables, you will then force everyone to use views and stored procedures to complete any data task. There will be more on stored procedures in the next chapter.

However taking a view on the data and assigning which role can have view access, or update access and so on, you are not only protecting the underlying tables, but also particular columns of data. This is all covered in the security sections of this chapter.

Security does not only encompass the protection of data, but also the protection of your system. There will be a time at some point as a developer when you will build a view and then someone else will come along and remove or alter a column from an underlying table that was used in the view. This causes problems; however, this chapter will show you how to get around this problem and secure the build of a view so that this sort of thing doesn't happen.

Imagine that we have a table holding specific security-sensitive information alongside general information – an example would be where we perhaps work for the licensing agency for driver licenses and alongside the name and address, there is a column to define the number of fines that have had to be paid. As you can see, this is information that should not be viewed by all employees within the organization. So, what do we do?

The simplest answer is to create a view on the data where we exclude the columns holding the sensitive data. In this way, we can restrict access on the table to the barest of minimum of roles or logins, and leave either a view, or a stored procedure as the only method of data retrieval allowed. This way, the information returned is restricted to only those columns that a general user is allowed to see.

It is also possible to place a `WHERE` statement within a view to restrict the rows returned. This could be useful when you don't wish all employee salaries to be listed: perhaps excluding the salaries of the top executives would be advised!

All of these methods give us, as developers, a method for protecting the physical data lying in the base tables behind the views. Combine this with what we learned with roles, and restricting table access, and we can really tighten down on the security surrounding our data.

Another method of securing views and the data is to encrypt the view.

Encrypting Views

As well as restricting access to certain tables or columns within a database, views also give the option of encrypting the query that is used to retrieve the data. Once a view is built and we are happy that it is functioning correctly, we would release that view to production; it is at this point that we would add the final area of security – we would encrypt the view.

The most common situation where we will find views encrypted is when the information returned by the view is of a privileged nature. To expand further, not only are we using a view to return specific information, we also don't wish anyone to see *how* that information was returned, for whatever reason. We would therefore encrypt the SQL code that makes up the view, which would mean that how the information was being returned would not be visible.

There is a downside to encrypting a view: once the process of encryption is completed, there is no way we can get back the details of the view. Therefore, if we need to modify the view, we will find that it is impossible: we have to delete the view and re-create it. If we build a view and encrypt it, we should make sure that we keep a copy of the source somewhere. This is why it is recommended that encrypted views should be used with care, and really should only be placed in production, or at worst, in user testing.

> **Always keep a copy of the original view, before encryption, in the company's source control system, for example SourceSafe, and make sure that there are regular backups.**

Now that we have touched upon the security issues behind views, it is time to start creating views for the database solution that we are building together.

Creating a View – Enterprise Manager

The first task for us is to create a view using Enterprise Manager. This is perhaps the simplest solution as it allows us to use "drag and drop" to build the view. This may be the slowest method for creating a new view, but it does give us the greatest visual flexibility for building the view, and this may also be the best method for dealing with views that already exist and require only minor modifications.

The view designer can aid you in the design, or modification of any view built. For example, it can assist if you trying to build a complex view from a simple view, or it can even be used as a trial and error tool while you are gaining your T-SQL knowledge.

However, enough of the background – let's take a look at how the View Designer works.

Try It Out – Creating a View in Enterprise Manager

1. Ensure that SQL Server Enterprise Manager is running, and that the `Wrox_Golf_Results` database is expanded.

2. Find the Views node, and right-click on it – this brings up the pop-up menu as shown below; from there select New View...

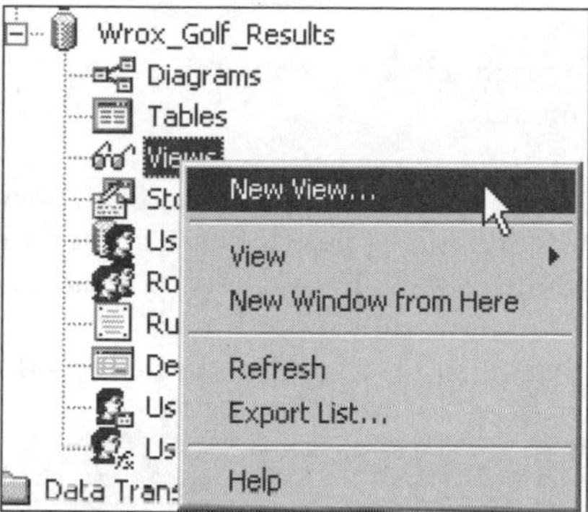

3. The next screen you will see is the **View Designer**. Although pretty empty at the moment, it is a busy screen with a lot of areas for information. It is within the View Designer that all of the information required to build a view will take its place. There are no tables in the view at this time, so there is nothing for the View Designer to show. For those of you who are familiar with Access, you will see that the View Designer is similar to the Access Query Designer, only a bit more sophisticated!

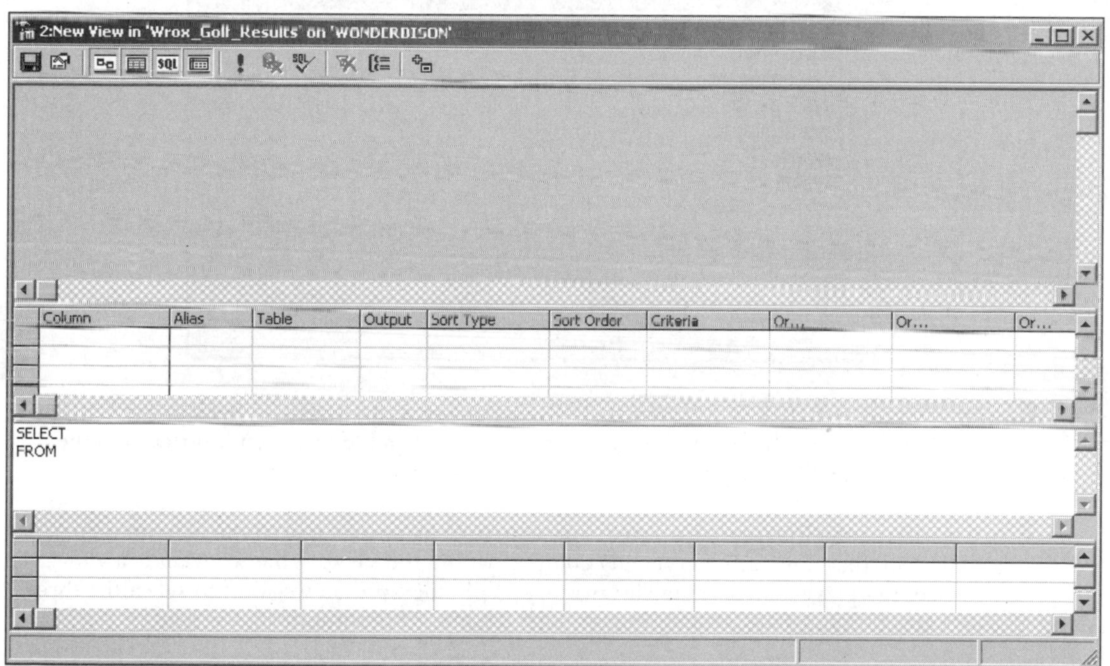

4. On the toolbar at the top of the view designer screen, the rightmost icon allows tables that exist within the Wrox_Golf_Results database to be added to the designer (as well as views and functions, but this is not our focus here). As indicated earlier in the chapter, you can also use tables from other databases; this book does not cover that, so we will be sticking with tables only from the Wrox_Golf_Results database. Click the icon so that you can add new tables.

This can also be done by right-clicking in the top pane (of this window) and selecting Add table from the pop-up menu.

5. The dialog for adding tables appears. Once again, SQL Server lists the system tables, without the ability to hide them in the dialog (recall that Chapter 9 mentioned that we could switch this option off for the whole server). Fortunately, our tables are at the top of the list with only one system table caught in the middle, and so they can be found very easily. The Players table is the one that we want, so highlight this and click Add.

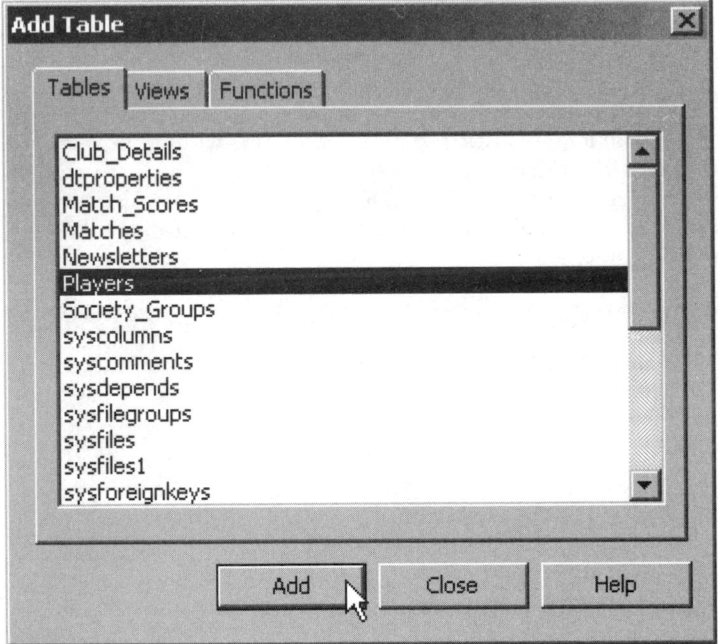

6. Once done, just click Close, which closes this dialog and places you back in the Enterprise Manager designer. You will then find that the Players table has been inserted into the Diagram pane.

7. We will see the Players table listed, but with no ticks against any of the column names, indicating that there are not yet any columns within the view. What we want is a view that will display the player's first name, last name, and photograph. So we want to select the three columns (Player_First_Name, Player_Last_Name, Photograph) shown next.

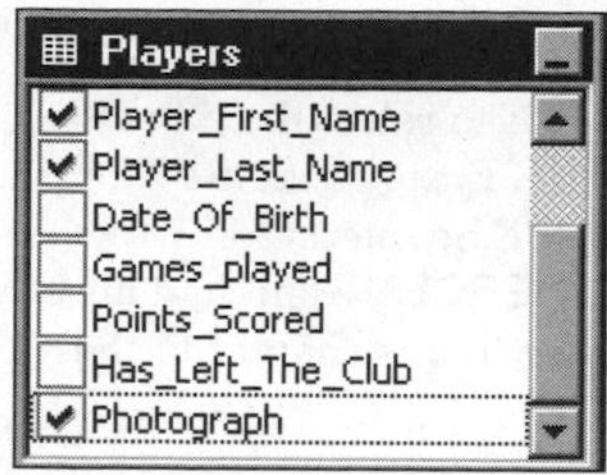

8. If we look lower down the View Designer we should notice some changes. Below the Diagram pane is the Grid pane. As we can see, the columns chosen are listed along with the table. Ensure that the Grid pane on your View Designer matches that below, by clicking on the Sort Type column corresponding to the Player_Last_Name row and selecting Ascending from the drop-down menu that appears. The Sort Order column will automatically default to 1, but make sure it is 1 anyway.

Column	Alias	Table	Output	Sort Type	Sort Order	Criteria
Player_First_Name		Players	✓			
Player_Last_Name		Players	✓	Ascending	1	
Photograph		Players	✓			

9. The pane below that is called the **SQL pane**. This is where we can see the SQL command resulting from our actions. There are two possibilities on the code that we see within this pane, depending on how the properties dialog is set up for building views. Notice that the only difference is the one has the `ORDER BY` clause and `TOP 100 Percent` clause and the other is a simple select. The differences are because of a setting in the properties dialog. We will look at this in more detail in Step 11 below.

```
SELECT     TOP 100 PERCENT Player_First_Name, Player_Last_Name, Photograph
FROM         dbo.Players
ORDER BY Player_Last_Name
```

Or you will see the following:

```
SELECT Player_First Name, Player_Last_Name, Photograph
FROM dbo.Players
```

10. There is more to do to this view before it is complete: we need to click the properties button found on the toolbar (the second button from the left),

first of all making sure that nothing is selected. This is also where you will see how the two queries above will differ.

11. As we might expect, this brings up the Properties dialog. First of all the Owner of the view needs to be set – the best option here is to select the database owner signified as dbo. Do not get confused with the db_owner ID. Ensure that the TOP command is also unchecked. If this option were already checked, this would be the reason why your query from an earlier point in the example would say TOP 100 PERCENT and had an ORDER BY clause. We will discuss when you want to use this option later in this chapter in the *CREATE VIEW Syntax* section.

> **There are differences between dbo and db_owner. The dbo ID is a built-in ID that can perform any function within a database. A login that is defined as a member of the sysadmin role is automatically a member of dbo. Any object created by a login that belongs to dbo will have a prefix of dbo. Any object created by a user that only belongs to db_owner, and not dbo, will have their user ID as the owner of the object.**

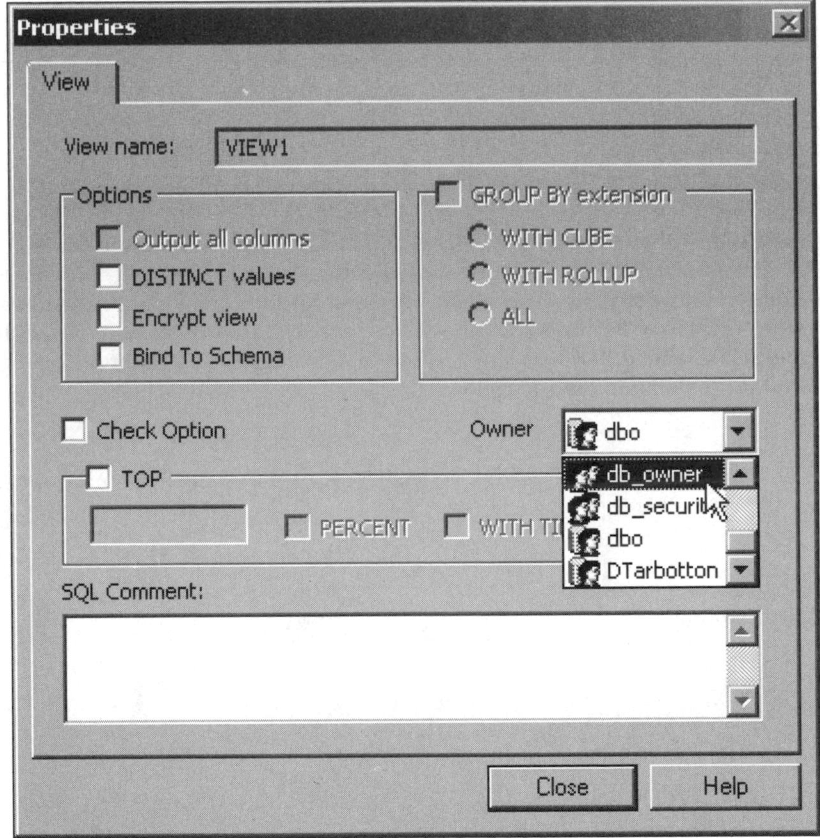

12. This is how the screen should end up looking. Having the options set as demonstrated will ensure that the right settings for the view are created and there will be no `TOP` option. Once done, click Close.

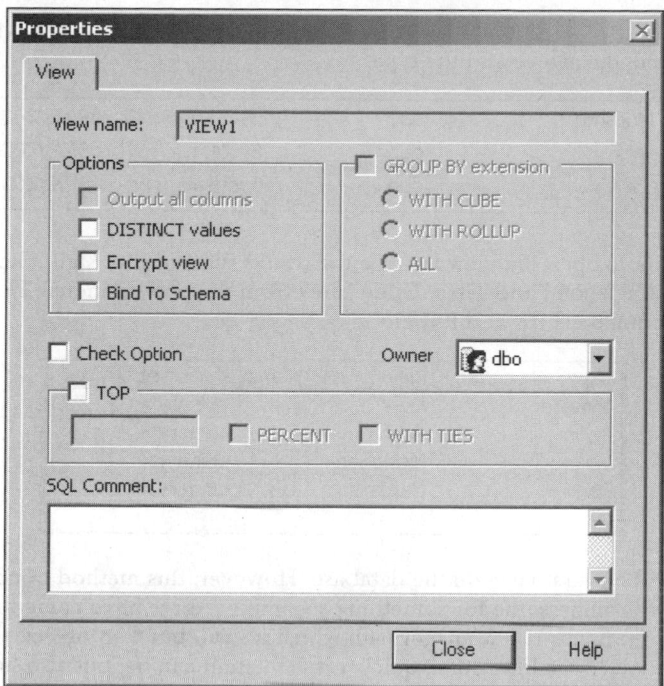

13. We are now finished, so close the view and observe the prompt for saving; obviously click Yes to save the changes.

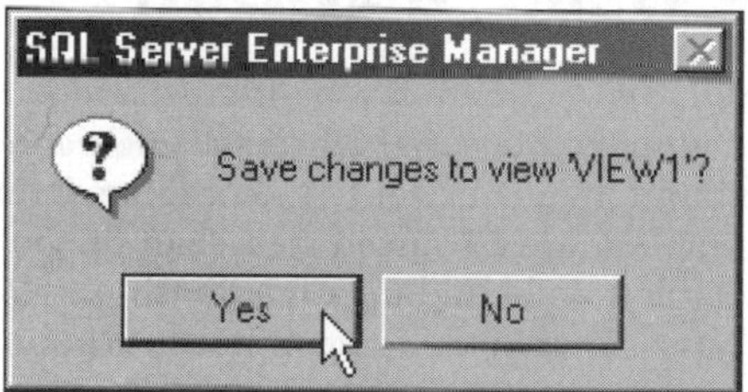

14. This then brings up the Save As dialog, as this is a new view. Type in a meaningful name; as we can see here, we have decided to use a naming convention where we prefix vw to the view name so that know instantly that Player_Mugshots is a view and not a real table. We will also see this sort of naming convention when we look at the system stored procedures in Chapter 18 – they are all prefixed with sp to show instantly that they are stored procedures.

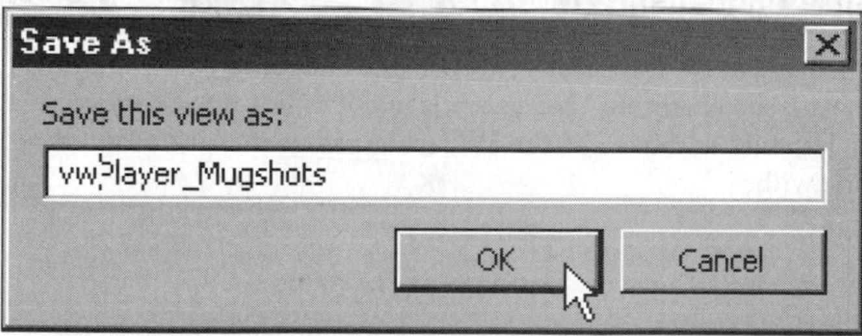

15. Moving back to SQL Server Enterprise Manager, you will see the new view, along with when it was created, the owner and the type.

vwPlayer_Mugshots	dbo	User	09/05/2001 16:57:14
sysconstraints	dbo	System	06/08/2000 01:29:12
syssegments	dbo	System	06/08/2000 01:29:12

16. Now we want to open the view and see the results that we get. Right-click on the view (vwPlayer_Mugshots) and select Open View from the pop-up menu. Then select Return all rows. You should get the results below:

Player_First_Name	Player_Last_Name	Photograph
Annette	Kelly	<Binary>
Jason	Atkins	<Binary>
Ian	McMahon	<Binary>
Glen	Harding	<Binary>

We have now created our first view on the database. However, this method of building a view could be seen as a bit slow and cumbersome for something so simple. As we have come to expect, there is another method within Enterprise Manager with which we can build an object: the Create View wizard. In the next section we will see how much quicker this method can be, but also how, despite how easy using a wizard can be, we can still go wrong.

Creating a View – Using a Wizard

As for several objects within SQL Server, there is a built-in wizard available for creating a view in Enterprise Manager. Wizards can make life easier when starting out by stepping through one stage at a time, gathering information to build up an answer to the problem being set. Keeping this in mind, this section is going to look at creating a more advanced view than previously, where the view will take information from two or more tables, and build up a relationship, called a join, between them to return the required information. We have covered the topic of joins earlier in the book, so here is our chance to use that knowledge.

The aim of this view is to be able to return and display the details of a specific player – these are the player's name, the number of games played, the number of points scored, and the description of the society group they belong to. This data will be sourced from the `Players` and the `Society_Groups` tables. So, let's start building the view by using the wizard.

Try It Out – Creating a View using a Wizard

1. As usual, ensure that SQL Server Enterprise Manager is running and that the server our database is on is also running. For this wizard, it is not necessary to select the Wrox_Golf_Results database as the Wizard gives us the option to choose the database we want to work with.

2. From the toolbar, select the wizard button. As expected, this brings up the now familiar Select Wizard form. Choose Create View Wizard, as seen in the next dialog, and click OK.

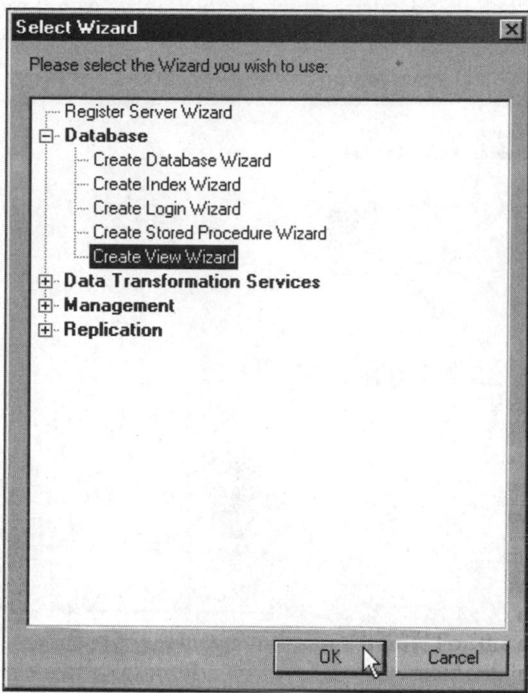

3. As usual, there is an introductory screen with the Wizard – read it and click Next.

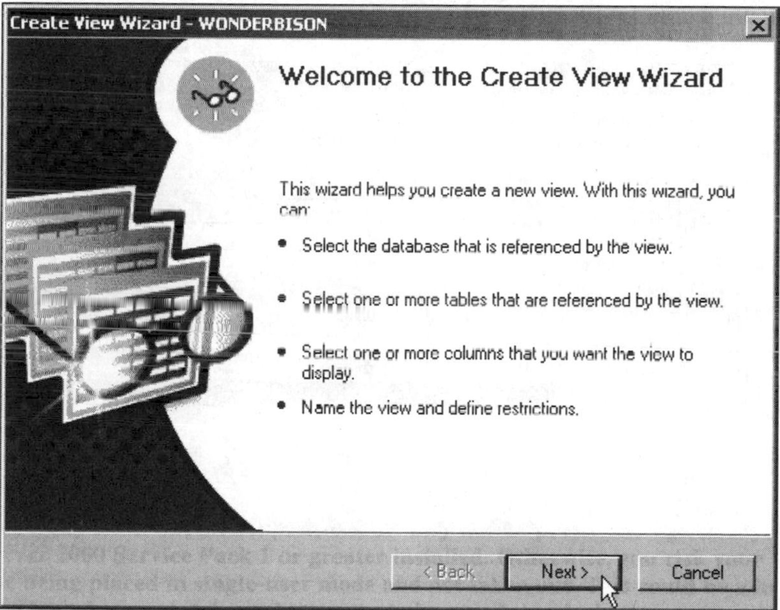

4. The next screen displayed allows us to choose which database the view is to be built from. This wizard was started while in the Wrox_Golf_Results database, but if we had started this from another database, then that database would be the one we would see in the combo box. Just ensure that Wrox_Golf_Results is the database chosen as the Database Name, then click Next.

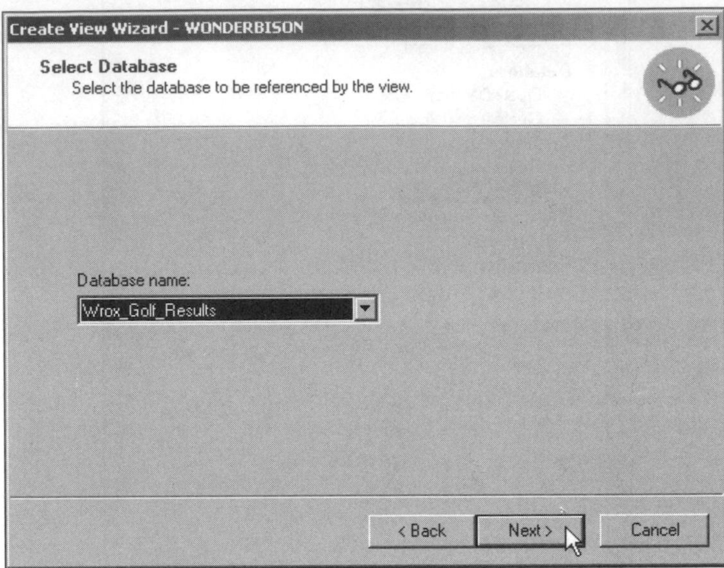

5. At the top of this section, we mentioned that two or more tables were going to be used, and that's just what the Select Objects screen will allow us to do. We will use just two tables – Society_Groups and Players – so place a tick in the check boxes next to these tables and click Next. Make sure that the Society_Group_Temp table created earlier in the book is not selected by mistake.

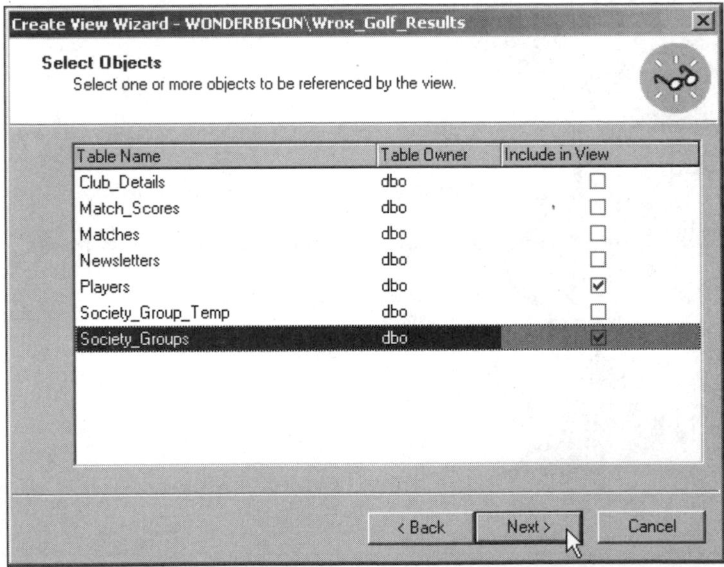

6. It is now time to select the columns to place in the view; there are a number of columns listed from the two tables. The columns that we need are Society_Group_Desc from the Society_Groups table, and Players_First_Name, Players_Last_Name, Games_Played, and Points_Scored from the Players table. We may have to scroll through the list to find all the columns. Once all the columns are selected, click Next.

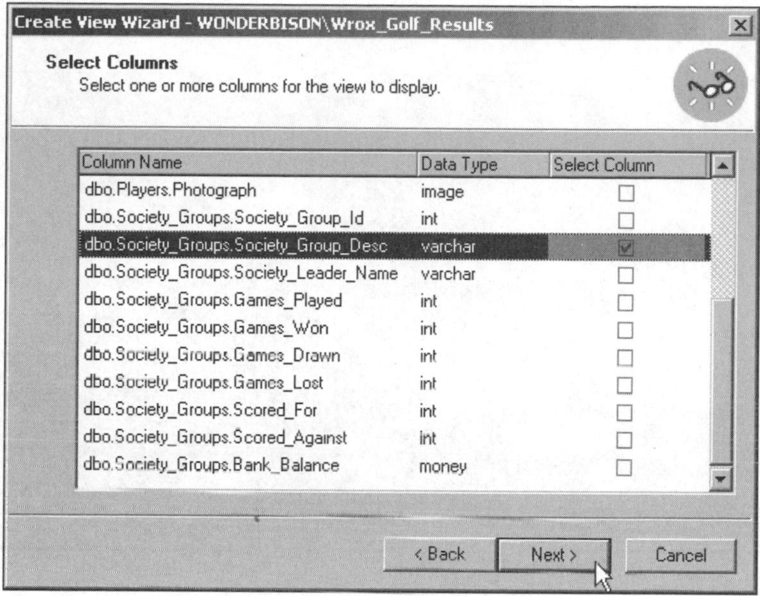

7. Ignore the next screen for the moment: we will come back to this later in the example. Just click Next.

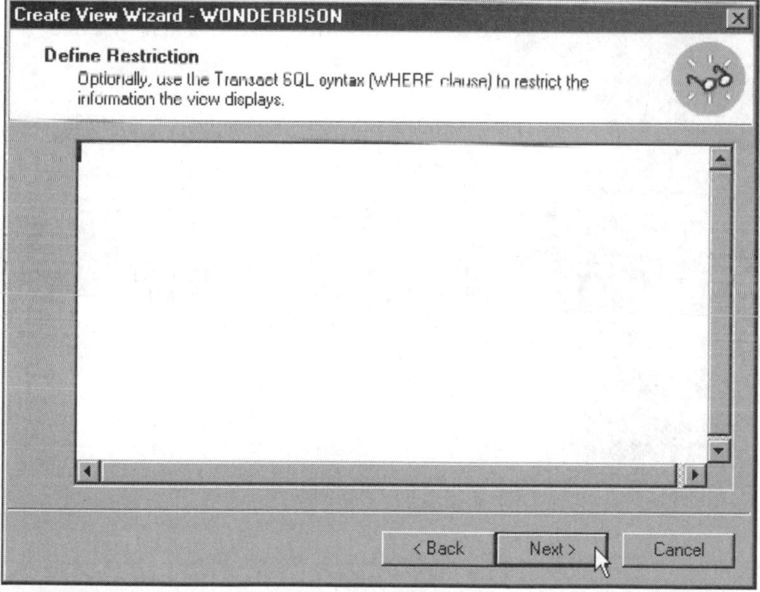

8. It is now time to name the view. Keep to the naming standard of prefixing the view with **vw**, then think of a meaningful name for it. Once you are happy with the name, click **Next**. We will choose the name **vwPlayers_Details** for this view.

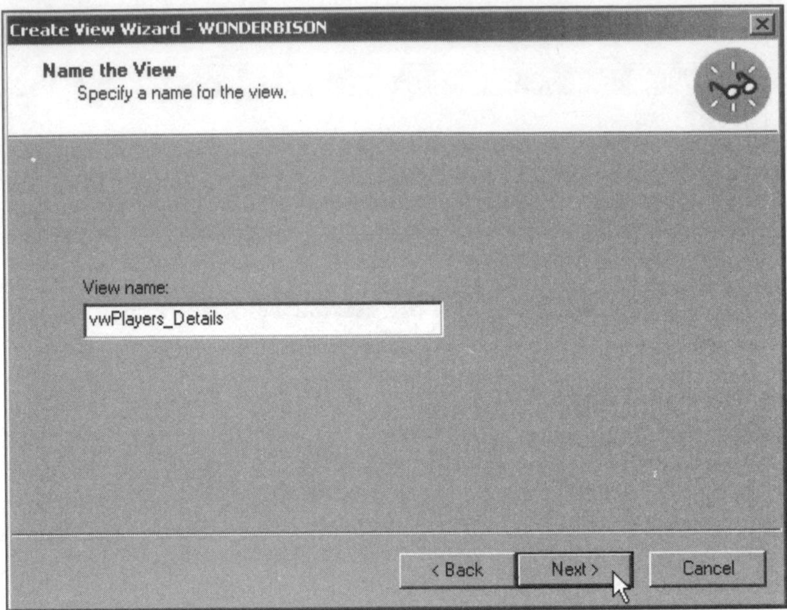

9. A summary screen is then displayed showing the SQL Syntax that has been generated for the creation of the view. When you have examined this, click **Finish**.

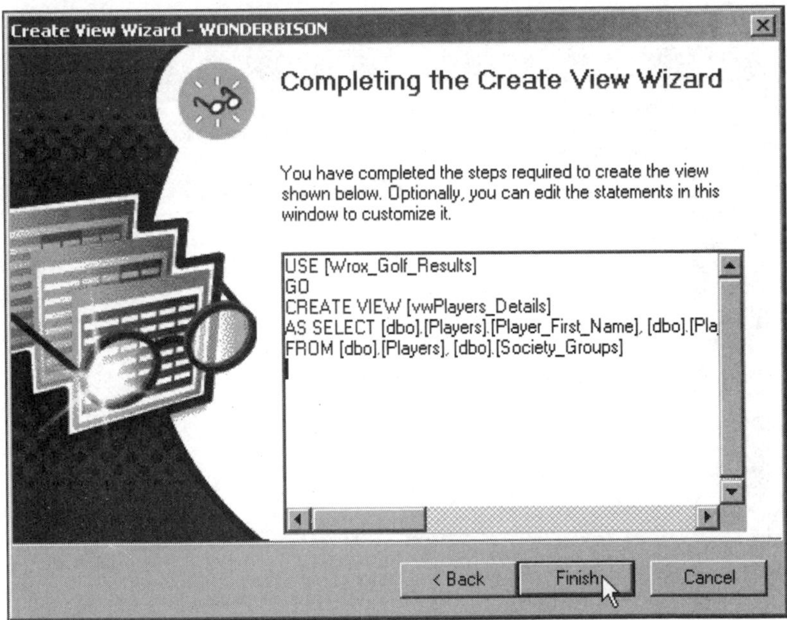

10. Finally, a message box is displayed informing us that the view has been created successfully.

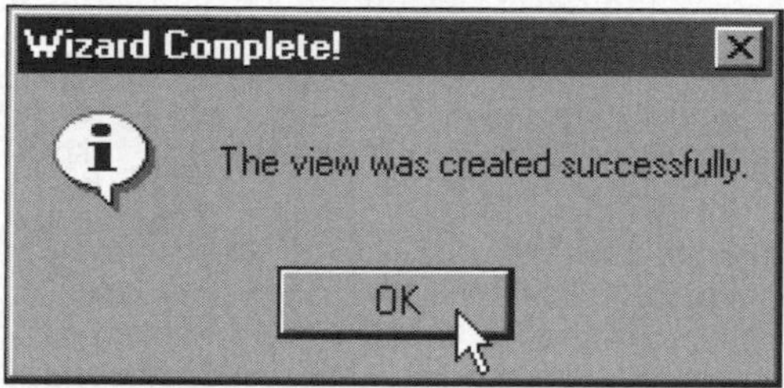

11. If we now look at Enterprise Manager, we should see the new view listed, much like the figure below.

Views 4 Items

Name	Owner	Type	Create Date
vwPlayers_Details	dbo	User	22/04/2001 14:34:58
vwPlayer_Mugshots	db_owner	User	27/03/2001 14:40:44
sysconstraints	dbo	System	06/08/2000 01:29:12
syssegments	dbo	System	06/08/2000 01:29:12

12. Time to test out the view to ensure that it works and returns the required information. From Enterprise Manager, right-click on the vwPlayers_Details view, select Open View and then Return All Rows.

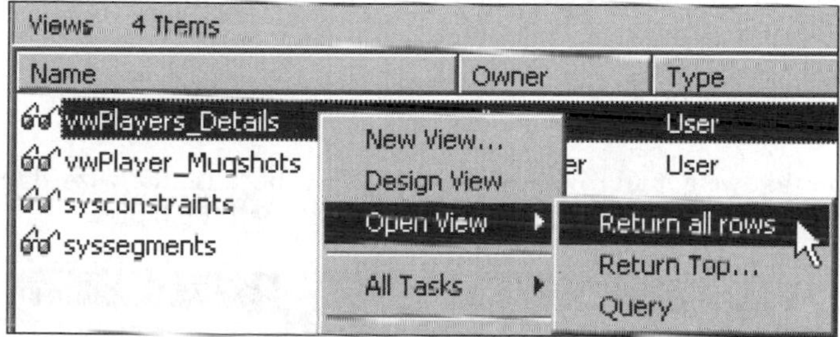

13. This will then return the output shown overleaf from the view as it stands. We should instantly see that this is just not right. What has happened is that every row in the Players table has been linked with every row in the Society Groups table. This is obviously wrong and not what we actually required. This is down to the fact that the view wizard did not place any joins automatically within it, and there were no `WHERE` statements created by us to build the join.

14. Let's take a look at the SQL that the wizard created. To do this right-click on the vwPlayers_Details view and select Design View from the menu.

Player_First_Name	Player_Last_Name	Games_played	Points_Scored	Society_Group_Desc
Annette	Kelly	0	0	Kojak Team
Annette	Kelly	0	0	Bedford Junior Blues
Annette	Kelly	0	0	The Upmarket Traders
Annette	Kelly	0	0	Gilbert's Golfers
Annette	Kelly	0	0	Security Blankets
Annette	Kelly	0	0	The Chieftan Coach
Jason	Atkins	0	0	Kojak Team
Jason	Atkins	0	0	Bedford Junior Blues
Jason	Atkins	0	0	The Upmarket Traders
Jason	Atkins	0	0	Gilbert's Golfers
Jason	Atkins	0	0	Security Blankets
Jason	Atkins	0	0	The Chieftan Coach
Ian	McMahon	0	0	Kojak Team
Ian	McMahon	0	0	Bedford Junior Blues
Ian	McMahon	0	0	The Upmarket Traders
Ian	McMahon	0	0	Gilbert's Golfers
Ian	McMahon	0	0	Security Blankets
Ian	McMahon	0	0	The Chieftan Coach
*				

Look at the SQL pane of the window, the SQL statement should be as follows:

```
SELECT dbo.Players.Player_First_Name, dbo.Players.Player_Last_Name,
       dbo.Players.Games_played, dbo.Players.Points_Scored,
       dbo.Society_Groups.Society_Group_Desc
FROM   dbo.Players CROSS JOIN
       dbo.Society_Groups
```

15. The reason that we got all rows from both tables is because the wizard built a cross join. Let's correct the problem by adding the correct join between the tables.

16. The two tables are in the designer as expected, along with the column selections and the SQL. What we are now going to do is show how to link two tables so that the data is returned correctly.

If the two tables had the same column names and were involved in primary and foreign keys, then the relationship would have been built automatically for this view. When this happens you need to check this relationship to make sure that it is the type of join you wanted.

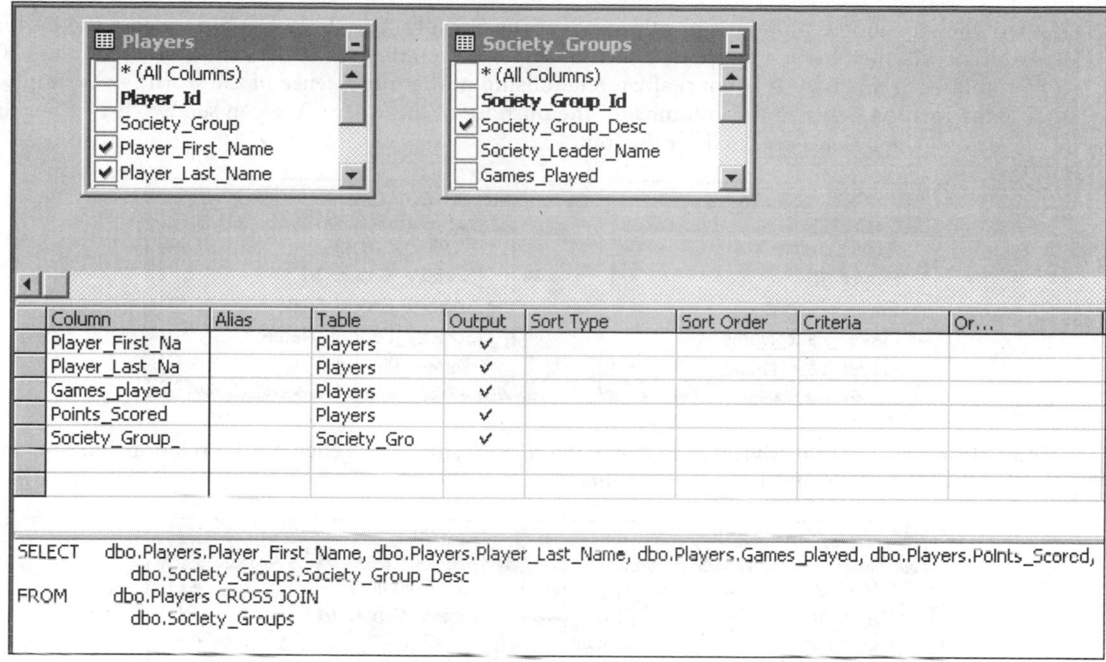

18. It is very easy to link the two tables together by dragging a column from one table to a column in another table. This is very similar to how the relationships are built in the Database Designer, as we saw earlier in the book. First of all click on the Society_Group column in the Players table.

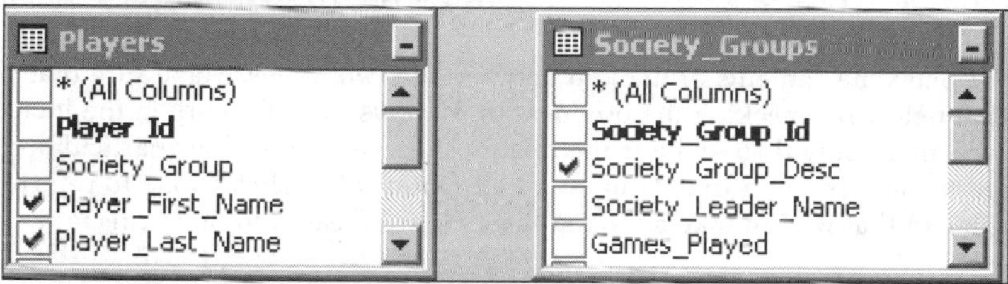

19. Keeping the mouse button clicked down, drag the mouse pointer from the Players tables over to the Society_Group_Id column in the Society_Groups table. You will see the mouse pointerlook like it does in the figure below.

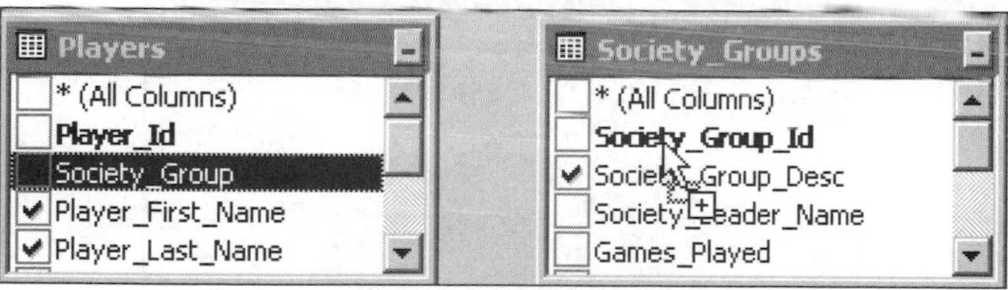

20. Once the mouse pointer is positioned over the Society_Group_Id column, release the button. This will then build a temporary relationship between the two tables, as we can see in the following diagram. It is not really a relationship in the truest sense of the word – it is simply the relation between the columns for the purpose of this query. We can see two gray lines that show which fields are used for the join.

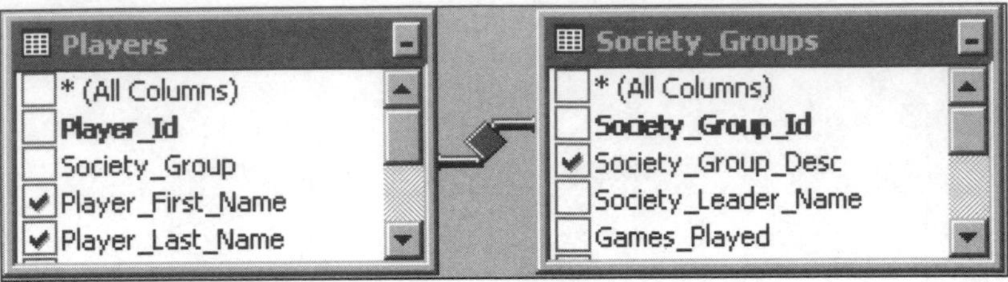

21. However, it is still advisable to check the relationship: right-click on the relationship line and select Properties from the pop-up menu.

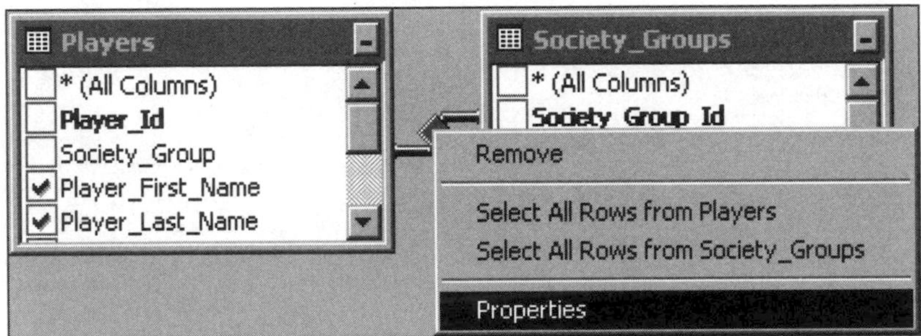

22. This displays the contents of the join between the two tables. Make sure that your screen looks like that below by checking the box next to All rows from Players in the Include rows section. This will make sure that we have the relationship we want for our particular query. This will change the join from an Inner Join to a Left Outer Join. Click Close to return to the View Designer so that we can take a look at the code we created to build this join.

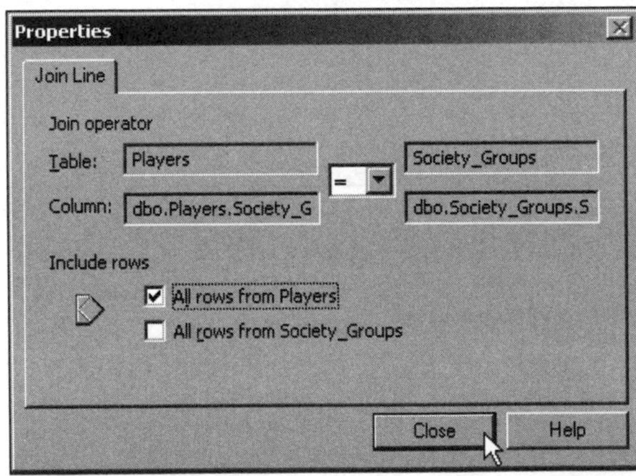

23. If you look at the bottom of the View Designer, you should see the T-SQL code built for the view. If this is cannot be viewed, then press the Show SQL Pane icon on the toolbar at the top.

24. Earlier in the example, we glossed over a screen in the Create View Wizard, where it asked us if we wanted to specify a `WHERE` statement to link the two tables together. We missed this out for a good reason – as we can see below, although we might expect a `WHERE` statement to link the two tables, this is not what has happened in the SQL when we specified a relationship linking the two tables in the view designer. Instead there are new keywords, LEFT OUTER JOIN. This is taking us into a deeper level of joining tables than this book will be covering. However, very simply, this syntax is informing the view that any records found in the table that is specified on the left-hand side of the equals sign (from the Players table), will still be returned, even when there are no matches found in the table specified on the right-hand side of the equals sign. So if a person appears in the Players table but has no entries in the Society_Groups table they will still be listed in this view.

```
SELECT   dbo.Players.Player_First_Name, dbo.Players.Player_Last_Name, dbo.Players.Games_played, dbo.Players.Points_Scored,
            dbo.Society_Groups.Society_Group_Desc
FROM     dbo.Players LEFT OUTER JOIN
            dbo.Society_Groups ON dbo.Players.Society_Group = dbo.Society_Groups.Society_Group_Id
```

25. Now that you are done, click the cross in the top right of the view, which will prompt you to save the changes to the view. Click Yes to save the changes for the relationship.

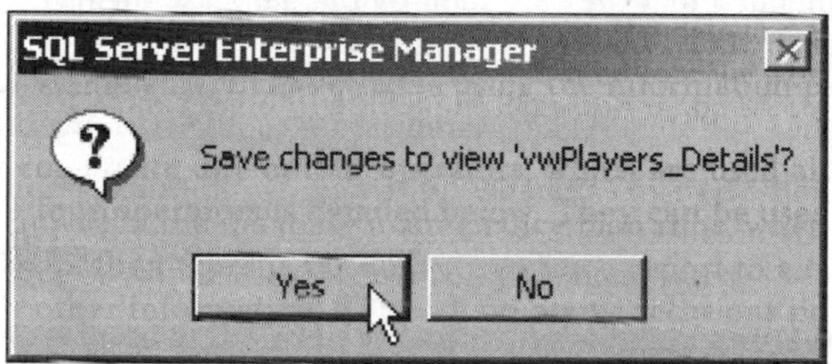

26. Let's make sure that the view returns the required information. From Enterprise Manager, right-click on the vwPlayers_Details view, select Open View, and then Return All Rows, which should produce the following output:

	Player_First_Name	Player_Last_Name	Games_played	Points_Scored	Society_Group_Desc
▶	Annette	Kelly	0	0	Kojak Team
	Jason	Atkins	0	0	The Upmarket Traders
	Ian	McMahon	0	0	Bedford Junior Blues
*					

CREATE VIEW Syntax

Here is the full syntax for the CREATE VIEW statement.

```
CREATE [ < owner > ] VIEW view_name [ ( column [ ,...n ] ) ]
 [ WITH < view_attribute > [ ,...n ] ]
AS
SELECT_statement
[ WITH CHECK OPTION ]
< view_attribute > ::=
{ ENCRYPTION | SCHEMABINDING | VIEW_METADATA }
```

In this chapter we will only be looking at the basic syntax. The basic CREATE VIEW syntax is very simple and straightforward. The following syntax is the most basic syntax of the CREATE VIEW statement.

```
CREATE VIEW [database_name.][owner.]view_name
WITH {ENCRYPTION | SCHEMABINDING}
AS
SELECT_statement
```

Taking a look at the first section of the syntax, we will see that the name of the view can be prefixed with the name of its owner, and the name of the database to which it belongs; however, the database name and the owner are optional. Providing that we are in the correct database and that we are logged in with the ID we wish to create the view for, these options are not required as they will be assumed from what the database knows. For production views, rather than views used purely by a single SQL Server user, it is recommended that they are built by the database owner.

Following on from these options comes the query, typically formed with a SELECT statement, that makes up the view itself. As we saw in the previous example, the SELECT statement can cover one or many tables, many columns, and as many filtering options using the WHERE statement as we wish. We can also order the data in a view; however, to place an ORDER BY clause on a SELECT statement within a view, it is necessary to use the TOP statement. We specified the TOP 100 PERCENT in our first example to get around this problem. Failure to do so will result in an error and the view will not be created. We also cannot reference any temporary variable or temporary table within a view, or create a new table from a view by using the INTO clause. To clarify, it is not possible to have a SELECT column INTO newtable.

The ENCRYPTION option will take the view created and encrypt the schema contained so that the view is secure and no one can see the underlying code or modify the contents of the SELECT statement within. However, do keep a backup of the contents of the view in a safe place in development in case any modifications are required.

The SCHEMABINDING option ensures that any column referenced within the view cannot be dropped from the underlying table without dropping the view built with SCHEMABINDING first. This, therefore, keeps the view secure with the knowledge that there will be no run-time errors when columns have been altered or dropped and the view not altered in line with those changes. There is one knock-on effect when using SCHEMABINDING: all tables or other views named within the SELECT statement must be prefixed with the name of the owner of the table or view, even if the owner of these objects is the same as the owner of the view.

Now that we are aware of the basic syntax for creating a view, the next example will take this knowledge and build a new view for the database.

Creating a View – Query Analyzer

Another method for creating views is by using T-SQL code in Query Analyzer. This can be a faster method for building views than using a wizard or Enterprise Manager, especially as we become more experienced with T-SQL commands. This section will demonstrate the T-SQL syntax required to create a view, which we will soon see is very straightforward.

The `SELECT` statement forms the basis for most views, so this is where most of the emphasis is placed when developing a view. By getting the `SELECT` statement correct and retrieving the required data, it can then be easily transformed into a view. This is how the view in the following example was created, so let's look at building a view using T-SQL and Query Analyzer. In the following example, we will create a view that returns match information (`Society_Group_Id`, `Match_Id`, `Date_Played`, `Opposition_Name`, `Home`, `Points_For`, `Points_Against`) from the `Matches` table with the most recent information first.

Try It Out – Creating a View in Query Analyzer

1. Ensure that SQL Server Query Analyzer is running and that there is an empty Query pane.

2. In the Query pane, enter the following code, ensuring of course you are in the `Wrox_Golf_Results` database.

```
CREATE VIEW dbo.vwMatches
AS
SELECT TOP 100 PERCENT Society_Group_Id, Match_Id, Date_Played, Opposition_Name,
Home, Points_For, Points_Against
FROM dbo.Matches
ORDER BY Date_Played DESC
```

3. Once done, execute the code by either pressing *F5*, *CTRL+E*, or the Execute button. You should then see the following success message:

The command(s) completed successfully.

4. Let's check the results that are returned by our view. From Enterprise Manager, right-click on the vwMatches, select Open View, and then Return All Rows:

Society_Group_Id	Match_Id	Date_Played	Opposition_Name	Home	Points_For	Points_Against
1	5	21/04/2001	Symington Junior G	0	1	1
1	4	14/04/2001	Bedford Charity Go	1	3	0
1	3	07/04/2001	The Scottish Claym	1	0	3
1	2	31/03/2001	The Vertigo Vikings	0	1	1
1	1	24/03/2001	The Wrox Hackers	1	3	0

How It Works

This view is a straightforward view with no ENCRYPTION or SCHEMABINDING options selected and was built in the Wrox_Golf_Results database with the dbo user ID.

The one complication within the view concerns the ORDER BY clause: one of the stipulations for this view is that it returns the data of matches played with the most recent game first. Therefore an ORDER BY statement is required on the Date_Played column to return the records in descending order. To avoid receiving an error message when building the view, it has been necessary to place a TOP option within the SELECT statement; in the case of the example, a TOP 100 PERCENT statement has been chosen so that all the records are returned.

The remainder of the SELECT statement syntax is very straightforward. To demonstrate a more complex view the next example will cover the use of the SCHEMABINDING option by building a view using a template and incorporating a more complex SELECT statement.

Creating a View – Using a Template

Building a view with a template is perhaps more time consuming than writing the view on its own, but the use of a template is good for learning T-SQL syntax.

The following example will bind the columns used in the view to the acutal tables that lie behind the view, so that if any column contained within the view is modified an error message will be displayed and the changes will be canceled. The error received will be shown so that we can see for ourselves what happens.

To also expand our knowledge of the SELECT statement, a join between two tables has been placed within the query; this is not a simple join like the one demonstrated in the SELECT chapter, but one step further where the join takes place to build up a specific column within the view.

First of all, let's build the view before going on to discuss the background.

Try It Out – Creating a View with a Template

1. Ensure that Query Analyzer is running, and click on the Templates tab at the bottom of the object browser.

2. Expand the Create View node, and double-click on the Create View with SCHEMABINDING option.

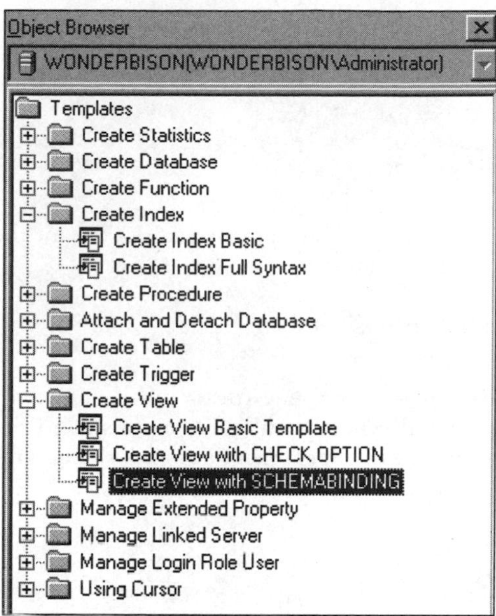

3. This brings up the code template to build a view using SQL Server Query Analyzer. Most of this will stay the same for our purposes.

```
-- =============================================
-- Create schemabinding view
-- =============================================
IF EXISTS (SELECT TABLE_NAME
      FROM   INFORMATION_SCHEMA.VIEWS
      WHERE  TABLE_NAME = N'<view_name, sysname, view_test>')
    DROP VIEW <view_name, sysname, view_test>
GO

CREATE VIEW <view_name, sysname, view_test> WITH SCHEMABINDING
AS
<select_statement, , SELECT au_id FROM dbo.authors>
--note: need to specify specific column names and owner of the table
--eg. SELECT column_1, column_2 FROM owner.table_or_view_name WHERE
search_condition
GO
```

4. The full SQL code for the `CREATE VIEW` statement reads as follows. Change the template code to resemble the code below – the highlighted sections are those you will need to modify.

```
-- =============================================
-- Create schemabinding view
-- =============================================
IF EXISTS (SELECT TABLE_NAME
   FROM   INFORMATION_SCHEMA.VIEWS
   WHERE  TABLE_NAME = 'vwSociety_Groups_Balances')
   DROP VIEW vwSociety_Groups_Balances
GO
```

```
CREATE VIEW vwSociety_Groups_Balances WITH SCHEMABINDING
AS
   SELECT Society_Group_Id, Society_Group_Desc, Bank_Balance,
      (SELECT COUNT(*) FROM dbo.Players
         WHERE Society_Group = Society_Group_Id) AS No_Of_Players
      FROM dbo.Society_Groups
GO
```

5. Once done, execute the code by either pressing *F5*, *Ctrl+E*, or the Execute button. We should then see the following success message:

```
The command(s) completed successfully.
```

6. Now that our `vwSociety_Groups_Balances` view is created, which we can check by looking in Enterprise Manager, it is possible to demonstrate what happens if we try to alter a column used in the view and so affect one of the underlying tables. Enter the following code, and then execute it.

```
ALTER TABLE Society_Groups
ALTER COLUMN Society_Group_Desc varchar (30) NOT NULL
GO
```

7. You will then see in the Results pane two error messages: the first shows that an alteration has been attempted on the `Society_Groups` table, which is not allowed, and the second shows that the alteration has been canceled.

```
Server: Msg 5074, Level 16, State 3, Line 1
The object 'vwSociety_Groups_Balances' is dependent on column 'Society_Group_Desc'.
Server: Msg 4922, Level 16, State 1, Line 1
ALTER TABLE ALTER COLUMN Society_Group_Desc failed because one or more objects
access this column.
```

8. Finally, to demonstrate what data is returned from this view and to test out the view, enter the following code and execute it.

```
SELECT *
FROM vwSociety_Groups_Balances
WHERE No_Of_Players > 0
```

9. This will then return three rows of data where the society group has a player associated with it.

```
Society_Group_Id Society_Group_Desc   Bank_Balance          No_Of_Players
---------------- -------------------- --------------------- -------------
1                Kojak Team           .0000                 1
2                Bedford Junior Blues .0000                 1
3                The Upmarket Traders .0000                 1

(3 row(s) affected)
```

Now that we have seen the example, we will look more closely at the code within.

How It Works

Using a template within Query Analyzer, whether to create a view, or another object, always starts along very similar lines. The code checks within SQL Server's system tables whether the object already exists; if the object does exist, the object is removed from SQL Server by using the `DROP` command. This is one area when using a template that we have to take care with. Dropping an object may not be the desired action: when an object is dropped from SQL Server, all permissions are lost. When dealing with inserting data earlier in the book, roles and permissions were discussed and demonstrated, along with how they work with objects within the database. Those objects were tables, but the same can be said for other objects, such as views.

So when building an object using a template, we must take care to ensure that removing the object is a desired action.

```
IF EXISTS (SELECT TABLE_NAME
   FROM    INFORMATION_SCHEMA.VIEWS
   WHERE   TABLE_NAME = 'vwSociety_Groups_Balances')
   DROP VIEW vwSociety_Groups_Balances
GO
```

Moving on to the code that creates the view, we see the introduction of the `WITH SCHEMABINDING` option. The `CREATE VIEW` command is entered to inform SQL Server what object is to be created. This is followed by the name of the view, and then the `WITH SCHEMABINDING` option. By having this option, it is ensuring that changes to the columns listed in the view below for the `Society_Groups` and `Players` tables cannot be made without dropping the view first. Columns within the `Society_Groups` table that are not listed in the view can be altered without any problem.

```
CREATE VIEW vwSociety_Groups_Balances WITH SCHEMABINDING
AS
```

Most of the `SELECT` statement is straightforward with three columns from the `Society_Groups` table listed. However, there is one complication with the `No_Of_Players` column: this column doesn't exist in any table, but is derived from a query created to build this column. We can have columns listed within a query that are not from any of the tables within the query, but, no matter how we build those columns, we will need to give the column an alias.

> *A column alias is assigned by using the `AS` keyword before the alias name. Any column can have an alias, providing that the `AS` keyword is placed after the column definition, followed by the alias name. We can also alias "real" columns, but if we do, we can no longer use their real name.*

The `No_Of_Players` column has been built up by using another `SELECT` statement within a set of brackets – this is known as a **subquery**. Providing that the query within the brackets returns a single value, the subquery will work. This could be a single column, or a mathematical function, like `COUNT`, which returns a single value. The subquery can be placed, as demonstrated, to create a column, or it can be placed in the `WHERE` statement to aid the joining of two tables.

What happens is that for each record within the `Society_Groups` table, the query will move to the `Players` table and count the number of players where the `Society_Group_Ids` match. No match will return a value of 0 – this is a design feature of our particular database.

```
SELECT Society_Group_Id, Society_Group_Desc, Bank_Balance,
   (SELECT COUNT(*) FROM dbo.Players
      WHERE Society_Group = Society_Group_Id) AS No_Of_Players
FROM dbo.Society_Groups
```

The view then returns the groups where there is at least one player within the society group by executing a query that selects all of the columns from the view and specifies that the `No_Of_Players` has to be greater than zero.

Setting Permissions on a View

You can set permissions on a view just like any other object in the database. Just like a table or any other object there will be times when you want to restrict access to the view to some users. In this example we will set full permissions for the vwPlayers_Details view to the Developers Role. We will do this in the Query Analyzer but you could do it in the Enterprise Manager as well.

Try It Out – Setting Permissions on a View

1. Make sure that Query Analyzer is open and that the `Wrox_Golf_Database` is selected. Enter the following code into an empty Query pane.

```
GRANT ALL
   ON vwPlayers_Details
   TO Developers
GO
```

2. Once done, execute the code by either pressing *F5*, *Ctrl+E*, or the Execute button. You should then see the following success message:

The command(s) completed successfully.

3. You can verify that the rights were granted by going into Enterprise Manager and checking the permissions on the view. To do this, right-click on the vwPlayers_Details view, and then select All Tasks from the pop-up menu. From the next menu, select Manage Permissions. The Developer role will have the SELECT, INSERT, UPDATE, DELETE and DRI permissions checked:

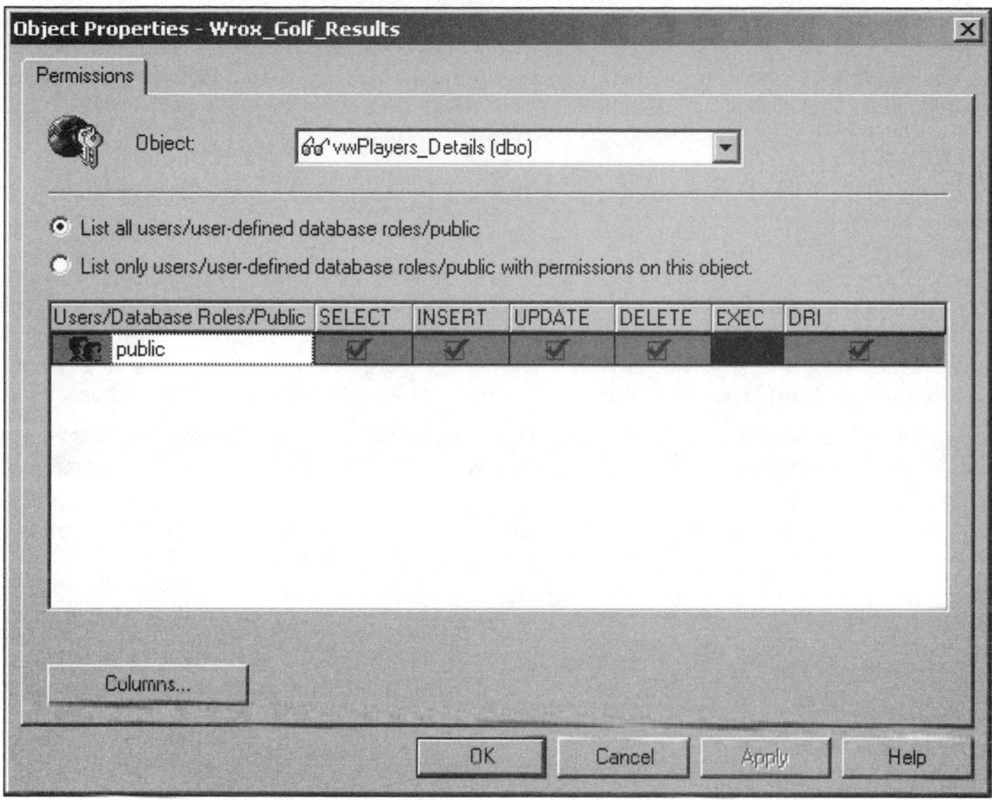

Indexing a View

Views can be indexed just as tables can be indexed. Rules in choosing columns to make indexes on a view are similar to those for a table.

There are also major speed implications of indexing views. If a view remains without an index, every time that the view is executed, the data behind the view, including any joins, is rebuilt and executed. SQL Server will use any indexes that we have on the tables when building the views. Indexing a view is most beneficial when the data in the underlying tables is not changing frequently and when the view is executed often. Keep in mind that a view is taking information from other tables and is not a table itself, and therefore any updates to the underlying tables will not be reflected in the view, until the view is rerun.

By placing an index on a view, not only are the columns named within the index stored within the database, but also all of the columns defined for the view will be stored within the database along with the data rows. Therefore any changes to the raw data within the native tables will also be reflected in the data stored for the view. Keep in mind the performance issues with this. Every data change in the tables used in the views requires SQL Server to evaluate the effect the change has on the view. This requires more processing by SQL Server causing a slowdown in performance. Temper this perceived gain of using an index with the downside of the extra processing required to keep the data up to date in two places for the table, and two places for the index for those columns involved in the view.

When building indexes on views, the first index to be created must be a unique clustered index. Once such an index has been built, further indexes on this view can then be created. This is also taken further, in that if we have a view with subsequent indexes on it, and we drop the unique clustered index, then all of the other indexes will automatically be dropped. Also, if we drop the view, as we would expect, the indexes are also dropped.

Now that we are aware of the pros and cons of building indexes on views, and how they differ from indexes for tables, it is time to build an index on our view.

The aim of this index is to locate a record in the view quickly. The loss of performance with the updates of the account balance and additional players will be minimal. Once a golf society is set up, we tend not to find that the players within the society change on a daily, or even weekly, basis. Also, the funds within the societies at Wrox do not move much as membership fees are annual. Building the index is very quick and very simple, especially as building indexes was covered earlier in the book.

Try It Out – Indexing a View

1. Creating the index is a straightforward process and the code is detailed below, or at least it should be. Make sure that Query Analyzer is open and that the Wrox_Golf_Database is selected. Enter the following code into an empty Query pane.

```
CREATE UNIQUE CLUSTERED INDEX IXvwBalances
ON vwSociety_Groups_Balances
   (Society_Group_Id)
GO
```

2. Now it is possible to execute the code. Press *CTRL+E*, *F5*, or the Execute button on the toolbar. This will in fact generate an error message, as you can see below:

Cannot index the view 'Wrox_Golf_Results.dbo.vwSociety_Groups_Balances'. It contains one or more disallowed constructs.

3. The reason behind this error lies in the fact that the view has a subquery within it. The subquery is counting the number of players into a column defined as `No_Of_Players`. So what can you do? You have two options. The first option is to remove the count from the view, meaning that the subquery would then have to be "attached" to any query using the view when you require the count to actually take place. Or, you can leave the view with no index. There are a number of restrictions on creating indexes on views, which are bulleted at the end of this example.

4. The only view that we have that can be indexed is the `vw_Players_Details`, but even this requires modification. When this was built within Enterprise Manager, the `Society_Groups` and the `Players` tables were joined together using the `JOIN` keyword. If you recall from the *Retrieving Data* chapter, Chapter 13, when we looked at joins, it was possible to use a `WHERE` clause in certain `JOIN` conditions when joining two tables. This is what we have to do in this instance. Therefore, we need to re-create the view to create the index. This is the sort of action you may have to perform yourself when indexing a view. The whole code for dropping the view, re-creating the view, and then indexing it, is shown next.

```
SET QUOTED_IDENTIFIER ON
GO
SET ANSI_NULLS ON
GO
DROP VIEW vwPlayers_Details
GO
CREATE VIEW vwPlayers_Details WITH SCHEMABINDING
AS
SELECT Players.Player_First_Name, Players.Player_Last_Name, Players.Games_played,
Players.Points_Scored, Society_Groups.Society_Group_Desc
FROM   dbo.Players, dbo.Society_Groups
WHERE  Players.Society_Group = Society_Groups.Society_Group_Id

GO
CREATE UNIQUE CLUSTERED INDEX ixPlayers_Details ON vwPlayers_Details
(Player_First_Name, Player_Last_Name)
go
SET QUOTED_IDENTIFIER OFF
GO
SET ANSI_NULLS ON
GO
```

5. Now when you execute the code you will receive no error messages and the view will be successfully built.

As was indicated above, there are a number of points within a view that you cannot have if you wish to place an index on it. These are as follows

- You must not have `TOP`, `DISTINCT`, `COMPUTE`, `HAVING`, or `UNION` statements within the query
- You cannot have a subquery
- You cannot have any wild cards, `DISTINCT`, `COUNT()`, `COUNT(<expression>)`, computed columns from the base tables, or scalar aggregates.
- Many aggregate functions are not allowed, like `MIN` and `MAX`, but you can have `SUM` when you have a `GROUP BY`
- No `OUTER JOIN` is allowed
- No `CONTAINS` or `FREETEXT` clauses are allowed

As you can see, there are a number of restrictions, but not to the point that no index can exist. You just have to think about what you are doing and if you have a query in your view that contains an item from the list above and you wish to create an index, you just have to find a way around it.

Summary

This chapter will have given you the confidence, when building your own view, of knowing which options and features of views you wish to use. We have covered: what a view is, how views can improve a database's security, how to encrypt your view, building a view using the Enterprise Manager and Query Analyer, how to join two tables within a view, and indexing a view.

Creating a view when there is more than one table to retrieve data from on a regular basis is quite often a sensible solution, with even more weight given to this argument when you wish to use views as a method of simplifying the database schema and abstracting the database data into a presentation layer for users.

Encrypting views may seem like a good idea to hide even further the schema of your database from potential users; however do use encrypted views with caution, and always keep a backup of the source in a safe and secure environment. It has even been known for people to keep a printout of the view just in case the source became corrupt. Use encrypted views sparsely, and only when really required.

Having had four different methods to build a view demonstrated, you should have found a method that suits you and your style of working. You may find that as time moves on, the tool used alters, as well as the methods within that tool. Never discount any tool or option within SQL Server and banish it to the annals of history: always keep each option and tool in mind, for one day that area may be your savior. When starting out, switch between each method for building a view so that you are fully conversant with each method.

You will find that in most cases when building views, the `SCHEMABINDING` option will be a good option to have on a view, ensuring that a view that works today will always work. It would only be when someone deliberately removed your view from the system to complete table changes, and then didn't correctly put it back, that you would find that a view has stopped working. Herein lies yet another scenario for keeping the code of encrypted views to hand: if you have encrypted views, along with `SCHEMABINDING`, and someone wishes to alter an underlying table, then you had better have the code to hand!

Finally, being aware of the differences between indexes on tables and indexes in views is crucial to a successful and well performing view. If you are unsure, try out the view with, and then without, an index within your development or testing environment.

We move on now to look at stored procedures.

Stored Procedures

Now that you know how to build queries of single executable lines of T-SQL code, it is time to look at how to place these into a stored procedure that will allow them to be stored within SQL Server, then to be run as often as they are required.

While we may save queries on a disk drive somewhere, we do not store them within SQL Server itself, nor do we save them as multiple units of work. Often, however, we need to execute multiple queries in series from SQL Server. To do this, we employ **Stored Procedures**. When a stored procedure is created, SQL Server assumes that this procedure will be run more than once. Therefore when it is saved, this is completed as a compiled unit of work.

It is also possible, just like any other database object, to assign security to a stored procedure, so that only specific users can run this stored procedure, lending added security over a one-time-only query saved to a hard drive.

The aim of this chapter is to build a simple stored procedure from the ground up, which will insert a single record, and then look at error handling and controlling the flow of execution within our procedure.

Therefore, this chapter will

- Describe what a stored procedure is
- Explain the advantages of a stored procedure over a view
- Cover the basic syntax for creating a stored procedure
- Show how to set values within variables
- Control the flow through a stored procedure

What is a Stored Procedure?

In the simplest terms, a **stored procedure** is a collection of compiled T-SQL commands that are directly accessible by SQL Server. The commands placed within a stored procedure are executed as one single unit, or **batch**, of work – the benefit of this is that network traffic is greatly reduced, as single SQL statements are not forced to travel over the network; hence this reduces network congestion. In addition to `SELECT`, `UPDATE`, or `DELETE` statements, stored procedures are able to call other stored procedures, use statements that control the flow of execution, and perform aggregate functions or other calculations.

Any developer with access rights to create objects within SQL Server can build a stored procedure. There are also hundreds of system stored procedures, all of which start with a prefix of `sp`, within SQL Server that complete tasks from actions that we initiate. Under no circumstances should we attempt to modify any system stored procedure that belongs to SQL Server as this could corrupt not only our database but also other databases and a full restore would have to be undertaken.

There is little point in building a stored procedure just to run a set of T-SQL statements only once; conversely, a stored procedure is ideal for when you wish to run a set of T-SQL statements many times. However, there is an exception when we would build a stored procedure to run a set of statements once: when a set of T-SQL statements would take a few seconds to run, the entire database's stability would benefit from the performance advantage of these statements being compiled. Unlike other queries, a stored procedure, when built, is **compiled** and the compiled version of the code is placed in SQL Server. Compiled code runs a lot faster than waiting for each line of T-SQL to be interpreted and then compiled each time it is processed. Furthermore, SQL Server will develop an execution plan based on indexing, offering even greater performance advantages.

The reasons for choosing a stored procedure are similar to those that would persuade us to choose a view rather than letting users access the table data directly.

> **Stored procedures give our application a single proven interface for accessing or manipulating our data such that data integrity is kept, the correct modifications or selections are made to the data, and ensuring that there is no need for users of the database to know structures, layouts, relationships, or connected processes required to perform a specific function.**

We can also validate any data input and ensure that the data brought into the stored procedure is correct.

Just like a view, we can grant very specific permission for users of stored procedures. Permissions may limit insertions, updates, and deletes, or any combination of these features. To prevent access to the source code, you can encrypt stored procedures. This is an important method for preserving intellectual property, but ensure you keep a copy of the source code safe so that you may apply future modifications.

Why Not Choose a View?

At this stage, we might be thinking that a view could complete the work of a stored procedure. After all, views can not only return data, but also modify it as well. Not only that, but a view can complete joins on tables and complete very complex queries. A view is ideal for these scenarios; however, the contents of the T-SQL commands that make up a view can only be contained within one T-SQL statement. Stored procedures may contain more than one T-SQL statement and offer more powerful programmatic features making them less restrictive than views.

Views enjoy an advantage over stored procedures when there are single T-SQL commands that are not particularly intensive, or when the frequency of use is relatively light. Stored procedures also take a little more effort to write compared to views, so may not be worth the effort unless the operation will be requested often.

CREATE PROCEDURE Syntax

Begin a stored procedure with a `CREATE PROCEDURE` statement. The `CREATE PROCEDURE` syntax offers a great many flexible options and extends T-SQL with some additional commands. The syntax generally appears as follows:

```
CREATE PROCEDURE procedure_name
[ { @parameter_name} datatype [= default_value] [OUTPUT]]
[ { WITH [RECOMPILE | ENCRYPTION | RECOMPILE, ENCRYPTION } ]
AS
[BEGIN]
   statements
[END]
```

First of all, it is necessary to inform SQL Server which action you wish to perform. Obviously this is a stored procedure that we wish to create, and so we need to supply a `CREATE PROCEDURE` statement.

The next part of the syntax is to give the procedure a name. It would be advisable, just as it is with any SQL Server object, to adhere to a naming standard. Everyone has their own standard within their installation, but if we prefix the name with `sp`, a very common naming convention, then we will know what that object is. Some people adopt a different naming convention where the prefix defines what the stored procedure will do; therefore an update would have a prefix of `up`, a deletion `dt`, and a selection `sl`. There are many different prefixes we could use, but once we have decided on our standard, we should stick with it.

Some procedures may require information to be provided in order for them to do their work; this is achieved by passing in a parameter. More than one parameter can be passed in: all we do is separate them with a comma. Any parameter defined must be prefixed with an `@` sign. Not all procedures will require parameters and so this is optional; however, if we do wish to pass in parameters to a stored procedure, we name the parameters and follow them with the data type and, where required, the length of the data to pass in. For example, the following specifies a parameter of name `L_Name`, with `varchar` data type of length `50`.

```
@L_Name varchar(50)
```

We can also specify a default value in the event that a user does not provide one at execution time. The value specified must be a constant value, like `DEFAULT`, or `24031964`, or it can be `NULL`. It is not possible to define a variable as a default value, since the procedure cannot resolve this when the procedure is built. For example, if your application is commonly, but not exclusively, used by the marketing department, you could make the department variable optional by setting a default of `marketing`:

```
@department varchar(50) = 'marketing'
```

Thus, in this example, if you were from marketing, you would not need to provide the department input. If you were from information services, however, you could simply provide an input for `department` that would override the default.

It is also possible to return a value from a stored procedure using a parameter to pass the information out. The parameter would still be defined as if it was for input, with one exception and one extra option. First of all, the exception: it is not possible to define a default value for this parameter. If we do define a default value, no errors will be generated, but the definition will be ignored. The extra syntax option that is required is to suffix the parameter with the keyword OUTPUT. This must follow the data type definition:

```
@calc_result varchar(50) OUTPUT
```

It is not required to place OUTPUT parameters after the input parameters; they can be intermixed. Conventionally, however, try to keep the OUTPUT parameters until last.

Before continuing, there is one last thing about parameters that needs to be discussed, and that is to do with executing the procedure and working with the defined parameters. When it comes to executing a stored procedure that has input parameters, there are two ways to run it.

The first method is to name the stored procedure and then pass the input values for the parameters in the same order that they are defined. SQL Server will then take each comma-delimited value set at the EXECUTE command, and assign it to the defined variable. However, this does make an assumption that the order of the parameters does not change, and that any default value defined parameters are also set with a value at the EXECUTE command prompt.

The second, and preferred, method of executing a stored procedure is to name the parameter, and follow this with the value to pass in. We are then ensuring that, at execution time, it doesn't matter what order the stored procedure has named the parameters, because SQL Server will be able to match the parameter defined in the EXECUTE line with the parameter defined within the stored procedure. We then don't need to define a value for parameters that already have default values. There will be examples of each of the two different methods of passing in values to parameters within this chapter.

Next come two options that define how the stored procedure is built. First of all, just to remind ourselves, a stored procedure, when created, is compiled and SQL Server stores the compiled code for subsequent executions. This is to save time and resources: each time a line of code is run within a stored procedure, it is not interpreted and altered to run as machine code.

However, the RECOMPILE option on a stored procedure dictates to SQL Server that every time the stored procedure is run, the whole procedure is recompiled. Typically, (in order to take advantage of newer indexing on target tables) you may want to add the RECOMPILE option to a stored procedure for a single execution with the new structure and subsequently remove it.

The second of the two options is the ENCRYPTION keyword. Just like a view, it is possible to encrypt a stored procedure so that the contents of the stored procedure cannot be viewed. Keep in mind that ENCRYPTION does not secure the data, but rather protects the source code from inspection and modification. Both ENCRYPTION and RECOMPILE are preceded by the WITH keyword and can be employed together when separated by a comma:

```
CREATE PROCEDURE sp_do_nothing
   @nothing int
   WITH ENCRYPTION, RECOMPILE
AS
   SELECT something FROM nothing
```

The keyword AS defines the start of the T-SQL code, which will be the basis of the stored procedure. AS has no other function, but is mandatory within the CREATE PROCEDURE command, defining the end of all variable definitions and procedure creation options. Once the keyword AS is defined, you can then start creating your T-SQL code.

Returning a Set of Records

One method of achieving output from a stored procedure is to return a set of records, also known as a **recordset**. This recordset may contain zero, one, or many records as a single batch of output. This is achieved through the use of the `SELECT` statement within a stored procedure – what is selected is returned as the output of the stored procedure. Don't be fooled into thinking, though, that we can only return one recordset within a stored procedure, as this is not true: we can return as many recordsets as we wish.

As soon as there is a `SELECT` statement placed within our stored procedure we may think that there will be a recordset generated. This is true with one exception: it is possible to assign a value to a variable using the `SELECT` statement, rather than the `SET` statement. For example, the next set of code will not produce any records as it is purely setting a value. Running the code as it stands will produce the same results as if it was within a stored procedure. Enter the following code and execute it and we will see that no set of rows is returned.

```
DECLARE @aa as varchar(20)
SELECT @aa = "122"
```

Compare this with the following code, which does return data, and so there will be a recordset produced.

```
SELECT "122"
```

Therefore, providing the `SELECT` statement is not setting a variable, a recordset is returned.

In this chapter we will see single recordsets of data returned and how these look within Query Analyzer. Returning single, or even multiple, recordsets should not really concern us at this stage, but is of more concern to developers in languages such as Visual Basic, C++, and so on, even .NET developers. Multiple recordsets will only concern us when we move on to more advanced stored procedures with multiple queries or the extended stored procedures of the next chapter.

Creating a Stored Proc – Enterprise Manager

Now that we have seen some of the merits of a stored procedure over other methods of working with data, it is time to create the first stored procedure in this chapter. This stored procedure will be built within Enterprise Manager to insert a player in to the `Players` table from the information passed to it. It will also expose an area where we could make a mistake with the image data type. This area will be addressed in the next chapter by modifying the stored procedure, once created. Ensure that SQL Server Enterprise Manager is running and let's get started.

Try It Out – Using Enterprise Manager

1. Navigate to the Wrox_Golf_Results database and right-click on Stored Procedures. From the pop-up menu, select New Stored Procedure...

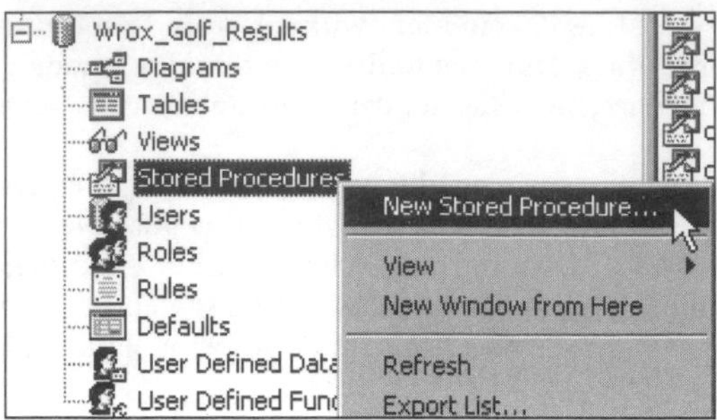

2. This opens a dialog box in which we can enter the SQL Syntax to build the stored procedure. As we can see, there isn't a great deal of room to enter any SQL commands; the form cannot be expanded to give more room either. This dialog doesn't give a great many options to us as a developer and already Enterprise Manager is making our task of building the stored procedure less easy. However, what it does allow is the building of a stored procedure within Enterprise Manager rather than having to use a second tool, like Query Analyzer, and having to swap between these two tools in our development.

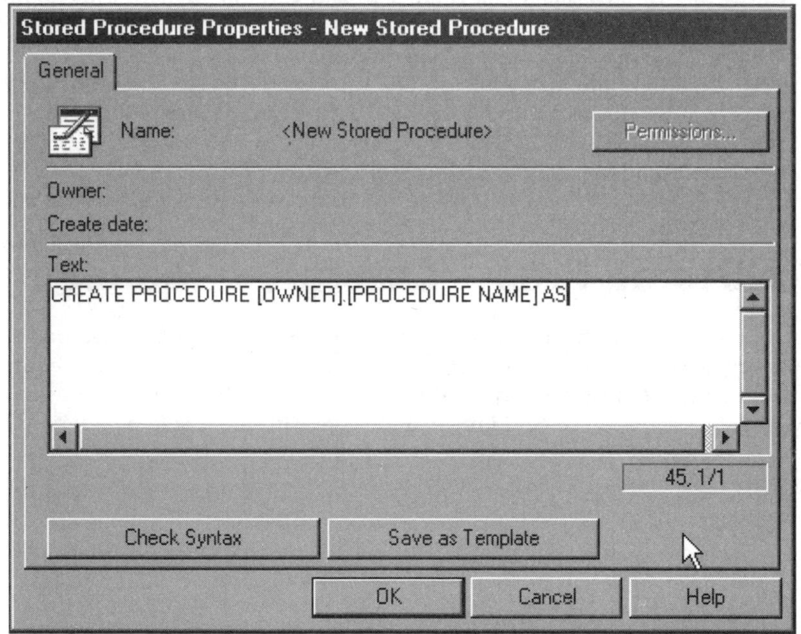

3. Enter the following SQL into the Text window. Follow it exactly, and yes, there is a deliberate error within the code! (There is a missing parenthesis at the start of the list of columns to insert.) This is to demonstrate what happens when we receive an error message when checking the syntax of our SQL code.

```
CREATE PROCEDURE [sp_Insert_A_Player]
   (@iSociety_Group        [int],
   @vPlayer_First_Name     [varchar](50),
   @vPlayer_Last_Name      [varchar](50),
   @sdDate_Of_Birth        [smalldatetime],
   @tiGames_played         [tinyint],
   @siPoints_Scored        [smallint],
   @imPhotograph           [image])
AS INSERT INTO Players
   [Society_Group],
   [Player_First_Name],
   [Player_Last_Name],
   [Date_Of_Birth],
   [Games_played],
   [Points_Scored],
   [Has_Left_The_Club],
   [Photograph])

VALUES
   (@iSociety_Group,
   @vPlayer_First_Name,
   @vPlayer_Last_Name,
   @sdDate_Of_Birth,
   @tiGames_played,
   @siPoints_Scored,
   0,
   @imPhotograph)
```

4. Now that we have entered this code, click the Check Syntax button on the dialog.

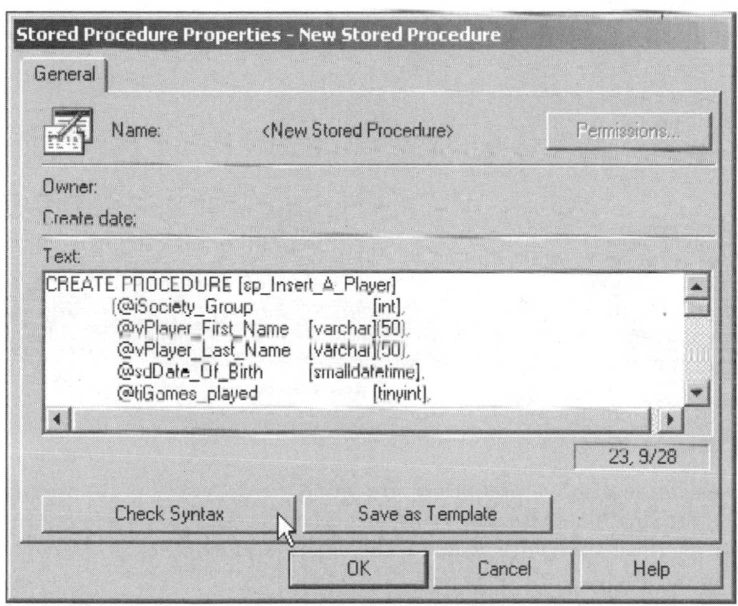

5. As mentioned above, there is a deliberate error within the code, and as expected, an error box has been displayed. If you have made a typing error other than that mentioned, you may well see a different message; however, you are given some clue as to what the error is and where it can be found, no matter what error you have made. Once you have noted the error, click **OK**.

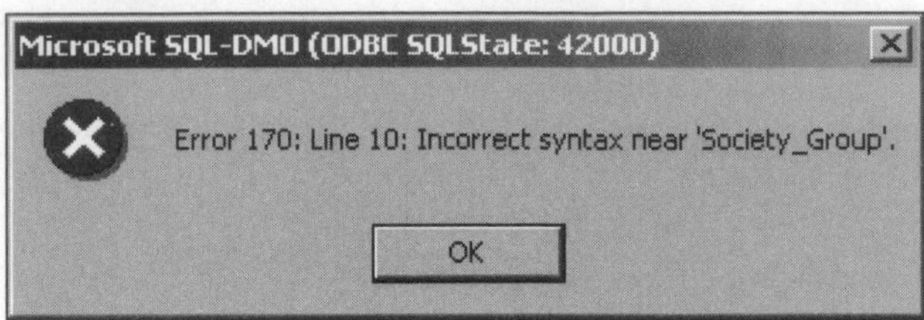

6. Make the correction as detailed below by placing a parenthesis within the `INSERT` command, and then click the **Check Syntax** button again. This time, hopefully, there will be no errors. However, if you have made errors, then you need to iterate this process until all the errors have disappeared.

```
CREATE PROCEDURE [sp_Insert_A_Player]
   (@iSociety_Group         [int],
    @vPlayer_First_Name     [varchar](50),
    @vPlayer_Last_Name      [varchar](50),
    @sdDate_Of_Birth      [smalldatetime],
    @tiGames_played         [tinyint],
    @siPoints_Scored      [smallint],
    @imPhotograph         [image])

AS INSERT INTO Players
    ( [Society_Group],
    [Player_First_Name],
    [Player_Last_Name],
    [Date_Of_Birth],
    [Games_played],
    [Points_Scored],
    [Has_Left_The_Club],
    [Photograph])

VALUES
   (@iSociety_Group,
    @vPlayer_First_Name,
    @vPlayer_Last_Name,
    @sdDate_Of_Birth,
    @tiGames_played,
    @siPoints_Scored,
    0,
    @imPhotograph)
```

7. Note our use of descriptive prefixes representing the data type of the variable, with v for varchar, sd for smalldatetime, ti for tinyinteger, and si for smallinteger. After resolving any further errors, if we click once again on the Check Syntax button, we should see the success message like below.

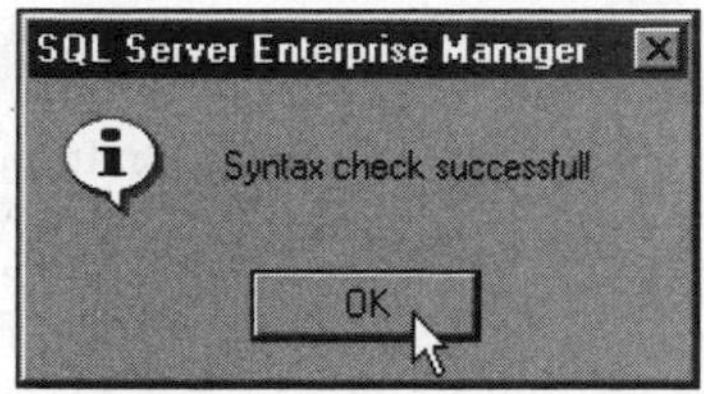

8. Click the **OK** button on the syntax check box, and click **OK** again, which will then commit the stored procedure to SQL Server. We will be brought back into Enterprise Manager and we should see the new stored procedure listed. Of course, it will be mixed in with the system stored procedures as this SQL Server instance has been set up to display all system objects. If we sort by **Create Date**, then you should see the stored procedure at the top of the list.

Stored Procedures 31 Items

Name	Owner	Type	Create Date
sp_Insert_A_Player	dbo	User	09/04/2001 19:47:29
dt_validateloginparams_u	dbo	System	12/11/2000 19:42:35
dt_whocheckedout_u	dbo	System	12/11/2000 19:42:35

This has now completed our first developer-built stored procedure within the system. Inserting data using the stored procedure will be demonstrated later in the chapter. Creating a stored procedure within Enterprise Manager, although straightforward, is not easy. This method of building stored procedures is unlikely to be used except for very quick and simple stored procedures similar to the one just demonstrated. However, Enterprise Manager does offer an excellent environment for editing stored procedures.

A better method of creating a stored procedure is demonstrated next, where the use of a wizard can help us build a stored procedure when we are still learning the syntax of T-SQL commands. However, we will still need to have some command of T-SQL, although a lot less than that required when using Enterprise Manager.

Creating a Stored Proc – Using a Wizard

As with so many of the wizards within Enterprise Manager, the wizard that builds stored procedures is very useful when we are unsure of what to do when building our task. Although the actual wizard only comprises a few screens, the last screen demonstrated is where the power of building the stored procedure comes from. However, don't start thinking that this is going to be the answer to all our problems for building every stored procedure that we will want; the power of the wizard comes from when we are building straightforward stored procedures that complete one action, which is either `UPDATE`, `DELETE`, or `INSERT`. For some reason, there is no ability to create a stored procedure surrounding the `SELECT` statement. However, we can create an `INSERT` stored procedure and, with a small amount of work, could alter it into a `SELECT` "style" stored procedure.

What the stored procedure wizard obviously lacks is the capability of building us a solution to a business problem, or slightly more complex queries where transactions are required, or more than one action at a time. The whole emphasis of the wizard is to build quick and simple stored procedures for the more common and straightforward tasks.

Time to demonstrate how simple building a stored procedure using the wizard is. The following stored procedure is to update the bank balance on a specific `Society_Group`.

Try It Out – Using a Wizard

1. Ensure that SQL Server Enterprise Manager is running. It is not necessary to be within a specific database, however, in the case of this example, SQL Server was positioned on the Wrox_Golf_Results database. Click the wizard button on the toolbar. The Select Wizard options dialog pops up waiting for our choice. Select Create Stored Procedure Wizard and click OK.

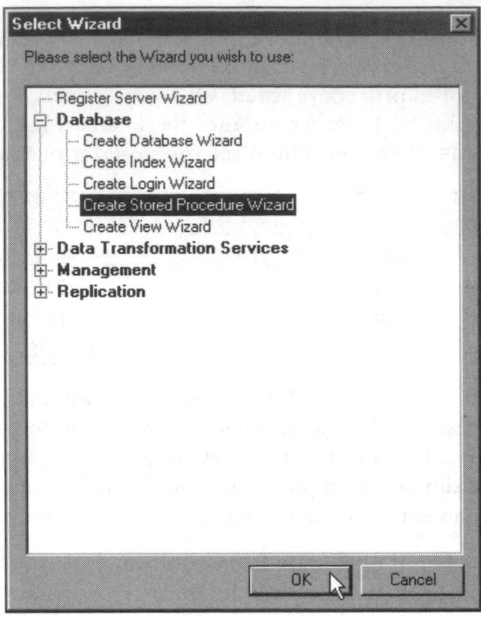

2. As ever, there is an opening screen informing us of what the aim of the wizard is. Read it and click Next.

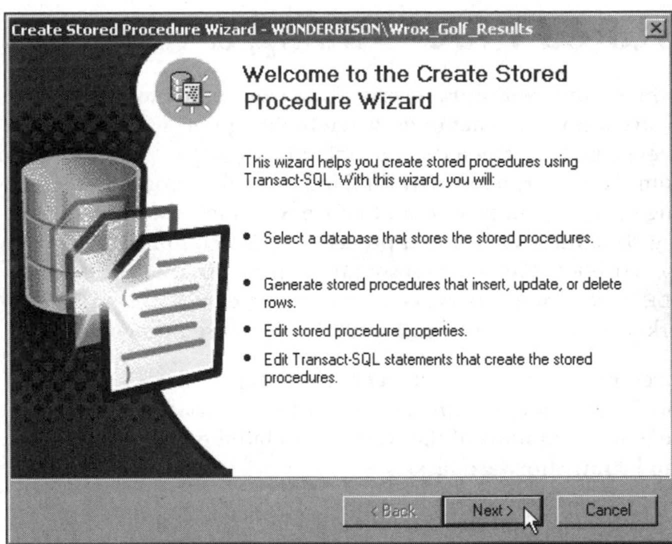

3. As in this example, the SQL Server Enterprise Manager was on the Wrox_Golf_Results database, so this is the selected database in the combo box. If you were positioned on another database, ensure that Wrox_Golf_Results is the value in the Database name. Once ready, click Next.

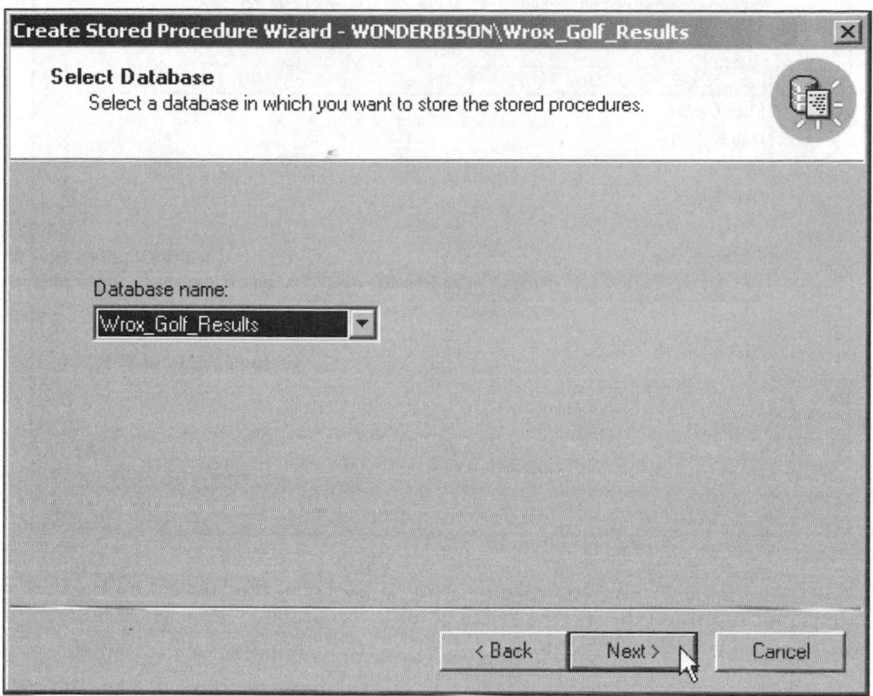

4. This example is a simple update of the bank balance field in the Society_Groups table. The screen shown overleaf allows for selection of one or more tables to be included within the stored procedure. In our case, just place a tick in the Update column for the Society_Groups table, and then click Next.

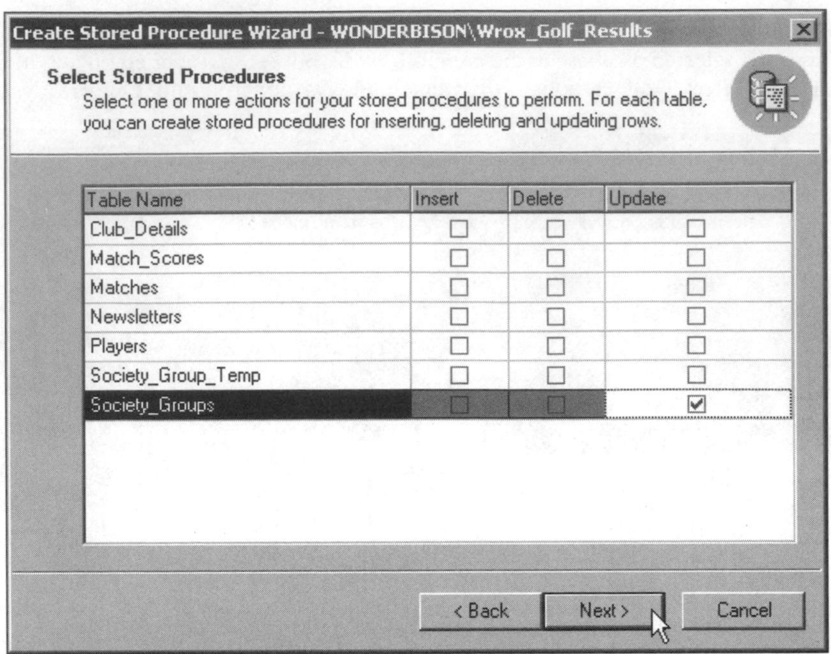

5. This brings us to the final screen of the wizard. However, how can it be the end when in fact we have not informed the wizard which columns to update, which parameters are coming in, and so on? To complete this information we need to click the Edit… button.

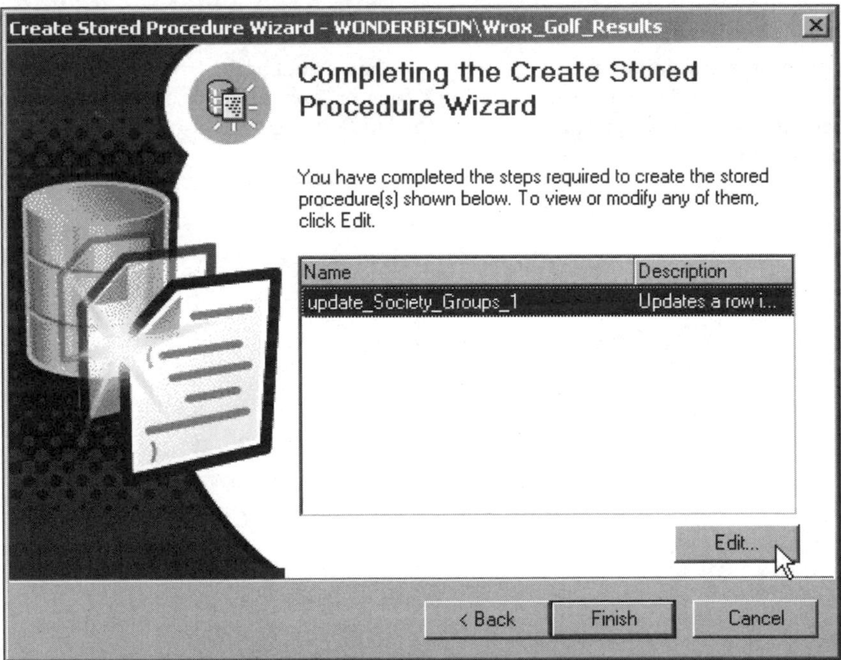

6. The screen that we are taken to is used to edit the properties and contents of the stored procedure we are building. The first task is to alter the stored procedure name to something more meaningful, such as sp_Update_Bank_Balance. Then, moving to the Include in Set Clause and Include in Where Clause columns below, this is where we inform the wizard which columns will be updated, and which columns will be used to find the relevant records. We can alter the columns for both of these situations by clicking and changing the columns selected under the relevant column heading.

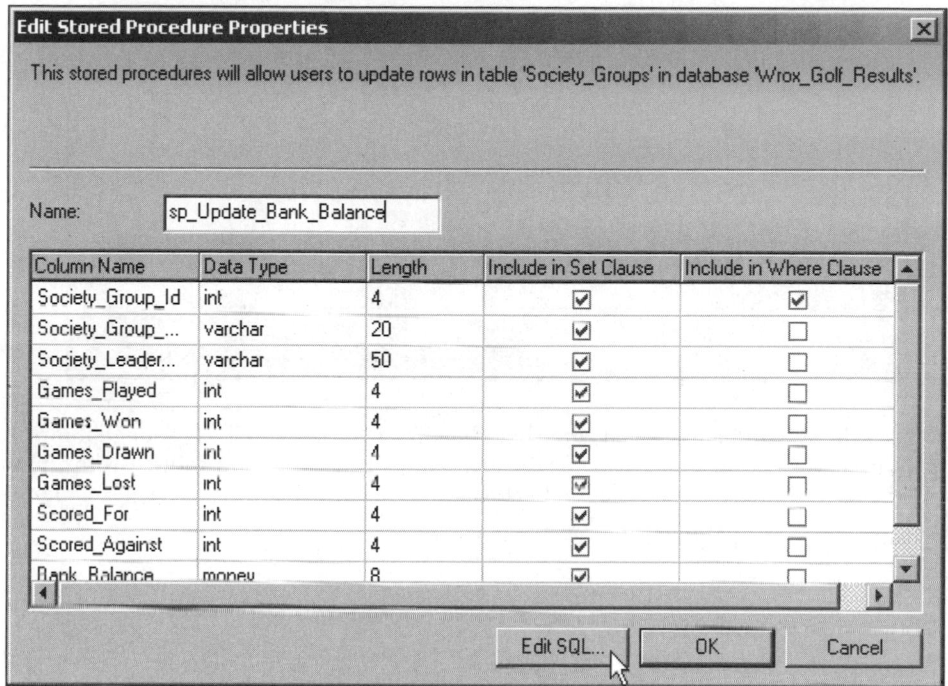

7. Alter the Edit Stored Procedure Properties screen to look like the following screenshot overleaf. Notice how the number of columns chosen in the Include in Set Clause column has been reduced to just the Bank_Balance column: this is the only column that will be updated. Let's take a look at the T-SQL that has been generated from this wizard. Click on the Edit SQL... command button at the bottom of the screen.

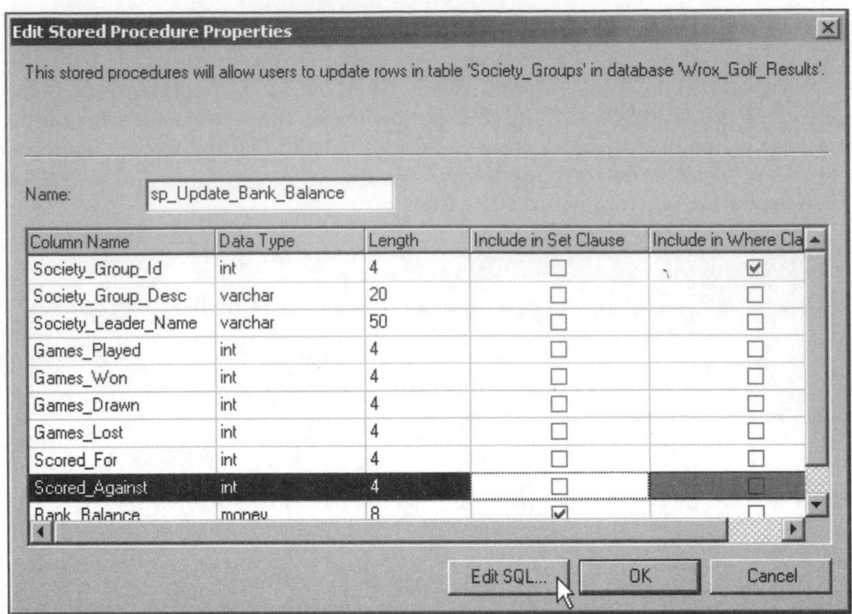

8. The code we will be presented with should be like that below. This is enough information if all that we are doing is replacing one value in the `Bank_Balance` column with another. However, this probably does not reflect what will actually happen in a real situation.

```
USE [Wrox_Golf_Results]
GO
CREATE PROCEDURE [sp_Update_Bank_Balance]
  (@Society_Group_Id_1    [int],
   @Bank_Balance_2    [money])

AS UPDATE [Wrox_Golf_Results].[dbo].[Society_Groups]

SET  [Bank_Balance]    = @Bank_Balance_2

WHERE
  ( [Society_Group_Id]    = @Society_Group_Id_1)
```

9. What is more likely to happen is that a value is passed in to the stored procedure which reflects the amount of a transaction, and the amount passed in is then used to reflect the value change within the bank balance. To complete this action, a minor modification is required to the stored procedure; this revolves around the SET statement. Make the modifications as detailed below within the code window.

```
USE [Wrox_Golf_Results]
GO
CREATE PROCEDURE [sp_Update_Bank_Balance]
  (@Society_Group_Id_1    [int],
   @Bank_Balance_2    [money])

AS UPDATE [Wrox_Golf_Results].[dbo].[Society_Groups]
```

```
SET [Bank_Balance]   = Bank_Balance + @Bank_Balance_2

WHERE
  ( [Society_Group_Id]   = @Society_Group_Id_1)
```

10. By clicking OK, we are informing the wizard that we have finished modifying the data, the column selection, and WHERE clauses are to our satisfaction, and the wizard can now proceed.

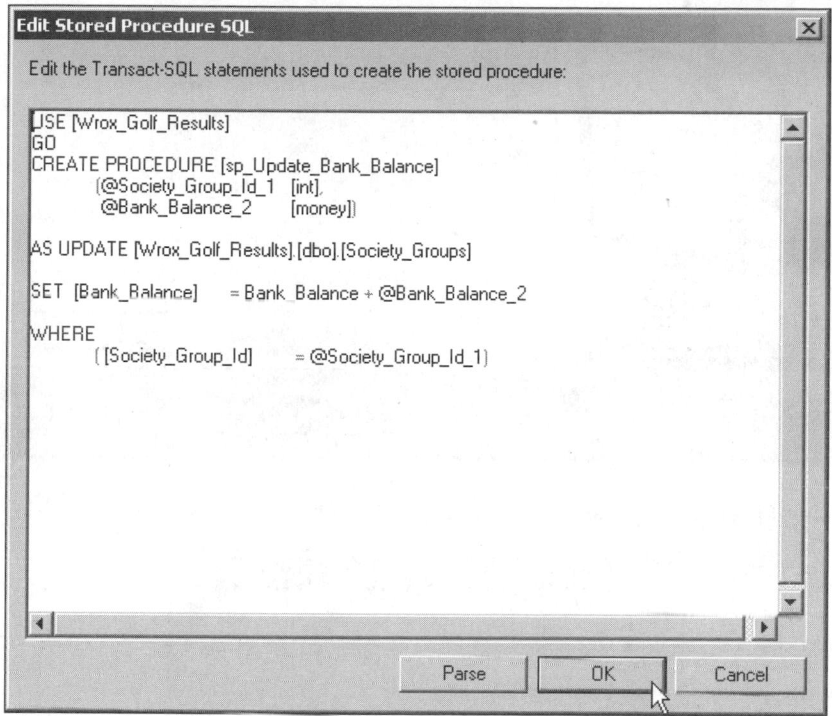

11. This brings us back to the final dialog. If we clicked Edit now, we would move to the Edit Stored Procedure SQL screen that we have just left, and not the screen from which we can choose columns. The reason for this is that the SQL has been generated and the wizard may not be able to rebuild any changes that we placed within the SQL. So the safest and easiest option is to take us straight in to the T-SQL editor. Click Finish, which will commit the stored procedure to the database.

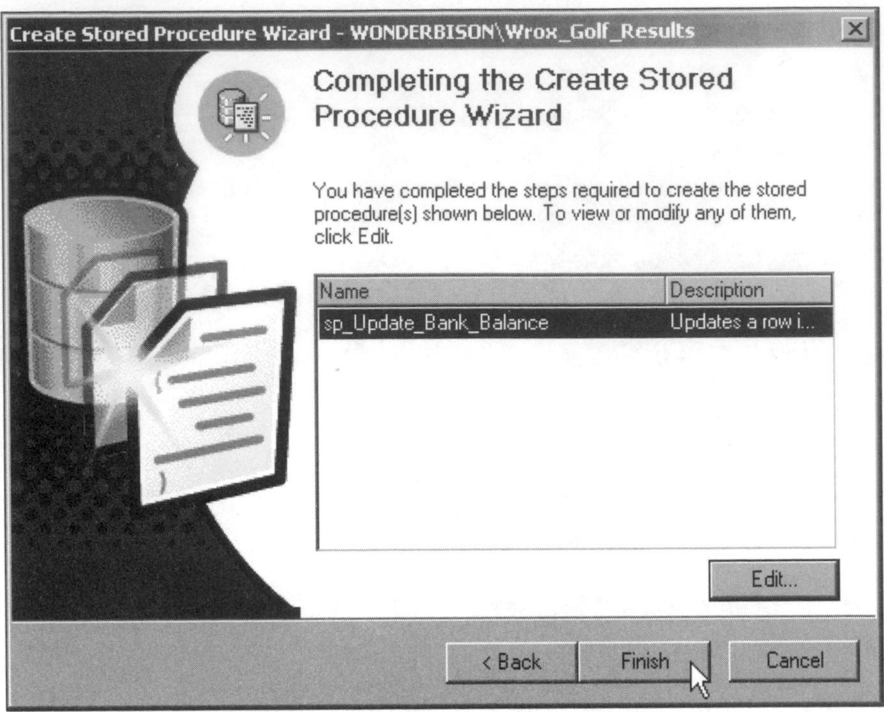

12. We should see the expected success dialog. Click **OK**.

13. This then brings us back into SQL Server Enterprise Manager; if we click on the **Stored Procedures** node under the `Wrox_Golf_Results` database, we will see the new stored procedure among all the existing procedures within our database.

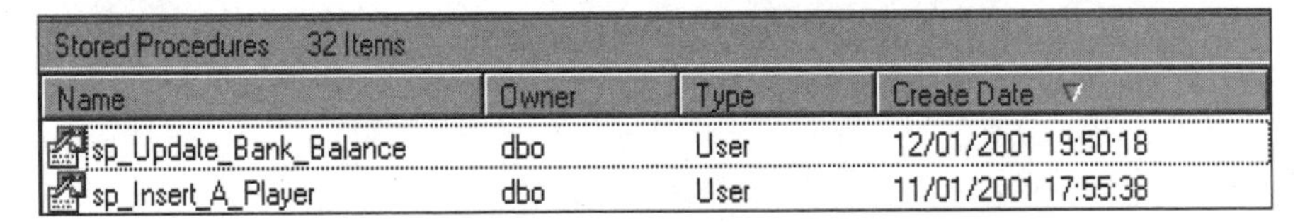

Stored Procedures 32 Items

Name	Owner	Type	Create Date
sp_Update_Bank_Balance	dbo	User	12/01/2001 19:50:18
sp_Insert_A_Player	dbo	User	11/01/2001 17:55:38

14. We can test this stored procedure straightaway. To do this, enter and execute the following code in Query Analyzer, making sure that the **Wrox_Golf_Results** database is selected. This code is passing in the parameters **1** and **1000** to the stored procedure unnamed, and in the correct order. This will add 1000 dollars onto the bank balance of the society with `Society_Group_Id` equal to `1`, namely the Kojak Team society.

```
sp_Update_Bank_Balance 1, 1000
SELECT Bank_Balance
FROM Society_Groups
WHERE Society_Group_Id = 1
```

15. This should return the following in the Results pane.

```
(1 row(s) affected)

Bank_Balance
---------------------
1000.0000

(1 row(s) affected)
```

16. We can also update the bank balance using named parameters, which is demonstrated next. As discussed earlier, the parameters will not need to be in the same order.

```
sp_Update_Bank_Balance @Bank_Balance_2 = 3000, @Society_Group_Id_1 = 2
SELECT Bank_Balance
FROM Society_Groups
WHERE Society_Group_Id = 2
```

17. When we execute this code, we will see similar results to that before.

```
(1 row(s) affected)

Bank_Balance
---------------------
3000.0000

(1 row(s) affected)
```

18. Currently there is no error handling in our stored procedure. In the example below, we attempt to update the bank balance of a non-existent society, as there is no society with a `Society_Group_Id` of 57. Therefore, no rows are updated, and no rows are returned in the `SELECT` statement either. However, there is also no error listed, so, to the untrained eye, it is possible to believe that a row has been updated. Overleaf, you will see the screenshot after the code has been executed:

```
sp_Update_Bank_Balance @Bank_Balance_2 = 3000, @Society_Group_Id_1 = 57
SELECT Bank_Balance
FROM Society_Groups
WHERE Society_Group_Id = 57
```

```
(0 row(s) affected)

Bank_Balance
--------------------

(0 row(s) affected)
```

19. Finally, we demonstrate another way to execute a stored procedure from within Query Analyzer, which saves on typing in a long function name and can be useful if you have forgotten the name of the procedure you wish to call. In the Object Browser, simply expand the Stored Procedures node under the Wrox_Golf_Results database and find the name of the procedure you wish to execute. In this case, we wish to execute the sp_Update_Bank_Balance procedure again. Left-click on the procedure, hold down the mouse button, move the mouse pointer back into the Query pane, and then release the mouse button. This will drag the name of the stored procedure into the Query pane, and we can then add the parameters onto the end of the line, 3 and 500 say, and then click the Execute button on the toolbar.

Returning an Error using RETURN

One method of returning a value from a stored procedure to signify an error is to use the RETURN statement. This statement immediately stops executing the code within a stored procedure, and passes control back out of the stored procedure. Therefore, any statements after the RETURN statement will not be executed.

It is not compulsory to have a RETURN statement within our code, really it is only necessary when we either wish to return an error code, or exit from a stored procedure without running any further code from that specific point. For example, if we were running a series of dependent queries, where subsequent queries depend upon earlier queries, we would want a graceful exit from the procedure should an early query fail. Otherwise, the remaining queries will cascade in errors, creating more problems.

By default, a setting of 0 is returned, which means that the stored procedure was successful. Any other integer value means that an unexpected result occurred and that we should check the return code. Notice that the word error wasn't mentioned, as it may be valid for a non-zero return code to come out of a stored procedure.

In this next example, not only is a stored procedure going to use a template to build the basis of the procedure, but the stored procedure will also use the RETURN value to demonstrate an error condition.

Use of the SET Statement

It is possible to assign a value to a variable through a `SELECT` statement. However, it is also possible to assign a value to a variable using the `SET` statement. This is different from using the `SET` statement within a `UPDATE` command, which assigns a value to a column within a table.

When assigning a value using `SET` or `SELECT` the syntax is exactly the same as that used within an `UPDATE` command, with the one exception that as this is not within an `UPDATE` command, there are no columns from any tables available to use to set a variable's value to. Therefore, we can only set the value of a variable from a static value, a value from another variable, or a combination of this that includes string or mathematical functions, (in other words, any valid expression). The next example demonstrates the setting of a value to a variable. However, before moving on to this, there are a couple of areas that need to be covered concerning the next example.

> *The `SET` statement is not valid to use to set a value to a variable if we are moving from SQL Server to another database, for example Sybase. Within these other databases, the only valid command is the `SELECT` statement.*

Creating a Stored Proc – Using a Template

In this example, we will create a stored procedure that will return an output parameter back to the calling procedure, indicating the bank balance of a specific society group. This differs from the previous example, as the output parameter will be set through a row returned from a recordset. To achieve this, the stored procedure will access the `Society_Groups` table and return the current bank balance for the society group passed in. The stored procedure will have error handling using the `RETURN` keyword. If no society groups are found, or more than one society group is found, the balance will be set to `0` and a numeric return value set.

Try It Out – Using a Template

1. Ensure that SQL Server Query Analyzer is running and that you are logged in with a user ID that allows updates to the `Wrox_Golf_Results` database.

2. Switch to the **Template** tab on the **Object Browser** and expand the **Create Procedure** node. Now double-click on the **Create Procedure with OUTPUT Parameter option**, which will create a new Query pane with the template details in it.

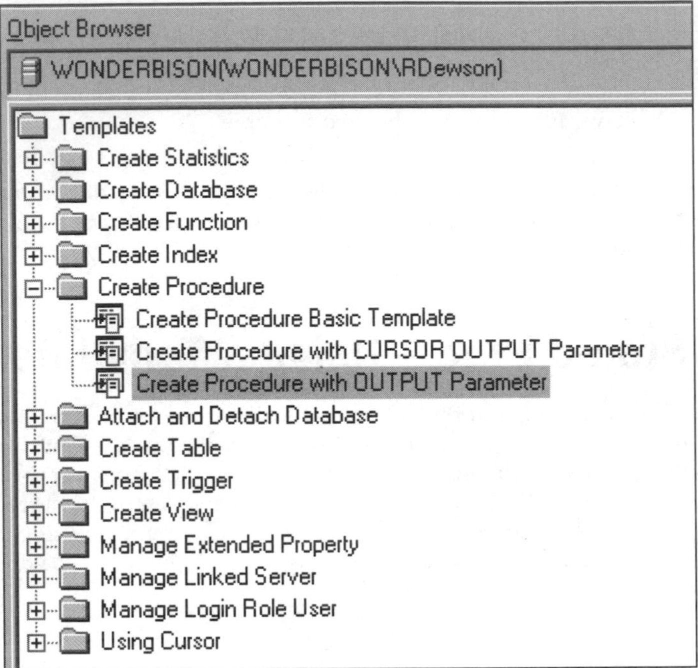

3. This will then give us a Query Analyzer that looks similar to the following. There are three batches to this template, denoted by the three `GO` statements within the code. Batches were covered in Chapter 12, *Inserting Data*. In the template below, the example will take each batch in turn and they will be covered in separate bullet points. When each batch is demonstrated, we will see the template populated with the correct code to build the stored procedure.

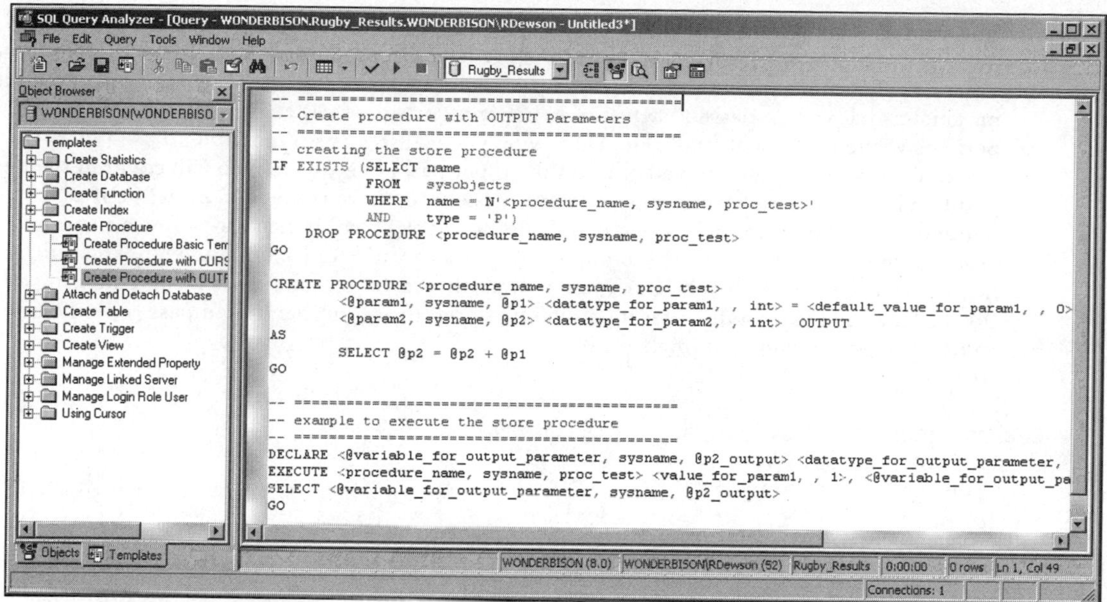

4. In the following steps, replace each section of code in the template with the relevant code listed below. First of all, the first batch within the template sets up checks to see if the stored procedure already exists, and if it does, deletes the procedure through the `DROP PROCEDURE` command. By running `DROP PROCEDURE`, just like dropping any object, when we then recreate the object, all of the permissions associated with that object are lost. For example, if a stored procedure had `EXECUTE` permission assigned to the `PUBLIC` role, then when the procedure is re-created, it will be necessary to give those rights back to that role. This will be covered later when the template is slightly modified to grant permissions. Within the code, we can see that the stored procedure has been named as `sp_Output_Society_Group_Bank_Balance`.

```
-- =============================================
-- Create procedure with OUTPUT Parameters
-- =============================================
-- creating the store procedure
IF EXISTS (SELECT name
        FROM   sysobjects
        WHERE  name = N'sp_Output_Society_Group_Bank_Balance'
        AND        type = 'P')
    DROP PROCEDURE sp_Output_Society_Group_Bank_Balance
GO
```

5. The second section is the code that creates the contents of the stored procedure and we'll go through each part of it in turn. Add each section to the procedure as we discuss it. This stored procedure takes two parameters: an input parameter of `Society_Group_Id`, and an output parameter that will be passed backed to either another stored procedure, or a program, perhaps written in Visual Basic, etc. Don't worry, because it is still possible to use Query Analyzer to demonstrate the value from the output parameter, which we will cover in the next point. When defining parameters in a stored procedure, there is no need to define if a parameter is set for input as this is the default; however, if we do need to define a parameter as an output parameter, we have to place `OUTPUT` as a suffix to each parameter. This will, in fact, allow the parameter to be input and output; therefore we could pass a value in using an `OUTPUT` defined parameter, alter it within our stored procedure, and then pass back the new value through the same parameter.

```
CREATE PROCEDURE sp_Output_Society_Group_Bank_Balance
   @Society_Group int,
   @Bank_Balance money OUTPUT
AS
   SELECT @Bank_Balance = Bank_Balance
      FROM Society_Groups
      WHERE Society_Group_Id = @Society_Group
```

6. Notice in the second section of the code shown below, the use of the keyword `@@ROWCOUNT`. This is a system-defined variable that is set to the number of rows that the previous statement has affected. This variable's setting will alter after each `SELECT`, `UPDATE`, `INSERT`, `DELETE` or `SET` statement. Therefore, we should immediately move the setting for system variables such as these straight to a variable, or use it immediately; more on this in the next chapter, but for the moment, as there are no statements in between then we will leave it as this.

```
   IF @@ROWCOUNT = 1
      RETURN
   SET @Bank_Balance = 0
   RETURN 1
GO
```

7. Before reaching the final batch, it is necessary to grant `EXECUTE` permissions on the stored procedure for those roles that might run the procedure in production. It is possible to avoid this section of work and the stored procedure would still run for us, as it was our login that created the stored procedure. The same is true for any `dbo` logins that are also able to run this stored procedure, if our login ID is a member of the `dbo` role too. However, with these roles, at present, nobody else could run the stored procedure. Therefore it is necessary to `GRANT EXECUTE` permissions to the roles we wish to allow to retrieve the society groups' bank balances. For the moment, let's assume that everyone can run this procedure. So insert the following into the template code:

```
GRANT EXECUTE ON sp_Output_Society_Group_Bank_Balance TO PUBLIC
GO
```

8. The final batch of the template demonstrates how to call the stored procedure, pass in the `Society_Group_ID` for which we wish to retrieve the balance, retrieve the value passed back from the stored procedure into a local variable, and then display it for us to see. Also the return status is checked and listed in a separate recordset. This first part of this code section will return a valid value.

```
-- =============================================
-- example to execute the store procedure - valid
-- =============================================
DECLARE @Bank_Bal money
DECLARE @Ret_Status int
EXECUTE @Ret_Status = sp_Output_Society_Group_Bank_Balance 1, @Bank_Bal OUTPUT
SELECT @Bank_Bal
SELECT @Ret_Status
GO
```

9. This second part of the code section will produce an error since it is passing `0` for the input parameter. The return code is set to `1`.

```
-- =============================================
-- example to execute the store procedure - invalid
-- =============================================
DECLARE @Bank_Bal money
DECLARE @Ret_Status int
EXECUTE @Ret_Status = sp_Output_Society_Group_Bank_Balance 0, @Bank_Bal OUTPUT
SELECT @Bank_Bal
SELECT @Ret_Status
GO
```

10. Now that the template has been altered, execute this by pressing *CTRL+E*, *F5*, or the Execute button on the toolbar. This will not only create the stored procedure, but also runs the examples at the end to demonstrate the procedure called. Of course, we can run this section of code as many times as we want because the whole scenario, from dropping and losing the stored procedure through re-creating the stored procedure, including the security aspects, is all there ready for us. The stored procedure will pass back its output parameter value to the `@Bank_Val` variable defined within the execution batch, and the return value to the `@Ret_Status` variable. From there, once the variable is set, the value can be printed out using a `SELECT` statement. This will produce the following output in the Results pane:

```
---------------------
1000.0000

(1 row(s) affected)


-----------
0

(1 row(s) affected)


---------------------
.0000

(1 row(s) affected)


-----------
1
```

Controlling the Flow

When working within a stored procedure, there will be times when it is necessary to control the flow of information through it. The main control of flow will be completed by the use of an IF...ELSE statement; however, the other method discussed in this chapter is the use of the CASE statement.

Controlling the flow through a stored procedure will probably be required when a procedure does anything more than working with one T-SQL statement. Controlling the flow will depend on our procedure taking an expression and making a true or false decision, and then taking two separate actions depending on the answer from the decision.

IF ... ELSE

There will be times when a logical expression needs to be evaluated and there will be only a true or false answer. This is where an IF...ELSE statement would be used. There are a large number of possible ways of making a True or False condition. Most of the possibilities surround the use of relational operators such as <, >, = and NOT; however, these can be combined with string functions, other mathematical equations, or comparisons between values in local variables, or even system-wide variables. It is also possible to place a SELECT statement within an IF...ELSE block, as long as a single value is returned.

A basic IF...ELSE would perhaps look like the following:

```
IF A=B
   Statement when True
ELSE
   Statement when False
```

IF...ELSE statements can also be nested and would look like the following; within the next example, you will see demonstrated how to include a SELECT statement within an IF decision.

```
IF A=B
   IF (SELECT AVG(SALARY) FROM Employees) > $20000
      Statement2 when True
   ELSE
      Statement2 when False
ELSE
   Statement when False
```

As you can see, there is only one statement within the `IF...ELSE` block. If we wish to have more than one line of executable code after the `IF` or the `ELSE`, we must include another control-of-flow statement, the `BEGIN...END` block.

BEGIN...END

To batch statements together within an `IF...ELSE`, we must surround the code with a `BEGIN...END` block. If we try to have more than one statement after the `IF`, the second and subsequent statements will run no matter what the setting of the `IF` statement is, if we don't have an `ELSE`. If we used an `ELSE` statement after a second or subsequent statement after an `IF`, we will get an error message. Therefore the only way around this is to use `BEGIN...END`.

An example of how the code would look follows:

```
IF A=B
   BEGIN
      Statement when True
      Another statement when True
      Yet Another True statement
   END
ELSE
   False statement
```

Notice how within the `ELSE` section, there is only one line of code; therefore no `BEGIN...END` is required.

The final method of controlling the flow in this section is to use a `CASE` statement.

CASE Statement

When there is more than a plain `True` or `False` answer – in other words, when there are several potential answers – the `CASE` statement would be used.

There are several parts to a `CASE` statement that can be placed within a stored procedure to control the flow, depending on each scenario. Let's take a look at all the parts to the `CASE` statement syntax:

```
CASE expression
WHEN value_matched THEN
   statement
[[WHEN value_matched2 THEN]
   [Statement2]]
[[ELSE]
   [catch_all_code]
END
```

First of all, next to the CASE keyword, the expression that is to be tested needs to be defined. This could be the value of a variable, or a column from a returned value from any column within the T-SQL statement, or any valid expression within SQL Server. This expression is then used to determine the values to be matched in each WHEN statement.

We can have as many WHEN statements as we wish within the CASE condition, and we do not need to cover every condition of possible value that could be placed within the condition. Once the value_matched condition is matched, then only the statements within that WHEN block will be executed. Of course, only the WHEN conditions that are defined will be tested. However, we can cover ourselves for any value within the expression that has not been defined with a WHEN statement by using an ELSE condition. This would be used as a **catch all** statement. Any value not matched would drop in to the ELSE condition and from there we could deal with any scenario that we desire.

A CASE statement does not need to be on its own like an IF...ELSE statement, but can form a decision making process within a SELECT or UPDATE statement. It is possible to set a value for a column within a recordset based on a CASE statement and the resultant value. Obviously, with this knowledge, a CASE statement cannot form part of a DELETE statement.

The CASE statement example is the second example in the series. The first example demonstrates the use of the IF...ELSE statement and the BEGIN...END blocking command.

Validating a Parameter – Using Query Analyzer

It is not necessary to just accept that a value coming in within a parameter is valid. One of the major areas of stored procedures is to assume that any parameter value passed in contains garbage. We should avoid this situation by validating every parameter to ensure that what we are receiving in the stored procedure is what we are expecting. Without validation we will find ourselves in the middle of a 'garbage in, garbage out' scenario.

Validating the data is not as tricky as how to report the error back. The following example will demonstrate how to return an error through an OUTPUT parameter.

Try It Out – Error Handling

1. Make sure Query Analyzer is connected to the Wrox_Golf_Results database. Enter the first section of code, which defines the procedure to create and the parameters to pass in.

```
CREATE PROCEDURE sp_Insert_New_Game
@SocietyGroup INT, @DatePlayed SMALLDATETIME, @Opposition VARCHAR(50), @Home BIT,
@Points_for INT, @Points_Against INT, @ErrorCode INT OUTPUT
AS
```

2. The next section of code deals with the validation of the parameters. All but the @Home parameter is validated: this is because we can only have a 0 or a 1 within the @Home variable, otherwise SQL Server returns an error. Therefore, any erroneous value won't even make it into our stored procedure. Every parameter will have to be validated and each parameter will have its own error value. From there we should know exactly where the problem lies. We first check that a positive @SocietyGroup value is supplied, otherwise we set @ErrorCode = 1. We then check that date of the match played is not in the future, setting @ErrorCode = 2 if DatePlayed is a date greater than today's date. The next check is to ensure that we have not passed an empty name for the opposition, using LEN(@Opposition), which gives us the length of the opposition's name. Finally, we check to see if a valid number of points have been supplied for @Points_For and @Points_Against.

```
IF @SocietyGroup < 1
   BEGIN
      SET @ErrorCode = 1
      RETURN -1
   END
IF @DatePlayed > GETDATE()
   BEGIN
      SET @ErrorCode = 2
      RETURN -1
   END
IF LEN(@Opposition) = 0
   BEGIN
      SET @ErrorCode = 3
      RETURN -1
   END
IF @Points_For < 0 OR @Points_For > 3
   BEGIN
      SET @ErrorCode = 4
      RETURN -1
   END
IF @Points_Against < 0 OR @Points_Against > 3
   BEGIN
      SET @ErrorCode = 5
      RETURN -1
   END
```

3. Now that all the parameters have been tested, it is possible to insert the match results. A simple INSERT statement is now all that is required.

```
INSERT INTO Matches (Society_Group_Id, Date_Played, Opposition_Name, Home,
Points_For, Points_Against)
       VALUES(@SocietyGroup, @DatePlayed, @Opposition, @Home, @Points_For,
@Points_Against)
```

4. This is the completion of the code for the stored procedure so let's build it, ready to test and insert some data. Execute the code above using any of the normal execution methods.

5. Time to test out the procedure. Below is a list of potential insertions, but each will produce a different error. They should produce an error number in an ascending sequence, denoting each of the five validation errors within the stored procedure. Notice how there are several errors in most of the lines of code, but once the first error is reached, the stored procedure exits. Enter the code below and execute it. Note, the `SELECT` statement will return the values for us, with the possible error number being stored in the `@Ret` parameter:

```
SET QUOTED_IDENTIFIER OFF

DECLARE @Ret INT
DECLARE @RetStatus INT
EXEC @RetStatus = sp_Insert_New_Game 0,"24 Mar 2003","",1,-1,4,@Ret OUTPUT
SELECT @RetStatus,@Ret
EXEC @RetStatus = sp_Insert_New_Game 1,"24 Mar 2003","",1,-1,4,@Ret OUTPUT
SELECT @RetStatus,@Ret
EXEC @RetStatus = sp_Insert_New_Game 1,"24 Mar 2001","",1,-1,4,@Ret OUTPUT
SELECT @RetStatus,@Ret
EXEC @RetStatus = sp_Insert_New_Game 1,"24 Mar 2001","Symington Junior
Golfers",1,-1,4,@Ret OUTPUT
SELECT @RetStatus,@Ret
EXEC @RetStatus = sp_Insert_New_Game 1,"24 Mar 2001","Symington Junior
Golfers",1,0,4,@Ret OUTPUT
SELECT @RetStatus,@Ret
```

6. You should see the following results denoting each of the errors being returned:

```
----------- -----------
-1          1

(1 row(s) affected)


----------- -----------
-1          2

(1 row(s) affected)


----------- -----------
-1          3

(1 row(s) affected)


----------- -----------
-1          4

(1 row(s) affected)


----------- -----------
-1          5

(1 row(s) affected)
```

7. Now that the procedure has tested that all the parameters that come in are valid, we can enter some matches, which will be used in a few moments' time. Enter the following matches as if they were real matches that had been played:

```
DECLARE @Ret INT
DECLARE @RetStatus INT
EXEC @RetStatus = sp_Insert_New_Game 1,"24 Mar 2001","The Wrox Hackers",1,3,0,@Ret
OUTPUT
SELECT @RetStatus,@Ret
EXEC @RetStatus = sp_Insert_New_Game 1,"31 Mar 2001","The Vertigo
Vikings",0,1,1,@Ret OUTPUT
SELECT @RetStatus,@Ret
EXEC @RetStatus = sp_Insert_New_Game 1,"7 Apr 2001","The Scottish
Claymores",1,0,3,@Ret OUTPUT
SELECT @RetStatus,@Ret
EXEC @RetStatus = sp_Insert_New_Game 1,"14 Apr 2001","Bedford Charity
Golfers",1,3,0,@Ret OUTPUT
SELECT @RetStatus,@Ret
EXEC @RetStatus = sp_Insert_New_Game 1,"21 apr 2001","Symington Junior
Golfers",0,1,1,@Ret OUTPUT
SELECT @RetStatus,@Ret
```

8. There should now be five matches, with results, entered in the `Matches` table. Normally, we would enter a player's individual result, which would then update this table, and this is covered in Chapter 20, when triggers are discussed. For the moment, view this as entering historical results.

Now that two of the three control-of-flow statements have been covered, time to look at the third, the `CASE` statement.

Using the CASE Statement

As we have just seen, five match results have just been placed into the system. This next example will take those results and, through the use of a `CASE` statement, decide if a particular match was a win, a draw, or a loss. Two parameters will be passed into this stored procedure: The first will be the date of the match, and the second will be the `Society_Group_ID`.

The `CASE` statement will form part of the `SELECT` statement and the result from the `CASE` statement will create one column within a single row of data that is then used as the output to display.

Also, this stored procedure will be encrypted to demonstrate protecting the stored procedure source code.

Try It Out – Using the CASE Statement

1. Find an empty Query pane within Query Analyzer. The following stored procedure is going to use double quotation marks as part of the query, therefore to make sure that entry of the code doesn't fail, ensure that Query Analyzer can cope with this by ensuring that the setting of the `QUOTED_IDENTIFIER` is correct. Execute the following code, just to make sure:

```
SET QUOTED_IDENTIFIER OFF
GO
```

2. Now enter the following stored procedure. Notice that the `Society_Group_ID` has a default value placed against it, and the use of the `ENCRYPTION` keyword. The two parameters will be validated to ensure that the data coming in is valid. Finally the crux of the procedure is where a check on the `Points_For` and the `Points_Against` columns is made to see if this particular result was a win, a loss, or a draw. There is no need for a catch all `ELSE` within the `CASE` as there was enough validation within the stored procedure that inserts the records to ensure that each value must be a win, loss, or draw.

```
CREATE PROCEDURE sp_Win_Lose_Or_Draw
   @Game_Date SMALLDATETIME,
   @Society_Group_ID INT = 1
WITH ENCRYPTION
AS
   IF @Game_Date > GETDATE()
      RETURN 1
   IF @Society_Group_ID < 0
      RETURN 2
   SELECT "Win_Lose_Or_Draw_Result" =
   CASE WHEN Points_For > Points_Against THEN
      "Win"
   WHEN Points_For = Points_Against THEN
      "Draw"
   WHEN Points_For < Points_Against THEN
      "Lost"
   END
      FROM Matches
      WHERE Society_Group_Id = @Society_Group_ID
        AND Date_Played = @Game_Date
GO
```

3. Execute this by pressing *CTRL+E*, *F5*, or the Execute button on the toolbar. This will create the stored procedure. You should see the following:

```
The command(s) completed successfully.
```

4. The following code will then test the stored procedure to ensure that it produces a set of results that match the golf results entered in the previous section. This example will test against the first match played for the 24th March, but it could be run against any of the dates that have matches. To illustrate the method of passing parameters to a stored procedure by using variables, we will declare two variables, `@Game_Date_In` and `@Society_Group_Id_In`, and pass in their values.

```
DECLARE @Game_Date_In smalldatetime
DECLARE @Society_Group_Id_In INT
SET @Game_Date_In = "24 March 2001"
SET @Society_Group_ID_In = 1
EXECUTE sp_Win_Lose_Or_Draw @Game_Date_In, @Society_Group_ID_In
```

5. When executed we should see the following result:

```
Win_Lose_Or_Draw_Result
-----------------------
Win

(1 row(s) affected)
```

How It Works – Using the CASE Statement

Using the CASE statement within a SELECT is purely including intelligent decision making on each row returned from a table. Although the example is working on a single row being returned, this is not a restriction on this clause. A CASE statement can be used on as many rows as necessary and will take each row in turn and make a decision.

As each row is being retrieved from the table, the CASE statement kicks in and instead of the column value being returned, it is the value from the decision making process that is inserted instead. This happens after the data has been retrieved and just before the rows returned are displayed in the Results pane. The actual value is returned initially from the table and is then validated through the CASE statement; once this is done, the value is discarded if no longer required.

We will now move our attention to how the ENCRYPTION keyword works. Move to the **Object Browser** pane and we should find the **sp_Win_Lose_Or_Draw** stored procedure listed. You may have to complete a **Refresh** on the **Object Browser** if you have not already done so, before you can see the procedure; pressing *F5* while the **Object Browser** has the focus can do this. If we expand the node for the stored procedure we will still be able to see the parameters to pass in. Right-click on the procedure we just created and select **Edit** – now we will see how the contents of the procedure are hidden.

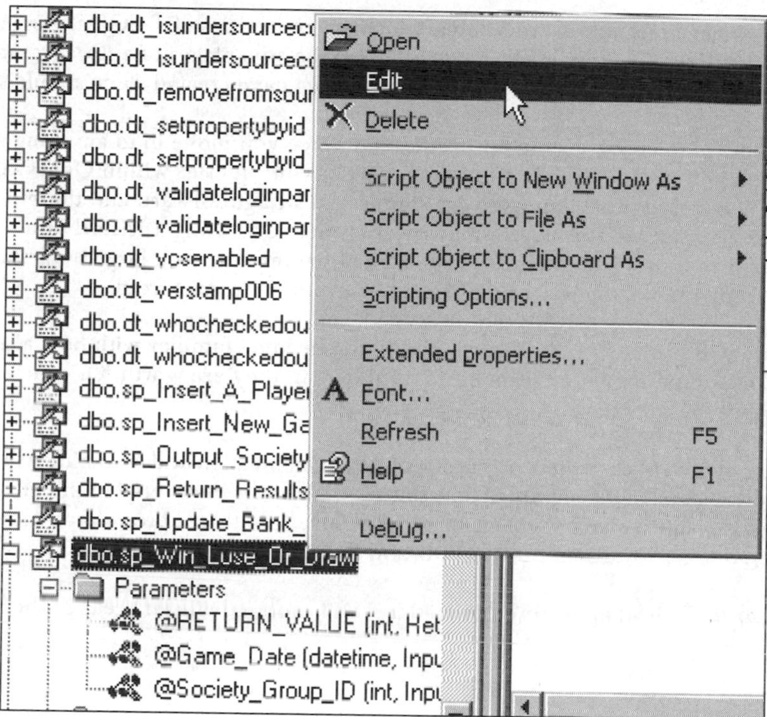

If we then look at the Query pane to the right of the **Object Browser**, we will see the following code. There is just no way that SQL Server will let that code out.

```
SET QUOTED_IDENTIFIER OFF
GO
SET ANSI_NULLS ON
GO

/****** Encrypted object is not transferable, and script can not be generated. ******/

GO
SET QUOTED_IDENTIFIER OFF
GO
SET ANSI_NULLS ON
GO
```

As always, make sure that a copy of the source code is kept elsewhere, just in case modifications need to be made.

Summary

In this chapter, we have met stored procedures, which are collections of T-SQL statements compiled and ready to be executed by SQL Server. We have discussed the advantages of a stored procedure over a view, covered the basic `CREATE PROCEDURE` syntax, and then we have created some simple stored procedures.

There are many ways to create a stored procedure but once you move in to anything more than a simple query, you will no doubt end up building most of your queries within Query Analyzer. The basics of building a stored procedure are very simple and straightforward and therefore building a stored procedure within Query Analyzer may be as attractive as using a wizard or a template. However, if you do have a stored procedure that requires a lot of parameters, or a large SQL statement that uses a lot of columns from a table, the wizard may be a better option to start from.

Using a template will probably only be useful until you become familiar with how a stored procedure is built up. After this point, they may seem more trouble than they are worth. Of course, it is always handy to have them there for reference.

Probably the largest area of code creation outside of data manipulation and searching will be through control-of-flow statements. Not all of the control-of-flow statements have been covered in this chapter: more are covered in the next chapter where we move on to more advanced stored procedures. However, the three statements covered here, `IF...ELSE`, `BEGIN...END`, and `CASE` will cover a large majority of situations.

The next chapter looks further at stored procedures and more advanced areas of their use.

Advanced Stored Procedures

Chapter 17 introduced stored procedures and provided the basic syntax for their use as well as some simple examples. Stored procedures encompass quite a bit more and deserve some additional attention. The syntax allows for sophisticated construction of related, interdependent operations as well as graceful error control.

Certainly, with the material covered in the last chapter you should be able to take advantage of stored procedures in many of your database tasks. This chapter will provide you with some important additional techniques with which to extend the capabilities of your own stored procedures.

In this chapter we will continue our foray into stored procedures by investigating the following:

- Using System Variables to extend Transact-SQL
- How to alter stored procedures
- Using the `RAISERROR` function to provide meaningful error handling and messages
- The System Stored Procedures
- The Extended Stored Procedures

System Variables

There are more than 30 system defined variables, also known as **globals**, within SQL Server, which can be used within queries or stored procedures. These can be used to provide information to a developer to make decisions on whether a process has had the desired results, to retrieve information about the last process, or to provide information about SQL Server. We have already seen one system variable in action, `@@ROWCOUNT`, which was used in the last chapter. Many system variables, such as `@@LANGUAGE`, which returns the name of the language currently used by the system, have little use in routine stored procedures. Some globals, such as `@@TRANCOUNT`, can assist in determining where you are within nested transactions. For most stored procedures, however, the only globals you are likely to use are `@@ROWCOUNT` and two additional variables, `@@ERROR` and `@@IDENTITY`. Appendix B describes all of the system global variables with a short example demonstrating how each can be used.

@@ERROR

With each and every statement executed within a query or stored procedure, it is possible that an error could occur. This could be from an invalid action, data type mismatches and so on, through to actual constraint errors. When an error is generated, it has an associated error number. The variable @@ERROR is set to this numerical value. If the statement is valid however, @@ERROR is set to 0.

After each statement @@ERROR is reset to the new value from the previous action. Therefore, it is imperative for @@ERROR to be placed immediately into a local variable to preserve the value of the previous error for later use. Most likely you will capture the error with the following syntax:

```
SET @err_temp = @@ERROR  -- set the @@ERROR to a local variable
IF NOT @err_temp = 0  -- if an error occurred
RETURN @err_temp.
```

We will explore @@ERROR in greater detail with examples that follow.

@@IDENTITY

Once a record, or batch of records, has been inserted into a table and the insertion command has completed, whether this is an INSERT or a SELECT INTO, the last row entered will set the @@IDENTITY value ready for inspection. If you recall when creating our Players table for example, we set the Player_Id column to be an identity column, which is an int data type that automatically increments when a new record is inserted. It is this value that will be placed in to the @@IDENTITY global. If there is no identity column involved in the insertion, this global will be set to NULL. Actually, every insertion updates the @@IDENTITY value; however, it is not until the query ends that we can get to inspect the value. This value can be used as a reference to pass back to another stored procedure or to indicate the value of the last record entered, for cross checking and validating that the correct number of records have been inserted. This also includes any bulk copy statement where data is loaded in bulk into the table. However, if you run an INSERT and there is an error, the @@IDENTITY global is set to NULL.

> **Although @@IDENTITY is set to NULL when an error occurs, don't forget that the value for the next identity value for a column does increase when there is an error. If you are inserting a record in a transaction, and you complete a ROLLBACK, the value of @@IDENTITY will still be set to that of the last inserted record, whether it is rolled back or not.**

There are quite a few uses for this special system-defined variable. In a relational database, the @@IDENTITY can provide a stored procedure with a foreign key for use in another table. For example, if you create a county in a table, and go on to insert towns in a table related to county, the identity of the newly inserted county can tie the towns to their parent. Without @@IDENTITY, you would have to find the last record inserted with a manual query.

There are some pitfalls to @@IDENTITY. First, you have to set it to a local variable immediately after inserting a record, just like @@ERROR. Subsequent inserts by either the current user or other users will compromise this value if you do not. To ensure the integrity of your insert, you may want to wrap the statement in a transaction block, as described in Chapter 14. For databases with numerous simultaneous users, such as those connected to a web server, locking this transaction block deserves considerable attention.

Setting Multiple Values

There may be times when a conflict of order of setting local variables happens. For example, @@ERROR is set after each statement; @@ROWCOUNT is set after every data access. What if we wanted to store both the @@ERROR value and the @@ROWCOUNT values to local variables? In this instance, we would use a single SELECT or SET statement to set both values, separated by a comma. If we used a seperate SELECT statement to set the @Err variable, this would reset @@ROWCOUNT to a value of 1, as there has been 1 "row" altered by the setting of @Err. To demonstrate:

```
DECLARE @Err int
DECLARE @RowC int
SELECT COUNT(*) FROM Players

SELECT @Err = @@ERROR, @RowC = @@ROWCOUNT
```

By completing the code this way, both settings are within one statement and therefore one local variable setting will not alter the value within another variable setting. Many people get confused when this scenario comes about, so now we are one step ahead of the game!

Now let's look at putting these areas into practice and also look at how to alter a stored procedure.

Altering a Stored Procedure

In the previous chapter, we inserted a record for a player that included an image parameter for the player. This would not work how we would have expected it to, as we would have had to pass in binary data for the image parameter to actually store the physical image within the column. If you want to type in all the binary bits that make up the image, then go ahead, but it will take you an extremely long time, and even then there is no guarantee that you will get it right!

However, it is possible and this is how Microsoft actually inserts images in to the Northwind database. If you want to see for yourself, take a look in C:\Program Files\Microsoft SQL Server\MSSQL\Install and check out instnwnd.sql. You don't have to scroll down far to where you will see a VERY large binary set of data, which is inserting an image in to the Categories table.

In our database, we don't actually hold the image, but a pointer to where the image resides. A pointer will reference the path to where the image is stored. With this information, we can retrieve the image. This next section will take the stored procedure that inserts players, alter it to receive a path to where the image is stored, and then insert the path into the photograph column.

Try It Out – Alter Procedure

1. Ensure Query Analyzer is still running. Navigate to the **Object Browser** and within the **Stored Procedures** of the **Wrox_Golf_Results** database, find **sp_Insert_A_Player**. Right-click and then select **Edit**.

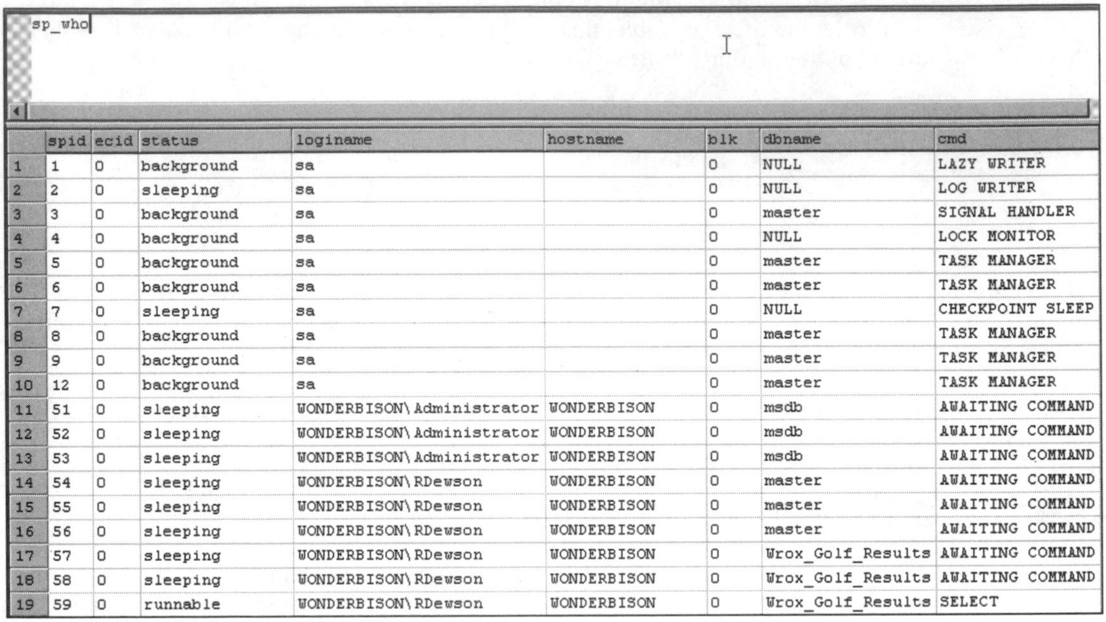

```
sp_who
```

	spid	ecid	status	loginame	hostname	blk	dbname	cmd
1	1	0	background	sa		0	NULL	LAZY WRITER
2	2	0	sleeping	sa		0	NULL	LOG WRITER
3	3	0	background	sa		0	master	SIGNAL HANDLER
4	4	0	background	sa		0	NULL	LOCK MONITOR
5	5	0	background	sa		0	master	TASK MANAGER
6	6	0	background	sa		0	master	TASK MANAGER
7	7	0	sleeping	sa		0	NULL	CHECKPOINT SLEEP
8	8	0	background	sa		0	master	TASK MANAGER
9	9	0	background	sa		0	master	TASK MANAGER
10	12	0	background	sa		0	master	TASK MANAGER
11	51	0	sleeping	WONDERBISON\Administrator	WONDERBISON	0	msdb	AWAITING COMMAND
12	52	0	sleeping	WONDERBISON\Administrator	WONDERBISON	0	msdb	AWAITING COMMAND
13	53	0	sleeping	WONDERBISON\Administrator	WONDERBISON	0	msdb	AWAITING COMMAND
14	54	0	sleeping	WONDERBISON\RDewson	WONDERBISON	0	master	AWAITING COMMAND
15	55	0	sleeping	WONDERBISON\RDewson	WONDERBISON	0	master	AWAITING COMMAND
16	56	0	sleeping	WONDERBISON\RDewson	WONDERBISON	0	master	AWAITING COMMAND
17	57	0	sleeping	WONDERBISON\RDewson	WONDERBISON	0	Wrox_Golf_Results	AWAITING COMMAND
18	58	0	sleeping	WONDERBISON\RDewson	WONDERBISON	0	Wrox_Golf_Results	AWAITING COMMAND
19	59	0	runnable	WONDERBISON\RDewson	WONDERBISON	0	Wrox_Golf_Results	SELECT

2. This will open up a new query pane with the existing code that makes up the stored procedure. The code will look like that below.

```
SET QUOTED_IDENTIFIER OFF
GO
SET ANSI_NULLS OFF
GO

ALTER  PROCEDURE [sp_Insert_A_Player]
    (@iSociety_Group     [int],
    @vPlayer_First_Name [varchar](50),
    @vPlayer_Last_Name  [varchar](50),
    @sdDate_Of_Birth     [smalldatetime],
    @tiGames_played      [tinyint],
    @siPoints_Scored     [smallint],
    @imPhotograph        [image])
AS INSERT INTO Players
    ( [Society_Group],
    [Player_First_Name],
    [Player_Last_Name],
    [Date_Of_Birth],
    [Games_played],
    [Points_Scored],
    [Has_Left_The_Club],
```

```
    [Photograph])

VALUES
    (@iSociety_Group,
    @vPlayer_First_Name,
    @vPlayer_Last_Name,
    @sdDate_Of_Birth,
    @tiGames_played,
    @siPoints_Scored,
    0,
    @imPhotograph)

GO
SET QUOTED_IDENTIFIER OFF
GO
SET ANSI_NULLS ON
GO
```

3. First of all, the stored procedure needs to be altered to accept the path to where the photograph is stored; the procedure will no longer try to accept an image as a parameter. Alter the line highlighted below:

```
SET QUOTED_IDENTIFIER OFF
GO
SET ANSI_NULLS OFF
GO

ALTER  PROCEDURE [sp_Insert_A_Player]
    (@iSociety_Group      [int],
    @vPlayer_First_Name  [varchar](50),
    @vPlayer_Last_Name   [varchar](50),
    @sdDate_Of_Birth     [smalldatetime],
    @tiGames_played      [tinyint],
    @siPoints_Scored     [smallint],
    @vPhotograph_Path    [varchar](100))
```

4. If you remember from when we were looking at inserting data in Chapter 12, it was necessary to find the pointer of the image and then place it in the new pointer. Now that we know about the `@@IDENTITY` system variable, this whole process of inserting a player can all be completed within the stored procedure. When a record is inserted, the identity value of that row will be returned and placed in the first local variable. The second local variable that needs to be defined is the variable that will hold the text pointer, the third variable will hold the error number from any SQL statement, and, finally, the fourth local variable will hold the number of rows affected by the last statement. Put the following code into the stored procedure before the final `SET QUOTED_IDENTIFIER OFF` statement.

```
DECLARE @New_Player_Id int
DECLARE @Photo_Pointer varbinary(16)
DECLARE @Error_Value int
DECLARE @Rows int
```

5. There will be no validation of parameters within this stored procedure, to allow the focus of the example to stay on altering a procedure and inserting an image, but we should always do this. The next change is the insertion of the `Players` details from the parameters. The only real alteration covers the insertion to the photograph column where a hexadecimal value will be inserted, as was discussed in Chapter 12 on *Inserting Data*. We will subsequently overwrite the hex value we are inserting with a `WRITETEXT` statement, so the 0xFFFFFF will simply provide a non-`NULL` value for `Photograph`.

```
AS INSERT INTO Players
   ( [Society_Group],
    [Player_First_Name],
    [Player_Last_Name],
    [Date_Of_Birth],
    [Games_played],
    [Points_Scored],
    [Has_Left_The_Club],
    [Photograph])

VALUES
   (@iSociety_Group,
    @vPlayer_First_Name,
    @vPlayer_Last_Name,
    @sdDate_Of_Birth,
    @tiGames_played,
    @siPoints_Scored,
    0,
    0xFFFFFF)
```

6. It is now time to move on to retrieving the `@@IDENTITY` value while checking the `@@ERROR` value. So which should come first? As we have discussed, we should store their values in local variables before they are tested. Since setting the `@@ERROR` variable does not involve inserting any records, we can be safe in assuming that storing `@@ERROR` will not interfere with value of `@@IDENTITY`. Consequently, we will set the error variable first. Once set, test the variable holding the error value, and if it is a non-zero value, then return this to the calling procedure or statement. If the value is zero, then it is safe to proceed. Enter this code after the variable declarations entered previously. We could of course, set both variables in one `SET` statement if we so desired as well. They have been split out here simply to aid discussion of the example.

```
SET @Error_Value = @@ERROR
IF NOT @Error_Value  = 0
   RETURN @Error_Value
```

7. The next area that has to be completed is the storing of the identity value generated by the insertion. This is straightforward and is purely setting the value to a variable. We will use the `@@IDENTITY` to keep track of the record we created that we will subsequently query to obtain the text pointer. Enter this after the previous section.

```
SET @New_Player_Id = @@IDENTITY
```

8. Now use this value to find our new record to retrieve the text pointer. The value is used within the WHERE statement, which should only return one record as the value is unique. A TEXTPTR() function, which provides a unique value for each image column of a row, will provide us a storage address for the image. As before, the pointer within the Photograph column is placed into the variable, which is used in a few moments when writing back the new pointer to the Players table. Enter this after the previous section:

```
SELECT @Photo_Pointer = TEXTPTR(Photograph)
FROM Players
WHERE Player_Id = @New_Player_Id
```

9. There is no need to check the @@ERROR global at this point. By checking the @@ROWCOUNT global, providing that this returns one, we know that the record has been found successfully. Enter this after the previous section:

```
SET @Rows = @@ROWCOUNT

IF NOT @Rows = 1
   RETURN -1
```

10. The last modification to the stored procedure is to write the new pointer to where the image is stored. The WRITETEXT statement uses the pointer created in the SELECT statement above, and then also uses the parameter that holds the path to where the image is stored. WRITETEXT allows updates of a database without SQL Server logging the event. This is an important advantage when manipulating image or text fields, since their substantial size could quickly lead to congestion of a transaction log. The syntax for the statement begins with the command WRITETEXT followed by the table name and column. The final attribute to assign is the data to be written, in this case represented by the variable @vPhotograph_Path. Again the @@ERROR global is checked to ensure that no errors have occurred. Enter this after the previous section:

```
WRITETEXT Players.Photograph @Photo_Pointer @vPhotograph_Path

SET @Error_Value = @@ERROR
IF NOT @Error_Value  = 0
   RETURN @Error Value
```

11. The stored procedure for inserting players is now ready for building and inserting into SQL Server and should look like the following:

```
SET QUOTED_IDENTIFIER OFF
GO
SET ANSI_NULLS OFF
GO

ALTER PROCEDURE [sp_Insert_A_Player]
   (@iSociety_Group       [int],
   @vPlayer_First_Name    [varchar](50),
   @vPlayer_Last_Name     [varchar](50),
   @sdDate_Of_Birth       [smalldatetime],
   @tiGames_played        [tinyint],
```

```
   @siPoints_Scored      [smallint],
   @vPhotograph_Path     [varchar] (100))
AS INSERT INTO Players
   ([Society_Group],
   [Player_First_Name],
   [Player_Last_Name],
   [Date_Of_Birth],
   [Games_played],
   [Points_Scored],
   [Has_Left_The_Club],
   [Photograph])

VALUES
   (@iSociety_Group,
   @vPlayer_First_Name,
   @vPlayer_Last_Name,
   @sdDate_Of_Birth,
   @tiGames_played,
   @siPoints_Scored,
   0,
   0xFFFFFF)

DECLARE @New_Player_Id int
DECLARE @Photo_Pointer varbinary(16)
DECLARE @Error_Value int
DECLARE @Rows int

SET @Error_Value = @@ERROR
IF NOT @Error_Value  = 0
   RETURN @Error_Value
SET @New_Player_Id = @@IDENTITY
SELECT @Photo_Pointer = TEXTPTR(Photograph)
FROM Players
WHERE Player_Id = @New_Player_Id
SET @Rows = @@ROWCOUNT

IF NOT @Rows = 1
   RETURN -1
WRITETEXT Players.Photograph @Photo_Pointer @vPhotograph_Path

SET @Error_Value = @@ERROR
IF NOT @Error_Value  = 0
   RETURN @Error_Value
GO

SET QUOTED_IDENTIFIER OFF
GO
SET ANSI_NULLS ON
GO
```

12. Execute the code and commit the changes to the system. There is no GRANT statement associated with this statement because the stored procedure was only altered, not dropped. Therefore the permissions associated with this object are still in place. If our permissions denied users UPDATE privileges, we would have to include a third statement with the QUOTED_IDENTIFIER and ANSI_NULLS to permit the action. Once executed, we should see the following message:

```
The command(s) completed successfully.
```

13. Time to test out the stored procedure. Jason Atkins already exists within the Players table but we will borrow his photograph to insert another player ID to test out the procedure. Of course, if this was in a live environment, then we should either use the right photograph or replace the photograph with the correct one as soon as possible. This was covered in Chapter 14, the *Updating Data and Transactions* chapter. Enter the following code into an empty pane and execute it.

```
sp_Insert_A_Player @iSociety_Group=1,
   @vPlayer_First_Name="Glen",
   @vPlayer_Last_Name="Harding",
   @sdDate_Of_Birth="23 September 1961",
   @tiGames_played=0,
   @siPoints_Scored=0,
   @vPhotograph_Path="C:\Program Files\Microsoft SQL
                        Server\MSSQL\Data\Wrox_Golf_Results\Images\ja.bmp"
```

14. If we then check the Players table, we will find that the record has been successfully inserted with the same pointer. Depending on what other player records you have added in, you may need to alter the query, but the basis is to list both Jason's and Glen's records.

```
SELECT Player_First_Name,Photograph FROM Players
WHERE  Player_Last_Name = "Atkins" OR Player_Last_Name = "Harding"
```

15. When we look at the results, we will see that both players' Photograph columns are identical

```
Player_First_Name  Photograph
--------------------------------------------------------------------------
Jason              0x433A5C50726F6772616D2046696C65735C4D6963726F736F6674
Glen               0x433A5C50726F6772616D2046696C65735C4D6963726F736F6674

(2 row(s) affected)
```

We now have built up a more advanced stored procedure where values returned from actions have been put to use elsewhere within a stored procedure. Before exploring more advanced examples, we need to take one last look at errors.

RAISERROR

There is one last area of error handling that has to be addressed before it is possible to leave it, and that is the ability to produce our own SQL Server error messages when running queries or stored procedures. We are not tied to just using error messages that come with SQL Server; we can set up our own messages and our own level of severity for those messages. It is also possible to determine whether the message is recorded in the Windows error log or not.

However, whether we wish to use our own error message or a system error message, we can still generate an error message from SQL Server as if SQL Server itself raised it. This gives an advantage over using a parameter or the `RETURN` keyword, as we can give back specific text with an error message as well as an error number, which means that the user will receive more useful information about what went wrong. To do this using the `RETURN` keyword is impossible, and it would require parameters to achieve. We also won't be able to log any errors into the Windows error log as we can with `RAISERROR`. Furthermore, it is also possible to pass in a parameter to a SQL Server error message, giving a more specific definition to a more general error message.

Enterprise environments typically experience the same errors on repeated occasions, since they employ SQL Server in very specific ways depending on their business model. With this in mind, attention to employing `RAISERROR` can have big benefits by providing more meaningful feedback as well as suggested solutions for users.

By using `RAISERROR` the whole SQL Server system will act as if SQL Server raised the error. This gives a great deal more power to our stored procedure.

`RAISERROR` can be used in one of two ways; looking at the syntax will make this clear.

```
RAISERROR ({msg_id|msg_str} {,severity,state}
          [,argument [ ,...n ] ])
          [WITH option [ ,...n ]]
```

You can either use a specific `msg_id` or provide an actual output string, `msg_str`, containing the error message that will be recorded. The `msg_id` references system and user-defined messages that already exist within the SQL Server error messages table. We will look at how to create a user-defined message shortly. There is also a system stored procedure `sp_addmessage` that can create a new global error message. We will look at this in more detail shortly.

Alternatively, you may specify a text message in the first parameter of the `RAISERROR` function. This is easier to write than creating a new message, but does not allow you to use some of the tools afforded in Enterprise Manager for extending error messages. The syntax for specifying a text message looks like:

```
RAISERROR('You made an error', 10, 1)
```

The next two parameters in the `RAISERROR` syntax are numerical and relate to how severe the error is and information about how the error was invoked. Severity levels range from 1 at the innocuous end to 25 at the fatal end. Severity levels of 2-14 are generally informational. Severity level 15 is for warnings and levels 16 or higher represent errors. Severity levels from 20-25 are considered fatal, and require the `WITH LOG` option, which will mean that the error is logged in the Windows error log and the connection terminated; quite simply, the stored procedure stops executing. The connection referred to here is the connection within Query Analyzer, or the connection made by an application using a data access method like ADO. Only for a most extreme error would we set the severity to this level; in most cases, we would use a number between 1 and 18.

The last parameter within the function specifies `state`. Use a 1 here for most implementations, although the legitimate range is from 1 to 127. You may use this to indicate which error was thrown by providing a different state for each `RAISERROR` function in your stored procedure. SQL Server will not act on any legitimate state value, but the parameter is required.

If `msg_str` has a parameter defined within the text, then placing the value, either statically or via a variable, after the last parameter that you define, will replace the message parameter with that value. This is demonstrated in the following example.

> *To place a parameter within a message string, where the parameter needs to be inserted, you would define this by a % sign followed by one of the following options:* `d` *or* `i` *for a signed integer,* `p` *for a pointer,* `s` *for a string,* `u` *for unsigned integer,* `x` *or* `X` *for unsigned hexadecimal, and* `o` *for unsigned octal. Note that float, double, and single are not supported as parameter types for messages.*

Finally, there are three options that could be placed at the end of the `RAISERROR` message. These are the `WITH` options: `LOG` will place the error message within the Windows error log, `NOWAIT` sends the error directly to the client, and `SETERROR` will reset the error number to 50000 within the message string only. When using any of these last `WITH` options, do take the greatest of care as their misuse can create more problems than they solve. For example, you may unnecessarily use `LOG` a great deal, filling up the Windows error log, which leads to further problems.

Time now to move to the next example, which will set up an error message that will then be used within the `sp_Insert_New_Game` procedure. We will replace the error codes by using the `RAISERROR` command as well as providing a text parameter giving details of the specific error that has occurred. Let's now take a look at how this all works.

Try It Out – RAISERROR

1. First of all, it is necessary to define an error message to return when a specific error has occurred. Error messages can be added to the system by one of two methods: this example will use the SQL Server method of adding a message, but it is also possible to use a system defined procedure, `sp_addmessage`. A quick look at `sp_addmessage` follows in the System Procedures section at the end of this chapter. To add a message in SQL Server, select **Tools | Manage SQL Server Messages…** from the menu within Enterprise Manager.

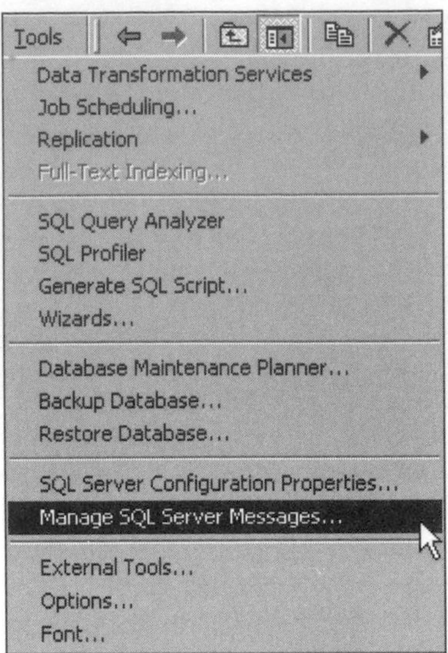

2. This will bring up the Manage SQL Server Messages screen. Clicking on the Messages tab will allow new messages to be entered. Any new message created will only be available for that SQL Server instance, and is not populated through every instance that Enterprise Manager is connected to. At the moment, there are no user-defined error messages. To add one, click on New...

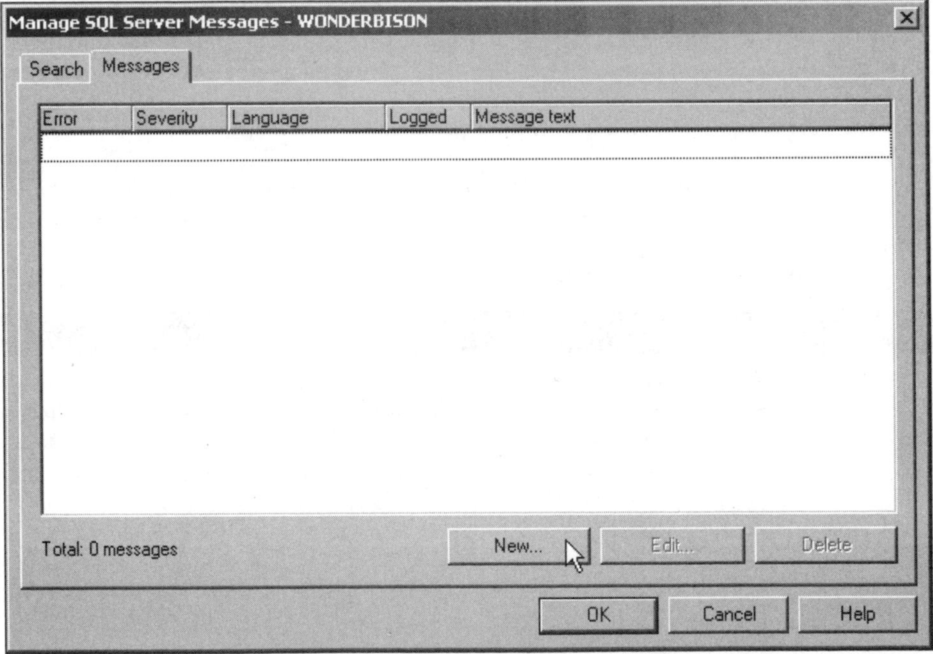

3. We can now add any new SQL Server message that we wish. Any user-defined error message must be greater than 50000 and so the first error message would normally be 50001. The New SQL Server Message screen enters this first available number for you. Ignore the Severity combo box for the moment as this will be covered in the next bullet point. Within the Message text box, enter the error message that you wish to output. We can define the Language of the error message and finally, whether we wish the error message to be written to the Windows eventlog. This option should only be checked when the error is of a severe enough nature that it needs recording within the event log. These error messages tend to be recorded when a fatal error occurs, and if we select a severity level of 20-25, this is checked and cannot be edited.

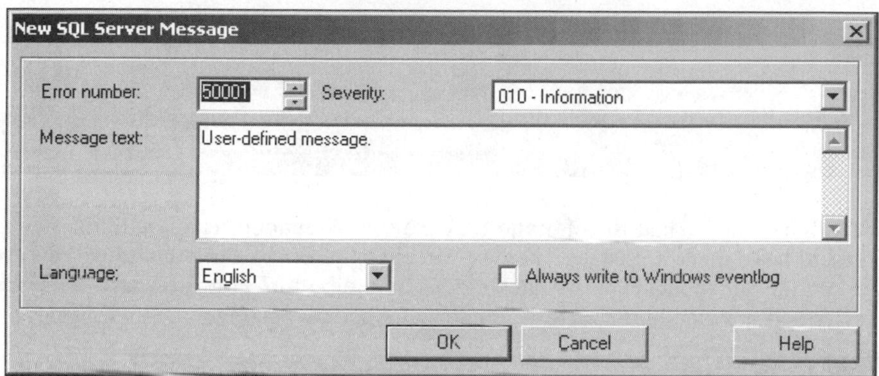

4. Moving back to the Severity: combo box, there is quite a large range of error levels that could be chosen for the error message. In the instance of this message, it is for informational purposes only, although if we look through the possible list, the range goes as high as fatal error severities. Choose the level of severity with care as it will determine how other developers perceive the message; the wrong setting could mean that the message is misused.

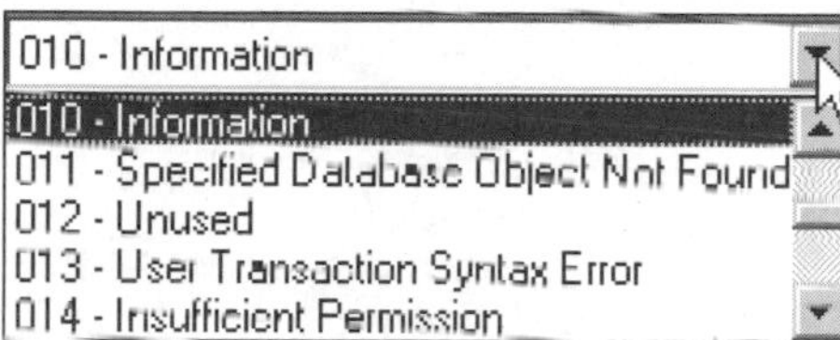

5. Enter the following text into the dialog box:

An error has occurred with a user passed parameter. Please correct and try again. The parameter in error is %s

Overleaf is the filled-in dialog box. Notice that the Message text is pretty general and could be applied in several scenarios. The key here is really a balance between the need to give the user sufficient information about what's gone wrong and the need to avoid too many similar messages. Now that all the details have been chosen and entered, click OK to add the message. Notice at the end of the message, there is a %s sign denoting a string: this will be used to define what is in the error parameter.

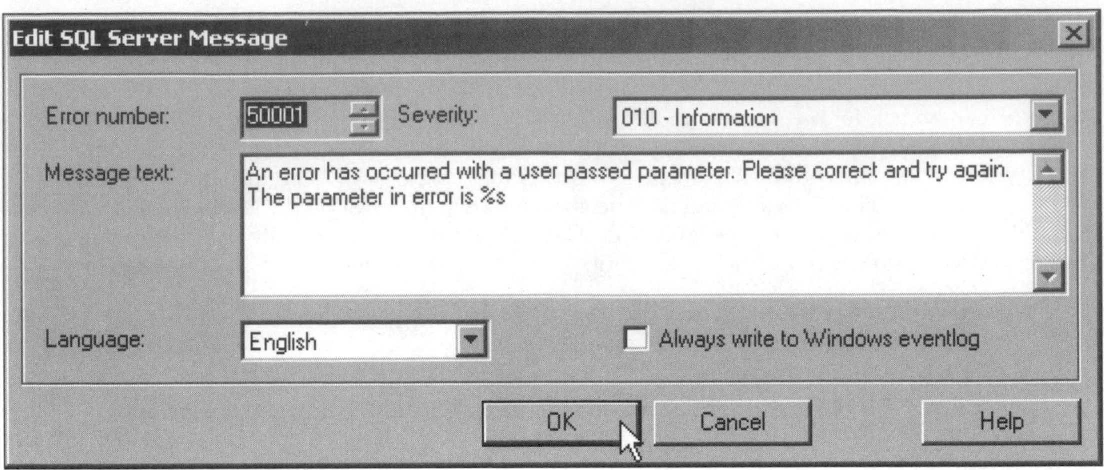

6. We will now be back at the **Manage SQL Server Messages** screen with the new message entered. If we made a mistake, then we can click the **Edit...** button, and we can also remove old and unwanted messages by clicking the **Delete** button. How to search for system error messages is covered in the `@@ERROR` entry of Appendix B.

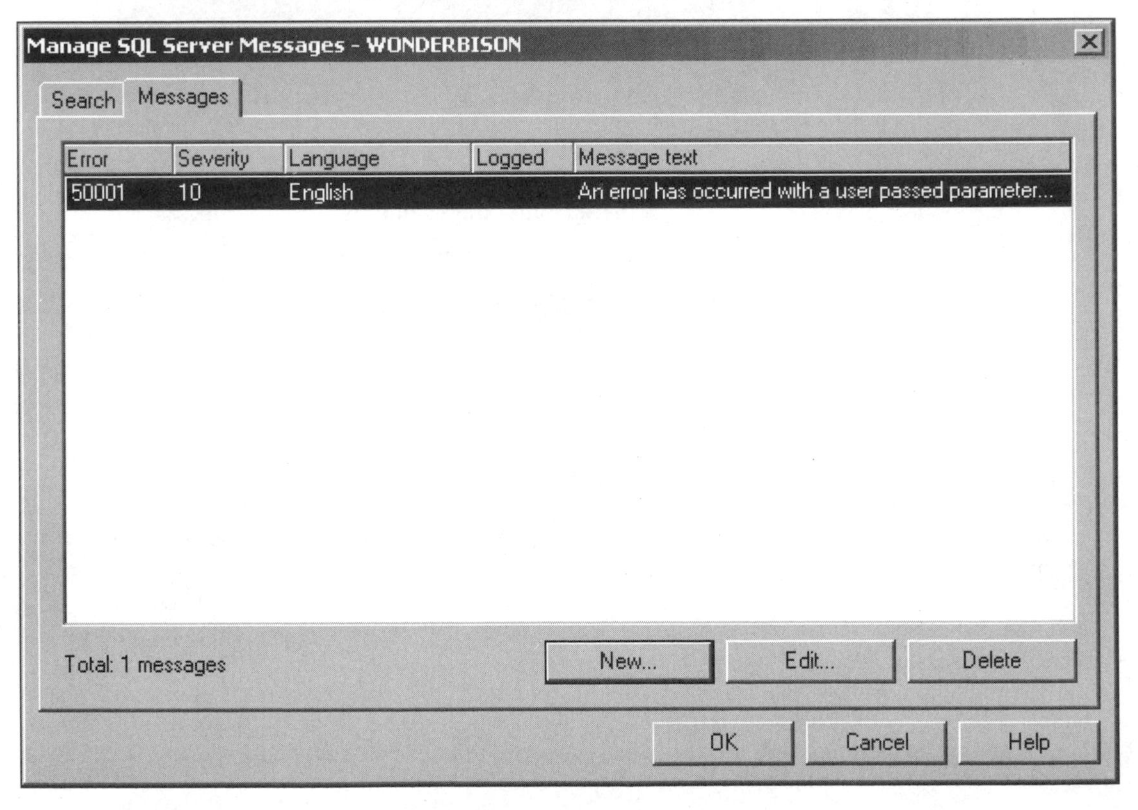

Manage SQL Server Messages - WONDERBISON

Search | Messages

Error	Severity	Language	Logged	Message text
50001	10	English		An error has occurred with a user passed parameter...

Total: 1 messages

New... | Edit... | Delete

OK | Cancel | Help

7. Now that the error message is set up, it's time to alter the procedure. Right-click on the procedure **sp_Insert_New_Game** in the **Object Browser** in Query Analyzer, and select **Edit**.

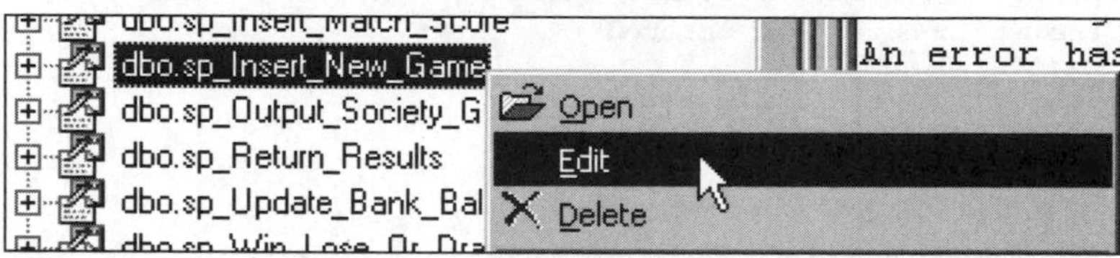

8. The code for the procedure is listed below with the changes to the procedure highlighted for you. Note that the `@ErrorCode` parameter has been commented out with `--`, and so have all lines that `SET @ErrorCode`. If you wish, you may remove these lines from the procedure, as the `@ErrorCode` parameter is no longer required. The `RAISERROR` command allows us to pass the parameter that has the error followed by a custom message that overrides the default message we set up in SQL Server.

```
SET QUOTED_IDENTIFIER OFF
GO
SET ANSI_NULLS ON
GO

ALTER      PROCEDURE sp_Insert_New_Game
@SocietyGroup INT, @DatePlayed SMALLDATETIME, @Opposition VARCHAR(50),
@Home BIT, @Points_For INT, @Points_Against INT = 0
 -- , @ErrorCode INT OUTPUT
AS
DECLARE @MatchId INT

IF @SocietyGroup < 1
   BEGIN
      RAISERROR(50001,16,1,"@SocietyGroup - Society Group < 1")
      -- SET @ErrorCode = 1
      RETURN  1
   END
IF @DatePlayed > GETDATE()
   BEGIN
      RAISERROR(50001,16,1,"@DatePlayed - Date Played is in the future")
      -- SET @ErrorCode = 2
      RETURN -1
   END
IF LEN(@Opposition) = 0
   BEGIN
      RAISERROR(50001,16,1,"@Opposition - No opposition has been entered")
      -- SET @ErrorCode = 3
      RETURN -1
   END
IF @Points_For < 0 OR @Points_For > 3
   BEGIN
      RAISERROR(50001,16,1,"@Points_For - The wrong number of points for the
         match have been entered")
      -- SET @ErrorCode = 4
      RETURN -1
   END
```

```
IF @Points_Against < 0 OR @Points_Against > 3
   BEGIN
      RAISERROR(50001,16,1,"@Points_Against - The wrong number of points for
         the match have been entered")
      -- SET @ErrorCode = 5
      RETURN -1
   END


-- All the parameters are okay, so proceed

INSERT INTO Matches (Society_Group_Id, Date_Played, Opposition_Name, Home,
         Points_For, Points_Against)
      VALUES(@SocietyGroup, @DatePlayed, @Opposition, @Home, @Points_For,
         @Points_Against)
```

9. As a final modification to the procedure, we will store the value of `@@IDENTITY` in `@MatchId`, which will be the value returned if the procedure has not already encountered an error.

```
SET @MatchId = @@IDENTITY

RETURN @MatchId

GO
SET QUOTED_IDENTIFIER OFF
GO
SET ANSI_NULLS ON
GO
```

10. The changes are as simple as that, so execute the code to commit the alterations to SQL Server. It is now time to test out the alterations made to ensure that the `RAISERROR` works. Enter the following code, which will test each of the parameters, into a Query pane. Note that since we have removed the `@ErrorCode` parameter from the procedure, we also need to list one less parameter.

```
SET QUOTED_IDENTIFIER OFF
GO

DECLARE @Ret INT
DECLARE @RetStatus INT
EXEC @RetStatus = sp_Insert_New_Game 0,"24 Mar 2003","",1,-1,4
SELECT @RetStatus
EXEC @RetStatus = sp_Insert_New_Game 1,"24 Mar 2003","",1,-1,4
SELECT @RetStatus
EXEC @RetStatus = sp_Insert_New_Game 1,"24 Mar 2001","",1,-1,4
SELECT @RetStatus
EXEC @RetStatus = sp_Insert_New_Game 1,"24 Mar 2001","Symington Junior
Golfers",1,-1,4
SELECT @RetStatus
EXEC @RetStatus = sp_Insert_New_Game 1,"24 Mar 2001","Symington Junior
Golfers",1,0,4
SELECT @RetStatus
```

11. When we execute this code, as expected, the error generated will match with the erroneous parameter. We should see the following output. Notice how much more information is given out using the `RAISERROR` method: we have the name of the procedure, the line the error occurred, plus the error that we expected from the messages.

```
Server: Msg 50001, Level 16, State 1, Procedure sp_Insert_New_Game, Line 11
An error has occurred with a user passed parameter. Please correct and try again. The
parameter in error is @SocietyGroup - Society Group < 1

-----------
-1

(1 row(s) affected)

Server: Msg 50001, Level 16, State 1, Procedure sp_Insert_New_Game, Line 16
An error has occurred with a user passed parameter. Please correct and try again. The
parameter in error is @DatePlayed - Date Played is in the future

-----------
-1

(1 row(s) affected)

Server: Msg 50001, Level 16, State 1, Procedure sp_Insert_New_Game, Line 21
An error has occurred with a user passed parameter. Please correct and try again. The
parameter in error is @Opposition - No opposition has been entered

-----------
-1

(1 row(s) affected)

Server: Msg 50001, Level 16, State 1, Procedure sp_Insert_New_Game, Line 26
An error has occurred with a user passed parameter. Please correct and try again. The
parameter in error is @Points_For - The wrong number of points for the match have been
entered

-----------
-1

(1 row(s) affected)
```

```
Server: Msg 50001, Level 16, State 1, Procedure sp_Insert_New_Game, Line 32
An error has occurred with a user passed parameter. Please correct and try again. The
parameter in error is @Points_Against - The wrong number of points for the match have been
entered

-----------
-1

(1 row(s) affected)
```

To exploit the `state` parameter, we could have assigned sequential states to the errors. This may have been more meaningful than the line number in understanding where the error was generated. Since our error messages are particularly descriptive, such an approach was unnecessary here.

The final area of stored procedures is to have a look at a handful of system stored procedures that exist within SQL Server. Although we have come across how to perform these actions using other methods, some people prefer to work within Query Analyzer and enter the information without using Enterprise Manager.

System Stored Procedures

Within SQL Server, there are already many useful stored procedures that even a beginner should be aware of. Of course, by this stage of the book, we have progressed further on from that! These stored procedures are very useful in providing information or allowing tasks to be completed without the need for SQL Server Enterprise Manager. Below is a list of what will probably be the most used stored procedure commands; this is by no means an exhaustive list. With almost five hundred system stored procedures within SQL Server, to provide an exhaustive list could well take up over a quarter of the size of this book, of which less than 10% would be used by everyone except administrators; however, all of these are covered in the SQL Server documentation. Many of the system stored procedures reside in the `master` database. Let's now take a look at some prominent stored procedures.

sp_addmessage

As we saw earlier, adding a user defined SQL Server message can be completed through Enterprise Manager. However it is also possible to add a message using T-SQL. You will recognize the `msg_id`, `severity`, `msg`, and `WITH LOG` parameters from the previous example. The last option, however, is the new option: `@replace`. We need to specify this option, and the syntax of `replace` as the value for the parameter, if the error message already exists and we wish to replace what was there before with the new values. Failure to do so will result in an error message.

Don't forget that user-defined error messages should start at 50001, since the earlier numbers belong to SQL Server. There are some possible numbers prior to 50000, but you are safer to avoid them, as they could be used by Microsoft at any point.

```
sp_addmessage [@msgnum=]msg_id ,
   [@severity=]severity ,
   [@msgtext=]'msg'
   [,[@lang=]'language' ]
   [,[@with_log=]'with_log' ]
   [,[@replace=]'replace' ]
```

sp_help

This system stored procedure provides helpful information about objects within a database. It cannot give information about the database itself, merely an object contained within it. It is not compulsory to name an object to use within sp_help; by not passing in an object name, we will receive a list of the objects within the database about which we can receive more information. These are, for example, the views and tables within the database. Triggers and constraints, for example, form parts of a table definition and so cannot be listed using sp_help.

Below is the syntax for sp_help, which may or may not take in the object name.

```
sp_help [[@objname=]name]
```

The screenshot below demonstrates sp_help with no object passed in. Notice that all the tables and the views from the database are listed, along with a few system objects. These can also be interrogated specifically as they do form part of the database; however, there is little or nothing to be gained from this, so it would be best if they were ignored.

	Name	Owner	Object_type
1	sysconstraints	dbo	view
2	syssegments	dbo	view
3	vwMatches	dbo	view
4	vwPlayer_Mugshots	db_owner	view
5	vwPlayers_Details	dbo	view
6	vwSociety_Groups_Balances	dbo	view
7	Club_Details	dbo	user table
8	dtproperties	dbo	user table
9	Match Scores	dbo	user table
10	Matches	dbo	user table
11	Newsletters	dbo	user table

However, if we use sp_help with an object, we will get a great deal more information. In the screenshot overleaf, we have performed an sp_help on the Matches table. Look at the vast amount of information passed across: from one command we can have virtually every piece of information about a table instantly available to us.

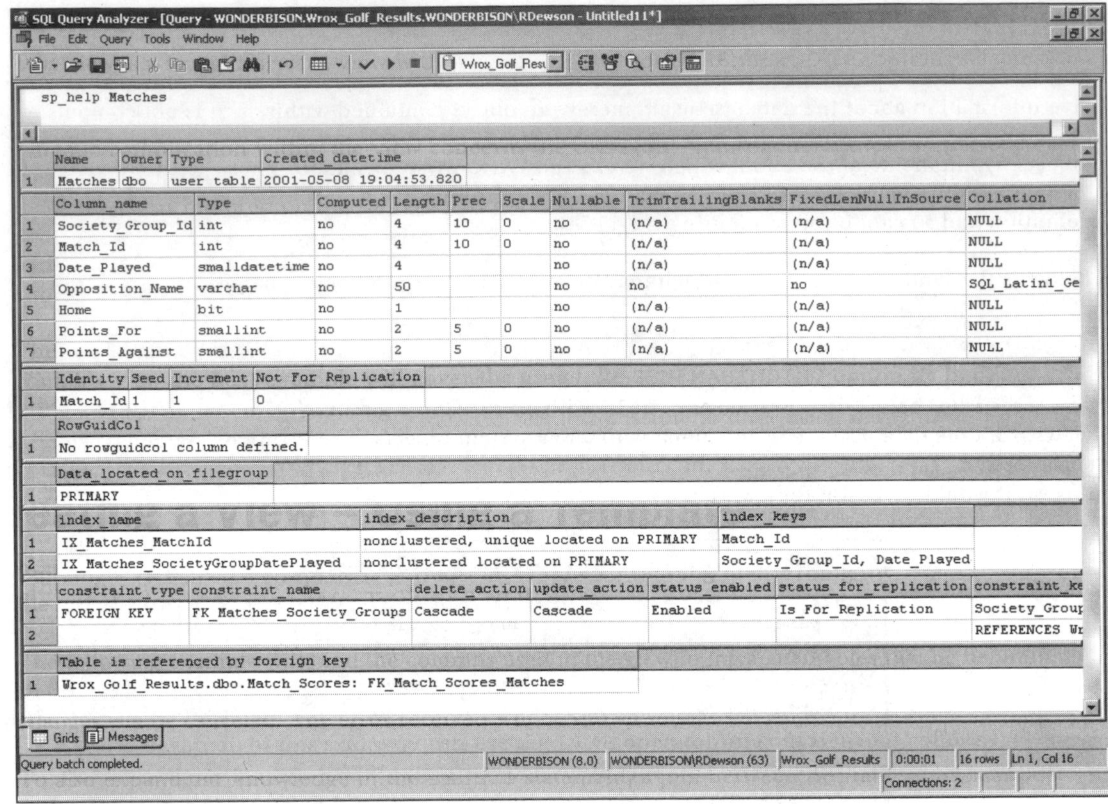

SQL Query Analyzer - [Query - WONDERBISON.Wrox_Golf_Results.WONDERBISON\RDewson - Untitled11*]
File Edit Query Tools Window Help
sp_help Matches
Name Owner Type Created_datetime
1 Matches dbo user table 2001-05-08 19:04:53.820
Column_name Type Computed Length Prec Scale Nullable TrimTrailingBlanks FixedLenNullInSource Collation
1 Society_Group_Id int no 4 10 0 no (n/a) (n/a) NULL
2 Match_Id int no 4 10 0 no (n/a) (n/a) NULL
3 Date_Played smalldatetime no 4 no (n/a) (n/a) NULL
4 Opposition_Name varchar no 50 no no no SQL_Latin1_Ge
5 Home bit no 1 no (n/a) (n/a) NULL
6 Points_For smallint no 2 5 0 no (n/a) (n/a) NULL
7 Points_Against smallint no 2 5 0 no (n/a) (n/a) NULL
Identity Seed Increment Not For Replication
1 Match_Id 1 1 0
RowGuidCol
1 No rowguidcol column defined.
Data_located_on_filegroup
1 PRIMARY
index_name index_description index_keys
1 IX_Matches_MatchId nonclustered, unique located on PRIMARY Match_Id
2 IX_Matches_SocietyGroupDatePlayed nonclustered located on PRIMARY Society_Group_Id, Date_Played
constraint_type constraint_name delete_action update_action status_enabled status_for_replication constraint_ke
1 FOREIGN KEY FK_Matches_Society_Groups Cascade Cascade Enabled Is_For_Replication Society_Grour
2 REFERENCES Wr
Table is referenced by foreign key
1 Wrox_Golf_Results.dbo.Match_Scores: FK_Match_Scores_Matches
Grids Messages
Query batch completed.
WONDERBISON (8.0) WONDERBISON\RDewson (63) Wrox_Golf_Results 0:00:01 16 rows Ln 1, Col 16
Connections: 2

sp_password

If we are using SQL Server logins, there will be times when we wish to set a new password to a user ID. We can change our own user ID password while within a successful login, or, if we have membership to the `sysadmin` roles, we can set anyone's password within that database. This procedure may only change standard logins.

Resetting a password is instantaneous and will be reflected at the next login attempt but will not affect a currently logged in user. The syntax is as follows:

```
sp_password [[@old=]'old_password',] {[@new=]'new_password'}
            [,[@loginame=]'login']
```

sp_who

There will be times when we will need to know who is logged on to our SQL Server instance and what they are doing. This could be for a number of reasons: when SQL Server has ground to a halt because a stored procedure is executing an infinite loop, or perhaps a query attempting to bring back a great deal of data has become stuck. By executing `sp_who`, we can see which IDs have connections, what their status is, which database they are working with, and what they are trying to perform.

```
sp_who
```

	spid	ecid	status	loginame	hostname	blk	dbname	cmd
1	1	0	background	sa		0	NULL	LAZY WRITER
2	2	0	sleeping	sa		0	NULL	LOG WRITER
3	3	0	background	sa		0	master	SIGNAL HANDLER
4	4	0	background	sa		0	NULL	LOCK MONITOR
5	5	0	background	sa		0	master	TASK MANAGER
6	6	0	background	sa		0	master	TASK MANAGER
7	7	0	sleeping	sa		0	NULL	CHECKPOINT SLEEP
8	8	0	background	sa		0	master	TASK MANAGER
9	9	0	background	sa		0	master	TASK MANAGER
10	12	0	background	sa		0	master	TASK MANAGER
11	51	0	sleeping	WONDERBISON\Administrator	WONDERBISON	0	msdb	AWAITING COMMAND
12	52	0	sleeping	WONDERBISON\Administrator	WONDERBISON	0	msdb	AWAITING COMMAND
13	53	0	sleeping	WONDERBISON\Administrator	WONDERBISON	0	msdb	AWAITING COMMAND
14	54	0	sleeping	WONDERBISON\RDewson	WONDERBISON	0	master	AWAITING COMMAND
15	55	0	sleeping	WONDERBISON\RDewson	WONDERBISON	0	master	AWAITING COMMAND
16	56	0	sleeping	WONDERBISON\RDewson	WONDERBISON	0	master	AWAITING COMMAND
17	57	0	sleeping	WONDERBISON\RDewson	WONDERBISON	0	Wrox_Golf_Results	AWAITING COMMAND
18	58	0	sleeping	WONDERBISON\RDewson	WONDERBISON	0	Wrox_Golf_Results	AWAITING COMMAND
19	59	0	runnable	WONDERBISON\RDewson	WONDERBISON	0	Wrox_Golf_Results	SELECT

If we inspect the data listed for `sp_who` above, the only real command that is performing any action is the last item in the list, which is performing a `SELECT`. This is running under system process ID, or spid, 59. Rows 11-13, spids 51, 52, and 53, are all logged in as the Adminstrator ID to the `msdb` database. These three connections relate to SQL Server Service Manager. The last seven rows of processes that are listed as running under the login sa are all processes which would be used by SQL Server when required. The other rows are connections that currently exist within Query Analyzer or Enterprise Manager (spids 57-59). You will be able to figure this out yourself, as each individual Query pane creates a new spid. However, working out which spid means what only comes from experience and investigative work. To gain that experience, create queries that take a few minutes to run, within Query panes in separate Query Analyzers if you wish. Each of these queries should process different tasks, for example a `SELECT`, another completing an `INSERT`, and so on. Of course, this should only be attempted in a development environment.

System Catalog Stored Procedures

System stored procedures are grouped into a dozen categories, including replication, security, system, and cursor procedures among others. An interesting group for database developers is the System Catalog stored procedures. These stored procedures provide a catalog of information about databases on your server. They can list all databases with `sp_databases`, identify foreign keys that reference primary keys in a linked server with `sp_pkeys`, and list all of the tables with `sp_tables`. For example, ensure that the Wrox_Golf_Results database is selected in Query Analyzer, enter the following into the query pane, and then execute the code.

```
sp_tables @table_type = "'TABLE'"
```

This stored procedure will return all the tables in the Wrox_Golf_Results database that are not system tables or views. At this point in the book, the output would look like:

	TABLE_QUALIFIER	TABLE_OWNER	TABLE_NAME	TABLE_TYPE
1	Wrox_Golf_Results	dbo	Club_Details	TABLE
2	Wrox_Golf_Results	dbo	dtproperties	TABLE
3	Wrox_Golf_Results	dbo	Match_Scores	TABLE
4	Wrox_Golf_Results	dbo	Matches	TABLE
5	Wrox_Golf_Results	dbo	Newsletters	TABLE
6	Wrox_Golf_Results	dbo	Players	TABLE
7	Wrox_Golf_Results	dbo	Society_Group_Temp	TABLE
8	Wrox_Golf_Results	dbo	Society_Groups	TABLE

If you are working on a complex query involving columns from tables, but cannot recall all of the specifics, stored procedures from this group can be tremendously valuable in helping you sort out your query. Other stored procedures in this group include: `sp_columns`, `sp_column_privileges`, `sp_fkeys`, `sp_server_info`, `sp_special_columns`, `sp_sproc_columns`, `sp_statistics`, `sp_stord_procedures`, and `sp_table_privileges`.

Extended Stored Procedures

Chances are, you will not author extended stored procedures often, but you may see them on occasion. Extended stored procedures offer developers an opportunity to use C or C++ routines that can be exploited by SQL Server. SQL Server dynamically executes DLL's containing the routines and can extend the limited language of Transact-SQL by exposing the rich offerings of C or C++.

Extended stored procedures usually begin with a prefix of `xp_`, although they may at times adopt the system stored procedure format of an `sp_` prefix. When selecting the properties of an extended stored procedure, instead of offering the procedure's syntax, SQL Server displays the path to the .DLL:

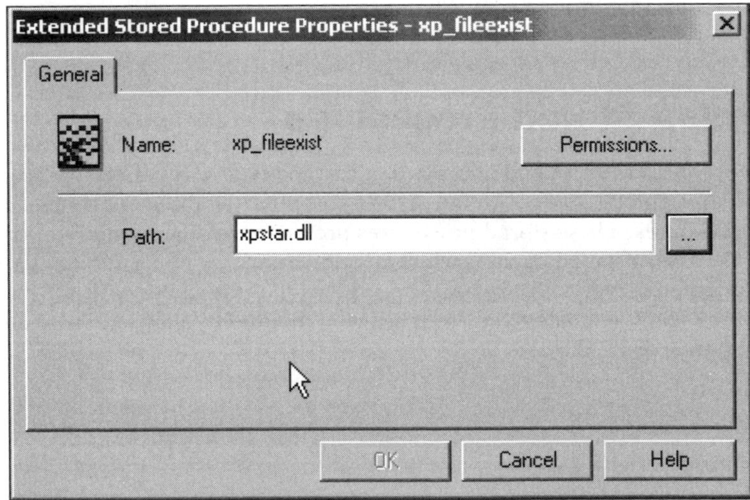

Given the power that some of the extended stored procedures offer, you may want to tighten permissions to exclude execution from certain groups. The **Permissions...** button will provide a familiar dialog with which to remove or grant various permissions.

SQL Server provides several extended stored procedures for your use, including the following:

- `xp_cmdshell` – Allows you to execute any command-line executable. This is very popular and facilitates integration of several outside technologies.
- `xp_sendmail` – This is one of a half-dozen extended stored procedures that compose SQL-Mail, SQL Server's integration with e-mail servers. These extended stored procedures allow messages to be generated from stored procedures or triggers, allowing your database to address and author the messages.

Be careful with the use of all user-created extended stored procedures. They run with full security rights on the server, and as such they can pose a security risk.

Summary

Stored procedures offer a powerful approach to database use. They can execute faster, perform more features, and reduce network load when compared to alternatives. SQL Server 2000 provides a solid collection of tools for the creation and management of stored procedures, and allows you to use their power in a wide variety of ways.

As more third-party tools integrate with SQL Server for web and enterprise requirements, stored procedures promise to become increasingly important. First they can offer a method of encapsulating database work, offloading the development of queries from software developers to database designers. They also offer centralized management of features, where a single stored procedure is available to multiple platforms. This facilitates easier maintenance or updates when required, since the database engineer may only have to manipulate a single object. Finally, the ability to send smaller requests over connections as well as exploit compiled code on the database server, improves the entire network's performance.

Stored procedures are not the perfect answer. They can be more cumbersome to develop than views, and require careful declarations and data type assignment. The syntax requires more from developers with the added complexity of variables in the query.

Understanding stored procedures is important for all who use SQL Server. A well architected database will certainly take advantage of this powerful tool.

XML and Data Retrieval

We're almost at the end of the book and by now you should be very proficient in working within SQL Server 2000 and be confident that you are able to easily deal with simple tasks, and have enough knowledge to attempt more complex ones. You are almost ready to move on to the next level of development within SQL Server and read *Professional SQL Server 2000.* However, there are just a couple of areas left to cover, the first deals with publishing data onto a web page using HTML and more importantly **XML**.

This whole chapter covers publishing data using SQL Server and how it is possible to use SQL queries directly entered from a web browser, pass these through to SQL Server, and retrieve and display information in an orderly manner. This task is not as straightforward as other tasks within the book and there is the potential for problems, especially for beginners. However, we meet these areas head on, deal with them, and give resolutions to the problems; so that you find this area of working with SQL Server and the Internet a much easier experience than others have found it.

The chapter covers XML in some depth, although you will only see data being retrieved from tables and displayed in browsers.

There is another method of producing data for web pages rather than having to enter SQL commands within the web browser by hand, and that is to set up a job within SQL Server that builds HTML files and places these in a predefined directory. This is quite a complex task and luckily, there is a wizard within SQL Server to help you with this. I think that this wizard is the best wizard within SQL Server for its usefulness, the power that it gives a database user, and also what the final achieved result is.

The aims of this chapter are therefore to:

- Give you a solid grounding in XML
- Ensure you know what is required to retrieve data from SQL Server
- Install IIS 5 on a Windows 2000 machine
- Test out the installation
- Build up the computer for use in retrieving data and publishing on a web browser
- Create a user able to utilize the SQL Server database for Internet access
- Retrieve and display data on a browser
- Use a wizard to build HTML pages when required

First of all though, it is necessary to know a bit about the background of the area this chapter is dealing with. This chapter gives a flavor of SQL Server and XML. Wrox have recently published a book entitled *"Professional SQL Server 2000 XML" (Wrox Press, ISBN 1-861005-46-6)*, which if this is an area you wish to work in, I wholly recommend buying. We also publish numerous XML-specific books, including *"Beginning XML" (Wrox Press, ISBN 1-861003-41-2)*, and the recently published *"Professional XML Second Edition" (Wrox Press, ISBN 1-861005-05-9)*.

HTML/XML background

HTML, you may already know about. It is what's known as a markup language, and is used to describe data so that it can be presented visually in a browser. Almost all of the tags merely describe how the data will look, not what it is.

HTML is short for **HyperText Markup Language** and is the basis for placing basic information on a web page to display in a browser.

XML is short for **Extensible Markup Language** and is a standard for data interchange. Any information passed will have a markup tag against it so that the recipient, whether this is a browser or another program, knows what the data is. XML can be used for almost any purpose. For instance, the vocabulary known as XHTML 1.0 is HTML 4 in an XML format. The contents produce the same results as HTML in a browser, but additionally, an XML parser can read the data.

XML is a textual, structured, hierarchical, standard for representing data. It looks similar to HTML, except the rules of XML have to be rigidly enforced – unlike with the varying implementations of HTML. The easiest way to explain what XML is is to show you a quick example of what XML data could contain. View the `xml_example.xml` below:

```
<?xml version="1.0" encoding="utf-8">
<book ISBN="1861005237">
   <title>Beginning SQL Server 2000</title>
   <author>Robin Dewson</author>
   <publisher>Wrox Press</publisher>
   <price unit="$">49.99</price>
   <stock>197</stock> <!-- Details how many units are in stock -->
</book>
```

The items between the < and > items are **tags**, and any tag can be used, providing it follows certain naming rules. The tag names you choose are called a **vocabulary**, and in the above case, the vocabulary I have chosen describes books in a bookstore; more specifically, this book. The tag at the beginning isn't a tag as such; it is the **XML declaration** - so that browsers know that XML content is being dealt with – which also passes some other useful information to the XML parser. The `encoding` attribute specifies that the text is 8-bit Unicode, which is a superset of ASCII or plain text. The `<!--...-->` tag is a **comment tag**, as it is in HTML, and is ignored in processing.

As well as its being very human readable, an XML parser can retrieve the data from this file quite easily, discovering all of the **elements** and **attributes** and what they contain. Attributes are items like `ISBN` in the above examples, and their values are contained in quotation marks. Elements in this example are `<book>`, `<title>`, `<author>`, `<price>`, and `<stock>`. Their respective values are everything up until their corresponding closing tags, which are prefixed with a `/`, for example, `</title>`. So the `<book>` element contains numerous other elements, and the `<publisher>` element contains `Wrox Press`. There are some basic rules that all XML documents have to follow to be called **well-formed**, which means that an XML parser can work with the data. We will cover some of these later, but a few essential rules are that all XML data has to be contained within an element (the `<book>` element in this case). Because the data is thought of as hierarchical, tags must be closed in sequence (`</stock>` had to be before `</book>`), and the values of all attributes, whether numerical or textual, have to be enclosed in quotes. XML is also case sensitive, so the `ISBN` attribute cannot also be written as `isbn`.

In addition to well-formed XML, we can also have **valid** XML. There are schemas that define which elements and attributes an XML document can contain, as well as the data types, or the contents, of these. The standard schema format built into the XML specification is based on a standard validation format known as **DTDs**. On May 2 2001, the W3C (who oversee all XML development) released a new XML-based schema format called **XML Schema**. SQL Server 2000 mostly uses an earlier standard, similar to XML Schema, called **XDR** or **XML Data Reduced** to validate its XML. These schemas define the structure of content of XML data; in the much the same way a table can define structure of data within a database.

Internet Explorer 5 comes with a built in parser for XML. It is this parser that is used when Internet Explorer receives data from SQL Server in an XML format and then automatically uses a technology called **XSLT** to transform the data into HTML, which shows this data in a hierarchical fashion on the web page. It is also possible to update SQL Server data using a set of data defined as an XML format; however, this will not be covered within this book (although data retrieval is).

In the next section you will see a demonstration of how HTML and XML work and we will expand on the differences within the relevant documents.

How does XML work?

As you have just read, there are similarities between HTML and XML. However there are also some major differences. HTML works by using tags indiscriminately to denote the start and end of formatting on a web page. To give an example, the following code is valid HTML, but not well-formed XML. It can be found in the code download as `5237_19_01.html`:

```
<html>
<head><title>An HTML Example</title></head>
<body>Start off with plain text.<br><b>Here is some bold text<br><i>now changed to
italics</b><br>bold has ended but there is still italics</i><br> and now back to
plain text.</body>
</html>
```

To clarify the tags if you have not used HTML before,

- `<b>` means bold
- `<br>` means new line
- `<i>` denotes italic

When this is displayed in a browser, it would look like the following. You can see that all the elements have been displayed as per the descriptions.

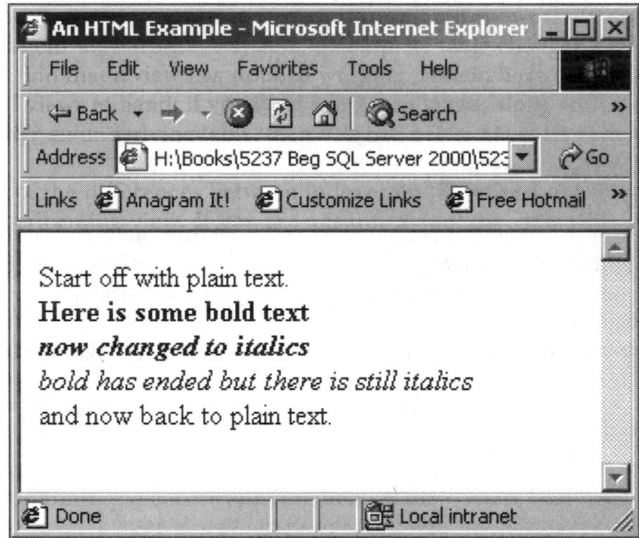

However, if you look closely at the code, you will see that the outer tag, `<b>`, ends before an inner tag, `<i>`, has ended. If this was an XML document, this text would fail because the parser would expect the `<b>` tag to end before the `<i>` tag started. If you tried to view the code for the HTML document as an XML document (by renaming it with a `.xml` extension), it would look as the screenshot below. The XML parser program stopped as soon as it reached an inconsistency with the positioning of tags, as it is not well-formed XML. An error was thrown and no more processing of the document has taken place:

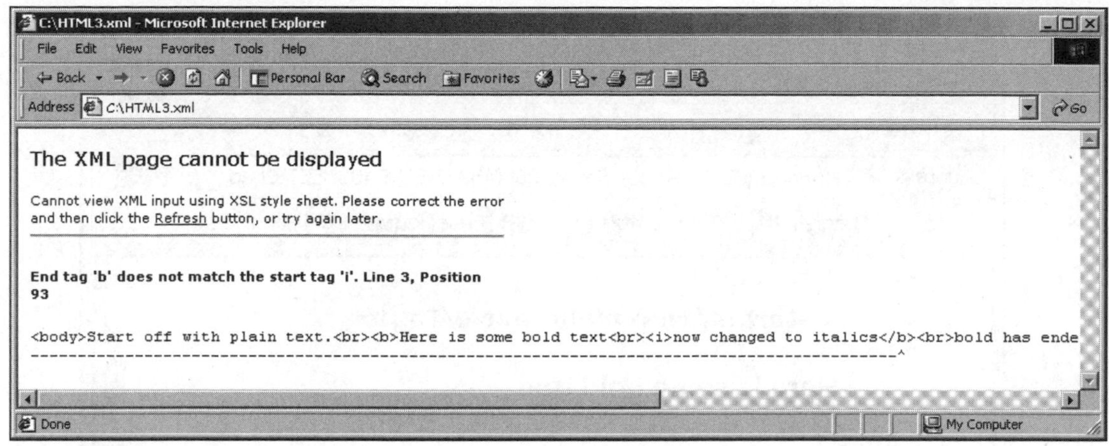

Formatting of XML could be defined within an XML style sheet, which could transform any XML data into XHTML or HTML as required just as when you view well-formed XML data in Internet Explorer, you can see only the results, and never the HTML that the XML has been transformed into. The XML document must have an element root – which in the code below is denoted by the tag `<Top>`, and was the `<book>` tag in the example above. The root node then surrounds all the other XML tags and is then closed off in the last line of code.

> **Remember that XML document tags are case sensitive so do take care when building an XML document that you keep this in mind.**

```
<Top>
<Tag1>Start off with plain text.</Tag1>
<Tag2><b>Here is some bold text</b></Tag2>
<Tag3><b><i>now changed to italics</i></b></Tag3>
<Tag4><i>bold has ended but there is still italics</i></Tag4>
<Tag5>and now back to plain text.</Tag5>
</Top>
```

There is at no point any overlap of tags, unlike that within the HTML code, but you are allowed to have tags within tags, although of course they are still not allowed to overlap. The above code was saved as a file with an XML suffix (`5237_19_02.xml`) to denote that the file is to be treated as an XML document.

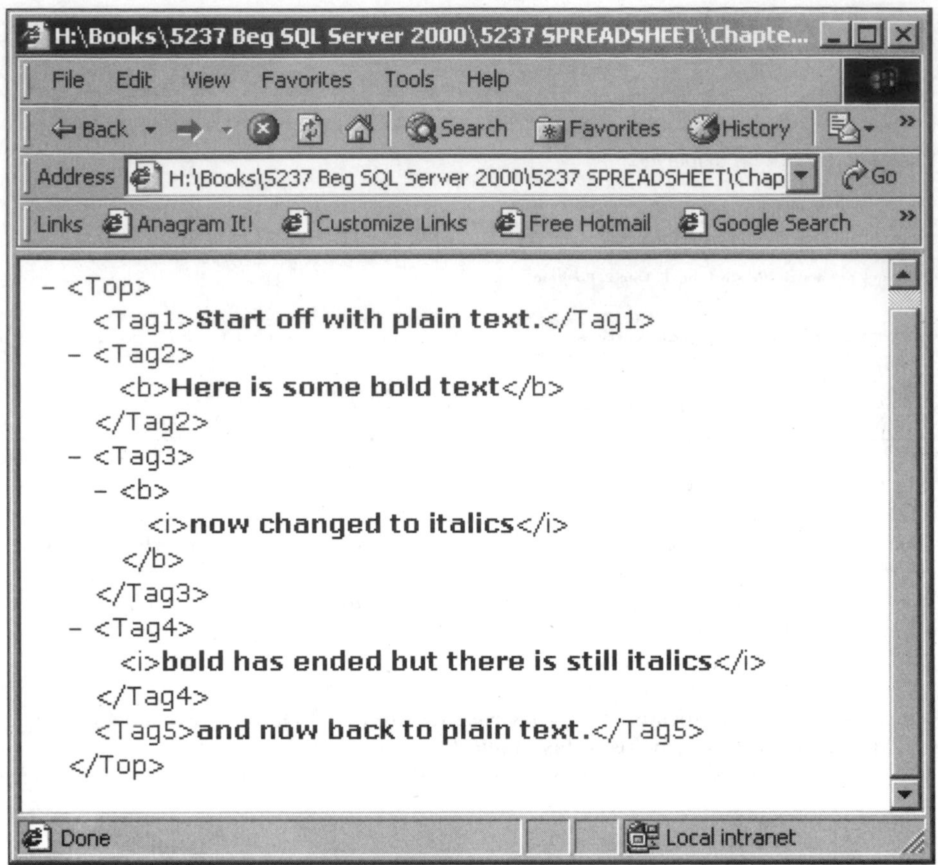

It really is not possible to do justice to how XML works in such a short space. If you require it, a more detailed XML primer can be found in *"Professional SQL Server 2000 Programming"* (Wrox Press, ISBN 1-861004-48-6).

To prove the point, Wrox has whole books on the subject, depending on what other technology you wish to use alongside XML. This lightning tour of XML might leave you wondering why we should bother with it. Basically, XML parsers are available for most programming languages and platforms, making it possible to read XML no matter what system any application is written on. This is useful as, for instance, a C developer might want to create an application on a FreeBSD system to access an MS SQL Server 2000 database on a Windows 2000 system. No driver exists to get at the data natively, but using XML, the application can request the data, parse the results, and transform it into whatever is desired. Also, as the XML standard is so rigidly defined, it is relatively simple to create a new parser in the language of your choice on obsolete or small-niche platforms, such as some embedded device.

What has been discussed is only a small part of how XML works. The remainder of the chapter will demonstrate XML further, along with the requirements to get XML working on your machine using SQL Server 2000. First of all though, it is necessary to ensure you have IIS 5 installed.

Installing IIS 5 on Windows 2000

It is necessary to have either Personal Web Server or Internet Information Services version 5 (IIS 5) installed on the machine that you are going to use to access SQL Server data through a web page. This next section will cover installing IIS 5 on Windows 2000 to enable our database example to retrieve information in XML format and display this on a web page. If you are running Windows 98/ME or Windows NT Workstation, then you will have to install Personal Web Server. This is not as powerful as IIS; but it will still allow you to work with XML and SQL Server solutions. However, it is recommended that if you want to be serious about XML with SQL Server, you should upgrade and use IIS and Windows 2000.

You may find the IIS 5 is already installed on your machine if your machine is used as any kind of server for displaying HTML/XML information, even for testing. You can check if you have IIS 5 already installed by looking to see it you have the Internet Services Manager option under Start | Programs | Administrative Tools. If you don't, then you will need to install IIS 5. Ensure that you have your Windows 2000 CDROM handy, or any CD that has IIS 5 installation files on it. Then you can safely follow the following installation.

This section will not be discussing the security issues surrounding IIS 5 installation and setup. Therefore I strongly suggest that you do not install IIS 5 on a production machine, or a machine that has a direct connection to the Internet, or a machine that has secure information that you don't wish other people in your organization to connect to.

Try It Out – Installing IIS 5

1. First of all, insert the Windows 2000 CD-ROM into your drive. This should start up the Windows 2000 setup routine automatically. If not, then open Windows Explorer, navigate to the CD-ROM drive, and double-click setup.exe. On the Windows 2000 CD, this will be in the root directory, however, you may find, if you are using a CD-ROM from MSDN for example, that you will have to search the CD to find the installation files. When setup starts, click Install Add-On Components.

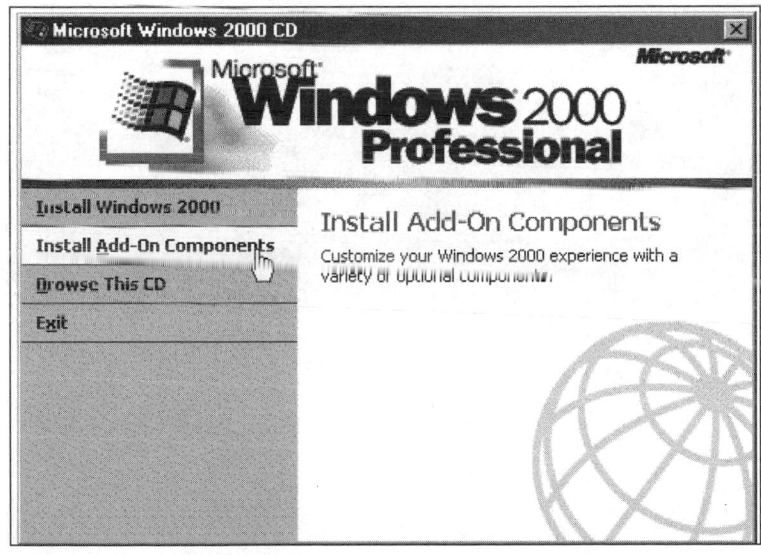

2. This then brings up the **Windows Components Wizard** listing the Windows components that can be installed onto Windows 2000. The items required to install IIS 5 will be already checked along with a couple of other options, and personally, I would leave what has been selected. Once you are ready, click **Next**.

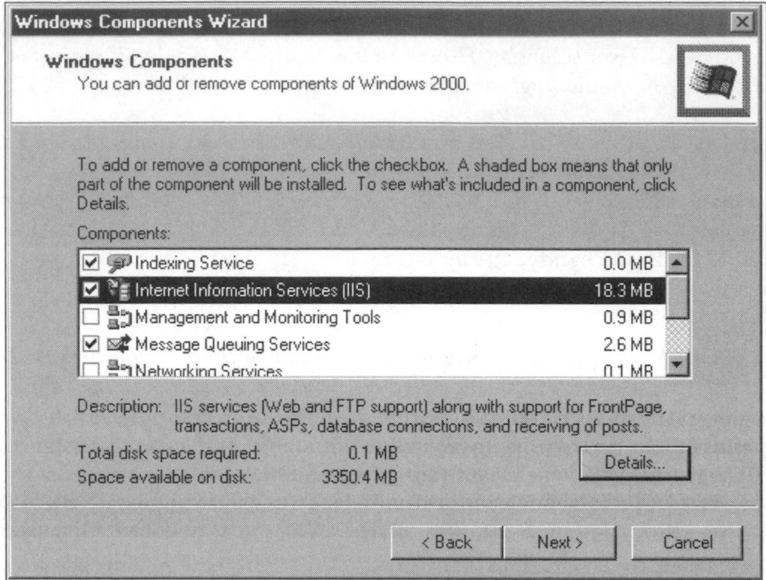

3. This will immediately start to configure and install the components selected; you will see this happening, and an update shown using the progress bar.

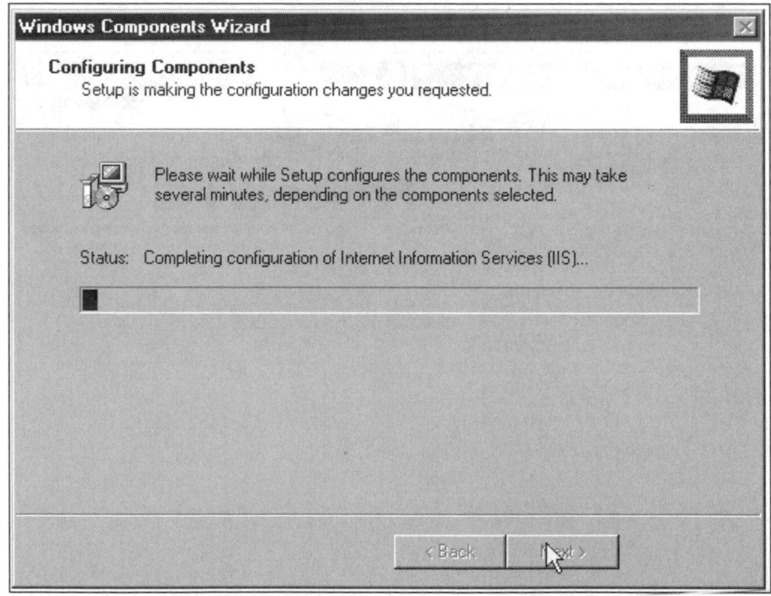

4. Once it has completed, you will see the final screen informing you of this. Click the **Finish** button.

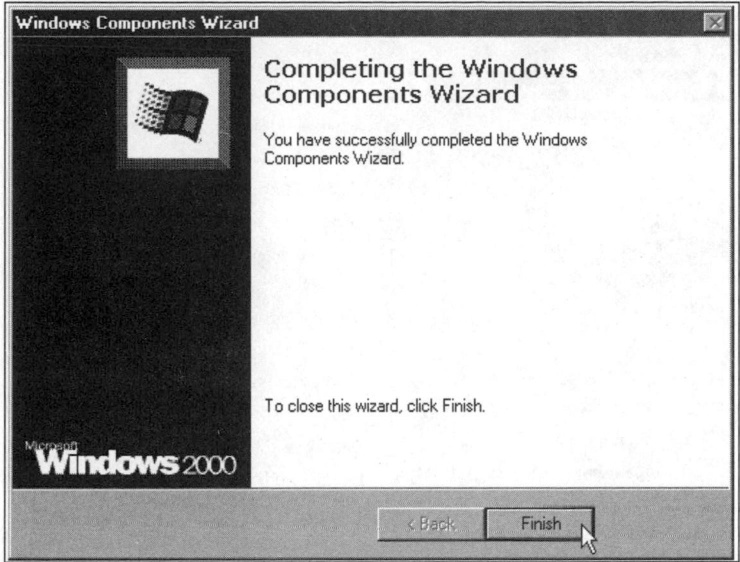

5. You will now need to restart your computer after installation. Once the system has restarted, the next stage is to create a directory and then to enter the details of this directory for IIS 5 to work with it. The IIS 5 installation will by default create a directory that it expects information for Internet services to reside within. Start up Windows Explorer, and the directory should be located at `E:\inetpub\wwwroot` (or a different drive as specified). It is now necessary to create a directory below this for the `Wrox_Golf_Results` application. I have chosen the name `Wrox_Golf` for this directory.

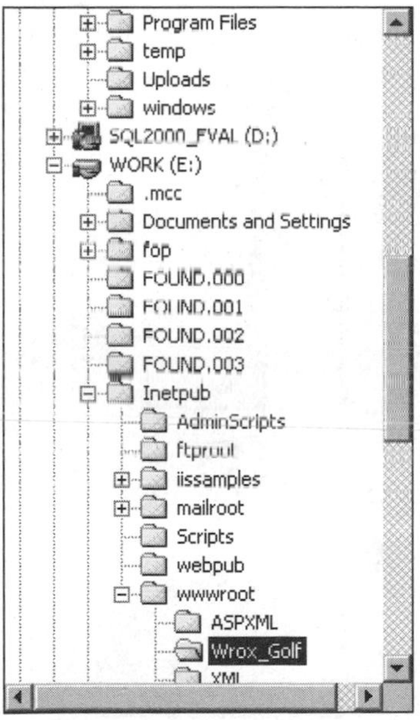

6. Now start up **Internet Services Manager** (**ISM**), which can be found in Start | Programs | Administrative Tools | Internet Services Manager.

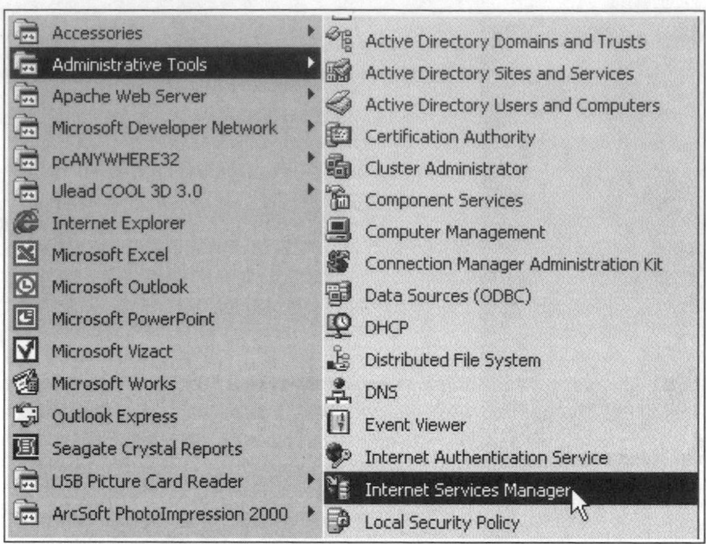

7. Once you start ISM, you will be presented with three collapsed nodes of Default FTP Site, Default Web Site, and Default SMTP Virtual Server, which will be residing under your computer name. Expand the Default Web Site node and you should see the Wrox_Golf directory created a few moments ago, automatically listed. Right-click on it and select Properties from the menu.

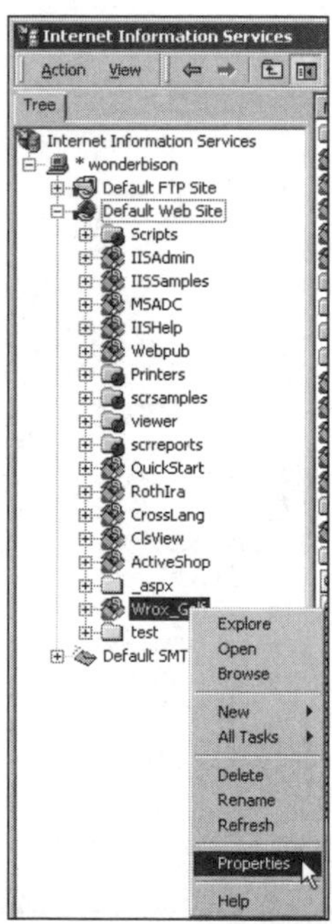

8. This then brings up a five-tabbed dialog where it is possible to set up the properties of the `Wrox_Golf` **Virtual Directory**. In the Directory tab, ensure that the properties are set as you can see below. There will be no executables in this directory, therefore, ensure that Scripts Only is selected.

A virtual directory is a directory that is referenced as a subdirectory of the main site. To explain further, when you go to a web site, the root of the web site will sit in a subdirectory within the main web site server. However, this subdirectory is seen as the main root directory for the web site. A virtual directory is a directory that can be anywhere on the system, which is used by IIS.

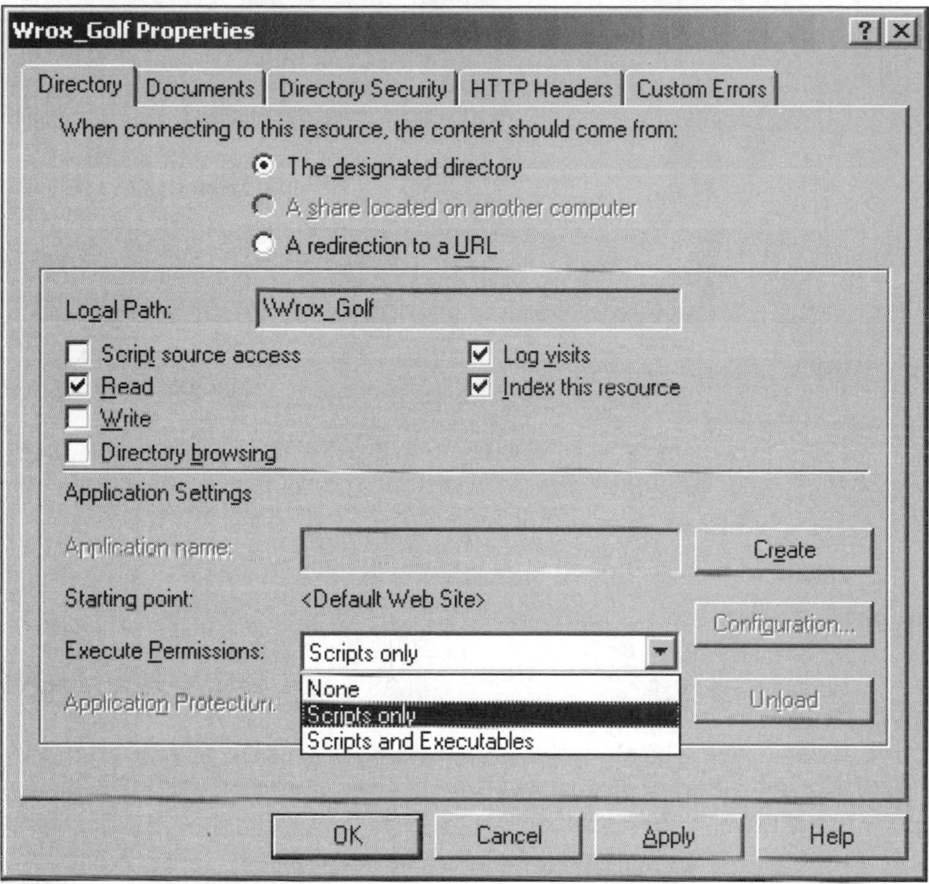

9. Now click on the **Create** button found under **Application Settings**, and enter a reasonable name. The dialog should now look like that below. A new default name has been entered, but it is now possible to also alter this further if you wish. In this instance, leave it as it is.

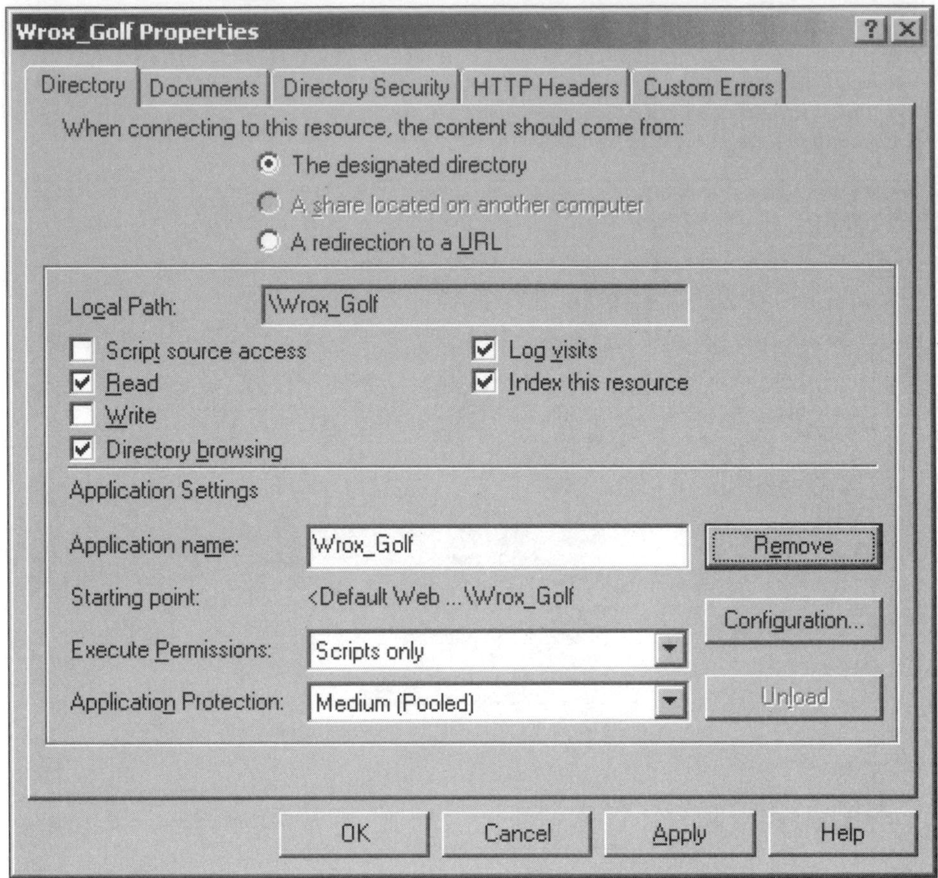

10. It is now necessary to build and set up the configuration for this web site, so click on the **Configuration...** button. The configuration will specify how the site works and behaves and further options as to how certain actions will respond.

11. Ignore the first tab, **App Mappings**, as there is nothing of interest or relevance to discuss in this chapter listed here. Click on to the **App Options** tab. Although the **App Options** tab does have options that are of use, and could be altered, we won't alter any of them as the settings are as they should be. However, there are a couple of options that you might wish to change. For example, you may wish your sessions to last longer than 20 minutes. These options can be set from here.

Certain sites, for example, online banking corporations, automatically force you to log in again to their site if there has been no activity for more than twenty minutes. This is set through the session timeout. Active Server Pages, or ASP, are web pages with programming attributes.

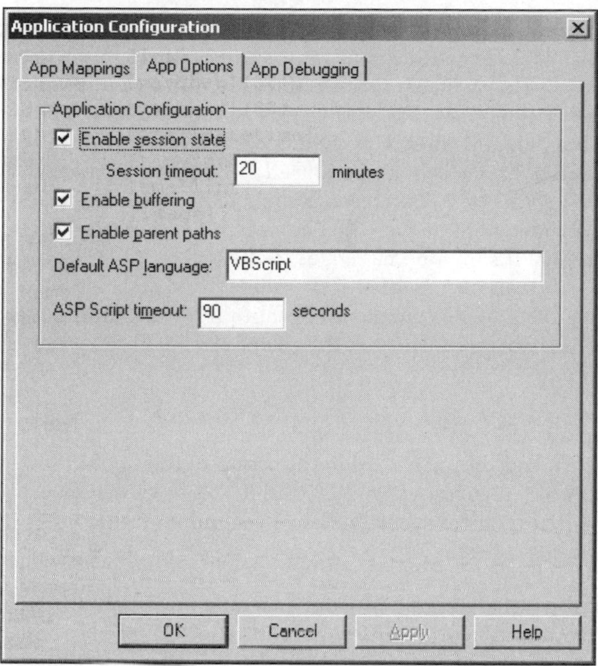

12. The final tab on the Application Configuration screen, the App Debugging tab, revolves around debugging and error messages within your web site. Ensure that the options in this tab are set like those below. When you are done, click OK.

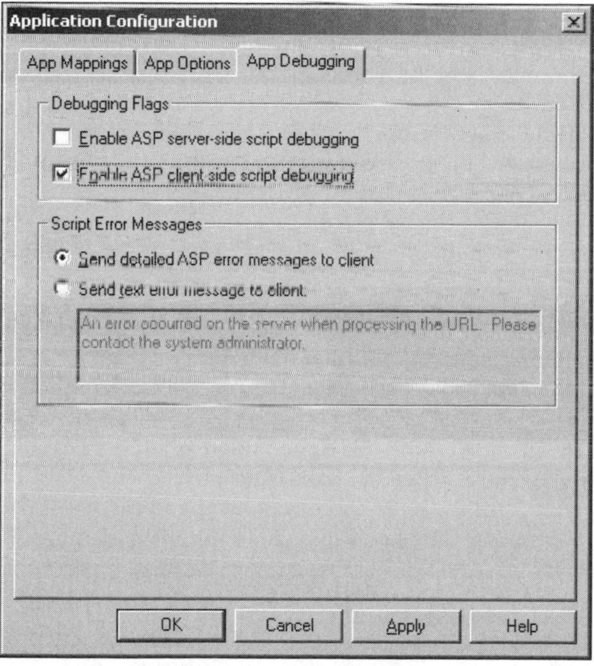

13. You are now taken back to the previous Properties dialog. Click on the Documents tab and you will see a list of three settings that can be used to bring up a default document, or home page, for this Wrox_Golf site. It is normal to add a fourth item, index.htm to this list, as quite often, many developers like to have this as their default. These choices are used, as these are frequently the defaults chosen. Some people may ask why we have chosen index.htm, and not index.html; this is because it used to be the case that on Windows systems, filenames could only have 8 characters as their main name, followed by 3 characters as the extension (the characters after the '.'). The practice has carried through even now. These four settings indicate that if someone navigates to the Wrox_Golf web site that we are currently building, IIS 5 will look for any one of the items listed to bring up as the default web page. A word of caution, keep this list small and do not put every combination of potential web page in this list. The less documents listed, the easier IIS 5 will find it to identify and display the correct start up page.

14. The remaining tabs will not be discussed as there is nothing to alter or to know about to make our example work and they are outside the scope of the book. However, they are very important from a site security viewpoint, and if you have installed or are required to install IIS 5 on a machine that requires security, then I recommend that you read more on the subject to ensure that your site is secure.

You have now successfully installed IIS 5 on your machine and should be ready to test out the installation to ensure that it is all working for your computer.

Testing Your IIS 5 Installation

This next section tests out your IIS 5 installation, and also completes your first simple Wrox_Golf web page. There is no database access in this section of the chapter as the main aim is to ensure that IIS is working correctly. The easiest way to test everything is all right is to view a web page, placed within the Wrox_Golf directory, through a web browser.

A very simple web page will be built using very basic HTML code, which even if you don't know HTML is very easy to follow and enter. If you wish to know more about HTML, take a look at *"HTML 4.01 Programmer's Reference"* (Wrox Press, ISBN1-861005-33-4).

Let's now try out the IIS installation.

Try It Out – Testing your Installation

1. Start up Notepad or a similar application that doesn't add any special codes to the start of a file. If you use WordPad, you must remember to save as plain text.

2. Enter the following code exactly as it is, into the text editor. The code will place a heading on the top of the web browser when the page is displayed, which will say IIS4 Installation Test HTML. The remainder of the code will place the text that starts If you can read this... in the main area of the browser. This can also be found in the code download in the file 5237_19_03.htm:

```
<HTML>
<HEAD>
<TITLE>
IIS 4 Installation Test HTML
</TITLE>
</HEAD>

<BODY>
<P>
<B><U>
If you can read this, then your IIS 4 installation is successful and
your Wrox_Golf site is up and running</U></B>
</P>
</BODY>
</HTML>
```

3. Once you have completed entering this code, save the file in to the directory created for the `Wrox_Golf` web site. If you have been following the example, then this will be `E:\Inetpub\wwwroot\Wrox_Golf`. Save this as `default.htm`.

4. Now open up Internet Explorer, or any other browser, and enter the following text in to the Address area: `http://localhost/Wrox_Golf/`. The browser does not need to be Internet Explorer. It could easily be Netscape, Opera, or any other browser.

5. When you press *Enter*, then providing the installation has worked, you should see the following screen displayed. However, don't be surprised if this is not displayed. The next bullet point demonstrates the most common error that you may encounter, and how to get around it.

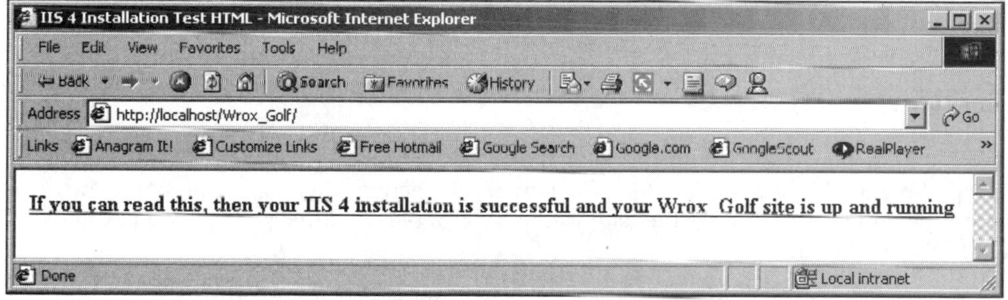

6. You may be presented with a modal dialog saying the page cannot be found offline. As the dialog says, just click Connect and you should find that the page comes up. The reason for this is that the page has not been stored as an offline page by your browser. It is therefore necessary to connect to a host to retrieve the page. Don't be alarmed and think that your browser is about to connect to the Internet. As the name of the web site is `localhost`, no dial up will take place and the browser will be connecting through to your web site defined using IIS 5.

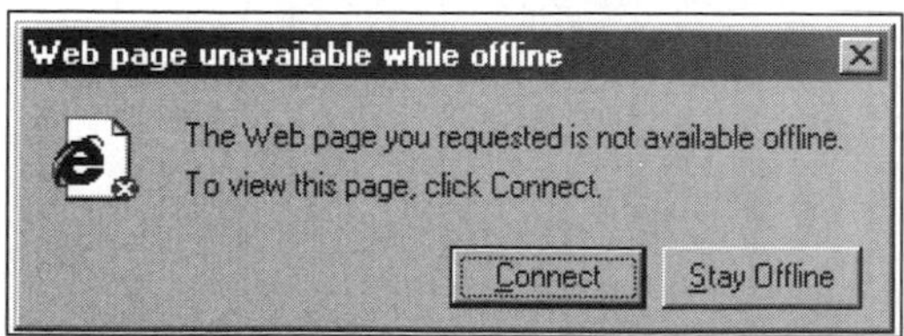

7. Another method to bring up the same information in Internet Explorer is to navigate to the file saved using Windows Explorer, and double-click on the file. Providing that you have your computer set up so that any file with an `.htm` suffix is automatically sent to a browser, then the page will be displayed.

8. If you check the Internet Explorer screenshot below, with the details on the one a few moments ago, you will notice that the Address bar contains differing information within it. The address bars on each browser point to the same item of data, but it was IIS 5 that translated the earlier address bar, to the information that you see below. So they are both completing the same task, except the first method needs IIS to make a translation for it.

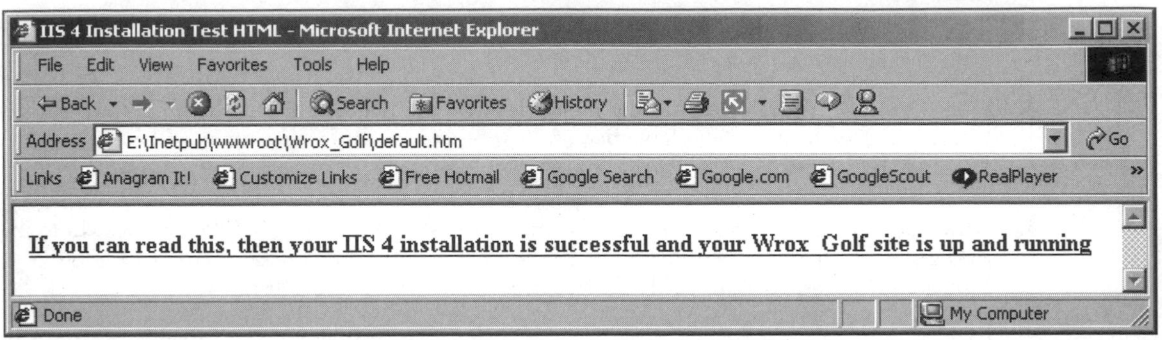

That's the installation tested, so you can close down Internet Explorer for the moment. Now that IIS is installed, and has been tested, it is possible to move on to look at how SQL Server interacts with IIS and a web browser so that it sends and receives information, and displays this information in an orderly fashion.

SQL Server and IIS

It is possible to display static web pages, however, it is still not possible to display any data, unless the data is typed manually in to a web page. The aim of this section, therefore, is to complete the solution and set up the computer to access the data within SQL Server and the `Wrox_Golf_Results` database through SQL commands.

Most of the background work has been completed. The SQL Server database is available with information, and IIS is working as has just been demonstrated. However, there are still a few missing pieces to the jigsaw before you can say that the installation is complete.

First of all there is more to set up within IIS using the IIS Virtual Directory Management for SQL Server, from directories to login information. This also leads to creating a specific user ID within SQL Server purely for web access.

However, the best way at this moment to retrieve and display data is to use XML. This chapter will take SQL Server data and use XML to display the information within Internet Explorer.

Try It Out – SQL Server and IIS 5

1. First of all, it is necessary to create the directories where the XML templates and XML schemas will reside. This is so that the web browser can use these files to format the information correctly. Open up Windows Explorer, and navigate to the C:\Inetpub\wwwroot directory. Add into the `Wrox_Golf_Data` directory two subdirectories called `Schemas` and `Templates`. You can leave the creation of these directories and complete this afterwards, as we will see later in this example, however, I tend to create the directories first. This is personal preference.

2. Whether you chose to create these directories or not, you can now start configuring support for XML within IIS for SQL Server. SQL Server 2000 provides a tool to let you do just that. From the Start menu, select Programs | Microsoft SQL Server | Configure SQL XML Support in IIS.

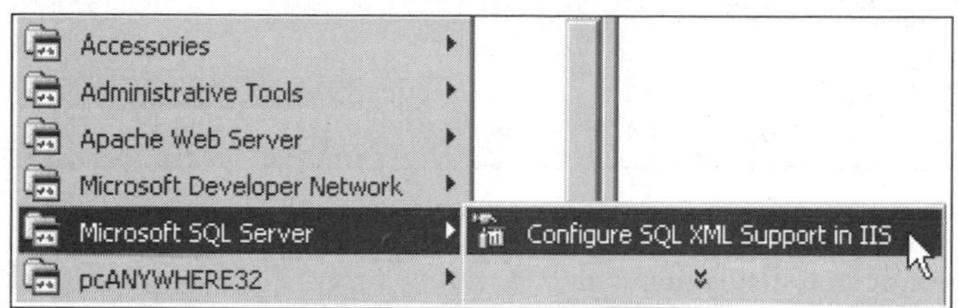

3. This then starts up Microsoft Management Console for IIS and SQL Server. The basis of the screenshot should not be too unfamiliar to you, as you should be used to the SQL Server management console by this point. As you can see, the name of my computer is listed, with a node below that called Default Web Site. I haven't set up any web sites yet on this computer, and so everything else is empty. If there had been web sites already set up, you would see these listed here.

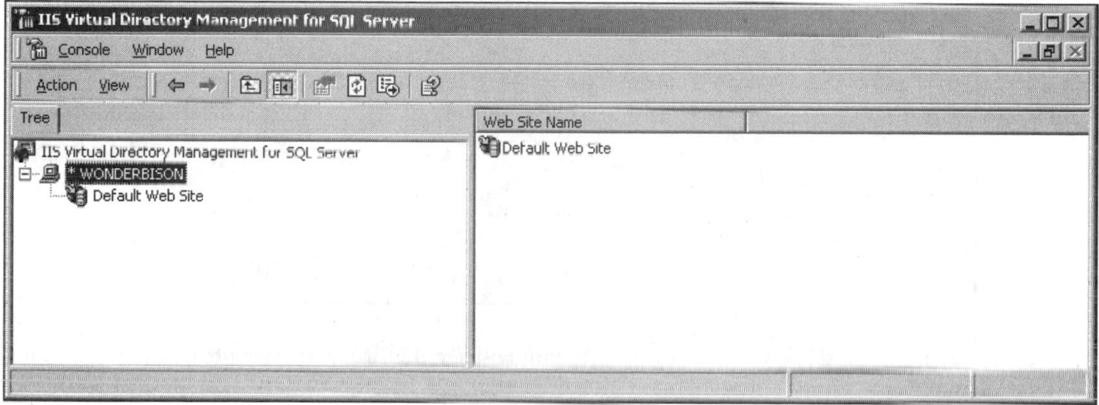

4. Right-click on Default Web Site icon, which brings up a pop-up menu. From there select New and then the only option, Virtual Directory.

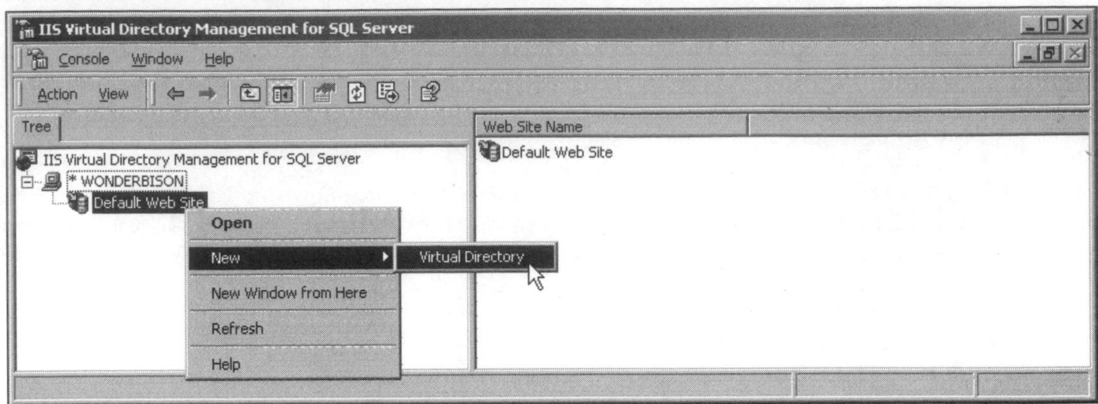

5. You will now see a six tabbed form that needs to be populated to get SQL Server and XML up and running and displaying data in a web browser. The first tab to look at is the General tab, and the top half of this tab displays that a name has to be given for the new Virtual Directory. I have entered the Virtual Directory Name as Wrox_Golf_Data.

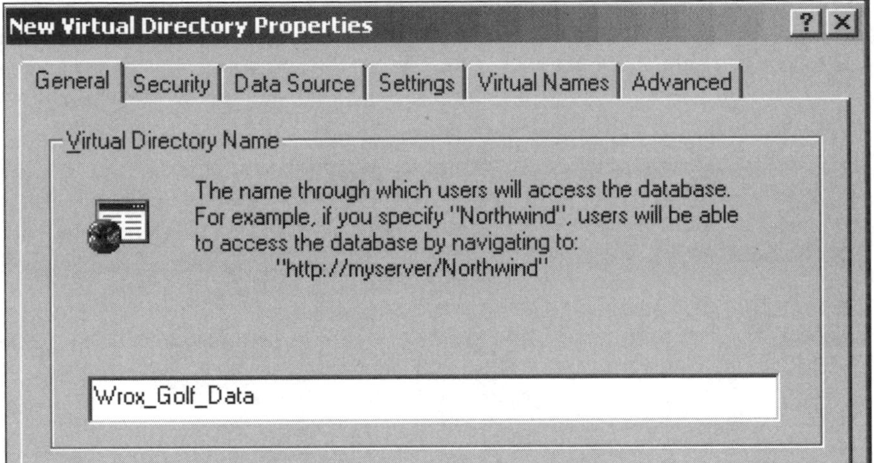

6. Moving on to the lower part of the tab, you will see that it is necessary to enter the path on the computer where the directory is defined for the SQL Server XML information. It is within this path that IIS will locate files denoting the schema or the templates of the XML data. Any information that IIS will use has to be placed in this path. Click on Browse... to point to the necessary Local Path.

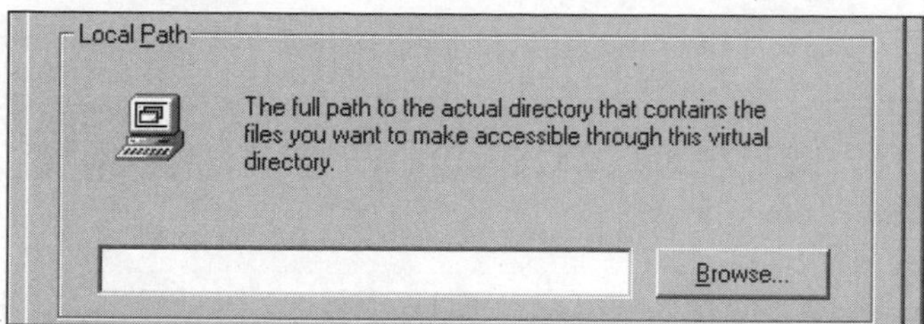

7. This then brings up a dialog for selecting the directory where the folder exists. There is a New Folder button that we could have used to build the directory structure – however, remember that we created our directory structure in the first point of this example. However you could have easily completed it at this point. Navigate to the Wrox_Golf directory and click OK.

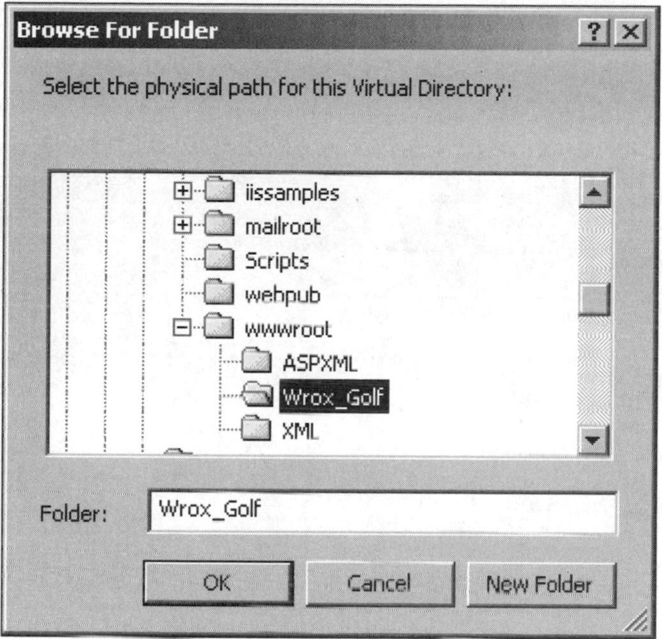

8. The first tab will now look as it does below, populated with the directory chosen.

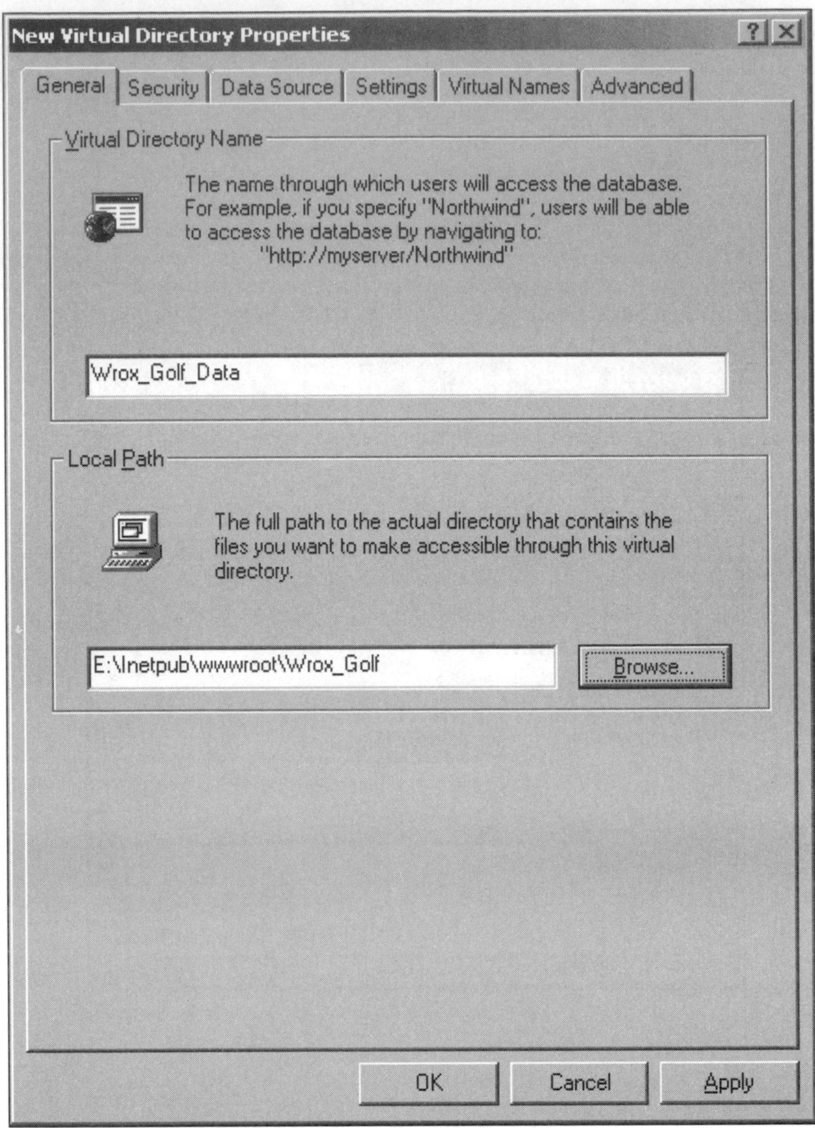

9. It is now time to move on to the second tab, the **Security** tab. Opposite you will see the tab as it is when you first move in. This tab will be set up so that whenever access to the `Wrox_Golf` web site is attempted, a login is established with an appropriate user ID. It is best not to use any SQL Server user ID already set up, but a new, specific ID. As this site could be put on the Internet, Windows Authentication should not be used with the login ID of your Internet machine, as this is both insecure and incompatible with different clients that might try to connect. It is therefore necessary to create a user ID for this site. To create this user ID, let's quickly go through it:

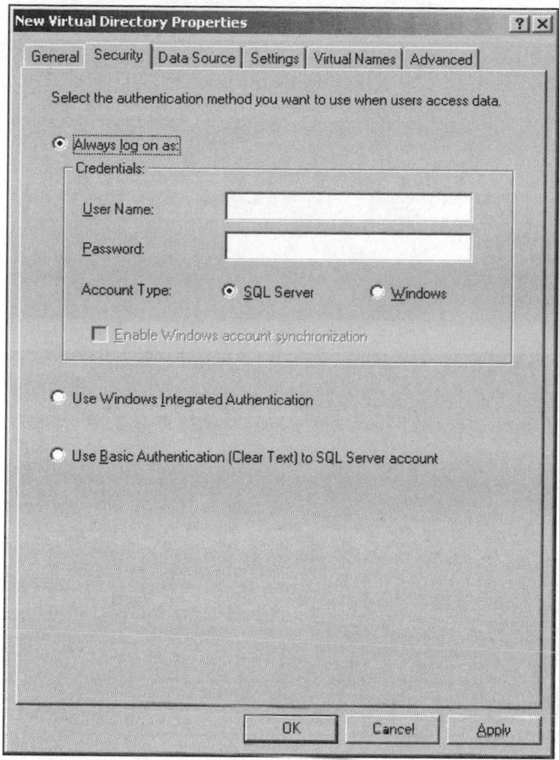

10. Open Enterprise Manager and navigate to Security, and find Logins.

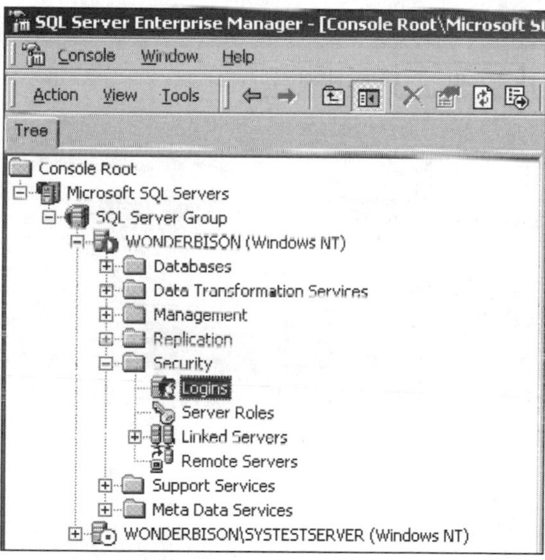

11. Now right-click and select New Login…

12. Enter a user **Name** of **Wrox_Golf_XML** and specify that you are using **SQL Server Authentication**. You then need to enter a password, and remember it. Finally, ensure **Wrox_Golf_Results** is set up as the default database.

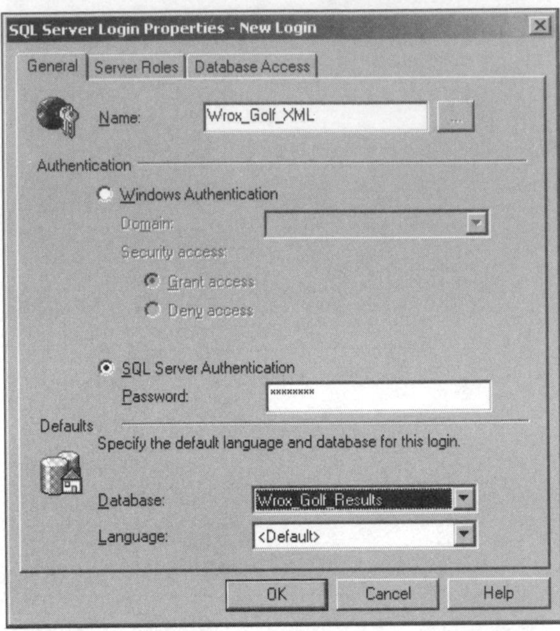

13. Skip the **Server Roles** tab and move to the **Database Access** tab; select **Wrox_Golf_Results**, then click **OK**.

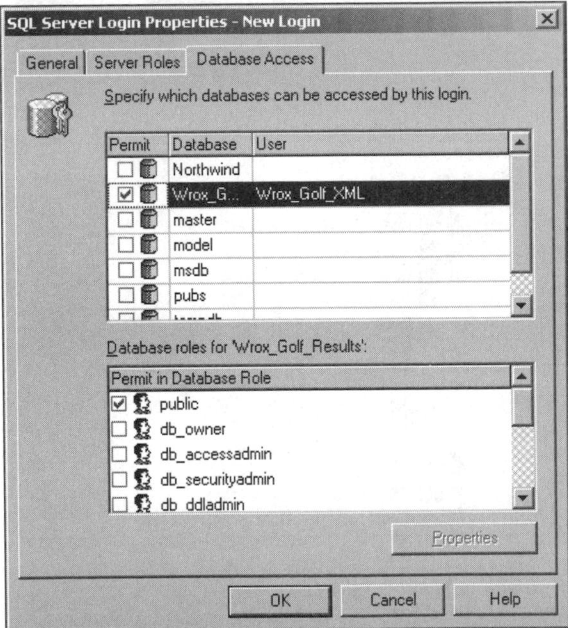

14. This brings up the Confirm new password dialog, so just re-enter the password entered earlier. Then click OK.

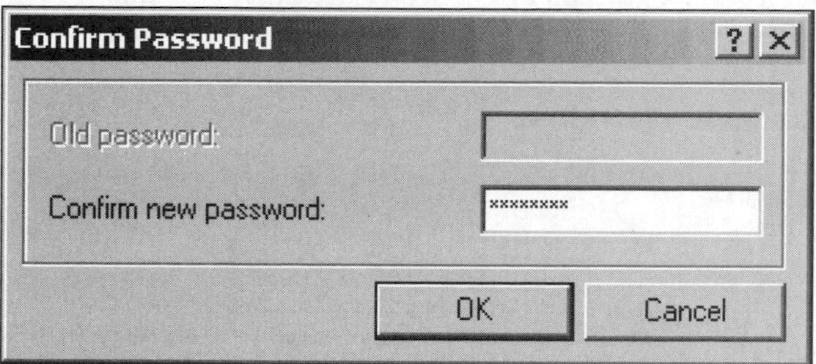

15. Now that the user is set up, go back to setting up the Virtual Directory within the IIS Virtual Directory Management for SQL Server console, and click the Account Type to SQL Server. Now enter the User Name just created as well as the Password.

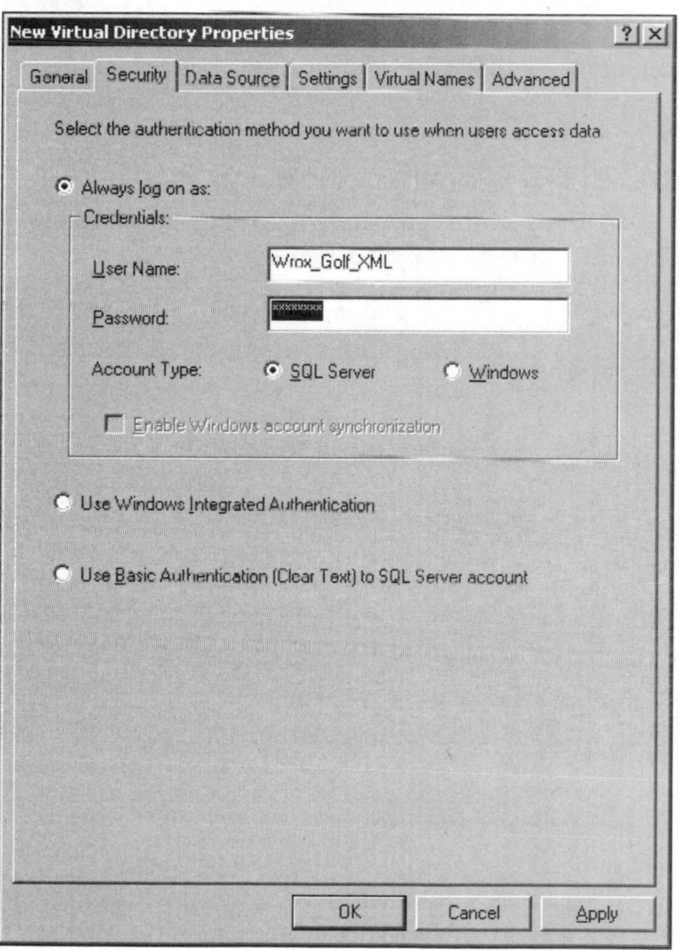

16. Time to look at the data source for this virtual directory. This is where the link is made between the virtual directory and where the physical data is stored. The Data Source tab knows that it has to look within a SQL Server database, providing you give it the name of the server and then the name of the database, Wrox_Golf_Results.

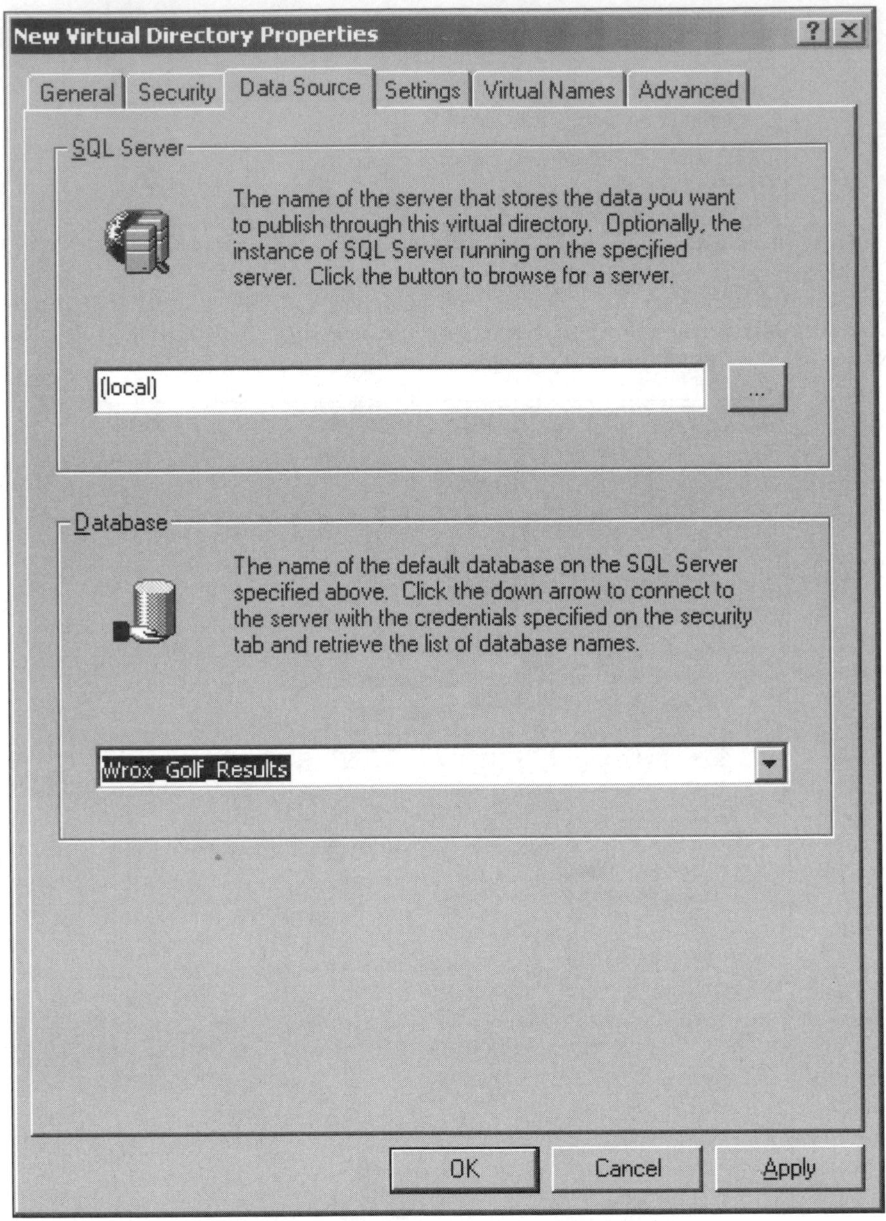

17. Moving on to the Settings tab, without getting in to detail here, this site would be best if it was as flexible as possible in allowing all kinds of data access methods, so click all the check boxes. I will demonstrate XPath and URL queries later in this chapter.

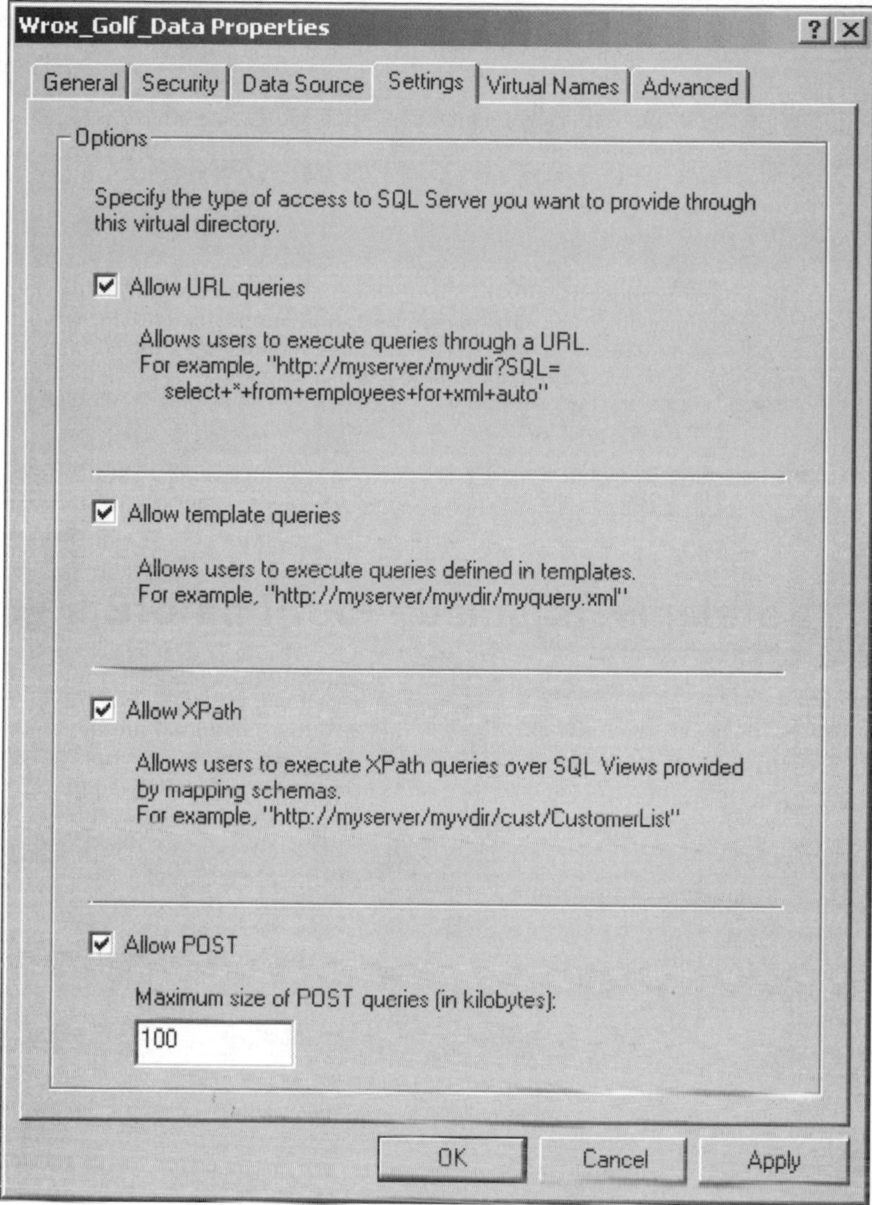
Wrox_Golf_Data Properties
General
Security
Data Source
Settings
Virtual Names
Advanced
Options
Specify the type of access to SQL Server you want to provide through this virtual directory.
Allow URL queries
Allows users to execute queries through a URL.
For example, "http://myserver/myvdir?SQL=
select+*+from+employees+for+xml+auto"
Allow template queries
Allows users to execute queries defined in templates.
For example, "http://myserver/myvdir/myquery.xml"
Allow XPath
Allows users to execute XPath queries over SQL Views provided by mapping schemas.
For example, "http://myserver/myvdir/cust/CustomerList"
Allow POST
Maximum size of POST queries (in kilobytes):
100
OK
Cancel
Apply

18. The Virtual Names tab lets you define where you wish XML templates and schemas to be stored, as well as where you define the name of the database objects.

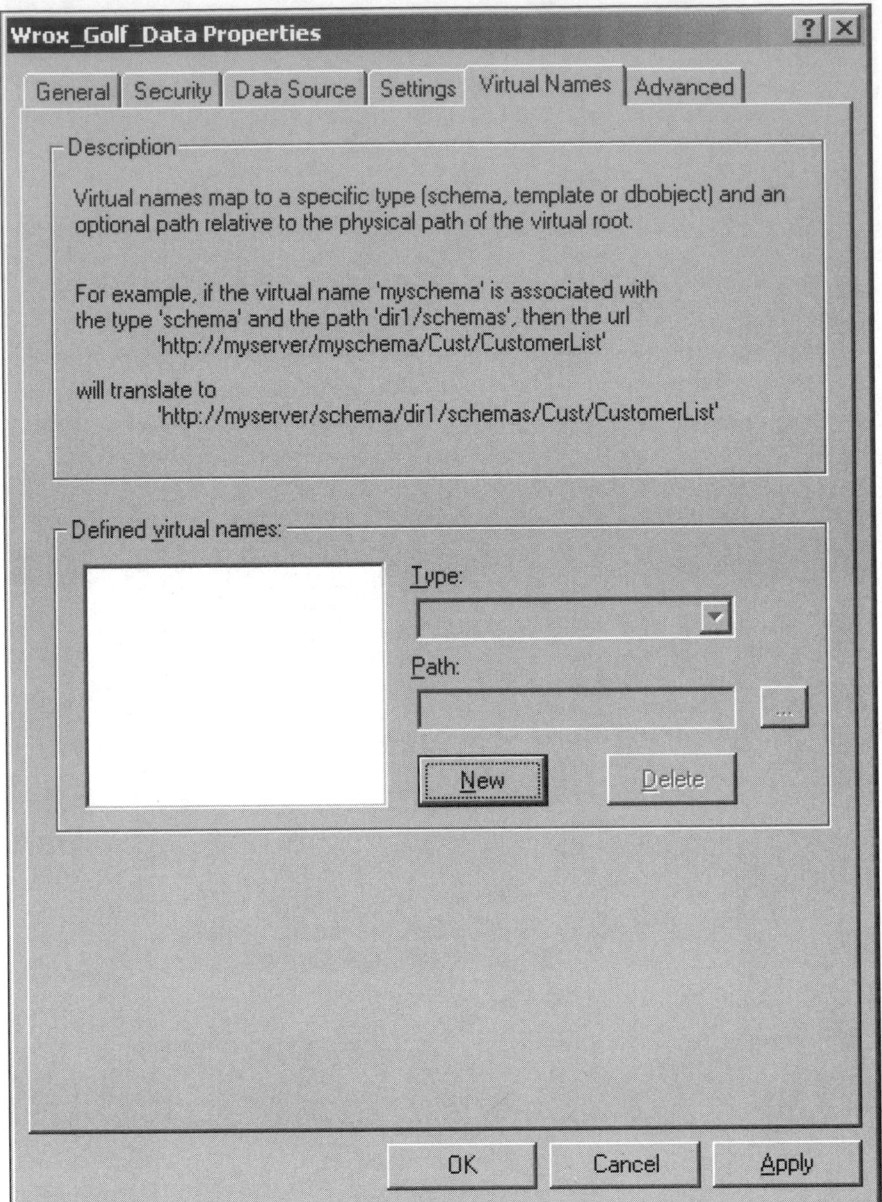

19. You add these by first clicking the New button.

20. Enter the **Virtual name** that you want to assign for the database object. You don't specify a path for this object. This is all worked out internally based on the login ID defined earlier and the default database setup. Once you have finished, click **Save**.

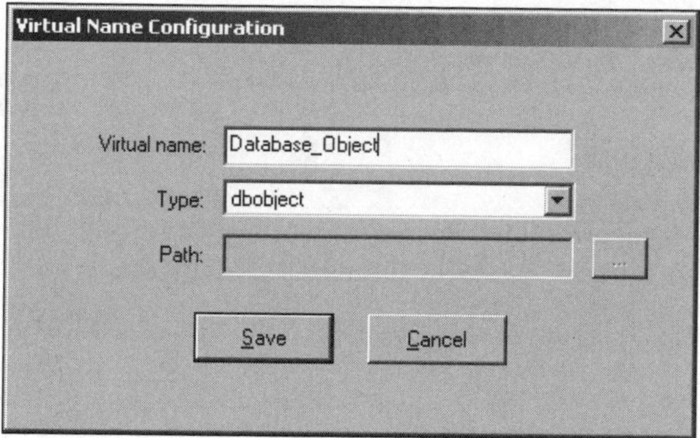

21. Click the **New** button again and define the **Virtual Name Configuration** for **Schemas**. This time, you need to enter a **Path**, which can either be done through the ... button and using the **Browse for Folder** screen, or by entering the full path. Locate the `Wrox_Golf_Results` path. Now you will have to append `\Schemas` to the **Path**: text entry box. The schemas and templates for the XML will be placed in different folders.

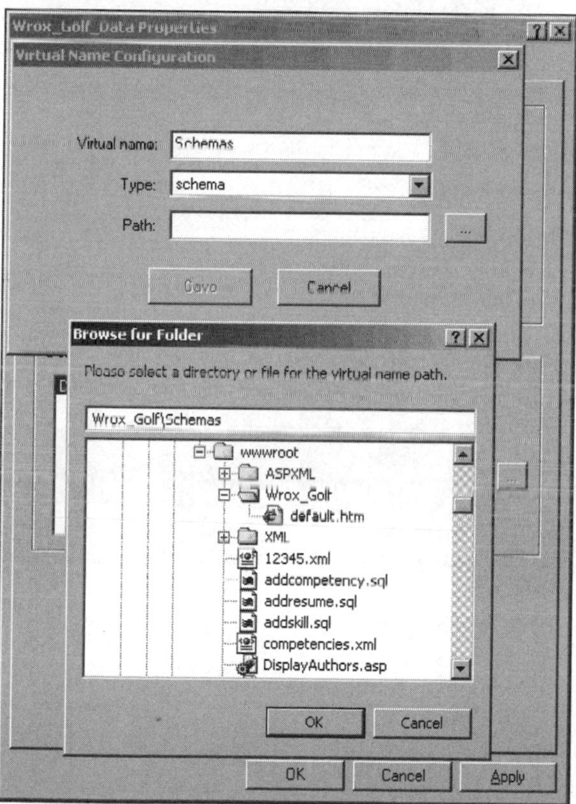

22. As you can see below, the Schemas virtual name should now show the path to the directory where the schemas will reside. As mentioned earlier, a schema describes how the XML document is structured and also any information within the XML document that has any constraints on it.

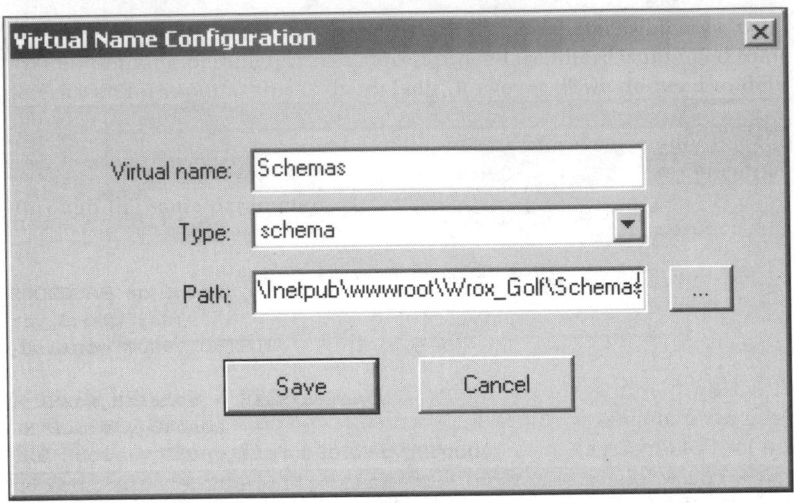

23. The final name is for the Templates. As you can see, instead of using the full path, the Path is using the relative name. Click Save on this as well.

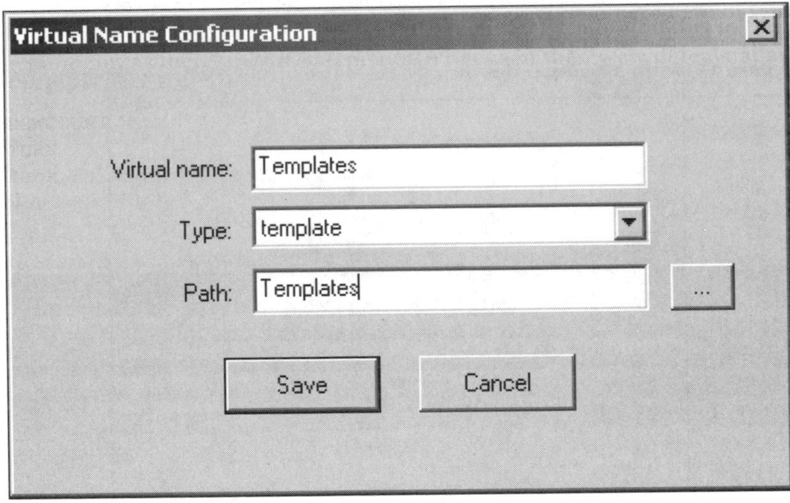

24. The Advanced tab will be left alone, as there is nothing to alter. So click Apply to finish off setting this up.

25. Once you come out of the Virtual Directory Properties dialog, you will see the web site defined in the Management Console.

26. This is the `Wrox_Golf` site set up for use with XML.

I have found that once a virtual directory has been set up, and you have then gone back and altered any of the security information, then this has not always been implemented without a reboot of the computer, or deleting the definition and rebuilding it all again. It seems as if once a connection to the server has been made, then no matter what, until you reboot, the connection remains, even if you use the ability to stop and restart the virtual directory.

Retrieving Data Through XML

Before proceeding in this section, be warned. This will have the greatest number of potential traps for a new developer to fall in to. If you have not set up the connection in the configuration section earlier and you need to go back and alter any items, then I have found on a local computer, that you really have to reboot. I have tried to track down if it is SQL Server, IIS 5, Windows 2000, or any other area, and have not been successful. Choosing to restart the application in the configuration tool, did not completely stop, clean out, and restart the connection. It really did seem as if the failed connection was constantly residing in memory. If anything at all requires altering, whether it is the path structure, the login, or any other area, then I do recommend that you reboot your machine. Obviously this is a real bind and painful, but until Microsoft posts a fix, it looks like you will be stuck with it.

Getting the address bar with the correct details and query syntax is also another potential area for problems, however this example will ensure that you know what details to enter and how to get it right and avoid any pitfalls. Even just working offline can cause confusion initially when Internet Explorer does not find the right page and prompts with a connection dialog. All of the problems you will probably encounter that as a beginner will be broached and solved so that when you do come across them in your own environment, you know where to go to solve them. This will be the main thrust of this section of the chapter, otherwise, retrieving data would be over in two screenshots and really, you would not be a great deal further forward in the understanding of using XML within SQL Server.

However, this section is not just about problems and problem solving. Retrieving data using IIS, SQL Server, XML, and placing the results in a browser correctly can be straightforward. With the system set up as it is, it is possible to retrieve and display data in a browser. It won't be very attractive, but it will form the basis of further examples within the chapter.

Try It Out – Retrieving Data Through XML

1. Start up Internet Explorer version 5 or above, and if you get the option, click Work Offline. Do make sure that you have the right version of Internet Explorer. Less than version 5 will not work with this example.

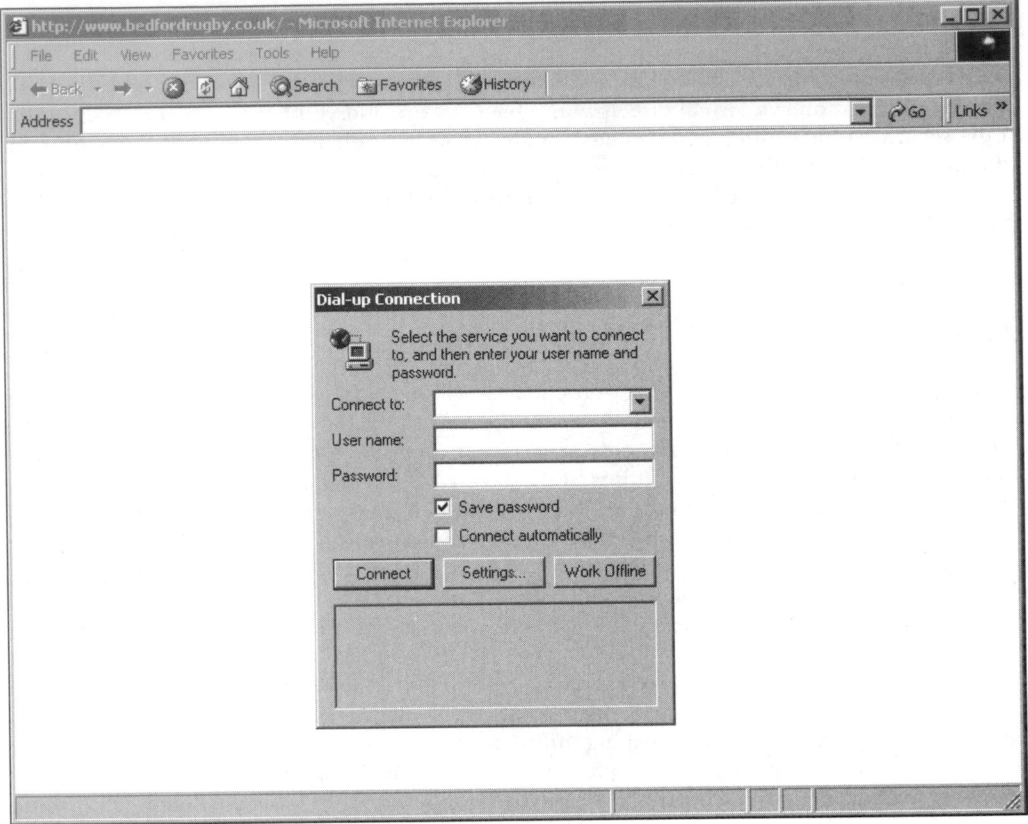

2. You can now enter in a query to run against your SQL Server database. Enter the following into the Address bar of Internet Explorer: http://localhost/wrox_golf_data?sql=SELECT Society_Group_Desc from Society_Groups for xml auto

   The above URL submits a SQL query that instructs the database server to transmit all the values in the `Society_Group_Desc` column in the `Society_Groups` table, and transmit them as XML. The `AUTO` keyword formats the output in a hierarchical fashion.

Note that within the `FOR XML` clause, you can specify one of three XML modes. These are `RAW`, `AUTO` and `EXPLICIT`. `RAW` is the most basic format – each row of data is sent back as a single data element, with the element name "row" and with each column as an attribute of the "row" element. `AUTO` recognizes the idea that our data has some underlying hierarchical notion that we want represented in the XML, and so tries to format things a little for us. `EXPLICIT` is the most complex option – it takes the most effort to set up, but provides us with a high degree of control over the structure of our final XML. It enables us to define each level of the hierarchy and how each level is going to look.

You should also find that the browser alters the URL after it is entered, replacing all spaces with %20. Don't worry about this – it is just impossible to have spaces in URLs, so the browser transforms it by giving the hexadecimal representation of the ASCII code value of the space character, or 32 (20 in hexadecimal).

3. You may be prompted if you want to Connect or Stay Offline. This will come up the first time that you try to run the above, or any, SQL command in Internet Explorer. Here is a potential trap. Where you may think that by pressing Connect, you will be connecting to the Internet, you won't. What you will be doing is connecting to your IIS 5 installation to retrieve the information stated in the SQL Query. So click the Connect button.

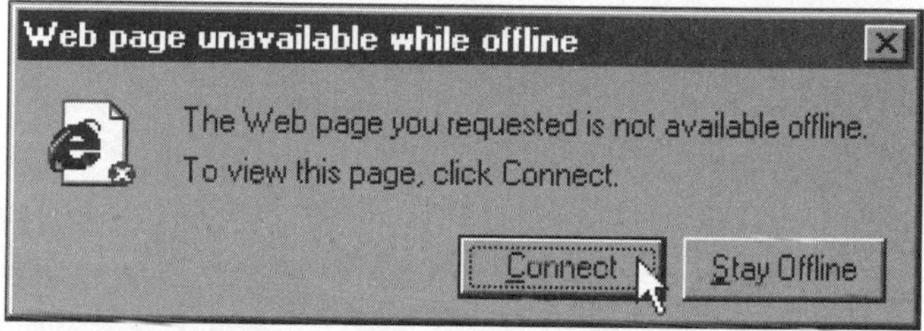

4. After a few moments, you should see a screen that looks not too dissimilar to one of the two shown below. Neither graphic is displaying any data, and both are showing what looks like
an XML error, which it is. XML needs to know where to start building its tree nodes from, and therefore needs to be told about its root. Recall earlier in the chapter how an XML document is structured. The second screen would be displayed if you had used a user ID to connect to the Wrox_Golf_Results database and the user had the authority to select data from the Matches table.

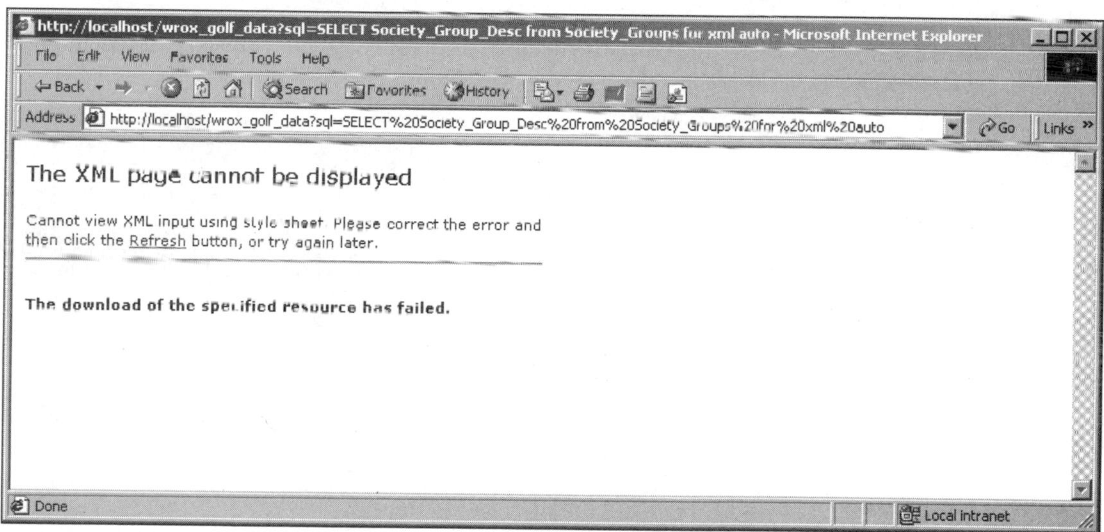

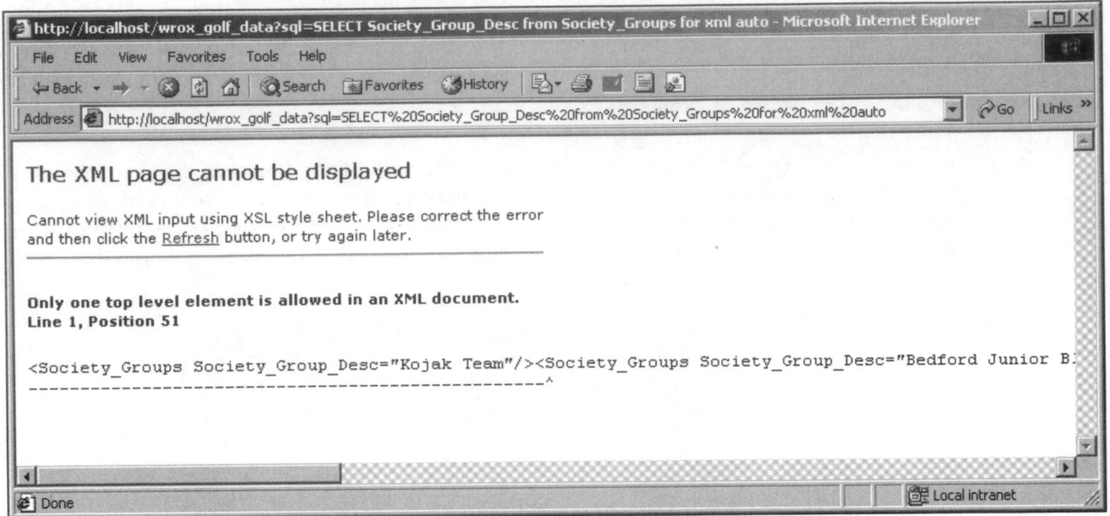

5. So now, change the query to read like the code below. This will solve the problem of missing the root node by defining the root node as the `Society_Group_Id`.

   http://localhost/wrox_golf_data?sql=SELECT Society_Group_Desc from Society_Groups for xml auto &root=Society_Group_Id

6. A new error message will now be displayed. Not the most helpful of statements, and doesn't really tell you anything useful straight away. The error message is in fact "Access denied". You can find these errors and what they mean by checking in MSDN (http://msdn.microsoft.com/) or within the Microsoft Knowledge Base online. If you remember when setting up the user `Wrox_Golf_XML` as a SQL Server user authentication, it was given access to `Wrox_Golf_Results` database. But it wasn't actually then given the powers to do anything in the database. It could connect and nothing more. So let's go back and give the ID some privileges.

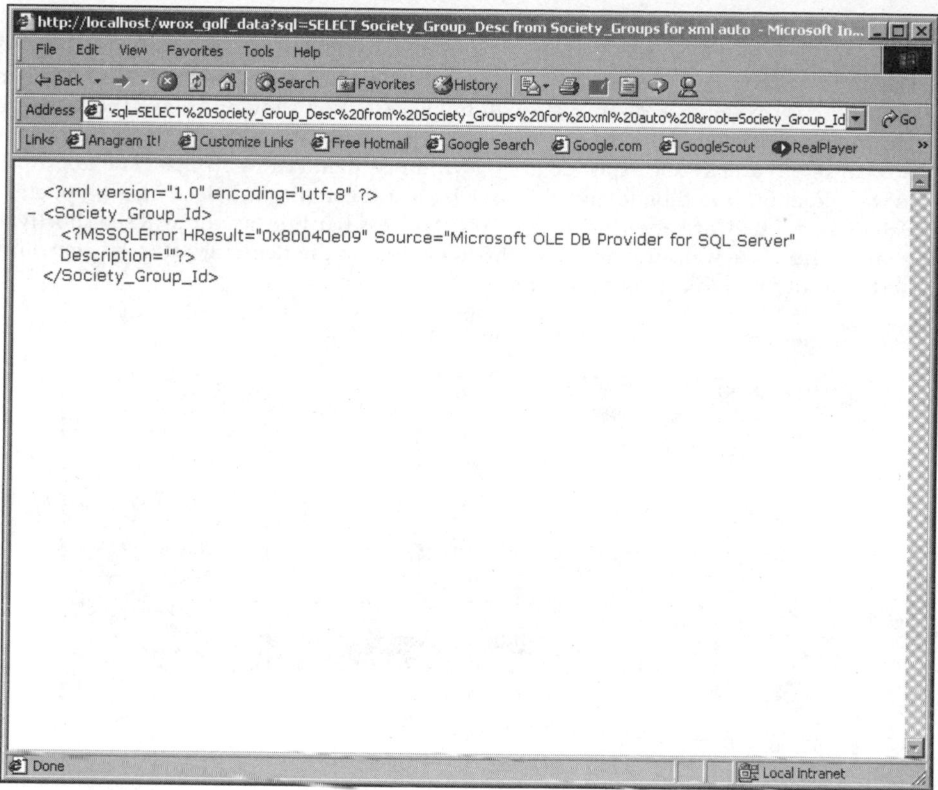

7. Ensure that SQL Server Enterprise Manager is running. Move to the Security section of Wrox_Golf_Results, click on Logins, find the Wrox_Golf_XML user ID, right-click, and select Properties.

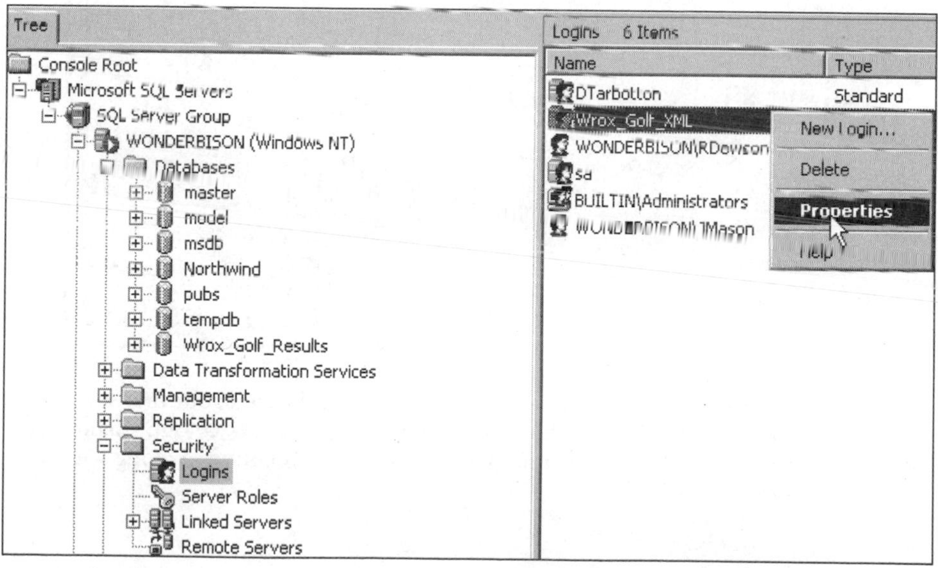

To demonstrate the code in this chapter, give this user System Administrators rights, which will allow this user ID to do anything. Although we will only be selecting the data using this ID, and displaying the information on the web page, it is easier and quicker for the moment to set up the Wrox_Golf_XML user ID with full access. You shouldn't leave the ID as this. However, rather than me take up 4 or 5 pages demonstrating how to do this now, you will see how to set up user IDs for specific access within Appendix E – *Security*. The appropriate thing in this situation would be to give this user ID just the ability to select, insert, update, and delete data if they are entering SQL on the Address bar line, as you will see shortly, or if this going to be a live web site, only give this ID access to the necessary stored procedures pertinent to the web site, or views used.

For now, let's just keep it if is. When finished, click OK.

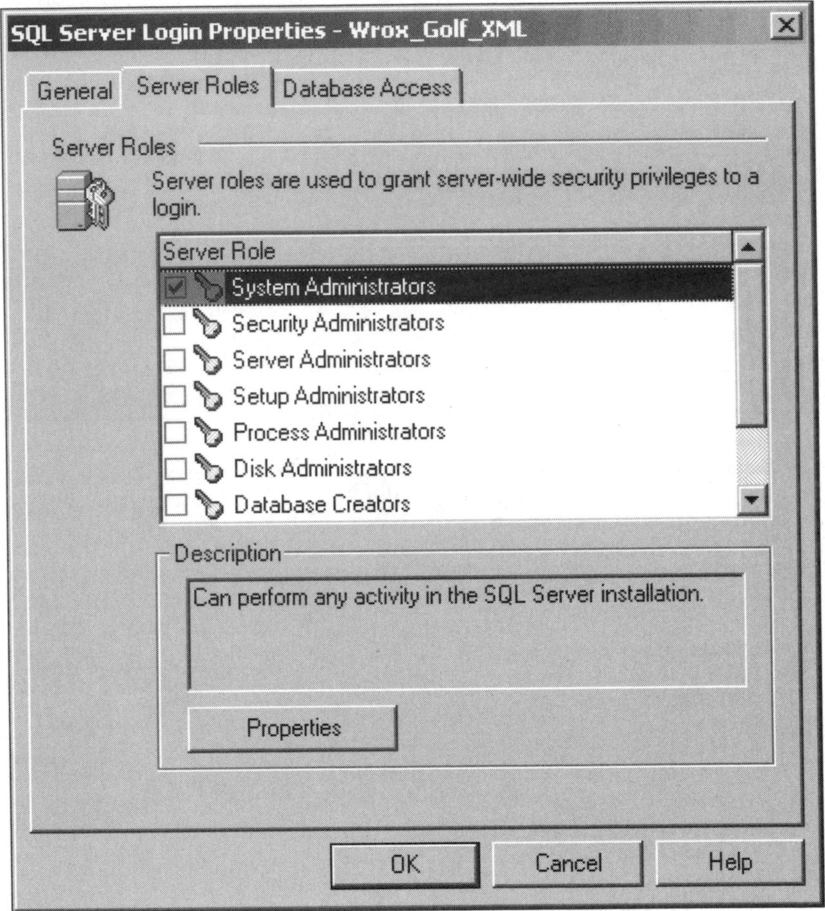

8. Now go back to Internet Explorer and refresh the page. Success; our first set of data returned via XML using SQL Server. All the records from the `Society_Groups` table have been returned, the column that the data has come from is also mentioned along with the information in each row.

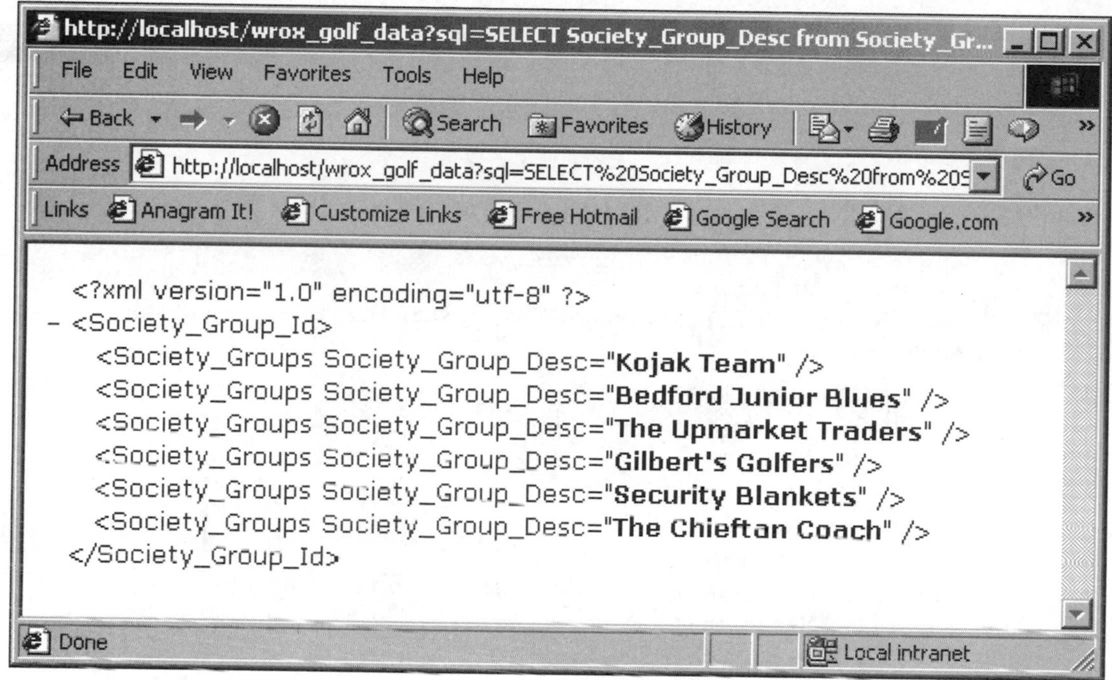

9. You can perform the `SELECT` with a `WHERE` statement that will be covered shortly, but for the moment, you have at least retrieved your first XML data from a SQL Server database.

Web Assistant Wizard

There is another way of publishing data for web pages, using a wizard. This is perhaps not the best way to deal with publishing data, however, it does allow a fast and effective way of getting data from your database onto a web site. This wizard creates a stored procedure within SQL Server that runs when a new web page has to be created. The stored procedure, which generates an HTML web page, is activated by either a job, something called a **trigger**, or whenever executed manually.

This wizard builds up the whole process for completing the automatic building of web pages, which although they are static, can be refreshed at specific times or when specific actions are performed. Although simplistic, this process can be a very powerful tool in exporting data to a web site. By including formatting you can build a very good web page.

The following example will take the `Players` table, and build web pages from the data, these will be rebuilt whenever the information within the `Players` table alters. This is completed through a trigger, which is a special feature within SQL Server that executes when an action happens on a table. Chapter 20 deals with triggers and these triggers will be discussed in more detail there. Time to dive in and start building our web pages. There will be one problematic area that this example demonstrates, and that deals with images. It is not possible to display graphics from this wizard.

Try It Out – Web Assistant Wizard

1. First of all, within Enterprise Manager, click the Wizard toolbar button.

2. From the Select Wizard options, choose Web Assistant Wizard found under the Management node.

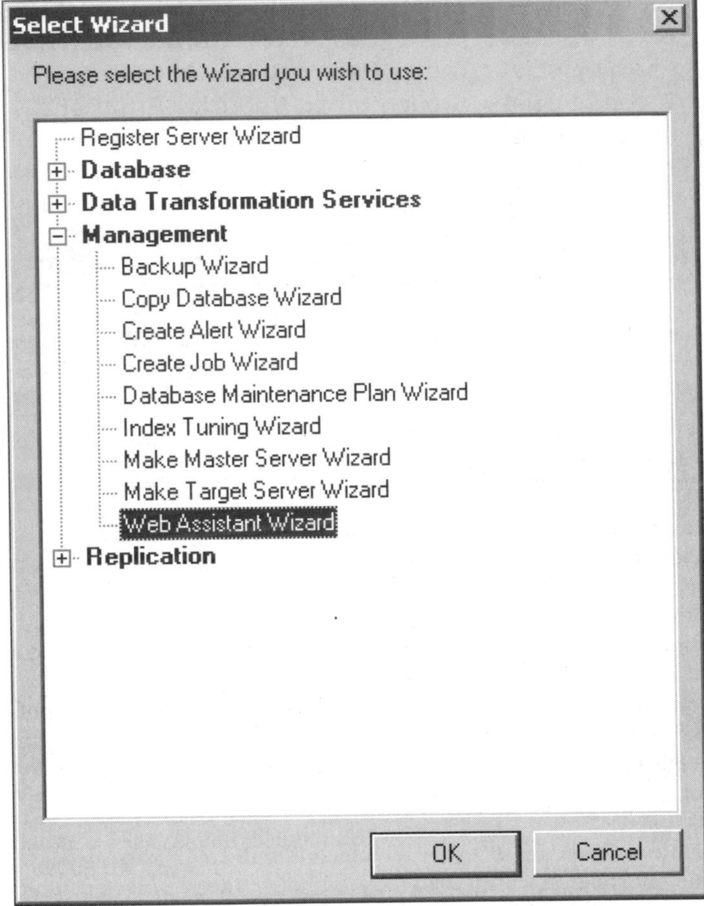

3. This then starts up the Web Assistant Wizard. The first screen gives a summary of what the aims of the wizard are. Click Next.

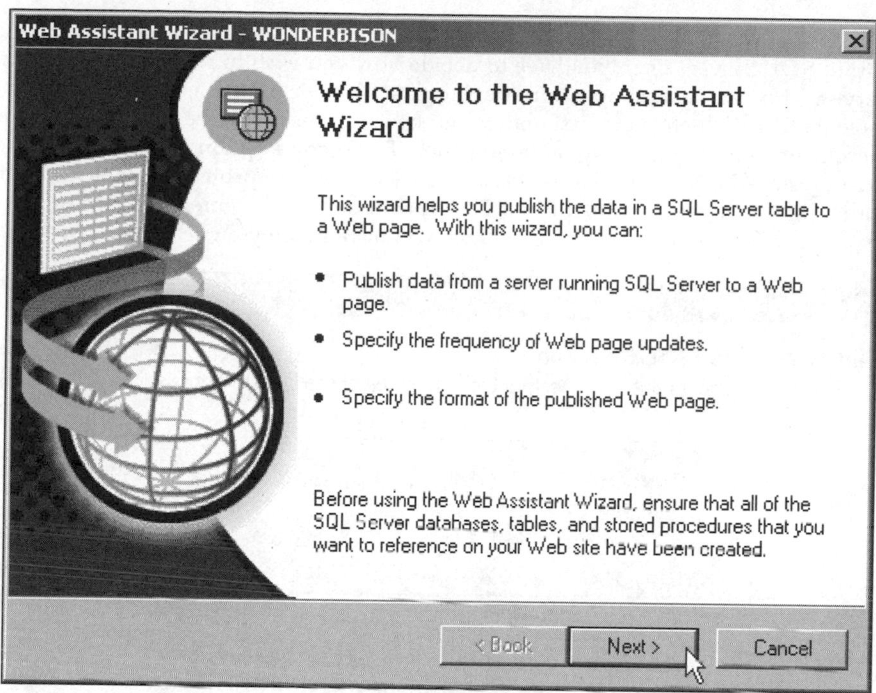

4. The first real decision to make is which database the web builder is to deal with. Of course, this will be the `Wrox_Golf_Results` database. Now click **Next**.

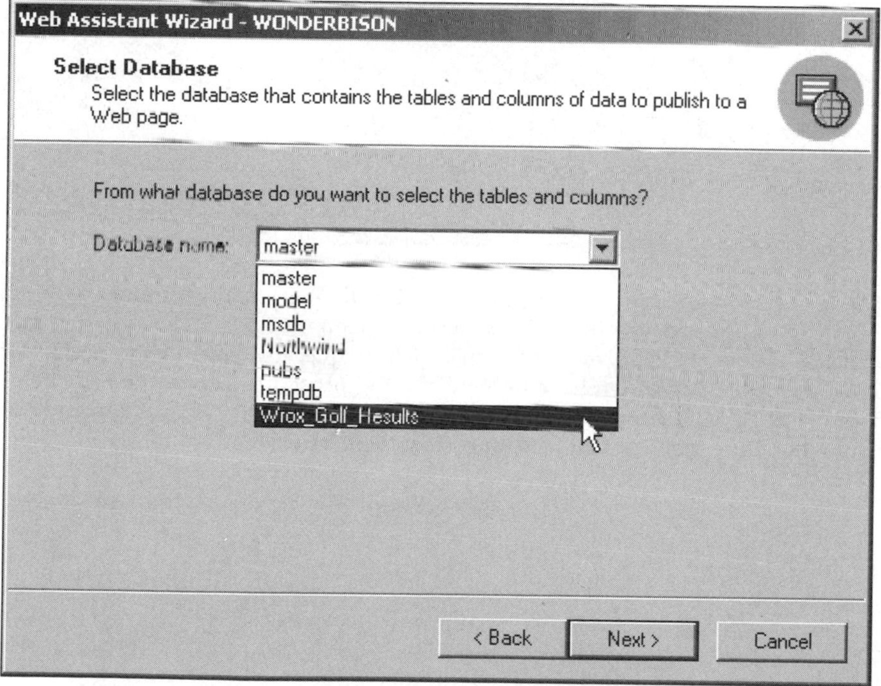

5. The next task is to give a name to the job that will be created. This has to be a unique name within SQL Server. Then you have to decide how you wish to retrieve the data from SQL Server. This can be as simple as retrieving data by selecting the columns you wish to retrieve the data from, which is the first option, but beware, this would be from a single table only and there is no ability to join two tables together. The second option is retrieving data from an existing stored procedure that builds a result set of data to print out. Finally the third option, which we will be using, is to allow a T-SQL command to be entered returning the data required to build up the web pages. Once you have made your selections, click Next.

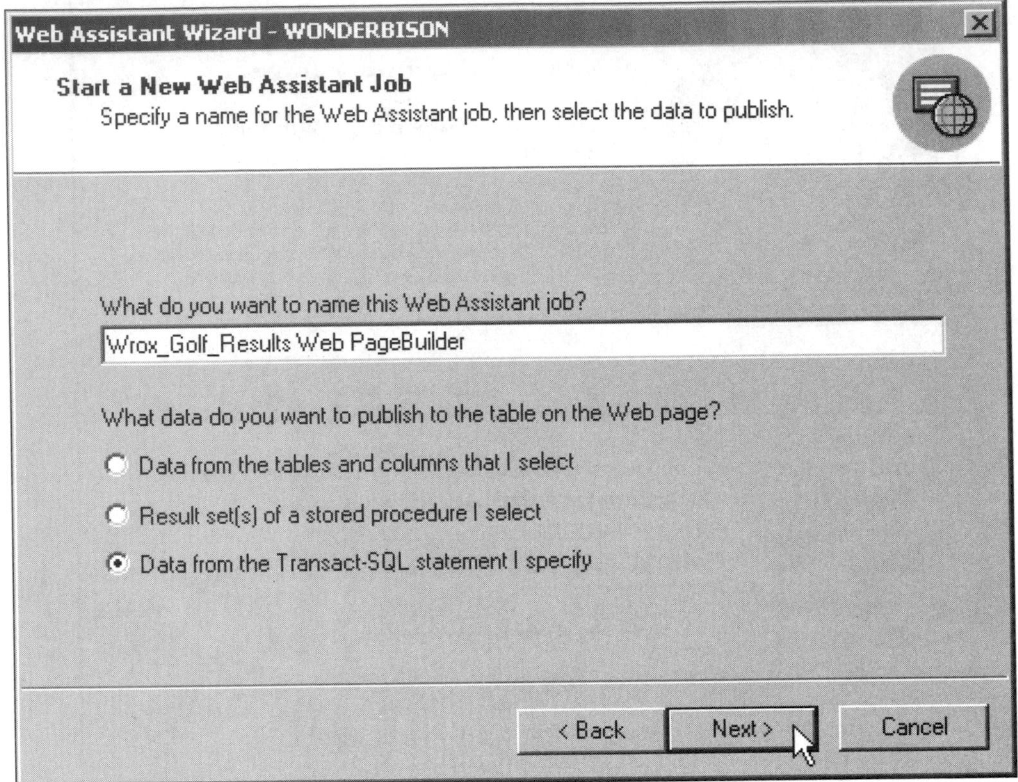

6. The next screen does allow the entry of any T-SQL query that will return a set of information. As you are informed, any text strings must be surrounded by single quotation marks. This screen will only allow the entry of a single T-SQL query. If you need to perform more than one query, then you would have to build a stored procedure. Enter the code below as you see it and click Next. Any errors are detected when you click the Next button and you will be notified of these and you will have to correct them before you can proceed:

```
SELECT Society_Group_Desc, Player_First_Name, Player_Last_Name, Photograph
FROM Players, Society_Groups
WHERE Society_Group = Society_Group_Id
```

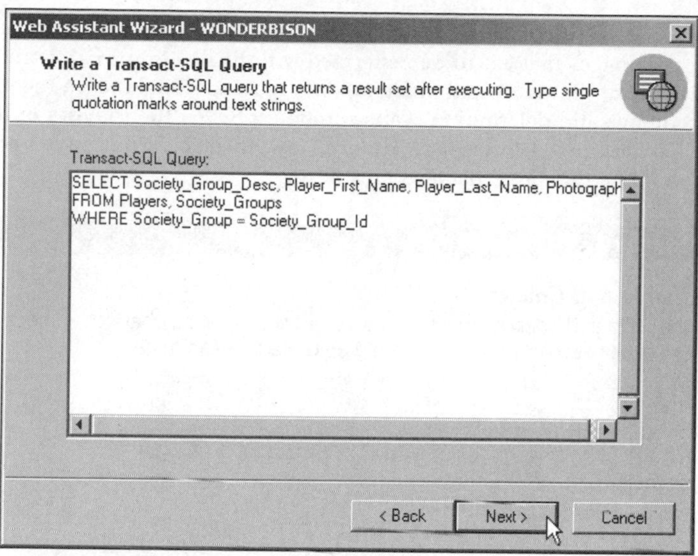

7. The next decision to make is how you wish the HTML pages to be generated. There are five options that can be chosen, each option producing different results within SQL Server. The first option will just produce the HTML and not create any further items within SQL Server. The second option builds the stored procedure that will be used to build the HTML and it will only run when executed manually, or when called from another action within SQL Server. The third option will generate the HTML once at a specific date and time. This will not run regularly. If you wish to run the generation at a scheduled time, then you need to set up a regular job within SQL Server, which is what the fifth option will do. The fourth option, the option that I would like you to use for this example, will create a trigger within SQL Server that will update the HTML pages when the data has been altered. The use of triggers that, as I have indicated, is covered in Chapter 20. Click **Next**.

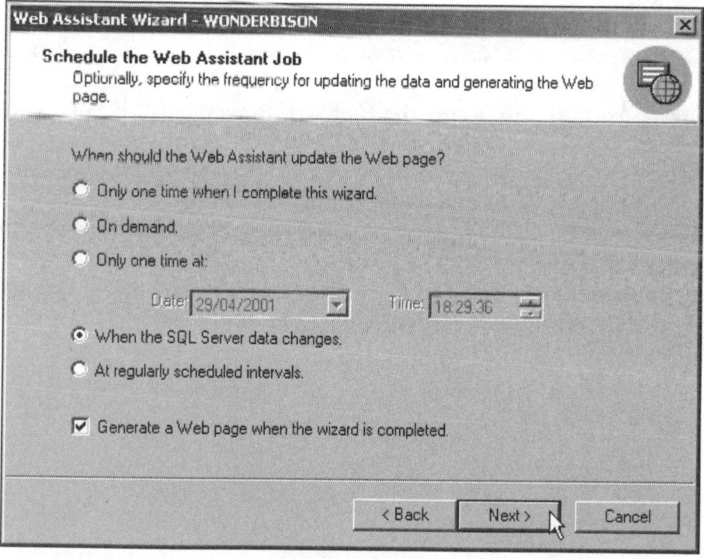

8. The option selected, indicates that the HTML will be produced when specific information alters. The web pages that are to be generated will display information about `Players`, therefore, if any of that information alters, then the pages need to be regenerated. This includes additions and deletions as well as updates. Select the **Players** option from the drop-down list. As you can see in the screenshot below, three columns have been chosen. Once you have chosen them, then as expected, click **Next**.

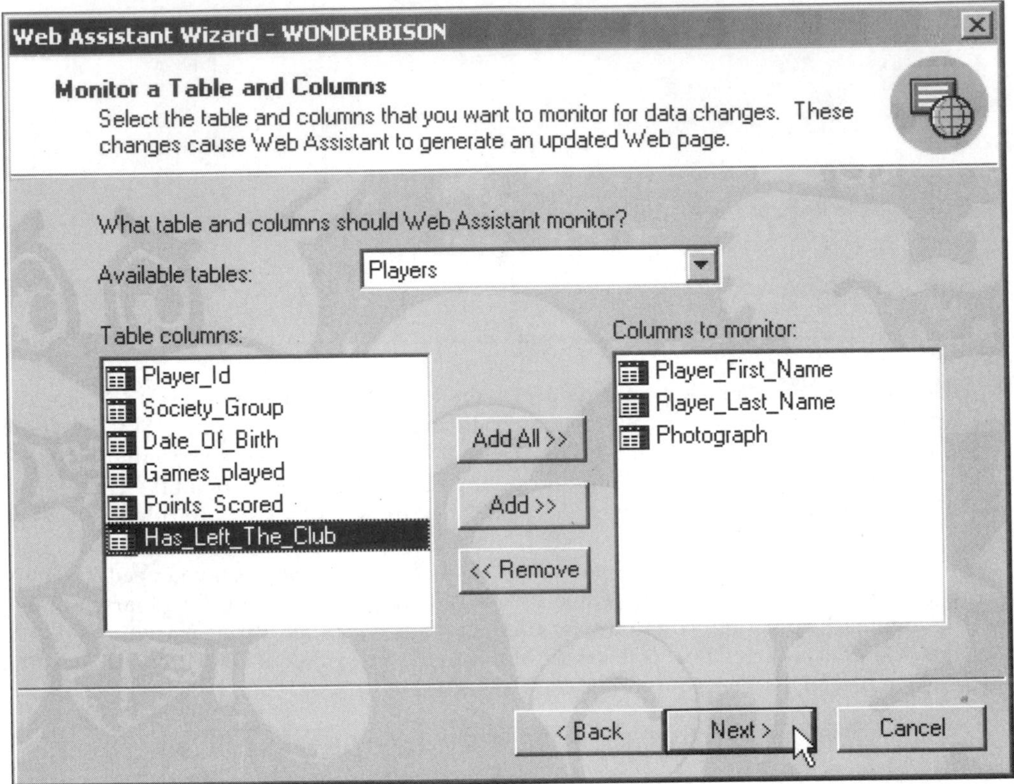

9. You are now asked to specify where the HTML is to be placed. Earlier within the chapter, a directory was set up to hold HTML pages. This is in `C:\Inetpub\wwwroot\Wrox_Golf`. It is in this directory that the web pages will be placed. The wizard places a directory location and the name of a web page in the **File name** box by default. However, click on the ellipsis button to the right of this to navigate to the correct directory, or enter the directory directly here.

10. By clicking on the ellipsis, you will be presented with a screen requesting you to **Specify the Output File Location** and the **File name**. Navigate to the `Wrox_Golf` directory and enter a filename of `Players.htm`. Then click **OK**.

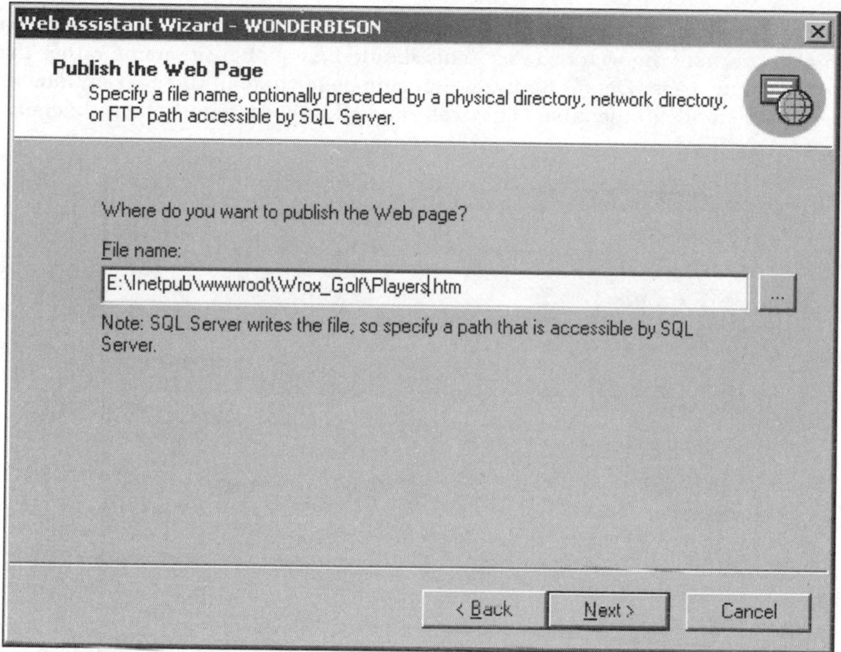

11. After clicking Next, you are then allowed to specify any formatting to put on to the web page. You could use an XML template to aid with the layout of the page, however, we will use the wizard to help with the layout. Leave the option Yes, help me format the Web page selected and click Next.

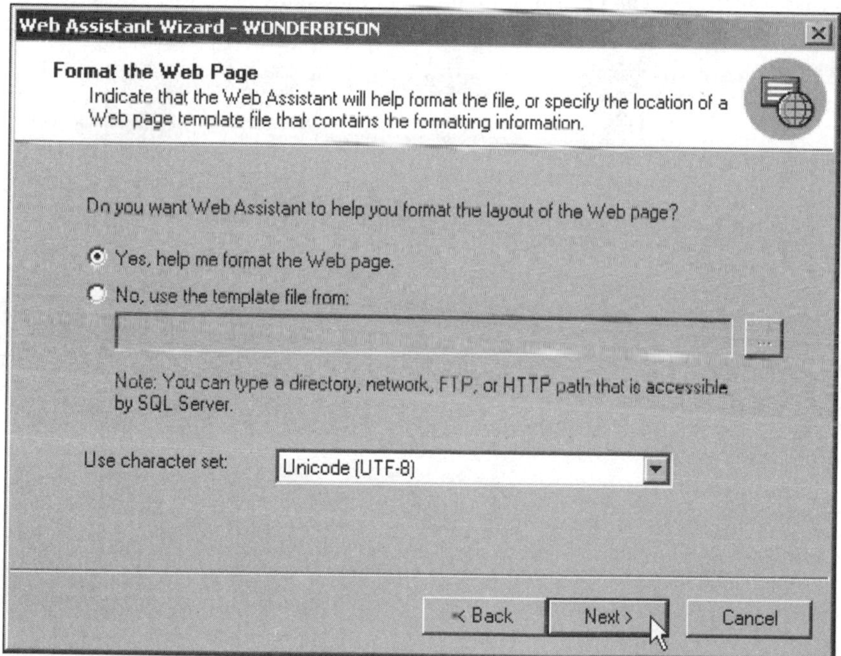

12. There are two titles to place on a web page. The first title is placed in the blue banner at the topmost portion of the web browser. This should be a global site name rather than any details about a specific page. Details about the specific page come in the next option, where you are asked to give a title to the table. This web site will only surround players' details so both titles reflect this. Click Next.

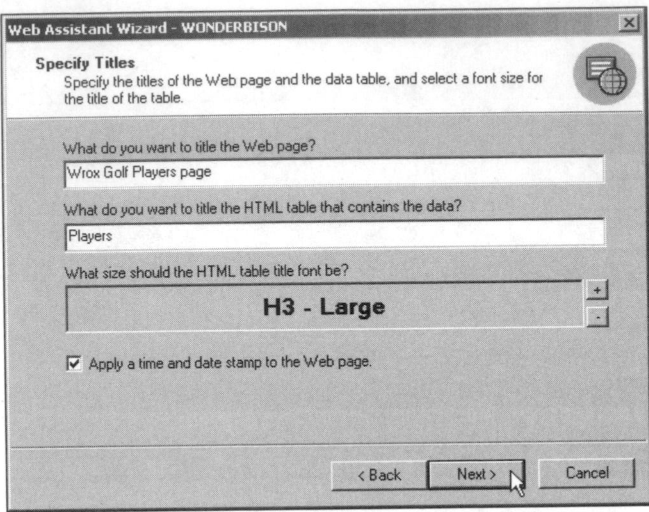

13. A table is generated from the results built up from the query earlier. Whether this query is from the query entry dialog, a stored procedure, or from a selection of columns, the data will still come out in a tabular format. You can then decide how this table is to be displayed. In this case, there are to be no column names, and the table is of a `Fixed` font made **Bold**. No border lines should be placed around the table. Click Next.

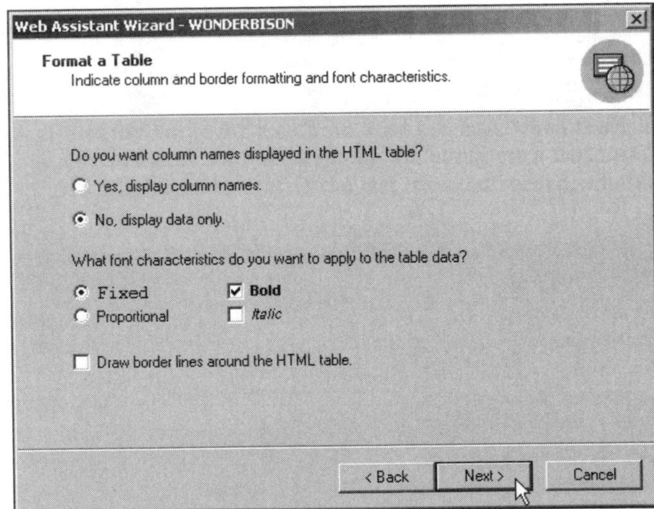

14. You can add links to any other site either by entering the details directly or by taking the links from a table that will hold the necessary information for creating the links. If you wish to retrieve links from a table, the `SELECT` statement would look something like what follows below:

```
SELECT label_column, hyperlink_column FROM hyperlinks_table
```

However we will only link to one site and so instead, enter it exactly as in the screenshot below. Click Next.

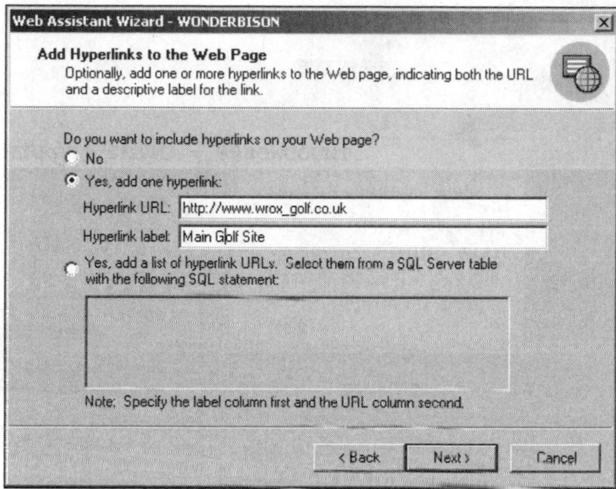

15. We're almost at the end now and the last questions asked are about the retrieval of the records and the number of records to be placed onto a web page. The first area surrounds the number of records to return. You can limit the number of rows, or place all the rows in the HTML page. In this case, No, return all rows of data is the chosen option. Move to the section where you can limit the number of rows displayed on each Web page. To demonstrate how this works, knowing that there are three records in the `Players` table, there will be two rows of data per web page. Click Next.

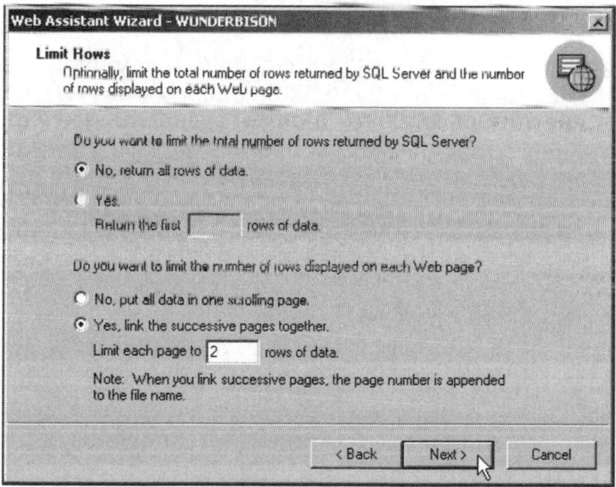

16. The final screen summarizes what has been achieved. If there are any problems, then click Back and alter them, otherwise click Finish. You can store the SQL built up through the wizard to a file to enter into SQL Server later, or perhaps store this within a source control system, ready to run on another server when required.

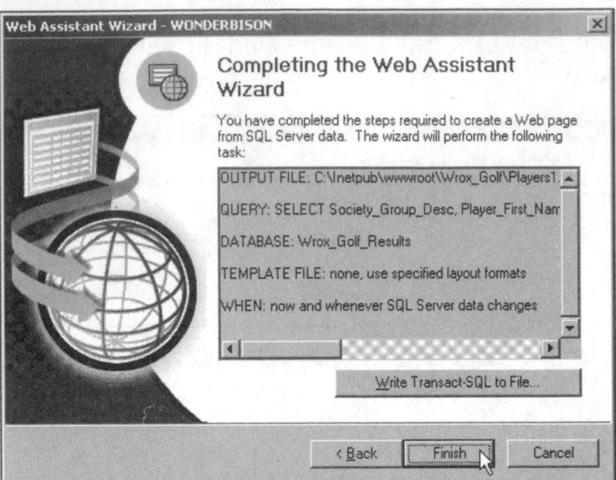

17. A message box indicating success should be displayed after pressing Finish, to inform you that the task of the wizard is completed. Click. OK.

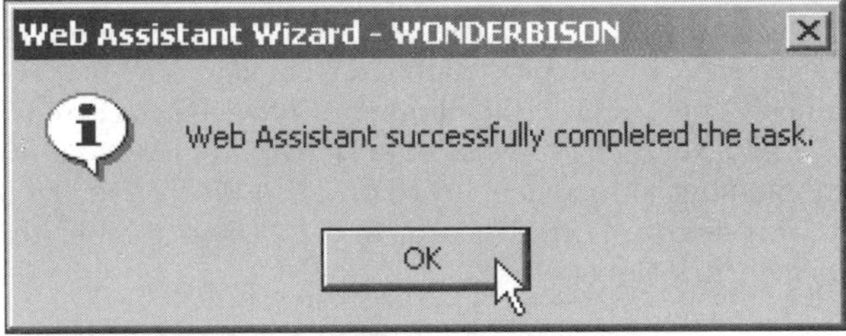

18. It's time to see what has been generated. Remember that in one of the screens, the option to generate the HTML initially when the wizard completes was selected, so therefore there should be something to see. Open up a browser, in this instance I will use Internet Explorer, and click File/Open...

19. This will bring up a screen to locate the file. Click Browse to find the file or enter the path directly here.

20. Locate the `Wrox_Golf` directory where, within the Wizard, you requested the web pages to be stored, and you will see the default.htm file from before, and two other pages. Both files are prefixed by `Players` but are suffixed with `1` and `2`. Recall that within the wizard, the pages were to be named Players. SQL Server being smart has realized that there is more than one page of data and so each page has a numerical suffix. Select Players1.htm and then click Open.

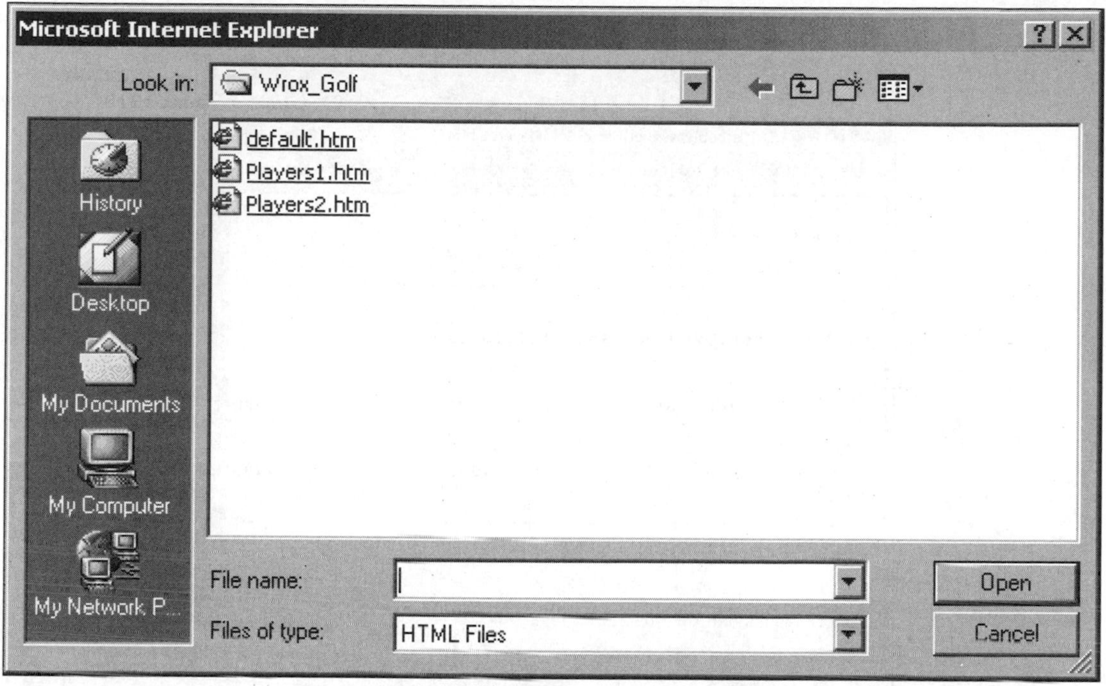

21. This brings you back to the Open screen, so just click OK.

22. This will then return the page selected and display the HTML holding the data from the web pages. Notice that there is a date and time stamp listed on the page, the players are listed, the page titles exist, and there is a link to the Main Golf Site. However, the main focus of attention surrounds the data returned, especially the large column of what looks like numbers and letters. This is actually the pointer to the photographs for these players. The wizard, as it stands, will not display any images. The only way around this is beyond the scope of this book I'm afraid, and would mean writing some ASP code. Notice at the foot of the page, there is a link titled Next. Clicking this will bring up the `Players2.htm` web page.

If you wish to know more about ASP, on the ASP Watch web site there is an article describing what is required. The link is
http://www.aspwatch.com/c/200037/d2D4C08CA8DFF11D4AEF900A0C9E95208.asp
For more information on ASP, see *"Beginning Active Server Pages 3.0" (Wrox Press, ISBN 1-861003-82-2).*

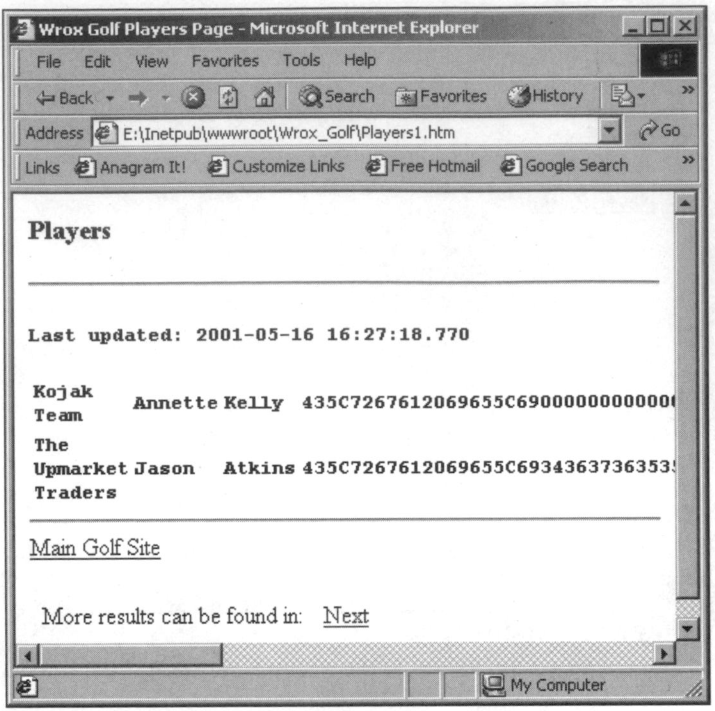

23. Clicking Next will produce the third record from the `Players` table:

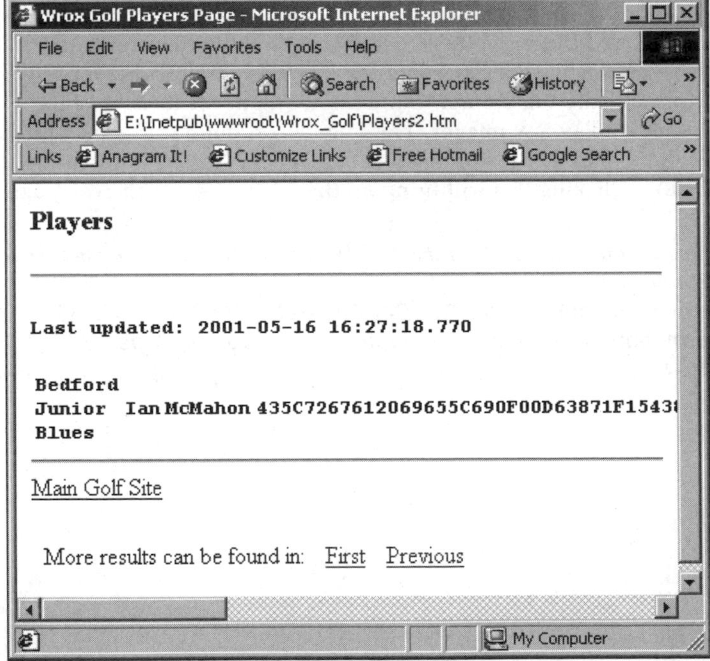

That is all there is to getting a web site up and running. The only real drawback of this method is that formatting is limited and you could be generating pages more often than required if you get the trigger or the scheduling of the job wrong. Don't forget that if you manually alter any pages after generation, when you regenerate the pages, through any method, your changes will be lost. Many SQL Server 2000 developers use this wizard to set up production of HTML and you can become very clever in getting the stored procedure generated to produce results that you require. However, this would be another very large section, beyond the scope of this book.

I would not be surprised if the wizard eventually included the ability to generate ASP and allow data updates to occur from the web pages generated. Other areas that could easily be modified, are the formatting of the output and data retrieval. However, it is already very powerful.

Retrieving images

As you have seen within the book, photographs have been placed within the `Players` table for the three players that exist. What is stored within the Photograph column is not the image itself, but a pointer to the image. The image itself is not actually stored within the column.

It is possible to bring back and convert the pointer to the location on your hard drive where the image is stored and this next section will demonstrate this. From this location, it is possible then to retrieve the image.

If however, the image was actually stored within the column, in other words, the image size was below 7KB and this was possible, you could actually retrieve the actual image and display it within the browser. If the example had been working with the `Northwind` database, the employee pictures are held within the column itself. This will also be demonstrated within this example.

To retrieve the image stored within our database for our players requires the building of XML templates and XML style sheets. This in itself would require another two chapters at least, so I'm afraid it isn't discussed here.

Try It Out – Retrieving Images

1. First of all, this example is going to bring back the reference for Player 2, Jason Atkins. To complete this a new method of retrieving data is going to be used. This is using an XML navigation technique called **XPath**. How this works will be explained very briefly at the end. Enter the following code into the address bar of a web browser:
   http://localhost/Wrox_Golf_Data/Database_Object/Players[@Player_Id='2']/@Photograph

2. Of course, if you are prompted to work offline, then, do this. The information returned is the path to where Jason's photograph resides.

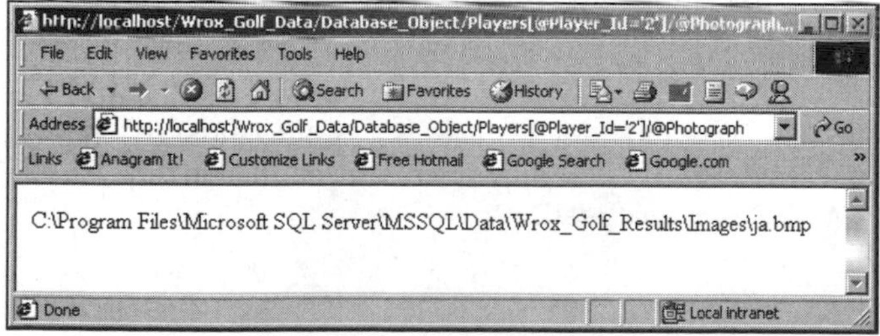

3. Another method, which will also return the path to where the image is stored, is to use a SQL query in the address bar. To retrieve the same information for Jason, enter the following URL: http://localhost/Wrox_Golf_Data?sql=SELECT+Photograph+FROM+Players+WHERE+Player_ID=2

   Images can be stored within the columns as found in `Northwind`. To retrieve an image from the `Northwind` database's `Employees` table, you would have to set up a virtual directory for `Northwind` along with the correct database access, just as you have completed for `Wrox_Golf_Results`. If you have completed this, then there are several ways to bring back the image. The first method is to use an XPath query. Enter the following code into Internet Explorer's address bar:
   http://localhost/northwind/dbobject/Employees[@EmployeeID='1']/@Photo

4. This will then display the following in the web browser. As the image is only 7KB in size, the quality is not very good. What is happening is that the actual binary data within the image column is being displayed; it just so happens the binary code in this instance makes up an image.

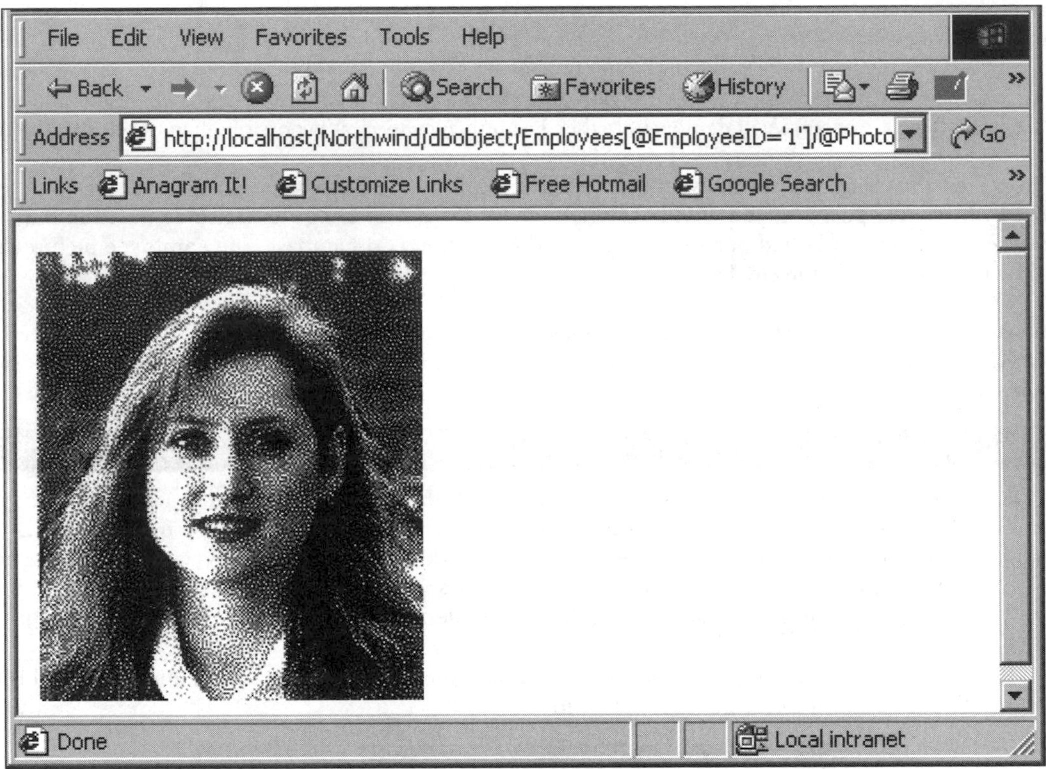

5. Another method is to use straight SQL. As long as there is only the photograph column being returned, then there should be no problem. The following SQL would bring back the photograph for `Employee_Id` 2: http://localhost/northwind?sql=SELECT+Photo+FROM+Employees+WHERE+EmployeeID=2

6. This then displays the correct photograph in the web browser just as before by converting the binary information into a physical image.

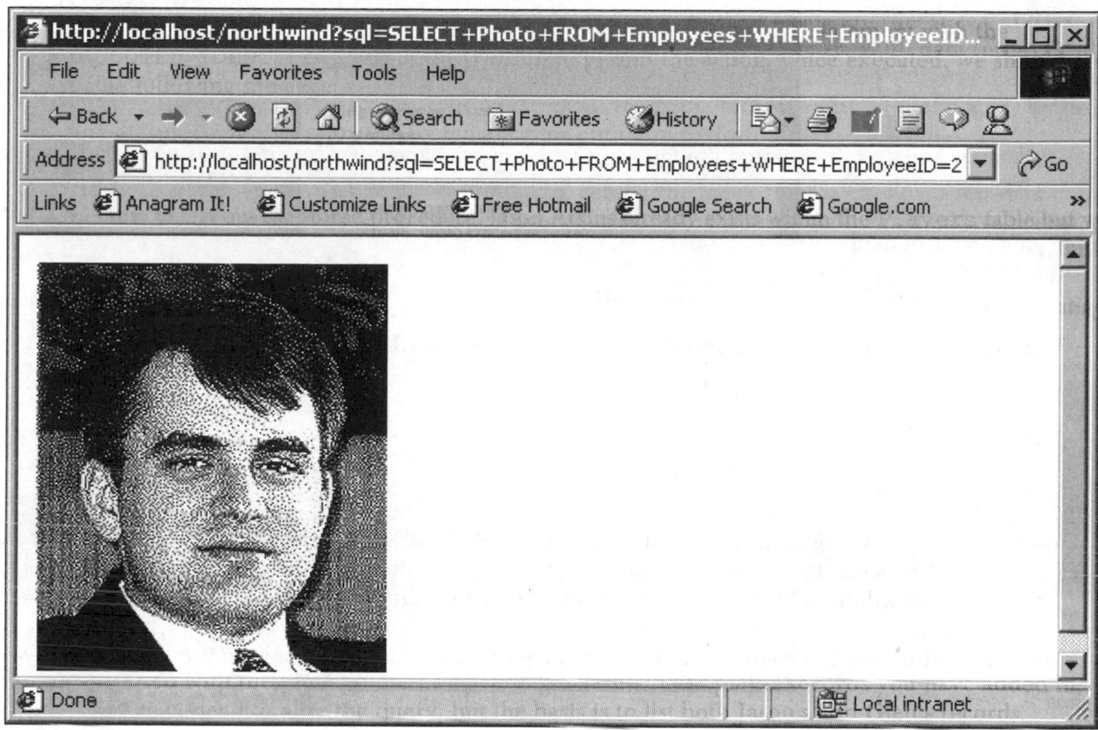

XPath Queries

An XPath query uses the IIS installation to pass information entered in the web browser to the database object, which then builds the SQL statements and passes them on to SQL Server. An XPath query can do a great deal more than has been demonstrated above, but this would take up a whole major section of the book on its own. However, it can be very useful when retrieving information, as detailed above.

The syntax of an XPath query is very straightforward:

```
//IISServer_Name/virtual_directory/dbobject_name/table_name[@column_name_to_
search=value]/@column_name_of_image
```

Using the command we entered to return Jason's photograph, the query would be translated into:

```
SELECT Photograph FROM Players WHERE Player_Id = 2
```

This is then executed against the `Wrox_Golf_Results` database; the value retrieved passed to the browser and displayed.

Summary

A great deal has been covered within this chapter and yet, it has not been possible to give XML the full coverage it deserves. The aim of this chapter though was to give you some exposure to XML, installing the necessary components to make XML work, how it works, and how to generate results on a web page using SQL statements and XPath.

Although only data retrieval and limited work with images have been covered, it is possible to modify data and even run stored procedures using XML. But where the real power of XML lies is with templates and stylesheets, which are beyond the scope of this chapter. In summary, the areas covered in varying levels of detail were:

- A brief overview and history of XML
- Setting up IIS and SQL Server to provide data via XML
- Retrieving data using XML
- Using the Web Assistant Wizard
- Retrieving images using XML

Do take care when using XML as a solution to passing data between applications. Self-describing data can be slow in processing compared to more conventional methods; however, what you do gain is more control over the validity of the information contained within the XML document.

Using the web wizard to produce HTML pages may seem like the better solution initially, and if you wish to go further with XML, then do read several XML books first. Try:

- *"Professional SQL Server 2000" (Wrox Press, ISBN 1-861004-48-6)*
- *"Professional SQL Server 2000 XML" (Wrox Press, ISBN 1-861005-46-6)*
- *"Beginning XML" (Wrox Press, ISBN 1-861003-41-2)*
- *"Professional XML Second Edition" (Wrox Press, ISBN 1-861005-05-9)*

More information is also available from the World Wide Web Consortium's web site, located at: http://www.w3c.org/.

Triggers

Although we have become quite proficient in using SQL Server 2000, there is one last area that really ought to be covered in this book. Triggers are that one last step, and this chapter is the missing link in the foundation of our knowledge and skill set.

There will be times when a modification to data somewhere within our database will require action on data elsewhere, either in our database, another database, or elsewhere within SQL Server; a trigger is the object that will do this for us. When a modification to our data occurs, a trigger can fire, which will then allow a specialized stored procedure to run, performing the actions that we desire. Triggers are similar to constraints but are more powerful, although requiring more system overhead that can lead to a reduction in performance. Triggers are most commonly used to perform business rules validation, cascading data modifications (changes on one table causing changes to be made on other tables), keeping track of changes for each record (audit trail), or any other processing that we require to be performed when data on a specific table is modified.

The aim of this chapter is to:

- Learn what a trigger is
- Detail potential problems surrounding triggers
- Show the `CREATE TRIGGER` T-SQL syntax
- Discuss when to use a constraint and when to use a trigger
- Show the system tables and functions specific to triggers
- Demonstrate the creation of a trigger through a template and straight T-SQL commands
- Talk about image data types and the problems that surround updating these columns and firing a trigger

First of all though, we really need to know what a trigger is.

What is a Trigger?

A trigger is a specialized stored procedure. Triggers are pieces of code attached to a specific table that are set to automatically run in response to an INSERT, DELETE, or UPDATE command. Unlike stored procedures, you cannot manually make a trigger run, you cannot use parameters with triggers, and you cannot use return values with triggers.

There are many uses for triggers. Perhaps the most common use for a trigger is to enforce a business rule, for example when a customer places an order, to check that they have sufficient funds, or that we have enough stock; if any of these checks fail, we can complete further actions or return error messages and rollback the update. Triggers can be used as a form of extra validation, for example to perform quite complex checks on data that a constraint could not achieve. Keep in mind that using constraints instead of triggers gives you better performance, but triggers are the better choice when dealing with complex data validation. Another use for a trigger is to make changes in another table based on what is about to happen within the original triggered table. Finally, triggers can be used to create an automated audit trail that creates a change history for each record.

We can create separate triggers for any table action except SELECT, or a trigger that will fire on any combination of table actions. Obviously, as there are no table modifications happening on a SELECT statement, it is impossible to create such a trigger. There are three main types of triggers:

- INSERT Trigger
- DELETE Trigger
- UPDATE Trigger

You can also have a combination of the three types of triggers.

Triggers can update tables within other databases if desired and it is also possible for triggers to span servers as well, so don't think the scope of triggers is limited to the current database.

It is possible for a trigger to fire another trigger. For example, imagine we have Table A, which has a trigger on it to fire a modification within Table B, and Table B, which has a trigger on it that fires a modification within Table C. If a modification is made to Table A, then Table A will fire a trigger in Table B, which will in turn fire a trigger in Table C. This nesting of triggers can go up to 32 triggers deep before we reach the limit set within SQL Server; however, if we start getting close to that sort of level we either have a very complex system, or perhaps we have been over zealous with our creation of triggers! It is possible to switch off any nesting of triggers, so that when one trigger fires no other trigger can fire; however this is not usually the norm. Be aware that your performance will suffer greatly when you start using nested triggers; use them only when necessary.

There is one statement that will stop a DELETE trigger from firing. If we issue a TRUNCATE TABLE T-SQL command, it is as if the table has been wiped without any logging. This also means that a DELETE trigger will not fire, as it is not a deletion per se that is happening.

Do take care when building triggers that, as with stored procedures, you don't create a potential endless loop where a trigger causes an update, which fires a trigger already fired earlier within the loop, so repeating the process.

CREATE TRIGGER Syntax

The creation of a trigger through T-SQL code can be quite complex if we use the full trigger syntax. However, the reduced version that is covered here is much more manageable and easier to demonstrate. When building a trigger, it can be created for a single action, or for multiple actions. To expand on this, a trigger can be for insertion of a record only, or it could cover inserting and updating the record.

Although this chapter will demonstrate triggers on tables, a trigger can also be placed on a view as well, so that when data is modified through a view, it too can fire a trigger if required.

Here is the syntax for creating a basic trigger:

```
CREATE TRIGGER trigger_name
ON {table|view}
[WITH ENCRYPTION]
{
{{FOR {[INSERT] [,] [UPDATE] [,] [DELETE]}
AS
[{IF UPDATE (column)
[{AND|OR} UPDATE (column)]]
sql_statements}}
```

We will now explore the options in this syntax more closely:

- `CREATE TRIGGER trigger_name` – First of all, as ever, we need to inform SQL Server what we are attempting to do, and in this instance, we wish to create a trigger. The name for the trigger must also follow the SQL Server standards for naming objects within a database. In this chapter we name the triggers starting with `tg` to indicate the object is a trigger, followed by the type of trigger (`ins` for insert, `del` for delete, and `upd` for update), and then the name of the root table the trigger will be associated with. An example of naming a trigger would be `tgInsMatch_Scores`: we can tell that this is an Insert (`Ins`) trigger (`tg`) that is on the `Match_Scores` table.
- `ON {table|view}` – It is then necessary to give the name of the single table or view that the trigger relates to, which is named after the `ON` keyword. Each trigger is attached to one table only.
- `[WITH ENCRYPTION]` – As with views and stored procedures, we can encrypt the trigger using the `WITH ENCRYPTION` options so that the code cannot be viewed by prying eyes.
- `{FOR {[INSERT] [,] [UPDATE] [,] [DELETE]}` – This section of the syntax determines on what action(s) the trigger will execute. This can be an `INSERT`, an `UPDATE`, or a `DELETE` T-SQL command. As mentioned earlier, the trigger can fire on one, two, or three of these commands, depending on what we wish the trigger to do. Therefore we need, at this point, to mention which combination of commands, separated by a comma, we wish to work with.
- `AS` – The keyword `AS` defines that the trigger code has commenced, just as the `AS` keyword defined the start of a stored procedure. After all, a trigger is just a specialized stored procedure.

- `[{IF UPDATE (column) [{AND|OR} UPDATE (column)]]` – There is one last option that can be used within a trigger that is not available within a stored procedure, and that is the test to check whether a specific column has been modified or not. This is through the use of the `UPDATE()` keyword. By placing the name of the column to test in between the parentheses, a logical `TRUE` or `FALSE` will be returned depending on whether the column has been updated or not. The deletion of a record will not set the `UPDATE` test to `TRUE` or `FALSE` as we are removing an item and not updating it. An `INSERT` or an `UPDATE` record manipulation will set the `UPDATE` test to the necessary value.
- `sql_statements` – We can then code the trigger just like any other stored procedure.

> **The main thought that must be kept in mind when building a trigger is that a trigger fires after each record is flagged to be modified, but before the modification is actually placed into the table. Therefore, if we have a statement that updates many rows, the trigger will fire after each record is flagged and not when all the records have been dealt with.**

Now that we know how to create a trigger, when would we use one?

Why Not Use a Constraint?

There is nothing stopping us from using a constraint to enforce a business rule, and in fact, constraints should be used to enforce data integrity. Constraints also give you better performance than triggers. However, they are limited in what they can achieve and what information is available to them to complete their job.

Triggers are more commonly used for validation of business rules, or for more complex data validation, which may or may not then go on to complete further updates of data elsewhere within SQL Server.

A constraint can also only validate data that is within the table that the constraint is being built for, or a specified value entered at design time. This is in contrast to a trigger, which can span databases, or even servers, and check against any data set at design time, or built from data collected from other actions against any table. This can happen if the necessary access rights are given to all objects involved.

However, constraints are the objects to use to ensure that data forming a key is correct, or when referential integrity needs to be enforced through a foreign key constraint.

There will be times when a fine line will exist between building a constraint and a trigger, when the trigger will perform a very simple validation task. In this case, if the decision deals with any form of data integrity, then use a constraint. This will give you better performance than using a trigger. If the object to be built is for business rules and may require complex validation, needs to handle multiple databases or servers, or requires advanced error handling, then build a trigger. For example, a trigger must be used if you need a change on one table to result in an action (update, detete, etc.) on a table that is located in another database. You might have this situation if you keep an audit trail (change history) database separate from your production database. It is doubtful that you would want to use a trigger if you are doing something simple like verifying that a date field only contains values within a certain range.

Deleted and Inserted Logical Tables

When a table is modified, whether this is by an insertion, modification, or removal, this action and what exactly has happened is recorded in two system logical tables. These tables do not actually physically exist within SQL Server so it is not possible to complete any further processing on these tables, which are called `DELETED` and `INSERTED`. You can, however, access these tables within a trigger to find out which records have been inserted, updated, or deleted.

When a record is inserted into a table within a database, a full copy of the insertion of the record is placed in to the `INSERTED` table. Every item of information placed into each column for the insertion is then available for checking. If a deletion is performed, a record of the row of data is placed in the `DELETED` table. Finally, when an update occurs on a row of data, a record of the row before the modification is placed in the `DELETED` table, and then a copy of the row of data after the modification is placed in the `INSERTED` table. Therefore, to check what columns have been modified, it would be possible to compare each and every column value between the two tables to see what information had been altered. Luckily, as was discussed in the syntax section, there is a function that can test if a column has been modified, which is the `UPDATE()` function.

The `INSERTED` and `DELETED` tables will by default only hold one record from each table at any one time, because as each insertion, modification, or row removal occurs, the trigger for the relevant action fires. Once the trigger has completed, the data for that table is removed from the relevant tables.

Now that we are fully up-to-date as to what a trigger is and how it works, it is time to create and test the first trigger within the database.

Creating a Trigger

It doesn't matter if we use SQL Server Enterprise Manager or Query Analyzer, the building of triggers is exactly the same. There are no wizards or shortcuts to building a trigger, only templates, so in all cases it is necessary to write the raw code. In this chapter, all code will be completed in Query Analyzer. The first trigger that will be created is for updating the match scores.

The scoring in this society is that there are 3 points for a win, 1 point for a draw and of course, no points if the player loses. The trigger will work like this: as each player comes to the end of their game, their score will be inserted into the `Match Scores` table. This will then fire a trigger that will update the `Matches` table as required. This will allow an up-to-date state of how the match is progressing. Let's proceed now to building the trigger in Query Analyzer

Try It Out – Creating a Trigger in Query Analyzer

1. Ensure that Query Analyzer is running and that you are logged in with an ID that can insert objects in to the database. In the **Object Browser**, switch to the **Templates** tab. Find the **Create Trigger** node, expand this, and then select the **Create Trigger Basic Template** option.

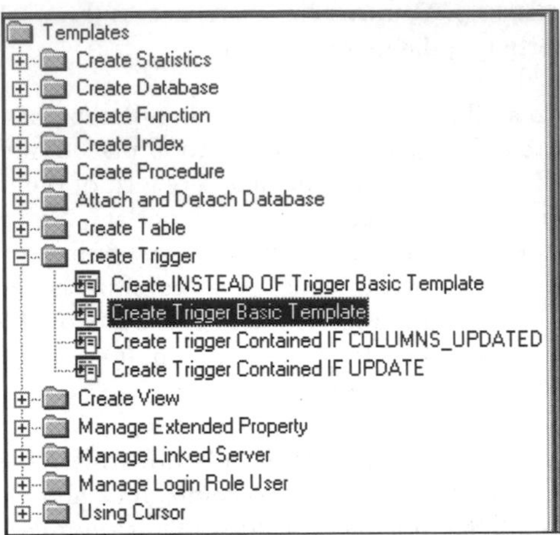

2. This gives the following trigger template code to work with.

```
-- ===============================================
-- Create trigger basic template(After trigger)
-- ===============================================
IF EXISTS (SELECT name
   FROM   sysobjects
   WHERE  name = N'<trigger_name, sysname, trig_test>'
   AND    type = 'TR')
    DROP TRIGGER <trigger_name, sysname, trig_test>
GO

CREATE TRIGGER <trigger_name, sysname, trig_test>
ON <table_name, sysname, pubs.dbo.sales>
FOR DELETE, INSERT, UPDATE
AS
BEGIN
   RAISERROR (50009, 16, 10)
END
GO
```

3. We won't demonstrate the replacing of the values for the template using the **Replace Template Values** screen as this has been demonstrated before. First of all, it is necessary to give the trigger a meaningful name. One naming convention is to use `tg` as a prefix, followed by the actions the trigger is dealing with, in this case `Ins` for Insert, and then the name of the root table that the trigger will sit on, which will be `Match_Scores`. So the trigger will be called `tgInsMatch_Scores`. As with other templates, this template checks for the existence of the trigger within SQL Server, and if it does exist, then it is dropped before the creation takes place. Alter the code to look like the following:

```
-- =============================================
-- Create trigger basic template(After trigger)
-- =============================================
IF EXISTS (SELECT name
   FROM   sysobjects
   WHERE  name = "tgInsMatch_Scores"
   AND    type = 'TR')
    DROP TRIGGER tgInsMatch_Scores
GO

CREATE TRIGGER tgInsMatch_Scores
ON Match_Scores
FOR INSERT
AS
BEGIN
   RAISERROR (50009, 16, 10)
END
GO
```

4. It is now time to enter the remainder of the code for the trigger. It is necessary to retrieve the `Points_Against`, `Points_For`, and `Match_Id` values from the `INSERTED` table to be able to use these in the update of the `Matches` table. The `CASE` statement is used to assign the `Points_Against` variable: if `Score_Points` is one, `Points_Against` is assigned to one; otherwise it is given the value three minus `Score_Points`. Once these values have been found, it is then possible to update the `Matches` table. Also note that the `RAISERROR` SQL statement at the end is of no real use for this trigger, and so its removal is necessary. We will be using the `RAISEERROR` statement in the next example and will cover it in detail there. Make sure you have run the `SET QUOTED_IDENTIFIER OFF` statement so that you can use the single quotes. This now leaves the full code for the trigger as follows:

```
-- =============================================
-- Create trigger basic template(After trigger)
-- =============================================
IF EXISTS (SELECT name
   FROM   sysobjects
   WHERE  name = "tgInsMatch_Scores"
   AND    type = 'TR')
    DROP TRIGGER tgInsMatch_Scores
GO

CREATE TRIGGER tgInsMatch_Scores
ON Match_Scores
FOR  INSERT
AS
BEGIN
   DECLARE @Points_Against int
   DECLARE @Points_For int
   DECLARE @Match_Id int
   SELECT @Points_Against =
      CASE WHEN Score_Points = 1
           THEN 1
           ELSE 3 - Score_Points
```

```
        END,
        @Points_For = Score_Points,
        @Match_Id = Match_Id
    FROM INSERTED

    -- There will be a Matches record already set up
    UPDATE Matches
        SET Points_For = Points_For + @Points_For,
            Points_Against = Points_Against + @Points_Against
        WHERE Match_Id = @Match_Id
END
GO
```

5. Execute the previous code to create the trigger. Now let's make this a nice rounded example by creating the necessary stored procedure to insert each match result as it comes in. This stored procedure will be a very simplistic procedure that will accept the player ID, the date and time the match score was made, and the number of points the player received. It will then insert a record in to the `Match_Scores` table recording these facts. The stored procedure will look like the following; execute the code after entering it:

```
CREATE PROCEDURE sp_Insert_Match_Score
    @Match_Id int, @Player_Id int, @Score_Time datetime, @Points tinyint
AS
BEGIN
    --insert the values into the (in order) match_id, player_id,
    --score_time and scored_points columns
    INSERT INTO Match_Scores VALUES
    (@Match_Id, @Player_Id, @Score_Time, @Points)

END
GO
```

6. So now we are ready to start inserting scores for players to test out the trigger. First of all, it is necessary to add a match. This stored procedure, called `sp_Insert_New_Game`, was covered in Chapter 17 and when covering parameter validation. However, this time, instead of setting up historical scores, the stored procedure will be used to set up the start of a new match. We are now going to add a new match to the Bedford Junior Blues (ID number 2) who will be playing The Chieftan Coach, and return back the match ID to use in the next section of adding in a score. Execute the code below.

```
DECLARE @Id INT
DECLARE @ErrorCode INT
EXEC @Id = sp_Insert_New_Game 2,"5 May 2001", "The Chieftan Coach",1,0,0
SELECT @Id
```

7. If you recall from Chapter 18, this procedure uses the `@@IDENTITY` global to return the last generated value for the `Match_Id` column. When this code is run, the value returned will vary on what test data we have already inserted, but in this case a match ID of 6 was returned, so this is what will be used in the first parameter. The golf match is in progress and the first result has come in, which happens to be for Player 1, just after half past two in the afternoon. Player 1 won their game, and so gains 3 points. Enter the following code and execute it. This will insert a new record in to the `Match_Scores` table. As an insertion is taking place, this will fire the trigger that we have just created, the `tgInsMatch_Scores` trigger. So this action will insert into one table, and update another.

```
sp_Insert_Match_Score    @Match_ID=6, @Player_Id=1, @Score_Time = "5 May 2001
14:32:27", @Points = 3
```

8. Now, to check what has happened, enter the following code, which will return the records from the `Match_Scores` table and the `Matches` table. Once entered, execute the code.

```
SELECT * FROM Match_Scores
SELECT Match_Id,Points_For, Points_Against from Matches
```

9. We should see similar results to the following, proving that the trigger has worked as we have an entry in the `Matches` table:

```
Match_Id    Player_Id   Score_Time                              Score_Points
----------- ----------- --------------------------------------- ------------
6           1           2001-05-05 14:32:27.000                 3

(1 row(s) affected)

Match_Id    Points_For Points_Against
----------- ---------- --------------
1           3          0
2           1          1
3           0          3
4           3          0
5           1          1
6           3          0

(6 row(s) affected)
```

Dealing with Table Updates

Earlier in the chapter, we discussed how to use the `INSERTED` and `DELETED` system tables to make a T_SQL `UPDATE` command work for a trigger. This next example builds on the trigger built above, by adding a trigger that will fire when the `Matches` table is updated. When a new match result is inserted, adding a record to the `Match_Scores` table, the trigger of the previous example updates the `Matches` table. This will fire the trigger to be built in this example, which will update the `Society_Groups` table from the information updated in the `Matches` table. This is a nesting of triggers.

The trigger itself is quite complex and makes full use of retrieving information from both the `DELETED` and `INSERTED` tables to find out what the information in the `Matches` table was before any updates, and what it is after the updates. Due to the complexity of the trigger, you will be taken through it a step at a time with full explanation of the code as we move along.

The aim of the trigger is to keep the state of play of a match up-to-date at all times, in respect of a team's win, draw, and loss rate, as well as the points for and against. Just to recap, a match may have multiple results, each of which – win, lose, or draw – is dynamic and updated for all results in a match. So, a Society Group may win three matches and lose two matches, and this would be seen as only one win overall. This is so that when each match finishes, the society group will be up to date as if that match was the final result and no extra processing is required to signify the end of a match.

Try It Out – Dealing with Updates

1. Query Analyzer should still be running and we should still be pointing to the `Wrox_Golf_Results` database. Clear the Query pane by pressing *Ctrl+Shift+Delete*. Once done, enter the following code. There is a large amount of code to enter so do take care when entering it.

2. First of all build the `CREATE TRIGGER` command, naming the trigger and defining that this is for an `UPDATE` on the `Matches` table. Notice that the name of the trigger has kept to the same naming standards as before. This trigger will not fire on a match insertion or deletion.

```
CREATE  TRIGGER tgUpdMatches
ON Matches
FOR  UPDATE
```

3. Continue with the declarations of the variables that will be used within the procedure. The variables and their uses will be discussed when they are set.

```
AS
BEGIN
   DECLARE @Points_Against_Before int,@Points_For_Before INT
   DECLARE @Points_Against_After int,@Points_For_After INT
   DECLARE @Game_Won_Before int, @Game_Drawn_Before INT
   DECLARE @Game_Lost_Before INT
   DECLARE @Game_Won_After INT, @Game_Drawn_After int, @Game_Lost_After INT
   DECLARE @Society_Group INT
```

4. We know that this is an update to the `Matches` table, therefore there will be entries in the `DELETED` and `INSERTED` table. Each of these tables will be dealt with one at a time rather than using a join, purely to demonstrate both of these tables in action separately. The first columns to be inspected will be those from the `DELETED` table and the necessary values of the data that was there in the `Matches` table before the update. This is where the first round of variables is set. If you recall, when a `Match_Score` record is inserted, the `Matches` table is updated from a trigger placed on that table. Therefore there will be a value within the `DELETED` table that contains all the details of what was in the `Matches` table before the update.

```
-- First take the details of what was there before
SELECT @Points_For_Before = Points_For,
   @Points_Against_Before = Points_Against,
   @Society_Group = Society_Group_Id
FROM DELETED
```

5. It is necessary to know what the state of play within the `Society_Groups` table was before the update happened. This will then give the number of games won, lost and drawn. To cover for the possibility of two out of three variables not being set when figuring out what the state of play was before, it is simpler to set all three to zero first. The reason behind this statement is quite simple. With the control of flow, which is covered in Point 6, depending on the result, you will fall in to one of the `IF` statements. As you can see, only one variable is set. Therefore two of the three variables will not be set, and therefore have a value of `NULL`. This is not what is required. It is possible that we could place the setting of the two variables not mentioned to zero in each `IF` statement, but this would be duplication of code. So it is easy to initialize all three variables to 0 at the start.

```
-- Required in case this is the first match. No DELETED record
SET @Game_Lost_Before = 0
SET @Game_Won_Before = 0
SET @Game_Drawn_Before = 0
```

6. Then we figure out what the type of result was before this match update. This is a simple process that looks at what the points for and the points against were before the update took place using the values just retrieved from the `DELETED` table. This process is only made slightly complex because we may have the situation where we do not have a previous match. We do need to take a bit more care when looking at the scenario where the points for and the points against are equal. If both of these are also set to zero, then there have been no match results recorded and therefore this is the first match of the meeting. This is a significant point that we will come to when we come to look at actually updating the `Society_Groups` table.

```
IF (@Points_For_Before < @Points_Against_Before)
   BEGIN
      SET @Game_Lost_Before = 1
   END
ELSE
   IF (@Points_For_Before > @Points_Against_Before)
      BEGIN
         SET @Game_Won_Before = 1
      END
   ELSE
      IF (@Points_For_Before = @Points_Against_Before
      AND @Points_For_Before > 0 AND @Points_Against_Before > 0)
         BEGIN
            SET @Game_Drawn_Before = 1
         END
```

7. Now that we know what the state of the game was before, we can move on and take a look at what the results of the table would be after the insertion. This is very similar to the code above for the DELETED table, but we now want to look at the number of points that the match would generate.

```
-- Now take what is there after which will give the difference
SELECT @Points_For_After = Points_For,
   @Points_Against_After = Points_Against,
   @Society_Group = Society_Group_Id
FROM INSERTED

-- cater for any backouts to make the score 0-0
SET @Game_Won_After = 0
SET @Game_Lost_After = 0
SET @Game_Drawn_After = 0
```

8. This code is also very similar to the code for the DELETED table inspection. From here it is possible to know what the new state of the match is. Again special attention is required for when the points are equal but there are no points recorded. You may be thinking that there is no need to check both the points for and the points against being greater than zero when performing an UPDATE trigger; however, this does cater for updates to the Matches table, for example, updating the opposition name before a match is played.

```
IF (@Points_For_After < @Points_Against_After)
   BEGIN
      SET @Game_Lost_After = 1
   END
ELSE
   IF (@Points_For_After > @Points_Against_After)
      BEGIN
         SET @Game_Won_After = 1
      END
   ELSE
      IF (@Points_For_After = @Points_Against_After
      AND @Points_For_After > 0 AND @Points_Against_After > 0)
         BEGIN
            SET @Game_Drawn_After = 1
         END
```

9. Now that we know what the overall match score was before the update, and how it looks after the update, we can apply this knowledge to the Society_Groups table. This is done by taking off the values that were there before, and adding in the values that were calculated after; for example, if the Society was winning, but is now drawing, we would subtract one from the winning total and add one to the drawing total. This whole UPDATE statement will perform this re-calculation of the scores

```
        UPDATE Society_Groups
        SET Games_Won = Games_Won + @Game_Won_After - @Game_Won_Before,
            Games_Drawn = Games_Drawn + @Game_Drawn_After - @Game_Drawn_Before,
            Games_Lost = Games_Lost + @Game_Lost_After - @Game_Lost_Before,
            Scored_For = Scored_For + (@Points_For_After - @Points_For_Before),
            Scored_Against = Scored_Against + _
                                 (@Points_Against_After - @Points_Against_Before)
    WHERE Society_Group_Id = @Society_Group

END
```

10. Now that all the code is in, execute the Query pane so that the trigger is created.

11. To test the code, more matches need to be entered; as each match is entered, the `Society_Groups` table will be updated. A minor problem that needs to be addressed first is that a match was entered earlier in the chapter for society group 2, but the `Society_Group` table was not updated. Therefore, first of all, let's update the `Society_Group` table so that everything is in alignment. Enter and execute the following code:

```
UPDATE Society_Groups
SET Games_Played = 1, Games_Won = 1,Scored_For = 3
WHERE Society_Group_Id = 2
```

12. Now to start entering further scores for the match on May 5th, match ID number 6; the first of the new entries is a loss by Player 3. Don't yet execute this code.

```
sp_Insert_Match_Score    @Match_ID=6, @Player_Id=3, @Score_Time = "5 May 2001
14:37:27", @Points = 0
```

13. Place in the same batch the following SQL, which will be used to watch the necessary tables to ensure that the triggers work. With this code and the code above, you should see the `Society_Groups` move from one win to no wins and one draw, and `Scored_Against` move from 0 to 3 points.

```
SELECT * FROM Match_Scores
SELECT Match_Id,Points_For, Points_Against
FROM Matches
SELECT Games_Won, Games_Drawn, Games_Lost, Scored_For, Scored_Against
FROM Society_Groups WHERE Society_Group_id = 2
```

14. Now it is possible to execute the code. The results we get should look similar to the following. We get three different listings of (1 row(s) affected) to cover the record inserted in to the `Match_Scores` table, the trigger just built in the previous section that is updating the `Matches` table from the `Match_Scores` insertion, and then the trigger just built which is updating the `Society_Groups` table. We then get three recordsets detailing the output from the three `SELECT` statements that follow the match insertion. As expected, the match is now being viewed as a draw, instead of a winning position, with 3 points each.

```
 (1 row(s) affected)


(1 row(s) affected)


(1 row(s) affected)

Match_Id    Player_Id   Score_Time                              Score_Points
----------- ----------- --------------------------------------- ------------
6           1           2001-05-05 14:32:27.000                 3
6           3           2001-05-05 14:37:27.000                 0

(2 row(s) affected)

Match_Id    Points_For Points_Against
----------- ---------- --------------
1           3          0
2           1          1
3           0          3
4           3          0
5           1          1
6           3          3

(6 row(s) affected)

Games_won   Games_Drawn Games_Lost  Scored_For  Scored_Against
----------- ----------- ----------- ----------- --------------
0           1           0           3           3

(1 row(s) affected)
```

15. To test the trigger further, we need to insert another `Match_Score`. Player 2 has now finished, and managed a win, which now puts the group back in a winning situation within the match. Watch the `Games_Lost` and `Games_Drawn` columns again from the `Society_Group` table, just as in the last query, and the `Points_For` in the query dealing with the `Matches` table. Below is the code for the next insertion.

```
sp_Insert_Match_Score 6,2,"5 May 2001 14:45:27",3

SELECT * from Match_Scores
SELECT Match_Id,Points_For, Points_Against
FROM Matches
SELECT Games_won, Games_Drawn, Games_Lost, Scored_For, Scored_Against
FROM Society_Groups WHERE Society_Group_id = 2
```

16. Once this has been executed, we will see the following results with the expected changes.

```
(1 row(s) affected)


(1 row(s) affected)
```

```
(1 row(s) affected)

Match_Id    Player_Id   Score_Time                              Score_Points
----------- ----------- --------------------------------------- ------------
6           1           2001-05-05 14:32:27.000                 3
6           3           2001-05-05 14:37:27.000                 0
6           2           2001-05-05 14:45:27.000                 3

(3 row(s) affected)

Match_Id    Points_For Points_Against
----------- ---------- --------------
1           3          0
2           1          1
3           0          3
4           3          0
5           1          1
6           6          3

(6 row(s) affected)


Games_won   Games_Drawn Games_Lost  Scored_For  Scored_Against
----------- ----------- ----------- ----------- --------------
1           0           0           6           3

(1 row(s) affected)
```

It is possible to continue testing the trigger for when the Society_Group loses the next two matches and therefore is in a losing position overall for the whole match. You could then move on to test further with another new match, which would be Match_Id number 7. You could then move through the scenarios again with inserting records to ensure that when altering match 7, the result record for match 6 does not alter. If this were for a production system, then it would be imperative for you to do this.

Now that you have seen a nested trigger, we can further examine the one problem found within it.

Using the UPDATE() Function

The above trigger can be altered to check whether the points columns in Matches have altered to save us from updating the Society_Groups table when there is no need. The trigger in the previous example is assuming that every time the Matches table has been updated, the Society_Groups table is also updated; in other words, a match has either been inserted, or modified. This may not be the case where perhaps a small refinement of the match has to be made without any changes to the actual score. An example of this would be perhaps a spelling mistake in the name of the opposition. A lot of time and effort would be saved by using the UPDATE() function first to check that the points won, lost, or drawn had altered as if they had not, then it would not be needed to recalculate the match scores. This next section demonstrates this statement and how to check whether a column has been updated or not.

The UPDATE() function is a very simple, yet powerful tool to a developer who is building a trigger. It is possible to check against a specific column, or a list of columns, to see whether a value has been inserted or updated within that column. It is not possible to check if a value has been deleted for a column, because quite simply, you cannot delete columns, you can only delete whole rows of data. If you wish to check more than one column at the same time, place them one after another with either an AND or an OR depending on what you wish to happen. Each individual UPDATE() will return TRUE if a value has been updated. For example

```
IF UPDATE(column1) [AND|OR UPDATE(column2)]
```

By simply checking each column as necessary, it is possible to see if an update is required to the Society_Groups table. This next example will take the trigger created a few moments ago and alter it through the ALTER TRIGGER command, which works just like the other ALTER object commands within the book. This will take the current trigger and keep the security settings already built, but allow the updates to the trigger that are required.

Try It Out – UPDATE() Function

1. In Query Analyzer, find the tgUpdMatches trigger, which as you can see, is under Triggers under the Matches table. As triggers are effectively objects belonging to a table, they will always be found underneath the table they are attached to in the Object Browser. When found, right-click and select Edit.

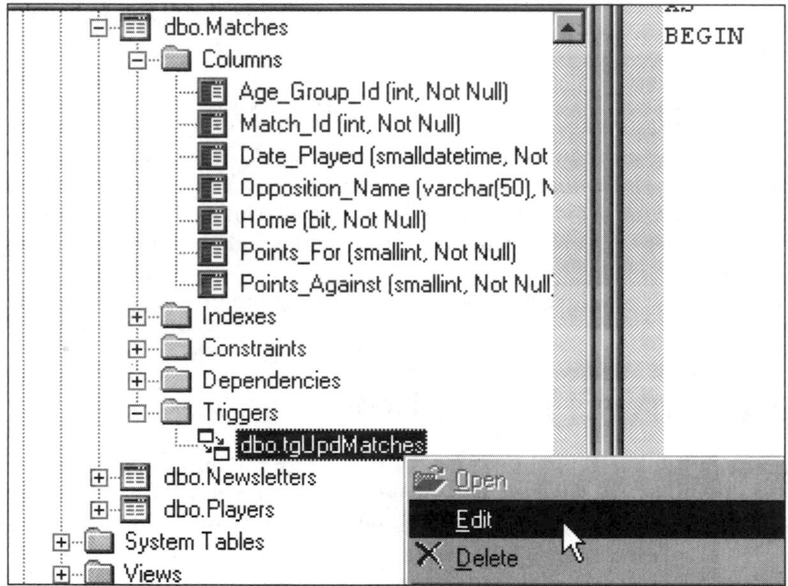

2. This then brings up the code for the trigger in the query pane. What we see should be very similar to the figure below.

```
SET QUOTED_IDENTIFIER OFF
GO
SET ANSI_NULLS ON
GO


ALTER   TRIGGER tgUpdMatches
ON Matches
FOR  UPDATE
AS
BEGIN
    DECLARE @Points_Against_Before INT,@Points_For_Before INT
    DECLARE @Points_Against_After INT,@Points_For_After INT
    DECLARE @Game_Won_Before INT, @Game_Drawn_Before INT, @Game_Lost_Before INT
    DECLARE @Game_Won_After INT, @Game_Drawn_After INT, @Game_Lost_After INT
    DECLARE @Society_Group INT

    -- First take the details of what was there before
    SELECT  @Points_For_Before = Points_For,
        @Points_Against_Before = Points_Against,
        @Society_Group = Society_Group_Id
    FROM DELETED
    -- Required in case this is the first match. No DELETED record
    SET @Game_Lost_Before = 0
    SET @Game_Won_Before = 0
```

3. It is now time to alter the code to check to see if the `Points_For` and the `Points_Against` columns have altered. It is worth the time and trouble to check these two columns before having to complete all the processing for updating the Society_Groups table for any changes in the match score. In the Query pane, alter the trigger so that it now reads as below. Notice as well that near the end there are two sets of comments. The first is a comment block which is using the `/*` and `*/` notation that we discussed in Chapter 3, and the second is a line of code we wish to remove using the `--` notation which was also discussed in Chapter 3. The comment block describes why the line of code from the trigger needs to be removed.

```
SET QUOTED_IDENTIFIER OFF
GO
SET ANSI_NULLS ON
GO


ALTER   TRIGGER tgUpdMatches
ON Matches
FOR  UPDATE
AS
   IF UPDATE(Points_For) OR UPDATE(Points_Against)
   BEGIN
      DECLARE @Points_Against_Before INT,@Points_For_Before INT
      DECLARE @Points_Against_After INT,@Points_For_After INT
      DECLARE @Game_Won_Before INT, @Game_Drawn_Before INT,
```

```
    @Game_Lost_Before INT
DECLARE @Game_Won_After INT, @Game_Drawn_After INT,
    @Game_Lost_After INT
DECLARE @Society_Group INT

-- First take the details of what was there before
SELECT    @Points_For_Before = Points_For,
    @Points_Against_Before = Points_Against,
    @Society_Group = Society_Group_Id
FROM DELETED
-- Required in case this is the first match. No DELETED record
SET @Game_Lost_Before = 0
SET @Game_Won_Before = 0
SET @Game_Drawn_Before = 0
IF (@Points_For_Before < @Points_Against_Before)
    BEGIN
        SET @Game_Lost_Before = 1
    END
ELSE
    IF (@Points_For_Before > @Points_Against_Before)
        BEGIN
            SET @Game_Won_Before = 1
        END
    ELSE
        IF (@Points_For_Before = @Points_Against_Before
        AND @Points_For_Before > 0 AND @Points_Against_Before > 0)
            BEGIN
                SET @Game_Drawn_Before = 1
            END
-- Now take what is there after which will give the difference
SELECT    @Points_For_After = Points_For,
    @Points_Against_After = Points_Against,
    @Society_Group = Society_Group_Id
FROM INSERTED

-- cater for any backouts to make the score 0-0
SET @Game_Won_After = 0
SET @Game_Lost_After = 0
SET @Game_Drawn_After = 0

IF (@Points_For_After < @Points_Against_After)
    BEGIN
        SET @Game_Lost_After = 1
    END
ELSE
    IF (@Points_For_After > @Points_Against_After)
        BEGIN
            SET @Game_Won_After = 1
        END
    ELSE
        IF (@Points_For_After = @Points_Against_After)
/*
This next line is not required any longer because we know for a fact that the
points have been updated and so therefore if the points match, then they must be
more than 0.
*/
--          AND @Points_For_After > 0 AND @Points_Against_After > 0)
```

```
               BEGIN
                  SET @Game_Drawn_After = 1
               END

            UPDATE Society_Groups
            SET Games_Won = Games_Won + @Game_Won_After - @Game_Won_Before,
                Games_Drawn = Games_Drawn + @Game_Drawn_After - @Game_Drawn_Before,
                Games_Lost = Games_Lost + @Game_Lost_After - @Game_Lost_Before,
                Scored_For = Scored_For + (@Points_For_After - @Points_For_Before),
                Scored_Against = Scored_Against + (@Points_Against_After -
@Points_Against_Before)
         WHERE Society_Group_Id = @Society_Group
   RAISERROR ('Updated Society Groups' ,0,1)
END

GO
SET QUOTED_IDENTIFIER OFF
GO
SET ANSI_NULLS ON
GO
```

4. Once the lines of code have been altered, it is necessary to execute this code for the ALTER TRIGGER to take effect. So go ahead and execute this by one of the usual methods. We should see the usual success message like that below:

```
The command(s) completed successfully.
```

5. With the RAISERROR message inserted at the end of the trigger, this will give the game away as to whether the UPDATE function has worked and as to whether the Society_Groups table has been modified. The logic behind this is that there is a check on the Points_For and Points_Against columns using the UPDATE() function and if either of these columns returns a TRUE, then the code moves into a BEGIN...END code block, which has the RAISERROR statement at the end. If neither of the columns returns TRUE, then the code block is not dropped into and, therefore, the RAISERROR will not be run. The RAISERROR is a testing statement only, and would be removed before the trigger went live, but the best time to remove it would be once the testing is completed. The first test to run is to ensure that the trigger still works as it did, using similar code to that built to test the trigger before. This code should alter the Society_Groups points and the Won/Drawn/Lost columns as before; however, this will now also raise an error to inform us that the update has taken place. Before executing this, it would be best to use a grid to display the output, so press *Ctrl+D*. Once done, execute the code below.

```
sp_Insert_Match_Score 6,4,"5 May 2001 14:54:27",0

SELECT * FROM Match_Scores
SELECT Match_Id,Points_For, Points_Against
FROM Matches
SELECT Games_won, Games_Drawn, Games_Lost, Scored_For, Scored_Against
FROM Society_Groups WHERE Society_Group_id = 2
```

6. On the grids tab, we will see that the `Society_Groups` table has been altered so that whereas the match was being won, it is now currently drawing with 6 points each. Here is the screenshot.

	Match_Id	Player_Id	Score_Time	Score_Points
1	6	1	2001-05-05 14:32:27.000	3
2	6	3	2001-05-05 14:37:27.000	0
3	6	2	2001-05-05 14:45:27.000	3
4	6	4	2001-05-05 14:54:27.000	0

	Match_Id	Points_For	Points_Against
1	1	3	0
2	2	1	1
3	3	0	3
4	4	3	0
5	5	1	1
6	6	6	6

	Games_won	Games_Drawn	Games_Lost	Scored_For	Scored_Against
1	0	1	0	6	6

7. As we can see, there is no message on this tab, but where is the `RAISERROR` message? Click on the **Messages** tab, and we will see all the messages the trigger and the code above created, which will not only be the `RAISEERROR` message, but, just as before, the records affected for each update performed. We should see the following details; sure enough, the `Updated Society Groups` message is displayed:

```
(1 row(s) affected)

Updated Society Groups

(1 row(s) affected)


(1 row(s) affected)


(4 row(s) affected)


(6 row(s) affected)


(1 row(s) affected)
```

8. Now to see what happens if the `Points_For` or the `Points_Against` columns are not updated. Using the code below, which changes the opposition but none of the points columns, we will see that no error message is generated; therefore the `Society_Group` table has not been altered. Enter the code below and then execute it.

```
UPDATE Matches
   Set Opposition_Name = "The Fat Belly's"
WHERE Match_Id = 6

SELECT * FROM Match_Scores
SELECT Match_Id,Points_For, Points_Against
FROM Matches
SELECT Games_won, Games_Drawn, Games_Lost, Scored_For, Scored_Against
FROM Society_Groups WHERE Society_Group_id = 2
```

9. Here is the grids tab, from which it is obvious that nothing has altered.

	Match_Id	Player_Id	Score_Time	Score_Points
1	6	1	2001-05-05 14:32:27.000	3
2	6	3	2001-05-05 14:37:27.000	0
3	6	2	2001-05-05 14:45:27.000	3
4	6	4	2001-05-05 14:54:27.000	0

	Match_Id	Points_For	Points_Against
1	1	3	0
2	2	1	1
3	3	0	3
4	4	3	0
5	5	1	1
6	6	6	6

	Games_won	Games_Drawn	Games_Lost	Scored_For	Scored_Against
1	0	1	0	6	6

10. However, we can't trust this figure: it is still possible the `Society_Groups` table has been altered, but the details have stayed the same. So we come to rely on the `RAISERROR` message and whether it was produced or not. If we now click on the **Messages** tab, we will find that there is no error message this time. Also, the number of row(s) affected messages has lessened as we've lost the two updates from the triggers. These two areas of proof, as well as the figure, should be enough to satisfy even the most ardent of doubters that the trigger has not updated the `Society_Groups` table.

```
(1 row(s) affected)

(5 row(s) affected)

(6 row(s) affected)

(1 row(s) affected)
```

So by using the inbuilt `UPDATE()` function for testing columns, processing time and unnecessary work is saved. It may also stave off producing erroneous results within a trigger if the trigger is expecting data to have altered on specific columns.

What About Image Data Types?

There is a problem with image data types and triggers: if we update the image column with binary data and use the `INSERT` or `UPDATE` commands, then the trigger will fire; however, if we use `WRITETEXT` and `UPDATETEXT` as we have covered within the book, then unfortunately no trigger will fire.

There are only two solutions to the problem, of which neither can be classified as a good solution. The first is to insert or update data within the image data type column, which will then fire the appropriate trigger, and after that, update the column with the correct information. This has an obvious downfall that a trigger is firing before a potential column that is being checked for an update has been altered.

The second option is to have a column within the table that has the image data type, which is only updated once the image data type has been updated. This pseudo-column, once updated, could be tested by using the `UPDATE()` function, which will then inform a trigger that the image has been altered. The downside to this solution is that the same trigger, or nest of triggers, could run twice; once for all columns except the data type, and once for the image data type.

However, this second solution would probably be the better option for us to use as we do have a bit more control over the triggers and what information has altered when they fire.

If at all possible though, avoid triggers on image or text data types. There won't be many, if any, business rules that surround these data types and therefore any alterations to these data types could be catered for within the stored procedure performing the relevant action.

Summary

Triggers should be seen as specialized and specific stored procedures set up to help your system with data integrity, cascading updates throughout a system or for enforcing business rules. If you take out the fact that there are two system tables, `INSERTED` and `DELETED`, and that you can check what columns have been modified, then the whole essence of a trigger is that it is a stored procedure that runs automatically when a set data modification condition arises on a specific table.

Coding a trigger is just like coding a stored procedure with the full control-of-flow, error handling, and processing that is available to you within a stored procedure object.

The aim of this chapter was to demonstrate how a trigger is fired, and how to use the information that is available to you within the system to update subsequent tables or to stop processing and rollback the changes.

The triggers built within this chapter have demonstrated how to use the system tables, as well as how to determine if a column has been modified. Finally, the chapter also discussed how to get around a potential problem concerning image data types and how problematic they can be when you need to fire a trigger if their data has altered.

You are now at the end of the book. After going through all the chapters and successfully reaching this point, you should take pride in the fact that you should no longer call yourself a beginner with SQL Server 2000, but are well on the road to becoming an accomplished and knowledgeable developer, who certainly knows their way around SQL Server and can start to look at more complex areas of development.

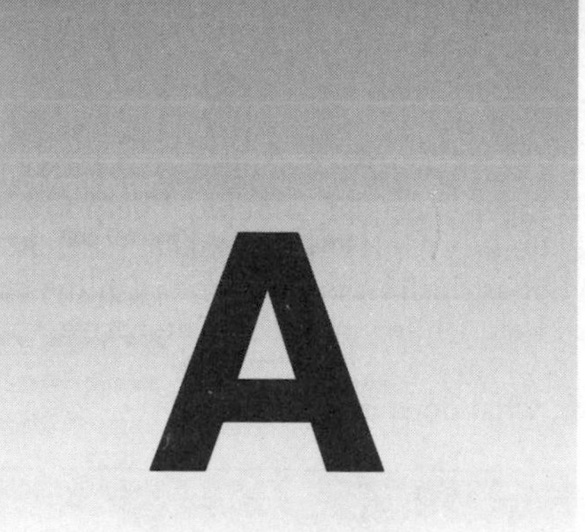

Further References

There will, of course, be times when you are developing your database that you become stuck and this book has not covered the scenario. Or perhaps you are receiving an error message that you don't understand. Who do you turn to for help? There are many, many resources around that may help you solve your problem where this book can't. This appendix points you in the direction of some of those resources, from resources that come with SQL Server, to resources on the Internet, and other books that may help.

Let's start with the most obvious first point of reference, SQL Server itself.

SQL Server Resources

SQL Server contains a comprehensive help file within it, available as an optional install, called Books Online. Let's see what it offers and how to use it.

Books Online

When you purchase SQL Server 2000, you are given probably the best resource for many of your immediate questions. Not only does Books Online give help with syntax for commands, but also help with every aspect of working with SQL Server.

Books Online can be started in one of three ways:

- Start | Programs | Microsoft SQL Server | Books Online – SQL Server does not have to be running to access Books Online in this way.
- Pressing *F1* while in Enterprise Manager or Query Analyzer – while in Enterprise Manager, pressing *F1* brings up contextual help, depending on what is highlighted on screen at the moment of pressing the key.

- Going to the **Help** menu and selecting **Contents and Index** in Query Analyzer. Using the **Help** menu in Enterprise Manager gives the contextual help for the Microsoft Management Console – you can get to Books Online from here (by selecting **SQL Server Enterprise Manager Help** in the left-hand pane) but as this just opens Books Online anyway, you are better off simply pressing *F1* if you need help while you are in Enterprise Manager.

Now we know how to get there, what does it look like?

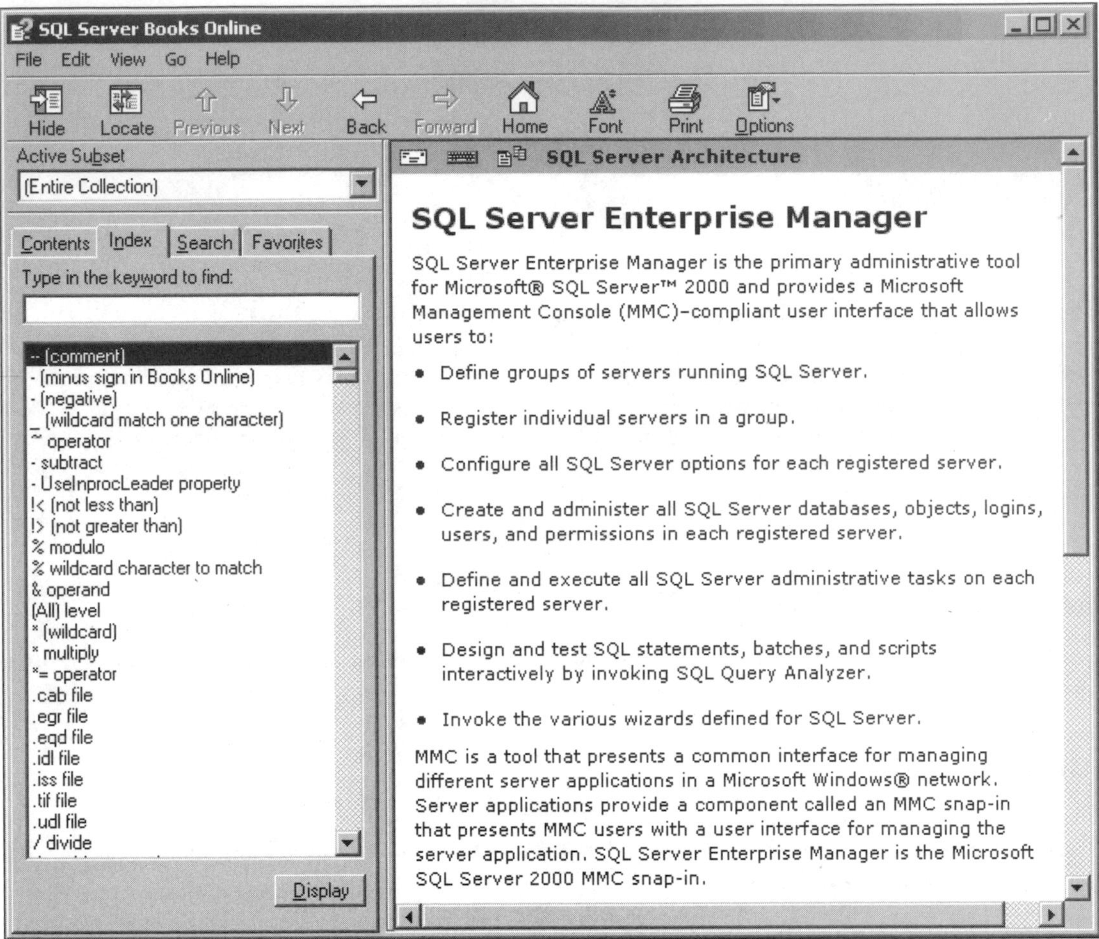

As you can see, like most Microsoft products, it is browser-based. The right hand pane displays the help files selected, while the left-hand pane is where you conduct your search for information.

There are a number of options to help you find the information you need; they are:

- Contents
- Index
- Search

The **Contents** tab provides a list of topic areas, into which you drill down until you find the help you need. For instance, in the next screenshot you can see how we have drilled down to find information about how to start SQL Server automatically.

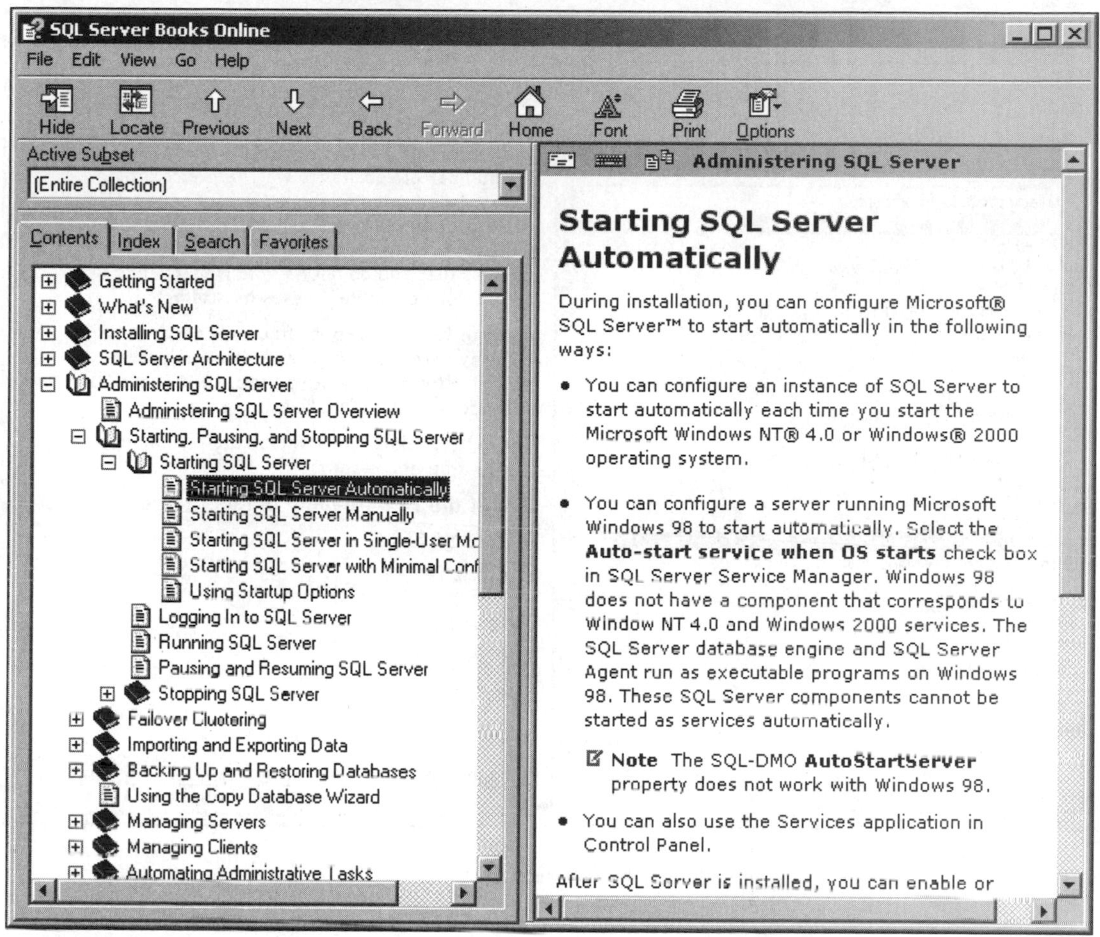

However, if you have no idea where the information might be, you could always look at the **Index**. On this tab, all the help topics are listed alphabetically; however, you don't have to look through everything to get to what you want, simply type in a letter and it will jump to the first topic matching what you have entered. However, you have to double-click on the topic to get it to display in the right-hand pane.

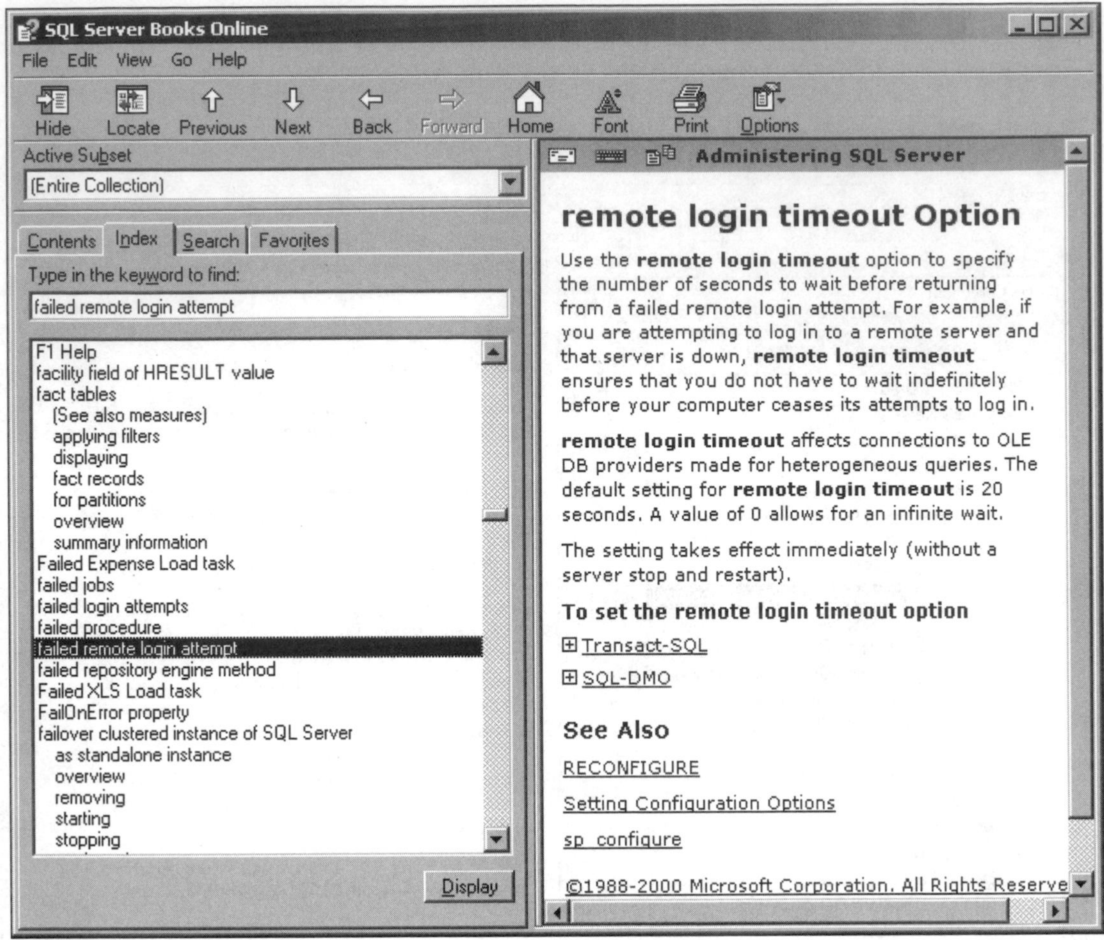
SQL Server Books Online
File Edit View Go Help
Hide Locate Previous Next Back Forward Home Font Print Options
Active Subset
(Entire Collection)
Contents Index Search Favorites
Type in the keyword to find:
failed remote login attempt
F1 Help
facility field of HRESULT value
fact tables
(See also measures)
applying filters
displaying
fact records
for partitions
overview
summary information
Failed Expense Load task
failed jobs
failed login attempts
failed procedure
failed remote login attempt
failed repository engine method
Failed XLS Load task
FailOnError property
failover clustered instance of SQL Server
as standalone instance
overview
removing
starting
stopping
Display
Administering SQL Server
remote login timeout Option
Use the remote login timeout option to specify the number of seconds to wait before returning from a failed remote login attempt. For example, if you are attempting to log in to a remote server and that server is down, remote login timeout ensures that you do not have to wait indefinitely before your computer ceases its attempts to log in.
remote login timeout affects connections to OLE DB providers made for heterogeneous queries. The default setting for remote login timeout is 20 seconds. A value of 0 allows for an infinite wait.
The setting takes effect immediately (without a server stop and restart).
To set the remote login timeout option
Transact-SQL
SQL-DMO
See Also
RECONFIGURE
Setting Configuration Options
sp_configure
©1988-2000 Microsoft Corporation. All Rights Reserve

If this still leaves you confused, you can always use the Search tab to find the information you need. As you can see, you enter what it is you are searching for, and you can also specify, at the bottom of the left-hand pane, how it should search for you.

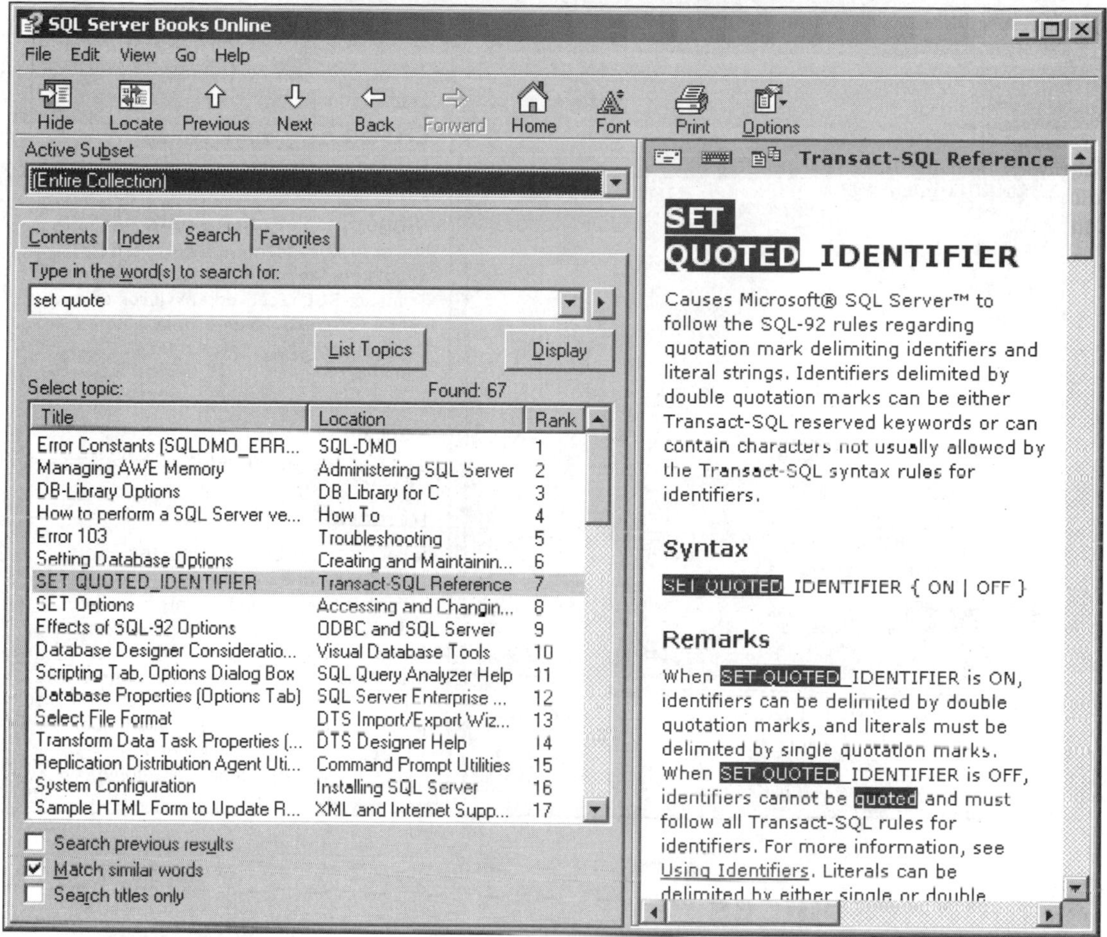

The Search finds a list of topics that you might find relevant, giving them a rank so that you can work your way down from what it thinks is the best matching topic to a lesser matching topic.

Now on to the Favorites tab. Say, for instance, that we always had trouble remembering the syntax for `SET QUOTED_IDENTIFIER` – we wouldn't want to have to go through a time consuming search every time we needed the information, especially if we needed to search on a regular basis. Well, Books Online gives us a place to store our most frequently visited help topics.

To add a topic to Favorites, all you have to do is find what you are looking for, by one of the methods we have just covered, make sure it is displayed in the right-hand pane, then go to the Favorites tab. The topic heading will be listed at the bottom of the screen, and when you click the Add button, the topic will be saved in an easy-to-access location, saving you precious time when you need to look at it again.

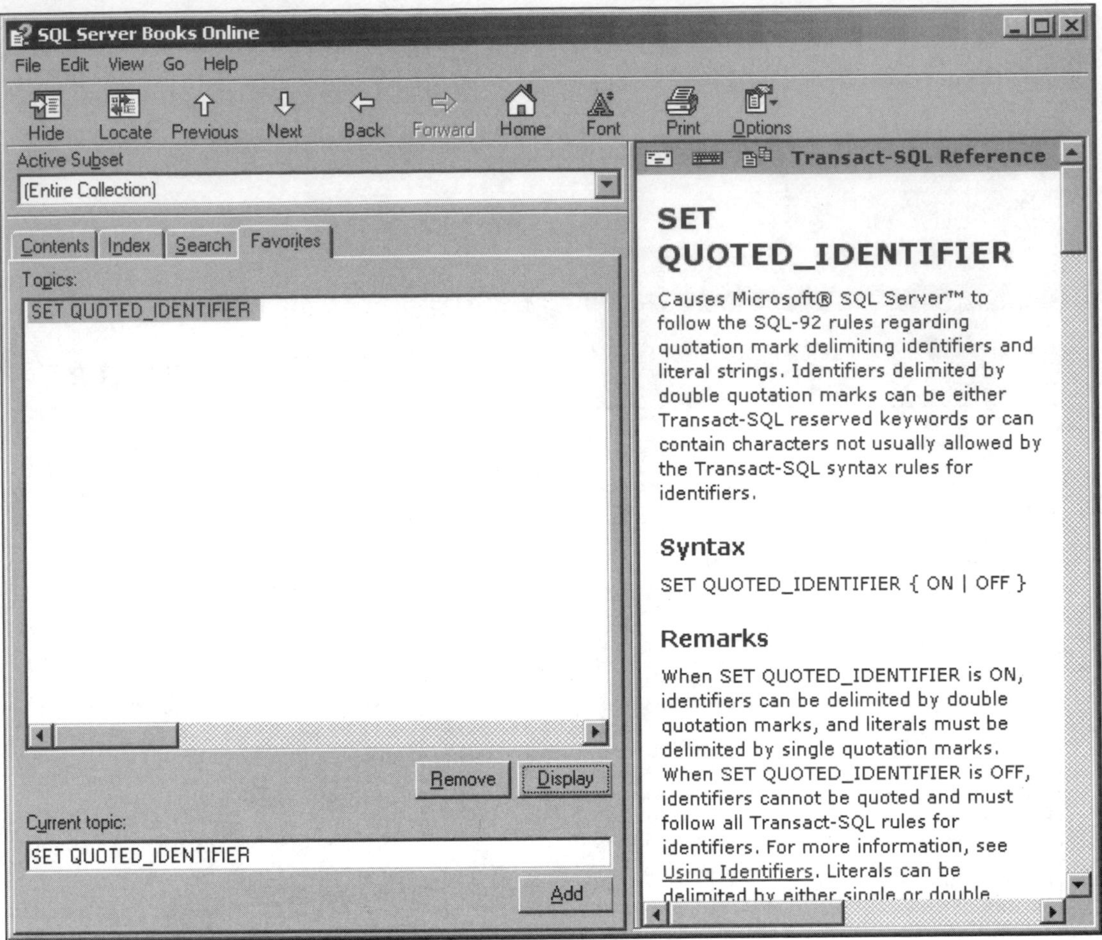

Internet Resources

We will now list some sites that may prove invaluable when you need that extra bit of help that Books Online can't provide – let's face it, the way that some topics are presented in Books Online can be a bit dry, so it sometimes helps to get a different slant on things. We won't go in depth into the sites – if you visit them you can see what they have to offer in more detail.

Microsoft Sites

The most obvious place to look for information about Microsoft SQL Server is at Microsoft. Microsoft has a whole host of sites relating to SQL Server, and we cover some of them here.

SQL Server

To find out more about SQL Server itself, browse to http://www.microsoft.com/sql/default.asp.

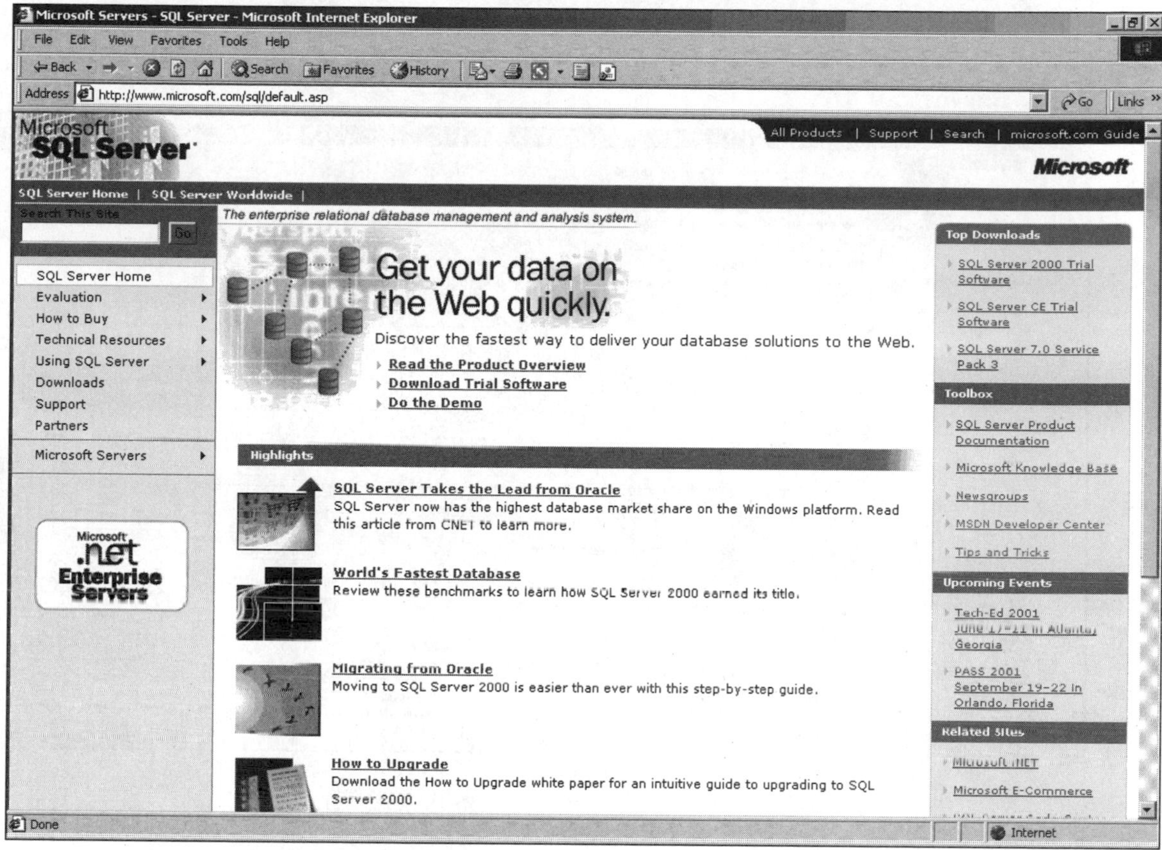

This page is dedicated solely to SQL Server, and includes such information as what is SQL Server, what it does, how to use it, and various download and support options. It also contains the SQL Server documentation, as well as infromation about any upcoming events featuring SQL Server that may be worth attending.

Although still on the dedicated site, a section worth a separate mention is the Tips and Tricks page. Here you will find, unsurprisingly, lots of tips and tricks on how to get the most out of SQL Server, ranging from how to build more efficient code, to administrative questions. The tips and tricks are supplied by SQL Server Most Valuable Professionals, so you can be sure that these people will know what they are talking about!

The Tips and Tricks section can be found at http://www.microsoft.com/sql/using/tips/default.asp.

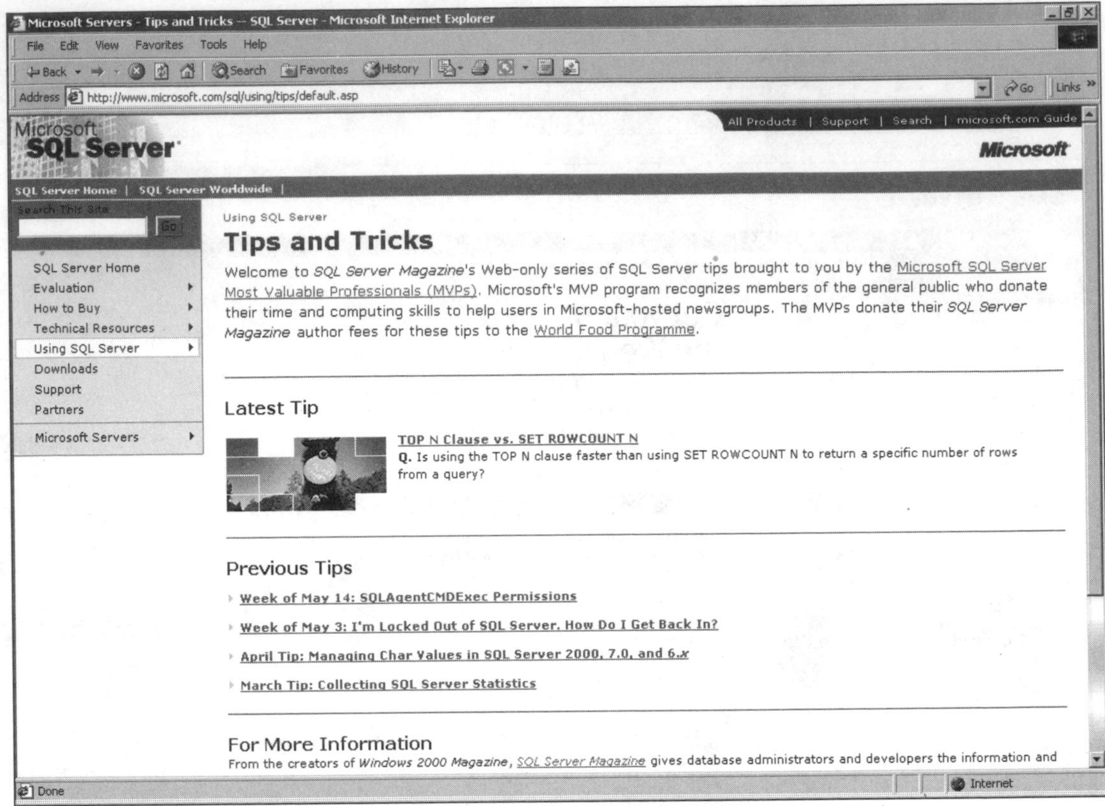

Technet

Technet is a Microsoft resource that you can subscribe to that not only provides technical solutions to problems that you might find with SQL Server 2000, but to every Microsoft product within the market place. This is a monthly CD or DVD that contains bug reports, solutions to queries, and background information about each product in the Microsoft stable, where you can find workarounds to problems that you might be encountering with the product. Technet can also be found online for each product; the URL for SQL Server is http://www.microsoft.com/technet/sql/default.asp.

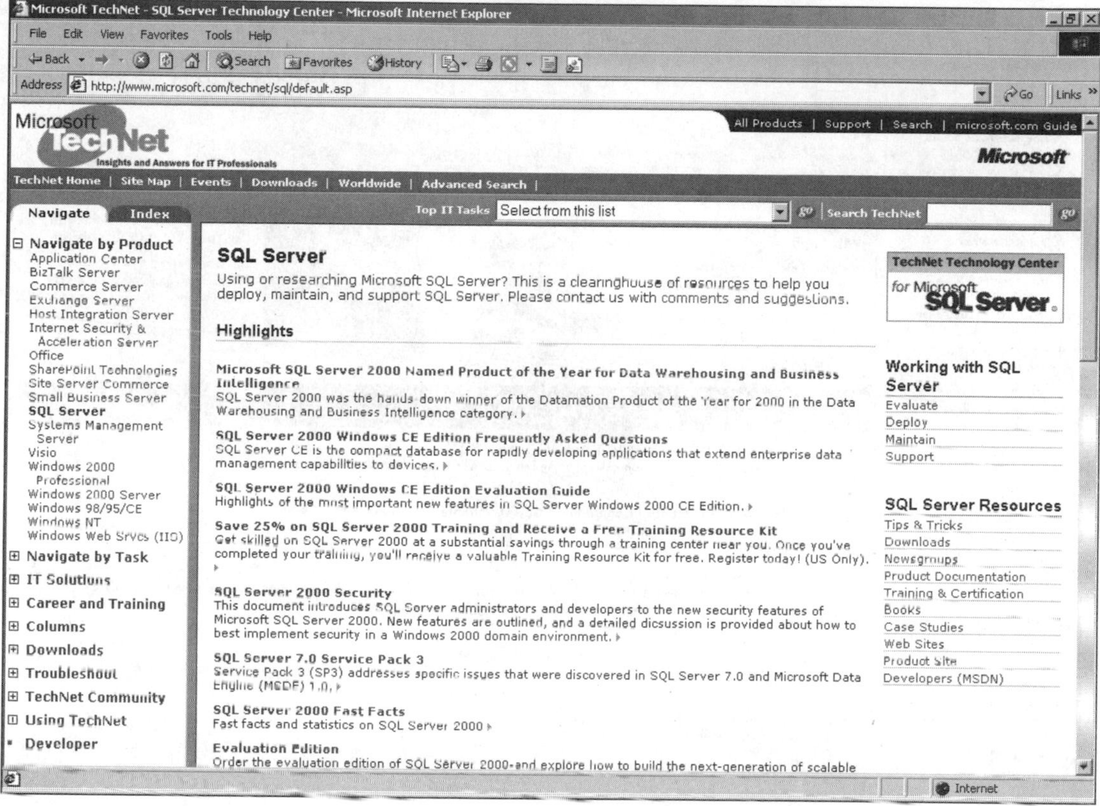

As you can see, it is best to visit this site to get the most out of what it has to offer.

MSDN

The MSDN Library can be bought as a quarterly subscription from Microsoft on CD or DVD, and it can also be found online at http://msdn.microsoft.com/sqlserver/.

MSDN contains the Books Online of many development tools, as well as beta information, white papers, and platform software development kit information. This is an excellent tool for learning inside information!

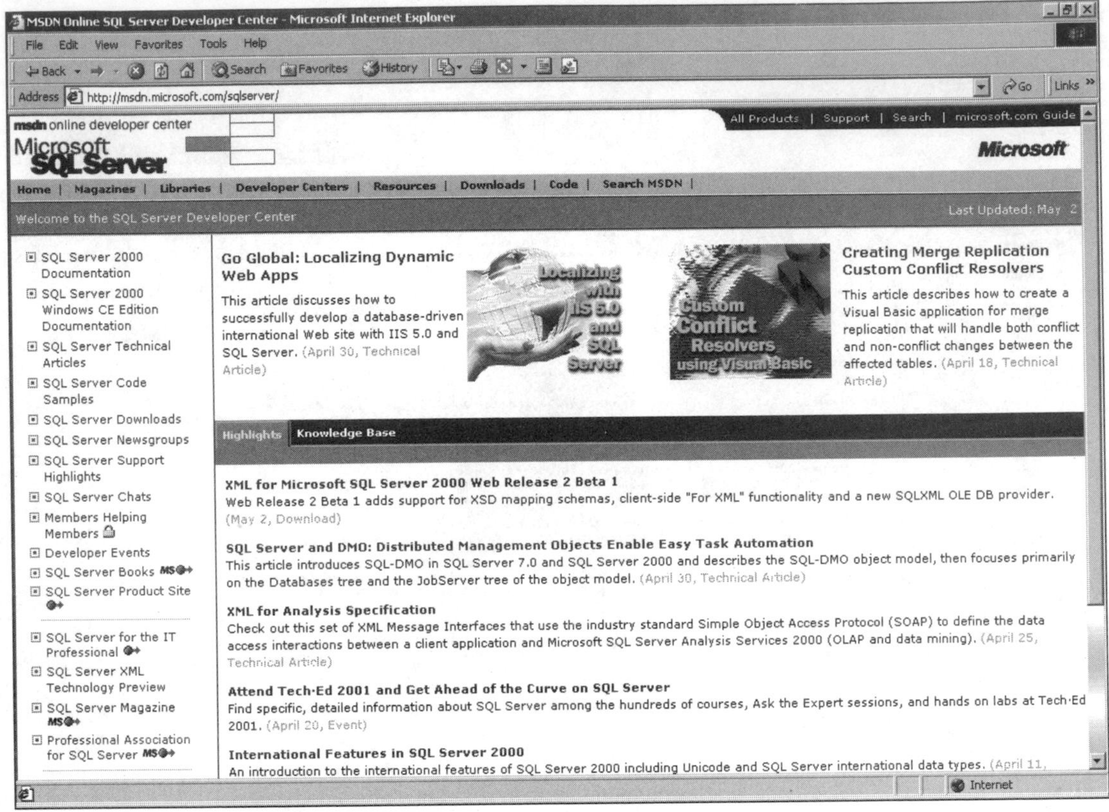

Also under the banner of MSDN is the SQL Server collection of newsgroups. These are a resource where users can post messages to each other and receive help from their peers. To get to these, browse to http://msdn.microsoft.com/newsgroups/default.asp?URL=/code/topic.asp?url=/msdn-files/028/201/073/topic.xml.

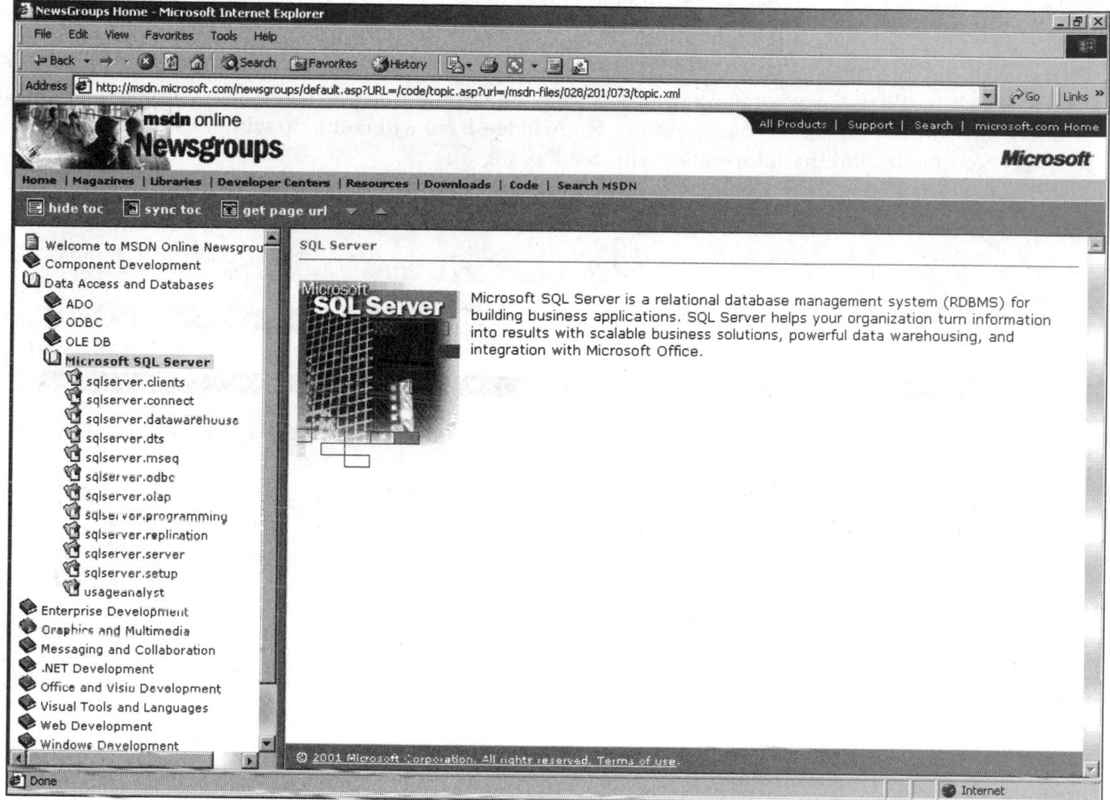

Microsoft Knowledge Base

Microsoft Knowledge Base is a collective resource of technical support information that you can search to find the information you need. The screenshot below was taken of http://search.support.microsoft.com/kb/c.asp?ln=en-us&sd=gn, but as you can see in the top left-hand corner, you can specify which country you are in to get tailored results.

There are a number of options that you can choose, depending on what it is you need to find. Your first stop is which product you are having trouble with, while the last option is the actual topic you need help with. When you have entered your question, Knowledge Base will come up with a list of suggestions as to where you might find the information you are looking for.

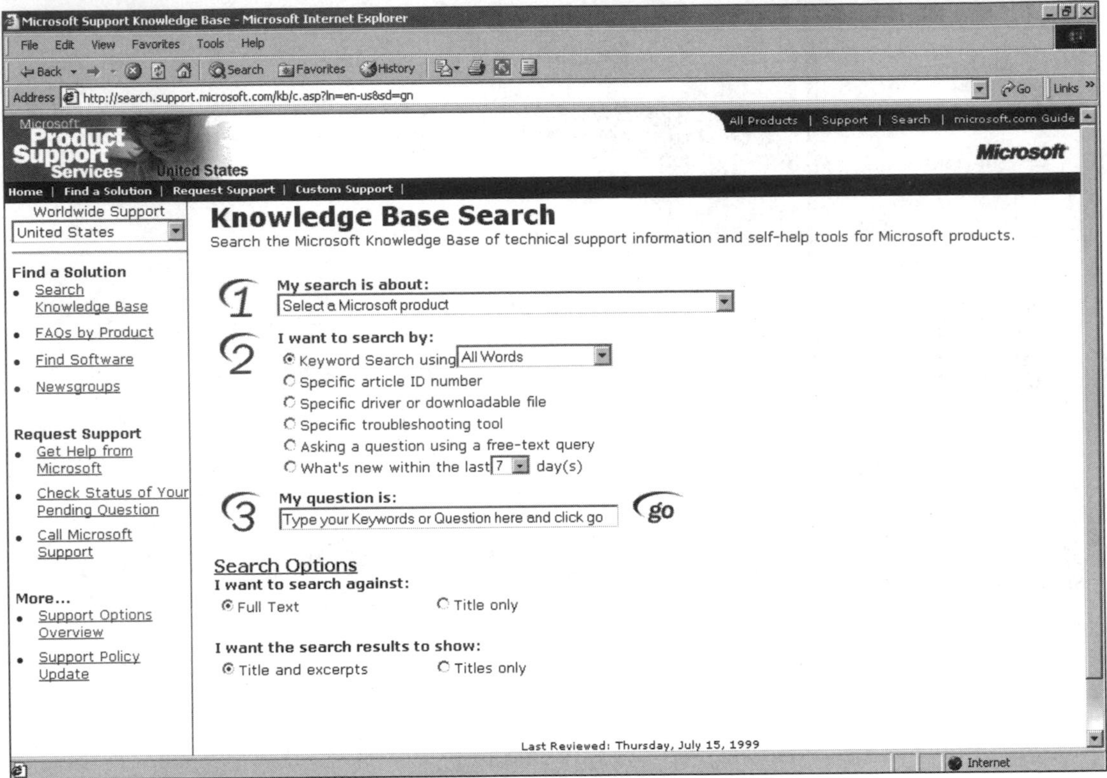

Non-Microsoft Sites

Although it is a Microsoft product, not all the sites out there that can help with SQL Server problems are run by Microsoft. The following are non-Microsoft resources that you migth find helpful.

Online Magazines

There are a number of sites that have a magazine format, with features and articles posted regularly.

One such site is SQL Mag, found at http://www.sqlmag.com/.

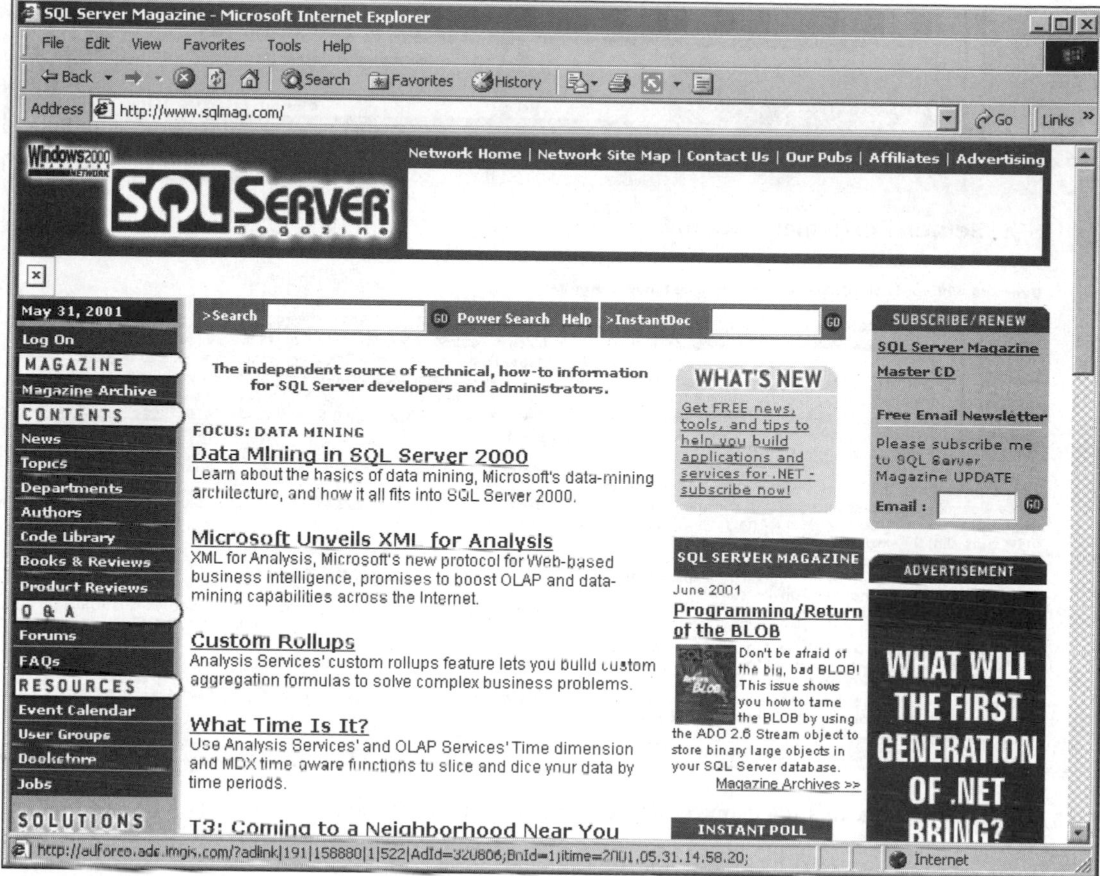

As you can see, this includes a vast number of topics related to SQL Server and how to use it.

Another such site is Performance, found at http://www.sql-server-performance.com/default.asp.

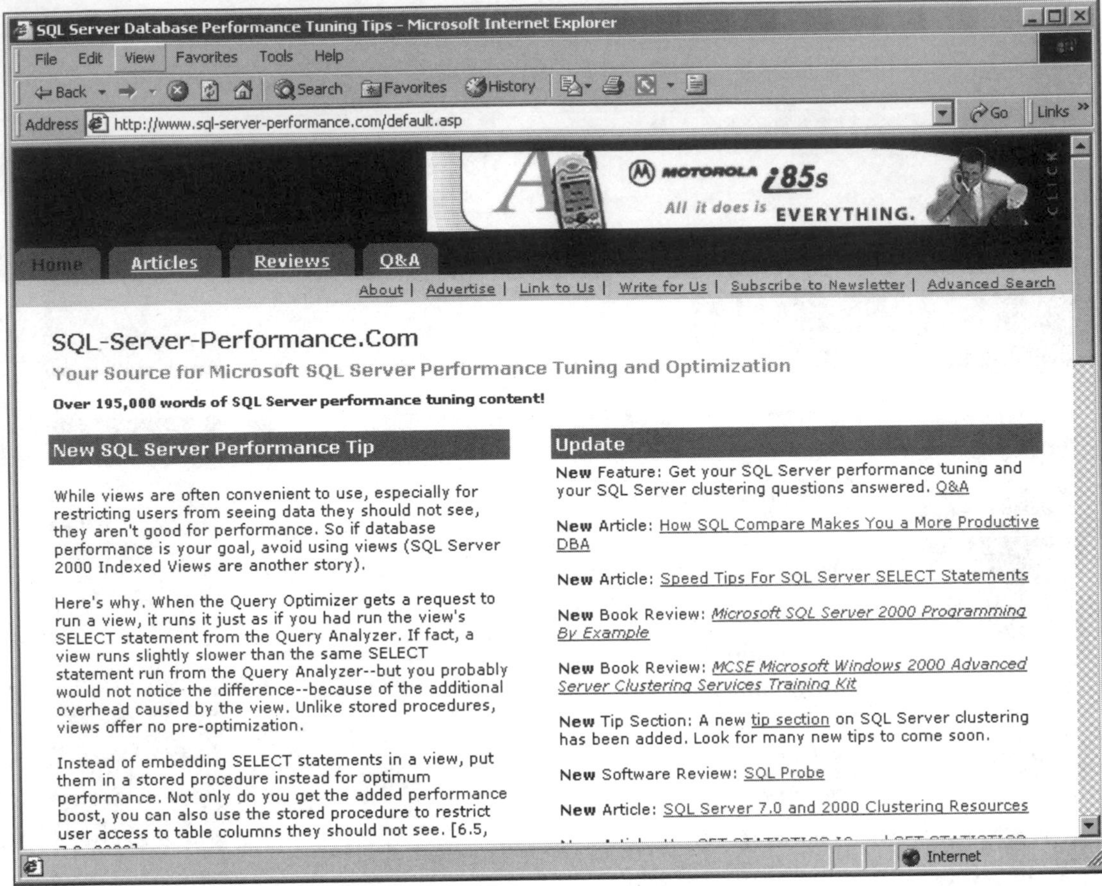

As its name suggests, this site is more focused on performance tuning and optimization.

There are many more sites like these out there, so have fun exploring!

User Groups

User groups are where users decide to get together and meet, or share resources, tips, and tricks in another way, mostly online. There are many, many, user groups out there, but to start you off, these are worth a look:

- Pacific Northwest SQL Server User Group – http://www.pnwssug.org/
- UK User Group – www.sql-server.co.uk
- Connecticut User Group – http://www.ctmsdev.net/SQL/
- List of user groups – http://www.sqlmag.com/UserGroups/

Books

There are a number of books out there that might help you, but if you have bought and enjoyed this book, then the style in which Wrox present their books will probably suit you best. There are many directions you can now take, or supplements to the knowledge you may already have; here are a few books that might suit you in your progression through working with SQL Server.

Professional SQL Server 2000 Programming

ISBN: 1-861004-48-6

This is, without a doubt, the definitive guide for the professional developer, something you can now consider yourself to be. Professional SQL Server 2000 builds on the knowledge you have gained from this book, looking at things more deeply and comprehensively. This is an obvious choice if you wish to learn even more about SQL Server, and expand your knowledge to include the more advanced features that it offers, such as Analysis Services and Data Transformation Services.

This is a book no SQL Server developer should be without.

Beginning SQL Server 2000 for Visual Basic Developers

ISBN: 1-861004-67-2

If you develop in Visual Basic and either need, or want, to learn how to incorporate data access into your VB applications, then this is the book for you. In this book you can learn how to take your SQL Server knowledge into VB, and use VB to manage and access the data within SQL Server.

Obviously you will need to know VB, but this book again looks at the fundamentals of SQL Server 2000, meaning that you will learn to develop more sophisticated systems, and even prepare your data for availability across the web.

Beginning SQL Programming

ISBN: 1-861001-80-0

We have seen a few SQL – Structured Query Language – statements in this book, but we have by no means tapped into the potential of this language.

SQL is the industry standard for querying data held in relational databases. SQL can be used to create and alter the structure of databases, add new data, and access or modify existing data. Beginning SQL Programming begins by looking at what SQL is, then moves on to teach you the fundamentals of ANSI SQL, using the familiar Northwind database that comes with versions of Microsoft Access and SQL Server.

Learning more about SQL will mean that you can access your data more readily, as you know exactly how a query should be formulated to return the correct results.

Professional Data Warehousing

ISBN: 1-861002-81-5

I'm sure that you are quite aware of the fact that, with the vast amounts of data flowing through the workplace on a daily basis, one standalone database is just not enough. This is where data warehouses have evolved, which cope with the huge volumes involved by separating the data used for reporting and decision making from the operational systems.

The purpose of the data warehouse is simply to store the raw data. The combination of this with OLAP enables the data to be transformed into useful information that reflects the real factors affecting that enterprise. OLAP techniques may range from simple navigation and browsing of the data to more serious analyses, such as time-series and complex modeling.

So, if you need to move on to a grander scale, this is the book for you.

Professional SQL Server 2000 Development with Access 2000

ISBN: 1-861004 83-4

While you have learned about SQL Server in this book, it is a fact that many developers are more familiar with Access, especially as it comes as part of the Office suite. However, do not let this deter you: you can still harness the power of the SQL Server range of database engines while working inside a familiar framework.

Rick Dobson's book concentrates on the use of Access 2000 projects with MSDE and SQL Server engines and will highlight the ease with which sophisticated, scalable database solutions may be constructed. Since the delivery of data over the Internet is becoming crucial, this book will also cover the approaches and technologies required to build database-driven web pages.

Professional SQL Server 2000 DTS

ISBN: 1-861004-41-9

If you want to move into Data Transformation Services, or DTS, then this is the book for you. DTS is the process of taking information from one source, whether it is a table in SQL Server, or an external source like Excel, and transporting it, transforming it, or working with it, and then moving the results to another source.

Professional SQL Server DTS provides a complete introduction to DTS fundamentals and architecture before exploring the more complex data transformations involved in moving data between different servers, applications, and providers. The book then focuses on DTS programming via the DTS object model, enabling developers to incorporate custom transformations and reporting capabilities into their applications.

Professional SQL Server 2000 XML

ISBN: 1-861005-46-6

The most important new features of SQL Server 2000 concern XML and the added functionality that it provides. This includes the ability to use XML documents to update your database, access SQL Server through HTTP, and retrieve data from your database in XML format.

We have touched upon XML in this book, but Professional SQL Server 2000 XML goes beyond just the key issues and provides blanket in-depth coverage of advanced topics, including the very latest XML schemas and new additions such as XML update-grams. So, if you want to take advantage of the very newest technologies, this book is for you.

Professional SQL Server 2000 Database Design

ISBN: 1-861004-76-1

Although this book did not focus too long on database design issues, it is an important area that must be investigated in order to develop an efficient database solution. Professional SQL Server 2000 Database Design is aimed at developers who have an interest in learning more about general relational database design issues.

The book provides an outline of the techniques that a designer can employ to make effective use of the full range of facilities that SQL Server 2000 offers. It attempts to move away from traditional texts on relational database design by considering design issues from a 'real-world' point of view.

System Functions

Introduction

There are a number of system-defined globally available variables, which used to be known as **globals**, or **global variables**, which can be used to retrieve either information about the last action performed or about the state of the system at that specific point in time.

A handful of these functions have been covered within the book, but in this appendix all the available system functions are listed with a short description about what each is and the type of value it returns.

Every system function should be immediately placed in to a locally defined variable at the point of execution and then tested for its value. This is so that between retrieving the information and using it, the value has not altered, giving spurious results. This is especially true when the system function is retrieving information about the last data action.

Some of the system functions are of more use than others and in fact, you may well find that there are some that you will never use, however, it is important that you are aware of their existence. Defining local variables with the same name as global variables may also create unexpected results.

> **A global variable is distinguished from a standard variable by the @@ prefix.**

@@CONNECTIONS

Returns an `integer` value of the number of attempts, successful or not, that have been made toconnect to the SQL Server instance, since SQL Server was last re-started.

This one is the total of all connection *attempts* made since the last time your SQL Server was started. The key thing to remember here is that we are talking about attempts, not actual connections, and that we are talking about connections as opposed to users.

Every attempt made to create a connection increments this counter regardless of whether that connection was successful or not. The only catch with this is that the connection attempt has to have made it as far as the server. If the connection failed because of NetLib differences or some other network issue, then your SQL Server wouldn't even know that it needed to increase the count – it only counts if the server saw the connection attempt. Whether the attempt succeeded or failed does not matter.

It's also important to understand that we're talking about connections instead of login attempts. Depending on your application, you may create several connections to your server, but you'll probably only ask the user for information once. Indeed, even Query Analyzer does this. When you click for a new window, it automatically creates another connection based on the same login information. This, like a number of other global variables, is better served by a system procedure, `sp_monitor`. This procedure, in one command, produces the information from the number of connections, CPU busy, through to the total number of writes by SQL Server.

A connection is made when an application or a user attempts to log in to a SQL Server instance.

@@CPU_BUSY

Returns the time in milliseconds that the CPU has been actively doing work since SQL Server was last started. This number is based on the resolution of the system timer – which can vary – and can therefore vary in accuracy.

This is another of the "since the server started" kind of system function. This means that you can't always count on the number going up as your application runs. It's possible, based on this number, to figure out a CPU percentage that your SQL Server is taking up. Realistically though, I'd rather tap right into the Performance Monitor for that if I had some dire need for it. The bottom line is that this is one of those really cool things from a "gee, isn't it swell to know that" point of view, but doesn't have all that many practical uses in most applications.

This returns an `integer` value and the value is based on cumulative CPU server time in ticks.

@@CURSOR_ROWS

One area not covered within the book is cursors within stored procedures. For more information on cursors look at *Professional SQL Server 2000* published by Wrox Press.

@@DATEFIRST

Returns the numeric value (as a `tinyint`) that corresponds to the day of the week that the system considers to be the first day of the week.

The default in the US is 7, which equates to Sunday. The values convert as follows:

- 1 – Monday (the first day for most of the world)
- 2 – Tuesday
- 3 – Wednesday
- 4 – Thursday
- 5 – Friday
- 6 – Saturday
- 7 – Sunday

This can be really handy when dealing with localization issues so you can properly layout any calendar or other day of week dependent information you have.

> **Use the** `SET DATEFIRST` **function to alter this setting.**

@@DBTS

Returns the last used timestamp for the current database (in `varbinary` format).

At first look this one seems to act an awful lot like `@@IDENTITY` in that it gives you the chance to get back the last value set by the system (this time, it's the last timestamp instead of the last identity value). The things to watch out for on this one include:

- The value changes based on any change in the database, not just the table you're working on
- The value is more of a true global than is `@@IDENTITY` – *any* timestamp change in the database is reflected, not just those for the current connection

Because you can't count on this value truly being the last one that you used (someone else may have done something that would change it), I personally find very little practical use for this one.

@@ERROR

This will be the most heavily used system function within the system and if it isn't, you should revisit your stored procedures!

Returns the error code for the last T-SQL statement that ran on the current connection (as an `integer`). If there is no error, then the value will be zero.

If you're going to be writing stored procedures or triggers, this is a bread and butter kind of system function – you pretty much can't live without it.

> **The thing to remember with `@@ERROR` is that its lifespan is just one statement. This means that, if you want to use it to check for an error after a given statement, then you either need to make your test the very next statement, or you need to move it into a holding variable.**

A listing of all the system errors can be viewed by using the `sysmessages` system table in the `master` database.

Sytem errors can also be cross-referenced within MSDN or TechNet or through SQL Server Enterprise Manager. Error messages can be found in Tools | Manage SQL Server Messages.

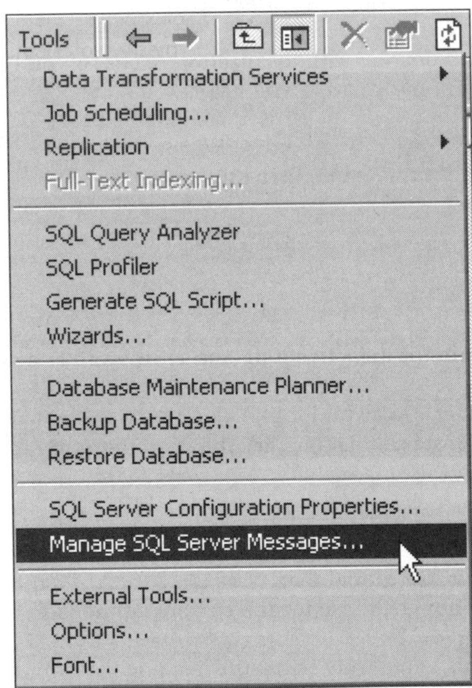

This brings up a dialog that allows the searching of messages. To find a message enter either a number or a partial description and click Find.

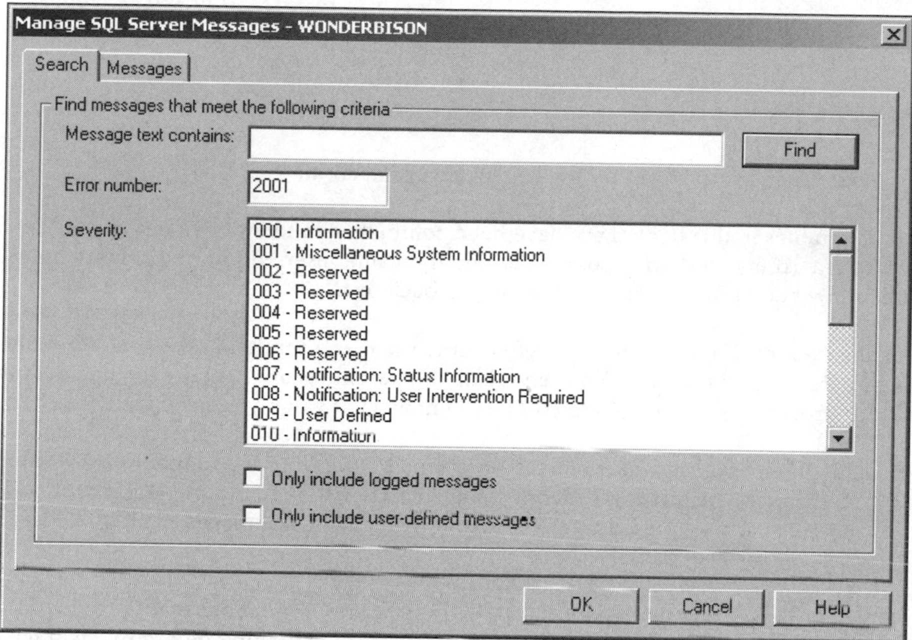

This will produce the relevant error in the Messages tab.

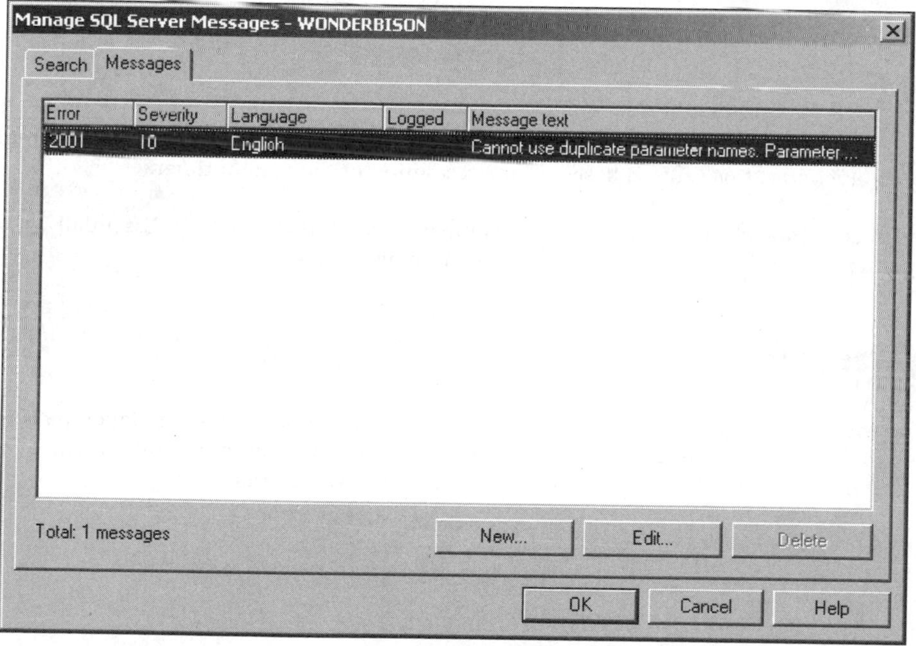

To create your own custom errors, use `sp_addmessage`.

@@FETCH_STATUS

This system variable deals with cursors and is covered in the *Professional SQL Server 2000* book.

@@IDENTITY

Returns the last identity value created by the current connection.

When building tables in this book there have been columns with identity values created by SQL Server at the time of record insertion. It is possible to find the value inserted into the column by using this system function whether the insertion is then rolled back or not.

If you're using identity columns and then referencing them as a foreign key in another table, you'll find yourself using this one all the time. You can create the parent record (usually the one with the identity you need to retrieve), then select `@@IDENTITY` to know what value you need to relate child records to.

A numeric data type of the last value entered is returned , therefore if a number of rows are inserted in one statement, then it is the last row's identity value which will be found in `@@IDENTITY`. Take care with this as this value is also altered by triggers, and the value is not placed back to the last successful value if an insertion is rolled back.

If you perform inserts into multiple tables with identity values, remember that the value in `@@IDENTITY` will only be for the *last* identity value inserted – anything before that will have been lost, unless you move the value into a holding variable after each insert. Also, if the last column you inserted into didn't have an identity column, then `@@IDENTITY` will be set to `NULL`.

@@IDLE

An `integer` data type is returned denoting how many milliseconds SQL Server has been idle since the last restart. Of course, this value is based on the resolution of the system timer.

You can think of this one as being something of the inverse of `@@CPU_BUSY`. Essentially, it tells you how much time your SQL Server has spent doing nothing.

@@IO_BUSY

Another variable used for monitoring system activity and angain an `integer` data type is returned. This time the number of milliseconds spent performing input and output operations since the last restart of SQL Server are returned (based on the resolution of the system timer).

@@LANGID

Returns a smallint data type denoting the local language identifier currently in use within SQL Server. These can be handy for figuring out if your product has been installed in a localization situation or not, and if so what language is the default.

For a full listing of the languages currently supported by SQL Server, run a SELECT * on the syslanguages table or use the system stored procedure, sp_helplanguage.

@@LANGUAGE

Returns an nvarchar holding the name of the language currently in use.

@@LOCK_TIMEOUT

Returns the current amount of time in milliseconds before the system will time-out waiting on a locked resource.

If a resource (a page, a row, a table, or whatever) is locked, your process will stop and wait for the lock to clear. This determines just how long your process will wait before the statement is canceled.

The default time to wait is 0 (which equates to indefinitely) unless someone has changed it at the system level (using sp_configure). Regardless of how the system default is set, you will get a value of -1 from this global unless you have manually set the value for the current connection using SET LOCK_TIMEOUT.

@@MAX_CONNECTIONS

There is a limit to the number of simultaneous connections that can exist within a SQL Server installation. @@MAX_CONNECTIONS returns an integer data type of the maximum number that can be connected.

Don't mistake this one to mean the same thing as you would see under the Maximum Connections property in the Enterprise Manager. This one is based on licensing, and will show a very high number if you have selected "per seat" licensing.

Note that the actual number of user connections allowed also depends on the version of SQL Server you are using and the limits of your application(s) and hardware.

@@MAX_PRECISION

Returns the level of precision currently set for decimal and numeric data types (as a tinyint).

The default is 38 places, but the value can be changed by using the /p option when you start your SQL Server. The /p can be added by starting SQL Server from a command line, or by adding it to the Startup parameters for the MSSQLServer service in the Windows NT or 2000 Services applet (if you're running NT or 2000).

@@NESTLEVEL

A stored procedure can call another stored procedure, which can call another stored procedure, and so the calling depth can go on until you reach the limit of 32 stored procedures. This function returns the current nesting level for nested stored procedures.

The first stored procedure (sproc) to run has an @@NESTLEVEL of 0. If that sproc calls another, then the second sproc is said to be nested in the first sproc (and @@NESTLEVEL is incremented to a value of 1). Likewise, the second sproc may call a third, and so on up to maximum of 32 levels deep (nest level 31). If you go past the level of 32 levels deep, not only will the transaction be terminated, but you should revisit the design of your application.

@@OPTIONS

A number of options for SQL Server connection can be modified within a query using the sp_configure system stored procedure. This global will return an integer data type. These options use bitwise operations to determine whether a value is set or not.

Returns information about options that have been applied using the SET command.

These options can be modified in a query using the sp_configure system stored procedure.

Since you only get one value back, but can have many options set, SQL Server uses binary flags to indicate what values are set. In order to test whether the option you are interested in is set, you must use the option value together with a bitwise operator. For example:

```
IF (@@OPTIONS & 2)
```

If this evaluates to True, then you know that IMPLICIT_TRANSACTIONS has been turned on for the current connection. The values are:

Bit	SET Option	Description
1	DISABLE_DEF_CNST_CHK	Interim vs. deferred constraint checking.
2	IMPLICIT_TRANSACTIONS	A transaction is started implicitly when a statement is executed.
4	CURSOR_CLOSE_ON_COMMIT	Controls behavior of cursors after a COMMIT operation has been performed.
8	ANSI_WARNINGS	Warns of truncation and NULL in aggregates.
16	ANSI_PADDING	Controls padding of fixed-length variables.
32	ANSI_NULLS	Determines handling of NULLS when using equality operators.
64	ARITHABORT	Terminates a query when an overflow or divide-by-zero error occurs during query execution.
128	ARITHIGNORE	Returns NULL when an overflow or divide-by-zero error occurs during a query.
256	QUOTED_IDENTIFIER	Differentiates between single and double quotation marks when evaluating an expression.
512	NOCOUNT	Turns off the row(s) affected message returned at the end of each statement.
1024	ANSI_NULL_DFLT_ON	Alters the session's behavior to use ANSI compatibility for nullability. Columns created with new tables or added to old tables without explicit null option settings are defined to allow nulls. Mutually exclusive with ANSI_NULL_DFLT_OFF.
2048	ANSI_NULL_DFLT_OFF	Alters the session's behavior not to use ANSI compatibility for nullability. New columns defined without explicit nullability are defined not to allow nulls. Mutually exclusive with ANSI_NULL_DFLT_ON.
4096	CONCAT_NULL_YIELDS_NULL	Returns a NULL when concatenating a NULL with a string.
8192	NUMERIC_ROUNDABORT	Generates an error when a loss of precision occurs in an expression.

@@PACK_RECEIVED

Returns integer data type of the number of network packets of data read from the network since the last SQL Server restart.

Primarily a network trouble-shooting tool.

@@PACK_SENT

Returns an `integer` data type of the number of network packets of data sent to the network since the last SQL Server restart.

@@PACKET_ERRORS

An `integer` data type that is the number of network packet errors that have occurred on read and send since the last SQL Server restart.

@@PROCID

Returns an `integer` data type of the stored procedure identifier giving the ID of the current procedure executing. Used when trying to determine which stored procedure is causing a lock. Also useful when a process is running and using up a large amount of resources. Used mainly as a DBA function.

@@REMSERVER

It is possible to return the name of the remote SQL Server database server as it appears in the login record. This returns an `nvarchar` data type and would be used to determine the name of the server the procedure has been run from (this is not necessarily the server that the procedure "lives on").

Used only in stored procedures. This one is handy when you want the sproc to behave differently depending on what remote server (often a geographic location) the sproc was called from.

@@ROWCOUNT

This is the number of rows affected by the last T-SQL statement, and returns an `integer` data type. If no rows have been affected, this number will be set to `0`.

One of the most used functions, the most common use for this one is to check for non run-time errors – that is, items that are logically errors to your program, but that SQL Server isn't going to see any problem with. An example would be a situation where we are performing an update based on a condition, but we find that it affects zero rows. Odds are that, if our client submitted a modification for a particular row, it was expecting that row to match the criteria given – zero rows affected is indicative of something being wrong.

However, if we test this global variable on any statement that does not return rows, then we will also return a value of `0`.

@@SERVERNAME

By using the `@@SERVERNAME`, you can return the name of the local server running SQL Server as an `nvarchar` data type. If we have multiple instances of SQL Server installed (a good example would be a web hosting service that uses a separate SQL Server installation for each client), then `@@SERVERNAME` returns the following local server name information if the local server name has not been changed since setup:

Instance	Server Information
Default instance	*<servername>*
Named instance	*<servername\instancename>*
Virtual server – default instance	*<virtualservername>*
Virtual server – named instance	*<virtualservername\instancename>*

@@SERVICENAME

Returns an `nvarchar` data type of the name of the registry key that SQL Server is running. Only returns something under Windows NT/2000, and (under either of these) should always return `MSSQLService` unless you've been playing games in the registry. Should return nothing if running under Win 9x (Win 9x doesn't have services, so SQL Server can't run as one).

@@SPID

Returns (as a `smallint` data type) the server process identifier, or SPID, of the current process executing. This can then be used using `sp_who` to cross reference to show which process is currently locked. What's nice is that we can tell the `SPID` for your current connection, which can be used by the DBA to monitor, and if necessary terminate, that task.

@@TEXTSIZE

Returns an `integer` data type of the current value that a text or image data type will return in a `SELECT` T-SQL statement.

The default is 4096 bytes (4KB). You can change this value by using the `SET TEXTSIZE` statement.

@@TIMETICKS

Returns an `integer` data type of the number of microseconds per tick on a computer.

@@TOTAL_ERRORS

Returns an integer number detailing the number of disk read/write errors that have occurred since SQL Server was recycled.

@@TOTAL_READ

Returns as an integer data type, the number of disk reads that have occurred since SQL Server has been restarted. This does not include any data pulled from the cache – only physical I/O.

@@TOTAL_WRITE

Returns – as an integer data type – the number of disk writes that have occurred since SQL Server has been restarted. This does not include any data pulled from the cache – only physical I/O.

@@TRANCOUNT

It is possible to nest transactions just as you can with triggers and stored procedures, and this system function will return the number of transactions that are currently active. BEGIN TRAN increments this by one and ROLLBACK TRAN / COMMIT TRAN decrement it by one. If you are about to end a connection, by checking this function, you will know if there are still any transactions to be committed. This is an integer data type.

This is a very big one when you are using transactions. There are times where nested transactions are difficult to avoid. As such, it can be important to know just where we are in the transaction nesting side of things (for example, you may have logic that only starts a transaction if we're not already in one).

If we're not in a transaction, then @@TRANCOUNT is 0. From there, let's look at a brief example:

```
SELECT @@TRANCOUNT As TransactionNestLevel       --This will be 0 at this point

BEGIN TRAN
SELECT @@TRANCOUNT As TransactionNestLevel       --This will be 1 at this point
  BEGIN TRAN
    SELECT @@TRANCOUNT As TransactionNestLevel   --This will be 2 at this point
  COMMIT TRAN
SELECT @@TRANCOUNT As TransactionNestLevel       --This will be back to 1
                                                 --at this point
ROLLBACK TRAN
SELECT @@TRANCOUNT As TransactionNestLevel       --This will be back to 0
                                                 --at this point
```

Note that, in this example, the @@TRANCOUNT at the end would also have reached 0 if we had a COMMIT as our last statement.

@@VERSION

Returns the current version of SQL Server as well as the processor type and OS architecture as an `nvarchar` data type.

For example:

```
SELECT @@VERSION
```

gives:

```
Microsoft SQL Server  2000 - 8.00.194 (Intel X86)
	Aug  6 2000 01:19:00
	Copyright (c) 1988-2000 Microsoft Corporation
	Developer Edition on Windows NT 5.0 (Build 2195: )


(1 row(s) affected)
```

Unfortunately, this doesn't return the information into any kind of structured field arrangement, so you have to parse it if you want to use it to test for specific information.

Consider using the `xp_msver` system sproc instead – it returns information in such a way that you can more easily retrieve specific information from the results.

Function Listing

This appendix introduces and provides details of some of SQL Server's string, date, and mathematical functions. Each function has a simple and clear overview of what it does, and then there is an example of each function for your reference. Most of the functions can be used in conjunction with one another, and it will not be long before you realize the full power that,these functions can hold when building queries, stored procedures, or any other operation that returns or manipulates data.

This list is not intended to be complete reference, and not all possible options for a function are shown or discussed; for further syntax details of the functions consult the SQL Servers Books Online. The examples presented in this appendix are intended to get you up and running with the particular function.

String Functions

To follow the string functions in this appendix, it is advisable to enter the following lines of code first:

```
SET QUOTED IDENTIFIER OFF
GO
```

This will ensure that SQL Server will correctly interpret strings delimited by " characters. Without setting this option, you will have to replace all " characters by ' characters in order to run the examples in this appendix at least.

ASCII

This will return the ASCII numeric value of the leftmost character of a string. *Only* the first character in the string is evaluated.

```
DECLARE @ASCII_STRING CHAR(5)
SET @ASCII_STRING = "ROBIN"
SELECT ASCII(@ASCII_STRING)
```

would return a value of 82, this being the ASCII value of R.

CHAR

This is the reverse of the ASCII function as it changes a numeric value in to an ASCII character.

```
DECLARE @ASCII_VALUE INT
SET @ASCII_VALUE = 82
SELECT CHAR(@ASCII_VALUE)
```

would return a value of R.

CHARINDEX

CHARINDEX returns the starting point of the first occurrence of one string of characters within another string. A value of 0 is returned if the string is not found. A further parameter informs the function to start looking from a certain point within the string.

CHARINDEX does not take into account whether the strings are upper or lower case. In the example below you would hope that the CHARINDEX function would find the last Wrox, but it actually finds the WROX before that.

```
DECLARE @STRING_TO_SEARCH_FOR varchar(4)
DECLARE @STRING_TO_SEARCH_WITHIN varchar(100)
SET @STRING_TO_SEARCH_FOR = "Wrox"
SET @STRING_TO_SEARCH_WITHIN = "Skip this Wrox. Start here. Not this WROX? Find me
this Wrox"
SELECT CHARINDEX(@STRING_TO_SEARCH_FOR, @STRING_TO_SEARCH_WITHIN, 16)
```

This will search for the string "Wrox" in @STRING_TO_SEARCH_WITHIN, starting its search 16 characters along in the string. The code returns a value of 38, since it locates the upper case "WROX".

DIFFERENCE

SQL Server is clever enough to work out when one string sounds similar to another string. This is often used in more advanced functions, such as when using SQL Server as a back-end database to a search engine. A user may enter one name, when they actually mean another. In the example below, the user is trying to find Dewson, but has entered Joosun, a similar sounding name. Applying the DIFFERENCE function to two strings returns a value between 0 and 4 that reflects how close a match there is between the two strings. A value of 0 means that the two strings aren't even close, and a value of 4 means a perfect match, with the higher the number returned meaning a closer match between the two strings.

```
DECLARE @STRING_DIFFERENCE1 varchar(6)
DECLARE @STRING_DIFFERENCE2 varchar(6)
SET @STRING_DIFFERENCE1 = "Dewson"
SET @STRING_DIFFERENCE2 = "Joosun"

SELECT DIFFERENCE(@STRING_DIFFERENCE1,@STRING_DIFFERENCE2)
```

This returns a value of 3. The actual comparison between the two strings is done by the SOUNDEX function, which is below.

LEFT

By using the LEFT function, you can return a number of characters from the left-hand side of a string. This can be from 1 character up to all the characters in the string.

```
DECLARE @LEFT_STRING char(100)
SET @LEFT_STRING = "Welcome to the Wrox Press Beginning SQL Server 2000 Book"

SELECT LEFT(@LEFT_STRING,10)
```

This produces a result of:

```
Welcome to
```

LEN

Returns the length of a string as an integer.

```
DECLARE @LEN_STRING varchar(100)
SET @LEN_STRING = "Welcome to the Wrox Press Beginning SQL Server 2000 Book"

SELECT LEN(@LEN_STRING)
```

Although the string has a length of up to 100 characters, only 56 characters have been used. Therefore the length is 56. This function will also give 56 if using a char data type.

LOWER

Translates all characters within the string to lower case.

```
DECLARE @LOWER_STRING CHAR(100)
SET @LOWER_STRING = "Welcome to the Wrox Press Beginning SQL Server 2000 Book"

SELECT LOWER(@LOWER_STRING)
```

This would then have a result of:

```
welcome to the wrox press beginning sql server 2000 book
```

LTRIM

Will remove leading spaces from a string. This will mean that the first character of the returned string is a non-space.

```
DECLARE @STRING_WITH_SPACES VARCHAR(30)
DECLARE @STRING_WITHOUT_SPACES VARCHAR(30)
SET @STRING_WITH_SPACES = "   Welcome to Wrox Press"

SET @STRING_WITHOUT_SPACES = LTRIM(@STRING_WITH_SPACES)

SELECT @STRING_WITH_SPACES
SELECT @STRING_WITHOUT_SPACES
```

This will return two rows of information demonstrating both sets of strings, with the second row being the string that has used LTRIM.

```
   Welcome to Wrox Press
Welcome to Wrox Press
```

NCHAR

Returns a Unicode character representing the number passed as a parameter.

```
SELECT NCHAR(105)
```

This will return the letter i.

PATINDEX

This function will search for a pattern of characters within a string. This is very much like CHARINDEX except this can also search through text data types. Also like CHARINDEX, it is not case sensitive, and will return 0 if no match is found. PATINDEX allows the handling of wildcards, unlike CHARINDEX.

```
SELECT PATINDEX("%Wrox%","This is wrox, more WROX, even more Wrox")
```

This will return the value 9, the first Wrox. As an example of a wildcard search, in the following example, _ represents any character. The value returned is once again 9.

```
SELECT PATINDEX("%Wr_x%","This is wrox, WROX, Wrox")
```

REPLACE

This function takes three strings as parameters, and all instances of the second string in the first are replaced by the third string.

The syntax is:

```
REPLACE(string to search, string to find, string to replace)
```

An example of this is as follows:

```
SELECT REPLACE("The author of the Wrox Press book, Beginning SQL Server 2000, is
Robin Dewson","Robin Dewson","Wonderbison")
```

This would return the following:

The author of the Wrox Press book, Beginning SQL Server 2000, is Wonderbison

QUOTENAME

This takes a character string and turns it in to a valid SQL Server identifier, which can be used as a name for a SQL Server object, such as a table, column, etc.

```
SELECT QUOTENAME("[bad] table name")
```

This will return:

[[bad]] table name]

REPLICATE

This is used if you wish to replicate the same string several times.

```
SELECT REPLICATE("Wrox is the best! ",5)
```

When this is run, you will receive the following output, professing how good Wrox is!

Wrox is the best! Wrox is the best! Wrox is the best! Wrox is the best! Wrox is the best!

REVERSE

This function takes the string input, and reverses the order of the information.

```
SELECT REVERSE("Wrox is the best!")
```

This will return

!tseb eht si xorW

RIGHT

By using the RIGHT function, you can return a number of characters from the right-hand side of a string. There are differences when using a fixed length data type, like char, to that of varchar. Don't forget that with char, any "unused" characters will be space filled.

```
DECLARE @RIGHT_STRING char(100)
SET @RIGHT_STRING = "Welcome to the Wrox Press Beginning SQL Server 2000 Book"

SELECT RIGHT(@RIGHT_STRING,10)
```

This produces a result of ten spaces, because the last 10 characters are space filled.

```
DECLARE @RIGHT_STRING varchar(100)
SET @RIGHT_STRING = "Welcome to the Wrox Press Beginning SQL Server 2000 Book"

SELECT RIGHT(@RIGHT_STRING,10)
```

This produces:

2000 Book

RTRIM

RTRIM will remove trailing spaces from a string. This will mean that the last character of the returned string is a non-space.

```
DECLARE @STRING_WITH_SPACES VARCHAR(30)
DECLARE @STRING_WITHOUT_SPACES VARCHAR(30)
SET @STRING_WITH_SPACES = "Welcome to Wrox Press    "

SET @STRING_WITHOUT_SPACES = RTRIM(@STRING_WITH_SPACES)

SELECT @STRING_WITH_SPACES + "!"
SELECT @STRING_WITHOUT_SPACES + "!"
```

This will return 2 rows of information demonstrating both sets of strings. To show the position of the spaces an exclamation mark is tagged on at the end.

```
Welcome to Wrox Press    !
Welcome to Wrox Press!
```

SOUNDEX

Used to check how similarly sounding two tested strings can be. Used mainly for searching a SQL Server column to see how similar a match can be found. It is, usually defined as `text` data type, though not solely that data type. This could be used when, as in the example below, someone is trying to find a name, but does not know how to spell the name and has perhaps used phonetics.

```
SELECT SOUNDEX("Robin Dewson"), SOUNDEX("Robyn Jewshoon")
```

When this is run, these two string values are close enough to return the same value R150, which is what is desired, since these two words do sound the same.

SPACE

This returns a set number of spaces, often used when placing a specific number of spaces between two sets of `char` type data. Do not use this function if the spaces to insert need to be in the Unicode format. Use `REPLICATE` instead.

```
SELECT "Robin"+SPACE(10)+"Dewson"
```

Will return:

```
Robin          Dewson
```

STR

This function takes a numeric value and changes the data type to a `char`. There are three parameters to this function; the syntax and explanation of `STR` is as follows.

```
STR(number_to_convert, length_of_string, [number_of_decimal_places])
```

The length of the resultant string will be left space filled where required to make the resultant string the correct length. The data type is therefore obviously a `char`. If the numeric value has three decimal places and you only ask for two decimal places within the string, the number is rounded up. If no decimal places are specified, then the number is automatically rounded up.

```
SELECT STR(100.325,7,2)
```

This will return (note that there is a space at the start):

 100.33

and the following will return   100 (note the 4 spaces):

```
SELECT STR(100.325,7)
```

STUFF

This takes two string parameters, and two numbers, specifying a start point and a length. At the specified starting point in the first string, `STUFF` deletes the required length of characters from this string and inserts the second string at this point.

The syntax for `STUFF` is as follows

```
STUFF(string_used_as_basis, start_point, length, string_to_insert)
```

For example, the following:

```
SELECT STUFF("Count Dracula is a vampire",20,7,"showoff")
```

will produce:

Count Dracula is a showoff

However, changing the `length` to 4 will produce:

Count Dracula is a showoffire

SUBSTRING

`SUBSTRING` is used to retrieve part of a string from another string. The syntax for the function is as follows:

```
SUBSTRING(string_to_remove_string_from, start_position, length)
```

Not surprisingly, the function will retrieve the `length` of characters from `string_to_remove_string_from`, starting at the `start_position`. For example,

```
SELECT SUBSTRING("Count Dracula is a vampire",20,7)
```

will return:

vampire

UNICODE

Returns the integer Unicode value of a single leftmost character in a string

```
SELECT UNICODE("Bedford Blues")
```

This will return the Unicode value for B, which is 66.

UPPER

Translates all characters within the string to upper case.

```
DECLARE @UPPER_STRING char(100)
SET @UPPER_STRING = "Welcome to the Wrox Press Beginning SQL Server 2000 Book"

SELECT UPPER(@UPPER_STRING)
```

This would then have a result of:

WELCOME TO THE WROX PRESS BEGINNING SQL SERVER 2000 BOOK

Data Type Conversions

These are more advanced functions, and are not covered within the book. They are here for the sake of completeness, as they will become more and more important to your SQL Server knowledge.

There will be many times through your queries where a value must be converted from one data type to another. This is most common when dealing with strings because you need to convert numbers to strings in order to put them into a `varchar` field. For instance, you may want to write out "Your order number is 134242" where 134242 is a numeric field in one of your tables. In order to do this operation you must be able to convert this from a number to a string or SQL will generate an error message.

We will be looking at the two ways to convert our data from one type to another using built-in SQL functions. As we will see, both of the conversion functions perform the same function and operate in very similar fashions with only a few minor differences.

CAST

The CAST function is the first data conversion function that we will look at. The reason why we have picked the CAST function first is that it is based on the SQL-92 standard and is the preferred method of converting data types. It is not always necessary to call CAST because SQL Server will perform implicit data conversion when possible. Implicit data conversions can occur between like data types within SQL. An example would be adding a float and an integer together. SQL will convert the integer to a float for the purpose of the addition operation.

There are many implicit conversions that can take place, but there are also certain conversions that can never take place. For instance, you cannot convert an image data type to an integer data type since the conversion would not make any sense and the information in an image data type contains binary data that cannot convert to a meaningful number.

When calling the CAST function you need to provide the data type that the initial value should be cast as.

```
CAST(expression AS data type(<length>))
```

The expression can be any valid SQL expression or variable. The data type must be a valid type and will change based on the database provider that you use. The optional length parameter is used for nchar, char, varchar, nvarchar, varbinary, and binary data types.

If you attempt to make a conversion from to a number to fewer decimal places than the expression, then the value will be truncated to fit the cast data type. For example, if we cast 2.78128 as an integer:

```
SELECT CAST(2.78128 AS integer)
```

then we would have 2 retuned. Notice that the number is not rounded up; rather it is truncated. If we converted the same value to money:

```
SELECT CAST(2.78128 AS money)
```

then we would get 2.7813 returned.

Here the results did round up. This seems to be a more meaningful conversion than the integer conversion since we would expect the data to be rounded appropriately. Be wary of converting floating point numbers to integers for the reason that we just demonstrated: you will not get a rounded number, you will actually get a truncated number.

Where else can the CAST function come in handy? Well, you cannot use the LIKE operator with numbers, but you can with strings. If you were looking for a product and you knew that it was something like $15.25 or $15.52, but you cannot for the life of you remember, you could write a series of conditional statements to look for these ranges; but then again we can use string operations. So, we convert the price to a string and then use the LIKE operator to find our data. Ensure that you are connected to the Northwind database, as we will use this database to demonstrate further.

```
SELECT
   ProductID,
   ProductName,
   UnitPrice
FROM Products
WHERE CAST(UnitPrice as varchar(10)) LIKE '15%'
```

	ProductID	ProductName	UnitPrice
1	15	Genen Shouyu	15.5000
2	70	Outback Lager	15.0000
3	73	Röd Kaviar	15.0000

As you can see, we have applied the conversion as part of our WHERE clause. We convert the number to a string and then compare against the search criteria. Keep in mind that this will return to us any data that starts with 15, so be careful how you search since you could return more results than you bargained for. We can also chain multiple cast operators together to correctly format our data.

CAST is the safe bet when you need to do a data conversion.

CONVERT

The CONVERT function is a bit more complex than the CAST operation since we can specify date styles as one of the parameters to the statement.

Let's first look at CONVERT to see what is in the function call:

```
CONVERT(data_ type(<length>), expression, <style>)
```

As with CAST, the length option is only used on the following data types: nchar, char, varchar, nvarchar, varbinary, and binary. The expression can be any valid SQL statement and the style is a date style for dealing with datetime and smalldatetime conversions as well as float, real, money, or smallmoney to string conversions.

Note that SQL Server interprets two digit years as follows: if the year is less than 49 then the year is considered to be 20XX while anything 50 and over is considered 19XX. In order to avoid any confusion or future date issues it is recommended that you implement four digit years wherever possible.

To verify this, try the following:

```
SELECT
   CAST('11/11/72' as smalldatetime) AS '11/11/72',
   CAST('6/5/40' as smalldatetime) as '6/5/40'
```

The result is what we expected:

	11/11/72	6/5/40
1	1972-11-11 00:00:00	2040-06-05 00:00:00

Let's look at some of the date conversions available. We will see some of the different styles that can be applied using the CONVERT statement.

```
SELECT
    CONVERT(varchar, getdate(), 1),
    CONVERT(varchar, getdate(), 2),
    CONVERT(varchar, getdate(), 3),
    CONVERT(varchar, getdate(), 4),
    CONVERT(varchar, getdate(), 5),
    CONVERT(varchar, getdate(), 6)
```

	(No column name)	(No column name)	(No column name)	(No column name)	(No column name)	(No column name)
1	02/14/01	01.02.14	14/02/01	14.02.01	14-02-01	14 Feb 01

Let's take a look at our price information query above and change the query to use the CONVERT function.

```
SELECT
    Orders.OrderID,
    Products.ProductName,
    'The total line item price is $' +
    CONVERT
    (varchar(10),
    CONVERT(money, ([Order Details].[UnitPrice]*[Quantity])*(1-[Discount])))
FROM
    Products
    INNER JOIN
    (
        Orders INNER JOIN [Order Details]
        ON Orders.OrderID = [Order Details].OrderID
    )
    ON Products.ProductID = [Order Details].ProductID;
```

Again, performing this query against the Northwind database will give us the following results:

	OrderID	ProductName	(No column name)
1	10248	Queso Cabrales	The total line item price is $168.00
2	10248	Singaporean Hokkien Fried Mee	The total line item price is $98.00
3	10248	Mozzarella di Giovanni	The total line item price is $174.00
4	10249	Tofu	The total line item price is $167.40
5	10249	Manjimup Dried Apples	The total line item price is $1696.00
...	...	...	...
2151	11077	Wimmers gute Semmelknödel	The total line item price is $64.51
2152	11077	Louisiana Hot Spiced Okra	The total line item price is $17.00
2153	11077	Röd Kaviar	The total line item price is $29.70
2154	11077	Rhönbräu Klosterbier	The total line item price is $31.00
2155	11077	Original Frankfurter grüne Soße	The total line item price is $26.00
	(2155 row(s) affected)		

As you can see, the results are the same. There is very little difference (with the exception of the conversion options) between CAST and CONVERT.

As you can see, SQL is very flexible with conversions. It is capable of handling many conversions on its own while it provides the flexibility needed to force conversions if the developer feels that it is necessary.

Date and Time Functions

Once again, it is advisable to enter the following lines of code first, to ensure proper recognition of ".

```
SET QUOTED IDENTIFIER OFF
GO
```

DATEADD

Will add or subtract a number of days, months, or years from a specific date. To subtract days, use a negative number in the second parameter

For example, to add 12 days to 24th March 1964 you would use the following:

```
SELECT DATEADD(dd,12,"24 March 1964")
```

This would return the following:

1964-04-05 00:00:00.000

The syntax for DATEADD requires 3 parameters.

```
DATEADD(what_to_add,number_to_add,date_to_add_it_to)
```

The first parameter can define what you are wishing to add to the date. A list of some of the possible options is a follows:

- Year – yy, yyyy
- Month – mm, m
- Week – wk, ww
- Day – dd, d
- Hour – hh
- Minute – mi, n

There are other options such as qq for quarter, dy for day of year, ss for seconds, and finally ms for milliseconds.

DATEDIFF

Used to return the difference between two dates. This difference, as with DATEADD can be calculated in days using dd, months using mm, and so on.

The syntax is:

```
DATEDIFF(what_to_return,first_date,second_date)
```

For example, to return the number of days between 24th March 1964 and 2001, you would use,

```
SELECT DATEDIFF(dd,"24 March 1964","24 March 2001")
```

This would return 13514, which is the number of days. Attempting to find the number of days between 24th March 2001 and 24th March 1964 using

```
SELECT DATEDIFF(dd, "24 March 2001",24 March 1964")
```

will return –135414.

DATENAME

Used to return the part of the date in a literal form. Excellent for use when making data more user friendly. This function has two parts, the first, like DATEADD, is which part of the date to return, in the example below, it is the month. The second part is the date.

```
SELECT DATENAME(mm,GETDATE())
```

This example will return a different value depending on which month you run it in. In this case, it was in May. Therefore the value returned is:

May

Combining this with DATEADD allows you to find out the month name in two months time:

```
SELECT DATENAME(mm,DATEADD(mm,2,GETDATE()))
```

which is of course, July.

DATEPART

This will return part of a date as an integer value. The syntax for DATEPART is very similar to DATENAME:

```
DATEPART(part_of_the_date_to_return, the_date)
```

The first option is just like DATEADD, in that this could be dd for day, yy for year, and so on.

To compare with the DATEADD example above, the following example returns the month as a number. Since this example was run in May, the value returned is 5.

```
SELECT DATEPART(dw,GETDATE())
```

DAY

This will return the day portion of a date as an integer. In the example below a specific date is used and so is pretty obvious, but you can also use the value in a variable, or the name of a column, instead of the specific date in the example.

```
SELECT DAY("24 March 1964")
```

This will return 24.

You can also use this with other functions, as you can with MONTH and YEAR. For example,

```
SELECT DAY(DATEADD(DAY,-14,'24 March 1964'))
```

This takes a date, subtracts 14 days and then gives the day part of the date, in this case, 10.

GETDATE

Returns the current local system date and time.

```
SELECT GETDATE()
```

This returns something like:

```
2001-04-11 15:07:50.047
```

GETUTCDATE

This returns the GMT, or Greenwich Mean Time at the current date and time, in the same format as GETDATE. This value is calculated from GETDATE. To demonstrate the difference, in the UK during the summer, there will be a 1 hour difference, when running the commands below:

```
SELECT GETDATE()
SELECT GETUTCDATE ()
```

This produces output of the form:

```
2001-05-31 15:48:12.490
2001-05-31 14:48:12.490
```

MONTH

This will return the month portion of a date. This is exactly like DAY in how to use it.

```
SELECT MONTH("24 March 1964")
```

This will return 3. This function is the equivalent of using mm in DATEPART.

YEAR

This will return the year portion of a date. This is exactly like DAY and MONTH in how to use it.

```
SELECT YEAR("24 March 1964")
```

This will return 1964. This function is the equivalent of using yy in DATEPART.

Mathematical Functions

ABS

Returns the absolute number of the given value, which is the value without its sign. The value returned is of the same data type as the value passed, unless we pass a `bit` value.

```
SELECT ABS(-321.22)
```

Will return:

321.22

ACOS

Returns as a `float` data type, the angle in radians that corresponds to the entered cosine, which must have values between –1 and 1. This function is the inverse of `COS`.

```
SELECT ACOS(0.33)
```

Returns:

1.2344927516409163

ASIN

Returns as a `float` data type, the angle in radians that corresponds to the entered sine, which must have values between –1 and 1. This function is the inverse of `SIN`.

```
SELECT ASIN(0.35)
```

Returns:

0.35757110384551026

ATAN

Returns as a `float` data type, the angle in radians that corresponds to the entered tangent. This is the inverse of `TAN`.

```
SELECT ATAN(0.87)
```

Returns:

0.71599111441630015

CEILING

Will return the next integer that is larger than the number entered.

```
SELECT CEILING(100.234)
SELECT CEILING(-98.9)
SELECT CEILING(-98.1)
```

This returns :

```
101
-98
-98
```

This is correct, since –98 is bigger than both –98.1 and –98.9.

COS

This function will return a `float` value that is the cosine of the angle passed in as a parameter. Note that this angle passed in must be in radians.

```
SELECT COS(1.2)
```

This returns:

```
0.36235775447667362
```

To demonstrate that ACOS is the inverse of COS:

```
SELECT COS(ACOS(0.5))
```

returns 0.50000000000000011.

COT

This function will return a `float` value that is the cotangent of the angle passed in as a parameter. Note that the angle passed in must be in radians.

```
SELECT COT(1.2)
```

This returns:

```
0.38877956936820496
```

DEGREES

This function converts a float value, which represents an angle in radians, into the value of this angle in degrees.

```
SELECT DEGREES(PI()/4)
```

returns 45.0, since PI() radians is the same as 180 degrees.

Once an angle has been calculated in radians, the `DEGREES` function can be used to convert that to an angle in degrees. For example, the following returns the angle in degrees that has a cosine value of 0.5.

```
SELECT DEGREES(ACOS(0.5))
```

Will return:

```
59.999999999999993
```

EXP

Returns a `float`, which is the exponential of the `float` value passed in as a parameter

```
SELECT EXP(4)
```

Returns:

```
54.598150033144236
```

FLOOR

This will return the largest integer less than the given value.

```
SELECT FLOOR(-145.677)
SELECT FLOOR(23.7)
```

Returns -146 and 23.

LOG

Takes one positive valued parameter, and returns the natural logarithm of this parameter as a `float` value.

```
SELECT LOG(5.67)
```

Returns:

```
1.7351891177396608
```

`LOG` is the inverse of `EXP`, and this can be demonstrated by:

```
SELECT LOG(EXP(2))
```

which returns 2.0

LOG10

Takes one parameter, and returns the base 10 logarithm of this parameter as a `float` value.

```
SELECT LOG10(5.67)
```

Returns:

0.75358305889290655

PI

Returns the value of the mathematical constant PI to 16 decimal places

```
SELECT PI()
```

Returns:

3.1415926535897931

POWER

Takes two parameters, and returns the value of the first parameter raised to the power of the second parameter.

```
SELECT POWER(3,2)
```

Returns 9.

RADIANS

Converts a value in degrees to a value in radians.

```
SELECT RADIANS(0.53543)
```

Returns:

.009345016413953240

RAND

Generates a random number between 0 and 1, which is returned as a `float`.

```
SELECT RAND()
```

Can return any number within the range but in this instance:

0.89619111523800699

ROUND

Rounds a value to the number of decimal places specified in the second parameter. Let's take a look at the syntax.

```
ROUND(number_to_round, number_of_places,[0|1])
```

The first parameter is obviously the number to round, the second is the number of decimal places to round to, with a negative number rounding to the left of the decimal point. The final parameter of a 0 will mean the number is rounded. A numeric of anything but 0 will mean the number is truncated.

```
SELECT ROUND(100.345678,5,0)
```

This returns:

```
100.345680
```

However,

```
SELECT ROUND(100.345678,5,1)
```

Returns:

```
100.345670
```

And finally,

```
SELECT ROUND(107.345678,-1,0)
```

Returns:

```
110.000000
```

SIGN

Will return a –1 if the number is negative, +1 if the number is positive, or 0 if the number is 0.

```
SELECT SIGN(-23)
```

Will return –1, since -23 is indeed a negative number.

SIN

This function will return a `float` value that is the sine of the angle passed in as a parameter. Note that the angle passed in must be in radians.

```
SELECT SIN(1.2)
```

This returns:

```
0.93203908596722629
```

SQUARE

Returns the square of the given number.

```
SELECT SQUARE(20)
```

Returns:

```
400.0
```

SQRT

Returns the square root of the given positive number.

```
SELECT SQRT(25)
```

Returns:

```
5.0
```

TAN

This function will return a `float` value that is the tangent of the angle passed in as a parameter. Note that this angle passed in must be in radians.

```
SELECT TAN(1.2)
```

This returns:

```
2.5721516221263188
```

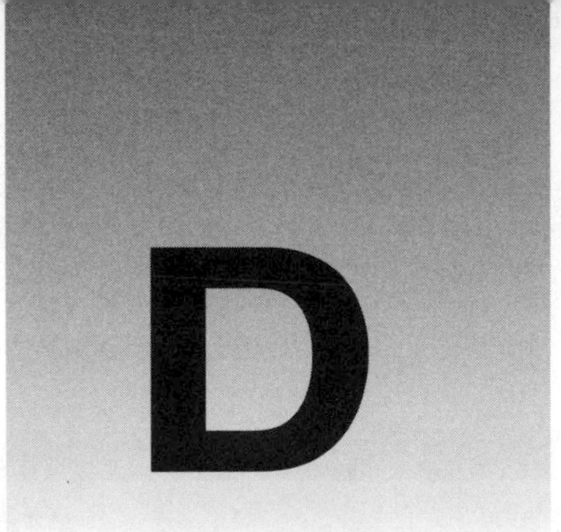

Access Upsizing

Due to the popularity of Access, given that it is highly available as part of certain Microsoft Office suites, it is quite likely that you will have started your foray into database development with Access. However, as your database grows, and the number of people wanting access to that data increases, you may find that Access is no longer suitable, and you need to move to a more scalable, more sophisticated database, such as SQL Server.

However, how do you make the move from Access to SQL Server?

Microsoft suggests several methods of converting your Access data to SQL Server 2000. These are summarized as:

- Use the Access Upsizing Wizard to create a SQL Server 7.0 database and then use SQL Server 2000 DTS to migrate the data from SQL 7 to SQL 2000
- Use SQL Server 2000 DTS to import the Access database in one step

Let's look at these methods in a bit more depth.

Access Upsizing Wizard

A few years ago, Microsoft brought out the Access Upsizing Wizard, which enables you to easily and cleanly create a SQL Server database from an Access database.

You would think that, because you want to create a SQL Server 2000 database, the Upsizing Wizard would allow you to do this in one step directly from Access. However, there is a known bug with this, documented at http://support.microsoft.com/support/kb/articles/Q272/3/84.ASP, which means that Microsoft recommends upsizing to SQL Server 7.0, then again to SQL Server 2000.

So, although we can't directly upsize to SQL Server 2000, it is still worth seeing what happens when we try. From within Access, the wizard is accessed by selecting the **Tools | Database Utilities** and selecting the **Upsizing Wizard** from the list.

You are able to specify a SQL Server 2000 server, the name for your new database, and a user ID and password combination as follows:

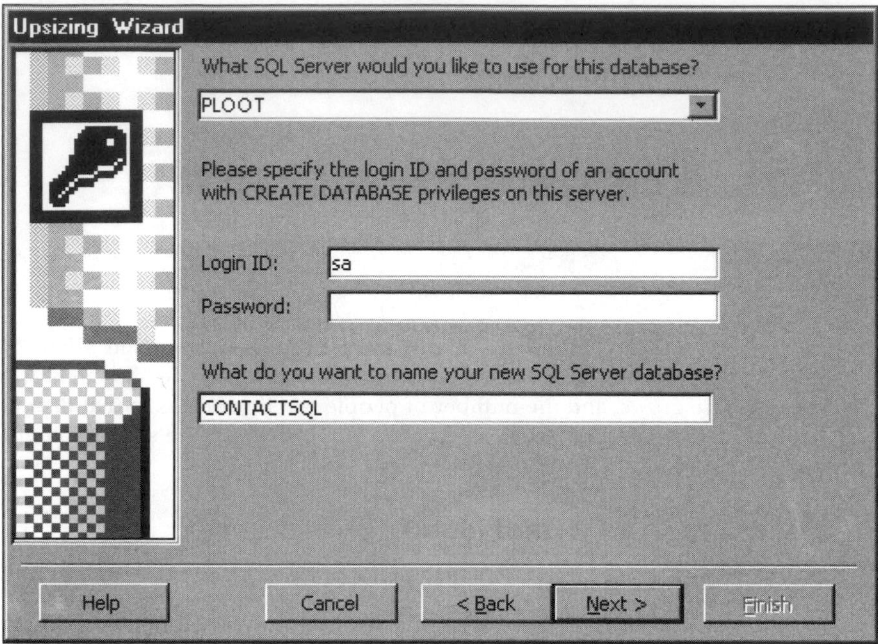

As soon as you press the **Next** button you get this unhelpful response:

Though this message doesn't give much away, it succeeds in stopping the wizard dead in its tracks. More information can be found at the URL mentioned previously.

So, Microsoft recommends that this wizard is used to upsize the data to SQL Server 7.0, then using SQL Server DTS to upsize to SQL Server 2000. However, as using SQL Server DTS is the second method that Microsoft suggests to upsize your data, it would make sense to make this the first method of choice.

SQL Server DTS

Unless you really need your data to exist as a SQL Server 7.0 database, you would normally use the second method of data conversion, which is what we'll now concentrate on. This process is really quite easy. In Enterprise Manager, right-click on **Databases | All Tasks** and select **Import Data**.

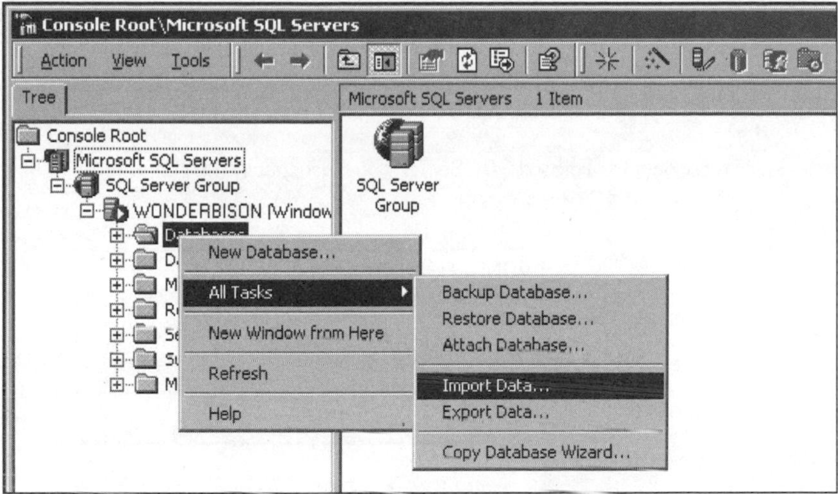

The import wizard then guides you through the process. First, you select your data source and the database you wish to upsize, providing the appropriate username and password details

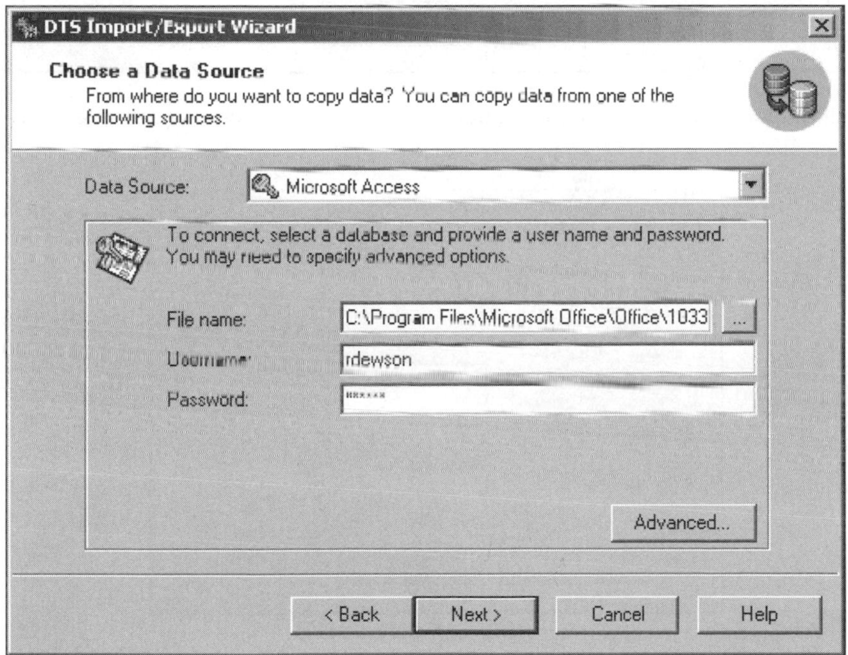

After pressing **Next** you will be able to specify where you wish to upsize to. Note that you do not even need to create a blank database first: simply select the <new> option from the database list:

DTS Import/Export Wizard

Choose a destination

To where do you want to copy data? You can copy data to one of the following destinations.

Destination: Microsoft OLE DB Provider for SQL Server

To connect to Microsoft SQL Server, you must specify the server, user name, and password.

Server: WONDERBISON

Use Windows Authentication

Use SQL Server Authentication

Username: rdewson

Password: ******

Database: <new> Refresh Advanced...

< Back Next > Cancel Help

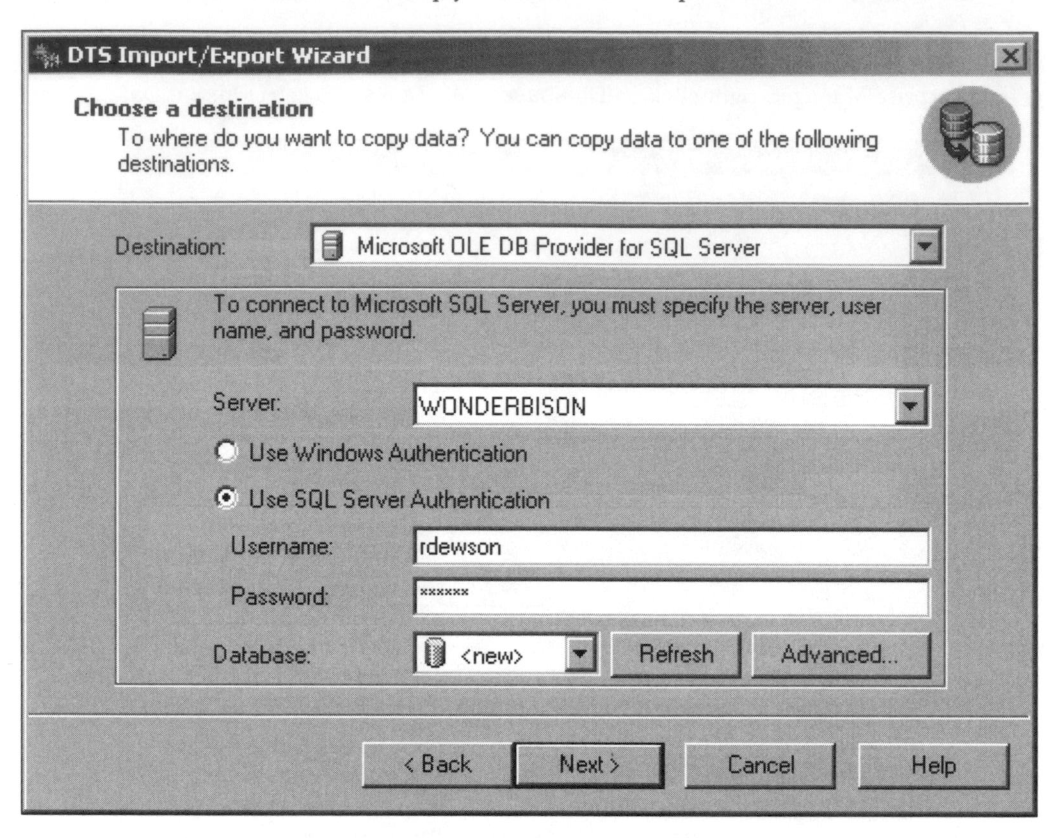

A window will pop up inviting you supply a name and, if you so wish, you can select the size of the data and log files.

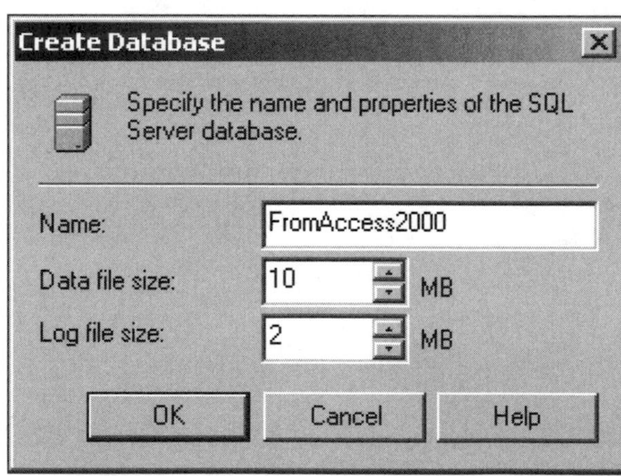

The next screen, after pressing OK and then Next, allows you to select the tables you want to import – this can either be all the tables in the Access database, or you can specify a query if you only want to import selected tables.

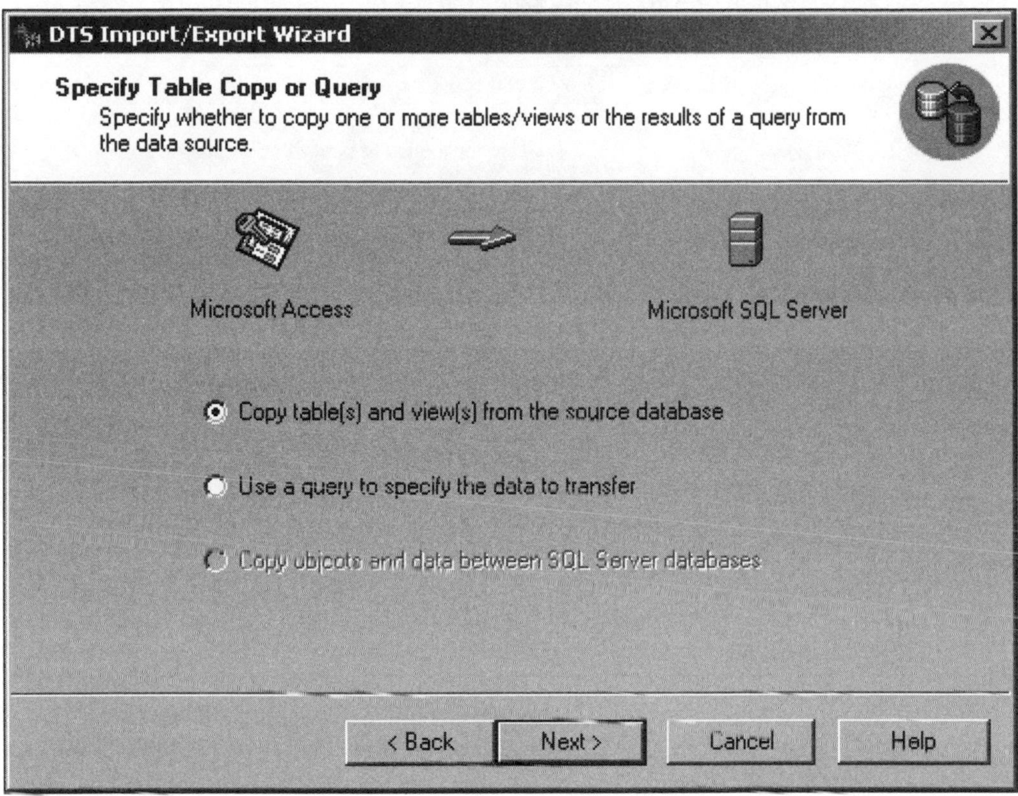

Obviously, as you are importing from Access, the last option will be grayed out as it deals with moving data between SQL Server databases.

- Specifying Copy tables(s) and views(s) from the source database means that we go straight to the next screen, which allows us to select which tables we want. Simply place a tick next to each table you want, or click the Select All button if you want to import everything.
- If you choose the Use a query to specify the data to transfer option, you will go through three or four screens that allow you to build the query to select the data you want to import, before returning to the screen that allows you to choose the query you have just built.

When you have chosen the tables, or query, that you want to use, click Next and you will reach the screen asking you when you want the import to run.

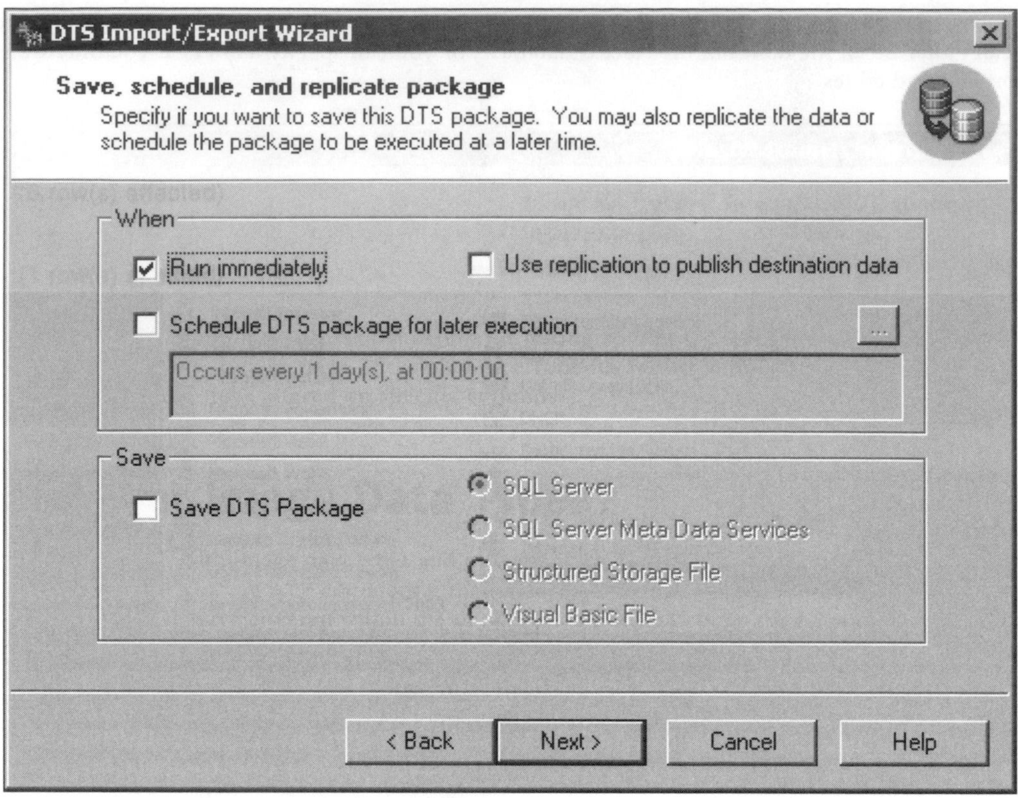

Basically, it is up to you to choose when to run the import process, but the options are:

- Run the package immediately – self explanatory
- Use replication to publish destination data – quite an advanced option and best left alone unless you fully understand replication
- Schedule DTS package for later execution – good to use when you know you need the data, but want it to run automatically at a later point in time
- Save DTS Package – meaning that you will have to run it manually at a later date; just remember where you saved it and that you still have to run it!

That is it! No matter what option you choose, clicking Next will bring you to the final screen where you get a reminder of the options you have chosen. Remember that you can go back to change any information you have given in any stage by clicking the Back button.

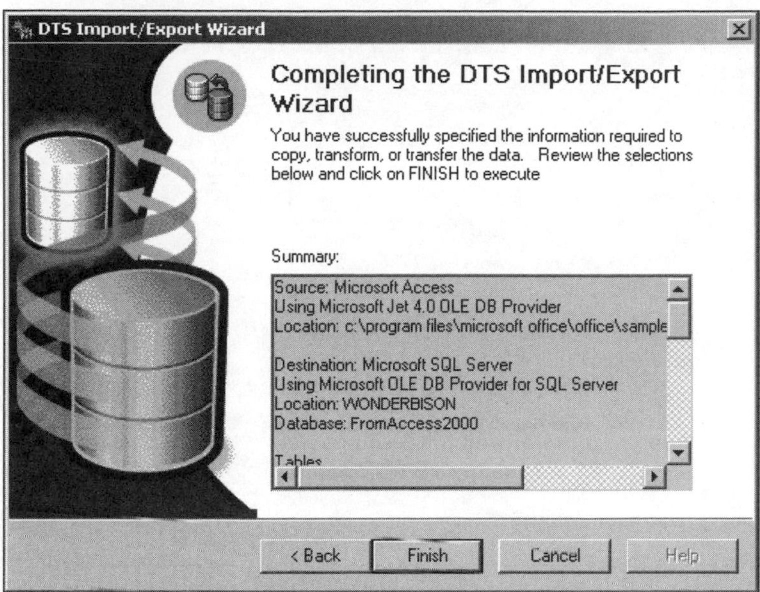

Clicking Finish means that SQL Server will either schedule your package to run automatically later on, save it to the location you specified if you saved it as a package to run manually, or run the import process if you specified that it was to run immediately. If you chose the Run immediately option, SQL Server then chugs away for a few moments and creates tables, keys, etc. and inserts data for you. All you have to do is perform a refresh of Enterprise Manager and you should see your new database in the list.

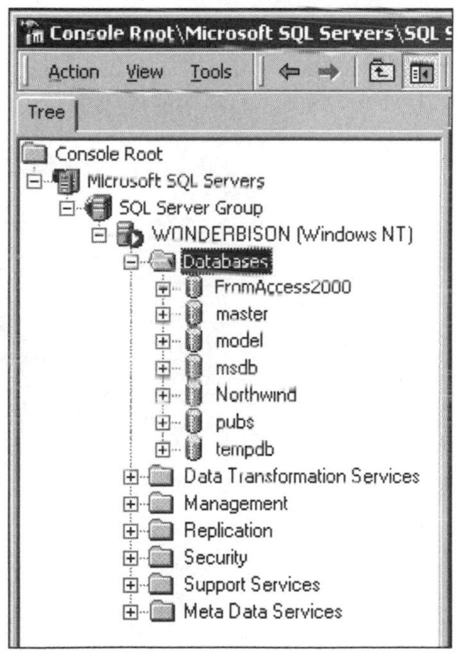

It's as simple as that!

Security

Security is important – if your database had no security measures in place, absolutely anyone could come along, steal or corrupt the data, and cause unmentionable amounts of havoc to you and your company. There are many ways that security can be enforced: by Windows itself, as we have seen earlier in the book, or by restricting users' access to sensitive data by means of views, or by specifically creating users, logins, and roles that explicitly state the level of access each is entitled to. It is this last method that is the focus of this appendix.

First of all, what do we mean by users, roles, and logins?

Users

Quite simply, a user within SQL Server is someone who can use a specific database. Each database has its own unique users – a user of one database is not necessarily the user of another database. However, users are not the objects used to log in to SQL Server: this is the function of logins.

Logins

A login, once created, can be associated with a user within the necessary database, which is then assigned permissions either as a user ID, or as a role. If a login is not associated with a user, then the login will be assigned to a special user ID, called **guest**. If guest doesn't exist, then that login cannot access the database.

Roles

A role is simply a collection of logins that all require the same level of access to a particular database. For instance, three people may need full access to a database, meaning that they can be grouped together, or three hundred people may need limited access, so they would be assigned a different role.

To create a role for the logins you wish to group, you must give it a meaningful name, and then place all the logins required into this role. Then, instead of having to assign permissions to each user for each database object, it is possible to assign the permissions once to the role. By doing this you will be giving the users within the role the necessary access in one single action. Also by using roles, it is simpler to keep security tight with a much smaller chance of an error being made with a login being missed when having to restrict access.

A login can belong to no roles, one role, or as many roles as desired, but if you do place a login within two or more roles then it will become confusing for you to ensure that the user is receiving the correct security. It would be better to create a role that placed users in one role only.

By creating roles, when a user moves jobs within an organization, it is a simple matter of moving that user from one role to another role and they would then immediately have all the correct access for their new role. If they did not belong to a role then you would have to revoke all their accesses for the database objects and then go through the necessary objects giving the right access. As you can see, this could be quite an extensive task.

Initial Permissions

When a database is created it is initially only the database owner who has any rights to complete any task on that database, whether it is to add a table, insert any data, or view any data. In the case of `Wrox_Golf_Results`, this would also have been the case. It is only when the database owner grants permissions to other users that they gain extra access to complete tasks.

This would then suggest that, in our case, only `RDewson`, the database owner, would be able to complete any data modifications on the `Wrox_Golf_Results` database. Earlier in the book, when creating the database, it was opened up to allow all users within the Administrators group to also have full access rights to the database. When mentioning Administrators here, don't forget that this relates to Windows NT/2000 users who have been assigned the Administrators group membership. With Windows 98 you can only log in using SQL Server Authentication and therefore there is no concept of being an Administrator. This can be checked by opening up the database in Enterprise Manager, moving to the Logins option found under the Security node, and then finding the Administrators ID in the list of logins. If we right-click and select Properties, we will be taken into the properties of Administrators.

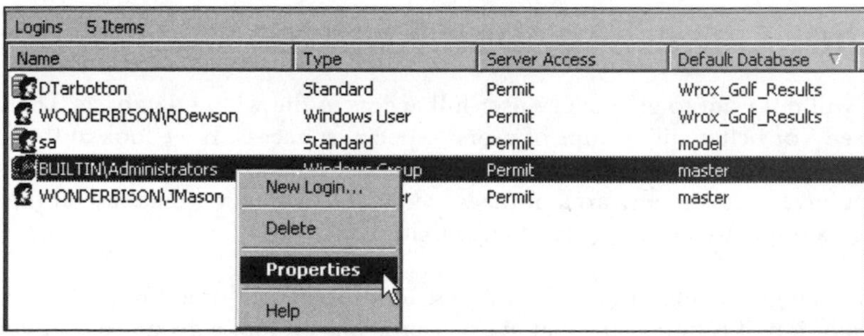

From there you can see all the properties of the login, in this case, the login group. Moving to the **Database Access** tab, you will see that the Administrators ID for **Wrox_Golf_Results** is a member of two totally separate and independent roles: the **public** group, but also the **db_owner** group. What this means is that this ID has also been defined as a database owner. Therefore any user defined as an Administrator can also have the same rights as the user ID `RDewson`. To clarify this point, this is because the Administrator ID is now included within the database owner role: any login that is included in the Administrators group will also become a database owner, just like `RDewson`. So already there is a set of users who can have access to your data.

> **Whenever you add a new login and allow it to have access to a database, it will automatically become a member of the public role for that database, and inherit any and all the rights that the public role possesses.**

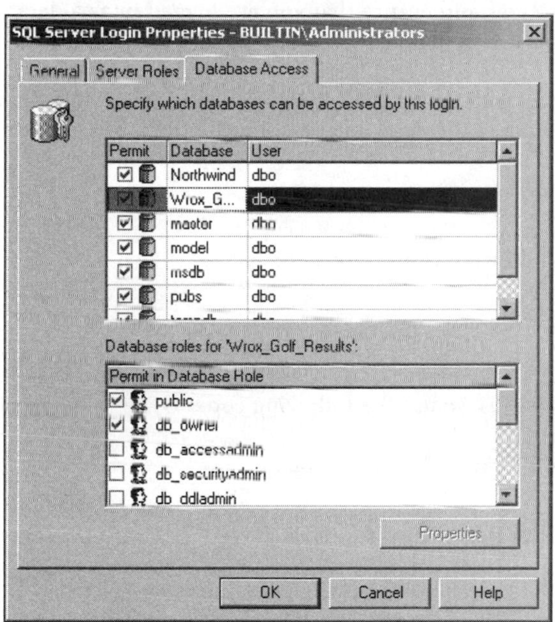

It is from the **Logins Properties** dialog, or through a T-SQL command that you grant authority to other users, or groups of users.

Giving Other Users Access Rights

Obviously you will not want to give every user full access to the whole database. Therefore you will give each specific user – or better still groups of users – specialist access. If we look at the users for our database and what their roles are, we can see that DTarbotton and JMason are not administrators and therefore do not have access to any area of the `Wrox_Golf_Results` database at this time. However, in the following example we are going to change that.

As indicated, we can grant different levels of access to a single user or a group of users. When building your database solution, it is important that every user is placed into a group so that you can control access to your database for each group of users. Giving access to your database to a single user at a time is a maintenance nightmare, and may give totally unrelated levels of authority for similar users. A user can belong to more than one role at a time; this is perfectly acceptable.

So, to understand this more fully we will look at an example. The first role that is usually built in a development environment is a role for Developers. There is no need for a developer to alter any table within a database, only manipulate and investigate the data contained. Any changes a developer needs to make should be made on a copy of a table in a test environment and not on the live database.

The following section will build a role definition and then add user DTarbotton to the role. The creation of the role will be completed through T-SQL commands, but it is just as straightforward when using Enterprise Manager.

Try It Out – Building a Role

1. Open Query Analyzer and ensure that you are logged in as a database owner (for example, RDewson) and accessing the `Wrox_Golf_Results` database.

2. Enter the following code into an empty Query pane. This will add a role called `Developers`. Once you have entered the code, execute it using the normal methods.

```
sp_addrole "Developers"
```

3. You will see the following result returned:

New role added.

4. Now that there is a role for developers, you can add users to this role. DTarbotton is the user ID to insert. To do this we use the following code. Once done, execute the code as normal.

```
sp_addrolemember "Developers","DTarbotton"
```

5. When executed, the following result is displayed:

'DTarbotton' added to role 'Developers'.

6. However, DTarbotton still has no authority at this point. Although he is within the database, and he is contained within a role, because the role has not been given any rights, then by default he still has not been given any rights. This next SQL statement redresses this and will give DTarbotton, and any other user added to the Developers role, full access to data manipulation. This includes any method of inserting, updating, or deleting data.

```
GRANT ALL ON Society_Groups TO Developers
```

7. Now that all of this has taken place, you can see the results and what has been achieved by moving into Enterprise Manager. Once in Enterprise Manager, navigate to the Roles option under the Wrox_Golf_Results database. You may have to complete a refresh, but on the right, you should see the new role for the Developers role group. Right-click on it and select Properties.

Notice in the following screenshot there is the option to create a New Database Role. Although we are using Query Analyzer to perform the addition of a new role, from this option within Enterprise Manager, the creation of a role could also have taken place.

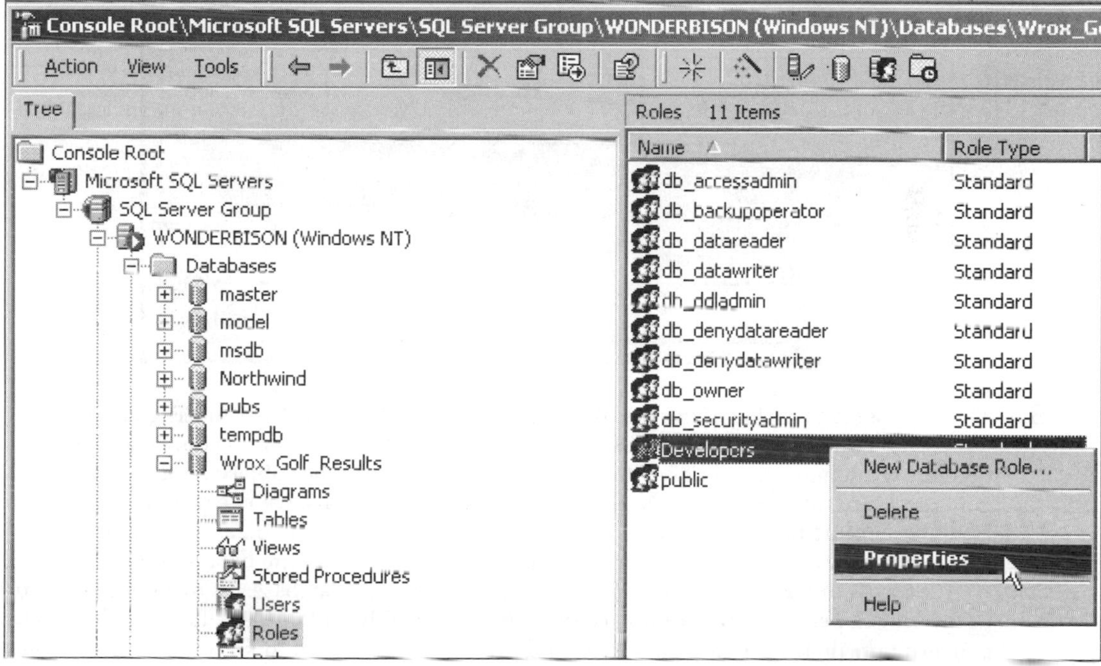

8. This takes us into the properties of the role. We can see the DTarbotton user ID listed. If you click on the Permissions... button at the top right of the screen, you will see what authority the Developers role will have.

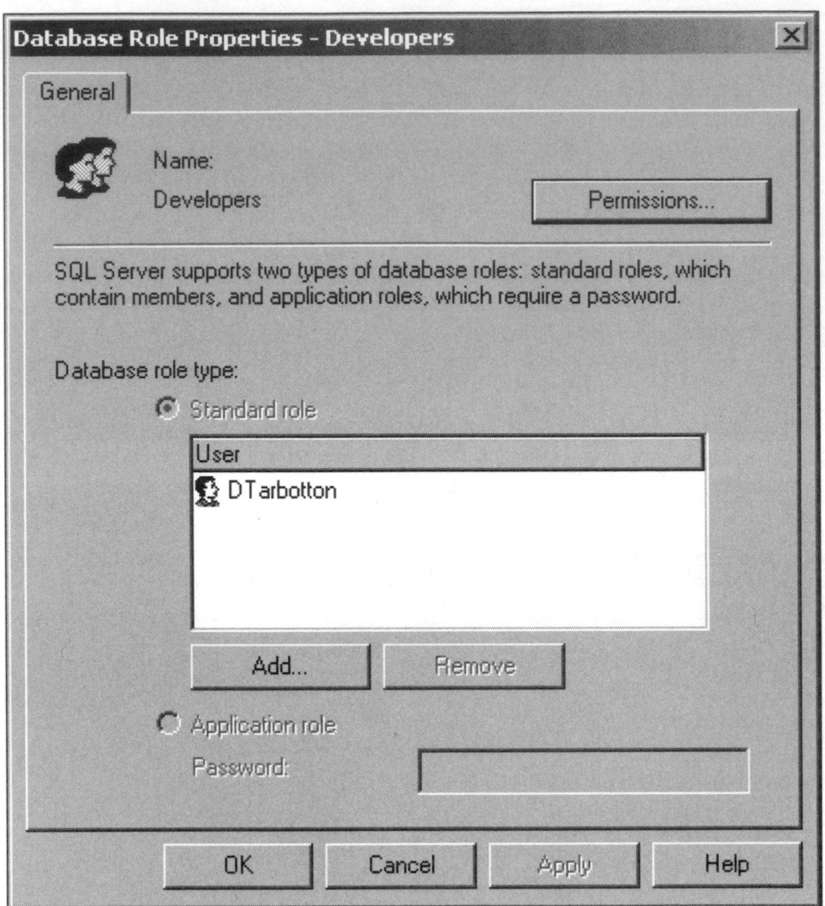

9. The Permissions dialog of the role doesn't just list the table that you can assign authority to, but all the tables within the database, as well as any views, various procedures, and other objects. From here you can give this role more authority to other objects. For now we are going to leave this role as it is. Notice that this user has ticks against every item for the Society_Groups table. This means that this role can complete any data retrieval or modification command in SQL Server to manipulate or retrieve the data on the `Society_Groups` table within the `Wrox_Golf_Results` database. At this point, everyone in the Developers role still has no access to any other table within the database. We won't concern ourselves with the other items in this dialog. If you want to know more about roles, I recommend you look at *"Professional SQL Server 2000 Programming" (Wrox Press, ISBN 1-861004-48-6).*

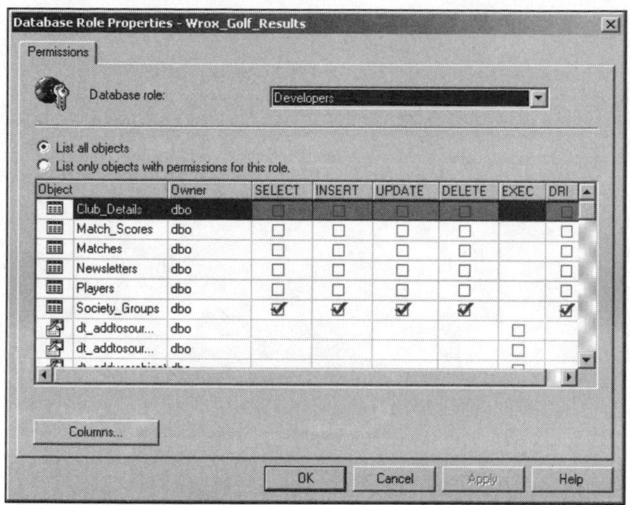

10. By pressing the Columns... button as shown on the previous dialog, it is possible to also give authority at a column level to this role. This functionality is to be used with care. It is easy to get carried away. The only real time that you should move to column level security for a table is when you wish developers to be able to work with a table that has secure information that you do not wish those developers to see or manipulate.

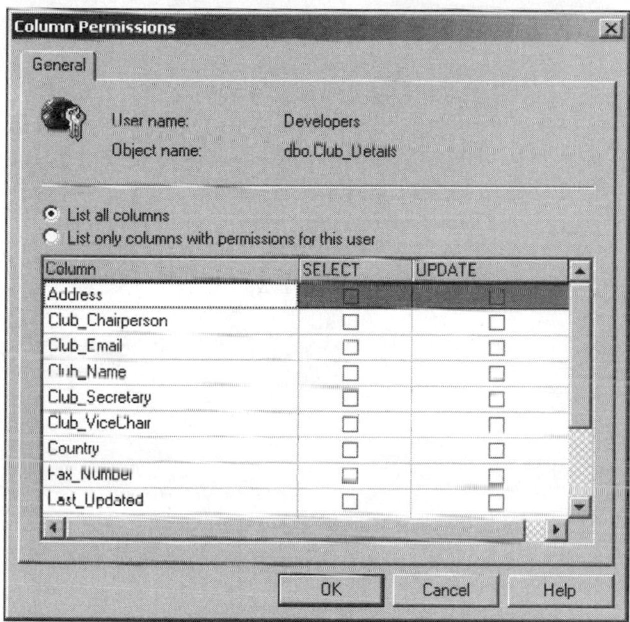

So, you can see now how using users, logins, and roles can help with protecting your data from prying eyes. Of course, you have to think carefully about what roles to create and what permissions to give, but roles and users make permissions, and unlawful access, much easier to manage. This leaves you in control of who can access what parts of your database, tightening up access to sensitive data so that everybody benefits.

Glossary of Terms

The aim of this glossary is to provide you with a quick and easy-to-use reference to many of the terms that you may come across in this book.

When beginning to study a new area of interest (especially in specialized areas), whether it be computing or not, it is very easy for a book, or any discussion for that matter, to get bogged down in new terminology, making it difficult for a new reader to advance in their knowledge of the subject at hand. Essentially, that's where this glossary comes in. Hopefully, this glossary will help you get to grips with SQL Server, and you may also find this to be a useful reference guide for use in meetings, or indeed any other area while you are starting out with SQL Server. So, without further ado, let's begin...

A

Alias

A substituted name for a database, table, column or other database object. If you have, for example, a table, or a column with a long name, or if you are joining two tables together, and both have a column name that is the same, or if perhaps, the name of a column doesn't lend itself to describing the contents of the data that it holds well enough for output displayed, then we could use an alias on the column name. In this way, we can assign a more descriptive name to the column, via the alias, thereby making it easier to see just what the data in the column actually represents. The alias on the column name would typically be used within `SELECT` statements or `WHERE` clauses of SQL commands.

You can also alias table names to make it easier when building queries joining two tables, so that the alias is used in defining the join conditions, rather than a long table name.

ANSI

Acronym for American National Standards Institute. A body of representatives from industry and business based in America, used to define standards in many areas, one of which deals with database standards.

Authentication

When logging-in to SQL Server, whether using Windows authentication, or SQL Server authentication, the process of verifying that the submitted user ID is valid for a given instance of SQL Server, and then allocating permissions to that user based upon their user profile is referred to as "authentication".

B

Back up device

Describes a hardware device, for example, a tape drive, that is used to back up a SQL Server database, making another copy for storage. If a tape drive is used, then the tape drive must be attached directly to the computer that the SQL Server database resides on, and cannot be a tape drive found on a remote computer elsewhere on the network. This can also refer to a hard drive on the same computer, or another server if required.

Batch

A set of T-SQL statements forming one group of actions. In Query Analyzer, we define the end of a batch by employing a `GO` statement. This would also determine the end of a transaction in any transaction processing. A batch allows you do put together a set of work which either has to be done because of the syntax of SQL Server, or you wish to "batch" together a set of work as one single unit. Finally, certain T-SQL commands must be placed in a batch on their own with no other T-SQL commands. These are statements like `CREATE TABLE`.

BEGIN TRAN[SACTION]

Is used to denote the start of a transaction of work, in which modifications will be made to data that once completed can either be placed in to the database, using a `COMMIT TRAN[SACTION]`, or rejected using a `ROLLBACK TRAN[SACTION]`.

Binary Large Object (BLOB)

Usually used to define a column in a table that is holding a very large amount of data, most commonly storing an image, although it is becoming more common to use this term in association with audio and video objects as well. This object is also known as a BLOB.

C

Checkpoint

This is a system function that is performed by SQL Server to write back pages of information to disk that have been modified by T-SQL commands, either since the last checkpoint, or since SQL Server started. The writing back of information can be controlled by a user, or SQL Server can be used to handle this automatically. For a user to issue a checkpoint, the `CHECKPOINT` T-SQL command can be employed.

Clustered index

An index on a table (or view) that defines the physical order in which the data will be stored on the table (or view).

COMMIT TRAN[SACTION]

Used to inform SQL Server that any data modifications performed within a transaction, by using the `BEGIN TRAN[SACTION]` statement (also `BEGIN TRAN`), are to be accepted as being valid and are to be committed to the database (that is permanently written).

Constraint

A constraint can be a check placed against a table column to ensure that the data entered is valid; a foreign key constraint identifies the relationship between two tables, while a primary key constraint identifies the column(s) that make a unique primary key on a table.

Control-of-flow language

This is the T-SQL language contained within a stored procedure, trigger, or batch of queries that determines the flow of execution of T-SQL statements. Contains commands such as `BEGIN...END`, and `IF...ELSE` among others.

Cursor

A special type of data repository, which holds rows and columns of data, just like a table. A cursor has no indexes, and is designed and built at run time to hold a transient resultset of data. A cursor can have the rows of data fetched one record at a time.

D

Data integrity

Ensuring that all the data stored within your database is valid, and that there are no inconsistencies between rows or tables of any information. Maintaining data integrity is paramount to the success of your database solution, and can be achieved through the use of constraints, keys and triggers.

Database

A repository of objects holding information that makes up a single unit of information. A database will not only hold rows and columns of information, but also how that information is stored within the database. A database will hold many different objects other than tables, including indexes and views through to stored procedures, logins, and many other objects.

Database diagram

A graphical representation, which can be generated by SQL Server, of all of the tables and relationships within a SQL Server database. A default database diagram can be specifically generated by a developer, and is displayed within Enterprise Manager when the database is selected. However there can be as many diagrams as desired containing any tables within the database.

Database object

A database object is an item that is held within a database, which is used in part to make the database solution. For example, a database object could be a table, a trigger, or a relationship.

Database owner

The user ID or user ID group that holds ownership of the database. This id has full system administration rights on the database. There can only be one user ID acting as database owner.

Database role

A database role is a grouping of users that have the same rights. When adding a new user who is to be allowed connection to the SQL Server, it is necessary for them to belong to what is known as a database role. Initially, when added, the new user will be held in a role called `public`, which has very few access or security rights. It is possible for the user to then be moved to a different database role, thus setting different access rights that are typically more appropriate to the user. Such rights may dictate whether the user has read-only access to the data, the privilege of being able to write to the data, or perhaps even full rights within the SQL Server database, such that the user can add or remove database objects as they see fit.

Deadlock

A deadlock occurs when there are two transactions trying to complete an update simultaneously, and when transaction one has updated one table (`TableA`), and is trying to update another table (`TableB`), the second transaction had updated `TableB`, and is waiting to update `TableA`. After a period of time, SQL Server will choose a deadlock victim, which is the update to be canceled and rolled back.

DEFAULT constraint

A specific value defined for a table column, that is used when no value is passed to the column during the insertion of a record.

Default database

When a user is created in SQL Server, a default database is automatically assigned to them. When no specific database is defined, the default database assignment is used to denote which database will be connected to when that specific user ID or group connects to SQL Server, through any application from Query Analyzer to an application written in Visual Basic or any other programming language. If you do not alter this setting, the user will default to connecting to the `master` database. As soon as possible, alter the default database to a more appropriate database.

Default instance

It is possible to have more than one instance of SQL Server installed within an organization and defined within Enterprise Manager. The instances installed within Enterprise Manager could all be on the same computer or on any remote computer. However, the default instance must reside on the local computer and is the instance that uses the name of the computer on which it is installed, as the name; for example, throughout the book, the default instance has been `WONDERBISON`.

DELETE query

This is a query that is built and created purely to delete records from a table within a SQL Server database.

Delimiter

Characters that denote the start and end of object names. Delimiter characters are either double quotation marks or square brackets.

De-normalize

This occurs when certain data within a table could be seen as redundant, and could be accessed through a relationship within another table because the same information is repeated several times in multiple rows. However, it exists as redundant data within a table for efficiency and performance.

Differential database backup

When a back up of a database is made, only the changes made to the database since the last full database back up are reflected. Used for speed.

E

Extent

Whenever a table or index requires more space, then SQL Server will allocate more space, which is known as an **extent**.

F

Foreign key (FK)

A foreign key is a column or set of columns that match the definition of a primary key or a unique key from another table. A foreign key is used to establish relationships between two tables through the correspondence between the foreign key and the primary key.

Foreign table

If a table has a foreign key, then the table is known as a **foreign table**, and the use of this term is most common when discussing relationships between tables.

Full backup

When a complete backup of all the data within a SQL Server database is taken. All data, including indexes are backed up.

G

GRANT statement

When we wish to give a user, or indeed, a group of users defined within a role, permissions to access or work with a database object, then we need to grant permission to them to perform the desired task using the `GRANT` statement.

H

HTML

HTML is short for HyperText Markup Language, which is the language used to display information within web browsers. HTML code consists of the data to be displayed, embedded in between two or more "tags". These tags simply mark the start and end of units of data, and specify what is to be done with the data within. For example, these tags can be used to format the data (which could be text data), or can even be sent as parameters to search engines. HTML is used as the basis for XML output in SQL Server and as such can be expanded with many areas such as cascading style sheets and templates.

I

Identity column

An identity column is a specialized column within a table that has its value automatically inserted by SQL Server each time a new record is inserted. This value cannot be altered. The value is unique for the table and is based upon a starting point and an increment for each insertion.

Index

By creating an index on a table, we can speed up access and data retrieval from a table or a view. An index consists of one or more columns from an associated table that can define the order data will be retrieved if that index is used. We can also use an index to enforce data integrity and uniqueness of rows within a table.

INSERT query

A T-SQL query that inserts information into a table.

Instance

An instance is an installation of SQL Server on a local or remote computer. It is possible to have multiple instances of SQL Server installed and running simultaneously on the same computer with some or all instances registered within Enterprise Manager.

ISO

Abbreviation for the International Organization for Standardization. This is one of the two international standards bodies responsible for developing international data communication standards. The other organization is the International Electrotechnical Commission (IEC). ISO and IEC are responsible for the SQL-92 standard for SQL. If a database is defined as SQL-92 compliant, this means it meets the requirements described in this standard, which is set by these two organizations.

J

JOIN condition

A T-SQL clause or a condition forms a relationship that is used to relate two tables and make them appear as one.

K

Key

A single column or combination of columns that defines a single row, like a primary key or unique key, or defines a relationship between two tables, a foreign key. Can also be used to build an index.

L

Local server

An example of local server is the type of server used throughout this book, and that is where the instance of SQL Server is running on the same computer as the application.

Local variable

Within a stored procedure or query, when wishing to store values without wishing to place them within a table, we can do this within a user-defined, locally-scoped variable, using the `DECLARE` statement. We can then assign a value using the `SELECT` or `SET` statement. As soon as the batch of work is complete, the local variable is no longer valid and the values within will have been destroyed.

Lock

When updating data, a lock is placed on the data stopping any other connection from being able to modify that data which has the lock, until such time as the process is finished and releases the lock. A lock is released when a transaction of work has been processed. Locks should be held for as short a time as possible to avoid a deadlock situation. A lock is released at the end of a transaction.

Login (account)

An identifier, or ID, that is used as a basis of checking a user's permission to work with objects within SQL Server.

Login security mode

There are two types of login security modes, Windows authentication, and Mixed mode authentication. You can set your database to allow access through either of these two modes.

M

Many-to-many relationship

Such a relationship becomes apparent when looking at the relationship between two tables where there are many records in one table that can be related, or linked, to many records in the other table.

Many-to-one relationship

In this case there are two tables that are linked, and there are many records in one table that can be linked to one record in another table. An example of this would be when the many table is driving the relationship, which could be found when looking at customer records and retrieving the country of residence from a cross reference number within the `customers`.

master database

This is the most important database within SQL Server as it serves as the database that controls user accounts, any processes that are in progress, environment settings, system error messages, and locking. This database should not be altered manually. Using commands or system stored procedures within SQL Server will alter the database but it is only through these system stored procedures, such as `sp_addrole`, that the `master` database should be altered.

Media set

All the media, whether it is tapes or disks, involved in the process of making a backup.

Mixed Mode

Uses both Windows and SQL Server authentication to connect to an instance of SQL Server though a Windows NT/2000 machine. (Not available on a Windows 9x system.).

model database

Used as the template from which all other databases and database objects are built. Details from within this database are copied when creating a new database, and when a new object is created, the details of the object initially come from the `model` database. Alter with care.

msdb

A system-defined database used by SQL Server Agent when dealing with automated jobs and alerts.

Multiple instances

More than one copy of SQL Server is running on the same computer, whether it be local or remote.

N

Named instance

This is an instance of SQL Server that has been given a name, since it is not the default instance.

Non-clustered index

An index where the columns listed within the index do not physically store the data in that order (as opposed to a clustered index).

NULL

A NULL value indicates that no data is stored in a column. This is a special entry within a column as it can be placed in any data type and yet means nothing. If you find this value within a column, you cannot compare it through a comparison with any other value, other than another NULL, which is a special comparison. To explain further, it is not less than or greater than any other value, or equal to any other value, even another NULL value.

Nullability

Expresses whether or not a column or a parameter can accept NULL values.

O

Object

An object is any component contained within a database. As such, an object can range from a database table, right through to a stored procedure.

One-to-many relationship

Similar to a many-to-one relationship, wherein there is one row in the master table being related to many rows in a child table. However, the difference here is that it is the master table that is driving the relationship. An example scenario might be a table for orders (one) with a table of order details (many).

One-to-one relationship

This relationship is rarely found, and exists when every record in one table has a relationship with a single record in another table, and vice versa. This could be when a single row in a table becomes split in two where data in one table is referenced frequently, and data in the other table is not so frequently referenced. This will then speed up data retrieval on the frequently referenced table.

P

Precision

The number of digits found in a non-integer number both to the left and to the right of the decimal point.

Primary key (PK)

A single column or a set of columns from a single table or view that can uniquely identify a row of data within that table or view. No two rows can have the same value within a primary key and no column defined for the primary key can contain a NULL value.

Q

Query

A single or set of T-SQL statements that deal with any aspect of data manipulation or retrieval. Queries can be run once, or run many times, and quite often are stored within stored procedures.

R

Record

A single, "horizontal" set of values that have come from one or more tables through a query, or a single, "horizontal" set of values from all columns within a table. This can also be called a row.

Referential integrity (RI)

A state where all the relationships between tables are valid, commonly achieved using constraints and keys, to ensure that the data integrity, hence the referential integrity remains valid. Preserving referential integrity will ensure that all data within the database is in alignment.

ROLLBACK TRAN[SACTION]

If, when working within a transaction, you decide that you no longer wish for any data modifications within the transaction to be committed to SQL Server, then you would issue a `ROLLBACK TRAN[SACTION]` (also `ROLLBACK TRAN`) statement that will restore the original values to all of the columns and all the rows that have been modified in the most recent transaction.

Row

A single, "horizontal" set of values that have come from one or more tables through a query, or a single, "horizontal" set of values from all columns within a table. This can also be called a record.

S

SELECT query

A `SELECT` query is a T-SQL query that is used to retrieve data from one or more tables or views. By also using the `INTO` keyword, it is also possible to create a new table from the returned rows of data. `SELECT` can also be used to define the value of a local variable.

SET

Used to define the value of a variable rather than using SELECT.

SQL (Structured Query Language) query

An action that will either manipulate, or retrieve data from objects within SQL Server or any other database that supports SQL, for example Oracle or Sybase.

SQL Server authentication

A method for validating login attempts to SQL Server using a user ID and password that are defined with SQL Server. This is the method used on Windows 9x machines as these do not support Windows Authentication.

SQL Server login

An account within SQL Server that enables users to connect using either SQL Server authentication or Windows authentication. This is known as the SQL Server login account.

SQL-92

The SQL standard published by the ISO/IEC in 1992. A system defined as SQL-92 compliant means that it meets all of the criteria within this standard, although many systems then branch from this, defining their own commands and procedure, for example through the use of T-SQL commands.

Stored procedure

A set of T-SQL statements grouped together and stored as a compiled object within SQL Server, associated to a particular table. Can contain control of flow statements.

Subquery

A `SELECT` statement that is used to aid data selection, by being nested within another SQL Query.

System administrator/s

People within an organization who will administer a SQL Server installation to ensure that there are enough resources for the installation. They may also be responsible for the security of the system.

T

Table

A database object that contains rows and columns of data. Each column will have a pre-defined data type and may also have constraints, indexes, and keys associated with it.

Table scan

Occurs when SQL Server scans every row within a table while performing a SQL command, rather than using an index.

tempdb

This is a transient database that will hold any temporary tables, indexes and any temporary storage needed by a query, or stored procedure, or any system process.

Temporary table

A table placed in the `tempdb`, which is then lost at the end of the session that built it.

Transact-SQL (T-SQL)

A language extension to the SQL-92 defined standards for a database to allow administrating data and objects within SQL Server.

Transaction

A logical unit of work, such that if it contains any data modifications, these modifications can be committed or rolled back depending upon a decision that can be made at any time within the transaction. Related to `BEGIN TRAN[SACTION]`, `COMMIT TRAN[SACTION]` and `ROLLBACK TRAN[SACTION]`.

Transaction log

A file separate from the database, which holds all of the data modifications made within a transaction. Used by SQL Server for recovery purposes.

Trigger

A specialized stored procedure that is executed when data in the table associated with the trigger is modified. Used to enforce referential integrity or business rules.

U

Unique index

An index that defines that no two rows within a table are the same.

UPDATE query

A T-SQL query that will update the data within a table.

User-defined data type

A data type based upon a SQL Server data type created by the user. Used when you wish to bind defaults or constraints to a specific data type. For example, you could create a user-defined data type that is set up for storing an order ID. You would create this as `OrderId` as `varchar(20)`. Then when it comes to creating tables with an `OrderId`, you would place this as a data type rather than `varchar(20)`. Then if you need to alter how an `OrderId` is stored, you only have to alter one place, the definition of the user-defined data type, rather than modifying several tables.

User-defined function

A new feature of SQL Server 2000, these are functions that can be created by a user to perform frequently used, or business-related, logic. They are different from stored procedures because these are like code snippets rather than full blown procedures.

V

Variables

Hold values used in queries or stored procedures, and although they can hold information from a column of data from a table, they are not actually part of any table. Variables are defined by using the `DECLARE` command and are prefixed with the `@` sign. Values are placed in to variables using the `SET` or the `SELECT` statement. These are local variables. Global variables are variables defined and set by SQL Server and are prefixed by `@@`.

View

A database object that can be used as a security measure when dealing with data that is sensitive, or to make a database scheme more friendly and usable for user-defined data queries. Acts in a similar fashion to a table, and although called a view, data can be updated and deleted providing specific conditions are met.

W

Windows authentication

A SQL Server database will have either Windows authentication or SQL Server authentication, or both, as the basis of any connections to the database. (This is for Windows NT/2000 machines. You cannot have Windows authentication on a Windows 9x machine.) Windows authentication uses the Windows user ID and logon as the basis of its connection to SQL Server. This is more secure than SQL Server authentication for connecting to SQL Server.

XML

Short for Extensible Markup Language, and is a technique for building self-describing data. This is can be used to pass data and information between systems, or to a web browser. Data can be retrieved from SQL Server in an XML format, and displayed in a browser.

Support, Errata, and P2P.Wrox.Com

One of the most irritating things about any programming book is when you find that bit of code you've just spent an hour typing simply doesn't work. You check it a hundred times to see if you've set it up correctly and then you notice the spelling mistake in the variable name on the book page. Of course, you can blame the authors for not taking enough care and testing the code, the editors for not doing their job properly, or the proofreaders for not being eagle-eyed enough, but this doesn't get around the fact that mistakes do happen.

We try hard to ensure no mistakes sneak out into the real world, but we can't promise that this book is 100% error free. What we can do is offer the next best thing by providing you with immediate support and feedback from experts who have worked on the book, and try to ensure that future editions eliminate these gremlins.

We also now commit to supporting you not just while you read the book, but once you start developing applications as well, through our online forums, where you can put your questions to the authors, reviewers, and fellow industry professionals.

In this appendix we'll look at how to:

- Enroll in the peer-to-peer forums at http://p2p.wrox.com
- Post and check for errata on our main site, http://www.wrox.com
- E-mail technical support with a query or feedback on our books in general

Between all three of these support procedures, you should get an answer to your problem very quickly.

The Online Forums at P2P.Wrox.Com

You can join the SQL mailing list (or any others which are of interest to you) for author and peer support. Our system provides **programmer to programmer™ support** on mailing lists, forums and newsgroups all in addition to our one-to-one e-mail system, which we'll look at in just a while. Be confident that your query is not just being examined by a support professional, but by the many Wrox authors and other industry experts present on our mailing lists.

How to Enroll for Online Support

Just follow this four-step system:

1. Go to p2p.wrox.com in your favorite browser. Here you'll find any current announcements concerning P2P – new lists created, any removed and so on.

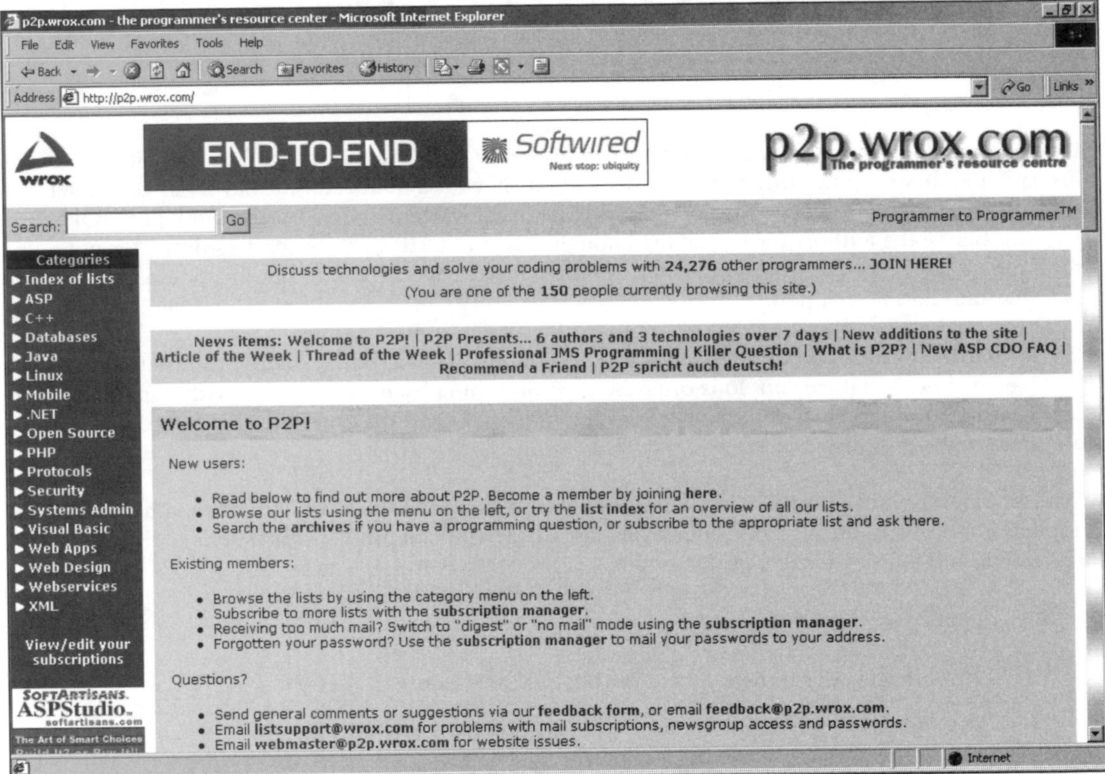

2. Click on the Databases button in the left hand column.

3. Choose to access the sql_server list.

4. If you are not a member of the list, you can choose to either view the list without joining it or create an account in the list, by hitting the respective buttons.

5. If you wish to join, you'll be presented with a form in which you'll need to fill in your e-mail address, name, and a password (of at least 4 digits). Choose how you would like to receive the messages from the list and then hit Save.

6. Congratulations. You're now a member of the sql_server mailing list.

Why this System Offers the Best Support

You can choose to join the mailing lists and you can receive a weekly digest of the list. If you don't have the time or facility to receive the mailing list, then you can search our online archives. You'll find the ability to search on specific subject areas or keywords. As these lists are moderated, you can be confident of finding good, accurate information quickly. Mails can be edited or moved by the moderator into the correct place, making this a most efficient resource. Junk and spam mail are deleted, and your own e-mail address is protected by the unique Lyris system from web-bots that can automatically hoover up newsgroup mailing list addresses. Any queries about joining, or leaving the lists, or any query about the list should be sent to: listsupport@p2p.wrox.com.

Support and Errata

The following section will take you step by step through the process of finding errata on our web site to get book-specific help. The sections that follow, therefore, are:

- Finding a list of existing errata on the web site
- Adding your own errata to the existing list

There is also a section covering how to e-mail a question for technical support. This comprises:

- What your e-mail should include
- What happens to your e-mail once it has been received by us

Finding an Erratum on the Web Site

Before you send in a query, you might be able to save time by finding the answer to your problem on our web site – http:\\www.wrox.com.

Each book we publish has its own page and its own errata sheet. You can get to any book's page by clicking on the Books link on the left-hand side of the page

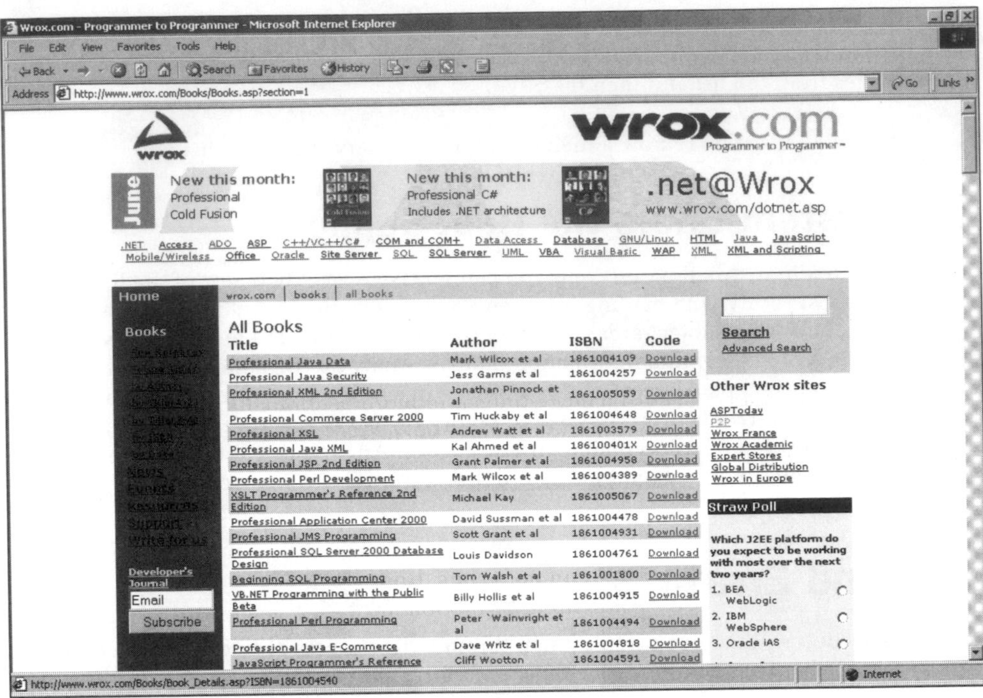

From here, find the book you are interested in and click the link. Towards the bottom of the page, underneath the book information at the right-hand side of the central column, is a link called Book Errata.

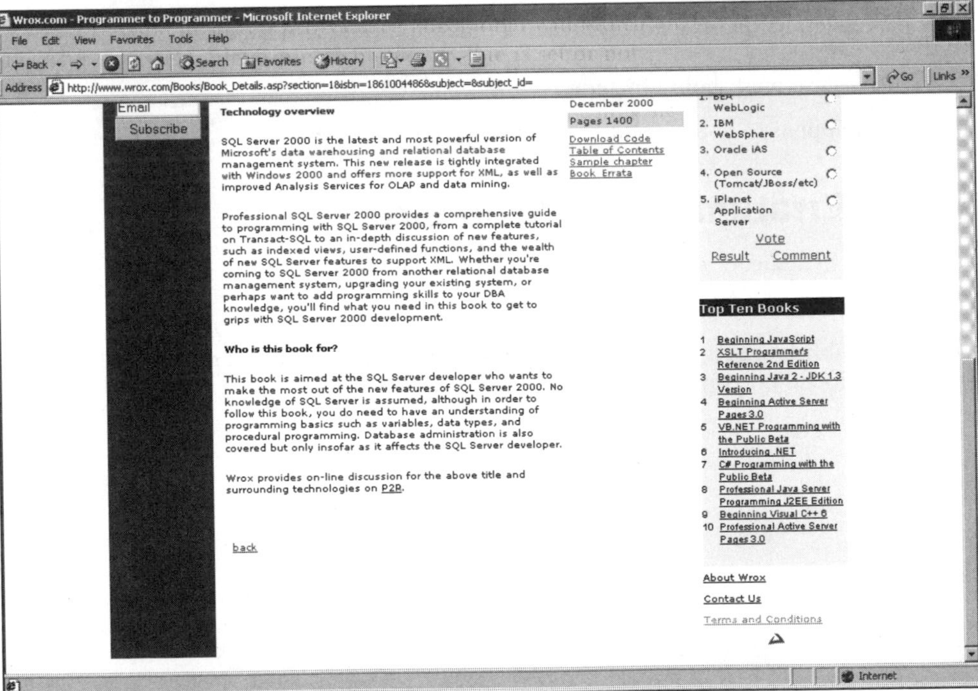

Simply click on this and you will be able to view a list of errata for that book:

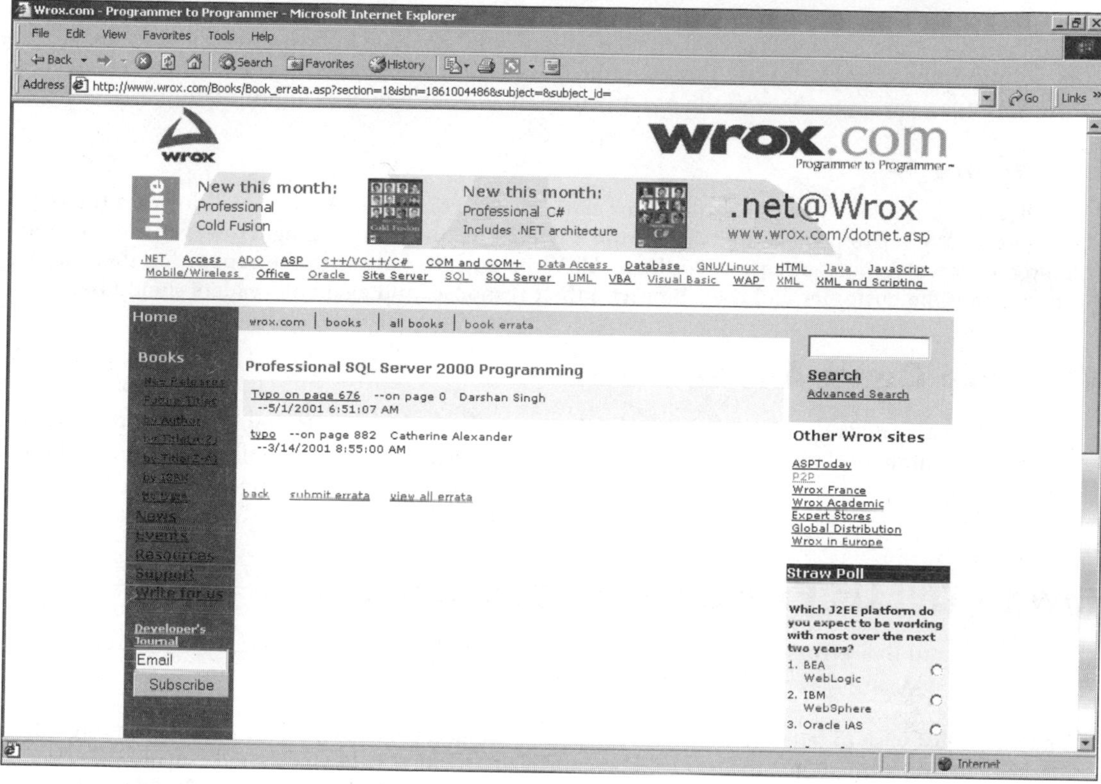

Add an Erratum: E-mail Support

If you wish to point out an erratum to put up on the web site, or directly query a problem in the book with an expert who knows the book in detail, then e-mail support@wrox.com. A typical e-mail should include the following things:

- The **book name**, **last four digits of the ISBN**, and **page number** of the problem in the Subject field
- Your **name**, **contact info**, and details of the **problem** in the body of the message

We won't send you junk mail. We need the details to save your time and ours. When you send us an e-mail it will go through the following chain of support.

Customer Support

Your message is delivered to one of our customer support staff, who are the first people to read it. They have files on most frequently asked questions and will answer anything general immediately. They answer general questions about the book and the web site.

Editorial

Deeper queries are forwarded to the technical editor responsible for that book. They have experience with the programming language or particular product and are able to answer detailed technical questions on the subject, directly related to the book's contents. Once an issue has been resolved, the editor can post errata to the web site or reply directly to your e-mail as appropriate.

The Authors

Finally, in the unlikely event that the editor can't answer your problem, they will forward the request to the author. We try to protect the author from any distractions from writing. However, we are quite happy to forward specific requests to them. All Wrox authors help with the support on their books. They'll mail the customer and the editor with their response, and again all readers should benefit.

What We Can't Answer

Obviously with an ever-growing range of books and an ever-changing technology base, there is an increasing volume of data requiring support. While we endeavor to answer all questions about the book, we can't solve bugs in your own programs that you've adapted from our code. However, do tell us if you're especially pleased with the routine you developed with our help.

How to Tell Us Exactly What You Think

We understand that errors can destroy the enjoyment of a book and can cause many wasted and frustrated hours, so we seek to minimize the distress that they can cause.

You might just wish to tell us how much you liked or loathed the book in question. Or you might have ideas about how this whole process could be improved. In either case you should e-mail feedback@wrox.com. You'll always find a sympathetic ear, no matter what the problem is. Above all you should remember that we do care about what you have to say and we will do our utmost to act upon it.

Index

A Guide to the Index

The index is arranged hierarchically, in alphabetical order, with symbols preceding the letter A. Most second-level entries and many third-level entries also occur as first-level entries. This is to ensure that users will find the information they require however they choose to search for it.

Symbols

A

B

C

D

E

I

J

K

L

M

N

O

R

S

U

V

W

X

Y

Beginning SQL Server 2000 Programming – Registration Card

Name ____________________
Address ____________________
____
____
____
City __________ State/Region __________
Country __________ Postcode/Zip __________
E-Mail ____________________
Occupation ____________________

How did you hear about this book?

- ☐ Book review (name) ____________
- ☐ Advertisement (name) ____________
- ☐ Recommendation ____________
- ☐ Catalog ____________
- ☐ Other ____________

Where did you buy this book?

- ☐ Bookstore (name) __________ City __________
- ☐ Computer store (name) ____________
- ☐ Mail order ____________
- ☐ Other ____________

What influenced you in the purchase of this book?

☐ Cover Design ☐ Contents ☐ Other (please specify):
____

How did you rate the overall content of this book?

☐ Excellent ☐ Good ☐ Average ☐ Poor

What did you find most useful about this book? ____________
____

What did you find least useful about this book? ____________
____

Please add any additional comments. ____________
____

What other subjects will you buy a computer book on soon?
____

What is the best computer book you have used this year?
____

Note: This information will only be used to keep you updated about new Wrox Press titles and will not be used for any other purpose or passed to any other third party.

5237

Check here if you DO NOT want to receive support for this book ☐ 5237

Note: If you post the bounce back card below in the UK, please send it to:

Wrox Press Limited, Arden House, 1102 Warwick Road,
Acocks Green, Birmingham B27 6HB. UK.

Computer Book Publishers

NO POSTAGE
NECESSARY
IF MAILED
IN THE
UNITED STATES

BUSINESS REPLY MAIL

FIRST CLASS MAIL PERMIT#64 CHICAGO, IL

POSTAGE WILL BE PAID BY ADDRESSEE

WROX PRESS INC.
29 S. LA SALLE ST.
SUITE 520
CHICAGO IL 60603-USA